REEDS

PRACTICAL Boat Owner
BRITAIN'S BIGGEST SELLING YACHTING MAGAZINE   SAIL AND POWER

SMALL CRAFT ALMANAC 2007

EDITORS

Neville Featherstone & Peter Lambie

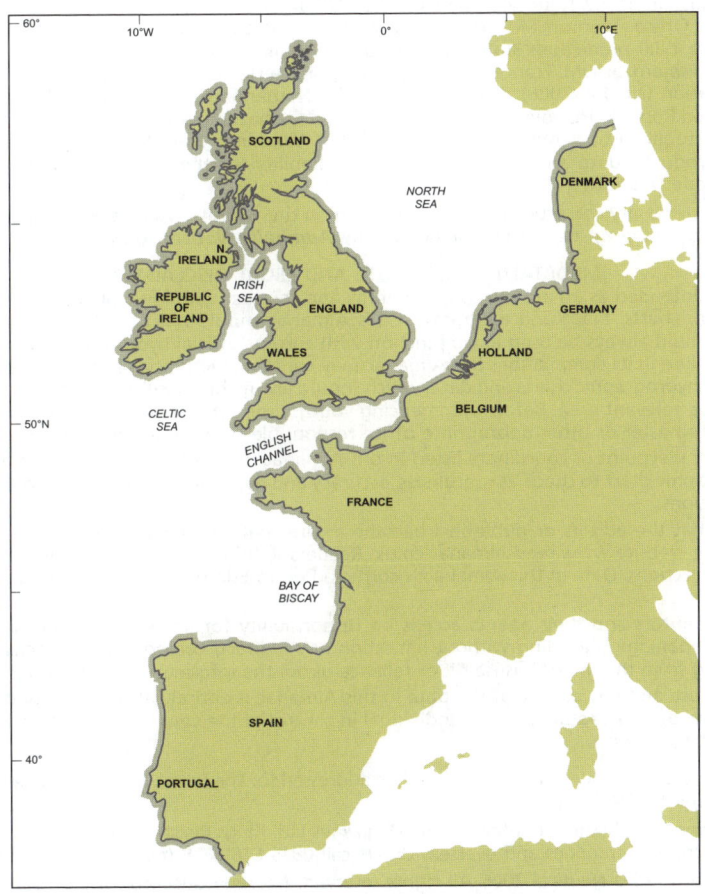

THE UNITED KINGDOM & IRELAND
AND DENMARK TO GIBRALTAR

PLEASE SEE IMPORTANT SAFETY NOTE ON PAGE 2

SMALL CRAFT ALMANAC 2007

Editors: Neville Featherstone & Peter Lambie

The Editors would like to thank the many official bodies who have kindly provided essential information in the preparation of this Almanac. They include the UK Hydrographic Office, Trinity House, Northern Lighthouse Board, Irish Lights, HM Nautical Almanac Office, HM Stationery Office, HM Customs, Meteorological Office and the Maritime and Coastguard Agency.

Information from the Admiralty List of Lights, Admiralty Tide Tables and the Admiralty List of Radio Signals is reproduced with the permission of the UK Hydrographic Office and the Controller of HMSO. Extracts from the following are published by permission of the Controller of HM Stationery Office: International Code of Signals, 1969; Meteorological Office Weather Services for Shipping. Phases of the Moon and Sun/Moon rising and setting times are derived from the current editions of the Channel and Eastern Almanacs, and are included by permission of HM Nautical Almanac Office. UK and Foreign tidal predictions are supplied by the UK Hydrographic Office, Taunton TA1 2DN. Acknowledgment is also made to the following authorities for permission to use tidal predictions stated: Royal Danish Administration of Navigation and Hydrography, Farvandsvæsnet: Esbjerg. SHOM, France: Dunkerque, Dieppe, Le Havre, Cherbourg, St Malo, Brest, Pointe de Grave, Authorisation (No 110/2006). Rijkswaterstaat, The Netherlands: Vlissingen, and Hoek van Holland. BSH, Hamburg and Rostock: Helgoland, Wilhelmshaven and Cuxhaven (BSH 11123/2005-09). Marina Institute Hidrográfico, Portugal: Lisboa, Authorisation (No 3/2006). **Warning:** The UK Hydrographic Office has not verified the reproduced data and does not accept any liability for the accuracy of reproduction or any modifications made thereafter.

Corrections Any necessary corrections will be published on the website www.reedsalmanac.co.uk. Data in this almanac is corrected up to Edition 25/2006 of the *Admiralty Notices to Mariners*.

IMPORTANT SAFETY NOTE AND LEGAL DISCLAIMER

This Almanac is intended as an aid to navigation only and to assist with basic planning for your journey. The information, charts, maps and diagrams in this Almanac should not be relied on for navigational purposes and should always be used in conjunction with current official hydrographic data. Whilst every care has been taken in its compilation, this Almanac may contain inaccuracies and is no substitute for the relevant official hydrographic charts and data, which should always be consulted in advance of, and whilst, navigating in the relevant area. Before commencing your journey you should also check local conditions with the harbourmaster or other appropriate office responsible for your intended area of navigation.

Before using any waypoint or coordinate listed in this Almanac it must first be plotted on an appropriate official hydrographic chart to check its usefulness, accuracy and appropriateness for the prevailing weather and tidal conditions.

To the extent that the editors or publishers become aware that corrections are required, these will be published on the website www.reedsalmanac.co.uk. Readers should therefore regularly check the website for any such corrections. Data in this Almanac is corrected up to Edition 25/2006 of the Admiralty Notices to Mariners.

The publishers, editors and their agents accept no responsibility for any errors or omission, or for any accident, loss or damage (including without limitation any indirect, consequential, special or exemplary damages) arising from the use or misuse of, or reliance upon, the information contained in this Almanac.

The decision to use and rely on any of the data in this Almanac is entirely at the discretion of, and is the sole responsibility of, the Captain or other individual in control of the vessel in connection with which it is being used or relied upon.

Correspondence Letters on nautical matters should be addressed to: The Editor, Reeds PBO Small Craft Almanac, 38 Soho Square, London W1D 3HB.

Practical Boat Owner is published monthly by IPC Magazines Ltd, Kings Reach Tower, Stamford Street, London SE1 9LS. For subscription enquiries and overseas orders call 0845 676 7778 (fax: 01444 445599).

Almanac manager: Chris Stevens
Cartography & production: Chris Stevens

Adlard Coles Nautical
38 Soho Square, London W1D 3HB
Tel: +44 (0)207 758 0200 Fax: +44 (0)207 758 0222
www.reedsalmanac.co.uk

FOREWORD

Every boat needs an almanac, and the Reeds/PBO Small Craft edition is the one most boat-owners choose.

Use this little book in conjunction with your charts and pilot books, and you have all the data you need to plan a day out or a long coastal cruise.

Many people only use the tide tables, tidal graphs and tidal gate information, but flick through and you'll find quick reference guides to how to make a distress call, lights and shapes, flag signals, first aid advice, the meanings of buoys, and much more.

The information is compiled and checked by the Almanac's editors at Adlard Coles, publishers of all the Reeds almanacs. They make every effort to ensure that the information is correct, but before making your passage plan please check the latest almanac updates on the Reeds website.

Check regularly for corrections and updates on:

www.reedsalmanac.co.uk

Wishing you happy boating in 2007

Sarah Norbury
Editor
Practical Boat Owner - Britain's biggest selling yachting magazine
www.pbo.co.uk

CONTENTS

Abbreviations 5
General vocabulary 6

CHAPTER 1 - NAVIGATION

Contents.. 8
Passage planning 9
Cross-Channel distance table 11
Lights, buoys & waypoints by Areas, with maps 12
Sunrise/set, moonrise/set.................................. 64
Speed, time & distance table 70
Distance off dipping/rising lights, table 71
Conversions table 72
Light characteristics.. 73

CHAPTER 2 - WEATHER

Contents.. 74
Beaufort scale & meteorological terms 75
UK shipping forecast areas/record 76
Weather sources in the UK................................ 78
Weather sources abroad 87
Weather vocabulary 98

CHAPTER 3 - COMMUNICATIONS

Contents... 100
Radio operation 101
Radio data 102
Ports & marinas: VHF & Tel details, plus VTS charts ... 104
Coast radio stations 117
Sound signals & shapes 119

CHAPTER 4 - SAFETY

Contents... 120
National Coastwatch Institution 121
Mayday. Helicopter rescue. Medical help 122
First Aid 124
GMDSS 128
Emergency VHF direction finding service 131
Coastguard services, UK and abroad 133

CHAPTER 5 - TIDES

Contents... 141
Dover tidal ranges 142
Brest tidal coefficients...................................... 143
Tidal calculations... 144
Bournemouth to Selsey, special instructions 148
Tidal stream charts 152
Tidal gates 190
Secondary ports: time/height differences 199
Standard ports: tidal curves & predictions 218

Index 414

ABBREVIATIONS

AC, ACA	Admiralty chart, chart agent
AC	Shore power (electrical)
ACN	Adlard Coles Nautical
Al	Alternating lt
ALL	Admiralty list of lights
ALRS	Admiralty list of radio signals
ASD	Admiralty sailing directions (Pilot)
ATT	Admiralty tide tables
ATT	Atterisage (landfall/SWM) buoy
Bcn, Bn	Beacon
Bkwtr	Breakwater
BST	British summer time (DST)
CD	Chart datum
Cf	Compare, cross-refer to
CG	Coastguard
Ch	Channel (VHF)
chan.	Channel (navigational)
CROSS	Centre régional opérationnel de surveillance et sauvetage (MRCC)
CRS	Coast radio station(s)
DF	Direction finding
Dia	Diaphone (fog signal)
Dir Lt	Directional light
DSC	Digital selective calling
DST	Daylight saving time
DZ	Danger zone (buoy)
E	East
ECM	East cardinal mark (buoy/beacon)
ED	Existence doubtful, European datum
EPIRB	Emergency position indicating radio bn
F	Fixed light. Beaufort wind force
FFL	Fixed and flashing lt
Fl	Flashing light
FM	Frequency modulation
FV	Fishing vessel
G	Green. Gravel
GMDSS	Global maritime distress & safety system
H, Hrs, h	Hour(s)
H24	Continuous
HAT	Highest astronomical tide
Hbr	Harbour
Hd	Head, headland
HF	High frequency
HJ	Day service, sunrise to sunset
HO	Office hours, Hydrographic office
ht	Height
HW	High water
HX	No fixed hours
Hz	Hertz
IALA	Int'l association of lt ho authorities
IDM	Isolated danger mark (buoy/bcn)
IMO	Int'l maritime organisation
Inmarsat	Int'l maritime satellite system
IPTS	Int'l port traffic signals
Is, I	Island, Islet
Iso	Isophase light
ITZ	Inshore traffic zone
Kn	Knot(s)
Lanby	Large automatic navigational buoy
Lat	Latitude
LB	Lifeboat
Ldg	Leading (lt)
LF	Low frequency
Long	Longitude
LT	Local time
Lt(s)	Light(s)
Lt F	Light float
Lt Ho	Lighthouse
Lt V	Light vessel
LW	Low water
M	Nautical mile(s)
m	Metre(s)
MCA	Maritime & Coastguard Agency
Météo	Météorologie/weather
MF	Medium frequency
MHWN	Mean HW neaps
MHWS	Mean HW springs
MHz	Megahertz
MLWN	Mean LW neaps
MLWS	Mean LW springs
MMSI	Maritime mobile service identity
Mo	Morse
MRCC	Maritime rescue co-ordination centre
MRSC	Maritime rescue sub-centre (not in UK)
MSI	Maritime safety information
N	North
NCM	North cardinal mark (buoy/bcn)
Oc	Occulting light
PHM	Port-hand mark (buoy/bcn)
Pt(e), (a)	Point(e), Punta
Q	Quick flashing
R	Red. River
Ra	Coast radar station
Racon	Radar transponder beacon
RG	Emergency RDF station
R/T	Radiotelephony
S	South
s	second(s) of time
SAR	Search and rescue
SCM	South cardinal mark (buoy/bcn)
SHM	Starboard-hand mark (buoy/bcn)
Sig Stn	Signal station
SMS	Short message service (texting)
SNSM	Société nationale de sauvetage en mer (French LB service)
SOG	Speed over the ground
SOLAS	Safety of life at sea (Convention)
SPM	Special mark (buoy/bcn)
SRR	SAR Region
SSB	Single sideband (radio)
Stn	Station
SWM	Safe water mark, landfall buoy
Tfc	Traffic
TSS	Traffic separation scheme
UQ	Ultra quick flashing lt
UT	Universal time
VHF	Very high frequency
VNF	Voie navigable de France (canals)
VQ	Very quick flashing lt
VTS	Vessel traffic service
W	West, White
WCM	West cardinal mark (buoy/bcn)
WGS	World geodetic system (datum)
WIP	Work in progress
WPT	Waypoint
Y	Yellow, orange, amber

GENERAL VOCABULARY. See also weather vocabulary in Chapter 2

ENGLISH	GERMAN	FRENCH	SPANISH	DUTCH
ASHORE				
Ashore	An Land	A terre	A tierra	Aan land
Airport	Flughafen	Aéroport	Aeropuerto	Vliegveld
Bank	Bank	Banque	Banco	Bank
Boathoist	Bootskran	Travelift	Travelift	Botenlift
Boatyard	Bootswerft	Chantier naval	Astilleros	Jachtwerf
Bureau de change	Wechselstelle	Bureau de change	Cambio	Geldwisselkantoor
Bus	Bus	Autobus	Autobús	Bus
Chandlery	Yachtausrüster	Shipchandler	Efectos navales	Scheepswinkel
Chemist	Apotheke	Pharmacie	Farmacia	Apotheek
Dentist	Zahnarzt	Dentiste	Dentista	Tandarts
Doctor	Arzt	Médecin	Médico	Dokter
Engineer	Motorenservice	Ingénieur/mécanique	Mecánico	Ingenieur
Ferry	Fähre	Ferry/transbordeur	Ferry	Veer/Pont
Garage	Autowerkstatt	Station service	Garage	Garage
Harbour	Hafen	Port	Puerto	Haven
Hospital	Krankenhaus	Hôpital	Hospital	Ziekenhuis
Mast crane	Mastenkran	Grue	Grúa	Masten kraan
Post office	Postamt	Bureau de poste/PTT	Correos	Postkantoor
Railway station	Bahnhof	Gare de chemin de fer	Estación de ferrocanil	Station
Sailmaker	Segelmacher	Voilier	Velero	Zeilmaker
Shops	Geschäfte	Boutiques	Tiendas	Winkels
Slip	Slip	Cale	Varadero	Helling
Supermarket	Supermarkt	Supermarché	Supermercado	Supermarkt
Taxi	Taxi	Taxi	Taxis	Taxi
Village	Ort	Village	Pueblo	Dorp
Yacht club	Yachtclub	Club nautique	Club náutico	Jacht club
NAVIGATION				
Abeam	Querab	A côté	Por el través	Naast
Ahead	Voraus	Avant	Avante	Voor
Astern	Achteraus	Arrière	Atrás	Achter
Bearing	Peilung	Cap	Maración	Peiling
Buoy	Tonne	Bouée	Boya	Boei
Binoculars	Fernglas	Jumelles	Prismáticos	Verrekijker
Channel	Kanal	Chenal	Canal	Kanaal
Chart	Seekarte	Carte	Carta náutica	Zeekaart
Compass	Kompass	Compas	Compás	Kompas
Compass course	Kompass Kurs	Cap du compas	Rumbo de aguja	Kompas koers
Current	Strömung	Courant	Coriente	Stroom
Dead reckoning	Koppelnavigation	Estime	Estimación	Gegist bestek
Degree	Grad	Degré	Grado	Graden
Deviation	Deviation	Déviation	Desvio	Deviatie
Distance	Entfernung	Distance	Distancia	Afstand
Downstream	Flußabwärts	En aval	Río abajo	Stroom afwaards
East	Ost	Est	Este	Oost
Ebb	Ebbe	Jusant	Marea menguante	Eb
Echosounder	Echolot	Sondeur	Sonda	Dieptemeter
Estimated position	Gegißte Position	Point estimé	Posición estimado	Gegiste positie
Fathom	Faden	Une brasse	Braza	Vadem
Feet	Fuß	Pieds	Pie	Voet
Flood	Flut	Flot	Flujo de marea	Vloed
Handbearing compass	Handpeilkompass	Compas de relèvement	Compás de marcaciones	Handpeil kompas

ENGLISH	GERMAN	FRENCH	SPANISH	DUTCH
Harbour guide	Hafenhandbuch	Guide du port	Guia del Puerto	Havengids
High water	Hochwasser	Peine mer	Altamer	Hoog water
Latitude	Geographische Breite	Latitude	Latitud	Breedte
Leading lights	Feuer in Linie	Alignement	Luz de enfilación	Geleide lichten
Leeway	Abdrift	Dérive	Hacia sotavento	Drift
Lighthouse	Leuchtturm	Phare	Faro	Vuurtoren
List of lights	Leuchtfeuer Verzeichnis	Liste des feux	Listude de Luces	Lichtenlijst
Log	Logge	Loch	Corredera	Log
Longitude	Geographische Länge	Longitude	Longitud	Lengte
Low water	Niedrigwasser	Basse mer	Bajamar	Laag water
Metre	Meter	Mètre	Metro	Meter
Minute	Minute	Minute	Minuto	Minuut
Nautical almanac	Nautischer Almanach	Almanach nautique	Almanaque náutico	Almanak
Nautical mile	Seemeile	Mille nautique	Milla marina	Zeemijl
Neap tide	Nipptide	Morte-eau	Marea muerta	Dood tij
North	Nord	Nord	Norte	Noord
Pilot	Lotse	Pilote	Práctico	Loods/Gids
Pilotage book	Handbuch	Instructions nautiques	Derrotero	Vaarwijzer
RDF	Funkpeiler	Radio gonio	Radio-gonió	Radio richtingzoeker
Radar	Radar	Radar	Radar	Radar
Radio receiver	Radio, Empfänger	Réceptor radio	Receptor de radio	Radio ontvanger
Radio transmitter	Sender	Emetteur radio	Radio-transmisor	Radio zender
River outlet	Flußmündung	Embouchure	Embocadura	Riviermond
South	Süd	Sud	Sud, Sur	Zuid
Spring tide	Springtide	Vive-eau	Marea viva	Springtij/ springvloed
Tide	Tide, Gezeit	Marée	Marea	Getijde
Tide tables	Tidenkalender	Annuaire des marées	Anuario de mareas	Getijdetafel
True course	Wahrer Kurs	Vrai cap	Rumbo	Ware Koers
Upstream	Flußaufwärts	En amont	Río arriba	Stroom opwaards
VHF	UKW	VHF	VHF	Marifoon
Variation	Mißweisung	Variation	Variación	Variatie
Waypoint	Wegpunkt	Point de rapport	Waypoint	Waypoint/Route punt
West	West	Ouest	Oeste	West

OFFICIALDOM

ENGLISH	GERMAN	FRENCH	SPANISH	DUTCH
Certificate of registry	Schiffszertifikat	Acte de franchisation	Doc de matrícuia	Zeebrief
Check in	Einklarieren	Enregistrement	Registrar	Check-in
Customs	Zoll	Douanes	Aduana	Douane
Declare	Verzollen	Déclarer	Declarar	Aangeven
Harbour master	Hafenmeister	Capitaine du port	Capitán del puerto	Havenmeester
Insurance	Versicherung	Assurance	Seguro	Verzekering
Insurance certificate	Versicherungspolice	Certificat d'assurance	Certificado deseguro	Verzekeringsbewijs
Passport	Paß	Passeport	Pasaporte	Paspoort
Police	Polizei	Police	Policía	Politie
Pratique	Verkehrserlaubnis	Pratique	Prático	Verlof tot ontscheping
Prohibited area	Sperrgebiet	Zone interdite	Zona de prohibida	Verboden gebied
Register	Register	Liste de passagers	Lista de tripulantes/rol	Register
Ship's log	Logbuch	Livre de bord	Cuaderno de bitácora	Logboek
Ship's papers	Schiffspapiere	Papiers de bateau	Documentos del barco	Scheepspapieren
Surveyor	Gutachter	Expert maritime	Inspector	Opzichter

CHAPTER 1 - NAVIGATION

CONTENTS

Passage planning 9
Distances across the English Channel 11
Selected lights, buoys and waypoints by Areas
  Area 1 - SW England and maps of Naval exercise areas 12
  Area 2 - S Central England 16
    Map of Area 2 18
  Area 3 - SE England 19
  Area 4 - E England 20
    Map of Areas 4 – 7 23
  Area 5 - E Scotland 24
  Area 6 - NW Scotland and map of Naval exercise areas 27
  Area 7 - SW Scotland 30
  Area 8 - NW England & Wales 32
    Map of Areas 1 and 8 – 10 34
  Area 9 - S Wales & SW England 35
  Area 10 - Ireland 37
  Area 11 - West Denmark 40
  Area 12 - Germany (North Sea coast) 41
    Map of Areas 11 – 13 43
  Area 13 - Netherlands & Belgium 44
  Area 14 - N France 46
  Area 15 - N Central France & Channel Is 48
    Map of Areas 14 – 17 50
  Area 16 - NW France & N Biscay 51
  Area 17 - S Biscay and map of Landes firing range 53
  Area 18 - N & NW Spain 56
    Map of Areas 18 – 20 58
  Area 19 - Portugal & The Azores 59
  Area 20 - SW Spain & Gibraltar 62
Tables
  Sunrise/set & Moonrise/set times 64
  Speed, time and distance 70
  Distance off dipping/rising lights 71
  Conversion table 72
  Light characteristics 73

PASSAGE PLANNING CHECKLIST

DATE .... FROM ....ETD .... VIA .... TO .... ETA ....

TIMES OF SUNRISE .... SUNSET .... MOON RISE .... MOONSET .... WATCH SYSTEM ☐

CHARTS ☐   DOCUMENTS ☐   CUSTOMS ☐   PAY DUES ☐   CG (T/R) ☐   FUEL ☐   WATER ☐   FOOD ☐

WEATHER FORECAST ....

DEPARTURE PORT VHF .... HM ☎ ....

BRIDGE TIMES ....

LOCK/GATE TIMES ....

BAR CROSSING TIMES ....

DEPARTURE WINDOW ....

DEPARTURE PROCEDURE ....

....

....

VTS DETAILS ....

....

....

STANDARD PORT, TIDES (SP/NP, HW/LW TIMES & HEIGHTS)

....

....

DEPARTURE PORT TIDES (HW/LW TIMES & HEIGHTS) ....

....

....

....

TIDAL STREAMS ON DEPARTURE ....

....

....

....

EN ROUTE

TIDAL STREAM ANALYSIS ....

....

....

....

....

TIDAL GATES (TIMES) ....

TIDE RACES ....

....

TRAFFIC SEPARATION SCHEMES ....

....

PROHIBITED AREAS/DANGERS ....

PRINCIPAL LIGHTS/MARKS ....

....

....

LEG DETAILS

FROM	TO	WPT	TRK°M	DIST	TIME	REMARKS

DESTINATION PORT VHF .... HM ☎ ....

ARRIVAL PROCEDURE ....

....

BAR CROSSING TIMES ....

LOCK/GATE/SILL TIMES ....

BRIDGE TIMES ....

ACCESS WINDOW ....

ALTERNATE PORT VHF .... HM ☎ ....

ARRIVAL PROCEDURE ....

....

BAR CROSSING TIMES ....

LOCK/GATE/SILL TIMES ....

BRIDGE TIMES ....

ACCESS WINDOW ....

PASSAGE PLANNING & SOLAS V

Before you start to navigate you need to plan: where you are going, how to get there and what factors may influence the plan. To most people this is commonsense, but now it is also the law; see Regulation 34 in chapter V of the International Convention for Safety of Life at Sea (SOLAS).

Regulation 34 **Safe Navigation and avoidance of dangerous situations** is actually quite short and bland. The MCA have provided extra guidance for small craft skippers at www.mcga.gov.uk.

Legally all voyages/passages by any vessel that goes to sea must be pre-planned. 'Going to sea' is defined as proceeding beyond sheltered waters. Even in very familiar waters every passage, however short, must be pre-planned, but for small craft the degree of planning may be less than for big ships.

The passage plan need not be in writing – which makes it hard to consult. However a written plan, in the event of legal action, is clear proof that planning has been done. A checklist, which when completed forms the passage plan, is therefore included on the previous page; it may be photocopied and enlarged to suit individual needs.

The MCA states that Regulation 34 does not herald a regime of pre-departure or spot checks on small craft. But obviously it might apply to an incident or accident involving a pleasure craft where it can be proved that the skipper did not carry out any form of passage planning; in which case the MCA would have clear authority to take action under the Merchant Shipping Act. For small craft skippers the emphasis on passage planning has shifted from good practice to a legal requirement.

SOLAS V, Regulation 34 (as paraphrased)

All passage plans, however short, should consider or better still answer the following questions:

- **Limitations of the vessel:** Is your craft suitable for the intended passage? Is proper safety equipment and enough fuel, water and stores onboard?
- **Crew:** Is the crew sufficiently experienced and physically capable? Cold, tiredness and seasickness can soon render crew incapable of performing their tasks properly, thus overburdening the skipper both physically and mentally.
- **Navigational dangers:** Are you aware of navigational dangers which may affect the passage? If not, check up-to-date charts, pilot books and the current PBO Almanac.
- **Tides:** Do you know times/heights of HW & LW at departure, destination and alternate ports? Are you aware of tidal streams and races expected on passage? Does your passage plan make best use of all tidal data?
- **Weather:** Before leaving, is the forecast suitable for the likely duration of the passage? Whilst at sea what updates can be obtained for destination and alternate?
- **Contingency plan:** Have you an alternative plan to cope with weather deterioration, gear failure, accident or injury? Which ports of refuge or bolt-holes are available?
- **GPS**: Do not become over-reliant on it. It *can* fail, usually at the most awkward moment. Can you navigate safely without it? Do you have a back-up set?
- **Information ashore:** Does someone ashore know your plans and what to do should he/she become concerned? If you get into difficulties the CG Voluntary Identification Scheme (CG66) helps the Coastguard to help you more quickly. It is easy to join – and free.

Passage planning checklist

Before reaching the checklist stage, much thought and study must go into drafting the plan. Any plan for any project goes through some or all of the following phases:

- Deciding the aim – not always obvious.
- Gathering the facts – time consuming but essential.
- Assessing the information now available.
- Formulating the plan. Think laterally.

A checklist ensures that the plan has been methodically prepared and minimises the risk of errors or omissions. Use a checklist in which the user must actively tick off items and/or insert data into boxes – rather than passively glancing at a screed and saying 'Yes, done all that'. That may well not be the case.

The following notes amplify some of the checklist items:

- Tidal streams around headlands tend to form gates, especially on a coastal passage. Note when the tides are fair or foul and the times of slack water.
- Times of entry/exit at a harbour may be affected by bars, sills and locks.
- A detailed pilotage plan/sketch for any unfamiliar harbour always helps.
- Involve your crew with passage plans.

DISTANCES (M) ACROSS THE ENGLISH CHANNEL

ENGLAND / FRANCE/CI	Longships	Falmouth	Fowey	Plymouth bkwtr	Salcombe	Dartmouth	Torbay	Weymouth	Poole Hbr Ent	Needles Lt Ho	Nab Tower	Littlehampton	Shoreham	Brighton	Newhaven	Eastbourne	Folkestone	Dover
Le Conquet	112	112	123	125	125	137	144	172	188	194	212	230	240	245	249	261	295	301
L'Aberwrac'h	102	97	106	107	105	117	124	153	168	174	192	211	219	224	228	239	275	280
Roscoff	110	97	101	97	91	100	107	130	144	149	165	184	193	197	200	211	246	252
Trébeurden	120	105	106	102	94	102	109	129	142	147	164	181	190	194	197	208	244	249
Tréguier	132	112	110	101	94	98	102	116	128	132	147	162	170	174	177	188	224	229
Lézardrieux	142	121	118	107	94	100	105	115	126	130	140	157	165	169	172	184	219	224
St Q.-Portrieux	159	137	135	124	111	115	121	127	135	135	146	162	171	174	178	189	225	230
St Malo	172	149	146	133	118	120	124	125	130	130	143	157	166	170	173	184	220	225
St Helier	155	130	123	108	93	95	100	99	104	104	115	132	140	144	147	158	194	199
St Peter Port	139	113	104	89	73	70	75	71	79	83	97	112	120	124	127	135	174	179
Braye (Alderney)	146	116	106	89	72	69	71	54	60	62	73	91	100	103	106	114	153	159
Cherbourg	168	138	125	107	92	87	88	66	64	63	68	81	90	92	96	102	140	145
St Vaast	194	164	150	132	116	111	112	83	76	72	71	80	87	88	90	96	132	138
Ouistreham	229	198	185	167	151	146	147	117	107	100	86	91	92	91	90	92	125	130
Deauville	236	205	192	174	158	153	154	122	111	104	88	89	88	87	85	87	120	125
Le Havre	231	200	187	169	153	148	148	118	105	97	82	82	83	82	79	80	115	120
Fécamp	242	212	197	179	163	157	157	120	105	96	75	71	68	65	62	62	90	95
Dieppe	268	237	222	204	188	180	180	142	125	117	91	80	75	70	64	63	70	75
Boulogne	290	258	242	224	208	198	195	153	135	127	97	81	71	66	59	47	28	25
Calais	305	272	257	239	223	213	210	168	150	141	111	96	86	81	74	62	26	22

NOTES

1. This Table applies to Areas 1–3, and 14–16, each of which also contains its own internal Distance Table. Approximate distances in nautical miles are by the most direct route, while avoiding dangers and allowing for Traffic Separation Schemes.

2. For ports within the Solent, add the appropriate distances given in Area 2 to those shown above under either Needles Light house or Nab Tower.

AREA 1 South West England - *Isles of Scilly to Anvil Point*

SELECTED LIGHTS, BUOYS & WAYPOINTS

Positions are referenced to WGS84

ISLES OF SCILLY

Bishop Rock ☆ Fl (2) 15s 44m **24M**; part obsc 204°-211°, obsc 211°-233° and 236°-259°; Gy ○ twr with helo platform; *Horn Mo (N) 90s;* ***Racon T, 18M, 254°-215°;*** 49°52'·37N 06°26'·74W.

Peninnis Hd ☆ Fl 20s 36m **17M**; 231°-117° but partially obsc 048°-083° within 5M; W ○ twr on B frame, B cupola; 49°54'·28N 06°18'·22W.

Spanish Ledge ⟨ Q (3) 10s; *Bell;* 49°53'·94N 06°18'·86W.

N Bartholomew ↝ Fl R 5s; 49°54'·49N 06°19'·99W.

Bacon Ledge ↝ Fl (4) R 5s; 49°55'·22N 06°19'·27W.

Little Rag Ledge ↥ Fl (2) R 5s; 49°56'·43N 06°20'·43W.

Bryher, Bar Quay ↥ Q(3) 10s, 49°57'·35N 06°20'·85W.

Spencers Ledge ⟨ Q (6) + L Fl 15s; 49°54'·78N 06°22'·06W.

St Agnes, Porth Conger quay ↯ QG, 49°53'·76N 06°20'·40W.

Steeple Rock ⟨ Q (9) 15s; 49°55'·46N 06°24'·24W.

Round Island ☆ Fl 10s 55m **18M**, also shown in reduced vis; 021°-288°; *Horn (4) 60s;* ***Racon M, 10M;*** 49°58'·74N 06°19'·40W.

St Martin's, Higher Town quay ↯ Fl R 5s, 49°57'·45N 06°16'·84W.

SCILLY TO LAND'S END

Seven Stones ↝ Fl (3) 30s 12m **25M**; H24; *Horn (3) 60s;* ***Racon O, 15M;*** 50°03'·62N 06°04'·34W.

Wolf Rock ☆ Fl 15s 34m **16M**; H24; *Horn 30s;* ***Racon T, 10M;*** 49°56'·72N 05°48'·57W.

Longships ☆ Fl (2) WR 10s 35m **W16M**, R11M; 189°-R-327°-W-189°; Gy ○ twr with helicopter platform; *Horn 10s;* 50°04'·01N 05°44'·81W.

Runnel Stone ⟨ Q (6) + L Fl 15s; *Whis;* 50°01'·19N 05°40'·36W.

Tater-du ☆ Fl (3) 15s 34m **20M**; 241°-074°; W ○ twr 50°03'·14N 05°34'·68W. Same twr FR 31m 13M, 060°-074° over Runnel Stone and in places 074°-077° (3°) within 4M; *Horn (2) 30s.*

NEWLYN and PENZANCE

S Pier ↯ Fl 5s 10m 9M; W ○ twr; 253°-336°; 50°06'·19N 05°32'·57W.

N Pier ↯ F WG 4m 2M; 238°-G-248°, W over hbr; 50°06'·19N 05°32'·62W.

Penzance S Pier ↯ Fl WR 5s 11m **W17M**, R12M; 159°-R-268°-W-344·5°-R-shore;   50°07'·07N 05°31'·68W.

Lizard ☆ Fl 3s 70m **26M**; H24; 250°-120°, partly visible 235°-250°; W 8-sided twr; *Horn 30s;* 49°57'·61N 05°12'·13W.

FALMOUTH

St Anthony Head ☆ Iso WR 15s 22m, **W16M,** R14M, H24; 295°-W-004°-R-022°-W-172°; W 8-sided twr; *Horn 30s;* 50°08'·47N 05°00'·96W.

Black Rock ⟨ Q (3) 10s; 50°08'·68N 05°01'·74W.

The Governor ⟨ VQ (3) 5s; 50°09'·15N 05°02'·40W.

MEVAGISSEY

Victoria Pier ↯ Fl (2) 10s 9m 12M; *Dia 30s;* 50°16'·15N 04°46'·93W.

FOWEY

Fowey ↯ L Fl WR 5s 28m W11M, R9M; 284°-R-295°-W-028°-R-054°; 50°19'·62N 04°38'·84W.

Whitehouse Pt ↯ Iso WRG 3s 11m W11M, R/G8M; 017°-G-022°- W-032°-R-037°; R col; 50°19'·98N 04°38'·24W.

POLPERRO

Spy House Pt ↯ Iso WR 6s 30m 7M; W288°-060°, R060°-288°; 50°19'·81N 04°30'·70W.

LOOE AND EDDYSTONE

Banjo Pier ☆ Oc WR 3s 8m **W15M**, R12M; 207°-R267°- W-313°-R-332°; 50°21'·05N 04°27'·06W.

Eddystone ☆ Fl (2) 10s 41m **17M**; Gy twr, helicopter platform; *Horn 30s;* ***Racon T, 10M,*** 50°10'·85N 04°15'·94W. Same twr, Iso R 10s 28m 8M; 110·5°-130·5° over Hand Deeps.

PLYMOUTH

Draystone ↝ Fl (2) R 5s; 50°18'·85N 04°11'·07W.

Plymouth bkwtr W ↯ Fl WR 10s 19m W12M, R9M; 262°-W-208°-R-262°; W ○ twr. Same twr, Iso 4s 12m 10M; vis 033°-037°; *Horn 15s;* 50°20'·07N 04°09'·53W.

The Bridge Channel. No 1, ↥ QG 4m; 50°21'·03N 04°09'·53W. No 2, ↥ QR 4m.

Bkwtr E ↥ L Fl WR 10s 9m W8M, R6M; 190°-R-353°-W-001°-R-018°-W-190°; 50°20'·01N 04°08'·25W.

Ldg lts 349°. Front, Mallard Shoal ↥ Q WRG 5m W10M, R/G3M; 233°-G-043°- R-067°-G-087°-W-099°-R-108°; 50°21'·60N 04°08'·33W. Rear, 396m from front, Hoe ↥ Oc G 1·3s 11m 3M; 310°-040°; W ▽, Or bands.

QAB (Queen Anne's Battery) ldg lts ↯ 048·5°. Front, FR; Or/W bcn; 50°21'·84N 04°07'·84W. Rear, Dir Oc WRG 7.5s 14m 3M; 038°-G-047·2°-W-049·7°-R-060·5°.

Sutton Hbr lock; IPTS; 50°21'·98N 04°07'·96W.

PYH (Plymouth Yacht Haven), outer bkwtr, E end, 2 FG (vert); 50°21'·59N 04°07'·15W.

Mayflower marina, outer bkwtr, E end, 2 FR (vert).

RIVER YEALM

The Sand Bar ⚓ Fl R 5s; 50°18'·59N 04°04'·12W.

SALCOMBE

Sandhill Pt Dir ⚡ 000°: Fl WRG 2s 27m W10M, R/G7M; 182·5°-G-357·5°-W-002·5°-R-182·5°; R/W ◇ on W mast; 50°13'·77N 03°46'·67W. 000° on with Pound Stone R/W ⎐, 230m S.

Start Pt ☆ Fl (3) 10s 62m **25M**; 184°-068°. Same twr: FR 55m 12M; 210°-255° over Skerries Bank; *Horn 60s;* 50°13'·33N 03°38'·54W.

DARTMOUTH

Kingswear Dir ⚡ 328°: Iso WRG 3s 9m 8M; 318°-G-325°-W-331°-R-340°; W ○ twr; 50°20'·81N 03°34'·10W.

Mewstone ⎇ VQ (6) + L Fl 10s; 50°19'·92N 03°31'·89W.

West Rock ⎇ Q (6) + L Fl 15s; 50°19'·86N 03°32'·47W.

Homestone ⚓ QR; 50°19'·61N 03°33'·55W.

Castle Ledge ⚑ Fl G 5s; 50°19'·99N 03°33'·12W.

BRIXHAM

Berry Head ☆ Fl (2) 15s 58m 14M; vis 100°-023°; W twr; 50°23'·97N 03°29'·01W. R lts on radio mast 5·7M NW, inland of Paignton.

Victoria bkwtr ⚡ Oc R 15s 9m 6M; W twr; 50°24'·33N 03°30'·78W.

Fairway Dir ⚡ 159°: Iso WRG 5s 4m 6M; 145°-G-157°- W-161°-R-173°; 50°23'·83N 03°30'·57W.

TORQUAY

⚑ QG (May-Sep); 50°27'·42N 03°31'·80W.

TEIGNMOUTH

Outfall ⚓ Fl Y 5, 288°/1·3M to hbr ent.

Spratt Sand ⚑ Fl G 2s; 50°32'·39N 03°29'·77W.

The Point ⎐ Oc G 6s 3M & FG (vert); 50°32'·42N 03°30'·05W.

RIVER EXE

E Exe ⎇ Q (3) 10s; 50°36'·00N 03°22'·38W.

Ldg lts 305°. Front, Iso 2s 6m 7M, 50°36'·99N 03°25'·34W. Rear, Q 12m 7M, 57m from front.

No. 10 ⚓ Fl R 3s; 50°36'·73N 03°24'·77W.

No. 12 Warren Pt ⚓ 50°36'·91N 03°25'·40W.

Straight Pt ⚡ Fl R 10s 34m 7M; 246°-071°; 50°36'·49N 03°21'·76W.

LYME REGIS

Outfall ⎇ Q (6) + L Fl 15s; 50°43'·17N 02°55'·66W.

Ldg lts 284°: Front, Victoria Pier ⚡ Oc WR 8s 6m, W9M, R7M; 296°-R-116°-W-296°; 50°43'·19N 02°56'·17W. Rear, FG 8m 9M, 240m from front.

WEST BAY (BRIDPORT)

W pier root, Dir ⚡ F WRG 5m 4M; 165°-G-331°-W-341°-R-165°; 50°42'·62N 02°45'·89W.

W pier ⚡ Iso R 2s 5m 4M; 50°42'·51N 02°45'·83W.

E pier ⚡ Iso G 2s 5m 4M; 50°42'·53N 02°45'·80W.

PORTLAND

Portland Bill lt ho ⚡ Fl (4) 20s 43m **25M**. vis 221°-244° (gradual change from 1 Fl to 4 Fl); 244°-117° (shows 4 Fl); 117°-141° (gradual change from 4 Fl to 1 Fl). W ○ twr; *Dia 30s;* 50°30'·85N 02°27'·38W. Same twr, FR 19m 13M; 271°-291° over Shambles.

W Shambles ⎇ Q (9) 15s; *Bell;* 50°29'·78N 02°24'·40W.

E Shambles ⎇ Q (3) 10s; *Bell;* 50°30'·78N 02°20'·08W.

Portland hbr, outer bkwtr (N end) ⚡ QR 14m 5M; 013°-268°; 50°35'·11N 02°24'·87W.

NE Bkwtr (A Hd) ⚡ Fl 2·5s 22m **20M**; 50°35'·16N 02°25'·07W.

NE Bkwtr (B Hd) ⚡ Oc R 15s 11m 5M; 50°35'·65N 02°25'·88W.

WEYMOUTH TO ANVIL POINT

Weymouth ldg lts 239·6°: both FR 5/7m 7M; Front 50°36'·46N 02°26'·87W, R ♦ on W post; rear 17m from front, R ♦ on W mast.

N Pier hd ⚡ 2 FG (vert) 9m 6M; 50°36'·59N 02°26'·63W.

S Pier hd ⚡ Q 10m 9M; 50°36'·57N 02°26'·49W. IPTS 190m SW.

Lulworth Cove, E point 50°37'·00N 02°14'·78W.

Anvil Pt ☆ Fl 10s 45m **19M**; vis 237°-076° (H24); W ○ twr and dwelling; 50°35'·51N 01°57'·60W.

		1															
1	Longships	1															
2	Scilly (Crow Rock)	22	2														
3	Penzance	15	35	3													
4	Lizard Point	23	42	16	4												
5	Falmouth	39	60	32	16	5											
6	Mevagissey	52	69	46	28	17	6										
7	Fowey	57	76	49	34	22	7	7									
8	Looe	63	80	57	39	29	16	11	8								
9	Plymouth (bkwtr)	70	92	64	49	39	25	22	11	9							
10	R. Yealm (ent)	72	89	66	49	39	28	23	16	4	10						
11	Salcombe	81	102	74	59	50	40	36	29	22	17	11					
12	Start Point	86	103	80	63	55	45	40	33	24	22	7	12				
13	Dartmouth	95	116	88	72	63	54	48	42	35	31	14	9	13			
14	Torbay	101	118	96	78	70	62	55	50	39	38	24	15	11	14		
15	Exmouth	113	131	107	90	82	73	67	61	51	49	33	27	24	12	15	
16	Lyme Regis	126	144	120	104	96	86	81	74	63	62	48	41	35	30	21	16
17	Portland Bill	135	151	128	112	104	93	89	81	73	70	55	49	45	42	36	22	17

NAVAL EXERCISE AREAS: Isles of Scilly to Start Point

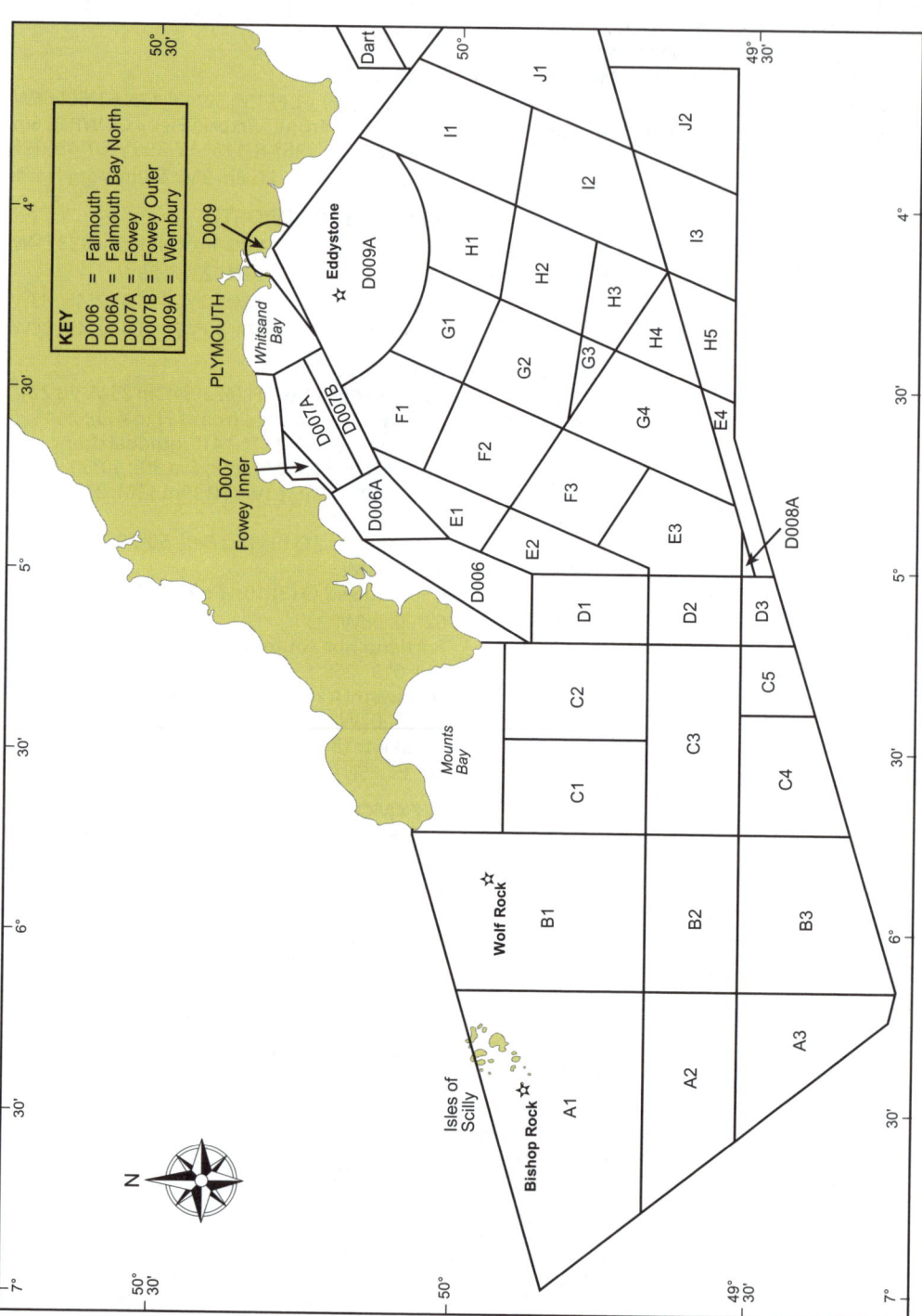

KEY

D006 = Falmouth
D006A = Falmouth Bay North
D007A = Fowey
D007B = Fowey Outer
D009A = Wembury

NAVAL EXERCISE AREAS: Berry Head to Selsey Bill

15

AREA 2 South Central England - *Anvil Point to Selsey Bill*

SELECTED LIGHTS, BUOYS & WAYPOINTS | Positions are referenced to WGS84

SWANAGE TO ISLE OF WIGHT

SWANAGE
Pier Hd ⚓ 2 FR (vert) 6m 3M; 50°36'·56N 01°56'·95W.
Peveril Ledge ≈ QR; 50°36'·41N 01°56'·10W.

POOLE HARBOUR AND APPROACHES
Poole Bar (No.1) ▲ QG; *Bell.*; 50°39·32N 01°55'·16W.

SWASH CHANNEL/EAST LOOE CHANNEL
South Hook ↓; 50°39'·70N 01°55'·20W.
No. 3 ▲ Fl G 3s; 50°39'·76N 01°55'·49W.
Training Bank ↓ 2 FR (vert); 50°39'·84N 01°55'·92W.
Channel (No. 8) ≈ Fl R 2s; 50°40'·45N 01°56'·26W.
Swash (No.9) ↓ Q (9) 15s; 50°40'·88N 01°56'·70W.
East Looe 1 ▲ Fl G 5s; 50°41'·09N 01°55'·82W.
East Looe 4 (Limit 10 knots) ≈ Fl R 2s; 50°41'·09N 01°56'·17W.

South Deep. Marked by lit and unlit Bns from ent South of Brownsea Castle to Furzey Is.

MIDDLE SHIP AND NORTH CHANNELS
Bell (No. 15) ↓ Q (6) + L Fl 15s; *Bell*; 50°41'·38N 01°57'·10W.
Marked by PHM and SHM Lt buoys.
Aunt Betty (No.22) ↓ Q (3)10s; 50°41'·96N 01°57'·39W.
Diver (No. 25) ↓ Q (9) 15s; 50°42'·28N 01°58'·34W.
Stakes (No. 29) ↓ Q (6) + L Fl 15s; 50°42'·43N 01°59'·01W.

WAREHAM CHANNEL
Wareham Chan initially m'kd by ▲'s and ≈'s and then by stakes.

WESTERN APPROACHES TO SOLENT

NEEDLES AND NORTH CHANNELS
Needles Fairway ↓ L Fl 10s; *Bell*; 50°38'·24N 01°38'·98W.
SW Shingles ↓Fl R 2·5s;50°38'·24N 01°38'·98W.
Bridge ↓ VQ (9) 10s; *Racon (T) 10M*; 50°39'·63N 01°36'·88W.

Needles 50°39'·73N 01°35'·50W; Oc (2) WRG 20s 24m **W17M**, R14M, R13M G14M; ○ Twr, R band and lantern; vis: shore-R-300°-W-083°-R (unintens)-212°-W-217°-G-224°. *Horn (2) 30s* H24. 01°33'·55W.
NE Shingles ↓ Q (3) 10s; 50°41'·96N 01°33'·41W.
Hurst Point ☆ 50°42'·48N 01°33'·03W; FL (4) WR 15s 23m W13M, R11M; W ○ Twr; vis:080°-W(unintens)-104°, 234°-W-244°-R-250°-W-053°.
Same structure, Iso WRG 4s 19m **W21M, R18M, G17M**; vis: 038·8°-G-040·8°-W-041·8°-R- 043·8°; By day W7M, R5M, G5M.
N Head ▲ Fl (3) G 10s; 50°42'·69N 01°35'·52W.

YARMOUTH/LYMINGTON
Sconce ↓ Q; *Bell*; 50°42'·53N 01°31'·43W.

Black Rock ▲ Fl G 5s; 50°42'·58N 01°30'·64W.
Y'mouth E F'wy ≈ Fl R 2s. 50°42'·64N 01°29'·88W.
Pier Head, centre, ⚓ 2 FR (vert) 2M; G col. High intensity FW (occas); 50°42'·51N 01°29'·97W.
Jack in the Basket ↓ Fl R 2s 9m; 50°44'·27N 01°30'·57W.
No. 1 ↓ Fl G 2s 2m 3M; G △ on pile; 50°44'·41N 01°30'·48W.
Lymington Bank ≈ Fl (2) R 5s. *Bell*; 50°43'·10N 01°30'·85W.
Solent Bank ≈ Fl (3) R 10s; 50°44'·23N 01°27'·37W.
Hamstead Ledge ▲ Fl (2) G 5s; 50°43'·87N 01°26'18W.
Newtown River ≈ Fl R 4s; 50°43'·75N 01°24'·91W.
W Lepe ≈ Fl R 5s; 50°45'·24N 01°24'·09W.
Salt Mead ▲ Fl (3) G 10s; 50°44'·51N 01°23'·04W.
Gurnard Ledge ▲Fl(4)G 15s; 50°45'·51N 01°20'·59W.
E Lepe ≈ Fl (2) R 5s; *Bell*; 50°45'·93N 01°21'·07W.
Lepe Spit ↓ Q (6) + L Fl 15s; 50°46'·78N 01°20'·64W.
Beaulieu Millenium Dir lt 334°. ⚓ Oc Q WRG 4s 13m W4M, R3M, G3M; vis: 321°-G-331°-W-337°-R-347°; 50°47'·12N 01°21'·90W.
NE Gurnard ▲ Fl (3) R 10s; 50°47'·06N 01°19'·42W.
W Bramble ↓ VQ (9) 10s; *Bell*; *Racon (T) 3M.*; 50°47'·20N 01°18'·65W.
W Knoll ▲ Fl Y 2·5s; 50°47'·43N 01°17'·84W.
Williams Ship'g ≈ (or) Fl Y 4s; 50°47'·11N 01°18'·08W.
S Bramble ▲ Fl G 2·5s; 50°46'·98N 01°17'·72W.

COWES
Gurnard ↓ Q; 50°46'·22N 01°18'·84W.
Prince Consort ↓ VQ; 50°46'·42N 01°17'·55W.
No. 1 ▲ Fl G 3s; 50°46'·07N 01°18'·03W.
No. 2 ≈ QR; 50°46'·07N 01°17'·87W.

SOUTHAMPTON WATER/RIVER HAMBLE
CALSHOT SPIT ⇌ Fl 5s 12m 11M; R hull, Lt Twr amidships; *Horn (2) 60s*; 50°48'·35N 01°17'·64W.
Calshot ↓ VQ; *Bell*; 50°48'·44N 01°17'·03W.
Black Jack ≈ Fl (2) R 4s; 50°49'·13N 01°18'·09W.
Hook ↓ QG; *Horn (1) 15s*; 50°49'·52N 01°18'·30W.
Bald Head ▲ 50°49'·90N 01°18'·25W.
Hamble Pt ↓ Q (6) + L Fl 15s; 50°50'·15N 01°18'·66W.
No. 1 ↓ QG 2m 2M; 50°50'·34N 01°18'·65W.
No. 2 ↓ Q (3) 10s 2m 2M; 50°50'·39N 01°18'·77W.
Greenland ▲ IQ G 10s; 50°51'·11N 01°20'·38W.
Weston Shelf ▲ Fl (3) G 15s; 50°52'·71N 01°23'·26W.
Hythe Pier Hd ⚓ 2 FR (vert) 12m 5M; 50°52'·49N 01°23'·61W.

SOUTHAMPTON/ITCHEN/TEST
Swinging Ground No. 1 ▲ Oc G 4s; 50°53'·00N 01°23'·44W.
Queen Elizabeth II Terminal, S end ⚓ 4 FG (vert) 16m 3M; 50°53'·00N 01°23'·71W.
Gymp ≈ QR; 50°53'·17N 01°24'·30W.

THE EAST SOLENT

NORTH CHANNEL/HILLHEAD
Hillhead ≈Fl R 2·5s; 50°48'·07N 01°16'·00W.
Hillhead ↓ Or Bn; 50°49'·06N 01°14'·78W.
E Bramble ↓ VQ (3) 5s; 50°47'·23N 01°13'·64W.

EASTERN SOLENT MARKS/WOOTTON
W Ryde Middle ↓ Q (9) 15s; 50°46'·48N 01°15'·79W.
Norris ≈ Fl (3) R 10s; 50°45'·97N 01°15'·51W.
N Ryde Middle ≈ Fl (4) R 20s; 50°46'·61N 01°14'·31W.
S Ryde Middle ▲ Fl G 5s; 50°46'·13N 01°14'·16W.
Peel Bank ≈ Fl (2) R 5s; 50°45'·49N 01°13'·35W.
SE Ryde Middle ↓ VQ (6)+L Fl 10s; 50°45'·93N 01°12'·10W.
NE Ryde Middle ≈ Fl (2) R 10s; 50°46'·21N 01°11'·88W.
Wootton Bn ↓ Q 1M; (NB); 50°44'·53N 01°12'·13W.
Mother Bank ≈ Fl R 3s; 50°45'·49N 01°11'·21W.
Browndown ▲ Fl G 15s; 50°46'·57N 01°10'·95W.

PORTSMOUTH AND APPROACHES
Horse Sand Ft ✠ Iso G 2s 21m 8M; 50°45'·01N 01°04'·34W.
Horse Sand ▲ Fl G 2·5s; 50°45'·53N 01°05'·27W.
Outer Spit ↓ Q (6) + L Fl 15s; 50°45'·58N 01°05'·50W.
Mary Rose ≈ Fl Y 5s; 50°45'·80N 01°06'·20W.
No. 1 Bar (NB) ▲ Fl (3) G 10s; 50°46'·77N 01°05'·81W.
No. 2 ≈ Fl (3) R 10s; 50°46'·69N 01°05'·97W.
No. 4 (NB) ≈ QR; 50°47'·01N 01°06'·36W.
BC Outer ↓ Oc R 15s; 50°47'·32N 01°06'·68W.
Fort Blockhouse ✠ Dir lt 320°; WRG 6m W13M, R5M, G5M; vis: 310°- Oc G-316°-Al WG(W phase incr with brg), 318·5°-Oc-321·5°-Al WR (R phase incr with brg), 324°-Oc R-330°. 2 FR (vert) 20m E; 50°47'·37N 01°06'·74W.
Ballast ↓ Fl R 2·5s; 50°47'·62N 01°06'·83W.

EASTERN APPROACHES TO THE SOLENT
Outer Nab 1 ↓ VQ (9) 10s; 50°38'·18N 00°56'·88W.
Outer Nab 2 ↓ VQ (3) 5s; 50°38'·43N 00°57'·70W.
Nab Tower ☆ 50°40'·08N 00°57'·15W; Fl 10s 27m **16M**, *Horn (2) 30s*; *Racon (T) 10M*.
N 2 ↓ Fl Y 2·5s. 6M; 50°41'·03N 00°56'·74W.
N 1 ↓ Fl Y (4)10s; 50°41'·26N 00°56'·52W.
N 7 ↓ Fl Y 2·5s; 50°42'·35N 00°57'·20W.
New Grounds ↓ VQ (3) 5s; 50°41'·84N 00°58'·49W.
Nab End ↓ Fl R 5s; *Whis*; 50°42'·63N 00°59'·49W.
Dean Tail ▲ Fl G 5s; 50°42'·99N 00°59'·17W.
Dean Tail S ↓ Q (6)+L Fl 10s; 50°43'·04N 00°59'·57W.
Dean Tail N ↓ Q; 50°43'·13N 00°59'·57W.
St Helens ≈ Fl (3) R 15s; 50°43'·36N 01°02'·41W.
Horse Elbow ▲QG; 50°44'·26N 01°03'·88W.
Cambrian Wreck ↓ 50°44'·43N 01°03'·43W.
Warner ↓ QR; *Whis*; 50°43'·87N 01°03'·99W.
W Princessa ↓ Q (9) 15s; 50°40'·16N 01°03'·65W.
Bembridge Ledge ↓ Q (3) 10s; 50°41'·15N 01°02'·81W
St Helen's Fort ☆ (IOW) Fl (3) 10s 16m 8M; large ○ stone structure; 50°42'·30N 01°05'·05W.

SE COAST OF THE ISLE OF WIGHT
St Catherine's Point ☆ 50°34'·54N 01°17'·87W; Fl 5s 41m **27M**; vis: 257°-117°; FR 35m **17M** (same Twr) vis: 099°-116°.
Ventnor Haven W Bwtr ✠ 2 FR (vert) 3M; 50°35'·50N 01°12'·30W.

LANGSTONE AND APPROACHES
Winner ↓; 50°45'·10N 01°00'·10W.
Langstone F'wy ↓ L Fl 10s; 50°46'·32N 01°01'·36W.

CHICHESTER ENTRANCE
West Pole ↓ Fl WR 5s W7M, R5M; vis: 321°-W-081°-R-321°; 50°45'·71N 00°56'·50W.
Chichester Bar ↓ Fl (2) R 10s 14m 2M; Tide gauge; 50°45'·92N 00°56'·46W.
Eastoke ↓ QR 2m 3M; 50°46'·66N 00°56'·16W.
West Winner ↓ QG; Tide gauge. 50°46'·88N 00°55'·98W.

		1	2	3	4	5	6	7	8	9	10	11	12	13	14	15	16	17	18
1	Portland Bill	**1**																	
2	Weymouth	8	**2**																
3	Swanage	22	22	**3**															
4	Poole Hbr ent	28	26	6	**4**														
5	Needles Lt Ho	35	34	14	14	**5**													
6	Lymington	42	40	20	24	6	**6**												
7	Yarmouth (IOW)	40	39	18	22	4	2	**7**											
8	Beaulieu R. ent	46	45	25	29	11	7	7	**8**										
9	Cowes	49	46	28	27	14	10	9	2	**9**									
10	Southampton	55	54	34	34	20	16	16	9	9	**10**								
11	R. Hamble (ent)	53	51	32	34	18	12	13	6	6	5	**11**							
12	Portsmouth	58	57	37	35	23	19	19	12	10	18	13	**12**						
13	Langstone Hbr	61	59	39	39	25	21	21	14	12	21	18	5	**13**					
14	Chichester Bar	63	62	42	42	28	23	24	17	15	23	18	8	5	**14**				
15	Bembridge	59	58	38	39	24	18	19	13	10	18	15	5	6	8	**15**			
16	Nab Tower	64	63	43	44	29	23	24	18	15	24	19	10	7	6	6	**16**		
17	St Catherine's Pt	45	44	25	25	12	19	21	27	15	36	29	20	20	19	17	15	**17**	
18	Littlehampton	79	79	60	61	46	44	45	38	36	45	42	31	28	25	28	22	35	**18**

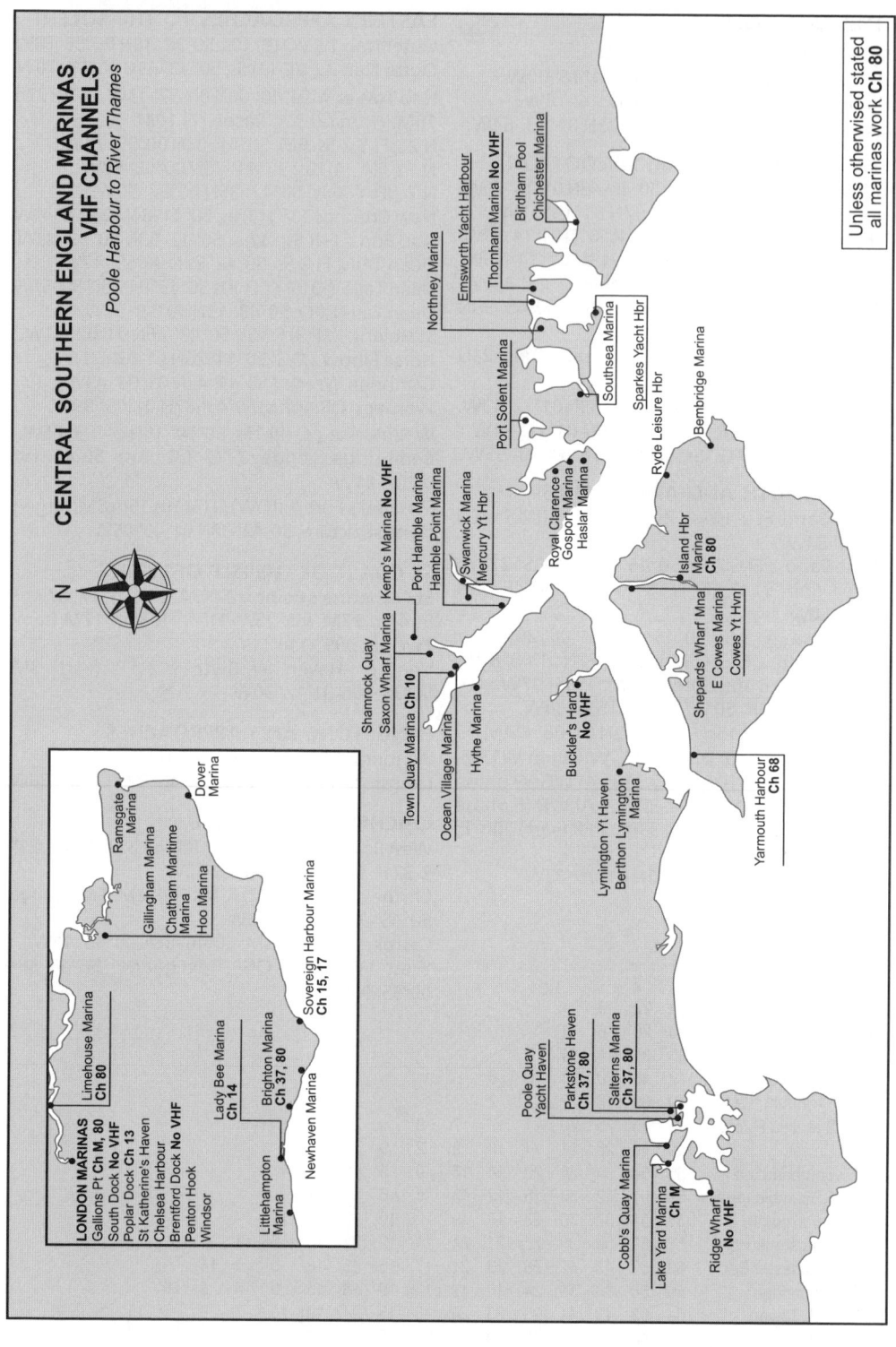

CENTRAL SOUTHERN ENGLAND MARINAS
VHF CHANNELS
Poole Harbour to River Thames

N

Unless otherwise stated all marinas work **Ch 80**

LONDON MARINAS
Gallions Pt **Ch M, 80**
South Dock **No VHF**
Poplar Dock **Ch 13**
St Katherine's Haven
Chelsea Harbour
Brentford Dock **No VHF**
Penton Hook
Windsor

Limehouse Marina **Ch 80**

Ramsgate Marina
Gillingham Marina
Chatham Maritime Marina
Hoo Marina
Dover Marina

Lady Bee Marina **Ch 14**

Brighton Marina **Ch 37, 80**

Sovereign Harbour Marina **Ch 15, 17**

Littlehampton Marina

Newhaven Marina

Poole Quay Yacht Haven

Parkstone Haven **Ch 37, 80**

Salterns Marina **Ch 37, 80**

Cobb's Quay Marina

Lake Yard Marina **Ch M**

Ridge Wharf **No VHF**

Shamrock Quay
Saxon Wharf Marina

Kemp's Marina **No VHF**

Port Hamble Marina
Hamble Point Marina
Swanwick Marina
Mercury Yt Hbr

Town Quay Marina **Ch 10**

Ocean Village Marina

Hythe Marina

Buckler's Hard **No VHF**

Lymington Yt Haven
Berthon Lymington Marina

Yarmouth Harbour **Ch 68**

Northney Marina
Emsworth Yacht Harbour
Thornham Marina **No VHF**
Birdham Pool
Chichester Marina

Southsea Marina

Sparkes Yacht Hbr

Bembridge Marina

Port Solent Marina

Royal Clarence
Gosport Marina
Haslar Marina

Ryde Leisure Hbr

Island Hbr Marina **Ch 80**

Shepards Wharf Mna
E Cowes Marina
Cowes Yt Hvn

18

SELECTED LIGHTS, BUOYS & WAYPOINTS | Positions are referenced to WGS84

SELSEY BILL TO NORTH FORELAND
SELSEY BILL AND THE OWERS
S Pullar ↙ VQ (6) + L Fl 10s; 50°38'·84N 00°49'·29W.
Boulder ⚓ Fl G 2·5s; 50°41'·56N 00°49'·09W.
Street ↙ QR; 50°41'·69N 00°48'·89W.
Mixon ↙ Fl R 5s; 50°42'·35N 00°46'·21W.
Owers ↙ Q (6) + L Fl 15s; *Whis*; *Racon (O) 10M.*; 50°38'·63N 00°41'·19W.
E'Boro Hd ↙ Q (3) 10s *Bell;* 50°41'·54N 00°39'·09W

LITTLEHAMPTON/SHOREHAM
Littlehampton W Pier Hd ↙QR 7m 6M; 50°47'·88N 00°32'·46W.
Shoreham E Bkwtr Hd ⚐ Fl G 5s 8M; *Siren 120s;* 50°49'·54N 00°14'·80W.

BRIGHTON MARINA
W Bkwtr Hd ⚐ QR 10m 7M; W ○ structure, R bands; *Horn (2) 30s;* 50°48'·50N 00°06'·38W.
E Bkwtr Hd ⚐ QG 8m 7M and Fl (4) WR 20s 16m W10M, R8M; W pillar, G bands; vis: 260°-R- 295°-W-100°; 50°48'·47N 00°06'·37W.

NEWHAVEN TO DUNGENESS
Newhaven Bkwtr Hd ⚐ Oc (2) 10s 17m 12M; 50°46'·56N 00°03'·50E.
GREENWICH ⚏ 50°24'·54N 00°00'·10E; Fl 5s 12m **15M**; Riding lt FW; R hull; *Racon (M) 10M*; *Horn 30s.*
Beachy Head ☆ 50°44'·03N 00°14'·49E; Fl (2) 20s 31m **20M**; W round twr, R band and lantern; vis: 248°-101°; (H24); *Horn 30s.*
Royal Sovereign ☆ Fl 20s 28m 12M; W ○ twr, R band on W cabin on col; *Horn (2) 30s;* 50°43'·45N 00°26'·09E.

SOVEREIGN HBR/RYE
Sovereign Hr Marina ⚐ Fl (3) 15s 12m 7M.; 50°47'·24N 00°19'·83E.
Rye Fairway , L Fl 10s; 50°54'·04N 00°48'·04E.

DUNGENESS - DOVER STRAIT
Dungeness ☆ 50°54'·81N 00°58'·56E; Fl 10s 40m **21M**; B ○ twr, W bands and lantern, floodlit; Part obsc 078°-shore; (H24). F RG 37m 10M (same twr); vis: 057°-R-073°-G-078°-196°-R-216°; *Horn (3) 60s;* FR Lts shown between 2·4M and 5·2M WNW when firing taking place. QR on radio mast 1·2M NW.
Folkestone Bkwtr Hd ⚐ 51°04'·56N 01°11'·69E; Fl (2) 10s 14m **22M**; *Dia (4) 60s.* In fog Fl 2s; vis: 246°-306°, intens 271·5°-280·5°.
VARNE ⚏ 51°01'·29N 01°23'·90E; Fl R 20s12m **19M**; *Racon (T)10M;* Horn 30s.

DOVER TO NORTH FORELAND
Dover Admiralty Pier Extension Hd ⚐ 51°06'·69N 01°19'·66E; Fl 7·5s 21m **20M**; W twr; vis: 096°-090°, obsc in The Downs by S Foreland inshore of 226°; *Horn 10s;* Int Port Tfc sigs.
Knuckle ☆ 51°07'·04N 01°20'·49E; Fl (4) WR 10s 15m **W15M**, R13M; W twr; vis: 059°-R-239°-W-059°.
SW Goodwin ↙ Q (6) + L Fl 15s; 51°07'·97N 01°28'·49E.
E GOODWIN ⚏ 51°13'·26N 01°36'·37E; Fl 15s 12m **23M**; R hull with lt twr amidships; *Racon (T) 10M;* Horn 30s.
NE Goodwin ↙ Q (3) 10s; *Racon (M) 10M.* 51°20'·31N 01°34'·16E.
Goodwin Fork ↙ Q (6) + L Fl 15s; *Bell;* 51°14'·33N 01°26'·86E.
NW Goodwin ↙ Q (9) 15s; *Bell;* 51°16'·57N 01°28'·57E.
Gull Stream ⚐ QR; 51°18'·26N 01°29'·69E.

RAMSGATE/BROADSTAIRS
RA ↙ Q(6) + L Fl 15s; 51°19'·60N 01°30'·13E.
E Brake ⚐ Fl R 5s; 51°19'·47N 01°29'·20E.
Broadstairs Knoll ⚐ Fl R 2·5s; 51°20'·88N 01°29'·48E.
North Foreland ☆ 51°22'·49N 01°26'·70E; Fl (5) WR 20s 57m **W19M, R16M, R15M**; W 8-sided twr; vis: shore-W-150°-R(**16M**)-181°-R(**15M**)-200°-W-011°; H24.

1	Nab Tower	1															
2	Boulder Lt Buoy	5	2														
3	Owers Lt Buoy	11	8	3													
4	Littlehampton	19	13	12	4												
5	Shoreham	32	24	21	13	5											
6	Brighton	35	28	24	17	5	6										
7	Newhaven	40	34	29	24	12	7	7									
8	Beachy Head Lt	46	41	36	30	20	14	8	8								
9	Eastbourne	51	45	40	34	24	19	12	7	9							
10	Rye	72	67	62	56	46	41	34	25	23	10						
11	Dungeness Lt	76	71	66	60	50	44	38	30	26	9	11					
12	Folkestone	92	84	81	76	65	60	53	43	40	23	13	12				
13	Dover	97	89	86	81	70	65	58	48	45	28	18	5	13			
14	Ramsgate	112	104	101	96	85	80	73	63	60	43	33	20	15	14		
15	N Foreland Lt	115	107	104	99	88	83	76	66	63	46	36	23	18	3	15	
16	Sheerness	146	139	135	132	119	114	107	97	96	79	67	54	49	34	31	16
17	London Bridge	188	184	177	177	161	156	149	139	141	124	109	96	91	76	73	45	17

AREA 4 East England - *North Foreland to Berwick-upon-Tweed*

SELECTED LIGHTS, BUOYS & WAYPOINTS | Positions are referenced to WGS84

THAMES ESTUARY – SOUTHERN

(Direction of buoyage generally East to West)

IMPORTANT NOTE. Regular changes are made to Thames Estuary buoyage. Check Notices to Mariners for the latest information.

OUTER APPROACHES

Foxtrot 3 ⌐ 51°23'·85N 02°00'·51E; Fl 10s 12m **15M**; *Racon (T) 10M*; Horn 10s.
Drill Stone ⌊ Q (3) 10s ; 51°25'·88N 01°42'·89E.
NE Spit ⌊ VQ (3) 5s; 51°27'·93N 01°29'·89E.

N KENT COAST/THE SWALE

East Margate ⌐ Fl R 2·5s; 51°27'·03N 01°26'·40E.
Foreness Pt O'fall ⌊ Fl R 5s; 51°24'·61N 01°26'·02E.
SE Margate ⌊ Q (3) 10s; 51°24'·05N 01°20'·40E.
Hook Spit ⌃ QG; 51°24'·08N 01°12'·26E.
Spaniard ⌊ Q (3) 10s; 51°26'·23N 01°04'·00E.
Spile ⌃ Fl G 2·5s; 51°26'·43N 00°55'·70E.
Whitstable Street ⌊ Q; 51°23'·85N 01°01'·59E.
Pollard Spit ⌐ QR; 51°22'·98N 00° 58'·57E.
Queenboro Spit ⌊ Q (3) 10s; 51°25'·81N 00°43'·93E.

PRINCES CHANNEL /MEDWAY/SEA REACH

Outer Tongue ⌊ L Fl 10s; *Racon (T) 10M*; *Whis*; 51°30'·73N 01°26'·40E.
Princes Appr ⌊ Mo (A) 10s; 51°28'·32N 01°23'·75E.
E Redsand ⌐ Fl (2) R 5s; 51°29'·41N 01°04'·05E.
Sea Reach 1 ⌊ Fl Y 2·5s; *Racon (T) 10M*; 51°29'·45N 00°52'·57E.
Medway ⌊ Mo (A) 6s; 51°28'·83N 00°52'·81E.

FOULGER'S - FISHERMAN'S GATS

Long Sand Inner ⌐ Mo 'A' 15s; 51°38'·80N 01°25'·60E.
Long Sand Outer ⌐ L Fl 10s; 51°36'·00N 01°26'·30E.
Outer Fisherman ⌊ Q (3) 10s; 51°33'·89N 01°25'·01E.
Inner Fisherman ⌐ Q R; 51°36'·07N 01°19'·87E.

THAMES ESTUARY – NORTHERN

KENTISH KNOCK

Kentish Knock ⌊ Q (3) 10s; *Whis*; 51°38'·53N 01°40·39E.
S Knock ⌊ Q (6) + L Fl 15s; *Bell*; 51°34'·13N 01°34'·29E.

BLACK DEEP

No. 9 ⌊ Q (6) + L Fl 15s; 51°35'·13N 01°15'·09E.
No. 2 ⌐ Fl (4) R 15s; 51°45'·63N 01°32'·20E.
Sunk Hd Tr ⌊ Q; *Whis*; 51°46'·63N 01°30'·51E.
Black Deep ⌐ QR. 51°47'·50N 01°35'·64E.
Long Sand Hd ⌊ VQ; *Bell*; 51°47'·90N 01°39'·42E.

BARROW DEEP

SW Barrow ⌊ Q(6) + L Fl 15s; *Bell*; 51°32'·29N 01°00'·31E.
Barrow No. 9 ⌊ VQ (3) 5s; 51°35'·34N 01°10'·30E.

Barrow No. 5 ⌃ Fl G 10s; 51°40'·03N 01°16'·20E.
Barrow No. 3 ⌊ Q (3) 10s; *Racon (M)10M*; 51°42'·02N 01°20'·24E.

WEST SWIN AND MIDDLE DEEP

Blacktail Spit ⌃ Fl (3) G 10s; 51°31'·47N 00°56'·74E.
Maplin ⌊ Q (3) 10s; *Bell*; 51°34'·03N 01°02'·30E.
W Swin ⌐ QR; 51°33'·40N 01°01'·97E.
Maplin Edge ⌃ 51°35'·33N 01°03'·64E.
Maplin Bank ⌐ Fl (3) R 10s; 51°35'·50N 01°04'·70E.

EAST SWIN (KING'S) CHANNEL

NE Maplin ⌃ Fl G 5s; *Bell*; 51°37'·43N 01°04'·90E.
S Whitaker ⌃ Fl (2) G 10s; 51°40'·23N 01°09'·05E.
W Sunk ⌊ Q (9) 15s; 51°44'·33N 01°25'·80E.
Gunfleet Spit ⌊ Q (6) + L Fl 15s; *Bell*; 51°45'·33N 01°21'·70E.
Gunfleet Old Lt Ho 51°46'·09N 01°20'·39E.

WHITAKER CHANNEL AND RIVER CROUCH

Whitaker ⌊ Q (3) 10s; *Bell*; 51°41'·43N 01°10'·51E.
Swin Spitway ⌊ Iso 10s; *Bell;* 51°41'·95N 01°08'·35E.
Whitaker ⌊ 51°39'·64N 01°06'·16E.
Ridge ⌐ Fl R 10s; 51°40'·13N 01°04'·87E.
Sunken Buxey ⌊ Q; 51°39'·54N 01°00'·59E.
Outer Crouch ⌊ Q(6)+LFl15s; 51°38'·38N 00°58'·48E.

GOLDMER GAT/WALLET/COLNE BAR

NE Gunfleet ⌊ Q (3) 10s; 51°49'·93N 01°27'·79E.
Wallet No. 2 ⌐ Fl R 5s; 51°48'·88N 01°22'·99E.
Wallet No. 4 ⌐ Fl (4) R 10s; 51°46'·53N 01°17'·23E.
Wallet Spitway ⌐ L Fl 10s; *Bell*; 51°42'·86N 01°07'·30E.
Knoll ⌊ Q; 51°43'·88N 01°05'·07E.
N Eagle ⌊ Q; 51°44'·71N 01°04'·32E.
NW Knoll ⌐ Fl (2) R 5s; 51°44'·35N 01°02'·17E.
Colne Bar ⌃ Fl (2) G 5s; 51°44'·61N 01°02'·57E.
Bench Head ⌃ Fl (3) G 10s; 51°44'·69N 01°01'·10E.
Inner Bench Hd ⌐ Fl (2) R 5s; 51°45'·96N 01°01'·74E.
Brightlingsea Spit ⌊ Q (6) + L Fl 15s; 51°48'·08N 01°00'·70E.

RIVER BLACKWATER/WALTON BACKWATERS

The Nass ⌊ VQ (3) 5s 6m 2M; 51°45'·83N 00°54'·83E.
Thirslet ⌃ Fl (3) G 10s; 51°43'·73N 00°50'·39E. 00°57'·10E.
Naze Tower; 51°51'·87N 01°17'·29E.
Pye End ⌐ L Fl 10s; 51°55'·03N 01°17'·90E.
Crab Knoll No. 3 ⌃ Fl G 5s; 51°54'·41N 01°16'·41E.
Island Point ⌊ Q; 51°53'·36N 01°15'·36E.

HARWICH APPROACHES

(Direction of buoyage North to South)

MEDUSA CHAN/CORK SAND/ROUGHS

Medusa ⌃ Fl G 5s; 51°51'·23N 01°20'·35E.
Stone Banks ⌐ FlR 5s; 51°53'·19N 01°19'·23E.
S Cork ⌊ Q (6) + L Fl 15s; 51°51'·33N 01°24'·09E.

Roughs Tr SE ⌐ Q (3) 10s; 51°53'·64N 01°28'·94E.
Cork Sand Yacht Bn ⌐ VQ ; 51°55'·21N 01°25'·20E.

HARWICH CHANNEL

SUNK ⌐ Fl (2) 20s 12m **16M**; R hull with lt twr;
Racon (T); *Horn (2) 60s*; 51°51'·03N 01°34'·89E.
S Shipwash ⌐⌐ 2 By(s) Q (6) + L Fl 15s; 51°52'·71N
01°33'·97E.
Outer Tidal Bn ⌐ Mo (U) 15s 2m 3M; 51°52'·85N
01°32'·34E.
SW Shipwash ⌐ Q (9)15s; 51°54'·75N 01°34'·21E.
Haven ⌐ Mo (A) 5s; 51°55'·76N 01°35'·56E.
HA ⌐ Iso 5s; 51°56'·75N 01°30'·66E.
Harwich Chan No. 1 ⌐ Fl Y 2·5s; *Racon (T)10M*;
51°56'·13N 01°27'·06E.
S Bawdsey ⌐ Q (6) + L Fl 15s; *Whis*; 51°57'·23N
01°30'·22E.
Platters ⌐ Q (6) + L Fl 15s; 51°55'·64N 01°20'·97E.
Rolling Ground ⌐ QG; 51°55'·55N 01°19'·75E.
Inner Ridge ⌐ QR; 51°55'·38N 01°20'·20E.
Landguard ⌐ Q; 51°55'·45N 01°18'·84E.

HARWICH TO ORFORDNESS

OFFSHORE MARKS

E Shipwash ⌐ VQ (3) 5s; 51°57'·08N 01°37'·89E.
N Shipwash ⌐ Q 7M; *Racon (M) 10M*; *Bell*;
52°01'·73N 01°38'·27E.
S Galloper ⌐ Q (6) L Fl 15s; *Racon (T)10M*; *Whis*.
51°43'·98N 01°56'·39E.
Outer Gabbard ⌐ Q (3) 10s; *Racon (O)10M*; *Whis*;
51°57'·83N 02°04'·19E.

DEBEN/ORE/SUFFOLK COAST

Woodbridge Haven ⌐ Mo(A)15s; 51°58'·20N
01°23'·85E.
Cutler ⌐ QG; 51°58'·51N 01°27'·48E.
SW Whiting ⌐ Q (6) + L Fl 10s; 52°00'·96N 01°30'·69E.
Orford Haven ⌐ L Fl 10s; *Bell*. 52°01'·62N 01°28'·00E.
NE Whiting ⌐ Q (3) 10s; 52°03'·61N 01°33'·32E.
NE Bawdsey ⌐ Fl G 10s; 52°01'·73N 01°36'·09E.

ORFORDNESS TO GT YARMOUTH

(Direction of buoyage is South to North)
Orford Ness ☆ 52°05'·03N 01°34'·46E; Fl 5s 28m
20M; W ○ twr, R bands. F WRG 14m **W17M**,
R13M, **G15M** (same twr). vis: R shore-210°, 038°-R-
047°-G-shore; *Racon (T) 18M*. FR 13m 12M vis:
026°- 038° over Whiting Bank.

Aldeburgh Ridge ⌐ QR; 52°06'·72N 01°36'·95E.
Southwold ☆ 52°19'·63N 01°40'·89E; Fl (4) WR
20s 37m **W16M, R12M**, R14M; vis 204°-R (intens)-
215°-W-001°.

LOWESTOFT/GT YARMOUTH APPROACHES

E Barnard ⌐ Q (3) 10s; 52°25'·14N 01°46'·38E .
Newcome Sand ⌐ QR; 52°26'·28N 01°46'·97E.
S Holm ⌐ VQ (6) + L Fl 10s; 52°27'·05N 01°47'·15E.

N Newcome ⌐ Fl (4) R 15s; 52°28'·39N 01°46'·37E.
Lowestoft ☆ 52°29'·22N 01°45'·35; Fl 15s 37m
23M; W twr; part obscd 347°- shore;
E Newcome ⌐ Fl (2) R 5s; 52°28'·51N 01°49'·21E.
Corton ⌐ Q (3) 10s; *Whis*; 52°31'·13N 01°51'·39E.
E. Holm ⌐ Fl (3) R 10s; 52°30'·64N 01°49'·72E.
S Corton ⌐ Q (6) + L Fl 15s; *Bell*; 52°32'·70N
01°49'·50E.
Holm Sand ⌐ Q. 52°33'·36N 01°46'·85E.
W Corton ⌐ Q (9) 15s; 52°34'·59N 01°46'·62E.
Gorleston South Pier Hd ⌐ Fl R 3s 11m 11M; vis:
235°-340°; *Horn (3) 60s*; 52°34'·33N 01°44'·28E.

GREAT YARMOUTH TO THE WASH

(Direction of buoyage ⌐ South to North)

GT YARMOUTH/COCKLE GATWAY/OFFSHORE

SW Scroby ⌐ Fl G 2·5s; 52°35'·82N 01°46'·26E.
Scroby Sands Wind Farm, 30 turbines centred on
52°39'·00N 01°47'·00E. NW, NE, SW, SE extremities
(F.R Lts) Fl Y 5s 5M Horn Mo (U) 30s.
N Scroby ⌐ VQ; 52°41'·39N 01°46'·47E.
Cockle ⌐ VQ (3) 5s; *Bell*; 52°44'·03N 01°43'·59E.
Winterton Church *Racon (T) 10M*; 52°42'·92N
01°41'·21E.
Cross Sand ⌐ L Fl 10s 6m 5M; *Racon (T)10M*;
52°37'·03N 01°59'·14E.
NE Cross Sand ⌐ VQ (3) 5s; 52°44'·22N 01° 58'·80E.
Smith's Knoll ⌐ Q (6) + L Fl 15s 7M; *Racon (T) 10M*;
52°43'·52N 02°17'·89E.
S Winterton Ridge ⌐ Q (6) + L Fl 15s; 52°47'·21N
02°03'·44E.
Newarp ⌐ L Fl 10s 7M; *Racon (O) 10M*; 52°48'·37N
01°55'·69E.
S Haisbro ⌐ Q (6) + L Fl 15s; *Bell*; 52°50'·82N
01°48'·29E.
N Haisbro ⌐ Q; *Racon (T) 10M*; *Bell*; 53°00'·22N
01°32'·29E.
Happisburgh ☆ Fl (3) 30s 41m 14M; 52°49'·21N
01°32'·18E.

N NORFOLK COAST/THE WASH

Cromer ☆ 52°55'·45N 01°19'·01E; Fl 5s 84m **21M**;
W 8-sided twr; vis: 102°-307° H24; *Racon (O) 25M*.
E Sheringham ⌐ Q (3) 10s; 53°02'·21N 01°14'·84E.
Blakeney O'falls ⌐ Fl (2) R 5s; *Bell;* 53°03'·01N 01°01'·37E.
Wells Fairway ⌐ L Fl 10s; 52°59'·67N 00°50'·36E.
S Race ⌐ Q (6) + L Fl 15s; *Bell;* 53°07'·81N 00°57'·34E.
S Inner Dowsing ⌐ Q (6) + L Fl 15s; *Bell;* 53°12'·12N
00°33'·69E.
Burnham Flats ⌐ Q (9) 15s; *Bell;* 53°07'·53N
00°34'·89E.
N Well ⌐ L Fl 10s; *Whis*; *Racon (T) 10M*;
53°03'·02N 00°27'·90E.
Roaring Middle ⌐ L Fl 10s 7m 8M; 52°58'·64N
00°21'·08E.
Sunk ⌐ Q (9) 15s; 52°56'·29N 00°23'·40E.
Boston Roads ⌐ L Fl 10s; 52°57'·66N 00°16'·04E.

THE WASH TO THE RIVER HUMBER

Dudgeon ⟨Q (9) 15s 7M; *Racon (O) 10M*; *Whis*; 53°16'·62N 01°16'·90E.

E Dudgeon ⟨ Q (3) 10s; 53°19'·72N 00°58'·69E.

N Outer Dowsing ⟨ Q; 53°33'·52N 00°59'·59E.

B.1D Platform Dowsing ⌑ 53°33'·68N 00°52'·63E; Fl (2) 10s 28m **22M**; Morse (U) R 15s 28m 3M; *Horn (2) 60s*; *Racon (T) 10M*.

Inner Dowsing ⟨ Q (3) 10s 7M, *Racon (T) 10M*; *Horn 60s*; 53°19'·10N 00°34'·80E.

Protector ⌇ Fl R 2·5s; 53°24'·84N 00°25'·12E.

Humber ⚓ L Fl 10s 7M; *Horn (2) 30s*; *Racon (T) 7M*; 53°38'·83N 00°20'·17E.

SPURN ⚓ Q (3) 10s 10m 8M; *Horn 20s*; *Racon (M) 5M*; 53°33'·56N 00°14'·20E.

RIVER HUMBER TO RIVER TYNE
BRIDLINGTON/FILEY

SW Smithic ⟨ Q (9) 15s; 54°02'·41N 00°09'·21W.

Flamborough Hd ☆ 54°06'·98N 00°04'·96W; Fl (4) 15s 65m **24M**; W ○ twr; *Horn (2) 90s*.

Filey Brigg ⟨ Q (3) 10s; *Bell*; 54°12'·74N 00°14'·60W.

SCARBOROUGH/WHITBY

Scarborough Pier ⚹ Iso 5s 17m 9M; W ○ twr; vis: 219°-039° (tide sigs); *Dia 60s*; 54°16'·91N 00°23'·40W.

Whitby ⟨ Q; *Bell*; 54°30'·33N 00°36'·58W.

Whitby High ☆ 54°28'·67N 00°34'·10W; Ling Hill Fl WR 5s 73m **18M**, R16M; W 8-sided twr and dwellings; vis: 128°-R-143°-W- 319°.

Salt Scar ⟨ 54°38'·12N 01°00'·12W VQ; *Bell*.

TEES BAY/HARTLEPOOL/SUNDERLAND

Tees Fairway ⟨ Iso 4s 8m 8M; *Racon (B) unknown range*; *Horn (1) 5s*; 54°40'·94N 01°06'·48W.

Bkwtr Hd S Gare ☆ 54°38'·85N 01°08'·27W; Fl WR 12s 16m **W20M, R17M**; W ○ twr; vis: 020°-W-274°-R-357°; Sig Stn; *Horn 30s*.

Longscar ⟨ Q (3) 10s; *Bell*; 54°40'·86N 01°09'·89W.

The Heugh ☆ 54°41'·79N 01°10'·56W; Fl (2) 10s 19m **19M**; W twr.

Hartlepool Old Pier Hd ⚹ Fl WG 3s 13m 7M; vis: 317°-W-325°-G- 317°; 54°41'·60N 01°11'·09W.

Sunderland Roker Pier Hd ☆ 54°55'·28N 01°21'·15W; Fl 5s 25m **23M**; W □ twr, 3 R bands and cupola: vis: 211°- 357°; *Siren 20s*.

TYNE ENTRANCE/NORTH SHIELDS

Ent North Pier Hd ☆ 55°00'·88N 01°24'·18W; Fl (3) 10s 26m **26M**; Gy □ twr, W lantern; *Horn 10s*.

RIVER TYNE TO BERWICK-ON-TWEED
BLYTH/COQUET ISLAND/ AMBLE

Blyth F'w'y ⚓ Fl G 3s; *Bell*; 55°06'·59N 01°28'·60W.

Blyth E Pier Hd ☆ 55°06'·98N 01°29'·37W; Fl (4) 10s 19m **21M**; W twr; same structure FR 13m 13M, vis:152°-249°; Horn (3) 30s.

Coquet ☆ 55°20'·03N 01°32'·39W; Fl (3) WR 30s 25m **W23M, R19M**; W □ twr, turreted parapet, lower half Gy; vis: 330°-R-140°-W-163°-R-180°-W-330°; sector boundaries are indeterminate and may appear as Alt WR; *Horn 30s*.

Amble N Pier Hd ⚹ Fl G 6s 12m 6M; 55°20'·39N 01°34'·25W.

BAMBURGH/FARNE ISLANDS

The Falls ⌇ Fl R 2·5s; 55°34'·61N 01°37'·12W.

Shoreston Outcars ⌇ QR; 55°35'·88N 01°39'·34W.

Bamburgh Black Rocks Point ☆ 55°36'·99N 01°43'·45W; Oc(2) WRG 8s 12m **W14M**, R11M, G11M; W bldg; vis: 122°-G-165°-W-175°-R-191°-W- 238°-R- 275°-W- 289°-G-300°.

Inner Farne ⚹ Fl (2) WR 15s 27m W10M, R7M; W ○ twr; vis: 119°-R-280°-W-119°; 55°36'·92N 01°39'·35W.

Longstone ☆ **W side** 55°38'·62N 01°36'·65W; Fl 20s 23m **24M**; R twr, W band; *Horn (2) 60s*.

Swedman ⚓ Fl G 2·5s; 55°37'·65N 01°41'·63W.

HOLY ISLAND

Ridge ⟨ Q (3) 10s; 55°39'·70N 01°45'·97W.

Triton ⚓ QG; 55°39'·59N 01°46'·82W.

Plough Seat ⚓ QR; 55°40'·37N 01°44'·97W.

Goldstone ⚓ QG; 55°40'·25N 01°43'·64W.

BERWICK-ON-TWEED

Bkwtr Hd ⚹ Fl 5s 15m 6M; vis: 201°-009°, (obscured 155°-201°); W ○ twr, R cupola and base; FG (same twr) 8m 1M; vis 009°-G-155°; 55°45'·88N 01°59'·06W.

No.	Port													Port	No.
1	Ramsgate	1	11	31	61	78	91	107	126	189	205	205	232	Berwick-upon-Tweed	11
2	Sheerness	34	2	10	27	42	65	81	102	157	176	185	203	Amble	10
3	Gravesend	56	22	3	9	16	36	51	70	138	149	156	180	Sunderland	9
4	London Bridge	76	45	23	4	8	24	39	58	122	137	140	169	Hartlepool	8
5	Burnham-on-Crouch	44	34	53	76	5	7	16	35	88	114	121	143	Whitby	7
6	Brightlingsea	41	28	47	71	22	6	6	20	81	98	105	130	Scarborough	6
7	Harwich	40	50	65	83	31	24	7	5	58	83	87	114	Bridlington	5
8	River Deben (ent)	45	55	71	89	35	38	6	8	4	72	75	113	Hull	4
9	Southwold	62	80	95	113	58	63	30	23	9	3	34	83	Boston	3
10	Lowestoft	72	90	105	123	68	73	40	33	10	10	2	85	King's Lynn	2
11	Great Yarmouth	79	97	112	130	76	80	52	41	18	7	11	1	Great Yarmouth	1

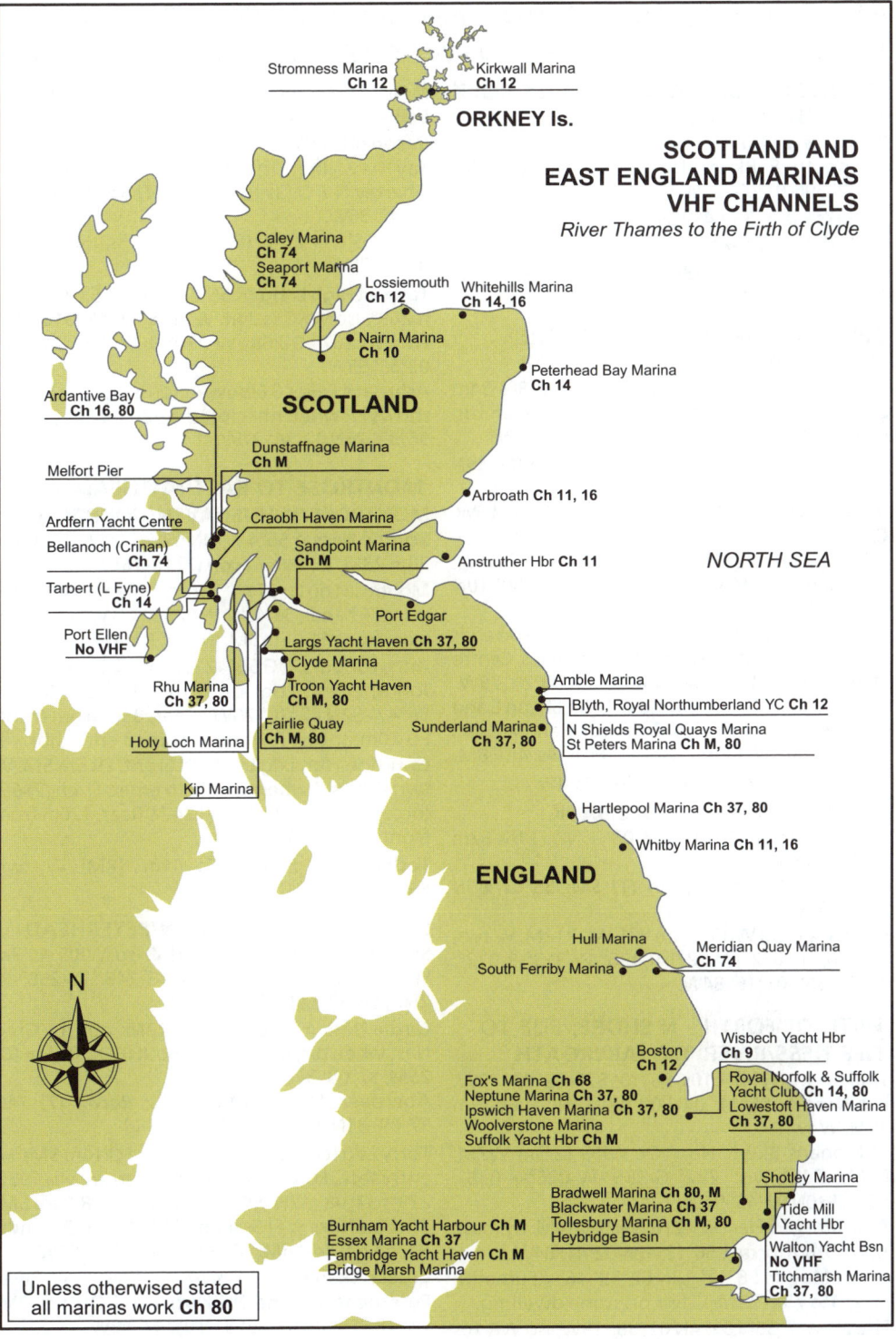

Stromness Marina **Ch 12**   Kirkwall Marina **Ch 12**

ORKNEY Is.

**SCOTLAND AND
EAST ENGLAND MARINAS
VHF CHANNELS**
River Thames to the Firth of Clyde

Caley Marina **Ch 74**
Seaport Marina **Ch 74**
Lossiemouth **Ch 12**   Whitehills Marina **Ch 14, 16**

Nairn Marina **Ch 10**

SCOTLAND

Peterhead Bay Marina **Ch 14**

Ardantive Bay **Ch 16, 80**

Dunstaffnage Marina **Ch M**

Melfort Pier

Ardfern Yacht Centre

Craobh Haven Marina

Arbroath **Ch 11, 16**

Bellanoch (Crinan) **Ch 74**

Sandpoint Marina **Ch M**

Anstruther Hbr **Ch 11**

NORTH SEA

Tarbert (L Fyne) **Ch 14**

Port Edgar

Port Ellen **No VHF**

Largs Yacht Haven **Ch 37, 80**

Rhu Marina **Ch 37, 80**

Clyde Marina

Troon Yacht Haven **Ch M, 80**

Amble Marina

Blyth, Royal Northumberland YC **Ch 12**

Holy Loch Marina

Fairlie Quay **Ch M, 80**

Sunderland Marina **Ch 37, 80**

N Shields Royal Quays Marina
St Peters Marina **Ch M, 80**

Kip Marina

Hartlepool Marina **Ch 37, 80**

Whitby Marina **Ch 11, 16**

ENGLAND

Hull Marina

Meridian Quay Marina **Ch 74**

South Ferriby Marina

N

Boston **Ch 12**

Wisbech Yacht Hbr **Ch 9**

Fox's Marina **Ch 68**
Neptune Marina **Ch 37, 80**
Ipswich Haven Marina **Ch 37, 80**
Woolverstone Marina
Suffolk Yacht Hbr **Ch M**

Royal Norfolk & Suffolk Yacht Club **Ch 14, 80**
Lowestoft Haven Marina **Ch 37, 80**

Shotley Marina

Bradwell Marina **Ch 80, M**
Blackwater Marina **Ch 37**
Tollesbury Marina **Ch M, 80**
Heybridge Basin

Tide Mill Yacht Hbr

Burnham Yacht Harbour **Ch M**
Essex Marina **Ch 37**
Fambridge Yacht Haven **Ch M**
Bridge Marsh Marina

Walton Yacht Bsn **No VHF**
Titchmarsh Marina **Ch 37, 80**

Unless otherwised stated
all marinas work **Ch 80**

AREA 5 E. Scotland - *Berwick-upon-Tweed to C Wrath & N Isles*

SELECTED LIGHTS, BUOYS & WAYPOINTS | Positions are referenced to WGS84

BERWICK-UPON-TWEED TO BASS ROCK
EYEMOUTH/ST ABB'S/DUNBAR
Blind Buss ⟨ Q; 55°52'·80N 02°05'·25E.

Eyemouth E Bkwtr Hd ⚓ Iso R 2s 8m 8M; 55°52'·50N 02°05'·29W.

St Abb's Hd ☆ 55°54'·96N 02°08'·29W; Fl 10s 68m **26M**; W twr; *Racon (T) 18M*.

Bass Rock, S side, ☆ Fl (3) 20s 46m 10M; W twr; vis: 241°-107°; 56°04'·61N 02°38'·48W.

FIRTH OF FORTH - SOUTH SHORE
SOUTH SIDE TO LEITH/PORT EDGAR
Fidra ☆ 56°04'·39N 02°47'·13W; Fl (4) 30s 34m **24M**; W twr; obsc by Bass Rk, Craig Leith & Lamb Is.

Wreck ⚓ Fl (2) R 10s; 56°04'·39N 02°52'·39W.

Inchkeith F'wy ⚓ Iso 2s; *Racon (T) 5M*; 56°03'·49N 03°00'·10W.

Narrow Deep ⚓ Fl (2) R 10s; 56°01'·46N 03°04'·59W.

Craigh Waugh ⟨ Q;56°00'·26N 03°04'·47W.

Leith Approach ⚓ Fl R 3s; 55°59'·95N 03°11'·51W.

Inch Garvie, NW ⚓ L Fl 5s 9m 11M; 56°00'·10N 03°23'·37W.

Forth Rail Br. Centres of spans have W Lts and ends of cantilevers R Lts, defining N and S chans. Centre Piers; 2 Aero FR 47m 5M; 56°00'·33N 03°21'·79W. Forth Road Br. N susp twr Iso G 4s 7m 6M on E and W sides. S susp twr Iso R 4s 7m 6M on E and W sides. Port Edgar W Bkwtr Hd ⚓ Fl R 4s 4m 8M; 55°59'·86N 03°24'·78W. W blockhouse

NORTH CHANNEL/MIDDLE BANK
Inchkeith ☆ 56°02'·01N 03°08'·17W; Fl 15s 67m **22M**; stone twr.

No. 7 ⚓ QG; *Bell*; *Racon (T) 5M*; 56°02'·80N 03°10'·97W.

Oxcars ☆ Fl (2) WR 7s 16m W13M, R12M; W twr, R band; vis: 072°-W-087°-R-196°-W-313°-R-072°; 56°01'·36N 03°16'·84W.

FIRTH OF FORTH - N SHORE; ELIE TO FIFE NESS/RIVER TAY/ARBROATH
Thill Rock ⚓ Fl (4) R 10s; 56°10'·87N 02°49'·70W.

Elie Ness ☆ 56°11'·04N 02°48'·77W; Fl 6s 15m **18M**; W twr.

St Monans Bkwtr Hd ⚓ Oc WRG 6s 5m W7M, R4M, G4M; vis: 282°-G-355°-W-026°-R-038°; 56°12'·20N 02°45'·94W.

Anstruther, W Pier Hd ⚓ 2 FR (vert) 5m 4M; Gy mast; *Horn (3) 60s (occas)*; 56°13'·18N 02°41'·84W.

Isle of May ☆ 56°11'·12N 02°33'·46W(Summit); Fl (2) 15s 73m **22M**; ☐ twr on stone dwelling.

Fife Ness ☆ 56°16'·74N 02°35'·19W; Iso WR 10s 12m **W21M, R20M**; W bldg; vis: 143°-W-197°-R-217°-W-023°.

N Carr ⟨ Q (3) 10s 3m 5M; 56°18'·05N 02°32'·94W.

Bell Rk ☆ 56°26'·08N 02°23'·21W; Fl 5s 28m **18M**; *Racon (M) 18M*.

Tay F'wy ⚓ L Fl 10s; 56°28'·30N 02°36'·60W.

Abertay N ⟨ Q (3) 10s; *Racon (T) 8M*; 56°27'·39N 02°40'·36W.

Horse Shoe ⟨ Q (6) + L Fl 15s; 56°27'·28N 02°50'·20W.

Tayport High Lt Ho ☆ 56°27'·17N 02°53'·96W; Dir lt 269°; Iso WRG3s 24m **W22M, R17M, G16M**; W twr; vis:267°-G-268°-W-270°-R-271°;56°27'·04N 02°56'·55W.

Arbroath E Pier S Elbow ⚓ Fl G 3s 8m 5M; W twr; shows FR when hbr closed; *Siren (3) 60s (occas)*; 56°33'·25N 02°34'·97W.

MONTROSE TO RATTRAY HEAD
MONTROSE/JOHNSHAVEN/GOURDON
Scurdie Ness ☆ 56°42'·10N 02°26'·24W; Fl (3) 20s 38m **23M**; W twr; *Racon (T) 14-16M*.

Montrose Ldg Lts 271·5°. Front, FR 11m 5M; W twin pillars, R bands; 56°42'·21N 02°27'·41W. Rear, 272m from front, FR 18m 5M; W twr, R cupola.

Annat Shoal ⚓ QG 56°42'·37N 02°25'·19W.

Johnshaven, Ldg Lts 316°. Front, FR 5m; 56°47'·62N 02°20'·26W . Rear, 85m from front, FG 20m; shows R when unsafe to enter hbr.

Gourdon Hbr, Ldg Lts 358°. Front, FR 5m 5M; W twr; shows G when unsafe to enter; *Siren (2) 60s (occas)*; 56°49'·69N 02°17'·24W. Rear, 120m from front, FR 30m 5M; W twr.

Todhead ☆ Fl (4) 30s 41m **18M**; W twr; 56°53'·00N 02°12'·97W.

STONEHAVEN/ABERDEEN/PETERHEAD
Stonehaven Outer Pier Hd ⚓ Iso WRG 4s 7m W11M, R7M, G8M; vis: 214°-G-246°-W-268°-R-280°; 56°57'·59N 02°12'·00W.

Girdle Ness ☆ Fl (2) 20s 56m **22M**; obsc by Greg Ness when brg more than about 020°; *Racon (G) 25M*; 57°08'·34N 02°02'·91W.

Aberdeen F'wy ⚓ Mo (A) 5s; *Racon (T) 7M*; 57°09'·31N 02°01'·95W.

Torry Ldg lts 235·7°. Front, FR or FG 14m 5M; FR entry safe, FG when entry dangerous; vis: 195°-279°; 57°08'·37N 02°04'·51W. Rear, FR 19m 5M.

Buchan Ness ☆ Fl 5s 40m **28M**; W twr, R bands; *Racon (O) 14-16M*; 57°28'·23N 01°46'·51W.

Cruden Skares ⚓ Fl R 10s; 57°23'·17N 01°50'·36W.

Peterhead Marina N Bkwtr Hd ⚓ QG 5m 2M; vis: 185°-300°; 57°29'·81N 01°47'·49W.

Rattray Hd ☆ 57°36'·61N 01°49'·03W; Fl (3) 30s 28m **24M**; W twr; *Racon (M) 15M*.

RATTRAY HEAD TO INVERNESS

Rattray Hd ☆ 57°36'·61N 01°49'·03W Fl (3) 30s 28m **24M**; W twr; **Racon (M) 15M**; *Horn (2) 45s.*

FRASERBURGH/MACDUFF/BANFF

Fraserburgh, Balaclava Bkwtr Head ⚓ Fl (2) G 8s 26m 6M; dome on W twr; vis: 178°-326°; 57°41'·51N 01°59'·70W.

Kinnaird Hd ☆ 57°41'·87N 02°00'·26W Fl 5s 25m **22M**; vis: 092°-297°.

Macduff Pier Hd ⚓ Fl (2) WRG 6s 12m W9M, R7M; W twr; vis: shore-G-115°-W-174°-R-210°; 57°40'·25N 02°30'·02W.

Banff N Pier Hd ⚓ Fl 4s; 57°40'·22N 02°31'·27W.

WHITEHILLS/PORTSOY/FINDOCHTY

Whitehills Pier Hd ⚓ 57°40'·80N 02°34'·88W Fl WR 3s 7m W9M, R6M; W twr; vis: 132°-R-212°-W-245°.
Portsoy Pier Ldg Lts 160°, Front F 12m 5M; twr; 57°41'·17N 02°41'·49W. Rear FR 17m 5M; mast.
Findochty Middle Pier Ldg Lts 166°, Front FR 6m 3M; 57°41'·90N 02°54'·20W. Rear FR 10m 3M.

BUCKIE/LOSSIEMOUTH/HOPEMAN

West Muck ⚓ QR 5m 7M; tripod; 57°41'·06N 02°58'·01W.

N Pier 60m from Hd ☆ 57°40'·9N 02°57'·5W Oc R 10s 15m **15M** W twr.

BURGHEAD/FINDHORN/NAIRN

Lossiemouth S Pier Hd ⚓ Fl R 6s 11m 5M; *Siren 60s;* 57°43'·42N 03°16'·69W.

Covesea Skerries ☆ 57°43'·47N 03°20'·45W Fl WR 20s 49m **W24M, R20M**; W twr; vis: 076°-W-267°-R-282°.

Hopeman W Pier Hd ⚓ Oc G 4s 8m 4M; 57°42'·69N 03°26'·29W.
Burghead N Bkwtr Hd ⚓ Oc 8s 7m 5M; 57°42'·09N 03°30'·03W.
Findhorn Landfall ⚓ LF 10s; 57°40'·33N 03°38'·94W.
Nairn W Pier Hd ⚓ QG 5m 1M; Gy post; 57°35'·60N 03°51'·63W.

INVERNESS FIRTH/CALEDONIAN CANAL

Navity Bk ⚓ Fl (3) G 15s; 57°38'·16N 04°01'·18W.
Riff Bank S ⚓ Q (6) + L Fl 15s; 57°36'·73N 04°00'·97W.
Craigmee ⚓ Fl R 6s 3m 4M; 57°35'·30N 04°05'·04W.

Chanonry ☆ 57°34'·44N 04°05'·57W Oc 6s 12m **15M**; W twr; vis: 148°-073°.
Kessock Bridge Centre , Or △; **Racon (K) 6M;** 57°29'·97N 04°13'·79W.

Clachnaharry, S Tr'ng Wall Hd ⚓ Iso G 4s 5m 2M; tfc sigs; 57°29'·43N 04°15'·86W.

INVERNESS TO DUNCANSBY HEAD

CROMARTY FIRTH

Fairway ⚓ L Fl 10s; **Racon (M) 5M**; 57°39'·96N 03°54'·19W.

Cromarty Bank ⚓ Fl (2) G 10s; 57°40'·66N 03°56'·78W.
Buss Bank ⚓ Fl R 3s 57°40'·97N 03°59'·54W.

The Ness ☆ 57°40'·98N 04°02'·20W Oc WR 10s 18m **W15M**, R11M; W twr; vis: 079°-R-088°-W-275°, obsc by N Sutor when brg less than 253°.
Three Kings ⚓ Q (3) 10s; 57°43'·73N 03°54'·25W.

DORNOCH FIRTH/LYBSTER/WICK

Tarbat Ness ☆ 57°51'·88N 03°46'·76W Fl (4) 30s 53m **24M**; W twr, R bands; *Racon (T) 14-16M*.
Lybster, S Pier Hd ⚓ Oc R 6s 10m 3M; 58°17'·79N 03°17'·41W.

Clyth Ness ☆ Fl (2) 30s 45m 14M; 58°18'·64N 03°12'·74W.

Wick S Pier Hd ⚓ Fl WRG 3s 12m W12M, R9M, G9M; W 8-sided twr; vis: 253°-G-270°-W-286°-R-329°; Bell (2) 10s (occas); 58°26'·34N 03°04'·73W.

Noss Hd ☆ 58°28'·71N 03°03'·09W Fl WR 20s 53m **W25M, R21M**; W twr; vis: shore-R-191°-W-shore.

DUNCANSBY HEAD TO CAPE WRATH

Duncansby Hd ☆ 58°38'·65N 03°01'·58W Fl 12s 67m **22M**; W twr; **Racon (T)**.
Pentland Skerries ☆ 58°41'·41N 02°55'·49W Fl (3) 30s 52m **23M**; W twr.
Lother Rock ⚓ Fl 2s 13m 6M; *Racon (M)10M;* 58°43'·79N 02°58'·69W.
Swona N Hd ⚓ Fl (3) 10s 16m 10M; 58°45'·11N 03°03'·10W.
Stroma ☆, Swilkie Point 58°41'·75N 03°07'·01W Fl (2) 20s 32m **26M**; W twr.
Dunnet Hd ☆ 58°40'·28N 03°22'·60W Fl (4) 30s 105m **23M**.
Scrabster Q. E. Pier Hd ⚓ Fl (2) 4s 8m 8M 58°36'·66N 03°32'·31W.
Strathy Pt ☆ 58°36'·04N 04°01'·12W Fl 20s 45m **26M**; W twr on W dwelling. F.R. on chy 100° 8·5M.
Sule Skerry ☆ 59°05'·09N 04°24'·38W Fl (2) 15s 34m **21M**; W twr; *Racon (T)*.
North Rona ☆ 59°07'·27N 05°48'·91W Fl (3) 20s 114m **24M**.
Sula Sgeir ⚓ Fl 15s 74m 11M; □ structure; 59°05'·61N 06°09'·57W.
Loch Eriboll, White Hd ⚓ Fl WR10s 18m W13M, R12M; W twr and bldg; vis: 030°-W-172°-R-191°-W-212°; 58°31'·01N 04°38'·90W.

Cape Wrath ☆ 58°37'·54N 04°59'·94W Fl (4) 30s 122m **22M**; W twr.

ORKNEY ISLANDS

Tor Ness ☆ 58°46'·78N 03°17'·86W Fl 5s 21m **17M**; W twr.

Cantick Hd (S Walls, SE end) ☆ 58°47'·23N 03°07'·88W Fl 20s 35m **18M**; W twr.

SCAPA FLOW AND APPROACHES

Ruff Reef, off Cantick Hd ⚓Fl 10s 10m 6M; 58°47'·43N 03°07'·80W.

Hoxa Hd ⚓ Fl WR 3s 15m W9M, R6M; W twr; vis: 026°-W-163°-R-201°-W-215°; 58°49'·31N 03°02'·09W.

Stanger Hd ⚓Fl R 5s 25m 8M 58°48'·96N 03°04'·74W.

CLESTRAN SOUND/HOY SOUND

Peter Skerry ▲ Fl G 6s; 58°55'·25N 03°13'·51W.

Riddock Shoal ⌇ Fl (2) R 12s; 58°55'·89N 03°15'·00W.

Graemsay Is Hoy Sound Low ☆ Ldg Lts 104°.
Front, 58°56'·42N 03°18'·60W Iso 3s 17m **15M**; W twr; vis: 070°-255°. **High Rear,** 1·2M from front, Oc WR 8s 35m **W20M, R16M**; W twr; vis: 097°-R-112°-W-163°-R-178°-W-332°; obsc on Ldg line within 0·5M.

STROMNESS

Stromness ⌇ QR; 58°57'·25N 03°17'·61W.

N Pier Hd ⚓ Fl R 3s 8m 5M; 58°57'·75N 03°17'·71W.

AUSKERRY/KIRKWALL

Copinsay ☆ 58°53'·77N 02°40'·35W Fl (5) 30s 79m **21M**; W twr.

Auskerry ☆ 59°01'·51N 02°34'·34W Fl 20s 34m **20M**; W twr.

Scargun Shoal v Q (3) 10s; 59°00'·69N 02°58'·58W.

Kirkwall Pier N end ☆ 58°59'·29N 02°57'·72W Iso WRG 5s 8m **W15M**, R13M, G13M; W twr; vis: 153°-G-183°-W-192°-R-210°.

WIDE FIRTH

Linga Skerry ⧘ Q (3) 10s; 59°02'·39N 02°57'·56W.

Boray Skerries ⧘ Q (6) + L Fl 15s; 59°03'·65N 02°57'·66W.

Skertours ⧘ Q; 59°04'·11N 02°56'·72W.

Galt Skerry ⧘ Q; 59°05'·21N 02°54'·20W.

Brough of Birsay ☆ 59°08'·19N 03°20'·41W Fl (3) 25s 52m **18M**.

Papa Stronsay NE end, The Ness Fl(4)20s 8m 9M; W twr; 59°09'·34N 02°34'·93W

STRONSAY, PAPA SOUND

Quiabow ▲ Fl (2) G 12s; 59°09'·82N 02°36'·30W.

No. 1 ▲ Fl G 5s; (off Jacks Reef) 59°09'·16N 02°36'·51W.

Whitehall Pier Hd ⚓ 2 FG (vert) 8m 4M; 50°08'·61N 02°35'·96W.

SANDAY ISLAND/NORTH RONALDSAY

Start Pt ☆ 59°16'·69N 02°22'·71W Fl (2) 20s 24m **18M**.

N Ronaldsay ☆ NE end, 59°23'·37N 02°23'·03W Fl 10s 43m **24M**; R twr, W bands; *Racon (T) 14-17M*.

WESTRAY/PIEROWALL

Noup Head ☆ 59°19'·86N 03°04'·23W Fl 30s 79m **20M**; W twr; vis: about 335°-282° but partially obsc 240°-275°.

Pierowall E Pier Head ⚓ Fl WRG 3s 7m W11M, R7M, G7M; vis: 254°-G-276°-W-291°-R-308°-G-215°; 59°19'·35N 02°58'·53W.

Papa Westray, Moclett Bay Pier Head ⚓Fl WRG 5s 7m W5M, R3M,G3M; vis: 306°-G-341°-W-040°-R-074°; 59°19'·60N 02°53'·52W.

SHETLAND ISLES

FAIR ISLE

Skadan South ☆, 59°30'·84N 01°39'·16W Fl (4) 30s 32m **22M**; W twr; vis: 260°-146°, obsc inshore 260°-282°; *Horn (2) 60s.*

Skroo ☆ N end 59°33'·13N 01°36'·58W Fl (2) 30s 80m **22M**; W twr; vis: 086·7°-358°.

MAINLAND, SOUTH

Sumburgh Head ☆ 59°51'·21N 01°16'·58W Fl (3) 30s 91m **23M**.

Pool of Virkie, Marina E Bkwtr Head ⚓ 2 FG (vert) 6m 5M; 59°53'·01N 01°17'·16W.

BRESSAY/LERWICK

Bressay, Kirkabister Ness ☆ 60°07'·20N 01°07'·29W; Fl (2) 20s 32m **23M**.

Soldian Rock ⧘ Q (6) + L Fl 15s 60°12'·51N 01°04'·73W.

Gremista Marina S Hd ⚓ Iso R 4s 3m 2M; 60°10'·20N 01°09'·61W.

Rova Hd ⚓ 60°11'·46N 01°08'·60W Fl (3) WRG 18s 12m W12M, R9M, G9M; W twr; vis: 090°-R-182°-W-191°-G-213°-R-241°-W-261·5°-G-009°-R-040°. Same structure and synhcronised: Fl (3) WRG 18s 14m **W16M**, R13M, G13M; vis: 176·5°-R-182°-W-191°-G-196·5°.

The Brethren Rock ⧘ Q (9) 15s; 60°12'·35N 01°08'·24W.

The Unicorn Rock ⧘ VQ (3) 5s; 60°13'·51N 01°08'·48W.

Dales Voe ⚓ Fl (2) WRG 8s 5m W4M, R3M, G3M; vis: 220°-G-227°-W-233°-R-240°; 60°11'·79N 01°11'·23W.

Dales Voe Quay ⚓ 2 FR (vert) 9m 3M; 60°11'·60N 01°10'·48W.

		1	2	3	4	5	6	7	8	9	10	11					
1	Berwick-upon-Tweed	1		11	155	79	47	76	104	144	126	120	125	145	Cape Wrath	11
2	Eyemouth	10	2		10	95	124	120	148	190	170	162	156	160	Lerwick	10
3	Dunbar	26	17	3		9	50	46	74	114	104	90	95	115	Kirkwall	9
4	Port Edgar	58	50	34	4		8	31	59	99	89	75	80	100	Scrabster	8
5	Methil	45	36	20	20	5		7	29	69	58	44	50	72	Wick	7
6	Fife Ness	38	29	17	34	16	6		6	43	32	26	44	74	Helmsdale	6
7	Dundee	58	49	37	54	36	20	7		5	13	34	59	90	Inverness	5
8	Montrose	59	51	43	61	43	27	27	8		4	23	48	79	Nairn	4
9	Stonehaven	72	66	60	78	60	44	45	20	9		3	25	56	Lossiemouth	3
10	Aberdeen	82	78	73	90	72	56	57	32	13	10		2	33	Banff/Macduff	2
11	Peterhead	105	98	93	108	94	78	80	54	35	25	11		1	Peterhead	1

AREA 6 NW Scotland - *C. Wrath to Oban including The Western Isles*

SELECTED LIGHTS, BUOYS & WAYPOINTS | Positions are referenced to WGS84

CAPE WRATH TO LOCH TORRIDON

Cape Wrath ☆ 58°37'·54N 04°59'·99W Fl (4) 30s 122m **22M**; W twr.

LOCH INCHARD/LOCH LAXFORD

Bodha Ceann na Saile ⌀ Q; 58°27'·24N 05°04'·01W.

Kinlochbervie Dir lt 327° ☆. 58°27'·49N 05°03'·08W WRG 15m **16M**; vis: 326°-FG-326·5°-Al GW-326·75°-FW-327·25°-Al RW-327·5°-FR-328°.

Stoer Head ☆ 58°14'·43N 05°24'·07W Fl 15s 59m **24M**; W twr.

LOCH INVER/SUMMER ISLES/ULLAPOOL

Soyea I ⌀ Fl (2) 10s 34m 6M; 58°08'·56N 05°19'·67W.

Glas Leac ⌀ Fl WRG 3s 7m 5M; 58°08'·68N 05°16'·36W.

Rubha Cadail ⌀ FlWRG 6s 11m W9M, R6M, G6M; W twr; vis: 311°-G-320°-W-325°-R-103°-W-111°-G-118°-W-127°-R-157°-W-199°; 57°55'·51N 05°13'·40W.

Ullapool Pt ⌀ QR; 57°53'·70N 05°10'·68W.

Cailleach Head ⌀ Fl (2) 12s 60m 9M; W twr; vis: 015°-236°; 57°55'·81N 05°24'·23W.

LOCH EWE/LOCH GAIRLOCH

Fairway ⌀ L Fl 10s; 57°51'·98N 05°40'·09W.

Rubha Reidh ☆ 57°51'·52N 05°48'·72W Fl (4) 15s 37m **24M**.

Glas Eilean ⌀Fl WRG 6s 9m W6M, R4M; vis: 080°-W-102°-R-296°-W-333°-G-080°; 57°42'·79N 05°42'·42W.

Gairloch Pier ⌀ 57°42'·59N 05°41'·03W QR 6m 2M.

OUTER HEBRIDES – EAST SIDE

LEWIS

Butt of Lewis ☆ 58°30'·89N 06°15'·84W Fl 5s 52m **25M**; R twr; vis: 056°-320°.

Tiumpan Head ☆ 58°15'·66N 06°08'·29W Fl (2) 15s 55m **25M**; W twr.

Reef Rock ⌀ QR; 58°11'·58N 06°21'·97W.

Arnish Point ☆ Fl WR 10s 17m W9M, R7M; W ○ twr; vis: 088°-W-198°-R-302°-W-013°; 58°11'·50N 06°22'·16W.

Rubh' Uisenis ⌀ Fl 5s 24m 11M; W twr; 57°56'·25N 06°28'·36W.

Shiants ▲ QG; 57°54'·57N 06°25'·70W.

Sgeir Inoe ▲ Fl G 6s; 57°50'·93N 06°33'·93W.

Scalpay, **Eilean Glas** ☆ 57°51'·41N 06°38'·55W Fl (3) 20s 43m **23M**; W twr, R bands; *Racon (T) 16-18M*.

Sgeir Bràigh Mor ▲ Fl G 6s; 57°51'·51N 06°43'·84W.

Sgeir Graidach ⌀ Q (6) + L Fl 15s; 57°50'·36N 06°41'·37W.

Tarbert ⌀ Oc WRG 6s 10m 5M; 57°53'·82N 06°47'·93W

SOUND OF HARRIS/BERNERAY

Fairway ⌀ L Fl 10s; 57°40'·35N 07°02'·15W.

Cabbage ⌀ Fl (2) R 6s; *Racon (T) 5M (3cm)*; 57°42'·13N 07°03'·96W.

Bo Stainan ⌀ 57°45'·76N 07°02'·40W VQ(6) + LF 10s.

Trench ▲ Q (3) G 10s; 57°41'·89N 07°09'·00W.

LOCH MADDY

Weaver's Pt ⌀ 57°36'·49N 07°06'·00W Fl 3s 24m 7M; W hut.

Glas Eilean Mòr ⌀ 57°35'·95N 07°06'·70W Fl (2) G 4s 8m 5M.

SOUTH UIST, LOCH CARNAN

Landfall ⌀ L Fl 10s; 57°22'·27N 07°11'·52W.

Ushenish ☆ (S Uist) 57°17'·89N 07°11'·58W Fl WR 20s 54m **W19M, R15M**; W twr; vis: 193°-W-356°-R-018°.

LOCH BOISDALE/BARRA/CASTLEBAY

MacKenzie Rk ⌀ Fl (3) R 15s 3m 4M; 57°08'·24N 07°13'·71W.

Calvay E End ⌀ Fl (2) WRG 10s 16m W7M, R4M, G4M; W twr; vis: 111°-W-190°-G-202°-W-286°-R-111°; 57°08'·53N 07°15'·38W.

Binch Rock ⌀ Q (6) + L Fl 15s; 57°01'·71N 07°17'·16W.

Bo Vich Chuan ⌀ Q (6) + L Fl 15s; *Racon (M) 5M*; 56°56'·15N 07°23'·31W.

Castle Bay S ⌀ Fl (2) R 8s; *Racon (T) 7M*; 56°56'·09N 07°27'·21W.

Barra Hd ☆ 56°47'·11N 07°39'·26W Fl 15s 208m **18M**; W twr; obsc by islands to NE.

OUTER HEBRIDES – WEST SIDE

Flannan I ☆, Eilean Mór 58°17'·32N 07°35'·23W Fl (2) 30s 101m **20M**; W twr; obsc in places by ls to W of Eilean Mór.

Haskeir I ☆ 57°41'·98N 07°41·36W Fl 20s 44m **23M**; W twr.

LOCH TORRIDON TO MULL

LITTLE MINCH/NORTH SKYE/RONA

Eugenie Rk ⌀ Q 6 + LF 15s; 57°46'·47N 06°27'·28W.

Eilean Trodday ⌀ Fl (2) WRG 10s 52m W12M, R9M, G9M; W Bn; vis: W062°-R088°-130°-W-322°-G-062°; 57°43'·64N 06°17'·89W.

Comet Rock ⌀ Fl R 6s; 57°44'·60N 06°20'·50W.

Rona NE Point £ 57°34'·68N 05°57'·56W Fl 12s 69m 19M; W twr; vis: 050°-358°.

CROWLIN ISLANDS/RAASAY

Sgeir Mhór ⌀ Fl G 5s; 57°24'·57N 06°10'·53W.

Eilean Beag ⌀ Fl 6s 32m 6M; W Bn; 57°21'·21N 05°51'·42W.

Eyre Pt ⌖ Fl WR 3s 6m W9M, R6M; W twr; vis: 215°-W-266°-R- 288°-W-063°; 57°20'·01N 06°01'·29W.

KYLE AKIN AND KYLE OF LOCH ALSH

Carragh Rk ▲ Fl (2) G 12s; *Racon (T) 5M*; 57°17'·18N 05°45'·36W.
Skye Br Centre ⌖ Oc 6s; 57°16'·57N 05°44'·58W.
String Rock ⌔ Fl R 6s; 57°16'·50N 05°42'·89W.
Sgeir-na-Caillich ⌖ Fl (2) R 6s 3m 4M; 57°15'·59N 05°38'·90W.

SOUND OF SLEAT

Kyle Rhea ⌖ Fl WRG 3s 7m W8M, R5M, G5M; W Bn; vis: shore-R-219-W-228°-G-338°-W-346°-R-shore; 57°14'·22N 05°39'·93W.
Ornsay, SE end ☆ 57°08'·59N 05°46'·88W Oc 8s 18m **15M**; W twr; vis: 157°-030°.
Pt. of Sleat ⌖ Fl 3s 20m 9M; W twr; 57°01'·08N 06°01'·08W.

MALLAIG

Sgeir Dhearg ▲ QG; 57°00'·74N 05°49'·50W.
N Pier, E end ⌖ Iso WRG 4s 6m W9M, R6M, G6M; Gy twr; vis: 181°-G-185°-W-197°-R-201°. Fl G 3s 14m 6M; same structure; 57°00'·47N 05°49'·50W.

NW SKYE

Neist Point ☆ 57°25'·41N 06°47'·30W Fl 5s 43m **16M**; W twr.

Hyskeir ☆ 56°58'·14N 06°40'·87W Fl (3) 30s 41m **24M**; W twr. *Racon (T) 14-17M*.
Bogha Ruadh⌖ Fl G 5s 4m 3M; 56°49'·56N 06°13'·05W.
Bo Faskadale ▲ Fl (3) G 18s; 56°48'·18N 06°06'·37W.
Ardnamurchan ☆ 56°43'·63N 06°13'·58W Fl (2) 20s 55m **24M**; Gy twr; vis: 002°-217°.

TIREE

Roan Bogha ⌕ Q (6) + L Fl 15s 3m 5M; 56°32'·23N 06°40'·18W.
Placaid Bogha ▲ Fl G 4s; 56°33'·22N 06°44'·06W.

Scarinish ☆, S side of ent 56°30'·01N 06°48'·27W Fl 3s 11m **16M**; W ☐ twr; vis: 210°-030°.
Skerryvore ☆ 56°19'·36N 07°06'·88W Fl 10s 46m **23M**; *Racon (M) 18M*; *Horn 60s*.

LOCH NA LÀTHAICH (LOCH LATHAICH)

Dubh Artach ☆ 56°07'·94N 06°38'·08W; Fl (2)30s 44m **20M**; Gy twr, R band.

LOCH SUNART/TOBERMORY/LOCH ALINE

Ardmore Pt ⌖ Fl (2) 10s 18m 13M; 56°39'·37N 06°07'·70W.
New Rks ▲ Fl G 6s 56°39'·05N 06°03'·30W.
Rubha nan Gall ☆ 56°38'·33N 06°04'·00W Fl 3s 17m **15M**; W twr.
Avon Rock ⌔ Fl (4) R 12s; 56°30'·78N 05°46'·80W.
Yule Rocks ⌔ Fl R 15s; 56°30'·01N 05°43'·96W.
Glas Eileanan Gy Rks ⌖ Fl 3s 11m 6M; W ○ twr on W base; 56°29'·77N 05°42'·83W.
Craignure Ldg Lts 240·9°. Front, FR 10m; 56°28'·26N 05°42'·28W. Rear, 150m from front, FR 12m; vis: 225·8°-255·8°.

Lismore ☆, SW end 56°27'·34N 05°36'·45W Fl 10s 31m **17M**; W twr; vis: 237°-208°.
Lady's Rk ⌕ Fl 6s 12m 5M; 56°26'·92N 05°37'·05W.
Duart Pt ⌖ Fl (3) WR 18s 14m W5M, R3M; vis: 162°-W-261°-R-275°-W-353°-R-shore; 56°26'·84N 05°38'·77W.

DUNSTAFFNAGE BAY

Pier Hd ⌖ NE end, 2 FG (vert) 4m 2M; 56°27'·21N 05°26'·18W.

OBAN

N spit of Kerrera ⌖ Fl R 3s 9m 5M; W col, R bands; 56°25'·49N 05°29'·56W.
Dunollie ⌖ Fl (2) WRG 6s 7m W5M, G4M, R4M; vis:G351°-W009°-R047°-W120°-G138°-143°; 56°25'·37N 05°29'·05W.
Corran Ledge ⌕ VQ (9) 10s; 56°25'·19N 05°29'·11W.
Oban N Pier Mid ⌖ 2 FG (vert) 8m 5M; 56°24'·87N 05°28'·49W.

		1	2	3	4	5	6	7	8	9	10	11	12	13	14	15	16	17
1	Cape Wrath	1																
2	Ullapool	54	2															
3	Stornoway	53	45	3														
4	East Loch Tarbert	75	56	33	4													
5	Portree	83	57	53	42	5												
6	Kyle of Lochalsh	91	63	62	63	21	6											
7	Mallaig	112	82	83	84	42	21	7										
8	Eigg	123	98	97	75	54	35	14	8									
9	Castlebay (Barra)	133	105	92	69	97	76	59	46	9								
10	Tobermory	144	114	115	87	74	53	32	20	53	10							
11	Loch Aline	157	127	128	100	87	66	45	33	66	13	11						
12	Fort William	198	161	162	134	121	98	75	63	96	43	34	12					
13	Oban	169	138	139	111	100	77	56	44	77	24	13	29	13				
14	Loch Melfort	184	154	155	117	114	93	69	61	92	40	27	45	18	14			
15	Craobh Haven	184	155	155	117	114	92	70	60	93	40	27	50	21	5	15		
16	Crinan	187	157	158	129	112	95	74	63	97	42	30	54	25	14	9	16	
17	Mull of Kintyre	232	203	189	175	159	143	121	105	120	89	87	98	72	62	57	51	17

NAVAL EXERCISE AREAS

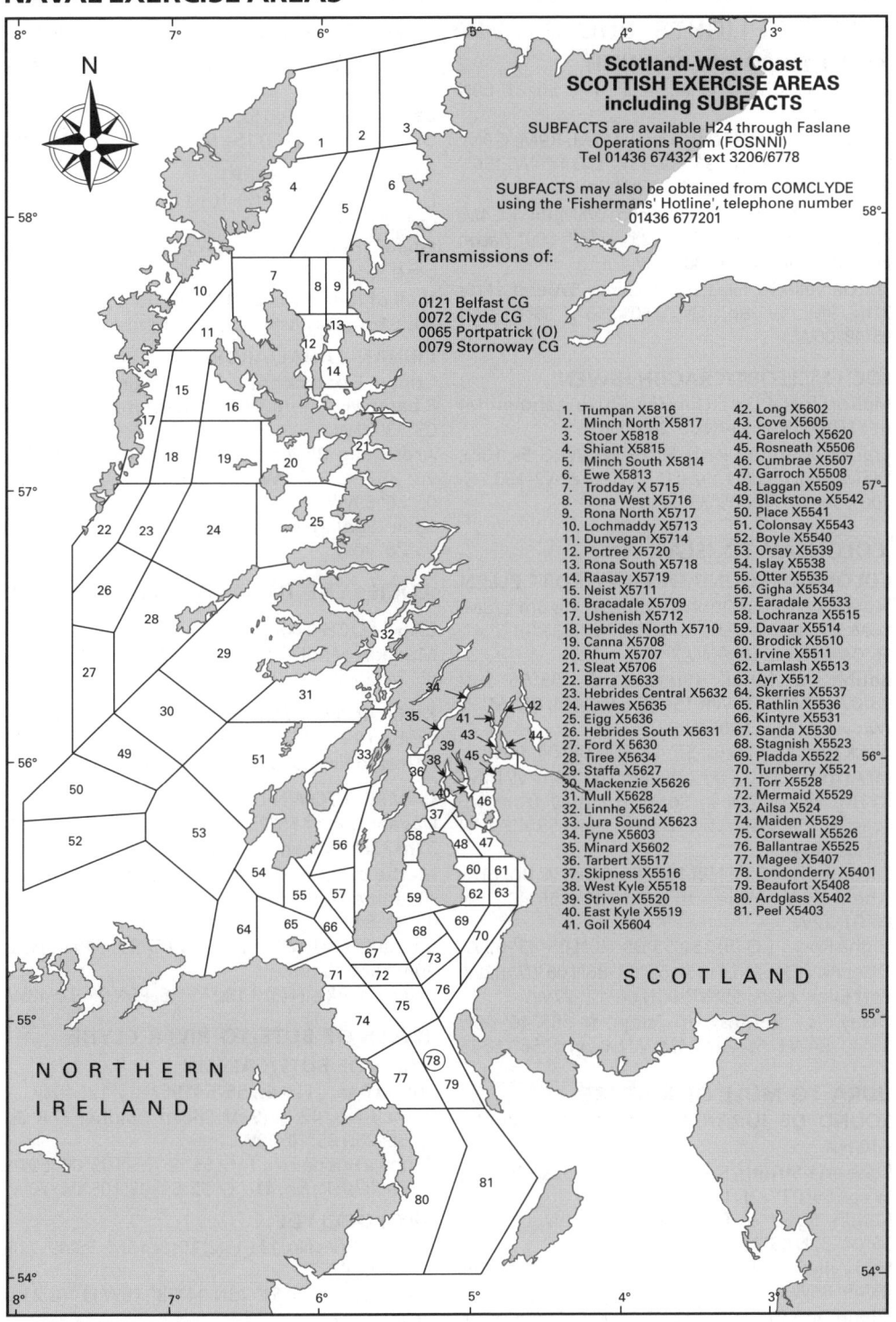

Scotland-West Coast
SCOTTISH EXERCISE AREAS
including SUBFACTS

SUBFACTS are available H24 through Faslane
Operations Room (FOSNNI)
Tel 01436 674321 ext 3206/6778

SUBFACTS may also be obtained from COMCLYDE
using the 'Fishermans' Hotline', telephone number
01436 677201

Transmissions of:

0121 Belfast CG
0072 Clyde CG
0065 Portpatrick (O)
0079 Stornoway CG

1. Tiumpan X5816
2. Minch North X5817
3. Stoer X5818
4. Shiant X5815
5. Minch South X5814
6. Ewe X5813
7. Trodday X 5715
8. Rona West X5716
9. Rona North X5717
10. Lochmaddy X5713
11. Dunvegan X5714
12. Portree X5720
13. Rona South X5718
14. Raasay X5719
15. Neist X5711
16. Bracadale X5709
17. Ushenish X5712
18. Hebrides North X5710
19. Canna X5708
20. Rhum X5707
21. Sleat X5706
22. Barra X5633
23. Hebrides Central X5632
24. Hawes X5635
25. Hebrides South X5631
26. Ford X 5630
27. Tiree X5634
28. Tiree X5634
29. Staffa X5627
30. Mackenzie X5626
31. Mull X5628
32. Linnhe X5624
33. Jura Sound X5623
34. Fyne X5603
35. Minard X5602
36. Tarbert X5517
37. Skipness X5516
38. West Kyle X5518
39. Striven X5520
40. East Kyle X5519
41. Goil X5604

42. Long X5602
43. Cove X5605
44. Gareloch X5620
45. Rosneath X5506
46. Cumbrae X5507
47. Garroch X5508
48. Laggan X5509
49. Blackstone X5542
50. Place X5541
51. Colonsay X5543
52. Boyle X5540
53. Orsay X5539
54. Islay X5538
55. Otter X5535
56. Gigha X5534
57. Earadale X5533
58. Lochranza X5515
59. Davaar X5514
60. Brodick X5510
61. Irvine X5511
62. Lamlash X5513
63. Ayr X5512
64. Skerries X5537
65. Rathlin X5536
66. Kintyre X5531
67. Sanda X5530
68. Stagnish X5523
69. Pladda X5522
70. Turnberry X5521
71. Torr X5528
72. Mermaid X5529
73. Ailsa X524
74. Maiden X5529
75. Corsewall X5526
76. Ballantrae X5525
77. Magee X5407
78. Londonderry X5401
79. Beaufort X5408
80. Ardglass X5402
81. Peel X5403

SCOTLAND

NORTHERN
IRELAND

29

AREA 7 SW. Scotland - *Oban to Kirkcudbright*

SELECTED LIGHTS, BUOYS & WAYPOINTS | Positions are referenced to WGS84

OBAN TO LOCH CRAIGNISH

Bogha Nuadh ⚓ Q (6) + LFl 15s; 56°21'·69N 05°37'·88W.

Fladda ⚡ Fl (2) WRG 9s 13m W11M, R9M, G9M; W twr; vis: 169°-R-186°-W-337°-G-344°-W-356°-R-026°; 56°14'·89N 05°40'·83W.

Dubh Sgeir (Luing) ⚡FlWRG 6s 9m W6M, R4M. G4M; W twr; vis: W000°- R010°- W025°- G199°-000°; *Racon (M) 5M*; 56°14'·76N 05°40'·20W.

The Garvellachs, Eileach an Naoimh, SW end ⚡ Fl 6s 21m 9M; W Bn; vis: 240°-215°; 56°13'·04N 05°49'·06W.

LOCH MELFORT/CRAOBH HAVEN

Melfort Pier ⚡ Dir FR 6m 3M; (Private shown 1/4 to 31/10); 56°16'·14N 05°30'·19W.

Craobh Marina Bkwtr Hd ⚡ Iso WRG 5s 10m, W5M, R3M, G3M ; vis:114°-G-162°-W-183°-R-200°; 56°12'·78N 05°33'·52W.

COLONSAY TO ISLAY

COLONSAY/SOUND OF ISLAY/PORT ELLEN

Scalasaig, Rubha Dubh ⚡ Fl (2) WR 10s 8m W8M, R6M; W bldg; vis: shore-R- 230°-W-337°-R-354°; 56°04'·01N 06°10'·90W.

Rhubh' a Mháil (Ruvaal) ☆ 55°56'·18N 06°07'·46W Fl (3) WR 15s 45m **W24M, R21M**; W twr; vis: 075°-R-180°-W-075°.

Black Rocks ⚓ Fl G 6s; 55°47'·50N 06°04'·09W.

McArthur's Hd ⚡ Fl (2) WR 10s 39m W14M, R11M; W twr; W in Sound of Islay from NE coast,159°-R-244°-W-E coast of Islay; 55°45'·84N 06°02'·90W.

Eilean a Chùirn ⚡ Fl (3) 18s 26m 8M; W Bn; obsc when brg more than 040°; 55°40'·12N 06°01'·22W.

Gigha Rocks ⚓ Q (9) 15s; 55°39'·20N 05°43'·65W.

Otter Rk ⚓ Q (6) + L Fl 15s; 55°33'·86N 06°07'·92W.

Port Ellen ⚓ QG; 55°37'·00N 06°12'·27W.

Orsay Is, **Rhinns of Islay** ☆ 55°40'·40N 06°30'·84W Fl 5s 46m **24M**; W twr; vis: 256°-184°.

JURA TO MULL OF KINTYRE

SOUND OF JURA/CRAIGHOUSE/L SWEEN/GIGHA

Reisa an t-Struith, S end of Is ⚡ Fl (2) 12s 12m 7M; W col; 56°07'·77N 05°38'·91W.

Ruadh Sgeir ⚡ Fl 6s 15m 9M; W ◯ twr; 56°04'·32N 05°39'·77W.

Skervuile ⚡ Fl 15s 22m 9M; W twr; 55°52'·46N 05°49'·85W.

Eilean nan Gabhar ⚡ Fl 5s 7m 8M; framework twr; vis: 225°-010°; 55°50'·04N 05°56'·25W.

Sgeir Gigalum ⚓ Fl G 6s 3m 4M; 55°39'·96N 05°42'·67W.

Cath Sgeir ⚓ Q (9) 15s; 55°39'·66N 05°47'·50W.

Gigalum Rks ⚓ Q (9) 15s; 55°39'·20N 05°43'·70W.

WEST LOCH TARBERT

Dunskeig Bay ⚡ Q (2) 10s 11m 8M; 55°45'·22N 05°35'·00W.

Eileen Tráighe (off S side) ⚓ Fl (2) R 5s 5m 3M; R post; 55°45'·37N 05°35'·75W.

Mull of Kintyre ☆ 55°18'·64N 05°48'·25W Fl (2) 20s 91m **24M**; W twr on W bldg; vis: 347°-178°.

CRINAN CANAL/ARDRISHAIG

Crinan, E of lock ent ⚡ Fl WG 3s 8m 4M; W twr, R band; vis: shore-W-146°-G-shore; 56°05'·48N 05°33'·37W.

Ardrishaig Bkwtr Hd ⚡ L Fl WRG 6s 9m 4M; vis: 287°-G-339°-W-350°-R-035°; 56°00'·76N 05°26'·59W.

Sgeir Sgalag No. 49 ⚓ Fl G 5s; 56°00'·36N 05°26'·30W.

LOCH FYNE TO SANDA ISLAND

EAST LOCH TARBERT

Madadh Maol ⚡ Fl R 2·5s 4m 3M; 55°52'·02N 05°24'·25W.

KILBRANNAN SOUND/CARRADALE BAY

Crubon Rk ⚓ Fl (2) R 12s; 55°34'·48N 05°27'·07W.

Otterard Rk ⚓ Q (3) 10s; 55°27'·07N 05°31'·11W.

CAMPBELTOWN LOCH

Davaar N Pt ☆ 55°25'·69N 05°32'·42W Fl (2) 10s 37m **23M**; W twr; vis: 073°-330°.

Methe Bk 'C' ⚓ Fl (2) 6s; 55°25'·30N 05°34'·42W.

Arranman's Barrels ⚓ Fl (2) R 12s; 55°19'·40N 05°32'·87W.

Sanda Island ☆ 55°16'·50N 05°35'·01W Fl 10s 50m **15M**; W twr.

Patersons Rk ⚓ Fl (3) R 18s; 55°16'·90N 05°32'·48W.

KYLES OF BUTE TO RIVER CLYDE

KYLES OF BUTE/CALADH

Rubha Ban ⚓ Fl R 4s; 55°54'·95N 05°12'·40W.

Burnt I No. 42 ⚓ (S of Eilean Buidhe) Fl R 2s; 55°55'·76N 05°10'·39W.

Rubha á Bhodaich ⚓ Fl G; 55°55'·38N 05°09'·59W.

Ardmaleish Pt No. 41 ⚓ Q; 55°53'·02N 05°04'·70W.

FIRTH OF CLYDE

Ascog Patches No. 13 ⚓ Fl (2) 10s 5m 5M; 55°49'·71N 05°00'·25W.

Toward Pt ☆ 55°51'·73N 04°58'·79W Fl 10s 21m **22M**; W twr.

Skelmorlie ⚓ Iso 5s; 55°51'·65N 04°56'·34W.

WEMYSS/INVERKIP/HOLY LOCH

Kip ⚓ QG; 55°54'·49N 04°52'·98W.
Warden Bank ⚓ Fl G 2s; 55°54'·77N 04°54'·54W.
Cowal ⚓ L Fl 10s; 55°56'·00N 04°54'·83W.
The Gantocks ⚓ Fl R 6s 12m 6M; ○ twr; 55°56'·45N 04°55'·08W.
Cloch Point ⚓ Fl 3s 24m 8M; W○ twr, B band, W dwellings; 55°56'·55N 04°52'·74W.
Holy Loch Marina 2 FR (vert) 4m 1M; 55°59'·00N 04°56'·80W.

LOCH LONG/LOCH GOIL/GOUROCK

Loch Long ⚓ Oc 6s; 55°59'·15N 04°52'·42W.
Ashton ⚓ Iso 5s; 55°58'·10N 04°50'·65W.
Whiteforeland ⚓ L Fl 10s; 55°58'·11N 04°47'·28W.
Rosneath Patch ⚓ Fl (2) 10s 5m 10M; 55°58'·52N 04°47'·45W.

ROSNEATH/RHU NARROWS/GARELOCH

Ldg Lts 356°. **Front, No. 7N** ⚓ 56°00'·05N 04°45'·36W
Dir lt 356°. WRG 5m **W16M**, R13M, G13M; vis: 353°-Al WG- 355°- FW-357°-Al WR-000°-FR-002°.
Dir lt 115° WRG 5m **W16M**, R13M, G13M; vis: 111°-Al WG-114°-FW- 116°-Al WR-119°-FR-121°.
Row ⚓ Fl G 5s; 55°59'·84N 04°45'·13W.
Cairndhu ⚓ Fl G 2·5s; 56°00'·35N 04°46'·00W.
Rhu SE ⚓ Fl G 3s; 56°00'·64N 04°47'·17W.
Rhu NE ⚓ QG; 56°01'·02N 04°47'·58W.
Rhu Spit ⚓ Fl 3s 6m 6M; 56°00'·84N 04°47'·34W.
8m 8M. are Fl G and Lts on N bank are Fl R.

CLYDE TO LOCH RYAN

LARGS/FAIRLIE

Approach ⚓ L Fl 10s; 55°46'·40N 04°51'·85W.
Largs Marina S Bkwtr Hd ⚓ Oc G 10s 4m 4M; 55°46'·36N 04°51'·73W.
Fairlie Patch ⚓ Fl G 1·5s; 55°45'·38N 04°52'·34W.

MILLPORT, GREAT CUMBRAE

The Eileans, W end ⚓ QG 5m 2M; 55°44'·89N 04°55'·59W.
Mountstuart ⚓ L Fl 10s; 55°48'·00N 04°57'·57W.

Portachur ⚓ Fl G 3s; 55°44'·35N 04°58'·52W.
Little Cumbrae Is, Cumbrae Elbow ⚓ Fl 6s 28m 14M; W twr; vis: 334°-193°; 55°43'·22N 04°58'·06W.

ARDROSSAN/TROON

Ardrossan N Bkwtr Hd ⚓ Fl R 5s 7m 5M; R gantry; 55°38'·53N 04°49'·64W.
W Crinan Rk ⚓ Fl R 4s; 55°38'·47N 04°49'·89W.
Eagle Rock ⚓ 55°38'·21N 04°49'·69W Fl G 5s.
Troon ⚓ Fl G 4s; 55°33'·06N 04°41'·35W.
Lady I ⚓ Fl 2s 19m 8M; W Bn; 55°31'·63N 04°44'·04W.

ARRAN/RANZA/LAMLASH

Hamilton Rk ⚓ Fl R 6s; 55°32'·63N 05°04'·90W.
Pillar Rk Pt ☆ (Holy Island), 55°31'·04N 05°03'·67W Fl (2) 20s 38m **25M**; W □ twr.
Pladda ☆ 55°25'·50N 05°07'·12W Fl (3) 30s 40m **17M**; W twr.

AYR/GIRVAN/LOCH RYAN

S. Nicholas ⚓ 55°28'·12N 04°39'·44W Fl G 2s.
Turnberry Point ☆, near castle ruins 55°19'·56N 04°50'·71W Fl 15s 29m **24M**; W twr.
Ailsa Craig ☆ 55°15'·12N 05°06'·52W Fl 4s 18m **17M**; W twr; vis: 145°-028°.
Girvan S Pier Hd °2 FG (vert) 8m 4M; W twr; 55°14'·72N 04°51'·90W.
Milleur Point ⚓ Q; 55°01'·28N 05°05'·66W.
Cairn Pt ⚓ Fl (2) R 10s 14m 12M; W twr; 54°58'·46N 05°01'·85W.

LOCH RYAN TO KIRKUDBRIGHT

Corsewall Point ☆ 55°00'·41N 05°09'·58W Fl (5) 30s 34m **22M**; W twr; vis: 027°-257°.
Killantringan Black Head ☆ 54°51'·70N 05°08'·85W Fl (2) 15s 49m **25M**; W twr.
Crammag Hd ☆ 54°39'·90N 04°57'·92W Fl 10s 35m **18M**; W twr.
Mull of Galloway ☆, SE end 54°38'·08N 04°51'·45W Fl 20s 99m **28M**; W twr; vis: 182°-105°.

KIRKCUDBRIGHT BAY

Hestan I, E end ⚓ Fl (2) 10s 42m 9M; 54°49'·95N 03°48'·53W.

		1	2	3	4	5	6	7	8	9	10	11	12	13	14
1	Loch Craignish	1													
2	Crinan	5	2												
3	Ardrishaig	14	9	3											
6	East Loch Tarbert	24	19	10	4										
5	Campbeltown	55	50	39	31	5									
6	Lamlash	48	43	34	25	24	6								
7	Largs	48	43	34	24	39	17	7							
8	Kip Marina	53	48	39	28	50	25	10	8						
9	Greenock	59	54	45	36	53	31	16	6	9					
10	Rhu (Helensburgh)	62	57	48	37	59	33	19	9	4	10				
11	Troon	54	49	40	33	33	16	20	29	34	38	11			
12	Girvan	67	62	53	43	29	20	33	46	49	51	21	12		
13	Stranraer	89	84	75	65	34	39	56	69	65	74	44	23	13	
14	Kirkcudbright	136	131	122	114	88	92	110	116	124	125	97	94	71	14

AREA 8 NW. England & Wales - *Kirkcudbright and IoMan to Swansea*

SELECTED LIGHTS, BUOYS & WAYPOINTS | Positions are referenced to WGS84

SOLWAY FIRTH TO BARROW-IN-FURNESS
SILLOTH/MARYPORT
Two Feet Bk ⌀ Q (9) 15s; 54°42'·90N 03°47'·10W.

Solway ⌀ Fl G 4s; 54°46'·80N 03°30'·14W.

Maryport S Pier Hd ⌀.Fl 1·5s 10m 6M;54°43'·07N 03°30'·64W.

S Workington ⌀ VQ (6) + L Fl 10s; 54°37'·01N 03°38'·58W.

Whitehaven W Pier Hd ⌀ Fl G 5s 16m 13M; W ○ twr; 54°33'·17N 03°35'·92W.

Saint Bees Hd ☆ 54°30'·81N 03°38'·23W Fl (2) 20s 102m **18M**; W○ twr; obsc shore-340°.

Selker ⌀ Fl (3) G 10s; *Bell;* 54°16'·14N 03°29'·58W.

Barrow Wind Farm ⌀ VQ (6) + L Fl 10s; 53°58'·20N 03°17'·40W.

Lightning Knoll ⌀ L Fl 10s; *Bell;* 53°59'·83N 03°14'·28W.

Isle of Walney ☆ 54°02'·92N 03°10'·64W Fl 15s 21m **23M**; stone twr; obsc 122°-127° within 3M of shore.

ISLE OF MAN
Whitestone Bk ⌀ Q (9) 15s; 54°24'·58N 04°20'·41W.

Point of Ayre ☆ 54°24'·94N 04°22'·13W Fl (4) 20s 32m **19M**; W twr, two R bands; *Racon (M) 13-15M.*

Low Lt ⌀ 54°25'·03N 04°21'·86W Fl 3s 10m 8M; R twr, lower part W, on B Base; part obsc 335°-341°.

Thousla Rk ⌀ Fl R 3s 9m 4M; 54°03'·73N 04°48'·05W.

Calf of Man ☆ W Pt 54°03'·19N 04°49'·78W Fl 15s 93m **26M**; W 8-sided twr; vis 274°-190°.

Chicken Rk ⌀ Fl 5s 38m 13M; twr; 54°02'·26N 04°50'·32W.

Douglas Head ☆ 54°08'·60N 04°27'·95W Fl 10s 32m **24M**; W twr; obsc brg more than 037°. FR Lts on radio masts 1 and 3M West.

Maughold Head ☆ 54°17'·72N 04°18'·58W Fl (3) 30s 65m **21M**.

Bahama ⌀ VQ (6) + L Fl 10s; 54°20'·01N 04°08'·57W.

King William Bank ⌀ Q (3) 10s; 54°26'·01N 04°00'·08W.

BARROW TO RIVERS MERSEY AND DEE
MORECAMBE/FLEETWOOD/RIVER RIBBLE
Morecambe ⌀ Q (9) 15s; *Whis;* 53°51'·99N 03°24'·10W.

Lune Deep ⌀ Q (6) + L Fl 15s; *Whis; Racon (T);* 53°55'·81N 03°11'·08W. 02°55'·80W.

R Lune ⌀ Q (9) 15s; 53°58'·63N 03°00'·03W. 53°58'·89N 02°52'·96W.

Gut ⌀ L Fl 10s; 53°41'·74N 03°08'·98W.

Jordan's Spit ⌀ Q (9) 15s; 53°35'·76N 03°19'·28W.

RIVER MERSEY APPROACHES
Bar ⌀ L Fl 10s; *Racon (T) 10M;* 53°32'·01N 03°20'·98W.

Q1 ⌀ VQ; 53°31'·00N 03°16'·72W.

Formby ⌀ Iso 4s 11m 6M; R hull, W stripes; 53°31'·13N 03°13'·50W.

Crosby ⌀ Oc 5s 11m 8M; R hull, W stripes; 53°30'·72N 03°06'·29W.

Brazil ⌀ QG; G hull; 53°26'·84N 03°02'·24W.

RIVER DEE
HE1 ⌀ Q (9) 15s; 53°26'·33N 03°18'·08W.

Hilbre I ⌀ Fl R 3s 14m 5M; W twr; 53°22'·99N 03°13'·72W.

Salisbury Mid ⌀ Fl (3) R 10s; 53°21'·30N 03°16'·39W.

Dee ⌀ Q (6) + L Fl 15s; 53°21'·99N 03°18'·68W.

N AND NW WALES COAST
RIVER DEE TO CONWY
N Hoyle ⌀ VQ; 53°26'·68N 03°30'·58W.

S Hoyle Outer ⌀ Fl R 2·5s; 53°21'·47N 03°24'·70W.

Prestatyn ⌀ QG; 53°21'·51N 03°28'·51W.

N Rhyl ⌀ Q; 53°22'·76N 03°34'·58W.

N Hoyle Wind Farm (30 turbines, see 9.10.5) centred on 53°25'·00N 03°27'·00W. NW, NE, SW, SE extremities (F.R Lts) Fl Y 2.5s 5M Horn Mo (U) 30s.

W Constable ⌀ Q (9) 15s; *Racon (M) 10M;* 53°23'·14N 03°49'·26W.

Conwy F'wy ⌀ L Fl 10s; 53°17'·95N 03°55'·58W.

C2 ⌀ Fl (2) R 10s; 53°17'·64N 03°54'·69W.

MENAI STRIAT - N APPROACHES
Trwyn-Du ⌀ Fl 5s 19m 12M; W○ castellated twr, B bands; vis: 101°-023°; *Bell (1) 30s,* sounded continuously; 53°18'·77N 04°02'·44W.

Ten Feet Bank ⌀ QR; 53°19'·47N 04°02'·82W.

ANGLESEY
Point Lynas ☆ 53°24'·98N 04°17'·35W Oc 10s 39m **18M**; W castellated twr; vis: 109°-315°; *Horn 45s;* H24 in periods of reduced visibility.

Archdeacon Rock ⌀ Q; 53°26'·71N 04°30'·87W.

The Skerries ☆ 53°25'·27N 04°36'·55W Fl (2) 15s 36m **20M**; W ○ twr, R band; *Racon (T) 25M.* Iso 4s 26m 10M; same twr; vis: 233°-253°; *Horn (2) 60s.* H24 in periods of reduced visibility.

Langdon ⌀ Q (9) 15s; 53°22'·74N 04°38'·74W.

Holyhead Bkwtr Hd ⌀ Fl (3) G 10s 21m 14M; W □ twr, B band; Fl Y vis: 174°-226°; *Siren 20s;* 53°19'·86N 04°37'·16W.

Marina Bkwtr Hd ⌀ 2 FR (vert); 53°18'·40N 04°38'·63W.

South Stack ☆ 53°19'·31N 04°41'·98W Fl 10s 60m **24M**; (H24); W ○ twr; obsc to N by N Stack and part obsc in Penrhos bay; *Horn 30s.* Fog Det lt vis: 145°-325°.

MENAI STRAIT TO BARDSEY ISLAND

CAERNARFON APPROACHES
(Direction of buoyage ⟳ SW to NE)

C2 ⬡ Fl R 10s; 53°07'·07N 04°24'·52W.

Llanddwyn I ⚡Fl WR 2·5s 12m W7M, R4M; W twr; vis: 280°-R- 015°-W-120°; 53°08'·05N 04°24'·79W.

Mussel Bank ⬡ Fl (2) R 5s; 53°07'·27N 04°20'·81W.

LLEYN PENINSULA/BARDSEY ISLAND
Porth Dinllaen, Careg y Chwislen ⬡ 52°56'·99N 04°33'·51W.

Bardsey I ☆ 52°44'·97N 04°48'·02W Fl (5) 15s 39m **26M**; W ☐ twr, R bands; obsc by Bardsey Is 198°-250° and in Tremadoc B when brg less than 260°; *Horn Mo (N) 45s*; H24.

CARDIGAN BAY

St Tudwal's ⚡Fl WR 15s 46m W14, R10M; vis: 349°-W-169°-R- 221°-W-243°-R-259°-W-293°-R-349°; obsc by East I 211°-231°; 52°47'·92N 04°28'·30W.

PWLLHELI/PORTHMADOG/BARMOUTH/ ABERDOVEY
Pwllheli App ⬡ Iso 2s; 52°53'·02N 04°23'·07W.

Porthmadog Fairway ⬡ L Fl 10s; 52°52'·97N 04°11'·18W.

Barmouth Outer ⬡ L Fl 10s; 52°42'·62N 04°04'·83W.

Sarn Badrig Causeway ⬡Q (9) 15s; *Bell;* 52°41'·19N 04°25'·36W.

Sarn-y-Bwch ⬡ VQ (9) 10s; 52°34'·81N 04°13'·58W.

Aberdovey Outer ⬡ Iso 4s; 52°32'·00N 04°05'·56W.

Patches ⬡ Q (9) 15s; 52°25'·83N 04°16'·41W.

ABERYSTWYTH/FISHGUARD
Aberystwyth S Bkwtr Hd ⚡ Fl (2) WG 10s 12m 10M; vis: 030°-G- 053°-W-210°; 52°24'·40N 04°05'·52W.

Fishguard N Bkwtr Hd ⚡ Fl G 4·5s 18m 13M; *Bell (1) 8s;* 52°00'·76N 04°58'·23W. 89m 5M.

Strumble Head ☆ 52°01'·79N 05°04'·43W Fl (4) 15s 45m **26M**;   vis: 038°-257°; (H24).

BISHOPS AND SMALLS
South Bishop ☆ 51°51'·14N 05°24'·74W Fl 5s 44m **16M**; W ○ twr;   *Horn (3) 45s; Racon (O)10M;* (H24).

The Smalls ☆ 51°43'·27N 05°40'·19W Fl (3) 15s 36m **18M**;   *Racon (T)* ;   *Horn (2) 60s.* Same twr, Iso R 4s 33m 13M; vis: 253°-285° over Hats & Barrels Rk; both Lts shown H24 in periods of reduced visibility.

Skokholm I ☆, 51°41'·64N 05°17'·22W Fl WR 10s 54m **W18M, R15M**; vis: 301°-W-154°-R-301°; partially obsc 226°-258°.

W & S WALES - BRISTOL CHANNEL

MILFORD HAVEN
St Ann's Head ☆ 51°40'·87N 05°10'·42W Fl WR 5s 48m **W18M, R17M**, R14M; W 8-sided twr; vis: 233°-W-247°-R-285°-R(intens)-314°-R-332°-W131°, partially obscured between 124°-129°; *Horn (2) 60s.*

W Blockhouse Pt ⬡ Ldg Lts 022·5°. Front, F 54m 13M; B stripe on W twr; vis: 004·5°-040·5°; intens on lead. By day 10M; vis: 004·5°-040·5°; *Racon (Q) range unknown*; 51°41'·31N 05°09'·56W.

Watwick Point Common Rear ☆, 0·5M from front, F 80m **15M**; vis: 013·5°-031·5°. By day 10M; vis: 013·5°-031·5°; *Racon (Y).*

St Ann's ⬡ Fl R 2·5s; 51°40'·25N 05°10'·51W.

Sheep ⬡ QG; 51°40'·06N 05°08'·31W.

Dakotian ⬡ Q (3) 10s; 51°42'·15N 05°08'·29W.

Turbot Bk ⬡ VQ (9) 10s; 51°37'·41N 05°10'·08W.

St Gowan ⬡ Q (6) + L Fl 15s, *Whis, Racon (T) 10M*; 51°31'·93N 04°59'·77W.

TENBY/CARMARTHEN BAY/BURRY INLET
Caldey I ⚡ Fl (3) WR 20s 65m W13M, R9M; vis: R173°- W212°- R088°-102°; 51°37'·90N 04°41'·08W.

Spaniel ⬡ Q (3) 10s; 51°38'·06N 04°39'·74W.

Tenby Pier Hd ⚡ FR 7m 7M; 51°40'·40N 04°41'·89W.

DZ7 ⬡ Fl Y 10s; 51°38'·09N 04°30'·12W.

DZ5 ⬡ Fl Y 2·5s; 51°36'·37N 04°24'·39W.

Burry Port ⚡51°40'·62N 04°15'·06W Fl 5s 7m **15M**.

W. Helwick (W HWK) ⬡ (9) 15s; *Racon (T) 10M; Whis;* 51°31'·40N 04°23'·65W Q.

E. Helwick ⬡ VQ (3) 5s; *Bell;* 51°31'·80N 04°12'·68W.

SWANSEA BAY
Ledge ⬡ VQ (6) + L Fl 10s; 51°29'·93N 03°58'·77W.

Mixon ⬡ Fl (2) R 5s; *Bell;* 51°33'·12N 03°58'·78W.

1	Portpatrick	**1**															
2	Mull of Galloway	16	**2**														
3	Kirkcudbright	48	32	**3**													
4	Maryport	65	49	26	**4**												
5	Workington	63	47	25	6	**5**											
6	Ravenglass	70	54	40	30	23	**6**										
7	Point of Ayre	38	22	28	37	31	34	**7**									
8	Peel	41	26	46	55	49	52	18	**8**								
9	Douglas	60	42	46	50	44	39	19	30	**9**							
10	Glasson Dock	101	85	74	66	60	37	64	85	63	**10**						
11	Fleetwood	95	79	68	59	53	30	58	80	57	10	**11**					
12	Liverpool	118	102	97	89	83	60	80	86	70	52	46	**12**				
13	Conwy	111	95	95	92	86	58	72	72	59	62	56	46	**13**			
14	Beaumaris	109	93	94	95	89	72	71	73	58	66	60	49	12	**14**		
15	Caernarfon	117	103	104	105	99	82	81	73	68	76	70	59	22	10	**15**	
16	Holyhead	93	81	94	96	90	69	68	62	50	79	73	68	36	32	26	**16**
17	Fishguard	171	158	175	175	169	160	153	140	134	153	147	136	100	88	78	89	**17**

IRELAND AND WEST UK MARINAS VHF CHANNELS
Solway Firth to Weymouth

N

Coleraine Marina **Ch M1**
Seaton's Marina **Ch M**
Ballycastle Marina

N. IRELAND

Glenarm Marina **No VHF**
Carrickfergus **Ch 37, 80**
Portaferry Marina **Ch M**
Bangor Marina **Ch 11, 80**

Maryport Marina **Ch 12, 16, 80**
Whitehaven **Ch 12**

REPUBLIC OF IRELAND

Carlingford Marina **Ch 37**
Ardglass Marina **Ch 37, 80**
Fleetwood Harbour Marina **Ch 12**
Glasson Dock **Ch 69**

IRISH SEA

Preston Marina

Holyhead Marina **Ch 37**
Malahide **Ch 37, 80**
Howth YC Marina **Ch 37A, 80**
Poolbeg Marina **Ch M**
Dun Laoghaire Marina **Ch M, M2, 16**

Liverpool Marina **Ch M**

Conwy Marina
Deganwy Marina

Pwllheli Marina

Dingle Marina **Ch M** Kilrush

Arklow Marina **Ch 12**

Fenit Marina **Ch M**

Waterford **Ch 12**

Aberystwyth
WALES

Cahersiveen **Ch M**

Kilmore Quay **Ch M**

Lawrence Cove **Ch 16**

Sharpness Marina **Ch 17**

Swansea Marina
Penarth Quays Marina
Portishead

Neyland Yacht Haven **Ch M, 80**
Milford Marina **Ch 18, 37**

Bristol Marina

Castlepark Marina **Ch M**
Kinsale YC Marina **Ch M**

CELTIC SEA

Watchet Hbr

Weymouth Marina
Weymouth Harbour **Ch 12**

Crosshaven BY Marina **Ch M**
East Ferry Marina **Ch M**
Royal Cork YC Marina **Ch M**
Salve Marine **Ch M**

Torquay Marina
Exmouth **Ch 14**
Bridport **Ch 11**

Penzance **Ch 12**

Fowey **Ch 12**

Brixham Marina

Falmouth Marina
Falmouth Visitors' Yt Haven **Ch 12**
Port Pendennis Marina
Mylor Yacht Harbour **Ch M**

Dart Hbr **Ch 11**
Dart/Noss-on-Dart Marinas
Darthaven Marina

Salcombe **Ch 14**

Plymouth Yt Haven
Q. Anne's Battery Marina
Sutton Harbour **Ch 12**
Mayflower Marina
Torpoint Yt Harbour

Unless otherwised stated all marinas work **Ch 80**

AREA 9 S.Wales & SW. England - *Swansea to Padstow*

SELECTED LIGHTS, BUOYS & WAYPOINTS | Positions are referenced to WGS84

BRISTOL CHANNEL (NORTH SHORE)

SWANSEA BAY/PORT TALBOT/PORTHCAWL

Mixon ⸾ Fl (2) R 5s; *Bell;* 51°33'·12N 03°58'·78W.
Grounds ⸾ VQ (3) 5s; 51°32'·81N 03°53'·47W.
Mumbles ☆ 51°34'·01N 03°58'·27W Fl (4) 20s 35m **15M**; W twr; *Horn (3) 60s.*
SW Inner Green Grounds ⸾ Q (6) + L Fl 15s; *Bell;* 51°34'·06N 03°57'·03W.
Cabenda ⸾ VQ (6) + L Fl 10s; *Racon (Q);* 51°33'·36N 03°52'·23W.
P Talbot N Outer ⸾ Fl R 5s; 51°33'·78N 03°51'·38W.
Kenfig ⸾ VQ (3) 5s; 51°29'·44N 03°46'·06W.
W Scar ⸾ Q (9) 15s, *Bell,* **Racon (T) 10M;** 51°28'·31N 03°55'·57W.
S Scar ⸾ Q (6) + L Fl 15s; 51°27'·61N 03°51'·58W.
E Scar ⸾ Q (3) 10s; *Bell;* 51°27'·98N 03°46'·76W.
Fairy ⸾ Q (9) 15s; *Bell;* 51°27'·86N 03°42'·07W.
Tusker ⸾ Fl (2) R 5s *Bell;* 51°26'·85N 03°40'·74W.
W Nash ⸾ VQ (9) 10s; *Bell;* 51°25'·99N 03°45'·95W.
East Nash ⸾ Q (3) 10s; 51°24'·06N 03°34'·10W.
Nash ☆ 51°24'·03N 03°33'·06W Fl (2) WR 15s 56m **W21M, R16M**; vis: 280°-R-290°-W-100°-R-120°-W-128°.

BARRY/CARDIFF/PENARTH/NEWPORT

Breaksea ⸾ L Fl 10s; *Racon (T) 10M;* 51°19'·88N 03°19'·08W.
Merkur ⸾ QR; 51°21'·88N 03°15'·95W.
Barry W Bkwtr Hd ⸹ Fl 2·5s 12m 10M; 51°23'·46N 03°15'·52W.
Lavernock Spit ⸾ VQ (6) + L Fl 10s; 51°23'·02N 03°10'·82W.
Mackenzie ⸾ QR; 51°21'·75N 03°08'·24W.
Wolves ⸾ VQ; 51°23'·13N 03°08'·88W.
Flat Holm ☆, SE Pt Fl (3) WR 10s 50m **W15M**, R12M; W ○ twr; vis: 106°-R-140°-W-151°-R-203°-W-106°; (H24). 51°22'·54N 03°07'·14W
Weston ⸾ Fl (2) R 5s; 51°22'·60N 03°05'·75W.
Monkstone Rk ⸹ Fl 5s 13m 12M; 51°24'·89N 03°06'·02W.
Ranie ⸾ Fl (2) R 5s; 51°24'·23N 03°09'·39W.
S Cardiff ⸾ Q (6) + L Fl 15s; *Bell;* 51°24'·18N 03°08'·57W.
Outer Wrach ⸾ Q (9) 15s; 51°26'·20N 03°09'·46W.
N Cardiff ⸁ QG; 51°26'·52N 03°07'·19W.
EW Grounds ⸾ L Fl 10s 7M; *Bell;* **Racon (T) 7M;** 51°27'·12N 02°59'·95W.
Newport Deep ⸁ Fl (3) G 10s; *Bell;* 51°29'·36N 02°59'·12W.
East Usk ☆ 51°32'·40N 02°58'·01W Fl (2) WRG 10s 11m W11M, R10M, G10M; vis: 284°-W-290° - obscured shore-324°-R- 017°-W-037°-G-115°-W-120°. Also Oc WRG 10s 10m W11M, R9M, G9M; vis:

018°-G-022°-W- 024°-R-028°.

SEVERN ESTUARY

THE SHOOTS

Lower Shoots ⸾ Q (9) 15s 6m 7M; 51°33'·85N 02°42'·05W.
2nd Severn Crossing, Centre span ⸹ Q Bu 5M; *Racon (O) (3cm) range unknown;* 51°34'·45N 02°42'·03W.
Old Man's Hd ⸾ VQ (9) W 10s 6m 7M; 51°34'·74N 02°41'·69W.
Lady Bench (Lts in line 234°) ⸾ QR 6m 6M; 51°34'·85N 02°42'·20W. Rear, Oc R 5s 38m 3M.
Charston Rk ⸹ Fl 3s 5m 8M; 51°35'·35N 02°41'·68W.
Chapel Rk ⸹ Fl WRG 2·6s 6m 8M, vis: W213°-G284°-W049°-R051·5°-160°; 51°36'·44N 02°39'·21W.

SEVERN BRIDGE TO SHARPNESS

Aust ⸹ 2 QG (vert) 11m 6M; 51°36'·16N 02°38'·00W.
West Tower ⸹ 3 QR (hor) on upstream/downstream sides; *Siren (3) 30s;* obscured 040°-065°; 51°36'·73N 02°38'·80W.
Centre of span ⸹ Q Bu, each side; 51°36'·59N 02°38'·43W.
Lyde Rock ⸹ Q WR 5m 5M; vis: 148°-R-237°-W-336°-R-067°; 51°36'·89N 02°38'·67W.
COUNTS ⸺ Q; 51°39'·48N 02°35'·84W .
LEDGES ⚓ 51°39'·77N 02°34'·15W Fl (3) G 10s.
Bull Rock ⸹ Fl 3s 6m 8M; 51°41'·80N 02°29'·89W.
Sharpness S Pier Hd ⸹ 2 FG (vert) 6m 3M; *Siren 20s;* 51°42'·97N 02°29'·12W.

BRISTOL CHANNEL (SOUTH SHORE)

BRISTOL DEEP

N Elbow ⸁ QG; *Bell;* 51°26'·97N 02°58'·65W.
S Mid Grounds ⸾ VQ (6) + L Fl 10s; 51°27'·62N 02°58'·68W.
E Mid Grounds ⸾ Fl R 5s; 51°28'·14N 02°53'·56W.
Clevedon ⸾ VQ; 51°27'·39N 02°54'·93W.
Welsh Hook ⸾ Q (6) + L Fl 15s; *Bell;* 51°28'·53N 02°51'·86W.
Avon ⸁ Fl G 2·5s; 51°27'·92N 02°51'·73W.
Black Nore Pt ☆ 51°29'·09N 02°48'·05W Fl (2) 10s 11m **17M**; obsc by Sand Pt when brg less than 049°; vis: 044°-243°.
Firefly ⸁ Fl (2) G 5s; 51°29'·96N 02°45'·35W.
Portishead Pt ☆ 51°29'·68N 02°46'·42W Q (3) 10s 9m **16M**; B twr, W base; vis: 060°-262°; *Horn 20s.*

AVONMOUTH/RIVER AVON

Royal Edward Dock N Pier Hd ⸹ Fl 4s 15m 10M; vis: 060°-228·5°; 51°30'·49N 02°43'·09W.
Avonmouth S Pier Hd ⸹ Oc RG 30s 9m 10M; vis: 294°-R-036°-G-194°; 51°30'·37N 02°43'·10W.

BRISTOL CHANNEL (SOUTH SHORE)

E Culver ⚓ Q (3) 10s; 51°18'·00N 03°15'·44W.
W Culver ⚓ VQ (9) 10s; 51°17'·37N 03°18'·68W.
Gore ⚓ Iso 5s; *Bell;* 51°13'·94N 03°09'·79W.

BURNHAM-ON-SEA/RIVER PARRETT

Lower Lt Ent ⚡ Fl 7·5s 7m 12M; vis: 074°-164°;
51°14'·89N 03°00'·36W. Dir lt 076°. F WRG 4m W12M,
R10M, G10M; vis: 071°-G-075°-W-077°-R-081°.
Bridgewater Bar No. 1 ⚓ QR; 51°14'·53N
03°03'·75W.

WATCHET/MINEHEAD

Watchet W Bkwtr Hd ⚡ Oc G 3s 9m 9M;
51°11'·03N 03°19'·74W.
Minehead Bkwtr Hd ⚡ Fl (2) G 5s 4M; vis: 127°-262°;
51°12'·81N 03°28'·36W.
Lynmouth Foreland ☆ 51°14'·73N 03°47'·21W Fl
(4) 15s 67m **18M**; W ○ twr; vis: 083°-275°; (H24).

LYNMOUTH/WATERMOUTH/ILFRACOMBE

Lynmouth Harbour Arm ⚡ 2 FG (vert) 6m 5M;
51°13'·92N 03°49'·84W.
Sand Ridge ⚓ Q G; 51°15'·01N 03°49'·77W.
Copperas Rock ⚓ 51°13'·78N 04°00'·60W.
Watermouth ⚡ Oc WRG 5s 1m 3M; W △; vis:
149·5°-G-151·5°-W- 154·5°-R-156·5°; 51°12'·93N
04°04'·60W.
Lantern Hill ⚡ Fl G 2·5s 39m 6M; 51°12'·66N
04°06'·78W.
Horseshoe ⚓ Q; 51°15'·02N 04°12'·96W.
Bull Point ☆ 51°11'·94N 04°12'·09W Fl (3) 10s 54m
20M; W ○ twr, obscd shore-056°. Same twr; FR 48m
12M; vis: 058°-096°.
Morte Stone ⚓ 51°11'·30N 04°14'·95W.
Baggy Leap ⚓ 51°08'·92N 04°16'·97W.

BIDEFORD, RIVERS TAW AND TORRIDGE

Bideford F'wy ⚓ L Fl 10s; *Bell;* 51°05'·25N 04°16'·25W.
Bideford Bar ⚓ Q G; 51°04'·96N 04°14'·83W.
Pulley ⚓ Fl G 10s; 51°04'·08N 04°12'·74W.
Instow ☆ Ldg Lts 118°. **Front,** 51°03'·62N
04°10'·67W Oc 6s 22m **15M**; vis: 104·5°-131·5°.
Rear, 427m from front, Oc 10s 38m **15M**; vis:
104°-132°; (H24).
Crow Pt ⚡ Fl WR 2. 5s 8m W6M R5M; vis: 225°-R-
232°-W-237°-R-358°-W-015°-R-045°; 51°03'·96N
04°11'·39W.

CLOVELLY/HARTLAND/LUNDY

Clovelly Hbr Quay Hd ⚡ 50°59'·92N 04°23'·83W
Fl G 5s 5m 5M.
Lundy Near North Pt ☆ 51°12'·10N 04°40'·65W Fl
15s 48m **17M**; vis: 009°-285°.
Lundy South East Pt ☆ 51°09'·72N 04°39'·37W Fl
5s 53m **15M**; vis: 170°-073°; *Horn 25s.*
Jetty Head ⚡ Fl R 3s 8m 3M; 51°09'·80N
04°39'·20W.
Hartland Point ☆ 51°01'·29N 04°31'·59W Fl (6)
15s 37m **25M**; (H24); *Horn 60s.*

NORTH CORNWALL
PADSTOW/NEWQUAY

Stepper Point ⚡ L Fl 10s 12m 4M; 50°34'·12N
04°56'·72W.
Greenaway ⚓ Fl (2) R 10s; 50°33'·78N 04°56'·06W.
Bar ⚓ Fl G 5s; 50°33'·46N 04°56'·12W.
Padstow N Quay Hd ⚡ 2 FG (vert) 6m 2M;
50°32'·50N 04°56'·16W.
Trevose Head ☆ 50°32'·94N 05°02'·13W Fl 7·5s
62m **21M**; *Horn (2) 30s.*
Newquay N Pier Hd ⚡ 2 FG (vert) 5m 2M;
50°25'·07N 05°05'·19W..

HAYLE/ST IVES

The Stones ⚓ Q; 50°15'·64N 05°25'·51W.
Godrevy I ⚡ Fl WR 10s 37m W12M, R9M; vis: 022°-
W-101°-R-145°-W-272°; 50°14'·54N 05°24'·04W.
Hayle App ⚓ QR; 50°12'·26N 05°26'·30W.
St Ives App ⚓ 50°12'·85N 05°28'·42W
East Pier Hd ⚡ 2 FG (vert) 8m 5M; 50°12'·80N
05°28'·61W.
West Pier Hd ⚡ 2 FR (vert) 5m 3M; 50°12'·77N
05°28'·73W.
Pendeen ☆ 50°09'·90N 05°40'·32W Fl (4) 15s
59m **16M**; vis: 042°-240°; in bay between
Gurnard Hd and Pendeen it shows to coast;
Horn 20s.

**For Lts further W see Area 1 SW England - *Isles
of Scilly to Anvil Point.***

#		1	2	3	4	5	6	7	8	9	10	11	12			
1	Aberystwyth	1	12	64	66	122	164	192	224	254	286	299	318	361	Kilrush	12
2	Fishguard	40	2	11	13	69	111	139	171	201	233	246	265	308	Dingle	11
3	Milford Haven	84	48	3	10	56	102	131	165	188	227	242	252	295	Valentia	10
4	Tenby	107	71	28	4	9	42	70	102	132	164	177	196	239	Baltimore	9
5	Swansea	130	94	55	36	5	8	35	69	95	135	150	168	202	Kinsale	8
6	Cardiff	161	125	86	66	46	6	7	34	65	100	115	133	172	Youghal	7
7	Sharpness	192	156	117	106	75	33	7	6	32	69	84	102	139	Dunmore East	6
8	Avonmouth	175	139	100	89	58	20	18	8	5	34	47	66	108	Rosslare	5
9	Burnham-on-Sea	169	133	94	70	48	53	50	33	9	4	15	36	75	Arklow	4
10	Ilfracombe	128	92	53	35	25	44	74	57	45	10	3	21	63	Wicklow	3
11	Padstow	142	106	70	70	76	97	127	110	98	55	11	2	48	Dun Laoghaire	2
12	Longships	169	133	105	110	120	139	169	152	140	95	50	12	1	Carlingford Lough	1

AREA 10 Ireland - *South and Westwards from Rockabill to Inisheer*

SELECTED LIGHTS, BUOYS & WAYPOINTS | Positions are referenced to WGS84

LAMBAY ISLAND TO TUSKAR ROCK

MALAHIDE/LAMBAY ISLAND/HOWTH
Taylor Rks ↓ Q; 53°30'·21N 06°01'·87W.
Rowan Rocks ↓ Q (3) 10s; 53°23'·88N 06°03'·27W.
Howth E Pier Hd ≤ Fl (2) WR 7·5s 13m W12M, R9M;
W twr; vis: W256°-R295°-256°; 53°23'·66N
06°04'·03W.
Baily ☆ 53°21'·70N 06°03'·14W Fl 15s 41m **26M**; twr.
Rosbeg E ↓ Q (3) 10s; 53°21'·02N 06°03'·45W.
Rosbeg S ↓ Q (6)+L Fl 15s; 53°20'·22N 06°04'·17W.
S Burford ↓ VQ (6) + L Fl 10s; *Whis*; 53°18'·07N
06°01'·27W.

PORT OF DUBLIN/DUN LAOGHAIRE
Dublin Bay ↓ Mo (A) 10s; *Racon (M)*; 53°19'·92N
06°04'·64W.
Great S Wall Hd Poolbeg ☆ Fl R 4s 20m
10M*(synchro with N.Bull)*; R ○ twr; *Horn (2)
60s*; 53°20'·53N 06°09'·08W
Dublin N Bank ☆ 53°20'·69N 06°10'·59W Oc G 8s
10m **16M**; G □ twr.
Dun Laoghaire E Bkwtr Hd ≤ 53°18'·15N
06°07'·62W Fl (2) R 10s 16m **17M**; twr, R lantern;
Horn 30s (or *Bell (1) 6s*).
Muglins ⚡Fl 5s 14m 11M; 53°16'·55N 06°04'·58W.
Bennett Bk ↓ Q (6)+L Fl 15s; 53°20'·17N 05°55'·11W.
Kish Bank ☆ 53°18'·64N 05°55'·48W Fl (2) 20s 29m
22M; W twr, R band; *Racon (T) 15M*; *Horn (2) 30s*.
S Codling ↓ VQ (6) + L Fl 10s; 53°04'·74N
05°49'·76W.
S India ↓ Q (6)+L Fl 15s; 53°00'·36N 05°53'·31W.
CODLING LANBY ⌐ 53°03'·02N 05°40'·76W Fl 4s
12m **15M**; tubular structure on By; *Racon
(G)10M*; *Horn 20s*.

WICKLOW/ARKLOW
Wicklow E Pier Hd ≤ Fl WR 5s 11m 6M; W twr,
R base and cupola; vis: 136°-R-293°-W-136°;
52°58'·99N 06°02'·07W.
Wicklow Head ☆ 52°57'·95N 05°59'·89W; Fl (3) 15s
37m **23M**; W twr.
N Arklow ↓ Q; 52°53'·86N 05°55'·21W.
Arklow Bank Wind Farm from 52°48'·47N
05°56'·57W to 52°46'·47N 05°57'·11W, N and S
Turbines Fl Y 5s14m 10M + Fl W Aero lts. AIS
transmitters. Other turbines Fl Y 5s.
S Arklow ↓ VQ (6) + L Fl 10s; 52°40'·82N
05°59'·21W.
ARKLOW LANBY ⌐ 52°39'·52N 05°58'·16W Fl
(2) 12s 12m **15M**; *Racon (O)10M*; *Horn Mo (A) 30s*.
No. 2 Glassgorman ⚓ Fl (4) R 10s; 52°44'·52N
06°05'·36W.
S Blackwater ↓ Q (6) + L Fl 15s; 52°22'·76N
06°12'·86W.

WEXFORD/ROSSLARE
S Long ↓ VQ (6) + L Fl 10s; 52°14'·84N
06°15'·64W.
Splaugh ⚓ Fl R 6s; 52°14'·37N 06°16'·76W.
Tuskar ☆ 52°12'·17N 06°12'·42W Q (2) 7·5s 33m
24M; W twr; *Horn (4) 45s, Racon (T) 18M*.

TUSKAR ROCK TO OLD HD OF KINSALE
S Rock ↓ Q (6)+L Fl 15s; 52°10'·80N 06°12'·84W.
Barrels ↓ Q (3) 10s; 52°08'·32N 06°22'·05W.

KILMORE/WATERFORD
St Patrick's Bridge ⚓ Fl R 6s; (Apr-Sep);
52°09'·30N 06°34'·71W
CONINGBEG ⟿ 52°02'·40N 06°39'·49W Fl (3) 30s
12m **24M**; R hull/twr, *Racon (M) 13M*; *Horn (3) 60s*.
Hook Hd ☆ 52°07'·32N 06°55'·85W Fl 3s 46m
23M; W twr, two B bands; *Racon (K) 10M vis:
237°-177°*; *Horn (2) 45s*.
Waterford ↓ Fl R 3s. Fl (3) R 10s; 52°08'·95N
06°57'·00W.
Dunmore East Pier Head ☆ 52°08'·93N
06°59'·37W Fl WR 8s 13m **W17M**, R13M; Gy twr;
vis: W225°-R310°-004°.

DUNGARVAN
Helvick ↓ Q (3) 10s; 52°03'·61N 07°32'·25W.
Mine Head ☆ 51°59'·52N 07°35'·25W Fl (4) 20s
87m **20M**; W twr, B band; vis: 228°-052°.

YOUGHAL/BALLYCOTTON
Youghal W side of ent ☆ 51°56'·57N 07°50'·53W
Fl WR 2·5s 24m **W17M**, R13M; W twr; vis: W183°-
R273°- W295°- R307°- W351°-003°.
Ballycotton ☆ 51°49'·52N 07° 59'·09W Fl WR 10s
59m **W21M, R17M**; B twr, within W walls, B lantern;
vis: W238°-R048°-238°; *Horn (4) 90s*.

CORK
Cork ↓ L Fl 10s; *Racon (T) 7M*; 51°42'·92N
08°15'·60W.
Fort Davis Ldg lts 354·1°. Front, 51°48'·82N
08°15'·80W Dir WRG 29m **17M**; vis: FG351·5°-
AlWG352·25°-FW353°-AlWR355°-FR355·75°-
356·5°. Rear, Dognose Quay, 203m from front,
Oc 5s 37m 10M; Or 3, synch with front.
Roche's Point ☆ 51°47'·59N 08°15'·29W Fl WR 3s
30m **W20M, R16M**; vis: Rshore- W292°- R016°-
033°, W(unintens) 033°- R159°- shore.

KINSALE/OYSTER HAVEN
Bulman ↓ Q (6)+L Fl 15s; 51°40'·14N 08°29'·74W.
Charle's Fort ≤ Fl WRG 5s 18m W9M, R6M, G7M;
vis: G348°- W358°- R004°-168°; H24; 51°41'·74N
08°29'·97W.

OLD HEAD OF KINSALE TO MIZEN HEAD

Old Head of Kinsale ☆, S point 51°36'·28N 08°32'·03W Fl (2) 10s 72m **20M**; B twr, two W bands; *Horn (3) 45s*.

Galley Head ☆ summit 51°31'·80N 08°57'·19W Fl (5) 20s 53m **23M**; W twr; vis: 256°-065°.

Kowloon Br ⛗ Q (6)+LFl15s; 51°27'·58N 09°13'·75W.

BALTIMORE/SCHULL/CROOKHAVEN

Barrack Pt ⛗ Fl (2) WR 6s 40m W6M, R3M; vis: R168°- W294°-038°; 51°28'·33N 09°23'·65W.

Fastnet ☆, W end 51°23'·35N 09°36'·19W Fl 5s 49m **27M**; Gy twr, *Horn (4) 60s*, *Racon (G) 18M*.

Mizen Head ☆ 51°27'·00N 09°49'·24W Iso 4s 55m **15M**; vis: 313°-133°.

MIZEN HEAD TO DINGLE BAY

Sheep's Hd ☆ 51°32'·60N 09°50'·95W Fl (3) WR 15s 83m **W18M, R15M**; W bldg; vis: 007°-R-017°-W-212°.

BANTRY BAY/KENMARE RIVER

Roancarrigmore ☆ 51°39'·19N 09°44'·83W Fl WR 3s 18m **W18M**, R14M; W ☐ twr, B band; vis: 312°-W-050°-R-122°-R(unintens)-242°-R-312°. Reserve lt W8M, R6M obsc 140°-220°.

Ardnakinna Pt ☆ 51°37'·11N 09°55'·08W Fl (2) WR 10s 62m **W17M**, R14M; W ○ twr; vis: 319°-R- 348°-W- 066°-R-shore.

Bull Rock ☆ 51°35'·51N 10°18'·08W Fl 15s 83m **21M**; W twr; vis: 220°-186°.

Skelligs Rock ☆ 51°46'·12N 10°32'·51W Fl (3) 15s 53m **19M**; W twr; vis: 262°-115°; part obsc within 6M 110°-115°.

VALENTIA/PORTMAGEE

Fort (Cromwell) Point ☆ 51°56'·02N 10°19'·27W Fl WR 2s 16m **W17M, R15M**; W twr; vis: 304°-R-351°,102°-W-304°; obsc from seaward by Doulus Head when brg more than 180°.

DINGLE BAY TO LOOP HEAD

DINGLE BAY/VENTRY/DINGLE/FENIT

Inishtearaght ☆, W end Blasket Islands 52°04'·55N 10°39'·68W Fl (2) 20s 84m **19M**; W twr; vis: 318°-221°; *Racon (O)*.

Little Samphire Is ☆ 52°16'·26N 09°52'·91W Fl WRG 5s 17m **W16M**, R13M; G13M; Bu ○ twr; vis: 262°-R-275°, 280-R-090°-G-140°-W- 152°-R-172°.

SHANNON ESTUARY

Ballybunnion ⛗ VQ; *Racon (M) 6M*; 52°32'·52N 09°46'·93W.

Kilcredaune Hd ☆ Fl 6s 41m **15M**; W twr; 52°34'·79N 09°42'·58W; obsc 224°-247° by hill within 1M. twr; vis: 208°-092°; 52°36'·32N 09°31'·03W.

Loop Head ☆ 52°33'·68N 09°55'·96W Fl (4) 20s 84m **23M**.

North and Westwards from Rockabill to Inisheer

LAMBAY ISLAND TO DONAGHADEE

Rockabill ☆ 53°35'·82N 06°00'·25W Fl WR 12s 45m **W22M, R18M**; W twr, B band; vis: 178°-W-329°-R-178°; H24.

DROGHEDA/DUNDALK

Drogheda Port Appr Dir lt 53°43'·30N 06°14'·73W WRG 10m **W19M, R15M**, G15M; vis: 268°-FG- 269°-Al WG-269·5°-FW-270·5°-Al WR-271°-FR-272°; H24.

Dundalk Pile Light ☆ 53°58'·56N 06°17'·70W Fl WR 15s 10m **W21M, R18M**; W Ho; vis: 124°-W-151°-R-284°-W-313°-R-124°. Fog Det lt VQ 7m, vis: when brg 358°; *Horn (3) 60s*.

CARLINGFORD LOUGH

Carlingford ⛗ L Fl 10s; 53°58'·76N 06°01'·06W.

Hellyhunter ⛗ Q (6) + L Fl 15s; *Racon*; 54°00'·35N 06°02'·10W.

Haulbowline ☆ 54°01'·19N 06°04'·74W Fl (3) 10s 32m **17M**; Gy twr; reserve lt 15M; Fog Det lt VQ 26m; vis: 330°. Turning lt ⛗ FR 21m 9M; same twr; vis: 196°-208°; *Horn 30s*.

DUNDRUM BAY

St John's Point ☆ 54°13'·61N 05°39'·30W Q (2) 7·5s 37m **25M**; B twr, Y bands; H24 when horn is operating. **Auxiliary Light** ☆ Fl WR 3s 14m **W15M**, R11M; same twr, vis: 064°-W-078°-R-shore; Fog Det lt VQ 14m vis: 270°; *Horn (2) 60s*.

STRANGFORD LOUGH/ARDS PENINSULA

Strangford ⛗ L Fl 10s; 54°18'·61N 05°28'·67W.

Bar Pladdy ⛗ Q (6) + L Fl 15s; 54°19'·34N 05°30'·51W.

Butter Pladdy ⛗ Q (3) 10s; 54°22'·45N 05°25'·74W.

SOUTH ROCK ⛴ 54°24'·49N 05°22'·02W Fl (3) R 30s 12m **20M**; R hull and lt twr, W Mast, *Horn (3) 45s, Racon (T) 13M*.

BALLYWATER/DONAGHADEE

Skulmartin ⛗ L Fl 10s; *Whis;* 54°31'·82N 05°24'·80W.

Donaghadee ☆, S Pier Hd 54°38'·70N 05°31'·86W Iso WR 4s 17m **W18M**, R14M; W twr; vis: shore-W-326°-R-shore; *Siren 12s*.

DONAGHADEE TO RATHLIN ISLAND

BELFAST LOUGH/BANGOR

Mew I ☆ NE end 54°41'·91N 05°30'·79W Fl (4) 30s 37m; B twr, W band; *Racon (O) 14M*.

S Briggs ⛗ 54°41'·19N 05°35'·72W Fl (2) R 10s.

BangorN Pier Hd ⛗ Iso R 12s 9m14M; 54°40'·03N 05°40'·34W.

Belfast Fairway ⛗ LFl10s; *Horn (1) 16s; Racon(G)*; 54°41'·71N 05°46'·24W

CARRICKFERGUS/LARNE

Carrickfergus Marina E Bkwtr Hd ⚡ QG 8m 3M; 54°42'·58N 05°48'·69W.

Black Hd ☆ 54°45'·99N 05°41'·33W Fl 3s 45m **27M**; W 8-sided twr.

N Hunter Rock ↓ Q; 54°53'·04N 05°45'·13W.

Larne Chaine Twr ☆ Iso WR 5s 23m **16M**; Gy twr; vis: 230°-W-240°-240°-R-shore; 54°51'·27N 05°47'·90W.

East Maiden ⚡ Fl (3) 20s 29m 24M; W twr, B band; *Racon (M) 11-21M.* Auxiliary lt Fl R 5s 15m 8M; 54°55'·74N 05°43'·65W; same twr; vis:142°-182° over Russel and Highland Rks.

RATHLIN ISLAND TO INISHTRAHULL

RATHLIN ISLAND

Altacarry Head Rathlin East ☆ 55°18'·06N 06°10'·30W Fl (4) 20s 74m **26M**; W twr, B band; vis: 110°-006° and 036°-058°; *Racon (G) 15-27M.*

Rathlin W 0·5M NE of Bull Pt ⚡ 55°18'·05N 06°16'·82W Fl R 5s 62m **22M**; W twr, lantern at base; vis: 015°-225°; H24.

LOUGH FOYLE

Foyle ↓ L Fl 10s; 55°15'·32N 06°52'·60W.

Inishowen ☆ 55°13'·56N 06°55'·75W Fl (2) WRG 10s 28m **W18M**, R14M, G14M; W twr, 2 B bands; vis: 197°-G-211°-W-249°-R-000°; *Horn (2) 30s.* Fog Det lt VQ 16m vis: 270°.

Inishtrahull ☆ 55°25'·86N 07°14'·62W Fl (3) 15s 59m **19M**; W twr; obscd 256°-261° within 3M; *Racon (T) 24M 060°-310°.*

INISHTRAHULL TO BLOODY FORELAND

L SWILLY/MULROY BAY/SHEEPHAVEN

Fanad Head ☆ 55°16'·57N 07°37'·91W Fl (5) WR 20s 39m **W18M**, R14M; W twr; vis 100°-R-110°-W-313°-R-345°-W-100°.

Limeburner ↓ Q Fl; 55°18'·54N 07°48'·40W.

Tory Island ☆ 55°16'·36N 08°14'·97W Fl (4) 30s 40m **27M**; B twr, W band; vis: 302°-277°; *Racon (M) 12-23M*; H24.

Bloody Foreland ⚡ Fl WG 7·5s 14m W6M, G4M; vis: 062°-W-232°-G-062°; 55°09'·51N 08°17'·03W.

BLOODY F'LD TO RATHLIN O'BIRNE

Aranmore, Rinrawros Pt ☆ 55°00'·90N 08°33'·66W Fl (2) 20s 71m **27M**; W twr; obsc by land about 234°-007° and about 013°. Auxiliary lt Fl R 3s 61m 13M, same twr; vis: 203°-234°.

Rathlin O'Birne, W side ☆ 54°39'·80N 08°49'·94W Fl WR 15s 35m **W18M**, R14M; W twr; vis: 195°-R-307°-W-195°; *Racon (O) 13M, vis 284°-203°.*

RATHLIN O'BIRNE TO EAGLE ISLAND

St John's Pt ⚡ Fl 6s 30m 14M; W twr; 54°34'·16N 08°27'·64W.

Rotten I ☆ 54°36'·97N 08°26'·41W; Fl WR 4s 20m **W15M**, R11M; W twr; vis:W255°-R008°-W039°-208°.

SLIGO

Wheat Rk ↓ Q (6) + LFl 15s; 54°18'·84N 08°39'·10W.

EAGLE ISLAND TO SLYNE HEAD

Eagle Is, W end ☆ 54°17'·02N 10°05'·56W Fl (3) 15s 67m **19M**; W twr.

Black Rk ☆ 54°04'·03N 10°19'·25W Fl WR 12s 86m **W20M**, R16M; W twr; vis: 276°-W-212°-R-276°.

BROAD HAVEN/BLACKSOD/CLEW BAYS

Gubacashel Pt ⚡ Iso WR 4s 27m W17M, R12M; 110°-R-133°-W-355°-R-021° W twr; 54°16'·06N 09°53'·33W.

Blacksod ↓ Q (3) 10s; 54°05'·89N 10°03'·01W.

Achillbeg I S Point ☆ 53°51'·51N 09°56'·85W Fl WR 5s 56m **W18M**, R18M, R15M; W ☐ twr on ☐ building; vis: 262°-R-281°-W-342°-R- 060°-W-092°-R(intens)-099°-W-118°.

Inishgort S Point ⚡ L Fl 10s 11m 10M; W twr. Shown H24; 53°49'·61N 09°40'·25W.

Slyne Hd, North twr, Illaunamid ☆ 53°23'·99N 10°14'·06W; Fl (2) 15s 35m **19M**; B twr.

SLYNE HEAD TO BLACK HEAD

GALWAY BAY/INISHMORE

Eeragh, Rock Is ☆ 53°08'·10N 09°51'·39W Fl 15s 35m **23M**; W twr, two B bands; vis: 297°-262°.

Straw Is ☆ 53°07'·06N 09°37'·85W Fl (2) 5s 11m **15M**; W twr.

Black Hd ⚡ Fl WR 5s 20m W11M, R8M, W ☐ twr; vis: 045°-R268°-276°; 53°09'·26N 09°15'·83W.

Inisheer ☆ 53°02'·78N 09°31'·58W Iso WR 12s 34m **W20M**, R16M; vis: 225°-W(partially vis >7M)-231°, 231°-W-245°-R-269°-W-115°; *Racon (K) 13M.*

See table on page 36 for distances anticlockwise between Kilrush and Carlingford Lough

		1	2	3	4	5	6	7	8	9	10	11	12	13	14	15
1	Strangford Lough	1														
2	Bangor	34	2													
3	Carrickfergus	39	6	3												
4	Larne	45	16	16	4											
5	Carnlough	50	25	26	11	5										
6	Portrush	87	58	60	48	35	6									
7	Lough Foyle	92	72	73	55	47	11	7								
8	L Swilly (Fahan)	138	109	104	96	81	48	42	8							
9	Burtonport	153	130	130	116	108	74	68	49	9						
10	Killybegs	204	175	171	163	148	115	109	93	43	10					
11	Sligo	218	189	179	177	156	123	117	107	51	30	11				
12	Eagle Island	234	205	198	193	175	147	136	123	72	62	59	12			
13	Westport	295	266	249	240	226	193	187	168	120	108	100	57	13		
14	Galway	338	309	307	297	284	253	245	227	178	166	163	104	94	14	
15	Kilrush	364	335	332	323	309	276	270	251	203	191	183	142	119	76	15

AREA 11 West Denmark - *Skagen to Rømø*

SELECTED LIGHTS, BUOYS & WAYPOINTS

| Positions are referenced to WGS84 |

SKAGEN

Skagen W ☆ Fl (3) WR 10s 31m **W17M**/R12M; 053°-W-248°-R-323°; W ○ twr; 57°44'·92N 10°35·66E.
Skagen ☆ Fl 4s 44m **23M**; Gy ○ twr; *Racon G, 20M*; 57°44'·11N 10°37'·76E.
Skagen No 1A ⚓ L Fl 10s; *Racon N*; 57°43'·42N 10°53'·51E.

HIRTSHALS

Hirtshals ☆ F Fl 30s 57m **F 18M**; **Fl 25M**; W ○ twr; approx 1M SSW of hbr ent; 57°35'·07N 09°56'·45E.
Outer W mole ⚓ Fl G 3s 14m 6M; G mast; *Horn 15s*; 57°35'·97N 09°57'·36E.

HANSTHOLM

Hanstholm ☆ Fl (3) 20s 65m **26M**; shown by day in poor vis; W 8-sided twr; 57°06'·65N 08°35'·74E, approx 1M S of the hbr ent.
Hanstholm ⚓ LFl 10s; 57°08'·10N 08°34'·94E.

THYBORØN

Landfall ⚓ L Fl 10s; *Racon T, 10m*; 56°42'·55N 08°08'·70E.
Approach ☆ Fl (3) 10s 24m 12M; 56°42'·49N 08°12'·90E.
Bovbjerg ☆ L Fl (2) 15s 62m **16M**; 56°30'·74N 08°07'·13E.

THORSMINDE HAVN (Positions approx)

Lt ho ⚓ F 30m 13M; 56°22'·34N 08°06'·99E.
S mole ⚓ Iso G 2s 9m 4M; 56°22'·26N 08°06'·92E.

HVIDE SANDE

Lyngvig ☆ Fl 5s 53m **22M**; 56°02'·95N 08°06'·17E.
N outer bkwtr ⚓ Fl R 3s 7m 8M; 55°59'·94N 08°06'·55E.
Lt ho ⚓ F 27m 14M; 56°00'·00N 08°07'·35E.

HORNS REV

Blåvands Huk ☆ Fl (3) 20s 55m **23M**; W □ twr; 55°33'·46N 08°04'·95E.

Horns Rev is encircled clockwise by:
Tuxen ⚓ Q; 55°34'·22N 07°41'·92E on the N side.
Vyl ⚓ Q (6) + L Fl 15s; 55°26'·22N 07°49'·99E.
No. 2 ⚓ L Fl 10s; 55°28'·74N 07°36'·49E, SW side.
Horns Rev W ⚓ Q (9) 15s; 55°34'·47N 07°26'·05E.
Slugen Channel (crosses Horns Rev ESE/WNW).
▲ L Fl G 10s; 55°33'·99N 07°49'·38E.
⚓ Fl (3) R 10s; 55°29'·42N 08°02'·56E.
Wind farm in □ 2·7M x 2·5M, centred on 55°29'·22N 07°50'·21E: 80 turbines all R lts, the 12 perimeter turbines are lit Fl (3) Y 10s. NE and SW turbines, *Racon (U)*.

APPROACHES TO ESBJERG

Grådyb ⚓ L Fl 10s; *Racon G, 10M*; 55°24'·63N 08°11'·59E.
Sædding Strand 053·8° triple ldg lts: to Nos 7/8 buoys; H24: **Front** Iso 2s 13m **21M**; 052°-056°; R bldg; 55°29'·74N 08°23'·87E.
Middle Iso 4s 26m **21M**; 051°-057°; R twr, W bands; 55°29'·94N 08°24'·33E, 630m from front.
Rear F 37m **18M**; 052°-056°; R twr; 55°30'·18N 08°24'·92E, 0·75M from front.
Ldg lts 067°, to Nos 9/10 buoys. Both FG 10/25m **16M**, H24. Front, Gy tripod; rear, Gy twr; 55°28'·76N 08°24'·70E.
Ldg lts 049°, to No 16 buoy/Jerg. Both FR 16/27m **16M**, H24. Front, W twr; rear, Gy twr, 55°29'·92N 08°23'·75E.

FANØ

Slunden outer ldg lts 242°, both Iso 2s 5/8m 3M; 227°-257°. Front, twr; 55°27'·20N 08°24'·53E. Rear, twr, 106m from front.
Nordby marina 55°26'·65N 08°24'·53E.

APPROACHES (Lister Tief) TO RØMØ

Rode Klit Sand ⚓ Q (9) 15s, 55°11'·11N 08°04'·88E, (130°/9M to Lister Tief ⚓).
Lister Tief ⚓ Iso 8s, *Whis*; 55°05'·32N 08°16'·80E.
Lister Landtief No 5 ▲ 55°03'·68N 08°24'·73E.
Rømø S mole ⚓ Fl R 3s 7m 2M; Gy twr; 55°05'·19N 08°34'·31E.

		1	2	3	4	5	6	7	8	9	10	11	12	13	14	15	16	17	18
1	Skagen	1																	
2	Hirtshals	33	2																
3	Hanstholm	85	52	3															
4	Thyborøn	114	84	32	4														
5	Torsminde	141	108	56	24	5													
6	Hvide Sande	162	179	77	45	24	6												
7	Esbjerg	200	174	122	90	76	54	7											
8	Fanø	210	177	125	93	79	57	3	8										
9	Rømø	233	200	148	116	94	73	30	33	9									
10	Hörnum	248	215	163	131	108	86	70	73	29	10								
11	Husum	275	247	195	163	152	131	95	98	68	45	11							
12	Kiel/Holtenau	261	233	281	249	232	208	180	183	189	126	129	12						
13	Bremerhaven	306	285	233	201	185	163	127	129	107	83	82	123	13					
14	Wilhelmshaven	414	296	242	310	184	162	125	128	106	82	82	123	45	14				
15	Helgoland	259	238	186	154	141	119	83	85	63	39	47	104	44	43	15			
16	Cuxhaven	304	284	232	200	162	138	110	113	85	56	66	70	58	56	38	16		
17	Wangerooge	283	262	210	178	168	147	109	112	94	68	52	108	38	27	24	42	17	
18	Hamburg	338	317	265	233	216	192	163	167	139	99	113	90	81	110	88	54	61	18

AREA 12 Germany (North Sea coast) - *List to Emden*

SELECTED LIGHTS, BUOYS & WAYPOINTS

SYLT

Lister Tief ⚓ Iso 8s; *Whis;* 55°05'·33N 08°16'·79E.
List West ⚓ Oc WRG 6s 19m W14M, R11M, G10M; 040°-R-133°-W-227°-R-266·4°-W-268°-G-285°-W-310°- W(unintens)-040°; W twr, R lantern; 55°03'·15N 08°24'·00E.
List Ost ⚓ Iso WRG 6s 22m W14M, R11M, G10M; 010·5°-W(unintens)-098°-W-262°-R-278°-W-296°-R-323·3°-W-324·5°-G-350°-W-010·5°; W twr, R band; 55°02'·93N 08°26'·58E.
List Hafen, N mole ⚓ FG 8m 4M; 218°-038°; G mast; 55°01'·03N 08°26'·52E.
Kampen, Rote Kliff ☆ L Fl WR 10s 62m **W20M, R16M**; 193°-W-260°- W (unintens)-339°-W-165°-R-193°; W twr, B band; 54°56'·76N 08°20'·38E.
Hörnum ☆ Fl (2) 9s 48m **20M**; 54°45'·23N 08°17'·47E. Hbr, N pier ⚓ FG 6m 4M, 024°-260°.
Vortrapptief ⚓ Iso 4s; 54°34'·88N 08°12'·97E.

AMRUM ISLAND

Norddorf ☆ Oc WRG 6s 22m **W15M**, R12M, G11M; 031-W-097°-R-176·5°-W-178·5°-G-188°; W ○ twr, R lantern; 54°40'·13N 08°18'·46E.
Amrum ☆ Fl 7·5s 63m **23M**; R twr, W bands; 54°37'·84N 08°21'·23E.

FÖHR ISLAND

Nieblum Dir lt ☆ Oc (2) WRG 10s 11m **W19M, R/ G15M**; 028°-G-031°-W-032·5°-R-035·5°; R twr, W band; 54°41'·10N 08°29'·20E.

DAGEBÜLL

Dagebüll Iso WRG 8s 23m **W18M, R/G15M**; 042°-G-043°-W-044·5°- R-047°; G mast; 54°43'·82N 08°41'·43E. FW lts on N and S moles.

RIVER HEVER

Hever ⚓ Iso 4s; *Whis;* 54°20'·41N 08°18'·82E.
Westerheversand ☆ Oc (3) WRG 15s 41m **W21M, R17M, G16M**; 012·2°-W-069°-G-079·5°-W-080·5°-R-107°-W-233°-R-248°; 54°22'·37N 08°38'·36E.

RIVER EIDER

Eider ⚓ Iso 4s; 54°14'·54N 08°27'·61E.
St Peter ☆ L Fl (2) WR 15s 23m **W15M**, R12M; 271°-R-280·5°-W-035°-R-055°-W-068°-R-091°-W-120°; R twr, B lantern; 54°17'·24N 08°39'·10E.

BÜSUM

Süderpiep ⚓ Iso 8s; *Whis;* 54°05'·82N 08°25'·70E.
Büsum ☆ Iso WR 6s 22m **W19M**, R12M; 248°-W-317°-R-024°-W-148°; 54°07'·60N 08°51'·48E.
GB Light V ▱ Iso 8s 12m **17M**; *Horn Mo (R) 30s; Racon T, 8M;* 54°10'·80N 07°27'·60E.

HELGOLAND

Helgoland ☆ Fl 5s 82m **28M**; brown □ twr, B lantern, W balcony; 54°10'·91N 07°52'·93E.
Vorhafen. Ostmole, S elbow ⚓ Oc WG 6s 5m W6M, G3M; 203°-W-250°-G-109°; G post; fog det lt; 54°10'·31N 07°53'·94E.
Düne. Ldg lts 020°. Front ⚓ Iso 4s 11m 8M; 54°10'·87N 07°54'·80E. Rear, Iso WRG 4s 17m W11M, R/G10M; synch; 010°-G-018·5°-W-021°-R-030; 106°-G-125°-W-130°-R-144°.

RIVER ELBE APPROACHES

Elbe ⚓ Iso 10s; *Racon T, 8M;* 53°59'·95N 08°06'·49E. No.1 ⚓ QG; 53°59'·21N 08°13'·20E.
Neuwerk ☆, S side, L Fl (3) WRG 20s 38m **W16M**, R12M, G11M; 165·3°-G-215·3°-W-238·8°-R-321°; 343°-R-100°; 53°54'·92N 08°29'·73E.

CUXHAVEN/OTTERNDORF

Marina, F WR & F WG ⚓; 53°52'·43N 08°42'·49E.
Medem ⚓ Fl (3) 12s 6m 5M; B △, on B col; 53°50'·15N 08°53'·85E.

BRUNSBÜTTEL

Ldg lts 065·5°: both Iso 3s 24/46m **16/21M**; synch; R twrs, W bands. Front ☆ 53°53'·32N 09°08'·47E. Alter Vorhafen ⚓ F WG 14m W10M, G6M; 266·3°-W-273·9°-G-088·8°; 53°53'·27N 09°08'·59E.

HAMBURG, WEDEL YACHT HAFEN

E ent ⚓ FG 5m 3M; 53°34'·25N 09°40'·79E.
City Sport Hafen ⚓ Iso Or 2s; 53°32'·52N 09°58'·81E.

RIVER WESER APPROACH CHANNELS

ALTE WESER

Schlüsseltonne ⚓ Iso 8s; 53°56'·25N 07°54'·76E.
Alte Weser ☆ F WRG 33m **W23M, R19M, G18M**; 288°-W-352°-R-003°-W-017°- G-045°-W-074°-G-118°- W-123°- R-140°-G-175°-W-183°-R-196°-W-238°; *Horn Mo (AL) 60s;* 53°51'·79N 08°07'·65E.

NEUE WESER

3/Jade 2 ⚓ Fl (2+1) G 15s; *Racon T, 8M;* 53°52'·40N 07°44'·00E.
Tegeler Plate ☆ Oc (3) WRG 12s 21m **W21M, R17M, G16M**; 329°-W-340°-R-014°-W-100°-G-116°-W-119°-R-123°-G-144°-W-147°-R-264°; 53°47'·87N 08°11'·45E.

BREMERHAVEN

No. 61 ⚓ QG; 53°32'·26N 08°33'·93E (Km 66·0).
Vorhafen S pier hd ⚓ FG 15m 5M; 355°-265°; 53°32'·09N 08°34'·50E.

BREMEN
Hasenbüren Sporthafen ⚓ 2 FY (vert); 53°07'·51N 08°40'·03E.

RIVER JADE APPROACHES
Jade-Weser ⚓ Oc 4s; *Racon T, 8M*; 53°58'·33N 07°38'·83E.
Mellumplate ☆ FW 28m **24M**; 116·1°-116·4°; R ☐ twr, W band; 53°46'·28N 08°05'·51E.

HOOKSIEL
No. 37/Hooksiel 1 ⚓ IQ G 13s; 53°39'·37N 08°06'·58E. Vorhafen ent ⚓ L Fl R 6s 9m 3M; 53°38'·63N 08°05'·25E.

WILHELMSHAVEN
Fluthafen N mole ⚓ F WG 9m,W6M, G3M; 216°-W-280°-G-010°-W-020°-G-130°; 53°30'·86N 08°09'·32E.

WANGEROOGE
Harle ⚓ Iso 8s; 53°49'·24N 07°48'·92E.
Buhne W bkwtr ⚓ FR 3m 4M; 53°46'·33N 07°51'·93E.

SPIEKEROOG
Otzumer Balje ⚓ Iso 4s; 53°47'·98N 07°37'·12E.
Spiekeroog ⚓ FR 6m 4M; 53°45'·0N 07°41'·3E.

LANGEOOG
Accumer Ee ⚓ Iso 8s; 53°46·81N 07°26·12E.
W mole ⚓ Oc WRG 6s 8m W7M, R5M, G4M; 064°-G-070°-W-074°-R-326°-W-330°-G-335°-R-064°; *Horn Mo (L) 30s*; 53°43'·42N 07°30'·13E .

NORDERNEY
Norderney N ⚓ Q; 53°46'·06N 07°17'·12E.
Dovetief ⚓ Iso 4s; 53°45'·25N 07°09'·13E.
Schluchter ⚓ Iso 8s; 53°44'·45N 07°02'·23E,.
W mole ⚓ Oc (2) R 9s 13m 4M; 53°41'·9N 07°09'·9E.
Norderney ☆ Fl (3) 12s 59m **23M**; unintens 067°-077° and 270°-280°; R 8-sided twr; 53°42'·58N 07°13'·83E.

BENSERSIEL
E training wall head ⚓ Oc WRG 6s 6m W5M, R3M, G2M; 110°-G-119°-W-121°-R-110°; R post & platform; 53° 41'·80N 07°32'·84E.
Ldg lts 138°, both Iso 6s 12/18m 9M.
Inner hbr, W mole hd FG; E mole hd FR.

DORNUMER-ACCUMERSIEL
AB3 ⚓ IQ G 13s; 53°41'·50N 07°29'·34E.
W bkwtr head, approx 53°41'·04N 07°29'·30E.

NESSMERSIEL
N mole ⚓ Oc 4s 6m 5M; G mast; 53°41'·9N 07°21'·7E.

NORDDEICH
W trng wall head ⚓ FG 8m 4M, 021°-327°; G framework twr; 53°38'·7N 07°09'·0E.
Outer ldg lts 144°, both B masts. Front, Iso WR 6s 6m W6M, R5M; 078°-R-122°-W-150°. Rear, Iso 6s 9m 6M; synch, 140m from front.

RIVER EMS APPROACHES
GW/EMS ⬚ Iso 8s 12m **17M**; *Horn Mo (R) 30s (H24)*; *Racon T, 8M*; 54°09'·96N 06°20'·72E.
Borkumriff ⚓ Oc 4s; *Racon T, 8M*; 53°47'·44N 06°22'·05E.
Osterems ⚓ Iso 4s; 53°41'·91N 06°36'·17E.
Riffgat ⚓ Iso 8s; 53°38'·96N 06°27'·07E.
Westerems ⚓ Iso 4s; *Racon T, 8M*; 53°36'·9N 06°19'·41E.
H1 ⚓ 53°34'·91N 06°17'·97E.

BORKUM
Borkum Grosser ☆ Fl (2) 12s 63m **24M**; 53°35'·32N 06°39'·64E. Same twr, ⚓ F WRG 46m **W19M, R/G15M**; 107·4°-G-109°-W-111·2°- R-112·6°.
Fischerbalje ☆ Oc (2) WRG 16s 15m **W16M**, R12M, G11M; 260°-R-313°-G-014°-W-068°-R-123°; 53°33'·16N 06°42'·86E.

EMDEN
Outer hbr, W pier ⚓ FR 10m 4M; R 8-sided twr; *Horn Mo (ED) 30s;* 53°20'·06N 07°10'·49E.
E pier ⚓ FG 7m 5M; 53°20'·05N 07°10'·84E.

1 Esbjerg	1																	
2 Hörnum Lt (Sylt)	47	2																
3 Husum	95	48	3															
4 Hamburg	163	112	113	4														
5 Kiel/Holtenau	179	128	129	90	5													
6 Brunsbüttel	126	75	76	37	53	6												
7 Cuxhaven	110	63	66	54	70	17	7											
8 Bremerhaven	127	80	82	81	131	78	58	8										
9 Wilhelmshaven	125	78	82	110	123	70	56	45	9									
10 Hooksiel	116	69	73	101	117	64	47	36	9	10								
11 Helgoland	83	38	47	88	104	51	38	44	43	35	11							
12 Wangerooge	109	60	52	61	108	55	42	38	27	19	24	12						
13 Langeoog	119	72	77	114	130	77	60	47	43	34	35	21	13					
14 Norderney	123	77	85	81	137	84	69	62	53	44	44	29	18	14				
15 Emden	165	129	137	174	190	137	120	115	106	97	85	80	63	47	15			
16 Borkum	133	97	105	104	163	110	95	88	80	71	67	55	46	31	32	16		
17 Delfzijl	155	119	127	159	173	120	105	100	89	83	81	65	56	41	10	22	17	
18 Den Helder	187	192	198	229	245	192	175	180	159	150	153	148	130	115	125	95	115	18

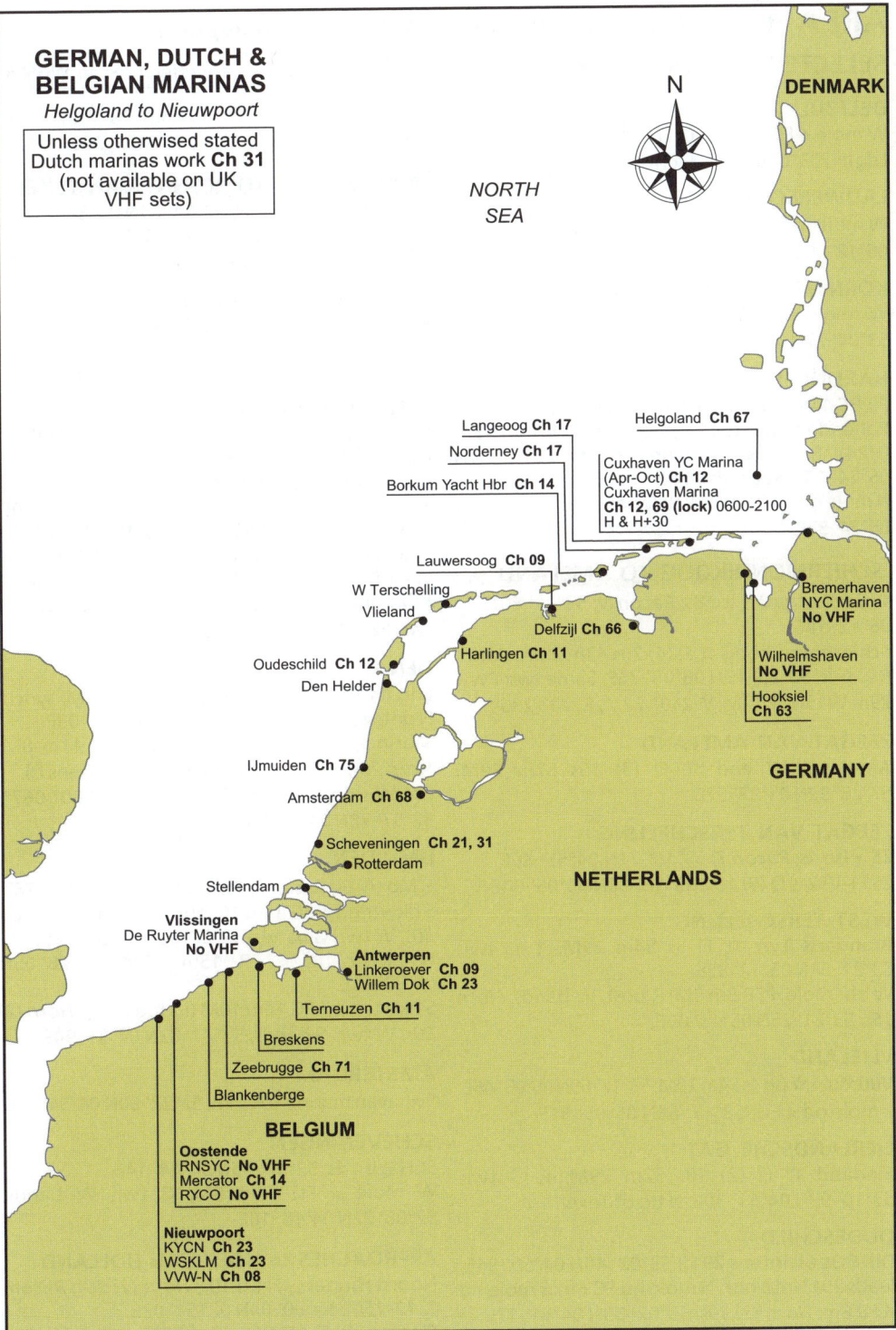

GERMAN, DUTCH & BELGIAN MARINAS
Helgoland to Nieuwpoort

Unless otherwised stated
Dutch marinas work **Ch 31**
(not available on UK
VHF sets)

N

DENMARK

NORTH SEA

Langeoog **Ch 17**

Helgoland **Ch 67**

Norderney **Ch 17**

Cuxhaven YC Marina
(Apr-Oct) **Ch 12**
Cuxhaven Marina
Ch 12, 69 (lock) 0600-2100
H & H+30

Borkum Yacht Hbr **Ch 14**

Lauwersoog **Ch 09**

W Terschelling

Bremerhaven
NYC Marina
No VHF

Vlieland

Delfzijl **Ch 66**

Oudeschild **Ch 12**

Harlingen **Ch 11**

Wilhelmshaven
No VHF

Den Helder

Hooksiel
Ch 63

IJmuiden **Ch 75**

GERMANY

Amsterdam **Ch 68**

Scheveningen **Ch 21, 31**

Rotterdam

NETHERLANDS

Stellendam

Vlissingen
De Ruyter Marina
No VHF

Antwerpen
Linkeroever **Ch 09**
Willem Dok **Ch 23**

Terneuzen **Ch 11**

Breskens

Zeebrugge **Ch 71**

Blankenberge

BELGIUM

Oostende
RNSYC **No VHF**
Mercator **Ch 14**
RYCO **No VHF**

Nieuwpoort
KYCN **Ch 23**
WSKLM **Ch 23**
VVW-N **Ch 08**

AREA 13 Netherlands & Belgium - *Delfzijl to Nieuwpoort*

SELECTED LIGHTS, BUOYS & WAYPOINTS | Positions are referenced to WGS84

DELFZIJL
W mole ⚓ FG; 53°19'·01N 07°00'·26E.
Ldg lts 203° both Iso 4s. Front, 53°18'·62N 07°00'·16E.

LAUWERSOOG
W mole head ⚓ FG 3M; *Horn (2) 30s;* 53°24'·68N 06°12'·00E.

KORNWERDERZAND SEALOCK
W mole ⚓ FG 9m 7M; *Horn Mo(N) 30s;* 53°04'·77N 05°20'·03E.

HARLINGEN
P9/BO44 ⚓ VQ; 53°10'·59N 05°23'·88E.
Pollendam ldg lts 112°, both Iso 6s 8/19m 13M (H24); B masts, W bands. Front, 53°10'·51N 05°24'·18E. Rear, vis 104·5°-119·5°.
N mole hd ⚓ FR 9m 4M; R/W pedestal; 53°10'·59N 05°24'·32E.

SCHIERMONNIKOOG TO AMELAND
WG (Westgat) ⚓ Iso 8s; *Racon N;* 53°31'·80N 06°12'·18E.
Schiermonnikoog ☆ Fl (4) 20s 43m **28M**; dark R ○ twr; 53°29'·19N 06°08'·76E. Same twr: FWR 29m **W15M**, R12M; W210°-221°, R221°-230°.

ZEEGAT VAN AMELAND
Ameland, W end ☆ Fl (3) 15s 57m **30M**; 53°26'·92N 05°37'·52E.

ZEEGAT VAN TERSCHELLING
ZS ⚓ Iso 4s; *Racon T;* 53°19'·71N 04°55'·86E.
ZS11-VS2 ⚓ Q (9) 15s; 53°18'·66N 05°05'·94E.

WEST TERSCHELLING
Brandaris Twr ☆ Fl 5s 54m **29M**, Y □ twr; 53°21'·61N 05°12'·85E.
W hbr mole ⚓ FR 5m 5M; R post, W bands; *Horn 15s;* 53°21'·25N 05°13'·09E.

VLIELAND
Vuurduin ☆ Iso 4s 54m **20M**; 53°17'·69N 05°03'·46E.
E mole hd ⚓ FG; 53°17'·68N 05°05'·51E.

EIERLANDSCHE GAT
Eierland ☆ Fl (2) 10s 52m **29M**; R ○ twr; 53°10'·93N 04°51'·30E, N tip of Texel.

OUDESCHILD
Dir ⚓ Oc 6s; intens 291°; 53°02'·40N 04°50'·94E; leads 291° into hbr. N mole hd FG 6m. S mole hd ⚓ FR 6m; *Horn (2) 30s;* 53°02'·33N 04°51'·17E.

DEN OEVER SEALOCK
LW ⚓ L Fl 10s; 52°59'·51N 04°55'·90E,.

Ldg lts 131°, both Oc 10s 6m 7M; 127°-137°. Front, 52°56'·32N 05°02'·98E. Rear, 280m SE.

APPROACHES TO ZEEGAT VAN TEXEL
ZH ⚓ VQ (6) + L Fl 10s; 52°54'·65N 04°34'·71E.
TX1 ⚓ Fl G 5s; 52°48'·01N 04°15'·50E.
Vinca G ⚓ Q (9) 15s; *Racon D;* 52°45'·93N 04°12'·35E.

MOLENGAT (from the N)
MG ⚓ Mo (A) 8s; 53°03'·91N 04°39'·36E.
MG1 ⚓ Iso G 4s; 53°02'·89N 04°40'·84E.
S14-MG17 ⚓ VQ (6) + L Fl 10s; 52°58'·50N 04°43'·60E.

SCHULPENGAT (from the SSW)
Ldg lts 026·5°, both Oc 8s **18M** (by day 9M); vis 024·5°-028·5°. **Front** ☆, 53°00'·85N 04°44'·42E (on Texel). Rear, **Den Hoorn** ☆.
SG ⚓ Mo (A) 8s; *Racon Z;* 52°52'·90N 04°37'·90E.
Schilbolsnol ☆ F WRG 27m **W15M**, R12M, G11M; 338°-W-002°-G-035°-W(ldg sector)-038°-R-051°-W-068°; post; 53°00'·50N 04°45'·68E (on Texel).
Kijkduin ☆ Fl (4) 20s 56m **30M**; vis 360°; brown twr; 52°57'·33N 04°43'·58E.

DEN HELDER
Ldg lts 191°, both Oc G 5s 15/24m 14M, synch. Front, vis 161°-221°; 52°57'·37N 04°47'·08E.
Marinehaven, W bkwtr head ⚓ QG 11m 8M; *Horn 20s;* 52°57'·95N 04°47'·07E (Harssens Is).
Ent W side, ⚓ Fl G 5s 9m 4M (H24); 180°-067°; 52°57'·78N 04°47'·08E.

IJMUIDEN
⚓ Mo (A) 8s; *Racon Y, 10M;* 52°28'·44N 04°23'·78E.
S bkwtr hd ⚓ FG 14m 10M (in fog Fl 3s); *Horn (2) 30s;* W twr, G bands; 52°27'·82N 04°31'·94E.
N bkwtr hd ⚓ FR 15m 10M; 52°28'·05N 04°32'·55E.
S bkwtr hd ⚓ FG 14m 10M (in fog Fl 3s); *Horn (2) 30s;* W twr, G bands; 52°27'·82N 04°31'·94E.

AMSTERDAM
Sixhaven marina ⚓ F & FR; 52°22'·90N 04°54'·37E.

SCHEVENINGEN
SCH ⚓ Iso 4s; 52°07'·75N 04°14'·14E.
W mole ⚓ FG 12m 9M; G twr, W bands; 52°06'·22N 04°15'·16E.

APPROACHES to HOEK VAN HOLLAND
Noord Hinder ⚓ Fl (2) 10s; *Horn (2) 30s; Racon T, 12-15M;* 52°00'·04N 02° 51'·03E.
Goeree ☆ Fl (4) 20s 32m **28M**; *Horn (4) 30s; Racon T, 12-15M;* 51°55'·42N 03°40'·03E.
Indusbank N ⚓ VQ; 52°02'·88N 04°03'·55E.

MO ℚ Mo (A) 8s; 52°00'·97N 03°58'·06E.
MVN ⌇ VQ; 51°59'·59N 04°00'·19E.
MV ⌇ Q (9) 15s; 51°57'·44N 03°58'·40E.
Westhoofd, 51°48'·78N 03°51'·82E, Fl (3) 15s
55m **30M**; R □ tr.

HOEK VAN HOLLAND
Nieuwe Waterweg ldg lts 107°: both Iso R 6s
29/43m **18M**; 099.5°-114.5°; Front, 51°58'·55N
04°07'·53E.
Maasvlakte ☆ Fl (5) 20s 67m **28M**, H24; 340°-267°;
51°58'·20N 04°00'·85E.
Nieuwe Zuiderdam ≰ FG 25m 10M; *Horn 10s;* G
twr, W bands; 51°59'·13N 04°02'·47E.

APPROACHES TO HARINGVLIET
West Schouwen ☆ Fl (2+1)15s 57m **30M**; Gy twr,
R diagonals; 51°42'·53N 03°41'·48E
SG ℚ Iso 4s; 51°51'·93N 03°51'·40E.

STELLENDAM
N mole ≰ FG; *Horn (2) 15s;* 51°49'·87N 04°02'·01E.

OOSTERSCHELDE APPROACHES
Schouwenbank ℚ Mo (A) 8s; *Racon O, 10M;*
51°44'·94N 03°14'·32E.
Westpit ℚ Iso 8s; 51°33'·65N 03°09'·92E.

ROOMPOTSLUIS
N bkwtr ≰ 51°37'·30N 03°40'·09E, FR 7m; *Horn(2) 30s.*
Kaloo ℚ Iso 8s; 51°35'·56N 03°23'·23E.
Westkapelle ☆, Common rear, Fl 3s 49m **28M**;
partially obsc'd; □ twr; 51°31'·75N 03°26'·80E.

VLISSINGEN
Koopmanshaven, W mole root, ≰ Iso WRG 3s
15m W12M, R10M, G9M; 253°-R-277°-W-284°-R-
297°-W-306·5°-G-013°-W-024°-G-033°-W-035°-
G-039°-W-055°-G-084·5°-R-092°-G-111°-W-114°;
R pylon; 51°26'·37N 03°34'·52E.
E mole ≰ FG 7m; W mast; 51°26'·32N 03°34'·66E.

BRESKENS
Yacht hbr, W mole ≰ FG 7m; 51°24'·04N
03°34'·06E. E mole ≰ FR 6m; 51°23'·95N 03°34'·09E.

TERNEUZEN
W mole ≰ Oc WRG 5s 15m W9M, R7M, G6M; 090°-
R-115°-W-120°-G-130°-W-245°-G-249°-W-279°-
R-004°; B & W post; 51°20'·54N 03°49'·58E.

BELGIUM

ANTWERPEN
Royerssluis, ldg lts 091°, both FR. FR/FG, ent to
Willemdok ④. Linkeroever marina ent, FR/FG.

ZEEBRUGGE
A2 ⌇ Iso 8s; 51°22'·42N 03°07'·05E.
Ldg lts 136°, both Oc 5s 22/45m 8M; 131°-141°;
H24, synch; W cols, R bands. Front, 51°20'·71N
03°13'·11E. Rear, 890m SE.
W outer mole ≰ Oc G 7s 31m 7M; *Horn (3) 30s;*
IPTS; 51°21'·73N 03°11'·17E.

BLANKENBERGE
Lt ho ☆ Fl (2) 8s 30m **20M**; 065°-245°; W twr, B
top; 51°18'·76N 03°06'·87E.
E pier ≰ FR 12m 11M; 290°-245°; W ○ twr; *Bell (2)
15s;* 51°18'·91N 03°06'·56E.
W pier ≰ FG 14m 11M; intens 065°-290°, unintens
290°-335°; W ○ twr; 51°18'·89N 03°06'·43E.

OOSTENDE
A1 ⌇ Iso 8s; 51°22'·37N 02°53'·34E.
Ldg lts 128°: both Iso 4s (triple vert) 22/32m 4M;
051°-201°. Front, 51°14'·13N 02°55'·55E.
Oostende lt ho ☆ Fl (3) 10s 65m **27M**; obsc
069·5°-071°; 51°14'·18N 02°55'·83E.
E pier ≰ FR 15m 12M; 333°-243°; W ○ twr; IPTS;
Horn Mo(OE) 30s; 51°14'·39N 02°55'·14E.

NIEUWPOORT
Lt ho ☆ Fl (2) R 14s 28m **16M**; R ○ twr, W bands;
51°09'·28N 02°43'·80E, 2 ca E of E pier root.
E pier ≰ FR 11m 10M; vis 025°-250° & 307°-347°;
Horn Mo (K) 30s; 51°09'·42N 02°43'·08E.
W pier ≰ FG 11m 9M; vis 025°-250° & 284°-324°;
IPTS; *Bell (2) 10s;* 51°09'·35N 02°43'·00E.

1	Delfzijl	1															
2	Terschelling	85	2														
3	Harlingen	102	19	3													
4	Den Oever	110	34	21	4												
5	Den Helder	115	39	30	11	5											
6	Amsterdam	159	83	81	62	51	6										
7	IJmuiden	146	70	68	49	38	13	7									
8	Scheveningen	171	95	93	74	63	38	25	8								
9	Rotterdam	205	129	127	108	97	72	59	34	9							
10	Hook of Holland	185	109	107	88	77	52	39	14	20	10						
11	Stellendam	201	125	123	104	93	68	55	30	36	16	11					
12	Roompotsluis	233	157	155	136	125	100	87	50	68	48	32	12				
13	Vlissingen	228	152	150	131	120	99	86	61	67	47	45	24	13			
14	Zeebrugge	239	163	161	142	131	106	93	68	74	54	50	28	16	14		
15	Blankenberge	244	168	166	147	136	111	98	73	79	59	55	33	21	5	15	
16	Oostende	239	163	161	142	131	110	106	81	87	67	72	40	29	13	9	16
17	Nieuwpoort	262	186	184	165	154	129	116	91	97	77	83	51	39	23	18	9	17

AREA 14, North France - *Dunkerque to Cap de la Hague*
SELECTED LIGHTS, BUOYS & WAYPOINTS | Positions are referenced to WGS84

OFFSHORE MARKS
WH Zuid ⚓ Q (6) + L Fl 15s; 51°22'·78N 02°26'·25E.
Bergues N ⚓ Q; 51°19'·92N 02°24'·50E.
Oostdyck radar twr; ☆ Mo (U) 15s 15m 12M;
Horn Mo (U) 30s; Racon O; 51°16'·49N 02°26'·83E.
Bergues ⚓ Fl G 4s; 51°17'·15N 02°18'·62E.
Ruytingen N ⚓ 51°13'·10N 02°10'·28E, VQ.
Ruytingen SE ⚓ VQ (3) 15s; 51°09'·20N 02°08'·92E.
Sandettié SW ⚓ Q (9) 15s 5M; 51°09'·72N 01°45'·60E.
Sandettié ⚓ Fl 5s 12m **15M**; R hull; *Horn 30s;*
Racon T, 10M; 51°09'·34N 01°47'·10E.

PASSE DE ZUYDCOOTE
E12 ⚓ VQ (6) + L Fl 10s; 51°07'·90N 02°30'·80E.
E11 ⚓ Fl G 4s; 51°06'·90N 02°30'·91E.
E9 ⚓ Fl (2) G 6s; 51°05'·66N 02°29'·68E.

PASSE DE L'EST
E6 ⚓ QR; 51°04'·86N 02°27'·08E.
E2 ⚓ Fl (2) R 6s; 51°04'·32N 02°22'·31E.
⚓ Q (6) + L Fl 15s; 51°04'·29N 02°21'·72E.

DUNKERQUE PORT EST
Jetée Est ☆ Fl (2) R 10s 12m **16M**; in fog Fl (2)
10s; 51°03'·59N 02°21'·20E.
Dunkerque lt ho ☆ Fl (2) 10s 59m **26M**; 51°02'·93N
02°21'·86E.

GRAVELINES
W jetty ⚓ Fl (2) WG 6s 9m W8M, G6M; 317°-W-
327°-G-085°-W-244°; 51°00'·94N 02°05'·48E.

DUNKERQUE, WEST APPROACH
DW29 ⚓ Fl (3) G 12s; 51°03'·85N 02°20'·21E.
DW18 ⚓ Fl (3) R 12s; 51°03'·47N 02°10'·37E.
RCE ⚓ Iso G 4s; 51°02'·43N 01°53'·21E.
Dyck ⚓ Fl 3s; *Racon B*; 51°02'·99N 01°51'·78E.

CALAIS
Jetée Est ☆ Fl (2) R 6s 12m **17M**; Gy twr, R top;
Horn (2) 40s; 50°58'·40N 01°50'·46E.
Jetée Ouest ⚓ Iso G 3s 12m 9M; W twr, G top; *Bell
5s;* 50°58'·24N 01°50'·40E.
Calais ☆ Fl (4) 15s 59m **22M**; vis 073°-260°; W 8-
sided twr, B top; 50°57'·68N 01°51'·21E.

CALAIS, WESTERN APPROACH
Calais Approche ⚓ VQ (9) 10s; 50°58'·89N 01°45'·10E.
CA2 ⚓ Fl R 4s; 50°58'·15N 01°45'·68E.
CA1 ⚓ Fl G 4s; 50°57'·64N 01°46'·14E.
Sangatte ⚓ Oc WG 4s 13m W8M, G5M; 065°-G-
089°-W-152°-G-245°; 50°57'·19N 01°46'·47E.
CA4 ⚓ Fl (2) R 6s; 50°58'·38N 01°48'·65E.
Cap Gris-Nez ☆ Fl 5s 72m **29M**; 005°-232°; W twr,
B top; *Horn 60s;* 50°52'·09N 01°34'·94E.

DOVER STRAIT TSS, French side
Ruytingen SW ⚓ Fl (3) G 12s; 51°04'·98N 01°46'·83E.
ZC2 ⚓ Fl (2+1) Y 15s; 50°53'·53N 01°30'·88E.
ZC1 ⚓ Fl (4) Y 15s; 50°44'·99N 01°27'·21E.
Vergoyer N ⚓ VQ; *Racon C, 5-8M*; 50°39'·64N
01°22'·18E.
Vergoyer E ⚓ VQ (3) 5s; 50°35'·74N 01°19'·65E.
Bassurelle ⚓ Fl (4) R 15s 6M; *Racon B, 5-8m*;
50°32'·74N 00°57'·69E.
Vergoyer SW ⚓ VQ (9) 10s; 50°26'·98N 01°00'·00E.

BOULOGNE
⚓ VQ (6) + L Fl 10s 8m 6M; *Whis;* 50°45'·31N
01°31'·07E.
Digue Carnot (S) ☆ Fl (2+1) 15s 25m **19M**; W twr,
G top; *Horn (2+1) 60s;* 50°44'·44N 01°34'·05E.
Cap d'Alprech ☆ Fl (3) 15s 62m **23M**; W twr, B
top; 50°41'·90N 01°33'·75E, 2·5M S of hbr ent.

LE TOUQUET and ÉTAPLES
Le Touquet ☆ Fl (2) 10s 54m **25M**; Or twr, brown
band, W&G top; 50°31'·43N 01°35'·49E.
Pointe du Haut-Blanc ☆ Fl 5s 44m **23M**; W twr, R
bands, G top; 50°23'·89N 01°33'·62E.

ST VALÉRY-SUR-SOMME
ATSO ⚓ Mo (A) 12s; 50°14'·00N 01°28'·08E.
Trng wall hd, ⚓ Fl G 2.5s 2m 1M; 50°12'·25N
01°35'·85E.
Cayeux-sur-Mer ☆ Fl R 5s 32m **22M**; W twr, R
top; 50°11'·65N 01°30'·67E.

LE TRÉPORT
Ault ☆ Oc (3) WR 12s 95m **W15M**, R11M; 040°-
W-175°-R-220°; W twr, R top; 50°06'·28N 01°27'·23E.
Jetée Ouest ☆ Fl (2) G 10s 15m **20M**; W twr, G
top; *Horn (2) 30s;* 50°03'·87N 01°22'·13E.

DIEPPE
DI ⚓ VQ (3) 5s; 49°57'·05N 01°01'·25E.
Jetée Ouest ⚓ Iso G 4s 11m 8M; W twr, G top;
Horn 30s; 49°56'·27N 01°04'·95E.
Pte d'Ailly ☆ Fl (3) 20s 95m **31M**; W ☐ twr, G top;
Horn (3) 60s; 49°54'·96N 00°57'·49E.

SAINT VALÉRY-EN-CAUX
Jetée Est ⚓ Fl (2) R 6s 8m 4M; 49°52'·40N 00°42'·70E.

FÉCAMP
Jetée Nord ☆ Fl (2) 10s 15m **16M**; Gy twr, R top;
Horn (2) 30s; 49°45'·93N 00°21'·78E.
Jetée Sud ⚓ QG 14m 9M; Gy twr, G top;
49°45'·88N 00°21'·80E.
Cap d'Antifer ☆ Fl 20s 128m **29M**; 021°-222°;
Gy 8-sided twr, G top; 49°41'·01N 00°09'·90E.

LE HAVRE

Cap de la Hève ☆ Fl 5s 123m **24M**; 225°-196°; W 8-sided twr, R top; 49°30'·74N 00°04'·15E.

LHA ⌐ Mo (A) 12s 10m 9M; R&W; *Racon, 8-10M*; 49°31'·38N 00°09'·88W.

Digue Nord ☆ Fl R 5s 15m **21M**; IPTS; W ○ twr, R top; *Horn 15s;* 49°29'·19N 00°05'·44E.

CHENAL DE ROUEN/HONFLEUR

No. 2 ↲ QR; *Racon T;* 49°27'·40N 00°01'·35E. Ratier NW ↲ Fl G 2·5s; 49°26'·85N 00°02'·50E. No. 20 ↲ QR; 49°25'·85N 00°13'·51E. Digue Ouest ↲ QG 10m 6M; 49°25'·68N 00°13'·81E.

DEAUVILLE/TROUVILLE

Ratelets ↲ Q (9) 15s; 49°25'·29N 00°01'·71E. E jetty ↲ Fl (4) WR 12s 8m W7M, R4M; 131°-W-175°-R-131°; 49°22'·22N 00°04'·33E.

DIVES-SUR-MER

DI ↲ L Fl 10s; 49°19'·18N 00°05'·84W. No. 1 ▲ 49°18'·50N 00°05'·67W. Dir lt 159·5°, Oc (2+1) WRG 12s 6m, W12M, R/G9M, 125°-G-157°-W-162°-R-194°; 49°17'·80N 00°05'·24W.

OUISTREHAM and CAEN

Ldg lts 185°, both Dir Oc (3+1) R 12s 10/30m **17M. Front**, 49°17'·09N 00°14'·80W.

Lt ho ☆ Oc WR 4s 37m **W17M**, R13M; 115°-R-151°-W-115°; 49°16'·85N 00°14'·80W.

COURSEULLES-SUR-MER

Courseulles ↲ Iso 4s; 49°21'·28N 00°27'·69W. W jetty ↲ Iso WG 4s 7m; W9M, G6M; 135°-W-235°-G-135°; 49°20'·41N 00°27'·37W.

Ver ☆ Fl (3)15s 42m **26M**; 49°20'·39N 00°31'·15W.

PORT-EN-BESSIN

W mole ↲ Fl WG 4s 14m, W10M, G7M; G065°-114·5°, W114·5°-065°; 49°21'·17N 00°45'·39W.

GRANDCAMP

Ldg lts 146°, both Dir Q 9/12m **15M**, 144·5°-147·5°. **Front** ☆, 49°23'·42N 01°02'·92W. Jetée Est ↲ Oc (2) R 6s 9m 9M; 49°23'·52N 01°02'·98W.

CARENTAN

C-I ↲ Iso 4s; 49°25'·44N 01°07'·08W. Trng wall ↲ Fl (4) G 15s; 49°21'·94N 01°09'·96W. Iles St-Marcouf ↲ VQ (3) 5s 18m 8M; □ Gy twr, G top; 49°29'·86N 01°08'·82W.

ST VAAST-LA-HOUGUE

Le Gavendest ↲ Q (6) + L Fl 15s; *Whis;* 49°34'·36N 01°13'·89W. Jetty ↲ Dir Oc (2) WRG 6s 12m W10M, R/G7M; 219°-R-237°-G-310°-W-350°-R-040°; *Siren Mo (N) 30s;* 49°35'·17N 01°15'·41W.

BARFLEUR

Ldg lts 219·5°, both Oc (3) 12s 7/13m 10M; synch. Front, W □ twr;49°40'·18N 01°15'·61W. W jetty ↲ Fl G 4s 8m 6M; 49°40'·32N 01°15'·57W.

Pte de Barfleur ☆ Fl (2) 10s 72m **29M**; Gy twr, B top; *Horn (2) 60s;* 49°41'·78N 01°15'·96W. Les Équets ↲ Q 8m 3M; 49°43'·62N 01°18'·36W. La Pierre Noire ↲ Q (9) 15s 8m 4M;49°43'·53N 01°29'·09W.

CHERBOURG

La Truite ↲ Fl (4) R 15s; 49°40'·33N 01°35'·50W. Fort de l'Est ↲ Iso G 4s 19m 9M; 49°40'·28N 01°35'·93W

Fort de l'Ouest ☆ Fl (3) WR 15s 19m **W24M, R20M**; 122°-W-355°-R-122°; Gy twr, R top; *Horn (3) 60s;* 49°40'·45N 01°38'·87W.

Fort de l'Ouest ☆ Fl (3) WR 15s 19m **W24M, R20M**; 122°-W-355°-R-122°; Gy twr, R top; *Horn (3) 60s;* 49°40'·45N 01°38'·87W. Marina W mole ↲ Fl (3) G 12s 7m 6M; G pylon; 49°38'·87N 01°37'·15W.

OMONVILLE-LA-ROGUE

L'Étonnard ▲ 49°42'·32N 01°49'·85W.

Cap de la Hague ☆ Fl 5s 48m **23M**; Gy twr, W top; *Horn 30s;* 49°43'·31N 01° 57'·28W.

		1	2	3	4	5	6	7	8	9	10	11	12	13	14	15	16	17	18	19
1	Dunkerque	1																		
2	Calais	22	2																	
3	Boulogne	42	20	3																
4	Étaples	51	32	12	4															
5	St Valéry-sur-Somme	69	50	30	19	5														
6	Dieppe	96	74	54	50	35	6													
7	St Valéry-en-Caux	103	81	61	58	45	16	7												
8	Fécamp	118	96	76	70	62	29	15	8											
9	Le Havre	143	121	101	90	85	54	38	25	9										
10	Honfleur	152	130	110	100	95	63	45	34	10	10									
11	Deauville/Trouville	150	128	108	100	95	61	44	32	10	8	11								
12	Dives-sur-Mer	151	129	108	117	97	67	55	39	17	13	7	12							
13	Ouistreham	160	138	115	110	103	68	58	39	24	19	14	8	13						
14	Courseulles	162	140	118	110	103	75	55	40	28	23	21	17	11	14					
15	Grandcamp-Maisy	190	168	135	130	125	94	80	64	50	45	43	38	35	25	15				
16	Carentan	192	170	145	140	132	105	88	72	62	56	56	51	46	37	13	16			
17	St Vaast	179	157	133	130	120	95	78	63	69	53	53	49	46	35	16	20	17		
18	Barfleur	170	148	128	124	120	94	77	64	56	62	56	53	46	39	21	26	10	18	
19	Cherbourg	182	160	142	134	130	108	82	82	80	76	70	69	66	54	41	39	26	20	19

47

AREA 15 N Central France (*Cap de la Hague to St Quay*) & Channel Is

SELECTED LIGHTS, BUOYS & WAYPOINTS | Positions are referenced to WGS84

DIELETTE

W bkwtr Dir lt 140°, Iso WRG 4s 12m W10M, R/G7M; 070°-G-135°-W-145°-R-180°; 49°33'·18N 01°51'·81W.
E bkwtr ⚓ Fl R 4s 6m 2M; 49°33'·21N 01°51'·78W.

CARERET

Cap de Carteret ☆ Fl (2+1) 15s 81m **26M**; Gy twr, G top; 49°22'·40N 01°48'·41W.
W bkwtr ⚓ Oc R 4s 7m 7M; W post, R top; 49°22'·17N 01°47'·30W.

PORTBAIL

PB ⚓ 49°18'·37N 01°44'·75W.
Ldg lts 042°: Front, Q 14m 10M, 49°19'·75N 01°42'·50W. Rear, Oc 4s 20m 10M; stubby ch spire.

PASSAGE DE LA DÉROUTE

Les Trois-Grunes ⚓ Q (9) 15s, 49°21'·84N 01°55'·21W.
Le Sénéquet ⚓ Fl (3) WR 12s 18m W13M, R10M; 083·5°-R-116·5°-W-083·5°; 49°05'·48N 01°39'·73W.
NE Minquiers ⚓ VQ (3) 5s; *Bell;* 49°00'·85N 01°55'·30W.
S Minquiers ⚓ Q (6) + L Fl 15s; 48°53'·09N 02°10'·10W.

ÎLES CHAUSEY

L'Enseigne, W twr, B top; 48°53'·67N 01°50'·37W.
Grande Île ☆ Fl 5s 39m **23M**; Gy □ twr, G top; *Horn 30s;* 48°52'·17N 01°49'·34W.
La Crabière Est ⚓ Oc WRG 4s 5m, W9M, R/G 6M; 079°-W-291°-G-329°-W-335°-R-079°; YB pylon; 48°52'·46N 01°49'·39W.

GRANVILLE

Pte du Roc ☆ Fl (4) 15s 49m **23M**; 48°50'·06N 01°36'·78W.
Le Loup ⚓ Fl (2) 6s 8m 11M; 48°49'·57N 01°36'·24W.
Marina S bkwtr ⚓ Fl (2) R 6s 12m 5M; W post, R top; *Horn (2) 40s;* 48°49'·89N 01°35'·90W.

CANCALE

Pierre-de-Herpin ☆ Oc (2) 6s 20m **17M**; *Siren Mo (N) 60s;* 48°43'·77N 01°48'·92W.
Jetty ⚓ Oc (3) G 12s 12m 7M; 48°40'·10N 01°51'·11W.

ST MALO, CHENAL DE LA PETITE PORTE

Outer ldg lts 129·7°: **Front, Le Grand Jardin** ☆ Fl (2) R 10s 24m **15M**, 48°40'·20N 02°04'·97W. Rear, **La Balue** ☆ FG 20m 22M; 48°37'·60N 02°00'·24W.
St Malo Fairway ⚓ Iso 4s; 48°41'·39N 02°07'·28W.
Inner ldg lts 128·6°, both Dir FG 20/69m **22/25M;** H24. Front, **Les Bas Sablons** ☆; W □ twr, B top; 48°38'·16N 02°01'·30W. Rear, **La Balue** ☆, above.

CHENAL DE LA GRANDE PORTE

Outer ldg lts 089·1°: **Front, Le Grand Jardin** ☆ (as

above). Rear, **Rochebonne** ☆ Dir FR 40m **24M;** 48°40'·26N 01°58'·71W. At Le Grand Jardin continue on inner 128·6° ldg line (above).
Môle des Noires hd ⚓ Fl R 5s 11m 13M; W twr, R top; *Horn (2) 20s;* 48°38'·52N 02°01'·91W.
Bas-Sablons marina ⚓ Fl G 4s 7m 5M; 48°38'·42N 02°01'·70W.

LA RANCE BARRAGE

La Jument ⚓ Fl G 4s 6m 4M; G twr, 48°37'·44N 02°01'·76W. Barrage lock, NW wall ⚓ Fl (2) G 6s 6m 5M, 191°-291°; 48°37'·06N 02°01'·73W.

ST CAST

Môle ⚓ Iso WG 4s 11m, W11M, G8M; 204°-W-217°-G-233°-W-245°-G-204°; 48°38'·41N 02°14'·61W.
Cap Fréhel ☆ Fl (2) 10s 85m **29M**; Gy □ twr, G lantern; *Horn (2) 60s;* 48°41'·05N 02°19'·13W.

ERQUY

S môle ⚓ Oc (2+1) WRG 12s 11m W11M, R/G8M; 055°-R-081°-W-094°-G-111°-W-120°-R-134°; W twr; 48°38'·07N 02°28'·66W.

DAHOUET

La Petite Muette ⚓ Fl WRG 4s 10m W9M, R/G6M; 055°-G-114°-W-146°-R-196°; 48°34'·82N 02°34'·19W.

BAIE DE SAINT BRIEUC and LE LÉGUÉ

Grand Léjon ☆ Fl (5) WR 20s 17m **W18M**, R14M; 015°-R-058°-W-283°-R-350°-W-015°; R twr, W bands; 48°44'·91N 02°39'·87W.
Le Rohein ⚓ VQ (9) WRG 10s 13m, W10M, R/G7M; 072°-R-105°-W-180°-G-193°-W-237°-G-282°-W-301°-G-330°-W-072°; Y twr, B band; 48°38'·80N 02°37'·77W.
Le Légué ⚓ Mo (A) 10s; 48°34'·32N 02°41'·15W.
Pte à l'Aigle ⚓ VQ G 13m 8M; 48°32'·12N 02°43'·11W.

BINIC

N môle ⚓ Oc (3) 12s 12m 11M; unintens 020°-110°; W twr, G lantern; 48°36'·07N 02°48'·92W.

SAINT QUAY-PORTRIEUX

La Roselière ⚓ VQ (6) + L Fl 10s; 48°37'·29N 02°46'·18W.
Herflux ⚓ Dir ⚓ 130°, Fl (2) WRG 6s 10m, W 8M, R/G 6M; 115°-G-125°-W-135°-R-145°; 48°39'·07N 02°47'·95W.
Île Harbour ⚓ Oc (2) WRG 6s 16m, W10M, R/G8M; 011°-R-133°-G-270°-R-306°-G-358°-W-011°; 48°39'·99N 02°48'·49W.
Marina, **NE mole elbow,** Dir lt 318·2°: Iso WRG 4s 16m **W15M**, R/G11M; 159°-W-179°-G-316°-W-320·5°-R-159°; 48°38'·99N 02°49'·09W.
NE môle hd ⚓ Fl (3) G 12s 10m 2M; 48°38'·84N 02°48'·91W.

CHANNEL ISLANDS

THE CASQUETS AND ALDERNEY

Casquets ☆ Fl (5) 30s 37m **24M**, H24; *Horn (2) 60s;* *Racon T, 25M*; 49°43'·32N 02°22'·63W.

Quenard Pt ☆ Fl (4) 15s 37m **23M**, H24; 085°-027°; *Horn 30s;* 49°43'·75N 02°09'·86W.

Braye, ldg lts 215°: both Q 8/17m 9/12M, synch; 210°-220°. Front, old pier, 49°43'·40N 02°11'·91W.

Admiralty bkwtr ⚓ L Fl 10s; 49°43'·82N 02°11'·67W.

LITTLE RUSSEL CHANNEL

Platte Fougère ☆ Fl WR 10s 15m **16M**; 155°-W-085°-R-155°; W 8-sided twr, B band; *Horn 45s;* *Racon P;* 49°30'·83N 02°29'·14W.

Roustel ⚓ Q 8m 7M; 49°29'·23N 02°28'·79W.

Platte ⚓, Fl WR 3s 6m, W7M, R5M; 024°-R-219°-W-024°; G conical twr; 49°29'·08N 02°29'·57W.

Brehon ⚓ Iso 4s 19m 9M, 49°28'·28N 02°29'·28W.

BIG RUSSEL

Noire Pute ⚓ Fl (2) WR 15s 8m 6M; 220°-W-040°-R-220°; on 2m high rock; 49°28'·21N 02°25'·02W.

Lower Heads ⚓ Q (6) + L Fl 15s; *Bell;* 49°25'·85N 02°28'·55W.

BEAUCETTE MARINA

Petite Canupe ⚓ Q (6) + L Fl 15s; 49°30'·20N 02°29'·14W.

Ldg lts 276°, both FR. Front, 49°30'·19N 02°30'·23W.

ST PETER PORT

Outer ldg lts 220°: **Front**, Castle bkwtr, Al WR 10s 14m **16M**; 187°-007°; *Horn 15s;* 49°27'·31N 02°30'·45W. Rear, Oc 10s 61m 14M; 179°-269°.

White Rock pier ⚓ Oc G 5s 11m 14M; tfc sigs; 49°27'·38N 02°31'·59W.

S Fairway ⚓ QG; 49°27'·30N 02°31'·76W.

HERM

Hbr ldg lts 078°: White drums. ⚓ 2F occas; 49°28'·25N 02°27'·11W.

SARK

Corbée du Nez ⚓ Fl (4) WR 15s 14m 8M; 057°-W-230°-R-057°; W structure; 49°27'·09N 02°22'·17W.

Point Robert ☆ Fl 15s 65m **20M**; W 8-sided twr; *Horn (2) 30s;* 49°26'·19N 02°20'·75W.

JERSEY (West and South coasts)

Grosnez Point ☆ Fl (2) WR 15s 50m **W19M, R17M;** 081°-W-188°-R-241°; 49°15'·50N 02°14'·80W.

La Corbière ☆ Iso WR 10s 36m **W18M, R16M;** shore-W-294°-R-328°-W-148°-R-shore; W ○ twr; *Horn Mo (C) 60s;* 49°10'·79N 02°15'·01W.

WESTERN PASSAGE

Ldg lts 082°. Front Oc 5s 23m 14M; 034°-129°; 49°10'·16N 02°05'·09W. Rear, Oc R 5s 46m 12M.

Noirmont Pt ⚓ Fl (4) 12s 18m 10M; B twr, W band; 49°09'·91N 02°10'·08W.

ST HELIER

Elizabeth marina: Dir ⚓ 106°: F WRG 4m 1M; 096°-G-104°-W-108°-R-119°; 49°10'·76N 02°07'·12W.

Marina ent ⚓ Oc G 4s 2M; 49°10'·83N 02°07'·13W.

Red & Green Passage, ldg lts 022·7° on dayglo R dolphins: Front, ⚓ Oc G 5s 10m 11M; 49°10'·63N 02°06'·94W. Rear, ⚓ Oc R 5s 18m 12M.

East Rock ⚓ QG; 49°09'·95N 02°07'·29W.

Victoria pier hd, Port control twr; IPTS; 49°10'·57N 02°06'·88W.

JERSEY (South-East coast)

Demie de Pas ⚓ Mo (D) WR 12s 11m, W14M, R10M; 130°-R-303°-W-130°; *Horn (3) 60s*; *Racon T, 10M*; B bn twr, Y top; 49°09'·01N 02°06'·15W.

Violet ⚓ L Fl 10s; 49°07'·81N 01°57'·14W.

GOREY

Ldg lts 298°: Front, ⚓ Oc RG 5s; 304°-R-353°-G-304°; 49°11'·80N 02°01'·34W. Rear, ⚓ Oc R 5s 24m 8M.

ST CATHERINE BAY

Verclut bkwtr ⚓ Fl 1·5s 18m 13M; 49°13'·34N 02°00'·64W. In line 315° with unlit turret, 49°13'·96N 02°01'·57W, on La Coupe Pt.

JERSEY (North coast)

Sorel Point ☆ L Fl WR 7·5s 50m **15M**; 095°-W-112°-R-173°-W-230°-R-269°-W-273°; 49°15'·60N 02°09'·54W.

		1															
1	Cherbourg	**1**															
2	Omonville	10	**2**														
3	Braye (Alderney)	25	15	**3**													
4	St Peter Port	44	34	23	**4**												
5	Creux (Sark)	37	29	22	10	**5**											
6	St Helier	64	51	46	29	24	**6**										
7	Carteret	41	29	28	31	23	26	**7**									
8	Portbail	49	33	32	35	27	25	5	**8**								
9	Iles Chausey	69	61	58	48	43	25	33	30	**9**							
10	Granville	75	67	66	55	50	30	38	35	9	**10**						
11	Dinan	102	91	85	66	64	50	62	59	29	35	**11**					
12	St Malo	90	79	73	54	52	38	50	47	17	23	12	**12**				
13	Dahouet	88	80	72	54	52	41	60	59	37	45	41	29	**13**			
14	Le Légué/St Brieuc	96	86	76	57	56	46	69	69	41	49	45	33	8	**14**		
15	Binic	95	84	75	56	55	46	70	70	43	51	45	33	10	8	**15**	
16	St Quay-Portrieux	88	80	73	56	51	46	64	64	47	54	47	35	11	7	4	**16**
17	Lézardrieux	88	80	68	48	38	47	68	71	53	54	61	49	33	32	30	21	**17**

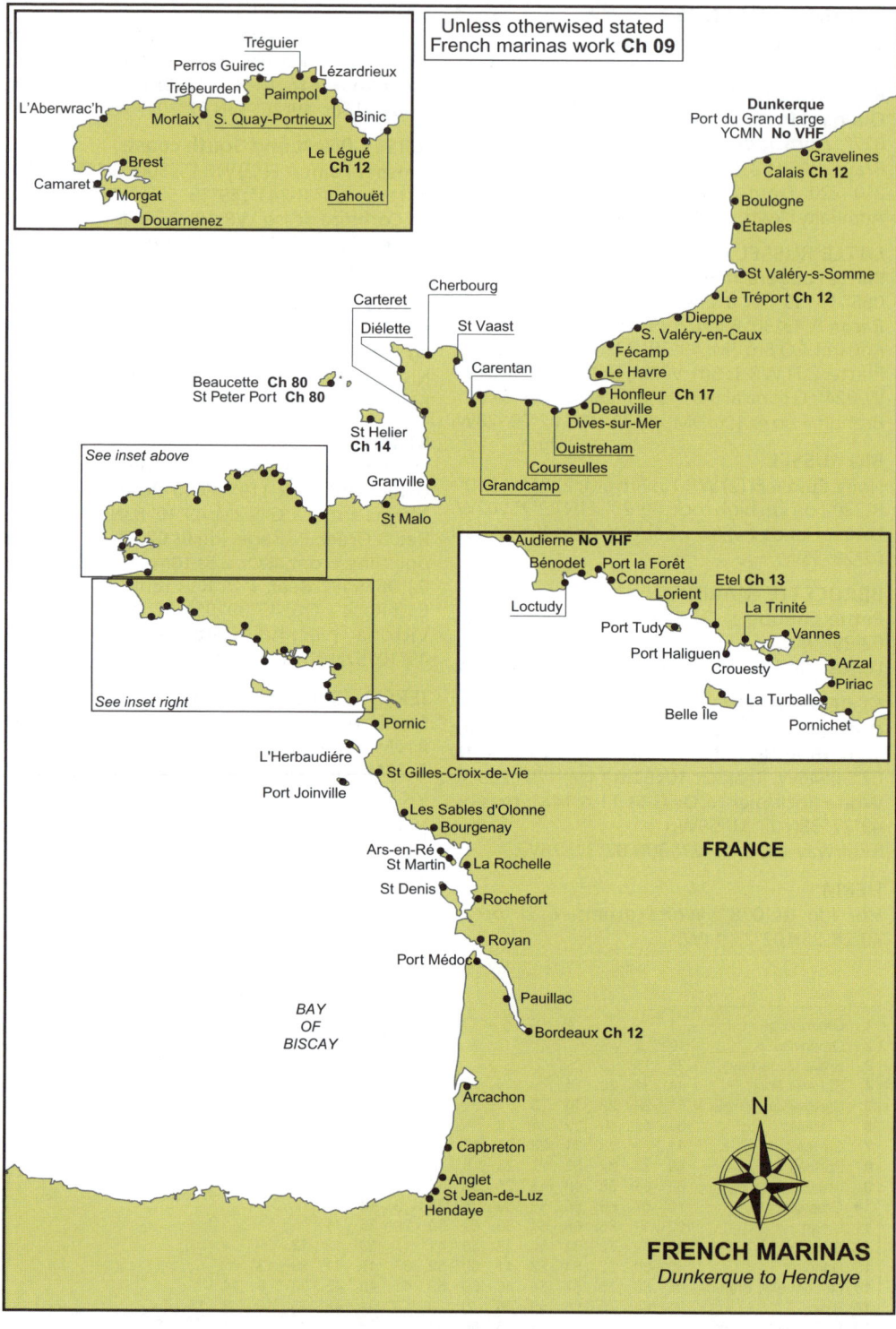

Tréguier
Perros Guirec   Lézardrieux
Trébeurden   Paimpol
L'Aberwrac'h
Morlaix   S. Quay-Portrieux   Binic
Brest   Le Légué **Ch 12**
Camaret
Morgat   Dahouët
Douarnenez

Unless otherwised stated
French marinas work **Ch 09**

Dunkerque
Port du Grand Large
YCMN **No VHF**
Gravelines
Calais **Ch 12**
Boulogne
Étaples
St Valéry-s-Somme
Le Tréport **Ch 12**
Dieppe
S. Valéry-en-Caux
Fécamp
Le Havre
Honfleur **Ch 17**
Deauville
Dives-sur-Mer
Ouistreham
Courseulles
Grandcamp

Cherbourg
Carteret
Diélette
St Vaast
Carentan

Beaucette **Ch 80**
St Peter Port **Ch 80**

St Helier
Ch 14

Granville
St Malo

See inset above

Audierne **No VHF**
Bénodet   Port la Forêt
Concarneau   Etel **Ch 13**
Lorient
Loctudy   La Trinité
Port Tudy   Vannes
Port Haliguen   Arzal
Crouesty   Piriac
La Turballe
Belle Île   Pornichet

See inset right

Pornic
L'Herbaudiére
St Gilles-Croix-de-Vie
Port Joinville

Les Sables d'Olonne
Bourgenay
Ars-en-Ré
St Martin   La Rochelle
St Denis
Rochefort

FRANCE

Royan
Port Médoc

*BAY
OF
BISCAY*

Pauillac

Bordeaux **Ch 12**

Arcachon

N

Capbreton
Anglet
St Jean-de-Luz
Hendaye

FRENCH MARINAS
Dunkerque to Hendaye

AREA 16 N and S Brittany - *Paimpol to Pornichet*

SELECTED LIGHTS, BUOYS & WAYPOINTS

> Positions are referenced to WGS84

OFFSHORE MARKS

Roches Douvres ☆ Fl 5s 60m **28M**; *Horn 60s*; 49°06'·28N 02°48'·89W.

PAIMPOL

L'Ost Pic ⚓ Oc WR 4s 20m, W11M, R8M; 105°-W-116°-R-221°-W-253°-R-291°-W-329°; 48°46'·76N 02°56'·44W. La Jument ⚓ 48°47'·34N 02°57'·97W. Ldg lts 262·2°, both QR 5/12m 7/14M. Front, Kernoa jetty; W & R hut; 48°47'·09N 03°02'·44W.

ÎLE DE BRÉHAT

Rosédo ☆ Fl 5s 29m **20M**; 48°51'·45N 03°00'·30W. Le Paon ⚓ F WRG 22m W11M, R/G8M; 033°-W-078°-G-181°-W-196°- R-307°-W-316°-R-348°; Y twr; 48°51'·93N 02°59'·17W.

LÉZARDRIEUX

Ldg lts 224·7°: Front, **La Croix** ☆ Dir Oc 4s 15m **19M**; 48°50'·22N 03°03'·24W. Rear **Bodic** ☆ Dir Q 55m **22M**.
Coatmer ldg lts 218·7°: Front, F RG 16m R/G9M; 200°-R-250°-G-053°; 48°48'·26N 03°05'·75W. Rear, FR 50m 9M; vis 197°-242°.

JAUDY (TRÉGUIER) RIVER

Les Héaux de Bréhat ☆ Oc (3) WRG 12s 48m, **W15M**, R/G11M; 227°-R-247°-W-270°-G-302°-W-227°; Gy ○ twr; 48°54'·50N 03°05'·18W.
Ldg lts 137°. Front, Oc 4s 12m 11M; 042°-232°; 48°51'·55N 03°07'·90W. Rear, Dir Oc R 4s 34m **15M**.
La Corne ⚓ Fl (3) WRG 12s 14m W11M, R/G8M; 052°-W-059°-R-173°-G-213°-W-220°-R-052°; W twr, R base; 48°51'·34N 03°10'·63W.

PERROS-GUIREC

Passe de l'Est, ldg lts 224·5°. Front ☆ Dir Oc (4) 12s 28m **15M**; 48°47'·87N 03°26'·66W. Rear ☆, Dir Q 79m **21M**; intens 221°-228°.

PLOUMANAC'H

Men-Ruz ⚓ Oc WR 4s 26m W12M, R9M; 226°-W-242°-R-226°; pink □ twr; 48°50'·26N 03°29'·03W.

TRÉBEURDEN

Ar Gouredec ⚓ VQ (6) + L Fl 10s; 48°46'·41N 03°36'·60W. NW bkwtr ⚓ Fl G 2·5s 8m 2M; IPTS; 48°46'·34N 03°35'·20W.

PRIMEL-TRÉGASTEL

Ldg lts 152°, both ⚓ QR 35/56m 7M, R vert stripe on W □. Front, 48°42'·45N 03°49'·20W.

BAIE DE MORLAIX

Chenal du Tréguier ldg lts 190·5°: Front, ⚓ Île Noire Oc (2) WRG 6s 15m, W11M, R/G8M; 051°-

G-135°-R-211°-W-051°; 48°40'·34N 03°52'·56W.
La Lande ☆ Fl 5s 85m **23M**; 48°38'·19N 03°53'·16W. Common rear for both channels.
Grande Chenal ldg lts 176·4°: Front, Île **Louet** ☆ Oc (3) WG 12s 17m **W15M**, G10M; 305°-W-244°-G-305°; W □ twr, B top; 48°40'·40N 03°53'·34W.

CANAL DE L'ÎLE DE BATZ

Ar-Chaden ⚓ Q (6) + L Fl WR 15s 14m, W8M, R6M; 262°-R-289·5°-W-293°-R-326°- W-110°; YB twr; 48°43'·93N 03°58'·26W.
Men-Guen-Bras ⚓ Q WRG 14m, W9M, R/G6M; 068°-W-073°-R-197°-W-257°-G-068°; BY twr; 48°43'·76N 03°58'·07W.
Lt ho ☆ Fl (4) 25s 69m **23M**; 48°44'·71N 04°01'·63W.

L'ABER WRAC'H

Île-Vierge ☆ Fl 5s 77m **27M**; 337°-325°; Gy twr; 48°38'·33N 04°34'·06W.
Libenter ⚓ Q (9) 15s 6M; 48°37'·50N 04°38'·37W.
Outer ldg lts 100·1°: Front ⚓ QR 20m 7M; 48°36'·88N 04°34'·56W. Rear ⚓ Dir Q 55m 12M.

CHENAUX DU FOUR ET DE LA HELLE

Le Four ☆ Fl (5) 15s 28m **18M**; Gy ○ twr; *Horn (3+2) 60s*; 48°31'·38N 04°48'·32W.
Ldg lts 158·5°. Front, **Kermorvan** ☆ Fl 5s 20m **22M**; W □ twr; *Horn 60s*; 48°21'·72N 04°47'·42W. Rear, **Pte de St Mathieu** ☆ Fl 15s 56m **29M**; W twr, R top; 48°19'·79N 04°46'·27W.
Grande Vinotière ⚓ L Fl R 10s; 48°21'·93N 04°48'·43W. Les Vieux-Moines ⚓ Fl R 4s 16m 5M; 280°-133°; R 8-sided twr; 48°19'·33N 04°46'·63W.

BREST AND APPROACHES

Pte du Toulinguet ☆ Oc (3) WR 12s **W15M**, R11M; shore-W-028°-R-090°-W-shore; 48°16'·82N 04°37'·73W.
Moulin Blanc ⚓ Fl (3) R 12s; 48°22'·79N 04°25'·99W.

CAMARET

N môle ⚓ Iso WG 4s 7m W12M, G9M; 135°-W-182°-G-027°; 48°16'·85N 04°35'·32W.

MORGAT

Pte de Morgat ☆ Oc (4) WRG 12s 77m **W15M**, R11M, G10M; Shore-W-281°-G-301°-W-021°-043°; 48°13'·17N 04°29'·81W.

DOUARNENEZ TO RAZ DE SEIN

Île Tristan ⚓ Oc (3) WR 12s 35m, W13M, R10M; shore-W-138°-R-153°-W-shore; 48°06'·14N 04°20'·25W.

RAZ DE SEIN

Tévennec ⚓ Q WR 28m W9M R6M; 090°-W-345°-R-090°; 48°04'·28N 04°47'·73W. Same twr, Dir ⚓

Fl 4s 24m 12M; intens 324°-332° (Raz de Sein).
La Vieille ☆ Oc (2+1) WRG 12s 33m **W18M**, R13M, G14M; 290°-W-298°-R-325°-W-355°-G-017°- W-035°-G-105°-W-123°-R-158°-W-205°; Gy □ twr; *Horn (2+1) 60s;* 48°02'·43N 04°45'·43W.
La Plate ⍌ VQ (9) 10s 8M; 48°02'·35N 04°45'·61W.

AUDIERNE

Kergadec Dir ⚡ 006°: Q WRG 43m 12/9M; 000°-G-005·3°-W-006·7°-R-017°; 48°00'·95N 04°32'·78W.

LOCTUDY

Pte de Langoz ☆ Fl (4) WRG 12s 12m, **W15M**, R/G11M; 115°-W-257°-G-284°-W-295°-R-318°-W-328°-R-025°; 47°49'·87N 04°09'·59W.

BENODET

Ldg lts 345·5°: Front Dir Oc (2+1) G 12s 11m **17M**; W ○ twr, G stripe; 47°52'·31N 04°06'·70W. Rear ⚡ Oc (2+1) 12s 48m 11M; 338°-016°, synch.

PORT-LA-FORÊT

Cap Coz ⚡ Fl (2) WRG 6s 5m, 7/5M; shore-R-335°-G-340°-W-346°-R-shore; 47°53'·48N 03°58'·28W.

ÎLES DE GLÉNAN

Penfret ☆ Fl R 5s 36m **21M**; W □ twr, R top; 47°43'·26N 03°57'·17W.

CONCARNEAU

Ldg lts 028·5°: Front, ⚡ Q 14m 13M; 006·5°-093°; 47°52'·15N 03°55'·08W. **Rear** ☆ Dir Q 87m **23M**; intens 026·5°-030·5°; spire, 1·34M from front. Marina ⚡ Fl (4) R 15s 3m 1M; 47°52'·20N 03°54'·72W.

ÎLE DE GROIX

Pen Men ☆ Fl (4) 25s 60m **29M**; 309°-275°; W □ twr, B top; 47°38'·86N 03°30'·54W.
Port Tudy, ⚡ Iso G 4s 12m 6M; 47°38'·70N 03°26'·74W.

LORIENT

Passe de l'Ouest ldg lts 057°: both Dir Q 11/22m 13/**18M**. Front, 47°42'·13N 03°21'·83W
Passe du Sud ldg lts 008·5°: both Dir QR 16/34m **17/16M**; 47°43'·76N 03°21'·74W .

BELLE ÎLE

Pte des Poulains ☆ Fl 5s 34m **23M**; 023°-291°; W □ twr and dwelling; 47°23'·28N 03°15'·17W.

Sauzon, ⚡ Fl G 4s 8m 8M; 47°22'·51N 03°13'·10W.
Le Palais, N jetty ⚡ Fl (2+1) G 12s 8m 7M; W twr, G top; 47°20'·82N 03°09'·08W.
La Teignouse ☆ Fl WR 4s 20m **W15M**, R11M; 033°-W-039°-R-033°; 47°27'·45N 03°02'·79W.

ÎLE DE HOUAT and ÎLE DE HOËDIC

Port St-Gildas N môle ⚡ Fl (2) WG 6s 8m W9M, G6M; 168°-W-198°-G-210°-W-240°-G-168°; W twr, G top; 47°23'·57N 02°57'·34W.
Port de l'Argol bkwtr ⚡ Fl WG 4s 10m W9M, G6M; 143°-W-163°-G-183°-W-194°-G-143°; W twr, G top; 47°20'·69N 02°52'·56W.

PORT HALIGUEN

E bkwtr hd ⚡ Oc (2) WR 6s 10m, W11M, R8M; 233°-W-240·5°-R-299°-W-306°-R-233°; W twr, R top; 47°29'·30N 03°05'·99W.

LA TRINITÉ-SUR-MER

Ldg lts 347°: Front, ⚡ Q WRG 11m W10M, R/G7M; 321°-G-345°-W-013·5°-R-080°; 47°34'·08N 03°00'·37W. **Rear,** Dir Q 21m **15M**; synch.
Marina ⚡ Iso R 4s 8m 5M; 47°35'·27N 03°01'·47W.

CROUESTY

Ldg lts 058°, Dir Q 10/27m **19M**: **Front**; 47°32'·54N 02°53'·94W. **Rear** ☆, grey lt ho.

VILAINE RIVER

Pte de Penlan ☆ Oc (2) WRG 6s 26m, **W15M**, R/G11M; 292·5°-R-025°-G-052°-W-060°-R-138°-G-180°; W twr, R bands; 47°30'·98N 02°30'·13W.

PIRIAC-SUR-MER

Inner mole ⚡ Oc (2) WRG 6s 8m, W10M, R/G7M; 066°-R-148°-G-194°-W-201°-R-221°; 47°22'·93N 02°32'·72W. *Siren 120s (occas), 35m SW.*

LA TURBALLE

Jetée de Garlahy ⚡ Fl (4) WR 12s 13m, W10M, R7M; 060°-R-315°-W-060°; W pylon, R top; 47°20'·70N 02°30'·93W.

PORNICHET (La Baule)

S bkwtr ⚡ Iso WRG 4s 11m, W10M, R/G7M; 303°-G-081°-W-084°-R-180°; 47°15'·49N 02°21'·15W.

1	Lézardrieux	1		12	16	18	24	42	43	45	72	97	100	105	124	Pornic	12
2	Tréguier	22	2		11	12	24	39	40	41	66	87	90	95	113	St Nazaire	11
3	Perros-Guirec	28	21	3		10	13	30	30	34	55	78	80	85	106	La Baule/Pornichet	10
4	Trébeurden	40	32	17	4		9	18	22	27	48	73	75	79	100	Le Croisic	9
5	Morlaix	60	46	36	23	5		8	28	36	57	78	80	84	105	Arzal/Camöel	8
6	Roscoff	54	41	28	17	12	6		7	16	37	58	60	64	85	Crouesty	7
7	L'Aberwrac'h	84	72	60	49	48	32	7		6	26	47	48	54	74	Le Palais (Belle Ile)	6
8	Le Conquet	106	98	83	72	68	55	29	8		5	32	33	38	61	Lorient	5
9	Brest (marina)	114	107	92	83	79	67	42	18	9		4	4	12	37	Concarneau	4
10	Morgat	126	118	103	92	88	75	49	20	24	10		3	12	36	Port-la-Forêt	3
11	Douarnenez	131	123	108	97	93	80	54	25	29	11	11		2	30	Loctudy	2
12	Audierne	135	128	113	102	98	86	55	30	34	27	30	12		1	Audierne	1

AREA 17 South Biscay - *River Loire to Spanish border*

SELECTED LIGHTS, BUOYS & WAYPOINTS

Positions are referenced to WGS84

Pte de Saint-Gildas ⚡ Q WRG 20m, W14M, R/G10M; 264°-R-308°-G-078°-W-088°-R-174°-W-180°-G-264°; col on W house; 47°08'·02N 02°14'·76W.

PORNIC

Appr buoy ⚓ L Fl 10s; 47°06'·45N 02°06'·64W.
Pte de Noëveillard ⚡ Oc (4) WRG 12s 22m W13M, R/G9M; Shore-G-051°-W-079°-R-shore; W ☐ twr, G top, W dwelling; 47°06'·62N 02°06'·92W.

ÎLE DE NOIRMOUTIER

Île du Pilier ☆ Fl (3) 20s 33m **29M**; Gy twr; 47°02'·55N 02°21'·61W. Same twr, ⚡ QR 10m 11M, 321°-034°.
Les Boeufs ⚓ VQ (9) 10s; 46°55'·04N 02°28'·02W.
L'Herbaudière, ldg lts 187·5°, both Q 5/21m 7M, Gy masts. Front, 47°01'·59N 02°17'·85W.
Martroger ⚓, Q WRG 11m W9M, R/G6M; 033°-G-055°-W-060°-R-095°-G-124°-W-153°-R-201°-W-240°-R-033°; 47°02'·60N 02°17'·12W.
W jetty ⚡ Oc (2+1) WG 12s 9m W10M, G7M; 187·5°-W-190°-G-187·5°; 47°01'·63N 02°17'·86W.
Noirmoutier-en-L'Île jetty ⚡ Oc (2) R 6s 6m 6M; W col, R top; 46°59'·27N 02°13'·14W.

ÎLE D'YEU

Petite Foule (main lt) ☆ Fl 5s 56m **24M**; W ☐ twr, G lantern; 46°43'·05N 02°22'·96W.
Port Joinville ldg lts 219°, both QR 11/16m 6M, 169°-269°: Front 46°43'·61N 02°20'·95W.
NW jetty ⚡ Oc (3) WG 12s 7m, W11M, G8M; Shore-G-150°-W-232°-G-279°-W-285°-G-shore; W 8-sided twr, G top; 46°43'·77N 02°20'·82W.
Pte des Corbeaux ☆ Fl (2+1) R 15s 25m **20M**; 083°-143° obsc by Île d'Yeu; 46°41'·42N 02°17'·11W.
Port de la Meule ⚡ Oc WRG 4s 9m, W9M, R/G6M; 007·5°-G-018°-W-027·5°-R-041·5°; Gy twr, R top; 46°41'·66N 02°20'·75W.

SAINT GILLES-CROIX-DE-VIE

Pte de Grosse Terre ☆ Fl (4) WR 12s 25m, **W18M, R15M**; 290°- R-339°-W-125°-R-145°; W truncated twr; 46°41'·54N 01°57'·92W.
Ldg lts 043·7°, Q 7/28m **15M**; 033·5°-053·5°: Front, 46°41'·85N 01°56'·67W
Pilours ⚓ Q (6) + L Fl 15s; *Bell;* 46°40'·98N 01°58'·10W.
Jetée de la Garenne ⚡ Fl G 4s 8m 6M; 46°41'·45N 01°57'·26W.

LES SABLES D'OLONNE

Les Barges ⚡ Fl (2) R 10s 25m 13M; Gy twr; 46°29'·70N 01°50'·50W.
L'Armandèche ☆ Fl (2+1) 15s 42m **24M**; 295°-130°; W 6-sided twr, R top; 46°29'·40N 01°48'·29W.

Nouch Sud ⚓ Q (6) + L Fl 15s; 46°28'·55N 01°47'·42W.
SW Pass, ldg lts 032·5°, Iso 4s 12/33m **16M**, H24: **Front** ☆, 46°29'·42N 01°46'·37W.
SE Pass, ldg lts 320°: Front ⚡ QG 11m 8M; 46°29'·44N 01°47'·51W. Rear ⚡ Q 33m 13M.
Jetée St Nicolas (W jetty) ⚡ QR 16m 8M; 143°-094°; W twr, R top; 46°29'·23N 01°47'·52W.

BOURGENAY

Ldg lts 040°, QG 9/19m 7M. Front; 46°26'·37N 01°40'·61W. Rear, 010°-070°; 162m from front.
Landfall ⚓ L Fl 10s; 46°25'·28N 01°41'·91W.
Ent ⚡ Fl R 4s & ⚡ Iso G 4s; 46°26'·29N 01°40'·75W.

ÎLE-DE-RÉ

Les Baleineaux ⚡ VQ 23m 7M; pink twr, R top; 46°15'·81N 01°35'·22W.
Les Baleines ☆ Fl (4) 15s 53m **27M**; conspic Gy 8-sided twr, R lantern; 46°14'·64N 01°33'·69W.
Chanchardon ⚡ Fl WR 4s 15m W11M, R8M; 118°-R-290°-W-118°; 46°09'·73N 01°28'·44W.
Chauveau ☆ Oc (3) WR 12s 27m **W15M**, R11M; 057°-W-094°-R-104°-W-342°-R-057°; W ○ twr, R top; 46°08'·03N 01°16'·42W.

ARS-EN-RÉ

Les Islattes ⚓ Q 13m 3M; BY bcn twr; 46°14'·03N 01°23'·33W.
Outer ldg lts 265·8°, ⚡ Iso 4s 5/13m 11/**15M**; synch: Front 46°14'·05N 01°28'·61W.
Le Fier d'Ars, inner ldg lts 232·5°: ⚡ Q 5/13m 9/11M; 46°12'·76N 01°30'·60W. Rear ⚡ Q 11M.

ST MARTIN DE RÉ

Rocha ⚓ Q; 46°14'·74N 01°20'·64W.
Lt ho, E of ent ⚡ Oc (2) WR 6s 18m W10M, R7M; Shore-W-245°-R-281°-W-shore; W twr, R top; 46°12'·44N 01°21'·89W.
W mole ⚡ Fl G 2·5s 10m 6M; 46°12'·49N 01°21'·89W.

LA ROCHELLE

Ldg lts 059°, both Dir Q 15/25m 13/14M; synch; by day Fl 4s. Front; 46°09'·35N 01°09'·16W.
Pte des Minimes ⚡ Fl (3) WG 12s 8m; W8M, G5M; 059°-W-213°; 313°-G-059°; 46°08'·33N 01°10'·68W.
Tour Richelieu ⚓ Fl R 4s 10m 9M; 46°08'·90N 01°10'·34W.
Marina ⚡ Fl (2)G 6s 9m 7M; 46°08'·82N 01°10'·15W.

LA CHARENTE

Ldg lts 115°, Dir QR 8/21m **19/20M**: Front ☆, 45°57'·96N 01°04'·38W.
Fort Boyard ⚡ Q (9) 15s; 45°59'·96N 01°12'·87W.
Île d'Aix ☆ Fl WR 5s 24m **W24M, R20M**; 103°-R-118°-W-103°; 46°00'·60N 01°10'·67W.

53

ÎLE D'OLÉRON
Chassiron ☆ Fl 10s **28M**; 46°02'·80N 01°24'·61W.
Antioche ⱡ Q 20m 11M; 46°03'·94N 01°23'·71W.

ST DENIS
Dir ⚡ 205°, Iso WRG 4s 14m, W11M, R/G8M; 190°-G-204°-W-206°-R-220°;46°01'·61N 01°21'·91W.
E jetty ⚡ Fl (2) WG 6s 6m, W9M, G6M; 205°-G-277°-W-292°-G-165°; 46°02'·10N 01°22'·06W.

GIRONDE, PASSE DE L'OUEST
Pte de la Coubre ☆ Fl (2) 10s 64m **28M**; 45°41'·78N 01°13'·99W. Also, F RG 42m, R12M, G10M; 030°-R-043°-G-060°-R-110°.
BXA ⱡ Iso 4s 8m 7M; *Whis*; *Racon* ; 45°37'·53N 01°28'·69W.
Ldg lts 081·5° (not valid E of Nos 4 & 5 buoys).
Front ☆, Dir Iso 4s 21m **20M**; 45°39'·56N 01°08'·76W. Same structure, Q (2) 5s 10m 3M.
La Palmyre, common rear ☆ Dir Q 57m **27M**; 45°39'·71N 01°07'·24W. Same twr, Dir FR **17M**.
Cordouan ☆ Oc (2+1) WRG 12s 60m, **W22M, R/G18M**; 014°-W-126°-G-178·5°-W-267°-R-294·5°-R-014°; 45°35'·16N 01°10'·39W.

PASSE SUD (or DE GRAVE)
Ldg lts 063°: **Front**, Dir QG 22m **16M**; 45°33'·72N 01°05'·03W. **Rear**, Oc WRG 4s 26m, **W19M, R/G15M**; 033°-W-233·5°-R-303°-W-312°-G-330°-W-341°-025°.
G ⱡ 45°30'·32N 01°15'·56W.
G3 ⱡ 45°32'·78N 01°07'·72W.
Ldg lts 041°, both Dir QR 33/61m **18M. Front, Le Chay** ☆ intens 039·5°-042·5°; W twr, R top; 45°37'·30N 01°02'·40W. **Rear, St Pierre** ☆, intens 039°-043°; R water twr, 0·97M from front.
G5 ⱡ 45°33'·97N 01°06'·39W.
G4 ⱡ 45°34'·70N 01°05'·79W.
G6 ⱡ 45°34'·88N 01°04'·81W.

ROYAN
R1 ⱡ Iso G 4s; 45°36'·56N 01°01'·96W.
NE jetty ⚡ Fl (3) G 12s 2m 5M; 45°37'·23N 01°01'·49W.

PORT-MÉDOC
N bkwtr ⚡ QG 4M; 45°33'·42N 01°03'·48W.
S bkwtr ⚡ QR 4M; 45°33'·37N 01°03'·44W.

PAUILLAC
Pauillac, NE elbow ⚡ Fl G 4s 7m 5M; 45°11'·96N 00°44'·61W.
Ent E side ⚡ QG 7m 4M; 45°11'·86N 00°44'·60W.

BORDEAUX
Lock into Bassins Nos 1 & 2, 44°51'·74N 00°32'·94W.

ARCACHON, PASSE NORD
Cap Ferret ☆ Fl R 5s 53m **27M**; W ○ twr, R top; 44°34'·05N 01°18'·71W. Same twr, ⚡ Oc (3) 12s.
ATT-ARC ⱡ L Fl 10s 8m 5M; 44°34'·05N 01°18'·71W.
Note: Buoys are moved as the channel shifts.
1N ⱡ 44°33'·99N 01°17'·80W.
3N ⱡ 44°34'·53N 01°16'·51W.
5N ⱡ 44°34'·78N 01°15'·92W.
7N ⱡ 44°35'·12N 01°15'·33W.
9N ⱡ 44°36'·96N 01°14'·34W.
11 ⱡ 44°37'·35N 01°14'·10W.
15 ⱡ 44°39'·85N 01°12'·04W.
Marina ⚡ QG 6m 6M; 44°39'·77N 01°09'·15W.

CAPBRETON
Digue Nord ⚡ Fl (2) R 6s 13m 12M; W ○ twr, R top; *Horn 30s;* 43°39'·38N 01°27'·01W.
Estacade Sud ⚡ Fl (2) G 6s 9m 12M; 43°39'·25N 01°26'·89W.

ANGLET/BAYONNE
BA ⱡ L Fl 10s; 43°32'·59N 01°32'·76W.
Outer S bkwtr ⱡ Q (9) 15s 15m 6M; 43°31'·60N 01°31'·68W.
Anglet marina ent ⚡ Fl G 2s 5m 2M; 43°31'·57N 01°30'·51W.

ST JEAN DE LUZ
Inner ldg lts 150·7°, both Dir QG 18/27m **16M**; intens 149·5°-152·2°. **Front, E jetty** ☆ W □ twr, R stripe; 43°23'·25N 01°40'·15W. **Rear** ☆, W □ twr, G stripe; at S corner of marina.

HENDAYE
Cabo Higuer ☆ Fl (2) 10s 63m **23M**; 43°23'·51N 01°47'·53W (in Spain).
W trng wall ⚡ Fl (3) G 9s 9m 5M; 43°22'·82N 01°47'·36W.

		1	2	3	4	5	6	7	8	9	10	11	12	13	14	15	16
1	Port Joinville	1															
2	St Gilles-C-de-Vie	18	2														
3	Sables d'Olonne	31	16	3													
4	Bourgenay	40	25	9	4												
5	St Martin (I de Ré)	55	44	27	20	5											
6	La Rochelle	66	51	36	29	12	6										
7	Rochefort	84	75	61	54	36	26	7									
8	R La Seudre	89	71	58	52	33	24	30	8								
9	Port St Denis	59	48	33	30	21	13	26	22	9							
10	Port Bloc/Royan	97	85	71	60	56	52	68	27	42	10						
11	Bordeaux	152	140	126	115	111	107	123	82	97	55	11					
12	Cap Ferret	138	130	113	110	102	98	114	75	88	68	123	12				
13	Capbreton	192	186	169	166	165	156	172	131	145	124	179	58	13			
14	Anglet/Bayonne	200	195	181	178	177	168	184	143	157	132	187	70	12	14		
15	Santander	212	210	204	204	206	202	218	184	192	180	235	133	106	103	15	
16	Cabo Finisterre	377	395	393	394	406	407	423	399	397	401	456	376	370	373	274	16

LANDES FIRING RANGE: Pointe de Grave to Capbreton

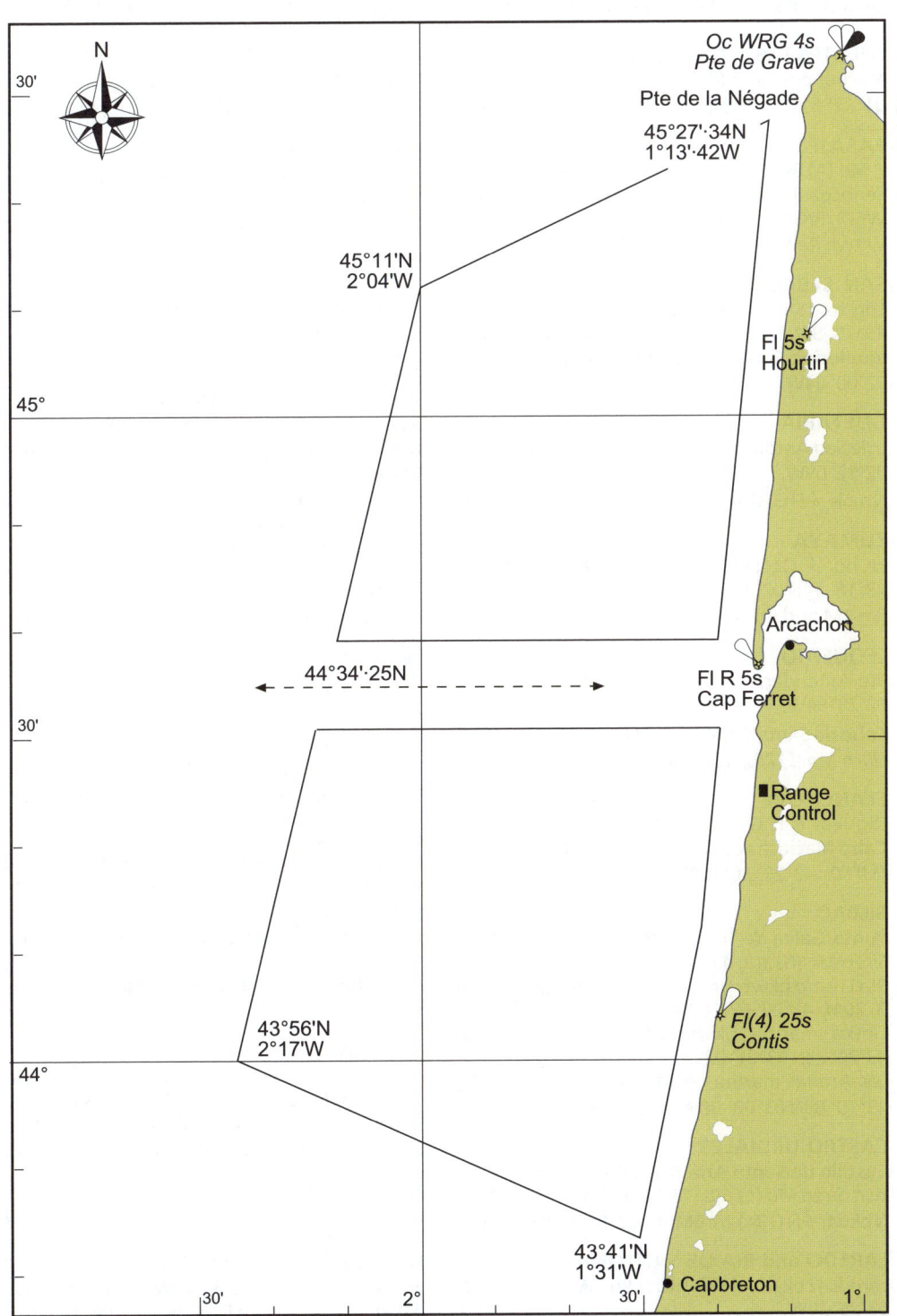

AREA 18 N & NW Spain - *French border to Portuguese border*

SELECTED LIGHTS, BUOYS & WAYPOINTS | Positions are referenced to WGS84

FUENTERRABIA (See Hendaye, facing page)
Marina ent, ⚡ Fl (4) G 11s 9m 3m; 43°22'·59N 01°47'·51W. ⚡ Fl (4) R 11s 9m 1M, close SW.

PASAJES
⚓ Mo (A) 6s 11M; 43°21'·19N 01°56'·12W.
Senocozulúa Dir ⚡ 155·75°: Oc (2) WRG 12s 50m W6M, R/G3M; 129·5°-G-154·5°-W-157°-R-190°; W twr; *Racon M*; 43°19'·90N 01°55'·61W.

SAN SEBASTIÁN
Ldg lts 158°: Front ⚡ QR 10m 7M; 143°-173°; 43°18'·89N 01°59'·47W. Rear ⚡ Oc R 4s 16m 7M.
Igueldo ☆ Fl (2+1) 15s 132m **26M**; 43°19'·35N 02°00'·64W.

GUETARIA
I. de San Antón ☆ Fl (4) 15s 91m **21M**; 43°18'·62N 02°12'·09W.
N mole ⚡ Fl (3) G 9s 11m 5M; 43°18'·26N 02°11'·91W.

ZUMAYA
Lt ho ⚡ Oc (1+3) 12s 39m 12M; Port sigs; 43°18'·14N 02°15'·07W. Marina ent, ⚡ Fl (3) R 9s 6m 1M and ⚡ Fl (2+1) G 10s 6m 1M.

LEQUEITIO
Pta Amandarri ⚡ Fl G 4s 8m 5M; 43°21'·99N 02°29'·94W.
Cabo de Santa Catalina ☆ Fl (1+3) 20s 44m **17M**; *Horn Mo (L) 20s*; 43°22'·67N 02°30'·69W.

ELANCHOVE
Digue N ⚡ Fl G 3s 8m 4M.
Cabo Machichaco ☆ Fl 7s 120m **24M**; *Siren Mo (M) 60s*; 43°27'·30N 02°45'·19W.

BILBAO
Punta Galea ☆ Fl (3) 8s 82m **19M**; 011°-227°; *Siren Mo (G) 30s*; 43°22'·30N 03°02'·14W.
Pta Lucero bkwtr head ⚡ Fl G 5s 21m 10M; *Racon X, 20M*; 43°22'·67N 03°05'·04W.
Getxo marina bkwtr ⚡QR 3m 2M, R col; 43°20'·23N 03°01'·02W.
Las Arenas marina (RCMA) ⚡ Oc G 4s 1m 1M; 43°19'·83N 03°00'·98W; and Oc R 4s 2m 1M.

CASTRO URDIALES
Castillo de Santa Ana ☆ Fl (4) 24s 47m **20M**; W twr; *Siren Mo (C) 60s*; 43°23'·06N 03°12'·89W.
N bkwtr ⚡ Fl G 3s 12m 6M; 43°22'·86N 03°12'·54W.

LAREDO and RIA DE SANTOÑA
Laredo N bkwtr ⚡ Fl (4) R 11s 9m 5M; 43°24'·89'N 03°25'·20W.

Santoña ldg lts 283·5°: Front, ⚡ Fl 2s 5m 8M; 43°26'·33N 03°27'·62W. Rear, ⚡ Oc (2) 5s 12m 11M.
C. Ajo ☆ Oc (3) 16s 69m **17M**; 43°30'·70N 03°35'·72W.

SANTANDER
Cabo Mayor ☆ Fl (2) 10s 89m **21M**; *Horn Mo (M) 40s*; 43°29'·37N 03°47'·51W.
Marina de Santander, ldg lts 235·6°: Front ⚡ Iso 2s 9m 2M; 43°25'·75N 03°48'·83W. Rear ⚡ Oc 5s. Marina ent QR and QG.
Pta del Torco de Afuera ☆ Fl (1+2) 24s 33m **22M**; W twr; 43°26'·51N 04°02'·61W.

RIBADESELLA
Pta del Caballo ⚡ Fl (4) R 11s 10m 5M; 278·4°-212·9°; ○ twr; 43°28'·08N 05°03'·98W.
Marina trng wall ⚓ Q; approx 43°27'·83N 05°03'·70W.
Somos ☆ Fl (2+1) 12s 113m **25M**; twr; 43°28'·08N 05°03'·98W.
C. Lastres ☆ Fl (5) 25s 116m **23M**. W ○ twr; 43°32'·03N 05°18'·07W.

GIJÓN
Piedra Sacramento ⚡ Fl (2) G 6s 9m 5M; 8-sided twr; 43°32'·90N 05°40'·21W.
Marina, N bkwtr ⚡ Fl (2) R 6s 7m 3M; 43°32'·85N 05°40'·08W.
Cabo de Torres ☆ Fl (2) 10s 80m **18M**; 43°34'·29N 05°41'·97W.
Cabo Peñas ☆ Fl (3) 15s 115m **35M**; Gy 8-sided twr; *Siren Mo (P) 60s*; 43°39'·31N 05°50'·90W.

CUDILLERO
Pta Rebollera ☆ Oc (4) 16s 42m **16M**; W 8-sided twr; *Siren Mo (D) 30s*; 43°33'·96N 06°08'·68W.
Ent, N bkwtr ⚡ Fl (3) G 9s 3m 2M.
Cabo Vidio ☆ Fl 5s 99m **25M**; *Siren Mo (V) 60s*; 43°35'·60N 06°14'·79W.
Cabo Busto ☆ Fl (4) 20s 84m **25M**; 43°34'·13N 06°28'·23W.

LUARCA
Punta Altaya ⚡ Oc (3) 15s 63m 14M; W □ twr; *Siren Mo (L) 30s*; 43°33'·03N 06°31'·85W.
Ldg lts 170°, W cols, R bands: Front ⚡ Fl 5s 18m 2M; 43°32'·78N 06°32'·11W. Rear ⚡ Oc 4s 25m 2M.

RÍA DE RIBADEO
Pta de la Cruz ⚡ Fl (4) R 11s 16m 7M; 43°33'·40N 07°01'·75W.
Isla Pancha ☆ Fl (3+1) 20s 26m **21M**; *Siren Mo (R) 30s*; 43°33'·39N 07°02'·53W, W side of entrance.
1st ldg lts 140°, both R ◇s, W twrs. Front ⚡ Iso R

18m 5M; 43°32'·83N 07°01'·53W. Rear ⸗ Oc R 4s.
2nd ldg lts 205°. Front, ⸗ VQ R 8m 3M; R ◊, W twr; 43°32'·49N 07°02'·24W. Rear ⸗ Oc R 2s 18m 3M.
Yacht hbr, ⸗ Fl G 5s 9m 3M; 43°32'·45N 07°02'·16W.

RÍA DE VIVERO
Pta de Faro ⸗ Fl R 5s 18m 7M; 43°42'·74N 07°35'·03W.
Pta Socastro ⸗ Fl G 5s 18m 7M; 43°43'·08N 07°36'·42W. Marina ent ⸗ Fl (3) G 9s 7m 1M; 43°40'·22N 07°35'·62W.
Pta de la Estaca de Bares ☆ Fl (2) 7·5s 99m **25M**; *Siren Mo (B) 60s;* 43°47'·21N 07°41'·14W.
Cabo Ortegal ☆ Oc 8s 122m **18M**; W ○ twr, R band; 43°46'·22N 07°52'·30W,.

RÍA DE CEDEIRA
Piedras de Media Mar ⸗ Fl (2) 5s 12m 4M; W ○ twr; 43°39'·37N 08°04'·80W.
Bkwtr ⸗ Fl (2) R 7s 10m 4M; 43°39'·30N 08°04'·20W.
Cabo Prior ☆ Fl (1+2) 15s 105m **22M**; 055·5°-310°; 6-sided twr; 43°34'·05N 08°18'·87W.

RÍA DE FERROL
Cabo Prioriño Chico ☆ Fl 5s 34m **23M**; 225°-129·5°; W 8-sided twr; 43°27'·52N 08°20'·40W.

RÍAs DE ARES & DE BETANZOS
Ares bkwtr ⸗ Fl (3) R 9s; 43°25'·35N 08°14'·27W.
Sada marina ⸗ Fl (4) G 11s; 43°21'·76N 08°14'·54W.

LA CORUÑA
Torre de Hércules ☆ Fl (4) 20s 104m **23M**; *Siren Mo (L) 30s;* 43°23'·15N 08°24'·39W.
Ldg lts 108·5°: Front ⸗ Oc WR 4s 54m, W8M R3M; 000°-R-023°; 100·5°-R-105·5°-W-114·5°-R-153°; *Racon M, 18M; 020°-196°;* 43°23'·00N 08°21'·28W. Rear ⸗ Fl 4s 79m 8M; 357·5°-177·5°.
Ldg lts 182°: Front, ⸗ Iso WRG 2s 27m, W10M, R/G7M; 146·4°-G-180°-W-184°-R-217·6°; *Racon X, 11-21M;* 43°20'·59N 08°22'·25W. Rear ⸗ Oc R 4s.
Darsena de la Marina ⸗ Fl G 5s 8m 2M; 43°21'·01N 08°23'·66W.

RÍA DE CORME Y LAGE
Pta Lage ☆ Fl (5) 20s 64m **20M**; 43°13'·88N 09°00'·83W. Lage, N mole ⸗ Fl G 3s 15m 4M; 43°13'·34N 08°59'·96W. Corme, mole ⸗ Fl (2) R 5s 12m 3M; 43°15'·64N 08°57'·83W.
C. Villano ☆ Fl (2) 15s 102m **28M**; *Siren Mo (V) 60s;*
Racon M, 35M; 43°09'·60N 09°12'·70W

1	Bilbao (ent)	1							
2	Santander	36	2						
3	Gijón	116	90	3					
4	Cabo Peñas	126	96	10	4				
5	Ría de Ribadeo	179	149	63	53	5			
6	Cabo Ortegal	214	184	98	88	40	6		
7	La Coruña	252	222	136	126	78	38	7	
8	Cabo Villano	284	254	168	158	110	70	43	8
9	Bayona	355	325	239	229	181	141	114	71	9

RÍA DE CAMARIÑAS
Ldg lts 081°: Front ⸗ Fl 5s 13m 9M; 43°07'·37N 09°11'·56W. Rear ⸗ Iso 4s 25m 11M.
Outer bkwtr ⸗ Fl R 5s 7m 3M; 43°07'·45N 09°10'·70W.
Cabo Toriñana ☆ Fl (2+1) 15s 63m **24M**; *Racon T, 35M (1.7M SE of ☆);* 43°03'·17N 09°18'·01W.
Cabo Finisterre ☆ Fl 5s 141m **23M**; *Racon O, 35M;* 42°52'·93N 09°16'·29W.

RÍA DE MUROS
Pta Queixal ⸗ Fl (2+1) 12s; 42°44'·36N 09°04'·75W.
Muros ⸗ Fl (4) R 13s 8m 4M; 42°46'·64N 09°03'·31W.
Portosin ⸗ Fl (3) G 9s 8m 5M; 42°45'·94N 08°56'·93W.
Pta Cabeiro ⸗ Oc WR 3s 35m 9/6M; 050°-R-054·5°-W-058·5°-R-099·5°-W-189·5°; 42°44'·37N 08°59'·44W.

RÍA DE AROUSA (Selected lights only)
Isla Sálvora ☆ Fl (3+1) 20s 38m **21M**; 42°27'·82N 09°00'·80W. Same twr, ⸗ Fl (3) 20s; 126°-160°.
Santa Uxia ⸗ Fl (2) R 7s 7m 4M; 42°33'·58N 08°59'·24W. 50m SE, ⸗ Fl R 5s 8m 5M.
Isla Rúa ⸗ Fl (2+1) WR 21s 24m 13M; 121·5°-R-211·5°-W-121·5°; *Racon K, 211°-121°, 10-20M;* 42°32'·95N 08°56'·38W.
Pobra do Caramiñal E bkwtr ⸗ Fl (3) G 9s 9m 5M; W ○ twr, G band; 42°36'·28N 08°55'·87W.
Villagarcia, N mole ⸗ Iso 2s 2m 10M; 42°36'·11N 08°46'·33W. Marina ent, QG & QR, both 6m 3M.
Piedras Negras marina ⸗ Fl (4) WR 11s 5m, W4M R3M; 305°-W-315°-R-305; 42°27'·49N 08°55'·11W.

RÍA DE PONTEVEDRA
Isla Ons ☆ Fl (4) 24s 125m **25M**; 8-sided twr; 42°22'·94N 08°56'·17W.
Sangenjo ⸗ QR 5m 4M; 42°23'·81N 08°48'·06W.
Combarro ⸗ Fl (2) R 8s 7m 3M; 42°25'·78N 08°42'·23W.
Aguete ⸗ Fl (4) G 11s 3M, 42°22'·66N 08°44'·21W.

RÍA DE VIGO
Ldg lts 129°: Front, ⸗ Fl 3s 36m 9M; 42°15'·15N 08°52'·37W. Rear ⸗ Oc 6s 53m 11M.
S Chan ldg lts 069·3°: **Front** ☆ Iso 2s 16m **18M**; *Horn Mo (V) 60s; Racon B, 22M;* 42°11'·12N 08°48'·89W. **Rear** Oc 4s 48m **18M**.
Marina, QG/QR, 10m 5M, 42°14'·56N 08°43'·41W.

BAYONA
Las Serralleiras ⸗ Q (9) 15s 4M; 42°09'·23N 08°53'·35W.
Ldg lts 084°: Front ⸗ Fl 6s 8m 10M; 42°08'·24N 08°50'·09W. Rear ⸗ Oc 4s 18m 9M.
C. Silleiro ☆ Fl (2+1) 15s 84m **24M**; W 8-sided twr, R bands; 42°06'·27N 08°53'·80W.

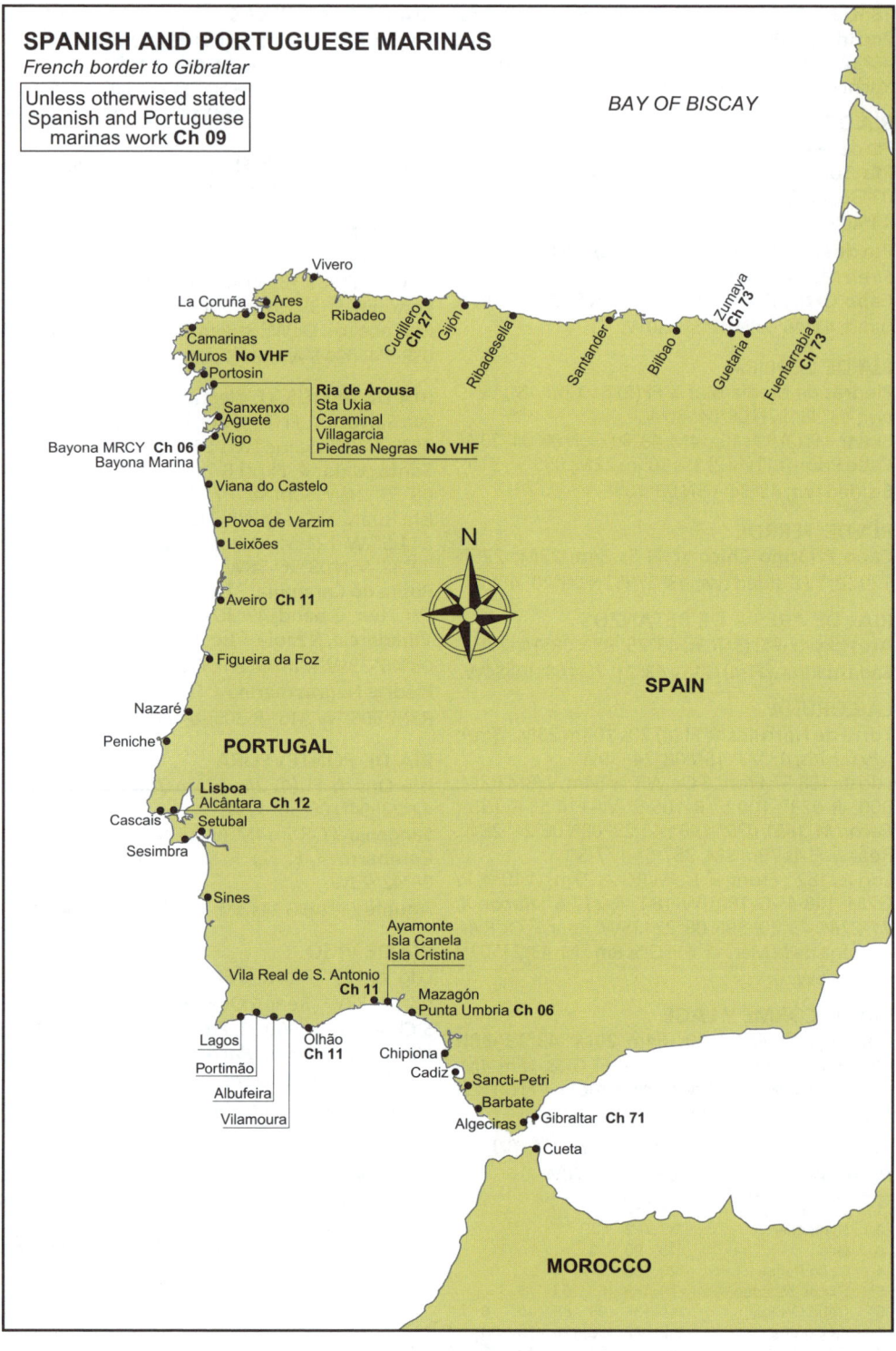

SPANISH AND PORTUGUESE MARINAS
French border to Gibraltar

Unless otherwised stated
Spanish and Portuguese
marinas work **Ch 09**

BAY OF BISCAY

Vivero

La Coruña • Ares
• Sada   Ribadeo   Cudillero **Ch 27** Gijón   Ribadesella   Santander   Bilbao   Guetaria   Zumaya **Ch 73**   Fuenterrabia **Ch 73**

Camarinas
Muros **No VHF**
• Portosin

Sanxenxo
• Aguete
• Vigo

Ria de Arousa
Sta Uxia
Caraminal
Villagarcia
Piedras Negras **No VHF**

Bayona MRCY **Ch 06**
Bayona Marina

• Viana do Castelo

• Povoa de Varzim

• Leixões

• Aveiro **Ch 11**

• Figueira da Foz

N

SPAIN

Nazaré •

Peniche •   **PORTUGAL**

Lisboa
Alcântara **Ch 12**
Cascais • Setubal

Sesimbra

• Sines

Ayamonte
Isla Canela
Isla Cristina

Vila Real de S. Antonio
Ch 11

Mazagón
Punta Umbria **Ch 06**

Lagos   Olhão
Portimão **Ch 11**   Chipiona
Albufeira   Cadiz • Sancti-Petri
Vilamoura   Barbate
                   Algeciras • Gibraltar **Ch 71**
                        • Cueta

MOROCCO

SELECTED LIGHTS, BUOYS & WAYPOINTS

Positions are referenced to WGS84

Montedor ☆ Fl (2) 9·5s 102m 22M; R twr; *Horn Mo (S) 25s;* 41°45'·09N 08°52'·49W.

VIANA DO CASTELO
Dir lt Oc WRG 4s 15m 8/6M; 350°-G-005°-W-010°-R-025°; 41°41'·12N 08°50'·21W.
Outer mole ≰ Fl R 3s 9M; *Horn 30s;* 41°40'·46N 08°50'·66W.
No. 2 ≈ Fl R 3s; 41°40'·53N 08°50'·48W.
E mole ≰ Fl G 3s 9M; 41°40'·67N 08°50'·25W.
No. 1 ▲ Fl G 3s; 41°40'·68N 08°50'·29W.
No. 3 ▲ Fl (2) G 3s; 41°40'·86N 08°50'·24W.
No. 4 ≈ Fl (2+1) R 5s; 41°40'·89N 08°50'·36W.
Nos. 5-13 ▲s are Fl G 3s. Nos. 6-14 ≈s are Fl R 3s.
No. 13 ▲ Fl G 3s; 41°41'·49N 08°49'·27W, SSE of marina ent at 41°41'·59N 08°49'·33W.

PÓVOA DE VARZIM
Molhe N ≰ Fl R 3s 14m 12M; *Siren 40s;* 41°22'·29N 08°46'·23W. Molhe S ≰ L Fl G 6s 4M.

LEIXÕES
Tanker mooring ⛽ Fl (3) 15s 6M; *Horn (U) 30s;* 41°12'·10N 08°45'·07W.
Leça ☆ Fl (3) 14s 56m **28M**; W twr, B bands; 41°12'·08N 08°42'·73W.
Outer N mole ≰ Fl WR 5s 23m W12M, R9M; 001°-R-180°-W-001°; *Horn 20s;* 41°10'·37N 08°42'·49W.
S mole ≰ Fl G 4s 16m 7M; 328°-285°; *Horn 30s;* 41°10'·68N 08°42'·35W.
Marina ≰ L Fl (2) R 12s 4m 2M; 41°11'·08N 08°42'·27W.

AVEIRO
Lt ho Aero ☆ Fl (4) 13s 65m **23M**; R/W twr; 40°38'·57N 08°44'·88W. Same twr ≰ Fl G 4s 53m 9M, rear 085·4° ldg lt. Front 085·4° ldg lt Fl G 3s 16m 9M; 40°38'·54N 08°45'·48W.
Ldg lts 065·6°: Front ≰ Oc R 3s 7m 9M; 40°38'·82N 08°44'·99W. Rear ≰ Oc R 6s 8M, 440m from front.
Molhe N ≰ Fl R 3s 11m 8M; W col, R bands; *Horn 15s;* 40°38'·61N 08°45'·81W.
Molhe S ≰ Fl G 3s 16m 9M; front 085·4° ldg lt.
Molhe Central ≰ L Fl G 5s; 40°38'·64N 08°44'·95W.

FIGUEIRA DA FOZ
Cabo Mondego ☆ Fl 5s 96m **28M**; W twr and house; *Horn 30s;* 40°11'·43N 08°54'·32W.
Ldg lts 081·5°, W cols, R bands: Front ≰ Iso R 5s 6m 8M; 40°08'·83N 08°51'·23W. Rear, ≰ Oc R 6s.
Molhe N ≰ Fl R 6s 14m 9M; *Horn 35s;* 40°08'·74N 08°52'·50W.
Molhe S ≰ Fl G 6s 13m 7M; 40°08'·59N 08°52'·41W.
Penedo da Saudade ☆ Fl (2) 15s 54m **30M**; □ twr, and house; 39°45'·84N 09°01'·89W.

NAZARÉ
Pontal da Nazaré ≰ Oc 3s 49m 14M; twr & bldg; *Siren 35s;* 39°36'·25N 09°05'·18W.
Molhe S ≰ L Fl G 5s 14m 8M; 39°35'·34N 09°04'·76W.

ILHA DA BERLENGA and PENICHE
Ilha da Berlenga ☆ Fl 10s 120m **27M**; W □ twr and houses; *Horn 28s;* 39°24'·90N 09°30'·63W.
Cabo Carvoeiro ☆ Fl (3) R 15s 56m **15M**; W □ twr; *Horn 35s;* 39°21'·61N 09°24'·51W.
Peniche molhe W ≰ Fl R 3s 13m 9M; W twr, R bands; *Siren 120s;* 39°20'·85N 09°22'·56W.
C. da Roca ☆ Fl (4) 18s 164m **26M**; W twr and bldgs; 38°46'·88N 09°29'·90W.
Cabo Raso ☆ Fl (3) 9s 22m **15M**; 324°-189°; R twr; *Horn Mo (I) 60s;* 38°42'·56N 09°29'·15W.

CASCAIS
Ldg lts 284·7°: Front, ☆ Oc WR 6s 24m **W18M**, R14M; 233°-R-334°-W-098°; *Horn 10s;* 38°41'·42N 09°25'·27W. Rear, ☆ Iso WR 2s **W19M, R16M**; 326°-W-092°; 278°-R-292°; W twr. Marina S mole ≰ Fl (3) R 4s 8m 6M; 38°41'·58N 09°24'·84W.

LISBOA
Triple ldg lts 047·1°: Front, ☆ Oc R 3s 30m **21M**; 38°41'·94N 09°15'·97W. Middle, ☆ Oc R 6s 81m **21M**; *Racon Q, 15M*. Rear, ☆ Iso 6s 153m **21M**; 38°43'·65N 09°13'·63W.
No. 1 ⌀ Fl G 2s; 38°39'·55N 09°18'·79W.
Forte Bugio ≰ Fl G 5s 27m 9M; ○ twr on fortress; *Horn Mo (B) 30s;* 38°39'·62N 09°17'·93W.
No. 5 ⌀ Fl G 4s; 38°40'·43N 09°17'·66W.
No. 7 ⌀ Fl G 5s; 38°40'·64N 09°16'·90W.
No. 9 ⌀ Fl G 6s; 38°40'·63N 09°14'·49W.
Ponte 25 de Abril. The N (38°41'·64N 09°10'·69W) and S pillars are lit Fl (3) G 9s and Fl (3) R 9s.
Cabo Espichel ☆ Fl 4s 167m **26M**; W 6-sided twr; *Horn 31s;* 38°24'·94N 09°13'·05W.

SESIMBRA
Ldg lts 003·5°, L Fl R 5s 9/21m 7/6M: Front, 38°26'·56N 09°06'·16W. Rear 34m from front.

SETÚBAL
Ldg lts 039·7°, both Iso Y 6s 12/60m **22M**. Front, R structure, W stripes; 38°31'·08N 08°54'·01W .
No. 1 ⌀ Fl G 3s 5M; 38°26'·98N 08°58'·18W.
No. 2 ⌀ Fl (2) R 10s 13m 9M; *Racon B, 15M;* 38°27'·21N 08°58'·45W.
Forte de Outão ≰ Oc R 6s 33m 12M; 38°29'·31N 08°56'·06W.
Pinheiro da Cruz ≰ Fl 3s; 38°15'·46N 08°46'·34W.

SINES

Cabo de Sines ☆ Fl (2) 15s 55m **26M**; 37°57'·56N 08°52'·83W.
W mole ⚡ Fl 3s 20m 12M; 37°56'·48N 08°53'·33W.
Sines W ⚓ Fl R 3s 6M; 37°56'·12N 08°53'·25W.
Marina mole ⚡ Fl G 4s 4M; W twr, G bands; 37°57'·03N 08°52'·03W.

C. Sardão ☆ Fl (3) 15s 67m **23M**; 37°35'·94N 08°49'·02W.

CAPE ST VINCENT/SAGRES

Cabo de São Vicente ☆ Fl 5s 84m **32M**; *Horn Mo (I) 30s;* 37°01'·36N 08°59'·78W.
Ponta de Sagres ⚡ Iso R 2s 52m 11M; 36°59'·66N 08°56'·94W.
Baleeira mole ⚡ Fl WR 4s 12m, W14M, R11M; 254°-W-355°-R-254°; 37°00'·67N 08°55'·46W.

LAGOS

Pta da Piedade ☆ Fl 7s 50m **20M**; 37°04'·81N 08°40'·20W.
W mole ⚡ Fl (2) R 6s 5M; W col, R bands; 37°05'·85N 08°40'·02W.
E mole ⚡ Fl (2) G 6s 5M; W col, G bands; 37°05'·96N 08°39'·96W.
Alvor ent, ⚡ Fl R/G 4s; W twrs, R/G bands; 37°07'·13N 08°37'·14W.

PORTIMÃO

Ponta do Altar ☆ L Fl 5s 31m **16M**; 290°-170°; W twr and bldg; 37°06'·34N 08°31'·17W.
Ldg lts 019·1°: Both ⚡ Iso R 6s 18/30m 6M; W cols, R bands. Front 37°07'·35N 08°31'·31W. Rear 54m from front.
E mole ⚡ Fl G 5s 9m 7M; 37°06'·50N 08°31'·59W.
W mole ⚡ Fl R 5s 9m 7M; 37°06'·52N 08°31'·77W.
No. 2 ⚓ Fl R 4s; 37°06'·96N 08°31'·53W.
Marina ent, S side ⚡ Fl R 6s 3M; 37°07'·10N 08°31'·58W.
N side ⚡ Fl G 6s 3M; 37°07'·14N 08°31'·58W.
N Mole ⚡ Iso R 4s 8m 3M; 37°07'·33N 08°31'·59W.

Pta de Alfanzina ☆ Fl (2) 15s 62m **29M**; 37°05'·22N 08°26'·59W.
Armacão de Pera ⚡ Oc R 5s 24m 6M; 37°05'·92N 08°21'·21W.

ALBUFEIRA

Ponta da Baleeira ⚡ Oc 6s 30m 11M; 37°04'·84N 08°15'·85W.
N bkwtr ⚡, Fl (2) G 5s 9m 4M, approx 37°04'·90N 08°15'·52W.
S bkwtr ⚡, Fl (2) R 5s 9m 4M.
Praia da Albufeira, E end of bay, Olhos de Água ⚡ L Fl 5s 29m 7M; 37°05'·47N 08°11'·40W.

VILAMOURA

Vilamoura ☆, Fl 5s 17m **19M**; 37°04'·50N 08°07'·42W.
Marina, W mole ⚡ Fl R 4s 13m 5M; 37°04'·19N 08°07'·49W.
E mole ⚡ Fl G 4s 13m 5M; 37°04'·22N 08°07'·42W.

FARO, OLHÃO and TAVIRA

Ent from sea: E mole ⚡ Fl G 4s 9m 6M; 36°57'·79N 07°52'·14W.
W mole ⚡ Fl R 4s 9m 6M; 37°57'·84N 08°52'·26W, appr on 352°.
Access ldg lts 020·9°: Front, Barra Nova ⚡ Oc 4s 8m 6M; 37°58'·22N 07°52'·00W. Rear, **Cabo de Santa Maria** ☆ Fl (4) 17s 49m **25M**; W ○ twr; 36°58'·48N 07°51'·88W.
No. 6 ⚓ Fl R 6s; 36°58'·49N 07°52'·12W (NW to Faro; NE to Olhão).
No. 20 ⚓ Fl R 6s, 37°00'·13N 07°55'·11W (edge of AC 83 approx 2M before **Faro** proper).
No. 8 ⚓ Fl R 3s; 36°59'·90N 07°51'·07W, thence N & E to **Olhão**.

Tavira ldg lts 325·9°: Front, ⚡ Fl R 3s 6m 4M. Rear, Iso ⚡ R 6s 9m 5M. W mole ⚡ Fl R 2·5s 7m 7M; 37°06'·79N 07°37'·10W.

VILA REAL DE SANTO ANTONIO

Lt ho ☆ Fl 6·5s 51m **26M**; W twr, B bands; 37°11'·23N 07°25'·00W.
R. Guadiano, Bar buoys ⚓ Q (3) G 6s; 37°08'·90N 07°23'·44W.
No. 2 ⚓ Fl R 4s; 37°08'·83N 07°23'·74W.
W bkwtr ⚡ Fl R 5s 4M; 37°09'·75N 07°24'·03W.
E trng wall ⚡ Fl G 3s 4M; 37°09'·93N 07°23'·63W.
Marina, QR at S corner; QR/QG at ent; QR at N corner.

See also Area 20 Distance Table

		1	2	3	4	5	6	7	8	9	10	11	12
1	Longships	1											
2	Ushant (Créac'h)	100	2										
3	La Coruña	418	338	3									
4	Cabo Villano	439	365	43	4								
5	Bayona	510	436	114	71	5							
6	Viana do Castelo	537	468	141	98	32	6						
7	Leixões (Pôrto)	565	491	169	126	63	33	7					
8	Nazaré	659	585	263	220	156	127	97	8				
9	Cabo Carvoeiro	670	596	274	231	171	143	114	22	9			
10	Cabo Raso	710	636	314	271	211	183	154	62	40	10		
11	Lisboa (bridge)	686	652	330	287	227	199	170	78	56	16	11	
12	Cabo Espichel	692	658	336	293	233	205	176	84	62	22	23	12

AZORES – SELECTED LIGHTS

Positions are referenced to WGS 84

ILHA DAS FLORES

Ponta do Albarnaz ☆, Fl 5s 103m 22M, 035°-258°; W twr, R cupola. 39°31'·20N 31°14'·12W.
Ponta das Lajes ☆, Fl (3) 28s 98m **26M**, 263°-054°; W twr, R cupola. 39°22'·56N 31°10'·59W.
PORTO DAS LAJES, ldg lts 250·8°: Front, L Fl G 7s 17m 2M, 39°22'·74N 31°10'·24W; rear Oc G 4s. Bkwtr hd ⚓ Oc R 6s 2M. 39°22'·75N 31°09'·94W.

ILHA DO FAIAL

Ponta dos Cedros ⚓, Fl 7s 144m 12M; 38°38'·29N 28°43'·36W.
Ponta da Ribeirinha ⚓, Fl (3) 20s 131m 12M; post; 38°35'·73N 28°36'·15W, E end of island.

HORTA

Boa Viagem ⚓ Iso G 1·5s 12m 9M; appr brg 285°; B column on R cupola; 38°32'·28N 28°37'·49W.

Bkwtr hd ⚓ Fl R 3s 20m 11M; W structure. 38°32'·03N 28°37'·27W.

Ldg lts 194·9°: both Iso G 2s 13/15m 2M; Red X on W posts, R bands. Front 38°31'·67N 28°37'·51W.

ILHA DO PICO (Pico mountain 38°28'·11N 28°23'·92W) Ponta de São Mateus ⚓ Fl 5s 33m 13M, 284°-118°; W twr, R cupola. 38°25'·35N 28°26'·93W, SW side of island.

ILHA DE SÃO JORGE

Ponta dos Rosais ⚓ Fl (2) 10s 259m 8M. 38°45'·24N 28°18'·71W, WNW tip of island.
Ponta da Topo ☆ Fl (3) 20s 57m **20M**, 133°-033°; W twr, R bldg. 38°32'·92N 27°45'·24W, E tip of island.

ILHA TERCEIRA

Ponta da Sereta ☆ Fl (3) 15s 95m **21M**; W col, R top; 38°45'·97N 27°22'·45W, NW end of island.
Lajes ☆ Aero Al Fl WG 10s 132m **W28M, G23M**.
Praia da Vitoria, N mole Fl G 5s 11m 6M; G lantern, Gy post; 38°43'·56N 27°03'·04W. S mole Fl R 3s 8M; W twr, R bands. 38°43'·24N 27°02'·92W.

Ponta das Contendas ☆ Fl (4) WR 15s 190m **W23M, R20M**; 220°-W-020°-R-044°-W-072°-R-093°; W twr, R top; 38°38'·62N 27°05'·07W.
Monte Brasil, Oc WR 10s 21m 12M; 191°-R-295°-W-057°; W col, R bands; 38°38'·60N 27°13'·04W.

ANGRA DO HEROISMO

Ldg lts 340·9°: front, Fl R 4s 29m 7M, R mast; 38°39'·25N 27°13'·09W. Rear, Oc R 6s 54m 7M. Marina ent, S side (Porto Pipas) ⚓ Fl G 3s 14m 6M. N mole, ⚓ Fl (2) R 6s 8m 3M; 38°39'·12N 27°12'·95W.

ILHA DE SAO MIGUEL

Ponta da Ferraria ☆ Fl (3) 20s 106m **27M**; 339°-174°; W twr, R cupola. 37°51'·21N 25°51'·02W.
Airport ☆ Aero Al Fl WG 10s 83m **W28M, G23M**; 282°-124°; control twr; 37°44'·64N 25°42'·46W.
Santa Clara ☆ L Fl 5s 26m **15M**; 282°-102°; R lantern; 37°43'·99N 25°41'·15W.
Ponta Garça ☆ L Fl WR 5s 100m **W16M**, R13M; 240°-W-080-R-100°; 37°42'·85N 25°22'·18W.
Ponta do Arnel ☆ Aeromarine Fl 5s 65m **25M**; 157°-355°; W twr on ho; 37°49'·43N 25°08'·12W.

PONTA DELGADA

Bkwtr head ⚓ Oc R 3s 16m 5M; W twr, R bands. 37°44'·18N 25°39'·37W, SSE of marina.
Outer ldg lts 320·5°: Front, Iso G 5s 14m 7M; B lamp on Y ho; hard to see by day; 37°44'·54N 25°39'·56W. Rear, Oc G 5s 48m 7M; B lamp on R/W post; may be obsc'd by vegetation.
Marina mole hd ⚓ Oc G 3s 12m 10M; W twr, G bands. 37°44'·37N 25°39'·55W.
Baixa de São Pedro ⚓ Q (6) + L Fl 15s 2M. 37°44'·27N 25°39'·72W.
Inner ldg lts 266·5°: both Oc R 6s 13/19m 9M. Front, W post, R bands; 37°44'·18N 25°40'·32W.
Ilhéus das Formigas ⚓ Fl (2) 12s 21m 9M; W twr. 37°16'·29N 24°46'·87W.

ILHA DE SANTA MARIA

Ponta do Castelo ☆ Aeromarine Fl (3) 13·5s 113m **25M**; 181°-089°; W □ twr and bldg. 36°55'·75N 25°00'·97W, SE corner of island.

NAVIGATION

1	Falmouth	**1**										
2	Brest	136	**2**									
3	La Coruña	440	350	**3**								
4	Bayona	554	456	114	**4**							
5	Leixões (Pôrto)	617	526	176	63	**5**						
6	HORTA	1235	1202	966	927	937	**6**					
7	PONTA DELGADA	1183	1145	862	813	815	151	**7**				
8	Lisboa	780	658	327	227	163	904	771	**8**			
9	Cabo São Vicente	888	757	426	318	263	934	794	102	**9**		
10	Cádiz	1022	901	560	452	397	1068	928	236	134	**10**	
11	Europa Point	1087	960	618	506	455	1125	984	294	192	72	**11**
12	Casablanca	1114	978	637	525	474	1065	918	313	211	187	188	**12**

1	131	152	190	282	320	Flores	1
2		48	69	152	191	Horta	2
3			44	138	185	Graciosa	3
4				94	143	Terceira	4
5					54	Ponta Delgada	5
6						Sta Maria	6

DISTANCE TABLES
Approx distances in nautical miles are by the most direct route allowing for dangers and TSS.

AREA 20 SW Spain & Gibraltar - *Ayamonte to Gibraltar and Ceuta*

SELECTED LIGHTS, BUOYS & WAYPOINTS

Positions are referenced to WGS84

AYAMONTE (E side of Rio Guadiana)

Bar buoys ⩘ Q (3) G 6s; 37°08'·90N 07°23'·44W.
⩘ Fl R 4s; 37°09'·14N 07°23'·82W.
W trng wall ⩘ Fl R 5s 4M; 37°09'·75N 07°24'·03W.
E trng wall ⩘ Fl G 3s 4M; 37°09'·93N 07°23'·63W.
Vila Real de Santo Antònio ☆ Fl 6·5s 51m **26M**;
W twr, B bands; 37°11'·23N 07°25'·00W (Portugal).
Marina ent, ⩘ QR & ⩘ QG; 37°12'·61N 07°24'·43W.

ISLA CANELA and ISLA CRISTINA

Appr ⩘ Fl 10s; 37°10'·51N 07°19'·49W.
W mole ⩘ VQ (2) R 5s 9m 4M; 37°10'·83N 07°19'·58W.
Ldg lts 313°: Front ⩘ Q 8m 5M; 37°11'·50N
07°20'·40W approx. Rear ⩘ Fl 4s 13m 5M.
Both marina entrances are QR and QG.

RIO DE LAS PIEDRAS

No 1 Bar ⩘ L Fl 10s; 37°11'·64N 07°03'·00W. The
shifting chan is marked by lateral lt buoys.
El Rompido ☆ Fl (2) 10s 41m **24M**; W twr, B
bands; 37°13'·12N 07°07'·69W.

RIA DE HUELVA

Punta Umbria, ⩘ L Fl 10s; 37°08'·78N 06°56'·74W.
No. 1 ⩘ Fl (2) G 10s; No. 2 ⩘ Fl (2) R 10s; 37°09'·14N
06°56'·60W.
Bkwtr hd ⩘ VQ (6) + L Fl 10s 8m 5M; 37°09'·85N
06°56'·93W.
Marina wavebreak, S hd, Fl (2) R 10s 1M; 37°10'·40N
06°56'·38W.
N head, Fl (3) R 15s 1M; 37°10'·40N 06°56'·48W.
Dir ⩘ 339·2°, WRG 59m 8M; 337·5°- Fl G-338°-FG-
338·6°-OcG-339·1°-FW-339·3°-OcR-339·8°-FR-
340·4°-Fl R-340·9°; W twr; 37°08'·57N 06°50'·66W.
No. 1 ⩘ Fl G 5s; 37°06'·26N 06°49'·46W.
No. 2 ⩘ Fl R 5s; 37°06'·33N 06°49'·72W.
Bkwtr hd ⩘ Fl (3+1) WR 20s 29m, W12M, R9M;
165°-W-100°-R-125°; *Racon K, 12M;* 37°06'·47N
06°49'·93W.
No. 3 ⩘ Fl (2) G 10s; 37°06'·87N 06°49'·77W.
No. 5 ⩘ Fl (3) G 15s; 37°07'·38N 06°50'·03W.
No. 7 ⩘ Fl (4) G 20s; 37°07'·77N 06°50'·29W.

MAZAGÓN

Picacho lt ho ☆ Fl (2+4) 30s 52m **25M**; 37°08'·10N
06°49'·56W.
Marina, S pier ⩘ QG 7m 2M; 37°07'·91N 06°50'·03W.
⩘ Fl (2) 10s; 37°04'·22N 06°43'·67W.
La Higuera ☆ Fl (3) 20s 45m **20M**; 37°00'·47N
06°34'·16W.

CHIPIONA

Bajo Salmedina ⩘ Q (9) 15s 9m 5M; 36°44'·27N
06°28'·64W.

Pta de Chipiona ☆ Fl 10s 67m **25M**; 36°44'·26N
06°26'·53W.
Marina, No. 2 ⩘ Fl (2) R 7s; 36°45'·14N 06°25'·59W.
N bkwtr ⩘ Fl (2) G 10s 6m 5M; 36°44'·96N 06°25'·70W.

RÍO GUADALQUIVIR

No. 1 ⩘ L Fl 10s; *Racon M, 10M;* 36°45'·74N
06°27'·03W.
Ldg lts 068·9°: Front ⩘ Q 28m 10M; 36°47'·84N
06°20'·24W. Rear, ⩘ Iso 4s 60m 10M.
No. 3 ⩘ Fl G 5s; 36°46'·16N 06°25'·36W.
Selected buoys in sequence as far as Bonanza:
No. 7 ⩘ Fl (3) G 10s; 36°46'·61N 06°24'·02W.
No. 8 ⩘ Fl (3) R 10s; 36°46'·67N 06°24'·12W.
No. 11 ⩘ Fl G 5s; 36°46'·96N 06°22'·90W.
No. 12 ⩘ Fl R 5s; 36°47'·05N 06°22'·94W.
No. 14 ⩘ Fl (2) R 6s; 36°47'·21N 06°22'·39W.
No.13 ⩘ Fl (2) G 6s; 36°47'·12N 06°22'·36W.
No.17 ⩘ Fl (4) G 12s; 36°47'·46N 06°21'·23W.
No. 20 ⩘ Fl R 5s; 36°47'·81N 06°20'·70W.
Bonanza lt ho Fl 5s 22m 6M; 36°48'·17N 06°20'·15W.

SEVILLA

No. 52 bcn ⩘ Fl (2+1) R 21s 9m 5M; 37°18'·97N
06°00'·83W.
Gelves marina Fl R 5s; 37°20'·42N 06°01'·39W;
and Fl G 3s.
Lock, 37°19'·86N 05°59'·74W, for city centre.
CN Sevilla pontoons, 37°22'·20N 05°59'·59W.

ROTA

Rota Aero ☆ Alt Fl WG 9s 79m **17M**; R/W
chequered water twr, conspic; 36°38'·13N
06°20'·84W.
Rota ⩘ Oc 4s 33m 13M; W lt ho, R band;
36°36'·96N 06°21'·44W.
Marina, S pier ⩘ Fl (3) R 10s 8m 9M; 36°36'·96N
06°21'·44W.

P'TO SHERRY/P'TO DE SANTA MARIA

Puerto Sherry marina, S bkwtr ⩘ Oc R 4s 4M;
36°34'·64N 06°15'·25W. N bkwtr ⩘ Oc G 5s 3M.
Santa María ldg lts 040°: Front ⩘ QG 16m 4M;
36°35'·77N 06°13'·36W. Rear ⩘ Iso G 4s 20m 4M.
W trng wall ⩘ Fl R 5s 10m 3M; 36°34'·34N 06°14'·96W.

CÁDIZ CITY and PUERTO AMERICA

⩘ L Fl 10s; 36°33'·99N 06°19'·80W.
No. 1 ⩘ Fl G 3s; 36°33'·12N 06°19'·07W.
No. 3 ⩘ Fl (2) G 4s; 36°33'·17N 06°18'·14W.
No. 5 ⩘ Fl (3) G 13s; 36°33'·03N 06°17'·38W.
San Felipe mole ⩘ Fl G 3s 10m 5M; G twr;
36°32'·56N 06°16'·77W.
P'to America marina, NE bkwtr, ⩘ Fl (4) G 16s 1M.

RCN pier ≮ FG; 36°32'·34N 06°17'·13W.
International Free Zone hbr: No. 1 ↓ Fl (3) G 9s; 36°30'·66N 06°15'·45W.
Puerto Elcano marina 36°30'·08N 06°15'·45W.
Castillo de San Sebastián ☆ Fl (2) 10s 38m **25M**; *Horn Mo (N) 20s;* 36°31'·70N 06°18'·97W.

SANCTI PETRI

Punta del Arrecife ≮ Q (9) 15s 7m 3M; 36°23'·71N 06°13'·58W.
Castle ≮ Fl 3s 18m 9M; 36°22'·75N 06°13'·33W.
Outer ldg lts 050°: Front ≮ Fl 5s 12m 6M. Rear ≮ Oc (2) 6s 16m 6M.
No. 1 ↓ Fl (3) G 9s; 36°22'·50N 06°12'·93W.
No. 2 ↓ Fl (3) R 9s; 36°22'·46N 06°12'·81W.
No. 3 ↓ Fl (4) G 11s; 36°22'·64N 06°12'·65W.
No. 4 ↓ Fl (4) R 11s; 36°22'·66N 06°12'·71W.
Inner ldg lts 346·5°: Front ≮ Fl 5s 11m 6M. Rear ≮ Oc (2) 6s 21m.
↓ Fl G 5s 8m 2M & ↓ Fl R 5s; 36°23'·10N 06°12'·65W.
Cabo Roche ☆ Fl (4) 24s 44m **20M**; 36°17'·75N 06°08'·59W.
Cabo Trafalgar ☆ Fl (2+1) 15s 50m **22M**; 36°10'·95N 06°02'·12W.

BARBATE

Lt ho ≮ Fl (2) WR 7s 22m, W10M, R7M; 281°-W-015°-R-095°; W twr, R bands; 36°11'·21N 05°55'·43W.
Ldg lts 297·5°, Q 3/8m 1M; 280·5°-310·5°; TE 2001.
SW mole ≮ Fl R 4s 11m 5M; 36°10'·78N 05°55'·56W.
Marina ent, Fl (2+1) R 21s 2M (anti-oil boom) and Fl R 4s 2M.
↓ Q; 36°10'·75N 05°55'·40W (1ca E of hbr ent) marks N end of a roughly △-shaped tunny net.
Torre de Gracia ≮ Oc (2) 5s 74m 13M; 36°05'·38N 05°48'·69W.

TARIFA

Tarifa ☆ Fl (3) WR 10s 40m **W26M, R18M**; 113°-W-089°-R-113°; W twr; *Siren Mo (O) 60s;* **Racon C, 20M**; 36°00'·06N 05°36'·60W.
Outer SE mole ≮ Fl G 5s 11m 5M; vis 249°-045°; G twr with statue; 36°00'·38N 05°36'·24W.

ALGECIRAS

Pta Carnero ☆ Fl (4) WR 20s 42m, **W16M**, R13M;

018°-W-325°-R-018°; *Siren Mo (K) 30s;* 36°04'·61N 05°25'·57W.
↓ Q (3) 10s; 36°06'·73N 05°24'·76W.
Marina, outer S jetty ≮ Q (3) R 9s 7m 3M; 36°07'·10N 05°26'·13W.

LA LÍNEA

↓ Fl (3) G 6s; 36°09'·53N 05°22'·03W.
Dique de Abrigo ≮ Fl (2) G 7s 8m 4M; 36°09'·51N 05°22'·05W.

GIBRALTAR

Aero ≮ Mo (GB) R 10s 405m **30M**; 36°08'·57N 05°20'·60W.
Europa Pt ☆ Iso 10s 49m **19/15M**; vis 197°-042° & 067°-125°; W twr, R band; 36°06'·58N 05°20'·69W.
Also ≮ FR 44m **15M**; 042°-067°; *Horn 20s.*
Same twr ≮ Oc R 10s 49m **15M**; 042°-067°.
'A' Head ☆ Fl 2s 18m **15M**; *Horn 10s;* 36°08'·03N 05°21'·85W.
'B' head ≮ QR 9m 5M; 36°08'·14N 05°21'·84W.
Queensway Quay marina, N ent ≮ FR/FG; 36°08'·16N 05°21'·39W.
Yacht fuelling station; 36°08'·90N 05°21'·37W.

MOROCCO (WEST TO EAST)

Cap Spartel ☆ Fl (4) 20s 95m **30M**; Y ☐ twr; *Dia (4) 90s;* 35°47'·47N 05°55'·43W.

TANGIER

Navaids are reported unreliable. They may be missing, unlit, off station or not as charted.
Monte Dirección (Le Charf) ☆ Oc (3) WRG 12s 88m **W16M**, R12M, G11M; 140°-G-174·5°-W-200°-R-225°; 35°45'·98N 05°47'·35W.
↓ L Fl 10s; 35°47'·66N 05°47'·03W.
N pier ≮ Fl (3) 12s 20m 14M; 35°47'·47N 05°47'·60W.
Jetée des Yachts ≮ Iso G 4s 6m 6M; 35°47'·23N 05°48'·14W.
Pta Malabata ☆ Fl 5s 77m **22M**. W ☐ twr; 35°48'·99N 05°44'·92W.
Pte Círes ≮ Fl (3) 10s 44m **18M**; 060°-330°; 35°54'·51N 05°28'·92W.

CEUTA (Spanish enclave)

Punta Almina ≮ Fl (2) 10s 148m 22M; 35°53'·90N 05°16'·85W.
W pier ≮ Fl G 5s 13m 10M; *Siren 15s;* **Racon O, 12M**; 35°53'·75N 05°18'·68W.
Marina ent ≮ Fl (4) R 11s 8m 1M; 35°53'·45N 05°18'·90W.

1	Nazaré	1											
2	Cabo Carvoeiro	22	2										
3	Cabo Raso	62	40	3									
4	Lisboa (bridge)	78	56	16	4								
5	Cabo Espichel	84	62	22	23	5							
6	Sines	118	96	54	57	34	6						
7	Cabo São Vicente	169	147	104	108	85	57	7					
8	Lagos	189	167	124	128	105	77	20	8				
9	Vilamoura	212	190	147	151	128	100	43	27	9			
10	Cádiz	303	281	238	242	219	191	134	120	95	10		
11	Cabo Trafalgar	320	298	255	259	236	208	151	139	115	28	11	
12	Tarifa	344	322	279	283	260	232	175	163	139	52	24	12
13	Gibraltar	360	338	295	299	276	248	191	179	155	68	40	16	13

56°N 00°E/W. Times are UT - for DST add 1 hour in non-shaded areas

2007 Sunrise and Sunset Time

The times are based on LAT 56°00'N   LONG 0° - add 4 min for every degree West and subtract 4 min for every degree East

	JAN Rise	JAN Set	FEB Rise	FEB Set	MAR Rise	MAR Set	APR Rise	APR Set	MAY Rise	MAY Set	JUN Rise	JUN Set
1	08 31	15 36	07 56	16 32	06 53	17 33	05 32	18 37	04 17	19 39	03 22	20 34
2	08 31	15 37	07 54	16 34	06 50	17 35	05 29	18 39	04 15	19 41	03 21	20 35
3	08 31	15 38	07 52	16 37	06 48	17 37	05 27	18 41	04 13	19 43	03 20	20 37
4	08 30	15 40	07 50	16 39	06 45	17 40	05 24	18 43	04 10	19 45	03 19	20 38
5	08 30	15 41	07 48	16 41	06 42	17 42	05 21	18 46	04 08	19 47	03 19	20 39
6	08 29	15 42	07 46	16 43	06 40	17 44	05 19	18 48	04 06	19 49	03 18	20 40
7	08 29	15 44	07 44	16 45	06 37	17 46	05 16	18 50	04 04	19 51	03 17	20 41
8	08 28	15 45	07 42	16 47	06 35	17 48	05 14	18 52	04 02	19 52	03 16	20 42
9	08 27	15 47	07 40	16 50	06 32	17 50	05 11	18 54	04 00	19 54	03 16	20 43
10	08 27	15 49	07 37	16 52	06 30	17 52	05 08	18 56	03 58	19 56	03 15	20 44
11	08 26	15 50	07 35	16 54	06 27	17 54	05 06	18 58	03 56	19 58	03 15	20 45
12	08 25	15 52	07 33	16 56	06 24	17 56	05 03	19 00	03 54	20 00	03 14	20 46
13	08 24	15 54	07 31	16 59	06 22	17 58	05 01	19 02	03 52	20 02	03 14	20 47
14	08 23	15 56	07 29	17 01	06 19	18 01	04 58	19 04	03 50	20 04	03 13	20 47
15	08 22	15 57	07 26	17 03	06 17	18 03	04 56	19 06	03 48	20 06	03 13	20 48
16	08 21	15 59	07 24	17 05	06 14	18 05	04 53	19 08	03 46	20 08	03 13	20 49
17	08 19	16 01	07 22	17 07	06 11	18 07	04 51	19 10	03 44	20 10	03 13	20 49
18	08 18	16 03	07 19	17 09	06 09	18 09	04 48	19 12	03 43	20 11	03 13	20 49
19	08 17	16 05	07 17	17 12	06 06	18 11	04 46	19 14	03 41	20 13	03 13	20 50
20	08 15	16 07	07 15	17 14	06 03	18 13	04 43	19 16	03 39	20 15	03 13	20 50
21	08 14	16 09	07 12	17 16	06 01	18 15	04 41	19 18	03 38	20 17	03 13	20 50
22	08 13	16 11	07 10	17 18	05 58	18 17	04 38	19 20	03 36	20 19	03 13	20 51
23	08 11	16 13	07 07	17 20	05 56	18 19	04 36	19 22	03 34	20 20	03 14	20 51
24	08 10	16 15	07 05	17 23	05 53	18 21	04 33	19 24	03 33	20 22	03 14	20 51
25	08 08	16 17	07 03	17 25	05 50	18 23	04 31	19 26	03 31	20 24	03 14	20 51
26	08 06	16 19	07 00	17 27	05 48	18 25	04 29	19 28	03 30	20 25	03 15	20 51
27	08 05	16 21	06 58	17 29	05 45	18 27	04 26	19 30	03 29	20 27	03 15	20 50
28	08 03	16 24	06 55	17 31	05 42	18 29	04 24	19 32	03 27	20 28	03 16	20 50
29	08 01	16 26			05 40	18 31	04 22	19 34	03 26	20 30	03 16	20 50
30	07 59	16 28			05 37	18 33	04 19	19 37	03 25	20 31	03 17	20 50
31	07 58	16 30			05 34	18 35			03 24	20 33		

	JUL Rise	JUL Set	AUG Rise	AUG Set	SEP Rise	SEP Set	OCT Rise	OCT Set	NOV Rise	NOV Set	DEC Rise	DEC Set
1	03 18	20 49	04 03	20 08	05 03	18 56	06 02	17 36	07 06	16 20	08 06	15 31
2	03 19	20 49	04 05	20 06	05 05	18 53	06 04	17 34	07 08	16 18	08 08	15 30
3	03 20	20 48	04 07	20 04	05 07	18 50	06 06	17 31	07 10	16 16	08 09	15 30
4	03 21	20 48	04 09	20 02	05 09	18 48	06 08	17 29	07 12	16 14	08 11	15 29
5	03 22	20 47	04 11	20 00	05 11	18 45	06 10	17 26	07 15	16 12	08 12	15 28
6	03 23	20 46	04 12	19 58	05 13	18 43	06 12	17 23	07 17	16 10	08 14	15 28
7	03 24	20 45	04 14	19 56	05 15	18 40	06 14	17 21	07 19	16 08	08 15	15 27
8	03 25	20 44	04 16	19 54	05 17	18 37	06 16	17 18	07 21	16 06	08 17	15 26
9	03 26	20 43	04 18	19 52	05 19	18 35	06 18	17 16	07 23	16 04	08 18	15 26
10	03 27	20 43	04 20	19 49	05 21	18 32	06 20	17 13	07 25	16 02	08 19	15 26
11	03 29	20 41	04 22	19 47	05 23	18 29	06 22	17 11	07 27	16 00	08 21	15 25
12	03 30	20 40	04 24	19 45	05 25	18 27	06 24	17 08	07 29	15 58	08 22	15 25
13	03 31	20 39	04 26	19 42	05 27	18 24	06 26	17 05	07 31	15 56	08 23	15 25
14	03 33	20 38	04 28	19 40	05 29	18 21	06 28	17 03	07 34	15 55	08 24	15 25
15	03 34	20 37	04 30	19 38	05 31	18 19	06 30	17 00	07 36	15 53	08 25	15 25
16	03 36	20 35	04 32	19 35	05 33	18 16	06 32	16 58	07 38	15 51	08 26	15 25
17	03 37	20 34	04 34	19 33	05 35	18 14	06 34	16 55	07 40	15 49	08 27	15 25
18	03 39	20 33	04 36	19 31	05 36	18 11	06 37	16 53	07 42	15 48	08 27	15 26
19	03 40	20 31	04 38	19 28	05 38	18 08	06 39	16 51	07 44	15 46	08 28	15 26
20	03 42	20 30	04 40	19 26	05 40	18 06	06 41	16 48	07 46	15 45	08 29	15 26
21	03 44	20 28	04 42	19 23	05 42	18 03	06 43	16 46	07 48	15 43	08 29	15 26
22	03 45	20 27	04 44	19 21	05 44	18 00	06 45	16 43	07 50	15 42	08 30	15 27
23	03 47	20 25	04 46	19 18	05 46	17 58	06 47	16 41	07 52	15 40	08 30	15 27
24	03 49	20 23	04 48	19 16	05 48	17 55	06 49	16 39	07 54	15 39	08 31	15 28
25	03 50	20 22	04 50	19 13	05 50	17 52	06 51	16 36	07 55	15 38	08 31	15 29
26	03 52	20 20	04 52	19 11	05 52	17 50	06 53	16 34	07 57	15 37	08 31	15 30
27	03 54	20 18	04 54	19 08	05 54	17 47	06 55	16 32	07 59	15 35	08 32	15 30
28	03 56	20 16	04 55	19 06	05 56	17 44	06 57	16 29	08 01	15 34	08 32	15 31
29	03 58	20 14	04 57	19 03	05 58	17 42	07 00	16 27	08 03	15 33	08 32	15 32
30	03 59	20 12	04 59	19 01	06 00	17 39	07 02	16 25	08 04	15 32	08 32	15 33
31	04 01	20 10	05 01	18 58			07 04	16 23			08 32	15 34

2007 Moonrise and Moonset Time

The times are based on **LAT 56°00'N   LONG 0°** - add 4 min for every degree West and subtract 4 min for every degree East

	JANUARY Rise h m	Set h m	FEBRUARY Rise h m	Set h m	MARCH Rise h m	Set h m	APRIL Rise h m	Set h m	MAY Rise h m	Set h m	JUNE Rise h m	Set h m
1	12 47	07 11	15 21	08 13	14 30	06 34	17 32	05 10	19 10	03 35	22 10	02 40
2	13 37	08 27	16 47	08 25	15 53	06 43	18 48	05 14	20 31	03 43	23 04	03 19
3	14 50	09 19	18 10	08 34	17 13	06 50	20 05	05 19	21 53	03 53	23 39	04 20
4	16 16	09 49	19 29	08 39	18 30	06 55	21 24	05 25	23 12	04 10	** **	05 38
5	17 45	10 07	20 46	08 44	19 46	06 59	22 46	05 33	** **	04 37	00 01	07 07
6	19 10	10 17	22 01	08 48	21 02	07 03	** **	05 44	00 18	05 22	00 15	08 38
7	20 31	10 25	23 17	08 53	22 19	07 08	00 08	06 03	01 06	06 28	00 24	10 09
8	21 48	10 30	** **	08 59	23 39	07 14	01 24	06 35	01 37	07 50	00 31	11 39
9	23 03	10 35	00 36	09 05	** **	07 23	02 25	07 26	01 55	09 20	00 38	13 09
10	** **	10 39	01 58	09 15	01 02	07 36	03 07	08 38	02 07	10 52	00 44	14 42
11	00 19	10 44	03 21	09 32	02 23	07 58	03 34	10 06	02 16	12 25	00 52	16 20
12	01 36	10 50	04 42	10 00	03 36	08 36	03 50	11 40	02 23	13 57	01 02	18 01
13	02 56	10 58	05 51	10 49	04 32	09 37	04 00	13 16	02 29	15 32	01 18	19 42
14	04 20	11 11	06 39	12 02	05 09	10 59	04 08	14 52	02 36	17 10	01 44	21 10
15	05 45	11 33	07 09	13 34	05 30	12 34	04 15	16 29	02 45	18 53	02 30	22 12
16	07 03	12 10	07 26	15 14	05 44	14 13	04 22	18 08	02 57	20 38	03 40	22 50
17	08 04	13 11	07 38	16 55	05 53	15 53	04 29	19 51	03 17	22 16	05 07	23 11
18	08 43	14 36	07 46	18 33	06 00	17 31	04 39	21 36	03 51	23 34	06 40	23 24
19	09 06	16 12	07 52	20 10	06 07	19 10	04 54	23 20	04 48	** **	08 09	23 32
20	09 20	17 52	07 58	21 47	06 14	20 51	05 20	** **	06 07	00 23	09 32	23 38
21	09 30	19 29	08 05	23 26	06 22	22 34	06 02	00 48	07 37	00 51	10 51	23 43
22	09 37	21 03	08 14	** **	06 33	** **	07 09	01 51	09 07	01 07	12 08	23 48
23	09 43	22 37	08 27	01 05	06 52	00 17	08 32	02 28	10 31	01 18	13 23	23 53
24	09 49	** **	08 48	02 42	07 22	01 52	10 00	02 49	11 51	01 25	14 40	** **
25	09 56	00 10	09 24	04 09	08 13	03 08	11 26	03 02	13 08	01 30	15 59	00 00
26	10 06	01 46	10 21	05 14	09 25	03 57	12 48	03 10	14 23	01 35	17 20	00 08
27	10 21	03 22	11 37	05 56	10 49	04 26	14 05	03 16	15 39	01 39	18 42	00 21
28	10 46	04 56	13 03	06 20	12 16	04 43	15 21	03 21	16 56	01 45	19 58	00 41
29	11 28	06 17			13 40	04 53	16 36	03 25	18 16	01 52	20 59	01 14
30	12 31	07 16			15 00	05 01	17 52	03 30	19 38	02 01	21 40	02 08
31	13 53	07 52			16 17	05 06			20 59	02 16		

	JULY Rise h m	Set h m	AUGUST Rise h m	Set h m	SEPTEMBER Rise h m	Set h m	OCTOBER Rise h m	Set h m	NOVEMBER Rise h m	Set h m	DECEMBER Rise h m	Set h m
1	22 06	03 23	20 56	07 07	19 37	11 02	18 56	13 29	21 57	14 12	23 51	12 46
2	22 22	04 51	21 03	08 39	19 52	12 42	19 55	14 40	23 24	14 24	** **	12 52
3	22 33	06 23	21 09	10 11	20 17	14 19	21 14	15 24	** **	14 32	01 08	12 57
4	22 40	07 55	21 17	11 45	20 59	15 44	22 43	15 50	00 46	14 38	02 24	13 03
5	22 47	09 25	21 28	13 21	22 04	16 45	** **	16 06	02 04	14 43	03 41	13 09
6	22 53	10 55	21 46	15 00	23 27	17 22	00 12	16 15	03 20	14 48	04 59	13 18
7	23 00	12 26	22 15	16 33	** **	17 44	01 36	16 22	04 36	14 54	06 18	13 31
8	23 09	14 00	23 04	17 52	00 57	17 57	02 57	16 28	05 53	15 01	07 38	13 50
9	23 22	15 37	** **	18 46	02 25	18 06	04 15	16 33	07 12	15 10	08 51	14 20
10	23 43	17 16	00 17	19 18	03 50	18 12	05 32	16 38	08 32	15 24	09 53	15 08
11	** **	18 48	01 45	19 36	05 11	18 17	06 48	16 43	09 51	15 46	10 36	16 14
12	00 18	20 01	03 16	19 48	06 29	18 22	08 06	16 51	11 01	16 20	11 05	17 33
13	01 17	20 47	04 44	19 56	07 46	18 27	09 26	17 01	11 57	17 13	11 23	18 58
14	02 38	21 14	06 08	20 02	09 03	18 33	10 46	17 16	12 36	18 23	11 35	20 25
15	04 10	21 30	07 29	20 07	10 22	18 41	12 04	17 41	13 01	19 44	11 44	21 51
16	05 41	21 40	08 46	20 11	11 42	18 52	13 11	18 20	13 16	21 11	11 51	23 17
17	07 08	21 47	10 03	20 16	13 03	19 10	14 02	19 19	13 27	22 39	11 57	** **
18	08 30	21 52	11 21	20 23	14 18	19 38	14 36	20 34	13 36	** **	12 04	00 45
19	09 49	21 57	12 41	20 32	15 21	20 25	14 57	22 00	13 43	00 07	12 12	02 17
20	11 05	22 02	14 02	20 45	16 07	21 32	15 11	23 30	13 49	01 36	12 24	03 53
21	12 22	22 07	15 22	21 07	16 35	22 56	15 21	** **	13 57	03 09	12 42	05 35
22	13 40	22 15	16 34	21 43	16 53	** **	15 28	01 02	14 07	04 46	13 13	07 14
23	15 01	22 25	17 32	22 39	17 05	00 28	15 35	02 34	14 21	06 30	14 05	08 40
24	16 22	22 42	18 10	23 57	17 14	02 02	15 42	04 09	14 45	08 15	15 24	09 39
25	17 41	23 09	18 33	** **	17 21	03 37	15 51	05 47	15 26	09 51	16 58	10 13
26	18 49	23 54	18 48	01 27	17 28	05 12	16 03	07 30	16 32	11 04	18 34	10 33
27	19 38	** **	18 58	03 02	17 35	06 49	16 21	09 16	17 59	11 49	20 05	10 45
28	20 10	01 01	19 06	04 38	17 44	08 29	16 51	10 58	19 33	12 14	21 30	10 54
29	20 29	02 26	19 12	06 13	17 58	10 13	17 43	12 23	21 05	12 29	22 51	11 00
30	20 41	03 59	19 19	07 47	18 20	11 56	18 58	13 20	22 30	12 39	** **	11 06
31	20 50	05 34	19 26	09 23			20 26	13 53			00 09	11 11

48°N 00°E/W. Times are UT - for DST add 1 hour in non-shaded areas

2007 Sunrise and Sunset Time

The times are based on **LAT 48°00′N   LONG 0°00′W** - add 4 min for every degree West and subtract 4 min for every degree East

	JANUARY Rise h m	JANUARY Set h m	FEBRUARY Rise h m	FEBRUARY Set h m	MARCH Rise h m	MARCH Set h m	APRIL Rise h m	APRIL Set h m	MAY Rise h m	MAY Set h m	JUNE Rise h m	JUNE Set h m
1	07 50	16 17	07 28	16 59	06 42	17 44	05 39	18 29	04 43	19 12	04 05	19 51
2	07 50	16 18	07 27	17 01	06 40	17 45	05 37	18 31	04 41	19 14	04 04	19 52
3	07 50	16 19	07 26	17 03	06 38	17 47	05 35	18 32	04 39	19 15	04 04	19 53
4	07 50	16 20	07 24	17 04	06 36	17 48	05 33	18 34	04 38	19 17	04 03	19 54
5	07 50	16 21	07 23	17 06	06 34	17 50	05 31	18 35	04 36	19 18	04 03	19 55
6	07 49	16 22	07 21	17 07	06 32	17 51	05 29	18 37	04 35	19 19	04 02	19 55
7	07 49	16 23	07 20	17 09	06 30	17 53	05 27	18 38	04 33	19 21	04 02	19 56
8	07 49	16 25	07 18	17 11	06 28	17 54	05 25	18 40	04 32	19 22	04 01	19 57
9	07 48	16 26	07 17	17 12	06 26	17 56	05 23	18 41	04 30	19 24	04 01	19 57
10	07 48	16 27	07 15	17 14	06 24	17 57	05 21	18 42	04 29	19 25	04 01	19 58
11	07 48	16 28	07 14	17 15	06 22	17 59	05 19	18 44	04 27	19 26	04 00	19 59
12	07 47	16 30	07 12	17 17	06 20	18 00	05 17	18 45	04 26	19 28	04 00	20 00
13	07 47	16 31	07 11	17 19	06 18	18 02	05 15	18 47	04 25	19 29	04 00	20 00
14	07 46	16 32	07 09	17 20	06 16	18 03	05 14	18 48	04 23	19 30	04 00	20 01
15	07 45	16 34	07 07	17 22	06 14	18 05	05 12	18 50	04 22	19 32	04 00	20 01
16	07 45	16 35	07 06	17 23	06 12	18 06	05 10	18 51	04 21	19 33	04 00	20 02
17	07 44	16 37	07 04	17 25	06 10	18 08	05 08	18 52	04 19	19 34	04 00	20 02
18	07 43	16 38	07 02	17 27	06 08	18 09	05 06	18 54	04 18	19 35	04 00	20 02
19	07 42	16 39	07 00	17 28	06 06	18 11	05 04	18 55	04 17	19 37	04 00	20 03
20	07 41	16 41	06 59	17 30	06 04	18 12	05 02	18 57	04 16	19 38	04 00	20 03
21	07 41	16 42	06 57	17 31	06 02	18 14	05 00	18 58	04 15	19 39	04 00	20 03
22	07 40	16 44	06 55	17 33	06 00	18 15	04 58	19 00	04 14	19 40	04 00	20 03
23	07 39	16 45	06 53	17 34	05 58	18 16	04 57	19 01	04 13	19 41	04 01	20 04
24	07 38	16 47	06 51	17 36	05 56	18 18	04 55	19 03	04 12	19 43	04 01	20 04
25	07 37	16 48	06 50	17 37	05 54	18 19	04 53	19 04	04 11	19 44	04 01	20 04
26	07 36	16 50	06 48	17 39	05 52	18 21	04 51	19 05	04 10	19 45	04 02	20 04
27	07 34	16 51	06 46	17 41	05 50	18 22	04 50	19 07	04 09	19 46	04 02	20 04
28	07 33	16 53	06 44	17 42	05 48	18 24	04 48	19 08	04 08	19 47	04 03	20 04
29	07 32	16 55			05 46	18 25	04 46	19 10	04 07	19 48	04 03	20 03
30	07 31	16 56			05 44	18 27	04 44	19 11	04 06	19 49	04 04	20 03
31	07 30	16 58			05 41	18 28			04 06	19 50		

	JULY Rise	JULY Set	AUGUST Rise	AUGUST Set	SEPTEMBER Rise	SEPTEMBER Set	OCTOBER Rise	OCTOBER Set	NOVEMBER Rise	NOVEMBER Set	DECEMBER Rise	DECEMBER Set
1	04 04	20 03	04 35	19 36	05 17	18 42	05 58	17 40	06 44	16 42	07 28	16 09
2	04 05	20 03	04 37	19 35	05 19	18 40	06 00	17 38	06 46	16 41	07 29	16 09
3	04 05	20 03	04 38	19 33	05 20	18 38	06 01	17 36	06 47	16 39	07 31	16 08
4	04 06	20 02	04 39	19 32	05 21	18 36	06 03	17 34	06 49	16 38	07 32	16 08
5	04 07	20 02	04 41	19 31	05 23	18 34	06 04	17 32	06 50	16 36	07 33	16 08
6	04 08	20 01	04 42	19 29	05 24	18 32	06 05	17 30	06 52	16 35	07 34	16 07
7	04 08	20 01	04 43	19 27	05 25	18 30	06 07	17 28	06 53	16 33	07 35	16 07
8	04 09	20 00	04 45	19 26	05 27	18 28	06 08	17 26	06 55	16 32	07 36	16 07
9	04 10	20 00	04 46	19 24	05 28	18 26	06 10	17 24	06 56	16 31	07 37	16 07
10	04 11	19 59	04 47	19 23	05 30	18 24	06 11	17 22	06 58	16 29	07 38	16 07
11	04 12	19 59	04 49	19 21	05 31	18 22	06 13	17 20	07 00	16 28	07 39	16 07
12	04 13	19 58	04 50	19 19	05 32	18 20	06 14	17 18	07 01	16 27	07 40	16 07
13	04 14	19 57	04 51	19 18	05 34	18 18	06 16	17 16	07 03	16 25	07 41	16 07
14	04 15	19 56	04 53	19 16	05 35	18 16	06 17	17 14	07 04	16 24	07 42	16 07
15	04 16	19 56	04 54	19 14	05 36	18 13	06 19	17 12	07 06	16 23	07 43	16 07
16	04 17	19 55	04 55	19 12	05 38	18 11	06 20	17 11	07 07	16 22	07 44	16 07
17	04 18	19 54	04 57	19 11	05 39	18 09	06 21	17 09	07 09	16 21	07 44	16 08
18	04 19	19 53	04 58	19 09	05 40	18 07	06 23	17 07	07 10	16 20	07 45	16 08
19	04 20	19 52	05 00	19 07	05 42	18 05	06 24	17 05	07 12	16 19	07 46	16 08
20	04 21	19 51	05 01	19 05	05 43	18 03	06 26	17 03	07 13	16 18	07 46	16 09
21	04 22	19 50	05 02	19 03	05 45	18 01	06 27	17 01	07 15	16 17	07 47	16 09
22	04 23	19 49	05 04	19 01	05 46	17 59	06 29	16 59	07 16	16 16	07 47	16 10
23	04 24	19 48	05 05	19 00	05 47	17 57	06 30	16 58	07 17	16 15	07 48	16 10
24	04 26	19 47	05 06	18 58	05 49	17 55	06 32	16 56	07 19	16 14	07 48	16 11
25	04 27	19 46	05 08	18 56	05 50	17 53	06 33	16 54	07 20	16 13	07 49	16 11
26	04 28	19 44	05 09	18 54	05 51	17 51	06 35	16 52	07 22	16 12	07 49	16 12
27	04 29	19 43	05 10	18 52	05 53	17 49	06 37	16 51	07 23	16 12	07 49	16 13
28	04 30	19 42	05 12	18 50	05 54	17 46	06 38	16 49	07 24	16 11	07 49	16 13
29	04 32	19 40	05 13	18 48	05 56	17 44	06 40	16 47	07 26	16 10	07 50	16 14
30	04 33	19 39	05 15	18 46	05 57	17 42	06 41	16 46	07 27	16 10	07 50	16 15
31	04 34	19 38	05 16	18 44			06 43	16 44			07 50	16 16

48°N 00°E/W. Times are UT - for DST add 1 hour in non-shaded areas

2007 Moonrise and Moonset Time

The times are based on **LAT 48°00'N   LONG 0°00'W** - add 4 min for every degree West and subtract 4 min for every degree East

	JANUARY Rise h m	JANUARY Set h m	FEBRUARY Rise h m	FEBRUARY Set h m	MARCH Rise h m	MARCH Set h m	APRIL Rise h m	APRIL Set h m	MAY Rise h m	MAY Set h m	JUNE Rise h m	JUNE Set h m
1	13 50	06 09	16 04	07 27	15 05	05 57	17 30	05 08	18 41	03 57	21 03	03 41
2	14 45	07 20	17 18	07 52	16 17	06 17	18 36	05 21	19 51	04 14	21 58	04 27
3	15 52	08 15	18 30	08 11	17 26	06 33	19 43	05 34	21 01	04 36	22 42	05 25
4	17 07	08 56	19 39	08 26	18 33	06 47	20 52	05 50	22 09	05 04	23 15	06 34
5	18 23	09 26	20 46	08 40	19 40	07 00	22 01	06 08	23 10	05 41	23 41	07 50
6	19 36	09 48	21 52	08 53	20 46	07 13	23 11	06 31	** **	06 30	** **	09 09
7	20 46	10 06	22 59	09 06	21 54	07 27	** **	07 01	00 01	07 32	00 02	10 27
8	21 54	10 20	** **	09 20	23 03	07 42	00 17	07 41	00 42	08 43	00 20	11 46
9	23 00	10 34	00 07	09 37	** **	08 02	01 16	08 34	01 13	10 00	00 36	13 05
10	** **	10 47	01 17	09 58	00 13	08 27	02 04	09 40	01 37	11 20	00 53	14 27
11	00 06	11 00	02 28	10 27	01 22	09 00	02 42	10 55	01 57	12 40	01 11	15 52
12	01 13	11 16	03 37	11 06	02 27	09 46	03 11	12 16	02 14	14 01	01 33	17 19
13	02 23	11 34	04 41	11 58	03 24	10 45	03 34	13 39	02 31	15 24	02 03	18 45
14	03 34	11 59	05 34	13 06	04 09	11 57	03 53	15 02	02 49	16 50	02 42	20 04
15	04 47	12 32	06 16	14 25	04 44	13 18	04 11	16 27	03 09	18 19	03 36	21 08
16	05 56	13 18	06 47	15 50	05 11	14 43	04 28	17 54	03 35	19 49	04 43	21 55
17	06 56	14 19	07 11	17 17	05 33	16 09	04 47	19 24	04 08	21 14	06 00	22 29
18	07 44	15 33	07 31	18 43	05 51	17 35	05 10	20 54	04 55	22 27	07 19	22 53
19	08 20	16 56	07 49	20 08	06 09	19 02	05 39	22 23	05 55	23 22	08 36	23 12
20	08 48	18 21	08 06	21 33	06 27	20 30	06 18	23 41	07 07	** **	09 49	23 28
21	09 09	19 46	08 24	22 58	06 47	21 59	07 10	** **	08 24	00 02	10 58	23 42
22	09 27	21 08	08 45	** **	07 11	23 27	08 14	00 45	09 41	00 30	12 05	23 55
23	09 44	22 30	09 11	00 24	07 43	** **	09 27	01 31	10 54	00 52	13 11	** **
24	10 01	23 52	09 45	01 47	08 26	00 49	10 43	02 04	12 04	01 08	14 18	00 09
25	10 19	** **	10 31	03 03	09 21	01 59	11 56	02 29	13 11	01 23	15 26	00 24
26	10 41	01 14	11 29	04 06	10 28	02 53	13 07	02 47	14 17	01 36	16 36	00 43
27	11 09	02 37	12 37	04 55	11 41	03 33	14 15	03 03	15 23	01 49	17 46	01 07
28	11 46	03 57	13 51	05 30	12 54	04 02	15 21	03 16	16 31	02 03	18 53	01 38
29	12 35	05 10			14 07	04 24	16 27	03 29	17 40	02 20	19 52	02 20
30	13 37	06 09			15 16	04 41	17 33	03 42	18 50	02 40	20 40	03 15
31	14 49	06 54			16 24	04 55			19 59	03 06		

	JULY Rise	JULY Set	AUGUST Rise	AUGUST Set	SEPTEMBER Rise	SEPTEMBER Set	OCTOBER Rise	OCTOBER Set	NOVEMBER Rise	NOVEMBER Set	DECEMBER Rise	DECEMBER Set
1	21 17	04 22	20 49	07 21	20 09	10 33	20 01	12 25	22 34	13 33	23 59	12 35
2	21 45	05 38	21 05	08 42	20 37	11 59	21 01	13 33	23 49	13 56	** **	12 49
3	22 07	06 57	21 22	10 02	21 15	13 22	22 13	14 25	** **	14 14	01 07	13 03
4	22 26	08 17	21 42	11 24	22 06	14 38	23 29	15 02	01 00	14 29	02 13	13 17
5	22 43	09 36	22 05	12 48	23 09	15 39	** **	15 30	02 09	14 43	03 20	13 33
6	22 59	10 54	22 35	14 12	** **	16 25	00 45	15 50	03 16	14 56	04 28	13 52
7	23 16	12 14	23 17	15 33	00 23	16 59	01 58	16 07	04 22	15 11	05 36	14 15
8	23 36	13 36	** **	16 45	01 39	17 24	03 09	16 22	05 30	15 27	06 44	14 44
9	** **	15 00	00 11	17 42	02 55	17 44	04 17	16 35	06 38	15 47	07 49	15 23
10	00 02	16 25	01 19	18 25	04 09	18 00	05 24	16 49	07 47	16 11	08 47	16 13
11	00 36	17 45	02 35	18 56	05 19	18 14	06 31	17 03	08 54	16 43	09 35	17 14
12	01 22	18 54	03 54	19 19	06 28	18 27	07 39	17 20	09 57	17 25	10 13	18 23
13	02 23	19 47	05 10	19 37	07 35	18 41	08 48	17 41	10 52	18 18	10 42	19 37
14	03 36	20 26	06 23	19 53	08 43	18 56	09 57	18 07	11 36	19 21	11 05	20 51
15	04 55	20 54	07 33	20 07	09 51	19 14	11 03	18 42	12 12	20 32	11 25	22 07
16	06 14	21 15	08 41	20 20	11 00	19 36	12 04	19 27	12 39	21 46	11 42	23 22
17	07 29	21 32	09 49	20 34	12 09	20 05	12 56	20 24	13 01	23 02	11 58	** **
18	08 41	21 47	10 57	20 50	13 14	20 43	13 38	21 30	13 20	** **	12 15	00 39
19	09 50	22 01	12 05	21 10	14 13	21 33	14 11	22 44	13 37	00 19	12 34	01 59
20	10 57	22 14	13 15	21 34	15 03	22 35	14 37	** **	13 53	01 37	12 57	03 23
21	12 04	22 29	14 23	22 07	15 42	23 48	14 58	00 02	14 12	02 59	13 28	04 51
22	13 12	22 46	15 28	22 50	16 12	** **	15 16	01 21	14 33	04 24	14 11	06 17
23	14 21	23 07	16 24	23 47	16 36	01 06	15 34	02 42	15 01	05 53	15 10	07 35
24	15 31	23 35	17 10	** **	16 56	02 27	15 51	04 05	15 38	07 24	16 24	08 37
25	16 39	** **	17 46	00 55	17 14	03 50	16 11	05 31	16 29	08 49	17 46	09 23
26	17 41	00 12	18 13	02 13	17 32	05 14	16 36	07 00	17 36	10 00	19 08	09 56
27	18 34	01 02	18 35	03 35	17 50	06 38	17 08	08 32	18 54	10 53	20 27	10 20
28	19 15	02 05	18 54	04 57	18 11	08 06	17 51	10 00	20 15	11 30	21 42	10 38
29	19 47	03 19	19 11	06 20	18 38	09 35	18 49	11 17	21 34	11 58	22 52	10 54
30	20 12	04 38	19 28	07 43	19 13	11 04	19 59	12 17	22 48	12 18	** **	11 08
31	20 32	06 00	19 47	09 07			21 16	13 01			00 01	11 23

67

40°N 00°E/W. Times are UT - for DST add 1 hour in non-shaded areas

2007 Sunrise and Sunset Time

The times are based on **LAT 40°00′N LONG 0°** - add 4 min for every degree West and subtract 4 min for every degree East

	JANUARY Rise h m	JANUARY Set h m	FEBRUARY Rise h m	FEBRUARY Set h m	MARCH Rise h m	MARCH Set h m	APRIL Rise h m	APRIL Set h m	MAY Rise h m	MAY Set h m	JUNE Rise h m	JUNE Set h m
1	07 22	16 45	07 09	17 19	06 34	17 51	05 45	18 24	05 01	18 54	04 33	19 22
2	07 22	16 46	07 08	17 20	06 33	17 52	05 43	18 25	04 59	18 55	04 33	19 23
3	07 22	16 47	07 07	17 21	06 31	17 54	05 42	18 26	04 58	18 56	04 33	19 24
4	07 22	16 48	07 06	17 22	06 30	17 55	05 40	18 27	04 57	18 57	04 32	19 25
5	07 22	16 49	07 05	17 23	06 28	17 56	05 38	18 28	04 56	18 58	04 32	19 25
6	07 22	16 50	07 04	17 25	06 27	17 57	05 37	18 29	04 55	18 59	04 32	19 26
7	07 22	16 50	07 03	17 26	06 25	17 58	05 35	18 30	04 54	19 00	04 31	19 26
8	07 22	16 51	07 02	17 27	06 23	17 59	05 34	18 31	04 52	19 01	04 31	19 27
9	07 22	16 52	07 01	17 28	06 22	18 00	05 32	18 32	04 51	19 02	04 31	19 28
10	07 22	16 53	07 00	17 29	06 20	18 01	05 31	18 33	04 50	19 03	04 31	19 28
11	07 21	16 54	06 58	17 31	06 19	18 02	05 29	18 34	04 49	19 04	04 31	19 29
12	07 21	16 55	06 57	17 32	06 17	18 03	05 28	18 35	04 48	19 05	04 31	19 29
13	07 21	16 57	06 56	17 33	06 16	18 04	05 26	18 36	04 47	19 06	04 31	19 30
14	07 21	16 58	06 55	17 34	06 14	18 05	05 24	18 37	04 46	19 07	04 31	19 30
15	07 20	16 59	06 54	17 35	06 12	18 06	05 23	18 38	04 45	19 08	04 31	19 31
16	07 20	17 00	06 52	17 36	06 11	18 07	05 21	18 39	04 44	19 09	04 31	19 31
17	07 19	17 01	06 51	17 38	06 09	18 08	05 20	18 40	04 43	19 10	04 31	19 31
18	07 19	17 02	06 50	17 39	06 08	18 09	05 19	18 41	04 43	19 11	04 31	19 31
19	07 18	17 03	06 48	17 40	06 06	18 11	05 17	18 42	04 42	19 12	04 31	19 32
20	07 18	17 04	06 47	17 41	06 04	18 12	05 16	18 43	04 41	19 13	04 31	19 32
21	07 17	17 06	06 46	17 42	06 03	18 13	05 14	18 44	04 40	19 14	04 31	19 32
22	07 17	17 07	06 44	17 43	06 01	18 14	05 13	18 45	04 39	19 14	04 31	19 32
23	07 16	17 08	06 43	17 45	05 59	18 15	05 11	18 46	04 39	19 15	04 32	19 33
24	07 15	17 09	06 41	17 46	05 58	18 16	05 10	18 47	04 38	19 16	04 32	19 33
25	07 15	17 10	06 40	17 47	05 56	18 17	05 09	18 48	04 37	19 17	04 32	19 33
26	07 14	17 11	06 39	17 48	05 55	18 18	05 07	18 49	04 37	19 18	04 33	19 33
27	07 13	17 13	06 37	17 49	05 53	18 19	05 06	18 50	04 36	19 19	04 33	19 33
28	07 12	17 14	06 36	17 50	05 51	18 20	05 05	18 51	04 35	19 19	04 33	19 33
29	07 12	17 15			05 50	18 21	05 03	18 52	04 35	19 20	04 34	19 33
30	07 11	17 16			05 48	18 22	05 02	18 53	04 34	19 21	04 34	19 33
31	07 10	17 17			05 46	18 23			04 34	19 22		

	JULY Rise	JULY Set	AUGUST Rise	AUGUST Set	SEPTEMBER Rise	SEPTEMBER Set	OCTOBER Rise	OCTOBER Set	NOVEMBER Rise	NOVEMBER Set	DECEMBER Rise	DECEMBER Set
1	04 35	19 33	04 58	19 14	05 27	18 32	05 56	17 43	06 28	16 58	07 02	16 35
2	04 35	19 33	04 59	19 13	05 28	18 31	05 57	17 42	06 30	16 57	07 03	16 35
3	04 36	19 33	05 00	19 12	05 29	18 29	05 58	17 40	06 31	16 56	07 04	16 35
4	04 36	19 32	05 01	19 11	05 30	18 28	05 59	17 38	06 32	16 55	07 05	16 35
5	04 37	19 32	05 02	19 10	05 31	18 26	06 00	17 37	06 33	16 54	07 06	16 35
6	04 37	19 32	05 03	19 09	05 32	18 24	06 01	17 35	06 34	16 53	07 07	16 35
7	04 38	19 32	05 03	19 08	05 33	18 23	06 02	17 34	06 35	16 52	07 08	16 35
8	04 38	19 31	05 04	19 06	05 34	18 21	06 03	17 32	06 37	16 50	07 09	16 35
9	04 39	19 31	05 05	19 05	05 35	18 19	06 04	17 30	06 38	16 49	07 10	16 35
10	04 40	19 31	05 06	19 04	05 36	18 18	06 05	17 29	06 39	16 49	07 10	16 35
11	04 40	19 30	05 07	19 03	05 37	18 16	06 06	17 27	06 40	16 48	07 11	16 35
12	04 41	19 30	05 08	19 01	05 38	18 15	06 07	17 26	06 41	16 47	07 12	16 35
13	04 42	19 29	05 09	19 00	05 39	18 13	06 08	17 24	06 42	16 46	07 13	16 35
14	04 43	19 29	05 10	18 59	05 39	18 11	06 09	17 23	06 43	16 45	07 14	16 35
15	04 43	19 28	05 11	18 57	05 40	18 10	06 10	17 21	06 45	16 44	07 14	16 36
16	04 44	19 28	05 12	18 56	05 41	18 08	06 11	17 20	06 46	16 43	07 15	16 36
17	04 45	19 27	05 13	18 55	05 42	18 06	06 12	17 18	06 47	16 43	07 16	16 36
18	04 46	19 26	05 14	18 53	05 43	18 05	06 13	17 17	06 48	16 42	07 17	16 37
19	04 47	19 26	05 15	18 52	05 44	18 03	06 14	17 15	06 49	16 41	07 17	16 37
20	04 47	19 25	05 16	18 50	05 45	18 01	06 15	17 14	06 50	16 40	07 18	16 37
21	04 48	19 24	05 17	18 49	05 46	18 00	06 16	17 13	06 51	16 40	07 18	16 38
22	04 49	19 23	05 18	18 48	05 47	17 58	06 17	17 11	06 53	16 39	07 19	16 38
23	04 50	19 23	05 19	18 46	05 48	17 56	06 18	17 10	06 54	16 39	07 19	16 39
24	04 51	19 22	05 20	18 45	05 49	17 55	06 20	17 08	06 55	16 38	07 20	16 39
25	04 52	19 21	05 21	18 43	05 50	17 53	06 21	17 07	06 56	16 38	07 20	16 40
26	04 52	19 20	05 22	18 42	05 51	17 51	06 22	17 06	06 57	16 37	07 20	16 40
27	04 53	19 19	05 23	18 40	05 52	17 50	06 23	17 04	06 58	16 37	07 21	16 41
28	04 54	19 18	05 23	18 39	05 53	17 48	06 24	17 03	06 59	16 36	07 21	16 42
29	04 55	19 17	05 24	18 37	05 54	17 46	06 25	17 02	07 00	16 36	07 21	16 43
30	04 56	19 16	05 25	18 35	05 55	17 45	06 26	17 01	07 01	16 36	07 21	16 43
31	04 57	19 15	05 26	18 34			06 27	16 59			07 22	16 44

40°N 00°E/W. Times are UT - for DST add 1 hour in non-shaded areas

2007 Moonrise and Moonset Time

The times are based on **LAT 40°00'N   LONG 0°00'W** - add 4 min for every degree West and subtract 4 min for every degree East

	JANUARY Rise (h m)	JANUARY Set (h m)	FEBRUARY Rise (h m)	FEBRUARY Set (h m)	MARCH Rise (h m)	MARCH Set (h m)	APRIL Rise (h m)	APRIL Set (h m)	MAY Rise (h m)	MAY Set (h m)	JUNE Rise (h m)	JUNE Set (h m)
1	14 29	05 31	16 32	06 57	15 28	05 31	17 28	05 07	18 21	04 13	20 23	04 19
2	15 26	06 39	17 39	07 28	16 33	05 58	18 27	05 26	19 24	04 36	21 18	05 07
3	16 31	07 36	18 44	07 54	17 35	06 21	19 28	05 46	20 27	05 04	22 05	06 05
4	17 40	08 22	19 46	08 16	18 36	06 41	20 29	06 07	21 30	05 39	22 45	07 10
5	18 48	08 59	20 46	08 36	19 36	07 01	21 32	06 26	22 29	06 21	23 18	08 19
6	19 54	09 28	21 45	08 56	20 35	07 20	22 35	07 02	23 22	07 12	23 46	09 30
7	20 58	09 52	22 45	09 15	21 36	07 40	23 37	07 38	** **	08 11	** **	10 40
8	21 58	10 13	23 46	09 36	22 38	08 02	** **	08 22	00 06	09 17	00 11	11 51
9	22 58	10 33	** **	10 00	23 41	08 29	00 34	09 16	00 44	10 27	00 35	13 02
10	23 57	10 52	00 49	10 28	** **	09 00	01 25	10 18	01 15	11 39	00 59	14 16
11	** **	11 12	01 54	11 02	00 45	09 39	02 08	11 28	01 43	12 51	01 25	15 32
12	00 57	11 34	02 58	11 46	01 46	10 27	02 44	12 40	02 08	14 04	01 56	16 51
13	02 00	12 00	03 59	12 40	02 42	11 26	03 15	13 55	02 33	15 18	02 33	18 10
14	03 04	12 31	04 54	13 45	03 32	12 34	03 42	15 10	02 58	16 35	03 19	19 24
15	04 10	13 10	05 41	14 58	04 13	13 47	04 08	16 26	03 27	17 55	04 16	20 28
16	05 15	13 59	06 20	16 15	04 48	15 04	04 33	17 44	04 00	19 17	05 23	21 20
17	06 15	15 00	06 52	17 33	05 18	16 21	05 01	19 04	04 42	20 35	06 34	22 00
18	07 06	16 10	07 20	18 50	05 44	17 38	05 32	20 26	05 34	21 46	07 46	22 32
19	07 50	17 25	07 46	20 07	06 10	18 56	06 09	21 47	06 36	22 44	08 55	22 58
20	08 25	18 42	08 11	21 23	06 36	20 15	06 55	23 01	07 45	23 29	10 00	23 20
21	08 54	19 57	08 37	22 40	07 05	21 35	07 51	** **	08 56	** **	11 03	23 40
22	09 20	21 12	09 06	23 56	07 38	22 55	08 54	00 04	10 05	00 05	12 03	** **
23	09 45	22 25	09 40	** **	08 17	** **	10 03	00 55	11 11	00 33	13 02	00 00
24	10 09	23 38	10 22	01 12	09 06	00 10	11 11	01 34	12 13	00 57	14 02	00 20
25	10 35	** **	11 12	02 22	10 03	01 17	12 18	02 05	13 14	01 17	15 04	00 42
26	11 05	00 53	12 10	03 25	11 07	02 14	13 21	02 31	14 13	01 37	16 07	01 07
27	11 40	02 07	13 15	04 16	12 14	02 58	14 22	02 53	15 12	01 56	17 11	01 38
28	12 24	03 21	14 22	04 58	13 21	03 34	15 21	03 13	16 13	02 17	18 13	02 15
29	13 16	04 29			14 26	04 02	16 20	03 32	17 15	02 40	19 11	03 00
30	14 17	05 28			15 28	04 26	17 20	03 51	18 18	03 07	20 02	03 56
31	15 24	06 18			16 29	04 47			19 22	03 39		

	JULY Rise (h m)	JULY Set (h m)	AUGUST Rise (h m)	AUGUST Set (h m)	SEPTEMBER Rise (h m)	SEPTEMBER Set (h m)	OCTOBER Rise (h m)	OCTOBER Set (h m)	NOVEMBER Rise (h m)	NOVEMBER Set (h m)	DECEMBER Rise (h m)	DECEMBER Set (h m)
1	20 44	05 00	20 43	07 31	20 32	10 12	20 41	11 46	22 59	13 05	** **	12 26
2	21 20	06 09	21 07	08 44	21 08	11 30	21 42	12 52	** **	13 36	00 04	12 47
3	21 49	07 21	21 32	09 56	21 53	12 46	22 50	13 47	00 07	14 01	01 05	13 07
4	22 15	08 32	21 59	11 10	22 47	13 57	23 59	14 30	01 11	14 23	02 05	13 28
5	22 39	09 43	22 30	12 25	23 49	14 59	** **	15 05	02 12	14 43	03 06	13 50
6	23 03	10 54	23 08	13 41	** **	15 49	01 08	15 32	03 13	15 03	04 06	14 15
7	23 28	12 05	23 55	14 55	00 58	16 29	02 14	15 56	04 12	15 23	05 08	14 44
8	23 56	13 19	** **	16 04	02 08	17 01	03 17	16 17	05 13	15 46	06 10	15 20
9	** **	14 35	00 52	17 03	03 16	17 28	04 19	16 37	06 14	16 12	07 11	16 02
10	00 29	15 52	01 58	17 50	04 22	17 51	05 19	16 57	07 16	16 43	08 07	16 54
11	01 11	17 06	03 08	18 28	05 25	18 11	06 19	17 18	08 18	17 20	08 57	17 52
12	02 02	18 13	04 19	18 59	06 27	18 31	07 20	17 41	09 17	18 05	09 39	18 56
13	03 04	19 10	05 28	19 24	07 28	18 51	08 22	18 09	10 11	18 58	10 15	20 03
14	04 13	19 54	06 34	19 46	08 28	19 13	09 24	18 41	10 59	19 58	10 45	21 10
15	05 25	20 30	07 37	20 07	09 30	19 38	10 26	19 20	11 39	21 03	11 11	22 18
16	06 36	20 58	08 38	20 27	10 32	20 06	11 24	20 08	12 13	22 10	11 35	23 26
17	07 44	21 22	09 39	20 47	11 34	20 41	12 16	21 03	12 42	23 18	11 58	** **
18	08 48	21 43	10 39	21 10	12 35	21 23	13 02	22 06	13 08	** **	12 22	00 35
19	09 50	22 03	11 41	21 36	13 32	22 14	13 40	23 13	13 32	00 28	12 49	01 47
20	10 51	22 23	12 44	22 06	14 23	23 14	14 13	** **	13 56	01 38	13 20	03 03
21	11 51	22 44	13 46	22 44	15 07	** **	14 42	00 23	14 22	02 51	13 59	04 21
22	12 52	23 08	14 47	23 31	15 44	00 21	15 08	01 35	14 52	04 08	14 49	05 41
23	13 54	23 36	15 43	** **	16 16	01 32	15 33	02 47	15 28	05 28	15 50	06 55
24	14 57	** **	16 32	00 27	16 44	02 45	15 58	04 02	16 13	06 51	17 01	07 59
25	16 00	00 10	17 14	01 32	17 09	04 00	16 26	05 19	17 09	08 10	18 17	08 50
26	17 00	00 52	17 49	02 43	17 35	05 15	16 59	06 40	18 16	09 20	19 32	09 30
27	17 54	01 43	18 19	03 57	18 01	06 31	17 39	08 02	19 29	10 17	20 43	10 01
28	18 40	02 44	18 45	05 11	18 31	07 50	18 29	09 23	20 43	11 01	21 50	10 27
29	19 19	03 53	19 10	06 25	19 06	09 10	19 29	10 37	21 54	11 35	22 54	10 50
30	19 51	05 05	19 35	07 40	19 48	10 30	20 37	11 38	23 01	12 03	23 55	11 11
31	20 18	06 18	20 02	08 55			21 49	12 27			** **	11 31

SPEED, TIME AND DISTANCE (NAUTICAL MILES)

Speed in knots

Time in minutes	1	2	3	4	5	6	7	8	9	10	15	20
1	0·0	0·0	0·1	0·1	0·1	0·1	0·1	0·1	0·2	0·2	0·3	0·3
2	0·0	0·1	0·1	0·1	0·2	0·2	0·2	0·3	0·3	0·3	0·5	0·7
3	0·1	0·1	0·2	0·2	0·3	0·3	0·4	0·4	0·5	0·5	0·8	1·0
4	0·1	0·1	0·2	0·3	0·3	0·4	0·5	0·5	0·6	0·7	1·0	1·3
5	0·1	0·2	0·3	0·3	0·4	0·5	0·6	0·7	0·8	0·8	1·3	1·7
6	0·1	0·2	0·3	0·4	0·5	0·6	0·7	0·8	0·9	1·0	1·5	2·0
7	0·1	0·2	0·4	0·5	0·6	0·7	0·8	0·9	1·1	1·2	1·8	2·3
8	0·1	0·3	0·4	0·5	0·7	0·8	0·9	1·1	1·2	1·3	2·0	2·7
9	0·2	0·3	0·5	0·6	0·8	0·9	1·1	1·2	1·4	1·5	2·3	3·0
10	0·2	0·3	0·5	0·7	0·8	1·0	1·2	1·3	1·5	1·7	2·5	3·3
11	0·2	0·4	0·6	0·7	0·9	1·1	1·3	1·5	1·7	1·8	2·8	3·7
12	0·2	0·4	0·6	0·8	1·0	1·2	1·4	1·6	1·8	2·0	3·0	4·0
13	0·2	0·4	0·7	0·9	1·1	1·3	1·5	1·7	2·0	2·2	3·3	4·3
14	0·2	0·5	0·7	0·9	1·2	1·4	1·6	1·9	2·1	2·3	3·5	4·7
15	0·3	0·5	0·8	1·0	1·3	1·5	1·8	2·0	2·3	2·5	3·8	5·0
16	0·3	0·5	0·8	1·1	1·3	1·6	1·9	2·1	2·4	2·7	4·0	5·3
17	0·3	0·6	0·9	1·1	1·4	1·7	2·0	2·3	2·6	2·8	4·3	5·7
18	0·3	0·6	0·9	1·2	1·5	1·8	2·1	2·4	2·7	3·0	4·5	6·0
19	0·3	0·6	1·0	1·3	1·6	1·9	2·2	2·5	2·9	3·2	4·8	6·3
20	0·3	0·7	1·0	1·3	1·7	2·0	2·3	2·7	3·0	3·3	5·0	6·7
21	0·4	0·7	1·1	1·4	1·8	2·1	2·5	2·8	3·2	3·5	5·3	7·0
22	0·4	0·7	1·1	1·5	1·8	2·2	2·6	2·9	3·3	3·7	5·5	7·3
23	0·4	0·8	1·2	1·5	1·9	2·3	2·7	3·1	3·5	3·8	5·8	7·7
24	0·4	0·8	1·2	1·6	2·0	2·4	2·8	3·2	3·6	4·0	6·0	8·0
25	0·4	0·8	1·3	1·7	2·1	2·5	2·9	3·3	3·8	4·2	6·3	8·3
30	0·5	1·0	1·5	2·0	2·5	3·0	3·5	4·0	4·5	5·0	7·5	10·0
35	0·6	1·2	1·8	2·3	2·9	3·5	4·1	4·7	5·3	5·8	8·8	11·7
40	0·7	1·3	2·0	2·7	3·3	4·0	4·7	5·3	6·0	6·7	10·0	13·3
45	0·8	1·5	2·3	3·0	3·8	4·5	5·3	6·0	6·8	7·5	11·3	15·0
50	0·8	1·7	2·5	3·3	4·2	5·0	5·8	6·7	7·5	8·3	12·5	16·7

DISTANCE (NAUTICAL MILES) OFF RISING/DIPPING LIGHTS

Height of light in metres	Height of eye in feet												
	2	3	4	5	6	7	8	9	10	20	30	40	50
2	4·6	4·9	5·2	5·5	5·7	6·0	6·2	6·4	6·6	8·1	9·2	10·2	11·0
3	5·2	5·6	5·9	6·2	6·4	6·6	6·8	7·0	7·2	8·7	9·9	10·8	11·7
4	5·8	6·1	6·4	6·7	6·9	7·2	7·4	7·6	7·8	9·3	10·4	11·4	12·2
5	6·3	6·6	6·9	7·2	7·4	7·7	7·9	8·1	8·3	9·8	10·9	11·9	12·7
6	6·7	7·1	7·4	7·6	7·9	8·1	8·3	8·5	8·7	10·2	11·3	12·3	13·2
7	7·1	7·5	7·8	8·0	8·3	8·5	8·7	8·9	9·1	10·6	11·8	12·7	13·6
8	7·5	7·8	8·2	8·4	8·7	8·9	9·1	9·3	9·5	11·0	12·1	13·1	14·0
9	7·8	8·2	8·5	8·8	9·0	9·2	9·5	9·7	9·8	11·3	12·5	13·5	14·3
10	8·2	8·5	8·8	9·1	9·4	9·6	9·8	10·0	10·2	11·7	12·8	13·8	14·6
11	8·5	8·9	9·2	9·4	9·7	9·9	10·1	10·3	10·5	12·0	13·1	14·1	15·0
12	8·8	9·2	9·5	9·7	10·0	10·2	10·4	10·6	10·8	12·3	13·4	14·4	15·3
13	9·1	9·5	9·8	10·0	10·3	10·5	10·7	10·9	11·1	12·6	13·7	14·7	15·6
14	9·4	9·7	10·0	10·3	10·6	10·8	11·0	11·2	11·4	12·9	14·0	15·0	15·8
15	9·6	10·0	10·3	10·6	10·8	11·1	11·3	11·5	11·6	13·1	14·3	15·3	16·1
16	9·9	10·3	10·6	10·8	11·1	11·3	11·5	11·7	11·9	13·4	14·6	15·5	16·4
17	10·2	10·5	10·8	11·1	11·3	11·6	11·8	12·0	12·2	13·7	14·8	15·8	16·6
18	10·4	10·8	11·1	11·4	11·6	11·8	12·0	12·2	12·4	13·9	15·1	16·0	16·9
19	10·7	11·0	11·3	11·6	11·8	12·1	12·3	12·5	12·7	14·2	15·3	16·3	17·1
20	10·9	11·3	11·6	11·8	12·1	12·3	12·5	12·7	12·9	14·4	15·5	16·5	17·3
25	12·0	12·3	12·6	12·9	13·2	13·4	13·6	13·8	14·0	15·5	16·6	17·6	18·4
30	13·0	13·3	13·6	13·9	14·1	14·4	14·6	14·8	15·0	16·5	17·6	18·6	19·4
40	14·7	15·1	15·4	15·7	15·9	16·1	16·3	16·5	16·7	18·2	19·4	20·3	21·2
50	16·3	16·6	16·9	17·2	17·4	17·7	17·9	18·1	18·3	19·8	20·9	21·9	22·7
60	17·7	18·0	18·3	18·6	18·8	19·1	19·3	19·5	19·7	21·2	22·3	23·3	24·1

CONVERSION TABLE

Sq inches to sq millimetres *multiply by* **645.20**	**Sq millimetres to sq inches** *multiply by* **0.0016**
Inches to millimetres *multiply by* **25.40**	**Millimetres to inches** *multiply by* **0.0394**
Sq feet to square metres *multiply by* **0.093**	**Sq metres to sq feet** *multiply by* **10.7640**
Inches to centimetres *multiply by* **2.54**	**Centimetres to inches** *multiply by* **0.3937**
Feet to metres *multiply by* **0.305**	**Metres to feet** *multiply by* **3.2810**
Nautical miles to kilometres *multiply by* **1.852**	**Kilometres to nautical miles** *multiply by* **0.5400**
Statute miles to kilometres *multiply by* **1.609**	**Kilometres to statute miles** *multiply by* **0.6214**
Statute miles to nautical miles *multiply by* **0.8684**	**Nautical miles to statute miles** *multiply by* **1.1515**
HP to metric HP *multiply by* **1.014**	**Metric HP to HP** *multiply by* **0.9862**
Pounds per sq inch to kg per sq centimetre *multiply by* **0.0703**	**Kg per sq centimetre to pounds per sq inch** *multiply by* **14.2200**
HP to kilowatts *multiply by* **0.746**	**Kilowatts to HP** *multiply by* **1.341**
Cu inches to cu centimetres *multiply by* **16.39**	**Cu centimetres to cu inches** *multiply by* **0.0610**
Imperial gallons to litres *multiply by* **4.540**	**Litres to imperial gallons** *multiply by* **0.2200**
Pints to litres *multiply by* **0.5680**	**Litres to pints** *multiply by* **1.7600**
Pounds to kilogrammes *multiply by* **0.4536**	**Kilogrammes to pounds** *multiply by* **2.2050**

LIGHT CHARACTERISTICS

CLASS OF LIGHT	International abbreviations	National abbreviations	Illustration Period shown ⊢————⊣
FIXED	F		
OCCULTING *(total duration of light longer than dark)*			
Single-occulting	Oc	Occ	
Group-occulting	eg Oc(2)	Gp Occ(2)	
Composite group-occulting	eg Oc(2+3)	Gp Occ(2+3)	
ISOPHASE *(light and dark equal)*	Iso		
FLASHING *(total duration of light shorter than dark)*			
Single-flashing	Fl		
Long-flashing *(flash 2s or longer)*		L Fl	
Group-flashing	eg Fl(3)	Gp Fl(3)	
Composite group-flashing	eg Fl(2+1)	Gp Fl(2+1)	
QUICK *(50 to 79, usually either 50 or 60, flashes per min.)*			
Continuous quick	Q	Qk Fl	
Group quick	eg Q(3)	Qk Fl(3)	
Interrupted quick	IQ	Int Qk Fl	
VERY QUICK *(80 to 159, usually either 100 or 120, flashes per min.)*			
Continuous very quick	VQ	V Qk Fl	
Group very quick	eg VQ(3)	V Qk Fl(3)	
Interrupted very quick	IVQ	Int V Qk Fl	
ULTRA QUICK *(160 or more, usually 240 to 300, flashes per min.)*			
Continuous ultra quick	UQ		
Interrupted ultra quick	IUQ		
MORSE CODE	eg Mo(K)		
FIXED AND FLASHING	F Fl		
ALTERNATING	eg Al. WR	Alt. WR	

COLOUR	International abbreviations	NOMINAL RANGE in miles	International abbreviations
White	W *(may be omitted)*	Light with single range	eg 15M
Red	R	Light with two different ranges	eg 15/10M
Green	G	Light with three or more ranges	eg 15-7M
Blue	Bu		
Violet	Vi	**PERIOD** is given in seconds	eg 90s
Yellow	Y	**DISPOSITION** horizontally disposed	(hor)
Orange	Y		
Amber	Y	**ELEVATION** is given in metres (m) or feet (ft) above MHWS	

CHAPTER 2 - WEATHER

CONTENTS

Beaufort scale & Met terminology 75

Map of UK shipping forecast areas 76

Shipping forecast record 77

Weather sources in the UK
  BBC Radio 4 broadcasts 78
  Navtex 79
  Telephone recordings, including European weather 81
  Fax messages, including European weather 82
  Mobile phones 83
  Other sources 84
  Broadcasts by HM Coastguard 84

Weather sources abroad
  Channel Islands 87
  Ireland 88
  Denmark 89
  Germany 90
  Netherlands 91
  Belgium 92
  France 92
  North and North West Spain 96
  Portugal & the Azores 96
  South West Spain 96
  Gibraltar 98

Five language weather vocabulary 98

Beaufort scale

Force	Wind speed (knots)	(km/h)	(m/sec)	Description	State of sea	Probable wave ht(m)
0	0–1	0–2	0–0·5	Calm	Like a mirror	0
1	1–3	2–6	0·5–1·5	Light airs	Ripples like scales are formed	0
2	4–6	7–11	2–3	Light breeze	Small wavelets, still short but more pronounced, not breaking	0·1
3	7–10	13–19	4–5	Gentle breeze	Large wavelets, crests begin to break; a few white horses	0·4
4	11–16	20–30	6–8	Moderate breeze	Small waves growing longer; fairly frequent white horses	1
5	17–21	31–39	8–11	Fresh breeze	Moderate waves, taking more pronounced form; many white horses, perhaps some spray	2
6	22–27	41–50	11–14	Strong breeze	Large waves forming; white foam crests more extensive; probably some spray	3
7	28–33	52–61	14–17	Near gale	Sea heaps up; white foam from breaking waves begins to blow in streaks	4
8	34–40	63–74	17–21	Gale	Moderately high waves of greater length; edge of crests break into spindrift; foam blown in well-marked streaks	5·5

Terminology used in forecasts
Pressure systems' speed of movement

Slowly	< 15 knots
Steadily	15–25 knots
Rather quickly	25–35 knots
Rapidly	35–45 knots
Very rapidly	> 45 knots

Visibility

Good	> 5 miles
Moderate	2–5 miles
Poor	1000 metres–2 miles
Fog	< 1000 metres

Barometric pressure tendency

Rising/falling slowly: Change of 0·1 to 1·5 hPa/mb in the preceding 3 hours.
Rising/falling: Change of 1·6 to 3·5 hPa/mb in the preceding 3 hours.
Rising/falling quickly: Change of 3·6 to 6 hPa/mb in the preceding 3 hours.
Rising/falling very rapidly: Change of > 6 hPa/mb in the preceding 3 hours.
Now rising/falling: Pressure has been falling (rising) or steady in the preceding 3 hours, but was definitely rising (falling) at the time of observation.

Gale warnings

A *Gale* warning means that winds of at least F8 (34-40kn) or gusts up to 43-51kn are expected somewhere within the area, but not necessarily over the whole area

Severe Gale means winds of at least F9 (41-47kn) or gusts reaching 52-60kn

Storm means winds of F10 (48-55kn) or gusts of 61-68kn

Violent Storm means winds of F11 (56-63kn) or gusts of 69+ kn

Hurricane Force means winds of F12 (64+ kn)

Gale warnings remain in force until amended or cancelled. If a gale persists for >24 hours the warning is re-issued.

Timing of gale warnings from time of issue

Imminent	<6 hrs
Soon	6–12 hrs
Later	>12 hrs

Strong wind warnings

Issued, if possible 6 hrs in advance, when winds F6 or more are expected up to 5M offshore; valid for 12 hrs.

MAP OF UK SHIPPING FORECAST AREAS

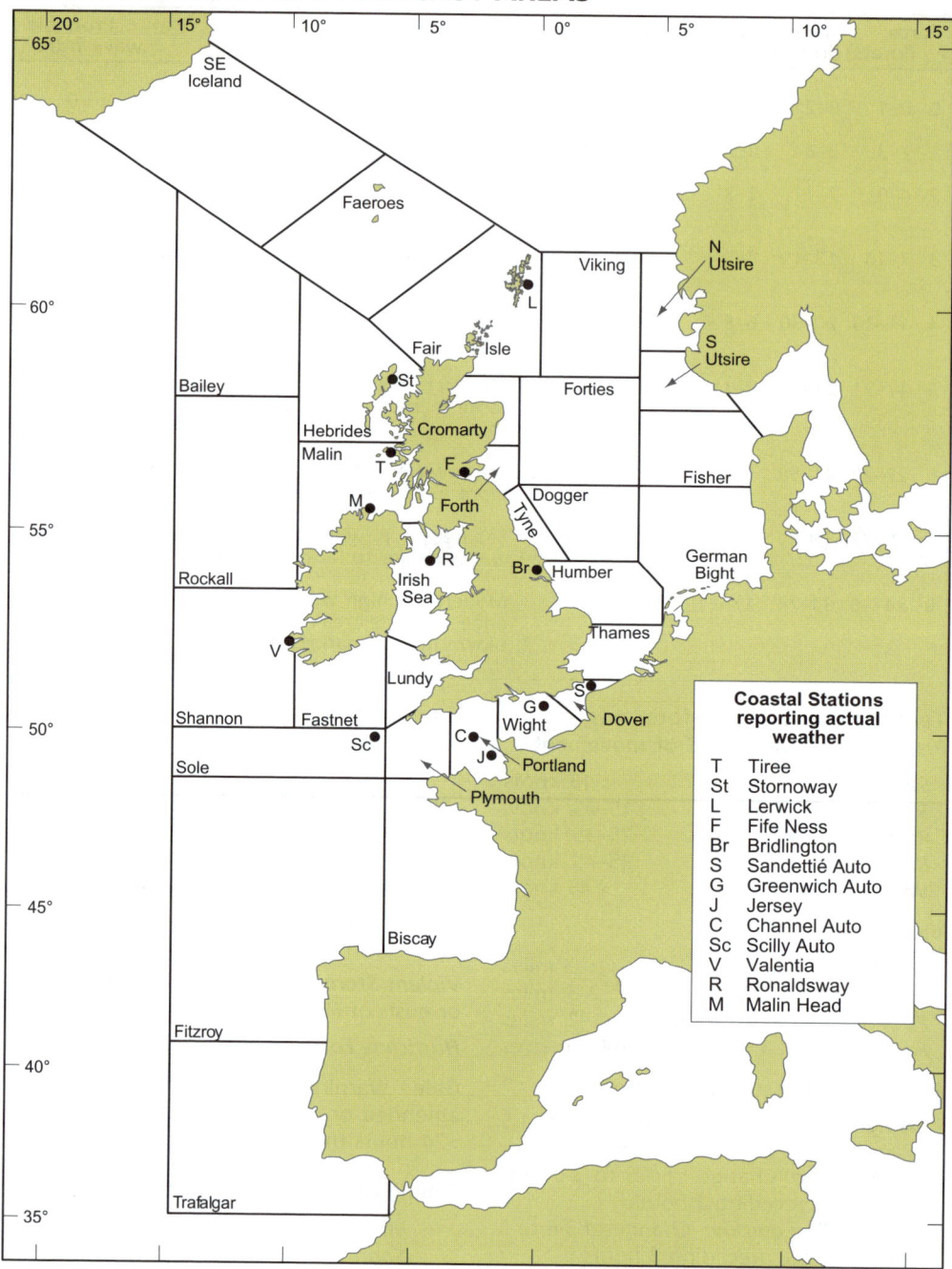

Coastal Stations reporting actual weather

T	Tiree
St	Stornoway
L	Lerwick
F	Fife Ness
Br	Bridlington
S	Sandettié Auto
G	Greenwich Auto
J	Jersey
C	Channel Auto
Sc	Scilly Auto
V	Valentia
R	Ronaldsway
M	Malin Head

SHIPPING FORECAST RECORD Time/Day/Date ....

GENERAL SYNOPSIS

at .... UT/BST

System position	Present position at	Movement	Forecast	

Gales	SEA AREA FORECAST	Wind		Weather	Visibility
		(At first)	(Later)		
	VIKING				
	NORTH UTSIRE				
	SOUTH UTSIRE				
	FORTIES				
	CROMARTY				
	FORTH				
	TYNE				
	DOGGER				
	FISHER				
	GERMAN BIGHT				
	HUMBER				
	THAMES				
	DOVER				
	WIGHT				
	PORTLAND				
	PLYMOUTH				
	BISCAY				
	FITZROY				
	TRAFALGAR				
	SOLE				
	LUNDY				
	FASTNET				
	IRISH SEA				
	SHANNON				
	ROCKALL				
	MALIN				
	HEBRIDES				
	BAILEY				
	FAIR ISLE				
	FAEROES				
	S E ICELAND				

COASTAL REPORTS BST at .... UTC	Wind Direction	Force	Weather	Visibility	Pressure	Change	COASTAL REPORTS	Wind Direction	Force	Weather	Visibility	Pressure	Change
Tiree (T)							Greenwich Lt V (G)						
Stornoway (St)							Jersey (J)						
Lerwick (L)							Channel auto (C)						
Fife Ness (F)							Scilly auto (Sc)						
Bridlington (Br)							Valentia (V)						
Sandettie auto (S)							Ronaldsway (R)						

WEATHER

SOURCES OF WEATHER INFORMATION IN THE UK

BBC Radio 4 Shipping forecasts
are broadcast at:

0048 LT[1]	LW, MW, FM
0520 LT[1]	LW, MW, FM
1201 LT	LW only
1754 LT	LW, FM (Sat/Sun)

[1] Includes weather reports from coastal stations

Frequencies

LW		198 kHz
MW	Tyneside	603 kHz
	London & N Ireland	720 kHz
	Redruth	756 kHz
	Plymouth & Enniskillen	774 kHz
	Aberdeen	1449 kHz
	Carlisle	1485 kHz
FM	England	92·4–94·6 MHz
	Scotland	91·3–96·1 MHz
		103·5–104·9 MHz
	Wales	92·8–96·1 MHz
		103·5–104·9 MHz
	N Ireland	93·2–96·0 MHz
		103·5–104·6 MHz
	Channel Islands	94·8 MHz

The Shipping forecast contains:

A summary of gale warnings in force at time of issue; a general synopsis of weather systems and their expected development over the next 24 hours; and a forecast of wind direction/force, weather and visibility in each sea area for the next 24 hours.

Gale warnings are also broadcast at the earliest juncture in Radio 4 programmes after receipt, as well as after the next news bulletin. Sea area **Trafalgar** is only included in the 0048 forecast.

Shipping forecasts cover large sea areas, and rarely include the detailed variations that may occur near land. The Inshore waters forecast can be more helpful to mariners on coastal passages.

Weather reports from coastal stations follow the 0048 and 0520 forecasts. They include wind direction and force, present weather, visibility, and sea-level pressure and tendency, if available. The stations are shown overleaf on the previous page.

BBC Radio 4 Inshore waters forecast

A forecast for inshore waters (up to 12M offshore) around the UK and N Ireland, valid until 1800, is broadcast after the 0048 and 0520 coastal station reports. It includes a general synopsis, forecasts of wind direction and force, visibility and weather for stretches of inshore waters. These are defined by well-known places and headlands from Cape Wrath clockwise via Orkney, Shetland, Rattray Hd, Berwick-upon-Tweed, Whitby, The Wash, North Foreland, Selsey Bill, St Catherine's Point, Land's End, Hartland Pt, Colwyn Bay, Mull of Galloway, Mull of Kintyre, Carlingford Lough, Lough Foyle and Ardnamurchan Pt.

Strong wind warnings are issued by the Met Office whenever winds of Force 6 or more are expected over coastal waters up to 5M offshore.

Reports of actual weather at the stations below are broadcast only after the 0048 Inshore waters forecast: Boulmer, *Bridlington*, Sheerness, St Catherine's Pt*, *Scilly**, Milford Haven, Aberporth, Valley, Liverpool/Crosby, *Ronaldsway*, Larne, Machrihanish*, Greenock, *Stornoway*, *Lerwick*, Wick*, Aberdeen and Leuchars. Asterisk* denotes an automatic station. Stations in italics also feature in the 0048 and 0520 shipping forecasts.

BBC general (land) forecasts

Land area forecasts may include an outlook period up to 48 hours beyond the shipping forecast, plus more details of frontal systems and weather along the coasts. The most comprehensive land area forecasts are broadcast by BBC Radio 4 on the frequencies above.

Land area forecasts – Wind strength

Wind descriptions used in land forecasts, with their Beaufort scale equivalents, are:

Calm	0	Fresh	5
Light	1–3	Strong	6–7
Moderate	4	Gale	8

Land area forecasts – Visibility

The following visibility definitions are used in land forecasts:

Mist	2000m–1000m
Fog	<1000m
Dense fog	< 50m

NAVTEX

Navtex uses a dedicated aerial, receiver and integral printer or LCD screen. The user programmes the receiver for the required station(s) and message categories. It automatically prints or displays MSI, ie weather, navigational and safety data.

Two frequencies are used: 518 kHz and *490 kHz*. 518 kHz messages are in English (occasionally in the national language as well), with excellent coverage of Europe. Interference between stations is avoided by time sharing and by limiting the range of transmitters to about 300M; see Fig. 5(4). Navtex information applies only to the geographic area for which each station is responsible.

490 kHz (for clarity shown in italics throughout this chapter) is used abroad for transmissions in the national language. In the UK it is used for inshore waters forecasts in English. Identification letters for 490 kHz stations differ from 518 kHz stations.

Weather information accounts for about 75% of all messages and Navtex is particularly valuable when out of range of other sources, otherwise occupied or if there is a language problem.

Messages

Each message is prefixed by a four-character group:

The first character is the code letter of the transmitting station (eg **E** for Niton).

The second character is the message category, see below.

The third and fourth are message serial numbers, running from 01 to 99 and then re-starting at 01.

The serial number 00 denotes urgent messages which are always printed.

Messages which are corrupt or have already been printed are rejected.

Weather messages, and certain other message types, are dated and timed.

Message categories

A*	Navigational warnings
B*	Meteorological warnings
C	Ice reports
D*	SAR info and piracy warnings
E	Weather forecasts
F	Pilot service
H	Loran-C
J	Satellite navigation
K	Other electronic navaids
L	Subfacts and Gunfacts (UK)
V	Amplifies Navwarnings initially sent under A; plus weekly oil/gas rig moves.
W-Y	Special service, trials
Z	No messages on hand at scheduled time

Missing category letters are unallocated.

*The receiver cannot reject these categories.

WEATHER

Navtex stations/areas – UK & W Europe

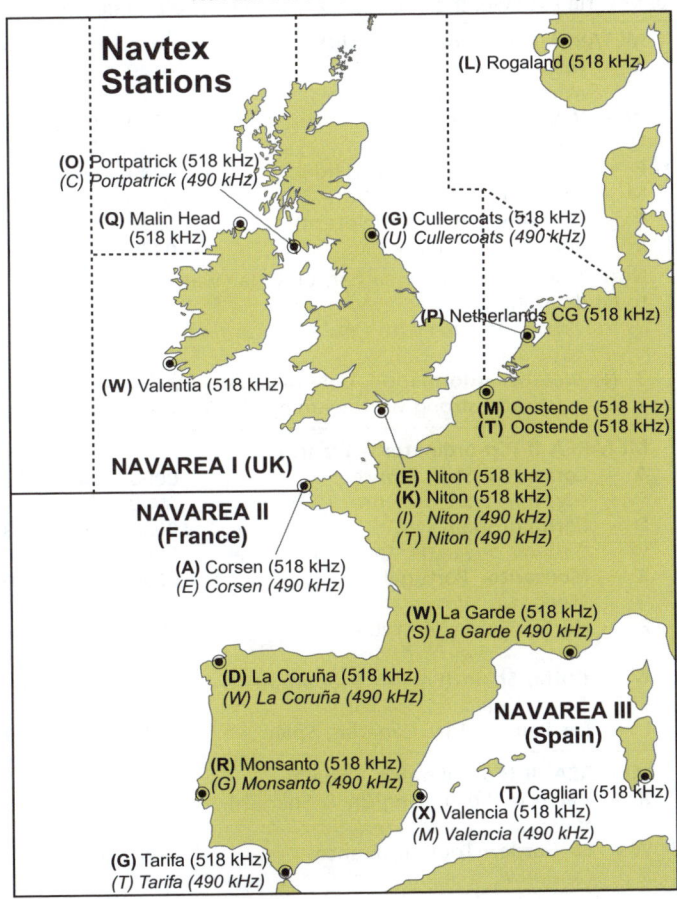

Navtex Stations

(L) Rogaland (518 kHz)

(O) Portpatrick (518 kHz)
(C) Portpatrick (490 kHz)

(Q) Malin Head (518 kHz)

(G) Cullercoats (518 kHz)
(U) Cullercoats (490 kHz)

(P) Netherlands CG (518 kHz)

(W) Valentia (518 kHz)

(M) Oostende (518 kHz)
(T) Oostende (518 kHz)

NAVAREA I (UK)

(E) Niton (518 kHz)
(K) Niton (518 kHz)
(I) Niton (490 kHz)
(T) Niton (490 kHz)

NAVAREA II (France)

(A) Corsen (518 kHz)
(E) Corsen (490 kHz)

(W) La Garde (518 kHz)
(S) La Garde (490 kHz)

(D) La Coruña (518 kHz)
(W) La Coruña (490 kHz)

NAVAREA III (Spain)

(R) Monsanto (518 kHz)
(G) Monsanto (490 kHz)

(T) Cagliari (518 kHz)
(X) Valencia (518 kHz)
(M) Valencia (490 kHz)

(G) Tarifa (518 kHz)
(T) Tarifa (490 kHz)

UK 518 kHz stations

The times (UT) of weather messages are in bold; the times of an extended outlook (a further 2 or 3 days beyond the shipping forecast period) are in italics. The Sea Areas covered follow the sequence on page 70.

G –	**Cullercoats**	*0100*	0500	**0900**	1300	1700	**2100**
	Fair Isle clockwise to Thames, excluding N & S Utsire, Fisher and German Bight.						
O –	**Portpatrick**	*0220*	**0620**	1020	1420	**1820**	2220
	Lundy clockwise to SE Iceland.						
E –	**Niton**	*0040*	0440	**0840**	1240	1640	**2040**
	Thames clockwise to Fastnet, excluding Trafalgar.						

UK 490 kHz stations

These provide forecasts for the Inshore waters (12M offshore) of the UK, including Shetland, plus a national 3 day outlook for inshore waters. Times are UT.

U –	*Cullercoats*	*Cape Wrath to North Foreland*	*0720*	*1920*	
C –	*Portpatrick*	*St David's Head to Cape Wrath*	*0820*	*2020*	
I –	*Niton*	*The Wash to Colwyn Bay*	*0520*	*1720*	

Navtex coverage abroad

Selected Navtex stations in Metareas I to III, with identity codes and transmission times, are listed below. Times of weather messages are shown in **bold**. Gale warnings are usually transmitted 4 hourly.

METAREA I (Co-ordinator – UK)	Transmission times (UT)					
K – **Niton** (Note 1)	0140	0540	0940	1340	1740	2140
T – Niton (Note 2)	*0310*	*0710*	*1110*	*1510*	*1910*	*2310*
W – **Valentia**, Eire	0340	**0740**	**1140**	1540	**1940**	2340
Q – **Malin Head**, Eire	0240	**0640**	**1040**	1440	**1840**	2240
P – **Netherlands CG**, Den Helder	**0230**	0630	1030	**1430**	1830	2230
M – **Oostende**, Belgium (Note 3)	**0200**	0600	1000	1400	1800	2200
T – **Oostende**, Belgium (Note 4)	**0310**	**0710**	1110	1510	**1910**	2310
L – **Rogaland**, Norway	**0150**	0550	0950	**1350**	1750	2150

Note 1 In English, no weather; only Nav warnings for the French coast from Cap Gris Nez to Île de Bréhat.
2 In French, weather info (and Nav warnings) for sea areas Humber to Ouessant (Plymouth).
3 No weather information, only Nav warnings for NavArea Juliett.
4 Forecasts and strong wind warnings for Thames and Dover, plus Nav info for Belgium.

METAREA II (Co-ordinator – France)						
A – **Corsen**, Le Stiff, France	**0000**	0400	0800	**1200**	1600	2000
E – Corsen, Le Stiff, France (In French)	*0040*	*0440*	*0840*	*1240*	*1640*	*2040*
D – **Coruña**, Spain	0030	0430	**0830**	1230	1630	**2030**
W – Coruña, Spain (in Spanish)	*0340*	*0740*	*1140*	*1540*	*1940*	*2340*
R – **Monsanto**, Portugal	**0250**	**0650**	**1050**	**1450**	**1850**	**2250**
G – Monsanto, Portugal (In Portuguese)	*0100*	*0500*	*0900*	*1300*	*1700*	*2100*
F – **Horta**, Açores, Portugal	**0050**	**0450**	**0850**	**1250**	**1650**	**2050**
J – Horta, Açores, (In Portuguese)	*0130*	*0530*	*0930*	*1330*	*1730*	*2130*
G – **Tarifa**, Spain (English & Spanish)	0100	0500	**0900**	1300	1700	**2100**
T – Tarifa, Spain (in Spanish)	*0310*	*0710*	*1110*	*1510*	*1910*	*2310*
I – **Las Palmas**, Islas Canarias, Spain	0120	0520	**0920**	1320	**1720**	2120

METAREA III (Co-ordinator – Spain)						
X – **Valencia**, Spain (English & Spanish)	0350	**0750**	1150	1550	**1950**	2350
M – Valencia, Spain (in Spanish)	*0200*	*0600*	*1000*	*1400*	*1800*	*2200*
W – **La Garde**, (Toulon), France	0340	0740	**1140**	1540	1940	**2340**
S – La Garde, (Toulon), France (In French)	*0300*	*0700*	*1100*	*1500*	*1900*	*2300*

WEATHER BY TELEPHONE

Marinecall offers 3 types of recorded forecasts as shown below. You can use Marinecall from any landline or mobile network within the UK (inc Channel Islands).

Actual weather

Current weather, updated hourly, gives hourly summaries for next 6 hours at over 160 locations around the UK. Dial **09068 969** + the required area number below.

5-day forecasts for Inshore waters

For UK inshore areas, call **09068 969** + **the Area number** shown below. For an inshore waters forecast covering the whole UK for 3 to 5 days ahead, dial **09068 969 640**.

Forecasts cover the waters out to 12M offshore for up to 5 days and include: General situation, strong wind or gale warnings in force, wind, weather, visibility, sea state, max air temp and mean sea temp.

The local inshore forecast for Shetland is only available from Shetland CG ☎ 01595 692976. 09068 calls cost 60p/min from a landline.

Offshore planning forecasts

For 2 to 5-day planning forecasts for offshore areas, updated by 0700, call **09068 969** + the number for the offshore area:

657 English Channel. **658** S North Sea. **659** Irish Sea. **660** Biscay. **661** NW Scotland **662** Northern North Sea

For further information contact:

Marinecall Customer Services, Avalon House, 57-63 Scrutton St, London EC2A 4PF. ☎ 0871 200 3985; 🖷 0870 600 4229. www.marinecall.co.uk marinecall@itouch.co.uk

European weather by phone and fax

Marinecall offers forecasts, updated 2x daily, of wind, cloud, temperature, visibility and general conditions for the European areas below.

For recorded bulletins call 09064 700 plus the 3 digit suffix below. Calls cost 60p/min.

For fax call 09065 501 and the 3 digit suffix. Calls cost £1.00/min.

NE France
☎ 421, 🖷 611
N France
☎ 422, 🖷 612
N Brittany
☎ 423, 🖷 613
S Brittany
☎ 424, 🖷 614
S Biscay
☎ 425, 🖷 615
N & W Spain
☎ 426, 🖷 616
SW Spain
☎ 427, 🖷 617
Portugal
☎ 428, 🖷 618

Telephone recordings
☎ 09068 969 + Area No

661

654 Ardnamurchan Point to Cape Wrath
641 Cape Wrath to Rattray Head
662
642 Rattray Head to Berwick-upon-Tweed
653 Mull of Kintyre to Ardnamurchan Point
652 Mull of Galloway to the Mull of Kintyre
643 Berwick-upon-Tweed to Whitby
655 Loch Foyle to Carlingford Lough
658
659
651 Colwyn Bay to the Mull of Galloway
644 Whitby to the Wash
645 The Wash to North Foreland
650 St Davids Head to Colwyn Bay
640 National Inshore Waters
649 Hartland Point St Davids Head
646 North Foreland to Selsey Bill
648 Lyme Regis to Hartland Point
647 Selsey Bill to Lyme Regis
660
656 Channel Islands
657

Inshore & offshore forecast areas by telephone

WEATHER

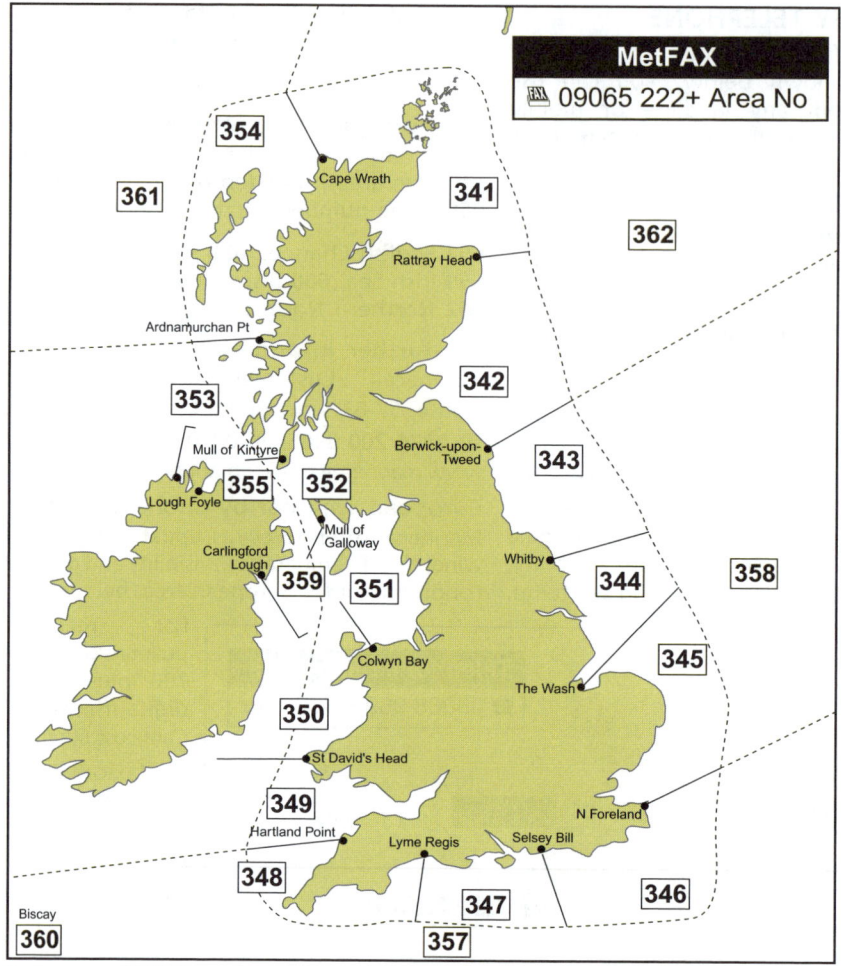

Inshore and Offshore forecast areas and codes by Fax

WEATHER BY FAX

Inshore and offshore forecasts by fax are available at Standard (£1/min) and Advance levels of service (£1.50/min). The Fax numbers given are for the Advance service.

Inshore waters forecasts

• The 2 page Standard inshore forecast is for up to 48 hrs and includes synoptic charts for today and tomorrow.

The forecast includes any gale and strong wind warnings, the general situation, wind speed/direction, strength of gusts, weather, visibility and sea state.

• The 3 page Advance inshore forecast includes the above, plus a tabulated hourly forecast over the next 6 hrs for 4 key places in the Area.

• To obtain the Advance inshore forecast dial 🖷 **09065 222** + the Area No above. For a National inshore 3–5 day forecast dial 🖷 **09065 222 340**.

Offshore planning forecasts

• The 2 page Standard offshore forecast includes 2–5 day planning forecasts and 2–5 day synoptic charts for the offshore Areas.

The forecast includes wind, weather, visibility and sea states.

• The 3 page Advance offshore forecast includes the above, plus four diagrams showing contours of significant wave heights in the forecast area. It takes about 6 mins to receive/print.

• To obtain the Advance offshore forecast dial 🖷 **09065 222** + Area Number required.

WEATHER BY MOBILE PHONE

Use your mobile to obtain forecasts by 3 different means:

- **SMS** (Short Message Service, or texting). A message includes: current weather and a forecast for 6 hrs later, at one of 161 coastal locations (below); updated hrly. Format: Location, date, time; max temp °C; mean wind direction/speed; visibility; % risk of precipitation. For example:

> Exmouth: 1/4/05
>
> 10am: 11c, WD 250d, WS 12kt, VIS 17.59km, RAIN 10%.
>
> 4pm: 12c, WD 290d, WS 14kt, VIS 13.50km, RAIN 12%.

To obtain this message, by return @ 25p per message, type **AC** and the location's name; then send it to 83141.

Or, for data received by 0900 daily @ £1.50 for 6 messages, type **AC Sub** and location's name; send it to 83141.

The message also contains an embedded Marinecall Tel No; press 'Dial' for a 2–5 day recorded forecast as in 5.8.2.

- Messages may also be received by **MMS** and **WAP**; the latter are shown in **bold**.

Coastal locations in Areas 1–11 and 15 are listed alphabetically below.

Area 1, SW England

Anvil Point	**Lyme Regis**
Brixham	Newton Ferrers, R Yealm
Darthaven, Dart marinas	Penzance
Exmouth	Plymouth
Falmouth	**Portland Bill**
Fowey	Salcombe
Helford River	Start Point
Lizard Point	Torquay
Longships	Weymouth

Area 2, S England

Beaulieu, Buckler's Hard	Poole
Bembridge Harbour	**Portsmouth**
Chichester, Birdham Pool	Ryde
Christchurch	**St Catherines Point**
Cowes	Southampton
Emsworth/Northney	Southsea marina
Hamble River	Sparkes Yacht harbour
Lymington	Wootton Creek
Needles Fairway buoy	Yarmouth, Isle of Wight

Area 3, SE England

Beachy Head	Newhaven
Brighton	**North Foreland**
Dover	Ramsgate
Dungeness	**Rye**
Eastbourne	**Selsey Bill**
Littlehampton	Shoreham

Area 4, E England

Aldeburgh	Orford Ness
Bradwell marina	Queenborough
Brightlingsea	Shotley Point marina
Burnham Yacht Harbour	Southend-on-sea
Essex marina	Southwold
Fox's marina	Suffolk Yacht harbour
Great Yarmouth	Tidemill Yacht harbour
Ipswich marina	Titchmarsh marina
Landguard Pt (Harwich)	Tollesbury
Lowestoft	Whitstable
Medway marinas	Woolverstone marina

Area 5, NE England

Amble	Holy Island
Berwick-upon-Tweed	**Hull**
Blyth	King's Lynn
Boston	Royal Quays, R Tyne
Bridlington	St Peter's marina, R Tyne
Cromer	**Spurn Head**
Flamborough Head	**Sunderland**
Grimsby	**Wells-next-the-Sea**
Hartlepool	**Whitby**

Area 6, SE Scotland

Aberdeen	Peterhead
Dundee	Port Edgar (Firth/ Forth)
Eyemouth	**Rattray Head**
Granton	St Abbs Head
Montrose	Stonehaven

Area 7, NE Scotland

Duncansby Head	**Whitehills**
Lossiemouth	Wick

Area 8, NW Scotland

Ardfern	Kip marina
Caledonia	Kirkcudbright
Cape Wrath	Largs
Craobh marina	**Oban**
Iona	**Tobermory**

Area 9, SW Scotland

Ardrossan	**Mull of Kintyre**
Campbeltown	**Portpatrick**
East Loch Tarbert	Rhu marina
Lamlash	Troon

Area 10, NW England

Beaumaris	Liverpool
Burrow Head	Maryport
Caernarfon	Morecambe Bay
Conwy	Port Dinorwic
Fleetwood (Wyre Dock)	Preston
Glasson Dock	**Whitehaven**
Holyhead	

Area 11, Wales – Land's End

Abersoch	Newquay
Aberystwyth	**Padstow**
Bangor	**Portishead**
Bardsey Island	Pwllheli
Bristol	**South Bishop (Lt ho)**
Cardiff (Penarth)	Swansea
Milford Haven	

Area 15, Channel Islands

Channel Isles	Jersey
Guernsey	

WEATHER

OTHER WEATHER SOURCES

Internet

www.metoffice.com (UK Met Office site) has 2 day and 3–5 day inshore forecasts, 2–5 day planning data, shipping forecasts, gale warnings, coastal reports, surface pressure charts and satellite images.

A pre-paid 'ticket' system (£10 for 20 tickets) pays for services used (MetWEB). To open a credit card account call ☎ 0845 300 0300 [+44 (0) 1344 855680 from abroad] or e-mail sales@metoffice.com

Other UK weather authorities and foreign Met Offices provide further information.

Press

Some national and regional papers include a synoptic chart which, in the absence of any other chart, can help to interpret the shipping forecast – unless the paper is already out of date when you buy it.

Television

Most TV forecasts show a synoptic chart and satellite pictures – a useful guide to the weather situation. In remote areas abroad a TV forecast in a bar, café or even shop window may be the best or only source of weather information.

In the UK Ceefax (BBC) gives the weather index on Ceefax page 400, weather warnings on page 405 and inshore waters forecasts on page 409.

Teletext (ITN) has general forecasts on page 151, shipping forecasts on page 157 and inshore waters forecasts on page 158. Antiope is the equivalent French system.

Broadcasts of shipping and inshore waters forecasts by HM Coastguard

Coastguard	Shipping f'cast areas	Inshore waters forecast areas	Broadcast times UT					
South Coast								
Falmouth	Plymouth, Lundy, Fastnet, Sole, FitzRoy	8 & 9	0140	0540	*0940*	1340	1740	*2140*
Brixham	Plymouth, Portland	8	0050	0450	*0850*	1250	1650	*2050*
Portland	Plymouth, Portland, Wight	7 & 8	0220	0620	*1020*	1420	1820	*2220*
Solent	Portland, Wight	6 & 7	0040	0440	*0840*	1240	1640	*2040*
Dover	Thames, Dover, Wight	5, 6 & 7	0105	0505	*0905*	1305	1707	*2105*
East Coast								
Thames	Thames, Dover	5	0010	0410	*0810*	1210	1610	*2010*
Yarmouth	Humber, Thames	5	0040	0440	*0840*	1240	1640	*2040*
Humber	Humber, Tyne, Dogger, German Bight	3 & 4	0340	*0740*	1140	1540	*1940*	2340
Forth	Forth, Tyne, Dogger, Forties	2	0205	0605	*1005*	1405	1805	*2205*
Aberdeen	Fair Is, Cromarty, Forth, Forties	1 & 2	0320	*0720*	1120	1520	*1920*	2320
Shetland	Faeroes, Fair Is, Viking	1 & 16	0105	0505	*0905*	1305	1705	*2105*
West Coast								
Stornoway	Fair Is, Faeroes, Bailey, Hebrides, Malin, Rockall	15	0110	0510	*0910*	1310	1710	*2110*
Clyde	Bailey, Hebrides, Rockall, Malin	13, 14 & 15	0020	0420	*0820*	1220	1620	*2020*
Belfast	Irish Sea, Malin	12	0305	*0705*	1105	1505	*1905*	2305
Liverpool	Irish Sea, Malin	11	0210	0610	*1010*	1410	1810	*2210*
Holyhead	Irish Sea	10	0235	*0635*	1035	1435	*1835*	2235
Milford Hvn	Lundy, Irish Sea, Fastnet	9 & 10	0335	*0735*	1135	1535	*1935*	2335
Swansea	Lundy, Irish Sea, Fastnet	9	0005	0405	*0805*	1205	1605	*2005*

CG transmitters and VHF channels

The VHF channels/positions of remote transmitters used for regular broadcasts of MSI are listed below. Thus the relevant (clearest) channel can be pre-selected and/or verified by listening to the prior announcement on Ch 16.

Falmouth MRCC

Trevose Head	86	50°33'N	05°02'W
St Mary's	23	49°56'N	06°18'W
Lizard	86	49°58'N	05°12'W
Falmouth	23	50°09'N	05°06'W

Brixham MRSC

Fowey	86	50°20'N	04°38'W
Rame Head	10	50°19'N	04°13'W
Salcombe	84	50°15'N	03°45'W
East Prawle	73	50°13'N	03°42'W
Dartmouth	23	50°21'N	03°35'W
Berry Head	86	50°24'N	03°29'W
Teignmouth	10	50°34'N	03°32'W
Beer Head	84	50°41'N	03°05'W

Portland MRSC

Beer Head	86	50°41'N	03°05'W
Bincleaves	23	50°36'N	02°27'W
Grove Pt (Portland)	84	50°33'N	02°25'W
Hengistbury Head	23	50°43'N	01°46'W

Solent MRSC

Needles	86	50°39'N	01°35'W
Boniface (Ventnor, IoW)	23	50°36'N	01°12'W
Newhaven	86	50°47'N	00°03'E

Dover MRCC

Fairlight (Hastings)	23	50°52'N	00°39'E
Langdon Battery (Dover)	86	51°08'N	01°21'E
North Foreland	86	51°23'N	01°27'E

Thames MRSC

Shoeburyness	23	51°31'N	00°47'E
Bradwell (R Blackwater)	86	51°44'N	00°53'E
Walton/Naze	73	51°51'N	01°17'E
Bawdsey (R Deben)	84	52°00'N	01°25'E

Yarmouth MRCC

Lowestoft	86	52°29'N	01°46'E
Yarmouth	84	52°36'N	01°43'E
Trimingham	23	52°54'N	01°21'E
Langham	86	52°57'N	00°58'E
Guy's Head	84	52°48'N	00°13'E
Skegness	23	53°09'N	00°21'E

Humber MRSC

Easington	84	53°39'N	00°06'E
Flamborough Head	23	54°07'N	00°05'W
Whitby	84	54°29'N	00°36'W
Hartlepool	23	54°42'N	01°10'W
Cullercoats (Blyth)	84	55°04'N	01°28'W
Newton	23	55°31'N	01°37'W

Forth MRSC

St Abbs/Cross Law	86	55°54'N	02°12'W
Craigkelly	86	56°04'N	03°14'W
Fife Ness	23	56°17'N	02°35'W
Tay Law (Dundee)	86	56°28'N	02°59'W
Inverbervie	23	56°51'N	02°16'W

Aberdeen MRCC

Greg Ness	86	57°08'N	02°03'W
Peterhead	86	57°31'N	01°46'W
Windyheads Hill	23	57°39'N	02°14'W
Banff	23	57°38'N	02°31'W
Foyers (Loch Ness)	86	57°14'N	04°31'W
Rosemarkie	86	57°38'N	04°05'W
Thrumster (Wick)	84	58°24'N	03°07'W
Noss Head (Wick)	84	58°29'N	03°03'W
Dunnet Hd (Thurso)	84	58°40'N	03°22'W
Ben Tongue	23	58°30'N	04°24'W
Durness (L Eriboll)	23	58°34'N	04°44'W

Shetland MRSC

Wideford Hill	23	58°59'N	03°01'W
Fitful Head	10	59°54'N	01°23'W
Shetland MRSC	84	60°10'N	01°08'W
Collafirth	73	60°32'N	01°23'W
Saxa Vord (Unst)	23	60°42'N	00°51'W

Stornoway MRSC

Butt of Lewis	10	58°28'N	06°14'W
Portnaguran	84	58°15'N	06°10'W
Forsneval	73	58°13'N	07°00'W
Melvaig (Loch Ewe)	67	57°50'N	05°47'W
Rodel (S Harris)	10	57°45'N	06°57'W
Clettreval (N Uist)	73	57°37'N	07°26'W
Skriag (Portree)	67	57°23'N	06°15'W
Drumfearn (Skye)	84	57°12'N	05°48'W
Barra	10	57°01'N	07°30'W
Arisaig	73	56°55'N	06°50'W

Clyde MRCC

Glengorm (N Mull)	23	56°38'N	06°08'W
Tiree	73	56°31'N	06°57'W
Torosay (E Mull)	10	56°27'N	05°43'W
Clyde MRCC	23	55°58'N	04°48'W
South Knapdale	23	55°55'N	05°28'W
Kilchiaran (W Islay)	84	55°46'N	06°27'W
Lawhill (Ardrossan)	86	55°42'N	04°50'W
Rhu Staffnish	10	55°22'N	05°32'W

Belfast MRSC

Navar	73	54°28'N	07°54'W
Limvady (L Foyle)	84	55°06'N	06°53'W
West Torr	73	55°12'N	06°06'W
Black Mountain	86	54°35'N	06°01'W
Orlock Point	84	54°40'N	05°35'W
Slievemartin	73	54°06'N	06°10'W

Liverpool MRSC

Caldbeck (Carlisle)	10	54°46'N	03°07'W
Snaefell (IoM)	86	54°16'N	04°28'W
Langthwaite	73	54°02'N	02°46'W
Moel-y-Parc	23	53°13'N	04°28'W

Holyhead MRSC

Great Ormes Head	84	53°20'N	03°51'W
Holyhead MRSC	10	53°19'N	04°38'W
Mynydd Rhiw	73	52°50'N	04°38'W

Milford Haven MRSC

Blaenplwyf	84	52°22'N	04°06'W
Dinas Hd	86	52°00'N	04°54'W
St Ann's Head	84	51°40'N	05°11'W
Tenby (Monkstone)	86	51°42'N	04°41'W

Swansea MRCC

Mumbles	84	51°34'N	03°59'W
St Hillary (Barry)	86	51°27'N	03°25'W
Severn Bridges	84	51°36'N	02°38'W
Combe Martin	86	51°12'N	04°03'W
Hartland Point	84	51°01'N	04°31'W

Inshore waters forecasts: Area boundaries used by the Coastguard

10°W 05°W 00°00'

15

Shetland 60°N

1 16 01°W

58° 58°

Cape Wrath

Stornoway

Rattray Head

Aberdeen 2

Ardnamurchan Pt

56° 56°

14 Forth

Clyde Berwick-upon-Tweed 3

Lough Foyle 13

Mull of Kintyre

Belfast Whitby

12

Carlingford Lough Humber 4 54°

54°

11

Colwyn Bay

Liverpool

Holyhead The Wash

Yarmouth

52° St David's Head Milford Haven Thames

10 Swansea 5

9 Solent Selsey Bill Dover

Lyme Regis Portland 6

Brixham 50°N

50°N Falmouth

Land's End 7

KEY:

■ MRCC

— Boundary of Inshore Waters Forecast

8 49°

CHANNEL ISLANDS

Jersey Meteorological department

From the CI and UK call ☎ 0900 665 0022 for the Channel Islands recorded shipping forecast. From France call ☎ +44 1534 492256. For Guernsey only, call ☎ 06969 8800; it is chargeable. For more detailed info call ☎ +44 1534 745550, ▨ 746351.

Forecasts include: general situation, 24hr forecast for wind, weather, vis, sea state, swell, sea temperature, plus 2 & 4 day outlooks and St Helier tide times/heights. The area is bounded by 50°N, 03°W and the mainland from Cap de la Hague to Ile de Bréhat.

Weather broadcasts and bulletins

BBC Radio Guernsey 93·2 MHz, 1116 kHz
Bulletins for the waters around Guernsey, Herm and Sark are broadcast Mon-Fri at 0630, 0730 and 0830 LT; Sat/Sun at 0730 and 0830 LT. They contain forecast, synopsis, coastal forecast, storm warnings and wind strength.

In the summer coastal reports are included from: Portland, Chan lt V, Alderney, Guernsey, Jersey, Cherbourg, Cap de la Hague and Dinard.

BBC Radio Jersey 1026 kHz, 88·8 MHz.
Storm warnings on receipt. Wind info for Jersey waters: Mon-Fri 0725, 0825, 1325, 1725 LT; Sat/Sun 0825.

Shipping forecast for local waters: Mon-Fri @ H+00 (0600-1900, after the news) and 0625 & 1825 LT; Sat/Sun @ H+00 (0700-1300, after the news) and 0725 LT.

Jersey Radio Ch 25, 82. Gale warnings at 0307, 0907, 1507 and 2107 UT. Gale warnings, synopsis, 24h forecast, outlook for next 24 hrs, plus reports from observation stations, are broadcast on request and at 0645*, 0745*, 0845*, 1245, 1845, 2245 UT; *broadcast 1 hr earlier when DST in force

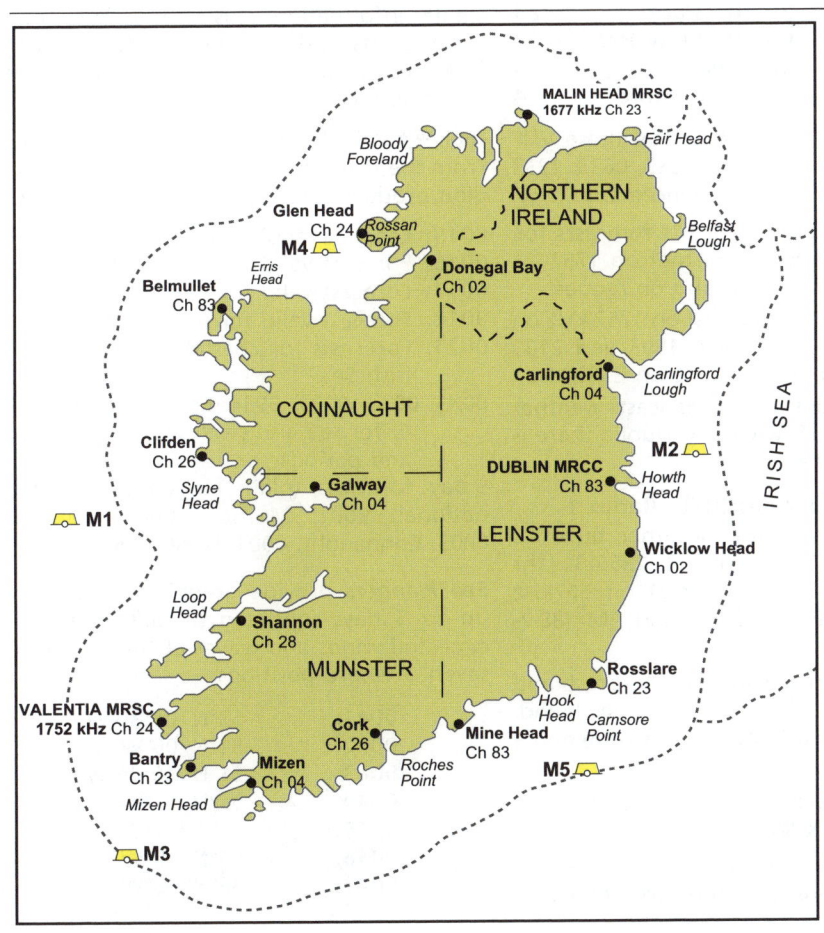

Provinces, headlands, sea areas and coastal stations referred to in weather broadcasts are shown here. Forecasts for coastal waters cover areas within 30M of the shore.

IRELAND

Met Éireann (Irish Met Office) is at Glasnevin Hill, Dublin 9, Ireland. ☎ 1 806 4250, 📠 1 806 4250, www.met.ie. General forecasting division: ☎ 1 806 4255, 📠 1 806 4275 (H24, charges may apply).

Coast radio stations

CRS and their VHF channels are listed below (anti-clockwise from Malin Head) and shown overleaf. Weather bulletins for 30M offshore and the Irish Sea are broadcast on VHF at 0103, 0403, 0703, 1003, 1303, 1603, 1903 and 2203UT after an announcement on Ch 16. Broadcasts are made 1 hour earlier when DST is in force. Bulletins include gale warnings, synopsis and a 24-hour forecast.

Malin Head	23	Bantry	23
Glen Head	24	Mizen Head	04
Donegal Bay	02	Cork	26
Belmullet	83	Mine Head	83
Clifden	26	Rosslare	23
Galway	04	Wicklow Head	02
Shannon	28	Dublin	83
Valentia	24	Carlingford	04

Gale warnings are broadcast on these VHF channels on receipt and at 0033, 0633, 1233 and 1833 UT, after an announcement Ch 16.

MF Valentia Radio broadcasts forecasts for sea areas Shannon and Fastnet on 1752 kHz at 0833 & 2033 UT, and on request.

Gale warnings are broadcast on 1752 kHz on receipt and at 0303, 0903, 1503 and 2103 (UT) after an announcement on 2182 kHz.

Malin Head does not broadcast weather information on 1677 kHz. At Dublin there is no MF transmitter.

Radio Telefís Éireann (RTE) Radio 1

RTE Radio 1 broadcasts weather bulletins daily at 0602, 1255, 1657 & 2355LT (1hr earlier when DST is in force) on 567kHz (Tullamore), 729kHz (Cork) and FM (88·2-95·2MHz).

Bulletins contain a situation, forecast and coastal reports. Forecasts include: wind, weather, vis, swell (if higher than 4m) and a 24 hrs outlook.

Gale warnings are included in hourly news bulletins on FM & MF.

Coastal reports include wind, weather, visibility, pressure and pressure tendency.

The change over the last 3 hrs is described as:

Steady	=	0–0·4hPa
Rising/falling slowly	=	0·5–1·9
Rising/falling	=	2·0–3·4
Rising/falling rapidly	=	3·5–5·9
Rising/falling very rapidly	=	> 6·0

Weather by telephone

The latest sea area forecast and gale warnings are available as recorded messages H24 from Weatherdial. Dial ☎ 1550 123 plus the suffixes below:

850	Munster
851	Leinster
852	Connaught
853	Ulster
854	Dublin (plus winds in Dublin Bay and HW times)
855	Coastal waters and Irish Sea.

Weather by fax

Similar information, plus isobaric, swell and wave charts and any small craft warnings (>F6 up to 10M offshore; Apr-Sep inc) is available H24 by Weatherdial Fax.

Dial 📠 1550 131 838 (from within Eire only). From the menu below select the required 4-digit product code (see 0400 for full listing):

0015: Latest analysis chart
0016: Forecast valid for next 24 hrs
0017: Forecast valid for next 36 hrs
0018: Forecast valid for next 48 hrs
0021: Forecasts for coastal waters and Irish Sea
0031, 0032, 0033, 0034: Forecast (days 1-4) for sea and swell wave heights and periods
5-day forecasts (plain language, farming/national) 0001: Munster. 0002: Leinster. 0003: Connaught. 0004: Ulster. 0005: Dublin.

Sea Planners provide graphic forecasts for up to 5 days (updated at 0430 daily) of expected winds and waves at the following seven offshore positions:

0041:	53°N 05°30'W
0042:	51°N 06°W
0043:	51°N 10°30'W
0044:	53°N 11°W
0045:	54°N 11°W
0046:	55°N 10°W
0047:	56°N 08°W

DENMARK

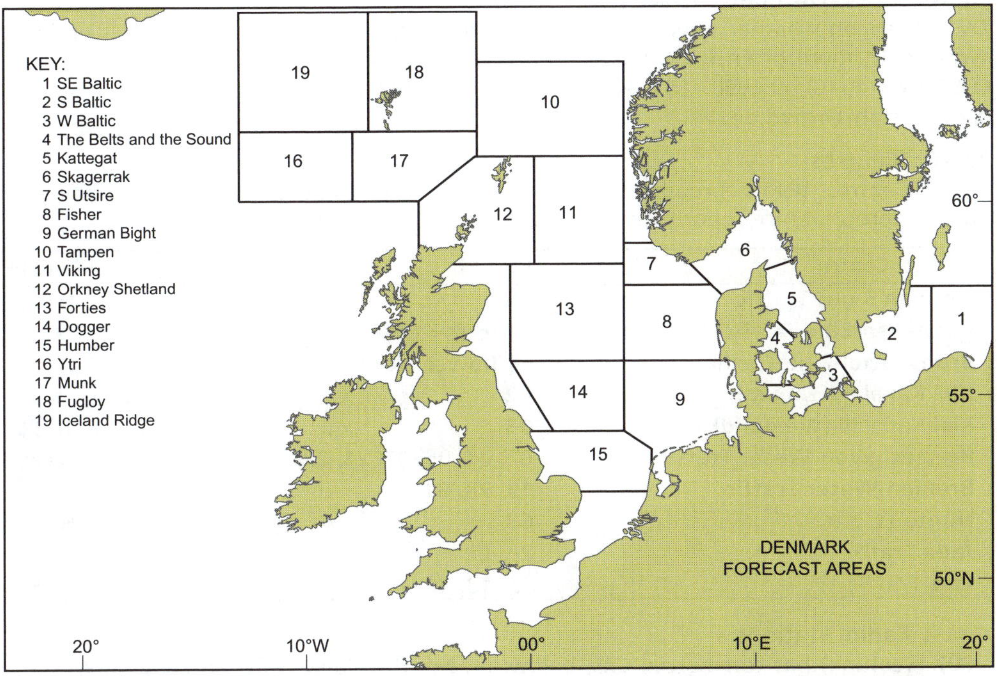

KEY:
1 SE Baltic
2 S Baltic
3 W Baltic
4 The Belts and the Sound
5 Kattegat
6 Skagerrak
7 S Utsire
8 Fisher
9 German Bight
10 Tampen
11 Viking
12 Orkney Shetland
13 Forties
14 Dogger
15 Humber
16 Ytri
17 Munk
18 Fugloy
19 Iceland Ridge
DENMARK
FORECAST AREAS
60°
55°
50°N
20°
10°W
00°
10°E
20°

Gale warnings & forecasts are broadcast on receipt, or on request, in Danish/English by remote CRS, callsign *Lyngby Radio:*

CRS	Chan/Freq	Areas
Skagen	04, 1758 kHz	4, 5, 6
Hirtshals	66	4, 5, 6, 8
Hanstholm	01	6, 8
Bovbjerg	02	6, 8, 9
Blåvand	23, 1734 kHz	8, 9

Forecast areas: see above. Skagen and Blåvand CRS broadcast on MF gale warnings for all areas on receipt.

8°
9°
10°E
11°
Skagen
Ch 04
1758 kHz
Hirtshals
Ch 66
Hanstholm
Ch 01
57°
Bovbjerg
Ch 02
56°
Blåvand
Ch 23
1734 kHz
55°N

Danmarks Radio broadcasts

Kalundborg (55°44'N 11°E) broadcasts on AM 243 and 1062 kHz at 0445, 0745, 1045, 1645 and 2145 UT:

Gale warnings, weather situation, outlook and coastal reports for areas 1–19.

A 5 day outlook for areas 2–9 and 13–15 and a 7 day outlook for Jutland & the Islands is broadcast only at 1045 & 1645.

Strong wind warnings (up to F6, 12m/sec) for Areas 2–5 & Limfjorden, plus the area south of Esbjerg (1 May – 31 Oct), are broadcast on every Hour by:

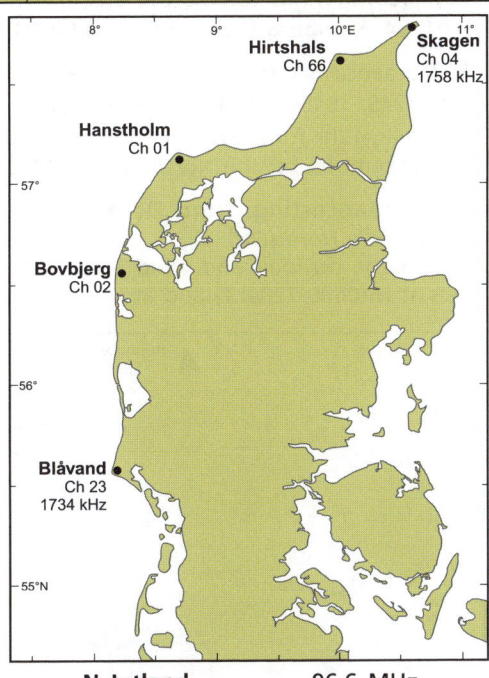

N Jutland	96·6 MHz
Thisted (Limfjord)	99·2 MHz
W Jutland	92·9 MHz
SW Jutland	92·3 MHz
S Jutland	97·2 MHz

GERMANY

Deutsche Wetterdienst (DWD)

DWD (German weather service) provides Met info through a databank which is updated twice daily; more often for weather reports and text forecasts.
DWD ☎ + 49 (0) 40 6690 1851. 📠 + 49 (0) 40 6690 1946. www.dwd.de seeschifffahrt@dwd.de.

Traffic Centres

Traffic Centres, below, broadcast local storm warnings, weather bulletins, visibility (and when appropriate ice reports) in German or **English** on request.

Traffic Centre	VHF Ch	Every
German Bight Traffic	80	H+00
Cuxhaven-Elbe Traffic	71 (outer Elbe)	H+35
Brunsbüttel-Elbe Traffic	68 (lower Elbe)	H+05
Kiel Kanal II (E-bound)	02	H+15 & H+45
Kiel Kanal III (W-bound)	03	H+20 & H+50
Bremerhaven-Weser Traffic	02, 04, 05, 07, 21, 22, 82	H+20
Bremen-Weser Traffic	19, 78, 81	H+30
Hunte Traffic	63	H+30
Jade Traffic	20, 63	H+10
Ems Traffic	15, 18, 20, 21	H+50

Coast Radio Stations

DP07 (Seefunk) has commercial CRS, below, at: **Nordfriesland (Sylt)** Ch 26. **Elbe-Weser** Ch 01, 24. **Hamburg** (Control centre) Ch 83. **Bremen** Ch 25. **Borkum** Ch 28.

DP07 broadcasts (only in German): gale and strong wind warnings on receipt. At 0745⊕, 0945, 1245, 1645 and 1945⊕ UT for Fisher, German Bight and Humber, DP07 broadcasts: a synopsis, 12hr forecast, 24hrs outlook and coastal station reports. ⊕summer only. Also a 4–5 day outlook for the North Sea (and Baltic) at 0945 and 1645.

Radio broadcasting: Nord Deutscher Rundfunk (NDR)

NDR 1 Welle Nord (FM)

A summary, outlook and wind forecast for the German Bight are broadcast after the news at H (0600-2200LT) and at H +30 (0530-17300LT) by: **Sylt** 90·9 MHz; **Helgoland** 88·9

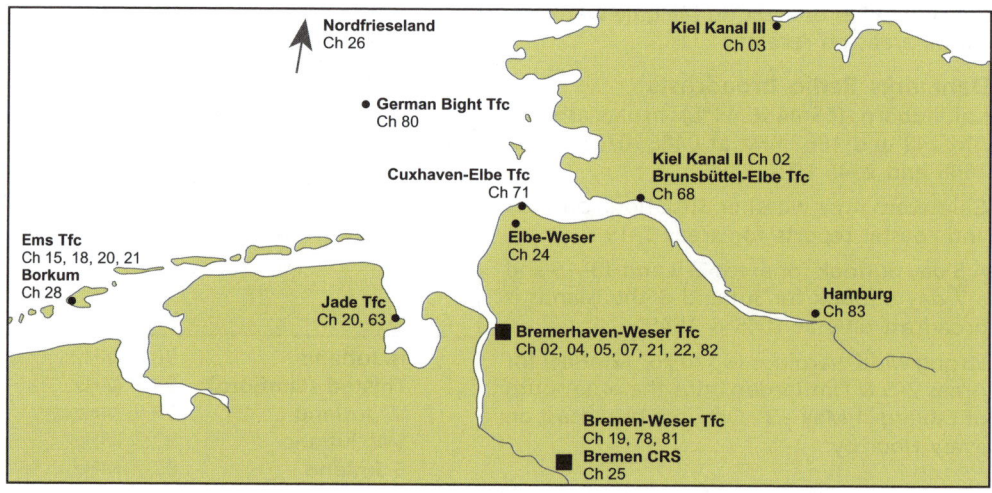

MHz; **Hamburg** 89·5 MHz; **Flensburg** 89·6 MHz; **Heide** 90·5 MHz; **Kiel** 91·3 MHz.

NDR Info (AM)
Synopsis, forecast and coastal station reports for the North Sea (and Baltic) are broadcast at 0005, 0830 and 2205 UT on 972 (Hamburg) & 702 (Flensburg) kHz.

Radio Bremen (MW and FM)
Warnings of extreme weather conditions in German Bight, with associated hazards, are broadcast after the news by: **Bremerhaven** 936 kHz; 89·3, 92·1, 95·4 & 100·8 MHz; and by **Bremen** 88·3, 93·8, 96·7 & 101·2 MHz.

Telephone forecasts (Marineweather)
For wind forecast and outlook (1 April – 30 Sept) call 0190 1160 (only within Germany) plus two digits for the following areas:

45	North Frisian Islands and Helgoland
46	R Elbe, Cuxhaven to Hamburg
47	Weser , Jade Bay and Helgoland
48	East Frisians and Ems Estuary
53	For pleasure craft

For year-round weather synopsis, forecast and outlook, call 0190 1169 plus two digits:

20	General information
21	North Sea and Baltic
22	German Bight, Fisher and SW North Sea
31	Reports for North Sea and Baltic

For the latest wind warnings (greater than F6) and storm warnings for individual areas of the North Sea coasts, call +49 40 66901209 (H24). If no warning is in force, a wind forecast for the German Bight, west and southern Baltic is given.

NETHERLANDS
Coastguard VHF weather broadcasts
Forecasts for Dutch coastal waters (up to 30M offshore) and inland waters (IJsselmeer, Markermeer, Oosterschelde) are broadcast in **English** and Dutch at 0805, 1305, 1905, 2305 LT on the VHF channels shown below, **without** prior announcement on Ch 16 or DSC 70.

Westkapelle	23	**Hoorn**	83
Woensdrecht	83	**Wezep**	23
Renesse	83	**Kornwerderzand**	23

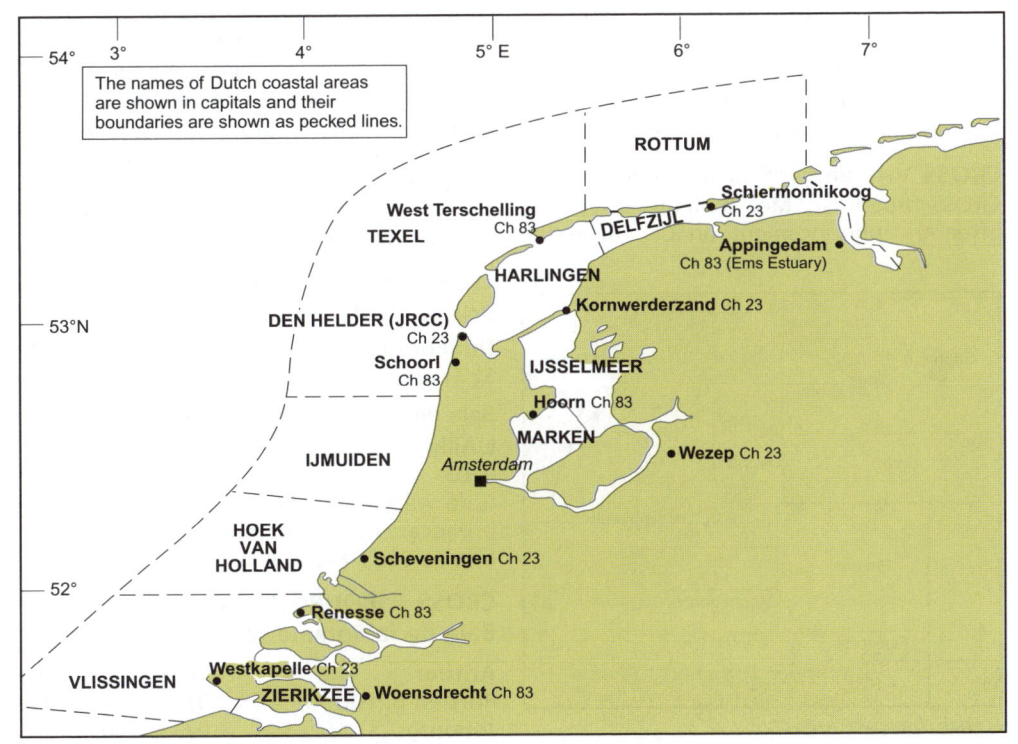

Scheveningen	23	West Terschelling	83
Schoorl	83	Schiermonnikoog	23
Den Helder	23	Appingedam	83

Gale warnings are broadcast on receipt and at 0333, 0733, 1133, 1533, 1933, 2333 UT.

MF weather broadcasts

Forecasts for areas Dover, Thames, Humber, German Bight, Dogger, Fisher, Forties and Viking are broadcast by Scheveningen in **English** at 0940 & 2140 UT on 3673 kHz. Gale warnings for these areas are broadcast in **English** on receipt and at 0333, 0733, 1133, 1533, 1933 and 2333 UT.

Radio Noord-Holland (FM)

Coastal forecasts for northern areas, gale warnings and wind strength are broadcast in Dutch, Mon-Fri at 0730, 0838, 1005, 1230 and 1705LT; Sat/Sun 1005, by: **Haarlem** 97.6 MHz and **Wieringermeer** 93.9 MHz.

Omroep Zeeland (FM)

Coastal forecasts for southern areas, synopsis, gale warnings and wind strength are broadcast in Dutch, Mon-Fri at 0715, 0915, 1215 and 1715LT; Sat/Sun 1015, by:

Philippine 97.8 MHz and **Goes** 101.9 MHz.

BELGIUM

Coast radio stations

Oostende Radio broadcasts in **English** and Dutch on VHF Ch 27 and 2761 kHz: Strong wind warnings on receipt and at 0820 and 1720 UT, together with a forecast for sea areas Thames and Dover.

Antwerpen Radio broadcasts in **English** and Dutch on VHF Ch 24 for the Schelde estuary: Gale warnings on receipt and at every odd H+05. Also strong wind warnings (F6+) on receipt and at every H+03 and H+48.

FRANCE

Le Guide Marine is a useful, free annual booklet which summarises the various means by which weather forecasts and warnings are broadcast or otherwise disseminated. It is available from marinas or Météo-France, 1 quai Branly, 75340 Paris. ☎ 01.45.56.74.36; 📠 01.45.56.71.70. marine@meteo.fr   www.meteo.fr

CROSS VHF and MF broadcasts

CROSS broadcasts Met bulletins in French, after an announcement on Ch 16. In the English Channel broadcasts can be given in English, on request Ch 16. Broadcasts include: Any gale warnings, general situation, 24 hrs forecast (actual weather, wind, sea state and vis) and further trends for coastal waters, which extend 20M offshore. VHF channels, remote stations and local times are shown below.

Gale warnings feature in Special Met Bulletins (*Bulletins Météorologique Spéciaux* or BMS). They are broadcast in French by all CROSS on VHF at H+03 and at other times on MF frequencies as shown below.

CROSS GRIS-NEZ Ch 79
Belgian border to Baie de la Somme

| Dunkerque | 0720, 1603, 1920 |
| St Frieux | 0710, 1545, 1910 |

Baie de la Somme to Cap de la Hague
L'Ailly
0703, 1533, 1903
Gale warnings for areas 12-13 are broadcast in French on MF 1650 & 2677 kHz at 0833 & 2033LT

CROSS JOBOURG Ch 80
Baie de la Somme to Cap de la Hague

Antifer	0803, 1633, 2003
Port-en-Bessin	0745, 1615, 1945
Jobourg	0733, 1603, 1933

French forecast areas

CROSS Jobourg *continued*
Cap de la Hague to Pointe de Penmarc'h
Jobourg   0715, 1545, 1915
Granville   0703, 1533, 1903
Gale warnings for areas 13-14 in **English** on receipt and at H+20 and H+50. No gale warnings on MF.

CROSS CORSEN Ch 79
Cap de la Hague to Pte de Penmarc'h
(Times in bold = 1 May to 30 Sep only).
Cap Fréhel   0545, 0803, **1203**, 1633, 2003
Bodic   0533, 0745, **1145**, 1615, 1945
Ile de Batz   0515, 0733, **1133**, 1603, 1933
Le Stiff   0503, 0715, **1115**, 1545, 1915

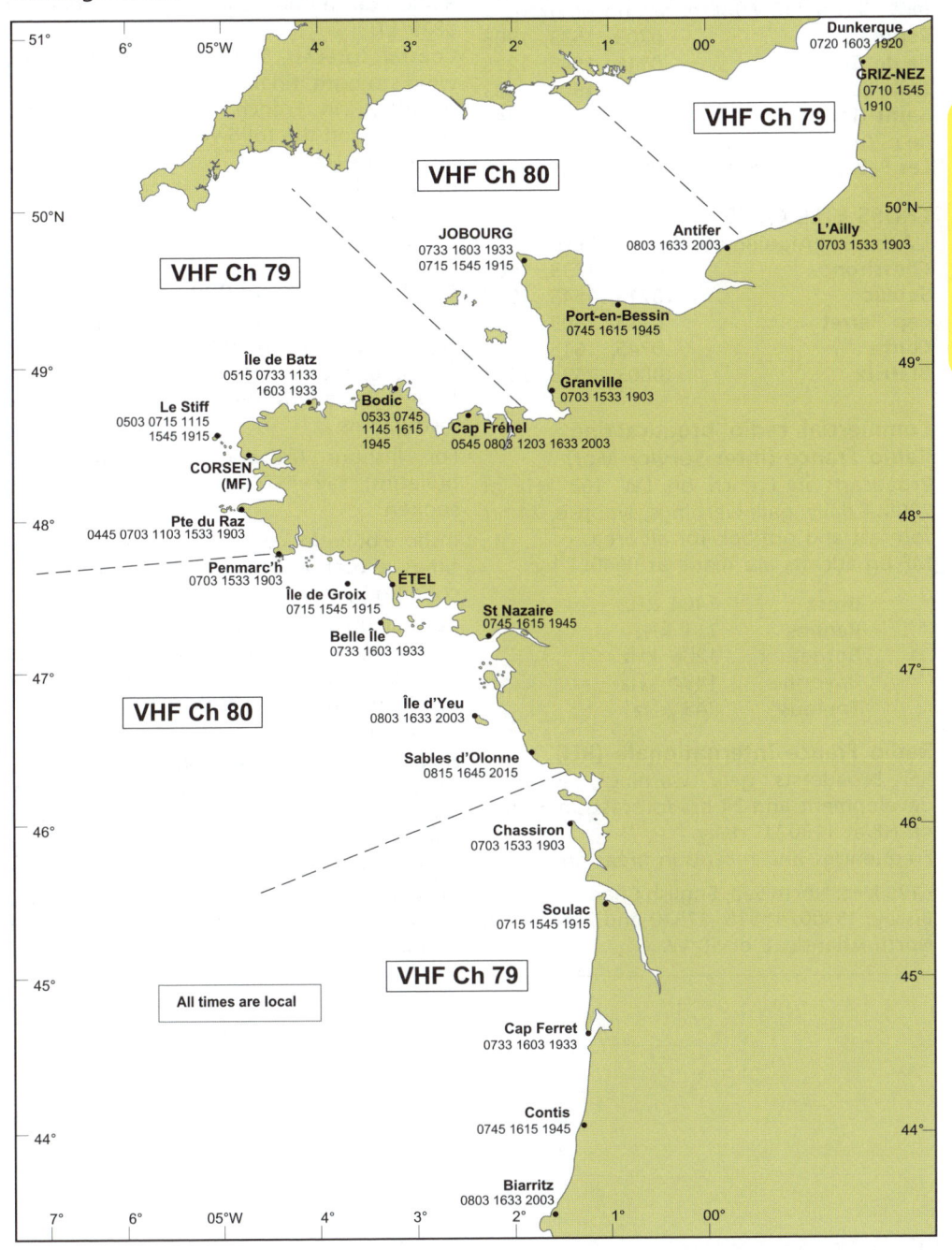

All times are local

WEATHER

93

Pte du Raz   0445, 0703, **1103**, 1533, 1903
Corsen broadcasts gale warnings for areas 13-22 in French at 0815 and 2015LT on MF 1650 & 2677 kHz.

CROSS ÉTEL Ch 80
Pte de Penmarc'h to l'Anse de l'Aiguillon
(46° 15'N 01°10'W). Étel has no MF freqs

Penmarc'h	0703,	1533,	1903
Ile de Groix	0715,	1545,	1915
Belle Ile	0733,	1603,	1933
Saint-Nazaire	0745,	1615,	1945
Ile d'Yeu	0803,	1633,	2003
Les Sables d'Olonne	0815,	1645,	2015

CROSS ÉTEL Ch 79
L'Anse de l'Aiguillon to Spanish border

Chassiron	0703,	1533,	1903
Soulac	0715,	1545,	1915
Cap Ferret	0733,	1603,	1933
Contis	0745,	1615,	1945
Biarritz	0803,	1633,	2003

Commercial radio broadcasting
Radio France (Inter-Service-Mer)
Broadcasts in French on LW 162 kHz at 2003LT daily: gale warnings, synopsis, 24 hrs forecast and outlook for all areas.
MF broadcasts are made at 0640LT by:

Brest	1404 kHz
Rennes	711 kHz
Bordeaux	1206 kHz
Bayonne	1494 kHz
Toulouse	945 kHz

Radio France Internationale (RFI)
RFI broadcasts gale warnings, synopsis, development and 24 hrs forecasts in French on HF at 1130 UT daily.

Frequencies and reception areas are:

6175 kHz: North Sea, English Channel, Bay of Biscay. 15300, 15515, 17570 and 21645 kHz: North Atlantic, E of 50°W.

See opposite for the High Seas forecast areas in the Eastern Atlantic.
Engineering bulletins giving any changes in frequency are transmitted between H+53 and H+00.

Local radio (FM)
Radio France Cherbourg broadcasts daily at 0829 LT:
Coastal forecast, gale warnings, visibility, wind strength, tidal information, small craft warnings, in French, for the Cherbourg peninsula on the following frequencies:

St Vaast-la-Hougue	85·0 MHz
Cherbourg	100·7 MHz
Cap de la Hague	99·8 MHz
Carteret	99·9 MHz

Forecasts by telephone
For recorded Inshore and Coastal forecasts. Dial 08·92·68·02·dd (dd is the number, as given, for the *département*); press the * key then 1 to access the main menu. Follow instructions ...

For Inshore (*rivage*) or Coastal (*côte*) bulletins, say "STOP" as your choice is spoken.

Inshore bulletins contain 7 day forecasts, tide times, actual reports, sea temperature, surf conditions, etc.

Coastal bulletins contain strong wind/gale warnings, general synopsis, 24 hrs forecast and outlook. Five bulletins cover the N & W coasts, out to 20M offshore.

For Offshore bulletins (*large*), out to 200M offshore, dial ☎ 08·92·68·08·77. Select one of three offshore areas (English Channel & southern North Sea, Bay of Biscay or the N part of the western Mediterranean) by saying "STOP" as it is named. Offshore bulletins contain strong wind/gale warnings, the general synopsis and forecast, and the outlook for up to 7 days.

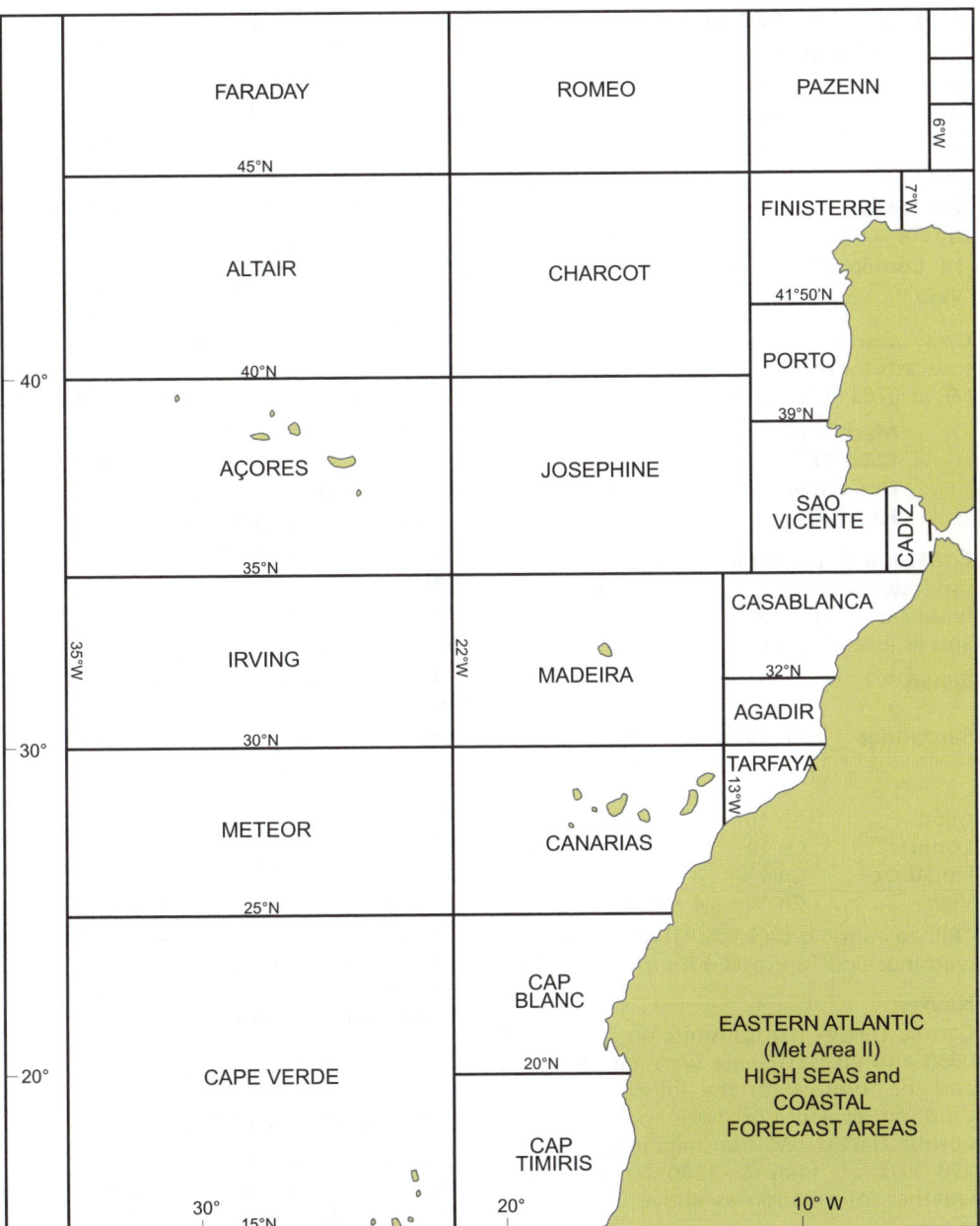

Forecast areas for the Eastern Atlantic and Coastal/Offshore Areas off France, Spain, Portugal and North West Africa

NORTH WEST SPAIN
Coast radio stations
VHF weather warnings and 48h coastal forecasts are broadcast in Spanish at 0840, 1240 and 2010 UT by:

Pasajes	Ch 27	Bilbao	Ch 26
Santander	Ch 24	Cabo Peñas	Ch 26
Navia	Ch 60	Cabo Ortegal	Ch 02
La Coruña	Ch 26	Finisterre	Ch 22
Vigo	Ch 65	La Guardia	Ch 21

Gale warnings, synopsis and 24h/48h forecasts for Atlantic areas are broadcast on MF at 0703, 1303 and 1903 UT by:

Machichaco	1707 kHz
Cabo Peñas	1677 kHz
La Coruña	1698 kHz
Finisterre	1764 kHz

Coastguard weather broadcasts
Gale warnings and coastal forecasts are broadcast in Spanish and English on receipt and as listed below:

Bilbao*	Ch 10	4 hrly from 0033, except 0633
Santander	Ch 74	0245, 0445, 0645, 0845, 1045, 1445, 1845, 2245
Gijón	Ch 10	2 hrly (0215-2215)
Coruña	Ch 10	4 hrly from 0005
Finisterre	Ch 11	4 hrly from 0233
Vigo	Ch 10	4 hrly from 0015

*Bilbao also broadcasts High Seas gale warnings and forecasts 4 hourly from 0233.

Navtex
Coruna Navtex (D) transmits on 518 kHz at 0830 and 2030 UT: gale warnings, synopsis and the forecast for the following 24 hrs, valid out to 450M offshore.
Coruna Navtex (W) transmits in Spanish on 490 kHz at 1140 & 1940 UT: the same weather information as above.

Radio Nacional de España (MW)
Broadcasts storm warnings, synopsis and 12h or 18h forecasts for Cantábrico and Galicia at 1100, 1400, 1800 & 2200 LT in Spanish. Stations/frequencies are:

San Sebastián	774 kHz
Bilbao	639 kHz
Santander	855 kHz
Oviedo	729 kHz
La Coruña	639 kHz

Recorded telephone forecasts
This service is only available within Spain and for vessels equipped with Autolink. For a recorded weather bulletin in Spanish, call:

☎ 906 365 372 for the coasts of Cantábrico and Galicia.
☎ 906 365 374 for High Seas bulletins.

PORTUGAL AND THE AZORES
Broadcasts by Radionaval Portugal
Broadcasts in Portuguese and **English** are on Ch 11 at the times (UT) below. They contain: Storm, gale and poor visibility warnings; synopsis and 24 hrs forecasts for three coastal zones out to 20M offshore; see opposite:

Leixões 0705, 1905
Coastal waters of N and Central zones.
Alges (also on MF 2657 kHz) 0905, 2105
Coastal waters of all 3 zones.
Faro 0805, 2005
Coastal waters of Central and S Zones.
Horta (Azores, LT) 0900, 2100
Waters off Faial, Pico, Graciosa, São Jorge and Terceira

Waters off Corvo and Flores 1000, 1900

Radiofusão Portuguesa
Broadcasts weather bulletins for coastal waters in Portuguese at 1100 UT. Stations (N-S) and frequencies are:

Porto	720 kHz
Viseu	666 kHz
Montemer (Coimbra)	630 kHz
Lisboa 1	666 kHz
Miranda do Douro	630 kHz
Elvas	720 kHz
Faro	97·6 MHz, 720 kHz

SOUTH WEST SPAIN
Coast radio stations
CRS broadcast gale warnings, synopsis, 24h and 48h forecasts for Atlantic and Mediterranean areas, in Spanish, at the times (UT) and on the VHF and MF frequencies shown below:

Chipiona	1656 kHz	0733	1233	1933
Cadiz	Ch 26	0833	1133	2003
Tarifa	Ch 81	0833	1133	2003
	1704 kHz	0733	1233	1933
Malaga	Ch 26	0833	1133	2003
Cabo Gata	Ch 27	0833	1133	2003

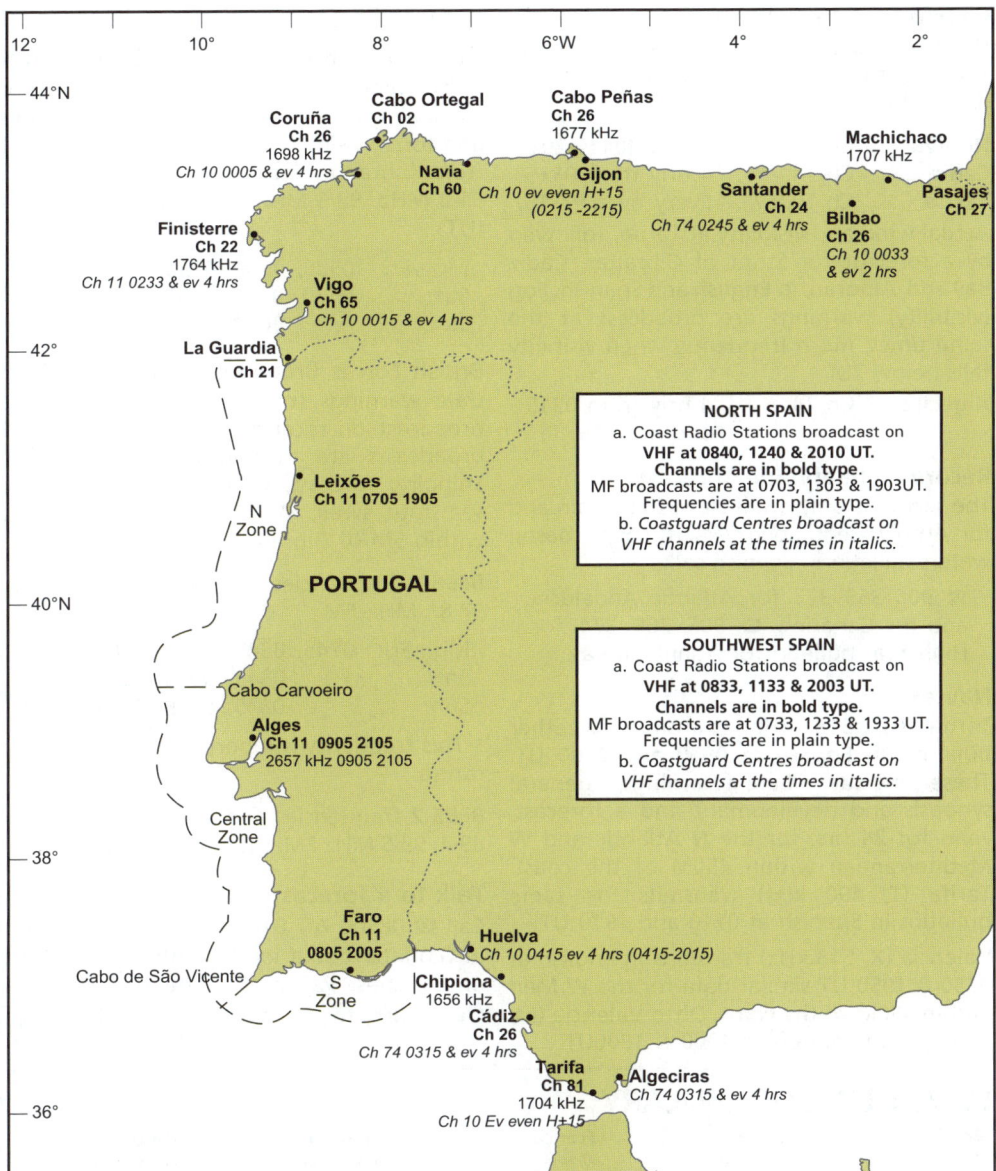

Cabo Ortegal
Ch 02

Cabo Peñas
Ch 26
1677 kHz

Coruña
Ch 26
1698 kHz
Ch 10 0005 & ev 4 hrs

Machichaco
1707 kHz

Navia
Ch 60

Gijon
Ch 10 ev even H+15
(0215 -2215)

Santander
Ch 24
Ch 74 0245 & ev 4 hrs

Bilbao
Ch 26
Ch 10 0033
& ev 2 hrs

Pasajes
Ch 27

Finisterre
Ch 22
1764 kHz
Ch 11 0233 & ev 4 hrs

Vigo
Ch 65
Ch 10 0015 & ev 4 hrs

La Guardia
Ch 21

N
Zone

Leixões
Ch 11 0705 1905

PORTUGAL

NORTH SPAIN
a. Coast Radio Stations broadcast on
VHF at 0840, 1240 & 2010 UT.
Channels are in bold type.
MF broadcasts are at 0703, 1303 & 1903UT.
Frequencies are in plain type.
b. *Coastguard Centres broadcast on*
VHF channels at the times in italics.

Cabo Carvoeiro

SOUTHWEST SPAIN
a. Coast Radio Stations broadcast on
VHF at 0833, 1133 & 2003 UT.
Channels are in bold type.
MF broadcasts are at 0733, 1233 & 1933 UT.
Frequencies are in plain type.
b. *Coastguard Centres broadcast on*
VHF channels at the times in italics.

Alges
Ch 11 0905 2105
2657 kHz 0905 2105

Central
Zone

Faro
Ch 11
0805 2005

Huelva
Ch 10 0415 ev 4 hrs (0415-2015)

Cabo de São Vicente

S
Zone

Chipiona
1656 kHz

Cádiz
Ch 26
Ch 74 0315 & ev 4 hrs

Tarifa
Ch 81
1704 kHz
Ch 10 Ev even H+15

Algeciras
Ch 74 0315 & ev 4 hrs

Spain and Portugal: MSI broadcasts by CRS and MRCCs/MRSCs (all times UT)

Coastguard broadcasts

Weather bulletins are broadcast in Spanish and **English** on the VHF channels and times (UT) below:

Huelva	Ch 10	4 hrly (0415-2015)
Cadiz	Ch 74	4 hrly from 0315
Tarifa	Ch 10, 67	Every even H+15.

Actual wind and visibility at Tarifa, followed by a forecast for Strait of Gibraltar, Cádiz Bay and Alborán, in **English** and Spanish. Fog (visibility) warnings are broadcast at the same times, more frequently when visibility falls below 2M.

Algeciras	Ch 74	4 hrly from 0315 and at 0515.

Recorded telephone forecasts

The service is only available within Spain and for Autolink-equipped vessels. For a coastal waters bulletin in Spanish call:

☎ 906 365 373 for Atlantic Andalucia and the Canaries. ☎ 906 365 374 for High Seas bulletin for Atlantic areas.

Navtex

Tarifa (G, 518 kHz) transmits weather bulletins in English at 0900 and 2100 UT. These include: Gale warnings, general synopsis and development and a forecast, valid for 24 hrs, for the N Atlantic and W Mediterranean within 450M of the coast. Tarifa (T, 490 kHz) transmits the same bulletins in Spanish at 0710 and 1910 UT.

Valencia (X, 518 kHz) transmits in English at 0750 & 1950 UT similar data for the W Med within 450M of the coast. Ditto Valencia (M, 490 kHz) in Spanish at 1000 & 1800UT.

GIBRALTAR

Gibraltar Broadcasting Corporation (GBC)

Gibraltar Radio broadcasts in English: General synopsis, situation, wind direction and force, visibility and sea state, radius 5M from Gibraltar. Frequencies are 1458 kHz, 91·3 MHz, 92·6 MHz and 100·5 MHz. Times (UT):

Mon-Fri:	0530, 0630, 0730, 1030, 1230
Sat:	0530, 0630, 0730, 1030
Sun:	0630, 0730, 1030

British Forces Broadcasting Service (BFBS)

Gale warnings for the Gibraltar area are broadcast on receipt by BFBS 1 and 2. All broadcasts are in English and comprise: Shipping forecast, wind, weather, visbility, sea state, swell, HW & LW times for waters within 5M of Gibraltar.

BFBS 1 frequencies and times (Local): 93·5, 97·8* MHz FM.

Mon-Fri:	0745, 0845, 1005, 1605
Sat:	0845, 0945, 1202
Sun:	0845, 0945, 1202, 1602

* This frequency is reported to have greater range.

BFBS 2 frequencies and time: 89·4, 99·5 MHz FM. Mon-Fri: 1200 Local time

Talk to a forecaster

Call ☎ 08700 767 818 to talk to a forecaster in Gibraltar about local weather in the Med or Canaries. Pay a flat rate of £17·00 by credit card, for a typical 5-10 mins briefing.

WEATHER VOCABULARY

English	German	French	Spanish	Dutch
Air mass	Luftmasse	Masse d'air	Massa de aire	Luchtmassa
Anticyclone	Antizyklonisch	Anticyclone	Anticiclón	Hogedrukgebied
Area	Gebiet	Zone	Zona	Gebied
Backing wind	Rückdrehender Wind	Vent reculant	Rolar el viento	Krimpende wind
Barometer	Barometer	Baromètre	Barómetro	Barometer
Breeze	Brise	Brise	Brisa	Bries
Calm	Flaute	Calme	Calma	Kalmte
Centre	Zentrum	Centre	Centro	Centum
Clouds	Wolken	Nuages	Nube	Wolken
Cold	Kalt	Froid	Frio	Koud
Cold front	Kaltfront	Front froid	Frente frio	Kou front
Cyclonic	Zyklonisch	Cyclonique	Ciclonica	Cycloonachtig
Decrease	Abnahme	Affaiblissement	Disminución	Afnemen
Deep	Tief	Profond	Profundo	Diep
Deepening	Vertiefend	Approfondissant	Ahondamiento	Verdiepend
Depression	Sturmtief	Dépression	Depresión	Depressie

English	German	French	Spanish	Dutch
Direction	Richtung	Direction	Direción	Richting
Dispersing	Auflösend	Se dispersant	Disipación	Oplossend
Disturbance	Störung	Perturbation	Perturbación	Verstoving
Drizzle	Niesel	Bruine	Lioviena	Motregen
East	Ost	Est	Este	Oosten
Extending	Ausdehnung	S'étendant	Extension	Uitstrekkend
Extensive	Ausgedehnt	Etendu	General	Uitgebreid
Falling	Fallend	Descendant	Bajando	Dalen
Filling	Auffüllend	Secomblant	Relleno	Vullend
Fog	Nebel	Brouillard	Niebla	Nevel
Fog bank	Nebelbank	Ligne de brouillard	Banco de niebla	Mist bank
Forecast	Vorhersage	Prévision	Previsión	Vooruitzicht
Frequent	Häufig	Fréquent	Frecuenta	Veelvuldig
Fresh	Frisch	Frais	Fresco	Fris
Front	Front	Front	Frente	Front
Gale	Sturm	Coup de vent	Temporal	Storm
Gale warning	Sturmwarnung	Avis de coup de vent	Aviso de temporal	Stormwaarschuwing
Good	Gut	Bon	Bueno	Goed
Gradient	Druckunterschied	Gradient	Gradiente	Gradiatie
Gust, squall	Bö	Rafalle	Ráfaga	Windvlaag
Hail	Hagel	Grêle	Granizo	Hagel
Haze	Diesig	Brume	Calina	Nevel
Heavy	Schwer	Abondant	Abunante	Zwaar
High	Hoch	Anticyclone	Alta presión	Hoog
Increasing	Zunehmend	Augmentant	Aumentar	Toenemend
Isobar	Isobar	Isobare	Isobara	Isobar
Isolated	Vereinzelt	Isolé	Aislado	Verspreid
Lightning	Blitze	Eclair de foudre	Relampago	Bliksem
Local	Örtlich	Locale	Local	Plaatselijk
Low	Tief	Dépression	Baja presión	Laag
Mist	Dunst	Brume légere	Nablina	Mist
Moderate	Mäßig	Modéré	Moderado	Matig
Moderating	Abnehmend	Se modérant	Medianente	Matigend
Moving	Bewegend	Se déplacant	Movimiento	Bewegend
North	Nord	Nord	Septentrional	Noorden
Occluded	Okklusion	Couvert	Okklusie	Bewolkt
Poor	Schlecht	Mauvais	Mal	Slecht
Precipitation	Niederschlag	Précipitation	Precipitación	Neerslag
Pressure	Druck	Pression	Presión	Druk
Rain	Regen	Pluie	Iluvia	Regen
Ridge	Hochdruckbrücke	Crête	Cresta	Rug
Rising	Ansteigend	Montant	Subiendo	Stijgen
Rough	Rauh	Agitée	Bravo o alborotado	Ruw
Sea	See	Mer	Mar	Zee
Seaway	Seegang	Haute mer	Alta mar	Zee
Scattered	Vereinzelt	Sporadiques	Difuso	Verspreid
Shower	Schauer	Averse	Aguacero	Bui
Slight	Leicht	Un peu	Leicht	Licht
Slow	Langsam	Lent	Lent	Langzaam
Snow	Schnee	Neige	Nieve	Sneeuw
South	Süd	Sud	Sur	Zuiden
Storm	Sturm	Tempête	Temporal	Storm
Sun	Sonne	Soleil	Sol	Zon
Swell	Schwell	Houle	Mar de fondo	Deining
Thunder	Donner	Tonnerre	Tormenta	Donder
Thunderstorm	Gewitter	Orage	Tronada	Onweer
Trough	Trog, Tiefausläufer	Creux	Seno	Trog
Variable	Umlaufend	Variable	Variable	Veranderlijk
Veering	Rechtdrehend	Virement de vent	Dextrogiro	Ruimende wind
Warm front	Warmfront	Front chaud	Frente calido	Warm front
Weather	Wetter	Temps	Tiempo	Weer
Wind	Wind	Vent	Viento	Wind
Weather report	Wetterbericht	Météo	Previsión	Weer bericht meteorologica

CHAPTER 3 - COMMUNICATIONS

CONTENTS

Radio operation 101

Radio data 102

Port and/or Marina VHF & Telephone details, including 4 VTS charts
  S England 104
  E England 105
     VTS Chart 1: Thames and Medway 106
     VTS Chart 2: Humber 107
  Scotland 108
  W England & Wales 109
  Ireland 110
  Denmark 110
  Germany 110
  Netherlands 111
     VTS Chart 3: Scheldemond and Westerschelde 112
     VTS Chart 4: Approaches to Nieuwe Waterweg 113
  Belgium 114
  N France 114
  Channel Islands 115
  W France 115
  N & NW Spain 116
  Portugal 116
  SW Spain 116
  Gibraltar & Morocco 116

VHF & MF coast radio stations
  Channel Islands 117
  Republic of Ireland 117
  Denmark 117
  Germany 117
  N Spain 118
  NW Spain 118
  Portugal 118
  Azores 118
  SW Spain 118

Sound signals and shapes 119

RADIO OPERATION

Avoiding interference

Before transmitting, first listen on the VHF channel. If occupied, wait for a break before transmitting, or choose another channel. If you cause interference you must comply immediately with any request from a Coastguard or Coast radio station to stop transmitting.

Control of communications

Ship-to-Shore: Communications between ship and shore stations are controlled by the latter, except in distress, urgency or safety cases.

Intership: The ship *called* controls communication. If you call another ship, then it has control. If you are called by a ship, you assume control. If a shore-based station breaks in, both ships must comply with instructions given.

Radio confidentiality

Private conversations heard on the radio must not be reproduced, passed on or otherwise used.

Making yourself understood

Clear R/T speech is vital. If a message cannot be understood by the receiver it is useless. Messages which have to be written down at the receiving station should be spoken slowly. This gives time for it to be written down by the receiving operator. If the transmitting operator himself writes it down all should be well. The average reading speed is 250 words a minute, whilst average writing speed is only 20.

When speaking, consider the following:

- **What** to say, ie *voice Procedure*
- **How** to say it, ie *voice Technique*

Voice Procedure is discussed below and overleaf. It includes procedural words, callsigns, making contact etc.

Voice Technique depends on a few simple rules:

Hold the microphone a few inches in front of the mouth and speak directly into it at a normal level. Speak clearly so that there can be no confusion. The voice should be pitched up at a higher level than normal. Do not drop the voice pitch at the end of a phrase or sentence. Emphasise words with weak syllables; 'Tower', if badly pronounced, could sound like 'tar'. People with strong regional or foreign accents must try to pronounce words as clearly as possible.

Difficult words may be spelled phonetically, preceded with 'I spell'. If the word can be pronounced, include it before and after it has been spelt. For example, the message 'I will berth on the yacht *Coila*' would be sent as: 'I will berth on the yacht *Coila* – I spell – Charlie Oscar India Lima Alfa – *Coila*'.

The phonetic alphabet

The syllables to emphasise are underlined

Letter	Morse	Phonetic	Spoken as
A	•—	Alfa	AL-fah
B	—•••	Bravo	BRAH-voh
C	—•—•	Charlie	CHAR-lee
D	—••	Delta	DELL-tah
E	•	Echo	ECK-oh
F	••—•	Foxtrot	FOKS-trot
G	——•	Golf	GOLF
H	••••	Hotel	hoh-TELL
I	••	India	IN-dee-ah
J	•———	Juliett	JEW-lee-ett
K	—•—	Kilo	KEY-loh
L	•—••	Lima	LEE-mah
M	——	Mike	MIKE
N	—•	November	no-VEM-ber
O	———	Oscar	OSS-car
P	•——•	Papa	pa-PAH
Q	——•—	Quebec	keh-BECK
R	•—•	Romeo	ROW-me-oh
S	•••	Sierra	see-AIR-rah
T	—	Tango	TANG-go
U	••—	Uniform	OO-nee-form
V	•••—	Victor	VIK-tah
W	•——	Whiskey	WISS-key
X	—••—	X-Ray	ECKS-ray
Y	—•——	Yankee	YANG-key
Z	——••	Zulu	ZOO-loo

Phonetic numerals

When numerals are transmitted, the following pronunciations make them easier to understand.

No	Morse	Spoken	No	Morse	Spoken
1	•————	WUN	6	—••••	SIX
2	••———	TOO	7	——•••	SEV-EN
3	•••——	TREE	8	———••	AIT
4	••••—	FOW-ER	9	————•	NIN-ER
5	•••••	FIFE	0	—————	ZERO

Numerals are transmitted digit by digit except that multiples of thousands may be spoken as follows:

Numeral	Spoken as
44	FOW-ER FOW-ER
90	NIN-ER ZERO
136	WUN TREE SIX
500	FIFE ZERO ZERO
1478	WUN FOW-ER SEV-EN AIT
7000	SEV-EN THOU-SAND

COMMUNICATIONS

Punctuation

Punctuation marks should be used only where their omission would cause confusion.

Mark	Word	Spoken as
.	Decimal	DAY-SEE-MAL
,	Comma	COMMA
.	Stop	STOP

Procedural words or 'prowords'

These are used to shorten transmissions

All after and **All before.** Used after proword *'say again'* to request repetition of a part of a message

Correct Reply to repeat of message that was preceded by prowords *'read back for check'* when it has been correctly repeated. Often said twice

Correction Cancel the last word or group of words. The correct word or group follows. Spoken when an error has been made in a transmission.

I say again I repeat the transmission or the part indicated (see 'All after' and 'All before').

I spell I shall spell the next word or group of letters phonetically

Out This is the end of working to you

Over Invitation to reply

Read back If the receiver is doubtful about accuracy of all or part of message he may repeat it back to the sending station, preceding the repetition with prowords *'I read back'*

Station calling Used when a station is uncertain of the calling station's identification/callsign

This is This transmission is from the station whose callsign or name immediately follows

Wait If a called station cannot accept traffic immediately, it will reply **'WAIT.......MINUTES'**, with reason if delay may exceed 10 minutes

Word after or Word before Used after the proword *'say again'* to request repetition

Wrong Reply to repetition of message preceded by prowords *'read back'* when it has been incorrectly repeated

Calls, calling and callsigns

Shore stations normally use a callsign of their geographic name followed by Coastguard or Radio, eg Solent Coastguard, Dublin Radio etc. Vessels usually identify themselves by the ship's name but the International callsign may be used in certain cases. If two yachts have the same or confusingly similar names, give your International callsign when starting communications, and thereafter use your ship's name as callsign.

'All ships' broadcast

Address used by Coastguard Radio where broadcast information is to be received or used by all who intercept it, eg gale warnings etc. No reply is needed.

Communicating with a coast radio station

Call initially on a working channel or very briefly on channel 16 to establish a working channel.

- Pause to check the working channel is clear before transmitting
- Use low power *(1 watt)* if close enough, ie up to 10 miles away. High power *(25 watts)* drains more from the battery
- The callsign of calling station up to three times only, and prowords 'This is'
- Say how many R/T calls you have to make
- Proword 'Over'

Using high power decreases battery state and the range your VHF will achieve. Continued calling also clutters up the channel and denies access to other users.

Aerial faults commonly reduce your transmitting range. Possibly the station aerial for the channel chosen is directionally orientated and you are on the wrong side. Try another channel or station. Call again when closer.

RADIO DATA

SHORT, MEDIUM and LONG RANGE RADIO COMMUNICATIONS

A suitable radio receiver on board will provide weather forecasts and time signals at scheduled times on a number of frequencies in various wavebands. With a maritime receiver you are not limited to the familiar BBC and commercial broadcasts. HM Coastguard transmit navigation warnings, storm warnings and weather messages for shipping in their respective sea areas.

Short range radiotelephony (RT) transmits and receives on VHF channels in the marine VHF (Very High Frequency) band. The equipment and procedures are simple, but range is normally limited to about 20 miles from ship to shore, rather less from ship to ship. Interconnection with national telephone systems is possible on certain VHF/RT channels when a yacht is within range of a Coast Radio Station, although there are now no such stations on the mainland of the UK, France or the Netherlands. Mobile telephones are now by far the most common form of ship to shore communication.

Medium range two-way communication operate in the marine MF (medium frequency) RT band, the 2MHz 'trawler band'. Single sideband techniques are employed on these medium frequencies and SSB equipment is essential. The effective range depends on the power of the transmitter and the sensitivity of the associated receiver; in general this might be up to 200 miles from certain (but not all) Coast Radio Stations.

THE MARINE VHF BAND

VHF is used by most vessels, Coast Radio Stations, CG centres and other rescue services. Its range is slightly better than the line of sight between the transmitting and receiving aerials. A good aerial, as high as possible, is most important.

In the Marine VHF band (156·00–174·00 MHz) the individual frequencies are separated from their neighbours by exactly 25kHz 'elbow-room' to eliminate mutual interference. Each frequency is given a channel number, not necessarily consecutive. Channels 29 to 59 are allocated to other purposes. Thus 55 channels are available, plus some with special purposes (see below).

VHF Channel Grouping

Channels are grouped for three main purposes, but some can be used for more than one purpose. They are listed below in their preferred order of usage:

• *Public correspondence* (ie link calls via CRS into the shore telephone system): Ch 26, 27, 25, 24, 23, 28, 04, 01, 03, 02, 07, 05, 84, 87, 86, 83, 85, 88, 61, 64, 65, 62, 66, 63, 60, 82, 78, 81.

• *Inter-ship:* Ch 06, 08, 10, 13, 09, 72, 73, 67, 69, 77, 15, 17. Remember these, so that if another vessel calls you, you can swiftly nominate a working channel from within this group.

• *Port Operations:* Ch 12, 14, 11, 13, 09, 68, 71, 74, 69, 73, 17, 15, 20, 22, 18, 19, 21, 05, 07, 02, 03, 01, 04, 78, 82, 79, 81, 80, 60, 63, 66, 62, 65, 64, 61, 84.

Special purposes. The following channels have one specific purpose only:

Ch 0 (156·00 MHz): SAR ops, not available to yachts.

Ch's 10 (156·500 MHz), **23** (161·750 MHz), **73** (156·675 MHz), **84** (161·825 MHz) and **86** (161·925 MHz): for MSI broadcasts by HMCG.

Ch 13 (156·650 MHz): Intership safety of navigation (sometimes referred to as bridge-to-bridge); a possible channel for calling a merchant ship if no contact on Ch 16.

Ch 16 (156·80 MHz): Distress, Safety and calling. *See Chapter 4 for Distress and Safety.* Ch 16 will be monitored by ships, CG centres (and, in some areas, any remaining Coast Radio Stations) for Distress and Safety until at least 2005, in parallel with DSC Ch 70. Yachts should monitor Ch 16.

After an initial call, the stations concerned **must** switch to a working channel, except for Safety matters.

Ch 67 (156·375 MHz): the Small Craft Safety channel in the UK, accessed via Ch 16.

Ch 70 (156·525 MHz): exclusively for digital selective calling for Distress and Safety purposes.

Ch 80 (157·025 MHz): the primary working channel between yachts and UK marinas.

Ch M (157·85 MHz): the secondary working channel between yachts and UK marinas; previously known as Ch 37.

Ch M2 (161·425 MHz): for race control, with Ch M as stand-by. YCs may apply to use Ch M2.

SILENCE PERIODS

The periods are the 3 minutes immediately after the whole and half hours, ie H to H+03 and H+30 to H+33, when no transmissions should be made.

MEDIUM RANGE MF RADIO

Single sideband MF/RT provides communications in the offshore waters of the UK and Western Europe where small craft may be out of VHF contact. A receiver alone gives the ability to hear weather bulletins, storm and navigation warnings for local sea areas broadcast from CRS in the 1.6 to 4.0MHz maritime band, ie on frequencies from 1605 to 4200 kHz.

MF transmissions tend to follow the curvature of the earth, which makes them suitable for direction-finding. For this reason, and because of their good range, the marine Distress R/T frequency (2182 kHz) is in the MF band.

TRAFFIC LISTS

If a Coast Radio station has messages for a vessel, but is unable to contact her, that vessel's name will be added to the Traffic List broadcast at (usually) two hour intervals. This is not a system much used by yachts and small craft.

LONG RANGE HF RADIO

HF radios use short wave frequencies in the 4, 8, 12, 16 and 22 MHz bands, as chosen to suit propagation conditions. HF is more expensive than MF and requires more power, but can provide worldwide coverage. A good installation and skilled operating techniques are essential for satisfactory results.

COMMUNICATIONS

PORT and/or MARINA VHF channels & Telephone numbers

NOTES. Ch 16 is almost universally guarded, so is omitted. *In larger ports it is sensible to monitor the VTS channel (if any) or the primary port channel (in bold) before changing to a marina channel.* Times are local, unless marked UT. Abbreviations are at the front of the book. Telephone codes are shown only once unless more than one applies.

ENGLAND – SOUTH COAST

ISLES OF SCILLY St Mary's HM Ch 14 (0800-1700); ☎ 01720 422768. *Falmouth CG* covers Scilly and the TSS off Land's End on Ch 23. **Tresco** HM ☎ 422849, mob 07778 601237.

NEWLYN HM Ch 09, **12** (M-F: 0800-1700, Sat: 0800-1200). ☎ 01736 362523.

PENZANCE HM Ch 09, **12** (M-F: 0830-1730 and HW –2 to +1). ☎ 01736 366113.

FALMOUTH *Falmouth Hbr Radio* Ch 11, **12**, 14 (M-F 0800-1700). ☎ 01326 312285. **Ch 80:** Falmouth ☎ 316620 and Port Pendennis marinas ☎ 311113. **Ch 12:** Visitors Yacht Haven ☎ 310991; St Mawes HM ☎ 270553. **Ch M** (HO): Mylor Yacht Hbr ☎ 372121.

TRURO HM *Carrick One* Ch 12. ☎ 01872 272130. **Ch M** (HO): Malpas Marine ☎ 271260.

MEVAGISSEY HM Ch 14 (Summer: 0900-2100, Winter: 0900-1700). ☎ 01726 843305.

CHARLESTOWN HM Ch 14, HW –2 to +1, only when a vessel is expected. ☎ 01726 70241.

PAR HM Ch 12 (HO). ☎ 01726 817337.

FOWEY HM Ch 12 (0900-1700); also Hbr Patrol (0900-2000). ☎ 01726 832471. Water taxi: Ch 06.

LOOE HM Ch 16, occas. ☎ 01503 262839.

PLYMOUTH *Long Room Port Control* Ch 14 H24, ☎ 01752 836528. **QAB** Ch 80, ☎ 671142. **Sutton Hbr lock:** Ch 12 H24, ☎ 204737. **Cattewater HM** Ch 14 (M-F 0900-1700), ☎ 836528. **Plymouth Yacht Haven**, Ch 80, M; ☎ 404231. **Mayflower marina**, Ch 80; ☎ 556633.

SALCOMBE HM & launch: Ch 14, May to mid-Sep: 7/7, 0600-2100; otherwise: M-F 0900-1600; ☎ 01548 843791. *Hbr Taxi* Ch 12. Fuel barge Ch 06, ☎ 07801 798862. *Egremont* (ICC) Ch M.

DARTMOUTH HM *Dartnav* Ch 11, 7/7 0730-dusk; ☎ 01803 832337. Darthaven marina Ch 80, ☎ 752545. Dart & Noss-on-Dart marinas Ch 80, ☎ 833351. Fuel barge Ch 06. Water taxi Ch 08.

TORBAY HBRS Brixham marina Ch 80, ☎ 01803 882929; YC, ☎ 853332, & Water taxi *Shuttle* Ch M. Torquay marina Ch 80, ☎ 200210. Fuel Ch M.

EXETER Exmouth marina Ch 14, ☎ 01395 269314. **Retreat BY:** Ch M, ☎ 01392 874720. **Port of Exeter** HM Ch 12, M-F: 0730-1730 and when vessel due; ☎ 274306.

LYME REGIS HM Ch 14. Summer 0800-2000, winter 1000-1500. ☎ 01297 442137.

BRIDPORT. HM Ch 11. ☎ 01308 423222.

PORTLAND PORT. Port Control Ch 74 (H24). ☎ 01305 824044. **Sailing Academy** ☎ 866000.

WEYMOUTH
HM & Town Bridge: Ch 12, M-F 0800-2000 summer & when vessel due; ☎ 01305 838423. **Marina** Ch 80, ☎ 767576. **Fuel** Ch 60.

POOLE
HM/bridge Ch 14 (H24); Code 01202 ☎ 440233. **Marinas Ch 80 M:** Salterns ☎ 709971. Parkstone YC ☎ 743610. Poole Quay ☎ 649488. Cobbs Quay ☎ 674299. **Poole Bay Fuels: Ch M** M-F: 0900-1730; Sat/Sun 0830-1800. ☎ 07768 71511.

YARMOUTH (IoW)
HM & Yar bridge **Ch 68** H24. ☎ 01983 760321. Water taxi **Ch 15.**

LYMINGTON
Marinas Ch 80, M: Yacht Haven ☎ 01590 677071. Berthon Marina ☎ 01590 673312.

COWES
Harbour Radio, Chain Ferry & Folly Inn Ch 69 Mon-Fri: 0800-1700. Marinas **Ch 80, M.** Tel code 01983: Yacht Haven ☎ 299975. Shepards ☎ 297821. East Cowes ☎ 293983. Island Hbr **Ch 80,** ☎ 822999. Water Taxi **Ch 06.**

NEWPORT HM & Yacht Hbr **Ch 69** 0800-1600. ☎ 01983 525994.

RYDE HM **Ch 80.** Summer 0900-2000, Winter HX. ☎ 01983 613879. Access HW±2.

BEMBRIDGE Marina **Ch 80,** ☎ 01983 872828. Hbr launch **Ch M.**

SOUTHAMPTON
Port Ops and VTS Ch 12 14. Marinas **Ch 80, M.** Tel code 02380: Hythe ☎ 207073. Ocean Village ☎ 229385. Shamrock Quay ☎ 229461. Kemp's ☎ 632323.

HAMBLE
Hbr Radio Ch 68 Apr-Sep daily 0600-2200; Oct-Mar 0700-1830. Marinas **Ch 80, M.** Tel code 02380: Hamble Pt ☎ 452464. Port Hamble ☎ 452741. Mercury ☎ 455994. Water Taxi **Ch 77,** ☎ 454512. Tel code 01489: Universal ☎ 574272. Swanwick ☎ 885000.

PORTSMOUTH
VTS **Ch 11** (& *QHM* if essential). Marinas **80.** Tel code 02392: Haslar ☎ 601201. Gosport ☎ 524811. Royal Clarence ☎ 523810. Port Solent ☎ 210765. THE CAMBER (Commercial Hbr): *Portsmouth Hbr Radio* **Ch 11** 14 (H24).

LANGSTONE HBR
HM **Ch 12**. Summer, daily 0830-1700; Winter, M-F 0830-1700; Sat/Sun 0830-1300. Southsea marina **Ch 80, M, ☎** 02392 822719.

CHICHESTER
HM *Chichester Hbr Radio* **Ch 14**. 1 Apr-Sep: M-Fri: 0830-1700. Sat: 0900-1300. 1 Oct - 31 Mar: 0900-1300, 1400-1700. Marinas **Ch 80, M**. Sparkes ☎ 02392 463572. Tel code 01243: Northney ☎ 466321. Emsworth Yacht Hbr ☎ 377727. Thornham ☎ 375335. Birdham Pool ☎ 512310. Chichester ☎ 512731.
Water taxi **Ch 08** 0900-1800, mobile 07970 378350

LITTLEHAMPTON
HM/Bridge **Ch 71** 0900-1700. Marina **Ch 80, M; ☎** 01903 241663.

SHOREHAM
HM & lock *Shoreham Hbr Radio* **Ch 14** (H24). Marina ☎ 01273 593801.

BRIGHTON
Marina *Brighton Control* **Ch M 80; ☎** 01273 819919.

NEWHAVEN
HM & Bridge *Newhaven Radio* **Ch 12**. Marina **Ch 80, M; ☎** 01273 513881.

EASTBOURNE
Sovereign Hbr, inc lock/berthing: **Ch 17**, 15. ☎ 01323 470099.

RYE
Hbr Radio, **Ch 14** 0900-1700 or when ship due. ☎ 01797 225225.

FOLKESTONE
Port Control **Ch 15** for entry; ☎ 01303 254597.

DOVER
Port Control **Ch 74** for entry. Marina **Ch 80; ☎** 01304 241663.

RAMSGATE
Port Control **Ch 14**. Marina **Ch 80; ☎** 01843 572110.

WHITSTABLE
Hbr Radio Ch 09 12, Mon-Fri: 0830-1700 and –3HW+1. ☎ 01227 274086.

MEDWAY
Medway Radio **Ch 74**. Kingsferry Bridge (W Swale) **Ch 10** H24. Marinas **Ch 80, M**. Tel code 01634: Gillingham ☎ 280022. Hoo ☎ 250311. Chatham ☎ 899200.

PORT OF LONDON
LONDON VTS: Ch 69 from sea to Sea Reach No 4 buoy. **Ch 68** Sea Reach No 4 to Crayford Ness. **Ch 14, 22**, W of Crayford Ness.
Thames Barrier Ch 14. ☎ 020 8855 0315.

RIVER THAMES
Patrol Launches *Thames Patrol* **Ch 06, 13, 14, 68**
King George V Dock lock *KG Control* **Ch 13.**
West India Dock lock **Ch 13**
Greenwich Yacht Club **Ch M**

Thames lock (Brentford) **Ch 74** Summer 0800-1800; Winter 0800-1630.
Cadogan Pier **Ch 14** 0900-1700.
Marinas Ch 80, M; Tel code 0207: Gallions Point ☎ 4767054. Poplar Dock ☎ 5151046. South Dock ☎ 2522244. Limehouse Basin ☎ 3089930. St Katherine Haven ☎ 2645312. Chelsea Hbr ☎ 2259100. Brentford Dock ☎ 0208 2328941.

RIVER ROACH
Havengore Bridge **Ch 72** *Shoe Bridge* HW±2. ☎ 01702 383436.

BURNHAM-ON-CROUCH
Ch 80: HM Launch 0900-1700. Yacht Hbr ☎ 01621 782150. Essex marina ☎ 01702 258531.

RIVER BLACKWATER
Marinas **Ch 80, M**; Tel code 01621: Tollesbury ☎ 869202. Bradwell ☎ 776235. **Ch M**: Blackwater ☎ 740264. Heybridge Lock, **Ch 80** ☎ 853506.

RIVER COLNE
Brightlingsea Hbr Radio **Ch 68** 0800-2000. ☎ 01206 302200, mob 07952 734814.

WALTON BACKWATERS
Titchmarsh marina **Ch 80,** ☎ 01255 672185.

RIVERS STOUR AND ORWELL
HARWICH VTS **Ch 71**, 11, 20, H24
SUNK VTS **Ch 14**, H24
Ipswich Port Radio (for R Orwell) **Ch 68,** H24
Marinas **Ch 80, M**. Tel code 01473: Shotley ☎ 788982. Suffolk Hbr ☎ 659240. Woolverstone ☎ 780206. Fox's ☎ 689111. Neptune ☎ 215204. Ipswich Haven ☎ 236644.

RIVER DEBEN
HM *Odd Times* **Ch 08**. Tidemill Yacht Hbr ☎ 01394 385745.

SOUTHWOLD
Port Radio **Ch 09** 12. HM ☎ 01502 724712.

LOWESTOFT
Hbr Control **Ch 11, 14**. HM ☎ 01502 572286. Royal Norfolk & Suffolk YC **Ch 80.** ☎ 566726. Haven Marina **Ch 80** ☎ 580300. **Mutford Bridge & Lock Ch** 09, **14** ☎ 531778.

GREAT YARMOUTH
Yarmouth Radio **Ch 12**. HM ☎ 01493 335511. *Haven & Breydon bridges* **Ch 12**.

WELLS-NEXT-THE-SEA
Wells Hbr **Ch 12**, HJ, HW±2 and when vessel expected. HM ☎ 01328 711646.

WISBECH
Ch 09 HW–3 when vessel expected. HM 01945 588059. Sutton Bridge **Ch 09**

KING'S LYNN
Harbour Radio **Ch 14** 11 Mon-Fri: 0800-1730 and –3HW+1. HM ☎ 01553 773411.

BOSTON
Port Control **Ch 11 12**. HM ☎ 01205 362328. *Grand Sluice* **Ch 74** only when lock operates. Marina ☎ 364420.

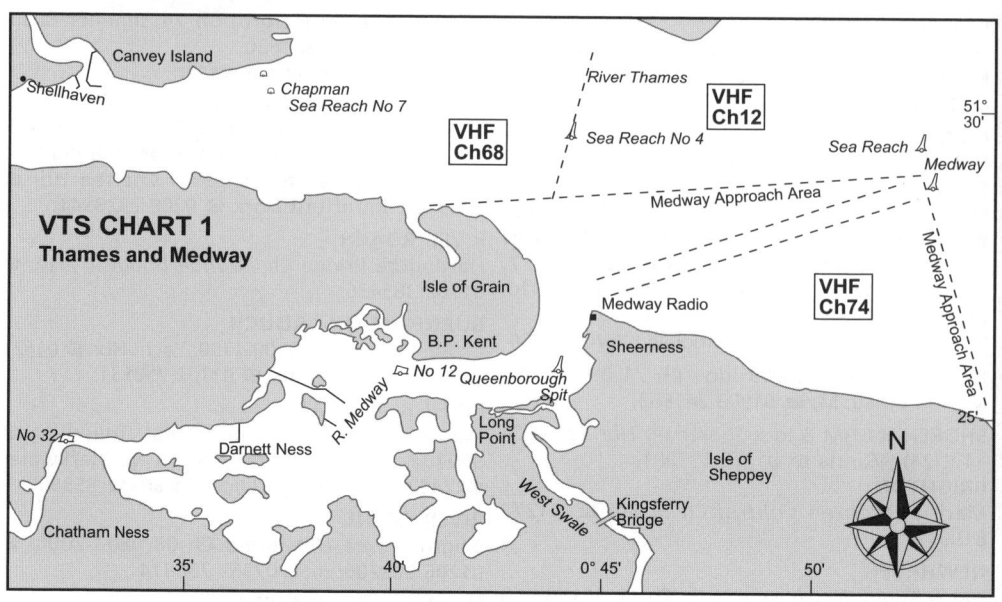

VTS CHART 1
Thames and Medway

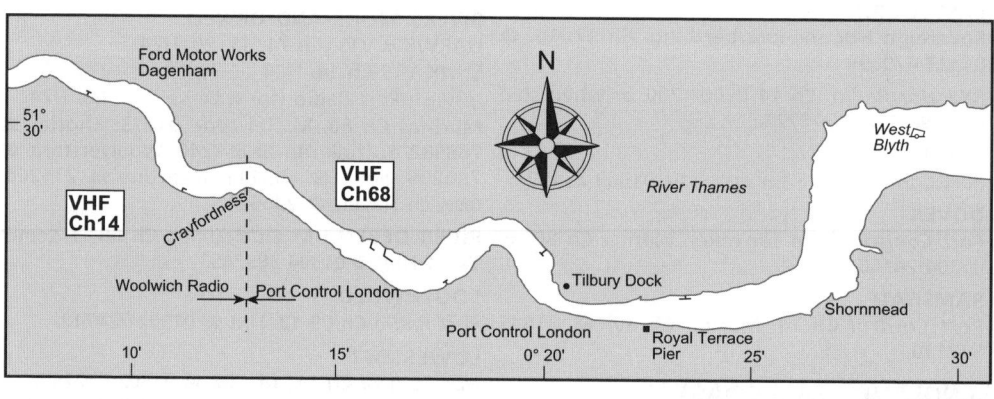

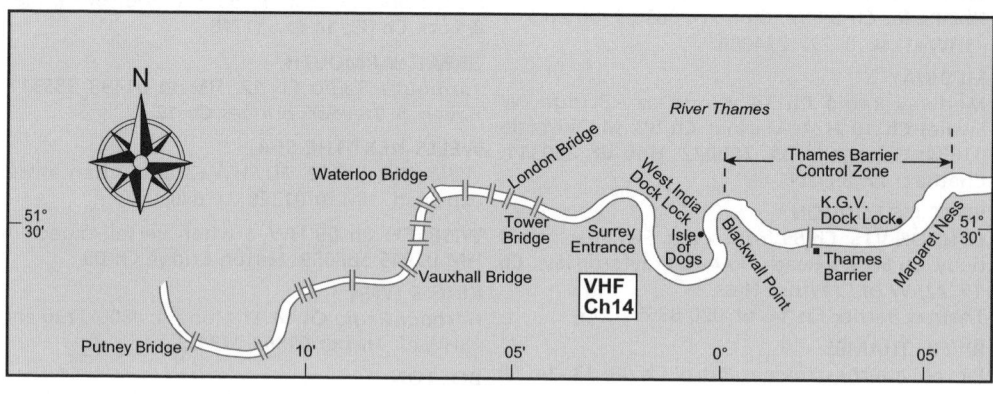

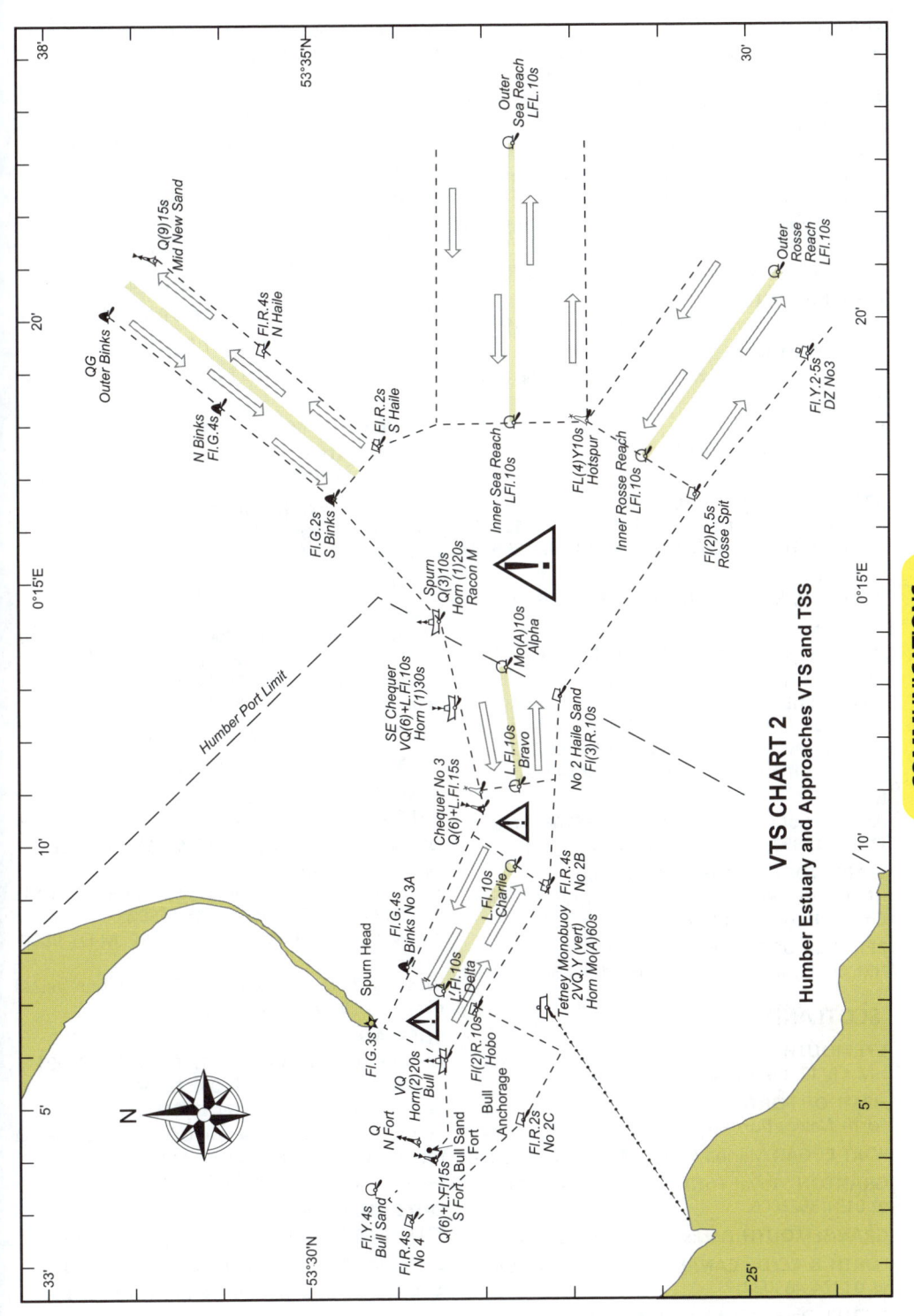

VTS CHART 2

Humber Estuary and Approaches VTS and TSS

Outer Sea Reach
LFl.10s

Q(9)15s
Mid New Sand

QG
Outer Binks

Fl.R.4s
N Haile

N Binks
Fl.G.4s

Fl.R.2s
S Haile

Fl.G.2s
S Binks

Outer
Rosse
Reach
LFl.10s

Fl.Y.2.5s
DZ No3

Humber Port Limit

Spurn
Q(3)10s
Horn (1)20s
Racon M

Inner Sea Reach
LFl.10s

Fl(4)Y10s
Hotspur

Inner Rosse Reach
LFl.10s

Fl(2)R.5s
Rosse Spit

Mo(A)10s
Alpha

SE Chequer
VQ(6)+L.Fl.10s
Horn (1)30s

L.Fl.10s
Bravo

No 2 Haile Sand
Fl(3)R.10s

Chequer No 3
Q(6)+L.Fl.15s

Fl.G.4s
Binks No 3A

L.Fl.10s
Charlie

Fl.R.4s
No 2B

L.Fl.10s
Delta

Tetney Monobuoy
2VQ.Y (vert)
Horn Mo(A)60s

Spurn Head

Fl.G.3s

VQ
Horn(2)20s
Bull

Fl(2)R.10s
Hobo

Bull
Anchorage

Fl.Y.4s
Bull Sand

Q
N Fort

Fl.R.2s
No 2C

Fl.R.4s
No 4

Q(6)+L.Fl15s
S Fort

Bull Sand
Fort

N

RIVER HUMBER

VTS 1, Ch 14 to seaward of Clee Ness Lt F

VTS 2, Ch 12 Clee Ness–Gainsborough (R Trent) & Goole (R Ouse). MSI broadcasts Ch 12 & 14 every 2 hrs from 0103LT.

Grimsby Docks Radio **Ch 74**; 18 79 H24

Marinas: Grimsby, Meridian Quay **Ch 74**, ☎ 01472 268424. **Hull**, **Ch 80**, ☎ 01482 330508.

South Ferriby: Sluice **Ch 74**. Marina **Ch 80**, ☎ 01652 635620. **Brough**, Humber Yawl club ☎ 01482 667224. **Goole** Boathouse ☎ 01405 763985.

BRIDLINGTON

HM, call Ch 16; work **Ch 12**. ☎ 01262 670148.

SCARBOROUGH

HM *Scarborough Lt Ho* **Ch 12** H24. ☎ 01723 373530.

WHITBY

HM, Bridge & marina **Ch 11**, 12 H24. ☎ 01947 602354.

RIVER TEES and HARTLEPOOL

Monitor *Tees Port control* **Ch 14**, 08, 11, 12, 22. Hartlepool marina **Ch 80, M** H24. ☎ 01429 865744.

SEAHAM

HM **Ch 12**, M-F 0800-1800. ☎ 0191 5161700.

SUNDERLAND

Hbr Radio **Ch 14** (H24). Marina **Ch 80, M.** ☎ 0191 5144721.

RIVER TYNE

Tyne Hbr Radio **Ch 12**, 08, 11, inc Info service. Royal Quays marina **Ch 80**. ☎ 0191 2728282. St Peter's marina **Ch M.** ☎ 0191 2654472.

BLYTH

Port control **Ch 12**, 11. ☎ 01670 352066. Marina ☎ 01670 353636 (R Northumberland YC).

WARKWORTH HARBOUR (Amble)

HM Ch 16, work **Ch 14**. ☎ 01665 710306. Marina **Ch 80**, ☎ 01665 712168.

BERWICK-UPON-TWEED

HM **Ch 12**, M-F 0800-1700. ☎ 01289 307404.

EYEMOUTH

HM **Ch 12**, 06 HO. ☎ 01890 750223.

FIRTH OF FORTH

Forth Navigation **Ch 71**; may work 12, 20.

PORT EDGAR Marina **Ch 80, M.** ☎ 0131 3313330.

GRANTON, Royal Forth YC, Call *Boswell* **Ch M.** ☎ 0131 5523006.

GRANGEMOUTH Docks **Ch 14**. ☎ 01324 498566.

FORTH & CLYDE CANAL *Carron Sea Lock* **Ch 74**. ☎ 01324 483034.

METHIL Docks **Ch 14**. ☎ 01324 498585.

ANSTRUTHER Ch 11. ☎ 01333 310836.

DUNDEE *Harbour Radio* **Ch 12**. ☎ 01382 224121. **Royal Tay YC Ch M.** ☎ 01382 477516.

PERTH *Perth Harbour* **Ch 09**. ☎ 01738 624056.

ARBROATH *Port Control* **Ch 11**. ☎ 01241 872166.

MONTROSE *Port Control* **Ch 12**. ☎ 01674 672302.

STONEHAVEN HM **Ch 11**. ☎ 01569 762741.

ABERDEEN VTS **Ch 12**, ☎ 01224 597000.

PETERHEAD *Peterhead Hbrs* **Ch 14** for cl'nce to enter/exit. Marina ☎ 01779 477868.

FRASERBURGH Ch 12 H24, ☎ 01346 515858.

MACDUFF Ch 12 H24, ☎ 01261 832236.

BANFF Ch 14 HX, ☎ 01261 815544 (part time).

WHITEHILLS *Whitehills Hbr Radio* **Ch 14**, ☎ 01261 861291.

BUCKIE Ch 12, 16 (H24), ☎ 01542 831700.

LOSSIEMOUTH

HM **Ch 12** 0700-1700. Marina, ☎ 01343 813066.

HOPEMAN and BURGHEAD

Same HM: *Burghead Radio* **Ch 14** HX, ☎ 01343 835337.

NAIRN HM/Marina ☎ 01667 454330. No VHF.

INVERNESS

HM & Longman Yacht Haven **Ch 12**, M-Fri 0900-1700; Tel code 01463: ☎ 715715.

Clachnaharry Sealock **Ch 74**, ☎ 713896. HW ±4. Seaport marina 239745. Caley marina 236539

HELMSDALE Ch 13, ☎ 01431 821692.

WICK Ch 14 HX, ☎ 01955 602030.

SCRABSTER

HM **Ch 12** H24. Call on arr/dep, ☎ 01847 892779.

ORKNEY HARBOURS NAVIGATION SERVICE

Orkney Harbour Radio **Ch 09 11** 12

Stromness HM **Ch 12** M-Fri 0900-1700; Tel code 01856: ☎ 850744. Marina, ☎ 465825.

Kirkwall *Hbr Radio* **Ch 12**, ☎ 872292. M-Fri, 0800-1700.

Westray Pier, *Pierowall Hbr* **Ch 14** when vessel expected. ☎ 01857 677216.

SHETLAND

Lerwick Hbr Radio **Ch 11, 12** ☎ 01595 692991.

Scalloway Hbr Radio **Ch 09, 12**, M-F 0700-1800, Sat 0900-1230. Piermaster ☎ 01595 880574.

Sullom Voe VTS **Ch 14** for tfc info, weather & radar assistance on request. ☎ 01806 242551.

Balta Sound Harbour **Ch 16, 20** HO

OUTER HEBRIDES

STORNOWAY HM **Ch 12** H24, ☎ 01851 702688.

Loch Maddy, N Uist Ch 12, ☎ 01876 500337.

St Kilda, *Kilda Radio* **Ch 16**, ☎ 01870 604406.

MAINLAND

Kinlochbervie Ch 14 HX, ☎ 01971 521235.

Loch Inver Ch 09 HX, ☎ 01571 844265.

ULLAPOOL Ch 14, ☎ 01854 612091.

Loch Gairloch Hbr Ch 16, ☎ 01445 712140.

ISLE OF SKYE
Portree Ch 12 (occas), ☎ 01478 612926.

Kyle Akin Ch 11, ☎ 01599 534167.

KYLE OF LOCH ALSH Ch 11, ☎ 01599 534589.

Mallaig Ch 09 HO, ☎ 01687 462154.

Tiree, Gott Bay Pier, Ch 31, ☎ 01879 230337.

Coll, Arinagour Pier, Ch 31, ☎ 01879 230347.

L Sunart, Salen Bay, Ch 16, ☎ 01967 431333.

ISLAND OF MULL
Tobermory, Ch 12, M HJ, ☎ 01688 302017.

Loch Lathaich; Sound of Iona; Craignure Pier.

Corpach basin & lock/Caledonian Canal Ch 74, ☎ 01397 772249.

DUNSTAFFNAGE Marina, Ch M, ☎ 01631 566555.

Oban North Bay Ch 12. Marina, ☎ 01631 565333.

L. Melfort, Kilmelford Haven, ☎ 01852 200248.

L. Shuna, Craobh marina, ☎ 01852 500222.

L. Craignish, Ardfern Ch 80, M, ☎ 01852 500247.

CRINAN CANAL, Ch 74. BWB, ☎ 01546 603210.

Islay, Port Ellen, ☎ 01496 300301; no VHF.

Tarbert, Loch Fyne Ch 14, ☎ 01880 820344.

CAMPBELTOWN Ch 12, 13, ☎ 01586 552552.

ROTHESAY, Bute Ch 12, ☎ 01700 500630.

LARGS Yacht Haven Ch 80, M, ☎ 01475 675333.

KIP Marina Ch 80, M, ☎ 01475 521485.

HOLY LOCH Marina Ch 80, M, ☎ 01369 701800.

RHU Marina Ch 80, M, ☎ 01436 820238.

ARDROSSAN Marina Ch 80, M, ☎ 01294 607077.

IRVINE HM/Bridge Ch 12, ☎ 01292 487286.

TROON Ch 14. Marina Ch 80, M, ☎ 01294 315553.

GIRVAN HM Ch 12, ☎ 01465 713648.

KIRKCUDBRIGHT HM Ch 12, ☎ 01557 331135.

ENGLAND W COAST & WALES

MARYPORT Marina Ch M, ☎ 01900 814431.

WORKINGTON HM Ch 14, ☎ 01900 602301.

WHITEHAVEN Marina Ch 12, ☎ 01946 692435.

ISLE OF MAN (Tel code 01624) If unable to contact IoM hbrs below, call Douglas.

Douglas Hbr Control Ch 12 H24.

Port St Mary HM Ch 12 HJ, ☎ 833205.

Peel HM Ch 12 HJ, ☎ 842338.

Ramsey HM Ch 12 HO, ☎ 812245.

MAINLAND
GLASSON DOCK Marina Ch 69, ☎ 01524 751491.

FLEETWOOD Dock Radio Ch 12 for Marina, ☎ 01253 879062.

PRESTON Lock Riversway Ch 14. Marina Ch 80, ☎ 01772 733595.

LIVERPOOL Mersey Radio Ch 12. Info Ch 09. Radar Ch 18. Liverpool marina (Brunswick Dock) Ch M, ☎ 0151 7076777. Albert Dock Ch M, ☎ 0151 7096558; access via Canning Dock lock.

CONWY HM Ch 14. Marinas, both Ch 80: Conwy, ☎ 01492 593000. Deganwy 576888.

MENAI STRAIT & ANGLESEY
Beaumaris/Menai HM Ch 69, ☎ 01248 712312.

Caernarfon, HM & Victoria Dock Ch 80, ☎ 01286 672118. Mon-Fri: 0900-1700 Sat: 0900-1200

HOLYHEAD Port Control Ch 14, ☎ 01407 606700. Marina 764242.

MAINLAND
PWLLHELI, HM Ch 12. Marina Ch 80, M, ☎ 01758 704081.

PORTHMADOG Hbr Ch 12, ☎ 01766 512927.

BARMOUTH HM Barmouth Hbr Ch 12, ☎ 01341 280671.

ABERDOVEY Aberdovey Hbr Ch 12, ☎ 01654 767626.

ABERYSTWYTH HM Ch 14. Marina Ch 80, ☎ 01970 611422.

FISHGUARD HM Ch 14, ☎ 01348 873369.

MILFORD HAVEN Monitor Port Control (and Patrol launch) Ch 12, whilst under way. Milford Docks Pierhead Ch 18. Milford Dock marina Ch M, ☎ 01646 696312. Neyland Yacht Haven Ch 80, M, ☎ 01646 601601.

Tenby Ch 80, ☎ 01834 842717.

Saundersfoot Ch 11

SWANSEA
Tawe Lock Ch 18. Marina Ch 80, ☎ 01792 470310.

BARRY Barry Radio Ch 11. HM ☎ 01446 732665.

CARDIFF Cardiff Radio Ch 14. Barrage control Ch 18. Penarth marina Ch 80, ☎ 02920 705021.

NEWPORT HM Ch 71, ☎ 0870 6096699.

SHARPNESS Sharpness Radio Ch 13 for lock. Marina, ☎ 01453 811476. Canal Ch 74

BRISTOL Bristol VTS Ch 12 with intentions. City Docks Radio Ch 14 (low power) to confirm. Bristol Floating Hbr Ch 73. Bristol marina Ch 80, ☎ 0117 9213198.

PORTISHEAD marina Ch 80, ☎ 0198 4631264.

BURNHAM-ON-SEA HM Ch 08, ☎ 01278 782180.

COMMUNICATIONS

WATCHET marina **Ch 80,** ☎ 01255 841941.

ILFRACOMBE HM **Ch 80,** ☎ 01271 862108.

APPLEDORE-BIDEFORD HM *Two Rivers* **Ch 12,** Appledore ☎ 01237 474569.

BUDE HM **Ch 12,** ☎ 01288 353111.

PADSTOW HM **Ch 12,** ☎ 01841 532239.

ST IVES HM **Ch 12,** ☎ 01736 795018.

IRELAND

ROSSAVEEL Ch 12, ☎ 091 572108.

GALWAY, HM **Ch 12,** ☎ 091 561874.

SHANNON ESTUARY *Shannon Ports Radio* **Ch 11** (HO), ☎ 087 2560427.

KILRUSH marina Ch 80, ☎ 06590 52072.

LIMERICK HBR Ch 12 13, ☎ 061 315377.

FENIT HM **Ch 14, M,** ☎ 066 7136231.

DINGLE HM **Ch 14** (no calls req'd), ☎ 066 9151629.

CAHERSIVEEN (Valentia) marina Ch 80, ☎ 066 9472777.

BANTRY BAY, Lawrence Cove marina **Ch M,** ☎ 027 75044.

CASTLETOWN BEARHAVEN ⚓, ☎ 027 70220.

CROOKHAVEN ⚓, ☎ 028 35319.

SCHULL ⚓, mobile ☎ 086 1039105.

BALTIMORE Ch 09, mobile 087 2351485.

GLANDORE HM **Ch 06,** ☎ 028 34737.

COURTMACSHERRY HM/RNLI ☎ 023 46170.

KINSALE HM **Ch 14** ☎ 021 4772503. Marinas **Ch M:** KYC ☎ 4772196. Castlepark ☎ 4774959.

CORK *Cork Hbr Radio* **Ch 12,** 14 H24. HM ☎ 021 4273125. Marinas **Ch M:** Crosshaven ☎ 4831161. Salve ☎ 4831145. Royal Cork YC ☎ 4831023. East Ferry ☎ 4813390.

YOUGHAL HM/Pilots **Ch 14,** ☎ 024 92577.

DUNMORE EAST HM/Pilots **Ch 14** ☎ 051 383166.

WATERFORD & **NEW ROSS Ch** 12, **14**. Marina **Ch M,** ☎ 051 873501.

KILMORE QUAY Ch 09. Marina, ☎ 053 29955.

ROSSLARE HM **Ch 12** H24, ☎ 053 33114.

WEXFORD Hbr Boat club. **Ch 16,** ☎ 053 22039.

ARKLOW HM **Ch 12,** ☎ 0402 32466. Marina 39901.

WICKLOW HM **Ch 14** 12, ☎ 0404 67455.

DUN LAOGHAIRE HM **Ch 14,** ☎ 01 2801130. YCs & Marina **Ch M:** Marina 2020040. National 2805725. R. St George 2801811. R. Irish 2809452. DL Motor YC 2801371.

DUBLIN HM and VTS *Port Radio* **Ch 12,** 13.

Poolbeg marina **Ch M,** ☎ 01 6689983. Lifting bridge *Eastlink* **Ch 12, 13.** City moorings, ☎ 01 8183300.

HOWTH HM **Ch 11.** Marina Ch M, 80, ☎ 01 8392777.

MALAHIDE Marina **Ch 80, M,** ☎ 01 8454129.

CARLINGFORDFORD LOUGH
Carlingford marina **Ch M,** ☎ 042 93730739.

Warrenpoint Ch 12, ☎ 028 41752878.

Kilkeel Ch 12, ☎ 028 41762287.

ARDGLASS (Phennick Cove) marina **Ch M, 80,** ☎ 028 44842332.

STRANGFORD LOUGH
HM **Ch 12 14,** ☎ 028 44881637.

Portaferry marina **Ch 80,** M, ☎ 07703 209780.

Donaghadee Copelands marina, ☎ 028 91882184.

BELFAST VTS *Belfast Hbr Radio* **Ch 12. Marinas Ch 80, M:** Carrickfergus, ☎ 028 93366666. Bangor, ☎ 028 91453217.

LARNE *Port Control* **Ch 14**, 11.

Glenarm HM/Marina, mobile ☎ 07703 606763.

Ballycastle HM/Marina, mob ☎ 07803 505084.

PORTRUSH HM **Ch 12,** ☎ 028 70822307.

COLERAINE HM **Ch 12.** Marina, ☎ 028 70832086.

LONDONDERRY *Hbr radio* **Ch 14,** ☎ 028 71860555.

L SWILLY Fahan marina, ☎ 074 9360008.

KILLYBEGS HM **Ch 14,** ☎ 07497 31032.

Burton Port HM **Ch** 06, 12, **14,** ☎ 075 42155.

SLIGO HM **Ch 12,** 14, ☎ 071 9161197.

DENMARK

Skagen HM **Ch 12** HX, ☎ 98 441346.

Hirtshals HM **Ch 12** 13 HX, ☎ 98 941422.

Torup Strand HM **Ch 12** 13 HX.

Hanstholm HM **Ch 12** 13 HX, ☎ 97 961833.

THYBORØN HM **Ch 12** 13 H24, ☎ 97 831188.

Thisted (Limfjord) Ch 12 13 HX, ☎ 97 911400.

Torsminde HM **Ch 12** 13, ☎ 24 233345.

Hvide Sande HM **Ch 12** HX, ☎ 97 311633.

ESBJERG *Hbr Control* **Ch 12** 13 14 H24, ☎ 75 124000. **Fanø** HM, ☎ 75 163100.

Rømø HM **Ch 10, 12, 13** HX, ☎ 74 755245.

GERMANY

HELGOLAND HM **Ch 67,** ☎ 04725 81593583.
May-Aug Mon-Thu 0700-1200, 1300-2000. Fri-Sun 0700-1200.

Sep-Apr Mon-Thu 0700-1200, 1300-1600. Fri 0700-1200.
List HM **Ch 11**, ☎ 046 51870374.
Hörnum HM **67**, ☎ 046 51881027.
Wyk HM **Ch 11**, ☎ 046 81500430.
Pellworm HM **Ch 11**, ☎ 048 44726.
Husum HM **Ch 11**, ☎ 048 16670.
R. Eider sealock **Ch 14**, ☎ 04833 4535211.
Büsum HM **Ch 11**, ☎ 048 413607.

INNER DEUTSCHE BUCHT (GERMAN BIGHT)
VTS, Eastern part **Ch 80**, ☎ 04421 489282.
VTS, Western part **Ch 79**
BRUNSBÜTTEL HM **Ch 06**, ☎ 04852 88418.

NORD-OSTSEE KANAL (KIEL CANAL)
VTS Canal I   **Ch 13**, ☎ 04852 885371.
VTS Canal II   **Ch 02**, ☎ 04852 885369.
VTS Canal III   **Ch 03**, ☎ 0431 3603456.
VTS Canal IV   **Ch 12**, ☎ 0431 3603465.
Brieholz, Ch 73
Ostermoor, Ch 73

RIVER ELBE
CUXHAVEN HM **Ch 69** HX, ☎ 04721 500150.
Cuxhaven marina, ☎ 37363. **YC** marina, ☎ 34111.
R. Stör Lock Ch 09 Bridge opens on request.
Glückstadt HM **Ch 08**, ☎ 04124 913200.

HAMBURG Port HM **Ch 12**, ☎ 040 7411540.
VTS *Hamburg Port Traffic* **Ch 13, 14, 74**. Wedel Yacht Hbr, ☎ 040 1034438. City Sporthafen, ☎ 040 364297.

BREMERHAVEN *Weser VTS* **Ch 22**. Port **Ch 12**, ☎ 0471 59613401. **Locks Ch 69, 70. Marinas** Weser YC, ☎ 23531. NYC, ☎ 77555. WVW, ☎ 73268.

BREMEN *Port Radio* **Ch 03**, ☎ 0421 3618504.

JADE VTS *Jade Traffic* **Ch 63, 20**.

WILHEMSHAVEN
Port **Ch 11**, ☎ 04421 154580. **Sealock Ch 13**.
Bridges **Ch 11**. **Marinas** Nassauhafen, ☎ 41439. Wiking Sportsboothafen, ☎ 41301.

HOOKSIEL Ch 63. Alterhafen marina.

WANGEROOGE HM **Ch 17**, ☎ 04469 630. Marina, ☎ 942126.

SPIEKEROOG HM No VHF, ☎ 04976 9193133.

DORNUMER-ACCUMERSIEL HM No VHF, ☎ 04933 2510. YC ☎ 2240.

LANGEOOG HM **Ch 17**, ☎ 04972 301.

NORDERNEY HM **Ch 17**, ☎ 04932 82826.

NORDDEICH HM **Ch 17**, ☎ 04931 81317.

BORKUM HM **Ch 14**, ☎ 04922 81317.

EMS VTS *Ems Traffic* **Ch 15, 18, 20, 21**

EMDEN HM & locks **Ch 13**, ☎ 04921 897260. YC marina, ☎ 997147. Mariners' Club, ☎ 953795. City marina, ☎ 8907211.

DELFZIJL/EEMSHAVEN VTS is not compulsory for leisure craft. **Delfzijl Radar Ch 03** gives radar assistance when visibility falls below 2000m. **Eemshaven Radar Ch 01**. **Port Control Ch 66** broadcasts info every even H+10.

DELFZIJL HBR HM **Ch 14**; ☎ 0596 640400. **Locks Ch 26**, M-Sat H24, Sun & hols on request; ☎ 693293. **Bridges:** Weiwerder **Ch 11**. Heemskes & Handelshaven **Ch 14**. **Farmsumerhaven**, **Ch 66**, ☎ 640494.

EEMSHAVEN HM **Ch 14**; ☎ 516142. Radar **Ch 19**.

LAUWERSOOG HM, *Havendienst*, **Ch 09**; ☎ 0519 39023. Mon 0000-1700; Tu-Wed 0800-1700; Th-Sat 0700-1500.

TERSCHELLING VTS Call/monitor *Brandaris* **Ch 02**; ☎ 0562 443100. **Marina**, **Ch 31**; ☎ 443337.

VLIELAND HM **Ch 12**. **Marina**, **Ch 31**; ☎ 0562 451729.

HARLINGEN HM **Ch 11** (not on Sun); ☎ 0517 413423. **Locks Ch 22**.

OUDESCHILD HM **Ch 12**; ☎ 0222 312710. **Marina**, **Ch 31**; ☎ 0222 321227. See Den Helder VTS.

DEN HELDER VTS Monitor *Tfc Centre* **Ch 62**, H24; broadcasts info and gives radar surveillance. **PORT CONTROL Ch 14**; ☎ 0223 62770. **Marina** ☎ 652645. **Bridge:** Moormanbrug **Ch 18**. **Lock:** Koopvaarders **Ch 22**.

IJSSELMEER Den Oever lock Ch 20, ☎ 0227 511383. **Port Ch 11**, ☎ 511303. Marina ☎ 511789. **Kornwerderzand lock Ch 18**, ☎ 0517 57441.

ENKHUIZEN Naviduct (also Krabbersgat) **Ch 22**.

IJMUIDEN VTS Traffic Centre Ch 07, Roads (W of IJmuiden buoy). Thence **Port Control Ch 61** to Noordzeesluizen (locks).
Seaport marina Ch 75, ☎ 0255 560300.

NORDZEEKANAAL VTS
Noordzeesluizen. *Sluis IJmuiden* **Ch 22**.
Noordzeekanaal. **Ch 03**, from locks to km 11·2.

AMSTERDAM
Port Control Ch 68 (Km 11·2 to Oranjesluisen).
Port Info Ch 14. Access to Standing Mast route: **Westerkeersluis Ch 22**. **Haarlem hbr Ch 18**. **Marinas:** Sixhaven, ☎ 020 6329429. **WV Aeolus**, ☎ 6360791. **Aquadam**, ☎ 6320616.
Access to Markermeer: **Oranjesluisen Ch 18**.

SCHEVENINGEN Traffic Centre & Port Ch 21; ☎ 070 3527711. **Marina Ch 31**; ☎ 070 3520017.

HOEK VAN HOLLAND ROADSTEAD
To cross the mouth of the Maas, call *Maas Entrance* **Ch 03**, with vessel's name, position and course. Follow a track close W of a line joining buoys MV, MVN and Indusbank N. See VTS Chart No 4. Whilst crossing, maintain continuous listening watch and keep a very sharp lookout.

COMMUNICATIONS

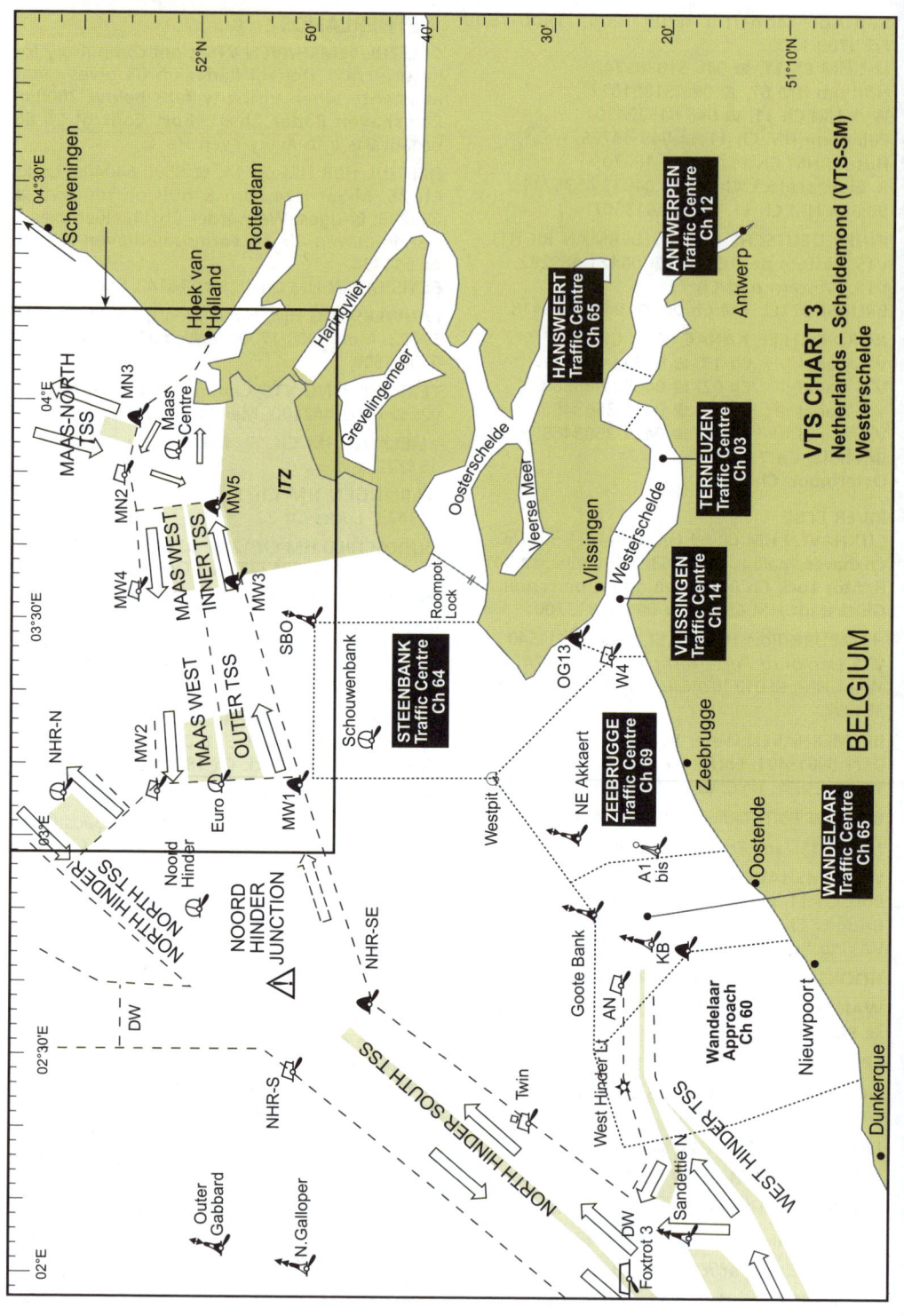

VTS CHART 3

Netherlands – Scheldemond (VTS-SM)

Westerschelde

BELGIUM

ANTWERPEN Traffic Centre	Ch 12
HANSWEERT Traffic Centre	Ch 65
TERNEUZEN Traffic Centre	Ch 03
VLISSINGEN Traffic Centre	Ch 14
STEENBANK Traffic Centre	Ch 64
ZEEBRUGGE Traffic Centre	Ch 69
WANDELAAR Traffic Centre	Ch 65

Wandelaar Approach Ch 60

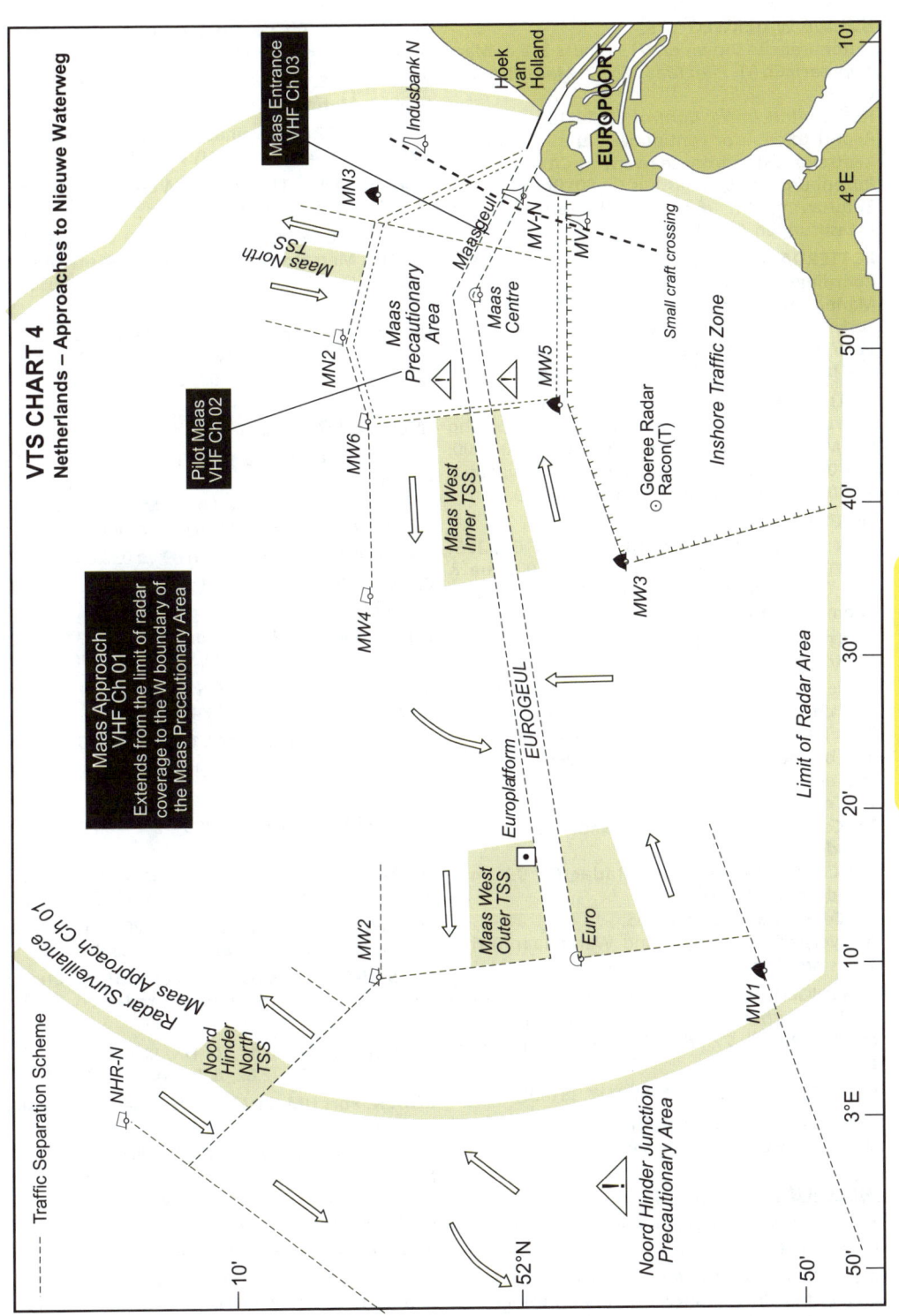

VTS CHART 4
Netherlands – Approaches to Nieuwe Waterweg

Maas Entrance
VHF Ch 03

Maas North
TSS

Maas Precautionary
Area

Pilot Maas
VHF Ch 02

MN3

MN2

Maasgeul

Maas
Centre

MV-N

MV-Z

Small craft crossing

Indusbank N

Hoek
van
Holland

EUROPOORT

4°E

10'

50'

Inshore Traffic Zone

○ Goeree Radar
○ Racon(T)

MW5

MW6

Maas Approach
VHF Ch 01
Extends from the limit of radar
coverage to the W boundary of
the Maas Precautionary Area

Maas West
Inner TSS

MW4

MW3

EUROGEUL

Europlatform

Limit of Radar Area

40'

30'

Maas West
Outer TSS

Euro

MW2

20'

10'

Radar Surveillance
Maas Approach Ch 07

Traffic Separation Scheme

Noord
Hinder
North
TSS

NHR-N

MW1

3°E

Noord Hinder Junction
Precautionary Area

52°N

10'

50'

50'

- - - - - Traffic Separation Scheme

COMMUNICATIONS

NIEUWE WATERWEG VTS.
Outer areas as shown on VTS Charts 3 & 4: *Maas Approach* Ch 01. *Pilot Maas* Ch 02. *Maas Entrance* Ch 03.
HCC *Central Traffic Control* Ch 14 19.
Report to/monitor continuously the relevant Tfc Centre, as listed from seaward to City marina:
Rozenburg Ch 65; Maassluis Ch 80; Botlek Ch 61; Eemhaven Ch 63; Waalhaven Ch 60; Maasbruggen Ch 81.

ROTTERDAM. Rotterdam Tfc Centre Ch 11. Hbr **Coordination Centre** (HCC) Ch 19.
Marinas/Yacht hbrs: Vlaardingen ☎ 010 4346786; Lock Ch 20. **Spuihaven** ☎ 4667765. Coolhaven ☎ 4738614. Veerhaven ☎ 4365446. **City marina** ☎ 0187 48540986, via Erasmus bridge Ch 18.

STELLENDAM. Haringvliet lock & lifting bridge: *Goereese Sluis* Ch 20, ☎ 0187 497350. Opening hrs: M-F 0000-2200. 1 Nov - 1 Apr: Sat 0800-2200; Sun 0800-1000, 1600-1800. 1 Apr - 1 Nov: Sat & Sun 0800-2000. **Marina** Ch 31, ☎ 493769.

OOSTERSCHELDE.
Lock *Roompotsluis* Ch 18, ☎ 0111 659265. Opening hours: Mon & Thu, 0000-2200; Tue & Sun, 0600-0000; Wed H24; Fri & Sat: 0600-2200. **Roompot marina** Ch 31.

WESTERSCHELDE VTS.
See VTS Chart No 3. Reporting is not compulsory for leisure craft, but they should monitor the VHF channel for the appropriate Traffic Area. Each Traffic Area is controlled by a Traffic Centre and bounded by buoys. *In emergency call the relevant Traffic Centre: Ch 67*.
Tfc Centre Steenbank **& Radar** Ch 64.
Tfc Centre Vlissingen Ch 14. **Radar** Ch 21. **Info broadcast** Ch 14 H+55.
Tfc Centre Terneuzen **& Radar** Ch 03. **Info broadcast** Ch 11 H+00.
Tfc Centre Hansweert Ch 65.
Antwerpen, Zeebrugge and Wandelaar Traffic Areas are listed under Belgium.

VLISSINGEN De Ruyter marina no VHF, ☎ 0118 414498. *Flushing Port Control* Ch 09. **Sealocks &** canal bridge Ch 22. **VVW Schelde marina** Ch 14, ☎ 465912.

BRESKENS Marina, Ch 31, ☎ 0117 381902.

TERNEUZEN Port control Ch 11. **Marina**, ☎ 0115 697089. **Oostsluis** (E lock, small craft) Ch 18.

BELGIUM

ANTWERPEN, *Tfc Centre Zandvliet* Ch 12. **Info broadcast** Ch 12 H+35.

ANTWERPEN PORT Calling and safety Ch 74. **Royerssluis** Ch 22. **Siberia & Londen bridges** Ch 62. **Willemdok marina** Ch 23, ☎ 03 2315066. **Linkeroever marina** Ch 09, ☎ 03 2190895.

ZEEBRUGGE. *Tfc Centre Zeebrugge* Ch 69. **Info broadcasts** Ch 69 H+15.

ZEEBRUGGE. Port Control Ch 71 H24, ☎ 050 546867. **Marina** Ch 71, ☎ 544903. **E lock** Ch 68.

BLANKENBERGE. Marinas: VNZ, ☎ 050 429150, & **SYCB**, ☎ 411420, Ch 31. **VVW** ☎ 417536, Ch 23.

WANDELAAR. **Tfc Centre Wandelaar** Ch 65. **Wandelaar Approach** Ch 60.

OOSTENDE. Port Control Ch 09 H24, ☎ 059 566313. **Mercator lock**, ☎ 321669, **& marina**, ☎ 705762: Ch 14 H24. **Marinas: RNSYC**, ☎ 505912. RYCO, ☎ 321452.

NIEUWPOORT. Port HM Ch 09 H24, ☎ 058 233000. **Marinas: KYCN**, Ch 23, ☎ 234413. **WSKLM**, Ch 23, ☎ 5233641. **VVW-N**, Ch 08, ☎ 235232.

NORTH FRANCE

DUNKERQUE. Port & VTS Ch 73, H24. The VTS does not affect leisure craft, but monitor Ch 73. **Marinas** Ch 09: Grande Large ☎ 03.28.63.23.00. **YCMN** ☎ 03.28.66.79.90. **Trystram lock** Ch 73.

GRAVELINES. HM/Marina, Ch 09, ☎ 03.28.23.19.45.

CALAIS. VTS, Port Control & Marina Ch 17 H24, ☎ 03.21.34.55.23.

BOULOGNE. *Boulogne Port*, ☎ 03.21.31.52.43, Ch 12, H24. **Marina** Ch 09, ☎ 03.21.31.70.01.

LE TOUQUET/ÉTAPLES-SUR-MER Ch 09, 77. **Étaples marina**, ☎ 03.21.84.54.03.

LE TRÉPORT. Marina/lock Ch 12, 72, ☎ 02.35.50.63.06

DIEPPE Port HM Ch 12, HO. **Marina** Ch 09, ☎ 02.35.40.19.79.

ST VALÉRY-EN-CAUX Entry gate & marina Ch 09, ☎ 02.35.97.01.30.

FÉCAMP Port HM, Ch 10, **12**, ☎ 02.35.28.25.53. **Marina & Bérigny lock**, Ch 09, ☎ 02.35.28.13.58.

LE HAVRE, *Control Tower* Ch **12**, 20. **Port Ops** Ch 67, 69. **Marina**, Ch 09, ☎ 02.35.21.23.95.

LA SEINE VTS Rouen Port Control Ch 73 (Estuary), 68 (River). **Honfleur radar** Ch 15, 19, **73**.

HONFLEUR. HM Ch **17**, 73 HX, ☎ 02.31.14.61.09. **Lock**, ☎ 02.31.98.72.82, **& Bridge** Ch 17 H24.

ROUEN. Port HM Ch **73**, 68 H24. **Halte Nautique**, ☎ 02.32.08.31.40.

ROUEN – PARIS, LOCKS. Amfreville Ch 18. **Notre-Dame-de-la-Garenne** Ch 22. **Mericourt** Ch 18. **Andrésy** Ch 22. **Bougival** Ch 22. **Chatou** Ch 18. **Suresnes** Ch 22.

PARIS-ARSENAL marina Ch 09, ☎ 01.43.41.39.32.

DEAUVILLE. Port Deauville lock, ☎ 02.31.88.95.66; marina ☎ 02.31.98.30.01, Ch 09 0800-1730. **Port Morny** gate ☎ 02.31.88.57.89; marina, Ch 09, ☎ 02.31.98.50.40.

DIVES-SUR-MER. Marina Ch 09, ☎ 02.31.24.48.00.

OUISTREHAM. Port 74; lock Ch 12, ☎ 02.31.36.22.00. Marina Ch 09, ☎ 02.31.96.91.37. **Canal** Ch 68. **CAEN** HM/marina Ch 74, ☎ 02.31.95.24.47.

COURSEULLES-SUR-MER. Marina Ch 09, ☎ 02.31.37.51.69.

PORT-EN-BESSIN. HM, ☎ 02.31.21.70.49. **Gate/ bridge** Ch 18, ☎ 02.31.21.71.77.

GRANDCAMP. Marina Ch 09, ☎ 02.31.22.63.16.

CARENTAN. Lock Ch 09, ☎ 02.33.71.10.85. Marina Ch 09, ☎ 02.33.42.24.44.

ST VAAST-LA-HOUGUE. Marina Ch 09, ☎ 02.33.21.61.00.

BARFLEUR. HM, ☎ 02.33.54.08.29. No VHF.

CHERBOURG. VTS (yachts to monitor) *Vigie du Homet* Ch 12 H24. **Marina** *Chantereyne* Ch 09, ☎ 02.33.87.65.70. **Gate** (B du Commerce) Ch 06.

OMONVILLE-LA-ROGUE. No VHF/Tel. 6 W 🙋s.

DIÉLETTE. Marina Ch 09, ☎ 02.33.53.68.78.

CARTERET. Marina Ch 09, ☎ 02.33.04.70.84.

PORTBAIL. Yacht hbr Ch 09, ☎ 02.33.04.83.48.

GRANVILLE. Port HM Ch 12. **Marina** Ch 09, ☎ 02.33.50.20.06.

ST MALO. Port HM Ch 12 H24. **Marinas** Ch 09: Bas Sablons, ☎ 02.99.81.71.34. **Bassin Vauban,** ☎ 02.99.56.51.91. **DINARD,** ☎ 02.99.46.65.55.

R. RANCE barrage lock Ch 13, ☎ 02.99.46.21.87. Chatelier lock Ch 14, ☎ 02.99.39.55.66.

DAHOUËT. Marina Ch 09, ☎ 02.96.72.82.85.

LE LÉGUÉ. HM/Marina Ch 12, ☎ 02.96.77.49.85.

BINIC. Marina Ch 09, ☎ 02.96.73.61.86.

ST QUAY-PORTRIEUX. Marina ☎ 02.96.70.81.30. Ch 09.

PAIMPOL. Lock/marina Ch 09, ☎ 02.96.20.47.65.

LÉZARDRIEUX. Marina Ch 09, ☎ 02.96.20.14.22.

PONTRIEUX. Lock/marina Ch 12, ☎ 02.96.95.34.87.

TRÉGUIER. Marina Ch 09, ☎ 02.96.92.42.37.

PERROS-GUIREC. Marina Ch 09, ☎ 02.96.49.80.50.

PLOUMANAC'H. Marina Ch 09, ☎ 02.96.91.44.31.

TRÉBEURDEN. Marina Ch 09, ☎ 02.96.23.64.00.

MORLAIX. Marina Ch 09, ☎ 02.98.62.13.14.

ROSCOFF. HM/S Basin Ch 09, ☎ 02.98.69.76.37.

BLOSCON. Ferry Port Ch 12, ☎ 02.98.61.27.84.

L'ABERWRACH. Marina Ch 09, ☎ 02.98.04.91.62.

CHANNEL ISLANDS

ALDERNEY, Braye Hbr, *Alderney Radio* Ch 74, ☎ 01481 822620. If no contact, try St Peter Port Radio.

GUERNSEY. Beaucette marina, Ch 80, ☎ 01481

245000. **St Sampson** Ch 12 H24 via **St Peter Port** Control Ch 12 H24, ☎ 720229.

Victoria marina Ch M, 80 HO, ☎ 725987. *St Peter Port Radio* Ch 20 H24 (only for link calls).

JERSEY. St Helier Port Control Ch 14 H24; 8M max range. **St Helier marina,** ☎ 01534 885508, has no VHF; call Ch 14 only if essential. **Gorey** Ch 74, ☎ 853616.

WEST FRANCE

BREST. VTS *Brest Port* Ch 08 H24. **Marina** Ch 09, ☎ 02.98.02.20.02.

CAMARET. Marina Ch 09, ☎ 02.98.27.95.99.

MORGAT. Marina Ch 09, ☎ 02.98.27.01.97.

DOUARNENEZ. HM Ch 12. **Marinas** Ch 09: Tréboul ☎ 02.98.74.02.56; Port Rhu ☎ 02.98.92.00.67.

AUDIERNE. No VHF. **Marina** ☎ 02.98.74.04.93. Ste Evette ☎ 02.98.70.00.28.

LOCTUDY. Marina Ch 09, ☎ 02.98.87.51.36.

BENODÉT. Marinas Ch 09: **Penfoul** ☎ 02.98.57.05.78. Ste Marine ☎ 02.98.56.38.72.

PORT-LA-FORÊT. Marina Ch 09, ☎ 02.98.56.98.45.

CONCARNEAU. Marina Ch 09, ☎ 02.98.97.57.96.

LORIENT. Port Ch 12. **Marinas** Ch 09: Ban-Gâvres ☎ 02.97.65.48.25. Kernével ☎ 02.97.65.48.25. Port Louis ☎ 02.97.83.59.55. Locmiquélic ☎ 02.97.33.59.51. Lorient ☎ 02.97.21.10.14.

PORT TUDY. Marina Ch 09, ☎ 02.97.86.54.62.

RIVER ÉTEL. Marina Ch 13, ☎ 02.97.55.46.62.

BELLE ILE. Sauzon HM Ch 09, ☎ 02.97.31.63.40. Le Palais HM Ch 09, ☎ 02.97.31.42.90.

PORT HALIGUEN. Marina Ch 09, ☎ 02.97.50.20.56.

LA TRINITÉ. Marina Ch 09, ☎ 02.97.55.71.49.

VANNES. Marina Ch 09, ☎ 02.97.54.16.08.

CROUESTY. Marina Ch 09, ☎ 02.97.53.73.33.

LA VILAINE. Arzal marina Ch 09, ☎ 02.97.45.02.97.

PIRIAC. Marina Ch 09, ☎ 02.40.23.52.32.

LA TURBALLE. Marina Ch 09, ☎ 02.40.23.41.65.

LE CROISIC. Marina Ch 09, ☎ 02.40.23.10.95.

LE POULIGUEN. Marina Ch 09, ☎ 02.40.11.97.97.

PORNICHET. Marina Ch 09, ☎ 02.40.61.03.20.

ST-NAZAIRE VTS *Loire Ports Control* Ch 14. **Port HM** Ch 14, ☎ 02.40.91.03.17.

PORNIC. Marina Ch 09, ☎ 02.40.82.05.40.

L'HERBAUDIÈRE. Marina Ch 09, ☎ 02.51.39.05.05.

PORT JOINVILLE. Marina Ch 09, ☎ 02.51.58.38.11.

ST GILLES-CROIX-DE-VIE. Marina Ch 09, ☎ 02.51.55.30.83.

LES SABLES D'OLONNE. Port HM Ch 12, ☎ 02.51.95.11.79. **Marina** Ch 09, ☎ 02.51.32.51.16.

BOURGENAY. Marina Ch 09, ☎ 02.51.22.20.36.

ILE DE RÉ. Ars-en-Ré Ch 09, ☎ 05.46.29.08.52. **St Martin** Ch 09, ☎ 05.46.09.26.69.

LA ROCHELLE. Marinas Ch 09: **Port des Minimes** ☎ 05.46.44.41.20. **Vieux Port** ☎ 05.46.41.32.05.

ROCHEFORT. Marina Ch 09, ☎ 05.46.83.99.06.

ILE D'OLÉRON. St Denis Ch 09, ☎ 05.46.47.97.97. **Boyardville** Ch 09, ☎ 05.46.76.48.56.

LA GIRONDE VTS Ch 12 (yachts to monitor). **Radar** *Bordeaux Port Control* Ch 12 on request. Depths in Gironde broadcast Ch 17 every 5 mins.

ROYAN. Marina Ch 09, ☎ 05.46.38.72.22.

PORT-MÉDOC. Marina Ch 09, ☎ 05.56.09.69.75.

PAUILLAC. Marina Ch 09, ☎ 05.56.59.12.16.

BORDEAUX. HM *Bordeaux Traffic* Ch 12, ☎ 05.56.31.58.64. **Bassin 2,** ☎ 05.56.90.59.57.

ARCACHON. Marina Ch 09, ☎ 05.56.22.36.75.

CAPBRETON. Marina Ch 09, ☎ 05.58.72.21.23.

ANGLET. Marina Ch 09, ☎ 05.59.63.05.45.

ST JEAN-DE-LUZ. Marina Ch 09, ☎ 05.59.47.26.81.

HENDAYE. Marina Ch 09, ☎ 05.59.48.06.10.

N & NW SPAIN

FUENTERRABIA. Marina Ch 73, ☎ 943 641711.

GUETARIA. Marina Ch 09, ☎ 943 580959.

ZUMAYA. Marina Ch 73, ☎ 943 860938.

BILBAO. *Port Control* Ch 12. **Marinas** Ch 09: **Getxo** ☎ 944 912367. **Las Arenas** ☎ 944 637600.

SANTANDER. Marina Ch 09, ☎ 942 369288.

GIJON. Marina Ch 09, ☎ 985 344543.

CUDILLERO. HM/Yacht hbr Ch 27, ☎ 985 591114.

RIBADEO. Marina Ch 09, ☎ 982 131444.

VIVERO. Marina Ch 09, ☎ 982 570610.

RÍA DE ARES. Marina Ch 09, ☎ 981 468787.

RÍA DE BETANZOS. Marina Ch 09, ☎ 981 619015.

LA CORUÑA. Marina Ch 09, ☎ 981 914142.

RÍA DE CAMARIÑAS. Marina Ch 09, ☎ 981 737130.

RÍA DE MUROS. HM Muros, ☎ 981 826005. **CN Portosin marina** Ch 09, ☎ 981 766598.

RÍA DE AROUSA. Marinas Ch 09: **Caraminal,** ☎ 981 830970. **Sta Uxia,** ☎ 981 873801. **Vilagarcia,** ☎ 986 511175. **Piedras Negras,** ☎ 986 738430.

RÍA DE PONTEVEDRA. Marinas Ch 09: **Sangenxo,** ☎ 986 720517. **Aguete,** ☎ 986 702373.

RÍA DE VIGO VTS *Vigo Traffic* Ch 10. **Marina** Ch 09, ☎ 986 449694.

BAYONA. MRCY Ch 06, ☎ 986 385000. **Bayona marina** Ch 09, ☎ 986 385107.

PORTUGAL

VIANA DO CASTELO. Marina Ch 09, ☎ 258 359546.

PÓVOA DE VARZIM. Marina Ch 09, ☎ 252 688121.

LEIXÕES. Port Ch 11. **Marina** Ch 09, ☎ 229 964895.

AVEIRO. Port HM Ch 11, 12, 13, ☎ 234 366250.

FIGUEIRA DA FOZ. Marina Ch 09, ☎ 233 402910.

NAZARÉ. Marina Ch 09, ☎ 262 561401.

PENICHE. Marina Ch 09, ☎ 262 783331.

CASCAIS. Marina Ch 09, ☎ 214 824800.

LISBOA. VTS *Lisboa Port Control* Ch 74. **Marina Doca de Alcântara** Ch 05, 09, 12, ☎ 213 922048.

SESIMBRA. Port Ch 11. **Marina** Ch 09, ☎ 212 233451.

SETÚBAL VTS (applies to yachts >15m LOA) *Port Control* Ch 73. **Marina** Ch 09, ☎ 265 452076.

SINES. Port Ch 11. **Marina** Ch 09, ☎ 269 860612.

LAGOS. Port Ch 11. **Marina** Ch 09, ☎ 282 770210.

PORTIMÃO. HM Ch 11. **Marina** Ch 09, ☎ 282 400680.

ALBUFEIRA. Marina Ch 09, ☎ 289 510180.

VILAMOURA. Marina Ch 09, ☎ 289 310560.

FARO ☎ 289 894990; **OLHÃO** ☎ 703160, Ch 11.

VILA REAL DE SANTO ANTÓNIO. Port Ch 11. **Marina** Ch 09, ☎ 281 541571.

SW SPAIN

AYAMONTE. Marina Ch 09, ☎ 959 321294.

IS CANELA, ☎ 959 479000; **CRISTINA,** ☎ 343501.

MAZAGON. Marina Ch 09, ☎ 959 536251.

CHIPIONA. Port Ch 12. **Marina** Ch 09, ☎ 956 373844.

SEVILLA. Port Ch 12. **Marinas** Ch 09: **Gelves** ☎ 955 761212. **Marina Yachting** ☎ 954 230326. **CN Sevilla** ☎ 954 454777.

CÁDIZ. Port *Cádiz Trafico* Ch 74. **Marinas** Ch 09: **Rota** ☎ 956 454777. **Pto Sherry** ☎ 870103. **Pto de Sta Maria** ☎ 852527. **Pto America** ☎ 223666.

SANCTI PETRI. Marina Ch 09, ☎ 956 496169.

BARBATE. Marina Ch 09, ☎ 956 431907.

TARIFA VTS. *Tarifa Traffic* Ch 10, ☎ 956 684757. **Info** Ch 67 (on request) inc weather in TSS/ITZ.

ALGECIRAS. Marina Ch 09, ☎ 956 572503.

GIBRALTAR & MOROCCO

GIBRALTAR. Port Ch 12, to be monitored whilst under way or at ⚓ in the Bay. **Marinas,** Ch 71: Queensway Quay, ☎ 350 44700; Marina Bay, ☎ 74322; Sheppards, ☎ 75148. **Customs** Ch 14. **Commercial Port** Ch 06.

TANGIER. Port Ch 16, ☎ (00 2129) 3993 7495.

CEUTA (Spain). Marina Ch 09, ☎ 956 513753.

COAST RADIO STATIONS

Coast Radio Stations (CRS) deal with public correspondence (and a few other things). They enable a yachtsman to be linked by radio into the public telephone system in order to converse with a subscriber ashore, ie he can make or receive a Link call.

However the mobile 'phone has to a great extent rendered Link calls obsolescent. Thus there are no longer any CRS in the UK, France and Netherlands. In Germany a limited service is provided by a commercial company (see below).

CRS still operate in the Channel Islands, Ireland, Denmark, Belgium, Spain and Portugal; see below. But they too may gradually be withdrawn.

Note that the term 'Coast Radio Station' now embraces, not only the original CRS, but also CG Centres, both in the UK and abroad. This is ambiguous and therefore confusing. Generally the CG does **not** handle Link calls, except in Ireland, Denmark and Belgium where the functions of CG and CRS have always been co-located.

CHANNEL ISLANDS

ST PETER PORT RADIO 49°27'·00N 02°32'00W
☎ 01481 720672 🖷 01534 714177
Link calls on **Ch 62** only. Ch 20 is used for navigation, pilotage and ships' business

JERSEY RADIO 49°10'·85N 02°14'30W ☎ 01534 885505 🖷 01534 499089
Link calls on **Ch 25** only

REPUBLIC OF IRELAND

A Coast Radio service is provided by the Dept of the Marine, Leeson Lane, Dublin 2, Eire. ☎ +353 (0)1 662 0922; ext 670 for enquiries. Broadcasts are made on a working channel/frequency following a prior announcement on Ch 16 and 2182 kHz. Ch 67 is used for Safety messages only. VHF calls to an Irish Coast Radio Station should be made on a working channel. Only use Ch 16 in case of difficulty or in emergency.

NW and SE Ireland

Stations broadcast at 0033, 0433, 0833, 1233, 1633 and 2033 UT on VHF Channels listed. Navwarnings and Traffic lists are broadcast at odd H+03 (except 0303 0703).

Clifden Radio	53°30'N 09°56'W	Ch 26
Belmullet Radio	54°16'N 10°03'W	Ch 83
Donegal Bay	54°22'N 08°31'W	Ch 02
Glen Head Radio	54°44'N 08°43'W	Ch 24
MALIN HD RADIO	55°22'N 07°21'W	Ch 23
MF 1677 kHz, ☎ +353 (0) 77 70103		
MMSI 002500100 DSC: 2187·5 kHz		

Carlingford Radio	54°05'N 06°19'W	Ch 04
Dublin Radio	53°23'N 06°04'W	Ch 83
Wicklow Hd Radio	52°58'N 06°00'W	Ch 02
Rosslare Radio	52°15'N 06°20'W	Ch 23
Mine Hd Radio	52°00'N 07°35'W	Ch 83

SW Ireland

Stations broadcast at 0233, 0633, 1033, 1433, 1833 and 2233 UT on VHF Channels listed. Navigational warnings and Traffic Lists are broadcast at every odd H+33 (except 0133 0533).

Cork Radio	51°51'N 08°29'W	Ch 26
Mizen Radio	51°34'N 09°33'W	Ch 04
Bantry Radio	51°38'N 10°00'W	Ch 23
VALENTIA RADIO	51°56'N 10°21'W	Ch 24
MF 1752 kHz, ☎ + 353 (0) 66947 6109		
MMSI 002500200, DSC: 2187·5 kHz		
Shannon Radio	52°31'N 09°36'W	Ch 28
Galway Bay Radio	53°18'N 09°07'W	Ch 04

DENMARK

All VHF/MF CRS are remotely controlled from Lyngby Radio (55°50N 11°25'E) (MMSI 002191000). The callsign for all stations is Lyngby Radio. Call on working frequencies to help keep Ch 16 clear. The stations listed below monitor Ch 16 H24 and Ch 70 DSC. Traffic lists are broadcast on all VHF channels every odd H+05. All MF stations, except Skagen, keep watch H24 on 2182 kHz. Blåvand, Skagen and Lyngby also monitor MF 2187·5 kHz DSC. MF DSC Public correspondence facilities are available from Blåvand and Skagen on 1624·5 and 2177 kHz.

Lyngby	55°50'N 11°25'E	Ch **07**, 85
	MF 1704, 2170·5 kHz	
Blåvand	55°33'N 08°07'E	Ch 23
	MF 1734, 1767, 2593	
Bovbjerg	56°32'N 08°10'E	Ch 02
	MF 1734, 1767, 2593	
Hanstholm	57°07'N 08°39'E	Ch 01
Hirtshals	57°31'N 09°57'E	Ch 66
Skagen	57°44'N 10°35'E	Ch 04
	MF 1758	

GERMANY

CRS: DPO7 – Seefunk (Hamburg) *(MMSI 002113100)*. All stns monitor DSC Ch 70 & 16. Traffic lists are broadcast: 0745, 0945, 1245, 1645, 1945 and H & H+30 on request Ch 16.

Hamburg	53°33'N 09°58'E	Ch 83
Borkum	53°35'N 06°40'E	Ch 28
Bremen	53°05'N 08°48'E	Ch 25
Elbe Weser	53°50'N 08°39'E	Ch 01,24
Nordfriesland	54°31'N 08°41'E	Ch 26

NORTH SPAIN

All stns guard DSC Ch 70 H24. Ch 16 is not continuously guarded. Call on the working channel below; the callsign is the name of the station followed by Radio; all are remotely controlled by Bilbao Comms Centre. Navigation warnings on VHF at 0840 & 2010 after weather broadcast.

Pasajes	43°17'N 01°55'W	Ch 27
Machichaco	43°27'N 02°45'W MF 1707 kHz	No VHF
BILBAO	43°22'N 03°02'W	Ch 26
Santander	43°25'N 03°36'W	Ch 24
Cabo Peñas	43°26'N 05°35'W MF 1677 kHz	Ch 23
Navia	43°25'N 06°50'W	Ch 60

NORTHWEST SPAIN

Details as for N Spain. All stations are remotely controlled by Coruña Comms Centre.

Cabo Ortegal	43°35'N 07°47'W	Ch 02, 63
CORUÑA	43°22'N 08°27'W MF 1698 kHz	Ch 26, 28
Finisterre	42°54'N 09°16'W	Ch 22, 85
Vigo	42°10'N 08°41'W	Ch 62, 65
La Guardia	41°53'N 08°52'W	Ch 21, 82

PORTUGAL

Stations are remotely controlled by Lisboa. All monitor Ch 16 H24. The callsign is the name of the station followed by Radio.

Arga	41°48'N 08°41'W	Ch 24, 25, 28
Arestal	40°46'N 08°21'W	Ch 24, 25, 26
Montejunto	39°10'N 09°03'W	Ch 24, 25, 27
LISBOA	38°33'N 09°11'W MF 2182 kHz.	Ch 23, 25, 26
Atalaia	38°10'N 08°38'W	Ch 23, 24, 25
Picos (Foia)	37°50'N 08°35'W	Ch 23, 24, 28
Estoi	37°10'N 07°50'W	Ch 24, 27, 28

AZORES

Stations are remotely controlled by Lisboa. All monitor Ch 16 H24. The callsign is the name of the station followed by Radio.

Flores	39°27'N 31°32'W	Ch 23
Faial	38°35'N 28°43'W	Ch 24, 25, 26
Pico	38°24'N 28°44'W	Ch 23, 24, 26
Sao Miguel	37°45'N 25°40'W	Ch 24, 25, 26

SOUTH WEST SPAIN

Stations are remotely controlled from Malaga. Initially call Ch 16 H24 using station callsign, ie name + Radio. Navwarnings 0833 & 2033 after the weather.

Chipiona	36°42'N 06°25'W MF 1656kHz	No VHF
Cádiz	36°22'N 06°17'W	Ch 26, 83
Tarifa	36°03'N 05°33'W MF 1704 kHz	Ch 81

NOTES

SOUND SIGNALS
MANOEUVRING AND WARNING SIGNALS (Rule 34)

Short blast ● = about 1 second. Long blast ▬▬ = about 5 seconds

●	I am altering course to **Starboard**
● ●	I am altering course to **Port**
● ● ●	My engines are going **Astern**
● ● ● ● ●	I do not understand your intentions/actions

In a narrow channel

▬▬ ▬▬ ●	I intend to overtake you on your **Starboard** side
▬▬ ▬▬ ● ●	I intend to overtake you on your **Port** side
▬▬ ● ▬▬ ●	In response to the above two signals - **Agreed**

Nearing a bend in the channel or an area where other vessels may be hidden by obstructions

▬▬	Warns of a vessel's presence
▬▬	Acknowledgement by any approaching vessel

VESSELS IN RESTRICTED VISIBILITY (Rule 35)

▬▬	Power vessel underway: every 2 mins
▬▬ ▬▬	Power vessel underway but stopped: every 2 mins
▬▬ ● ●	Vessels not under command, restricted in their ability to manoeuvre, constrained by draught, sailing, fishing or towing: every 2 mins
▬▬ ● ● ●	Last vessel in tow: immediately after tug's signal
♤ 5 seconds	At anchor: bell, every minute
♤ 5 seconds + ☉ 5 seconds	At anchor over 100m: bell forward, gong aft, every minute
● ▬▬ ●	At ⚓, as well as above, to warn an approaching vessel. **Yachts under 12m** are not obliged to sound the fog signals listed above, but if they do not, they *must* make some efficient noise every two minutes

SHAPES

▼	Sailing vessel under sail *and* power. **Rule 25**	◆	Towing vessel - length of tow over 200m. **Rule 24**
●	Vessel at anchor. **Rule 30**	● ◆ ●	Vessel restricted in her ability to manoeuvre. **Rule 27**
▼▲	Vessel fishing or trawling. **Rule 26**	● ●	Vessel not under command. **Rule 27**
▼▲ + ▲	Vessel fishing with outlying gear over 150m long.	▮	Vessel constrained by her draught **Rule 28**

CHAPTER 4 - SAFETY

CONTENTS

The National Coastwatch Institution 121

How to make a distress call 122

MAYDAY relay 122

Helicopter rescue 123

Medical help 123

First aid 124
   Essential information 124
   General medical information 125
   First aid kit 127

GMDSS
   Purpose 128
   Sea areas 128
   Functions 128
   Distress alerting 128
   Digital selective calling 129
   Maritime safety information 129
   Inmarsat 129
   Cospas/Sarsat 130
   EPIRBs 130

Emergency VHF direction finding
   UK 131
   Map of UK & French D/F sites 132

Coastguard services
   UK 133
   Channel Islands and Republic of Ireland 134
   Denmark 135
   Germany and Netherlands 136
   Belgium and France 137
   Spain 139
   Portugal and the Azores 140

THE NATIONAL COASTWATCH INSTITUTION (NCI)

There can be few more quintessentially English activities than to watch the sea and the coast. It is the very epitome of our island mentality. For centuries men and women have watched from towers and lookout posts around our shores. They still do.

Today a dedicated band of men and women feel so strongly about a Coastwatch that they have joined the NCI. This was founded in 1994 after HM Coastguard (CG) had moved towards an electronic image of radio, radar and digital everything else – and a brilliant job the CG do. But the Mark One Eyeball still has a role to play - hence NCI.

NCI originated in Cornwall where 13 of its 30 operational stations are; the rest range east and north as far as Sunderland. A Welsh station at Barry near Cardiff was due to open in late 2006. Most of the stations are former Coastguard lookout posts which have been renovated and equipped with radios, in many cases radar, an electric kettle and above all People.

Trained volunteers man these stations up to 365 days a year during daylight hours. Their task is not merely watching the sea, but perhaps more importantly the small craft which navigate across it. Sometimes these may stray dangerously close inshore, even losing their rudder or mast in a tidal race. Chances are that a friendly pair of binoculars are trained upon such craft. If that craft is you, look up at the looming cliff top or nearby headland and you may see · · – (U = *You are standing into danger*) being flashed at you by Aldis lamp. '*As if I don't know it*' you mutter, but you also may not know that the NCI watchkeeper has already alerted the CG who in turn have called out the lifeboat – another potential fatality averted.

Recently I visited 3 NCI stations in Dorset. At Peveril Point near Swanage the lady watchkeeper enthused about her job; she was fresh from completing a Round the World yacht rally.

Next at St Alban's Head, after the usual friendly greeting, the watchkeepers showed me their grandstand view from Anvil Point to Portland Bill with the potentially dangerous St Alban's race literally below their feet.

Finally at Portland Bill, where the even more dangerous race is always at the forefront of their minds, the well-informed watchkeeper turned out to be a retired Admiral and former Director of the Royal Institute of Navigation. He and a local fisherman shared the watch.

Is this something you could do? If so, scan the list of NCI stations below, before visiting www.nci.org.uk. Then join this worthwhile band of men and women.

NCI stations operational in 2006

Gwennap Head ⓡ	01736 871351
Penzance	01736 367063
Bass Point (Lizard) ⓡ	01326 290212
Portscatho (Falmouth East)	01872 580180
Charlestown ⓡ	01726 817068
Polruan (Fowey) ⓡ	01726 870291
Rame Head (Plymouth) ⓡ	01752 823706
Prawle Point (Salcombe) ⓡ	01548 511259
Froward Point (Dartmouth)	07871 426883
Teignmouth	01626 772377
Exmouth	01395 222492
Portland Bill ⓡ	01305 860178
St Alban's Head ⓡ	01929 439220
Peveril Pt (Swanage) ⓡ	01929 422596
Newhaven	01273 516464
Folkestone	01303 227132
Herne Bay	01227 743208
Whitstable	07932 968707
Holehaven (Canvey Island)	01268 696971
Southend	07815 945210
Felixstowe	01394 670808
Gorleston (Gt Yarmouth) ⓡ	01493 440384
Mundesley (Norfolk) ⓡ	01263 722399
Ingoldmells Pt (Skegness)	01754 874723
Hartlepool ⓡ	01429 274931
Sunderland (NCI Affiliate)	0191 5292651
Boscastle (N Cornwall) ⓡ	01840 250965
Stepper Pt (Padstow) ⓡ	07810 898041
St Ives ⓡ	01736 799398
Cape Cornwall (Land's End)	01736 787890

ⓡ = Radar equipped

DEFINITIONS OF DISTRESS, URGENCY AND SAFETY

MAYDAY, the distress call, is used to request *immediate assistance for a ship or person in grave and imminent danger*. This includes a man overboard, if not immediately recovered.

PAN-PAN, the urgency prefix, is used when *the safety of a ship or person is at risk*, or medical advice is urgently required.

SECURITÉ, the safety prefix, is used typically by coast stations to announce *navigation or weather warnings.* Or ships might use it to report hazards, eg a buoy adrift.

SAFETY

HOW TO MAKE A DISTRESS CALL

- Switch on the VHF Radio
- Select Channel 16
- Select **HIGH POWER (25W)**
- Switch off DUAL WATCH
- Holding down the button on microphone or handset, say slowly and clearly:
- **MAYDAY, MAYDAY, MAYDAY**
- This is.....................................(Say your boat's name 3 times)
- MAYDAY...........(Say the boat's name once only)
- My position is....................

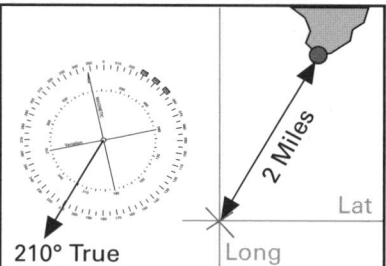

210° True   Lat   Long

Give your position either as:

Lat and Long (from the GPS); or as

Bearing and distance <u>from</u> a known landmark or feature:

For example 'My position is 2 miles SSW of Portland Bill'

Say if you are not sure of position– do not guess!

- ***Tell them what is wrong:*** For example, the boat is sinking; how many people (including you) on board; if you have fired flares; if you are abandoning ship, etc. If there is time, repeat your position
- **I require immediate assistance.** Over - This means: please reply
- Release the microphone button and listen
- Only if you can't hear clearly, adjust the *VOLUME* and/or *SQUELCH*

   If there is no reply, check the radio switches and repeat the message

MAYDAY RELAY

- **If you hear a MAYDAY CALL, write it down**
- If practicable, give assistance

- If the MAYDAY is not answered, pass it on like this:
- Select VHF Channel 16
- Select HIGH POWER (25W)
- Switch off DUAL WATCH

- Then, holding down the button on microphone or handset, say slowly and clearly:
MAYDAY RELAY, MAYDAY RELAY, MAYDAY RELAY
- This is......................(say your boat's name 3 times)
- **State the MAYDAY message, exactly as you wrote it down**
- **Over** - This means: please reply
- Release the button and listen

HELICOPTER RESCUE

- **COMMUNICATE ON CHANNEL 16**
- Use flares or smoke when helicopter is seen or heard
- Pilot may ask you to drop sails and motor an **EXACT COURSE**
- You may be asked to stream tender astern with casualty in
- Brief crew early (too noisy when helicopter is close)
- **HELM MUST KEEP ON COURSE** and not be distracted
- Weighted line lowered
- Let it touch boat or water first (to earth any static charge)
- Take in slack line only
- **PULL IN AS DIRECTED**
- **DO NOT SECURE IT TO THE BOAT**
- **DO AS YOU ARE TOLD**
  Note: The text and sketch relate to a Hi-line transfer, one of several techniques which may be used

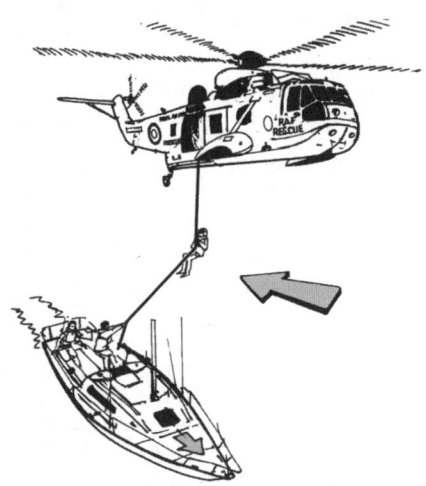

MEDICAL HELP

- **CH 16, High power, Dual watch off**
- **PAN PAN** .... (repeat 3 times)
- **ALL STATIONS** .... (repeat 3 times)
- **This is** ....(repeat 3 times)
- Over
  Next message should contain:
  Yacht's name, callsign, nationality
  Yacht's position and nearest harbour
  Patient's details, symptoms and advice wanted
  The medication you have on board

MEDICAL ADVICE BY RADIO

European countries covered by this Almanac will give free medical advice on request. Messages are usually sent via Coastguard or Coast Radio Stations of the country concerned.

Medical Advice (UK) can be obtained by contacting the nearest CG Centre on VHF 16, VHF DSC, or MF DSC, requesting medical advice. In a particularily urgent situation, broadcast an urgency alert using the pro-words 'PAN PAN'.

Priority is given to Medical Advice requests. A Medilink service doctor will be connected by telephone - VHF(usually Ch's 23,84,86) or MF link to the vessel. As this call is being placed the CG will request relevant additional information. The doctor will advise of suitable action and this call may be monitored by the CG. for operational reasons. If evacuation is necessary, then the CG is bound to act upon it. A Medilink service call (free of charge) will always precede a request for medical evacuation.

REPUBLIC OF IRELAND Call nearest Coast Radio Station by name. Procedures are similar to UK.

DENMARK Call 'Radiomedical Lyngby': English, Danish, Norwegian, Swedish, French or German are spoken.

GERMANY Call nearest Coast Radio Station using 'Funkarzt. . . (name of station)'. English or German are spoken.

NETHERLANDS Call 'Netherlands Coastguard, Radio medical advice'. English and Dutch are spoken. Expect transfer to working Ch 23 or 83 for duty doctor.

BELGIUM Call 'Radiomedical Ostend': English, French, Dutch or German are spoken.

FRANCE Call nearest CROSS, eg 'Radiomedical CROSS Jobourg' with PAN-PAN prefix. French, English or International Code of Signals. SAMU (Urgent Medical Aid Service) in Toulouse may be contacted by the CROSS to advise on treatment and/or possible evacuation. CROSS Etel specialises in providing medical advice.

SPAIN Call 'Medrad ... (any Coast Radio Station)': Spanish.

PORTUGAL Call 'Radiomedical Lisboa': English, French, Portuguese are spoken.

FIRST AID

First ensure your own safety and that of the vessel.

GETTING HELP

Recognising signs of serious injury is not usually difficult, but it is always better to ask advice if not sure. This is available by making a **PAN-PAN** call by R/T or VHF radio, which will normally be processed by a Coast Radio Station and/or the Coastguard. You will be connected to a local doctor or hospital for advice and, if assistance is required, it will be co-ordinated by the Coastguard (see LH column).

FIRST STEPS

A - AIRWAY - NOT BREATHING: Know how to achieve and maintain an airway in all unconscious patients, by:

- Clearing any seaweed, excess saliva, vomit, false teeth, etc from mouth and nose.
- Lifting the chin to prevent choking by tongue and soft palate falling back.

B - BREATHING - Sealing mouth with own mouth and pinching nose, then blow slowly and gently until the casualty's chest rises. Ten inflations should improve colour, then continue after 2-4 seconds another 10 ventilations, then re-assess. You can use mouth to nose ventilation if the casualty's mouth cannot be opened enough to breath into. The best position for maintaining spontaneous breathing after restarting is in the semi-prone or coma position. The casualty is rolled carefully on his side keeping head and neck in line.

C - CIRCULATION - HEART NOT BEATING: You can revive an unconscious or possibly near dead patient by external cardiac massage, if there is no pulse. The best place to find a pulse is in the neck beside the Trachea (Windpipe).

The patient must be lying on a firm surface. First ventilate 1–2 breaths. Then apply cardiac massage by pressure over the lower third of the sternum (breastbone). The heel of one hand should be placed two fingers width above the lower extremity of the sternum, and the heel of the other hand placed on top, with the fingers interlocked, keeping the elbows straight. Press down firmly on the sternum using just enough force to depress it (4.5cm), then release keeping hands in place. Continue by pressing firmly over the sternum with both hands, one on top of the other, with intermittent mouth to mouth respiration. The rate should be 80 compresses per minute, and the ratio of breaths to pressure should be 2:15. This should be continued until either colour improves, breathing starts or a pulse becomes palpable in the neck. Then place the patient in the recovery position.

BLEEDING: Know how to deal with severe haemorrhage.

EXTERNAL BLEEDING:

- Remove any loose foreign bodies from wounds.
- Press a folded handkerchief or soft pad directly on to wound, adding more padding if this becomes soaked.
- If possible raise bleeding part.
- If pressure is used to control bleeding check colour and temperature of parts distal to pressure pad to ensure adequate blood supply, releasing pressure frequently.

INTERNAL BLEEDING: Apparent when blood appears from the mouth or rectum, or suspected when a person collapses with pallor, sweating and a fast pulse.

All that can be done is to place the victim in the semi-prone position and prevent heat loss by covering with a blanket or sleeping bag. Supervision is necessary. *ADVICE SHOULD BE SOUGHT AS SOON AS POSSIBLE BY RADIO* (Make VHF **PAN-PAN** call).

LIVES CAN BE SAVED in all cases of injury by attending to the **A**IRWAY, **B**REATHING, **C**IRCULATION AND CONSCIOUS LEVEL of injured crew and doing this in an organised method. Using a check list prevents less important factors taking precedent. Always keep checking on anyone who has had an injury or been in the water.

GENERAL MEDICAL INFO

ARREST of heart's action can be caused by near drowning, by blood loss and by illness such as heart attack. It is not hard to recognise as the victim is obviously near death and a pulse cannot be found.

Refer to resuscitation above and perform external cardiac massage with patient on a firm surface such as deck or cabin sole, and with mouth to mouth resuscitation in a ratio of roughly 2 breaths to 15 chest pressings. Start with 2 breaths of expired air.

BREATHING: In conscious patients, problems can be caused by pain from injured ribs or chest infection. Help is given by pain killing tablets and/or antibiotics. Crew members with asthma will usually have their own medication and should be kept propped up. Keep checking. In an unconscious patient the airway must be cleared, the jaw tipped up and mouth to mouth breathing started if necessary, or if the patient is able to breath by himself he must be placed in the semi-prone position and carefully watched

in case the airway gets blocked by his tongue or by vomit or saliva.

CIRCULATION: Problems of central (the heart/pump) and peripheral (blood vessels/distribution) should be tackled as follows:

- Central: Failure of heart's action - dealt with by External Cardiac Massage (see above)
- Peripheral: Attempt to stop haemorrhage by method described above (see Bleeding)

BROKEN BONES: Principles are immobilisation and observation of circulation to the part beyond the probable fracture.

Skull: suspect fracture in severe blows to the head, especially if the patient is unconscious.

Priorities are (a) airway clearance and maintenance and cardiac massage if required (b) pressure if scalp bleeding is severe (c) monitoring of conscious or unconscious state (d) remember the possibility of neck injuries, keep neck and shoulders in line.

Spine: possible in falls from a height. Priority is always airway clearance and maintenance. *DO NOT USE EXCESSIVE CHIN TILT*, but if possible try to roll or lift patient from danger with head and back in a straight line – for example on a board large enough to stretch from head to buttocks with a rolled towel around the neck to minimise movement. The head should be held steady at all times in line with body in horizontal and vertical planes. *THIS IS ESSENTIAL TO PROTECT THE SPINAL CORD*.

Ribs: are often fractured in crush injuries and falls and do not take precedent over skull or spine injuries. If they appear to be the only injury then pain relief is essential to allow free movement of the chest for efficient breathing. Consider internal bleeding if patient becomes pale, clammy and collapsed. Possible internal damage if he becomes breathless.

Upper limbs: can be splinted to the trunk whether the fracture is closed or if bone is protruding. The bone should be immobilised at the joint above and below the fracture and padding should be inserted below any bandage or strapping. This should not be too tight and the part of the limb beyond should be checked regularly for changes in colour and temperature and for swelling which can restrict the blood flow. If this happens the bindings must be loosened. If the bone is protruding, cut clothing away and if possible cover with sterile gauze. Pain killers and, in the case of open fracture, antibiotics should be given as soon as possible.

Lower limbs: immobilise at point above and below fracture if possible. Check circulation in limb. Give pain relief or antibiotic cover for open fractures. The other limb, or an oar, is a suitable splint. Strapping should be added and distal circulation monitored.

BURNS: Best treatment is immediate immersion of affected part in clean, cold sea water for at least 10 minutes. Severe burns will swell a lot so any tight clothing or jewellery should be cut open or removed. The swelling around the burn is fluid from the body, which is then lost from the circulation so the victim can be shocked and dehydrated and fluid replacement is essential.

Burned tissue is easily infected and should not be handled, removed or blisters pricked. If clothing is stuck it should be left. Sunburn is a form of burn and can result in severe dehydration and shock.

BRUISES can cause a lot of pain under a finger or toenail. These can be treated safely by flaming the end of a piece of wire (such as a paper clip) and burning through the nail, just enough to release the blood.

COLD INJURY: Hypothermia should be suspected after any accidental immersion. Treat, whether apparent or not, by gradual re-warming. Shelter, dry clothes, gentle warmth from another person or handwarm heat source in a sleeping bag will help. *RESUSCITATION MAY BE REQUIRED*. Continual observation is essential.

CHOKING can be relieved by a sharp blow to the back preferably in the head down position. Alternatively grasp the victim from behind and pull clasped hands into the upper abdomen.

COLLAPSE can complicate injuries involving loss of blood, pain and loss of fluid. If the patient is unconscious then airway clearance, resuscitation and treatment of blood loss, followed by maintenance in the semi-prone position is paramount. Heat loss must be prevented but no active heating should be used. If the patient is conscious, loosen tight clothes and elevate the lower limbs. Fluids should be given (if conscious) frequently in small amounts.

CUTS: If deep, remove any foreign body and treat bleeding with compression. Clean and dry cut. Bring the edges together using Steristrips (or adhesive tape) to hold them closed, starting in mid-cut and working to ends. Reinforce middle strips to prevent bursting.

DROWNING: Try all the resuscitation techniques in the introduction, according to need.

A - Airway: clearance and maintenance

B - Breathing: by mouth to mouth or mouth to nose

C - Circulation: External Cardiac Massage may be required.

If successful, monitor level of consciousness and check airway. Maintain semi-prone position and keep under observation.

Hypothermia: usually complicates cold water immersion. Remove wet clothes and put patient in a dry sleeping bag with either a handwarm hot water bottle or a warm dry person. Look after patient out of wind, chill and rain and warm the cabin if possible. It can help to raise lower limbs and wrap towel round abdomen. Remember to watch for deterioration during warming.

DIARRHOEA should be treated by oral fluids only; no solid food for 24/48 hours.

EYE INJURIES - Foreign body(ies):

- Try to flush out with plenty of clean water.
- Try pulling upper lid over lower then releasing to remove foreign body from under upper lid.
- Raise upper, then lower lid, asking casualty to look all around. The upper lid can be turned back on itself over a matchstick. The speck can usually be seen and removed with a Q-tip or clean handkerchief.

If the foreign body cannot be removed it may have penetrated the eye and no further attempts should be made to remove it. The eye should be covered and both eyes rested. If pain persists after the speck is removed there may be a concealed abrasion and the eyes should be rested and Chloromycetin eye drops or a solution of 1 teaspoonful salt to 1 pint of boiled cooled water inserted.

Lost contact lenses can sometimes be lodged under upper lid in upper outer part of eye. It is possible to see them by turning back the lid and massaging them back into position through the lid.

FISH HOOKS can penetrate the skin and may have to be pushed right through until the barb can be cut off with pliers and the hook withdrawn.

HEART ATTACK: Though often hard to be sure, the following treatment should at least do no harm. If the patient is conscious, make them comfortable in the half-sitting position and give the strongest available pain killers. If the patient becomes semi-conscious place them in the recovery position, and observe carefully for maintenance of clear airway, and commence resuscitation should it be necessary.

HYPOTHERMIA nearly always complicates cold water immersion and should be considered even when not apparent. If conscious the victim may be confused and appear drunk, seeming lethargic and remote from what is going on. Shivering fits may or may not occur and poor colour, vomiting or faintness can develop. The treatment is mentioned under Cold Injury above and consists of gradual rewarming by removal from wet and cold, replacement of wet clothing and if conscious rewarming in a warm sleeping bag. Priority must be given to attention to airway and the semi-prone position if the victim is unconscious.

INTERNAL INJURIES may occur in any of the accidents which cause broken bones and bleeding and should be suspected when the patient seems unduly distressed, collapsed or blood appears from the body openings. The abdomen may appear rigid.

The priorities are airway clearance and maintenance and the adoption of the semi-prone position with careful observation to ensure prompt treatment of respiratory or cardiac arrest. The victim should be covered to prevent heat loss.

JOINTS can be strained and sprained on decks and winches. The treatment is rest and time, but supporting crepe bandages can be comforting.

SEASICKNESS is best avoided by starting treatment such as Stugeron or your favourite at least 12 hours before sailing. All these drugs may cause drowsiness. Alcohol must be avoided and hangovers predispose to seasickness.

ALL SEASICK CREW ON DECK SHOULD WEAR A HARNESS and should not be allowed to vomit over the side. Oral rehydration with very small amounts of rehydration fluids should be started, and fresh air and the ability to see the horizon can help. The danger of cold should not be ignored. Stemetil anti-sickness suppositories can be useful.

SWALLOWING: Accidentally swallowed objects can usually be left to nature. Dangerous objects such as watch batteries and open safety pins should be treated as emergencies.

STINGS from jellyfish are treated by oral antihistamines.

TOOTHACHE: Caused by abscess and accompanied by swelling can be treated with antibiotics and painkillers. You can buy dental kits over the counter.

VOMITING: Attempts should be made at rehydration using small amounts of fluid, preferably oral rehydration packs.

The information in the above list should give a casualty the best possibility of recovering until help arrives.

FIRST AID KIT

*Asterisked items require a prescription from a General Practitioner, who will have his/her own preferences and opinion on the need for a prescription. The following are mainly for guidance:

ANALGESICS – for pain relief
Paracetamol (Panadol) tabs 500mg. Dose; 2 tabs 4-6 hours for medium to moderate pain.

*Dihydrocodeine tabs. Dose: 1 tab 4-6 hourly for moderate to severe pain. Cause constipation with long term use. Can be used at night for cough or in the treatment of diarrhoea. Pharmacists will discuss other over the counter painkillers which are used for moderate pain.

ANTACIDS – for heartburn and indigestion. Gaviscon tabs. Dose; 2 tabs chewed and swallowed 3/4 times daily.

ANTIBIOTICS – for infections.
*Amoxycillin capsules 250mg. Dose: 2 caps three times daily. Check for allergy, otherwise safe.

*Erythromycin tablets 250mg for infection if allergic to Penicillin. Dose: 1 tab four times daily.

DIARRHOEALS – Imodium capsules after each loose stool. Up to 6 per day in conjunction with oral rehydration and avoiding solid food.

ANTIEMETICS – for seasickness. Prevention - Stugeron or other proprietory preparation.

*Stemetil suppositories along with oral rehydration in severe cases.

ANTIHISTAMINES – for stings, bites and hay fever. Newer Antihistamine - Loratadine, 1 tablet daily is less likely to cause drowsiness.

Piriton tablets 4mg - cause drowsiness

ANTISEPTICS – Savlon, TCP, Dettol etc.

DRESSINGS – Melolin Sterile Squares 10cm x 10cm. Put shiny side to wound, can be cut up and secured with Elastoplast or Micropore Tape. Crepe bandages - assorted widths for dressings, sprains or for securing splints. Steristrips for wound closure.

EYE DROPS – for sticky, gritty or red eyes. *Chloromycetin drop.

ORAL REHYDRATION – for vomiting and diarrhoea. Rehidrat or Diarolyte Powders in sachets with instructions. Start with small amounts then give freely to replace lost fluid in vomiting, diarrhoea, burns and sunburn.

GMDSS

The Global Maritime Distress and Safety System (GMDSS) is a sophisticated, but complex, semi-automatic, third-generation communications system. Although not compulsory for yachts, its potential for saving life, particularly when far offshore and out of VHF range, is so great that every yachtsman should consider it most seriously. Equipment costs continue to fall. Training courses, leading to the award of the Short Range Certificate (SRC) of Competence, are widely available. The Long Range Certificate covers MF, HF, SatCom, EPIRBs and SART.

Recommended reading:

- *ALRS, Vol 5* (UK Hydrographic Office)
- *GMDSS: a user's handbook* (Bréhaut/ACN)
- *GMDSS for small craft* (Clemmetsen/Fernhurst)
- *Reeds VHF/DSC Handbook* (Fletcher/ACN)

Purpose

GMDSS enables a coordinated SAR operation to be mounted rapidly and reliably anywhere at sea. To this end, terrestrial and satellite communications and navigation equipment is used to alert SAR authorities ashore and ships in the vicinity to a Distress incident or Urgency situation. GMDSS also promulgates Maritime Safety Information.

Sea areas

For the purposes of GMDSS, the world's sea areas are divided into 4 categories (A1-4), defined mainly by the range of radio communications. These are:

A1 An area within R/T coverage of at least one VHF Coastguard or Coast radio station in which continuous VHF alerting is available via DSC. Range: 20–50M from the CG/CRS.

A2 An area, excluding sea area A1, within R/T coverage of at least one MF CG/CRS in which continuous DSC alerting is available. Range: approx 50–250M from the CG/CRS.

A3 An area between 70°N and 70°S, excluding sea areas A1 and A2, within coverage of HF or an Inmarsat satellite in which continuous alerting is available.

A4 An area outside sea areas A1, A2 and A3, ie the polar regions, within coverage of HF.

In each category of sea area certain types of radio equipment must be carried. In A1 areas VHF DSC; A2 areas MF or HF DSC; A3 areas SatCom; A4 MF/HF.

Most UK yachtsmen will operate in A1 areas (the English Channel, for example, is an A1 area) where a simple VHF radio and a Navtex receiver will initially meet GMDSS requirements. As equipment becomes more affordable, yachtsmen may decide to fit GMDSS. This will become increasingly necessary as the present system for sending and receiving Distress calls is run down. The CG will continue a loudspeaker watch on VHF Ch 16 until further notice.

Functions

Regardless of the sea areas in which they operate, vessels complying with GMDSS must be able to perform certain functions:

- transmit ship-to-shore Distress alerts by two independent means
- receive shore-to-ship Distress alerts
- transmit & receive ship-to-ship Distress alerts
- transmit signals for locating incidents
- transmit and receive communications for SAR co-ordination
- transmit/receive maritime safety info, eg navigation and weather warnings

Distress alerts

A Distress alert is simply a Distress call using DSC. It is transmitted on Ch 70 and is automatically repeated five times. Whenever possible, a Distress alert should always include the last known position and time in UT. The position is normally entered automatically from an interfaced GPS, but can be entered manually if required. The nature of the distress can also be selected from the receiver's menu. The vessel's identity (MMSI number) is automatically included.

GMDSS requires participating ships to be able to send Distress alerts by two out of three independent means. These are:

- Digital Selective Calling (DSC) using terrestrial communications, ie VHF Ch 70,

MF 2187·5 kHz, or HF distress and alerting frequencies in the 4, 6, 8,12 and 16 MHz bands.

- Emergency Position Indicating Radio Beacons (EPIRBs), either float-free or manually released, using the Cospas/Sarsat satellites on 406 MHz with homing on 121·5 MHz; or those using Inmarsat satellites in the 1·6 GHz band. Both types transmit Distress messages which include the position and identification of the vessel in distress. See below for further details of EPIRBs.
- Inmarsat, via ship terminals.

Digital Selective Calling

DSC is an essential component of GMDSS. It is so called because information is sent by a burst of digital code; selective because it can be addressed to a specific DSC-equipped vessel or to a selected group of vessels.

In all DSC messages every vessel and relevant shore station has a 9-digit identification number, or MMSI (Maritime Mobile Service Identity), which is in effect an automatic, electronic callsign.

DSC is used to transmit Distress alerts from ships, to receive Distress acknowledgements from ships or shore stations; to send Urgency and Safety alerts; to relay Distress alerts; and for routine calling & answering. A thorough working knowledge is needed.

Using the procedures and switches applicable to your particular VHF/DSC radio, a VHF/DSC Distress alert might be sent as follows:

- Momentarily press the (red, guarded) Distress button. The set automatically switches to Ch 70 (DSC Distress chan) and transmits a basic Distress alert with position & time. It then reverts to Ch I6.
- If time permits, select from the DSC menu the nature of the distress, eg Collision. Then press the Distress button for 5 seconds to send a full Distress alert.

A CG/CRS automatically sends a Distress acknowledgement on Ch 70, before replying on Ch 16. Ships in range should reply directly on Ch 16.

If a Distress acknowledgement is not received from a CG/CRS, the Distress alert will automatically be repeated every four minutes.

- When a DSC Distress acknowledgement has been received, or after about 15 seconds, the vessel in distress should transmit a MAYDAY message by voice on Ch 16, adding its MMSI.

NB: If a Distress alert is inadvertently transmitted, an All stations DSC message cancelling the false alert (by date and time) must be sent at once.

Maritime Safety Information (MSI)

MSI consists of the vital navigational, weather and safety messages which traditionally were sent to vessels at sea by CRS in Morse, but by R/T on VHF and MF in more recent years – and now by GMDSS. For navigation and weather warnings see this and chapter 2 respectively.

GMDSS transmits MSI in English by two independent but complementary means, Navtex and SafetyNet.

- Navtex on MF (518 kHz and 490 kHz) which can be received out to about 300 miles offshore, see Chapter 2.
- SafetyNet uses Inmarsat-C satellites to cover beyond MF range. Enhanced Group Calling (EGC) is a part of SafetyNet which enables MSI to be sent to selected groups of users in any of the four oceans.

SATELLITES FOR SAR

Inmarsat (International Maritime Satellite system) and COSPAS/SARSAT (joint Russian-American system) provide satellite alerts and communications for SAR.

Inmarsat

Near-global communications are provided by four Inmarsat geostationary satellites, each positioned 19,300M above the four oceans (Pacific, Indian, East Atlantic & West Atlantic). The polar regions, ie N of about 70°N and S of 70°S, are not covered. Inmarsat-E enables distress alerting in the L-band 1.6 GHz frequency. From pressing the red button in a yacht to reception at an MRCC usually takes less than 2 minutes. From 1 Feb 2009 the 121·5 MHz service will be discontinued.

COSPAS/SARSAT (C/S)

These Russian/US C/S satellites were specifically designed for SAR operations. They not only detect a 406 MHz Distress alert transmitted by an EPIRB, but also locate it with a high degree of accuracy. There are 10 ground receiving stations in 9 countries worldwide.

There are four geostationary satellites (GEOSAR) in a 24 hr orbit at 19,400M above the equator, ie apparently fixed in relation to the earth. Four more low earth orbit (LEOSAR) satellites, about 450M high, pass over both poles every 100 minutes.

These 8 satellites give global coverage and receive both 406 and 121.5 MHz signals. But coverage is not quite continuous due to possible delays in detection by the LEOSAR system; waiting time is greater in equatorial regions.

LEOSAR satellites calculate an EPIRB's position by Doppler effect. GEOSAR satellites cannot do this since there is no Doppler shift between beacon and satellite. However this problem is solved by newer (and dearer) EPIRBs which have a built-in GPS receiver to provide location directly and with continuous updating.

EPIRBS

These are best categorised by their frequencies, ie:

- 406 MHz, as specifically designed to be processed by C/S. They emit a powerful and frequency-stable signal which ensures proven success in detection and location. C/S has established its own beacon specification and issues type approvals.

- 1·6 GHz, as used exclusively with Inmarsat satellites. L-band EPIRBs, known as Inmarsat-E, provide global distress alerting (as an alternative to 406 MHz EPIRBs in the C/S system). Inmarsat-E EPIRBs can also be equipped with an optional 121·5 MHz locator beacon for homing purposes and/or a Search and Rescue Radar Transponder (SART).

- 121·5 MHz (civilian aeronautical distress). These simple, inexpensive beacons are mainly used in conjunction with 406 MHz beacons for homing purposes. However their outdated technology was never designed to be detected by satellites. As a result from 1 Feb 2009 they will no longer be used at sea for satellite alerting.

If you own a basic 121·5 MHz beacon, do not throw it away; it can still be detected at long range by overflying airliners/Nimrods and at short range by homing lifeboats and helicopters.

- 243·0 MHz (military aeronautical distress). These too will be phased out from 1 Feb 2009 since their limitations are similar to 121·5 MHz beacons.

EPIRBs can be hand-held or float-free. Hand-held are popular in small craft because of their smaller size and portability. Many have lanyards for securing them to a liferaft or person in the water; these must not be secured to the yacht.

Float-free must be correctly installed so that they can indeed float free without snagging on a sinking vessel.

Most modern EPIRBs have a built-in GPS and a 48 hrs battery life. Costs range from £500 to £1200 for float-free, built-in GPS models. Inmarsat-E beacons cost about £1500.

Accuracy

All frequencies can be detected by C/S satellites. The processed positions are automatically passed to a Mission Control Centre (MCC) for assessment of any SAR action required; the UK MCC is co-located with the ARCC at Kinloss, NE Scotland.

C/S location accuracy is normally better than 5 km on 406 MHz, but no better than 20 km on 121·5 and 243·0 MHz. Dedicated SAR aircraft can home on 121·5 MHz and 243·0 MHz, but not on 406 MHz. Typically a helicopter at 1000 feet can receive homing signals from about 30M range whilst fixed-wing aircraft at higher altitudes can home from about 60M.

Best results will invariably be obtained from those 406 MHz EPIRBs with a built-in GPS receiver which transmits continuously updated positions.

UK EMERGENCY VHF DIRECTION FINDING SERVICE

VHF DF is for emergency use only, ie 'one stage down' from real distress. It is remotely controlled H24 by a CG Centre (MRCC) and is not a free navigational service. After contact on Ch 16, invariably Ch 67 is used for the DF procedure; this may be a count from 1-10. Note that the bearing obtained is in °True *from the station to the vessel*.

VHF-DF stations are marked on charts by a dot and magenta circle, suffixed 'RG'.

STATION	CONTROLLED BY MRCC	POSITION	
Barra	Stornoway	57°00'·81N	07°30'·42W
Bawdsey	Thames	51°59'·60N	01°25'·00E
Berry Head	Brixham	50°23'·97N	03°29'·05W
Boniface	Solent	50°36'·21N	01°12'·03W
Compass Head	Shetland	59°52'·05N	01°16'·30W
Crosslaw	Forth	55°54'·48N	02°12'·31W
Cullercoats	Humber	55°04'·00N	01°28'·00W
Dunnet Head	Aberdeen	58°40'·31N	03°22'·52W
Easington	Humber	53°39'·13N	00°05'·90E
East Prawle	Brixham	50°13'·10N	03°42'·50W
Fairlight	Dover	50°52'·19N	00°38'·74E
Fife Ness	Forth	56°16'·70N	02°35'·30W
Flamborough	Humber	54°07'·08N	00°05'·21W
Great Ormes Head	Holyhead	53°19'·96N	03°51'·25W
Grove Point	Portland	50°32'·93N	02°25'·20W
Hartland Pt	Swansea	51°01'·22N	04°31'·40W
Hartlepool	Humber	54°41'·79N	01°10'·57W
Hengistbury Head	Portland	50°42'·95N	01°45'·64W
Inverbervie	Forth	56°51'·10N	02°15'·65W
Kilchiaran	Clyde	55°45'·90N	06°27'·19W
Lands End	Falmouth	50°08'·13N	05°38'·19W
Landgon Battery	Dover	51°07'·97N	01°20'·59E
Law Hill	Clyde	55°41'·76N	04°50'·46W
Lizard	Falmouth	49°57'·60N	05°12'·06W
Lowestoft	Yarmouth	52°28'·60N	01°42'·20E
Newhaven	Solent	50°46'·93N	00°03'·01E
Newton	Humber	55°31'·01N	01°37'·10W
North Foreland	Dover	51°22'·53N	01°26'·72E
Noss Head	Aberdeen	58°28'·80N	03°03'·00W
Rame Head	Brixham	50°19'·03N	04°13'·20W
Rhiw	Holyhead	52°50'·00N	04°37'·82W
Rodel	Stornoway	57°44'·90N	06°57'·41W
St Ann's Head	Milford Haven	51°40'·97N	05°10'·52W
St Mary's, Isles of Scilly	Falmouth	49°55'·73N	06°18'·25W
Sandwick	Stornoway	58°12'·65N	06°21'·27W
Selsey	Solent	50°43'·80N	00°48'·22W
Shoeburyness	Thames	51°31'·38N	00°46'·50E
Skegness	Yarmouth	53°09'·00N	00°21'·00E
Snaefell	Liverpool	54°15'·84N	04°27'·66W
Tiree	Clyde	56°30'·62N	06°57'·68W
Trevose Head	Falmouth	50°32'·91N	05°01'·99W
Trimingham	Yarmouth	52°54'·57N	01°20'·60E
Tynemouth	Humber	55°01'·07N	01°24'·99W
Walney Island	Liverpool	54°06'·61N	03°16'·00W
Whitby	Humber	54°29'·40N	00°36'·30W
Wideford Hill	Shetland	58°59'·29N	03°01'·40W
Windyhead	Aberdeen	57°38'·90N	02°14'·50W
CHANNEL ISLANDS			
Guernsey	Ship transmits on Ch 16 (Distress only)	49°26'·27N	02°35'·77W
Jersey	or Ch 67 (Guernsey) or Ch 82 (Jersey)	49°10'·85N	02°14'·30W
NORTHERN IRELAND			
Orlock Head	Belfast	54°40'·41N	05°34'·97W
West Torr	Belfast	55°11'·70N	06°05'·20W

SAFETY

VHF EMERGENCY DIRECTION FINDING SERVICES

United Kingdom	Ch 16 (Distress only) Ch 67
Guernsey	Ch 16 (Distress) Ch 67
Jersey	Ch 16 (Distress) Ch 82
France	Ch 16 11 67

HM COASTGUARD - MRCC CONTACT DETAILS

EASTERN REGION

PORTLAND COASTGUARD
50°36'N 02°27'W. DSC MMSI 002320012
Custom House Quay, Weymouth DT4 8BE.
☎ 01305 760439. 🖷 01305 760451.
Area: Topsham to Chewton Bunney
(50°44'N 01°42'W).

SOLENT COASTGUARD
50°48'N 01°12'W. DSC MMSI 002320011
44A Marine Parade West, Lee-on-Solent,
PO13 9NR. ☎ 02392 552100. 🖷 02392
554131. Area: Chewton Bunney to Beachy
Hd. Call on Ch 67 to keep Ch 16 clear.

DOVER COASTGUARD
50°08'N 01°20'E. DSC MMSI 002320010
Langdon Battery, Dover CT15 5NA.
☎ 01304 210008. 🖷 01304 225762.
Area: Beachy Head to Reculver Towers
(51°23'N 01°12'E). Operates Channel
Navigation Information Service.

THAMES COASTGUARD
51°51'N 01°17'E. MMSI 002320009
East Terrace, Walton-on-the-Naze CO14
8PY. ☎ 01255 675518. 🖷 01255 679415.
Area: Reculver Towers to Southwold.

LONDON COASTGUARD
51°30'N 00°03'E. MMSI 002320063
Thames Barrier Navigation Centre, Unit 28,
34 Bowater Rd, Woolwich, London SE18 5TF.
☎ 0208 312 7380. 🖷 0208 309 8196.
Area: River Thames from Shell Haven Pt (N
bank) & Egypt Bay (S bank) up-river to
Teddington Lock.

YARMOUTH COASTGUARD
52°37'N 01°43'E. MMSI 002320008
Haven Bridge House, North Quay, Great
Yarmouth NR30 1HZ.
☎ 01493 851338. 🖷 01493 331975.
Area: Southwold to Haile Sand Fort.

†HUMBER COASTGUARD
54°06'N 00°11'W. MMSI 002320007
Lime Kiln Lane, Bridlington, N Humberside
YO15 2LX.
☎ 01262 672317. 🖷 01262 400779.
Area: Haile Sand Fort to Scottish border.

SCOTLAND & NORTHERN IRELAND

FORTH COASTGUARD
56°17'N 02°35'W. MMSI 002320005

Fifeness, Crail, Fife KY10 3XN.
☎ 01333 450666. 🖷 01333 450703.
Area: English border to Doonies Pt
(57°01'N 02°10'W).

†ABERDEEN COASTGUARD
57°08'N 02°05'W. MMSI 002320004
Marine House, Blaikies Quay, Aberdeen
AB11 5PB.
☎ 01224 592334. 🖷 01224 575920.
Area: Doonies Pt to Cape Wrath, incl
Pentland Firth.

†SHETLAND COASTGUARD
60°09'N 01°08'W. MMSI 002320001
Knab Road, Lerwick ZE1 0AX.
☎ 01595 692976. 🖷 01595 693634.
Area: Orkney, Fair Isle and Shetland.

†*STORNOWAY COASTGUARD
58°12'N 06°22'W. MMSI 002320024
Battery Pt, Stornoway, Isle of Lewis H51 2RT.
☎ 01851 702013. 🖷 01851 706796.
Area: Cape Wrath to Ardnamurchan Pt,
Western Isles and St Kilda.

†*CLYDE COASTGUARD
55°58'N 04°48'W. MMSI 002320022
Navy Bldgs, Eldon St, Greenock PA16 7QY.
☎ 01475 729988. 🖷 01475 888095.
Area: Ardnamurchan Pt to Mull of
Galloway inc islands.

*BELFAST COASTGUARD
54°40'N 05°40'W. MMSI 002320021
Bregenz House, Quay St, Bangor, Co Down
BT20 5ED.
☎ 02891 463933. 🖷 02891 469854.
Area: Carlingford Lough to Lough Foyle.

WESTERN REGION

LIVERPOOL COASTGUARD
53°30'N 03°03'W. MMSI 002320019
Hall Rd West, Crosby, Liverpool L23 8SY.
☎ 0151 9313341. 🖷 0151 9320978
Area: Mull of Galloway to Queensferry
(near Chester).

†HOLYHEAD COASTGUARD
53°19'N 04°38'W. MMSI 002320018
Prince of Wales Rd, Holyhead, Anglesey
LL65 1ET.
☎ 01407 762051. 🖷 01407 761613
Area: Queensferry to Friog (1·6M S of
Barmouth).

SAFETY

†MILFORD HAVEN COASTGUARD
51°42'N 05°03'W. MMSI 002320017
Gorsewood Drive, Hakin, Milford Haven,
SA73 2HD.
☎ 01646 690909. 📠 01646 697287.
Area: Friog to River Towy (11M N of
Worms Head).

SWANSEA COASTGUARD
51°34'N 03°58'W. MMSI 002320016
Tutt Head, Mumbles, Swansea SA3 4EX.
☎ 01792 366534. 📠 01792 368371.
Area: River Towy to Marsland Mouth (near
Bude).

†*FALMOUTH COASTGUARD
50°09'N 05°03'W. MMSI 002320014
Pendennis Point, Castle Drive, Falmouth
TR11 4WZ.
☎ 01326 317575. 📠 01326 315610.
Area: Marsland Mouth (near Bude) to
Dodman Point.

*BRIXHAM COASTGUARD
50°24'N 03°31'W. DSC MMSI 002320013
King's Quay, Brixham TQ5 9TW.
☎ 01803 882704. 📠 01803 859562.
Area: Dodman Point to Topsham (R. Exe).

NOTES: †Monitors DSC MF 2187.5 kHz.
*Broadcasts Gunfacts/Subfacts.

THE CHANNEL ISLANDS
There is no CG in the Channel Islands. The HMs
at St Peter Port and St Helier direct SAR
operations within the Northern and Southern
areas respectively.

Communications on VHF, MF and DSC are
provided by St Peter Port Radio and Jersey
Radio (Coast radio stations).

Close liaison is maintained with adjacent
French SAR authorities. A distress situation
may be controlled by the Channel Islands or
France, whichever is more appropriate. For
example a British yacht in difficulty in French
waters may be handled by St Peter Port or
Jersey so as to avoid language problems; and
vice versa for a French yacht.

ST PETER PORT RADIO 49°27'·00N
02°32'00W. DSC MMSI 002320064. ☎
01481 720672. 📠 714177. Area: Channel
Islands North.

JERSEY RADIO 49°10'·85N 02°14'30W.
DSC MMSI 002320060. ☎: 01534 741121.
📠: 499089. Area: Channel Islands South.

SEARCH AND RESCUE ABROAD THE IRISH REPUBLIC
The Irish CG co-ordinates SAR operations
around the coast of Eire via Dublin MRCC,
Malin Head and Valentia MRSCs and remote
sites. It may liaise with the UK and France
during any rescue operation within 100M of
the Irish coast. It is part of the Dept of Marine,
Leeson Lane, Dublin 2. ☎ (01) 6620922;
📠 (01) 6620795. The Irish EPIRB Registry is co-
located; ☎ (01) 6199280; 📠 (01) 6621571.

The MRCC/MRSCs are co-located with the
Coast radio stations of the same name and
manned by the same staff. All stations keep
watch H24 on VHF Ch 16 and DSC Ch 70. If
ashore dial 999 or 112 in an emergency and

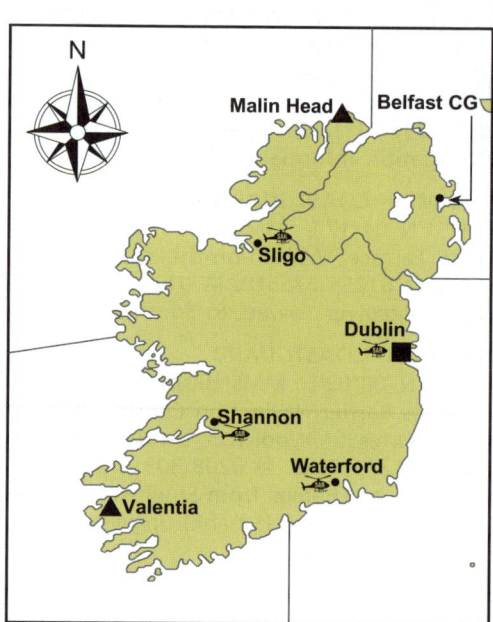

Irish Coastguard centres

ask for Marine Rescue.

Details of the MRCC/MRSCs are as follows:

DUBLIN (MRCC)
53°20'N 06°15W. DSC MMSI 002500300
(+2187·5 kHz).
☎ +353 1 662 0922/3; 📠 +353 1 662 0795.
Area: Carlingford Lough to Youghal.

VALENTIA (MRSC)
51°56'N 10°21'W.DSC MMSI 002500200
(+2187·5 kHz).
☎ +353 669 476 109; 📠 +353 669 476 289.
Area: Youghal to Slyne Head.

MALIN HEAD (MRSC)

55°22'N 07°20W. DSC MMSI 002500100 (+2187·5 kHz).

☎ +353 77 70103; 📠 +353 77 70221.
Area: Slyne Head to Lough Foyle.

SAR resources

The Irish CG provides some 50 units around the coast and is on call H24. The RNLI maintains 4 stations around the coast and operates 42 lifeboats; six community-run inshore rescue boats are also available.

Sikorsky S-61 helicopters, based at Dublin, Waterford, Shannon and Sligo, can respond within 15 to 45 minutes and operate to a radius of 200M. They are equipped with infrared search equipment and can uplift 30 survivors.

Military and civilian aircraft and vessels, together with the Garda and lighthouse service, can also be called upon.

Some stations provide specialist cliff climbing services. They are manned by volunteers, who are trained in first aid and equipped with inflatables, breeches buoys, cliff ladders etc. Their ☎ numbers (the Leader's residence) are given, where appropriate, under each port.

DENMARK

The national SAR agency is: Ministry of Defence, 42 Holmens Kanal, DK-1060 København K, Denmark.

☎ +45 339 23320; 📠 +45 333 20655.

The SAR coordinator for Denmark is MRCC Århus, ☎ +45 894 33099 ext 3203; 📠 +45 894 33230; mrcc@sok.dk. Århus has no direct communications with vessels in distress, but operates via two MRSCs and several Coast radio stations (CRS). MRSC Kattegat, ☎ +45 992 22255; 📠 +45 992 22838, deals with the W coast of Denmark.

Lyngby Radio

This is the main Danish CRS and is DSC VHF/MF/HF equipped (☎ +45 452 89800; 📠 +45 458 82485, lyngby-radio@tdc.dk MMSI 002191000).

It operates through remote sites at Skagen, Hirtshals, Hantsholm, Bovbjerg and Blavand, all of which guard Ch 16 H24 and use callsign *Lyngby Radio*. Their VHF and MF frequencies are shown in the chartlet opposite.

There are at least 12 lifeboats stationed at the major harbours along the west coast. They are designed to double up as Pilot boats.

Firing practice areas

There are 4 such areas on the W coast as in the chartlet and listed below. Firing times are broadcast daily by Danmarks Radio 1 after the weather at 1645UT. Times can also be obtained from the Range office Ch 16 or ☎.

Ⓐ Tranum & Blokhus ☎ 982 35088 or call *Tranum.*

Ⓑ Nymindegab ☎ 752 89355 or call *Nymindegab.*

Ⓒ Oksbøl ☎ 765 41213 or call *Oksbøl.*

Ⓓ Rømø E ☎ 747 55219; Rømø W ☎ 745 41340 – or call *Fly Rømø.*

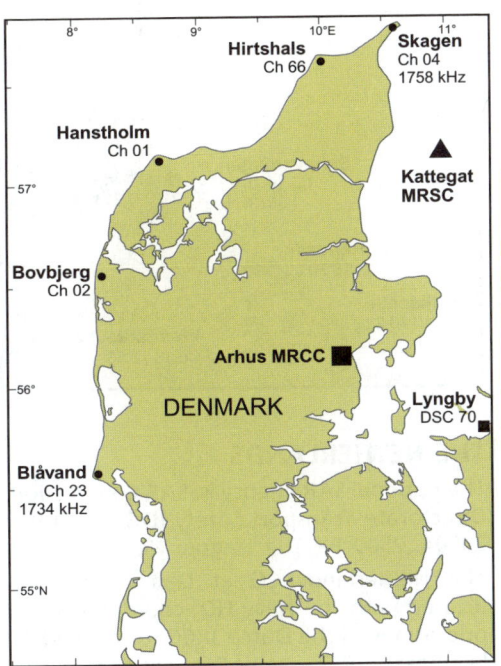

Danish Coastguard centres

GERMANY

The national SAR agency is: *Deutsche Gesellschaft zur Rettung Schiffbrüchiger* (DGzRS), the German Sea Rescue Service. Werderstrasse 2, Hermann-Helms-Haus, D-28199 Bremen. mail@mrcc-bremen.de. ☎ 421 537 070; 📠 421 537 0714.

DGzRS is responsible for coordinating SAR operations, supported by ships and SAR helicopters of the German Navy.

Bremen MRCC (☎ 421 536870; 📠 421 5368714; MMSI 002111240), using callsign *Bremen Rescue Radio,* maintains an H24 watch on Ch 16 and DSC Ch 70 via remote Coast radio stations at:

Sylt, Nordfriesland, Eiderstedt, Helgoland, Elbe-Weser, Hamburg and Norddeich.

There are 21 offshore lifeboats, LOA 23–

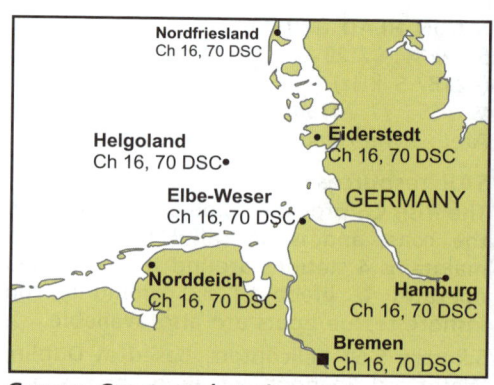

German Coastguard stations

44m, and 21 smaller <10m lifeboats, based at List, Amrum, Helgoland, Cuxhaven, Bremerhaven, Wilhelmshaven, Langeoog, Norderney and Borkum. There are also many inshore lifeboats.

Netherlands Coastguard stations

The JRCC keeps a listening watch H24 on DSC Ch 70, and MF DSC 2187·5 kHz (but not on 2182 kHz); MMSI 002442000.

Coastguard Operations can be contacted H24 via:

In emergency:
☎ + 31 9000 111 or dial 112.
Operational telephone number:
☎ + 31 223 542300. 📠 + 31 223 658358; ccc@kustwacht.nl If using a mobile phone, call 9000 111, especially if the International emergency number 112 is subject to delays.
Admin/info (HO)
☎+ 31 223 658300. 📠+31 223 658303. info@kustwacht.nl PO Box 10000, 1780 CA Den Helder.

THE NETHERLANDS

The national SAR agency is: SAR Commission, Directorate Transport Safety (DGG), PO Box 20904, 2500 EX The Hague, Netherlands.

The Netherlands CG at Den Helder, co-located with the Navy HQ, coordinates SAR operations as the Dutch JRCC for A1 and A2 Sea Areas. (JRCC = Joint Rescue Coordination Centre – marine & aeronautical.) Callsign is *Netherlands Coastguard,* but *Den Helder Rescue* during SAR operations.

Remote CG stations are shown above. Working channels are VHF 23 and 83.

BELGIUM

The Belgian CG coordinates SAR operations from Oostende MRCC, callsign *Coastguard Oostende*. The MRCC and *Oostende Radio* (Coast radio rtation) both keep listening watch H24 on Ch 16, 2182 kHz and DSC Ch 70 and 2187·5 kHz.

Coastguard stations

MRCC OOSTENDE
☎ +32 59 701000; 📠 +32 59 703605.
MMSI 002050480.
MRSC Nieuwpoort
☎ +32 58 230000; 📠 +32 58 231575.
MRSC Zeebrugge
☎ +32 50 550801; 📠 +32 50 547400.
RCC Brussels (COSPAS/SARSAT agency)
☎ +32 2 7200338; 📠 +32 2 7524201.

Coast Radio Stations

OOSTENDE Radio
☎ 59 702438; 📠 59 701339.
Ch 16, DSC Ch 70 and MF DSC 2187·5 kHz.
MMSI 002050480.

Antwerpen Radio (remotely controlled by Oostende CRS) MMSI 002050485. Ch 16, DSC Ch 70.

Resources

Offshore and inshore lifeboats are based at Nieuwpoort, Oostende and Zeebrugge.

The Belgian Air Force provides helicopters from Koksijde near the French border. The Belgian Navy also participates in SAR operations as required.

FRANCE – CROSS

Four CROSS (Centres Régionaux Opérationnels de Surveillance et de Sauvetage, ie an MRCC) provide a permanent, H24, all weather operational presence along the N and W coasts and liaise with foreign CGs.

CROSS' main functions include:

- Co-ordinating SAR operations.
- Navigational surveillance.
- Broadcasting navigational warnings.
- Broadcasting weather information.
- Anti-pollution control.
- Marine and fishery surveillance.

CROSS locations and areas of responsibility

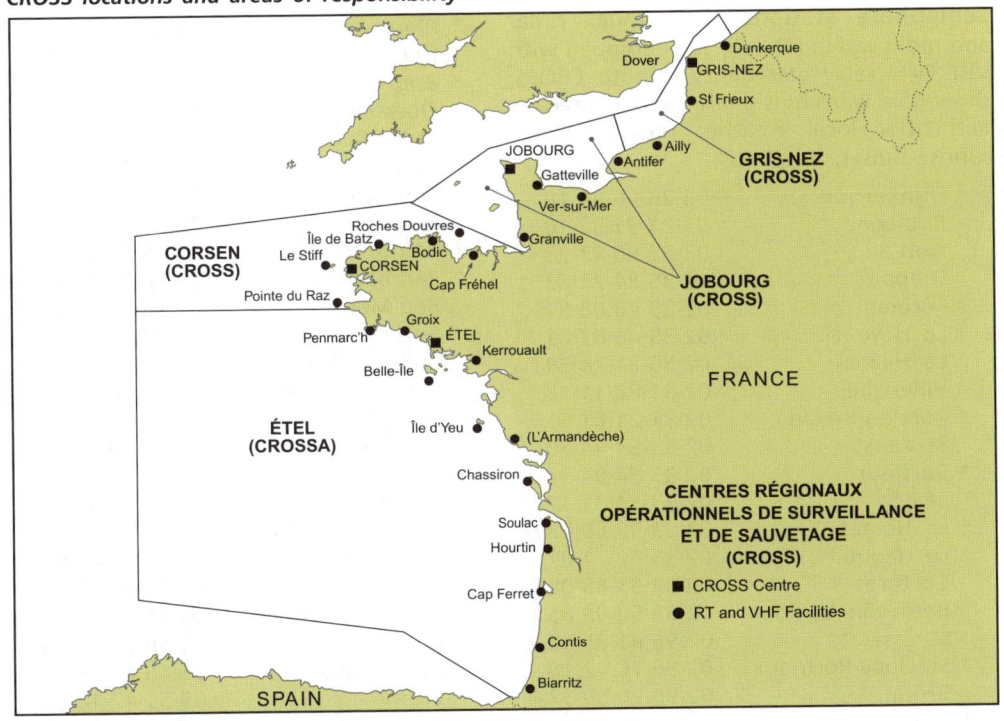

All centres keep watch on VHF Ch 16 as well as Ch 70 (DSC)and co-ordinate SAR on Ch 15, 67, 68, 73. They also broadcast gale warnings, weather forecasts and local navigational warnings.

CROSSA Étel specialises in medical advice and responds to alerts from Cospas/Sarsat satellites.

CROSS can be contacted by R/T, by ☎, through Coast Radio Stations, via the National Gendarmerie or Affaires Maritimes, or via a Semaphore station. Call *Semaphore* stations on Ch 16 (working Ch 10) or by ☎ as listed later in this section.

CROSS also monitor TSS in the Dover Strait, off Casquets and off Ouessant using, for example, the callsign *Corsen Traffic*.

For medical advice call CROSS which will contact a doctor or SAMU (Service d'Aide Médicale Urgente). In harbour/marina SAMU responds faster to a medical emergency than calling a doctor. Simply dial 15.

CROSS stations (Emergency ☎ 1616).

CROSS Gris-Nez
50°52'N 01°35'E   MMSI 002275100
☎ 03 21 87 21 87; ✉ 03 21 87 78 55
Belgian border to Cap d'Antifer.

NavWarnings Ch 79 at every H+10 via Dunkerque, Saint-Frieux and L'Ailly.

CROSS Jobourg
49°41'N 01°54'W   MMSI 002275200
☎ 02 33 52 72 13; ✉ 02 33 52 71 72
Cap de la Hague to Mont St Michel

NavWarnings Ch 80 every H+20 and H+50 via Antifer, Ver-sur-Mer, Gatteville, Jobourg, Granville and Roche Douvres.

CROSS Corsen
48°24'N 04°47'W   MMSI 002275300
☎ 02 98 89 31 31; ✉ 02 98 89 65 75
Mont St Michel to Pointe de Penmarc'h.

NavWarnings Ch 79 every H+10 and H+40 via Cap Fréhel, Bodic, Ile de Batz, Le Stiff and Pte du Raz.

CROSS Étel
47°39'N 03°12'W   MMSI 002275000
☎ 02 97 55 35 35; ✉ 02 97 55 49 34
Pte de Penmarc'h to the Spanish border

NavWarnings Ch 79 for Landes range activity via Chassiron 1903; Soulac 1915; Cap Ferret 1933; Contis 1945; and Biarritz 2003.

Semaphore stations keep visual, radar and radio watch (Ch 16); are equipped with VHF DF; relay emergency calls to CROSS; show gale warning signals, repeat forecasts and offer local weather reports. Hours sunrise-sunset, but * H24.

* Dunkerque	03·28·66·86·18
Boulogne	03·21·31·32·10
Ault	03·22·60·47·33
Dieppe	02·35·84·23·82
* Fécamp	02·35·28·00·91
* La Hève	02·35·46·07·81
* Le Havre	02·35·21·74·39
Villerville	02·31·88·11·13
* Port-en-Bessin	02·31·21·81·51
St-Vaast	02·33·54·44·50
* Barfleur	02·33·54·04·37
Lévy	02·33·54·31·17
* Le Homet	02·33·92·60·08
La Hague	02·33·52·71·07
Carteret	02·33·53·85·08
Barneville Le Roc	02·33·50·05·85
St-Cast	02·96·41·85·30
* St Quay-Portrieux	02·96.70.42.18
Bréhat	02·96·20·00·12

* Ploumanac'h	02·96·91·46·51
Batz	02·98·61·76·06
* Brignogan	02·98·83·50·84
* Ouessant Stiff	02·98·48·81·50
* St-Mathieu	02·98·89·01·59
* Portzic (Ch 08)	02·98·22·21·47
Toulinguet	02·98·27·90·02
Cap-de-la-Chèvre	02·98·27·09·55
* Pointe-du-Raz	02·98·70·66·57
* Penmarc'h	02·98·58·61·00
Beg Meil	02·98·94·98·92
* Port-Louis	02·97·82·52·10
Étel Mât Fenoux	02·97·55·35·35
Beg Melen (Groix)	02·97·86·80·13
Talut (Belle-Île)	02·97·31·85·07
St-Julien	02·97·50·09·35
Piriac-sur-Mer	02·40·23·59·87
* Chemoulin	02·40·91·99·00
St-Sauveur (Yeu)	02·51·58·31·01
Les Baleines (Ré)	05·46·29·42·06
Chassiron (Oléron)	05·46·47·85·43
* Pointe-de-Grave	05·56·09·60·03
Cap Ferret	05·56·60·60·03
Messanges	05·58·48·94·10
* Socoa	05·59·47·18·54

EMERGENCY VHF DF SERVICE

A yacht in emergency can call CROSS on VHF Ch 16, 11 or 67 to obtain a true bearing of the yacht *from* the DF station. These monitor Ch 16 and other continuously scanned frequencies, which include Ch 1-29, 36, 39, 48, 50, 52, 55, 56 and 60-88. The Semaphore stations overleaf are also equipped with VHF DF.

HJ = Day service only.

VHF DF stations, are listed below geographically from NE to W then S:

Station	Lat/Long	Hrs
Dunkerque	51°03'.40N 02°20'.40E	H24
*Gris-Nez	50°52'.20N 01°35'.01E	H24
Boulogne	50°44'.00N 01°36'.00E	HJ
Ault	50°06'.50N 01°27'.50E	HJ
Dieppe	49°56'.00N 01°05'.20E	HJ
Fécamp	49°46'.10N 00°22'.20E	H24
La Hève	49°30'.60N 00°04'.20E	H24
Villerville	49°23'.20N 00°06'.50E	HJ
Port-en-Bessin	49°21'.10N 00°46'.30W	H24
Saint-Vaast	49°34'.50N 01°16'.50W	HJ
Barfleur	49°41'.90N 01°15'.90W	H24
Levy	49°41'.70N 01°28'.20W	HJ
†Homet	49°39'.50N 01°37'.90W	H24
*Jobourg	49°41'.50N 01°54'.50W	H24
La Hague	49°43'.60N 01°56'.30W	HJ
Carteret	49°22'.40N 01°48'.30W	HJ
Le Roc	48°50'.10N 01°36'.90W	HJ
Grouin/Cancale	48°42'.60N 01°50'.60W	HJ
Saint-Cast	48°38'.60N 02°14'.70W	HJ
St-Quay-Port'x	48°39'.30N 02°49'.50W	H24
Bréhat	48°51'.30N 03°00'.10W	HJ
Ploumanac'h	48°49'.50N 03°28'.20W	H24
Batz	48°44'.80N 04°00'.60W	HJ
Brignogan	48°40'.60N 04°19'.70W	H24
Creac'h (Ushant)	48°27'.60N 05°07'.70W	HJ

*Creac'h	48°27'.60N 05°07'.80W	H24
†Saint-Mathieu	48°19'.80N 04°46'.20W	H24
Toulinguet	48°16'.80N 04°37'.50W	HJ
Cap de la Chèvre	48°10'.20N 04°33'.00W	HJ
Pointe du Raz	48°02'.30N 04°43'.80W	H24
Penmarc'h	47°47'.90N 04°22'.40W	H24
Beg-Meil	47°51'.30N 03°58'.40W	HJ
Beg Melen	47°39'.20N 03°30'.10W	HJ
†Port-Louis	47°42'.60N 03°21'.80W	H24
*Etel	47°39'.80N 03°12'.00W	H24
Saint-Julien	47°29'.70N 03°07'.50W	HJ
Taillefer	47°21'.80N 03°09'.00W	HJ
Le Talut	47°17'.70N 03°13'.00W	HJ
Piriac	47°22'.50N 02°33'.40W	HJ
Chemoulin	47°14'.10N 02°17'.80W	H24
Saint-Sauveur	46°41'.70N 02°18'.80W	HJ
Les Baleines	46°14'.60N 01°33'.70W	HJ
Chassiron	46°02'.80N 01°24'.50W	HJ
La Coubre	45°41'.90N 01°13'.40W	H24
Pointe de Grave	45°34'.30N 01°03'.90W	HJ
Cap Ferret	44°37'.50N 01°15'.00W	HJ
Messanges	43°48'.80N 01°23'.90W	HJ
Socoa	43°23'.30N 01°41'.10W	H24

Lifeboats

The lifeboat service Société National de Sauvetage en Mer (SNSM) comes under CROSS, but ashore it is best to contact local lifeboat stations direct. A hefty charge may be levied if a SNSM lifeboat attends a vessel not in distress.

Navigation warnings

Long-range warnings are broadcast by SafetyNet for Navarea II, which includes the W coast of France. The N coast is in Navarea I.

Avurnavs (AVis URgents aux NAVigateurs) are regional, coastal and local warnings issued by Cherbourg and Brest and broadcast by Niton and Brest Navtex and on MF. Warnings are prefixed by 'Sécurité Avurnav'.

SAFETY

SPAIN

The Society for Maritime Rescue and Safety (Sociedad de Salvamento y Seguridad Maritima – SASEMAR) is the national agency for SAR operations (and the prevention of pollution); akin to MCA in the UK.

MRCC Madrid coordinates SAR operations via 3 MRCCs (Bilbao, Gijon and Finisterre) on the N coast and Tarifa MRCC on the SW coast – as listed below.

All Centres monitor (H24) VHF Ch 16, MF 2182 kHz and DSC Ch 70, 2187·5 kHz. They also broadcast weather as shown in Chapter 2 and Nav warnings; but do *not* handle commercial link calls.

North and North West Spain

In N and NW Spain CG Centres do not keep continuous watch on Ch 16, so call on a working channel.

Spanish & Portuguese Coastguard Radio Stations

MADRID MRCC
MMSI 002241008 ☎ 91 7559 132/3; 🖷 9l 5261440.

Bilbao MRCC
43°21'N 03°02'W   MMSI 002240996
☎ 944 839411; 🖷 944 83 9161.

Santander MRSC
43°28'N 03°43'W   MMSI 002241009
☎ 942 213 030; 🖷 942 213 638.

Gijón MRCC
43°34'N 05°42'W   MMSI 002240997
☎ 985 326050; 🖷 985 320908.

Finisterre MRCC
42°42'N 08°59'W   MMSI 002240993
☎ 981 767320; 🖷 981 767740.

Coruña MRSC
43°22'N 08°23'W   MMSI 002241022
☎ 981 209541; 🖷 981 209518.

Vigo MRSC
42°10'N 08°41'W   MMSI 002240998
☎ 986 222230; 🖷 986 228957.

PORTUGAL
The Portuguese Navy coordinates SAR in two regions, Lisboa and Santa Maria (Azores) via MRCCs at Lisboa, Ponta Delgada (Azores) and one planned at Horta (Azores). A network of CRS maintains an H24 listening watch on all distress frequencies.

The Naval HQ (Estado Maior da Armada, 3 Divisao) is at: Praca do Comercio, 1188 Lisboa Codex, Portugal.
☎ 21 346 8965. 🖷 21 347 9591.

MAINLAND
Lisboa MRCC
38°41'N 09°19'W   MMSI 002630100
☎ 21 4401919; 🖷 21 4401954.
mrcclisboa@netc.pt
Planned DSC Ch 70; 2187·5 kHz

Remotely controlled MF DSC stations are planned (2005) at:
Apulia 41°28'N 08°45'W. MMSI 002630200.
Sagres 37°00'N 08°56'W. MMSI 002630400.

AZORES
Ponta Delgada MRCC
37°44'N 25°40'W   MMSI 002040100
☎ 296 281777; 🖷 296 281999
mrccdelgada@mail.telepac.pt
Planned DSC Ch 70; 2187·5 kHz.

SOUTH-WEST SPAIN
Tarifa MRCC coordinates SAR in SW Spain and the Gibraltar Strait.

Tarifa MRCC
36°01'N 05°35'W   MMSI 002240994
☎ 956 684740; 🖷 956 680 606.

Huelva MRSC
37°13'N 07°07'W   MMSI 002241012
☎ 959 243000; 🖷 959 242103.

Cadiz MRSC
36°32'N 06°18'W   MMSI 002241011
☎ 956 214253; 🖷 956 226091.

Algeciras MRSC
(controlled by Malaga MRCC)
36°08'N 05°26'W   MMSI 002241001
☎ 956 580930; 🖷 956 585402.

CHAPTER 5 - TIDES

CONTENTS

Dover ranges and times of HW 142

Brest tidal coefficients 143

Tidal calculations 144

Special instructions: Bournemouth to Selsey Bill 148
Tidal curves Bournemouth to Selsey Bill

Tidal stream charts 152
*English Channel & S Brittany, Portland, Isle of Wight, Channel Islands,
North Sea, Scotland, West UK and Ireland,*

Tidal gates 190

Secondary ports: time & height differences 199

Standard ports: curves & predictions

   Southern England 218
   *Falmouth, Plymouth, Dartmouth, Portland, Poole, Southampton,
   Portsmouth, Shoreham, Dover*

   Eastern England 254
   *Sheerness, London Bridge, Burnham-on-Crouch, Walton-on-the-Naze,
   Lowestoft, Immingham, River Tyne*

   Scotland 282
   Leith, Aberdeen, Wick, Lerwick, Stornoway, Ullapool, Oban, Greenock

   Western England and Wales 314
   Liverpool, Holyhead, Milford Haven, Avonmouth

   Ireland 330
   Dublin, Belfast, Galway, Cobh

   Denmark 346
   Esbjerg

   Germany 350
   Helgoland, Cuxhaven, Wilhelmshaven

   Netherlands 362
   Hoek van Holland, Vlissingen

   Northern France 370
   Dunkerque, Dieppe, Le Havre, Cherbourg, St Malo

   Channel Islands 390
   St Peter Port, St Helier

   Western France 398
   Brest, Pointe de Grave

   Portugal & Gibraltar 406
   Lisboa, Gibraltar

TIDES

DOVER RANGES & TIMES OF HW 2007

January

Day	HW	Range	HW
1	0859	4.4	2134
2	0956	4.8	2225
3	1047	5.1	2309
4	1132	5.2	2351
5	1213	5.2	
6	0031	5.1	1252
7	0110	4.9	1330
8	0148	4.7	1408
9	0225	4.4	1445
10	0300	4.1	1525
11	0339	3.6	1611
12	0426	3.2	1712
13	0530	2.9	1824
14	0642	2.9	1930
15	0748	3.2	2028
16	0845	3.7	2119
17	0935	4.3	2204
18	1020	4.8	2245
19	1103	5.3	2326
20	1145	5.5	
21	0006	5.7	1227
22	0048	5.8	1308
23	0130	5.8	1351
24	0215	5.7	1437
25	0302	5.1	1528
26	0354	4.5	1627
27	0455	3.8	1740
28	0611	3.5	1903
29	0737	3.3	2023
30	0858	3.7	2132
31	1003	4.3	2223

February

Day	HW	Range	HW
1	1051	4.8	2304
2	1130	5.1	2341
3	1204	5.3	
4	0017	5.3	1237
5	0051	5.3	1308
6	0123	5.1	1337
7	0150	4.9	1403
8	0214	4.6	1427
9	0240	4.2	1455
10	0316	3.6	1535
11	0405	2.9	1637
12	0537	2.5	1846
13	0715	2.8	2000
14	0824	3.4	2058
15	0920	4.2	2146
16	1007	4.9	2229
17	1050	5.6	2310
18	1131	6.0	2350
19	1210	6.3	
20	0029	6.4	1249
21	0110	6.4	1330
22	0152	6.1	1413
23	0236	5.4	1500
24	0325	4.5	1556
25	0426	3.6	1708
26	0545	3.0	1838
27	0730	2.8	2017
28	0905	3.4	2128

March

Day	HW	Range	HW
1	1002	4.3	2214
2	1043	4.9	2250
3	1116	5.3	2324
4	1145	5.4	2356
5	1213	5.4	
6	0027	5.4	1241
7	0054	5.3	1305
8	0115	5.2	1324
9	0133	4.9	1343
10	0158	4.5	1412
11	0232	3.9	1451
12	0316	3.1	1542
13	0427	2.4	1805
14	0650	2.5	1931
15	0803	3.3	2033
16	0900	4.3	2123
17	0948	5.2	2207
18	1030	5.8	2248
19	1110	6.3	2327
20	1148	6.6	
21	0007	6.7	1227
22	0048	6.5	1308
23	0129	6.1	1351
24	0214	5.3	1439
25	0304	4.3	1536
26	0407	3.3	1646
27	0528	2.6	1814
28	0727	2.7	2000
29	0853	3.5	2105
30	0941	4.3	2148
31	1018	4.9	2224

April

Day	HW	Range	HW
1	1048	5.2	2257
2	1117	5.3	2329
3	1144	5.3	2358
4	1211	5.3	
5	0022	5.3	1234
6	0041	5.1	1251
7	0100	4.9	1313
8	0127	4.6	1345
9	0203	4.1	1426
10	0250	3.3	1522
11	0407	2.7	1729
12	0625	2.8	1857
13	0736	3.5	2001
14	0833	4.4	2053
15	0921	5.3	2138
16	1004	5.9	2221
17	1045	6.3	2303
18	1125	6.5	2344
19	1205	6.4	
20	0026	6.3	1249
21	0110	5.8	1334
22	0157	5.0	1425
23	0251	4.2	1521
24	0354	3.4	1626
25	0508	2.9	1741
26	0653	3.0	1914
27	0814	3.5	2023
28	0902	4.1	2110
29	0940	4.5	2149
30	1012	4.8	2224

May

Day	HW	Range	HW
1	1042	4.9	2256
2	1112	5.1	2325
3	1141	5.0	2351
4	1206	5.0	
5	0013	4.9	1229
6	0039	4.8	1257
7	0111	4.5	1333
8	0152	4.1	1420
9	0246	3.6	1524
10	0412	3.4	1654
11	0551	3.5	1815
12	0701	3.9	1921
13	0759	4.6	2017
14	0850	5.1	2107
15	0937	5.6	2154
16	1021	5.9	2240
17	1105	6.0	2326
18	1150	5.9	
19	0012	5.8	1236
20	0059	5.4	1323
21	0148	4.8	1413
22	0240	4.3	1505
23	0337	3.7	1600
24	0439	3.3	1702
25	0552	3.2	1812
26	0708	3.4	1923
27	0805	3.7	2020
28	0851	4.0	2106
29	0930	4.3	2145
30	1006	4.6	2221
31	1041	4.8	2254

June

Day	HW	Range	HW
1	1114	4.8	2326
2	1146	4.8	2358
3	1219	4.8	
4	0032	4.8	1254
5	0110	4.8	1335
6	0155	4.6	1423
7	0248	4.3	1519
8	0352	4.1	1621
9	0505	4.1	1729
10	0616	4.1	1836
11	0721	4.4	1940
12	0819	4.7	2039
13	0914	5.0	2135
14	1006	5.3	2229
15	1056	5.4	2319
16	1143	5.5	
17	0007	5.4	1228
18	0054	5.3	1313
19	0139	5.1	1358
20	0224	4.7	1443
21	0311	4.3	1529
22	0401	3.9	1618
23	0456	3.5	1713
24	0557	3.3	1813
25	0700	3.3	1917
26	0758	3.4	2015
27	0849	3.8	2105
28	0934	4.1	2149
29	1015	4.4	2230
30	1054	4.8	2309

July

Day	HW	Range	HW
1	1131	4.9	2347
2	1208	5.0	
3	0026	5.2	1247
4	0106	5.2	1328
5	0147	5.2	1411
6	0233	5.1	1459
7	0324	4.8	1551
8	0422	4.4	1650
9	0529	4.2	1757
10	0645	3.9	1911
11	0758	4.0	2024
12	0904	4.3	2132
13	1003	4.7	2232
14	1053	5.1	2322
15	1137	5.3	
16	0005	5.5	1219
17	0045	5.3	1258
18	0123	5.3	1337
19	0200	4.9	1415
20	0237	4.7	1453
21	0316	4.3	1530
22	0359	3.7	1613
23	0452	3.2	1709
24	0559	2.9	1818
25	0710	2.9	1929
26	0814	3.2	2033
27	0908	3.8	2126
28	0954	4.3	2211
29	1034	4.8	2252
30	1112	5.2	2331
31	1151	5.5	

August

Day	HW	Range	HW
1	0010	5.7	1230
2	0048	5.8	1309
3	0127	5.8	1350
4	0209	5.5	1434
5	0255	5.1	1522
6	0349	4.4	1619
7	0456	3.7	1729
8	0621	3.3	1856
9	0749	3.4	2027
10	0905	3.8	2141
11	1004	4.5	2236
12	1048	5.1	2318
13	1126	5.4	2354
14	1202	5.6	
15	0026	5.6	1238
16	0058	5.4	1312
17	0129	5.2	1343
18	0158	4.8	1411
19	0224	4.4	1437
20	0250	3.9	1508
21	0326	3.3	1556
22	0440	2.6	1729
23	0630	2.5	1857
24	0743	2.8	2008
25	0843	3.6	2105
26	0930	4.4	2151
27	1010	5.1	2231
28	1049	5.5	2309
29	1127	6.0	2346
30	1205	6.2	
31	0023	6.3	1245

September

Day	HW	Range	HW
1	0102	6.2	1325
2	0144	5.7	1408
3	0229	5.1	1457
4	0324	4.2	1556
5	0436	3.3	1714
6	0606	2.9	1853
7	0745	3.1	2037
8	0903	3.8	2140
9	0953	4.6	2225
10	1031	5.3	2300
11	1105	5.6	2330
12	1138	5.6	2359
13	1211	5.5	
14	0028	5.4	1242
15	0056	5.2	1308
16	0118	4.9	1327
17	0135	4.5	1347
18	0158	4.1	1417
19	0232	3.4	1458
20	0322	2.5	1626
21	0553	2.3	1832
22	0711	2.7	1942
23	0812	3.7	2038
24	0900	4.5	2124
25	0941	5.3	2204
26	1021	5.9	2242
27	1059	6.3	2319
28	1138	6.4	2357
29	1218	6.4	
30	0037	6.2	1300

October

Day	HW	Range	HW
1	0121	5.7	1345
2	0209	4.9	1437
3	0308	3.9	1543
4	0421	3.1	1705
5	0547	2.7	1851
6	0729	3.2	2025
7	0840	4.0	2119
8	0926	4.6	2159
9	1003	5.1	2231
10	1037	5.4	2259
11	1110	5.4	2328
12	1141	5.4	2356
13	1209	5.2	
14	0023	5.1	1232
15	0043	4.9	1250
16	0100	4.6	1313
17	0127	4.2	1345
18	0205	3.5	1428
19	0257	2.8	1540
20	0506	2.5	1801
21	0630	2.9	1909
22	0733	3.7	2005
23	0824	4.5	2052
24	0908	5.3	2134
25	0950	5.9	2213
26	1031	6.3	2253
27	1112	6.3	2334
28	1155	6.2	
29	0017	6.0	1240
30	0105	5.4	1329
31	0157	4.8	1426

November

Day	HW	Range	HW
1	0256	3.8	1532
2	0402	3.3	1648
3	0516	3.1	1822
4	0644	3.3	1946
5	0757	3.7	2040
6	0847	4.3	2120
7	0928	4.7	2154
8	1004	5.0	2225
9	1038	5.1	2257
10	1110	5.1	2327
11	1139	5.1	2355
12	1204	4.9	
13	0019	4.8	1228
14	0043	4.6	1256
15	0115	4.3	1332
16	0156	3.8	1419
17	0250	3.3	1527
18	0409	3.2	1713
19	0537	3.3	1826
20	0646	3.8	1926
21	0743	4.4	2017
22	0834	5.0	2104
23	0921	5.5	2149
24	1008	5.9	2234
25	1054	6.0	2320
26	1142	6.0	
27	0007	5.7	1231
28	0056	5.3	1322
29	0147	4.8	1416
30	0240	4.3	1514

December

Day	HW	Range	HW
1	0336	3.7	1617
2	0437	3.5	1727
3	0544	3.3	1839
4	0655	3.4	1941
5	0756	3.7	2031
6	0846	4.0	2114
7	0929	4.3	2153
8	1008	4.6	2229
9	1043	4.8	2304
10	1116	4.8	2336
11	1148	4.8	
12	0007	4.8	1220
13	0038	4.8	1253
14	0113	4.6	1330
15	0153	4.4	1413
16	0240	4.2	1505
17	0335	4.0	1608
18	0440	3.8	1723
19	0551	3.9	1838
20	0701	4.1	1943
21	0804	4.4	2042
22	0903	4.9	2137
23	0959	5.3	2229
24	1051	5.5	2318
25	1141	5.6	
26	0004	5.6	1229
27	0049	5.4	1315
28	0134	5.1	1400
29	0219	4.8	1447
30	0305	4.3	1535
31	0353	3.8	1628

BREST TIDAL COEFFICIENTS 2007

Date	Jan am	Jan pm	Feb am	Feb pm	Mar am	Mar pm	Apr am	Apr pm	May am	May pm	June am	June pm	July am	July pm	Aug am	Aug pm	Sept am	Sept pm	Oct am	Oct pm	Nov am	Nov pm	Dec am	Dec pm
1	66	70	74	78	62	68	80	83	77	78	73	74	74	77	93	95	100	95	87	78	51	46	50	46
2	73	76	82	84	74	79	85	86	80	80	74	74	78	79	95	94	89	81	69	59	42	40	44	43
3	79	81	86	87	83	86	87	87	80	80	74	73	80	80	92	89	73	64	50	43	41		43	
4	83	84	87	87	88	89	86	85	79	77	71	70	80	79	84	79	55	48	38	37	44	48	45	47
5	84	83	85	83	90	90	83	81	75	73	67	65	77	75	73	67	42	39	39		52	57	49	52
6	82	80	80	77	89	87	78	75	69	66	63	60	73	70	61	55	39		44	50	61	65	55	58
7	78	75	73	69	85	82	70	66	61	57	58	57	67	64	50	47	43	49	56	63	69	72	61	63
8	71	67	64	59	78	74	61	55	53	49	55	55	61	59	46		56	63	68	73	74	76	66	68
9	63	59	53	48	69	64	49	43	45	42	56	57	57		48	52	69	75	78	81	77	78	69	71
10	54	50	43	37	59	53	38	33	42	43	59		56	57	57	63	80	84	84	86	78	78	72	73
11	45	41	33	29	47	40	31	32	46		62	66	59	61	68	74	87	90	87	87	78	76	73	73
12	38	35	28		35	29	37		51	57	70	74	65	69	79	83	91	91	86	85	75	73	73	72
13	34		30	34	27		43	52	63	71	78	82	73	77	86	89	91	89	84	81	70	67	70	69
14	34	35	41	48	27	32	61	71	77	84	84	87	80	83	90	91	87	84	79	75	64	60	67	64
15	38	43	56	65	39	48	79	88	90	94	89	89	85	87	90	89	81	77	72	67	56	52	62	60
16	48	54	73	81	58	68	96	102	98	100	89	89	87	87	87	83	73	67	63	57	48	44	57	55
17	59	65	88	95	77	86	107	111	102	101	87	85	86	84	80	75	62	56	52	47	41	40	53	52
18	71	76	101	105	95	102	112	112	100	97	82	78	82	78	71	65	50	44	41	36	40	41	52	53
19	81	86	108	110	108	113	110	107	93	88	75	70	75	70	60	54	38	32	31	29	45		55	
20	90	93	110	108	115	116	102	95	82	76	66	62	66	61	48	42	27	24	29	33	50	56	58	62
21	95	96	105	100	115	112	88	79	70	64	57	53	56	51	37	32	25		39		63	69	66	71
22	96	95	94	86	107	101	71	62	58	53	49	46	46	41	28	26	30	37	47	55	76	82	76	80
23	93	90	78	68	93	84	54	46	48	45	43	41	37	34	27		45	54	64	73	88	93	84	88
24	86	80	59	50	75	65	41	37	43	42	40		33		32	37	63	72	81	89	97	99	91	92
25	75	68	43	38	55	46	37		42		40	41	33	35	45	52	80	88	96	101	100	100	93	93
26	62	55	36		39	34	38	42	44	46	43	46	38	43	60	68	96	102	106	108	99	96	92	90
27	50	47	38	43	33		47	51	49	51	49	52	48	53	76	83	107	110	109	109	93	88	88	84
28	45		49	55	37	42	56	61	55	58	56	59	59	65	89	95	112	112	106	103	83	77	80	75
29	46	49			48	55	65	69	61	63	63	66	70	76	100	103	110	107	97	91	71	65	70	65
30	54	59			61	67	72	75	66	68	69	72	81	85	106	107	101	95	83	75	59	54	59	54
31	64	69			72	76			70	72			89	91	106	104			67	59			49	45

These tidal coefficients indicate at a glance the magnitude of the tide on any particular day by assigning a non-dimensional coefficient to the twice-daily range of tide. The coefficient is based on a scale of 45 for mean neap (morte eau) and 95 for mean spring (vive eau) ranges at Brest. The coefficient is 70 for an average tide. A very small neap tide may have a coefficient of only 20, whilst a very big spring tide might be as high as 120. The ratio of the coefficients of different tides equals the ratio of their ranges; the range, for example, of the largest spring tide (120) is six times that of the smallest neap tide (20). The table above is for Brest, but holds good elsewhere along the Channel and Atlantic coasts of France.

French translations of common tidal terms are as follows:

HW	Pleine mer (PM)	MHWS	Pleine mer moyenne de VE
LW	Basse mer (BM)	MHWN	Pleine mer moyenne de ME
Springs	Vive eau (VE)	MLWN	Basse mer moyenne de ME
Neaps	Morte eau (ME)	MLWS	Basse mer moyenne de VE

TIDES

143

TIDAL CALCULATIONS

Find the height at a given time (STANDARD PORT)

1. On Standard Curve diagram, plot heights of HW and LW occuring either side of required time and join by sloping line.
2. Enter HW Time and sufficient others to bracket required time.
3. From required time, proceed vertically to curves, using heights plotted in (1) to help interpolation between Spring and Neaps. Do NOT extrapolate.
4. Proceed horizontally to sloping line, thence vertically to Height scale.
5. Read off height.

EXAMPLE:

Find the height of tide at ULLAPOOL at 1900 on 6th January

From tables	JANUARY	
ULLAPOOL	**6** 0420	4.6
	1033	1.6
	1641	4.6
	F 2308	1.2

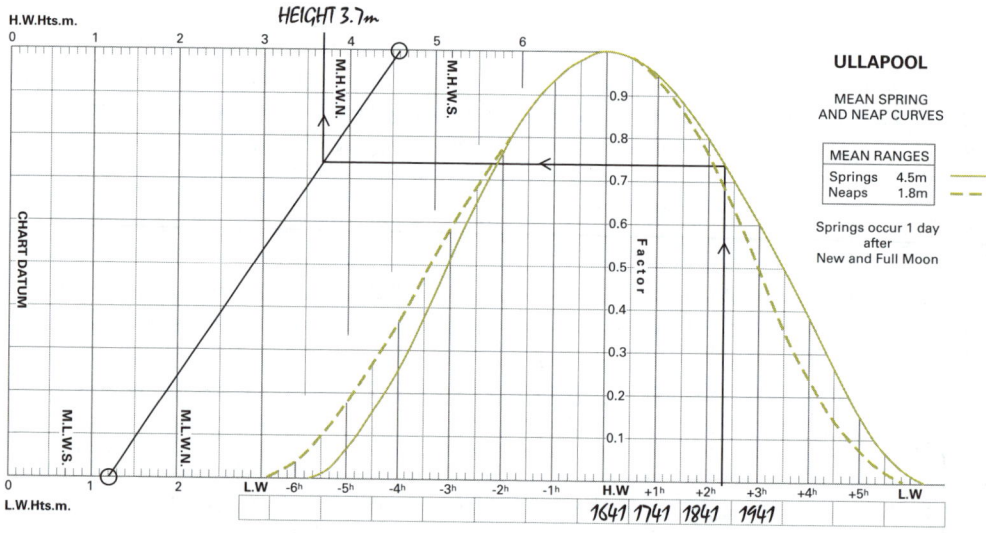

HEIGHT 3.7m

ULLAPOOL

MEAN SPRING AND NEAP CURVES

MEAN RANGES
Springs 4.5m
Neaps 1.8m

Springs occur 1 day after New and Full Moon

1641 1741 1841 1941

Find the time for a given height (STANDARD PORT)

1. On Standard Curve diagram, plot heights of HW and LW occurring either side of required event and join by sloping line.
2. Enter HW time and those for half-tidal cycle covering required event.
3. From required height, proceed vertically to sloping line, thence horizontally to curves, using heights plotted in (1) to assist interpolation between Spring and Neaps. Do NOT extrapolate.
4. Proceed vertically to Time scale.
5. Read off time.

EXAMPLE:

Find the time at which the afternoon tide at ULLAPOOL falls to 3.7m on 6 January

From tables	JANUARY	
ULLAPOOL	**6** 0420	4.6
	1033	1.6
	1641	4.6
	F 2308	1.2

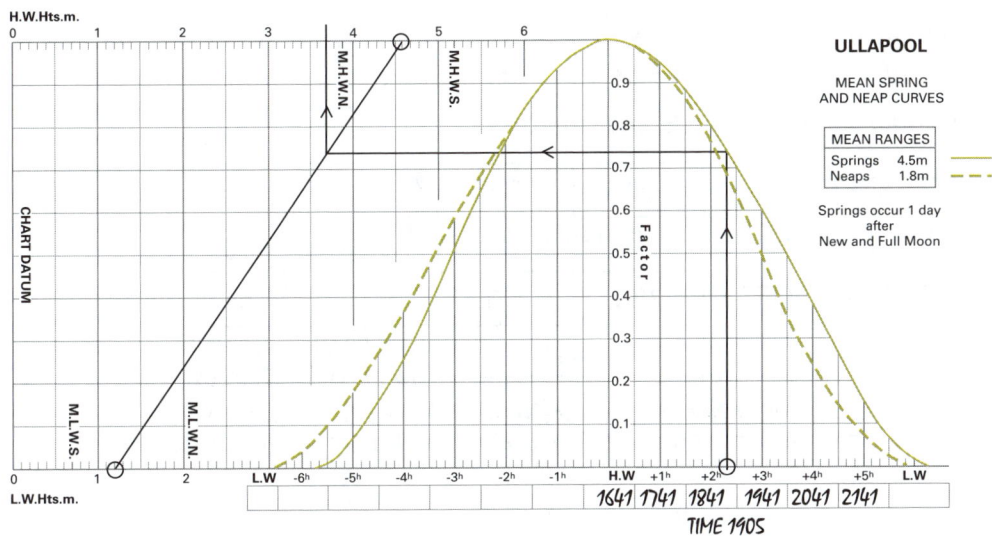

Find the time and height of HW and LW at a Secondary Port

EXAMPLE:

Find the time and height of the afternoon HW and LW at ST MARY's (Isles of Scilly) on 14th July (BST)
Note: *The data used in this example do not refer to the year of these tables.*

From tables	JULY	
PLYMOUTH (DEVONPORT)	**14** 0309	1.0
	0927	5.3
	1532	1.1
	SA 2149	5.0

From tables										
Location	Lat	Long	High Water		Low Water		MHWS	MHWN	MLWN	MLWS
DEVONPORT *Standard port*	50°22'N	4°11'W	0000 and 1200	0600 and 1800	0000 and 1200	0600 and 1800	5.5	4.4	2.2	0.8
St Mary's, *Scilly*	49° 55'N	6°19'W	−0035	−0100	−0040	−0025	+0.2	−0.1	−0.2	−0.1

TIDAL PREDICTION FORM (NP 204)

STANDARD PORT ....._Devonport_..... TIME/HEIGHT REQUIRED......._pm_

SECONDARY PORT ...._St Mary's_.... DATE _14 July_ TIME ZONE...._B.S.T_

	TIME		HEIGHT		
STANDARD PORT	HW	LW	HW	LW	RANGE
	1 2149	2 1532	3 5.0	4 1.1	5 3.9
Seasonal change	Standard Ports -		6 0.0	6 0.0	
DIFFERENCES	7* -0044	8 -0032	9 0.1	10 -0.1	
Seasonal change *	Secondary Ports +		11 0.0	11 0.0	
SECONDARY PORT	12 2105	13 1500	14 5.1	15 1.0	
Duration	16 0605		LW 1500 UT = 1600 BST HW 2105 UT = 2205 BST		

* The seasonal changes are generally less than ± 0.1m and for most purposes can be ignored. See Admiraly Tide Tables Vol 1. for details

INTERMEDIATE TIMES/HEIGHTS (SECONDARY PORT)

These are the same as the appropriate calculations for a Standard Port except that the Standard Curve diagram for the Standard Port must be entered with HW and LW heights and times for the Secondary Port obtained on Form N.P. 204. When interpolating between the Spring and Neap curves the Range at the Standard Port must be used.

EXAMPLE:
Find the height of the tide at PADSTOW at 1100 on 28th February. Find the time at which the morning tide at PADSTOW falls to 4.9m on 28th February.

Notes:
The data in these examples do not refer to the year of these tables.

From tables	FEBRUARY	
MILFORD HAVEN	**28** 0315	1.1
	0922	6.6
	1538	1.3
	TU 2145	6.3

Location	Lat	Long	High Water		Low Water		MHWS	MHWN	MLWN	MLWS
			0100	0700	0100	0700				
MILFORD HAVEN	51°42'N	5°03'W	and	and	and	and	7.0	5.2	2.5	0.7
Standard port			1300	1900	1300	1900				
River Camel										
Padstow	50°33'N	4°56'W	−0055	−0050	−0040	−0050	+0.3	+0.4	+0.1	+0.1
Wadebridge	50°31'N	4°50'W	−0052	−0052	+0235	+0245	−3.8	−3.8	−2.5	−0.4

TIDAL PREDICTION FORM (NP 204)

STANDARD PORT ... *Milford Haven* ... TIME/HEIGHT REQUIRED ... *1100 : 4.9*

SECONDARY PORT ... *Padstow* ... DATE *28 Feb* ... TIME ZONE ... *UT*

	TIME		HEIGHT		
STANDARD PORT	HW	LW	HW	LW	RANGE
	1 0922	2 1538	3 6·6	4 1·3	5 5·3
Seasonal change	Standard Ports +		6 0·0	6 0·0	
DIFFERENCES	7* −0052	8 —	9 +0·3	10 +0·1	
*Seasonal change *	Secondary Ports -		11 0·0	11 0·0	
SECONDARY PORT	12 0830	13 —	14 6·9	15 1·4	
Duration	16 —				

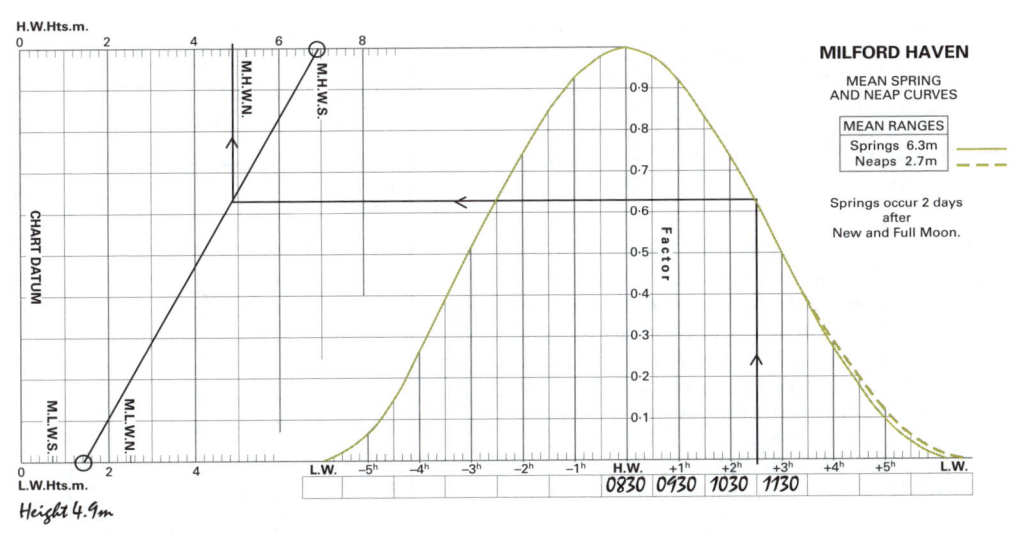

MILFORD HAVEN

MEAN SPRING
AND NEAP CURVES

MEAN RANGES
Springs 6.3m
Neaps 2.7m

Springs occur 2 days
after
New and Full Moon.

H.W.Hts.m.

CHART DATUM

M.L.W.S.
M.L.W.N.
M.H.W.N.
M.H.W.S.

Factor

L.W. −5h −4h −3h −2h −1h H.W. +1h +2h +3h +4h +5h L.W.

0830 0930 1030 1130

L.W.Hts.m.

Height 4.9m

SPECIAL INSTRUCTIONS FOR PLACES BETWEEN BOURNEMOUTH AND SELSEY BILL

• Owing to the rapid change of tidal characteristics and distortion of the tidal curve in this area, curves are shown for individual ports. It is a characteristic of the tide here that Low Water is more sharply defined than High Water and these curves have therefore been drawn with their times relative to that of Low Water.

• Apart from differences caused by referring the times to Low Water the procedure for obtaining intermediate heights at places whose curves are shown is identical to that used for normal Secondary Ports.

• The **height** differences for ports between Bournemouth and Yarmouth always refer to the higher High Water, i.e. that which is shown as reaching a factor of 1.0 on the curves. Note that the **time** differences, which are not required for this calculation, also refer to the higher High Water.

• The tide at ports between Bournemouth and Christchurch shows considerable change of shape and duration between Springs and Neaps and it is not practical to define the tide with only two curves. A third curve has therefore been drawn for the range at Portsmouth at which the two High Waters are equal at the port concerned – this range being marked on the body of the graph. Interpolation here should be between this 'critical' curve and either the Spring or Neap curve as appropriate.

Note that while the critical curve extends throughout the tidal cycle the Spring and Neap curves stop at the higher High Water. Thus for a range at Portsmouth of 3.5m the factor for 7 hours after LW at Bournemouth should be referred to the following Low Water, whereas had the range at Portsmouth been 2.5, it should be referred to the preceding Low Water.

NOTES

1. NEWPORT. Owing to the constriction of the River Medina, Newport requires slightly different treatment since the harbour dries out at 1.4m. The calculation should be performed using the Low Water Time and Height Differences for Cowes and the High Water Height Differences for Newport. Any calculated heights which fall below 1.4m should be treated as 1.4m

2. CHRISTCHURCH (Tuckton). Low Waters do not fall below 0.7m except under very low river flow conditions.

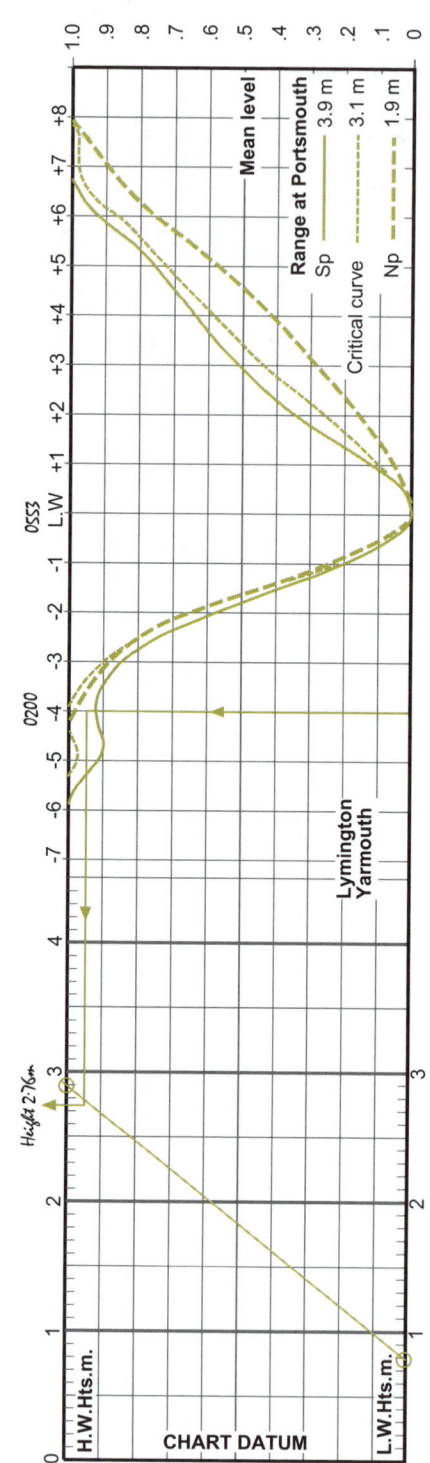

To find the Height of tide at a given time at any Secondary Port between Bournemouth and Selsey Bill

1. Complete top section of N.P. 204 (as below). Omit HW time column (Boxes 1,7,12)
2. On Standard Curve diagram (previous page), plot Secondary Port HW and LW heights and join by sloping line.
3. From the time required, using Secondary Port LW time, proceed vertically to curve, interpolating as necessary using Range at Portsmouth. Do NOT extrapolate.
4. Proceed horizontally to sloping line, thence vertically to Height Scale.
5. Read off height.

EXAMPLE:

Find the height of tide at LYMINGTON at 0200 UT on 18th November

From tables	NOVEMBER		
PORTSMOUTH	**18**	0110	4.6
		0613	1.1
		1318	4.6
	SA	1833	1.0

From tables Location	Lat	Long	High Water		Low Water		MHWS	MHWN	MLWN	MLWS
			0000	0600	0500	1100				
PORTSMOUTH	50°48'N	1°07'W	and	and	and	and	4.7	3.8	1.9	0.8
Standard port			1200	1800	1700	2300				
Lymington	50°46'N	1°32'W	-0110	+0005	-0020	-0020	-1.7	-1.2	-0.5	-0.1

STANDARD PORT ..... *Portsmouth* ..... TIME/HEIGHT REQUIRED *0200*

SECONDARY PORT ..... *Lymington* ..... DATE *18 Nov* ..... TIME ZONE ..... *UT*

	TIME		HEIGHT		
STANDARD PORT	HW	LW	HW	LW	RANGE
	1 —	2 0613	3 4·6	4 1·1	5 3·5
Seasonal change	Standard Ports -		6 0·0	6 0·0	
DIFFERENCES	7* —	8 -0020	9 -1·7	10 -0·2	
Seasonal change *	Secondary Ports +		11 0·0	11 0·0	
SECONDARY PORT	12 —	13 0553	14 2·9	15 0·9	
Duration	16 —				

* The Seasonal changes are generally less than ± 0.1m and for most purposes can be ignored. See Admiralty Tide Tables Vol 1 for full details.

TIDES

TIDAL CURVES -
BOURNEMOUTH TO FRESHWATER

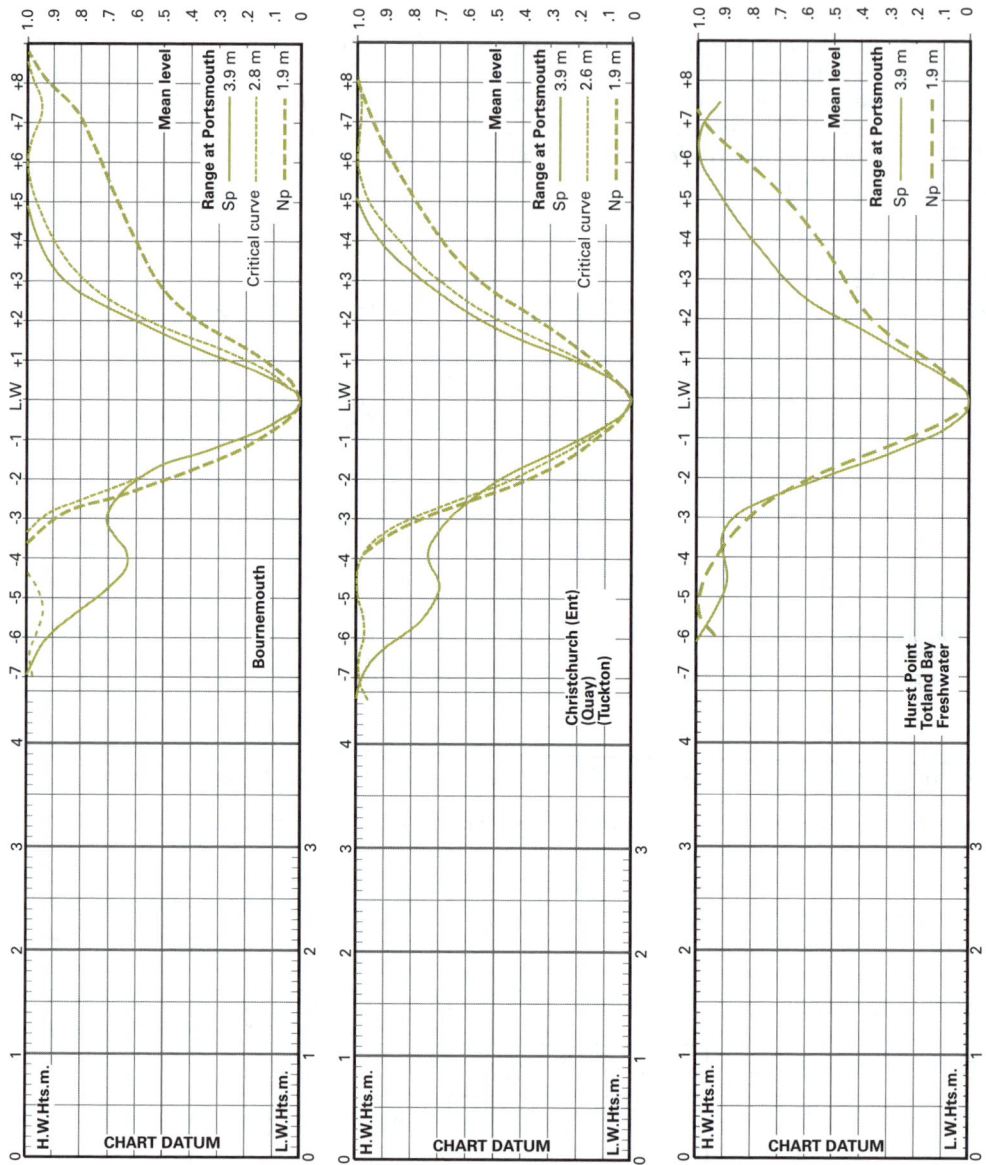

Note: The curves for Lymington and Yarmouth are on page 148, together with a worked example.

TIDAL CURVES -
BUCKLERS HARD TO SELSEY BILL

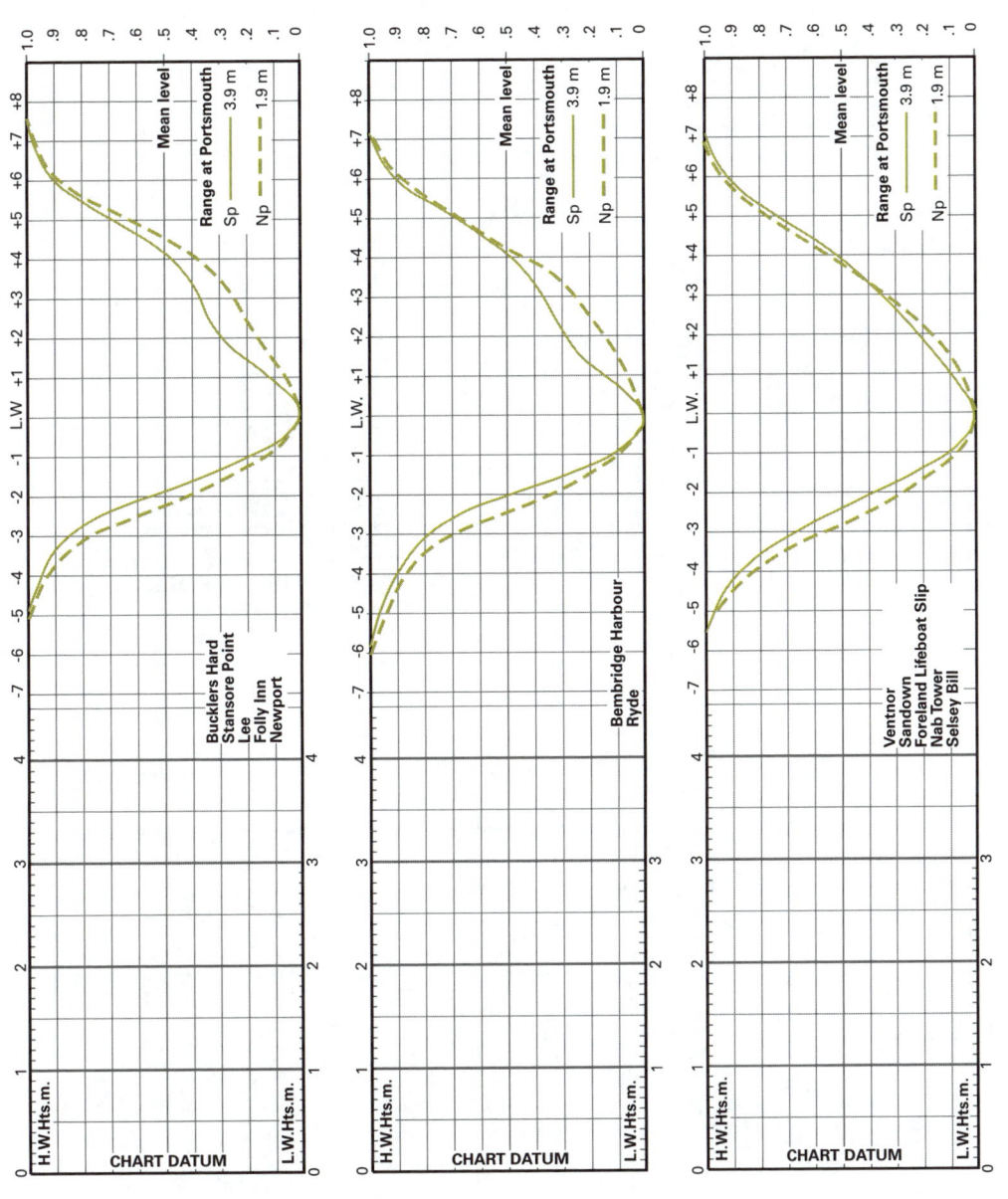

ENGLISH CHANNEL AND SOUTH BRITTANY

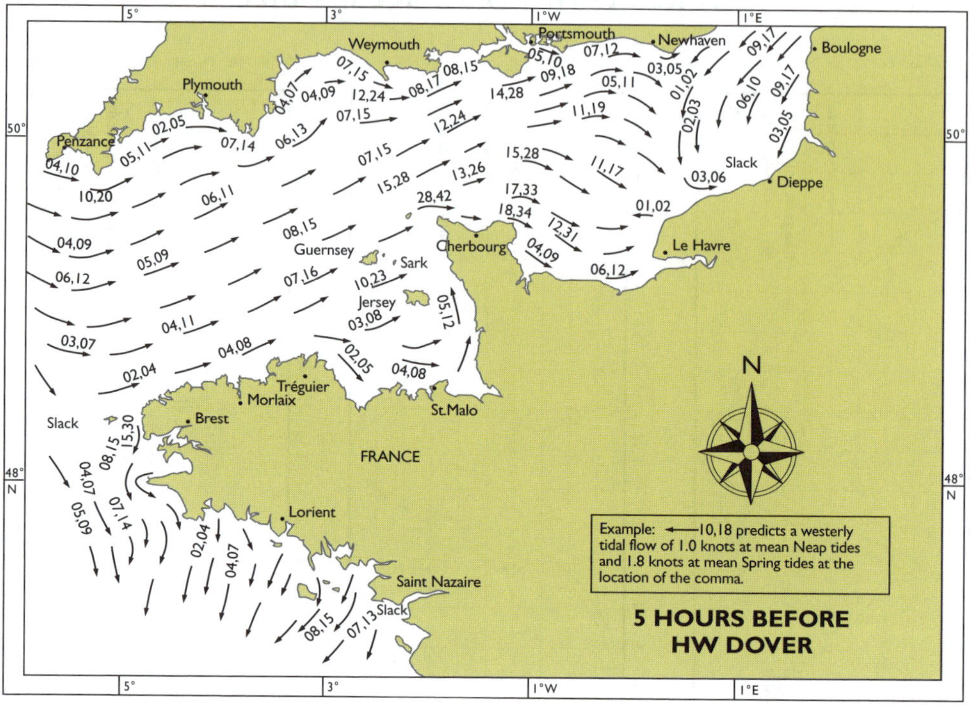

Map 1

Weymouth, Portsmouth, Newhaven, Boulogne, Plymouth, Penzance, Dieppe, Slack, Le Havre, Cherbourg, Guernsey, Sark, Jersey, Tréguier, Morlaix, Brest, St.Malo, Slack, FRANCE, Lorient, Saint Nazaire, Slack

Tidal values: 07,15 04,07 04,09 12,24 08,17 08,15 14,28 05,10 09,18 07,12 03,05 09,17 01,02 06,10 09,17 03,05 05,11 11,19 02,03 07,14 06,13 07,15 12,24 15,28 13,26 17,33 11,17 03,06 10,20 06,11 07,15 15,28 28,42 18,34 12,31 01,02 04,09 08,15 04,09 06,12 05,09 07,16 10,23 03,08 05,12 06,12 03,07 04,11 02,05 04,08 02,04 04,08 08,15 15,30 04,07 05,09 07,14 02,04 04,07 08,15 07,13

N

Example: ◄——10,18 predicts a westerly tidal flow of 1.0 knots at mean Neap tides and 1.8 knots at mean Spring tides at the location of the comma.

5 HOURS BEFORE HW DOVER

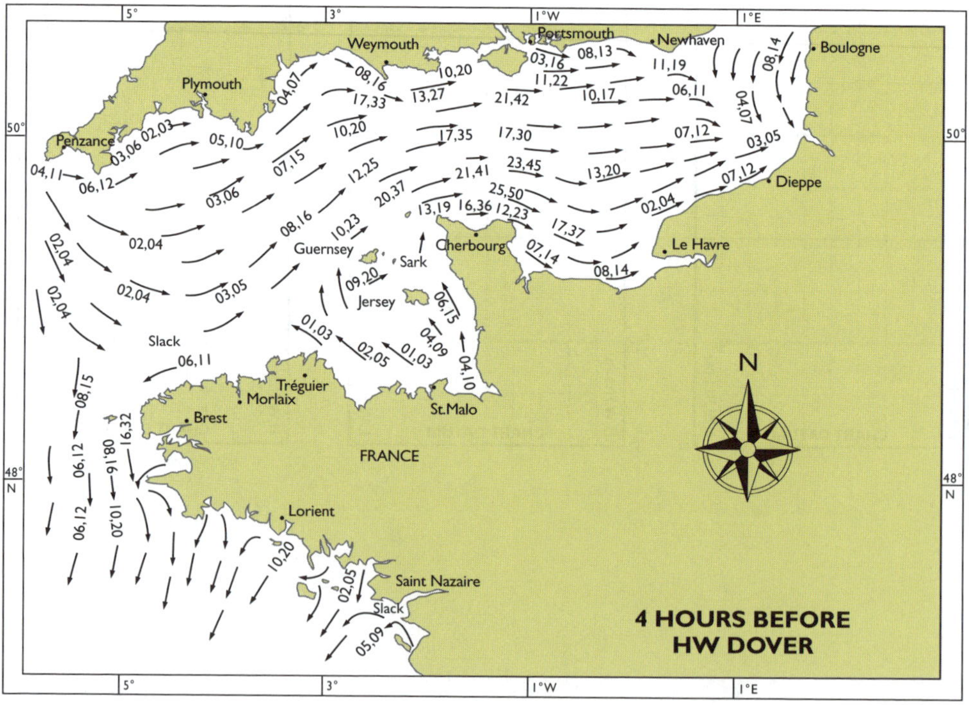

5° 3° 1°W 1°E
50° 48°N

Map 2

Weymouth, Portsmouth, Newhaven, Boulogne, Plymouth, Penzance, Dieppe, Le Havre, Cherbourg, Guernsey, Sark, Jersey, Tréguier, Morlaix, Brest, St.Malo, Slack, FRANCE, Lorient, Saint Nazaire, Slack

Tidal values: 04,07 08,16 10,20 03,16 08,13 11,19 08,14 17,33 13,27 21,42 10,17 06,11 04,07 03,06 02,03 05,10 10,20 11,22 07,12 03,05 04,11 06,12 17,35 17,30 07,12 02,04 03,06 07,15 12,25 21,41 23,45 13,20 08,16 10,23 20,37 25,50 17,37 02,04 02,04 13,19 16,36 12,23 07,14 08,14 02,04 03,05 09,20 06,13 01,03 02,05 04,09 01,03 04,10 06,11 08,15 16,32 06,12 08,10 06,12 10,20 10,20 02,05 05,09

N

4 HOURS BEFORE HW DOVER

5° 3° 1°W 1°E
50° 48°N

152

ENGLISH CHANNEL AND SOUTH BRITTANY

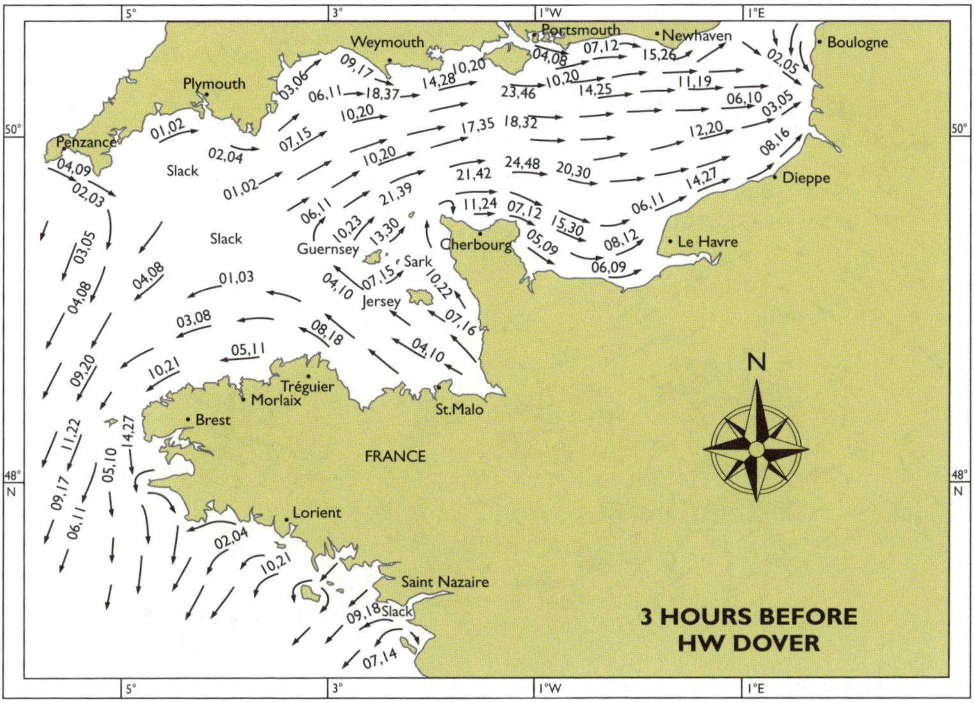

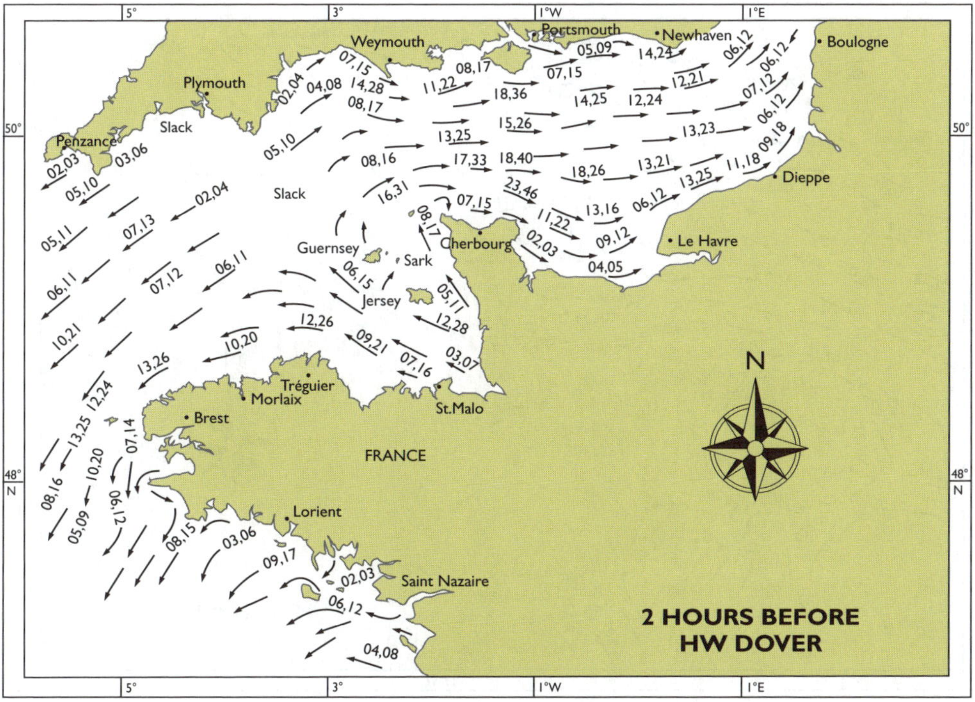

TIDES

ENGLISH CHANNEL AND SOUTH BRITTANY

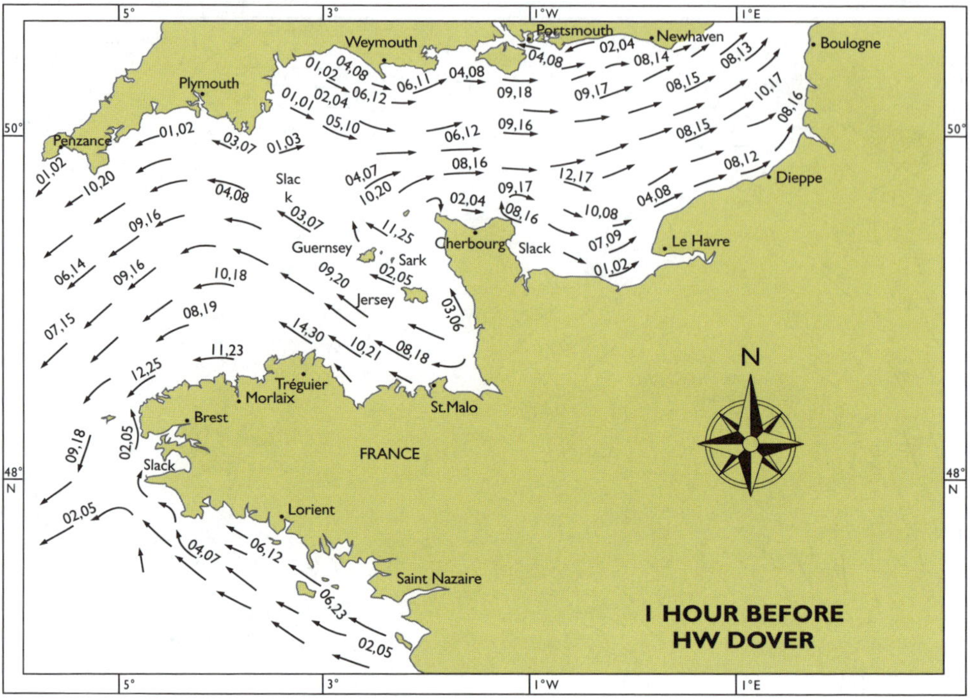

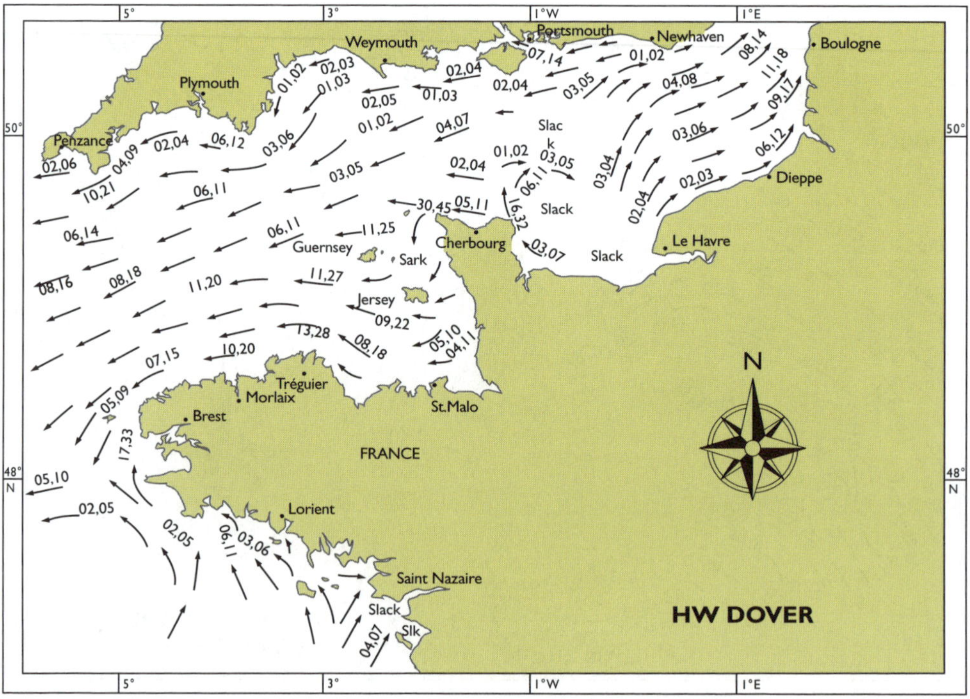

Map 1:

Weymouth · Portsmouth · Newhaven · Boulogne

Plymouth

Penzance

01,02 01,02 04,08 06,11 04,08 02,04 08,14 08,13

01,01 02,04 05,10 09,18 09,17 08,15 10,17

03,07 01,03 06,12 09,16 08,15 08,16

Slack 04,07 08,16 12,17 08,12

k 03,07 10,20 02,04 09,17 04,08 · Dieppe

11,25 08,16 10,08

Guernsey 09,20 Sark 07,09 Le Havre

02,05 Cherbourg Slack 01,02

Jersey 03,06

14,30 10,21 08,18

11,23 12,25

Tréguier Morlaix St.Malo

Brest

09,18 02,05 FRANCE

Slack

02,05

Lorient

04,07 06,12

06,23

02,05 Saint Nazaire

1 HOUR BEFORE HW DOVER

01,02 10,20 09,16 06,14 09,16 07,15 08,19

Map 2:

Weymouth · Portsmouth · Newhaven · Boulogne

Plymouth

01,02 02,03 02,04 07,14 01,02 08,14 11,18

01,03 02,04 03,05 04,08 09,17

02,05 01,03

Penzance 01,02 04,07 Slac 03,06 06,12

02,06 02,04 06,12 03,05 k 03,05

04,09 01,02 04,07 02,04 03,04 02,03 · Dieppe

10,21 06,11 03,05 01,02 05,11 06,11 03,07

06,11 11,25 30,45 16,32 Slack

Guernsey 06,14 Sark Cherbourg Slack

08,16 08,18 11,20 11,27 Le Havre

Jersey 09,22

13,28 08,18 05,10 04,11

07,15 10,20

05,09 Tréguier Morlaix St.Malo

17,33 Brest FRANCE

05,10

02,05 Lorient

02,05 06,11 03,06

Saint Nazaire

Slack

Slk

04,07

HW DOVER

154

1 HOUR AFTER HW DOVER

2 HOURS AFTER HW DOVER

TIDES

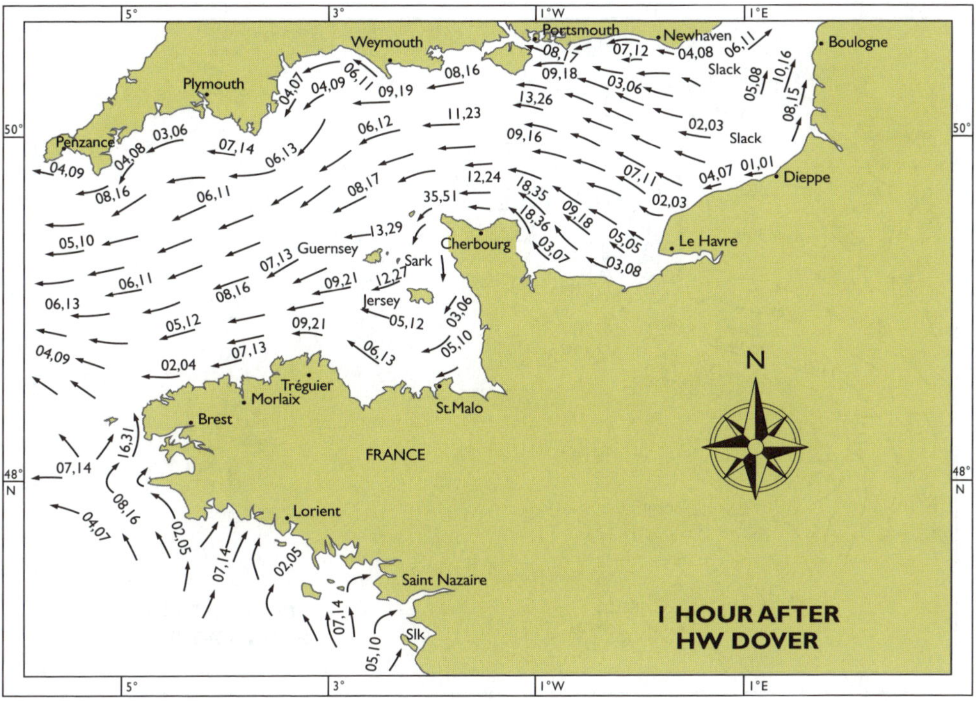

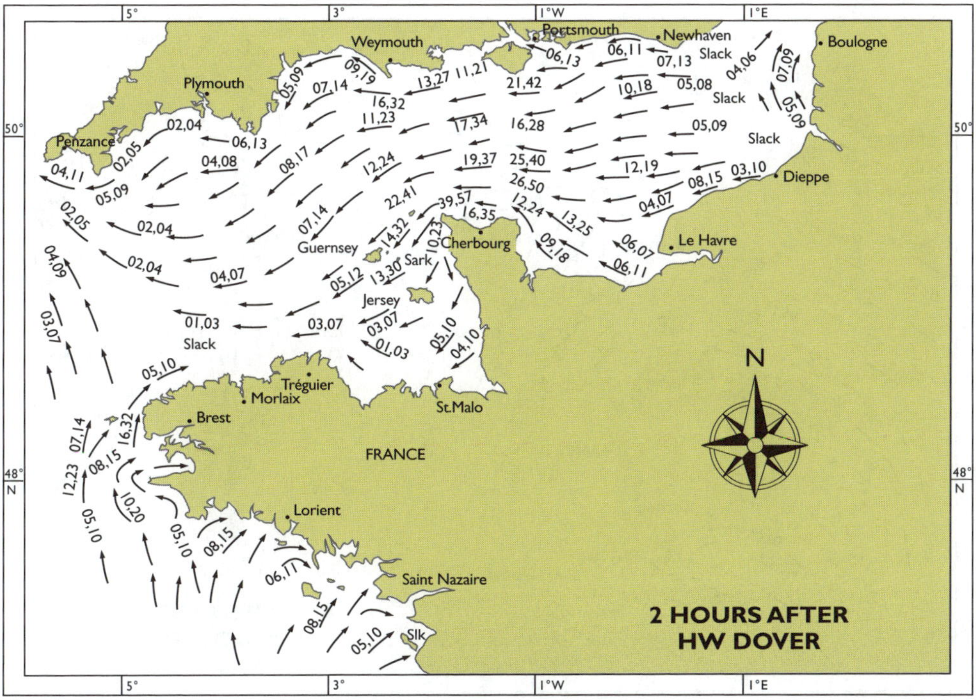

ENGLISH CHANNEL AND SOUTH BRITTANY

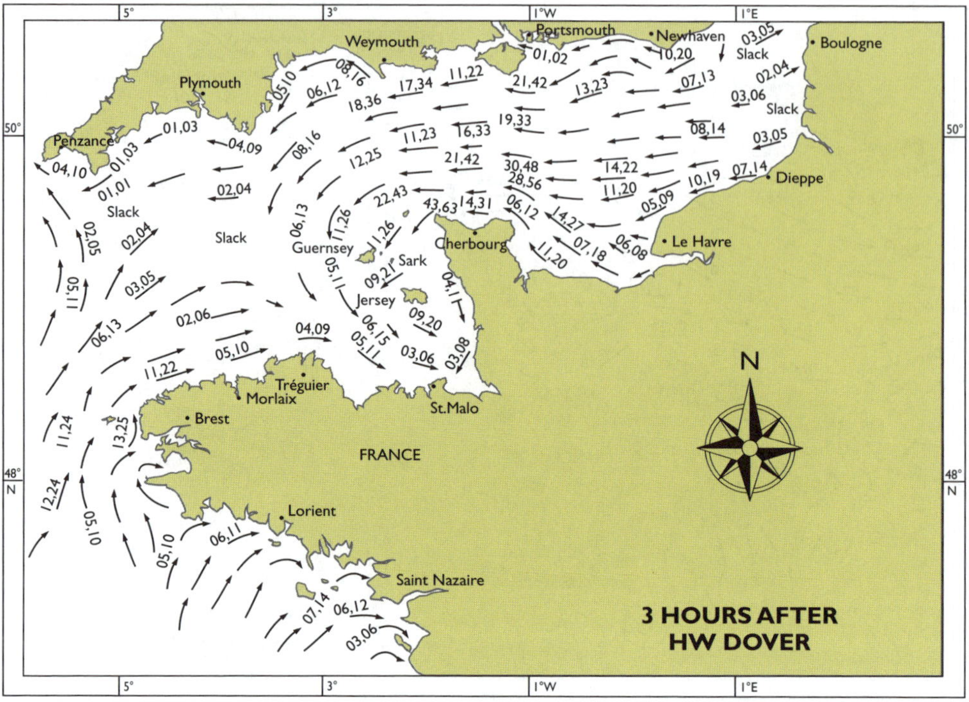

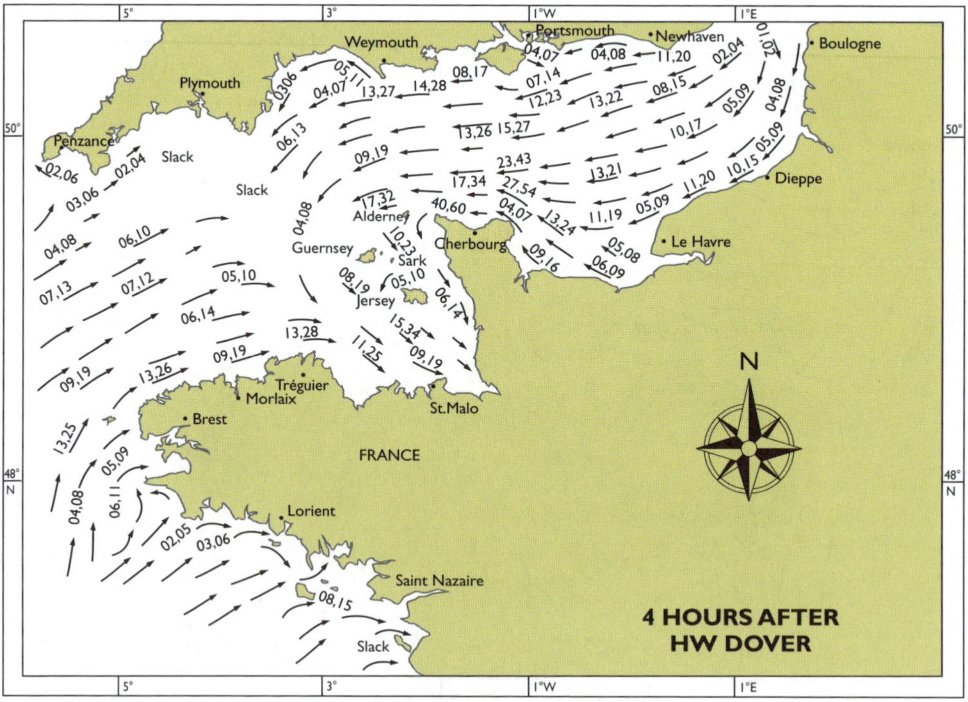

3 HOURS AFTER HW DOVER

4 HOURS AFTER HW DOVER

ENGLISH CHANNEL AND SOUTH BRITTANY

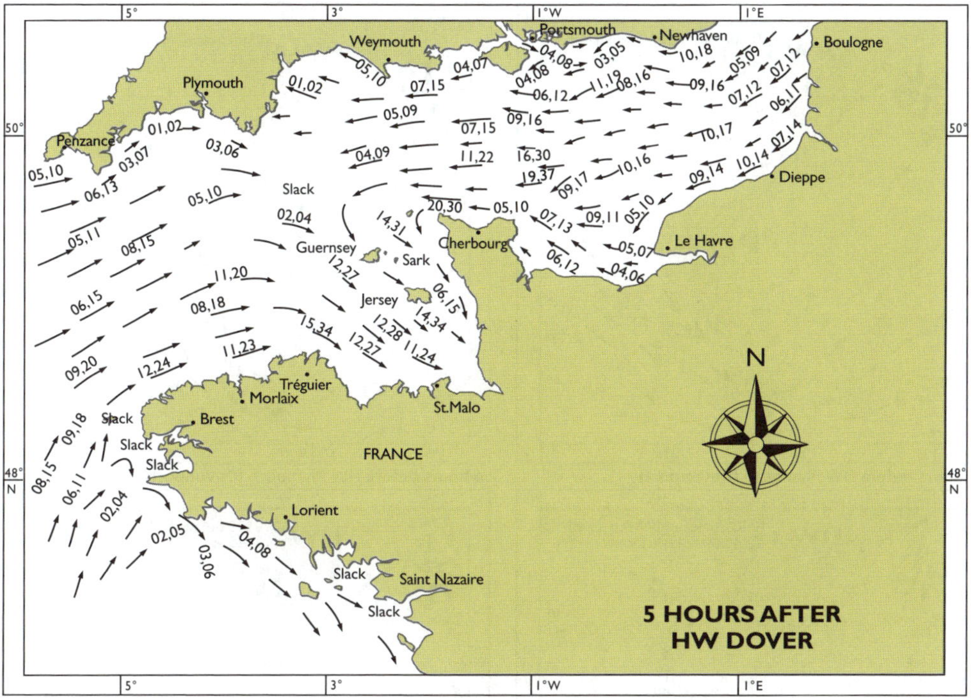

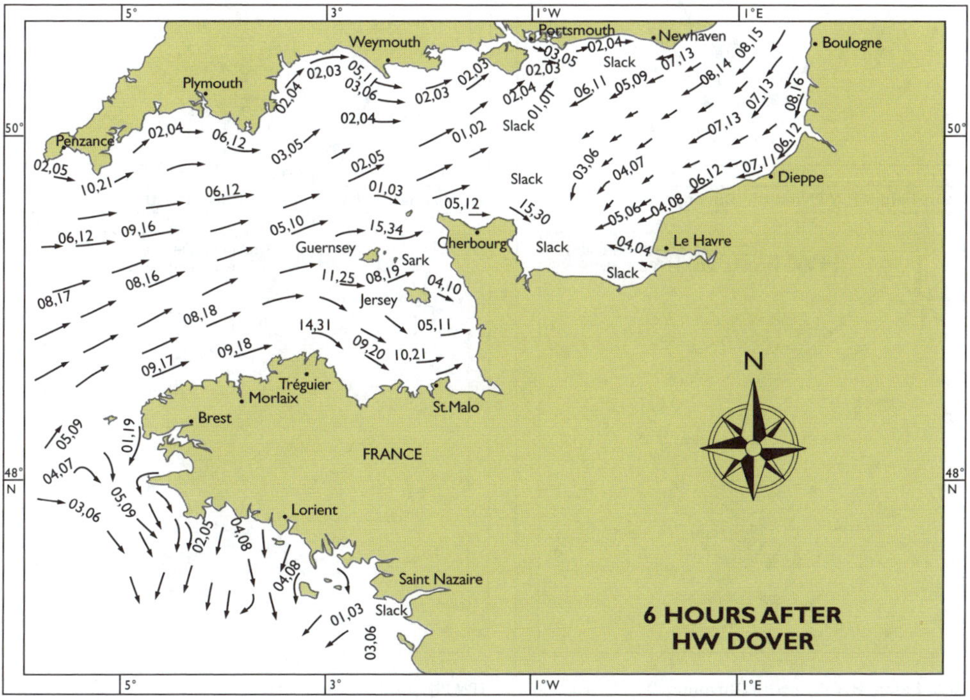

5 HOURS AFTER HW DOVER

6 HOURS AFTER HW DOVER

PORTLAND

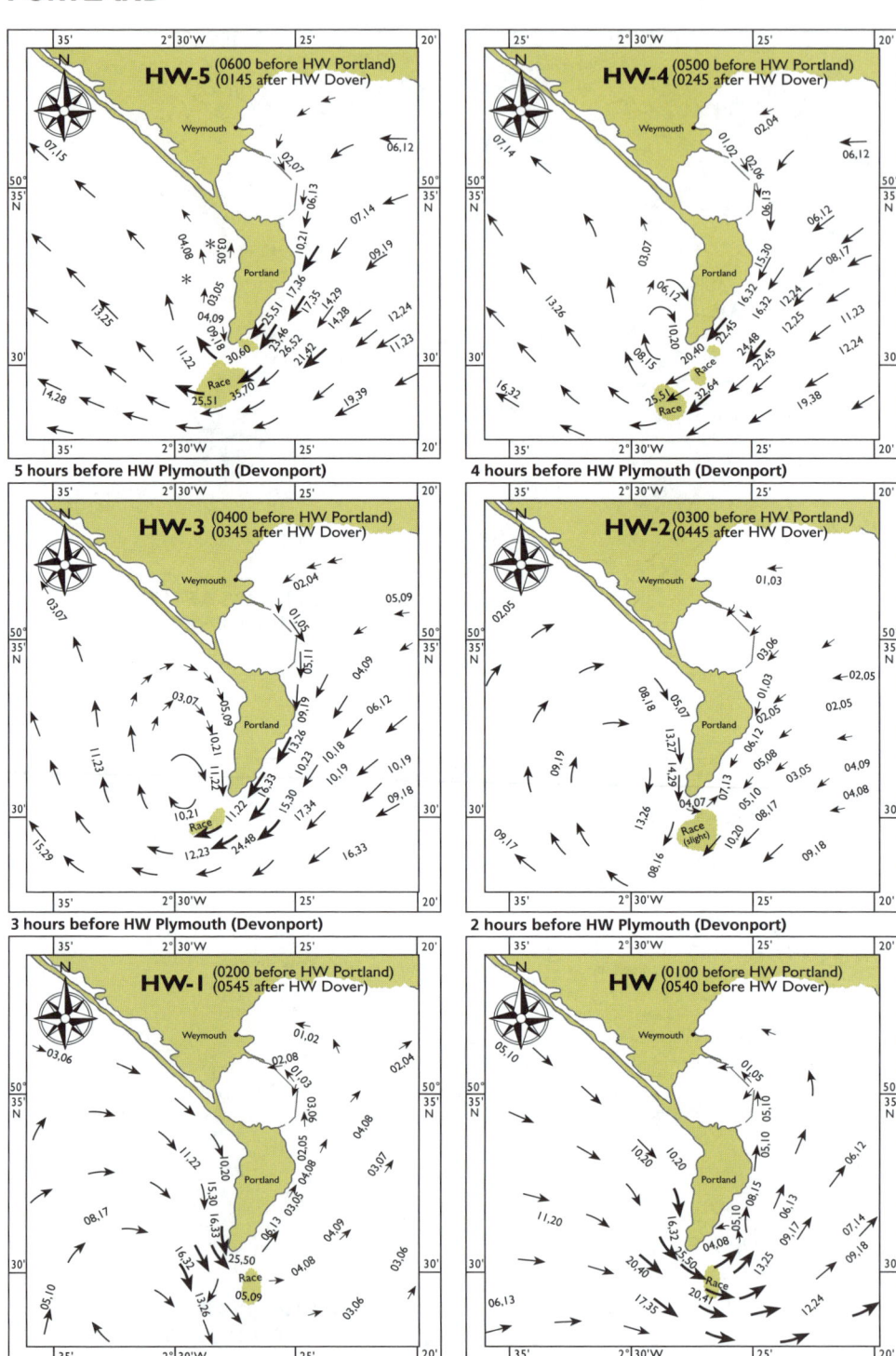

5 hours before HW Plymouth (Devonport)

4 hours before HW Plymouth (Devonport)

3 hours before HW Plymouth (Devonport)

2 hours before HW Plymouth (Devonport)

1 hour before HW Plymouth (Devonport)

HW Plymouth (Devonport)

PORTLAND

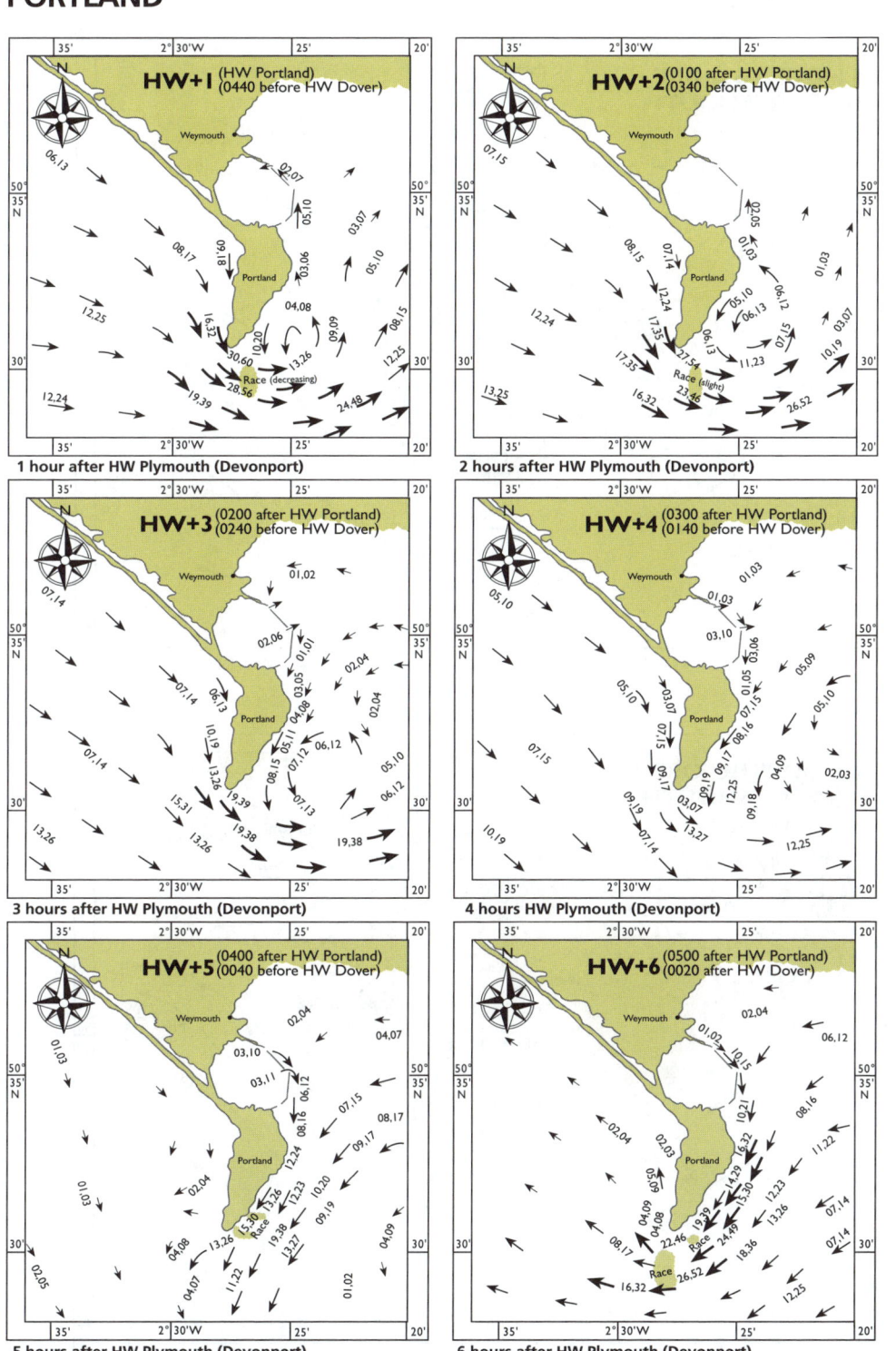

HW+1 (HW Portland) (0440 before HW Dover)

1 hour after HW Plymouth (Devonport)

HW+2 (0100 after HW Portland) (0340 before HW Dover)

2 hours after HW Plymouth (Devonport)

HW+3 (0200 after HW Portland) (0240 before HW Dover)

3 hours after HW Plymouth (Devonport)

HW+4 (0300 after HW Portland) (0140 before HW Dover)

4 hours HW Plymouth (Devonport)

HW+5 (0400 after HW Portland) (0040 before HW Dover)

5 hours after HW Plymouth (Devonport)

HW+6 (0500 after HW Portland) (0020 after HW Dover)

6 hours after HW Plymouth (Devonport)

TIDES

159

ISLE OF WIGHT

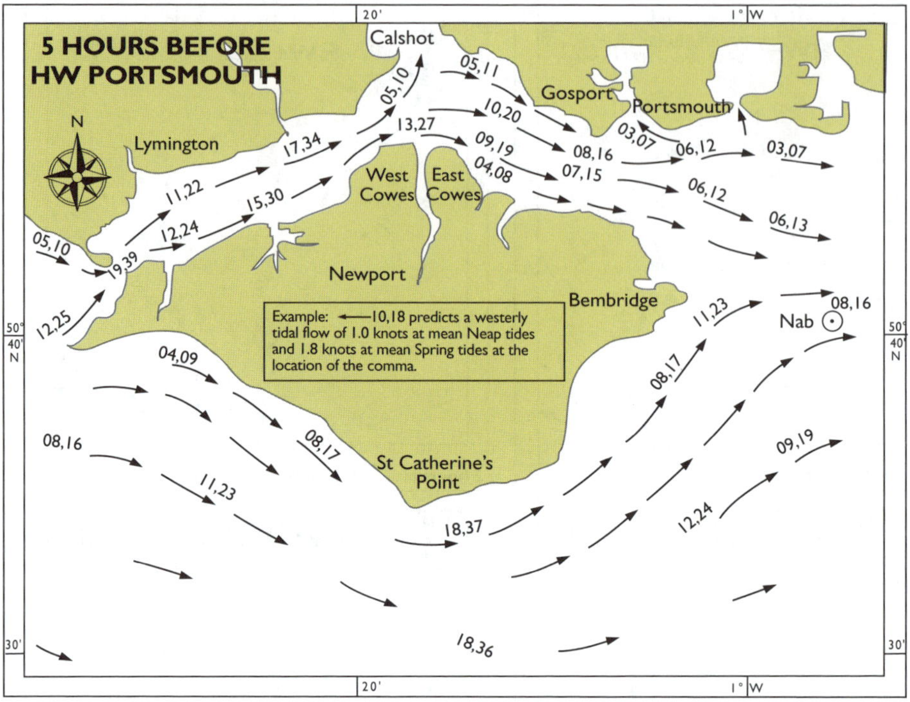

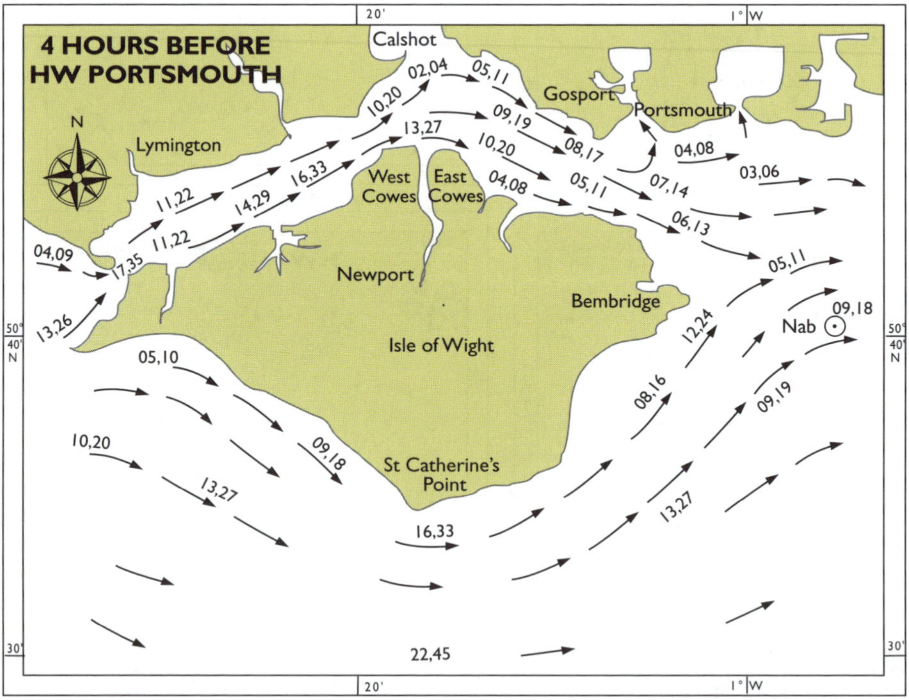

5 HOURS BEFORE HW PORTSMOUTH

N

Calshot
Lymington
05,10
05,11
Gosport
Portsmouth
13,27
10,20
03,07
17,34
09,19
08,16
06,12
03,07
11,22
15,30
West Cowes
East Cowes
04,08
07,15
06,12
12,24
06,13
05,10
9,39
Newport
Bembridge
12,25
11,23
Nab ⊙
08,16
04,09
08,17
08,16
08,17
St Catherine's Point
11,23
09,19
18,37
12,24
18,36

Example: ◄——10,18 predicts a westerly tidal flow of 1.0 knots at mean Neap tides and 1.8 knots at mean Spring tides at the location of the comma.

50' 40' N

50' 40' N

30'

30'

20'

1° W

4 HOURS BEFORE HW PORTSMOUTH

N

Calshot
02,04
05,11
Gosport
Portsmouth
10,20
09,19
Lymington
13,27
08,17
04,08
10,20
11,22
14,29
16,33
West Cowes
East Cowes
04,08
05,11
07,14
03,06
11,22
06,13
04,09
17,35
Newport
05,11
13,26
Isle of Wight
Bembridge
12,24
Nab ⊙
09,18
05,10
08,16
09,19
10,20
09,18
13,27
St Catherine's Point
13,27
16,33
22,45

50' 40' N

50' 40' N

30'

30'

20'

1° W

160

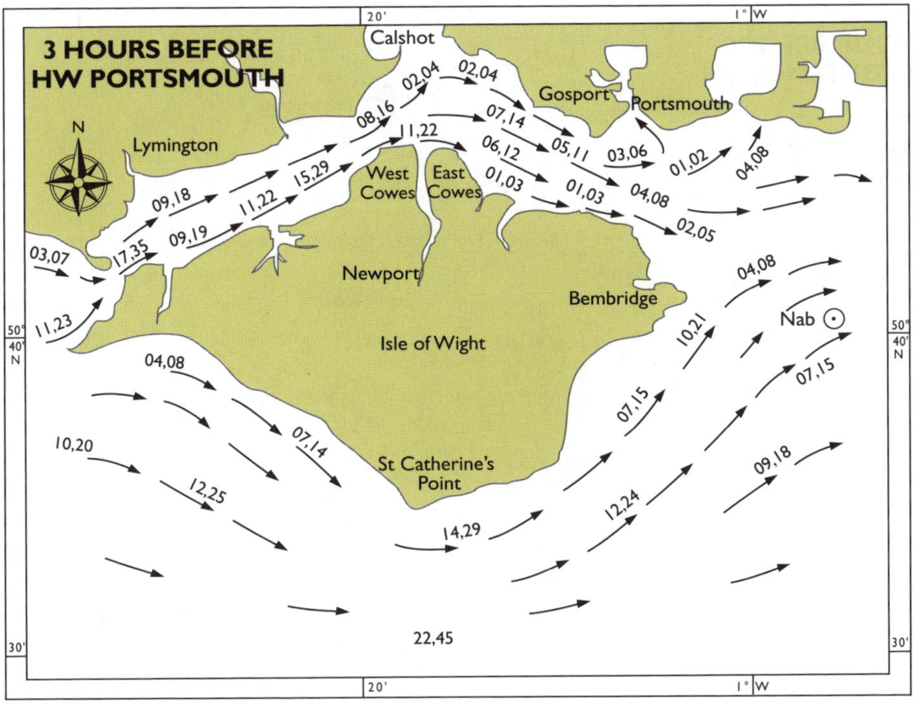

ISLE OF WIGHT

3 HOURS BEFORE HW PORTSMOUTH

N

Calshot
Lymington
02,04 02,04
Gosport Portsmouth
08,16 11,22 07,14 05,11 03,06 01,02 04,08
09,18 11,22 15,29 West Cowes East Cowes 06,12 01,03 01,03 04,08
09,19 01,03 02,05
03,07 17,35
11,23
Newport
Bembridge
04,08
Isle of Wight
Nab
10,21 04,08
04,08
07,15 07,15
10,20 07,14
12,25 St Catherine's Point 07,15
14,29 12,24 09,18
22,45

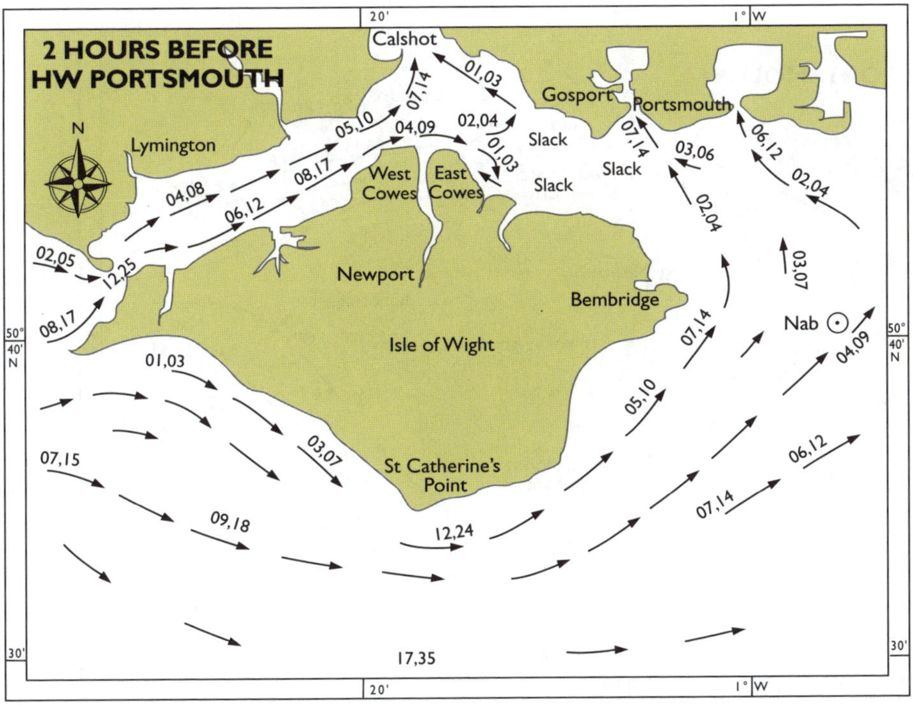

2 HOURS BEFORE HW PORTSMOUTH

N

Calshot
01,03
07,14
Gosport Portsmouth
05,10 04,09 02,04 Slack 07,14 03,06 06,12 02,04
Lymington 08,17 West Cowes East Cowes 01,03 Slack Slack
04,08 06,12 Slack 02,04
02,05 12,25 03,07
08,17 Newport Bembridge
01,03 07,14 Nab 04,09
05,10 06,12
07,15 03,07 St Catherine's Point 07,14
09,18 12,24
17,35

TIDES

161

ISLE OF WIGHT

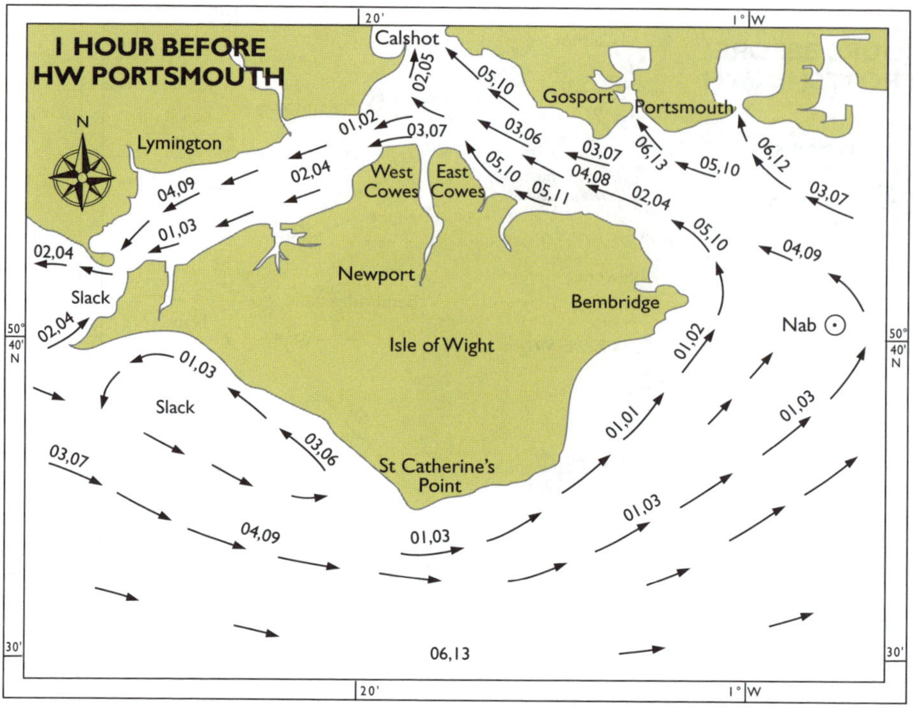

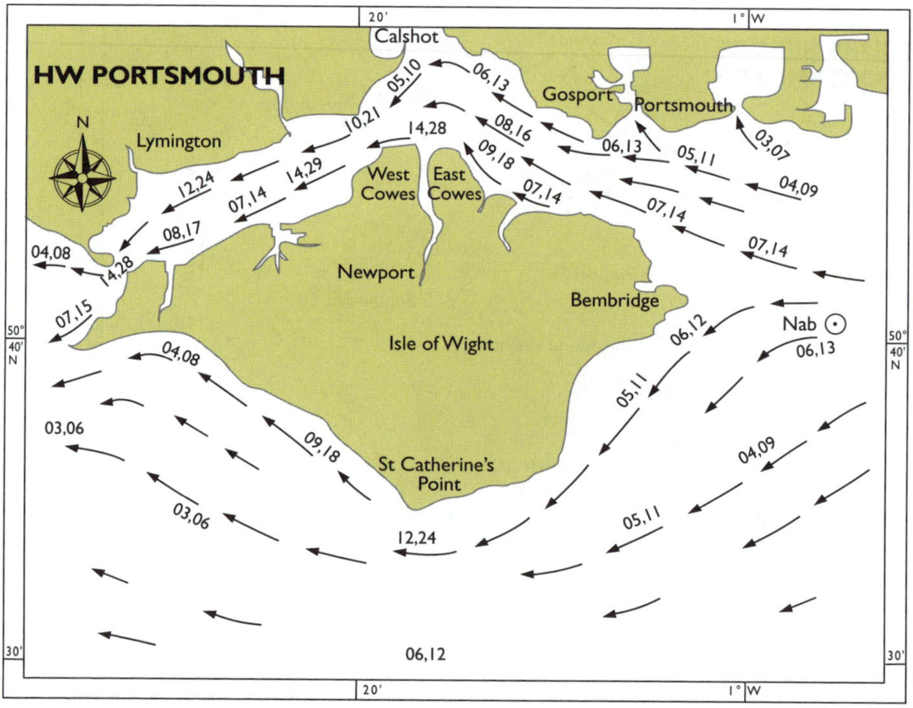

I HOUR BEFORE HW PORTSMOUTH

N

Calshot
Gosport
Portsmouth
Lymington
02,05
05,10
01,02
03,07
03,06
03,07
06,13
06,12
05,10
03,07
04,09
02,04
05,10
05,11
04,08
02,04
05,10
04,09
01,03
West Cowes
East Cowes
02,04
Newport
Bembridge
Slack
02,04
Nab ⊙
Isle of Wight
01,02
01,03
01,03
Slack
03,06
01,01
03,07
04,09
01,03
01,03
St Catherine's Point
01,03
06,13

50° 40' N
20'
1° W
30'

HW PORTSMOUTH

N

Calshot
Gosport
Portsmouth
Lymington
05,10
06,13
10,21
14,28
08,16
06,13
05,11
03,07
12,24
14,29
09,18
04,09
07,14
07,14
07,14
08,17
07,14
West Cowes
East Cowes
04,08
14,28
Newport
Bembridge
07,15
Nab ⊙
04,08
06,12
06,13
Isle of Wight
03,06
09,18
05,11
04,09
03,06
05,11
St Catherine's Point
12,24
06,12

50° 40' N
20'
1° W
30'

ISLE OF WIGHT

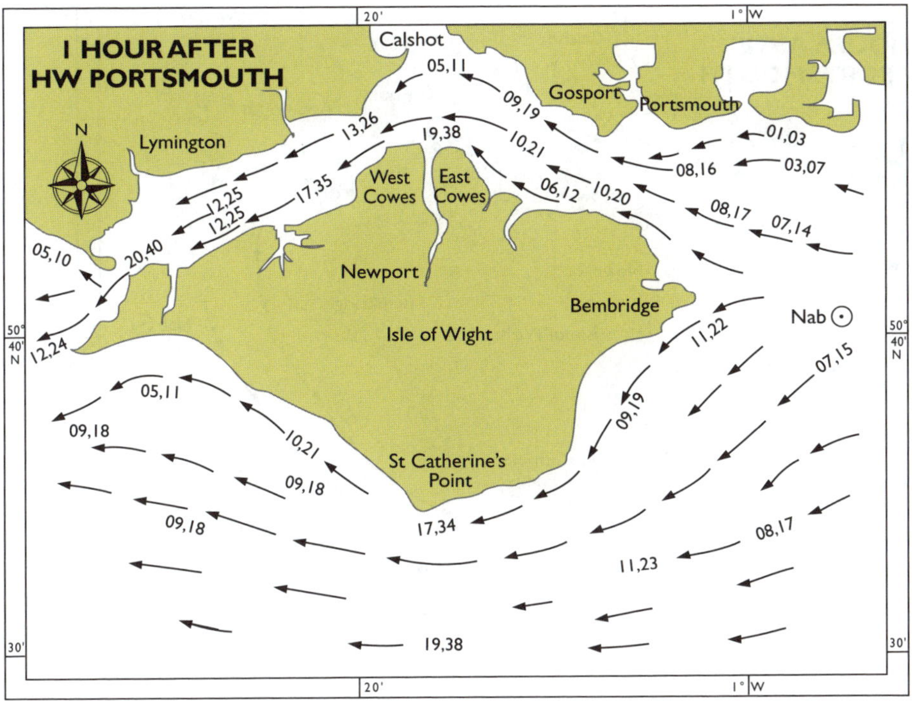

20'
1° W
1 HOUR AFTER HW PORTSMOUTH
N
Calshot
05,11
Gosport
Portsmouth
09,19
01,03
13,26
19,38
10,21
08,16
03,07
Lymington
West Cowes
East Cowes
06,12
10,20
08,17
07,14
12,25
12,25
17,35
05,10
20,40
Newport
Bembridge
Nab
11,22
50° 40' N
12,24
Isle of Wight
07,15
05,11
09,19
09,18
10,21
St Catherine's Point
09,18
09,18
17,34
08,17
11,23
19,38
30'

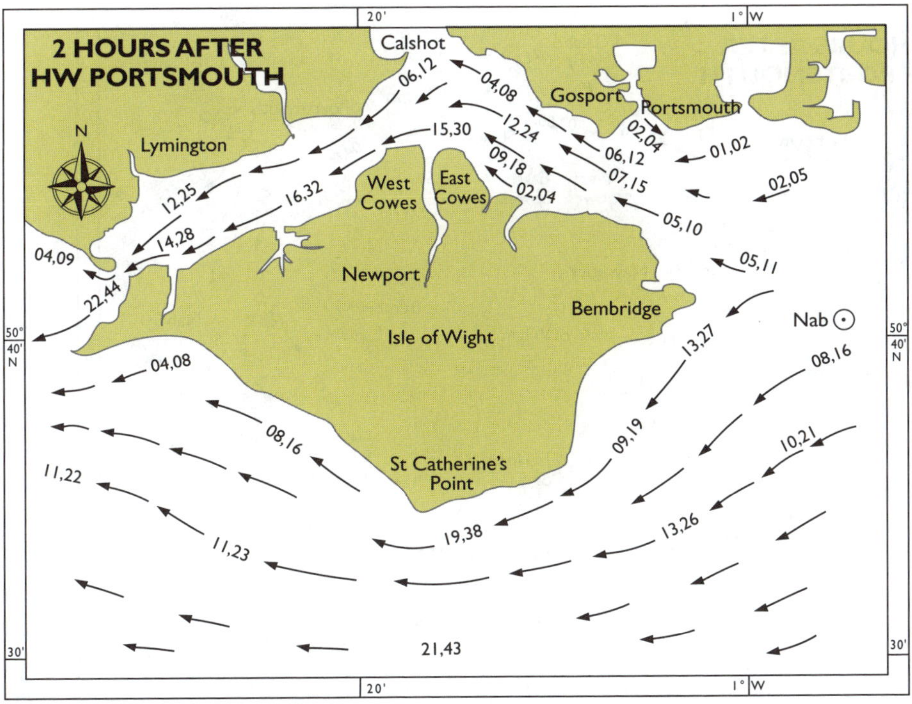

20'
1° W
2 HOURS AFTER HW PORTSMOUTH
N
Calshot
06,12
04,08
Gosport
Portsmouth
12,24
02,04
15,30
06,12
01,02
Lymington
09,18
07,15
West Cowes
East Cowes
02,04
02,05
12,25
16,32
05,10
14,28
04,09
Newport
05,11
22,44
Bembridge
Nab
50° 40' N
Isle of Wight
13,27
04,08
08,16
08,16
09,19
10,21
11,22
St Catherine's Point
19,38
13,26
11,23
21,43
30'

ISLE OF WIGHT

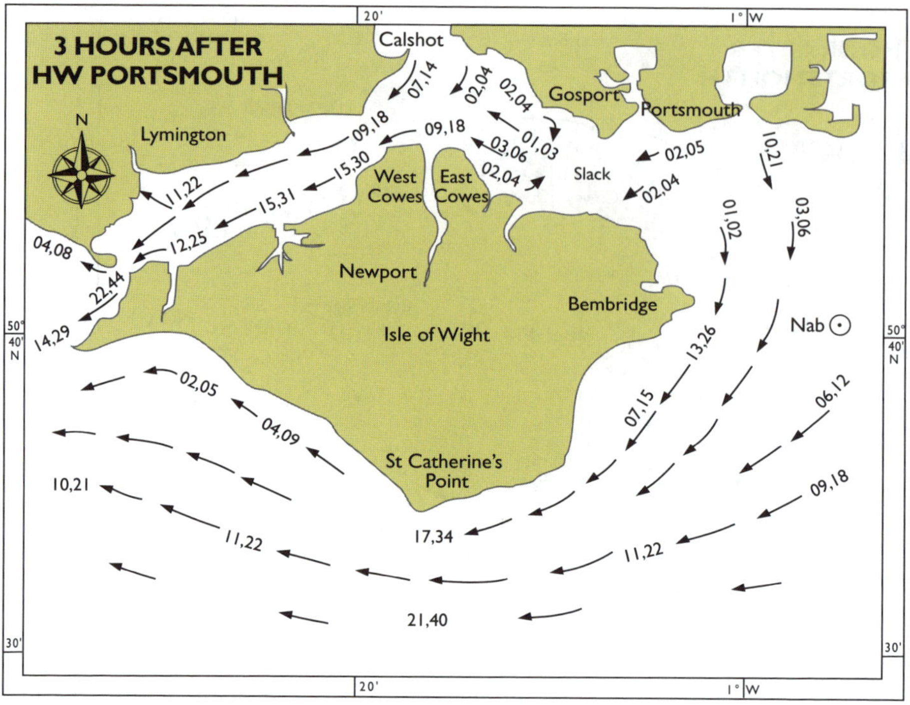

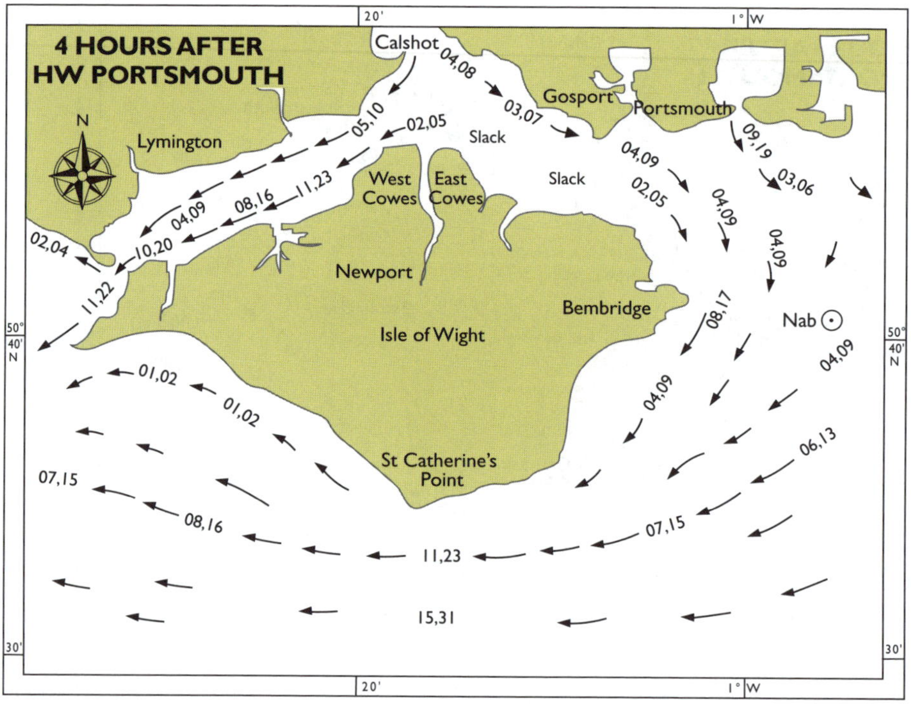

3 HOURS AFTER HW PORTSMOUTH

N

Calshot

Lymington

07,14
02,04 02,04
Gosport
Portsmouth
09,18 09,18
03,06 01,03
15,30 02,05
West East 02,04 Slack
Cowes Cowes 02,04
15,31 10,21
11,22 03,06
12,25 01,02
04,08
22,44 Newport
14,29 Bembridge 13,26
Isle of Wight Nab ⊙
St Catherine's 07,15 06,12
02,05 Point
04,09 09,18
10,21
17,34 11,22
11,22
21,40

50° 40' N
50° 40' N

20' 1° W
30' 30'

4 HOURS AFTER HW PORTSMOUTH

N

Calshot
04,08
03,07
Gosport
05,10 Portsmouth
02,05 Slack 09,19
11,23 04,09 03,06
Lymington 08,16 Slack 02,05
04,09 West East 04,09
02,04 Cowes Cowes 04,09
10,20
11,22 Newport
08,17
Bembridge
Isle of Wight Nab ⊙
04,09
01,02 04,09
01,02 St Catherine's
07,15 Point 06,13
08,16 04,09 07,15
11,23
15,31

50° 40' N
50° 40' N

20' 1° W
30' 30'

164

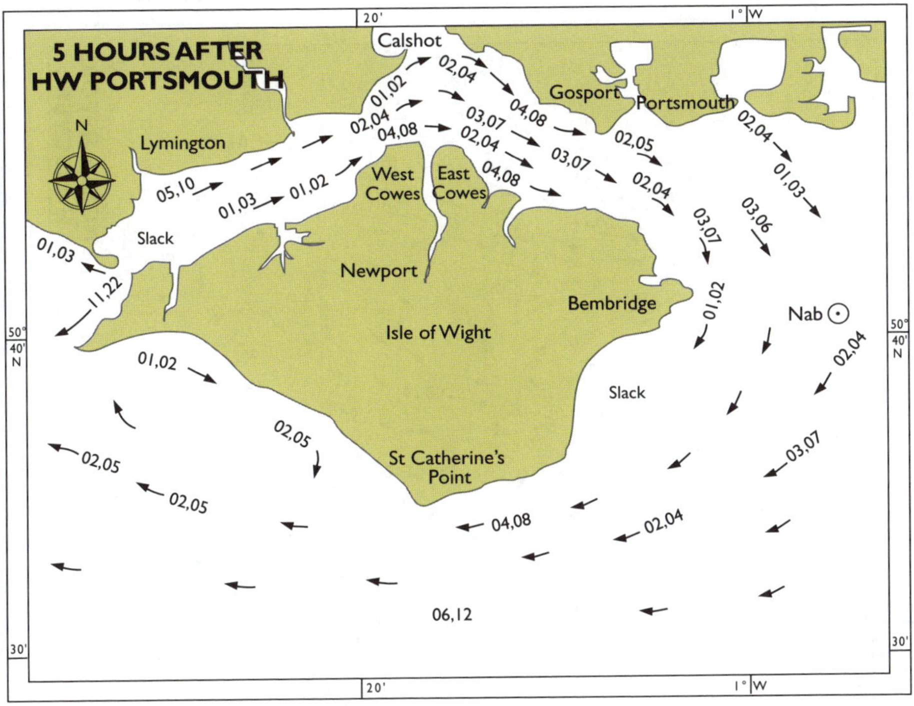

ISLE OF WIGHT

5 HOURS AFTER HW PORTSMOUTH

Calshot
Gosport
Portsmouth
Lymington
West Cowes
East Cowes
Newport
Bembridge
Isle of Wight
Nab ⊙
St Catherine's Point
Slack
Slack

N

20'   1° W
50°40'N
30'

01,02   02,04   04,08
02,04   03,07   02,04
04,08   02,04   03,07   02,05
05,10   01,03   01,02   02,04
01,03   03,07   03,06
Slack   01,03   04,08
11,22   01,02
01,02
02,05
02,05   02,05
04,08   02,04
06,12
02,04
03,07

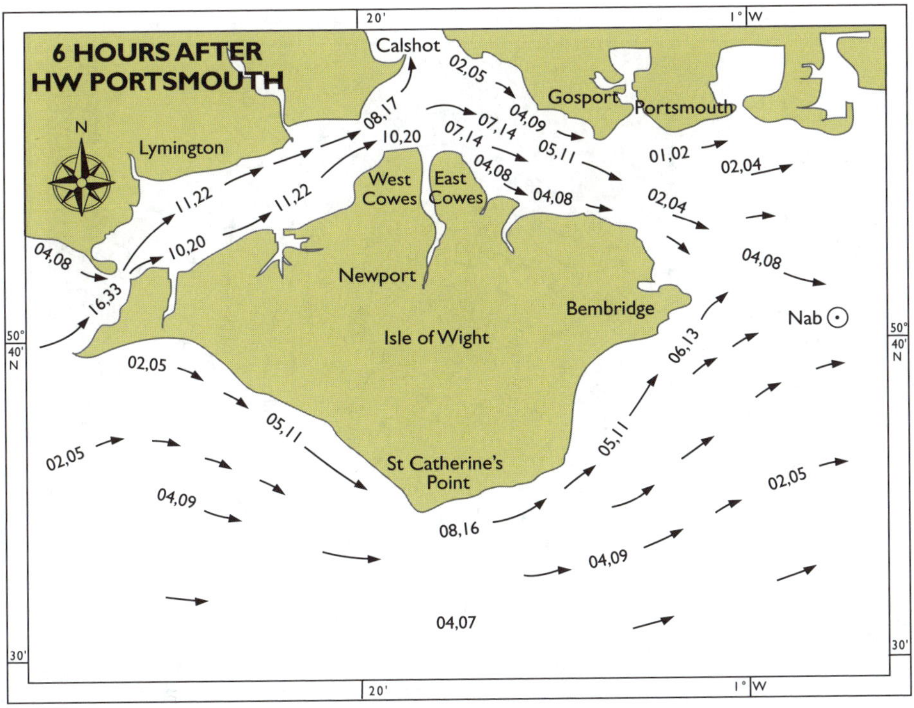

6 HOURS AFTER HW PORTSMOUTH

Calshot
Gosport
Portsmouth
Lymington
West Cowes
East Cowes
Newport
Bembridge
Isle of Wight
Nab ⊙
St Catherine's Point

N

20'   1° W
50°40'N
30'

02,05   04,09
08,17   07,14   05,11   01,02   02,04
10,20   07,14   04,08   04,08   02,04
11,22   11,22   04,08
04,08   10,20   06,13
16,33   05,11
02,05   05,11   02,05
02,05   05,11
04,09   08,16
04,09
04,07

CHANNEL ISLANDS

Example: ←—10,18 predicts a westerly tidal flow of 1.0 knots at mean
Neap tides and 1.8 knots at mean Spring tides at the location of the comma.

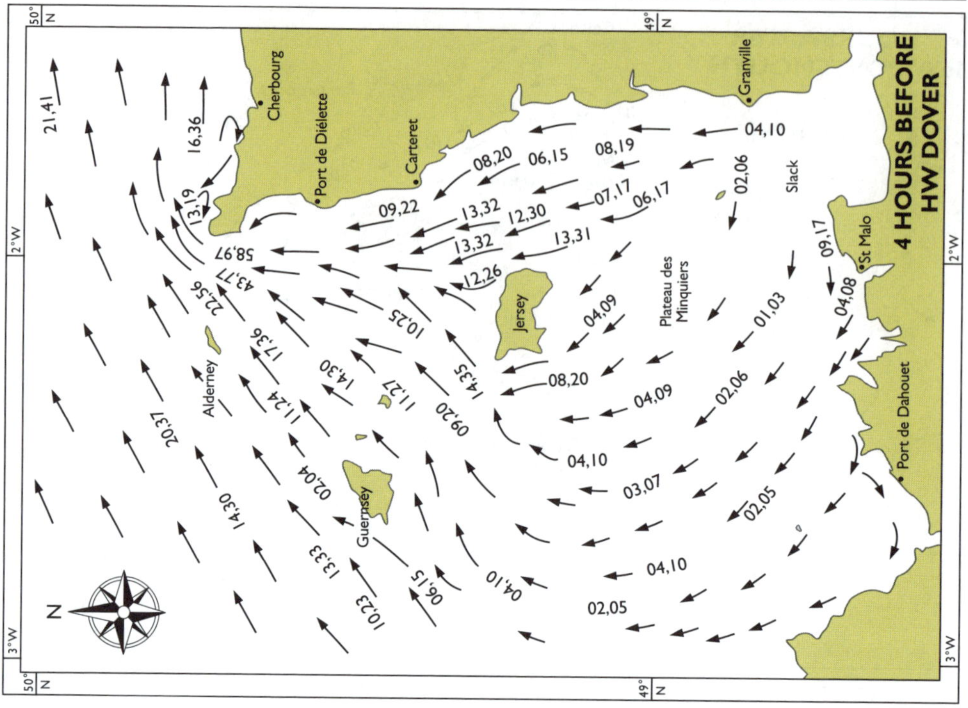

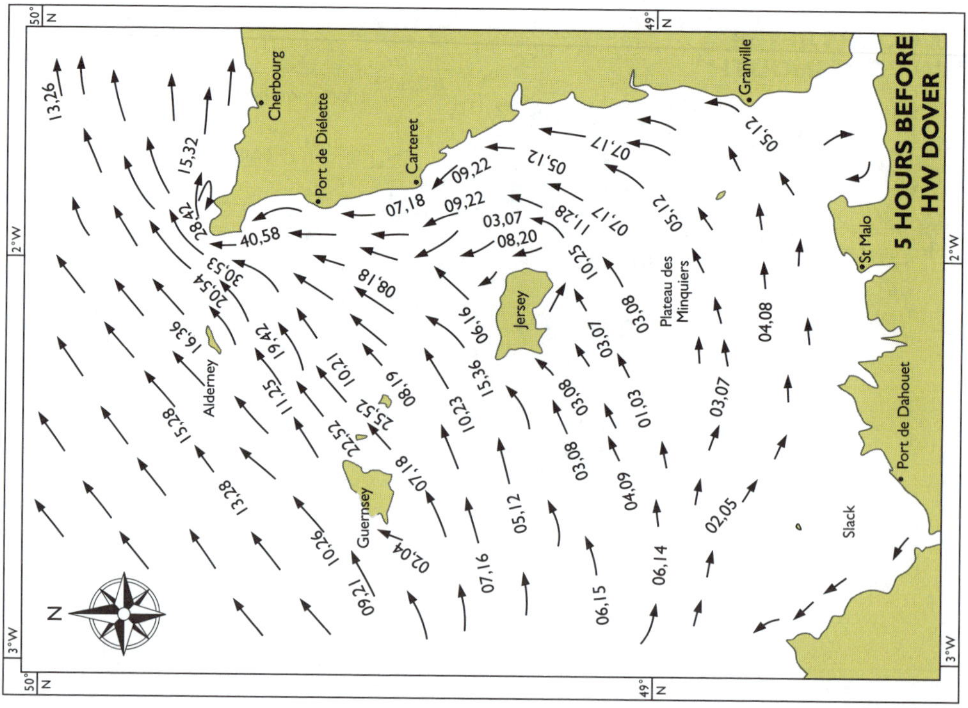

4 HOURS BEFORE HW DOVER

Cherbourg
Port de Diélette
Carteret
Granville
Jersey
Plateau des Minquiers
St Malo
Port de Dahouet
Alderney
Guernsey
Slack
N

21,41 16,36 13,19 08,20 06,15 08,19 04,10 02,06
09,22 13,32 12,30 07,17 06,17
58,97 13,32 13,31 09,17
43,77 12,26 04,08
22,56 17,36 10,25 04,09 01,03
20,37 17,24 14,30 11,27 08,20 04,09 02,06
14,30 13,24 09,20 04,10 02,05
13,33 02,04 14,35 03,07
10,23 06,15 04,10 04,10
02,05

5 HOURS BEFORE HW DOVER

Cherbourg
Port de Diélette
Carteret
Granville
Jersey
Plateau des Minquiers
St Malo
Port de Dahouet
Alderney
Guernsey
Slack
N

13,26 15,32 28,42 09,22 05,12 07,17 05,12
40,58 07,18 09,22 07,17
30,53 08,18 03,07 11,28 05,12
20,54 06,19 08,20 10,25
16,36 19,42 15,35 03,08 04,08
15,28 22,52 10,21 10,23 03,08 01,03 03,07
13,28 23,52 07,18 08,08 03,08
10,26 02,04 05,12 04,09 02,05
09,21 07,16 06,14 06,15

CHANNEL ISLANDS

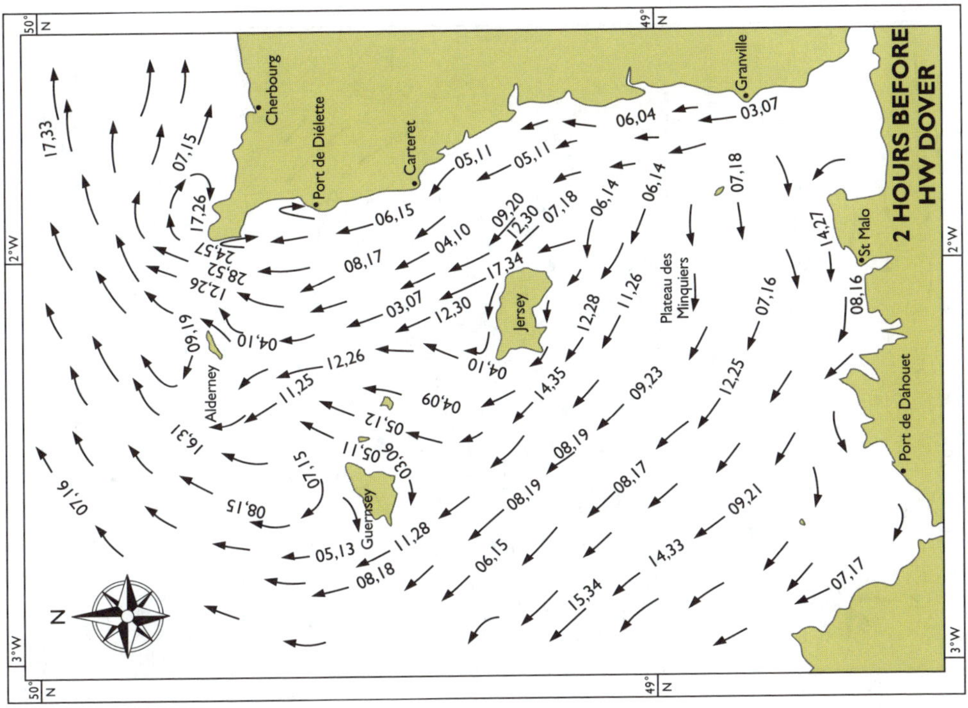

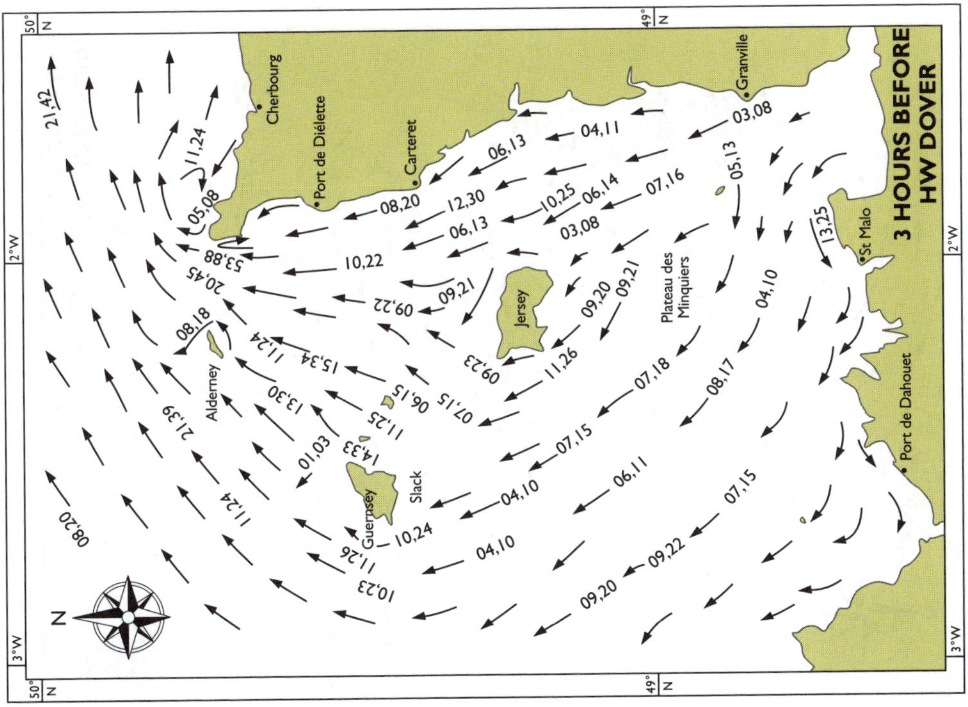

2 HOURS BEFORE HW DOVER

3 HOURS BEFORE HW DOVER

TIDES

CHANNEL ISLANDS

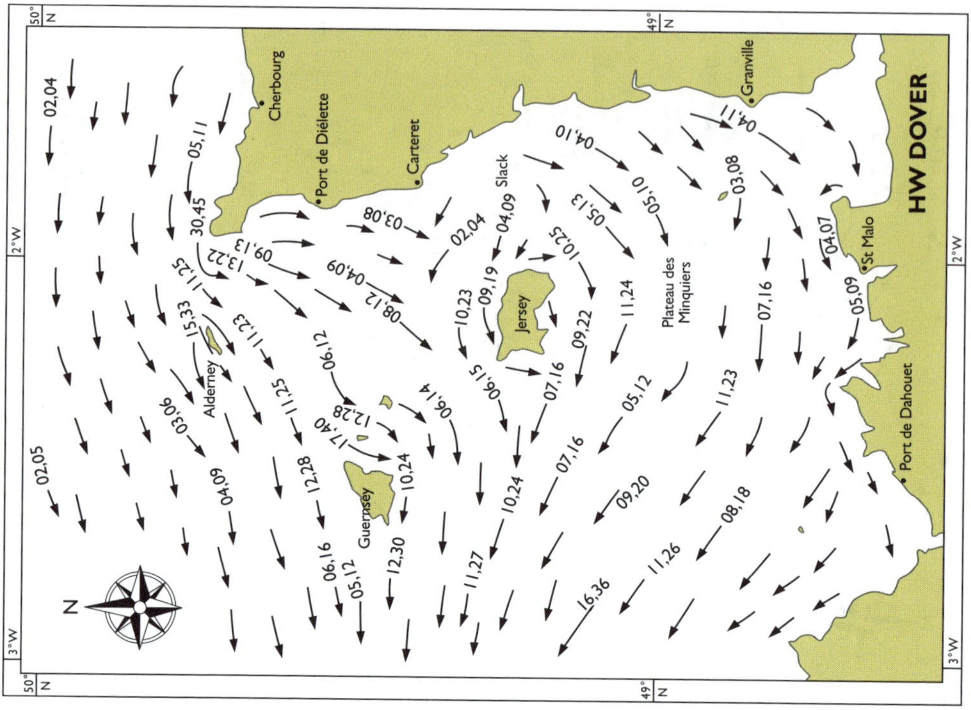
HW DOVER
Cherbourg
Port de Diélette
Carteret
Granville
St Malo
Port de Dahouet
Alderney
Guernsey
Jersey
Plateau des Minquiers
Slack
50°N
49°N
2°W
3°W
N

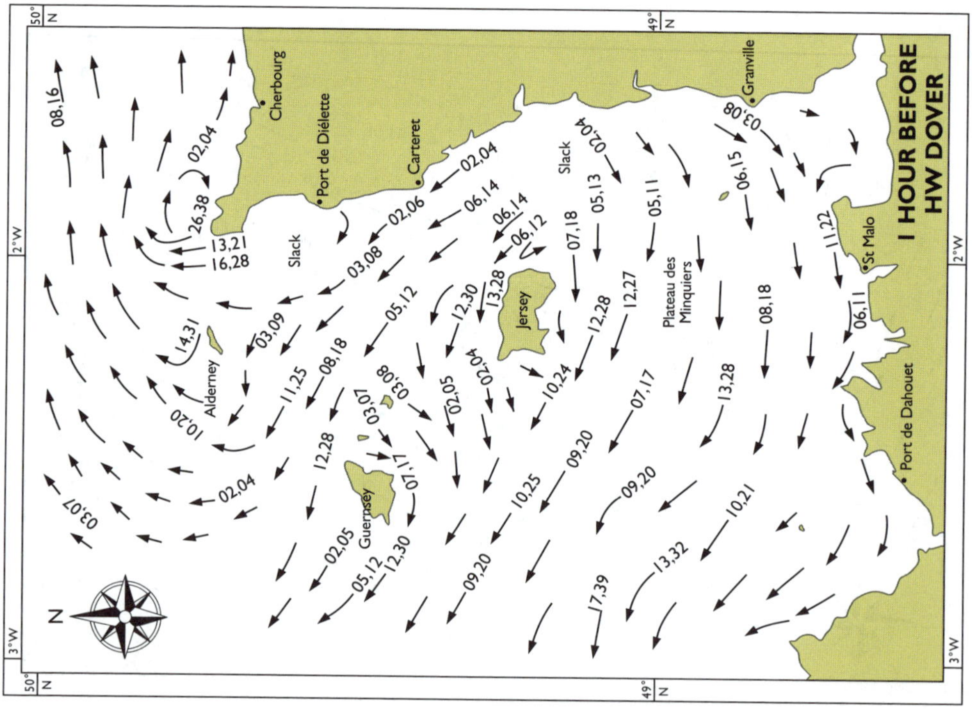
1 HOUR BEFORE HW DOVER
Cherbourg
Port de Diélette
Carteret
Granville
St Malo
Port de Dahouet
Alderney
Guernsey
Jersey
Plateau des Minquiers
Slack
50°N
49°N
2°W
3°W
N

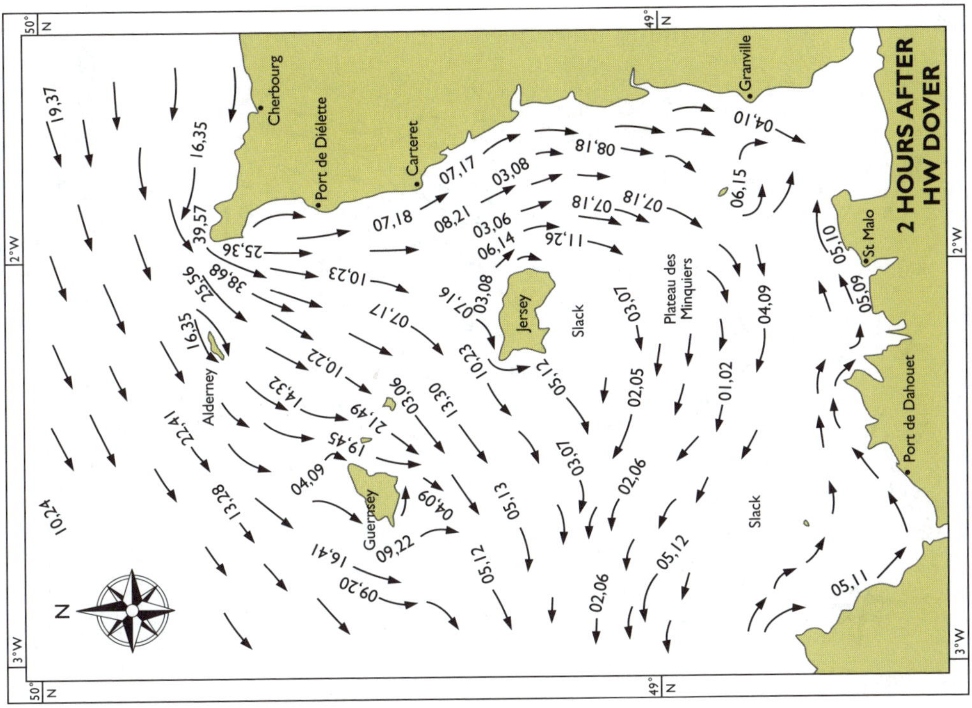

CHANNEL ISLANDS

2 HOURS AFTER HW DOVER

Cherbourg
Port de Diélette
Carteret
Granville
St Malo
Port de Dahouet
Alderney
Guernsey
Jersey
Slack
Plateau des Minquiers
Slack

19,37 · 16,35 · 39,57 · 25,36 · 38,68 · 35,56 · 16,35 · 22,41 · 13,28 · 10,24
07,17 · 03,08 · 08,18 · 07,18 · 07,18 · 06,15 · 04,10 · 05,10 · 05,09
07,18 · 08,21 · 03,06 · 06,14 · 11,26 · 04,09
10,23 · 07,17 · 03,08 · 07,16 · 03,07 · 02,05 · 01,02
10,22 · 03,06 · 13,30 · 10,23 · 05,12 · 02,06 · 05,12
14,32 · 21,49 · 04,09 · 03,07 · 05,11
19,45 · 04,09 · 05,13 · 02,06
16,41 · 09,22 · 05,12
09,20

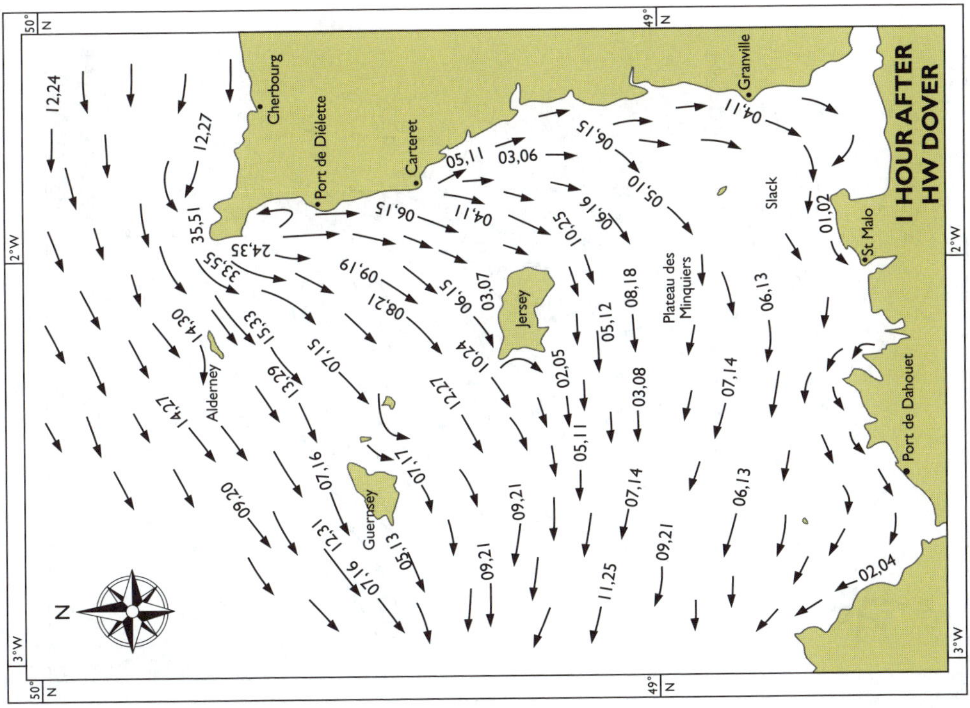

1 HOUR AFTER HW DOVER

Cherbourg
Port de Diélette
Carteret
Granville
St Malo
Port de Dahouet
Alderney
Guernsey
Jersey
Slack
Plateau des Minquiers

12,24 · 12,27 · 35,51 · 24,35 · 33,55 · 15,33 · 14,30 · 13,29 · 14,27
05,11 · 03,06 · 06,15 · 05,10 · 04,11 · 01,02
06,15 · 04,11 · 06,16 · 05 · 06,13
09,19 · 08,21 · 06,15 · 10,25 · 08,18 · 07,14
07,15 · 03,07 · 10,24 · 05,12 · 03,08 · 06,13
12,27 · 02,05 · 05,11 · 07,14 · 02,04
07,17 · 05,11 · 09,21 · 07,14 · 09,21
07,16 · 12,31 · 05,13 · 09,21 · 11,25
09,20

CHANNEL ISLANDS

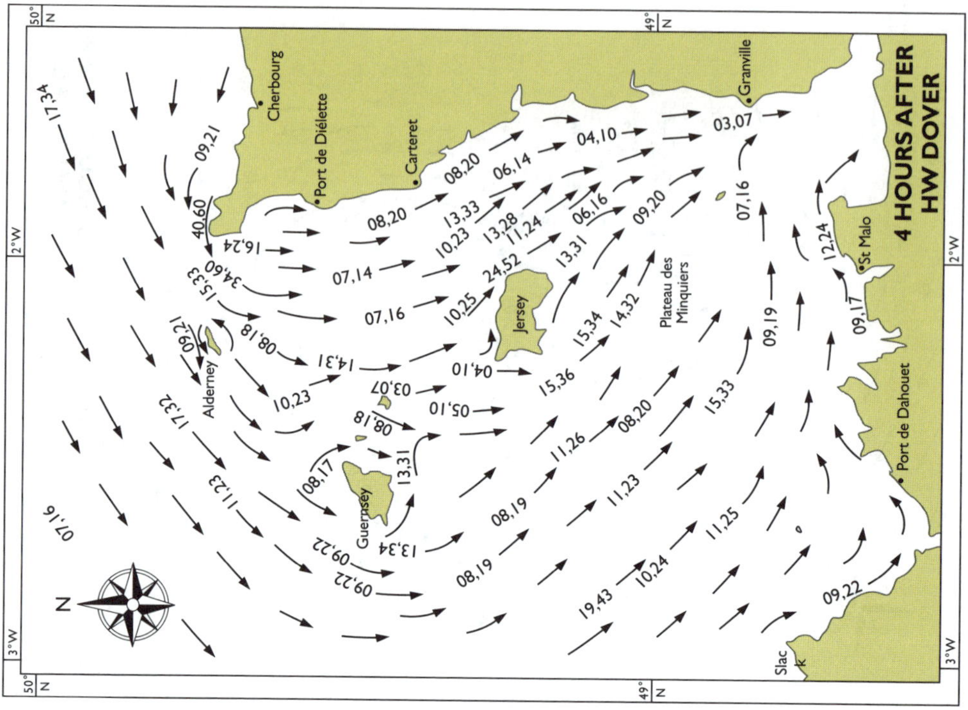

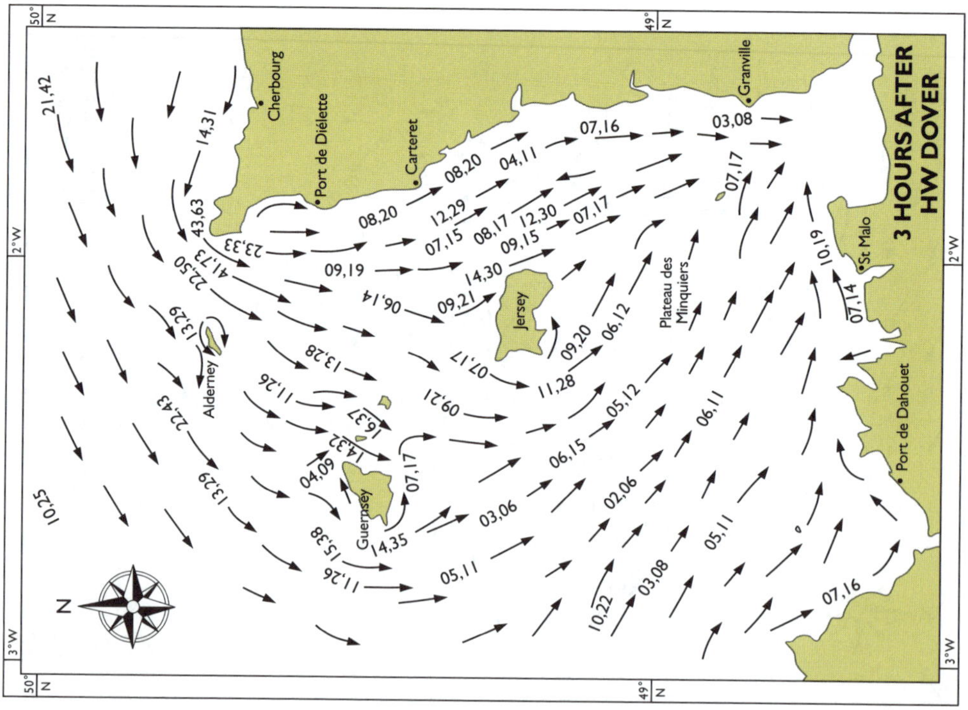

4 HOURS AFTER HW DOVER

A tidal stream chart of the Channel Islands region showing flow directions and rates. Locations marked include Cherbourg, Port de Diélette, Carteret, Granville, St Malo, Port de Dahouet, Alderney, Guernsey, Jersey, and Plateau des Minquiers. Tidal stream values shown along arrows:

17,34 · 09,21 · 40,60 · 16,24 · 34,60 · 15,33 · 06,21 · 08,18 · 17,32 · 11,33 · 07,16 · 08,20 · 07,14 · 13,33 · 10,23 · 13,28 · 11,24 · 24,52 · 13,31 · 07,16 · 10,25 · 14,31 · 03,07 · 08,17 · 10,23 · 08,18 · 03,07 · 05,10 · 04,10 · 15,36 · 15,34 · 14,32 · 13,31 · 06,14 · 04,10 · 09,20 · 07,16 · 12,24 · 09,17 · 09,19 · 15,33 · 08,20 · 11,26 · 11,23 · 11,25 · 08,19 · 08,19 · 19,43 · 10,24 · 09,22 · 13,34 · 09,22 · 09,22 · Plateau des Minquiers · Slac K

3 HOURS AFTER HW DOVER

A tidal stream chart of the Channel Islands region showing flow directions and rates. Locations marked include Cherbourg, Port de Diélette, Carteret, Granville, St Malo, Port de Dahouet, Alderney, Guernsey, Jersey, and Plateau des Minquiers. Tidal stream values shown along arrows:

21,42 · 14,31 · 43,63 · 23,33 · 41,73 · 22,50 · 13,29 · 22,43 · 13,29 · 10,25 · 08,20 · 08,20 · 09,19 · 12,29 · 07,15 · 08,17 · 12,30 · 09,15 · 07,17 · 14,30 · 06,14 · 09,21 · 04,11 · 07,16 · 03,08 · 07,17 · 13,28 · 11,26 · 16,37 · 14,32 · 09,40 · 15,38 · 11,26 · 07,17 · 04,35 · 09,21 · 07,17 · 09,20 · 11,28 · 06,12 · 05,12 · 06,11 · 10,19 · 07,14 · 03,06 · 06,15 · 02,06 · 05,11 · 05,11 · 10,22 · 03,08 · 07,16 · Plateau des Minquiers

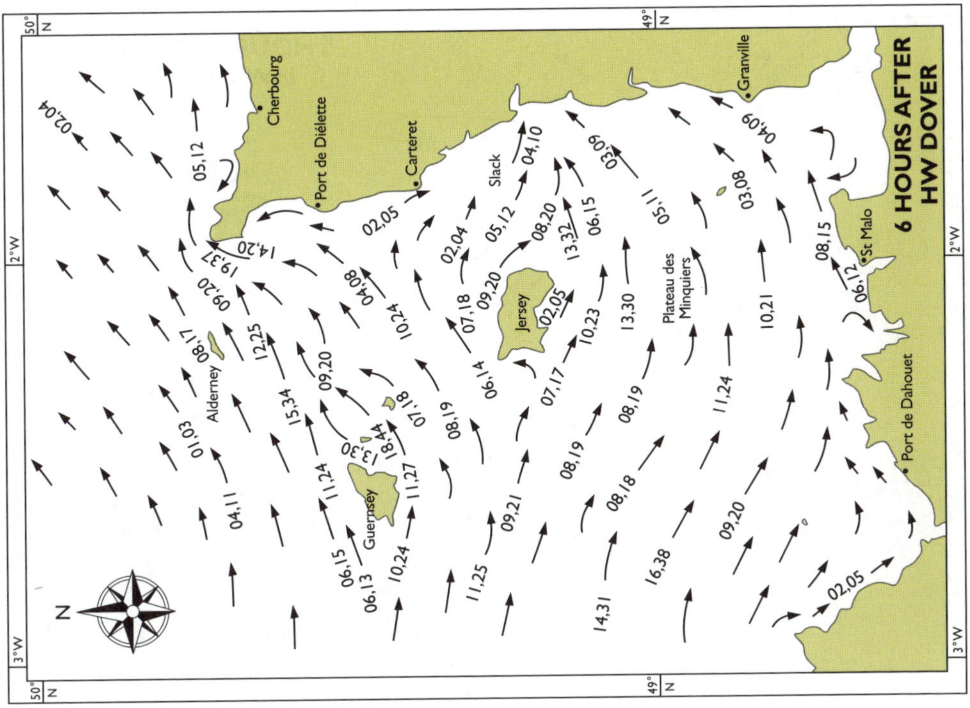

CHANNEL ISLANDS

6 HOURS AFTER HW DOVER

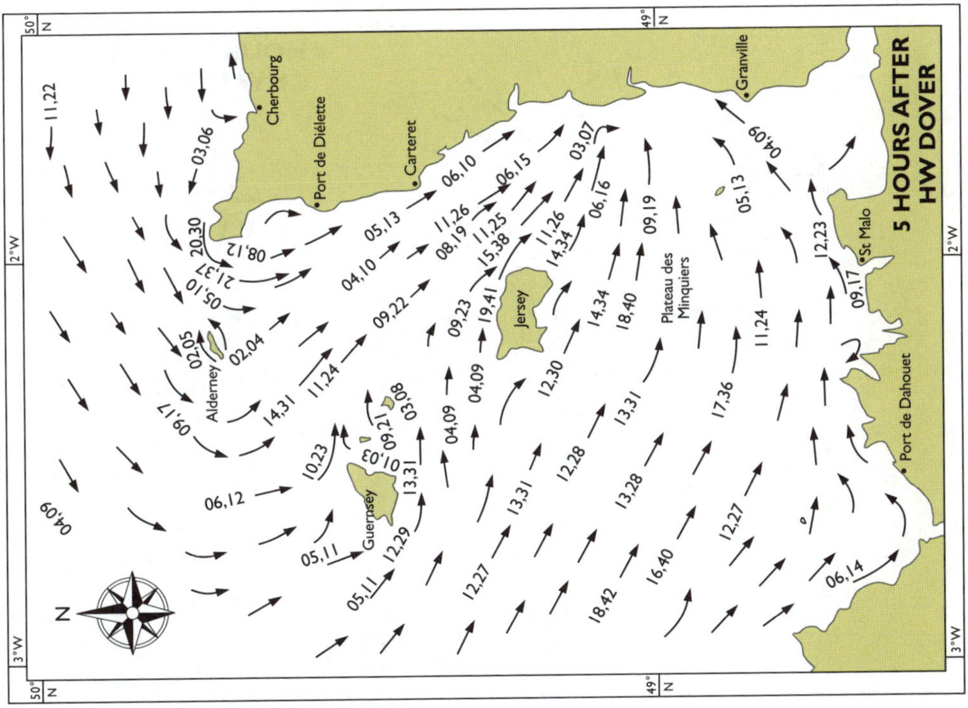

5 HOURS AFTER HW DOVER

NORTH SEA

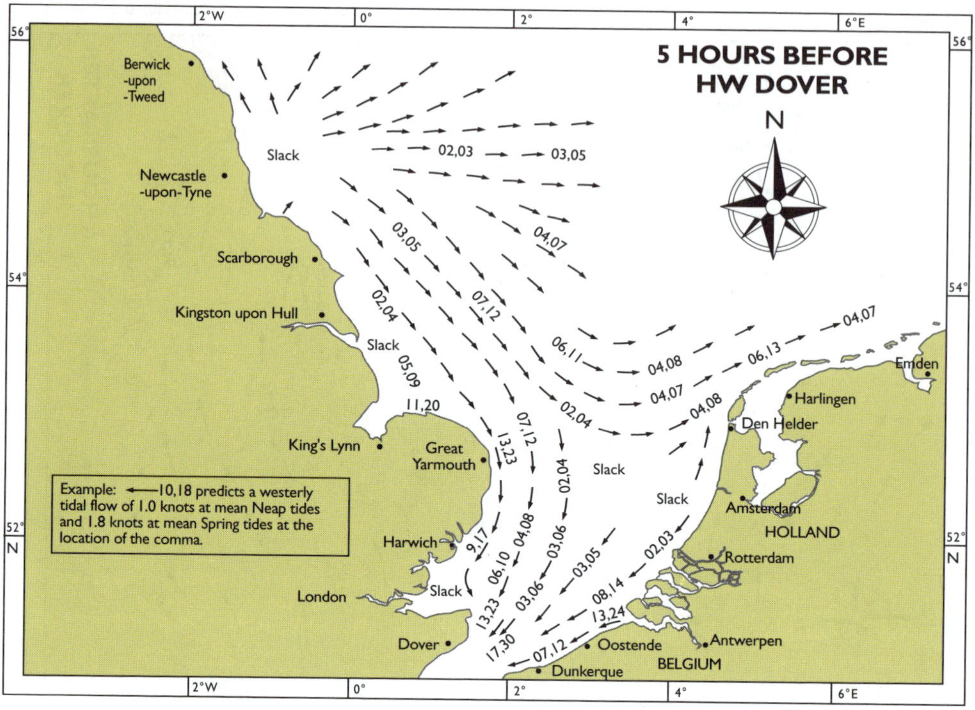

5 HOURS BEFORE HW DOVER

N

Berwick-upon-Tweed
Newcastle-upon-Tyne
Slack
02,03 → 03,05
03,05
04,07
Scarborough
03,05
02,04
07,12
04,07
Kingston upon Hull
Slack
05,09
06,11
04,08
04,08
06,13
Emden
11,20
04,07
Harlingen
King's Lynn
Great Yarmouth
07,12
13,23
02,04
02,04
Slack
Den Helder
Slack
Amsterdam
HOLLAND
Harwich
9,17
07,12
04,08
03,06
03,05
02,03
Rotterdam
London
Slack
13,23
06,10
03,06
08,14
13,24
Antwerpen
17,30
07,12
Oostende
Dover
Dunkerque
BELGIUM

Example: ←—10,18 predicts a westerly tidal flow of 1.0 knots at mean Neap tides and 1.8 knots at mean Spring tides at the location of the comma.

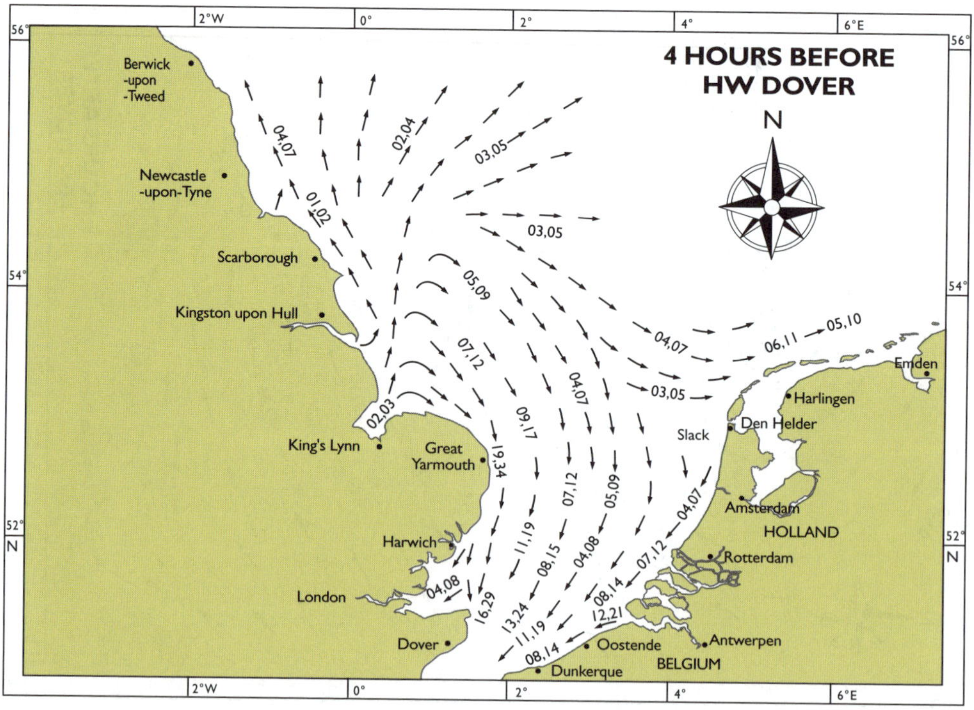

4 HOURS BEFORE HW DOVER

N

Berwick-upon-Tweed
04,07
02,04
03,05
Newcastle-upon-Tyne
01,02
03,05
Scarborough
05,09
Kingston upon Hull
04,07
06,11
05,10
07,12
03,05
Emden
02,03
04,07
Harlingen
King's Lynn
Great Yarmouth
09,17
04,07
Slack
Den Helder
19,34
07,12
05,09
04,07
Amsterdam
Harwich
11,19
08,15
04,08
08,14
07,12
HOLLAND
London
04,08
13,24
11,19
12,21
Rotterdam
16,29
08,14
Oostende
Antwerpen
Dover
Dunkerque
BELGIUM

NORTH SEA

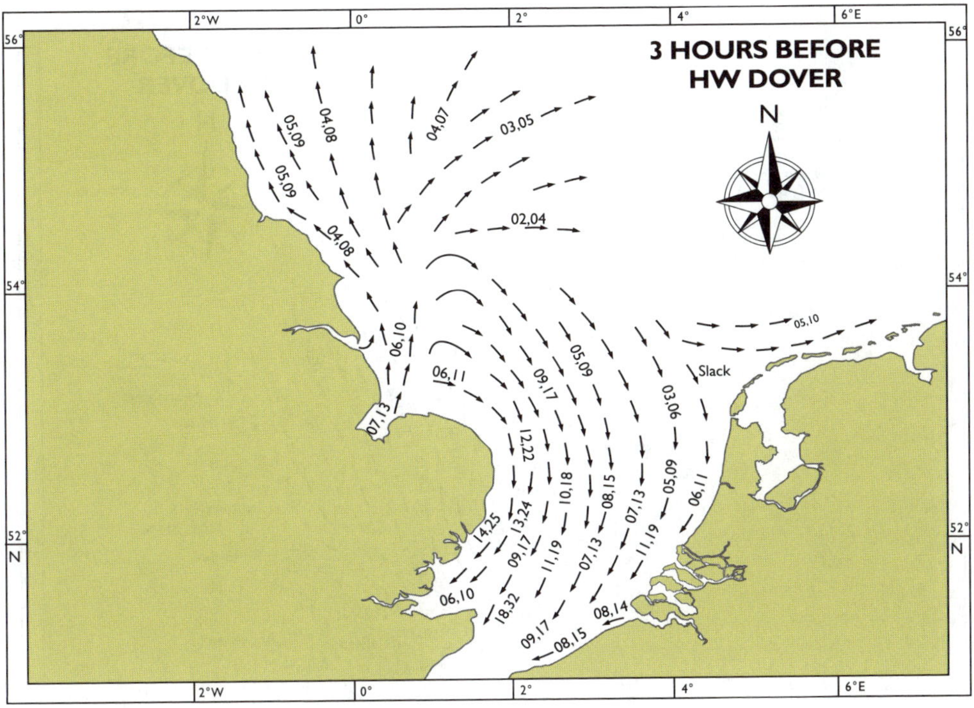

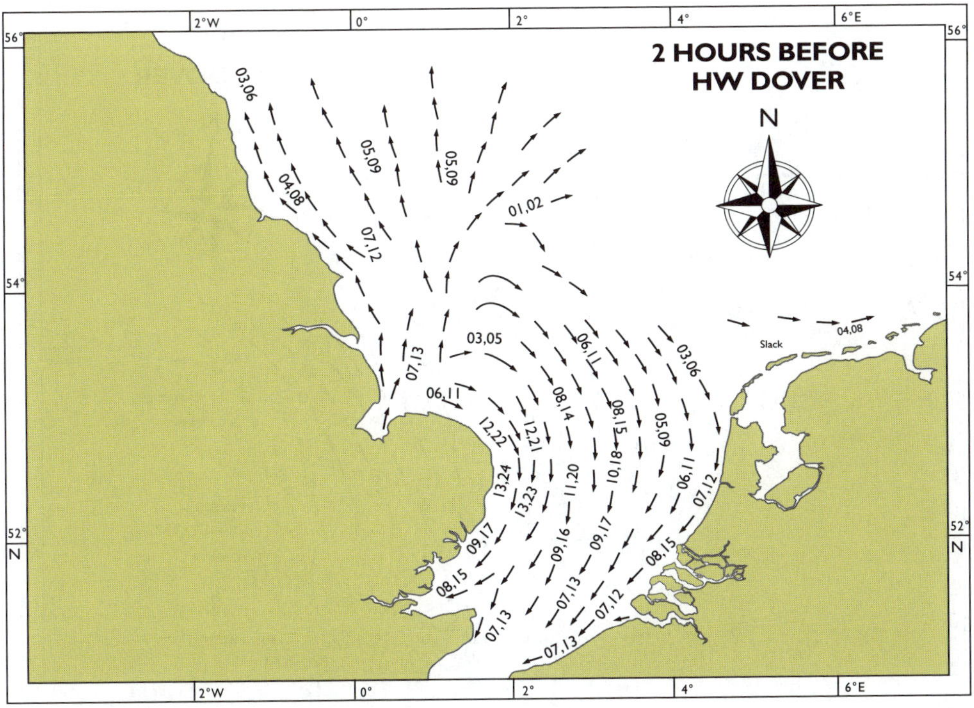

NORTH SEA

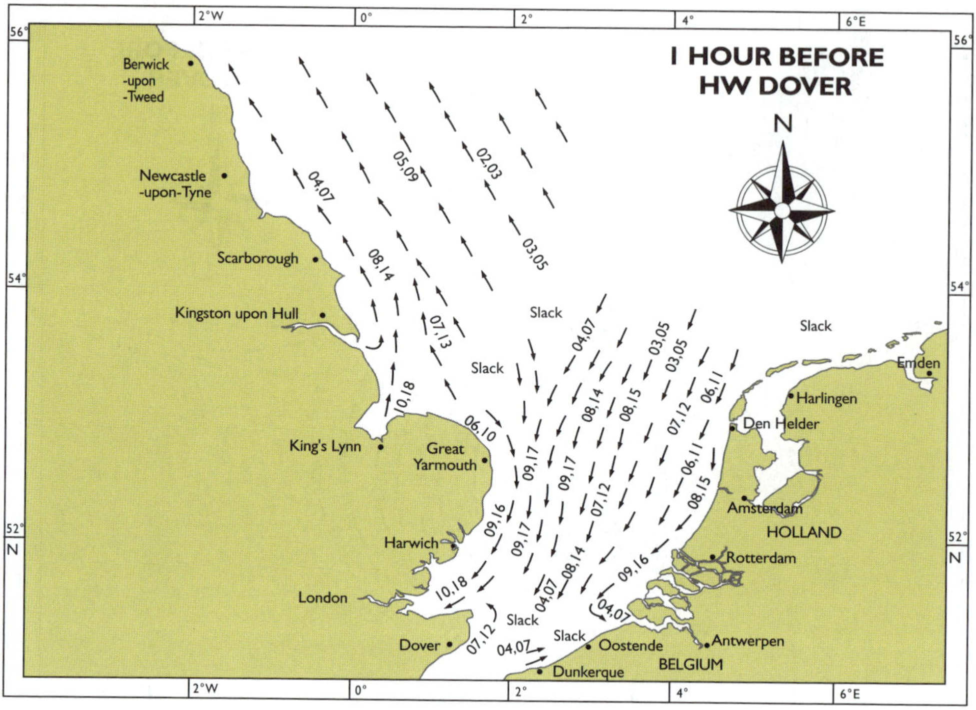

I HOUR BEFORE HW DOVER

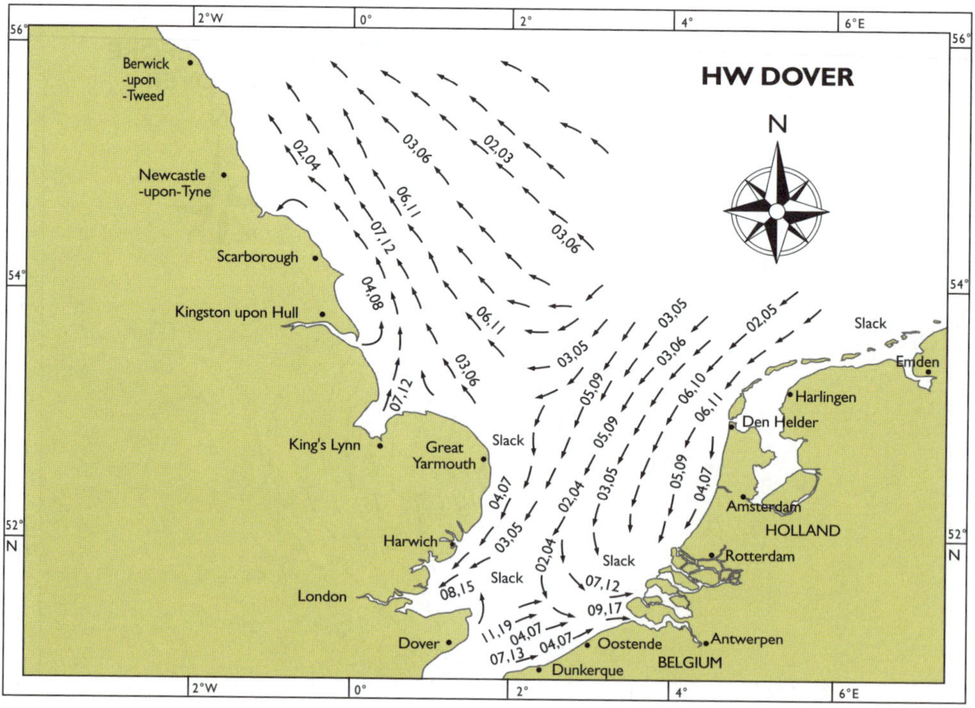

HW DOVER

NORTH SEA

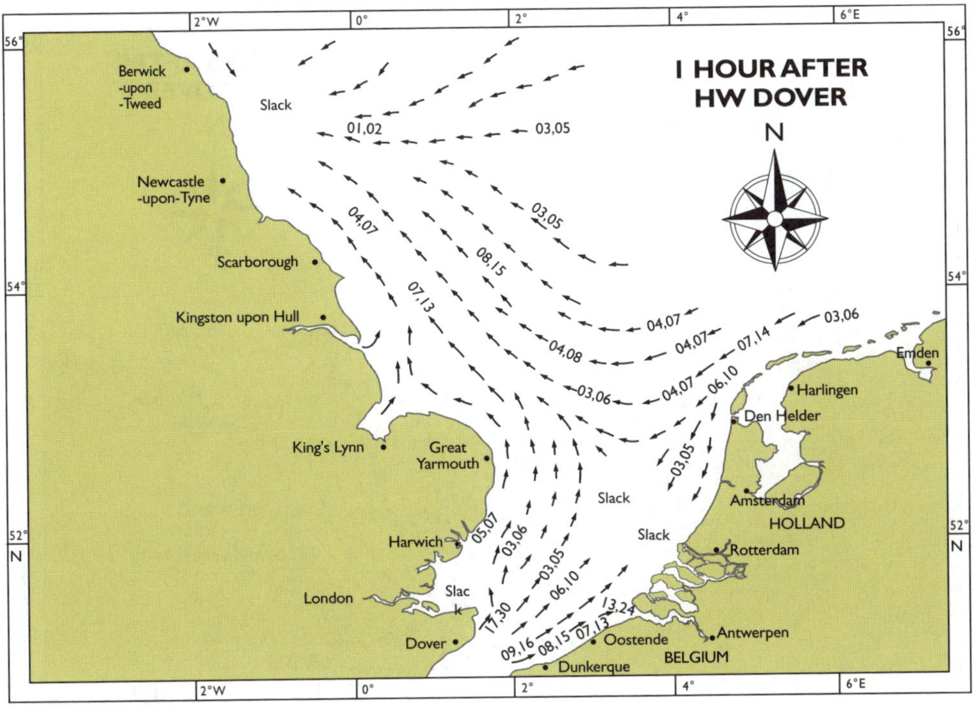

I HOUR AFTER HW DOVER

N

2°W | 0° | 2° | 4° | 6°E

56°

Berwick-upon-Tweed

Slack

01,02   03,05

Newcastle-upon-Tyne

04,07

03,05

Scarborough

08,15

03,05

54°

07,13

Kingston upon Hull

04,07   04,07   03,06

04,08   04,07   06,10   07,14   Emden

03,06   04,07   06,10   Harlingen

Den Helder

King's Lynn   Great Yarmouth   03,05

Slack   Amsterdam

HOLLAND

52°N   Harwich   05,07   03,06   Slack   Rotterdam

London   Slack   03,05

17,30   06,10   13,24

Dover   09,16 08,15 07,13   Oostende   Antwerpen

Dunkerque   BELGIUM

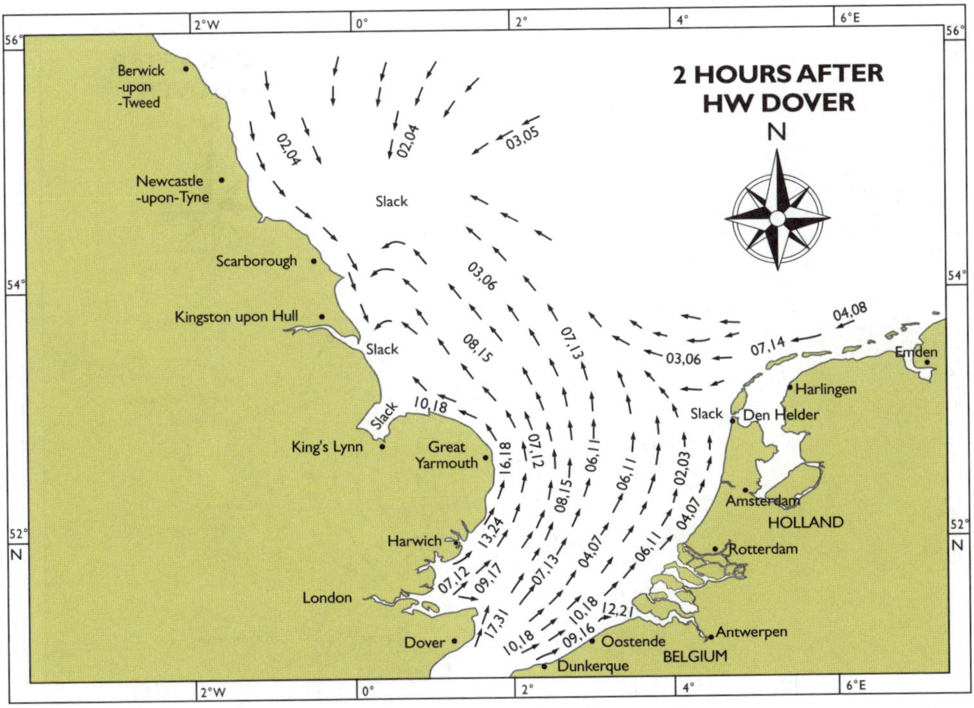

2 HOURS AFTER HW DOVER

N

2°W | 0° | 2° | 4° | 6°E

56°

Berwick-upon-Tweed

02,04   02,04   03,05

Newcastle-upon-Tyne

Slack

Scarborough

03,06

54°

08,15   07,13   04,08

Kingston upon Hull

03,06   07,14   Emden

Slack   Harlingen

10,18   Slack   Den Helder

King's Lynn   Great Yarmouth   16,18   07,12   06,11   02,03   Amsterdam

HOLLAND

52°N   Harwich   13,24   08,15   04,07   06,11   04,07   Rotterdam

07,12   07,13   06,11

London   09,17

17,31   10,18   12,21

Dover   10,18   09,16   Oostende   Antwerpen

Dunkerque   BELGIUM

TIDES

175

NORTH SEA

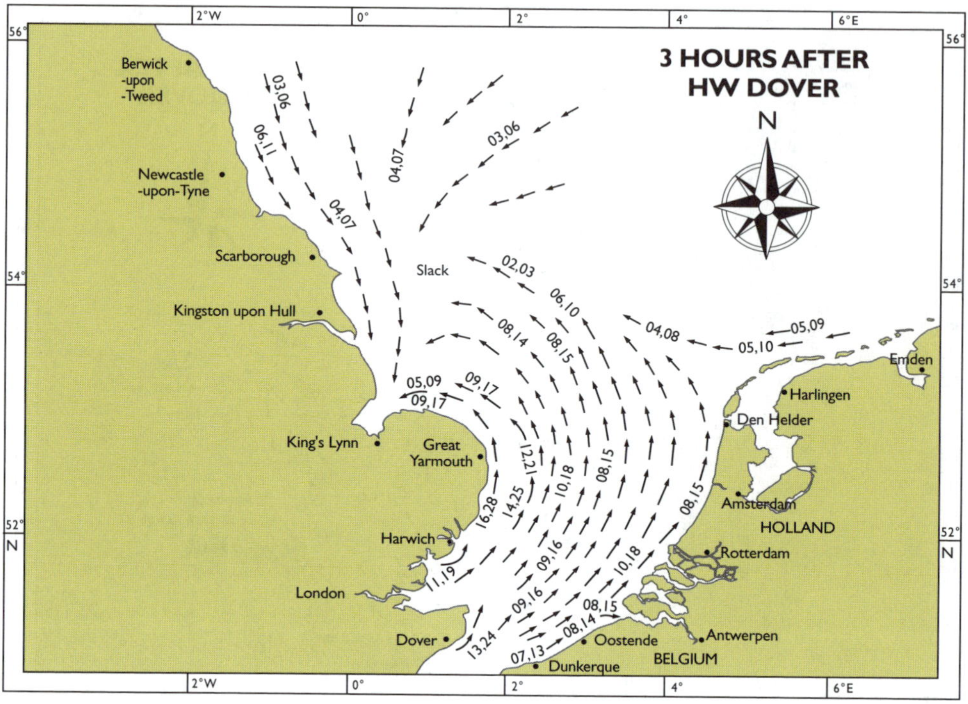
3 HOURS AFTER HW DOVER
N
Berwick -upon -Tweed
Newcastle -upon-Tyne
Scarborough
Kingston upon Hull
King's Lynn
Great Yarmouth
Harwich
London
Dover
Dunkerque
Oostende
BELGIUM
Antwerpen
Rotterdam
HOLLAND
Amsterdam
Den Helder
Harlingen
Emden
Slack
03,06
06,11
04,07
04,07
03,06
02,03
06,10
08,14
08,15
04,08
05,10
05,09
05,09
09,17
09,17
12,21
10,18
08,15
08,15
16,28
14,25
11,19
09,16
09,16
10,18
08,15
08,14
07,13
13,24
2°W
0°
2°
4°
6°E
56°
54°
52° N

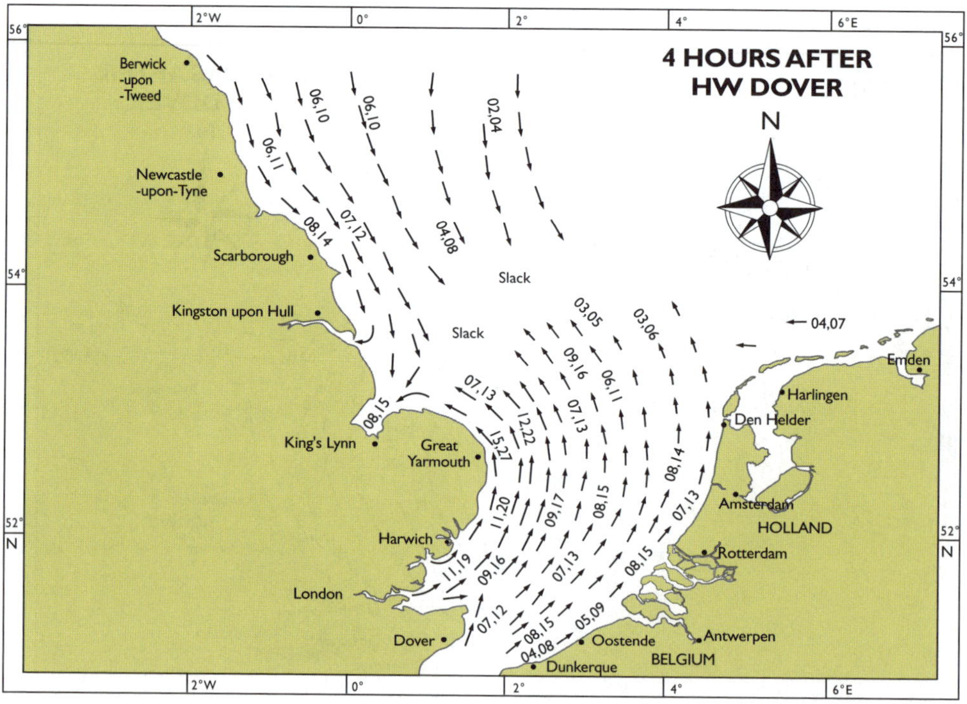
4 HOURS AFTER HW DOVER
N
Berwick -upon -Tweed
Newcastle -upon-Tyne
Scarborough
Kingston upon Hull
King's Lynn
Great Yarmouth
Harwich
London
Dover
Dunkerque
Oostende
BELGIUM
Antwerpen
Rotterdam
HOLLAND
Amsterdam
Den Helder
Harlingen
Emden
Slack
Slack
06,10
06,10
02,04
06,11
07,12
08,14
04,08
03,05
03,06
04,07
09,16
06,11
07,13
07,13
12,22
15,27
08,15
08,14
11,20
09,17
08,15
07,13
11,19
09,16
07,13
08,15
07,12
08,15
05,09
04,08
2°W
0°
2°
4°
6°E
56°
54°
52° N

NORTH SEA

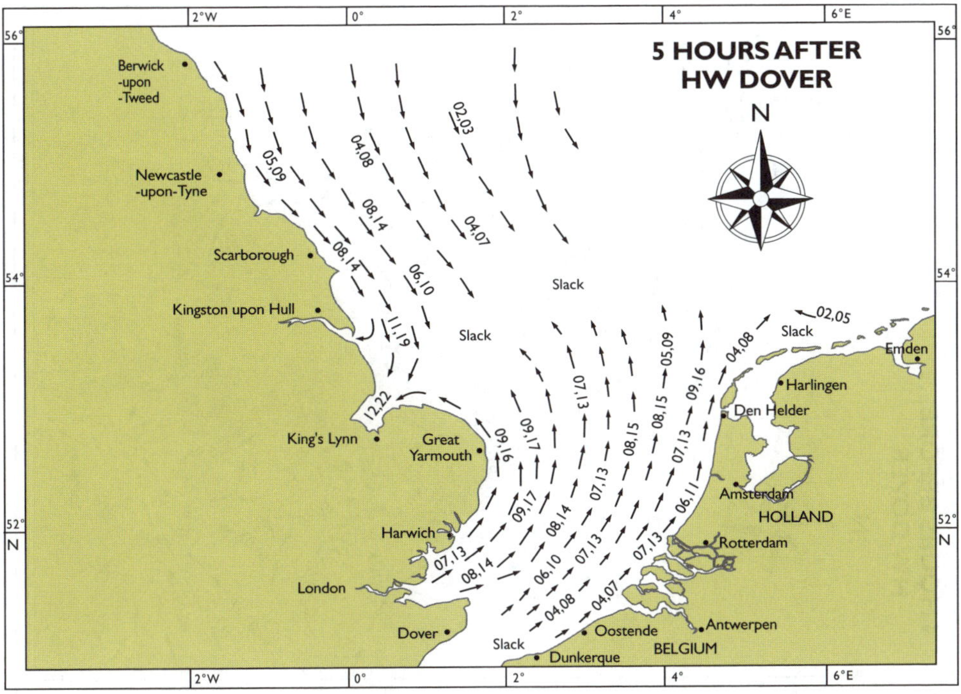

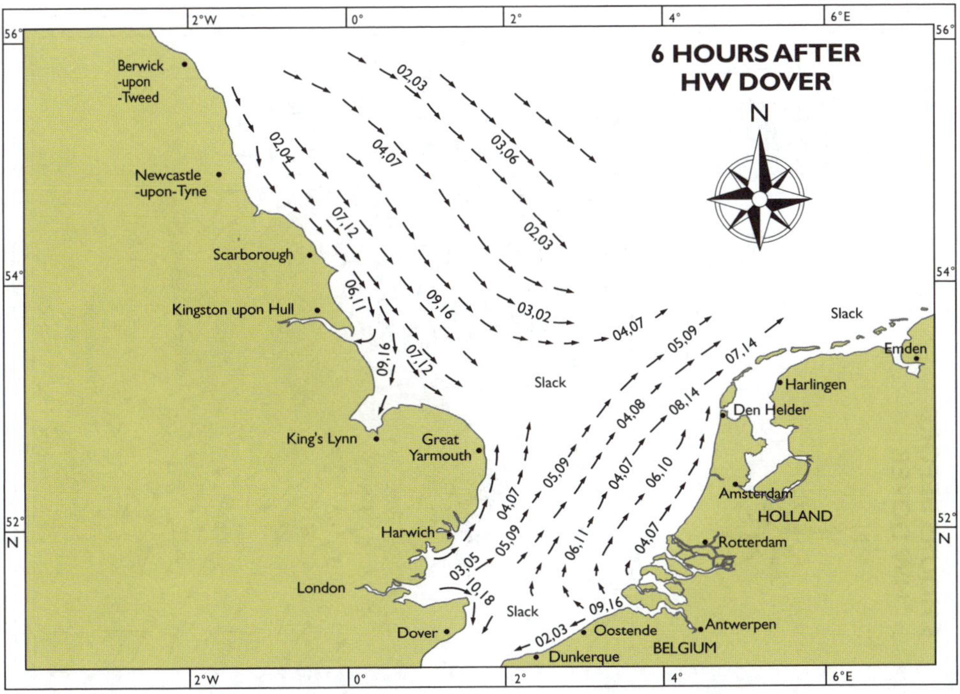

5 HOURS AFTER HW DOVER

6 HOURS AFTER HW DOVER

TIDES

177

SCOTLAND

Example: ◄—10,18 predicts a westerly tidal flow of 1.0 knots at mean
Neap tides and 1.8 knots at mean Spring tides at the location of the comma.

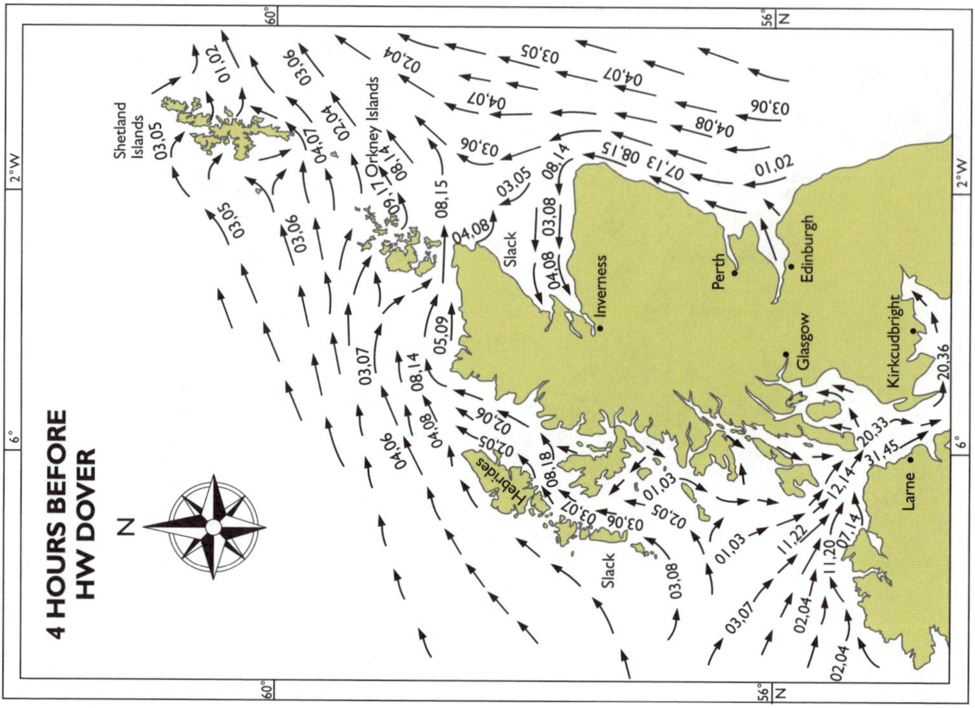

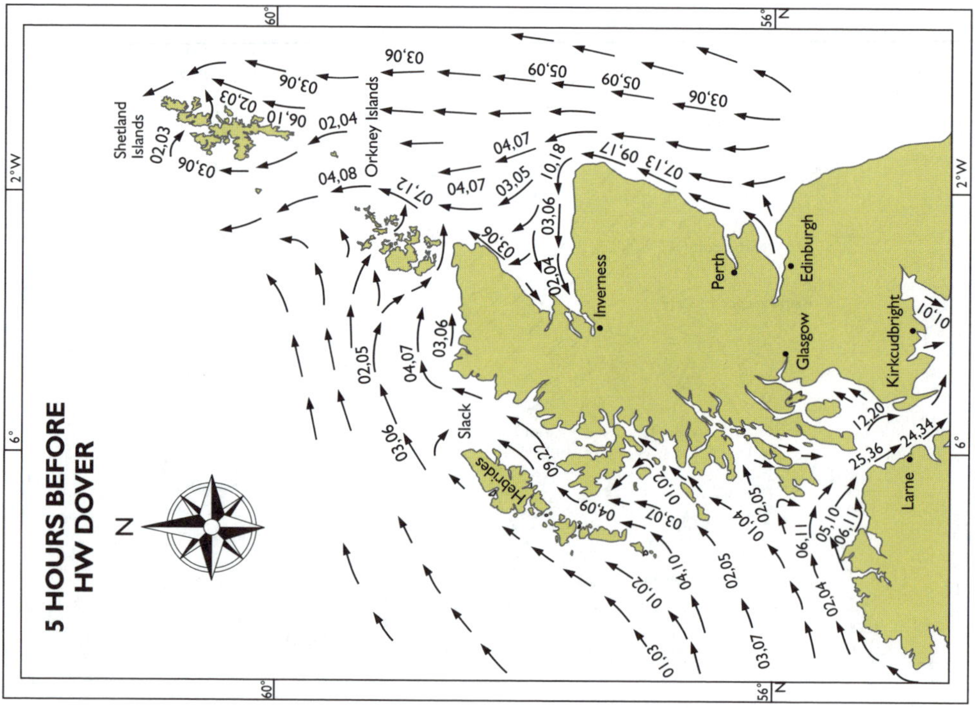

4 HOURS BEFORE HW DOVER

N

Shetland Islands

Orkney Islands

Inverness

Perth

Edinburgh

Glasgow

Kirkcudbright

Larne

Hebrides

Slack

Slack

01,02
03,06
03,05
04,07
04,07
04,08
03,06
07,13 08,13 08,15
08,14
03,08
03,05
04,08
04,08 03,08
03,05
Slack
02,06
05,09
08,14
04,08
04,06
03,07
02,05
08,18
03,06
03,07
01,03
03,06
02,05
01,03
03,08
03,07
02,04
11,22
11,20
02,04
01,14
12,14
31,45
20,33
20,36
01,02
02,02
03,06
03,05
03,06
04,07
02,04
08,14
08,15
03,05
03,06
03,06

5 HOURS BEFORE HW DOVER

N

Shetland Islands

Orkney Islands

Inverness

Perth

Edinburgh

Glasgow

Kirkcudbright

Larne

Hebrides

Slack

03,06
05,09
05,09
03,06
07,13 09,17
10,18
04,07
03,05
03,06
04,07
04,07
04,08
07,12
02,04
03,06
03,06
02,05
04,07
03,06
09,22
04,09
03,07
01,02
01,04
02,05
02,05
02,04
06,11
05,10
06,11
12,20
25,36
24,34
10,10
04,10
01,02
01,03
03,07
02,03
06,10
02,04
03,06
02,03

SCOTLAND

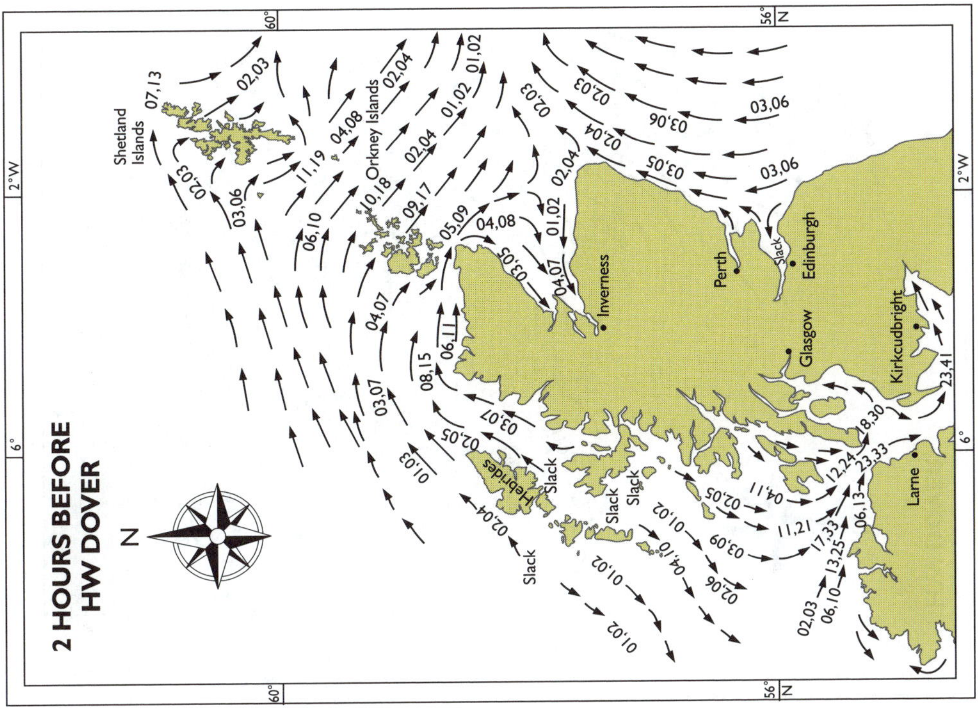

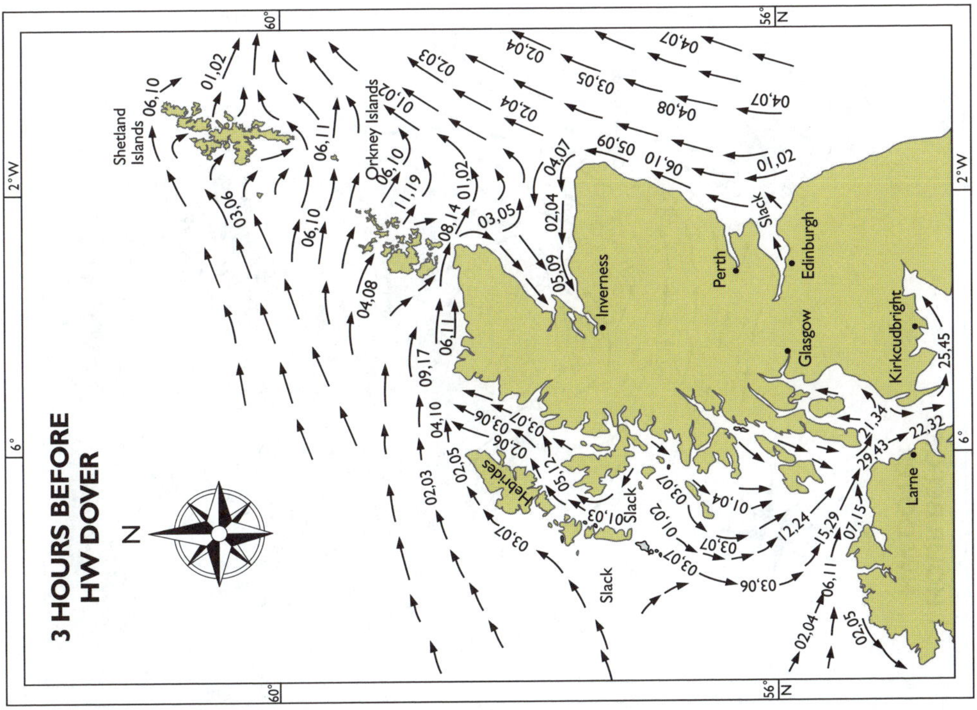

2 HOURS BEFORE HW DOVER

N

Shetland Islands 07,13

02,03
02,03
03,06
11,19 04,08
06,10 10,18 Orkney Islands 02,04 01,02 01,02
09,17 02,04
05,09 02,04
04,08 01,02 02,03 02,03
04,07 01,02 02,04 03,06 03,06
03,05 02,04 03,05
Inverness 04,07 03,06
Perth Slack Edinburgh
06,11
08,15
03,07
02,05 03,07
01,03 Slack Hebrides Slack Glasgow
02,04 Slack Slack 02,05 04,11 Kirkcudbright 23,41
01,02 03,09 11,21 18,30
Slack 02,06 01,02 04,10 17,33 12,24 23,33
01,02 13,25 06,13 Larne
02,03 06,10
01,02

3 HOURS BEFORE HW DOVER

N

Shetland Islands 06,10

01,02
06,11
03,06 06,10 06,11
04,08 11,19 Orkney Islands 01,02
06,10
08,14 01,02
03,05
02,04 04,07 02,03 02,04 04,07
05,09 04,07
06,10 03,05
05,09 04,08 04,07
02,04 01,02
Inverness 06,10
Perth Slack Edinburgh
09,17
06,11
04,10
02,03 02,05 03,06
03,07 03,07 Slack
Hebrides 03,07 Glasgow
05,12 01,04 Kirkcudbright 25,45
03,07 01,02 1,34
03,07 03,01 12,24 29,43 22,32
Slack 15,29 Larne
03,06 07,15
02,04 06,11
02,05

TIDES

179

SCOTLAND

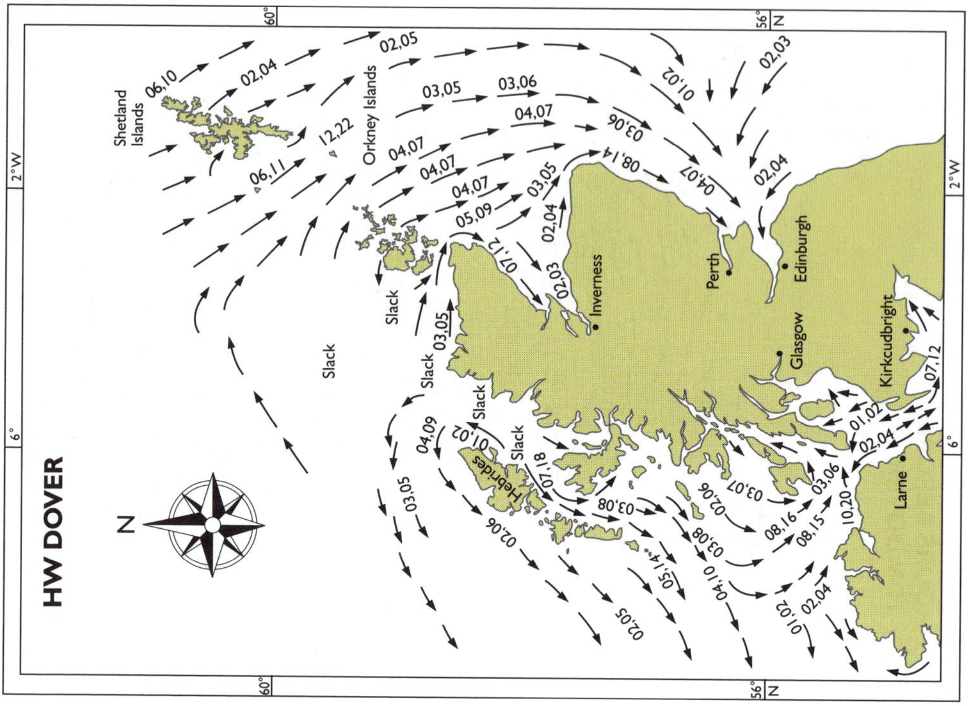

HW DOVER

1 HOUR BEFORE
HW DOVER

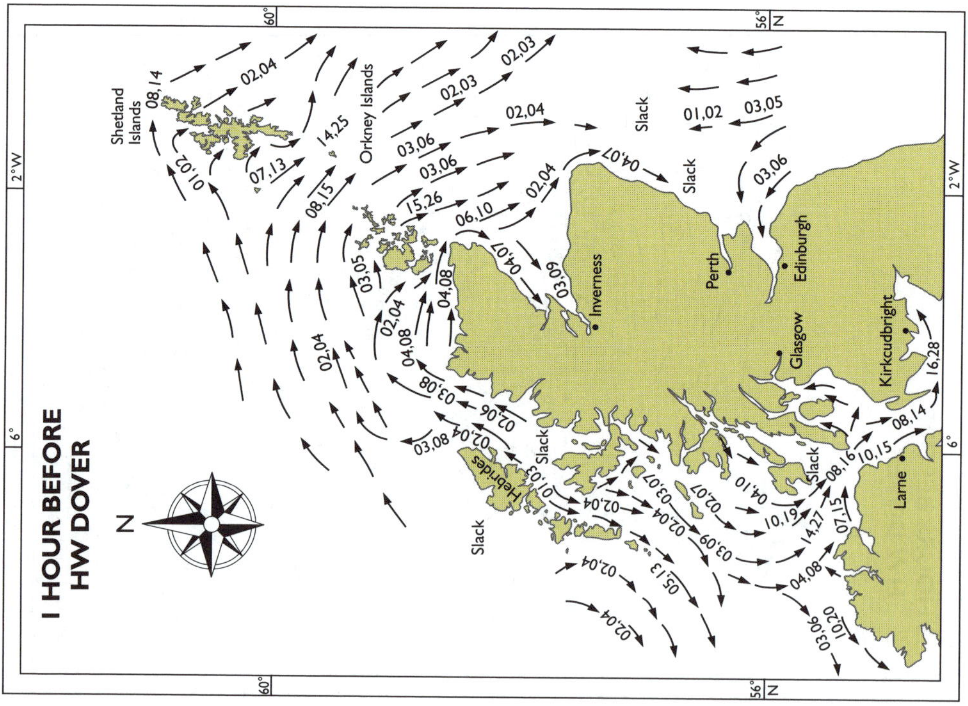

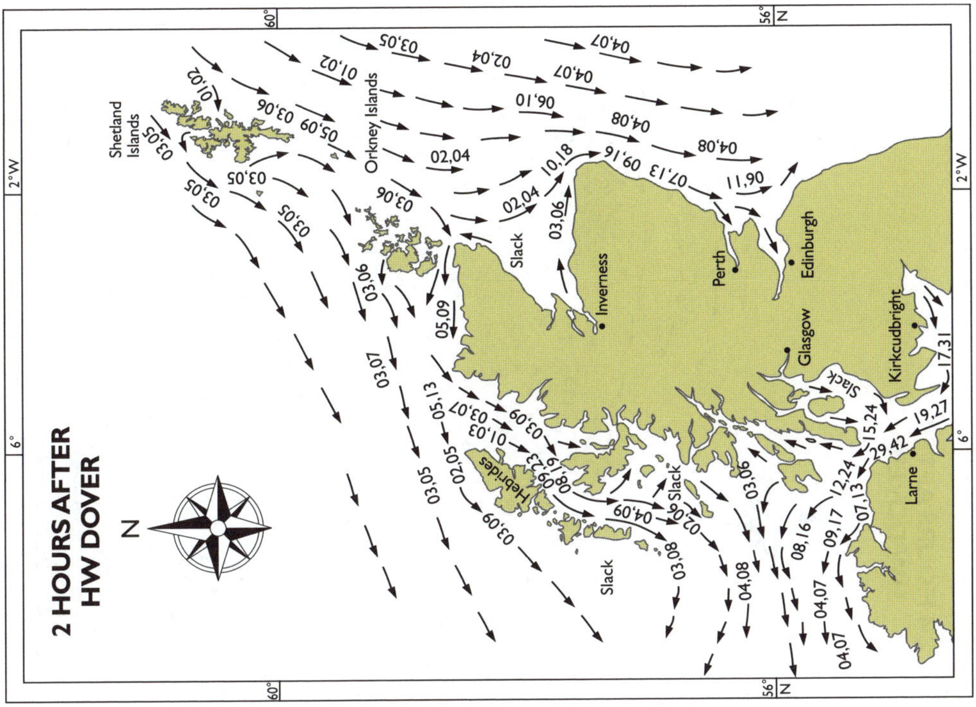

2 HOURS AFTER HW DOVER

N

Shetland Islands

Orkney Islands

Hebrides

Slack

Inverness

Perth

Edinburgh

Glasgow

Slack

Kirkcudbright

Larne

01,02
03,05
03,06
05,09
03,05
03,05
03,05
01,02
03,05
03,06
03,06
03,07
03,05
02,04
02,04
02,05
01,03
03,07
03,09
03,08
04,09
03,06
04,08
05,13
08,19
08,23
03,09
02,04
03,06
10,18
09,16
07,13
11,90
04,08
04,08
06,10
02,04
02,04
04,07
04,07
04,07
04,07
04,07
04,07
08,16
09,17
07,13
12,24
15,24
19,27
29,42
17,31

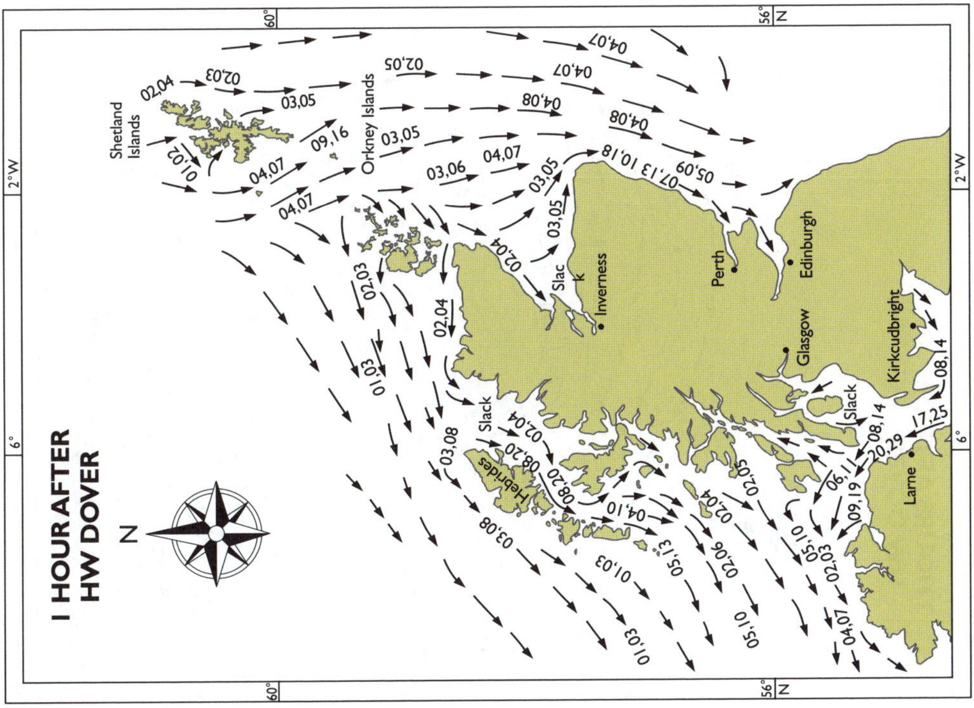

1 HOUR AFTER HW DOVER

N

Shetland Islands

Orkney Islands

Hebrides

Slack

Inverness

Perth

Edinburgh

Glasgow

Slack

Kirkcudbright

Larne

02,04
02,03
03,05
09,16
01,02
04,07
04,07
03,05
03,05
03,06
04,07
02,03
02,04
03,10
03,08
08,20
08,20
02,04
01,03
03,08
05,13
04,10
02,04
02,05
03,05
03,05
02,04
04,08
05,09
07,13
10,18
04,07
04,07
02,05
05,10
01,10
01,03
04,07
02,03
09,19
06,11
08,14
08,14
20,29
17,25
08,14
01,03
03,06

TIDES

181

SCOTLAND

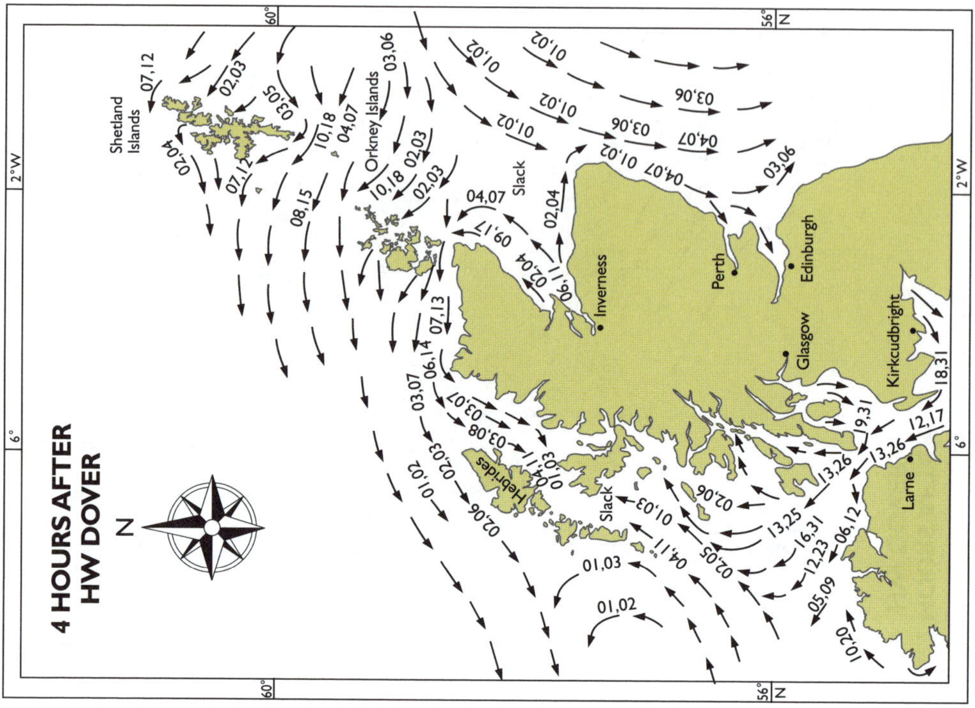

4 HOURS AFTER HW DOVER

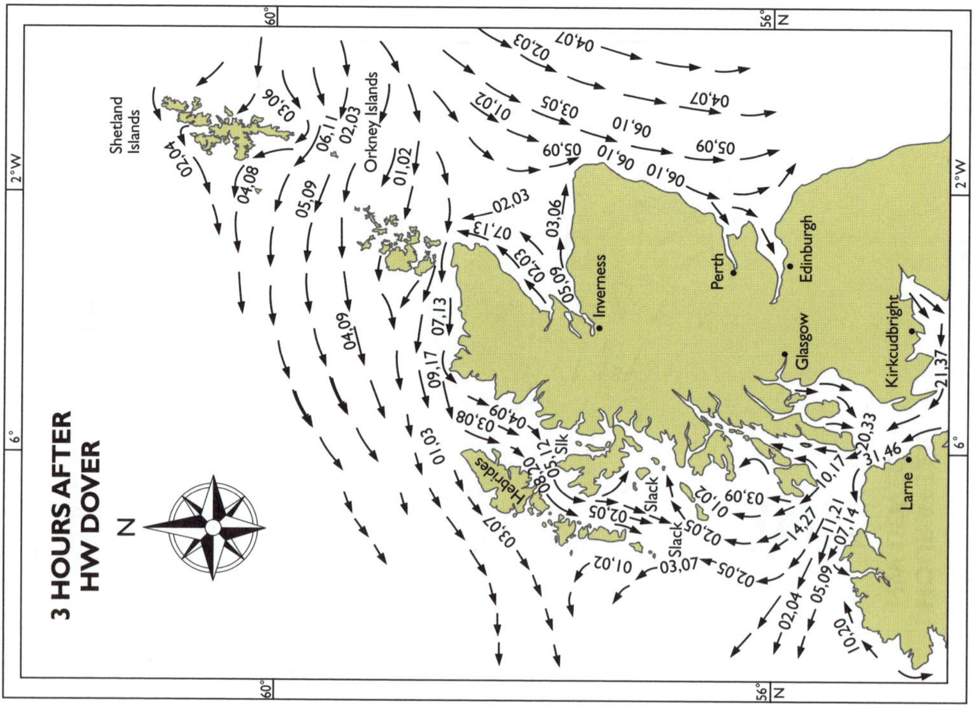

3 HOURS AFTER HW DOVER

SCOTLAND

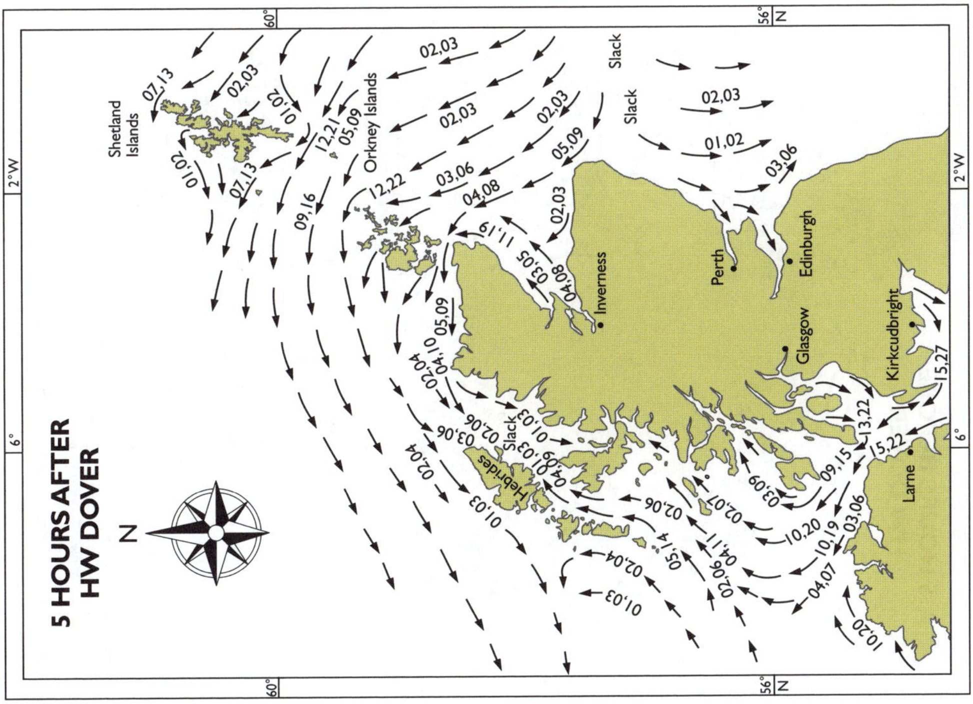

5 HOURS AFTER HW DOVER
N
Shetland Islands
Orkney Islands
Hebrides
Inverness
Perth
Edinburgh
Glasgow
Kirkcudbright
Larne
Slack
60°
56° N
6°
2° W

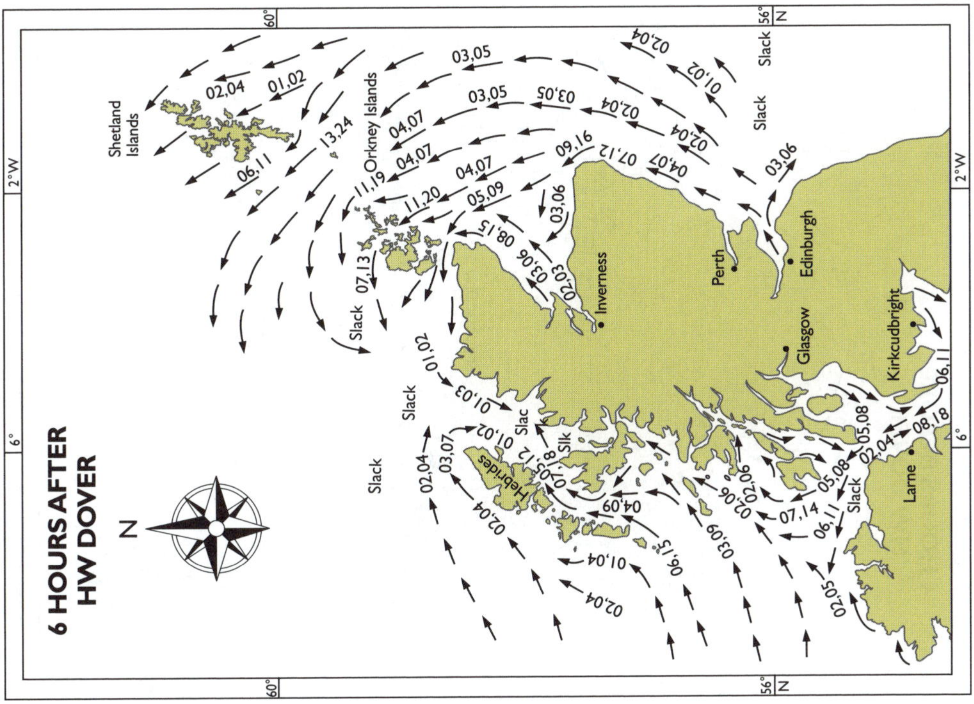

6 HOURS AFTER HW DOVER
N
Shetland Islands
Orkney Islands
Hebrides
Inverness
Perth
Edinburgh
Glasgow
Kirkcudbright
Larne
Slack
60°
56° N
6°
2° W

TIDES

WEST UK AND IRELAND

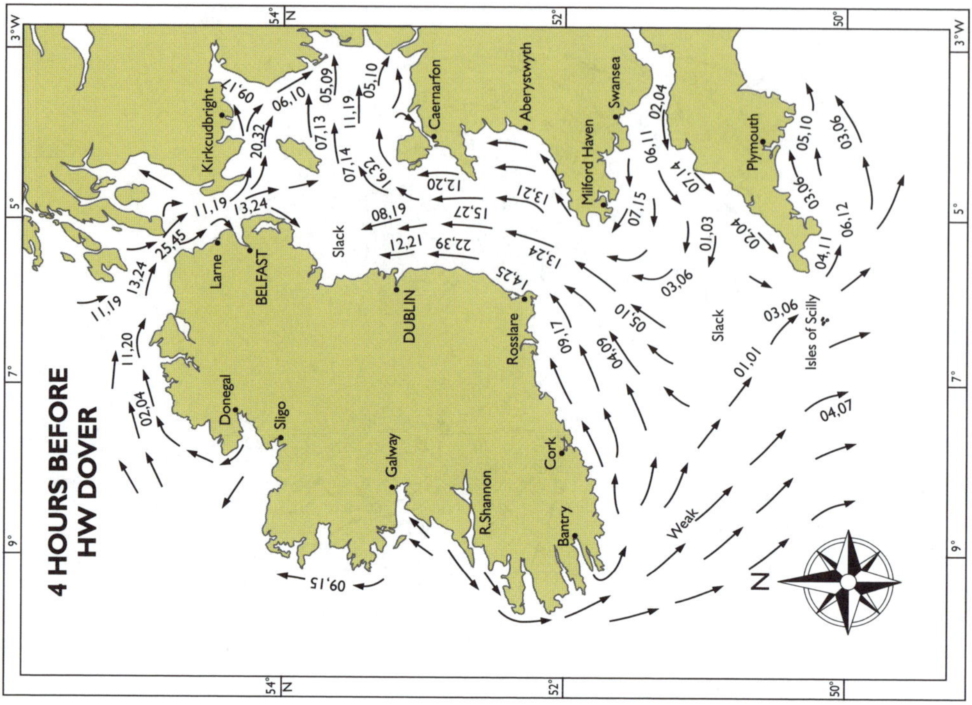

4 HOURS BEFORE HW DOVER

Kirkcudbright, Caernarfon, Aberystwyth, Swansea, Milford Haven, Plymouth, Larne, BELFAST, DUBLIN, Rosslare, Donegal, Sligo, Galway, R.Shannon, Cork, Bantry, Isles of Scilly

Slack, Slack, Weak

N

5 HOURS BEFORE HW DOVER

Kirkcudbright, Caernarfon, Aberystwyth, Swansea, Milford Haven, Plymouth, Larne, BELFAST, DUBLIN, Rosslare, Donegal, Sligo, Galway, R.Shannon, Cork, Bantry, Isles of Scilly

Slack, Weak

N

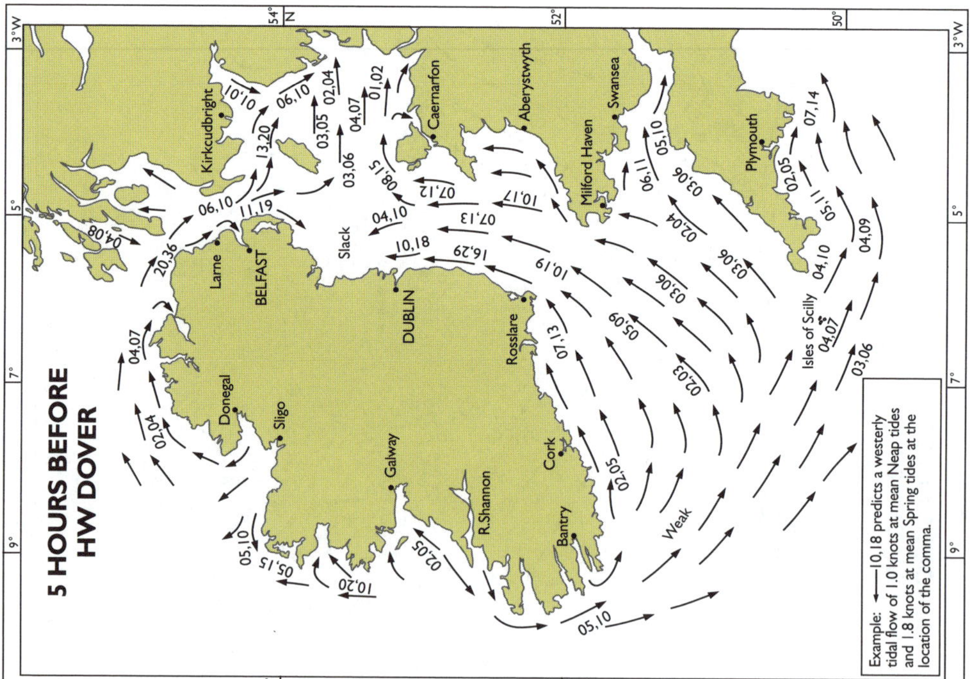

Example: ——— 10,18 predicts a westerly tidal flow of 1.0 knots at mean Neap tides and 1.8 knots at mean Spring tides at the location of the comma.

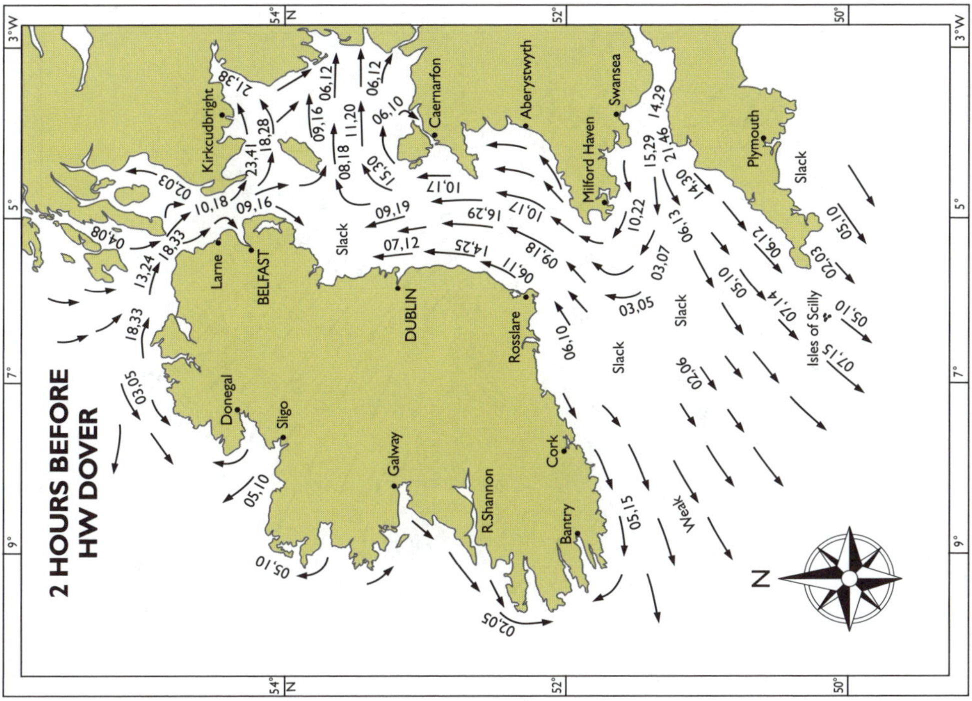

2 HOURS BEFORE HW DOVER

Kirkcudbright, Larne, BELFAST, Donegal, Sligo, Galway, R.Shannon, Bantry, Cork, DUBLIN, Rosslare, Caernarfon, Aberystwyth, Milford Haven, Swansea, Plymouth, Isles of Scilly

Slack, Weak

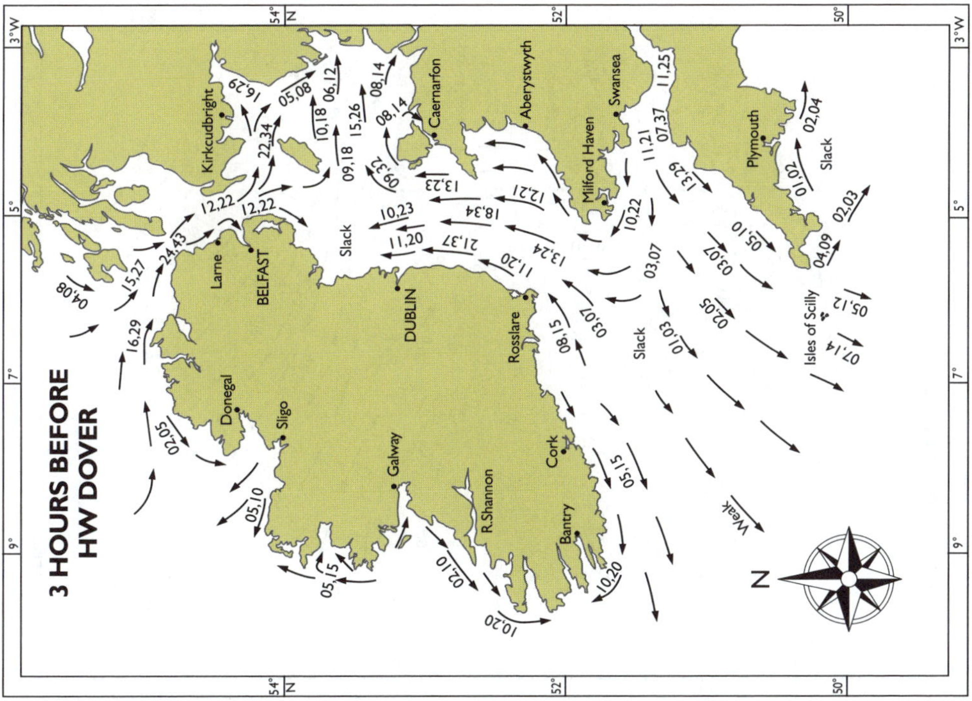

3 HOURS BEFORE HW DOVER

Kirkcudbright, Larne, BELFAST, Donegal, Sligo, Galway, R.Shannon, Bantry, Cork, DUBLIN, Rosslare, Caernarfon, Aberystwyth, Milford Haven, Swansea, Plymouth, Isles of Scilly

Slack, Weak

WEST UK AND IRELAND

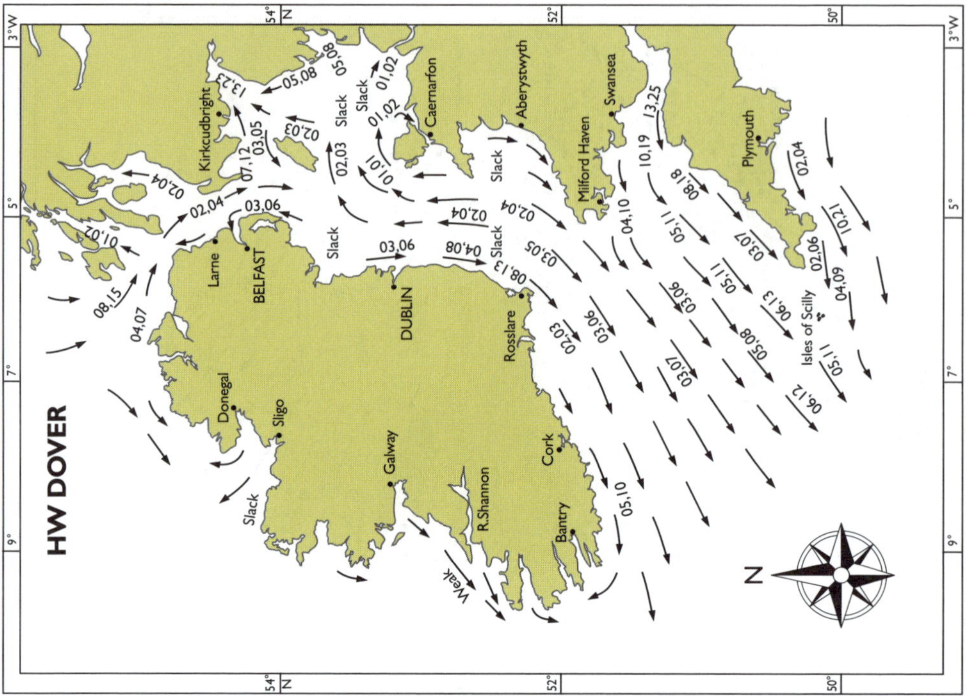

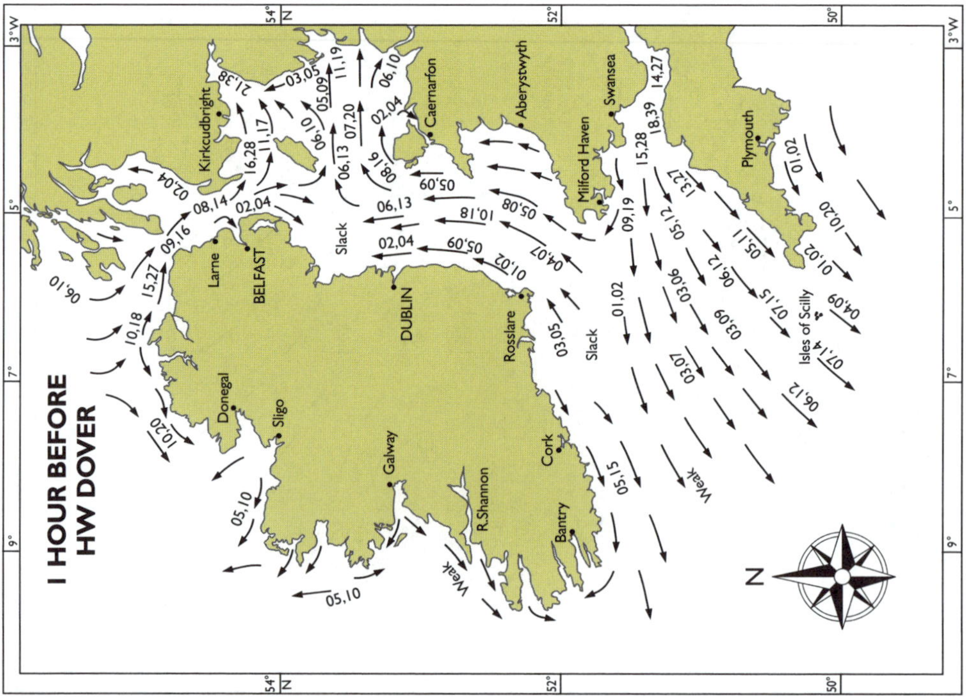

HW DOVER

Kirkcudbright 13.23, 05.08, 05.08, 03.05, 07.12, 02.03, 02.03, Slack, Slack, 01.02, Caernarfon, Aberystwyth, Swansea, 13.25, Milford Haven, 10.19, 08.18, Plymouth, 02.04, Slack, 02.04, 01.02, 10.01, Slack, 02.04, 04.10, 05.10, 11.07, 02.04, 03.06, 03.05, 03.07, Isles of Scilly, 04.09, Larne, BELFAST, Slack, 03.06, 04.08, Slack, 08.13, 03.07, 03.06, 06.13, 05.08, 06.12, DUBLIN, Rosslare, 02.03, 05.11, 02.04, 01.10, 02.04, 08.15, 04.07, Donegal, Sligo, Galway, R.Shannon, Cork, Bantry, 05.10, Slack, Weak

N

1 HOUR BEFORE HW DOVER

Kirkcudbright 21.38, 03.05, 05.09, 11.19, 06.10, 16.28, 11.17, 06.10, 07.20, 02.04, Caernarfon, Aberystwyth, Swansea, 14.27, 18.39, 15.28, Milford Haven, 09.19, Plymouth, 01.02, Larne, 08.14, 02.04, 06.13, 07.20, 09.16, 05.09, 05.08, 10.18, 05.12, 13.27, 05.11, 01.02, BELFAST, Slack, 02.04, 05.09, 04.07, 01.02, 03.05, 02.04, 09.16, 15.27, 06.10, 01.02, Slack, 01.02, 06.09, 03.06, 05.10, 07.15, Isles of Scilly, 04.09, 10.18, DUBLIN, Rosslare, 03.05, 03.07, 06.12, 07.14, 10.20, Donegal, Sligo, Galway, R.Shannon, Cork, Bantry, 05.15, Weak, 05.10, Weak, 05.10

N

2 HOURS AFTER HW DOVER

Kirkcudbright
Caernarfon
Aberystwyth
Swansea
Milford Haven
Plymouth
Slac
Larne
BELFAST
Slack
DUBLIN
Rosslare
Isles of Scilly
Donegal
Sligo
Galway
Cork
R.Shannon
Bantry
Slack
Weak

N

1 HOUR AFTER HW DOVER

Kirkcudbright
Caernarfon
Aberystwyth
Swansea
Milford Haven
Plymouth
Slack
Larne
BELFAST
Slack
DUBLIN
Rosslare
Isles of Scilly
Donegal
Sligo
Galway
Cork
R.Shannon
Bantry

N

TIDES

187

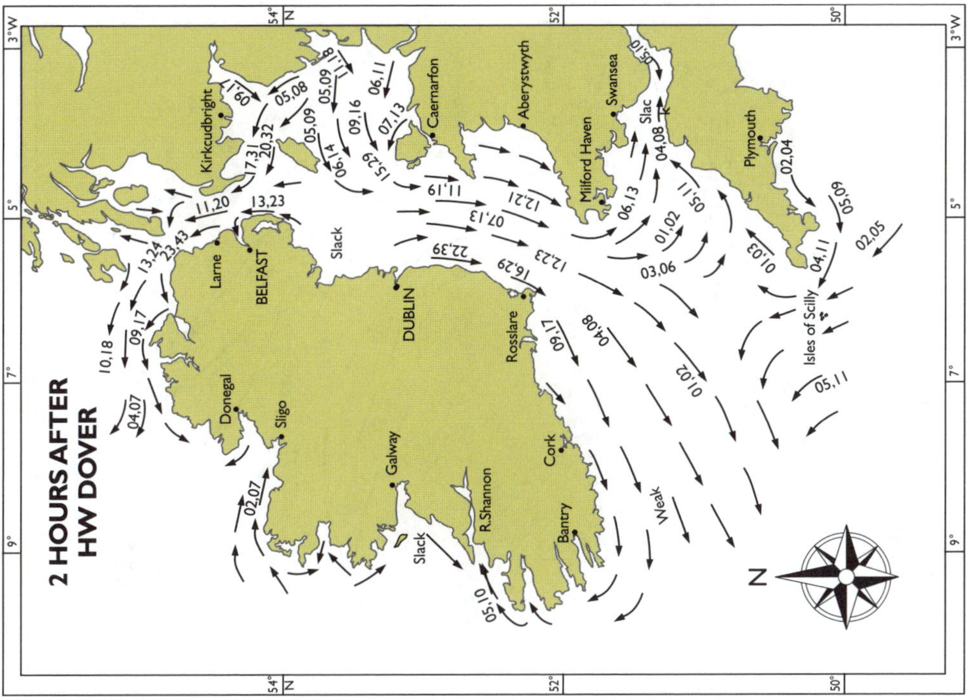

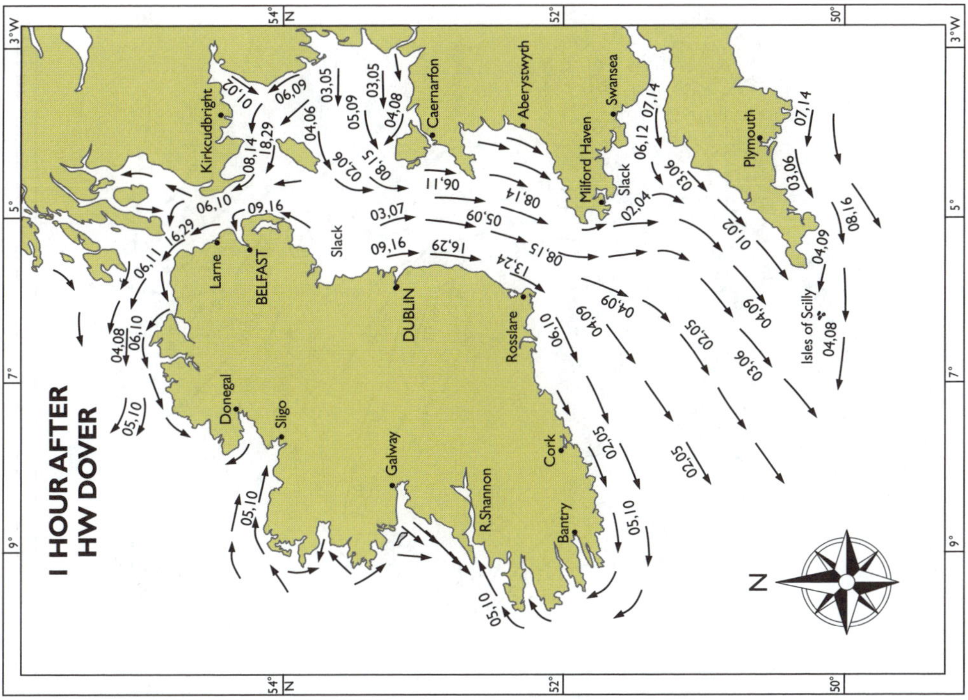

WEST UK AND IRELAND

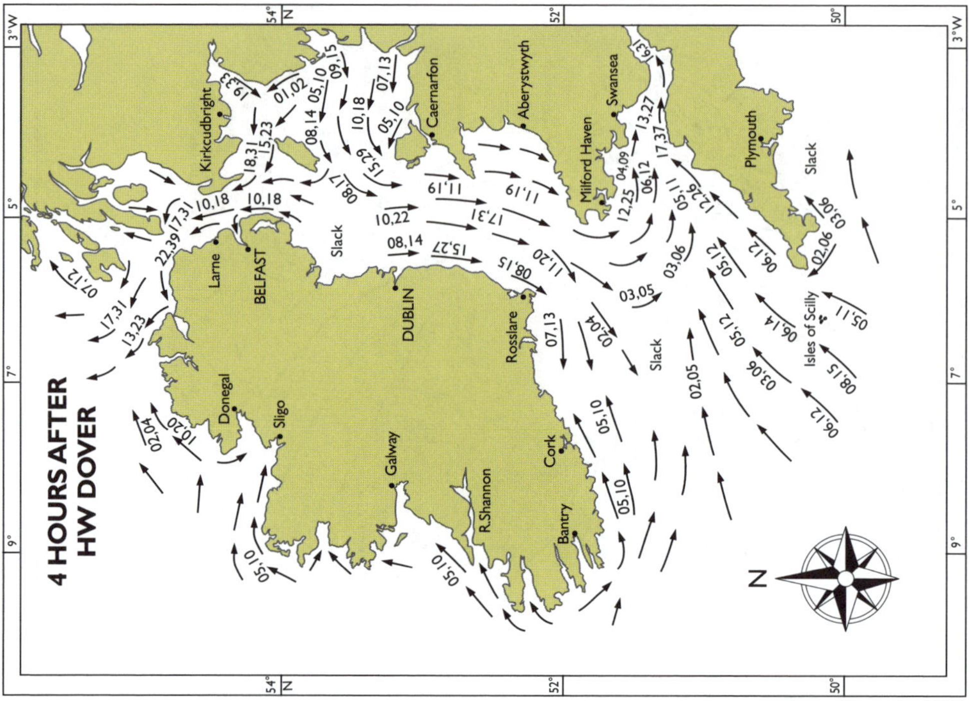

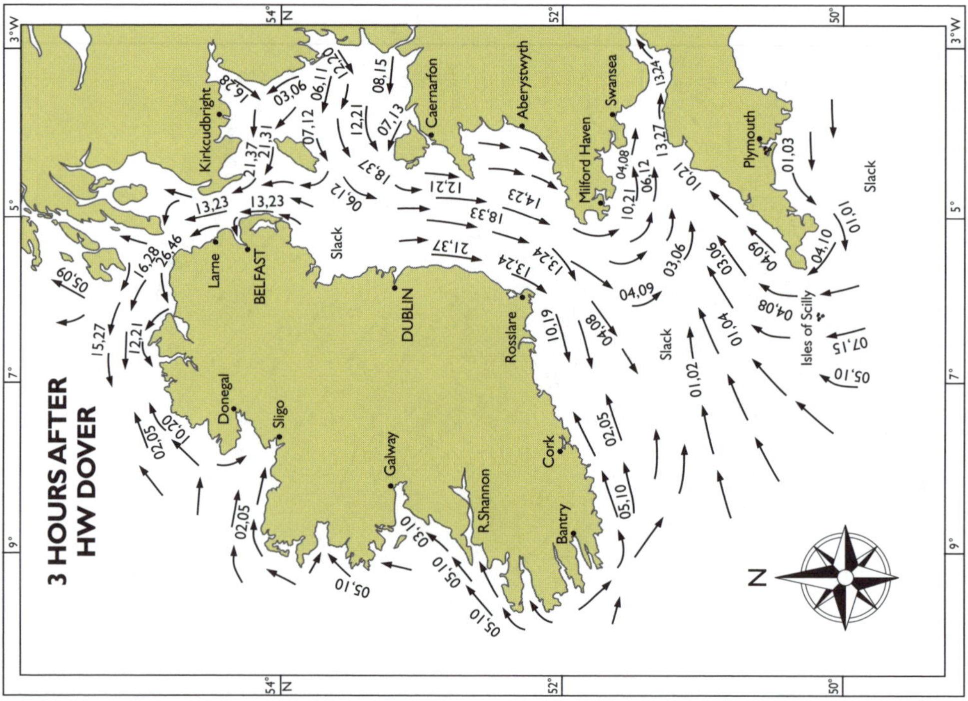

4 HOURS AFTER HW DOVER

Kirkcudbright, Larne, BELFAST, Caernarfon, Aberystwyth, Milford Haven, Swansea, Plymouth, Isles of Scilly, Slack, DUBLIN, Rosslare, Donegal, Sligo, Galway, R.Shannon, Cork, Bantry

3 HOURS AFTER HW DOVER

Kirkcudbright, Larne, BELFAST, Caernarfon, Aberystwyth, Milford Haven, Swansea, Plymouth, Isles of Scilly, Slack, DUBLIN, Rosslare, Donegal, Sligo, Galway, R.Shannon, Cork, Bantry

WEST UK AND IRELAND

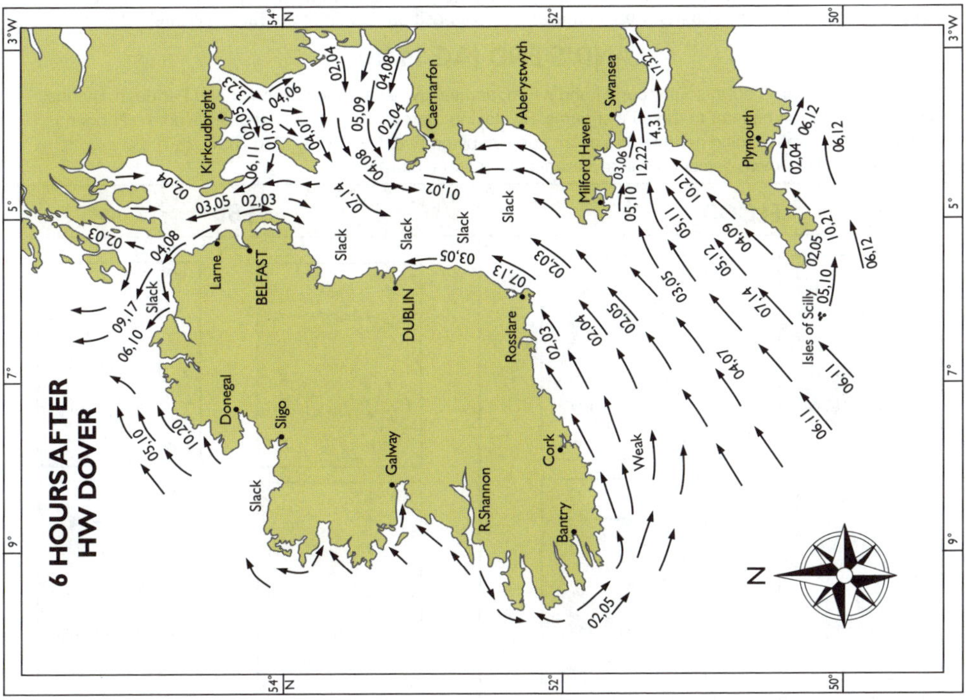

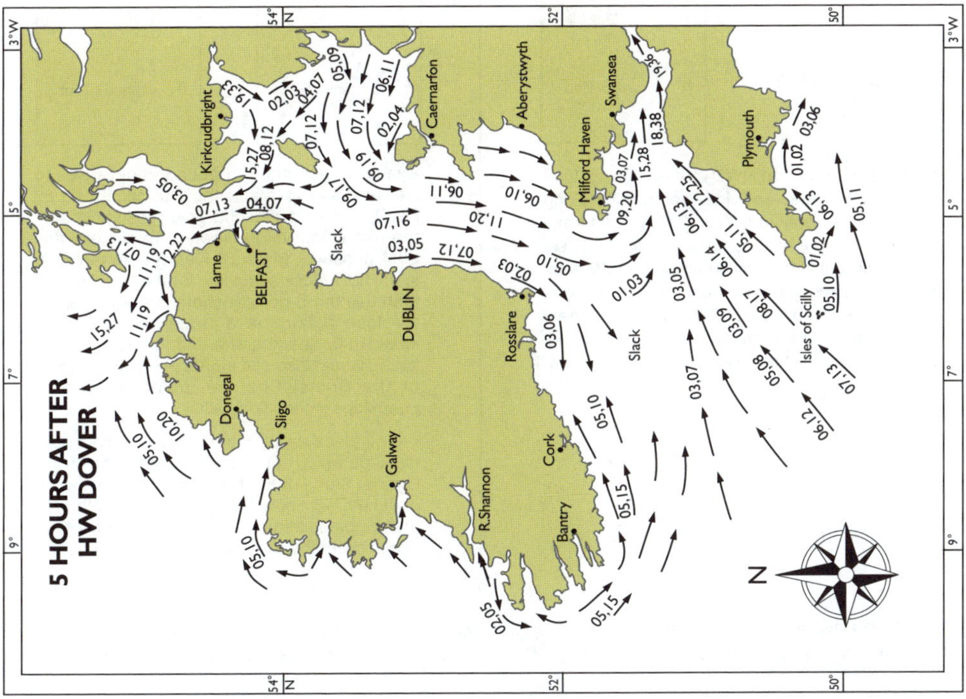

6 HOURS AFTER HW DOVER

5 HOURS AFTER HW DOVER

TIDAL GATES - SOUTHERN ENGLAND

A guide to the time of tide turn at tidal gates, the approximate maximum strength of the tidal flow (spring rates shown - neaps are approximately 60% of these), and the position and timing of races, counter tides, etc.

LAND'S END (AC 1148)

Tidal streams set hard north/south round Land's End, and east/west around Gwennap and Pendeen. But the inshore currents run counter to the tidal streams. By staying close inshore, this tidal gate favours a N-bound passage. With careful timing nearly 9½hrs of fair tide can be carried, from HWD−3 to HWD+5. The chartlets, referenced to HW Dover, depict both tidal streams and inshore currents.

FLOOD	EBB

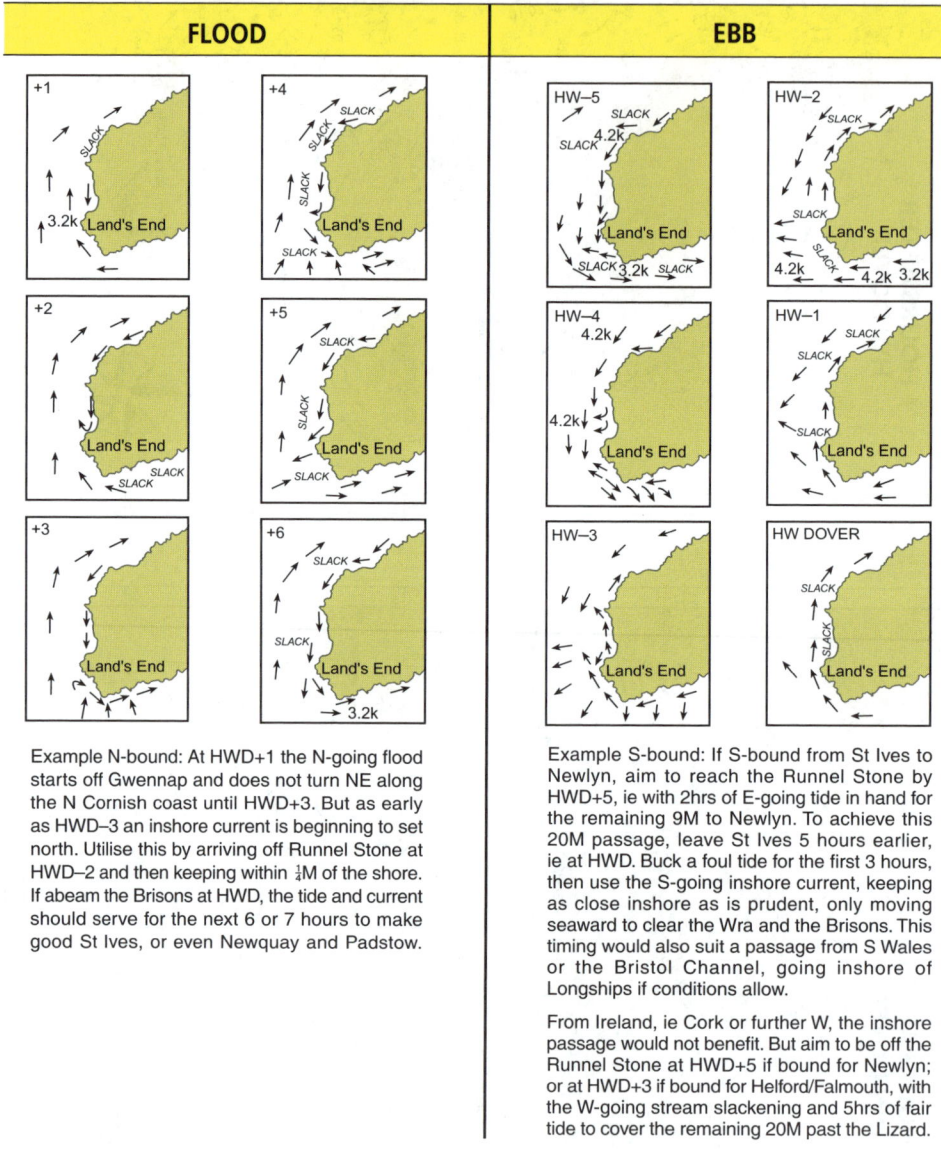

Example N-bound: At HWD+1 the N-going flood starts off Gwennap and does not turn NE along the N Cornish coast until HWD+3. But as early as HWD−3 an inshore current is beginning to set north. Utilise this by arriving off Runnel Stone at HWD−2 and then keeping within ¼M of the shore. If abeam the Brisons at HWD, the tide and current should serve for the next 6 or 7 hours to make good St Ives, or even Newquay and Padstow.

Example S-bound: If S-bound from St Ives to Newlyn, aim to reach the Runnel Stone by HWD+5, ie with 2hrs of E-going tide in hand for the remaining 9M to Newlyn. To achieve this 20M passage, leave St Ives 5 hours earlier, ie at HWD. Buck a foul tide for the first 3 hours, then use the S-going inshore current, keeping as close inshore as is prudent, only moving seaward to clear the Wra and the Brisons. This timing would also suit a passage from S Wales or the Bristol Channel, going inshore of Longships if conditions allow.

From Ireland, ie Cork or further W, the inshore passage would not benefit. But aim to be off the Runnel Stone at HWD+5 if bound for Newlyn; or at HWD+3 if bound for Helford/Falmouth, with the W-going stream slackening and 5hrs of fair tide to cover the remaining 20M past the Lizard.

With acknowledgements to the Royal Cruising Club Pilotage Foundation for their kind permission to use the tidal stream chartlets and text written by Hugh Davies, as first published in Yachting Monthly *magazine.*

TIDAL GATES - SOUTHERN ENGLAND

A guide to the time of tide turn at tidal gates, the approximate maximum strength of the tidal flow (spring rates shown - neaps are approximately 60% of these), and the position and timing of races, counter tides, etc.

FLOOD	EBB

THE LIZARD (AC 777, 2345)

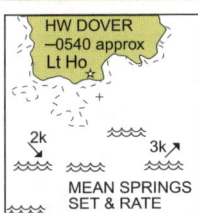 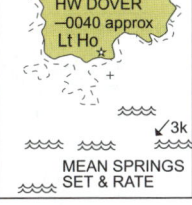

Drying rocks lie approx 5 cables S of the Lizard lt ho and extend westwards. 49°57'N is about as far N as yachts may safely pass inshore of the Race, which extends 2-3M to seaward of these rocks. Race conditions may also exist SE of the Lizard with short, heavy seas in westerlies. If passing S of the Race, route via 49°55'N 05°13'W to clear the worst of the Race.

Inshore the E-going Channel flood, 2kn max @ springs, begins at HW Dover +0145; and outside the Race at approx HWD +0300.	Inshore the W-going Channel ebb, 3kn max @ springs, begins at HW Dover –0345; and outside the Race at HWD –0240.

START POINT (AC 1634)

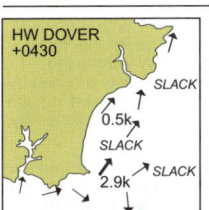 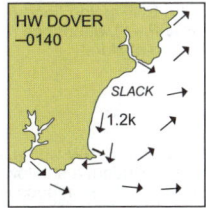

Start Pt, and to a lesser extent Prawle Pt (3.3M WSW), can be slow to round when W-bound with a fair tide against a W'ly wind raising a bad sea. Drying rocks extend 3 cables SSE of the lt ho and a Race may extend up to 1.7M ESE and 1.0M S of the lt ho. It is safe to pass between the Race and the rocks, but in bad weather wiser to go outside the Race. The Skerries Bank (least depth 2.1m) lies 8 cables NE of Start Pt. On both the flood and the ebb back eddies form between Start Pt and Hallsands, 1M NW.

The NE-going Channel flood, 3.1kn max @ springs, begins at HW Dover +0430.	The SW-going Channel ebb, 2.2kn max @ springs, begins at HW Dover –0140, but an hour earlier it is possible to round Start Pt close inshore using the back eddy.

PORTLAND (AC 2255)

A dangerous Race forms between 200 metres and 2 miles south of Portland Bill. The Race shifts westward on the W-going stream and eastward on the E-going stream. In the latter case it is not advisable to pass between the Race and the Shambles Bank. Study carefully the hourly tidal stream chartlets on pp.184-185 or in NP 257. The Race may be avoided either by passing to seaward of it, ie 3-5M south of the Bill and east of the Shambles; or by using the inshore passage – if conditions suit.

Seaward of the Race.

E-bound: The Channel flood sets east from HW Dover +6 to HWD –1.	W-bound: The ebb sets west from HW Dover to HWD +5½.

The inshore passage, (a narrow stretch of relatively smooth water between the Bill and the Race), should be started, in either direction, from a position 2M north of the Bill, keeping close inshore to the Portland peninsula. It should not be used at night (due to pot floats), nor in winds >F4/5, nor at springs especially with wind against tide.

If E-bound via the inshore passage, slackish water or a fair stream occurs around the Bill from HW Portland –3 to +1. The passage across Lyme Bay should be specifically timed to meet this critical window.	W-bound, similar conditions occur from HW Portland +4 to –6. The W-bound timing is easy if you have started from Weymouth, Portland harbour or Lulworth Cove.

ST ALBAN'S HEAD (AC 2610)

A sometimes vicious Race forms over St Alban's Ledge, a rocky dorsal ridge (least depth 8.5m) which extends approx 4M SW from St Alban's Head. Three yellow naval target buoys (DZ A, B and C) straddle the middle and outer sections, but are only occasionally used. In settled weather and at neaps the Race may be barely perceptible in which case it can be crossed with impunity. Avoid it either by keeping to seaward via 50°31'.40N 02°07'.80W; or by using the narrow inshore passage at the foot of St Alban's Head.

Based on a position 1M S of St Alban's Head, the tidal stream windows are:

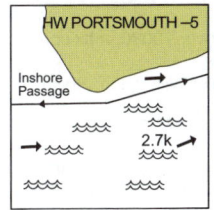 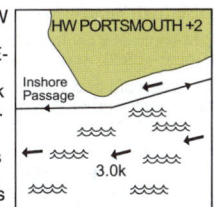

ESE-going stream starts at HW Portsmouth +0530. Spring rates are the same, max 4kn. Along the W side of St Alban's Head the stream runs almost continuously SE due to a back eddy.	WNW-going stream starts at HW Portsmouth. Overfalls extend 2.5M further SW than on the E-going stream and are more dangerous to small craft. Slack water lasts barely half an hour.

The inshore passage lies as close to the foot of St Alban's Head as feels comfortable. It may be hard to see the width of clear water in the inshore passage until committed to it, but except in onshore gales when it is better to stay offshore, the passage will be swiftly made with only a few, if any, overfalls. The NCI station on the Head (☎ 01929 439220) may advise on conditions.

TIDES

191

TIDAL GATES - SOUTHERN ENGLAND

A guide to the time of tide turn at tidal gates, the approximate maximum strength of the tidal flow (spring rates shown - neaps are approximately 60% of these), and the position and timing of races, counter tides, etc.

FLOOD	EBB

THE NEEDLES CHANNEL (AC 2035)

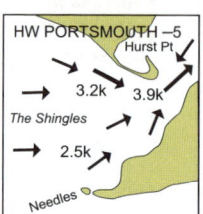

The Needles Channel lies between the SW Shingles PHM buoy and the Bridge WCM buoy. Once through this narrow section the channel widens with the Island shore to starboard and the long, drying 1.2m, Shingles bank to port. Abeam Hurst Castle the channel again narrows (assisted by The Trap, a shoal spit south of Hurst Castle) before opening out into the west Solent.

Study carefully the hourly tidal stream chartlets for the Isle of Wight on pp.186-191 and the values shown on AC 2035 at tidal diamonds B, C, D and E.

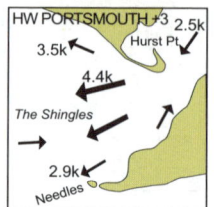

The ENE-going flood runs from HW Portsmouth +5 until HW P −1½, at springs reaching 3.1kn at The Bridge and 3.9kn at Hurst.	The WSW-going ebb runs from HW P −1 until HW P +4½, reaching 4.4kn at Hurst and 3.4kn at The Bridge, both spring rates. The ebb sets strongly WSW across the Shingles which with adequate rise is routinely crossed by racing yachts; but cruisers should stay clear even in calm conditions when any swell causes the sea to break heavily.

Prevailing W/SW winds, even if only F4, against the ebb raise dangerous breaking seas in the Needles Channel and at The Bridge, a shallow ridge extending 9 cables west from the Needles light. Worst conditions are often found just after LW slack. In such conditions it is safer to go via the North Channel to Hurst. In W/SW gales avoid the Needles altogether by sheltering at Poole or going east-about via Nab Tower.

ON PASSAGE UP CHANNEL

The following 3 tidal gates (The Looe, Beachy Head and Dungeness) are components in the tidal conveyor belt which, if stepped onto at the outset, can enable a fastish yacht to carry a fair tide for 88M from Selsey Bill to Dover. Go through the Looe at slackish water, HW Portsmouth +4½ (HW Dover +5). Based on a mean SOG of 7 knots, Beachy Head will be passed at HW D −1, Dungeness at HW D +3 and Dover at HW +5½, only bucking the first of the ebb in the last hour. A faster boat could make Ramsgate. The down-Channel passage is less rewarding and many yachts will pause at Brighton.

THE LOOE (AC 2045, 1652)

This channel is little shorter than the detour south of the Owers, but is much used by yachts on passage from/to points east of the Solent. Although adequately lit, it is best not attempted at night due to many lobster floats; nor in onshore gales as searoom is limited by extensive shoals on which the sea breaks.

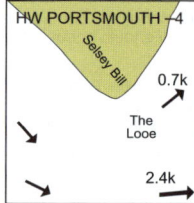

The E-going flood runs from HW Portsmouth +4½ (HW Dover +5) until HW P −1½ (HW D −1), at springs reaching 2.4kn near the Boulder and Street light buoys which mark its narrow western end; they may be hard to see in other than good visibility. Max neap rate is 1.2kn.	The W-going ebb runs from HW P −1½ (HW D −1) until HW P +4½ (HW D +5), at springs reaching 2.6kn near Boulder and Street. Max neap rate is 1.3kn.

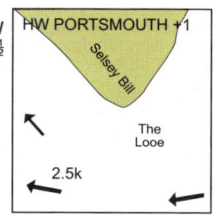

At the wider eastern end of the channel (near E Borough Head buoy) rates are greatly reduced.

BEACHY HEAD (AC 1652, 536)

Stay at least 5 cables to seaward of the towering chalk cliffs to avoid isolated boulders and rocky, part-drying ridges such as Head Ledge. The lt ho stands on a drying rock ledge. Close inshore many fishing floats are a trap for the unwary. In bad weather stay 2M offshore to avoid overfalls caused by a ridge of uneven ground which extends 1M SSE from Beachy Head.

2M south of Beachy Head the E-going flood starts at HW Dover +0530, max spring rate 2.6kn.	The W-going ebb starts at HW Dover +0030, max spring rate 2.0kn.

Between 5M and 7M east of Beachy Head avoid breakers and eddies caused by the Horse of Willingdon, Royal Sovereign and other shoals.

DUNGENESS (AC 536, 1892)

Tidal stream atlases: Dungeness is on the east and west edges respectively of NP 250 (English Channel) and NP 233 (Dover Strait). The nearest tidal stream diamond (2.2M SE of Dungeness) is 'H' on AC 536 and 'B' on AC 1892; their positions and values are the same.

The NE-going flood starts at HW Dover −0100, max spring rate 1.9kn.	The SW-going ebb starts at HW Dover +0430, max spring rate 2.1kn.

TIDAL GATES - NORTH EAST SCOTLAND

A guide to the time of tide turn at tidal gates, and in straits and estuaries, showing the approximate strength of the tidal flow (spring rates shown - neaps are approximately 60% of these), and the position and timing of races, counter tides etc.

FLOOD	EBB

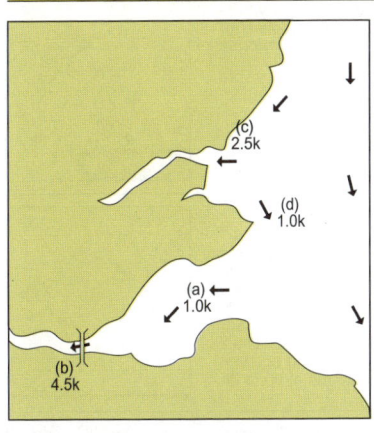
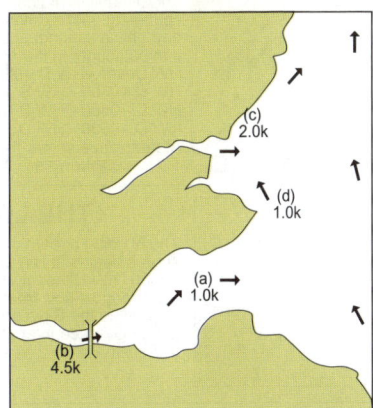

FIRTHS of FORTH (AC 175) & TAY (AC 1481)

Tidal streams are quite weak in the outer part of the Firth, increasing as the narrows at islands and the bridges are approached.
Apart from the stream of the Tay, which attains 5 knots in most places, the coastwise tidal streams between Fife Ness and Arbroath are weak.

(a) Dover −0225 to Dover +0330
(b) Dover −0200 to Dover +0400
(c) Dover −0210 to Dover +0420
(d) Dover −0110 to Dover +0520

(a) Dover +0330 to Dover −0225
(b) Dover +0400 to Dover −0200
(c) Dover +0420 to Dover −0210
(d) Dover +0520 to Dover −0110

PASSAGES FROM FORTH & TAY

Northbound. Leave before HW (Dover +0400) to be at N Carr at Dover +0600. Bound from Forth to Tay aim to arrive at Abertay By at LW slack (Dover −0200).
Southbound. Leave before LW (Dover -0200) to be at Bass Rk at HW Dover. Similar timings if bound from Tay to Forth, leave late in ebb to pick up early flood off St Andrews to N Carr and into Forth.

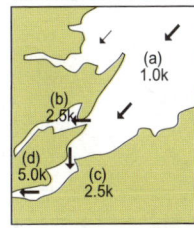
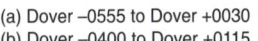
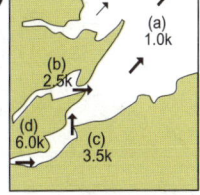

INVERNESS & CROMARTY FIRTHS (AC 1077)

Tidal streams in the Inverness Firth and approaches are not strong, except in the Cromarty Firth Narrows, the Fort George Narrows and the Kessock Road, including off the entrance to the Caledonian Canal.

(a) Dover −0555 to Dover +0030 | (a) Dover +0030 to Dover −0555
(b) Dover −0400 to Dover +0115 | (b) Dover +0115 to Dover −0400
(c) Dover −0400 to Dover −0220 | (c) Dover +0115 to Dover −0440
(d) Dover −0430 to Dover +0100 | (d) Dover −0130 to Dover +0545

PENTLAND FIRTH & ORKNEYS (AC 1954)

The tide flows strongly around and through the Orkney Islands. The Pentland Firth is a dangerous area for all craft, tidal flows reach 12 knots between Duncansby Head and S Ronaldsay. W of Dunnet Hd & Hoy is less violent. There is little tide within Scapa Flow.

(a) Dover −0500 to Dover +0100 | (a) Dover +0115 to Dover −0535
(b) Dover +0500 to Dover −0110 | (b) Dover −0110 to Dover +0050
(c) Dover −0530 to Dover +0040 | (c) Dover +0040 to Dover −0530

SHETLAND ISLANDS (AC 219)

The tidal flow around the Shetland Islands rotates as the cycle progresses. When the flood begins, at −0400 HW Dover, the tidal flow is to the E, at HW Dover it is S, at Dover +0300 it is W, and at −0600 Dover it is N.

(a) Dover −0410 to Dover +0020 | (a) Dover +0050 to Dover −0410
(b) Dover −0400 to Dover +0030 | (b) Dover +0130 to Dover −0500
(c) Dover −0530 to Dover +0100 | (c) Dover +0100 to Dover −0530
(d) Dover −0400 to Dover −0200 | (d) Dover +0200 to Dover +0500

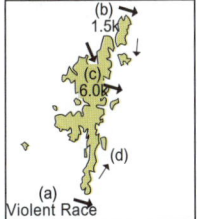
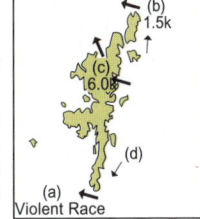

TIDES

TIDAL GATES - NORTH WEST SCOTLAND

A guide to the time of tide turn at tidal gates, the approximate maximum strength of the tidal flow (spring rates shown - neaps are approximately 60% of these), and the position and timing of races, counter tides, etc.

FLOOD	EBB

SOUND OF HARRIS (AC 2642)

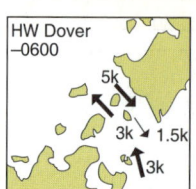

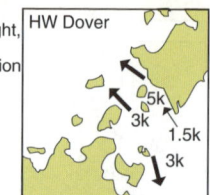

The behaviour of tidal streams in the Sd of Harris varies from day to night, springs to neaps, and winter to summer. The following data applies to daylight, in summer at spring tides in the Cope Channel. Further information can be sought in the Admiralty West of Scotland Pilot.
HW Dover - HW D +0200: SE stream.
HW D +0300 - HW D +0600: Incoming stream from both ends.
HW D −0600 - HW D −0500: NW stream.
HW D −0500 - HW Dover: Outgoing stream from both ends.
At neaps in summer the stream will run SE for most of the day.
Tide rates shown are the maxima likely to be encountered at any time.

THE LITTLE MINCH (AC 1795)

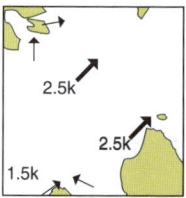

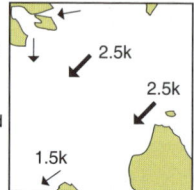

The N going stream on both shores begins at HW Dover +0430 (HW Ullapool -0345), with the strongest flow from mid channel to the Skye coast. There is a W going counter tide E of Vaternish Point.

The S going stream on both shores begins at HW Dover −0130 (HW Ullapool +0240), with the strongest flow from mid channel to the Skye coast. The E going stream in Sound of Scalpay runs at up to 2k.The E going flood and W going ebb in Sound of Scalpay run at up to 2k.

KYLE OF LOCHALSH & KYLERHEA (AC 2540)
NOTE: THESE STREAMS ARE SUBJECT TO VARIATION

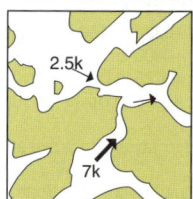

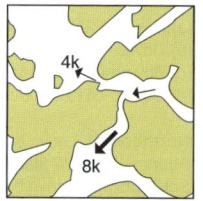

N going stream in Kyle Rhea begins HW Dover +0140 (HW Ullapool +0555) and runs for 6 hours. The E going stream in Kyle Akin begins (Sp) HW Dover +0350 (HW Ullapool −0415). (Nps) HW Dover −0415 (HW Ullapool).

S going stream in Kyle Rhea begins HW Dover -0415 (HW Ullapool) and runs for 6 hours. The W going stream in Kyle Akin begins (Sp) HW Dover −0015 (HW Ullapool +0400). (Nps) HW Dover +0140 (HW Ullapool +0555).

ARDNAMURCHAN POINT (AC 2171)

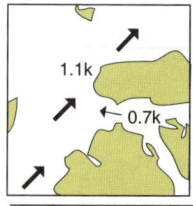

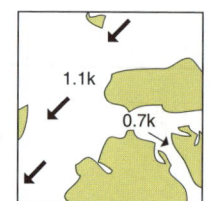

The N going stream off Ardnamurchan begins at HW Dover +0130 (HW Oban −0525). The E going stream in the Sound of Mull begins at HW Dover +0555 (HW Oban −0100).

The S going stream off Ardnamurchan begins at HW Dover −0430 (HW Oban +0100). The W going stream in the Sound of Mull begins at HW Dover −0130 (HW Oban +0400).

SOUND OF MULL - EAST (AC 2171)

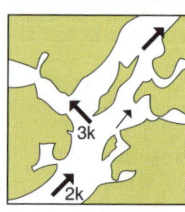

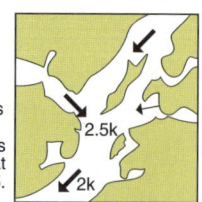

The N going stream in the Firth of Lorne begins at HW Dover −0100 (HW Oban +0430). The W going stream in the Sound of Mull begins at HW Dover +0105 (HW Oban −0550). The ingoing tides at Lochs Feochan, Etive and Creran begin at HW Dover +0300, −0100 & +0030.

The S going stream in the Firth of Lorne begins at HW Dover +0500 (HW Oban −0155). The E going stream in the Sound of Mull begins at HW Dover +0555 (HW Oban −0025). The outgoing tides at Lochs Feochan, Etive and Creran begin at HW Dover −0500, −0520 & −0505.

SOUND OF LUING & DORUS MOR (AC 2343)

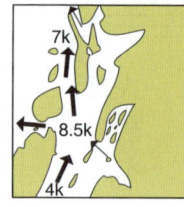

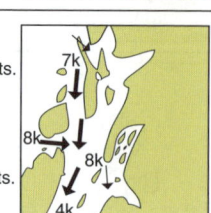

The N or W going stream begins as follows:
Dorus Mor: HW Dover −0200 (HW Oban +0330). Springs: 8 knots.
Corryvreckan: HW D −0120 (HW O +0410). Sp: 8.5 knots.
Cuan Sound: HW D −0110 (HW O +0420). Sp: 6 knots.
Sound of Jura: HW D −0130 (HW O +0400). Sp: 4 knots.
Sound of Luing: HW D −0100 (HW O +0430). Sp: 7 knots.
The S or E going stream begins as follows:
Dorus Mor: HW Dover +0440 (HW Oban −0215). Springs: 8 knots.
Corryvreckan: HW D +0445 (HW O −0210). Sp: 8.5 knots.
Cuan Sound: HW D +0455 (HW O −0200). Sp: 6 knots.
Sound of Jura: HW D +0450 (HW O −0205). Sp: 4 knots.
Sound of Luing: HW D +0500 (HW O −0155). Sp: 7 knots.

TIDAL GATES - SOUTH WEST SCOTLAND

A guide to the time of tide turn at tidal gates, the approximate maximum strength of the tidal flow (spring rates shown - neaps are approximately 60% of these), and the position and timing of races, counter tides, etc.

FLOOD	EBB

SOUNDS OF ISLAY AND GIGHA (AC 2168)

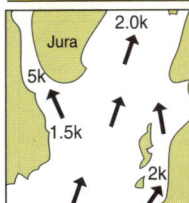

Main flood begins +0015 HW Dover (HW Oban +0545). Streams turn approx 1 hr earlier in Gigha Sd & at Kintyre & Jura shores. S going stream for 9hrs close inshore between Gigha and Machrihanish starting HW Dover (HW Oban –0530).

Main ebb begins HW Dover –0545 (HW Oban –0015). Streams turn 1 hr earlier in Gigha Sd, Kintyre & Jura shores. Overfalls off McArthur's Hd.

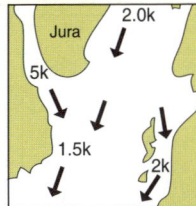

NORTH CHANNEL - NORTH (AC 2798)

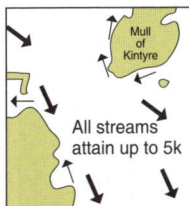

Main flood begins HW Dover –0600 (HW Greenock +0505). Races off Mull of Kintyre, Altacarry Hd & Fair Hd. Counter tides in bays of Antrim coast. W-going streams in Rathlin Sd, counter tide from Sanda Sd to Machrihanish last 1h30 - 2 hrs.

Main ebb begins HW Dover (HW Greenock –0120). Races off Mull of Kintyre & Altacarry Hd. Counter tides in bays of Antrim coast, counter tide from Macrihanish to Sanda Sd last 1h30 - 2 hrs.

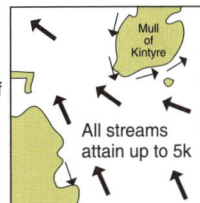

NORTH CHANNEL - SOUTH (AC 2198)

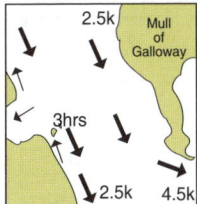

Irish coast - flood begins HW Dover +0610 (HW Belfast –0600). Scottish coast - HW Dover +0430 (HW Greenock +0310). Races off Copeland Is. & Mull of Galloway. Counter tide off Donaghadee and Island Magee last 3 hrs of flood.

Irish coast - ebb begins HW Dover –0015 (HW Belfast). Scottish coast - HW Dover –0130 (HW Greenock –0250). Races off Copeland Is. & Mull of Galloway. Flood begins 2 hrs early close inshore N of Mull of Galloway.

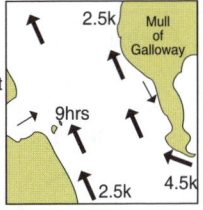

APPROACHES TO STRANGFORD LOUGH (AC 2156)

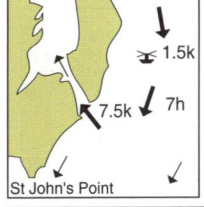

The tide cycle is approx 3 hours later than in the N Channel

Flood runs for 6 hours from HW Dover –0345 (HW Belfast –0330), with a maximum rate of 7.5 knots at Rue Point. The strong flow flattens the sea in onshore winds and entrance can be made in strong winds.

Ebb runs for 6 hours from HW Dover +0215 (HW Belfast +0230), max rate 7.5k, E of Angus Rk. If entering against ebb use West Channel with care. Smoothest water near Bar Pladdy Buoy when leaving.

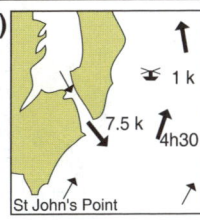

ISLE OF MAN - NORTH (AC 2094)

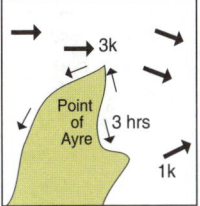

E going stream at Point of Ayre begins HW Dover –0545 (HW Liverpool –0600). Counter tide inside banks E of Point. In Ramsey Bay the S Going tide runs for 3h from +0530 Dover (+0515 Liverpool).

W going stream at Point of Ayre begins HW Dover +0015 (HW Liverpool). Counter tide inside banks W of Point. In Ramsey Bay the N going tide runs for 9h from –0330 Dover (–0345 Liverpool).

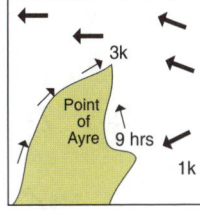

ISLE OF MAN - SOUTH (AC 2094)

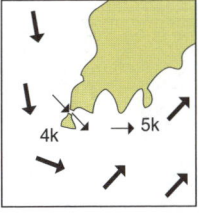

E going stream begins –0600 Dover (Liverpool +0610). Overfalls and race E of Chicken Rock. Calf Sound: The E going stream begins earlier, at approximately Dover +0400 (Liverpool +0345).

W going stream begins +0015 Dover (HW Liverpool). Overfalls and race N of Chicken Rock. Calf Sound: The W going stream begins earlier, at approximately –0130 Dover (–0145 Liverpool). Note: all times may vary due to weather conditions.

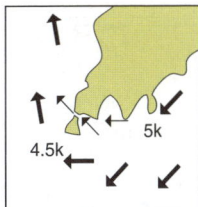

TIDES

TIDAL GATES - IRISH SEA

A guide to the time of tide turn at tidal gates, the approximate strength of the tidal flow (spring rates shown — neaps are approximately 60% of these), and the position and timing of races, counter tides, etc.

FLOOD	EBB

DUBLIN BAY (AC 1415)

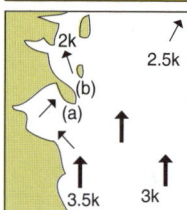

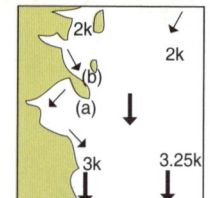

Tide between Rosbeg bank and Howth Hd (a) runs NE from HW Dublin +0300 for 9h30. In Howth Sd (b) the stream is NW going from +0430 to −0130. New flood and ebb tides begin close to the S shore and N of Baily up to 1h before HW Dublin .

The tide between Rosbeg bank and Howth Hd (a) runs SW from HW Dublin for 3h. In Howth Sd (b) the stream is SE going from −0130 to +0430. Strengths of streams increase S of Dublin Bay, and decrease N of it.

N W ANGLESEY (AC 1977)

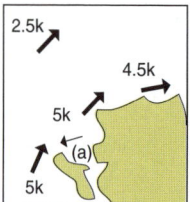

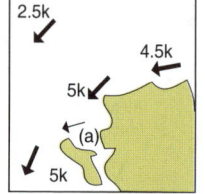

Flood tide close to the coast runs at over 5k springs, and at about 2.5k 7 miles offshore. The brief period of slack water offshore is 1h before HW Dover (1h15 before HW L'pool). Slack water lasts longer in Holyhead Bay.

Ebb tide close to the coast runs at over 5k springs, and at about 2.5k 7 miles offshore. Slack water is 5h after HW Dover (4h45 after HW L'pool). There is no significant counter tide in Holyhead Bay, but the ebb starts first there, giving about 9h W-going tide N of the harbour (a).

BARDSEY SOUND (AC 1971)

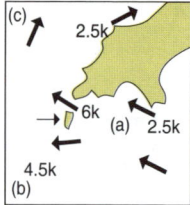

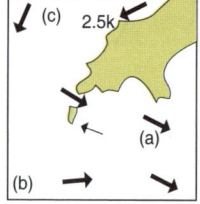

The tide turns to the NW or NE (flood) as follows:
at (a): HW Dover +0300;
at (b): HW D +0500;
at (c): −0545 HW D.
These times are approximate. There is a strong eddy down tide of Bardsey Island and overfalls throughout the area.

The tide turns to the SW or SE (ebb) as follows:
at (a): HW Dover −0300;
at (b): HW D −0100 ;
at (c): at HW D −0030.
These times are approximate. There is a strong eddy down tide of Bardsey Island and overfalls throughout the area.

S W WALES (AC 1478)

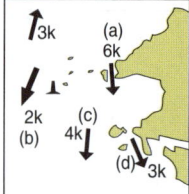

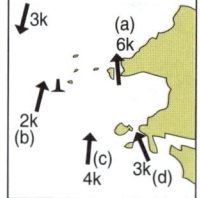

The tide turns to the S or SE (Bristol Channel flood) as follows:
at (a): HW Dover −0200;
at (b) & (c): HW D −0100 ;
at (d): −0300 HW D

The tide turns to the N or NW (Bristol Channel ebb) as follows:
at (a): HW Dover +0400;
at (b) & (c): HW D +0500 ;
at (d): +0300 HW D

CARNSORE POINT (AC 2049)

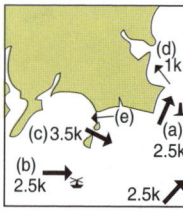

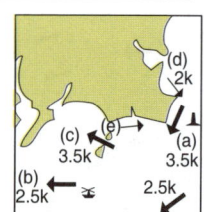

The tide turns to the NE or N (Irish Sea flood) as follows:
at (a): HW Dover +0500; at (b): HW D +0520; at (c): HW D +0600; at (d): −0600 HW D. NE going streams are shorter in duration and weaker than SE going - careful passage planning is essential.

The tide turns to the SW or S as follows:
at (a): −0200 HW D ; at (b): HW D −0020; at (c): −0015 HW D; at (d): −0300 HW Dover. Leaving Rosslare at −0300 HW D a yacht can carry a fair tide for about 8h until HW D +0515 off Hook Head.

NOTE: The tide turns on St Patrick's Bridge (e) up to 2 hours earlier than in Saltee Sound

CORK COAST (AC 2049)

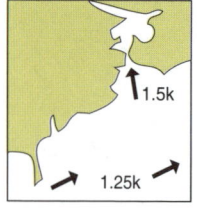

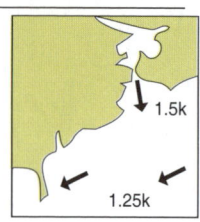

The tide, which flows coastwise, turns to the NE at HW Dover +0045. There is an eddy 5 miles ESE of Old Head of Kinsale at HW Dover +0400. The ingoing Cork Harbour tide begins at HW Dover +0055.

The tide turns SW at HW Dover +0500. The outgoing Cork Harbour tide begins at HW Dover −0540.

MENAI STRAIT (AC 1464) – TIDAL GATES

FLOOD

(T) : turning   → : < 2k   ➡ : 2-4k   ⫸ : 4k +

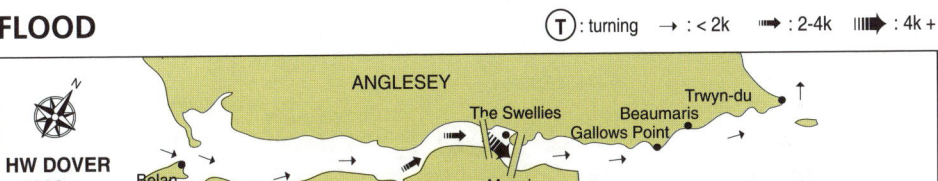

HW DOVER – 0600

LOCAL LW: Caernarfon: HW Dover –0555. Port Dinorwic: –0620. Menai: –0540. Beaumaris: –0605.

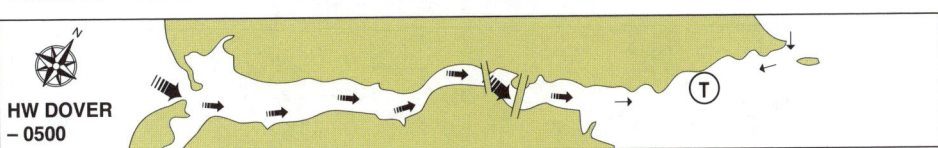

HW DOVER – 0500

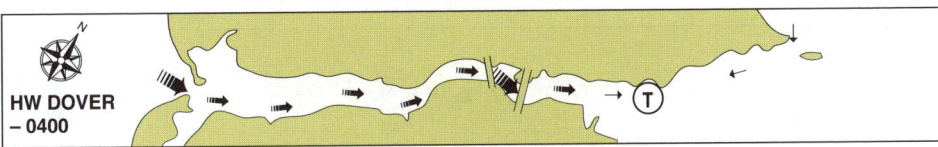

HW DOVER – 0400

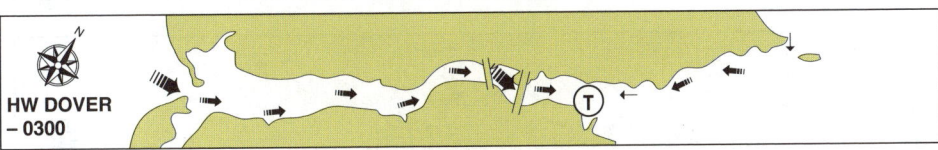

HW DOVER – 0300

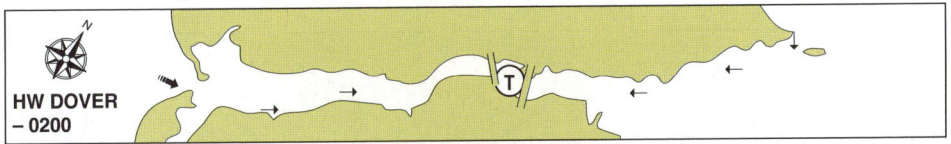

HW DOVER – 0200

SLACK WATER IN THE SWELLIES: HW Dover –0200 to –0230.

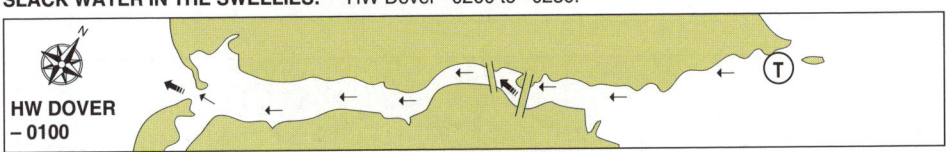

HW DOVER – 0100

LOCAL HW: Belan: HW Dover –0115.   Caernarfon: –0105.   Port Dinorwic: –0050.

THE SWELLIES

WESTBOUND: Leave or pass Beaumaris in time to arrive at the Swellies by HW Dover –0230 to –0200. If in doubt about passage speed, leave early; the adverse tide will check your progress. For a first time passage this is useful, as the yacht's speed over the ground is reduced. Late arrival will mean a faster passage, but with perhaps less control.

EASTBOUND: Leave or pass Port Dinorwic in time to arrive at Menai Bridge by HW Dover –0230 to –0200. Progress towards the Swellies should be closely monitored, as you are travelling with the last of the flood. Early arrival will mean a fast, perhaps dangerous passage, being late may make it impossible.

MENAI STRAIT (AC 1464) – TIDAL GATES *contd*

EBB

(T) : turning → : < 2k ⟹ : 2-4k ⟾ : 4k +

LOCAL HW TIMES: Menai: Dover – 0005.   Beaumaris: Dover – 0010

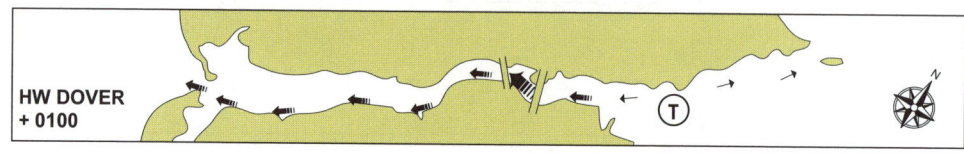

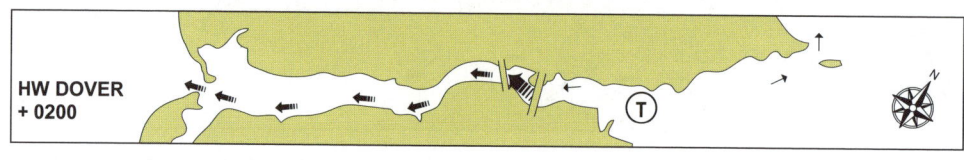

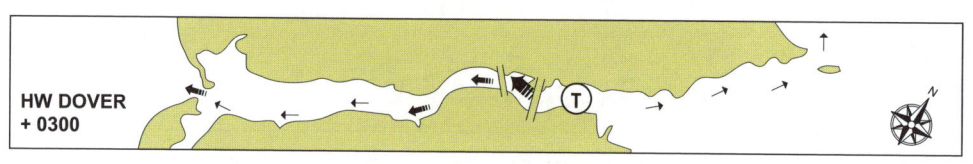

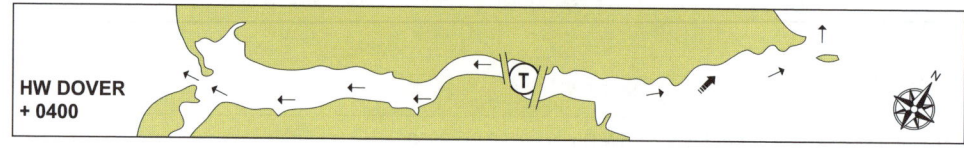

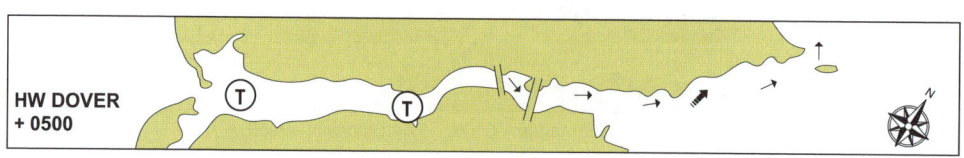

LOCAL LW TIMES: Belan: Dover + 0520.

CAERNARFON BAR

CAERNARFON BAR is without question highly dangerous in certain conditions. Buoys are located to suit changing channel; positions obtainable from Caernarfon Port Radio - VHF Ch 16; 06, 12: 2h–HW, or when vessel expected. Beware cross track tides near high water. Bar impassable during or after fresh or strong onshore weather. Keep strictly in channel.

OUTWARD BOUND: Do not leave Belan Narrows after half tide, better as soon as possible after the ebb commences, which gives maximum depth and duration of fair tide if bound S & W.

INWARD BOUND: Locating the bar buoys may be difficult; head for Llanddwyn I. until they are located. Only cross after half tide (HW Dover –0400), which inevitably limits onward passage to max of 3 hours.

SECONDARY PORTS – TIME & HEIGHT DIFFERENCES
SOUTH COAST OF ENGLAND *Time Zone UT*

Location	Lat	Long	High Water		Low Water		MHWS	MHWN	MLWN	MLWS
			0000	0600	0000	0600				
PLYMOUTH (DEVONPORT)	50 22N	4 11W	and	and	and	and	5.5	4.4	2.2	0.8
Standard port			1200	1800	1200	1800				
Isles of Scilly, St Mary's	49 55N	6 19W	−0035	−0100	−0040	−0025	+0.2	−0.1	−0.2	−0.1
Penzance & Newlyn	50 06N	5 33W	−0040	−0110	−0035	−0025	+0.1	0.0	−0.2	0.0
Porthleven	50 05N	5 19W	−0045	−0105	−0030	−0025	0.0	−0.1	−0.2	0.0
Lizard Point	49 57N	5 12W	−0045	−0100	−0030	−0030	−0.2	−0.2	−0.3	−0.2
Coverack	50 01N	5 05W	−0030	−0050	−0020	−0015	−0.2	−0.2	−0.3	−0.2
Helford River Entrance	50 05N	5 05W	−0030	−0035	−0015	−0010	−0.2	−0.2	−0.3	−0.2
FALMOUTH	50 09N	5 03W	*Standard port (no secondaries)*							
Truro	50 16N	5 03W	−0020	−0025	*Dries*	*Dries*	−2.0	−2.0	*Dries*	
Mevagissey	50 16N	4 47W	−0015	−0020	−0010	−0005	−0.1	−0.1	−0.2	−0.1
Par	50 21N	4 42W	−0010	−0015	−0010	−0005	−0.4	−0.4	−0.4	−0.2
Fowey	50 20N	4 38W	−0010	−0015	−0010	−0005	−0.1	−0.1	−0.2	−0.2
Lostwithiel	50 24N	4 40W	+0005	−0010	*Dries*	*Dries*	−4.1	−4.1	*Dries*	
Looe	50 21N	4 27W	−0010	−0010	−0005	−0005	−0.1	−0.2	−0.2	−0.2
Whitsand Bay	50 20N	4 15W	0000	0000	0000	0000	0.0	+0.1	−0.1	+0.2
River Tamar										
Saltash	50 24N	4 12W	0000	+0010	0000	−0005	+0.1	+0.1	+0.1	+0.1
Cargreen	50 26N	4 12W	0000	+0010	+0020	+0020	0.0	0.0	−0.1	0.0
Cotehele Quay	50 29N	4 13W	0000	+0020	+0045	+0045	−0.9	−0.9	−0.8	−0.4
Lopwell, R Tavy	50 28N	4 09W	*No data*	*No data*	*Dries*	*Dries*	−2.6	−2.7	*Dries*	
Jupiter Point	50 23N	4 14W	+0010	+0005	0000	−0005	0.0	0.0	+0.1	0.0
St Germans	50 23N	4 18W	0000	0000	+0020	+0020	−0.3	−0.1	0.0	+0.2
Turnchapel	50 22N	4 07W	0000	0000	+0010	−0015	0.0	+0.1	+0.2	+0.1
Bovisand Pier	50 20N	4 08W	0000	−0020	0000	−0010	−0.2	−0.1	+0.1	+0.1
River Yealm Entrance	50 18N	4 04W	+0006	+0006	+0002	+0002	−0.1	−0.1	−0.1	−0.1
			0100	0600	0100	0600				
PLYMOUTH (DEVONPORT)	50 22N	4 11W	and	and	and	and	5.5	4.4	2.2	0.8
Standard port			1300	1800	1300	1800				
Salcombe	50 13N	3 47W	0000	+0010	+0005	−0005	−0.2	−0.3	−0.1	−0.1
Start Point	50 13N	3 39W	+0015	+0015	+0005	+0010	−0.1	−0.2	+0.1	+0.2
River Dart										
DARTMOUTH	50 21N	3 34W	*Standard port (no secondaries)*							
Greenway Quay	50 23N	3 35W	+0030	+0045	+0025	+0005	−0.6	−0.6	−0.2	−0.2
Totnes	50 26N	3 41W	+0030	+0040	+0115	+0030	−2.0	−2.1	*Dries*	
Torquay	50 28N	3 31W	+0025	+0045	+0010	0000	−0.6	−0.7	−0.2	−0.1
Teignmouth Approaches	50 33N	3 29W	+0020	+0050	+0025	0000	−0.9	−0.8	−0.2	−0.1
Teignmouth New Quay	50 33N	3 30W	+0025	+0055	+0040	+0005	−0.8	−0.8	−0.2	+0.1
Exmouth Approaches	50 36N	3 23W	+0030	+0050	+0015	+0005	−0.9	−1.0	−0.5	−0.3
River Exe										
Exmouth Dock	50 37N	3 25W	+0035	+0055	+0050	+0020	−1.5	−1.6	−0.9	−0.6
Starcross	50 38N	3 27W	+0040	+0110	+0055	+0025	−1.4	−1.5	−0.8	−0.1
Topsham	50 41N	3 28W	+0045	+0105	*No data*	*No data*	− 1.5	−1.6	*No data*	
Lyme Regis	50 43N	2 56W	+0040	+0100	+0005	−0005	−1.2	−1.3	−0.5	−0.2
Bridport West Bay	50 42N	2 45W	+0025	+0040	0000	0000	−1.4	−1.4	−0.6	−0.2
Chesil Beach	50 37N	2 33W	+0040	+0055	−0005	+0010	−1.6	−1.5	−0.5	0.0
Chesil Cove	50 34N	2 28W	+0035	+0050	−0010	+0005	−1.5	−1.6	−0.5	−0.2
			0100	0700	0100	0700				
PORTLAND	50 34N	2 26W	and	and	and	and	2.1	1.4	0.8	0.1
Standard port			1300	1900	1300	1900				
Lulworth Cove	50 37N	2 15W	+0005	+0015	−0005	0000	+0.1	+0.1	+0.2	+0.1
Mupe Bay	50 37N	2 13W	+0005	+0015	−0005	0000	+0.1	+0.1	+0.2	+0.1
			—	—	0500	1100				
POOLE HARBOUR	50 42N	1 59W			and	and	2.2	1.7	1.2	0.6
Standard port			—	—	1700	2300				
Swanage	50 37N	1 57W	—	—	−0045	+0055	−0.2	−0.1	0.0	−0.1
Poole Harbour Entrance	50 41N	1 57W	—	—	−0025	−0010	0.0	0.0	0.0	0.0
Ro-Ro terminal	50 42N	1 59W	*Standard port*							
Pottery Pier	50 42N	1 59W	—	—	−0010	0000	−0.2	0.0	+0.1	+0.2
Wareham, River Frome	50 41N	2 06W	—	—	+0130	+0145	0.0	0.0	0.0	+0.3
Cleavel Point	50 40N	2 00W	—	—	−0005	−0005	−0.1	−0.2	0.0	*No data*
			0000	0600	0500	1100				
PORTSMOUTH	50 48N	1 07W	and	and	and	and	4.7	3.8	1.9	0.8
Standard port			1200	1800	1700	2300				

Location	Lat	Long	High Water		Low Water		MHWS	MHWN	MLWN	MLWS
Bournemouth	50 43N	1 52W	−0240	+0055	−0050	−0030	−2.7	−2.2	−0.8	−0.3
Christchurch Entrance	50 43N	1 45W	−0230	+0030	−0035	−0035	−2.9	−2.4	−1.2	−0.2
Christchurch Quay	50 44N	1 47W	−0210	+0100	+0105	+0055	−2.9	−2.4	−1.0	0.0
Christchurch, Tuckton	50 44N	1 47W	−0205	+0110	+0110	+0105	−3.0	−2.5	−1.0	+0.1
Hurst Point	50 42N	1 33W	−0115	−0005	−0030	−0025	−2.0	−1.5	−0.5	−0.1
Lymington	50 46N	1 32W	−0110	+0005	−0020	−0020	−1.7	−1.2	−0.5	−0.1
Bucklers Hard	50 48N	1 25W	−0040	−0010	+0010	−0010	−1.0	−0.8	−0.2	−0.3
Stansore Point	50 47N	1 20W	−0050	−0010	−0005	−0010	−0.8	−0.5	−0.3	−0.1
Isle of Wight										
Yarmouth	50 42N	1 30W	−0105	+0005	−0025	−0030	−1.7	−1.2	−0.3	0.0
Totland Bay	50 41N	1 33W	−0130	−0045	−0035	−0045	−2.2	−1.7	−0.4	−0.1
Freshwater	50 40N	1 31W	−0210	+0025	−0040	−0020	−2.1	−1.5	−0.4	0.0
Ventnor	50 36N	1 12W	−0025	−0030	−0025	−0030	−0.8	−0.6	−0.2	+0.2
Sandown	50 39N	1 09W	0000	+0005	+0010	+0025	−0.6	−0.5	−0.2	0.0
Foreland Lifeboat Slip	50 41N	1 04W	−0005	0000	+0005	+0010	+0.1	+0.1	0.0	+0.1
Bembridge Harbour	50 42N	1 07W	+0020	0000	+0100	+0020	−1.5	−1.4	−1.3	−1.0
Ryde	50 44N	1 10W	−0010	+0010	−0005	−0005	−0.1	0.0	0.0	0.0
Medina River										
Cowes	50 46N	1 18W	−0015	+0015	0000	−0020	−0.5	−0.3	−0.1	0.0
Folly Inn	50 44N	1 17W	−0015	+0015	0000	−0020	−0.6	−0.4	−0.1	+0.2
Newport	50 42N	1 17W	No data	No data	No data	No data	−0.6	−0.4	+0.1	+0.8
SOUTHAMPTON	50 53N	1 24W	0400 and 1600	1100 and 2300	0000 and 1200	0600 and 1800	4.5	3.7	1.8	0.5
Standard port										
Calshot Castle	50 49N	1 18W	0000	+0025	0000	0000	0.0	0.0	+0.2	+0.3
Redbridge	50 55N	1 28W	−0020	+0005	0000	−0005	−0.1	−0.1	−0.1	−0.1
River Hamble										
Warsash	50 51N	1 18W	+0020	+0010	+0010	0000	0.0	+0.1	+0.1	+0.3
Bursledon	50 53N	1 18W	+0020	+0020	+0010	+0010	+0.1	+0.2	+0.2	+0.2
PORTSMOUTH	50 48N	1 07W	0500 and 1700	1000 and 2200	0000 and 1200	0600 and 1800	4.7	3.8	1.9	0.8
Standard port										
Lee-on-the-Solent	50 48N	1 12W	−0005	+0005	−0015	−0010	−0.2	−0.1	+0.1	+0.2
Chichester Harbour Entrance	50 47N	0 56W	−0010	+0005	+0015	+0020	+0.2	+0.2	0.0	+0.1
Northney	50 50N	0 58W	+0010	+0015	+0015	+0025	+0.2	0.0	−0.2	−0.3
Bosham	50 50N	0 52W	0000	+0010	No data	No data	+0.2	+0.1	No data	
Itchenor	50 48N	0 52W	−0005	+0005	+0005	+0025	+0.1	0.0	−0.2	−0.2
Dell Quay	50 49N	0 49W	+0005	+0015	no data	No data	+0.2	+0.1	No data	
Selsey Bill	50 43N	0 47W	+0010	−0010	+0035	+0020	+0.5	+0.3	−0.1	−0.2
Nab Tower	50 40N	0 57W	+0015	0000	+0015	+0015	−0.2	0.0	+0.2	0.0
SHOREHAM	50 50N	0 15W	0500 and 1700	1000 and 2200	0000 and 1200	0600 and 1800	6.3	4.8	1.9	0.6
Standard port										
Pagham	50 46N	0 43W	+0015	0000	−0015	−0025	−0.7	−0.5	−0.1	−0.1
Bognor Regis	50 47N	0 40W	+0010	−0005	−0005	−0020	−0.6	−0.5	−0.2	−0.1
River Arun										
Littlehampton Entrance	50 48N	0 33W	+0010	0000	−0005	−0010	−0.4	−0.4	−0.2	−0.2
Littlehampton UMA wharf	50 49N	0 33W	+0015	+0005	0000	+0045	−0.7	−0.7	−0.3	+0.2
Arundel	50 51N	0 33W	No data	+0120	No data	No data	−3.1	−2.8	No data	
Worthing	50 48N	0 22W	+0010	0000	−0005	−0010	−0.1	−0.2	0.0	0.0
Brighton	50 49N	0 08W	0000	−0005	0000	0000	+0.3	+0.2	+0.1	0.0
Newhaven	50 47N	0 04E	−0015	−0010	0000	0000	+0.2	+0.1	−0.1	−0.2
Eastbourne	50 46N	0 17E	−0010	−0005	+0015	+0020	+1.1	+0.6	+0.2	+0.1
DOVER	51 07N	1 19E	0000 and 1200	0600 and 1800	0100 and 1300	0700 and 1900	6.8	5.3	2.1	0.8
Standard port										
Hastings	50 51N	0 36E	0000	−0010	−0030	−0030	+0.8	+0.5	+0.1	−0.1
Rye Approaches	50 55N	0 47E	+0005	−0010	No data	No data	+1.0	+0.7	No data	
Rye Harbour	50 56N	0 48E	+0005	−0010	Dries	Dries	−1.4	−1.7	Dries	
Dungeness	50 55N	0 58E	−0010	−0015	−0020	−0010	+1.0	+0.6	+0.4	+0.1
Folkestone	51 05N	1 12E	−0020	−0005	−0010	−0010	+0.4	+0.4	0.0	−0.1
Deal	51 13N	1 25E	+0010	+0020	+0010	+0005	−0.6	−0.3	0.0	0.0
Richborough	51 18N	1 21E	+0015	+0015	+0030	+0030	−3.4	−2.6	−1.7	−0.7
Ramsgate	51 20N	1 25E	+0030	+0030	+0017	+0007	−1.6	−1.3	−0.7	−0.2

EAST COAST ENGLAND *Time Zone UT*

Location	Lat	Long	High Water		Low Water		MHWS	MHWN	MLWN	MLWS
SHEERNESS	51 27N	0 45E	0200 and 1400	0800 and 2000	0200 and 1400	0700 and 1900	5.8	4.7	1.5	0.6
Standard port										

Location	Lat	Long	High Water		Low Water		MHWS	MHWN	MLWN	MLWS
Margate	51 23N	1 23E	−0050	−0040	−0020	−0050	−0.9	−0.9	−0.1	0.0
Herne Bay	51 23N	1 07E	−0025	−0015	0000	−0025	−0.5	−0.5	−0.1	−0.1
Whitstable approaches	51 22N	1 02E	−0008	−0011	+0005	0000	−0.3	−0.3	0.0	−0.1
River Swale										
Grovehurst Jetty	51 22N	0 46E	−0007	0000	0000	+0016	0.0	0.0	0.0	−0.1
Faversham	51 19N	0 54E	No data	No data	No data	No data	−0.2	−0.2	No data	
River Medway										
Bee Ness	51 25N	0 39E	+0002	+0002	0000	+0005	+0.2	+0.1	0.0	0.0
Bartlett Creek	51 23N	0 38E	+0016	+0008	No data	No data	+0.1	0.0	No data	
Darnett Ness	51 24N	0 36E	+0004	+0004	0000	+0010	+0.2	+0.1	0.0	−0.1
Chatham, Lock approaches	51 24N	0 33E	+0010	+0012	+0012	+0018	+0.3	+0.1	−0.1	−0.2
Upnor	51 25N	0 32E	+0015	+0015	+0015	+0025	+0.2	+0.2	−0.1	−0.1
Rochester, Strood Pier	51 24N	0 30E	+0018	+0018	+0018	+0028	+0.2	+0.2	−0.2	−0.3
Wouldham	51 21N	0 27E	+0030	+0025	+0035	+0120	−0.2	−0.3	−1.0	−0.3
New Hythe	51 19N	0 28E	+0035	+0035	+0220	+0240	−1.6	−1.7	−1.2	−0.3
Allington Lock	51 17N	0 30E	+0050	+0035	No data	No data	−2.1	−2.2	−1.3	−0.4
River Thames										
Southend–on–Sea	51 31N	0 43E	−0005	−0005	−0005	−0005	0.0	0.0	−0.1	−0.1
Coryton	51 30N	0 31E	+0005	+0010	+0010	+0010	+0.4	+0.3	0.0	0.0
LONDON BRIDGE	51 30N	0 05W	0300 and 1500	0900 and 2100	0400 and 1600	1100 and 2300	7.1	5.9	1.3	0.5
Standard port										
Tilbury	51 27N	0 22E	−0055	−0040	−0050	−0115	−0.7	−0.5	+0.1	0.0
North Woolwich	51 30N	0 05E	−0020	−0020	−0035	−0045	−0.1	0.0	+0.2	0.0
Albert bridge	51 29N	0 10W	+0025	+0020	+0105	+0110	−0.9	−0.8	−0.7	−0.4
Hammersmith bridge	51 29N	0 14W	+0040	+0035	+0205	+0155	−1.4	−1.3	−1.0	−0.5
Kew bridge	51 29N	0 17W	+0055	+0050	+0255	+0235	−1.8	−1.8	−1.2	−0.5
Richmond lock	51 28N	0 19W	+0105	+0055	+0325	+0305	−2.2	−2.2	−1.3	−0.5
SHEERNESS	51 27N	0 45E	0200 and 1400	0700 and 1900	0100 and 1300	0700 and 1900	5.8	4.7	1.5	0.6
Standard port										
Thames Estuary Shivering Sand	51 30N	1 05E	−0025	−0019	−0008	−0026	−0.6	−0.6	−0.1	−0.1
WALTON-ON-THE-NAZE	51 51N	1 17E	0000 and 1200	0600 and 1800	0500 and 1700	1100 and 2300	4.2	3.4	1.1	0.4
Standard port										
Whitaker Beacon	51 40N	1 06E	+0022	+0024	+0033	+0027	+0.6	+0.5	+0.2	+0.1
Holliwell Point	51 38N	0 56E	+0034	+0037	+0100	+0037	+1.1	+0.9	+0.3	+0.1
River Roach Rochford	51 35N	0 43E	+0050	+0040	Dries	Dries	−0.8	−1.1	Dries	
River Crouch										
BURNHAM-ON-CROUCH	51 37N	0 48E	Not a Standard port, but see full predictions page 263							
North Fambridge	51 38N	0 41E	+0115	+0050	+0130	+0100	+1.1	+0.8	0.0	−0.1
Hullbridge	51 38N	0 38E	+0115	+0050	+0135	+0105	+1.1	+0.8	0.0	−0.1
Battlesbridge	51 37N	0 34E	+0120	+0110	Dries	Dries	−1.8	−2.0	Dries	
River Blackwater										
Bradwell Waterside	51 45N	0 54E	+0035	+0023	+0047	+0004	+1.0	+0.8	+0.2	0.0
Osea Island	51 43N	0 46E	+0057	+0045	+0050	+0007	+1.1	+0.9	+0.1	0.0
Maldon	51 44N	0 42E	+0107	+0055	No data	No data	−1.3	−1.1	No data	
West Mersea	51 47N	0 54E	+0035	+0015	+0055	+0010	+0.9	+0.4	+0.1	+0.1
River Colne										
Brightlingsea	51 48N	1 00E	+0025	+0021	+0046	+0004	+0.8	+0.4	+0.1	0.0
Colchester	51 53N	0 56E	+0035	+0025	Dries	Dries	0.0	−0.3	Dries	
Clacton–on–Sea	51 47N	1 10E	+0012	+0010	+0025	+0008	+0.3	+0.1	+0.1	+0.1
Bramble Creek	51 53N	1 14E	+0010	−0007	−0005	+0010	+0.3	+0.3	+0.3	+0.3
Sunk Head	51 47N	1 30E	0000	+0002	−0002	+0002	−0.3	−0.3	−0.1	−0.1
Harwich	51 57N	1 17E	+0007	+0002	−0010	−0012	−0.2	0.0	0.0	0.0
Mistley	51 57N	1 05E	+0032	+0027	−0010	−0012	0.0	0.0	−0.1	−0.1
Ipswich	52 03N	1 10E	+0022	+0027	0000	−0012	0.0	0.0	−0.1	−0.1
WALTON–ON–THE–NAZE	51 51N	1 17E	0100 and 1300	0700 and 1900	0100 and 1300	0700 and 1900	4.2	3.4	1.1	0.4
Standard port										
Felixstowe Pier	51 57N	1 21E	−0005	−0007	−0018	−0020	−0.5	−0.4	0.0	0.0
River Deben										
Woodbridge Haven	51 59N	1 24E	0000	−0005	−0020	−0025	−0.5	−0.5	−0.1	+0.1
Woodbridge	52 05N	1 19E	+0045	+0025	+0025	−0020	−0.2	−0.3	−0.2	0.0
Bawdsey	52 01N	1 26E	−0016	−0020	−0030	−0032	−0.8	−0.6	−0.1	−0.1
Orford Haven										
Bar	52 02N	1 28E	−0026	−0030	−0036	−0038	−1.0	−0.8	−0.1	0.0

Location	Lat	Long	High Water		Low Water		MHWS	MHWN	MLWN	MLWS
Orford Quay	52 05N	1 32E	+0040	+0040	+0055	+0055	−1.4	−1.1	0.0	+0.2
Slaughden Quay	52 08N	1 36E	+0105	+0105	+0125	+0125	−1.3	−0.8	−0.1	+0.2
Iken Cliffs	52 09N	1 31E	+0130	+0130	+0155	+0155	−1.3	−1.0	0.0	+0.2
LOWESTOFT *Standard port*	52 28N	1 45E	0300 and 1500	0900 and 2100	0200 and 1400	0800 and 2000	**2.4**	**2.1**	**1.0**	**0.5**
Orford Ness	52 05N	1 35E	+0135	+0135	+0135	+0125	+0.4	+0.6	−0.1	0.0
Aldeburgh	52 09N	1 36E	+0130	+0130	+0115	+0120	+0.3	+0.2	−0.1	−0.2
Minsmere Sluice	52 14N	1 38E	+0110	+0110	+0110	+0110	0.0	−0.1	−0.2	−0.2
Southwold	52 19N	1 40E	+0105	+0105	+0055	+0055	0.0	0.0	−0.1	0.0
Great Yarmouth										
Gorleston-on-Sea	52 34N	1 44E	−0035	−0035	−0030	−0030	0.0	0.0	0.0	0.0
Britannia Pier	52 36N	1 45E	−0105	−0100	−0040	−0055	+0.1	+0.1	0.0	0.0
Caister-on-Sea	52 39N	1 44E	−0120	−0120	−0100	−0100	0.0	−0.1	0.0	0.0
Winterton-on-Sea	52 43N	1 42E	−0225	−0215	−0135	−0135	+0.8	+0.5	+0.2	+0.1
IMMINGHAM *Standard port*	53 38N	0 11W	0100 and 1300	0700 and 1900	0100 and 1300	0700 and 1900	**7.3**	**5.8**	**2.6**	**0.9**
Cromer	52 56N	1 18E	+0050	+0030	+0050	+0130	−2.1	−1.7	−0.5	−0.1
Blakeney Bar	52 59N	0 59E	+0035	+0025	+0030	+0040	−1.6	−1.3	*No data*	
Blakeney	52 57N	1 01E	+0115	+0055	*No data*	*No data*	−3.9	−3.8	*No data*	
Wells Bar	52 59N	0 49E	+0020	+0020	+0020	+0020	−1.3	−1.0	*No data*	
Wells	52 57N	0 51E	+0035	+0045	+0340	+0310	−3.8	−3.8	*Not below*	
⊙										
Burnham Overy Staithe	52 58N	0 48E	+0045	+0055	*No data*	*No data*	−5.0	−4.9	*No data*	
The Wash										
Hunstanton	52 56N	0 29E	+0010	+0020	+0105	+0025	+0.1	−0.2	−0.1	0.0
West Stones	52 50N	0 21E	+0025	+0025	+0115	+0040	−0.3	−0.4	−0.3	+0.2
King's Lynn	52 45N	0 24E	+0030	+0030	+0305	+0140	−0.5	−0.8	−0.8	+0.1
Wisbech Cut	52 48N	0 13E	+0020	+0010	+0120	+0055	−0.3	−0.7	−0.4	*No data*
Port Sutton bridge	52 46N	0 12E	+0030	+0020	+0130	+0105	−0.3	−0.6	−0.6	+0.3
Wisbech	52 40N	0 09E	+0055	+0040	*Dries*	*Dries*	−0.2	−0.6	*Dries*	*Dries*
Lawyer's Creek	52 53N	0 05E	+0010	+0020	*No data*	*No data*	−0.3	−0.6	*No data*	
Tabs Head	52 56N	0 05E	0000	+0005	+0125	+0020	+0.2	−0.2	−0.2	−0.2
Boston	52 58N	0 01W	0000	+0010	+0140	+0050	−0.5	−1.0	−0.9	−0.5
Skegness	53 09N	0 21E	+0010	+0015	+0030	+0020	−0.4	−0.5	−0.1	0.0
Inner Dowsing Light Tower	53 19N	0 35E	0000	0000	+0010	+0010	−0.9	−0.7	−0.1	+0.3
River Humber										
Bull Sand Fort	53 34N	0 04E	−0020	−0030	−0035	−0015	−0.4	−0.3	+0.1	+0.2
Grimsby	53 35N	0 04W	−0012	−0012	−0015	−0015	−0.2	−0.1	0.0	+0.2
Hull, King George Dock	53 44N	0 16W	+0010	+0010	+0021	+0017	+0.3	+0.2	−0.1	−0.2
Hull, Albert Dock	53 44N	0 21W	+0019	+0019	+0033	+0027	+0.3	+0.1	−0.1	−0.2
Humber Bridge	53 43N	0 27W	+0027	+0022	+0049	+0039	−0.1	−0.4	−0.7	−0.6
River Trent										
Burton Stather	53 39N	0 42W	+0105	+0045	+0335	+0305	−2.1	−2.3	−2.3	*Dries*
Flixborough Wharf	53 37N	0 42W	+0120	+0100	+0400	+0340	−2.3	−2.6	*Dries*	
Keadby	53 36N	0 44W	+0135	+0120	+0425	+0410	−2.5	−2.8	*Dries*	
Owston Ferry	53 29N	0 46W	+0155	+0145	*Dries*	*Dries*	−3.5	−3.9	*Dries*	
River Ouse										
Blacktoft	53 42N	0 43W	+0100	+0055	+0325	+0255	−1.6	−1.8	−2.2	−1.1
Goole	53 42N	0 52W	+0130	+0115	+0355	+0350	−1.6	−2.1	−1.9	−0.6
R. TYNE, NORTH SHIELDS *Standard port*	55 00N	1 26W	0200 and 1400	0800 and 2000	0100 and 1300	0800 and 2000	**5.0**	**3.9**	**1.8**	**0.7**
Bridlington	54 05N	0 11W	+0119	+0109	+0109	+0104	+1.1	+0.8	+0.5	+0.4
Filey Bay	54 13N	0 16W	+0101	+0101	+0101	+0048	+0.8	+1.0	+0.6	+0.3
Scarborough	54 17N	0 23W	+0059	+0059	+0044	+0044	+0.7	+0.7	+0.5	+0.2
Whitby	54 29N	0 37W	+0034	+0049	+0034	+0019	+0.6	+0.4	+0.1	+0.1
Middlesborough Dock ent	54 35N	1 13W	+0019	+0021	+0014	+0011	+0.6	+0.6	+0.3	+0.1
Hartlepool	54 42N	1 12W	+0015	+0015	+0008	+0008	+0.4	+0.3	0.0	+0.1
Seaham	54 50N	1 19W	+0004	+0004	−0001	−0001	+0.2	+0.2	+0.2	0.0
Sunderland	54 55N	1 22W	+0002	−0002	−0002	−0002	+0.2	+0.3	+0.2	+0.1
Newcastle-upon-Tyne	54 58N	1 36W	+0003	+0003	+0008	+0008	+0.3	+0.2	+0.1	+0.1
Blyth	55 07N	1 29W	+0005	−0007	−0001	+0009	0.0	0.0	−0.1	+0.1
Coquet Island	55 20N	1 32W	−0010	−0010	−0020	−0020	+0.1	+0.1	0.0	+0.1
Amble	55 20N	1 34W	−0013	−0013	−0016	−0020	0.0	0.0	+0.1	+0.1
North Sunderland	55 35N	1 39W	−0048	−0044	−0058	−0102	−0.2	−0.2	−0.2	0.0
Holy Island	55 40N	1 48W	−0043	−0039	−0105	−0110	−0.2	−0.2	−0.3	−0.1
Berwick	55 46N	1 59W	−0053	−0053	−0109	−0109	−0.3	−0.1	−0.5	−0.1

Location	Lat	Long	High Water		Low Water		MHWS	MHWN	MLWN	MLWS

SCOTLAND *Time Zone UT*

Location	Lat	Long	High Water		Low Water		MHWS	MHWN	MLWN	MLWS
			0300	0900	0300	0900				
LEITH	55 59N	3 11W	and	and	and	and	**5.6**	**4.4**	**2.0**	**0.8**
Standard port			1500	2100	1500	2100				
Eyemouth	55 52N	2 05W	−0005	+0007	+0012	+0008	−0.4	−0.3	0.0	+0.1
Dunbar	56 00N	2 31W	−0005	+0003	+0003	−0003	−0.3	−0.3	0.0	+0.1
Fidra	56 04N	2 47W	−0001	0000	−0002	+0001	−0.2	−0.2	0.0	0.0
Cockenzie	55 58N	2 57W	−0007	−0015	−0013	−0005	−0.2	0.0	*No data*	
Granton	55 59N	3 13W	0000	0000	0000	0000	0.0	0.0	0.0	0.0
River Forth Grangemouth	56 02N	3 41W	+0015	+0010	−0050	−0045	0.0	−0.1	−0.2	−0.2
Kincardine	56 04N	3 43W	+0015	+0030	−0030	−0030	0.0	−0.2	−0.5	−0.3
Alloa	56 06N	3 48W	+0040	+0040	+0025	+0025	−0.2	−0.5	*No data*	−0.7
Stirling	56 07N	3 56W	+0100	+0100	*No data*		−2.9	−3.1	−2.3	−0.7
Firth of Forth										
Burntisland	56 03N	3 14W	+0013	+0004	−0002	+0007	+0.1	0.0	+0.1	+0.2
Kirkcaldy	56 09N	3 09W	+0005	0000	−0004	−0001	−0.3	−0.3	−0.2	−0.2
Methil	56 11N	3 00W	−0005	−0001	−0001	−0001	−0.1	−0.1	−0.1	−0.1
Anstruther Easter	56 13N	2 42W	−0018	−0012	−0006	−0008	−0.3	−0.2	0.0	0.0
			0000	0600	0100	0700				
ABERDEEN	57 09N	2 04W	and	and	and	and	**4.3**	**3.4**	**1.6**	**0.6**
Standard port			1200	1800	1300	1900				
River Tay										
Bar	56 28N	2 38W	+0100	+0100	+0050	+0110	+0.9	+0.8	+0.3	+0.1
Dundee	56 27N	2 58W	+0140	+0120	+0055	+0145	+1.3	+0.9	+0.4	+0.2
Newburgh	56 21N	3 14W	+0215	+0200	+0250	+0335	−0.2	−0.4	−1.1	−0.5
Perth	56 24N	3 25W	+0220	+0225	+0510	+0530	−0.9	−1.4	−1.2	−0.3
Arbroath	56 33N	2 35W	+0056	+0037	+0034	+0055	+1.0	+0.8	+0.4	+0.2
Montrose	56 42N	2 28W	+0055	+0055	+0030	+0040	+0.5	+0.4	+0.2	0.0
Stonehaven	56 58N	2 12W	+0013	+0008	+0013	+0009	+0.2	+0.2	+0.1	0.0
Peterhead	57 30N	1 46W	−0035	−0045	−0035	−0040	−0.4	−0.3	+0.1	+0.1
Fraserburgh	57 41N	2 00W	−0105	−0115	−0120	−0110	−0.6	−0.5	−0.2	0.0
			0200	0900	0400	0900				
ABERDEEN	57 09N	2 04W	and	and	and	and	**4.3**	**3.4**	**1.6**	**0.6**
Standard port			1400	2100	1600	2100				
Banff	57 40N	2 31W	−0100	−0150	−0150	−0050	−0.4	−0.2	−0.1	+0.2
Whitehills	57 41N	2 35W	−0122	−0137	−0117	−0127	−0.4	−0.3	+0.1	+0.1
Buckie	57 41N	2 57W	−0130	−0145	−0125	−0140	−0.2	−0.2	0.0	+0.1
Lossiemouth	57 43N	3 18W	−0125	−0200	−0130	−0130	−0.2	−0.2	0.0	0.0
Burghead	57 42N	3 29W	−0120	−0150	−0135	−0120	−0.2	−0.2	0.0	0.0
Nairn	57 36N	3 52W	−0120	−0150	−0135	−0130	0.0	−0.1	0.0	+0.1
McDermott Base	57 36N	3 59W	−0110	−0140	−0120	−0115	−0.1	−0.1	+0.1	+0.3
			0300	1000	0000	0700				
ABERDEEN	57 09N	2 04W	and	and	and	and	**4.3**	**3.4**	**1.6**	**0.6**
Standard port			1500	2200	1200	1900				
Inverness Firth										
Fortrose	57 35N	4 08W	−0125	−0125	−0125	−0125	0.0	0.0	*No data*	
Inverness	57 30N	4 15W	−0050	−0150	−0200	−0150	+0.5	+0.3	+0.2	+0.1
Cromarty Firth										
Cromarty	57 42N	4 03W	−0120	−0155	−0155	−0120	0.0	0.0	+0.1	+0.2
Invergordon	57 41N	4 10W	−0105	−0200	−0200	−0110	+0.1	+0.1	+0.1	+0.1
Dingwall	57 36N	4 25W	−0045	−0145	*No data*	*No data*	+0.1	+0.2	*No data*	
			0300	0800	0200	0800				
ABERDEEN	57 09N	2 04W	and	and	and	and	**4.3**	**3.4**	**1.6**	**0.6**
Standard port			1500	2000	1400	2000				
Dornoch Firth										
Portmahomack	57 50N	3 50W	−0120	−0210	−0140	−0110	−0.2	−0.1	+0.1	+0.1
Meikle Ferry	57 51N	4 08W	−0100	−0140	−0120	−0055	+0.1	0.0	−0.1	0.0
Golspie	57 58N	3 59W	−0130	−0215	−0155	−0130	−0.3	−0.3	−0.1	0.0
			0000	0700	0200	0700				
WICK	58 26N	3 05W	and	and	and	and	**3.5**	**2.8**	**1.4**	**0.7**
Standard port			1200	1900	1400	1900				
Helmsdale	58 07N	3 39W	+0025	+0015	+0035	+0030	+0.4	+0.3	+0.1	0.0
Duncansby Head	58 39N	3 02W	−0115	−0115	−0110	−0110	−0.4	−0.4	*No data*	
Orkney Islands										
Muckle Skerry	58 41N	2 55W	−0025	−0025	−0020	−0020	−0.9	−0.8	−0.4	−0.3
Burray Ness	58 51N	2 52W	+0005	+0005	+0015	+0015	−0.2	−0.3	−0.1	−0.1

TIDES

TIDES

Location	Lat	Long	High Water		Low Water		MHWS	MHWN	MLWN	MLWS
Deer Sound	58 58N	2 50W	−0040	−0040	−0035	−0035	−0.3	−0.3	−0.1	−0.1
Kirkwall	58 59N	2 58W	−0042	−0042	−0041	−0041	−0.5	−0.4	−0.1	−0.1
Egilsay	59 09N	2 57W	−0125	−0125	−0125	−0125	−0.1	0.0	+0.2	+0.1
Whitehall	58 09N	2 36W	−0030	−0030	−0025	−0030	−0.1	0.0	+0.2	+0.2
Loth	59 11N	2 42W	−0045	−0045	−00558	−0105	−0.4	−0.3	+0.1	+0.2
Kettletoft Pier	59 14N	2 36W	−0030	−0025	−0025	−0025	0.0	0.0	+0.2	+0.2
Rapness	59 15N	2 52W	−0205	−0205	−0205	−0205	+0.1	0.0	+0.2	0.0
Pierowall	59 19N	2 59W	−0150	−0150	−0145	−0145	+0.2	0.0	0.0	−0.1
Tingwall	59 05N	3 03W	−0200	−0125	−0145	−0125	−0.4	−0.4	−0.1	−0.1
Stromness	58 58N	3 18W	−0225	−0135	−0205	−0205	+0.1	−0.1	0.0	0.0
St Mary's	58 54N	2 55W	−0140	−0140	−0140	−0140	−0.2	−0.2	0.0	−0.1
Widewall Bay	58 49N	3 01W	−0155	−0155	−0150	−0150	+0.1	−0.1	−0.1	−0.3
Bur Wick	58 44N	2 58W	−0100	−0100	−0150	−0150	−0.1	−0.1	+0.2	+0.1
			0000	**0600**	**0100**	**0800**				
LERWICK	60 09N	1 08W	and	and	and	and	**2.1**	**1.7**	**0.9**	**0.5**
Standard port			**1200**	**1800**	**1300**	**2000**				
Fair Isle	59 32N	1 36W	−0006	−0015	−0031	−0037	+0.1	0.0	+0.1	+0.1
Shetland Islands										
Sumburgh (Grutness Voe)	59 53N	1 17W	+0006	+0008	+0004	−0002	−0.3	−0.3	−0.2	−0.1
Dury Voe	60 21N	1 10W	−0015	−0015	−0010	−0010	0.0	−0.1	0.0	−0.2
Out Skerries	60 25N	0 45W	−0025	−0025	−0010	−0010	+0.1	0.0	0.0	−0.1
Toft Pier	60 28N	1 12W	−0105	−0100	−0125	−0115	+0.2	+0.1	−0.1	−0.1
Burra Voe (Yell Sound)	60 30N	1 03W	−0025	−0025	−0025	−0025	+0.2	+0.1	0.0	−0.1
Mid Yell	60 36N	1 03W	−0030	−0020	−0035	−0025	+0.3	+0.2	+0.2	+0.1
Balta Sound	60 46N	0 50W	−0055	−0055	−0045	−0045	+0.2	+0.1	0.0	−0.1
Burra Firth	60 48N	0 52W	−0110	−0110	−0115	−0115	+0.4	+0.2	0.0	0.0
Bluemull Sound	60 42N	1 00W	−0135	−0135	−0155	−0155	+0.5	+0.2	+0.1	0.0
Sullom Voe	60 27N	1 18W	−0135	−0125	−0135	−0120	0.0	0.0	−0.2	−0.2
Hillswick	60 29N	1 29W	−0220	−0220	−0200	−0200	−0.1	−0.1	−0.1	−0.1
Scalloway	60 08N	1 16W	−0150	−0150	−0150	−0150	−0.5	−0.4	−0.3	0.0
Bay of Quendale	59 54N	1 21W	−0025	−0025	−0030	−0030	−0.4	−0.3	0.0	+0.1
Foula	60 07N	2 03W	−0140	−0130	−0140	−0120	−0.1	−0.1	0.0	0.0
			0200	**0700**	**0100**	**0700**				
WICK	58 26N	3 05W	and	and	and	and	**3.5**	**2.8**	**1.4**	**0.7**
Standard port			**1400**	**1900**	**1300**	**1900**				
Stroma	58 40N	3 08W	−0115	−0115	−0110	−0110	−0.4	−0.5	−0.1	−0.2
Gills Bay	58 38N	3 10W	−0150	−0150	−0202	−0202	+0.7	+0.7	+0.6	+0.3
Scrabster	58 37N	3 33W	−0255	−0225	−0240	−0230	+1.5	+1.2	+0.8	+0.3
Sule Skerry	59 05N	4 24W	−0320	−0255	−0315	−0250	+0.4	+0.3	+0.2	+0.1
Loch Eriboll Portnancon	58 30N	4 42W	−0340	−0255	−0315	−0255	+1.6	+1.3	+0.8	+0.4
Kyle of Durness	58 36N	4 47W	−0350	−0350	−0315	−0315	+1.1	+0.7	+0.4	−0.1
Rona	59 08N	5 49W	−0410	−0345	−0330	−0340	−0.1	−0.2	−0.2	−0.1
			0100	**0700**	**0300**	**0900**				
STORNOWAY	58 12N	6 23W	and	and	and	and	**4.8**	**3.7**	**2.0**	**0.7**
Standard port			**1300**	**1900**	**1500**	**2100**				
Outer Hebrides										
Loch Shell	58 00N	6 25W	−0013	0000	0000	−0017	0.0	−0.1	−0.1	0.0
E. Loch Tarbert	57 54N	6 48W	−0025	−0010	−0010	−0020	+0.2	0.0	+0.1	+0.1
Leverburgh	57 46N	7 02W	−0041	−0020	−0015	−0025	−0.2	−0.2	−0.2	−0.1
Bays Loch	57 43N	7 10W	−0038	−0013	−0014	−0027	−0.1	−0.2	−0.2	−0.1
Loch Maddy	57 36N	7 09W	−0044	−0014	−0016	−0030	0.0	−0.1	−0.1	0.0
Loch Carnan	57 22N	7 16W	−0050	−0010	−0020	−0040	−0.3	−0.5	−0.1	−0.1
Loch Skiport	57 20N	7 16W	−0100	−0025	−0024	−0024	−0.2	−0.4	−0.3	−0.2
Loch Boisdale	57 09N	7 16W	−0055	−0030	−0020	−0040	−0.7	−0.7	−0.3	−0.2
Barra (North Bay)	57 00N	7 24W	−0103	−0031	−0034	−0048	−0.6	−0.5	−0.2	−0.1
Castle Bay	56 57N	7 29W	−0115	−0040	−0045	−0100	−0.5	−0.6	−0.3	−0.1
Barra Head	56 47N	7 38W	−0115	−0040	−0045	−0055	−0.8	−0.7	−0.2	+0.1
Shillay	57 32N	7 42W	−0103	−0043	−0047	−0107	−0.6	−0.7	−0.7	−0.3
Balivanich	57 29N	7 23W	−0103	−0017	−0031	−0045	−0.7	−0.6	−0.5	−0.2
Scolpaig	57 39N	7 29W	−0033	−0033	−0040	−0040	−1.0	−0.9	−0.5	0.0
W. Loch Tarbert	57 55N	6 55W	−0015	−0015	−0046	−0046	−1.1	−0.9	−0.5	0.0
Little Bernera	58 16N	6 52W	−0021	−0011	−0017	−0027	−0.5	−0.6	−0.4	−0.2
Carloway	58 17N	6 47W	−0040	+0020	−0035	−0015	−0.6	−0.5	−0.4	−0.1
St Kilda Village Bay	57 48N	8 34W	−0040	−0040	−0045	−0045	−1.4	−1.2	−0.8	−0.3
Flannan Isles	58 17N	7 35W	−0026	−0016	−0016	−0026	−0.9	−0.7	−0.6	−0.2
Rockall	57 36N	13 41W	−0055	−0055	−0105	−0105	−1.8	−1.5	−0.9	−0.2

Location	Lat	Long	High Water		Low Water		MHWS	MHWN	MLWN	MLWS
			0000	0600	0300	0900				
ULLAPOOL	57 54N	5 09W	and	and	and	and	5.2	3.9	2.1	0.7
Standard port			1200	1800	1500	2100				
Loch Bervie	58 27N	5 03W	+0020	+0010	+0010	+0020	−0.4	−0.3	−0.2	−0.1
Loch Laxford	58 24N	5 05W	+0015	+0015	+0005	+0005	−0.3	−0.4	−0.2	0.0
Eddrachillis Bay										
Badcall Bay	58 19N	5 08W	+0005	+0005	+0005	+0005	−0.7	−0.5	−0.5	+0.2
Loch Nedd	58 14N	5 10W	0000	0000	0000	0000	−0.3	−0.2	−0.2	0.0
Loch Inver	58 09N	5 18W	−0005	−0005	−0005	−0005	−0.2	0.0	0.0	+0.1
Summer Isles Tanera Mor	58 01N	5 24W	−0005	−0005	−0010	−0010	−0.1	+0.1	0.0	+0.1
Loch Ewe Mellon Charles	57 51N	5 38W	−0010	−0010	−0010	−0010	−0.1	−0.1	−0.1	0.0
Loch Gairloch Gairloch	57 43N	5 41W	−0020	−0020	−0010	−0010	0.0	+0.1	−0.3	−0.1
Loch Torridon Shieldaig	57 31N	5 39W	−0020	−0020	−0015	−0015	+0.4	+0.3	+0.1	0.0
Inner Sound Applecross	57 26N	5 49W	−0010	−0015	−0010	−0010	0.0	0.0	0.0	+0.1
Loch Carron Plockton	57 21N	5 39W	+0005	−0025	−0005	−0010	+0.5	+0.5	+0.5	+0.2
Rona Loch a' Bhraige	57 35N	5 58W	−0020	0000	−0010	0000	−0.1	−0.1	−0.1	−0.2
Skye										
Broadford Bay	57 15N	5 54W	−0015	−0015	−0010	−0015	+0.2	+0.1	+0.1	0.0
Portree	57 24N	6 11W	−0025	−0025	−0025	−0025	+0.1	−0.2	−0.2	0.0
Loch Snizort (Uig Bay)	57 35N	6 22W	−0045	−0020	−0005	−0025	+0.1	−0.4	−0.2	0.0
Loch Dunvegan	57 27N	6 38W	−0105	−0030	−0020	−0040	0.0	−0.1	0.0	0.0
Loch Harport	57 20N	6 25W	−0115	−0035	−0020	−0100	−0.1	−0.1	0.0	+0.1
Soay Camus nan Gall	57 09N	6 13W	−0055	−0025	−0025	−0045	−0.4	−0.2	No data	
Loch Alsh										
Kyle of Lochalsh	57 17N	5 43W	−0040	−0020	−0005	−0025	+0.1	0.0	0.0	−0.1
Dornie Bridge	57 17N	5 31W	−0040	−0010	−0005	−0020	+0.1	−0.1	0.0	0.0
Kyle Rhea Glenelg Bay	57 13N	5 38W	−0105	−0035	−0035	−0055	−0.4	−0.4	−0.9	−0.1
Loch Hourn	57 06N	5 34W	−0125	−0050	−0040	−0110	−0.2	−0.1	−0.1	+0.1
			0000	0600	0100	0700				
OBAN	56 25N	5 29W	and	and	and	and	4.0	2.9	1.8	0.7
Standard port			1200	1800	1300	1900				
Loch Nevis										
Inverie Bay	57 02N	5 41W	+0030	+0020	+0035	+0020	+1.0	+0.9	+0.2	0.0
Mallaig	57 00N	5 50W	+0017	+0017	+0017	+0017	+1.0	+0.7	+0.3	+0.1
Eigg Bay of Laig	56 55N	6 10W	+0015	+0030	+0040	+0005	+0.7	+0.6	−0.2	− 0.2
Loch Moidart	56 47N	5 53W	+0015	+0015	+0040	+0020	+0.8	+0.6	− 0.2	−0.2
Coll Loch Eatharna	56 37N	6 31W	+0025	+0010	+0015	+0025	+0.4	+0.3	No data	
Tiree Gott Bay	56 31N	6 48W	0000	+0010	+0005	+0010	0.0	+0.1	0.0	0.0
			0100	0700	0100	0800				
OBAN	56 25N	5 29W	and	and	and	and	4.0	2.9	1.8	0.7
Standard port			1300	1900	1300	2000				
Mull										
Carsaig Bay	56 19N	5 58W	−0015	−0005	−0030	+0020	+0.1	+0.2	0.0	−0.1
Iona	56 20N	6 23W	−0010	−0005	−0020	+0015	0.0	+0.1	−0.3	−0.2
Bunessan	56 19N	6 14W	−0015	−0015	−0010	−0015	+0.3	+0.1	0.0	−0.1
Ulva Sound	56 29N	6 08W	−0010	−0015	0000	−0005	+0.4	+0.3	0.0	−0.1
Loch Sunart Salen	56 43N	5 47W	−0015	+0015	+0010	+0005	+0.6	+0.5	−0.1	−0.1
Sound of Mull										
Tobermory	56 37N	6 04W	+0025	+0010	+0015	+0025	+0.4	+0.4	0.0	0.0
Salen	56 31N	5 57W	+0045	+0015	+0020	+0030	+0.2	+0.2	−0.1	0.0
Loch Aline	56 32N	5 46W	+0012	+0012	No data	No data	+0.5	+0.3	No data	
Craignure	56 28N	5 42W	+0030	+0005	+0010	+0015	0.0	+0.1	−0.1	−0.1
Loch Linnhe										
Corran	56 43N	5 14W	+0007	+0007	+0004	+0004	+0.4	+0.4	−0.1	0.0
Corpach	56 51N	5 07W	0000	+0020	+0040	0000	0.0	0.0	−0.2	−0.2
Loch Eil Head	56 51N	5 20W	+0025	+0045	+0105	+0025	No data		No data	
Loch Leven Head	56 43N	5 00W	+0045	+0045	+0045	+0045	No data		No data	
Loch Linnhe Port Appin	56 33N	5 25W	−0005	−0005	−0030	0000	+0.2	+0.2	+0.1	+0.1
Loch Creran										
Barcaldine Pier	56 32N	5 19W	+0010	+0020	+0040	+0015	+0.1	+0.1	0.0	+0.1
Loch Creran Head	56 33N	5 16W	+0015	+0025	+0120	+0020	−0.3	−0.3	−0.4	−0.3
Loch Etive										
Dunstaffnage Bay	56 27N	5 26W	+0005	0000	0000	+0005	+0.1	+0.1	+0.1	+0.1
Connel	56 27N	5 24W	+0020	+0005	+0010	+0015	−0.3	−0.2	−0.1	+0.1
Bonawe	56 27N	5 13W	+0150	+0205	+0240	+0210	−2.0	−1.7	−1.3	−0.5
Seil Sound	56 18N	5 35W	−0035	−0015	−0040	−0015	−1.3	−0.9	−0.7	−0.3
Colonsay Scalasaig	56 04N	6 11W	−0020	−0005	−0015	+0005	−0.1	−0.2	−0.2	−0.2
Jura Glengarrisdale Bay	56 07N	5 47W	−0020	0000	−0010	0000	−0.4	−0.2	0.0	−0.2

Location	Lat	Long	High Water		Low Water		MHWS	MHWN	MLWN	MLWS
Islay										
Rubha A'Mhail	55 56N	6 07W	−0020	0000	+0005	−0015	−0.3	−0.1	−0.3	−0.1
Ardnave Point	55 52N	6 20W	−0035	+0010	0000	−0025	−0.4	−0.2	−0.3	−0.1
Orsay	55 41N	6 31W	−0110	−0110	−0040	−0040	−1.4	−0.6	−0.5	−0.2
Bruichladdich	55 46N	6 22W	−0105	−0035	−0110	−0110	−1.8	−1.3	−0.4	+0.1
Port Ellen	55 38N	6 11W	−0530	−0050	−0045	−0530	−3.1	−2.1	−1.3	−0.4
Port Askaig	55 51N	6 06W	−0110	−0030	−0020	−0020	−1.9	−1.4	−0.8	−0.3
Sound of Jura										
Craighouse	55 50N	5 57W	−0230	−0250	−0150	−0230	−3.0	−2.4	−1.3	−0.6
Loch Melfort	56 15N	5 29W	−0055	−0025	−0040	−0035	−1.2	−0.8	−0.5	−0.1
Loch Beag	56 09N	5 36W	−0110	−0045	−0035	−0045	−1.6	−1.2	−0.8	−0.4
Carsaig Bay	56 02N	5 38W	−0105	−0040	−0050	−0050	−2.1	−1.6	−1.0	−0.4
Sound of Gigha	55 41N	5 44W	−0450	−0210	−0130	−0410	−2.5	−1.6	−1.0	−0.1
Machrihanish	55 25N	5 45W	−0520	−0350	−0340	−0540	*Mean range 0.5 metres*			
			0000	**0600**	**0000**	**0600**				
GREENOCK	55 57N	4 46W	and	and	and	and	**3.4**	**2.8**	**1.0**	**0.3**
Standard port			**1200**	**1800**	**1200**	**1800**				
Firth of Clyde										
Southend, Kintyre	55 19N	5 38W	−0030	−0010	+0005	+0035	−1.3	−1.2	−0.5	−0.2
Campbeltown	55 25N	5 36W	−0025	−0005	−0015	+0005	−0.5	−0.3	+0.1	+0.2
Carradale	55 36N	5 28W	−0015	−0005	−0005	+0005	−0.3	−0.2	+0.1	+0.1
Loch Ranza	55 43N	5 18W	−0015	−0005	−0010	−0005	−0.4	−0.3	−0.1	0.0
Loch Fyne										
East Loch Tarbert	55 52N	5 24W	−0005	−0005	0000	−0005	+0.2	+0.1	0.0	0.0
Inveraray	56 14N	5 04W	+0011	+0011	+0034	+0034	−0.1	+0.1	−0.5	−0.2
Kyles of Bute										
Rubha a'Bhodaich	55 55N	5 09W	−0020	−0010	−0007	−0007	−0.2	−0.1	+0.2	+0.2
Tighnabruich	55 55N	5 13W	+0007	−0010	−0002	−0015	0.0	+0.2	+0.4	+0.5
Firth of Clyde – continued										
Millport	55 45N	4 56W	−0005	−0025	−0025	−0005	0.0	−0.1	0.0	+0.1
Rothesay Bay	55 50N	5 03W	−0020	−0015	−0010	−0002	+0.2	+0.2	+0.2	+0.2
Wemyss Bay	55 53N	4 53W	−0005	−0005	−0005	−0005	0.0	0.0	+0.1	+0.1
Loch Long										
Coulport	56 03N	4 53W	−0011	−0011	−0008	−0008	0.0	0.0	0.0	0.0
Lochgoilhead	56 10N	4 54W	+0015	0000	−0005	−0005	−0.2	−0.3	−0.3	−0.3
Arrochar	56 12N	4 45W	−0005	−0005	−0005	−0005	0.0	0.0	−0.1	−0.1
Gare Loch										
Rosneath	56 00N	4 47W	−0005	−0005	−0005	−0005	0.0	−0.1	0.0	0.0
Faslane	56 04N	4 49W	−0010	−0010	−0010	−0010	0.0	0.0	−0.1	−0.2
Garelochhead	56 05N	4 50W	0000	0000	0000	0000	0.0	0.0	0.0	−0.1
River Clyde										
Helensburgh	56 00N	4 44W	0000	0000	0000	0000	0.0	0.0	0.0	0.0
Port Glasgow	55 56N	4 41W	+0010	+0005	+0010	+0020	+0.2	+0.1	0.0	0.0
Bowling	55 56N	4 29W	+0020	+0010	+0030	+0055	+0.6	+0.5	+0.3	+0.1
Clydebank (Rothesay Dock)	55 54N	4 24W	+0025	+0015	+0035	+0100	+1.1	+0.9	+0.6	+0.3
Glasgow	55 51N	4 16W	+0025	+0015	+0035	+0105	+1.3	+1.1	+0.7	+0.4
Firth of Clyde – continued										
Brodick Bay	55 35N	5 08W	−0013	−0013	−0008	−0008	−0.2	−0.1	0.0	+0.1
Lamlash	55 32N	5 07W	−0016	−0036	−0024	−0004	−0.2	−0.2	*No data*	
Ardrossan	55 38N	4 49W	−0020	−0010	−0010	−0010	−0.2	−0.2	+0.1	+0.1
Irvine	55 36N	4 42W	−0020	−0020	−0030	−0010	−0.3	−0.3	−0.1	0.0
Troon	55 33N	4 41W	−0025	−0025	−0020	−0020	−0.2	−0.2	0.0	0.0
Ayr	55 28N	4 39W	−0025	−0025	−0030	−0015	−0.4	−0.3	+0.1	+0.1
Girvan	55 15N	4 52W	−0025	−0040	−0035	−0010	−0.3	−0.3	−0.1	0.0
Loch Ryan Stranraer	54 55N	5 02W	−0030	−0025	−0010	−0010	−0.2	−0.1	0.0	+0.1
			0000	**0600**	**0200**	**0800**				
LIVERPOOL	53 24N	3 01W	and	and	and	and	**9.3**	**7.4**	**2.9**	**0.9**
Standard port			**1200**	**1800**	**1400**	**2000**				
Portpatrick	54 51N	5 07W	+0018	+0026	0000	−0035	−5.5	−4.4	−2.0	−0.6
Luce Bay										
Drummore	54 42N	4 53W	+0030	+0040	+0015	+0020	−3.4	−2.5	−0.9	−0.3
Port William	54 46N	4 35W	+0030	+0030	+0025	0000	−2.9	−2.2	−0.8	*No data*
Wigtown Bay										
Isle of Whithorn	54 42N	4 22W	+0020	+0025	+0025	+0005	−2.4	−2.0	−0.8	−0.2
Garlieston	54 47N	4 22W	+0025	+0035	+0030	+0005	−2.3	−1.7	−0.5	*No data*
Solway Firth										
Kirkcudbright Bay	54 48N	4 04W	+0015	+0015	+0010	0000	−1.8	−1.5	−0.5	−0.1
Hestan Islet	54 50N	3 48W	+0025	+0025	+0020	+0025	−1.0	−1.1	−0.5	0.0
Southerness Point	54 52N	3 36W	+0030	+0030	+0030	+0010	−0.7	−0.7	*No data*	

Location	Lat	Long	High Water		Low Water		MHWS	MHWN	MLWN	MLWS
Annan Waterfoot	54 58N	3 16W	+0050	+0105	+0220	+0310	−2.2	−2.6	−2.7	
Torduff Point	54 58N	3 09W	+0105	+0140	+0520	+0410	−4.1	−4.9		
Redkirk	54 59N	3 06W	+0110	+0215	+0715	+0445	−5.5	−6.2		

WEST COAST OF ENGLAND

Location	Lat	Long	High Water		Low Water		MHWS	MHWN	MLWN	MLWS
Silloth	54 52N	3 24W	+0030	+0040	+0045	+0055	−0.1	−0.3	−0.6	−0.1
Maryport	54 43N	3 30W	+0017	+0032	+0020	+0005	−0.7	−0.8	−0.4	0.0
Workington	54 39N	3 34W	+0020	+0020	+0020	+0010	−1.2	−1.1	−0.3	0.0
Whitehaven	54 33N	3 36W	+0005	+0015	+0010	+0005	−1.3	−1.1	−0.5	+0.1
Tarn Point	54 17N	3 25W	+0005	+0005	+0010	0000	−1.0	−1.0	−0.4	0.0
Duddon Bar	54 09N	3 20W	+0003	+0003	+0008	+0002	−0.8	−0.8	−0.3	0.0

Location	Lat	Long	High Water		Low Water		MHWS	MHWN	MLWN	MLWS
LIVERPOOL	53 24N	3 01W	0000 and 1200	0600 and 1800	0200 and 1400	0700 and 1900	9.3	7.4	2.9	0.9
Standard port										
Barrow-in-Furness	54 06N	3 12W	+0015	+0015	+0015	+0015	0.0	−0.3	+0.1	+0.2
Ulverston	54 11N	3 04W	+0020	+0040	No data	No data	0.0	−0.1	No data	
Arnside	54 12N	2 51W	+0100	+0135	No data	No data	+0.5	+0.2	No data	
Morecambe	54 04N	2 53W	+0005	+0010	+0030	+0015	+0.2	0.0	0.0	+0.2
Heysham	54 02N	2 55W	+0005	+0005	+0015	0000	+0.1	0.0	0.0	+0.2
River Lune Glasson Dock	54 00N	2 51W	+0020	+0030	+0220	+0240	−2.7	−3.0	No data	
Lancaster	54 03N	2 49W	+0110	+0030	*Dries*	*Dries*	−5.0	−4.9	*Dries*	
River Wyre										
Wyre Lighthouse	53 57N	3 02W	−0010	−0010	+0005	0000	−0.1	−0.1	No data	
Fleetwood	53 56N	3 00W	−0008	−0008	−0003	−0003	−0.1	−0.1	+0.1	+0.3
Blackpool	53 49N	3 04W	−0015	−0005	−0005	−0015	−0.4	−0.4	−0.1	+0.1
River Ribble Preston	53 45N	2 45W	+0010	+0010	+0335	+0310	−4.0	−4.1	−2.8	−0.8
Liverpool Bay										
Southport	53 39N	3 01W	−0020	−0010	No data	No data	−0.3	−0.3	No data	
Formby	53 32N	3 07W	−0015	−0010	−0020	−0020	−0.3	−0.1	0.0	+0.1
River Mersey										
Gladstone Dock	53 27N	3 01W	−0003	−0003	−0003	−0003	−0.1	−0.1	0.0	−0.1
Eastham	53 19N	2 57W	+0010	+0010	+0009	+0009	+0.3	+0.1	−0.1	−0.3
Hale Head	53 19N	2 48W	+0030	+0025	No data	No data	−2.4	−2.5	No data	
Widnes	53 21N	2 44W	+0040	+0045	+0400	+0345	−4.2	−4.4	−2.5	−0.3
Fiddler's Ferry	53 22N	2 40W	+0100	+0115	+0540	+0450	−5.9	−6.3	−2.4	−0.4
River Dee										
Hilbre Island	53 23N	3 14W	−0015	−0012	−0010	−0015	−0.3	−0.2	+0.2	+0.4
Chester	53 12N	2 54W	+0105	+0105	+0500	+0500	−5.3	−5.4	*Dries*	
Connah's Quay (Wales)	53 13N	3 03W	0000	+0015	+0355	+0340	−4.6	−4.4	*Dries*	
Mostyn Docks (Wales)	53 19N	3 16W	−0020	−0015	−0020	−0020	−0.8	−0.7	No data	
Isle of Man Peel	54 14N	4 42W	+0005	+0005	−0015	−0025	−4.1	−3.1	−1.4	−0.5
Ramsey	54 19N	4 22W	+0005	+0015	−0005	−0015	−1.9	−1.5	−0.6	0.0
Douglas	54 09N	4 28W	+0005	+0015	−0015	−0025	−2.4	−2.0	−0.5	−0.1
Port St Mary	54 04N	4 44W	+0005	+0015	−0010	−0030	−3.4	−2.6	−1.3	−0.4
Calf Sound	54 04N	4 48W	+0005	+0015	−0015	−0025	−3.2	−2.6	−0.9	−0.3
Port Erin	54 05N	4 46W	−0005	+0015	−0010	−0050	−4.1	−3.2	−1.3	−0.5

WALES

Location	Lat	Long	High Water		Low Water		MHWS	MHWN	MLWN	MLWS
Colwyn Bay	53 18N	3 43W	−0020	−0020	No data	No data	−1.5	−1.3	No data	
Llandudno	53 20N	3 50W	−0020	−0020	−0035	−0040	−1.7	−1.4	−0.7	−0.3

Location	Lat	Long	High Water		Low Water		MHWS	MHWN	MLWN	MLWS
HOLYHEAD	53 19N	4 37W	0000 and 1200	0600 and 1800	0500 and 1700	1100 and 2300	5.6	4.4	2.0	0.7
Standard port										
Conwy	53 17N	3 50W	+0025	+0035	+0120	+0105	+2.3	+1.8	+0.6	+0.4
Menai Strait										
Beaumaris	53 16N	4 05W	+0025	+0010	+0055	+0035	+2.0	+1.6	+0.5	+0.1
Menai Bridge	53 13N	4 10W	+0030	+0010	+0100	+0035	+1.7	+1.4	+0.3	0.0
Port Dinorwic	53 11N	4 13W	−0015	−0025	+0030	0000	0.0	0.0	0.0	+0.1
Caernarfon	53 09N	4 16W	−0030	−0030	+0015	−0005	−0.4	−0.4	−0.1	−0.1
Fort Belan	53 07N	4 20W	−0040	−0015	−0025	−0005	−1.0	−0.9	−0.2	−0.1
Trwyn Dinmor	53 19N	4 03W	+0025	+0015	+0050	+0035	+1.9	+1.5	+0.5	+0.2
Moelfre	53 20N	4 14W	+0025	+0020	+0050	+0035	+1.9	+1.4	+0.5	+0.2
Amlwch	53 25N	4 20W	+0020	+0010	+0035	+0025	+1.6	+ 1.3	+0.5	+0.2
Cemaes Bay	53 25N	4 27W	+0020	+0025	+0040	+0035	+1.0	+0.7	+0.3	+0.1
Trearddur Bay	53 16N	4 37W	−0045	−0025	−0015	−0015	−0.4	−0.4	0.0	+0.1
Porth Trecastell	53 12N	4 30W	−0045	−0025	−0005	−0015	−0.6	−0.6	0.0	0.0
Llanddwyn Island	53 08N	4 25W	−0115	−0055	−0030	−0020	−0.7	−0.5	−0.1	0.0
Trefor	53 00N	4 25W	−0115	−0100	−0030	−0020	−0.8	−0.9	−0.2	−0.1
Porth Dinllaen	52 57N	4 34W	−0120	−0105	−0035	−0025	−1.0	−1.0	−0.2	−0.2
Porth Ysgaden	52 54N	4 39W	−0125	−0110	−0040	−0035	−1.1	−1.0	−0.1	−0.1
Bardsey Island	52 46N	4 47W	−0220	−0240	−0145	−0140	−1.2	−1.2	−0.5	−0.1

TIDES

Location	Lat	Long	High Water		Low Water		MHWS	MHWN	MLWN	MLWS
MILFORD HAVEN	51 42N	5 03W	0100 and 1300	0800 and 2000	0100 and 1300	0700 and 1900	7.0	5.2	2.5	0.7
Standard port										
Cardigan Bay										
Aberdaron	52 48N	4 43W	+0210	+0200	+0240	+0310	−2.4	−1.9	−0.6	−0.2
St Tudwal's Roads	52 49N	4 29W	+0155	+0145	+0240	+0310	−2.2	−1.9	−0.7	−0.2
Pwllheli	52 53N	4 24W	+0210	+0150	+0245	+0320	−2.0	−1.8	−0.6	−0.2
Criccieth	52 55N	4 14W	+0210	+0155	+0255	+0320	−2.0	−1.8	−0.7	−0.3
Porthmadog	52 55N	4 08W	+0235	+0210	No data	No data	−1.9	−1.8	No data	
Barmouth	52 43N	4 03W	+0215	+0205	+0310	+0320	−2.0	−1.7	−0.7	0.0
Aberdovey	52 33N	4 03W	+0215	+0200	+0230	+0305	−2.0	−1.7	−0.5	0.0
Aberystwyth	52 24N	4 05W	+0145	+0130	+0210	+0245	−2.0	−1.7	−0.7	0.0
New Quay	52 13N	4 21W	+0150	+0125	+0155	+0230	−2.1	−1.8	−0.6	−0.1
Aberporth	52 08N	4 33W	+0135	+0120	+0150	+0220	−2.1	−1.8	−0.6	−0.1
Port Cardigan	52 07N	4 41W	+0140	+0120	+0220	+0130	−2.3	−1.8	−0.5	0.0
Cardigan (Town)	52 05N	4 40W	+0220	+0150	No data	No data	−2.2	−1.6	No data	
Fishguard	52 01N	4 59W	+0115	+0100	+0110	+0135	−2.2	−1.8	−0.5	+0.1
Porthgain	51 57N	5 11W	+0055	+0045	+0045	+0100	−2.5	−1.8	−0.6	0.0
Ramsey Sound	51 53N	5 19W	+0030	+0030	+0030	+0030	−1.9	−1.3	−0.3	0.0
Solva	51 52N	5 12W	+0015	+0010	+0035	+0015	−1.5	−1.0	−0.2	0.0
Little Haven	51 46N	5 07W	+0010	+0010	+0025	+0015	−1.1	−0.8	−0.2	0.0
Martin's Haven	51 44N	5 15W	+0010	+0010	+0015	+0015	−0.8	−0.5	+0.1	+0.1
Skomer Island	51 44N	5 17W	−0005	−0005	+0005	+0005	−0.4	−0.1	0.0	0.0
Dale Roads	51 42N	5 09W	−0005	−0005	−0008	−0008	0.0	0.0	0.0	−0.1
Cleddau River										
Neyland	51 42N	4 57W	+0002	+0010	0000	0000	0.0	0.0	0.0	0.0
Black Tar	51 45N	4 54W	+0010	+0020	+0005	0000	+0.1	+0.1	0.0	−0.1
Haverfordwest	51 48N	4 58W	+0010	+0025	Dries	Dries	−4.8	−4.9	Dries	
Stackpole Quay	51 37N	4 54W	−0005	+0025	−0010	−0010	+0.9	+0.7	+0.2	+0.3
Tenby	51 40N	4 42W	−0015	−0010	−0015	−0020	+1.4	+1.1	+0.5	+0.2
Towy River										
Ferryside	51 46N	4 22W	0000	−0010	+0220	0000	−0.3	−0.7	−1.7	−0.6
Carmarthen	51 51N	4 18W	+0010	0000	Dries	Dries	−4.4	−4.8	Dries	
Burry Inlet										
Burry Port	51 41N	4 15W	+0003	+0003	+0007	+0007	+1.6	+1.4	+0.5	+0.4
Llanelli	51 40N	4 10W	−0003	−0003	+0150	+0020	+0.8	+0.6	No data	
Mumbles	51 34N	3 58W	+0005	+0010	−0020	−0015	+2.3	+1.7	+0.6	+0.2
River Neath Entrance	51 37N	3 51W	+0002	+0011	Dries	Dries	+2.7	+2.2	Dries	
Port Talbot	51 35N	3 49W	+0003	+0005	−0010	−0005	+2.8	+2.2	+1.0	+0.5
Porthcawl	51 28N	3 42W	+0005	+0010	−0010	−0005	+2.9	+2.3	+0.8	+0.3
BRISTOL, AVONMOUTH	51 30N	2 44W	0600 and 1800	1100 and 2300	0300 and 1500	0800 and 2000	13.2	9.8	3.8	1.0
Standard port										
Barry	51 23N	3 16W	−0025	−0025	−0130	−0045	−1.7	−1.0	−0.2	0.0
Flat Holm	51 23N	3 07W	−0015	−0015	−0035	−0035	−1.4	−1.0	−0.5	0.0
Steep Holm	51 20N	3 06W	−0020	−0020	−0040	−0040	−1.7	−1.1	−0.5	−0.4
Cardiff	51 27N	3 10W	−0015	−0015	−0100	−0030	−1.0	−0.5	0.0	0.0
Newport	51 33N	2 59W	−0020	−0010	0000	−0020	−1.1	−0.9	−0.6	−0.6
River Wye Chepstow	51 39N	2 40W	+0020	+0020	No data	No data	No data		No data	
BRISTOL, AVONMOUTH	51 30N	2 44W	0000 and 1200	0600 and 1800	0000 and 1200	0700 and 1900	13.2	9.8	3.8	1.0
Standard port										

WEST COAST OF ENGLAND

Location	Lat	Long	High Water		Low Water		MHWS	MHWN	MLWN	MLWS
River Severn										
Sudbrook	51 35N	2 43W	+0010	+0010	+0025	+0015	+0.2	+0.1	−0.1	+0.1
Beachley (Aust)	51 36N	2 38W	+0010	+0015	+0040	+0025	−0.2	−0.2	−0.5	−0.3
Inward Rocks	51 39N	2 37W	+0020	+0020	+0105	+0045	−1.0	−1.1	−1.4	−0.6
Narlwood Rocks	51 39N	2 36W	+0025	+0025	+0120	+0100	−1.9	−2.0	−2.3	−0.8
White House	51 40N	2 33W	+0025	+0025	+0145	+0120	−3.0	−3.1	−3.6	−1.0
Berkeley	51 42N	2 30W	+0030	+0045	+0245	+0220	−3.8	−3.9	−3.4	−0.5
Sharpness Dock	51 43N	2 29W	+0035	+0050	+0305	+0245	−3.9	−4.2	−3.3	−0.4
Wellhouse Rock	51 44N	2 29W	+0040	+0055	+0320	+0305	−4.1	−4.4	−3.1	−0.2
Epney	51 42N	2 24W	+0130	No data	No data	No data	−9.4	No data	No data	
Minsterworth	51 50N	2 23W	+0140	No data	No data	No data	−10.1	No data	No data	
Llanthony	51 51N	2 21W	+0215	No data	No data	No data	−10.7	No data	No data	
BRISTOL, AVONMOUTH	51 30N	2 44W	0200 and 1400	0800 and 2000	0300 and 1500	0800 and 2000	13.2	9.8	3.8	1.0
Standard port										
River Avon										
Shirehampton	51 29N	2 41W	0000	0000	+0035	+0010	−0.7	−0.7	−0.8	0.0

Location	Lat	Long	High Water		Low Water		MHWS	MHWN	MLWN	MLWS
Sea Mills	51 29N	2 39W	+0005	+0005	+0105	+0030	−1.4	−1.5	−1.7	−0.1
Cumberland Basin Entrance	51 27N	2 37W	+0010	+0010	Dries	Dries	−2.9	−3.0	Dries	
Portishead	51 30N	2 45W	−0002	0000	No data	No data	−0.1	−0.1	No data	
Clevedon	51 27N	2 52W	−0010	−0020	−0025	−0015	−0.4	−0.2	+0.2	0.0
St Thomas Head	51 24N	2 56W	0000	0000	−0030	−0030	−0.4	−0.2	+0.1	+0.1
English & Welsh Grounds	51 28N	2 59W	−0008	−0008	−0030	−0030	−0.5	−0.8	−0.3	0.0
Weston-super-Mare	51 21N	2 59W	−0020	−0030	−0130	−0030	−1.2	−1.0	−0.8	−0.2
River Parrett										
Burnham-on-Sea	51 14N	3 00W	−0020	−0025	−0030	0000	−2.3	−1.9	−1.4	−1.1
Bridgwater	51 08N	3 00W	−0015	−0030	+0305	+0455	−8.6	−8.1	Dries	
Hinkley Point	51 13N	3 08W	−0020	−0025	−0100	−0040	−1.7	−1.4	−0.2	−0.2
Watchet	51 11N	3 20W	−0035	−0050	−0145	−0040	−1.9	−1.5	+0.1	+0.1
Minehead	51 13N	3 28W	−0037	−0052	−0155	−0045	−2.6	−1.9	−0.2	0.0
Porlock Bay	51 13N	3 38W	−0045	−0055	−0205	−0050	−3.0	−2.2	−0.1	−0.1
Lynmouth	51 14N	3 50W	−0055	−0115	No data	No data	−3.6	−2.7	No data	
			0100	**0700**	**0100**	**0700**				
MILFORD HAVEN	51 42N	5 03W	and	and	and	and	**7.0**	**5.2**	**2.5**	**0.7**
Standard port			**1300**	**1900**	**1300**	**1900**				
Ilfracombe	51 13N	4 07W	−0016	−0016	−0041	−0031	+2.3	+1.8	+0.6	+0.3
Rivers Taw & Torridge										
Appledore	51 03N	4 12W	−0020	−0025	+0015	−0045	+0.5	0.0	−0.9	−0.5
Yelland Marsh	51 04N	4 10W	−0010	−0015	+0100	−0015	+0.1	−0.4	−1.2	−0.6
Fremington	51 05N	4 07W	−0010	−0015	+0030	−0030	−1.1	−1.8	−2.2	−0.5
Barnstaple	51 05N	4 04W	0000	−0015	−0155	−0245	−2.9	−3.8	−2.2	−0.4
Bideford	51 01N	4 12W	−0020	−0025	0000	0000	−1.1	−1.6	−2.5	−0.7
Clovelly	51 00N	4 24W	−0030	−0030	−0020	−0040	+1.3	+1.1	+0.2	+0.2
Lundy	51 10N	4 39W	−0025	−0025	−0020	−0035	+0.9	+0.7	+0.3	+0.1
Bude	50 50N	4 33W	−0040	−0040	−0035	−0045	+0.7	+0.6	No data	
Boscastle	50 41N	4 42W	−0045	−0010	−0110	−0100	+0.3	+0.4	+0.2	+0.2
Port Isaac	50 35N	4 50W	−0100	−0100	−0100	−0100	+0.5	+0.6	0.0	+0.2
River Camel										
Padstow	50 33N	4 56W	−0055	−0050	−0040	−0050	+0.3	+0.4	+0.1	+0.1
Wadebridge	50 31N	4 50W	−0052	−0052	+0235	+0245	−3.8	−3.8	−2.5	−0.4
Newquay	50 25N	5 05W	−0100	−0110	−0105	−0050	0.0	+0.1	0.0	−0.1
Perranporth	50 21N	5 09W	−0100	−0110	−0110	−0050	−0.1	0.0	0.0	+0.1
St Ives	50 13N	5 29W	−0050	−0115	−0105	−0040	−0.4	−0.3	−0.1	+0.1
Cape Cornwall	50 08N	5 42 W	−0130	−0145	−0120	−0120	−1.0	−0.9	−0.5	−0.1
Sennen Cove	50 05N	5 42W	−0130	−0145	−0125	−0125	−0.9	−0.4	No data	
IRELAND			**0000**	**0700**	**0000**	**0500**				
DUBLIN, NORTH WALL	53 21N	6 13W	and	and	and	and	**4.1**	**3.4**	**1.5**	**0.7**
Standard port			**1200**	**1900**	**1200**	**1700**				
Courtown	52 39N	6 13W	−0328	−0242	−0158	−0138	−2.8	−2.4	−0.5	0.0
Arklow	52 48N	6 08W	−0315	−0201	−0140	−0134	−2.7	−2.2	−0.6	−0.1
Wicklow	52 59N	6 02W	−0019	−0019	−0024	−0026	−1.4	−1.1	−0.4	0.0
Greystones	53 09N	6 04W	−0008	−0008	−0008	−0008	−0.5	−0.4	No data	
Dun Laoghaire	53 18N	6 08W	−0006	−0001	−0002	−0003	0.0	0.0	0.0	+0.1
Dublin Bar	53 21N	6 09W	−0006	−0001	−0002	−0003	0.0	0.0	0.0	+0.1
Howth	53 23N	6 04W	−0007	−0005	+0001	+0005	0.0	−0.1	−0.2	−0.2
Malahide	53 27N	6 09W	+0002	+0003	+0009	+0009	+0.1	−0.2	−0.4	−0.2
Balbriggan	53 37N	6 11W	−0021	−0015	+0010	+0002	+0.3	+0.2	No data	
River Boyne Bar	53 43N	6 14W	−0005	0000	+0020	+0030	+0.4	+0.3	−0.1	−0.2
Dunany Point	53 52N	6 14W	−0028	−0018	−0008	−0006	+0.7	+0.9	No data	
Dundalk Soldiers Point	54 00N	6 21W	−0010	−0010	0000	+0045	+1.0	+0.8	+0.1	−0.1
NORTHERN IRELAND										
Carlingford Lough										
Cranfield Point	54 01N	6 04W	−0027	−0011	+0005	−0010	+0.7	+0.9	+0.3	+0.2
Warrenpoint	54 06N	6 15W	−0020	−0010	+0025	+0035	+1.0	+0.7	+0.2	+0.0
Newry (Victoria Lock)	54 09N	6 19W	+0005	+0015	+0045	Dries	+1.2	+0.9	+0.1	Dries
			0100	**0700**	**0000**	**0600**				
BELFAST	54 36N	5 55W	and	and	and	and	**3.5**	**3.0**	**1.1**	**0.4**
Standard port			**1300**	**1900**	**1200**	**1800**				
Kilkeel	54 03N	5 59W	+0040	+0030	+0010	+0010	+1.2	+1.1	+0.4	+0.4
Newcastle	54 12N	5 53W	+0025	+0035	+0020	+0040	+1.6	+1.1	+0.4	+0.1
Killough Harbour	54 15N	5 38W	0000	+0020	No data	No data	+1.8	+1.6	No data	
Ardglass	54 16N	5 36W	+0010	+0015	+0005	+0010	+1.7	+1.2	+0.6	+0.3
Strangford Lough										
Killard Point	54 19N	5 31W	+0011	+0021	+0005	+0025	+1.0	+0.8	+0.1	+0.1
Strangford	54 22N	5 33W	+0147	+0157	+0148	+0208	+0.1	+0.1	−0.2	0.0
Quoile Barrier	54 22N	5 41W	+0150	+0200	+0150	+0300	+0.2	+0.2	−0.3	−0.1

Location	Lat	Long	High Water		Low Water		MHWS	MHWN	MLWN	MLWS
Killyleagh	54 24N	5 39W	+0157	+0207	+0211	+0231	+0.3	+0.3	No data	
South Rock	54 24N	5 25W	+0023	+0023	+0025	+0025	+1.0	+0.8	+0.1	+0.1
Portavogie	54 27N	5 26W	+0010	+0020	+0010	+0020	+1.2	+0.9	+0.3	+0.2
Donaghadee	54 39N	5 32W	+0020	+0020	+0023	+0023	+0.5	+0.4	0.0	+0.1
Carrickfergus	54 43N	5 48W	+0005	+0005	+0005	+0005	−0.3	−0.3	−0.2	−0.1
Larne	54 51N	5 48W	+0005	0000	+0010	−0005	−0.7	−0.5	−0.3	0.0
Red Bay	55 04N	6 03W	+0022	−0010	+0007	−0017	−1.9	−1.5	−0.8	−0.2
Cushendun	55 08N	6 02W	+0010	−0030	0000	−0025	−1.7	−1.5	−0.6	−0.2
Portrush	55 12N	6 40W	−0433	−0433	−0433	−0433	−1.6	−1.6	−0.3	0.0
Coleraine	55 08N	6 40W	−0403	−0403	−0403	−0403	−1.3	−1.2	−0.2	0.0
GALWAY	53 16N	9 03W	0200 and 1400	0900 and 2100	0200 and 1400	0800 and 2000	**5.1**	**3.9**	**2.0**	**0.6**
Standard port										
Londonderry	55 00N	7 19W	+0254	+0319	+0322	+0321	−2.4	−1.8	−0.8	−0.1

IRELAND

Location	Lat	Long	High Water		Low Water		MHWS	MHWN	MLWN	MLWS
Inishtrahull	55 26N	7 14W	+0100	+0100	+0115	+0200	−1.8	−1.4	−0.4	−0.2
Bulbinbeg	55 22N	7 20W	+0120	+0120	+0135	+0135	−1.3	−1.1	−0.4	−0.1
Trawbreaga Bay	55 19N	7 23W	+0115	+0059	+0109	+0125	−1.1	−0.8	No data	
Lough Swilly										
Rathmullan	55 06N	7 32W	+0125	+0050	+0126	+0118	−0.8	−0.7	−0.1	−0.1
Fanad Head	55 17N	7 38W	+0115	+0040	+0125	+0120	−1.1	−0.9	−0.5	−0.1
Mulroy Bay										
Bar	55 15N	7 46W	+0108	+0052	+0102	+0118	−1.2	−1.0	No data	
Fanny's Bay	55 12N	7 49W	+0145	+0129	+0151	+0207	−2.2	−1.7	No data	
Seamount Bay	55 11N	7 44W	+0210	+0154	+0226	+0242	−3.1	−2.3	No data	
Cranford Bay	55 09N	7 42W	+0329	+0313	+0351	+0407	−3.7	−2.8	No data	
Sheephaven										
Downies Bay	55 11N	7 50W	+0057	+0043	+0053	+0107	−1.1	−0.9	No data	
Inishbofin Bay	55 10N	8 10W	+0040	+0026	+0032	+0046	−1.2	−0.9	No data	
GALWAY	53 16N	9 03W	0600 and 1800	1100 and 2300	0000 and 1200	0700 and 1900	**5.1**	**3.9**	**2.0**	**0.6**
Standard port										
Gweedore Harbour	55 04N	8 19W	+0048	+0100	+0055	+0107	−1.3	−1.0	−0.5	−0.1
Burtonport	54 59N	8 26W	+0042	+0055	+0115	+0055	−1.2	−1.0	−0.6	−0.1
Loughros More Bay	54 47N	8 30W	+0042	+0054	+0046	+0058	−1.1	−0.9	No data	
Donegal Bay										
Killybegs	54 38N	8 26W	+0040	+0050	+0055	+0035	−1.0	−0.9	−0.5	0.0
Donegal Hbr, Salt Hill Quay	54 38N	8 12W	+0038	+0050	+0052	+0104	−1.2	−0.9	No data	
Mullaghmore	54 28N	8 27W	+0036	+0048	+0047	+0059	−1.4	−1.0	−0.4	−0.2
Sligo Hbr (Oyster Island)	54 18N	8 34W	+0043	+0055	+0042	+0054	−1.0	−0.9	−0.5	−0.1
Ballysadare Bay, Culleenamore	54 16N	8 36W	+0059	+0111	+0111	+0123	−1.2	−0.9	No data	
Killala Bay (Inishcrone)	54 13N	9 06W	+0035	+0055	+0030	+0050	−1.3	−1.2	−0.7	−0.2
Broadhaven	54 16N	9 53W	+0040	+0050	+0040	+0050	−1.4	−1.1	−0.4	−0.1
Blacksod Bay										
Blacksod Quay	54 06N	10 04W	+0025	+0035	+0040	+0040	−1.2	−1.0	−0.6	−0.2
Inishbiggle	54 00N	9 53W	+0055	+0100	+0125	+0110	−1.3	− 0.9	−0.5	0.0
Clare Island	53 48N	9 57W	+0015	+0021	+0039	+0027	−0.6	−0.4	−0.1	+0.2
Clew Bay										
Inishgort	53 50N	9 40W	+0035	+0045	+0115	+0100	−0.7	−0.5	−0.2	+0.2
Killary Harbour	53 38N	9 53W	+0021	+0015	+0035	+0029	−1.0	−0.8	−0.4	−0.1
Inishbofin Bofin Harbour	53 37N	10 12W	+0013	+0009	+0021	+0017	−1.0	−0.8	−0.4	−0.1
Clifden Bay	53 29N	10 04W	+0005	+0005	+0016	+0016	−0.7	−0.5	No data	
Slyne Head	53 24N	10 14W	+0002	+0002	+0010	+0010	−0.7	−0.5	No data	
Roundstone Bay	53 23N	9 55W	+0003	+0003	+0008	+0008	−0.7	−0.5	−0.3	−0.1
Kilkieran Cove	53 19N	9 44W	+0005	+0005	+0016	+0016	−0.3	−0.2	−0.1	0.0
Aran Islands Killeany Bay	53 07N	9 40W	−0008	−0008	+0003	+0003	−0.4	−0.3	−0.2	−0.1
Liscannor	52 56N	9 23W	−0003	−0007	+0006	+0002	−0.4	−0.3	No data	
Seafield Point	52 48N	9 30W	−0006	−0014	+0004	−0004	−0.5	−0.4	No data	
Kilrush	52 38N	9 30W	−0006	+0027	+0057	−0016	−0.1	−0.2	−0.3	−0.1
Limerick Dock	52 40N	8 38W	+0135	+0141	+0141	+0219	+1.0	+0.7	−0.8	−0.2
COBH	51 51N	8 18 W	0500 and 1700	1100 and 2300	0500 and 1700	1100 and 2300	**4.1**	**3.2**	**1.3**	**0.4**
Standard port										
Tralee Bay Fenit Pier	52 16N	9 52W	−0057	−0017	−0029	−0109	+0.5	+0.2	+0.3	+0.1
Smerwick Harbour	52 12N	10 24W	−0107	−0027	−0041	−0121	−0.3	−0.4	No data	
Dingle Harbour	52 07N	10 15W	−0111	−0041	−0049	−0119	−0.1	0.0	+0.3	+0.4

Location	Lat	Long	High Water		Low Water		MHWS	MHWN	MLWN	MLWS
Castlemaine Hbr										
Cromane Point	52 08N	9 54W	−0026	−0006	−0017	−0037	+0.4	+0.2	+0.4	+0.2
Valentia Harbour										
Knights Town	51 56N	10 18W	−0118	−0038	−0056	−0136	−0.6	−0.4	−0.1	0.0
Ballinskelligs Bay										
Castle	51 49N	10 16W	−0119	−0039	−0054	−0134	−0.5	−0.5	−0.1	0.0
Kenmare River										
West Cove	51 46N	10 03W	−0113	−0033	−0049	−0129	−0.6	−0.5	−0.1	0.0
Dunkerron Harbour	51 52N	9 39W	−0117	−0027	−0050	−0140	−0.2	−0.3	+0.1	0.0
Coulagh Bay										
Ballycrovane Hbr	51 43N	9 57W	−0116	−0036	−0053	−0133	−0.6	−0.5	−0.1	0.0
Black Ball Harbour	51 36N	10 02W	−0115	−0035	−0047	−0127	−0.7	−0.6	−0.1	+0.1
Bantry Bay										
Castletown Bearhaven	51 39N	9 54W	−0048	−0012	−0025	−0101	−0.9	−0.6	−0.1	0.0
Bantry	51 41N	9 28W	−0045	−0025	−0040	−0105	−0.7	−0.6	−0.2	+0.1
Dunmanus Bay										
Dunbeacon Harbour	51 37N	9 33W	−0057	−0025	−0032	−0104	−0.8	−0.7	−0.3	−0.1
Dunmanus Harbour	51 32N	9 40W	−0107	−0031	−0044	−0120	−0.7	−0.6	−0.2	0.0
Crookhaven	51 28N	9 44W	−0057	−0033	−0048	−0112	−0.8	−0.6	−0.4	−0.1
Skull	51 31N	9 32W	−0040	−0015	−0015	−0110	−0.9	−0.6	−0.2	0.0
Baltimore	51 29N	9 23W	−0025	−0005	−0010	−0050	−0.6	−0.3	+0.1	+0.2
Castletownshend	51 32N	9 10W	−0020	−0030	−0020	−0050	−0.4	−0.2	+0.1	+0.3
Clonakilty Bay	51 35N	8 50W	−0033	−0011	−0019	−0041	−0.3	−0.2	No data	
Courtmacsherry	51 38N	8 43W	−0025	−0008	−0008	−0015	−0.1	−0.1	−0.0	+0.1
Kinsale	51 42N	8 31W	−0019	−0005	−0009	−0023	−0.2	0.0	+0.1	+0.2
Roberts Cove	51 45N	8 19W	−0005	−0005	−0005	−0005	−0.1	0.0	0.0	+0.1
Cork Harbour										
Ringaskiddy	51 50N	8 19W	+0005	+0020	+0007	+0013	+0.1	+0.1	+0.1	+0.1
Marino Point	51 53N	8 20W	0000	+0010	0000	+0010	+0.1	+0.1	0.0	0.0
Cork City	51 54N	8 27W	+0005	+0010	+0020	+0010	+0.4	+0.4	+0.3	+0.2
Ballycotton	51 50N	8 01W	−0011	+0001	+0003	−0009	0.0	0.0	−0.1	0.0
Youghal	51 57N	7 51W	0000	+0010	+0010	0000	−0.2	−0.1	−0.1	−0.1
Dungarvan Harbour	52 05N	7 34W	+0004	+0012	+0007	−0001	0.0	+0.1	−0.2	0.0
Waterford Harbour										
Dunmore East	52 09N	6 59W	+0008	+0003	0000	0000	+0.1	0.0	+0.1	+0.2
Cheekpoint	52 16N	7 00W	+0022	+0020	+0020	+0020	+0.3	+0.2	+0.2	+0.1
Kilmokea Point	52 17N	7 00W	+0026	+0022	+0020	+0020	+0.2	+0.1	+0.1	+0.1
Waterford	52 16N	7 07W	+0057	+0057	+0046	+0046	+0.4	+0.3	−0.1	+0.1
New Ross	52 24N	6 57W	+0100	+0030	+0055	+0130	+0.3	+0.4	+0.3	+0.4
Baginbun Head	52 10N	6 50W	+0003	+0003	−0008	−0008	−0.2	−0.1	+0.2	+0.2
Great Saltee	52 07N	6 37W	+0019	+0009	−0004	+0006	−0.3	−0.4	No data	
Carnsore Point	52 10N	6 22W	+0029	+0019	−0002	−0008	−1.1	−1.0	No data	
Rosslare Europort	52 15N	6 21W	+0045	+0035	+0015	−0005	−2.2	−1.8	−0.5	−0.1
Wexford Harbour	52 20N	6 27W	+0126	+0126	+0118	+0108	−2.1	−1.7	−0.3	+0.1

DENMARK *Time Zone −0100*

Location	Lat	Long	High Water		Low Water		MHWS	MHWN	MLWN	MLWS
			0300	0700	0100	0800				
ESBJERG	55 28N	8 27E	and	and	and	and	1.9	1.5	0.5	0.1
Standard port			1500	1900	1300	2000				
Hirtshals	57 36N	9 58E	+0055	+0320	+0340	+0100	−1.6	−1.3	−0.4	−0.1
Hanstholm	57 08N	8 36E	+0100	+0340	+0340	+0130	−1.6	−1.2	−0.4	−0.1
Thyborøn	56 42N	8 14E	+0120	+0230	+0410	+0210	−1.5	−1.2	−0.4	−0.1
Torsminde	56 22N	8 07E	+0045	+0050	+0040	+0010	−1.3	−1.0	−0.4	−0.1
Hvide Sande	56 00N	8 08E	0000	+0010	−0015	−0025	−1.1	−0.8	−0.3	−0.1
Blavands Huk	55 33N	8 05E	−0120	−0110	−0050	−0100	−0.1	−0.1	−0.2	−0.1
Gradyb Bar	55 26N	8 15E	−0130	−0115	No data	No data	−0.4	−0.3	−0.2	−0.1
Havneby (Rømø)	55 05N	8 34E	−0040	−0005	0000	−0020	0.0	+0.1	−0.2	−0.2
Hojer	54 58N	8 40E	−0020	+0015	No data	No data	+0.5	+0.6	−0.1	−0.1

GERMANY *Time Zone −0100*

Location	Lat	Long	High Water		Low Water		MHWS	MHWN	MLWN	MLWS
			0100	0600	0100	0800				
HELGOLAND	54 11N	7 53E	and	and	and	and	2.7	2.4	0.4	0.0
Standard port			1300	1800	1300	2000				
Lister Tief, List	55 01N	8 26E	+0252	+0240	+0201	+0210	−0.7	−0.6	−0.2	0.0
Hörnum	54 45N	8 18E	+0223	+0218	+0131	+0137	−0.4	−0.3	−0.1	0.0
Amrum–Hafen	54 38N	8 23E	+0138	+0137	+0128	+0134	+0.2	+0.2	0.0	0.0
Dagebüll	54 44N	8 41E	+0226	+0217	+0211	+0225	+0.5	+0.5	−0.1	0.0
Suderoogsand	54 25N	8 30E	+0116	+0102	+0038	+0122	+0.5	+0.4	+0.1	0.0
Hever, Husum	54 28N	9 01E	+0205	+0152	+0118	+0200	+1.1	+1.0	0.0	0.0
Suederhoeft	54 16N	8 42E	+0103	+0056	+0051	+0112	+0.7	+0.6	−0.1	0.0
Eidersperrwerk	54 16N	8 51E	+0120	+0115	+0130	+0155	+0.7	+0.6	0.0	0.0

Location	Lat	Long	High Water		Low Water		MHWS	MHWN	MLWN	MLWS
Linnenplate	54 13N	8 40E	+0047	+0046	+0034	+0046	+0.7	+0.6	0.0	−0.1
Büsum	54 07N	8 52E	+0054	+0049	−0001	+0027	+0.9	+0.8	+0.1	+0.1
CUXHAVEN Standard port River Elbe	53 52N	8 43E	0200 and 1400	0800 and 2000	0200 and 1400	0900 and 2100	**3.3**	**3.0**	**0.5**	**0.1**
Großer Vogelsand	54 00N	8 29E	−0044	−0046	−0101	−0103	0.0	−0.1	0.0	0.0
Scharhörn	53 58N	8 28E	−0045	−0047	−0101	−0103	+0.1	0.0	0.0	+0.1
Otterndorf	53 50N	8 52E	+0025	+0025	+0022	+0022	0.0	−0.1	−0.1	0.0
Brunsbüttel	53 53N	9 08E	+0057	+0105	+0121	+0112	−0.2	−0.3	−0.2	+0.1
Glückstadt	53 47N	9 25E	+0205	+0214	+0220	+0213	−0.3	−0.3	−0.3	+0.1
Krautsand	53 45N	9 23E	+0216	+0216	+0214	+0214	−0.2	−0.2	−0.2	+0.1
Stadersand	53 38N	9 32E	+0241	+0245	+0300	+0254	0.0	0.0	−0.3	0.0
Schulau	53 34N	9 42E	+0304	+0315	+0337	+0321	+0.1	+0.1	−0.3	−0.1
Seemannshoeft	53 32N	9 53E	+0324	+0332	+0403	+0347	+0.2	+0.3	−0.5	−0.1
Hamburg	53 33N	9 58E	+0338	+0346	+0422	+0406	+0.3	+0.3	−0.5	−0.2
Harburg	53 28N	10 00E	+0344	+0350	+0430	+0416	+0.4	+0.3	−0.5	−0.2
WILHELMSHAVEN Standard port River Weser	53 31N	8 09E	0200 and 1400	0800 and 2000	0200 and 1400	0900 and 2100	**4.3**	**3.8**	**0.6**	**0.0**
Alter Weser Lt Ho	53 32N	8 08E	−0055	−0048	−0015	−0029	−1.1	−0.9	−0.2	0.0
Dwarsgat	53 43N	8 18E	−0015	+0002	−0006	−0001	−0.6	−0.5	−0.2	0.0
Bremerhaven	53 33N	8 34E	+0029	+0046	+0033	+0038	−0.2	−0.1	−0.2	0.0
Nordenham	53 28N	8 29E	+0051	+0109	+0055	+0058	−0.2	−0.1	−0.4	−0.2
Brake	53 19N	8 29E	+0120	+0119	+0143	+0155	−0.3	−0.2	−0.4	−0.2
Elsfleth	53 16N	8 29E	+0137	+0137	+0206	+0216	−0.2	−0.1	−0.3	0.0
Vegesack	53 10N	8 37E	+0208	+0204	+0250	+0254	−0.2	−0.2	−0.5	−0.2
Bremen	53 07N	8 43E	+0216	+0211	+0311	+0314	−0.1	−0.1	−0.6	−0.3
River Jade										
Wangerooge East	53 46N	7 59E	−0058	−0053	−0024	−0034	−0.9	−0.9	−0.1	0.0
Wangerooge West	53 47N	7 52E	−0101	−0058	−0035	−0045	−1.1	−1.0	−0.2	0.0
Schillig	53 42N	8 03E	−0031	−0025	−0006	−0014	−0.7	−0.6	0.0	0.0
Hooksiel	53 39N	8 05E	−0023	−0022	−0008	−0012	−0.5	−0.4	0.0	0.0
HELGOLAND Standard port East Frisian Islands and coast	54 11N	7 53E	0200 and 1400	0700 and 1900	0200 and 1400	0800 and 2000	**2.7**	**2.4**	**0.4**	**0.0**
Spiekeroog	53 45N	7 41E	+0003	−0003	−0031	−0012	+0.4	+0.3	0.0	0.0
Neuharlingersiel	53 42N	7 42E	+0014	+0008	−0024	−0013	+0.5	+0.4	0.0	−0.1
Langeoog	53 43N	7 30E	+0003	−0001	−0034	−0018	+0.4	+0.2	0.0	0.0
Norderney (Riffgat)	53 42N	7 09E	−0024	−0030	−0056	−0045	+0.1	0.0	0.0	0.0
Norddeich Hafen	53 39N	7 09E	−0018	−0017	−0029	−0012	+0.1	+0.1	0.0	−0.1
Juist	53 40N	7 00E	−0026	−0032	−0019	−0008	+0.6	+0.5	+0.5	+0.4
River Ems										
Memmert	53 38N	6 54E	−0032	−0038	−0114	−0103	+0.5	+0.5	+0.5	+0.4
Borkum (Fischerbalje)	53 33N	6 45E	−0048	−0052	−0124	−0105	+0.4	+0.4	+0.4	+0.4
Emshorn	53 30N	6 50E	−0037	−0041	−0108	−0047	+0.5	+0.5	+0.4	+0.4
Knock	53 20N	7 02E	+0018	+0005	−0028	+0004	+0.6	+0.6	0.0	0.0
Emden	53 20N	7 11E	+0041	+0028	−0011	+0022	+0.9	+0.8	0.0	0.0

NETHERLANDS Time Zone −0100

	Lat	Long	High Water		Low Water		MHWS	MHWN	MLWN	MLWS
HELGOLAND Standard port	54 11N	7 53E	0200 and 1400	0700 and 1900	0200 and 1400	0800 and 2000	**2.7**	**2.4**	**0.4**	**0.0**
Nieuwe Statenzijl	53 14N	7 13E	+0101	+0045	+0026	+0026	+1.0	+0.8	+0.9	+0.6
Delfzijl	53 20N	6 56E	+0020	−0005	−0040	0000	+0.8	+0.8	+0.2	+0.2
Eemshaven	53 26N	6 52E	−0025	−0045	−0115	−0045	+0.5	+0.4	+0.3	+0.3
Schiermonnikoog	53 28N	6 12E	−0120	−0130	−0240	−0220	+0.1	+0.1	+0.3	+0.3
Waddenzee										
Lauwersoog	53 25N	6 12E	−0130	−0145	−0235	−0220	+0.1	+0.1	+0.2	+0.2
Nes	53 26N	5 47E	−0135	−0150	−0245	−0225	+0.1	0.0	+0.2	+0.2
West Terschelling	53 22N	5 13E	−0220	−0250	−0335	−0310	−0.4	−0.4	+0.1	+0.2
Vlieland–Haven	53 18N	5 06E	−0250	−0320	−0355	−0330	−0.4	−0.4	+0.1	+0.2
Harlingen	53 10N	5 25E	−0155	−0245	−0210	−0130	−0.5	−0.5	−0.1	+0.2
Kornwerderzand	53 04N	5 20E	−0210	−0315	−0300	−0215	−0.5	−0.5	−0.1	+0.2
Den Oever	52 56N	5 02E	−0245	−0410	−0400	−0305	−0.8	−0.7	0.0	+0.2
Oudeschild	53 02N	4 51E	−0310	−0420	−0445	−0400	−1.0	−0.8	0.0	+0.2

Location	Lat	Long	High Water		Low Water		MHWS	MHWN	MLWN	MLWS
Den Helder	52 58N	4 45E	−0410	−0520	−0520	−0430	−1.0	−0.8	0.0	+0.2
Noordwinning (Platform K13–A)	53 13N	3 13E	−0420	−0430	−0520	−0530	−1.1	−1.1	+0.1	+0.1
			0300	0900	0400	1000				
VLISSINGEN	51 27N	3 36E	and	and	and	and	4.7	3.8	0.8	0.2
Standard port			1500	2100	1600	2200				
IJmuiden	52 28N	4 35E	+0145	+0140	+0305	+0325	−2.6	−2.1	−0.5	0.0
Scheveningen	52 06N	4 16E	+0105	+0100	+0220	+0245	−2.6	−2.1	−0.6	0.0
Europlatform	52 00N	3 17E	+0005	−0005	−0030	−0055	−2.6	−2.1	−0.5	0.0
Nieuwe Waterweg										
HOEK VAN HOLLAND			*Standard port*							
Maassluis	51 55N	4 15E	+0155	+0115	+0100	+0310	−2.7	−2.1	−0.6	0.0
Nieuwe Maas, Vlaardingen	51 54N	4 21E	+0150	+0120	+0130	+0330	−2.6	−2.1	−0.6	0.0
Lek										
Krimpen Aan de Lek	51 53N	4 38E	+0225	+0200	+0325	+0445	−3.1	−2.5	−0.7	0.0
Schoonhoven	51 57N	4 51E	+0415	+0315	+0435	+0545	−3.1	−2.3	−0.4	+0.2
Oude Maas										
Spijkenisse	51 52N	4 20E	+0145	+0120	+0145	+0310	−2.9	−2.3	−0.6	0.0
Goidschalxoord	51 50N	4 27E	+0200	+0140	+0240	+0410	−3.3	−2.7	−0.7	0.0
Merwede										
Dordrecht	51 49N	4 39E	+0220	+0210	+0420	+0510	−3.7	−3.0	−0.7	−0.1
Werkendam	51 49N	4 53E	+0425	+0410	+0550	+0650	−4.0	−3.2	−0.5	+0.1
Moerdijk	51 42N	4 36E	+0525	+0450	+0520	+0605	−4.2	−3.3	−0.6	+0.1
Haringvlietsluizen	51 50N	4 02E	+0015	+0015	+0015	−0020	−1.7	−1.6	−0.4	+0.1
Brouwershavensche Gat	51 45N	3 49E	0000	+0010	0000	−0030	−1.5	−1.3	−0.3	+0.1
Ooster Schelde										
Roompot Buiten	51 37N	3 40E	−0015	+0005	+0005	−0020	−1.1	−0.9	−0.2	+0.1
Stavenisse	51 36N	4 01E	+0150	+0120	+0055	+0115	−1.2	−0.8	−0.4	+0.1
Bergse Diepsluis (West)	51 30N	4 12E	+0145	+0125	+0105	+0115	−0.6	−0.3	−0.2	+0.1
Zijpe, Philipsdam (West)	51 40N	4 11E	+0215	+0125	+0100	+0110	−1.1	−0.7	−0.4	0.0
Walcheren, Westkapelle	51 31N	3 27E	−0025	−0015	−0010	−0025	−0.5	−0.5	−0.1	+0.1
Westerschelde										
Terneuzen	51 20N	3 50E	+0020	+0020	+0020	+0030	+0.4	+0.4	0.0	+0.1
Hansweert	51 27N	4 00E	+0100	+0050	+0040	+0100	+0.6	+0.7	0.0	+0.1
Bath	51 24N	4 13E	+0125	+0115	+0115	+0140	+1.0	+1.0	0.0	+0.1

BELGIUM *Time Zone –0100*

Location	Lat	Long	High Water		Low Water		MHWS	MHWN	MLWN	MLWS
Antwerpen	51 21N	4 14E	+0128	+0116	+0121	+0144	+1.2	+1.0	+0.1	+0.1
Zeebrugge	51 21N	3 12E	−0035	−0015	−0020	−0035	+0.2	+0.2	+0.4	+0.2
Blankenberge	51 19N	3 07E	−0040	−0040	−0040	−0040	−0.3	0.0	+0.3	+0.2
Oostende	51 14N	2 56E	−0055	−0040	−0030	−0045	+0.5	+0.5	+0.4	+0.2
Nieuwpoort	51 09N	2 43E	−0110	−0050	−0035	−0045	+0.7	+0.6	+0.5	+0.2

FRANCE *Time Zone –0100*

Location	Lat	Long	High Water		Low Water		MHWS	MHWN	MLWN	MLWS
			0200	0800	0200	0900				
DUNKERQUE	51 03N	2 22E	and	and	and	and	6.0	5.0	1.5	0.6
Standard port			1400	2000	1400	2100				
Gravelines	51 01N	2 06E	−0010	−0015	−0010	−0005	+0.4	+0.3	−1.0	0.0
Sandettie Bank	51 09N	1 47E	−0015	−0025	−0020	−0005	+0.1	−0.1	−0.1	−0.1
Calais	51 58N	1 51E	−0020	−0030	−0015	−0005	+1.2	+0.9	+0.6	+0.3
Wissant	50 53N	1 40E	−0035	−0050	−0030	−0010	+1.9	+1.5	+0.8	+0.4
			0100	0600	0100	0700				
DIEPPE	49 56N	1 05E	and	and	and	and	9.3	7.4	2.5	0.8
Standard port			1300	1800	1300	1900				
Boulogne	50 44N	1 35E	+0014	+0027	+0035	+0033	−0.4	−0.2	+0.1	+0.3
Le Touquet, Étaples	50 31N	1 35E	+0005	+0015	+0030	+0030	+0.2	+0.3	+0.4	+0.4
Berck	50 24N	1 34E	+0007	+0017	+0028	+0028	+0.5	+0.5	+0.4	+0.4
La Somme										
Le Hourdel	50 13N	1 34E	+0020	+0020	*no data*	*no data*	+0.8	+0.6	*no data*	
St Valéry	50 11N	1 37E	+0035	+0035	*no data*	*no data*	+0.9	+0.7	*no data*	
Cayeux	50 11N	1 29E	0000	+0005	+0015	+0010	+0.4	+0.5	+0.5	+0.5
Le Tréport	50 04N	1 22E	+0005	0000	+0007	+0007	+0.1	+0.1	+0.1	+0.1
St Valéry–en–Caux	49 52N	0 42E	−0005	−0005	−0015	−0020	−0.5	−0.4	−0.1	−0.1
Fécamp	49 46N	0 22E	−0015	−0010	−0030	−0040	−1.0	−0.6	+0.3	+0.4
Etretat	49 42N	0 12E	−0020	−0020	−0045	−0050	−1.2	−0.8	+0.3	+0.4
			0000	0500	0000	0700				
LE HAVRE	49 29N	0 07E	and	and	and	and	7.9	6.6	2.8	1.2
Standard port			1200	1700	1200	1900				
Antifer (Le Havre)	49 39N	0 09E	+0025	+0015	+0005	−0007	+0.1	0.0	0.0	0.0

Location	Lat	Long	High Water		Low Water		MHWS	MHWN	MLWN	MLWS
La Seine										
Honfleur	49 25N	0 14E	−0135	−0135	+0015	+0040	+0.1	+0.1	+0.1	+0.3
Tancarville	49 28N	0 28E	−0105	−0100	+0105	+0140	−0.1	−0.1	0.0	+1.0
Quilleboeuf	49 28N	0 32E	−0045	−0050	+0120	+0200	0.0	0.0	+0.2	+1.4
Vatteville	49 29N	0 40E	+0005	−0020	+0225	+0250	0.0	−0.1	+0.8	+2.3
Caudebec	49 32N	0 44E	+0020	−0015	+0230	+0300	−0.3	−0.2	+0.9	+2.4
Heurteauville	49 27N	0 49E	+0110	+0025	+0310	+0330	−0.5	−0.2	+1.1	+2.7
Duclair	49 29N	0 53E	+0225	+0150	+0355	+0410	−0.4	−0.3	+1.4	+3.3
Rouen	49 27N	1 06E	+0440	+0415	+0525	+0525	−0.2	−0.1	+1.6	+3.6
Trouville	49 22N	0 05E	−0100	−0010	0000	+0005	+0.4	+0.3	+0.3	+0.1
Dives	49 18N	0 05W	−0100	−0010	0000	0000	+0.3	+0.2	+0.2	+0.1
Ouistreham	49 17N	0 15W	−0045	−0010	−0005	0000	−0.3	−0.3	−0.2	−0.3
Courseulles-sur-Mer	49 20N	0 27W	−0045	−0015	−0020	−0025	−0.5	−0.5	−0.1	−0.1
Arromanches	49 21N	0 37W	−0055	−0025	−0027	−0035	−0.6	−0.6	−0.2	−0.2
Port-en-Bessin	49 21N	0 45W	−0055	−0030	−0030	−0035	−0.7	−0.7	−0.2	−0.1
Alpha-Baie de Seine	49 49N	0 20W	+0030	+0020	−0005	−0020	−1.0	−0.9	−0.4	−0.2
CHERBOURG	49 39N	1 38W	0300 and 1500	1000 and 2200	0400 and 1600	1000 and 2200	**6.4**	**5.0**	**2.5**	**1.1**
Standard port										
Rade de la Capelle	49 25N	1 05W	+0115	+0050	+0130	+0117	+0.8	+0.9	+0.1	+0.1
Iles Saint Marcouf	49 30N	1 08W	+0118	+0052	+0125	+0110	+0.6	+0.7	+0.1	+0.1
St Vaast–la–Hougue	49 34N	1 16W	+0120	+0050	+0120	+0115	+0.3	+0.5	0.0	−0.1
Barfleur	49 40N	1 15W	+0110	+0055	+0052	+0052	+0.1	+0.3	0.0	0.0
Omonville	49 42N	1 50W	−0010	−0010	−0015	−0015	−0.1	−0.1	0.0	0.0
Goury	49 43N	1 57W	−0100	−0040	−0105	−0120	+1.7	+1.6	+1.0	+0.3

CHANNEL ISLANDS *Time Zone UT*

Location	Lat	Long	High Water		Low Water		MHWS	MHWN	MLWN	MLWS
ST HELIER	49 11N	2 07W	0300 and 1500	0900 and 2100	0200 and 1400	0900 and 2100	**11.0**	**8.1**	**4.0**	**1.4**
Standard port										
Alderney, Braye	49 43N	2 12W	+0050	+0040	+0025	+0105	−4.8	−3.4	−1.5	−0.5
Sark, Maseline Pier	49 26N	2 21W	+0005	+0015	+0005	+0010	−2.1	−1.5	−0.6	−0.3
Guernsey, St PETER PORT	49 27N	2 31W	*Standard port (no secondaries)*							
Jersey										
St Catherine Bay	49 13N	2 01W	0000	+0010	+0010	+0010	0.0	−0.1	0.0	+0.1
Bouley Bay	49 14N	2 05W	+0002	+0002	+0004	+0004	−0.3	−0.3	−0.1	−0.1
Les Ecrehou	49 17N	1 56W	+0005	+0009	+0011	+0009	−0.2	+0.1	−0.2	0.0
Les Minquiers	48 57N	2 08W	−0014	−0018	−0001	−0008	+0.5	+0.6	+0.1	+0.1

FRANCE *Time Zone −0100*

Location	Lat	Long	High Water		Low Water		MHWS	MHWN	MLWN	MLWS
ST MALO	48 38N	2 02W	0100 and 1300	0800 and 2000	0300 and 1500	0800 and 2000	**12.2**	**9.3**	**4.2**	**1.5**
Standard port										
Les Ardentes	48 58N	1 52W	+0010	+0010	+0020	+0010	0.0	−0.1	0.0	−0.1
Iles Chausey	48 52N	1 49W	+0005	+0005	+0015	+0015	+0.8	+0.7	+0.6	+0.4
Diélette	49 33N	1 52W	+0045	+0035	+0020	+0035	−2.5	−1.9	−0.7	−0.3
Carteret	49 22N	1 47W	+0030	+0020	+0015	+0030	−1.6	−1.2	−0.5	−0.2
Portbail	49 18N	1 45W	+0030	+0025	+0025	+0030	−0.8	−0.6	−0.2	−0.1
St Germain sur Ay	49 14N	1 36W	+0025	+0025	+0035	+0035	−0.7	−0.5	0.0	+0.1
Le Sénéquet	49 05N	1 40W	+0015	+0015	+0023	+0023	−0.3	−0.3	+0.1	+0.1
Regnéville sur Mer	49 01N	1 33W	+0010	+0010	+0030	+0020	+0.4	+0.3	+0.2	0.0
Granville	48 50N	1 36W	+0005	+0005	+0025	+0025	+0.7	+0.5	+0.3	+0.1
Cancale	48 40N	1 51W	−0002	−0002	+0010	+0010	+0.8	+0.6	+0.3	+0.1
Ile des Hebihens	48 37N	2 11W	−0002	−0002	−0005	−0005	−0.2	−0.2	−0.1	−0.1
St Cast	48 38N	2 15W	−0002	−0002	−0005	−0005	−0.2	−0.2	−0.1	−0.1
Erquy	48 38N	2 28W	−0010	−0005	−0023	−0017	−0.6	−0.5	0.0	0.0
Dahouët	48 35N	2 34W	−0010	−0010	−0025	−0020	−0.9	−0.7	−0.2	−0.2
Le Légué (Buoy)	48 34N	2 41W	−0010	−0005	−0020	−0015	−0.8	−0.5	−0.2	−0.1
Binic	48 36N	2 49W	−0008	−0008	−0030	−0015	−0.8	−0.7	−0.2	−0.2
St Quay-Portrieux	48 38N	2 49W	−0010	−0005	−0025	−0020	−0.9	−0.7	−0.2	−0.1
Paimpol	48 47N	3 02W	−0010	−0005	−0035	−0025	−1.4	−1.0	−0.4	−0.2
Ile de Bréhat	48 51N	3 00W	−0015	−0010	−0045	−0035	−1.9	−1.4	−0.6	−0.3
Les Héaux de Bréhat	48 55N	3 05W	−0020	−0015	−0055	−0035	−2.4	−1.7	−0.7	−0.3
Lézardrieux	48 47N	3 06W	−0020	−0015	−0055	−0045	−1.7	−1.3	−0.5	−0.2
Port–Béni	48 51N	3 10W	−0025	−0025	−0105	−0050	−2.4	−1.7	−0.6	−0.2
Tréguier	48 47N	3 13W	−0020	−0020	−0100	−0045	−2.3	−1.6	−0.6	−0.2
Perros–Guirec	48 49N	3 28W	−0040	−0045	−0120	−0105	−2.9	−2.0	−0.8	−0.3
Ploumanac'h	48 50N	3 29W	−0035	−0040	−0120	−0100	−2.9	−2.0	−0.7	−0.2

Location	Lat	Long	High Water		Low Water		MHWS	MHWN	MLWN	MLWS
			0000	0600	0000	0600				
BREST	48 23N	4 30W	and	and	and	and	7.0	5.5	2.7	1.1
Standard port			1200	1800	1200	1800				
Trébeurden	48 46N	3 35W	+0100	+0110	+0120	+0100	+2.2	+1.8	+0.8	+0.3
Locquirec	48 42N	3 38W	+0058	+0108	+0120	+0100	+2.1	+1.7	+0.7	+0.2
Anse de Primel	48 43N	3 50W	+0100	+0110	+0120	+0100	+2.0	+1.6	+0.7	+0.2
Chateau du Taureau (Morlaix)	48 41N	3 53W	+0055	+0105	+0115	+0055	+1.9	+1.6	+0.7	+0.2
Roscoff	48 43N	3 58W	+0055	+0105	+0115	+0055	+1.9	+1.5	+0.7	+0.2
Ile de Batz	48 44N	4 00W	+0045	+0100	+0105	+0055	+1.9	+1.5	+0.8	+0.3
Brignogan	48 40N	4 19W	+0040	+0045	+0058	+0038	+1.4	+1.1	+0.5	+0.1
L'Aber Vrac'h, Ile Cézon	48 36N	4 34W	+0030	+0030	+0040	+0035	+0.7	+0.6	+0.1	−0.1
Aber Benoit	48 35N	4 37W	+0022	+0025	+0035	+0020	+0.8	+0.6	+0.2	0.0
Portsall	48 34N	4 43W	+0015	+0020	+0025	+0015	+0.5	+0.4	0.0	−0.1
L'Aber Ildut	48 28N	4 45W	+0010	+0010	+0023	+0010	+0.3	+0.2	−0.1	−0.1
Ouessant, Baie de Lampaul	48 27N	5 06W	+0010	+0010	0000	+0005	−0.1	−0.1	−0.1	−0.1
Molene	48 24N	4 58W	+0012	+0012	+0017	+0017	+0.2	+0.1	0.0	−0.1
Le Conquet	48 22N	4 47W	−0005	0000	+0007	+0007	−0.2	−0.2	−0.2	−0.1
Le Trez Hir	48 21N	4 42W	−0010	−0005	−0008	−0008	−0.4	−0.4	−0.2	−0.1
Camaret	48 17N	4 35W	−0010	−0010	−0013	−0013	−0.4	−0.4	−0.2	−0.1
Morgat	48 13N	4 30W	−0008	−0008	−0020	−0010	−0.5	−0.5	−0.3	−0.1
Douarnenez	48 06N	4 19W	−0010	−0015	−0018	−0008	−0.6	−0.6	−0.4	−0.2
Ile de Sein	48 02N	4 51W	−0005	−0005	−0010	−0005	−0.8	−0.7	−0.3	−0.2
Audierne	48 01N	4 33W	−0035	−0030	−0035	−0030	−1.8	−1.4	−0.7	−0.3
Le Guilvinec	47 48N	4 17W	−0010	−0025	−0025	−0015	−1.9	−1.5	−0.7	−0.2
Lesconil	47 48N	4 13W	−0008	−0028	−0028	−0018	−2.0	−1.5	−0.7	−0.2
Pont l'Abbe River, Loctudy	47 50N	4 10W	−0010	−0030	−0030	−0020	−2.1	−1.7	−0.8	−0.4
Odet River										
Bénodet	47 53N	4 07W	0000	−0020	−0023	−0013	−1.9	−1.5	−0.7	−0.3
Corniguel	47 58N	4 06W	+0015	+0010	−0015	−0010	−2.1	−1.7	−1.1	−0.8
Concarneau	47 52N	3 55W	−0010	−0030	−0030	−0020	−2.0	−1.6	−0.8	−0.3
Iles de Glenan, Ile de Penfret	47 44N	3 57W	−0005	−0030	−0028	−0018	−2.0	−1.6	−0.8	−0.3
Port Louis	47 42N	3 21W	+0004	−0021	−0022	−0012	−1.9	−1.5	−0.7	−0.2
Lorient	47 45N	3 21W	+0003	−0022	−0020	−0010	−1.9	−1.5	−0.7	−0.3
Hennebont	47 48N	3 17W	+0015	−0017	+0005	+0003	−2.0	−1.6	−0.9	−0.3
Ile de Groix, Port Tudy	47 39N	3 27W	0000	−0025	−0025	−0015	−1.9	−1.5	−0.7	−0.2
Port d'Etel	47 39N	3 12W	+0020	−0010	+0030	+0010	−2.1	−1.4	−0.5	+0.4
Port–Haliguen	47 29N	3 06W	+0015	−0020	−0015	−0010	−1.9	−1.5	−0.8	−0.5
Port Maria	47 29N	3 08W	+0010	−0025	−0025	−0015	−1.7	−1.4	−0.7	−0.2
Belle–Ile, Le Palais	47 21N	3 09W	+0007	−0028	−0025	−0020	−1.9	−1.5	−0.8	−0.4
Crac'h River, La Trinité	47 35N	3 01W	+0020	−0020	−0015	−0005	−1.6	−1.2	−0.6	−0.3
Golfe du Morbihan										
Port-Navalo	47 33N	2 55W	+0030	−0005	−0010	−0005	−2.1	−1.6	−0.9	−0.4
Auray	47 40N	2 59W	+0055	0000	+0020	+0005	−2.1	−1.5	−0.9	−0.3
Arradon	47 37N	2 50W	+0155	+0145	+0145	+0130	−3.8	−2.8	−1.7	−0.6
Vannes	47 39N	2 46W	+0220	+0200	+0200	+0125	−3.7	−2.8	−1.7	−0.6
St Armel (Le Passage)	47 36N	2 43W	+0205	+0200	+0210	+0140	−3.6	−2.6	−1.6	−0.6
Le Logeo	47 33N	2 51W	+0155	+0140	+0145	+0125	−3.8	−2.8	−1.7	−0.6
Port du Crouesty	47 32N	2 54W	+0013	−0022	−0017	−0012	−1.7	−1.3	−0.7	−0.4
Ile de Houat	47 24N	2 57W	+0010	−0025	−0020	−0015	−1.8	−1.4	−0.7	−0.3
Ile de Hoedic	47 20N	2 52W	+0010	−0035	−0027	−0022	−1.9	−1.5	−0.8	−0.4
Pénerf	47 31N	2 37W	+0020	−0025	−0015	−0015	−1.6	−1.2	−0.7	−0.4
Tréhiguier	47 30N	2 27W	+0035	−0020	−0005	−0010	−1.5	−1.1	−0.6	−0.4
Le Croisic	47 18N	2 31W	+0015	−0040	−0020	−0015	−1.6	−1.2	−0.7	−0.4
Le Pouliguen	47 17N	2 25W	+0020	−0025	−0020	−0025	−1.6	−1.2	−0.7	−0.4
Le Grand–Charpentier	47 13N	2 19W	+0015	−0045	−0025	−0020	−1.6	−1.2	−0.7	−0.4
Pornichet	47 16N	2 21W	+0020	−0045	−0022	−0022	−1.5	−1.1	−0.6	−0.3
La Loire St Nazaire	47 16N	2 12W	+0030	−0040	−0010	−0010	−1.2	−0.9	−0.5	−0.3
Donges	47 18N	2 05W	+0035	−0035	+0005	+0005	−1.1	−0.8	−0.6	−0.5
Cordemais	47 17N	1 54W	+0055	−0005	+0105	+0030	−0.8	−0.6	−0.8	−0.5
Le Pellerin	47 12N	1 46W	+0110	+0010	+0145	+0100	−0.8	−0.6	−1.0	−0.5
Nantes (Chantenay)	47 12N	1 35W	+0135	+0055	+0215	+0125	−0.7	−0.4	−0.9	−0.2
			0500	1100	0500	1100				
BREST	48 23N	4 30W	and	and	and	and	7.0	5.5	2.7	1.1
Standard port			1700	2300	1700	2300				
Pointe de Saint–Gildas	47 08N	2 15W	−0045	+0025	−0020	−0020	−1.4	−1.1	−0.6	−0.3
Pornic	47 06N	2 07W	−0050	+0030	−0010	−0010	−1.2	−0.9	−0.5	−0.3
Ile de Noirmoutier, L'Herbaudière	47 02N	2 18W	−0047	+0023	−0020	−0020	−1.5	−1.1	−0.6	−0.3
Fromentine	46 54N	2 10W	−0050	+0020	−0020	+0010	−1.7	−1.3	−0.8	−0.1
Ile de Yeu, Port Joinville	46 44N	2 21W	−0040	+0015	−0030	−0035	−2.0	−1.5	−0.8	−0.4

Location	Lat	Long	High Water		Low Water		MHWS	MHWN	MLWN	MLWS
St Gilles–Croix–de–Vie	46 41N	1 56W	−0030	+0015	−0032	−0032	−1.9	−1.4	−0.7	−0.4
Les Sables d'Olonne	46 30N	1 48W	−0030	+0015	−0035	−0035	−1.8	−1.4	−0.7	−0.4
POINTE DE GRAVE *Standard port*	45 34N	1 04W	0000 and 1200	0600 and 1800	0500 and 1700	1200 and 2400	**5.4**	**4.4**	**2.1**	**1.0**
Ile de Ré, St Martin	46 12N	1 22W	+0015	−0030	−0025	−0020	+0.6	+0.5	+0.3	−0.1
La Pallice	46 10N	1 13W	+0015	−0030	−0025	−0020	+0.6	+0.5	+0.3	−0.1
La Rochelle	46 09N	1 09W	+0015	−0030	−0025	−0020	+0.6	+0.5	+0.3	−0.1
Ile d'Aix	46 01N	1 10W	+0015	−0040	−0030	−0025	+0.7	+0.5	+0.3	−0.1
La Charente, Rochefort	45 57N	0 58W	+0035	−0010	+0030	+0125	+1.1	+0.9	+0.1	−0.2
Le Chapus	45 51N	1 11W	+0015	−0040	−0025	−0015	+0.6	+0.6	+0.4	+0.2
La Cayenne	45 47N	1 08W	+0030	−0015	−0010	−0005	+0.2	+0.2	+0.3	0.0
Pointe de Gatseau	45 48N	1 14W	+0005	−0005	−0015	−0025	−0.1	−0.1	+0.2	+0.2
Cordouan	45 35N	1 10W	−0010	−0010	−0015	−0025	−0.5	−0.4	−0.1	−0.2
La Gironde Royan	45 37N	1 01W	0000	−0005	−0005	−0005	−0.3	−0.2	0.0	0.0
Richard	45 27N	0 56W	+0018	+0018	+0028	+0033	−0.1	−0.1	−0.4	−0.5
Lamena	45 20N	0 48W	+0035	+0045	+0100	+0125	+0.2	+0.1	−0.5	−0.3
Pauillac	45 12N	0 45W	+0100	+0100	+0135	+0205	+0.1	0.0	−1.0	−0.5
La Reuille	45 03N	0 36W	+0135	+0145	+0230	+0305	−0.2	−0.3	−1.3	−0.7
La Garonne Le Marquis	45 00N	0 33W	+0145	+0150	+0247	+0322	−0.3	−0.4	− 1.5	−0.9
Bordeaux	44 52N	0 33W	+0200	+0225	+0330	+0405	−0.1	−0.2	−1.7	−1.0
La Dordogne, Libourne	44 55N	0 15W	+0250	+0305	+0525	+0540	−0.7	−0.9	−2.0	−0.4
Bassin d' Arcachon										
Cap Ferret	44 37N	1 15W	−0015	+0005	−0005	+0015	−1.4	−1.2	−0.8	−0.5
Arcachon (Eyrac)	44 40N	1 10W	+0010	+0025	0000	+0020	−1.1	−1.0	−0.8	−0.6
L'Adour, Boucau	43 31N	1 31W	−0030	−0035	−0025	−0040	−1.2	−1.1	−0.4	−0.3
St Jean de Luz, Socoa	43 23N	1 40W	−0040	−0045	−0030	−0045	−1.1	−1.1	−0.6	−0.4

SPAIN *Time Zone −0100*

Location	Lat	Long	High Water		Low Water		MHWS	MHWN	MLWN	MLWS
Pasajes	43 20N	1 56W	−0050	−0030	−0015	−0045	−1.2	−1.3	−0.5	−0.5
San Sebastian	43 19N	1 59W	−0110	−0030	−0020	−0040	−1.2	−1.2	−0.5	−0.4
Guetaria	43 18N	2 12W	−0110	−0030	−0020	−0040	−1.0	−1.0	−0.5	−0.4
Lequeitio	43 22N	2 30W	−0115	−0035	−0025	−0045	−1.2	−1.2	−0.5	−0.4
Bermeo	43 25N	2 43W	−0055	−0015	−0005	−0025	−0.8	−0.7	−0.5	−0.4
Abra de Bilbao	43 21N	3 02W	−0125	−0045	−0035	−0055	−1.2	−1.2	−0.5	−0.4
Portugalete (Bilbao)	43 20N	3 02W	−0100	−0020	−0010	−0030	−0.7	−1.2	−0.2	−0.6
Castro Urdiales	43 23N	3 13W	−0040	−0120	−0020	−0110	−1.4	−1.5	−0.6	−0.6
Ria de Santona	43 26N	3 28W	−0005	−0045	+0015	−0035	−0.7	−1.2	−0.3	−0.7
Santander	43 28N	3 47W	−0020	−0100	0000	−0050	−0.7	−1.2	−0.3	−0.7
Ria de Suances	43 27N	4 03W	0000	−0030	+0020	−0020	−1.5	−1.5	−0.6	−0.6
San Vicente de la Barquera	43 23N	4 24W	−0020	−0100	0000	−0050	−1.5	−1.5	−0.6	−0.6
Ria de Tina Mayor	43 24N	4 31W	−0020	−0100	0000	−0050	−1.4	−1.5	−0.6	−0.6
Ribadesella	43 28N	5 04W	+0005	−0020	+0020	−0020	−1.4	−1.3	−0.6	−0.4
Gijon	43 34N	5 42W	−0005	−0030	+0010	−0030	−1.0	−1.4	−0.4	−0.7
Luanco	43 37N	5 47W	−0010	−0035	+0005	−0035	−1.4	−1.3	−0.6	−0.4
Aviles	43 35N	5 56W	−0100	−0040	−0015	−0050	−1.2	−1.6	−0.5	−0.7
San Esteban de Pravia	43 34N	6 05W	−0005	−0030	+0010	−0030	−1.4	−1.3	−0.6	−0.4
Luarca	43 33N	6 32W	+0010	−0015	+0025	−0015	−1.2	−1.1	−0.5	−0.3
Ribadeo	43 33N	7 02W	+0010	−0015	+0025	−0015	−1.3	−1.5	−0.7	−0.8
Burela	43 39N	7 21W	+0010	−0015	+0025	−0015	−1.5	−1.5	−0.7	−0.6
Ria de Vivero	43 43N	7 36W	+0010	−0015	+0025	−0015	−1.4	−1.3	−0.6	−0.4
Santa Marta de Ortigueira	43 41N	7 51W	−0020	0000	+0020	−0010	−1.3	−1.2	−0.6	−0.4
El Ferrol del Caudillo	43 28N	8 16W	−0045	−0100	−0010	−0105	−1.6	−1.4	−0.7	−0.4
La Coruna	43 22N	8 24W	−0110	−0050	−0030	−0100	−1.6	−1.6	−0.6	−0.5
Ria de Corme	43 16N	8 58W	−0025	−0005	+0015	−0015	−1.7	−1.6	−0.6	−0.5
Ria de Camarinas	43 08N	9 11W	−0115	−0055	0000	−0105	−1.6	−1.6	−0.6	−0.5
LISBOA *Standard port*	38 42N	9 07W	0500 and 1700	1000 and 2200	0300 and 1500	0800 and 2000	**3.9**	**3.0**	**1.5**	**0.6**
Corcubion	42 57N	9 12W	+0055	+0110	+0120	+0135	−0.5	−0.4	−0.3	−0.1
Muros	42 46N	9 03W	+0050	+0105	+0115	+0130	−0.3	−0.3	−0.2	−0.1
Ria de Arosa, Villagarcia	42 37N	8 47W	+0040	+0100	+0110	+0120	−0.3	−0.2	−0.2	−0.1
Ria de Pontevedra, Marin	42 24N	8 42W	+0050	+0110	+0120	+0130	−0.5	−0.4	−0.3	−0.1
Vigo	42 15N	8 43W	+0040	+0100	+0105	+0125	−0.4	−0.3	−0.2	−0.1
Bayona	42 07N	8 51W	+0035	+0050	+0100	+0115	−0.3	−0.3	−0.2	−0.1
La Guardia	41 54N	8 53W	+0040	+0055	+0105	+0120	−0.5	−0.4	−0.3	−0.2

Location	Lat	Long	High Water		Low Water		MHWS	MHWN	MLWN	MLWS
LISBOA	38 42N	9 07W	**0400** and **1600**	**0900** and **2100**	**0400** and **1600**	**0900** and **2100**	**3.9**	**3.0**	**1.5**	**0.6**
Standard port										

PORTUGAL *Time Zone UT*

Location	Lat	Long	High Water		Low Water		MHWS	MHWN	MLWN	MLWS
Viana do Castelo	41 41N	8 50W	−0020	0000	+0010	+0015	−0.4	−0.4	−0.1	0.0
Esposende	41 32N	8 47W	−0020	0000	+0010	+0015	−0.6	−0.5	−0.2	−0.1
Povoa de Varzim	41 22N	8 46W	−0020	0000	+0010	+0015	−0.3	−0.3	−0.1	−0.1
Porto de Leixoes	41 11N	8 42W	−0025	−0010	0000	+0010	−0.4	−0.4	−0.1	0.0
Rio Douro Entrance	41 09N	8 40W	−0010	+0005	+0015	+0025	−0.6	−0.5	−0.2	−0.1
Oporto (Porto)	41 08N	8 37W	+0002	+0002	+0040	+0040	−0.5	−0.4	−0.2	0.0
Porto de Aveiro	40 39N	8 45W	+0005	+0010	+0010	+0015	−0.6	−0.4	−0.1	0.0
Figueira da Foz	40 09N	8 51W	−0015	0000	+0010	+0020	−0.4	−0.4	−0.1	0.0
Nazare (Pederneira)	39 35N	9 04W	−0030	−0015	−0005	+0005	−0.5	−0.4	−0.1	0.0
Peniche	39 21N	9 22W	−0035	−0015	−0005	0000	−0.4	−0.4	−0.1	0.0
Ericeira	38 58N	9 25W	−0040	−0025	−0010	−0010	−0.4	−0.3	−0.1	0.0
River Tagus Cascais	38 42N	9 25W	−0040	−0025	−0015	−0010	−0.3	−0.3	0.0	+0.1
Paco de Arcos	38 41N	9 18W	−0020	−0030	−0005	−0005	−0.4	−0.4	−0.2	−0.1
Pedroucos	38 42N	9 13W	−0010	−0015	0000	0000	−0.2	−0.1	−0.1	−0.1
Alfeite	38 40N	9 09W	+0005	0000	0000	+0005	0.0	0.0	−0.1	−0.1
Alcochete	38 45N	8 58W	+0010	+0010	+0010	+0010	+0.5	+0.4	+0.1	0.0
Vila Franca de Xira	38 57N	8 59W	+0045	+0040	+0100	+0140	+0.3	+0.2	−0.2	+0.3
Sesimbra	38 26N	9 07W	−0045	−0030	−0020	−0010	−0.4	−0.4	−0.1	0.0
Setubal	38 30N	8 54W	−0020	−0015	−0005	+0005	−0.4	−0.4	−0.1	−0.1
Porto de Sines	37 57N	8 53W	−0050	−0030	−0020	−0010	−0.4	−0.4	−0.1	0.0
Milfontes	37 43N	8 47W	−0040	−0030 *no data*	*no data*	−0.1	−0.1	0.0	+0.1
Arrifana	37 17N	8 52W	−0030	−0020 *no data*	*no data*	−0.1	0.0	−0.1	+0.1
Enseada de Belixe	37 01N	8 58W	−0050	−0030	−0020	−0015	+0.3	+0.2	+0.2	+0.2
Lagos	37 06N	8 40W	−0100	−0040	−0030	−0025	−0.4	−0.4	−0.1	0.0
Portimao	37 07N	8 32W	−0100	−0040	−0030	−0025	−0.5	−0.4	−0.1	+0.1
Ponta do Altar	37 06N	8 31W	−0100	−0040	−0030	−0025	−0.3	−0.3	−0.1	0.0
Enseada de Albufeira	37 05N	8 15W	−0035	+0015	−0005	0000	−0.2	−0.2	0.0	+0.1
Porto de Faro-Olhao	36 59N	7 52W	−0050	−0030	−0015	+0005	−0.4	−0.4	−0.1	0.0
Rio Guadiana										
Vila Real de Santo António	37 12N	7 25W	−0050	−0015	−0010	0000	−0.4	−0.4	−0.1	+0.1

Location	Lat	Long	High Water		Low Water		MHWS	MHWN	MLWN	MLWS
LISBOA	38 42N	9 07W	**0500** and **1700**	**1000** and **2200**	**0500** and **1700**	**1100** and **2300**	**3.9**	**3.0**	**1.5**	**0.6**
Standard port										

SPAIN *Time Zone −0100*

Location	Lat	Long	High Water		Low Water		MHWS	MHWN	MLWN	MLWS
Ayamonte	37 13N	7 25W	+0005	+0015	+0025	+0045	−0.7	−0.6	−0.1	−0.2
Ria de Huelva Bar	37 08N	6 52W	0000	+0015	+0035	+0030	−0.1	−0.6	−0.1	−0.4
Huelva, Muelle de Fabrica	37 15N	6 58W	+0010	+0025	+0045	+0040	−0.3	−0.3	−0.3	−0.1
Rio Guadalquivir Bar	36 45N	6 26W	−0005	+0005	+0020	+0030	−0.6	−0.5	−0.2	−0.2
Bonanza	36 48N	6 20W	+0025	+0040	+0100	+0120	−0.8	−0.6	−0.4	−0.1
Corta de los Jerónimos	37 08N	6 06W	+0210	+0230	+0255	+0345	−1.2	−0.9	−0.5	−0.1
Sevilla	37 23N	6 00W	+0400	+0430	+0510	+0545	−1.7	−1.2	−0.6	−0.1
Rota	36 37N	6 21W	−0010	+0010	+0025	+0015	−0.7	−0.6	−0.3	−0.1
Puerto de Santa Maria	36 36N	6 13W	+0006	+0006	+0027	+0027	−0.6	−0.4	−0.4	−0.1
Bay of Cadiz										
Puerto Cadiz	36 32N	6 17W	0000	+0020	+0040	+0025	−0.5	−0.5	−0.3	0.0
La Carraca	36 30N	6 11W	+0020	+0050	+0100	+0040	−0.5	−0.4	−0.1	0.0
Cabo Trafalgar	36 11N	6 02W	−0003	−0003	+0026	+0026	−1.4	−1.1	−0.6	−0.1
Barbate	36 11N	5 56W	+0016	+0016	+0045	+0045	−1.9	−1.5	−0.5	+0.1
Punta Camarinal	36 05N	5 48W	−0007	−0007	+0013	+0013	−1.7	−1.4	−0.7	−0.2

Location	Lat	Long	High Water		Low Water		MHWS	MHWN	MLWN	MLWS
GIBRALTAR *Time Zone −0100*	36 08N	5 21W	**0000** and **1200**	**0700** and **1900**	**0100** and **1300**	**0600** and **1800**	**1.0**	**0.7**	**0.3**	**0.1**
Standard port										
Tarifa	36 00N	5 36W	−0038	−0038	−0042	−0042	+0.4	+0.3	+0.3	+0.2
Punta Carnero	36 04N	5 26W	−0010	−0010	0000	0000	0.0	+0.1	+0.1	+0.1
Algeciras	36 07N	5 27W	−0010	−0010	−0010	−0010	+0.1	+0.2	+0.1	+0.1
Sandy Bay (Gibraltar)	36 08N	5 20W	−0011	−0011	−0016	−0016	−0.2	−0.1	0.0	0.0

MOROCCO *Time Zone UT*

Location	Lat	Long	High Water		Low Water		MHWS	MHWN	MLWN	MLWS
Tangier	35 47N	5 48W	−0030	−0030	−0020	−0020	+1.3	+1.0	+0.5	+0.3
Pointe Ciris	35 55N	5 29W	−0109	−0109	−0104	−0104	+0.2	+0.2	+0.2	+0.1
Ceuta	35 53N	5 167W	−0045	−0045	−0050	−0050	0.0	+0.1	+0.1	+0.1

TIDES

217

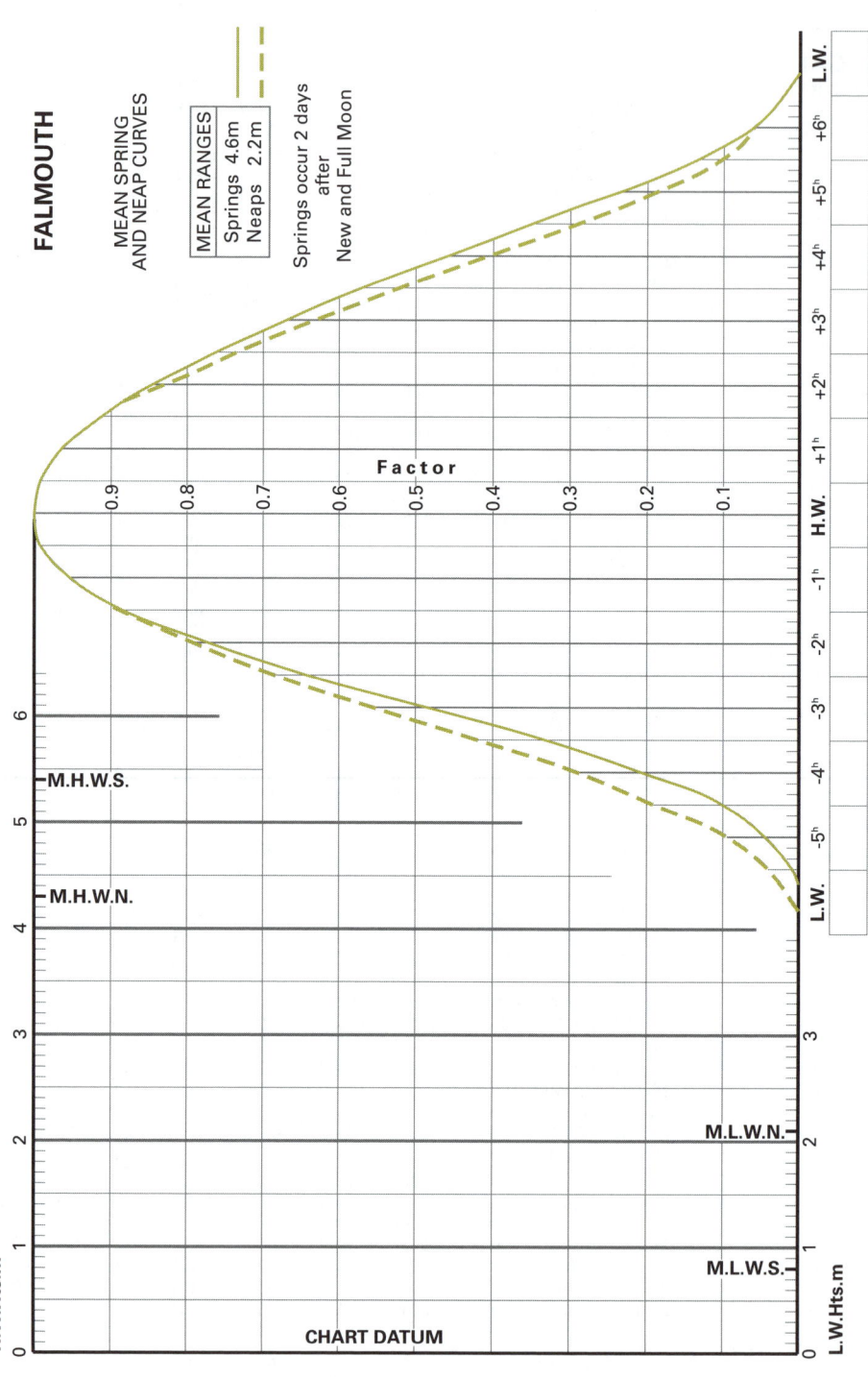

FALMOUTH

MEAN SPRING
AND NEAP CURVES

MEAN RANGES
Springs 4.6m
Neaps 2.2m

Springs occur 2 days
after
New and Full Moon

TIME ZONE (UT)
For Summer Time add ONE hour in **non-shaded areas**

ENGLAND – FALMOUTH

LAT 50°09′N   LONG 5°03′W

TIMES AND HEIGHTS OF HIGH AND LOW WATERS

Dates in amber are **SPRINGS**
Dates in yellow are **NEAPS**

2007

JANUARY

Day	Time m	Day	Time m
1 M	0254 4.8 / 0939 1.5 / 1523 4.8 / 2206 1.5	16 TU	0244 4.5 / 0913 1.9 / 1512 4.5 / 2138 1.7
2 TU	0351 5.0 / 1036 1.4 / 1619 4.9 / 2259 1.3	17 W	0339 4.8 / 1010 1.6 / 1605 4.7 / 2232 1.5
3 W	0441 5.2 / 1127 1.2 / 1708 5.0 / ○ 2346 1.2	18 TH	0427 5.0 / 1102 1.4 / 1653 4.9 / 2322 1.3
4 TH	0524 5.3 / 1214 1.1 / 1753 5.0	19 F	0510 5.2 / 1151 1.1 / 1738 5.0 ●
5 F	0030 1.2 / 0607 5.3 / 1258 1.1 / 1836 5.0	20 SA	0009 1.1 / 0555 5.4 / 1238 0.9 / 1824 5.1
6 SA	0111 1.2 / 0647 5.3 / 1338 1.1 / 1915 4.9	21 SU	0055 0.9 / 0640 5.5 / 1323 0.7 / 1909 5.2
7 SU	0148 1.3 / 0724 5.2 / 1414 1.2 / 1949 4.8	22 M	0138 0.8 / 0724 5.5 / 1404 0.7 / 1952 5.2
8 M	0222 1.4 / 0758 5.1 / 1447 1.4 / 2022 4.7	23 TU	0218 0.8 / 0807 5.5 / 1444 0.8 / 2033 5.1
9 TU	0253 1.5 / 0832 4.9 / 1517 1.5 / 2056 4.6	24 W	0257 1.0 / 0851 5.3 / 1523 1.0 / 2115 5.0
10 W	0323 1.7 / 0907 4.8 / 1548 1.7 / 2133 4.4	25 TH	0336 1.2 / 0934 5.1 / 1604 1.3 / ☽ 2159 4.8
11 TH	0356 1.9 / 0947 4.6 / 1622 1.9 / ☽ 2217 4.3	26 F	0419 1.5 / 1022 4.8 / 1650 1.5 / 2252 4.5
12 F	0438 2.1 / 1034 4.4 / 1710 2.1 / 2312 4.2	27 SA	0513 1.8 / 1124 4.5 / 1751 1.9
13 SA	0540 2.2 / 1134 4.2 / 1818 2.2	28 SU	0002 4.4 / 0629 2.0 / 1243 4.3 / 1917 2.1
14 SU	0019 4.2 / 0656 2.3 / 1247 4.2 / 1931 2.2	29 M	0123 4.3 / 0811 2.1 / 1405 4.3 / 2051 2.0
15 M	0137 4.3 / 0808 2.1 / 1407 4.3 / 2038 2.0	30 TU	0239 4.5 / 0933 1.8 / 1516 4.5 / 2200 1.7
		31 W	0341 4.8 / 1032 1.5 / 1613 4.7 / 2253 1.5

FEBRUARY

Day	Time m	Day	Time m
1 TH	0431 5.0 / 1121 1.2 / 1700 4.8 / 2339 1.2	16 F	0406 5.0 / 1047 1.2 / 1637 4.9 / 2309 1.1
2 F	0513 5.2 / 1205 1.0 / 1742 4.9 ○	17 SA	0452 5.3 / 1137 0.8 / 1721 5.1 / ● 2357 0.8
3 SA	0020 1.0 / 0552 5.3 / 1246 0.8 / 1819 5.0	18 SU	0537 5.5 / 1224 0.5 / 1807 5.3
4 SU	0058 0.9 / 0629 5.3 / 1321 0.9 / 1852 5.0	19 M	0042 0.5 / 0624 5.6 / 1307 0.3 / 1851 5.4
5 M	0131 1.0 / 0702 5.2 / 1353 0.9 / 1922 4.9	20 TU	0123 0.4 / 0708 5.7 / 1347 0.3 / 1932 5.4
6 TU	0159 1.1 / 0733 5.2 / 1419 1.1 / 1952 4.9	21 W	0202 0.4 / 0751 5.6 / 1425 0.4 / 2011 5.3
7 W	0223 1.2 / 0803 5.0 / 1441 1.3 / 2021 4.8	22 TH	0238 0.6 / 0831 5.4 / 1501 0.7 / 2050 5.1
8 TH	0245 1.4 / 0833 4.8 / 1501 1.4 / 2051 4.6	23 F	0314 0.9 / 0910 5.1 / 1537 1.2 / 2128 4.8
9 F	0307 1.5 / 0903 4.6 / 1523 1.6 / 2124 4.4	24 SA	0353 1.4 / 0952 4.7 / 1618 1.6 / ☽ 2213 4.5
10 SA	0335 1.8 / 0938 4.4 / 1556 1.9 / ☽ 2206 4.2	25 SU	0442 1.8 / 1051 4.3 / 1714 2.0 / 2326 4.2
11 SU	0419 2.1 / 1030 4.2 / 1650 2.2 / 2310 4.1	26 M	0556 2.2 / 1226 4.0 / 1845 2.3
12 M	0546 2.3 / 1146 4.0 / 1836 2.3	27 TU	0105 4.1 / 0808 2.2 / 1359 4.0 / 2048 2.2
13 TU	0036 4.1 / 0726 2.3 / 1324 4.1 / 2002 2.2	28 W	0228 4.3 / 0930 1.8 / 1512 4.3 / 2152 1.7
14 W	0210 4.3 / 0844 1.9 / 1449 4.3 / 2114 1.8		
15 TH	0315 4.7 / 0950 1.5 / 1548 4.6 / 2216 1.5		

MARCH

Day	Time m	Day	Time m
1 TH	0329 4.6 / 1022 1.5 / 1604 4.6 / 2241 1.4	16 F	0248 4.6 / 0929 1.5 / 1526 4.6 / 2155 1.4
2 F	0416 4.9 / 1106 1.1 / 1644 4.8 / 2322 1.1	17 SA	0342 5.0 / 1026 1.0 / 1614 5.0 / 2248 0.9
3 SA	0454 5.1 / 1146 0.8 / 1719 5.0 ○	18 SU	0429 5.3 / 1115 0.6 / 1659 5.2 / 2336 0.6
4 SU	0000 0.9 / 0529 5.3 / 1223 0.7 / 1752 5.0	19 M	0514 5.6 / 1201 0.3 / 1743 5.4 ●
5 M	0035 0.8 / 0602 5.3 / 1256 0.7 / 1823 5.1	20 TU	0020 0.3 / 0600 5.7 / 1244 0.2 / 1826 5.5
6 TU	0105 0.8 / 0634 5.2 / 1323 0.8 / 1851 5.1	21 W	0101 0.2 / 0645 5.7 / 1324 0.2 / 1908 5.5
7 W	0130 0.9 / 0704 5.2 / 1346 1.0 / 1920 5.0	22 TH	0140 0.3 / 0728 5.6 / 1402 0.4 / 1946 5.4
8 TH	0151 1.1 / 0733 5.0 / 1404 1.2 / 1948 4.9	23 F	0217 0.5 / 0809 5.3 / 1437 0.8 / 2023 5.2
9 F	0210 1.2 / 0800 4.8 / 1421 1.4 / 2012 4.7	24 SA	0253 0.9 / 0849 5.0 / 1513 1.2 / 2059 4.9
10 SA	0230 1.4 / 0826 4.6 / 1443 1.5 / 2039 4.6	25 SU	0333 1.4 / 0930 4.5 / 1555 1.7 / ☽ 2140 4.5
11 SU	0257 1.6 / 0857 4.4 / 1514 1.8 / 2118 4.3	26 M	0423 1.8 / 1031 4.1 / 1652 2.1 / 2255 4.2
12 M	0337 1.9 / 0949 4.1 / 1600 2.1 / ☽ 2223 4.1	27 TU	0540 2.2 / 1220 3.9 / 1827 2.4
13 TU	0447 2.2 / 1108 3.9 / 1744 2.4 / 2350 4.1	28 W	0050 4.1 / 0758 2.2 / 1347 4.0 / 2029 2.2
14 W	0655 2.2 / 1250 4.0 / 1935 2.2	29 TH	0208 4.3 / 0909 1.8 / 1451 4.3 / 2128 1.7
15 TH	0135 4.3 / 0820 1.9 / 1427 4.3 / 2052 1.8	30 F	0305 4.6 / 0957 1.4 / 1539 4.6 / 2214 1.4
		31 SA	0349 4.9 / 1039 1.1 / 1616 4.8 / 2254 1.1

APRIL

Day	Time m	Day	Time m
1 SU	0426 5.1 / 1117 0.9 / 1649 5.0 / 2331 0.9	16 M	0401 5.3 / 1047 0.5 / 1631 5.3 / 2309 0.5
2 M	0500 5.2 / 1152 0.8 / 1720 5.1 ○	17 TU	0448 5.5 / 1134 0.3 / 1714 5.4 / ● 2355 0.3
3 TU	0004 0.8 / 0531 5.2 / 1223 0.8 / 1750 5.1	18 W	0534 5.6 / 1218 0.2 / 1758 5.5
4 W	0033 0.8 / 0604 5.2 / 1249 0.9 / 1821 5.1	19 TH	0038 0.3 / 0622 5.6 / 1300 0.3 / 1841 5.5
5 TH	0058 0.9 / 0635 5.1 / 1312 1.0 / 1849 5.1	20 F	0119 0.4 / 0707 5.4 / 1339 0.6 / 1922 5.4
6 F	0120 1.1 / 0705 5.0 / 1331 1.2 / 1917 5.0	21 SA	0158 0.7 / 0750 5.1 / 1418 0.9 / 2000 5.2
7 SA	0141 1.2 / 0732 4.8 / 1351 1.4 / 1942 4.8	22 SU	0238 1.0 / 0833 4.8 / 1457 1.4 / 2038 4.9
8 SU	0204 1.4 / 0800 4.6 / 1416 1.5 / 2011 4.7	23 M	0321 1.5 / 0920 4.4 / 1542 1.7 / 2122 4.5
9 M	0234 1.5 / 0836 4.4 / 1450 1.7 / 2054 4.5	24 TU	0415 1.8 / 1028 4.1 / 1639 2.1 / ☽ 2233 4.2
10 TU	0317 1.8 / 0932 4.1 / 1539 2.1 / ☽ 2157 4.3	25 W	0528 2.1 / 1202 3.9 / 1801 2.3
11 W	0431 2.1 / 1047 4.0 / 1718 2.3 / 2320 4.2	26 TH	0020 4.2 / 0712 2.1 / 1315 4.0 / 1940 2.2
12 TH	0629 2.1 / 1221 4.0 / 1907 2.1	27 F	0132 4.3 / 0826 1.8 / 1413 4.3 / 2045 1.8
13 F	0055 4.3 / 0752 1.7 / 1355 4.3 / 2024 1.7	28 SA	0226 4.5 / 0917 1.5 / 1459 4.5 / 2134 1.5
14 SA	0215 4.7 / 0900 1.3 / 1455 4.7 / 2127 1.3	29 SU	0311 4.9 / 1000 1.3 / 1538 4.7 / 2216 1.3
15 SU	0312 5.0 / 0957 0.9 / 1545 5.0 / 2221 0.9	30 M	0351 4.9 / 1039 1.1 / 1613 4.9 / 2254 1.1

Chart Datum: 2·91 metres below Ordnance Datum (Newlyn)

TIME ZONE (UT)	ENGLAND – FALMOUTH	Dates in amber are SPRINGS
For Summer Time add ONE hour in **non-shaded areas**	LAT 50°09'N LONG 5°03'W	Dates in yellow are NEAPS
	TIMES AND HEIGHTS OF HIGH AND LOW WATERS	**2007**

MAY

Day	Time m	Time m	Time m	Time m		Day	Time m	Time m	Time m	Time m
1 TU	0427 5.0	1114 1.0	1646 5.3	2328 1.0		16 W	0423 5.3	1107 0.6	1648 5.3	●2330 0.6
2 W	0501 5.0	1146 1.0	1719 5.1	○2359 1.0		17 TH	0512 5.4	1154 0.6	1733 5.4	
3 TH	0535 5.0	1215 1.1	1752 5.1			18 F	0017 0.5	0601 5.3	1239 0.6	1820 5.4
4 F	0028 1.1	0609 5.0	1241 1.2	1824 5.1		19 SA	0102 0.6	0650 5.2	1322 0.8	1904 5.3
5 SA	0055 1.2	0643 4.9	1307 1.3	1854 5.0		20 SU	0145 0.8	0737 5.0	1405 1.1	1946 5.1
6 SU	0122 1.3	0715 4.7	1334 1.4	1924 4.9		21 M	0229 1.1	0825 4.7	1447 1.4	2027 4.9
7 M	0152 1.4	0749 4.6	1405 1.5	1959 4.8		22 TU	0315 1.4	0914 4.4	1533 1.6	2111 4.7
8 TU	0229 1.5	0830 4.4	1444 1.7	2044 4.6		23 W	0404 1.6	1011 4.2	1624 1.9	◑2207 4.4
9 W	0318 1.7	0925 4.2	1540 1.9	2143 4.5		24 TH	0502 1.9	1120 4.1	1723 2.1	2324 4.3
10 TH	0430 1.8	1032 4.1	1703 2.0	◑2255 4.4		25 F	0608 1.9	1223 4.1	1831 2.1	
11 F	0559 1.8	1153 4.2	1833 1.9			26 SA	0035 4.3	0717 1.9	1319 4.2	1939 2.0
12 SA	0017 4.5	0717 1.6	1313 4.4	1948 1.6		27 SU	0133 4.4	0817 1.7	1408 4.4	2038 1.8
13 SU	0134 4.7	0824 1.3	1416 4.7	2053 1.4		28 M	0223 4.5	0908 1.5	1452 4.6	2128 1.6
14 M	0237 5.0	0924 1.0	1511 5.0	2150 1.0		29 TU	0309 4.6	0952 1.5	1534 4.8	2211 1.5
15 TU	0332 5.2	1018 0.8	1601 5.2	2242 0.8		30 W	0352 4.8	1032 1.4	1613 4.9	2250 1.4
						31 TH	0432 4.8	1108 1.3	1651 5.0	2327 1.3

JUNE

Day	Time m	Time m	Time m	Time m		Day	Time m	Time m	Time m	Time m
1 F	0511 4.9	1144 1.3	1727 5.0	○		16 SA	0003 0.8	0547 5.1	1225 0.9	1804 5.3
2 SA	0003 1.2	0550 4.9	1218 1.3	1804 5.1		17 SU	0051 0.8	0638 5.0	1311 1.0	1850 5.2
3 SU	0038 1.2	0629 4.8	1253 1.3	1839 5.0		18 M	0137 0.9	0727 4.9	1355 1.1	1934 5.1
4 M	0115 1.3	0707 4.7	1329 1.4	1915 5.0		19 TU	0221 1.0	0813 4.7	1437 1.3	2015 5.0
5 TU	0153 1.3	0746 4.7	1408 1.5	1955 4.9		20 W	0303 1.2	0855 4.6	1517 1.5	2053 4.8
6 W	0235 1.4	0830 4.6	1451 1.5	2040 4.8		21 TH	0343 1.5	0935 4.4	1557 1.6	2131 4.6
7 TH	0323 1.5	0920 4.5	1542 1.6	2133 4.8		22 F	0425 1.6	1017 4.3	1640 1.8	◑2216 4.5
8 F	0419 1.5	1018 4.4	1642 1.7	◑2233 4.7		23 SA	0510 1.8	1106 4.2	1729 2.0	2310 4.3
9 SA	0525 1.5	1124 4.4	1753 1.7	2344 4.6		24 SU	0603 1.9	1204 4.2	1827 2.0	
10 SU	0635 1.5	1232 4.5	1906 1.6			25 M	0014 4.3	0701 1.9	1303 4.2	1928 2.0
11 M	0056 4.7	0745 1.5	1339 4.6	2017 1.5		26 TU	0122 4.3	0801 1.9	1402 4.4	2029 1.9
12 TU	0204 4.8	0851 1.3	1440 4.8	2121 1.3		27 W	0224 4.4	0858 1.7	1455 4.6	2125 1.7
13 W	0306 4.9	0951 1.1	1536 5.0	2219 1.1		28 TH	0318 4.5	0949 1.6	1543 4.7	2215 1.5
14 TH	0403 5.0	1046 1.0	1628 5.2	2313 0.9		29 F	0407 4.6	1036 1.5	1627 4.9	2301 1.4
15 F	0456 5.1	1137 0.9	1716 5.3	●		30 SA	0451 4.8	1120 1.4	1709 5.0	○2345 1.3

JULY

Day	Time m	Time m	Time m	Time m		Day	Time m	Time m	Time m	Time m
1 SU	0534 4.8	1203 1.3	1750 5.1			16 M	0043 0.8	0626 5.0	1301 0.9	1836 5.3
2 M	0028 1.2	0619 4.9	1246 1.2	1830 5.1		17 TU	0126 0.8	0710 4.9	1341 0.9	1916 5.2
3 TU	0111 1.1	0702 4.9	1328 1.2	1911 5.2		18 W	0205 0.9	0749 4.8	1418 1.1	1951 5.1
4 W	0152 1.0	0744 4.8	1408 1.2	1952 5.1		19 TH	0240 1.0	0822 4.7	1451 1.2	2022 5.0
5 TH	0233 1.1	0826 4.8	1449 1.2	2034 5.1		20 F	0311 1.3	0852 4.8	1521 1.5	2053 4.8
6 F	0315 1.1	0909 4.7	1531 1.3	2120 5.0		21 SA	0341 1.5	0924 4.5	1551 1.6	2127 4.6
7 SA	0359 1.3	0957 4.7	1617 1.5	◑2211 4.8		22 SU	0412 1.7	1001 4.4	1627 1.9	◑2208 4.4
8 SU	0450 1.4	1052 4.6	1714 1.6	2310 4.7		23 M	0451 1.9	1050 4.2	1718 2.1	2300 4.2
9 M	0552 1.5	1156 4.5	1824 1.7			24 TU	0551 2.1	1152 4.1	1828 2.2	
10 TU	0021 4.5	0706 1.6	1306 4.5	1944 1.7		25 W	0010 4.1	0702 2.1	1309 4.2	1940 2.1
11 W	0139 4.5	0823 1.6	1416 4.6	2101 1.6		26 TH	0139 4.1	0812 2.0	1421 4.4	2047 1.9
12 TH	0250 4.6	0934 1.5	1519 4.8	2207 1.4		27 F	0251 4.3	0915 1.8	1518 4.6	2148 1.6
13 F	0353 4.7	1035 1.3	1615 5.0	2305 1.2		28 SA	0347 4.5	1012 1.6	1607 4.9	2242 1.4
14 SA	0447 4.9	1128 1.1	1705 5.2	●2356 1.0		29 SU	0435 4.7	1104 1.4	1650 5.1	2331 1.1
15 SU	0537 4.9	1217 1.0	1751 5.2			30 M	0518 4.9	1151 1.1	1733 5.2	○
						31 TU	0017 0.9	0603 5.0	1236 1.0	1817 5.3

AUGUST

Day	Time m	Time m	Time m	Time m		Day	Time m	Time m	Time m	Time m
1 W	0101 0.8	0648 5.1	1318 0.9	1900 5.4		16 TH	0140 0.8	0713 5.0	1350 0.9	1918 5.2
2 TH	0142 0.7	0730 5.1	1357 0.8	1940 5.4		17 F	0208 0.9	0740 4.9	1417 1.1	1947 5.1
3 F	0220 0.7	0810 5.1	1434 0.9	2021 5.3		18 SA	0232 1.2	0809 4.8	1440 1.3	2016 4.9
4 SA	0257 0.8	0850 5.0	1511 1.0	2102 5.1		19 SU	0252 1.4	0838 4.7	1500 1.5	2046 4.7
5 SU	0335 1.1	0932 4.8	1552 1.3	◑2146 4.9		20 M	0311 1.6	0911 4.5	1524 1.8	◑2119 4.4
6 M	0418 1.4	1020 4.6	1640 1.6	2239 4.6		21 TU	0338 1.9	0951 4.3	1601 2.1	2206 4.2
7 TU	0513 1.7	1124 4.4	1748 1.9	2357 4.3		22 W	0424 2.2	1050 4.1	1722 2.3	2314 4.0
8 W	0633 2.0	1245 4.3	1925 2.0			23 TH	0611 2.4	1214 4.1	1903 2.3	
9 TH	0129 4.2	0812 2.0	1407 4.4	2058 1.8		24 F	0056 4.0	0739 2.2	1351 4.3	2020 2.0
10 F	0248 4.4	0931 1.7	1514 4.7	2206 1.5		25 SA	0232 4.2	0852 1.9	1456 4.6	2127 1.6
11 SA	0352 4.6	1030 1.4	1608 5.0	2259 1.2		26 SU	0328 4.5	0953 1.5	1546 4.9	2223 1.3
12 SU	0441 4.8	1119 1.1	1654 5.2	●2345 0.9		27 M	0415 4.8	1046 1.2	1630 5.2	2312 0.9
13 M	0524 5.0	1203 0.9	1735 5.3			28 TU	0459 5.0	1133 0.9	1712 5.4	○2358 0.7
14 TU	0027 0.7	0605 5.0	1243 0.8	1814 5.3		29 W	0542 5.2	1218 0.7	1756 5.5	
15 W	0106 0.7	0641 5.0	1319 0.8	1847 5.3		30 TH	0041 0.5	0625 5.3	1259 0.6	1839 5.6
						31 F	0121 0.4	0707 5.3	1337 0.5	1921 5.6

Chart Datum: 2·91 metres below Ordnance Datum (Newlyn)

TIME ZONE (UT)
For Summer Time add ONE hour in **non-shaded areas**

Dates in amber are **SPRINGS**
Dates in yellow are **NEAPS**

SEPTEMBER

Day	Time m	Day	Time m
1 SA	0158 0.5 / 0747 5.3 / 1414 0.7 / 2001 5.4	**16** SU	0151 1.2 / 0731 5.0 / 1359 1.3 / 1940 4.9
2 SU	0234 0.8 / 0825 5.2 / 1449 1.0 / 2040 5.2	**17** M	0207 1.4 / 0759 4.8 / 1417 1.5 / 2008 4.7
3 M	0310 1.1 / 0904 4.9 / 1528 1.4 / 2123 4.8	**18** TU	0225 1.6 / 0829 4.6 / 1440 1.7 / 2040 4.5
4 TU	0350 1.5 / 0950 4.6 / 1615 1.7 / 2215 4.4	**19** W	0252 1.8 / 0907 4.4 / 1515 2.0 / 2128 4.2
5 W	0444 2.0 / 1057 4.3 / 1727 2.2 / 2348 4.1	**20** TH	0333 2.2 / 1006 4.2 / 1616 2.4 / 2238 4.0
6 TH	0614 2.3 / 1236 4.2 / 1930 2.2	**21** F	0504 2.5 / 1128 4.1 / 1832 2.4
7 F	0132 4.1 / 0817 2.2 / 1403 4.4 / 2100 1.9	**22** SA	0017 3.9 / 0712 2.4 / 1315 4.3 / 1956 2.1
8 SA	0250 4.3 / 0926 1.8 / 1508 4.7 / 2157 1.5	**23** SU	0209 4.2 / 0828 2.0 / 1429 4.6 / 2102 1.6
9 SU	0345 4.6 / 1017 1.4 / 1556 5.0 / 2243 1.1	**24** M	0305 4.6 / 0929 1.5 / 1519 5.0 / 2158 1.2
10 M	0427 4.9 / 1101 1.1 / 1636 5.2 / 2324 0.8	**25** TU	0351 4.9 / 1021 1.1 / 1604 5.3 / 2247 0.8
11 TU ●	0503 5.1 / 1140 0.8 / 1711 5.3	**26** W ○	0434 5.2 / 1109 0.8 / 1647 5.5 / 2332 0.5
12 W	0002 0.7 / 0535 5.1 / 1217 0.7 / 1744 5.4	**27** TH	0515 5.4 / 1153 0.6 / 1730 5.7
13 TH	0037 0.7 / 0606 5.2 / 1249 0.8 / 1815 5.3	**28** F	0015 0.4 / 0557 5.5 / 1235 0.4 / 1815 5.7
14 F	0107 0.8 / 0635 5.1 / 1317 0.9 / 1844 5.2	**29** SA	0056 0.4 / 0640 5.5 / 1314 0.5 / 1859 5.6
15 SA	0131 1.0 / 0703 5.1 / 1340 1.1 / 1913 5.1	**30** SU	0134 0.6 / 0720 5.5 / 1352 0.7 / 1940 5.4

OCTOBER

Day	Time m	Day	Time m
1 M	0211 0.9 / 0800 5.3 / 1430 1.0 / 2022 5.1	**16** TU	0134 1.5 / 0729 4.9 / 1349 1.5 / 1942 4.7
2 TU	0248 1.3 / 0840 5.0 / 1511 1.5 / 2105 4.7	**17** W	0156 1.6 / 0759 4.7 / 1415 1.7 / 2017 4.5
3 W ◑	0330 1.7 / 0927 4.7 / 1602 1.9 / 2203 4.3	**18** TH	0226 1.9 / 0839 4.5 / 1453 2.0 / 2106 4.2
4 TH	0428 2.2 / 1038 4.3 / 1719 2.3 / 2349 4.0	**19** F ◑	0309 2.2 / 0937 4.3 / 1555 2.3 / 2215 4.1
5 F	0607 2.5 / 1226 4.2 / 1926 2.2	**20** SA	0429 2.5 / 1052 4.2 / 1757 2.3 / 2343 4.0
6 SA	0125 4.1 / 0801 2.2 / 1346 4.4 / 2041 1.9	**21** SU	0637 2.4 / 1223 4.4 / 1923 2.0
7 SU	0233 4.4 / 0903 1.8 / 1445 4.7 / 2132 1.5	**22** M	0125 4.3 / 0756 2.0 / 1347 4.7 / 2030 1.6
8 M	0321 4.7 / 0951 1.5 / 1530 5.0 / 2215 1.2	**23** TU	0229 4.6 / 0858 1.5 / 1444 5.0 / 2126 1.2
9 TU	0359 4.9 / 1032 1.2 / 1608 5.2 / 2254 1.0	**24** W	0318 5.0 / 0952 1.2 / 1534 5.3 / 2217 0.9
10 W	0433 5.1 / 1110 1.0 / 1642 5.3 / 2330 0.9	**25** TH	0403 5.3 / 1041 0.9 / 1621 5.5 / 2304 0.6
11 TH ●	0503 5.2 / 1145 0.9 / 1713 5.3	**26** F ○	0447 5.5 / 1127 0.6 / 1706 5.6 / 2348 0.5
12 F	0003 0.9 / 0531 5.3 / 1216 0.9 / 1743 5.3	**27** SA	0530 5.6 / 1211 0.5 / 1752 5.6
13 SA	0031 1.0 / 0601 5.2 / 1243 1.0 / 1814 5.2	**28** SU	0031 0.6 / 0615 5.6 / 1253 0.6 / 1838 5.5
14 SU	0054 1.1 / 0631 5.2 / 1306 1.2 / 1844 5.1	**29** M	0113 0.7 / 0659 5.5 / 1335 0.8 / 1924 5.3
15 M	0114 1.3 / 0701 5.1 / 1327 1.4 / 1913 4.9	**30** TU	0153 1.1 / 0741 5.3 / 1417 1.1 / 2009 5.0
		31 W	0234 1.5 / 0825 5.1 / 1503 1.5 / 2059 4.6

NOVEMBER

Day	Time m	Day	Time m
1 TH ◐	0321 1.8 / 0915 4.8 / 1556 1.9 / 2203 4.3	**16** F	0219 1.8 / 0824 4.7 / 1452 1.9 / 2055 4.4
2 F	0418 2.2 / 1025 4.5 / 1708 2.1 / 2333 4.1	**17** SA ◑	0306 2.0 / 0918 4.6 / 1551 2.0 / 2155 4.3
3 SA	0540 2.4 / 1157 4.4 / 1844 2.2	**18** SU	0414 2.2 / 1023 4.5 / 1715 2.1 / 2308 4.2
4 SU	0051 4.2 / 0716 2.3 / 1309 4.5 / 1959 1.9	**19** M	0548 2.2 / 1139 4.5 / 1839 1.9
5 M	0152 4.4 / 0822 2.0 / 1407 4.7 / 2053 1.6	**20** TU	0028 4.4 / 0711 2.0 / 1256 4.7 / 1949 1.6
6 TU	0241 4.6 / 0913 1.6 / 1453 4.9 / 2138 1.5	**21** W	0141 4.6 / 0820 1.7 / 1404 4.9 / 2051 1.4
7 W	0321 4.9 / 0956 1.5 / 1533 5.0 / 2218 1.3	**22** TH	0241 4.9 / 0919 1.4 / 1502 5.2 / 2146 1.1
8 TH	0357 5.0 / 1036 1.3 / 1610 5.1 / 2255 1.2	**23** F	0333 5.2 / 1013 1.1 / 1555 5.3 / 2237 0.9
9 F ●	0430 5.2 / 1111 1.2 / 1643 5.1 / 2327 1.2	**24** SA ○	0422 5.4 / 1103 0.9 / 1645 5.4 / 2326 0.8
10 SA	0502 5.2 / 1144 1.2 / 1716 5.0 / 2357 1.2	**25** SU	0509 5.5 / 1152 0.8 / 1734 5.4
11 SU	0533 5.3 / 1213 1.2 / 1750 5.1	**26** M	0012 0.8 / 0555 5.6 / 1239 0.8 / 1825 5.4
12 M	0024 1.3 / 0606 5.2 / 1241 1.3 / 1823 5.0	**27** TU	0058 0.9 / 0643 5.5 / 1325 0.9 / 1914 5.2
13 TU	0049 1.4 / 0638 5.1 / 1308 1.5 / 1855 4.9	**28** W	0143 1.1 / 0730 5.4 / 1411 1.1 / 2003 5.0
14 W	0115 1.5 / 0710 5.0 / 1336 1.5 / 1928 4.7	**29** TH	0227 1.4 / 0817 5.2 / 1458 1.4 / 2054 4.7
15 TH	0144 1.6 / 0744 4.9 / 1409 1.7 / 2006 4.5	**30** F	0313 1.6 / 0906 4.9 / 1547 1.6 / 2147 4.5

DECEMBER

Day	Time m	Day	Time m
1 SA ◐	0402 1.9 / 0959 4.7 / 1640 1.9 / 2249 4.3	**16** SU	0306 1.7 / 0904 4.9 / 1540 1.6 / 2136 4.5
2 SU	0459 2.1 / 1104 4.5 / 1742 2.0 / 2355 4.2	**17** M ◑	0356 1.8 / 0957 4.8 / 1636 1.7 / 2234 4.5
3 M	0605 2.2 / 1212 4.5 / 1850 2.0	**18** TU	0458 1.9 / 1100 4.7 / 1745 1.8 / 2343 4.5
4 TU	0055 4.3 / 0716 2.2 / 1311 4.5 / 1954 2.0	**19** W	0615 1.9 / 1211 4.7 / 1901 1.7
5 W	0147 4.4 / 0819 2.0 / 1405 4.6 / 2049 1.8	**20** TH	0054 4.5 / 0736 1.8 / 1324 4.7 / 2013 1.6
6 TH	0236 4.6 / 0912 1.8 / 1452 4.7 / 2136 1.6	**21** F	0204 4.7 / 0848 1.5 / 1433 4.9 / 2119 1.5
7 F	0318 4.8 / 0957 1.6 / 1536 4.8 / 2217 1.5	**22** SA	0307 5.0 / 0951 1.4 / 1536 5.0 / 2218 1.3
8 SA	0359 5.0 / 1038 1.5 / 1617 4.9 / 2254 1.5	**23** SU	0403 5.2 / 1048 1.1 / 1632 5.1 / 2311 1.1
9 SU ●	0437 5.1 / 1115 1.5 / 1655 5.0 / 2329 1.4	**24** M ○	0454 5.4 / 1141 1.0 / 1724 5.2
10 M	0513 5.2 / 1151 1.4 / 1733 5.0	**25** TU	0002 1.0 / 0544 5.5 / 1231 0.8 / 1816 5.2
11 TU	0002 1.4 / 0550 5.2 / 1225 1.4 / 1810 5.0	**26** W	0050 1.0 / 0633 5.5 / 1319 0.8 / 1907 5.1
12 W	0036 1.5 / 0626 5.2 / 1300 1.4 / 1848 4.9	**27** TH	0135 1.0 / 0720 5.4 / 1404 0.9 / 1953 5.0
13 TH	0110 1.5 / 0702 5.1 / 1335 1.5 / 1924 4.8	**28** F	0218 1.5 / 0805 5.3 / 1446 1.1 / 2036 4.9
14 F	0145 1.5 / 0737 5.0 / 1413 1.5 / 2003 4.7	**29** SA	0257 1.7 / 0846 5.1 / 1525 1.3 / 2114 4.7
15 SA	0223 1.6 / 0818 4.9 / 1453 1.6 / 2047 4.6	**30** SU	0336 1.8 / 0923 4.9 / 1604 1.5 / 2151 4.5
		31 M ◑	0415 1.8 / 1001 4.7 / 1645 1.8 / 2233 4.4

Chart Datum: 2·91 metres below Ordnance Datum (Newlyn)

TIDES

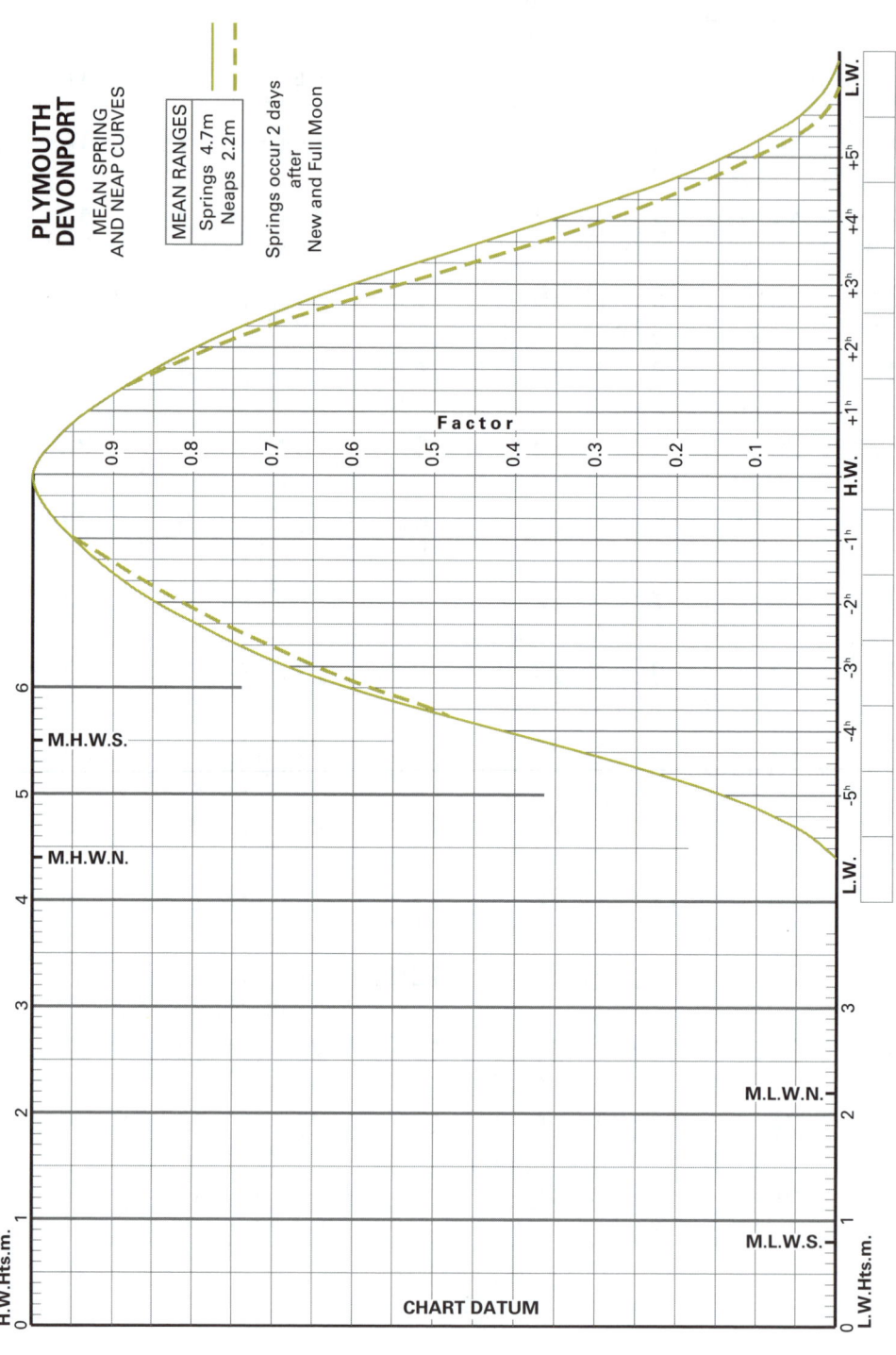

PLYMOUTH DEVONPORT

MEAN SPRING AND NEAP CURVES

MEAN RANGES
Springs 4.7m
Neaps 2.2m

Springs occur 2 days after New and Full Moon

Factor

0.9 0.8 0.7 0.6 0.5 0.4 0.3 0.2 0.1

H.W.Hts.m.

M.H.W.S.

M.H.W.N.

CHART DATUM

L.W.Hts.m.

M.L.W.N.

M.L.W.S.

H.W.

L.W.

ENGLAND – PLYMOUTH

LAT 50°22'N   LONG 4°11'W

TIMES AND HEIGHTS OF HIGH AND LOW WATERS

Dates in amber are **SPRINGS**
Dates in yellow are **NEAPS**

2007

JANUARY

Time	m	Time	m
1 0325	4.9	**16** 0315	4.6
0949	1.6	0923	2.0
M 1555	4.9	TU 1543	4.6
2216	1.5	2148	1.8
2 0423	5.1	**17** 0411	4.9
1046	1.4	1020	1.7
TU 1652	5.0	W 1638	4.8
2309	1.3	2242	1.6
3 0514	5.3	**18** 0500	5.1
1137	1.2	1112	1.4
W 1742	5.1	TH 1727	5.0
○ 2356	1.2	2332	1.3
4 0559	5.4	**19** 0545	5.3
1224	1.1	1201	1.1
TH 1827	5.1	F 1813	5.1
		●	
5 0040	1.2	**20** 0019	1.1
0641	5.4	0629	5.5
F 1308	1.1	SA 1248	0.9
1909	5.1	1857	5.2
6 0121	1.2	**21** 0105	0.9
0720	5.4	0713	5.6
SA 1348	1.1	SU 1333	0.7
1947	5.0	1941	5.3
7 0158	1.3	**22** 0148	0.8
0756	5.3	0756	5.6
SU 1424	1.2	M 1414	0.7
2020	4.9	2023	5.3
8 0232	1.4	**23** 0228	0.8
0829	5.2	0838	5.6
M 1457	1.4	TU 1454	0.8
2052	4.8	2103	5.2
9 0303	1.6	**24** 0307	1.0
0902	5.0	0920	5.4
TU 1527	1.6	W 1533	1.0
2125	4.7	2144	5.1
10 0333	1.8	**25** 0346	1.2
0936	4.9	1002	5.2
W 1558	1.8	TH 1614	1.3
2201	4.5	◐ 2227	4.9
11 0406	2.0	**26** 0429	1.5
1015	4.7	1049	4.9
TH 1632	2.0	F 1700	1.6
◐ 2244	4.4	2318	4.6
12 0448	2.2	**27** 0523	1.9
1101	4.5	1149	4.6
F 1720	2.2	SA 1801	2.0
2338	4.3		
13 0550	2.3	**28** 0028	4.5
1159	4.3	0639	2.1
SA 1828	2.3	SU 1310	4.4
		1927	2.2
14 0046	4.3	**29** 0151	4.4
0706	2.4	0821	2.2
SU 1314	4.4	M 1434	4.4
1941	2.3	2101	2.1
15 0205	4.4	**30** 0309	4.6
0818	2.2	0943	1.9
M 1436	4.4	TU 1548	4.6
2048	2.1	2210	1.8
		31 0413	4.9
		1042	1.5
		W 1646	4.8
		2303	1.5

FEBRUARY

Time	m	Time	m
1 0504	5.1	**16** 0439	5.1
1131	1.2	1057	1.2
TH 1734	4.9	F 1710	5.0
2349	1.2	2319	1.1
2 0548	5.3	**17** 0526	5.4
1215	1.0	1147	0.8
F 1816	5.0	SA 1756	5.2
○		●	
3 0030	1.0	**18** 0007	0.8
0626	5.4	0612	5.6
SA 1256	0.9	SU 1234	0.5
1852	5.1	1841	5.4
4 0108	0.9	**19** 0052	0.5
0702	5.4	0657	5.7
SU 1331	0.9	M 1317	0.3
1925	5.1	1924	5.5
5 0141	1.0	**20** 0133	0.4
0734	5.3	0740	5.8
M 1403	0.9	TU 1357	0.3
1954	5.0	2004	5.5
6 0209	1.1	**21** 0212	0.4
0805	5.3	0822	5.7
TU 1429	1.1	W 1435	0.4
2023	5.0	2042	5.4
7 0233	1.2	**22** 0248	0.6
0834	5.1	0901	5.5
W 1451	1.3	TH 1511	0.7
2051	4.9	2119	5.2
8 0255	1.4	**23** 0324	0.9
0903	4.9	0939	5.2
TH 1511	1.5	F 1547	1.2
2120	4.7	2156	4.9
9 0317	1.6	**24** 0403	1.4
0920	4.8	1020	4.8
F 1533	1.7	SA 1628	1.7
2152	4.5	◐ 2240	4.6
10 0345	1.9	**25** 0452	1.9
1006	4.5	1117	4.4
SA 1606	2.0	SU 1724	2.1
◐ 2233	4.3	2351	4.3
11 0429	2.2	**26** 0606	2.3
1057	4.3	1253	4.1
SU 1700	2.3	M 1855	2.4
2336	4.2		
12 0556	2.4	**27** 0133	4.2
1211	4.1	0818	2.3
M 1846	2.4	TU 1428	4.1
		2058	2.3
13 0103	4.2	**28** 0258	4.4
0736	2.4	0940	1.9
TU 1352	4.2	W 1543	4.4
2012	2.3	2202	1.8
14 0239	4.4		
0854	2.0		
W 1520	4.4		
2124	1.9		
15 0347	4.8		
1000	1.6		
TH 1620	4.7		
2226	1.5		

MARCH

Time	m	Time	m
1 0401	4.7	**16** 0319	4.7
1032	1.5	0939	1.5
TH 1637	4.7	F 1558	4.7
2251	1.4	2205	1.4
2 0449	5.0	**17** 0414	5.1
1116	1.1	1036	1.0
F 1718	4.9	SA 1647	5.1
2332	1.1	2258	0.9
3 0528	5.2	**18** 0502	5.4
1156	0.8	1125	0.6
SA 1754	5.1	SU 1733	5.3
○		2346	0.6
4 0010	0.9	**19** 0549	5.7
0604	5.4	1211	0.3
SU 1233	0.7	M 1817	5.5
1826	5.1	●	
5 0045	0.8	**20** 0030	0.3
0636	5.4	0634	5.8
M 1306	0.7	TU 1254	0.1
1856	5.2	1859	5.6
6 0115	0.8	**21** 0111	0.2
0707	5.3	0718	5.8
TU 1333	0.8	W 1334	0.2
1924	5.2	1940	5.6
7 0140	0.9	**22** 0150	0.3
0736	5.3	0800	5.7
W 1356	1.0	TH 1412	0.4
1952	5.1	2017	5.5
8 0201	1.1	**23** 0227	0.5
0805	5.1	0840	5.4
TH 1414	1.2	F 1447	0.8
2019	5.0	2053	5.3
9 0220	1.2	**24** 0303	0.9
0831	4.9	0918	5.1
F 1431	1.4	SA 1523	1.2
2043	4.8	2128	5.0
10 0240	1.4	**25** 0343	1.4
0856	4.7	0958	4.6
SA 1453	1.6	SU 1605	1.8
2109	4.7	◐ 2208	4.6
11 0307	1.7	**26** 0433	1.9
0926	4.5	1058	4.2
SU 1524	1.9	M 1702	2.3
2146	4.4	2321	4.3
12 0347	2.0	**27** 0550	2.3
1017	4.2	1247	4.0
M 1610	2.2	TU 1837	2.5
◐ 2250	4.2		
13 0457	2.3	**28** 0117	4.2
1134	4.0	0808	2.3
TU 1754	2.5	W 1416	4.1
		2039	2.3
14 0016	4.2	**29** 0237	4.4
0705	2.3	0919	1.9
W 1317	4.1	TH 1522	4.4
1945	2.3	2138	1.8
15 0203	4.4	**30** 0336	4.7
0830	2.0	1007	1.4
TH 1457	4.4	F 1611	4.7
2102	1.9	2224	1.4
		31 0421	5.0
		1049	1.1
		SA 1649	4.9
		2304	1.1

APRIL

Time	m	Time	m
1 0459	5.2	**16** 0434	5.4
1127	0.9	1057	0.5
SU 1723	5.1	M 1704	5.4
2341	0.9	2319	0.5
2 0534	5.3	**17** 0522	5.6
1202	0.8	1144	0.3
M 1755	5.2	TU 1749	5.5
○		●	
3 0014	0.8	**18** 0005	0.3
0606	5.3	0609	5.7
TU 1233	0.8	W 1228	0.2
1824	5.2	1832	5.6
4 0043	0.8	**19** 0048	0.3
0638	5.3	0655	5.7
W 1259	0.9	TH 1310	0.3
1854	5.2	1914	5.6
5 0108	0.9	**20** 0129	0.4
0708	5.2	0739	5.5
TH 1322	1.0	F 1349	0.6
1922	5.2	1954	5.5
6 0130	1.1	**21** 0208	0.7
0737	5.1	0821	5.2
F 1341	1.2	SA 1428	0.9
1949	5.1	2031	5.3
7 0151	1.2	**22** 0248	1.0
0804	4.9	0903	4.9
SA 1401	1.4	SU 1507	1.4
2014	4.9	2108	5.0
8 0214	1.4	**23** 0331	1.5
0831	4.7	0948	4.5
SU 1426	1.6	M 1552	1.8
2042	4.8	2150	4.6
9 0244	1.6	**24** 0425	1.9
0906	4.5	1055	4.2
M 1500	1.8	TU 1649	2.2
2123	4.6	◐ 2300	4.3
10 0327	1.9	**25** 0538	2.2
1000	4.2	1228	4.0
TU 1549	2.2	W 1811	2.4
◐ 2225	4.4		
11 0441	2.2	**26** 0047	4.3
1114	4.1	0722	2.2
W 1728	2.4	TH 1343	4.1
2345	4.3	1950	2.3
12 0639	2.2	**27** 0200	4.4
1248	4.1	0836	1.9
TH 1917	2.2	F 1442	4.4
		2055	1.9
13 0122	4.4	**28** 0256	4.6
0802	1.8	0927	1.6
F 1424	4.4	SA 1530	4.6
2034	1.8	2144	1.6
14 0244	4.8	**29** 0342	4.8
0910	1.3	1010	1.3
SA 1526	4.8	SU 1610	4.8
2137	1.3	2226	1.3
15 0343	5.1	**30** 0423	5.0
1007	0.9	1049	1.1
SU 1617	5.1	M 1646	5.0
2231	0.9	2304	1.1

Chart Datum: 3·22 metres below Ordnance Datum (Newlyn)

TIDES

TIDES

ENGLAND – PLYMOUTH

LAT 50°22'N   LONG 4°11'W

TIMES AND HEIGHTS OF HIGH AND LOW WATERS

Dates in amber are SPRINGS
Dates in yellow are NEAPS

2007

(Time in hours/minutes, heights in metres)

MAY

Day	Time m	Time m	Time m	Time m
1 TU	0500 5.1	1124 1.0	1720 5.1	2338 1.0
2 W ○	0535 5.1	1156 1.0	1754 5.2	
3 TH	0009 1.0	0610 5.1	1225 1.1	1826 5.2
4 F	0038 1.1	0643 5.1	1251 1.2	1857 5.2
5 SA	0105 1.2	0716 5.0	1317 1.3	1927 5.1
6 SU	0132 1.3	0747 4.8	1344 1.4	1956 5.0
7 M	0202 1.4	0820 4.7	1415 1.6	2030 4.9
8 TU	0239 1.6	0900 4.5	1454 1.8	2114 4.7
9 W	0328 1.8	0953 4.3	1550 2.0	2211 4.6
10 TH ◑	0440 1.9	1059 4.2	1713 2.1	2321 4.5
11 F	0609 1.9	1219 4.3	1843 2.0	
12 SA	0043 4.6	0727 1.7	1341 4.5	1958 1.7
13 SU	0202 4.8	0834 1.3	1446 4.8	2103 1.4
14 M	0307 5.1	0934 1.0	1542 5.1	2200 1.0
15 TU	0404 5.3	1028 0.8	1634 5.3	2252 0.8
16 W ●	0456 5.4	1117 0.6	1722 5.4	2340 0.6
17 TH	0547 5.5	1204 0.6	1808 5.5	
18 F	0027 0.5	0635 5.4	1249 0.6	1853 5.5
19 SA	0112 0.6	0723 5.3	1332 0.8	1936 5.4
20 SU	0155 0.8	0809 5.1	1415 1.1	2017 5.2
21 M	0239 1.1	0855 4.8	1457 1.4	2057 5.0
22 TU	0325 1.4	0943 4.5	1543 1.7	2140 4.8
23 W ◑	0414 1.7	1038 4.3	1634 2.0	2234 4.5
24 TH	0512 2.0	1133 4.2	1733 2.2	2349 4.4
25 F	0618 2.0	1250 4.2	1841 2.2	
26 SA	0102 4.4	0727 2.0	1347 4.3	1949 2.1
27 SU	0201 4.5	0827 1.8	1437 4.5	2048 1.9
28 M	0253 4.6	0918 1.6	1523 4.7	2138 1.7
29 TU	0340 4.7	1002 1.5	1606 4.9	2221 1.5
30 W	0424 4.9	1042 1.4	1646 5.0	2300 1.4
31 TH	0505 4.9	1118 1.3	1725 5.1	2337 1.3

JUNE

Day	Time m	Time m	Time m	Time m
1 F ○	0546 5.0	1154 1.3	1802 5.1	
2 SA	0013 1.2	0624 5.0	1228 1.3	1838 5.2
3 SU	0048 1.2	0702 4.9	1303 1.3	1912 5.1
4 M	0125 1.3	0739 4.8	1339 1.4	1947 5.1
5 TU	0203 1.3	0817 4.8	1418 1.5	2026 5.0
6 W	0245 1.4	0900 4.7	1501 1.6	2110 4.9
7 TH	0333 1.5	0948 4.6	1552 1.7	2201 4.9
8 F ◑	0429 1.6	1045 4.5	1652 1.8	2300 4.8
9 SA	0535 1.6	1149 4.5	1803 1.8	
10 SU	0009 4.7	0645 1.6	1259 4.6	1916 1.7
11 M	0123 4.8	0755 1.5	1407 4.7	2027 1.5
12 TU	0233 4.9	0901 1.3	1510 4.9	2131 1.3
13 W	0337 5.0	1001 1.1	1608 5.1	2229 1.1
14 TH	0436 5.1	1056 1.0	1701 5.3	2323 0.9
15 F	0530 5.2	1147 0.9	1751 5.4	
16 SA	0013 0.8	0621 5.2	1235 0.9	1838 5.4
17 SU	0101 0.8	0711 5.1	1321 1.0	1923 5.3
18 M	0147 0.9	0759 5.0	1405 1.1	2006 5.2
19 TU	0231 1.0	0844 4.8	1447 1.3	2045 5.1
20 W	0313 1.2	0924 4.7	1527 1.5	2122 4.9
21 TH	0353 1.5	1003 4.5	1607 1.7	2159 4.7
22 F ◑	0435 1.7	1044 4.4	1650 1.9	2243 4.6
23 SA	0520 1.9	1132 4.3	1739 2.1	2336 4.4
24 SU	0613 2.0	1230 4.3	1837 2.1	
25 M	0040 4.4	0711 2.0	1331 4.3	1938 2.1
26 TU	0150 4.4	0811 2.0	1431 4.5	2039 2.0
27 W	0254 4.5	0908 1.8	1526 4.7	2135 1.8
28 TH	0350 4.6	0959 1.7	1615 4.8	2225 1.6
29 F	0440 4.7	1046 1.5	1700 5.0	2311 1.4
30 SA ○	0525 4.9	1130 1.4	1743 5.1	2355 1.3

JULY

Day	Time m	Time m	Time m	Time m
1 SU	0609 4.9	1213 1.3	1824 5.2	
2 M	0038 1.2	0652 5.0	1256 1.2	1903 5.2
3 TU	0121 1.1	0734 5.0	1338 1.2	1943 5.3
4 W	0202 1.0	0815 4.9	1418 1.2	2023 5.2
5 TH	0243 1.1	0856 4.9	1459 1.2	2104 5.2
6 F	0325 1.1	0938 4.8	1541 1.3	2148 5.1
7 SA	0409 1.3	1025 4.8	1627 1.4	2238 4.9
8 SU	0500 1.4	1118 4.7	1724 1.7	2336 4.8
9 M	0602 1.6	1222 4.6	1834 1.8	
10 TU	0048 4.6	0716 1.7	1334 4.6	1954 1.8
11 W	0207 4.6	0833 1.7	1446 4.7	2111 1.7
12 TH	0321 4.7	0944 1.5	1551 4.9	2217 1.4
13 F	0425 4.8	1045 1.3	1648 5.1	2315 1.2
14 SA ●	0521 5.0	1138 1.1	1739 5.3	
15 SU	0006 1.0	0612 5.0	1227 1.0	1825 5.3
16 M	0053 0.8	0659 5.1	1311 0.9	1909 5.4
17 TU	0136 0.8	0742 5.0	1351 1.0	1948 5.3
18 W	0215 0.9	0820 4.9	1428 1.1	2022 5.2
19 TH	0250 1.0	0901 4.8	1501 1.2	2052 5.1
20 F	0321 1.3	0921 4.7	1531 1.5	2122 4.9
21 SA	0351 1.5	1001 4.6	1601 1.7	2155 4.7
22 SU ◑	0422 1.8	1029 4.5	1637 2.0	2235 4.5
23 M	0501 2.0	1116 4.3	1728 2.2	2326 4.3
24 TU	0601 2.2	1218 4.2	1838 2.3	
25 W	0036 4.2	0712 2.2	1337 4.3	1950 2.2
26 TH	0207 4.2	0822 2.1	1451 4.5	2057 2.0
27 F	0322 4.4	0925 1.9	1550 4.7	2158 1.7
28 SA	0419 4.6	1022 1.6	1640 5.0	2252 1.4
29 SU	0508 4.8	1114 1.4	1724 5.2	2341 1.1
30 M ○	0553 5.0	1201 1.1	1808 5.3	
31 TU	0027 0.9	0637 5.1	1246 1.0	1850 5.4

AUGUST

Day	Time m	Time m	Time m	Time m
1 W	0111 0.8	0721 5.2	1328 0.9	1932 5.5
2 TH	0152 0.7	0802 5.2	1407 0.8	2012 5.5
3 F	0230 0.7	0841 5.2	1444 0.9	2051 5.4
4 SA	0307 0.8	0919 5.1	1521 1.0	2131 5.2
5 SU ◑	0345 1.1	1000 4.9	1602 1.3	2214 5.0
6 M	0428 1.4	1047 4.7	1650 1.7	2306 4.7
7 TU	0523 1.8	1149 4.5	1758 2.0	
8 W	0023 4.4	0643 2.1	1312 4.4	1935 2.1
9 TH	0157 4.3	0822 2.1	1436 4.5	2108 1.9
10 F	0319 4.5	0941 1.8	1546 4.8	2216 1.6
11 SA	0424 4.7	1040 1.4	1641 5.1	2309 1.2
12 SU ●	0515 4.9	1129 1.1	1728 5.3	2355 0.9
13 M	0559 5.1	1213 0.9	1810 5.4	
14 TU	0037 0.7	0639 5.1	1253 0.8	1847 5.4
15 W	0116 0.7	0714 5.1	1329 0.8	1920 5.4
16 TH	0150 0.8	0745 5.1	1401 0.9	1950 5.3
17 F	0218 0.9	0812 5.0	1427 1.1	2018 5.2
18 SA	0242 1.2	0840 4.9	1450 1.3	2046 4.8
19 SU	0302 1.4	0908 4.8	1510 1.6	2115 4.8
20 M ◑	0321 1.7	0940 4.6	1534 1.9	2147 4.5
21 TU	0348 2.0	1019 4.4	1611 2.2	2233 4.3
22 W	0434 2.3	1116 4.2	1732 2.4	2340 4.1
23 TH	0621 2.5	1240 4.2	1913 2.4	
24 F	0123 4.1	0749 2.5	1420 4.4	2030 2.3
25 SA	0302 4.3	0902 2.0	1527 4.7	2137 1.7
26 SU	0400 4.6	1003 1.6	1618 5.0	2233 1.3
27 M	0448 4.9	1056 1.2	1703 5.3	2322 0.9
28 TU ○	0533 5.1	1143 0.9	1747 5.5	
29 W	0008 0.7	0616 5.3	1228 0.7	1830 5.6
30 TH	0051 0.5	0658 5.4	1309 0.6	1912 5.7
31 F	0131 0.4	0739 5.4	1347 0.5	1953 5.7

Chart Datum: 3·22 metres below Ordnance Datum (Newlyn)

TIME ZONE (UT)		
For Summer Time add ONE hour in **non-shaded areas**	**ENGLAND – PLYMOUTH** **LAT 50°22′N LONG 4°11′W** TIMES AND HEIGHTS OF HIGH AND LOW WATERS	Dates in amber are **SPRINGS** Dates in yellow are **NEAPS** **2007**

SEPTEMBER

Day	Time m	Time m	Time m	Time m
1 SA	0208 0.5	0818 5.4	1424 0.7	2032 5.5
2 SU	0244 0.8	0855 5.3	1459 1.0	2110 5.3
3 M	0320 1.1	0933 5.0	1538 1.4	2151 4.9
4 TU	0400 1.6	1018 4.7	1625 1.8	2242 4.5 ☽
5 W	0454 2.1	1123 4.4	1737 2.3	
6 TH	0013 4.2	0624 2.4	1303 4.3	1940 2.3
7 F	0200 4.2	0827 2.3	1432 4.5	2110 2.0
8 SA	0321 4.4	0936 1.9	1539 4.8	2207 1.5
9 SU	0417 4.7	1027 1.4	1628 5.1	2253 1.1
10 M	0500 5.0	1111 1.1	1709 5.3	2334 0.8
11 TU ●	0537 5.2	1150 0.8	1746 5.4	
12 W	0012 0.7	0610 5.2	1227 0.7	1818 5.5
13 TH	0047 0.7	0640 5.3	1259 0.8	1848 5.4
14 F	0117 0.8	0708 5.2	1327 1.0	1917 5.3
15 SA	0141 1.0	0735 5.2	1350 1.1	1945 5.2
16 SU	0201 1.2	0803 5.1	1409 1.3	2012 5.0
17 M	0217 1.4	0830 4.9	1427 1.6	2039 4.8
18 TU	0235 1.7	0859 4.7	1450 1.8	2110 4.6
19 W ◐	0302 1.9	0936 4.5	1525 2.1	2156 4.3
20 TH	0343 2.3	1033 4.3	1626 2.5	2305 4.1
21 F	0514 2.6	1153 4.2	1842 2.5	
22 SA	0043 4.0	0722 2.5	1343 4.4	2006 2.2
23 SU	0238 4.3	0838 2.1	1459 4.7	2112 1.7
24 M	0336 4.7	0939 1.6	1551 5.1	2208 1.2
25 TU	0423 5.0	1031 1.1	1637 5.4	2257 0.8
26 W ○	0507 5.3	1119 0.8	1721 5.6	2342 0.5
27 TH	0550 5.5	1203 0.6	1805 5.8	
28 F	0025 0.4	0631 5.6	1245 0.4	1848 5.8
29 SA	0106 0.4	0713 5.6	1324 0.5	1931 5.7
30 SU	0144 0.6	0752 5.6	1402 0.7	2012 5.5

OCTOBER

Day	Time m	Time m	Time m	Time m
1 M	0221 0.9	0831 5.4	1440 1.0	2052 5.2
2 TU	0258 1.3	0910 5.1	1521 1.5	2134 4.8
3 W	0340 1.8	0955 4.8	1612 2.0	2230 4.4
4 TH	0438 2.3	1105 4.4	1729 2.4 ☽	
5 F	0015 4.1	0617 2.6	1253 4.3	1936 2.3
6 SA	0153 4.2	0811 2.3	1415 4.5	2051 2.0
7 SU	0303 4.5	0913 1.9	1516 4.8	2142 1.5
8 M	0353 4.8	1001 1.5	1602 5.1	2225 1.2
9 TU	0432 5.0	1042 1.2	1641 5.3	2304 1.0
10 W	0506 5.2	1051 0.9	1716 5.4	2340 0.6
11 TH ●	0537 5.3	1155 0.9	1748 5.4	
12 F	0013 0.9	0606 5.4	1226 0.9	1817 5.4
13 SA	0041 1.0	0635 5.3	1253 1.0	1847 5.3
14 SU	0104 1.1	0704 5.3	1316 1.2	1917 5.2
15 M	0124 1.3	0733 5.2	1337 1.4	1945 5.0
16 TU	0144 1.5	0801 5.0	1359 1.6	2014 4.8
17 W	0206 1.7	0830 4.8	1425 1.8	2047 4.6
18 TH ◐	0236 2.0	0909 4.6	1503 2.1	2135 4.3
19 F ☽	0319 2.3	1005 4.4	1605 2.4	2242 4.2
20 SA	0439 2.6	1118 4.3	1807 2.4	
21 SU	0008 4.1	0647 2.5	1250 4.5	1933 2.1
22 M	0153 4.4	0806 2.1	1416 4.8	2040 1.7
23 TU	0259 4.7	0908 1.6	1515 5.1	2136 1.2
24 W	0350 5.1	1002 1.2	1606 5.4	2227 0.9
25 TH	0436 5.4	1051 0.9	1654 5.6	2314 0.6
26 F ○	0521 5.6	1137 0.6	1740 5.7	2358 0.5
27 SA	0605 5.7	1221 0.5	1826 5.7	
28 SU	0041 0.6	0648 5.7	1303 0.6	1911 5.6
29 M	0123 0.7	0731 5.6	1345 0.8	1956 5.4
30 TU	0203 1.1	0813 5.4	1427 1.1	2040 5.1
31 W	0244 1.5	0855 5.1	1513 1.6	2128 4.7

NOVEMBER

Day	Time m	Time m	Time m	Time m
1 TH ☽	0331 1.9	0944 4.9	1606 2.0	2230 4.4
2 F	0428 2.3	1052 4.6	1718 2.2	2358 4.2
3 SA	0550 2.5	1223 4.5	1854 2.3	
4 SU	0118 4.3	0726 2.4	1337 4.6	2009 2.0
5 M	0221 4.5	0832 2.1	1436 4.8	2103 1.7
6 TU	0311 4.7	0923 1.7	1526 5.1	2148 1.5
7 W	0353 5.0	1006 1.5	1605 5.1	2228 1.3
8 TH	0430 5.1	1046 1.3	1643 5.2	2305 1.2
9 F ●	0503 5.3	1121 1.2	1717 5.3	2337 1.0
10 SA	0536 5.3	1154 1.2	1751 5.3	
11 SU	0007 1.2	0608 5.4	1223 1.2	1824 5.4
12 M	0034 1.3	0640 5.3	1251 1.3	1856 5.1
13 TU	0059 1.4	0711 5.2	1318 1.5	1928 5.0
14 W	0125 1.6	0742 5.1	1346 1.6	2000 4.8
15 TH	0154 1.7	0815 5.0	1419 1.8	2037 4.6
16 F	0229 1.9	0854 4.8	1502 2.0	2124 4.5
17 SA ☽	0316 2.1	0946 4.7	1601 2.1	2223 4.4
18 SU	0424 2.3	1050 4.6	1725 2.2	2334 4.3
19 M	0558 2.3	1204 4.6	1849 2.0	
20 TU	0055 4.5	0721 2.1	1323 4.8	1959 1.7
21 W	0209 4.7	0830 1.8	1433 5.0	2101 1.4
22 TH	0311 5.0	0929 1.4	1533 5.3	2156 1.1
23 F	0405 5.3	1023 1.1	1627 5.4	2247 0.9
24 SA ○	0455 5.5	1113 0.9	1719 5.5	2336 0.8
25 SU	0543 5.6	1202 0.8	1809 5.5	
26 M	0022 0.8	0629 5.7	1249 0.8	1858 5.5
27 TU	0108 0.9	0716 5.6	1335 0.9	1946 5.3
28 W	0153 1.1	0802 5.5	1421 1.1	2034 5.1
29 TH	0237 1.4	0847 5.3	1508 1.4	2123 4.8
30 F	0323 1.7	0935 5.0	1557 1.7	2215 4.6

DECEMBER

Day	Time m	Time m	Time m	Time m
1 SA ☽	0412 2.0	1027 4.8	1650 2.0	2315 4.4
2 SU	0509 2.2	1130 4.6	1752 2.1	
3 M	0021 4.3	0615 2.3	1238 4.6	1900 2.1
4 TU	0122 4.4	0726 2.3	1339 4.6	2004 2.1
5 W	0216 4.5	0829 2.1	1434 4.7	2059 1.9
6 TH	0306 4.7	0922 1.9	1523 4.8	2146 1.7
7 F	0350 4.9	1007 1.7	1608 4.9	2227 1.6
8 SA	0432 5.1	1048 1.6	1650 5.0	2304 1.5
9 SU ●	0510 5.2	1125 1.5	1729 5.1	2339 1.4
10 M	0548 5.3	1201 1.4	1808 5.1	
11 TU	0012 1.4	0624 5.3	1235 1.4	1844 5.1
12 W	0046 1.5	0659 5.3	1310 1.4	1921 5.0
13 TH	0120 1.5	0734 5.2	1345 1.5	1956 4.9
14 F	0155 1.6	0809 5.1	1423 1.5	2034 4.8
15 SA	0233 1.7	0848 5.0	1503 1.6	2116 4.7
16 SU ◐	0316 1.8	0933 5.0	1550 1.7	2204 4.6
17 M ☽	0406 1.9	1025 4.9	1646 1.8	2301 4.6
18 TU	0508 2.0	1126 4.8	1755 1.9	
19 W	0008 4.6	0625 2.0	1237 4.8	1911 1.8
20 TH	0121 4.6	0746 1.9	1352 4.8	2023 1.7
21 F	0233 4.8	0858 1.7	1503 5.0	2129 1.5
22 SA	0338 5.1	1001 1.4	1608 5.1	2228 1.3
23 SU	0436 5.3	1058 1.1	1705 5.3	2321 1.1
24 M ○	0528 5.5	1151 1.0	1759 5.3	
25 TU	0012 1.0	0618 5.6	1241 0.8	1849 5.3
26 W	0100 1.0	0706 5.6	1329 0.8	1939 5.2
27 TH	0145 1.0	0752 5.5	1414 0.9	2024 5.1
28 F	0228 1.1	0836 5.4	1456 1.1	2106 5.0
29 SA	0307 1.3	0915 5.2	1535 1.3	2143 4.8
30 SU	0346 1.6	0951 5.0	1614 1.6	2219 4.6
31 M ☽	0425 1.9	1029 4.8	1655 1.9	2300 4.5

Chart Datum: 3·22 metres below Ordnance Datum (Newlyn)

TIDES

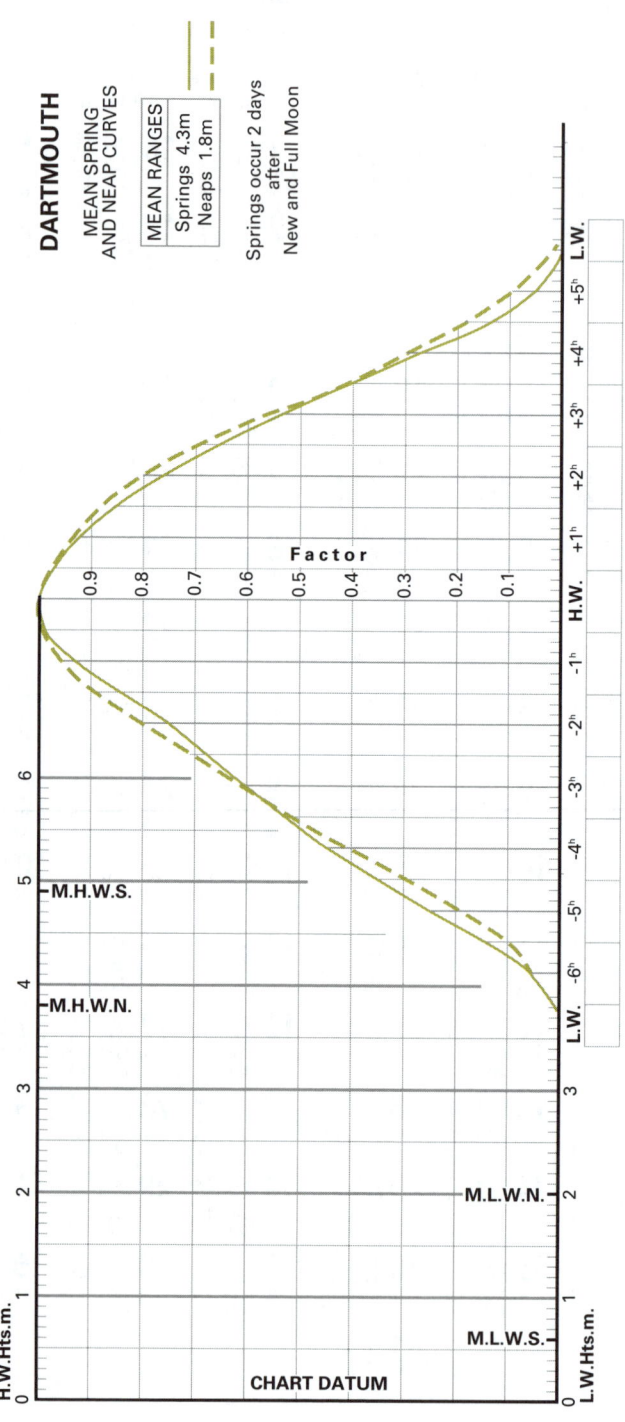

DARTMOUTH

MEAN SPRING
AND NEAP CURVES

MEAN RANGES
Springs 4.3m
Neaps 1.8m

Springs occur 2 days
after
New and Full Moon

ENGLAND - DARTMOUTH

LAT 50°21'N LONG 3°34'W

TIMES AND HEIGHTS OF HIGH AND LOW WATERS

Dates in amber are **SPRINGS**
Dates in yellow are **NEAPS**

2007

JANUARY

Date	Time	m	Time	m	Time	m	Time	m	Phase
1 M	0345	4.3	0947	1.4	1616	4.3	2214	1.3	
2 TU	0445	4.5	1045	1.2	1715	4.4	2308	1.1	
3 W	0537	4.7	1136	1.0	1806	4.5	2355	1.0	○
4 TH	0624		1223	0.9	1852	4.5			
5 F	0040	1.0	0705	4.8	1308	0.9	1933	4.5	
6 SA	0121	1.0	0743	4.8	1347	0.9	2009	4.4	
7 SU	0157	1.1	0818	4.7	1423	1.0	2042	4.3	
8 M	0230	1.2	0851	4.6	1455	1.2	2113	4.2	
9 TU	0301	1.4	0923	4.4	1525	1.4	2145	4.1	
10 W	0330	1.6	0956	4.3	1555	1.6	2220	3.9	
11 TH	0403	1.8	1034	4.1	1628	1.8	2302	3.8	◐
12 F	0444	2.0	1119	3.9	1716	2.0	2355	3.7	
13 SA	0545	2.1	1215	3.7	1823	2.1			
14 SU	0101	3.7	0702	2.2	1329	3.7	1937	2.1	
15 M	0222	3.8	0814	2.0	1454	3.8	2045	1.9	
16 TU	0335	4.0	0920	1.8	1603	4.0	2146	1.6	
17 W	0432	4.3	1018	1.5	1700	4.2	2241	1.4	
18 TH	0523	4.5	1111	1.2	1751	4.4	2331	1.1	
19 F	0610	4.7	1200	0.9	1838	4.5			●
20 SA	0018	0.9	0654	4.9	1248	0.7	1921	4.6	
21 SU	0105	0.7	0737	5.0	1332	0.5	2004	4.7	
22 M	0147	0.6	0818	5.0	1413	0.5	2045	4.7	
23 TU	0227	0.6	0858	5.0	1452	0.6	2124	4.6	
24 W	0305	0.8	0940	4.8	1530	0.8	2204	4.5	
25 TH	0343	1.0	1021	4.6	1611	1.1	2246	4.3	◑
26 F	0426	1.3	1107	4.3	1656	1.4	2335	4.0	
27 SA	0519	1.7	1205	4.0	1756	1.8			
28 SU	0044	3.9	0635	1.9	1325	3.8	1923	2.0	
29 M	0208	3.8	0817	2.0	1452	3.8	2058	1.9	
30 TU	0328	4.0	0941	1.7	1609	4.0	2208	1.6	
31 W	0434	4.3	1041	1.3	1709	4.2	2302	1.3	

FEBRUARY

Date	Time	m	Time	m	Time	m	Time	m	Phase
1 TH	0527	4.5	1130	1.0	1758	4.3	2348	1.0	
2 F	0613	4.7	1214	0.8	1841	4.4			○
3 SA	0030	0.8	0651	4.8	1256	0.7	1916	4.5	
4 SU	0108	0.7	0726	4.8	1330	0.7	1948	4.5	
5 M	0140	0.8	0757	4.7	1402	0.7	2016	4.4	
6 TU	0208	0.9	0827	4.7	1428	0.9	2045	4.4	
7 W	0231	1.0	0855	4.5	1449	1.1	2112	4.3	
8 TH	0253	1.2	0924	4.3	1509	1.3	2140	4.1	
9 F	0315	1.4	0952	4.1	1530	1.5	2211	3.9	
10 SA	0342	1.7	1025	3.9	1603	1.8	2251	3.7	
11 SU	0426	2.0	1115	3.7	1656	2.1	2353	3.6	
12 M	0551	2.2	1227	3.5	1842	2.2			
13 TU	0118	3.6	0732	2.2	1409	3.6	2008	2.1	
14 W	0257	3.8	0851	1.8	1540	3.8	2121	1.7	
15 TH	0408	4.2	0958	1.4	1642	4.1	2224	1.3	
16 F	0501	4.5	1056	1.0	1733	4.4	2318	0.9	
17 SA	0550	4.8	1146	0.6	1821	4.6			●
18 SU	0006	0.6	0637	5.0	1234	0.3	1905	4.8	
19 M	0052	0.3	0721	5.1	1317	0.1	1947	4.9	
20 TU	0132	0.2	0803	5.2	1356	0.1	2026	4.9	
21 W	0211	0.2	0844	5.1	1433	0.2	2103	4.8	
22 TH	0246	0.4	0922	4.9	1509	0.5	2139	4.6	
23 F	0322	0.7	0959	4.6	1544	1.0	2215	4.3	
24 SA	0400	1.2	1039	4.2	1625	1.5	2258	4.0	◐
25 SU	0448	1.7	1134	3.8	1720	1.9			
26 M	0007	3.7	0601	2.1	1308	3.5	1851	2.2	
27 TU	0149	3.6	0814	2.1	1446	3.5	2055	2.1	
28 W	0317	3.8	0938	1.7	1603	3.8	2200	1.6	

MARCH

Date	Time	m	Time	m	Time	m	Time	m	Phase
1 TH	0422	4.1	1031	1.3	1659	4.1	2250	1.2	
2 F	0512	4.4	1115	0.9	1742	4.3	2331	0.9	
3 SA	0552	4.6	1155	0.6	1819	4.5			○
4 SU	0009	0.7	0629	4.8	1233	0.5	1851	4.5	
5 M	0045	0.6	0700	4.8	1306	0.5	1920	4.6	
6 TU	0115	0.6	0731	4.7	1332	0.6	1947	4.6	
7 W	0139	0.7	0759	4.7	1355	0.8	2014	4.5	
8 TH	0200	0.9	0827	4.5	1413	1.0	2041	4.4	
9 F	0219	1.0	0852	4.3	1429	1.2	2104	4.2	
10 SA	0238	1.2	0917	4.0	1451	1.4	2130	4.1	
11 SU	0305	1.5	0946	3.9	1522	1.7	2205	3.8	
12 M	0344	1.8	1036	3.6	1607	2.0	2308	3.6	◑
13 TU	0453	2.1	1151	3.4	1749	2.3			
14 W	0032	3.6	0701	2.1	1333	3.5	1941	2.1	
15 TH	0220	3.8	0827	1.8	1516	3.8	2059	1.7	
16 F	0339	4.1	0937	1.3	1619	4.1	2203	1.2	
17 SA	0435	4.5	1035	0.8	1710	4.5	2257	0.7	
18 SU	0525	4.8	1124	0.4	1757	4.7	2345	0.4	
19 M	0614	5.1	1210	0.1	1842	4.9			●
20 TU	0030	0.1	0658	5.2	1254	-0.1	1923	5.0	
21 W	0111	0.0	0741	5.2	1333	0.0	2003	5.0	
22 TH	0149	0.1	0822	5.1	1411	0.2	2039	4.9	
23 F	0226	0.3	0901	4.8	1445	0.6	2114	4.7	
24 SA	0301	0.7	0938	4.5	1521	1.0	2148	4.4	
25 SU	0340	1.2	1017	4.0	1602	1.6	2227	4.0	◑
26 M	0429	1.7	1116	3.6	1658	2.1	2338	3.7	
27 TU	0545	2.1	1302	3.4	1833	2.3			
28 W	0133	3.6	0804	2.1	1434	3.5	2036	2.1	
29 TH	0255	3.8	0916	1.7	1542	3.8	2136	1.6	
30 F	0356	4.1	1005	1.2	1632	4.1	2222	1.2	
31 SA	0443	4.4	1048	0.9	1712	4.3	2303	0.9	

APRIL

Date	Time	m	Time	m	Time	m	Time	m	Phase
1 SU	0522	4.6	1126	0.7	1747	4.5	2340	0.7	
2 M	0558	4.7	1201	0.6	1820	4.6			○
3 TU	0013	0.6	0631	4.7	1233	0.6	1849	4.6	
4 W	0043	0.6	0702	4.7	1259	0.7	1918	4.6	
5 TH	0108	0.7	0732	4.6	1322	0.8	1945	4.6	
6 F	0129	0.9	0800	4.5	1340	1.0	2011	4.5	
7 SA	0150	1.0	0826	4.3	1400	1.2	2036	4.3	
8 SU	0213	1.2	0852	4.1	1425	1.4	2103	4.2	
9 M	0242	1.4	0927	3.9	1458	1.6	2143	4.0	
10 TU	0325	1.7	1019	3.6	1546	2.0	2244	3.8	◑
11 W	0437	2.0	1132	3.5	1724	2.2			
12 TH	0001	3.7	0635	2.0	1303	3.5	1913	2.0	
13 F	0138	3.8	0758	1.6	1442	3.8	2031	1.6	
14 SA	0302	4.2	0907	1.1	1546	4.2	2135	1.1	
15 SU	0403	4.5	1005	0.7	1639	4.5	2230	0.7	
16 M	0456	4.8	1056	0.3	1727	4.8	2318	0.3	
17 TU	0546	5.0	1143	0.1	1814	4.9			●
18 W	0004	0.1	0634	5.1	1227	0.0	1856	5.0	
19 TH	0048	0.1	0719	5.1	1310	0.1	1938	5.0	
20 F	0129	0.2	0802	4.9	1348	0.4	2016	4.9	
21 SA	0207	0.5	0843	4.6	1427	0.7	2052	4.7	
22 SU	0246	0.8	0924	4.3	1505	1.2	2129	4.4	
23 M	0328	1.3	1007	3.9	1549	1.6	2209	4.0	
24 TU	0422	1.7	1113	3.6	1645	2.0	2318	3.7	◐
25 W	0533	2.0	1244	3.4	1806	2.2			
26 TH	0102	3.7	0718	2.0	1359	3.5	1946	2.1	
27 F	0217	3.8	0833	1.7	1500	3.8	2052	1.7	
28 SA	0315	4.0	0924	1.4	1550	4.0	2142	1.4	
29 SU	0402	4.2	1008	1.1	1631	4.2	2224	1.1	
30 M	0445	4.4	1048	0.9	1709	4.4	2303	0.9	

Chart Datum: 2·62 metres below Ordnance Datum (Newlyn)

TIDES

TIME ZONE (UT)
For Summer Time add ONE hour in **non-shaded areas**

ENGLAND - DARTMOUTH

LAT 50°21'N   LONG 3°34'W

TIMES AND HEIGHTS OF HIGH AND LOW WATERS

Dates in amber are SPRINGS
Dates in yellow are NEAPS

2007

MAY

Day	Time	m	Time	m
1 TU	0523 / 1123 / 1744 / 2337	4.5 / 0.8 / 4.5 / 0.8	16 W 0519 / 1116 / 1746 / ●2339	4.8 / 0.4 / 4.8 / 0.4
2 W ○	0559 / 1155 / 1819	4.5 / 0.8 / 4.6	17 TH 0612 / 1203 / 1833	4.9 / 0.4 / 4.9
3 TH	0008 / 0635 / 1224 / 1851	0.8 / 4.5 / 0.9 / 4.6	18 F 0026 / 0659 / 1249 / 1917	0.3 / 4.8 / 0.4 / 4.9
4 F	0038 / 0707 / 1251 / 1921	0.9 / 4.5 / 1.0 / 4.6	19 SA 0112 / 0746 / 1331 / 1959	0.4 / 4.7 / 0.6 / 4.8
5 SA	0105 / 0739 / 1317 / 1950	1.0 / 4.4 / 1.1 / 4.4	20 SU 0154 / 0831 / 1414 / 2039	0.6 / 4.5 / 0.9 / 4.5
6 SU	0131 / 0809 / 1343 / 2018	1.1 / 4.2 / 1.2 / 4.4	21 M 0237 / 0916 / 1455 / 2118	0.9 / 4.2 / 1.2 / 4.4
7 M	0201 / 0842 / 1414 / 2051	1.2 / 4.1 / 1.4 / 4.3	22 TU 0323 / 1003 / 1540 / 2200	1.2 / 3.9 / 1.5 / 4.2
8 TU	0237 / 0921 / 1452 / 2135	1.4 / 3.9 / 1.6 / 4.1	23 W 0411 / 1056 / 1630 / ◐2252	1.5 / 3.7 / 1.8 / 3.9
9 W	0326 / 1012 / 1547 / 2230	1.6 / 3.7 / 1.8 / 4.0	24 TH 0508 / 1201 / 1728	1.8 / 3.6 / 2.0
10 TH	0436 / 1117 / 1709 / ◐2338	1.7 / 3.6 / 1.9 / 3.9	25 F 0005 / 0613 / 1305 / 1837	3.8 / 1.8 / 3.6 / 2.0
11 F	0604 / 1235 / 1839	1.7 / 3.7 / 1.8	26 SA 0117 / 0723 / 1404 / 1945	3.8 / 1.8 / 3.7 / 1.9
12 SA	0058 / 0723 / 1357 / 1954	4.0 / 1.5 / 3.9 / 1.5	27 SU 0218 / 0823 / 1455 / 2045	3.9 / 1.6 / 3.9 / 1.7
13 SU	0219 / 0831 / 1505 / 2100	4.2 / 1.1 / 4.2 / 1.2	28 M 0312 / 0915 / 1543 / 2136	4.0 / 1.4 / 4.1 / 1.5
14 M	0326 / 0932 / 1602 / 2158	4.5 / 0.8 / 4.5 / 0.8	29 TU 0400 / 1000 / 1627 / 2219	4.1 / 1.3 / 4.3 / 1.3
15 TU	0425 / 1026 / 1656 / 2251	4.7 / 0.6 / 4.7 / 0.6	30 W 0446 / 1041 / 1709 / 2259	4.3 / 1.2 / 4.4 / 1.2
			31 TH 0528 / 1117 / 1749 / 2336	4.3 / 1.1 / 4.5 / 1.1

JUNE

Day	Time	m	Time	m
1 F ○	0611 / 1153 / 1827	4.4 / 1.1 / 4.5	16 SA 0012 / 0646 / 1235 / 1902	0.6 / 4.6 / 0.7 / 4.8
2 SA	0012 / 0649 / 1227 / 1902	1.0 / 4.4 / 1.1 / 4.6	17 SU 0101 / 0735 / 1321 / 1946	0.6 / 4.5 / 0.8 / 4.7
3 SU	0048 / 0726 / 1303 / 1936	1.0 / 4.3 / 1.1 / 4.5	18 M 0146 / 0821 / 1404 / 2028	0.7 / 4.4 / 0.9 / 4.6
4 M	0125 / 0802 / 1338 / 2009	1.1 / 4.2 / 1.2 / 4.5	19 TU 0229 / 0905 / 1445 / 2106	0.8 / 4.2 / 1.1 / 4.5
5 TU	0202 / 0839 / 1417 / 2048	1.1 / 4.2 / 1.3 / 4.4	20 W 0311 / 0944 / 1525 / 2142	1.0 / 4.1 / 1.3 / 4.3
6 W	0243 / 0921 / 1459 / 2131	1.2 / 4.1 / 1.4 / 4.3	21 TH 0350 / 1022 / 1604 / 2218	1.3 / 3.9 / 1.5 / 4.1
7 TH	0330 / 1007 / 1549 / 2220	1.3 / 4.0 / 1.5 / 4.3	22 F 0431 / 1102 / 1646 / ◑2301	1.5 / 3.8 / 1.7 / 4.0
8 F	0426 / 1103 / 1648 / ◑2318	1.4 / 3.9 / 1.6 / 4.2	23 SA 0516 / 1149 / 1734 / 2353	1.7 / 3.7 / 1.9 / 3.8
9 SA	0530 / 1205 / 1758	1.4 / 3.9 / 1.6	24 SU 0608 / 1245 / 1833	1.8 / 3.7 / 1.9
10 SU	0025 / 0641 / 1314 / 1912	4.1 / 1.4 / 4.0 / 1.5	25 M 0055 / 0707 / 1347 / 1934	3.8 / 1.8 / 3.7 / 1.9
11 M	0139 / 0751 / 1424 / 2023	4.2 / 1.3 / 4.1 / 1.3	26 TU 0207 / 0807 / 1449 / 2036	3.8 / 1.8 / 3.9 / 1.6
12 TU	0251 / 0858 / 1529 / 2129	4.3 / 1.1 / 4.3 / 1.1	27 W 0313 / 0905 / 1546 / 2133	3.9 / 1.6 / 4.1 / 1.4
13 W	0357 / 0959 / 1637 / 2227	4.4 / 0.9 / 4.5 / 0.9	28 TH 0411 / 0957 / 1637 / 2223	4.0 / 1.5 / 4.2 / 1.4
14 TH	0458 / 1055 / 1724 / 2322	4.5 / 0.8 / 4.7 / 0.7	29 F 0502 / 1045 / 1723 / 2310	4.1 / 1.3 / 4.4 / 1.2
15 F ●	0554 / 1146 / 1816	4.6 / 0.7 / 4.8	30 SA 0549 / 1129 / 1807 / ○2354	4.3 / 1.2 / 4.5 / 1.1

JULY

Day	Time	m	Time	m
1 SU	0634 / 1212 / 1849	4.3 / 1.1 / 4.6	16 M 0053 / 0723 / 1311 / 1933	0.6 / 4.5 / 0.7 / 4.8
2 M	0038 / 0716 / 1256 / 1927	1.0 / 4.4 / 1.0 / 4.6	17 TU 0135 / 0805 / 1350 / 2010	0.6 / 4.4 / 0.7 / 4.7
3 TU	0121 / 0757 / 1337 / 2006	0.9 / 4.4 / 1.0 / 4.7	18 W 0214 / 0842 / 1427 / 2044	0.7 / 4.3 / 0.9 / 4.6
4 W	0201 / 0837 / 1417 / 2045	0.8 / 4.3 / 1.0 / 4.6	19 TH 0248 / 0913 / 1459 / 2113	0.8 / 4.2 / 1.0 / 4.5
5 TH	0241 / 0917 / 1457 / 2125	0.9 / 4.3 / 1.0 / 4.6	20 F 0319 / 0941 / 1528 / 2142	1.1 / 4.1 / 1.3 / 4.3
6 F	0323 / 0958 / 1538 / 2207	0.9 / 4.2 / 1.1 / 4.5	21 SA 0348 / 1011 / 1558 / 2214	1.3 / 4.0 / 1.5 / 4.1
7 SA	0406 / 1044 / 1624 / ◑2256	1.1 / 4.2 / 1.3 / 4.3	22 SU 0419 / 1048 / 1633 / ◑2253	1.6 / 3.9 / 1.8 / 3.9
8 SU	0456 / 1135 / 1720 / 2353	1.2 / 4.1 / 1.5 / 4.2	23 M 0457 / 1133 / 1724 / 2343	1.8 / 3.7 / 2.0 / 3.7
9 M	0557 / 1238 / 1830	1.4 / 4.0 / 1.6	24 TU 0556 / 1234 / 1834	2.0 / 3.6 / 2.1
10 TU	0103 / 0712 / 1350 / 1950	4.0 / 1.5 / 4.0 / 1.6	25 W 0051 / 0708 / 1353 / 1946	3.6 / 2.0 / 3.7 / 2.0
11 W	0224 / 0830 / 1505 / 2108	4.0 / 1.5 / 4.1 / 1.5	26 TH 0224 / 0818 / 1510 / 2054	3.6 / 1.9 / 3.9 / 1.8
12 TH	0341 / 0942 / 1612 / 2215	4.1 / 1.3 / 4.3 / 1.2	27 F 0342 / 0922 / 1611 / 2156	3.8 / 1.7 / 4.1 / 1.5
13 F	0447 / 1044 / 1711 / 2314	4.2 / 1.1 / 4.5 / 1.0	28 SA 0441 / 1020 / 1702 / 2251	4.0 / 1.4 / 4.4 / 1.2
14 SA ●	0545 / 1137 / 1748	4.4 / 0.9 / 4.7	29 SU 0531 / 1113 / 1748 / 2340	4.2 / 1.2 / 4.6 / 0.9
15 SU	0005 / 0637 / 1226 / 1850	0.8 / 4.4 / 0.8 / 4.7	30 M ○ 0618 / 1200 / 1833	4.4 / 0.9 / 4.7
			31 TU 0026 / 0701 / 1246 / 1914	0.7 / 4.5 / 0.8 / 4.8

AUGUST

Day	Time	m	Time	m
1 W	0111 / 0744 / 1328 / 1955	0.6 / 4.6 / 0.7 / 4.9	16 TH 0149 / 0807 / 1359 / 2012	0.6 / 4.5 / 0.7 / 4.7
2 TH	0151 / 0824 / 1406 / 2034	0.5 / 4.6 / 0.6 / 4.9	17 F 0217 / 0834 / 1426 / 2040	0.7 / 4.4 / 0.9 / 4.6
3 F	0228 / 0902 / 1442 / 2112	0.5 / 4.6 / 0.7 / 4.8	18 SA 0240 / 0901 / 1448 / 2107	1.0 / 4.3 / 1.1 / 4.4
4 SA	0305 / 0939 / 1519 / 2151	0.6 / 4.5 / 0.8 / 4.6	19 SU 0300 / 0929 / 1508 / 2135	1.2 / 4.2 / 1.4 / 4.2
5 SU	0342 / 1019 / 1559 / ◑2233	0.9 / 4.3 / 1.1 / 4.4	20 M 0319 / 1000 / 1531 / ◑2206	1.5 / 4.0 / 1.7 / 3.9
6 M	0425 / 1105 / 1646 / 2324	1.2 / 4.1 / 1.5 / 4.1	21 TU 0345 / 1038 / 1608 / 2251	1.8 / 3.8 / 2.0 / 3.7
7 TU	0519 / 1205 / 1753	1.6 / 3.9 / 1.8	22 W 0430 / 1133 / 1727 / 2357	2.1 / 3.6 / 2.2 / 3.5
8 W	0039 / 0639 / 1327 / 1931	3.8 / 1.9 / 3.8 / 1.9	23 TH 0616 / 1255 / 1909	2.3 / 3.6 / 2.2
9 TH	0214 / 0818 / 1454 / 2105	3.7 / 1.9 / 3.9 / 1.7	24 F 0139 / 0745 / 1438 / 2027	3.5 / 2.1 / 3.8 / 1.9
10 F	0339 / 0939 / 1607 / 2214	3.9 / 1.6 / 4.2 / 1.4	25 SA 0321 / 0859 / 1547 / 2135	3.7 / 1.8 / 4.1 / 1.5
11 SA	0446 / 1039 / 1703 / 2308	4.1 / 1.2 / 4.5 / 1.0	26 SU 0421 / 1001 / 1640 / 2232	4.0 / 1.4 / 4.4 / 1.1
12 SU	0539 / 1128 / 1752 / ●2354	4.3 / 0.9 / 4.7 / 0.7	27 M 0511 / 1055 / 1726 / 2321	4.3 / 1.0 / 4.7 / 0.7
13 M	0624 / 1212 / 1835	4.5 / 0.7 / 4.8	28 TU ○ 0557 / 1142 / 1812	4.5 / 0.7 / 4.9
14 TU	0037 / 0703 / 1253 / 1911	0.5 / 4.5 / 0.6 / 4.8	29 W 0007 / 0641 / 1227 / 1854	0.5 / 4.7 / 0.5 / 5.0
15 W	0116 / 0738 / 1329 / 1943	0.5 / 4.5 / 0.6 / 4.8	30 TH 0051 / 0722 / 1309 / 1936	0.3 / 4.8 / 0.4 / 5.1
			31 F 0130 / 0802 / 1346 / 2015	0.2 / 4.8 / 0.3 / 5.1

Chart Datum: 2·62 metres below Ordnance Datum (Newlyn)

ENGLAND - DARTMOUTH

LAT 50°21′N   LONG 3°34′W

TIMES AND HEIGHTS OF HIGH AND LOW WATERS

Dates in amber are **SPRINGS**
Dates in yellow are **NEAPS**

2007

SEPTEMBER

Time m	Time m
1 0207 0.3 / 0840 4.8 / SA 1423 0.5 / 2053 4.9	**16** 0200 1.0 / 0825 4.5 / SU 1408 1.0 / 2034 4.4
2 0242 0.6 / 0916 4.7 / SU 1457 0.8 / 2131 4.7	**17** 0216 1.2 / 0851 4.3 / M 1426 1.1 / 2100 4.2
3 0318 0.9 / 0953 4.6 / M 1535 1.2 / 2210 4.3	**18** 0233 1.5 / 0920 4.1 / TU 1448 1.6 / 2131 4.0
4 0357 1.4 / 1037 4.1 / TU 1622 1.6 / ☽ 2300 3.9	**19** 0300 1.7 / 0956 3.9 / W 1523 1.9 / ☾ 2215 3.7
5 0450 1.9 / 1140 3.8 / W 1732 2.1 / 2323 3.5	**20** 0340 2.1 / 1051 3.7 / TH 1623 2.3
6 0029 3.6 / 0619 2.2 / TH 1318 3.7 / 1936 2.1	**21** 0510 2.4 / 1209 3.6 / F 1838 2.3
7 0217 3.6 / 0823 2.1 / F 1450 3.9 / 2107 1.8	**22** 0058 3.4 / 0718 2.3 / SA 1359 3.8 / 2002 2.0
8 0341 3.8 / 0934 1.7 / SA 1559 4.2 / 2205 1.3	**23** 0256 3.7 / 0835 1.9 / SU 1518 4.1 / 2109 1.5
9 0439 4.1 / 1025 1.2 / SU 1650 4.5 / 2252 0.9	**24** 0356 4.1 / 0937 1.2 / M 1612 4.5 / 2206 1.0
10 0523 4.4 / 1110 0.9 / M 1732 4.7 / 2333 0.6	**25** 0445 4.4 / 1030 0.9 / TU 1659 4.8 / 2256 0.6
11 0601 4.6 / 1149 0.6 / TU 1811 4.8 / ●	**26** 0530 4.7 / 1118 0.6 / W 1745 5.0 / ○ 2341 0.3
12 0011 0.5 / 0635 4.6 / W 1226 0.5 / 1843 4.9	**27** 0615 4.9 / 1202 0.4 / TH 1830 5.2
13 0047 0.5 / 0704 4.7 / TH 1259 0.6 / 1912 4.8	**28** 0024 0.2 / 0655 5.0 / F 1245 0.2 / 1912 5.2
14 0117 0.6 / 0732 4.6 / F 1327 0.7 / 1940 4.7	**29** 0106 0.2 / 0737 5.0 / SA 1324 0.3 / 1954 5.1
15 0140 0.8 / 0758 4.6 / SA 1349 0.9 / 2007 4.6	**30** 0143 0.4 / 0814 5.0 / SU 1401 0.5 / 2034 4.9

OCTOBER

Time m	Time m
1 0220 0.7 / 0852 4.8 / M 1438 0.8 / 2113 4.6	**16** 0143 1.3 / 0823 4.4 / TU 1358 1.4 / 2036 4.2
2 0256 1.1 / 0931 4.5 / TU 1519 1.3 / 2154 4.2	**17** 0205 1.5 / 0851 4.2 / W 1424 1.6 / 2108 4.0
3 0337 1.6 / 1014 4.2 / W 1609 1.8 / ☽ 2248 3.8	**18** 0234 1.8 / 0930 4.0 / TH 1501 1.9 / 2155 3.7
4 0434 2.1 / 1123 3.8 / TH 1725 2.2	**19** 0317 2.1 / 1024 3.8 / F 1602 2.2 / ☾ 2300 3.6
5 0031 3.5 / 0612 2.4 / F 1308 3.7 / 1932 2.1	**20** 0435 2.4 / 1135 3.7 / SA 1802 2.2
6 0210 3.6 / 0807 2.1 / SA 1433 3.9 / 2048 1.8	**21** 0024 3.5 / 0643 2.3 / SU 1305 3.9 / 1929 1.9
7 0322 3.9 / 0910 1.7 / SU 1540 4.2 / 2140 1.3	**22** 0210 3.8 / 0802 1.9 / M 1434 4.2 / 2037 1.5
8 0414 4.2 / 0959 1.3 / M 1623 4.5 / 2223 1.0	**23** 0318 4.1 / 0905 1.4 / TU 1535 4.5 / 2134 1.0
9 0454 4.4 / 1041 1.0 / TU 1703 4.7 / 2303 0.8	**24** 0411 4.5 / 1000 1.0 / W 1627 4.8 / 2225 0.7
10 0529 4.6 / 1110 0.9 / W 1740 4.8 / 2339 0.7	**25** 0458 4.8 / 1050 0.7 / TH 1717 5.0 / 2313 0.4
11 0601 4.7 / 1154 0.7 / TH 1813 4.8 / ●	**26** 0545 5.0 / 1136 0.4 / F 1804 5.1 / ○ 2357 0.3
12 0012 0.7 / 0631 4.8 / F 1225 0.7 / 1842 4.8	**27** 0630 5.1 / 1220 0.3 / SA 1851 5.1
13 0041 0.8 / 0659 4.7 / SA 1253 0.8 / 1911 4.7	**28** 0041 0.4 / 0712 5.1 / SU 1303 0.4 / 1935 5.0
14 0104 0.9 / 0728 4.7 / SU 1316 1.0 / 1940 4.6	**29** 0123 0.5 / 0754 5.0 / M 1344 0.6 / 2018 4.8
15 0124 1.1 / 0756 4.6 / M 1336 1.2 / 2007 4.4	**30** 0202 0.9 / 0835 4.8 / TU 1426 0.9 / 2101 4.5
	31 0242 1.3 / 0916 4.6 / W 1511 1.4 / 2148 4.1

NOVEMBER

Time m	Time m
1 0328 1.7 / 1004 4.3 / TH 1603 1.8 / ☽ 2248 3.8	**16** 0228 1.7 / 0915 4.2 / F 1500 1.8 / 2144 3.9
2 0425 2.1 / 1110 4.0 / F 1714 2.0	**17** 0314 1.9 / 1005 4.1 / SA 1558 1.9 / ☾ 2242 3.8
3 0014 3.6 / 0545 2.3 / SA 1239 3.9 / 1850 2.1	**18** 0421 2.1 / 1108 4.0 / SU 1721 2.0 / 2351 3.7
4 0134 3.7 / 0722 2.2 / SU 1353 4.0 / 2005 1.8	**19** 0553 2.1 / 1220 4.0 / M 1845 1.8
5 0239 3.9 / 0829 1.9 / M 1454 4.2 / 2100 1.5	**20** 0110 3.9 / 0717 1.9 / TU 1339 4.2 / 1955 1.5
6 0330 4.1 / 0920 1.5 / TU 1544 4.4 / 2146 1.3	**21** 0226 4.1 / 0827 1.6 / W 1451 4.4 / 2058 1.2
7 0414 4.4 / 1004 1.3 / W 1626 4.5 / 2225 1.1	**22** 0330 4.4 / 0926 1.2 / TH 1553 4.7 / 2154 0.9
8 0452 4.5 / 1045 1.1 / TH 1705 4.6 / 2304 1.0	**23** 0426 4.7 / 1021 0.9 / F 1649 4.8 / 2246 0.7
9 0526 4.7 / 1120 1.0 / F 1741 4.7 / ● 2336 1.0	**24** 0518 4.9 / 1112 0.7 / SA 1743 4.9 / ○ 2335 0.6
10 0600 4.7 / 1153 1.0 / SA 1816 4.7	**25** 0607 5.0 / 1201 0.6 / SU 1834 4.9
11 0006 1.1 / 0633 4.8 / SU 1222 1.0 / 1849 4.6	**26** 0021 0.6 / 0654 5.1 / M 1249 0.6 / 1922 4.9
12 0034 1.1 / 0704 4.7 / M 1251 1.1 / 1920 4.5	**27** 0108 0.7 / 0739 5.0 / TU 1334 0.7 / 2008 4.7
13 0059 1.2 / 0735 4.6 / TU 1318 1.3 / 1951 4.4	**28** 0152 0.9 / 0824 4.9 / W 1420 0.9 / 2055 4.5
14 0125 1.4 / 0805 4.5 / W 1345 1.4 / 2022 4.2	**29** 0235 1.2 / 0908 4.7 / TH 1506 1.2 / 2143 4.2
15 0153 1.5 / 0837 4.4 / TH 1418 1.6 / 2058 4.0	**30** 0321 1.5 / 0955 4.4 / F 1554 1.5 / 2234 4.0

DECEMBER

Time m	Time m
1 0409 1.8 / 1046 4.2 / SA 1646 1.8 / ☽ 2332 3.8	**16** 0314 1.6 / 0953 4.4 / SU 1547 1.5 / 2223 4.0
2 0505 2.0 / 1147 4.0 / SU 1747 1.9	**17** 0403 1.7 / 1044 4.3 / M 1642 1.6 / ☾ 2319 4.0
3 0037 3.7 / 0610 2.1 / M 1253 4.0 / 1856 1.9	**18** 0504 1.8 / 1143 4.2 / TU 1750 1.7
4 0138 3.8 / 0722 2.1 / TU 1355 4.0 / 2000 1.9	**19** 0024 4.0 / 0620 1.8 / W 1252 4.2 / 1907 1.6
5 0234 3.9 / 0825 1.9 / W 1452 4.1 / 2056 1.9	**20** 0137 4.0 / 0742 1.7 / TH 1409 4.2 / 2019 1.5
6 0325 4.1 / 0919 1.7 / TH 1543 4.2 / 2144 1.5	**21** 0251 4.2 / 0855 1.5 / F 1522 4.4 / 2126 1.3
7 0411 4.3 / 1005 1.5 / F 1629 4.3 / 2225 1.4	**22** 0358 4.5 / 0959 1.2 / SA 1629 4.5 / 2226 1.1
8 0454 4.5 / 1047 1.4 / SA 1713 4.4 / 2303 1.3	**23** 0458 4.7 / 1057 0.9 / SU 1728 4.6 / 2320 0.9
9 0533 4.6 / 1124 1.3 / SU 1753 4.5 / ● 2338 1.4	**24** 0552 4.9 / 1150 0.8 / M 1824 4.7 / ○
10 0613 4.7 / 1200 1.2 / M 1833 4.5	**25** 0011 0.8 / 0643 5.0 / TU 1241 0.6 / 1913 4.7
11 0011 1.2 / 0649 4.7 / TU 1235 1.2 / 1908 4.5	**26** 0100 0.8 / 0730 5.0 / W 1329 0.6 / 2002 4.6
12 0046 1.3 / 0723 4.7 / W 1310 1.2 / 1944 4.4	**27** 0144 0.8 / 0814 4.9 / TH 1413 0.7 / 2046 4.5
13 0120 1.3 / 0757 4.6 / TH 1344 1.3 / 2018 4.3	**28** 0227 1.0 / 0857 4.8 / F 1454 0.9 / 2127 4.4
14 0154 1.4 / 0831 4.5 / F 1422 1.3 / 2055 4.2	**29** 0305 1.1 / 0935 4.6 / SA 1532 1.1 / 2203 4.2
15 0231 1.5 / 0909 4.4 / SA 1501 1.4 / 2136 4.1	**30** 0343 1.4 / 1010 4.4 / SU 1611 1.4 / 2238 4.0
	31 0422 1.7 / 1048 4.2 / M 1651 1.7 / ☽ 2318 3.9

Chart Datum: 2·62 metres below Ordnance Datum (Newlyn)

TIDES

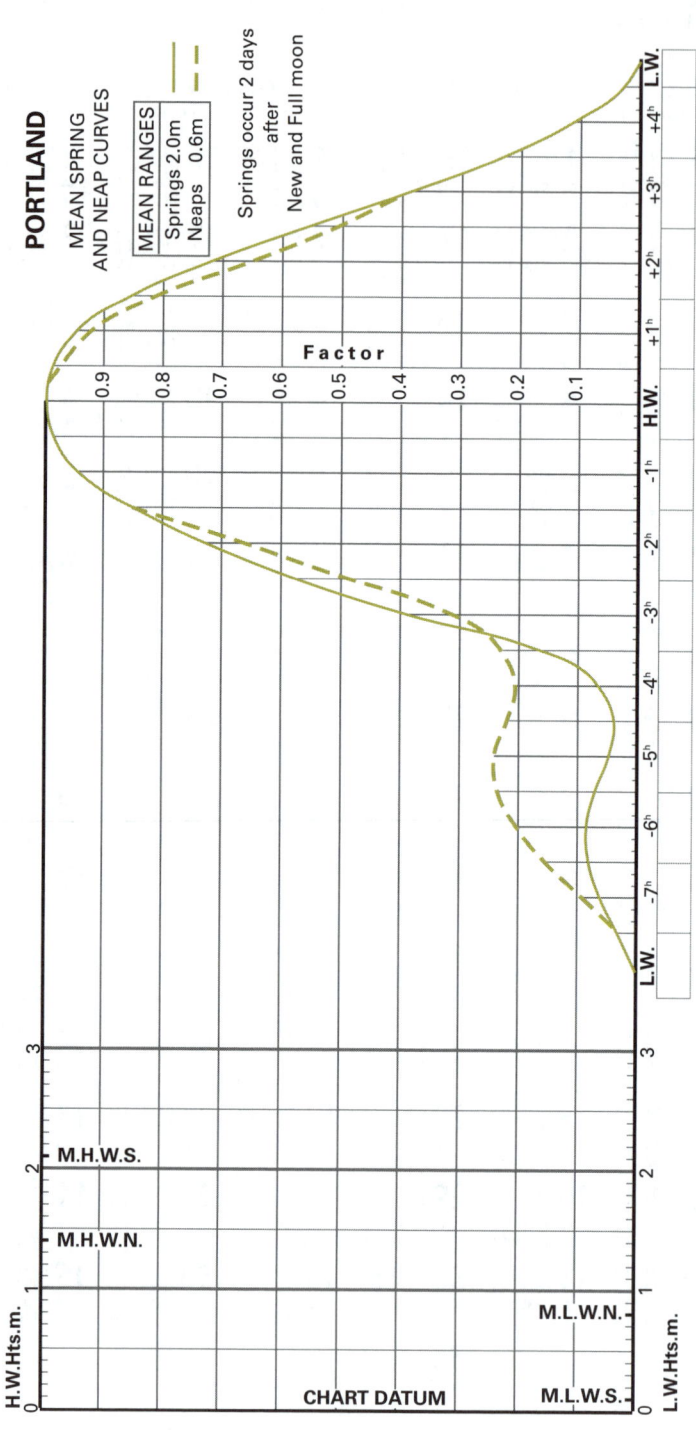

PORTLAND

MEAN SPRING
AND NEAP CURVES

MEAN RANGES
Springs 2.0m
Neaps 0.6m

Springs occur 2 days
after
New and Full moon

Factor

0.9
0.8
0.7
0.6
0.5
0.4
0.3
0.2
0.1

L.W. +4ʰ +3ʰ +2ʰ +1ʰ H.W. -1ʰ -2ʰ -3ʰ -4ʰ -5ʰ -6ʰ -7ʰ L.W.

H.W.Hts.m.

M.H.W.S.

M.H.W.N.

CHART DATUM

M.L.W.N.

M.L.W.S.

L.W.Hts.m.

Note - Double LWs occur at Portland. The predictions
are for the first LW. The second LW occurs from 3 to
4 Hrs later and may, at Springs, on occasions be lower
than the first.

ENGLAND – PORTLAND

LAT 50°34'N   LONG 2°26'W

TIMES AND HEIGHTS OF HIGH AND LOW WATERS

Dates in amber are **SPRINGS**
Dates in yellow are **NEAPS**

2007

JANUARY

Time	m		Time	m
1 M	0418 1.7 / 0941 0.6 / 1649 1.7 / 2204 0.5		**16** TU	0403 1.7 / 0923 0.7 / 1623 1.5 / 2132 0.5
2 TU	0518 1.9 / 1039 0.6 / 1750 2.0 / 2257 0.5		**17** W	0501 1.8 / 1016 0.6 / 1725 1.6 / 2227 0.4
3 W	0611 2.0 / 1129 0.5 / 1844 1.9 / ○ 2343 0.4		**18** TH	0554 1.9 / 1104 0.5 / 1822 1.8 / 2317 0.3
4 TH	0658 2.1 / 1214 0.4 / 1932 1.9		**19** F ●	0644 2.1 / 1149 0.3 / 1914 1.9
5 F	0026 0.4 / 0740 2.1 / 1256 0.3 / 2014 1.9		**20** SA	0004 0.3 / 0731 2.2 / 1233 0.2 / 2000 2.0
6 SA	0105 0.4 / 0817 2.1 / 1335 0.3 / 2049 1.8		**21** SU	0049 0.2 / 0816 2.2 / 1317 0.2 / 2042 2.0
7 SU	0142 0.4 / 0848 2.0 / 1412 0.3 / 2118 1.7		**22** M	0132 0.1 / 0856 2.2 / 1359 0.1 / 2119 2.0
8 M	0217 0.4 / 0914 1.9 / 1447 0.4 / 2144 1.6		**23** TU	0214 0.2 / 0934 2.1 / 1442 0.1 / 2153 1.9
9 TU	0247 0.5 / 0941 1.8 / 1518 0.4 / 2212 1.5		**24** W	0254 0.2 / 1010 2.0 / 1525 0.2 / 2228 1.8
10 W	0313 0.6 / 1010 1.6 / 1544 0.5 / 2244 1.4		**25** TH ◑	0335 0.3 / 1047 1.8 / 1611 0.3 / 2307 1.7
11 TH ◐	0338 0.6 / 1042 1.5 / 1610 0.6 / 2324 1.4		**26** F	0420 0.5 / 1128 1.7 / 1703 0.4 / 2354 1.5
12 F	0415 0.7 / 1121 1.4 / 1652 0.6		**27** SA	0516 0.6 / 1220 1.5 / 1806 0.6
13 SA	0019 1.3 / 0514 0.8 / 1220 1.3 / 1755 0.6		**28** SU	0056 1.5 / 0632 0.7 / 1335 1.4 / 1925 0.7
14 SU	0135 1.3 / 0644 0.8 / 1343 1.3 / 1914 0.7		**29** M	0228 1.5 / 0816 0.8 / 1521 1.4 / 2052 0.7
15 M	0255 1.4 / 0815 0.8 / 1510 1.4 / 2029 0.6		**30** TU	0402 1.6 / 0945 0.7 / 1647 1.6 / 2200 0.6
			31 W	0511 1.7 / 1041 0.6 / 1751 1.6 / 2251 0.5

FEBRUARY

Time	m		Time	m
1 TH	0605 1.9 / 1125 0.4 / 1842 1.7 / 2334 0.4		**16** F	0539 1.9 / 1053 0.3 / 1814 1.8 / 2306 0.3
2 F ○	0651 2.0 / 1204 0.3 / 1925 1.8		**17** SA ●	0632 2.1 / 1137 0.2 / 1904 1.9 / 2352 0.1
3 SA	0013 0.3 / 0731 2.1 / 1241 0.2 / 2002 1.9		**18** SU	0720 2.2 / 1220 0.0 / 1948 2.1
4 SU	0050 0.2 / 0805 2.1 / 1317 0.1 / 2033 1.9		**19** M	0035 0.0 / 0803 2.3 / 1302 -0.1 / 2027 2.1
5 M	0126 0.2 / 0833 2.1 / 1351 0.1 / 2058 1.8		**20** TU	0117 -0.1 / 0842 2.3 / 1343 -0.1 / 2102 2.1
6 TU	0158 0.2 / 0858 2.0 / 1422 0.2 / 2121 1.7		**21** W	0156 -0.1 / 0918 2.2 / 1423 -0.1 / 2134 2.0
7 W	0226 0.2 / 0922 1.8 / 1444 0.2 / 2144 1.6		**22** TH	0234 0.0 / 0952 2.1 / 1502 0.1 / 2206 1.9
8 TH	0245 0.3 / 0947 1.7 / 1458 0.3 / 2207 1.5		**23** F	0311 0.2 / 1026 1.8 / 1542 0.2 / 2240 1.7
9 F	0302 0.4 / 1010 1.5 / 1626 0.5 / 2230 1.4		**24** SA ◐	0351 0.4 / 1103 1.6 / 1626 0.5 / 2320 1.5
10 SA ◐	0328 0.5 / 1034 1.4 / 1546 0.5 / 2303 1.3		**25** SU	0440 0.6 / 1150 1.4 / 1725 0.7 / ◑ 2303 1.3
11 SU	0407 0.6 / 1113 1.3 / 1634 0.6		**26** M	0016 1.4 / 0603 0.8 / 1308 1.3 / 1901 0.8
12 M	0000 1.3 / 0514 0.7 / 1223 1.2 / 1754 0.7		**27** TU	0200 1.4 / 0834 0.8 / 1529 1.3 / 2049 0.8
13 TU	0142 1.3 / 0717 0.8 / 1420 1.2 / 1952 0.7		**28** W	0356 1.5 / 0949 0.7 / 1652 1.4 / 2152 0.7
14 W	0326 1.4 / 0908 0.7 / 1605 1.4 / 2119 0.6			
15 TH	0440 1.7 / 1006 0.5 / 1716 1.6 / 2217 0.4			

MARCH

Time	m		Time	m
1 TH	0502 1.7 / 1032 0.5 / 1743 1.6 / 2236 0.5		**16** F	0414 1.6 / 0947 0.4 / 1700 1.6 / 2159 0.4
2 F	0551 1.8 / 1108 0.4 / 1826 1.7 / 2314 0.4		**17** SA	0517 1.9 / 1032 0.2 / 1754 1.8 / 2247 0.2
3 SA ○	0633 2.0 / 1142 0.2 / 1904 1.9 / 2350 0.2		**18** SU	0610 2.1 / 1116 0.0 / 1841 2.0 / 2331 0.0
4 SU	0710 2.1 / 1216 0.1 / 1938 1.9		**19** M ●	0657 2.3 / 1158 -0.1 / 1924 2.2
5 M	0027 0.1 / 0742 2.1 / 1251 0.0 / 2007 2.0		**20** TU	0013 -0.1 / 0740 2.4 / 1240 -0.2 / 2002 2.2
6 TU	0102 0.1 / 0809 2.1 / 1324 0.0 / 2031 1.9		**21** W	0055 -0.1 / 0820 2.4 / 1320 -0.2 / 2038 2.2
7 W	0134 0.1 / 0834 2.0 / 1352 0.1 / 2054 1.8		**22** TH	0133 -0.1 / 0856 2.2 / 1359 -0.1 / 2112 2.1
8 TH	0159 0.1 / 0859 1.9 / 1410 0.1 / 2116 1.7		**23** F	0211 0.1 / 0931 2.0 / 1437 0.1 / 2144 1.9
9 F	0216 0.2 / 0921 1.7 / 1423 0.2 / 2134 1.6		**24** SA ◐	0248 0.2 / 1006 1.8 / 1514 0.3 / 2217 1.7
10 SA	0232 0.3 / 0941 1.5 / 1439 0.3 / 2152 1.5		**25** SU ◑	0329 0.4 / 1044 1.5 / 1556 0.5 / 2255 1.5
11 SU	0254 0.4 / 1002 1.4 / 1504 0.4 / 2218 1.4		**26** M	0421 0.6 / 1134 1.3 / 1655 0.7 / 2351 1.4
12 M ◐	0327 0.5 / 1036 1.3 / 1542 0.5 / 2306 1.3		**27** TU ◑	0555 0.8 / 1320 1.2 / 1841 0.9
13 TU	0425 0.7 / 1143 1.2 / 1653 0.7		**28** W	0151 1.4 / 0837 0.8 / 1530 1.3 / 2033 0.8
14 W	0035 1.3 / 0648 0.8 / 1345 1.2 / 1936 0.7		**29** TH	0336 1.5 / 0932 0.6 / 1631 1.4 / 2128 0.7
15 TH	0247 1.4 / 0851 0.6 / 1550 1.3 / 2103 0.6		**30** F	0434 1.6 / 1006 0.5 / 1715 1.6 / 2207 0.5
			31 SA	0520 1.8 / 1037 0.3 / 1755 1.8 / 2244 0.4

APRIL

Time	m		Time	m
1 SU	0600 1.9 / 1110 0.2 / 1831 1.9 / 2320 0.2		**16** M	0538 2.1 / 1048 0.0 / 1810 2.1 / 2305 0.1
2 M ○	0637 2.0 / 1144 0.1 / 1904 2.0 / 2357 0.1		**17** TU ●	0628 2.2 / 1132 -0.1 / 1854 2.2 / 2349 0.0
3 TU	0709 2.0 / 1219 0.0 / 1934 2.0		**18** W	0714 2.3 / 1215 -0.1 / 1936 2.3
4 W	0033 0.1 / 0738 2.0 / 1252 0.0 / 2000 2.0		**19** TH	0030 -0.1 / 0756 2.3 / 1256 0.0 / 2014 2.2
5 TH	0105 0.1 / 0806 1.9 / 1319 0.1 / 2025 1.9		**20** F	0111 0.0 / 0836 2.2 / 1336 0.0 / 2051 2.1
6 F	0130 0.2 / 0833 1.8 / 1338 0.2 / 2047 1.8		**21** SA	0151 0.1 / 0914 2.0 / 1414 0.2 / 2126 2.0
7 SA	0149 0.2 / 0857 1.7 / 1353 0.3 / 2106 1.7		**22** SU	0232 0.3 / 0953 1.7 / 1453 0.4 / 2201 1.8
8 SU	0207 0.3 / 0918 1.5 / 1412 0.4 / 2125 1.6		**23** M	0317 0.5 / 1035 1.5 / 1537 0.6 / 2240 1.6
9 M	0231 0.4 / 0943 1.4 / 1437 0.5 / 2152 1.5		**24** TU ◑	0414 0.6 / 1134 1.3 / 1636 0.8 / 2335 1.5
10 TU ◐	0307 0.5 / 1022 1.3 / 1515 0.6 / 2238 1.4		**25** W	0540 0.8 / 1322 1.3 / 1805 0.9
11 W	0411 0.7 / 1132 1.2 / 1634 0.8		**26** TH	0119 1.4 / 0753 0.7 / 1454 1.3 / 1945 0.9
12 TH	0004 1.4 / 0631 0.7 / 1330 1.2 / 1915 0.8		**27** F	0251 1.5 / 0848 0.6 / 1550 1.5 / 2045 0.7
13 F	0209 1.4 / 0817 0.6 / 1521 1.4 / 2036 0.6		**28** SA	0348 1.6 / 0923 0.5 / 1634 1.6 / 2128 0.6
14 SA	0339 1.6 / 0915 0.4 / 1628 1.6 / 2132 0.4		**29** SU	0434 1.7 / 0956 0.4 / 1713 1.7 / 2207 0.5
15 SU	0443 1.9 / 1003 0.2 / 1721 1.9 / 2220 0.2		**30** M	0516 1.8 / 1031 0.3 / 1749 1.8 / 2246 0.3

Chart Datum: 0·93 metres below Ordnance Datum (Newlyn)

TIDES

TIME ZONE (UT)
For Summer Time add ONE hour in **non-shaded areas**

ENGLAND – PORTLAND

LAT 50°34'N   LONG 2°26'W

TIMES AND HEIGHTS OF HIGH AND LOW WATERS

Dates in amber are **SPRINGS**
Dates in yellow are **NEAPS**

2007

MAY

Time	m		Time	m
1 TU	0554 1.9 / 1108 0.2 / 1824 1.9 / 2325 0.3	**16** W	0559 2.1 / 1106 0.1 / 1825 2.1 / ● 2326 0.1
2 W ○	0631 1.9 / 1144 0.2 / 1857 2.0	**17** TH	0650 2.1 / 1152 0.1 / 1911 2.2
3 TH	0002 0.2 / 0706 1.9 / 1218 0.2 / 1928 2.0	**18** F	0011 0.1 / 0737 2.1 / 1237 0.1 / 1954 2.2
4 F	0035 0.2 / 0739 1.9 / 1246 0.2 / 1958 1.9	**19** SA	0056 0.2 / 0822 2.0 / 1319 0.2 / 2035 2.1
5 SA	0103 0.3 / 0810 1.8 / 1311 0.3 / 2024 1.9	**20** SU	0140 0.2 / 0905 1.9 / 1401 0.3 / 2115 2.0
6 SU	0127 0.3 / 0838 1.7 / 1335 0.4 / 2048 1.8	**21** M	0224 0.3 / 0948 1.7 / 1442 0.5 / 2152 1.8
7 M	0154 0.4 / 0905 1.6 / 1401 0.5 / 2112 1.7	**22** TU	0310 0.5 / 1033 1.5 / 1525 0.6 / 2229 1.7
8 TU	0227 0.4 / 0938 1.5 / 1435 0.6 / 2145 1.6	**23** W	0402 0.6 / 1126 1.4 / 1616 0.8 / ◑ 2313 1.5
9 W	0311 0.5 / 1024 1.4 / 1524 0.7 / 2234 1.5	**24** TH	0505 0.7 / 1234 1.3 / 1720 0.8
10 TH ◑	0422 0.6 / 1132 1.3 / 1652 0.8 / 2351 1.5	**25** F	0011 1.5 / 0618 0.7 / 1349 1.3 / 1835 0.8
11 F	0601 0.6 / 1308 1.3 / 1839 0.7	**26** SA	0123 1.4 / 0728 0.6 / 1450 1.4 / 1943 0.8
12 SA	0132 1.5 / 0730 0.5 / 1438 1.5 / 1957 0.6	**27** SU	0232 1.5 / 0821 0.6 / 1539 1.5 / 2039 0.7
13 SU	0258 1.6 / 0835 0.4 / 1546 1.7 / 2058 0.5	**28** M	0330 1.5 / 0906 0.5 / 1621 1.6 / 2127 0.6
14 M	0405 1.8 / 0929 0.2 / 1644 1.9 / 2150 0.3	**29** TU	0420 1.6 / 0948 0.4 / 1702 1.8 / 2211 0.5
15 TU	0504 2.0 / 1019 0.1 / 1736 2.0 / 2239 0.2	**30** W	0508 1.7 / 1029 0.4 / 1743 1.9 / 2253 0.4
		31 TH	0554 1.8 / 1108 0.3 / 1823 1.9 / 2332 0.4

JUNE

Time	m		Time	m
1 F ○	0638 1.8 / 1146 0.3 / 1902 2.0	**16** SA	0003 0.3 / 0727 2.0 / 1227 0.3 / 1943 2.2
2 SA	0009 0.4 / 0718 1.8 / 1222 0.3 / 1938 2.0	**17** SU	0050 0.3 / 0816 2.0 / 1311 0.3 / 2027 2.1
3 SU	0043 0.4 / 0757 1.8 / 1257 0.4 / 2013 1.9	**18** M	0135 0.3 / 0901 1.9 / 1352 0.4 / 2107 2.0
4 M	0117 0.4 / 0833 1.7 / 1332 0.4 / 2045 1.8	**19** TU	0217 0.3 / 0942 1.8 / 1431 0.4 / 2142 1.9
5 TU	0154 0.4 / 0907 1.7 / 1410 0.5 / 2117 1.8	**20** W	0258 0.4 / 1019 1.6 / 1510 0.5 / 2213 1.8
6 W	0234 0.4 / 0944 1.6 / 1451 0.6 / 2154 1.7	**21** TH	0340 0.4 / 1053 1.5 / 1550 0.6 / 2243 1.6
7 TH	0321 0.4 / 1029 1.5 / 1541 0.6 / 2240 1.6	**22** F	0424 0.5 / 1129 1.4 / 1634 0.7 / ◑ 2320 1.5
8 F	0419 0.5 / 1125 1.5 / 1644 0.6 / ◑ 2340 1.6	**23** SA	0512 0.6 / 1215 1.4 / 1729 0.8
9 SA	0528 0.5 / 1233 1.5 / 1757 0.7	**24** SU	0007 1.4 / 0608 0.6 / 1313 1.3 / 1835 0.8
10 SU	0053 1.6 / 0641 0.5 / 1349 1.5 / 1911 0.6	**25** M	0106 1.4 / 0708 0.6 / 1419 1.4 / 1943 0.8
11 M	0212 1.6 / 0751 0.4 / 1502 1.6 / 2019 0.6	**26** TU	0215 1.4 / 0807 0.6 / 1522 1.5 / 2044 0.7
12 TU	0327 1.7 / 0855 0.4 / 1608 1.8 / 2122 0.5	**27** W	0325 1.4 / 0901 0.6 / 1618 1.6 / 2138 0.6
13 W	0435 1.8 / 0954 0.3 / 1708 1.9 / 2219 0.4	**28** TH	0428 1.5 / 0952 0.5 / 1708 1.8 / 2226 0.6
14 TH	0537 1.9 / 1049 0.3 / 1804 2.0 / 2313 0.3	**29** F	0525 1.6 / 1039 0.5 / 1757 1.9 / 2310 0.5
15 F ●	0635 1.9 / 1139 0.3 / 1856 2.1	**30** SA ○	0618 1.7 / 1124 0.4 / 1844 2.0 / 2352 0.4

JULY

Time	m		Time	m
1 SU	0707 1.8 / 1208 0.4 / 1928 2.0	**16** M	0044 0.3 / 0809 1.9 / 1300 0.3 / 2018 2.2
2 M	0032 0.4 / 0753 1.8 / 1250 0.3 / 2010 2.0	**17** TU	0124 0.2 / 0849 1.9 / 1338 0.3 / 2054 2.1
3 TU	0112 0.3 / 0835 1.8 / 1331 0.3 / 2049 2.0	**18** W	0202 0.2 / 0923 1.9 / 1414 0.3 / 2123 2.0
4 W	0153 0.3 / 0912 1.8 / 1411 0.3 / 2125 1.9	**19** TH	0238 0.2 / 0950 1.7 / 1448 0.4 / 2147 1.9
5 TH	0234 0.3 / 0948 1.8 / 1452 0.3 / 2201 1.9	**20** F	0311 0.3 / 1014 1.6 / 1519 0.4 / 2211 1.7
6 F	0317 0.3 / 1024 1.7 / 1535 0.4 / 2239 1.8	**21** SA	0341 0.4 / 1040 1.5 / 1547 0.5 / 2238 1.6
7 SA	0404 0.3 / 1106 1.6 / 1622 0.5 / ◑ 2323 1.7	**22** SU	0404 0.5 / 1113 1.4 / 1614 0.6 / ◑ 2309 1.4
8 SU	0458 0.4 / 1157 1.6 / 1719 0.6	**23** M	0432 0.6 / 1156 1.3 / 1657 0.7 / 2351 1.3
9 M	0017 1.6 / 0600 0.5 / 1300 1.5 / 1827 0.6	**24** TU	0518 0.6 / 1259 1.3 / 1813 0.8
10 TU	0126 1.5 / 0712 0.5 / 1418 1.5 / 1946 0.7	**25** W	0058 1.3 / 0634 0.7 / 1421 1.4 / 1956 0.8
11 W	0252 1.5 / 0830 0.5 / 1541 1.6 / 2107 0.7	**26** TH	0233 1.3 / 0812 0.7 / 1539 1.5 / 2112 0.7
12 TH	0417 1.6 / 0943 0.5 / 1653 1.8 / 2216 0.6	**27** F	0358 1.4 / 0925 0.6 / 1642 1.7 / 2208 0.6
13 F	0529 1.7 / 1043 0.4 / 1755 1.9 / 2312 0.5	**28** SA	0506 1.5 / 1021 0.5 / 1738 1.8 / 2254 0.5
14 SA ●	0631 1.8 / 1134 0.4 / 1849 2.1	**29** SU	0606 1.7 / 1109 0.4 / 1830 2.0 / 2337 0.4
15 SU	0000 0.4 / 0724 1.9 / 1219 0.3 / 1936 2.1	**30** M ○	0659 1.8 / 1154 0.3 / 1919 2.1
		31 TU	0019 0.2 / 0745 1.9 / 1237 0.2 / 2002 2.2

AUGUST

Time	m		Time	m
1 W	0100 0.1 / 0826 2.0 / 1318 0.1 / 2042 2.2	**16** TH	0137 0.1 / 0853 1.9 / 1349 0.2 / 2055 2.1
2 TH	0141 0.1 / 0902 2.0 / 1358 0.1 / 2118 2.1	**17** F	0210 0.1 / 0915 1.8 / 1420 0.2 / 2116 1.9
3 F	0221 0.1 / 0935 1.9 / 1437 0.2 / 2151 2.0	**18** SA	0237 0.2 / 0935 1.7 / 1445 0.3 / 2138 1.7
4 SA	0301 0.1 / 1007 1.8 / 1516 0.3 / 2224 1.9	**19** SU	0255 0.3 / 0957 1.6 / 1502 0.4 / 2200 1.6
5 SU	0343 0.2 / 1042 1.7 / 1557 0.4 / ◑ 2301 1.7	**20** M	0306 0.4 / 1020 1.5 / 1519 0.6 / ◑ 2220 1.4
6 M	0429 0.4 / 1124 1.6 / 1646 0.5 / 2346 1.6	**21** TU	0327 0.5 / 1048 1.4 / 1550 0.7 / 2249 1.3
7 TU	0527 0.5 / 1220 1.5 / 1755 0.7	**22** W	0404 0.6 / 1136 1.3 / 1649 0.8 / 2344 1.2
8 W	0051 1.4 / 0646 0.7 / 1345 1.5 / 1934 0.8	**23** TH	0512 0.7 / 1308 1.3 / 1911 0.9
9 TH	0239 1.4 / 0827 0.7 / 1532 1.5 / 2117 0.7	**24** F	0140 1.2 / 0736 0.8 / 1503 1.4 / 2057 0.8
10 F	0422 1.5 / 0944 0.6 / 1651 1.7 / 2220 0.6	**25** SA	0342 1.3 / 0909 0.7 / 1620 1.6 / 2151 0.6
11 SA	0533 1.6 / 1038 0.5 / 1750 1.9 / 2307 0.5	**26** SU	0455 1.5 / 1004 0.5 / 1719 1.8 / 2235 0.4
12 SU ●	0627 1.8 / 1122 0.4 / 1839 2.1 / 2348 0.3	**27** M	0551 1.7 / 1050 0.3 / 1811 2.0 / 2317 0.3
13 M	0712 1.9 / 1202 0.3 / 1922 2.2	**28** TU ○	0641 1.9 / 1133 0.2 / 1859 2.2 / 2358 0.1
14 TU	0025 0.2 / 0751 2.0 / 1240 0.2 / 1959 2.2	**29** W	0725 2.1 / 1215 0.1 / 1942 2.3
15 W ○	0102 0.1 / 0825 2.0 / 1315 0.2 / 2030 2.2	**30** TH	0039 0.0 / 0804 2.1 / 1257 0.0 / 2021 2.3
		31 F	0119 0.0 / 0839 2.1 / 1336 0.0 / 2057 2.3

Chart Datum: 0·93 metres below Ordnance Datum (Newlyn)

TIME ZONE (UT)
For Summer Time add ONE hour in **non-shaded areas**

ENGLAND – PORTLAND

LAT 50°34'N   LONG 2°26'W

TIMES AND HEIGHTS OF HIGH AND LOW WATERS

Dates in **amber** are **SPRINGS**
Dates in **yellow** are **NEAPS**

2007

SEPTEMBER

Day	Time m	Time m	Day	Time m	Time m
1 SA	0159 0.0 / 0912 2.1 / 1414 0.1 / 2130 2.1		**16** SU	0158 0.2 / 0858 1.8 / 1410 0.3 / 2105 1.8	
2 SU	0237 0.1 / 0943 2.0 / 1452 0.2 / 2203 1.9		**17** M	0210 0.3 / 0918 1.7 / 1422 0.4 / 2125 1.6	
3 M	0317 0.3 / 1017 1.8 / 1532 0.4 / 2239 1.7		**18** TU	0221 0.4 / 0935 1.6 / 1438 0.5 / 2143 1.4	
4 TU	0400 0.5 / 1057 1.6 / 1622 0.6 / ☽ 2325 1.5		**19** W	0239 0.5 / 0958 1.5 / 1505 0.7 / ☾ 2211 1.3	
5 W	0459 0.7 / 1152 1.5 / 1742 0.8		**20** TH	0308 0.6 / 1040 1.4 / 1556 0.8 / 2308 1.2	
6 TH	0040 1.3 / 0636 0.8 / 1336 1.4 / 1959 0.8		**21** F	0401 0.8 / 1202 1.3 / 1852 0.9	
7 F	0307 1.3 / 0833 0.8 / 1536 1.6 / 2125 0.7		**22** SA	0109 1.2 / 0719 0.9 / 1422 1.4 / 2034 0.7	
8 SA	0432 1.5 / 0938 0.7 / 1642 1.7 / 2211 0.6		**23** SU	0330 1.4 / 0847 0.7 / 1551 1.6 / 2125 0.6	
9 SU	0523 1.7 / 1022 0.6 / 1732 1.9 / 2248 0.4		**24** M	0435 1.6 / 0939 0.5 / 1650 1.9 / 2208 0.3	
10 M	0606 1.8 / 1100 0.4 / 1815 2.1 / 2322 0.3		**25** TU	0526 1.8 / 1024 0.3 / 1742 2.1 / 2249 0.2	
11 TU	0646 2.0 / 1136 0.3 / 1854 2.2 / ● 2357 0.2		**26** W	0612 2.0 / 1107 0.2 / 1829 2.3 / ○ 2330 0.2	
12 W	0721 2.0 / 1211 0.2 / 1929 2.2		**27** TH	0655 2.2 / 1149 0.1 / 1913 2.4	
13 TH	0031 0.1 / 0751 2.1 / 1247 0.1 / 1956 2.1		**28** F	0012 -0.1 / 0734 2.3 / 1230 0.0 / 1954 2.4	
14 F	0105 0.1 / 0816 2.0 / 1320 0.1 / 2020 2.0		**29** SA	0052 -0.1 / 0811 2.3 / 1310 0.0 / 2032 2.3	
15 SA	0136 0.1 / 0838 1.9 / 1349 0.2 / 2043 1.9		**30** SU	0132 0.0 / 0845 2.2 / 1349 0.1 / 2108 2.1	

OCTOBER

Day	Time m	Time m	Day	Time m	Time m
1 M	0210 0.2 / 0919 2.0 / 1428 0.3 / 2143 1.9		**16** TU	0132 0.4 / 0845 1.8 / 1351 0.5 / 2057 1.6	
2 TU	0249 0.4 / 0954 1.9 / 1511 0.5 / 2223 1.6		**17** W	0147 0.5 / 0903 1.7 / 1411 0.6 / 2120 1.5	
3 W	0332 0.6 / 1035 1.7 / 1609 0.7 / ☾ 2316 1.4		**18** TH	0207 0.6 / 0927 1.6 / 1441 0.7 / 2154 1.4	
4 TH	0435 0.8 / 1134 1.5 / 1747 0.9		**19** F	0237 0.7 / 1007 1.5 / 1537 0.8 / ☾ 2255 1.3	
5 F	0111 1.3 / 0625 1.0 / 1343 1.5 / 2009 0.8		**20** SA	0330 0.9 / 1124 1.4 / 1813 0.8	
6 SA	0314 1.4 / 0822 0.9 / 1518 1.6 / 2109 0.7		**21** SU	0052 1.2 / 0643 0.9 / 1333 1.5 / 1953 0.7	
7 SU	0413 1.6 / 0916 0.8 / 1614 1.8 / 2145 0.6		**22** M	0258 1.4 / 0813 0.6 / 1511 1.7 / 2047 0.5	
8 M	0455 1.7 / 0954 0.6 / 1659 1.9 / 2216 0.4		**23** TU	0401 1.7 / 0907 0.6 / 1613 1.9 / 2133 0.3	
9 TU	0533 1.9 / 1028 0.5 / 1739 2.0 / 2247 0.3		**24** W	0451 1.9 / 0954 0.4 / 1706 2.1 / 2217 0.2	
10 W	0609 2.0 / 1103 0.4 / 1816 2.1 / 2321 0.2		**25** TH	0538 2.1 / 1038 0.3 / 1756 2.2 / 2300 0.1	
11 TH	0642 2.1 / 1138 0.3 / 1849 2.1 / ● 2355 0.2		**26** F	0622 2.2 / 1121 0.2 / 1843 2.3 / ○ 2343 0.0	
12 F	0712 2.1 / 1203 0.1 / 1918 2.1		**27** SA	0704 2.3 / 1203 0.1 / 1927 2.3	
13 SA	0029 0.2 / 0737 2.1 / 1248 0.2 / 1944 2.0		**28** SU	0025 0.1 / 0744 2.3 / 1246 0.1 / 2009 2.2	
14 SU	0058 0.2 / 0801 2.0 / 1317 0.3 / 2011 1.9		**29** M	0106 0.2 / 0823 2.2 / 1328 0.3 / 2050 2.0	
15 M	0119 0.5 / 0824 1.9 / 1336 0.4 / 2035 1.7		**30** TU	0147 0.3 / 0900 2.1 / 1411 0.4 / 2131 1.8	
			31 W	0228 0.5 / 0938 1.9 / 1500 0.6 / 2217 1.6	

NOVEMBER

Day	Time m	Time m	Day	Time m	Time m
1 TH	0313 0.7 / 1021 1.7 / 1602 0.7 / ☽ 2320 1.4		**16** F	0203 0.6 / 0918 1.7 / 1444 0.6 / 2152 1.4	
2 F	0413 0.9 / 1121 1.6 / 1731 0.8		**17** SA	0241 0.7 / 1000 1.6 / 1545 0.7 / ☾ 2252 1.4	
3 SA	0107 1.4 / 0541 1.0 / 1309 1.5 / 1926 0.8		**18** SU	0346 0.9 / 1105 1.5 / 1724 0.7	
4 SU	0238 1.4 / 0732 1.0 / 1434 1.6 / 2024 0.7		**19** M	0020 1.4 / 0547 0.9 / 1242 1.5 / 1854 0.7	
5 M	0333 1.6 / 0834 0.9 / 1530 1.7 / 2100 0.6		**20** TU	0203 1.5 / 0720 0.8 / 1420 1.6 / 2000 0.5	
6 TU	0415 1.7 / 0914 0.7 / 1614 1.8 / 2132 0.5		**21** W	0315 1.7 / 0825 0.7 / 1531 1.8 / 2054 0.4	
7 W	0452 1.8 / 0950 0.6 / 1654 1.9 / 2206 0.4		**22** TH	0412 1.9 / 0919 0.5 / 1631 1.9 / 2144 0.3	
8 TH	0527 1.9 / 1027 0.5 / 1731 1.9 / 2242 0.3		**23** F	0504 2.0 / 1009 0.4 / 1726 2.1 / 2232 0.2	
9 F	0600 2.0 / 1105 0.4 / 1806 1.9 / 2318 0.3		**24** SA	0553 2.2 / 1057 0.3 / 1818 2.1 / ○ 2319 0.2	
10 SA	0631 2.1 / 1143 0.4 / 1840 1.9 / 2353 0.3		**25** SU	0640 2.3 / 1144 0.3 / 1908 2.1	
11 SU	0702 2.1 / 1218 0.4 / 1914 1.9		**26** M	0005 0.2 / 0725 2.3 / 1231 0.3 / 1955 2.0	
12 M	0023 0.4 / 0732 2.1 / 1248 0.4 / 1946 1.8		**27** TU	0050 0.3 / 0809 2.3 / 1318 0.3 / 2042 2.0	
13 TU	0049 0.4 / 0800 2.0 / 1313 0.5 / 2015 1.7		**28** W	0133 0.4 / 0851 2.1 / 1404 0.4 / 2127 1.8	
14 W	0111 0.5 / 0825 1.9 / 1336 0.5 / 2043 1.6		**29** TH	0216 0.5 / 0932 2.0 / 1453 0.5 / 2214 1.7	
15 TH	0135 0.6 / 0849 1.8 / 1405 0.6 / 2113 1.5		**30** F	0301 0.7 / 1013 1.8 / 1546 0.6 / 2306 1.5	

DECEMBER

Day	Time m	Time m	Day	Time m	Time m
1 SA	0350 0.8 / 1057 1.7 / 1647 0.7 / ☽		**16** SU	0259 0.6 / 1006 1.7 / 1542 0.5 / 2243 1.5	
2 SU	0009 1.4 / 0450 0.9 / 1151 1.6 / 1755 0.7		**17** M	0350 0.7 / 1056 1.6 / 1644 0.6 / 2343 1.5	
3 M	0123 1.4 / 0603 0.9 / 1259 1.5 / 1900 0.7		**18** TU	0459 0.7 / 1201 1.6 / 1757 0.6	
4 TU	0229 1.5 / 0717 0.9 / 1410 1.6 / 1954 0.5		**19** W	0056 1.5 / 0619 0.7 / 1320 1.6 / 1907 0.5	
5 W	0320 1.5 / 0818 0.8 / 1508 1.6 / 2040 0.6		**20** TH	0217 1.6 / 0736 0.7 / 1443 1.6 / 2014 0.5	
6 TH	0402 1.7 / 0908 0.7 / 1557 1.6 / 2123 0.5		**21** F	0331 1.7 / 0845 0.6 / 1558 1.7 / 2116 0.4	
7 F	0441 1.8 / 0953 0.6 / 1643 1.7 / 2204 0.5		**22** SA	0435 1.9 / 0948 0.5 / 1704 1.8 / 2214 0.4	
8 SA	0519 1.9 / 1036 0.6 / 1728 1.8 / 2245 0.4		**23** SU	0532 2.0 / 1046 0.5 / 1804 1.9 / 2308 0.3	
9 SU	0558 2.0 / 1117 0.5 / 1812 1.8 / ● 2324 0.4		**24** M	0626 2.2 / 1138 0.4 / 1900 2.0 / ○ 2357 0.3	
10 M	0637 2.0 / 1155 0.5 / 1854 1.8		**25** TU	0716 2.2 / 1228 0.3 / 1951 2.0	
11 TU	0000 0.4 / 0714 2.0 / 1231 0.5 / 1934 1.8		**26** W	0043 0.3 / 0803 2.2 / 1314 0.3 / 2038 2.0	
12 W	0035 0.4 / 0750 2.0 / 1303 0.5 / 2011 1.8		**27** TH	0127 0.3 / 0846 2.2 / 1358 0.3 / 2121 1.9	
13 TH	0109 0.5 / 0823 2.0 / 1336 0.5 / 2045 1.7		**28** F	0207 0.4 / 0924 2.1 / 1440 0.4 / 2159 1.8	
14 F	0143 0.5 / 0854 1.9 / 1412 0.5 / 2118 1.6		**29** SA	0246 0.5 / 0957 2.0 / 1521 0.4 / 2232 1.6	
15 SA	0219 0.6 / 0927 1.8 / 1452 0.5 / 2156 1.6		**30** SU	0324 0.5 / 1026 1.8 / 1604 0.5 / 2305 1.5	
			31 M	0404 0.7 / 1059 1.6 / 1649 0.6 / ☽ 2343 1.4	

Chart Datum: 0·93 metres below Ordnance Datum (Newlyn)

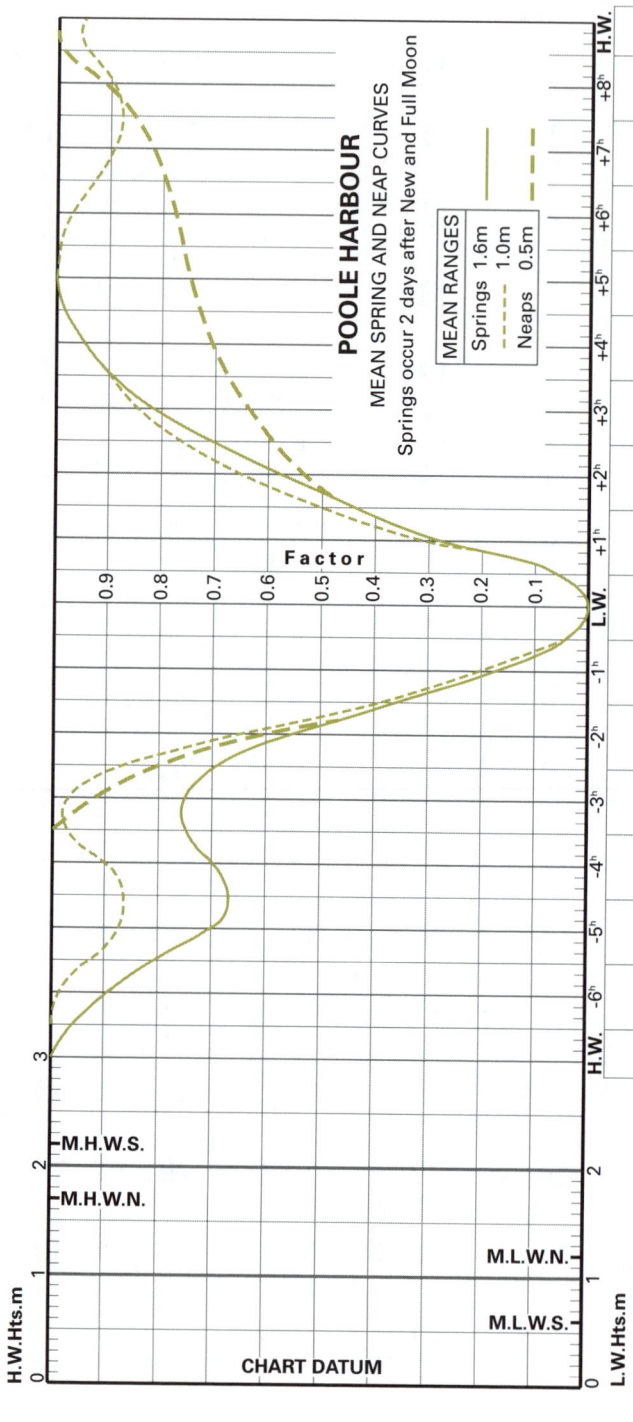

POOLE HARBOUR

MEAN SPRING AND NEAP CURVES

Springs occur 2 days after New and Full Moon

MEAN RANGES	
Springs	1.6m
	1.0m
Neaps	0.5m

Note - HW times are not shown because they cannot be predicted with reasonable accuracy. Approximate times can be gained using LW times and the Tidal Curves at the start of this section.

ENGLAND – POOLE HARBOUR

LAT 50°42'N   LONG 1°59'W

TIMES AND HEIGHTS OF HIGH AND LOW WATERS

Dates in amber are **SPRINGS**
Dates in yellow are **NEAPS**

2007

JANUARY

#	Time	m	#	Time	m
1 M	0159 / 1438	1.0 / 2.1 / 0.9 / 2.0	**16** TU	0153 / 1427	1.2 / 1.9 / 1.0 / 1.9
2 TU	0257 / 1531	0.9 / 2.1 / 0.8 / 2.1	**17** W	0246 / 1514	1.0 / 2.0 / 0.9 / 2.0
3 W ○	0349 / 1619	1.0 / 2.1 / 0.7 / 2.1	**18** TH	0332 / 1558	0.9 / 2.1 / 0.8 / 2.1
4 TH	0435 / 1704	0.8 / 2.1 / 0.7	**19** F ●	0416 / 1642	0.8 / 2.1 / 0.7 / 2.1
5 F	0518 / 1744	2.1 / 2.1 / 0.7	**20** SA	0459 / 1725	0.7 / 2.1 / 0.6
6 SA	0558 / 1822	2.1 / 2.1 / 0.7	**21** SU	0542 / 1807	2.2 / 0.7 / 0.5
7 SU	0637 / 1858	2.1 / 2.0 / 0.8	**22** M	0625 / 1850	2.2 / 0.6 / 0.5
8 M	0714 / 1933	0.9 / 1.9 / 0.8	**23** TU	0709 / 1933	2.2 / 0.7 / 0.6
9 TU	0750 / 2007	1.0 / 1.9 / 0.9	**24** W	0754 / 2017	0.7 / 2.1 / 0.6
10 W	0828 / 2043	1.1 / 1.9 / 1.0	**25** TH ☽	0842 / 2105	2.1 / 0.8 / 2.0 / 0.8
11 TH ☾	0909 / 2126	1.2 / 1.7 / 1.1	**26** F	0936 / 2200	2.0 / 0.9 / 1.9 / 0.9
12 F	1000 / 2220	1.8 / 1.3 / 1.6 / 1.2	**27** SA	1041 / 2310	1.9 / 1.0 / 1.8 / 1.1
13 SA	1107 / 2331	1.8 / 1.3 / 1.6 / 1.3	**28** SU	1203	1.8 / 1.2 / 1.7
14 SU	1225	1.8 / 1.3 / 1.6	**29** M	0034 / 1325	1.2 / 1.8 / 1.1 / 1.8
15 M	0049 / 1333	1.3 / 1.8 / 1.2 / 1.8	**30** TU	0153 / 1432	1.1 / 1.9 / 1.0 / 2.0
			31 W	0255 / 1526	1.0 / 2.0 / 0.9 / 2.0

FEBRUARY

#	Time	m	#	Time	m
1 TH	0345 / 1611	0.9 / 2.0 / 0.8 / 2.1	**16** F	0319 / 1543	0.9 / 2.0 / 0.7 / 2.1
2 F ○	0428 / 1652	0.8 / 2.1 / 0.7 / 2.1	**17** SA ●	0403 / 1627	0.7 / 2.1 / 0.6 / 2.2
3 SA	0507 / 1729	0.8 / 2.1 / 0.6	**18** SU	0445 / 1709	0.6 / 2.2 / 0.4
4 SU	0542 / 1802	2.1 / 0.7 / 0.6	**19** M	0527 / 1750	2.3 / 0.5 / 2.2 / 0.4
5 M	0615 / 1833	2.1 / 0.8 / 2.0 / 0.7	**20** TU	0608 / 1831	2.3 / 0.4 / 2.3 / 0.4
6 TU	0646 / 1902	2.1 / 0.8 / 0.7	**21** W	0650 / 1912	2.3 / 0.4 / 2.2 / 0.4
7 W	0714 / 1929	2.0 / 1.9 / 0.8	**22** TH	0731 / 1953	2.3 / 0.6 / 2.1 / 0.6
8 TH	0742 / 1956	0.9 / 1.9 / 0.9	**23** F	0815 / 2037	2.1 / 0.7 / 2.0 / 0.8
9 F	0813 / 2030	1.9 / 1.0 / 1.8 / 1.0	**24** SA	0905 / 2132	2.0 / 0.9 / 1.9 / 1.0
10 SA	0852 / 2113	1.8 / 1.2 / 1.2	**25** SU	1011 / 2248	1.8 / 1.1 / 1.7 / 1.2
11 SU	0946 / 2220	1.7 / 1.3 / 1.3	**26** M	1143	1.7 / 1.2 / 1.6
12 M	1114	1.6 / 1.3 / 1.6	**27** TU	0026 / 1316	1.3 / 1.6 / 1.2 / 1.8
13 TU	0007 / 1302	1.4 / 1.6 / 1.3 / 1.6	**28** W	0153 / 1425	1.2 / 1.8 / 1.0 / 1.9
14 W	0135 / 1408	1.3 / 1.7 / 1.1 / 1.8			
15 TH	0232 / 1458	1.1 / 1.9 / 0.9 / 2.0			

MARCH

#	Time	m	#	Time	m
1 TH	0252 / 1514	1.0 / 1.9 / 0.9 / 2.0	**16** F	0213 / 1435	1.0 / 1.9 / 0.8 / 2.0
2 F	0336 / 1555	0.9 / 2.0 / 0.7 / 2.1	**17** SA ●	0300 / 1520	0.8 / 2.0 / 0.6 / 2.1
3 SA ○	0413 / 1631	0.8 / 2.0 / 0.7 / 2.1	**18** SU	0342 / 1603	0.6 / 2.1 / 2.3
4 SU	0447 / 1705	0.7 / 2.0 / 0.6	**19** M ●	0424 / 1646	0.4 / 2.2 / 0.3 / 2.3
5 M	0519 / 1736	2.1 / 0.6 / 0.6	**20** TU	0506 / 1728	0.3 / 2.3 / 0.3
6 TU	0549 / 1805	2.1 / 2.0 / 0.6	**21** W	0547 / 1808	2.4 / 0.3 / 2.3 / 0.3
7 W	0616 / 1830	2.1 / 2.0 / 0.7	**22** TH	0628 / 1849	2.3 / 0.4 / 2.3 / 0.4
8 TH	0640 / 1854	0.7 / 2.0 / 0.7	**23** F	0709 / 1930	2.3 / 0.5 / 2.1 / 0.6
9 F	0704 / 1920	2.0 / 0.8 / 1.9 / 0.8	**24** SA	0752 / 2015	2.1 / 0.7 / 2.0 / 0.8
10 SA	0733 / 1951	1.9 / 0.9 / 1.9 / 0.9	**25** SU ☽	0842 / 2112	2.0 / 0.9 / 1.9 / 1.0
11 SU	0809 / 2033	1.9 / 1.1 / 1.8 / 1.2	**26** M	0950 / 2234	1.8 / 1.1 / 1.7 / 1.3
12 M ☾	0859 / 2136	1.7 / 1.2 / 1.6 / 1.3	**27** TU	1124	1.6 / 1.2 / 1.6
13 TU	1022 / 2336	1.6 / 1.6 / 1.2 / 1.4	**28** W	0014 / 1258	1.3 / 1.6 / 1.2 / 1.8
14 W	1231	1.6 / 1.3 / 1.6	**29** TH	0140 / 1404	1.2 / 1.8 / 1.0 / 1.9
15 TH	0115 / 1344	1.3 / 1.7 / 1.0 / 1.8	**30** F	0234 / 1449	1.0 / 1.9 / 0.9 / 2.0
			31 SA	0313 / 1527	0.9 / 1.9 / 0.8 / 2.1

APRIL

#	Time	m	#	Time	m
1 SU	0347 / 1601	0.7 / 2.0 / 0.7 / 2.1	**16** M	0314 / 1534	0.6 / 2.1 / 0.4 / 2.3
2 M ○	0420 / 1634	0.7 / 2.0 / 0.6 / 2.1	**17** TU ●	0358 / 1618	0.4 / 2.2 / 0.4 / 2.3
3 TU	0451 / 1706	0.6 / 2.0 / 0.6	**18** W	0442 / 1702	0.4 / 2.3 / 0.4
4 W	0520 / 1734	2.1 / 0.6 / 2.0 / 0.7	**19** TH	0524 / 1745	2.4 / 0.3 / 2.3 / 0.4
5 TH	0546 / 1800	2.1 / 2.0 / 0.7	**20** F	0607 / 1828	2.3 / 0.4 / 2.3 / 0.6
6 F	0609 / 1825	2.1 / 2.0 / 0.8	**21** SA	0650 / 1912	2.3 / 0.5 / 2.1 / 0.7
7 SA	0635 / 1852	0.8 / 2.0 / 0.9	**22** SU	0735 / 2000	2.1 / 0.7 / 2.0 / 0.9
8 SU	0705 / 1926	0.9 / 1.9 / 1.0	**23** M	0827 / 2059	1.9 / 0.9 / 1.9 / 1.1
9 M	0744 / 2011	1.9 / 1.0 / 1.2	**24** TU ☽	0932 / 2214	1.8 / 1.0 / 1.8 / 1.3
10 TU ☽	0836 / 2117	1.8 / 1.2 / 1.7 / 1.3	**25** W ☽	1055 / 2342	1.6 / 1.2 / 1.8 / 1.3
11 W ☽	0958 / 2303	1.6 / 1.6 / 1.4	**26** TH	1219	1.6 / 1.2 / 1.8
12 TH	1150	1.6 / 1.2 / 1.7	**27** F	0101 / 1323	1.2 / 1.7 / 1.0 / 1.9
13 F	0039 / 1308	1.2 / 1.7 / 1.0 / 1.9	**28** SA	0156 / 1410	1.0 / 1.8 / 0.9 / 2.0
14 SA	0141 / 1402	1.1 / 1.9 / 0.8 / 2.0	**29** SU	0237 / 1448	0.9 / 1.9 / 0.8 / 2.0
15 SU	0230 / 1449	0.8 / 2.0 / 0.6 / 2.2	**30** M	0312 / 1524	0.8 / 1.9 / 0.8 / 2.0

TIDES

Chart Datum: 1·40 metres below Ordnance Datum (Newlyn)

TIDES

TIME ZONE (UT)
For Summer Time add ONE hour in **non-shaded areas**

ENGLAND – POOLE HARBOUR

LAT 50°42′N   LONG 1°59′W

TIMES AND HEIGHTS OF HIGH AND LOW WATERS

Dates in amber are **SPRINGS**
Dates in yellow are **NEAPS**

2007

MAY

Day	R1	R2	R3	R4
1 TU	0346 0.7	2.0	1559 0.7	2.1
2 W	0419 0.7	2.0	1632 0.7	2.1
3 TH	0450 0.7	2.0	1704 0.7	
4 F	0518 2.1	0.7	1733 2.0	0.8
5 SA	0545 2.1	0.7	1802 2.0	0.8
6 SU	0615 2.0	0.8	1835 2.0	0.9
7 M	0651 2.0	0.8	1915 1.9	1.0
8 TU	0734 1.9	0.9	2004 1.9	1.1
9 W	0830 1.8	1.0	2109 1.8	1.2
10 TH	0942 1.8	1.1	2229 1.8	1.2
11 F	1104 1.7	1.8	2350 1.1	
12 SA	1219 1.8	0.9	1.9	
13 SU	0057 0.9	1.9	1321 0.8	2.1
14 M	0153 0.8	2.0	1414 0.7	2.2
15 TU	0244 0.7	2.1	1503 0.6	2.3
16 W	0332 0.6	2.2	1552 0.5	2.3
17 TH	0420 0.5	2.3	1639 0.5	2.3
18 F	0507 0.4	2.3	1726 0.6	
19 SA	0552 2.3	0.5	1812 2.2	0.7
20 SU	0638 2.2	0.6	1858 2.1	0.8
21 M	0724 2.1	0.7	1947 2.0	0.9
22 TU	0813 1.9	0.9	2041 1.9	1.0
23 W	0908 1.8	1.0	2142 1.8	1.2
24 TH	1011 1.7	1.1	2250 1.7	1.2
25 F	1118 1.6	1.1	1.8	
26 SA	0000 1.2	1.6	1222 1.1	1.8
27 SU	0101 1.2	1.7	1315 1.0	1.9
28 M	0149 0.9	1.8	1401 1.0	1.9
29 TU	0231 0.9	1.8	1443 0.9	2.0
30 W	0309 0.9	1.9	1523 0.9	2.0
31 TH	0346 0.8	2.0	1601 0.8	2.0

JUNE

Day	R1	R2	R3	R4
1 F	0422 0.8	2.0	1638 0.8	
2 SA	0456 0.8	2.0	1713 0.8	
3 SU	0530 2.0	0.8	1749 2.0	0.9
4 M	0606 2.0	0.8	1827 2.0	0.9
5 TU	0646 2.0	0.8	1911 2.0	0.9
6 W	0732 2.0	0.8	2000 2.0	1.0
7 TH	0824 1.9	0.9	2055 1.9	1.0
8 F	0922 1.9	0.9	2158 1.9	1.0
9 SA	1026 1.8	0.9	2305 1.9	1.0
10 SU	1133 1.9	0.9	2.0	
11 M	0014 0.9	1.9	1240 0.9	2.0
12 TU	0119 0.9	2.0	1342 0.8	2.1
13 W	0219 0.8	2.0	1439 0.8	2.1
14 TH	0314 2.1	1534 0.7	2.2	
15 F	0406 0.6	2.1	1625 0.7	2.2
16 SA	0455 0.6	2.2	1714 0.7	
17 SU	0542 0.6	2.2	1800 0.7	
18 M	0627 0.6	2.1	1845 0.8	
19 TU	0710 2.0	0.7	1930 2.1	0.9
20 W	0752 2.0	0.8	2014 2.0	0.9
21 TH	0835 1.9	0.9	2101 1.9	1.0
22 F	0921 1.8	0.9	2152 1.9	1.2
23 SA	1012 1.7	1.1	2249 1.8	1.2
24 SU	1109 1.6	1.2	2352 1.8	1.2
25 M	1212 1.6	1.2	1.8	
26 TU	0054 1.2	1.6	1312 1.2	1.8
27 W	0148 1.1	1.8	1405 1.1	1.9
28 TH	0236 1.0	1.9	1453 1.0	2.0
29 F	0320 0.9	1.9	1537 0.9	2.0
30 SA	0401 0.8	2.0	1619 0.9	2.0

JULY

Day	R1	R2	R3	R4
1 SU	0441 0.8	2.0	1659 0.8	2.0
2 M	0520 0.7	2.1	1739 0.8	
3 TU	0600 2.1	0.7	1820 2.1	0.8
4 W	0641 2.0	0.7	1902 2.1	0.8
5 TH	0724 2.0	0.7	1947 2.1	0.8
6 F	0809 2.0	0.7	2036 2.1	0.8
7 SA	0859 2.0	0.8	2129 2.0	0.9
8 SU	0954 1.9	0.8	2230 2.0	0.9
9 M	1056 0.9	1.9	2340 1.9	
10 TU	1208 1.8	1.0	1.9	
11 W	0056 1.0	1.9	1322 1.0	2.0
12 TH	0206 0.9	1.9	1429 0.9	2.0
13 F	0306 0.8	2.0	1526 0.9	2.1
14 SA	0359 0.7	2.1	1618 0.8	2.1
15 SU	0447 0.7	2.1	1705 0.8	
16 M	0531 0.6	2.1	1747 0.7	
17 TU	0611 0.6	2.1	1828 0.7	
18 W	0649 0.7	2.1	1905 0.7	
19 TH	0724 2.0	0.7	1941 2.1	0.8
20 F	0757 1.9	0.7	2017 2.0	0.9
21 SA	0832 1.9	0.8	2055 1.9	1.0
22 SU	0910 1.8	0.9	2139 1.9	1.2
23 M	0958 1.7	1.0	2238 1.8	1.3
24 TU	1105 1.6	1.3	2357 1.7	1.3
25 W	1227 1.6	1.3	1.7	
26 TH	0113 1.2	1.7	1337 1.3	1.8
27 F	0212 1.1	1.8	1432 1.2	1.9
28 SA	0301 0.9	1.9	1519 1.0	2.0
29 SU	0344 0.8	2.0	1603 0.9	2.0
30 M	0426 0.7	2.1	1644 0.8	2.1
31 TU	0506 0.6	2.1	1725 0.7	

AUGUST

Day	R1	R2	R3	R4
1 W	2.1	0546 0.6 / 2.2	1805 0.6	
2 TH	2.1	0626 0.5 / 2.2	1846 0.6	
3 F	0707 0.5	2.2	1928 0.6	
4 SA	0748 2.1	0.6	2012 2.1	0.7
5 SU	0833 2.0	0.7	2101 2.1	0.8
6 M	0925 1.9	0.9	2201 2.0	1.0
7 TU	1029 1.8	1.0	2318 1.9	1.1
8 W	1153 1.7	1.2	1.8	
9 TH	0047 1.1	1.8	1319 1.2	1.9
10 F	0204 1.0	1.9	1429 1.0	2.0
11 SA	0303 0.9	2.0	1524 0.9	2.0
12 SU	0352 0.7	2.1	1609 0.8	2.1
13 M	0434 0.6	2.1	1650 0.7	2.1
14 TU	0513 0.6	2.1	1728 0.7	
15 W	0548 0.6	2.1	1803 0.7	
16 TH	2.1	0620 0.6 / 2.1	1835 0.7	
17 F	0650 0.7	2.0	1904 0.8	
18 SA	0717 0.8	2.0	1933 0.9	
19 SU	0745 1.9	0.9	2003 1.9	1.0
20 M	0817 1.8	1.0	2039 1.8	1.1
21 TU	0858 1.7	1.2	2130 1.7	1.3
22 W	1001 1.6	1.4	2256 1.6	1.4
23 TH	1152 1.6	1.4	1.6	
24 F	0046 1.3	1.6	1318 1.5	1.8
25 SA	0153 1.2	1.8	1416 1.2	1.9
26 SU	0242 0.9	2.0	1501 1.0	2.0
27 M	0325 0.8	2.1	1543 0.8	2.1
28 TU	0405 0.6	2.1	1623 0.7	2.1
29 W	0445 0.5	2.3	1703 0.6	2.2
30 TH	0525 0.4	2.3	1744 0.5	
31 F	0604 0.4	2.3	1824 0.5	

Chart Datum: 1·40 metres below Ordnance Datum (Newlyn)

TIME ZONE (UT)
For Summer Time add ONE hour in **non-shaded areas**

ENGLAND – POOLE HARBOUR

LAT 50°42′N   LONG 1°59′W

TIMES AND HEIGHTS OF HIGH AND LOW WATERS

Dates in amber are **SPRINGS**
Dates in yellow are **NEAPS**

2007

SEPTEMBER

Day	Time	m	Day	Time	m
1 SA	0644 / 1905	2.2 0.4 / 2.3 / 0.6	16 SU	0640 / 1853	2.0 0.8 / 2.1 / 0.8
2 SU	0724 / 1948	0.6 / 2.2 / 0.7	17 M	0706 / 1921	2.0 0.9 / 2.0 / 0.9
3 M	0808 / 2036	2.1 0.8 / 0.9	18 TU	0736 / 1955	1.0 1.9 / 1.1
4 TU	0901 / ◗ 2138	1.9 1.0 / 1.9 / 1.0	19 W	0815 / ◗ 2043	1.3 1.8 / 1.8 / 1.3
5 W	1014 / 2306	1.8 1.8 / 1.2	20 TH	0917 / 2205	1.6 1.4 / 1.6 / 1.4
6 TH	1150	1.7 1.7	21 F	1121	1.6 1.5 / 1.6
7 F	0044 / 1321	1.2 1.8 / 1.3 / 1.8	22 SA	0015 / 1255	1.4 1.6 / 1.4 / 1.7
8 SA	0200 / 1426	1.0 1.9 / 1.1 / 2.0	23 SU	0126 / 1351	1.2 1.8 / 1.2 / 1.9
9 SU	0253 / 1513	0.9 2.1 / 0.9 / 2.0	24 M	0215 / 1436	0.9 2.0 / 0.9 / 2.0
10 M	0335 / 1552	0.7 2.1 / 0.8 / 2.1	25 TU	0257 / 1516	0.7 2.1 / 0.7 / 2.1
11 TU	0412 / 1628 ●	0.6 2.2 / 0.7 / 2.1	26 W	0337 / 1556 ○	0.6 2.3 / 0.6 / 2.3
12 W	0447 / 1702	0.6 2.2 / 0.7 / 2.1	27 TH	0418 / 1637	0.4 2.3 / 0.5 / 2.3
13 TH	0519 / 1733	0.6 2.1 / 0.7	28 F	0458 / 1718	0.4 2.4 / 0.4
14 F	0548 / 1801	2.1 0.6 / 2.1 / 0.7	29 SA	0538 / 1759	2.3 0.4 / 2.4 / 0.4
15 SA	0616 / 1828	0.7 2.1 / 0.8	30 SU	0619 / 1841	2.3 0.5 / 2.3 / 0.6

OCTOBER

Day	Time	m	Day	Time	m
1 M	0702 / 1926	2.2 0.7 / 2.2 / 0.7	16 TU	0636 / 1850	2.0 1.0 / 2.0 / 1.0
2 TU	0749 / 2017	0.8 2.1 / 0.9	17 W	0708 / 1926	1.1 1.9 / 1.1
3 W	0847 / ◗ 2123	1.1 1.9 / 1.1	18 TH	0750 / 2015	1.3 1.9 / 1.2
4 TH	1006 / 2253	1.8 1.7 / 1.3	19 F	0852 / ◗ 2131	1.4 1.8 / 1.7 / 1.3
5 F	1142	1.7 1.7	20 SA	1036 / 2321	1.5 1.7 / 1.6 / 1.3
6 SA	0029 / 1309	1.2 2.0 / 1.3 / 1.8	21 SU	1212	1.8 1.7
7 SU	0141 / 1407	1.1 2.0 / 1.1 / 2.0	22 M	0041 / 1313	1.1 1.9 / 1.2 / 1.9
8 M	0229 / 1449	0.9 2.1 / 0.9 / 2.0	23 TU	0136 / 1400	0.9 2.0 / 0.9 / 2.0
9 TU	0307 / 1525	0.8 2.1 / 0.7 / 2.1	24 W	0221 / 1444	0.8 2.2 / 0.7 / 2.1
10 W	0342 / 1559	0.7 2.2 / 0.7 / 2.1	25 TH	0304 / 1527	0.6 2.3 / 0.6 / 2.3
11 TH	0415 / 1631 ●	0.7 2.2 / 0.7 / 2.1	26 F	0347 / 1610 ○	0.5 2.4 / 0.5 / 2.3
12 F	0447 / 1701	0.7 2.2 / 0.7 / 2.1	27 SA	0431 / 1654	0.5 2.4 / 0.5 / 2.4
13 SA	0517 / 1730	0.7 2.1 / 0.7	28 SU	0515 / 1739	0.5 2.4 / 0.5
14 SU	0544 / 1755	0.8 2.1 / 0.8	29 M	0559 / 1824	2.3 0.6 / 2.3 / 0.6
15 M	0609 / 1821	0.9 2.1 / 0.9	30 TU	0645 / 1911	2.2 0.7 / 2.2 / 0.7
			31 W	0736 / 2004	2.1 0.9 / 2.0 / 0.9

NOVEMBER

Day	Time	m	Day	Time	m
1 TH	0836 / ◗ 2108	2.0 1.1 / 1.9 / 1.1	16 F	0738 / 2002	1.2 1.9 / 1.1
2 F	0949 / 2226	1.3 1.9 / 1.2	17 SA	0836 / ● 2107	1.3 1.8 / 1.2
3 SA	1114 / 2350	1.3 1.8 / 1.2	18 SU	0951 / 2224	1.3 1.8 / 1.2
4 SU	1233	1.9 1.9 / 1.8	19 M	1112 / 2340	1.3 1.8 / 1.1
5 M	0059 / 1331	1.1 2.0 / 1.1 / 1.9	20 TU	1221	1.9 1.9
6 TU	0150 / 1415	1.0 2.0 / 1.0 / 1.9	21 W	0045 / 1320	1.0 2.0 / 1.0 / 2.0
7 W	0230 / 1452	0.9 2.1 / 0.9 / 2.0	22 TH	0141 / 1412	0.8 2.2 / 0.8 / 2.1
8 TH	0306 / 1526	0.8 2.1 / 0.8 / 2.0	23 F	0232 / 1501	0.7 2.3 / 0.7 / 2.2
9 F	0340 / 1600	0.8 2.1 / 0.8 / 2.1	24 SA	0321 / 1549 ○	0.7 2.4 / 0.6 / 2.3
10 SA	0414 / 1632	0.8 2.1 / 0.8 / 2.1	25 SU	0409 / 1638	0.6 2.4 / 0.6 / 2.3
11 SU	0447 / 1703	0.8 2.1 / 0.8	26 M	0457 / 1726	0.6 2.3 / 0.6 / 2.1
12 M	0517 / 1731	2.1 0.9 / 2.1 / 0.8	27 TU	0545 / 1814	2.3 0.7 / 2.1 / 0.6
13 TU	0546 / 1800	2.1 0.9 / 2.1 / 0.9	28 W	0634 / 1902	2.2 0.9 / 2.1 / 0.7
14 W	0617 / 1833	2.1 1.0 / 2.0 / 0.9	29 TH	0725 / 1952	2.1 0.9 / 2.0 / 0.8
15 TH	0653 / 1912	2.0 1.1 / 2.0 / 1.0	30 F	0819 / 2046	2.0 1.0 / 1.9 / 1.0

DECEMBER

Day	Time	m	Day	Time	m
1 SA	0919 / ◗ 2145	2.0 1.2 / 1.8 / 1.1	16 SU	0819 / 2044	2.0 1.1 / 1.9 / 0.9
2 SU	1025 / 2249	1.3 1.9 / 1.2	17 M	0916 / 2142	1.9 1.1 / 1.9 / 1.0
3 M	1135 / 2354	1.3 1.9 / 1.2	18 TU	1021 / 2248	1.9 1.2 / 1.0
4 TU	1238	1.9 1.9 / 1.8	19 W	1131 / 2357	2.0 1.1 / 1.0
5 W	0054 / 1330	1.2 2.0 / 1.2 / 1.8	20 TH	1242	2.0 1.9 / 1.9
6 TH	0144 / 1414	1.1 2.0 / 1.0 / 1.9	21 F	0106 / 1347	0.9 2.0 / 0.9 / 2.0
7 F	0227 / 1454	1.0 2.0 / 1.0 / 1.9	22 SA	0208 / 1445	0.9 2.1 / 0.8 / 2.1
8 SA	0308 / 1532	1.0 2.1 / 0.9 / 2.0	23 SU	0305 / 1539	0.8 2.3 / 0.7 / 2.2
9 SU	0347 / 1609	0.9 2.1 / 0.9 / 2.0	24 M	0359 / 1631 ○	0.8 2.3 / 0.6 / 2.3
10 M	0424 / 1644	0.9 2.1 / 0.9 / 2.1	25 TU	0449 / 1720	0.7 2.3 / 0.6 / 2.3
11 TU	0459 / 1718	0.9 2.1 / 0.8	26 W	0537 / 1806	2.3 0.7 / 2.3 / 0.6
12 W	0532 / 1751	2.1 0.9 / 2.1 / 0.8	27 TH	0624 / 1851	2.3 0.8 / 2.1 / 0.7
13 TH	0607 / 1827	2.1 0.9 / 2.0 / 0.8	28 F	0709 / 1933	2.2 0.8 / 2.1 / 0.7
14 F	0645 / 1907	2.0 1.0 / 2.0 / 0.9	29 SA	0754 / 2015	2.1 1.0 / 2.0 / 0.8
15 SA	0729 / 1952	2.0 1.0 / 1.9 / 0.9	30 SU	0839 / 2058	2.0 1.0 / 1.9 / 0.9
			31 M	0928 / ◗ 2146	1.9 1.2 / 1.8 / 1.0

Chart Datum: 1·40 metres below Ordnance Datum (Newlyn)

TIDES

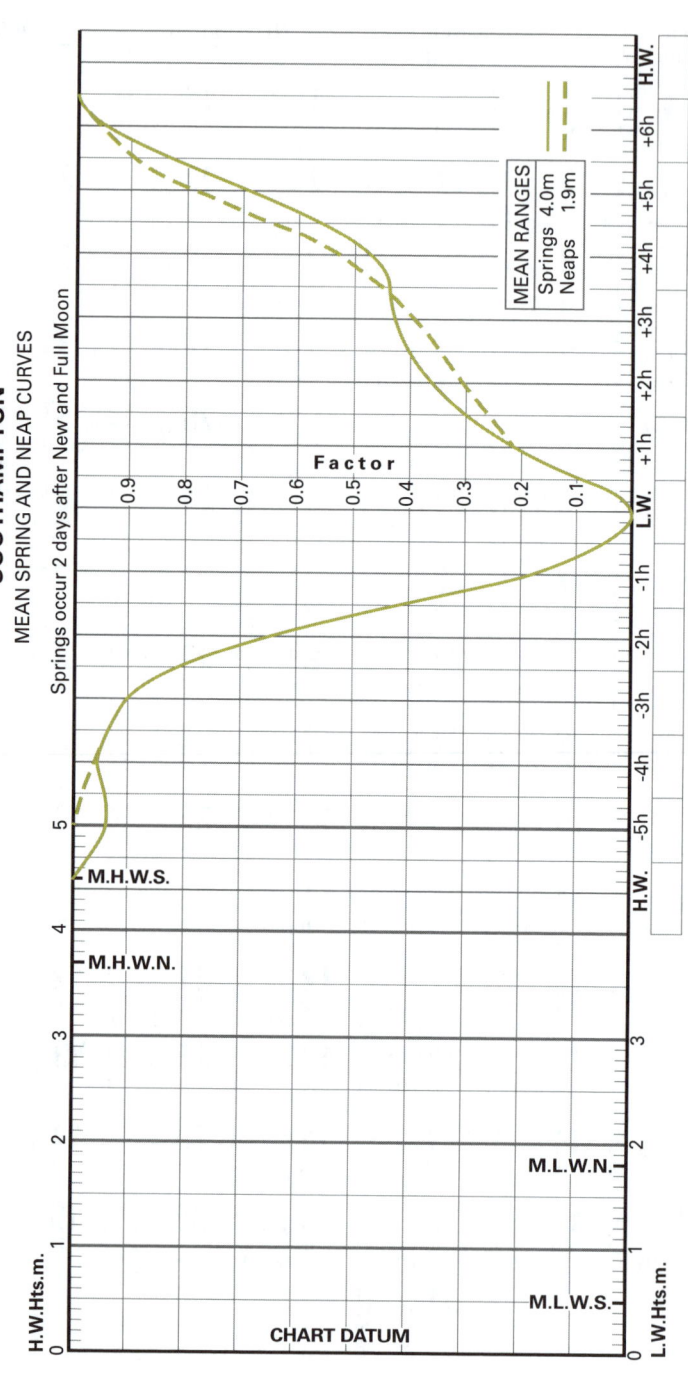

SOUTHAMPTON
MEAN SPRING AND NEAP CURVES

Springs occur 2 days after New and Full Moon

MEAN RANGES
Springs 4.0m
Neaps 1.9m

Factor

0.9 0.8 0.7 0.6 0.5 0.4 0.3 0.2 0.1

H.W.   +6h +5h +4h +3h +2h +1h L.W. -1h -2h -3h -4h -5h H.W.

H.W.Hts.m.

M.H.W.S.

M.H.W.N.

CHART DATUM

M.L.W.N.

M.L.W.S.

L.W.Hts.m.

Note - Double HWs occur at Southampton. The predictions are for the first HW.

ENGLAND – SOUTHAMPTON

LAT 50°54′N   LONG 1°24′W

TIMES AND HEIGHTS OF HIGH AND LOW WATERS

Dates in amber are SPRINGS
Dates in yellow are NEAPS

2007

JANUARY

Day	Time	m	Day	Time	m
1 M	0201 / 0836 / 1439 / 2105	1.4 / 4.3 / 1.3 / 4.2	16 TU	0157 / 0831 / 1431 / 2103	1.8 / 4.0 / 1.6 / 4.0
2 TU	0300 / 0930 / 1533 / 2159	1.3 / 4.4 / 1.1 / 4.3	17 W	0250 / 0920 / 1519 / 2149	1.6 / 4.2 / 1.3 / 4.2
3 W ○	0352 / 1019 / 1622 / 2247	1.2 / 4.5 / 0.9 / 4.4	18 TH	0337 / 1003 / 1604 / 2230	1.3 / 4.4 / 1.0 / 4.4
4 TH	0440 / 1104 / 1707 / 2331	1.1 / 4.5 / 0.8 / 4.4	19 F ●	0422 / 1045 / 1648 / 2311	1.1 / 4.5 / 0.8 / 4.5
5 F	0524 / 1145 / 1749	1.0 / 4.5 / 0.8	20 SA	0506 / 1126 / 1730 / 2352	0.9 / 4.6 / 0.6 / 4.6
6 SA	0012 / 0605 / 1224 / 1826	4.4 / 1.0 / 4.4 / 0.8	21 SU	0549 / 1207 / 1812	0.8 / 4.6 / 0.5
7 SU	0051 / 0644 / 1302 / 1902	4.4 / 1.1 / 4.3 / 0.9	22 M	0034 / 0631 / 1249 / 1853	4.6 / 0.7 / 4.6 / 0.5
8 M	0129 / 0720 / 1339 / 1934	4.3 / 1.2 / 4.2 / 1.1	23 TU	0117 / 0713 / 1332 / 1935	4.6 / 0.7 / 4.6 / 0.6
9 TU	0206 / 0755 / 1416 / 2007	4.2 / 1.4 / 4.1 / 1.3	24 W	0202 / 0756 / 1416 / 2018	4.5 / 0.9 / 4.4 / 0.8
10 W	0244 / 0831 / 1455 / 2043	4.1 / 1.5 / 3.9 / 1.5	25 TH ☽	0249 / 0842 / 1504 / 2105	4.4 / 1.1 / 4.3 / 1.0
11 TH ☽	0326 / 0912 / 1539 / 2126	4.0 / 1.7 / 3.8 / 1.7	26 F	0340 / 0935 / 1559 / 2200	4.2 / 1.3 / 4.0 / 1.4
12 F	0414 / 1004 / 1632 / 2223	3.8 / 1.9 / 3.6 / 1.9	27 SA	0440 / 1039 / 1707 / 2310	4.0 / 1.6 / 3.8 / 1.8
13 SA	0513 / 1112 / 1741 / 2338	3.8 / 2.0 / 3.6 / 2.1	28 SU	0554 / 1159 / 1831	3.9 / 1.7 / 3.7
14 SU	0623 / 1228 / 1900	3.7 / 2.0 / 3.6	29 M	0033 / 0716 / 1323 / 1957	1.8 / 3.9 / 1.6 / 3.8
15 M	0054 / 0732 / 1335 / 2009	2.0 / 3.9 / 1.8 / 3.8	30 TU	0153 / 0830 / 1434 / 2106	1.7 / 4.0 / 1.5 / 4.0
			31 W	0257 / 0929 / 1530 / 2159	1.5 / 4.2 / 1.2 / 4.2

FEBRUARY

Day	Time	m	Day	Time	m
1 TH	0349 / 1016 / 1616 / 2243	1.3 / 4.3 / 1.0 / 4.3	16 F	0323 / 0946 / 1549 / 2213	1.3 / 4.3 / 0.9 / 4.4
2 F ○	0433 / 1057 / 1657 / 2321	1.0 / 4.4 / 0.8 / 4.4	17 SA ●	0408 / 1028 / 1633 / 2253	0.9 / 4.5 / 0.5 / 4.6
3 SA	0513 / 1132 / 1734 / 2355	0.9 / 4.4 / 0.6 / 4.4	18 SU	0452 / 1108 / 1716 / 2333	0.6 / 4.7 / 0.3 / 4.7
4 SU	0550 / 1205 / 1808	0.8 / 4.4 / 0.6	19 M	0534 / 1148 / 1757	0.4 / 4.8 / 0.1
5 M	0027 / 0623 / 1237 / 1838	4.4 / 0.8 / 4.4 / 0.7	20 TU	0014 / 0614 / 1229 / 1836	4.8 / 0.3 / 4.8 / 0.1
6 TU	0058 / 0653 / 1309 / 1905	4.4 / 0.9 / 4.3 / 0.8	21 W	0055 / 0654 / 1310 / 1915	4.8 / 0.3 / 4.7 / 0.3
7 W	0130 / 0720 / 1340 / 1930	4.3 / 1.0 / 4.2 / 1.0	22 TH	0136 / 0734 / 1353 / 1954	4.7 / 0.5 / 4.5 / 0.6
8 TH	0201 / 0747 / 1413 / 1957	4.2 / 1.2 / 4.0 / 1.3	23 F	0220 / 0816 / 1438 / 2036	4.5 / 0.8 / 4.3 / 1.0
9 F	0235 / 0817 / 1448 / 2029	4.0 / 1.5 / 3.9 / 1.5	24 SA ☽	0307 / 0903 / 1530 / 2127	4.2 / 1.2 / 4.0 / 1.4
10 SA ☽	0312 / 0855 / 1529 / 2112	3.9 / 1.7 / 3.7 / 1.9	25 SU	0405 / 1005 / 1639 / 2240	3.9 / 1.6 / 3.7 / 1.9
11 SU	0401 / 0950 / 1630 / 2219	3.7 / 2.0 / 3.5 / 2.1	26 M	0525 / 1136 / 1819	3.7 / 1.9 / 3.6
12 M	0512 / 1119 / 1800	3.6 / 2.1 / 3.4	27 TU	0024 / 0707 / 1318 / 1959	2.0 / 3.6 / 1.8 / 3.7
13 TU	0004 / 0642 / 1257 / 1934	2.2 / 3.6 / 2.0 / 3.6	28 W	0155 / 0829 / 1430 / 2105	1.8 / 3.8 / 1.6 / 4.0
14 W	0131 / 0802 / 1407 / 2041	2.0 / 3.8 / 1.7 / 3.9			
15 TH	0233 / 0859 / 1501 / 2130	1.6 / 4.1 / 1.3 / 4.1			

MARCH

Day	Time	m	Day	Time	m
1 TH	0255 / 0924 / 1521 / 2151	1.5 / 4.1 / 1.2 / 4.2	16 F	0210 / 0832 / 1436 / 2104	1.6 / 4.0 / 1.2 / 4.2
2 F	0340 / 1006 / 1601 / 2229	1.2 / 4.3 / 0.9 / 4.3	17 SA	0301 / 0921 / 1525 / 2147	1.1 / 4.3 / 0.7 / 4.5
3 SA	0418 / 1040 / 1637 / 2301	0.9 / 4.3 / 0.7 / 4.4	18 SU ○	0347 / 1004 / 1610 / 2229	0.7 / 4.5 / 0.3 / 4.7
4 SU	0453 / 1111 / 1711 / 2330	0.7 / 4.4 / 0.5 / 4.4	19 M ●	0431 / 1045 / 1653 / 2309	0.4 / 4.7 / 0.1 / 4.8
5 M	0526 / 1140 / 1742 / 2357	0.6 / 4.4 / 0.5 / 4.4	20 TU	0513 / 1126 / 1734 / 2349	0.1 / 4.8 / 0.0 / 4.9
6 TU	0557 / 1208 / 1810	0.6 / 4.4 / 0.6	21 W	0554 / 1207 / 1814	0.1 / 4.8 / 0.0
7 W	0025 / 0623 / 1237 / 1834	4.4 / 0.7 / 4.3 / 0.7	22 TH	0030 / 0633 / 1249 / 1852	4.8 / 0.2 / 4.7 / 0.3
8 TH	0054 / 0646 / 1307 / 1856	4.3 / 0.8 / 4.2 / 0.9	23 F	0112 / 0712 / 1332 / 1931	4.7 / 0.4 / 4.5 / 0.6
9 F	0123 / 0709 / 1336 / 1920	4.2 / 1.0 / 4.1 / 1.2	24 SA	0155 / 0753 / 1418 / 2013	4.4 / 0.8 / 4.2 / 1.1
10 SA	0152 / 0736 / 1408 / 1949	4.1 / 1.3 / 3.9 / 1.5	25 SU ☽	0243 / 0840 / 1513 / 2106	4.1 / 1.2 / 3.9 / 1.6
11 SU	0225 / 0810 / 1445 / 2027	3.9 / 1.5 / 3.8 / 1.8	26 M	0342 / 0943 / 1628 / 2226	3.8 / 1.7 / 3.6 / 2.0
12 M	0308 / 0858 / 1541 / 2128	3.7 / 1.8 / 3.6 / 2.1	27 TU ☽	0507 / 1120 / 1815 / 2128	3.5 / 1.9 / 3.5 / 2.1
13 TU	0415 / 1020 / 1713 / 2319	3.5 / 2.1 / 3.5 / 2.2	28 W	0017 / 0655 / 1302 / 1948	2.1 / 3.6 / 1.8 / 3.7
14 W	0556 / 1217 / 1858	3.5 / 2.0 / 3.6	29 TH	0143 / 0812 / 1409 / 2046	1.9 / 3.8 / 1.6 / 4.0
15 TH	0104 / 0728 / 1339 / 2012	2.0 / 3.7 / 1.6 / 3.9	30 F	0236 / 0903 / 1454 / 2127	1.5 / 4.0 / 1.3 / 4.2
			31 SA	0316 / 0941 / 1532 / 2202	1.2 / 4.2 / 1.0 / 4.3

APRIL

Day	Time	m	Day	Time	m
1 SU	0351 / 1014 / 1606 / 2231	0.9 / 4.2 / 0.7 / 4.4	16 M	0319 / 0936 / 1540 / 2201	0.6 / 4.5 / 0.4 / 4.7
2 M ○	0424 / 1043 / 1639 / 2258	0.7 / 4.3 / 0.6 / 4.4	17 TU ●	0404 / 1019 / 1625 / 2243	0.3 / 4.7 / 0.2 / 4.8
3 TU	0456 / 1110 / 1710 / 2324	0.6 / 4.3 / 0.6 / 4.4	18 W	0448 / 1103 / 1708 / 2325	0.1 / 4.8 / 0.1 / 4.9
4 W	0525 / 1137 / 1738 / 2351	0.6 / 4.3 / 0.7 / 4.4	19 TH	0531 / 1146 / 1750	0.1 / 4.7 / 0.2
5 TH	0552 / 1206 / 1803	0.7 / 4.3 / 0.8	20 F	0008 / 0612 / 1231 / 1831	4.8 / 0.2 / 4.6 / 0.5
6 F	0020 / 0615 / 1237 / 1826	4.3 / 0.8 / 4.2 / 1.0	21 SA	0052 / 0653 / 1317 / 1913	4.6 / 0.5 / 4.4 / 0.8
7 SA	0050 / 0640 / 1308 / 1852	4.2 / 1.0 / 4.1 / 1.2	22 SU	0137 / 0737 / 1407 / 1959	4.3 / 0.9 / 4.2 / 1.3
8 SU	0121 / 0709 / 1342 / 1923	4.1 / 1.2 / 4.0 / 1.5	23 M	0227 / 0825 / 1506 / 2055	4.0 / 1.3 / 3.9 / 1.7
9 M	0156 / 0745 / 1423 / 2005	4.0 / 1.4 / 3.8 / 1.8	24 TU ☽	0328 / 0928 / 1620 / 2213	3.8 / 1.6 / 3.7 / 2.0
10 TU ☽	0241 / 0835 / 1522 / 2109	3.8 / 1.7 / 3.7 / 2.0	25 W	0447 / 1052 / 1751 / 2348	3.6 / 1.8 / 3.7 / 2.0
11 W	0348 / 0953 / 1648 / 2251	3.6 / 1.9 / 3.6 / 2.1	26 TH	0619 / 1219 / 1911	3.5 / 1.8 / 3.8
12 TH	0522 / 1139 / 1823	3.6 / 1.8 / 3.7	27 F	0104 / 0732 / 1324 / 2007	1.9 / 3.7 / 1.6 / 4.2
13 F	0029 / 0651 / 1302 / 1936	1.9 / 3.7 / 1.5 / 4.0	28 SA	0157 / 0825 / 1411 / 2049	1.6 / 3.9 / 1.4 / 4.1
14 SA	0137 / 0758 / 1402 / 2031	1.5 / 4.0 / 1.1 / 4.3	29 SU	0238 / 0905 / 1451 / 2124	1.3 / 4.0 / 1.2 / 4.2
15 SU	0231 / 0850 / 1453 / 2118	1.0 / 4.3 / 0.7 / 4.6	30 M	0314 / 0939 / 1527 / 2155	1.1 / 4.1 / 1.0 / 4.3

Chart Datum: 2·74 metres below Ordnance Datum (Newlyn)

TIDES

TIME ZONE (UT)
For Summer Time add ONE hour in **non-shaded areas**

ENGLAND – SOUTHAMPTON

LAT 50°54'N   LONG 1°24'W

TIMES AND HEIGHTS OF HIGH AND LOW WATERS

Dates in amber are **SPRINGS**
Dates in yellow are **NEAPS**

2007

MAY

Day	Readings (Time, m)
1 TU	0349 0.9 / 1010 4.2 / 1602 0.9 / 2224 4.3
2 W ○	0422 0.8 / 1040 4.2 / 1635 0.8 / 2252 4.3
3 TH	0453 0.8 / 1110 4.2 / 1707 0.9 / 2322 4.3
4 F	0523 0.8 / 1141 4.2 / 1736 1.0 / 2354 4.3
5 SA	0551 0.9 / 1214 4.2 / 1805 1.1
6 SU	0027 4.2 / 0620 1.0 / 1251 4.2 / 1835 1.3
7 M	0103 4.1 / 0654 1.2 / 1330 4.1 / 1913 1.5
8 TU	0144 4.0 / 0736 1.3 / 1417 4.0 / 2001 1.7
9 W	0233 3.9 / 0829 1.5 / 1517 3.8 / 2106 1.9
10 TH ☽	0337 3.8 / 0940 1.6 / 1631 3.8 / 2228 1.9
11 F	0455 3.7 / 1103 1.6 / 1749 3.9 / 2349 1.7
12 SA	0614 3.8 / 1219 1.4 / 1859 4.1
13 SU	0057 1.4 / 0721 4.0 / 1323 1.1 / 1956 4.3
14 M	0155 1.1 / 0817 4.2 / 1418 1.1 / 2047 4.5
15 TU	0248 0.8 / 0908 4.4 / 1509 0.6 / 2134 4.7
16 W	0337 0.5 / 0956 4.5 / 1558 0.5 / 2220 4.7
17 TH	0425 0.4 / 1043 4.6 / 1645 0.6 / 2305 4.7
18 F	0511 0.4 / 1130 4.6 / 1731 0.6 / 2351 4.6
19 SA	0556 0.5 / 1218 4.5 / 1816 0.8
20 SU	0037 4.5 / 0640 0.7 / 1308 4.3 / 1902 1.0
21 M	0125 4.3 / 0725 0.9 / 1400 4.2 / 1950 1.3
22 TU	0216 4.1 / 0813 1.2 / 1455 4.0 / 2043 1.6
23 W ☽	0310 3.8 / 0907 1.5 / 1556 3.9 / 2146 1.8
24 TH	0412 3.7 / 1010 1.7 / 1703 3.8 / 2256 1.9
25 F	0522 3.6 / 1118 1.7 / 1811 3.8
26 SA	0004 1.9 / 0631 3.6 / 1222 1.7 / 1910 3.9
27 SU	0102 1.7 / 0731 3.7 / 1316 1.6 / 1959 4.0
28 M	0150 1.5 / 0820 3.8 / 1403 1.6 / 2041 4.1
29 TU	0232 1.4 / 0902 3.9 / 1446 1.3 / 2118 4.2
30 W	0311 1.2 / 0939 4.0 / 1526 1.2 / 2152 4.2
31 TH	0349 1.1 / 1014 4.1 / 1604 1.1 / 2226 4.3

JUNE

Day	Readings (Time, m)
1 F ○	0425 1.0 / 1048 4.2 / 1641 1.1 / 2300 4.3
2 SA	0500 0.9 / 1124 4.2 / 1717 1.1 / 2336 4.3
3 SU	0535 0.9 / 1201 4.2 / 1753 1.2
4 M	0014 4.3 / 0611 1.0 / 1241 4.2 / 1830 1.3
5 TU	0055 4.2 / 0650 1.1 / 1324 4.2 / 1912 1.4
6 W	0138 4.1 / 0734 1.2 / 1412 4.1 / 2001 1.5
7 TH	0227 4.0 / 0825 1.3 / 1506 4.1 / 2057 1.6
8 F	0323 4.0 / 0923 1.3 / 1607 4.0 / 2201 1.6
9 SA	0427 3.9 / 1029 1.4 / 1713 4.1 / 2310 1.5
10 SU	0536 3.9 / 1137 1.3 / 1820 4.1
11 M	0017 1.4 / 0644 4.0 / 1244 1.2 / 1922 4.3
12 TU	0121 1.2 / 0747 4.1 / 1346 1.1 / 2019 4.4
13 W	0220 1.0 / 0845 4.2 / 1444 1.0 / 2112 4.5
14 TH	0316 0.8 / 0940 4.3 / 1538 0.9 / 2203 4.5
15 F ●	0408 0.7 / 1032 4.4 / 1630 0.9 / 2253 4.5
16 SA	0458 0.6 / 1123 4.4 / 1720 0.9 / 2341 4.5
17 SU	0546 0.6 / 1211 4.4 / 1808 0.9
18 M	0027 4.4 / 0630 0.7 / 1259 4.4 / 1853 1.1
19 TU	0113 4.3 / 0713 0.8 / 1346 4.3 / 1938 1.2
20 W	0158 4.1 / 0755 1.0 / 1432 4.2 / 2022 1.4
21 TH	0243 4.0 / 0837 1.3 / 1518 4.0 / 2108 1.6
22 F ☽	0329 3.8 / 0921 1.5 / 1607 3.9 / 2158 1.7
23 SA	0420 3.7 / 1012 1.7 / 1700 3.8 / 2255 1.8
24 SU	0519 3.6 / 1111 1.8 / 1759 3.8 / 2357 1.9
25 M	0625 3.6 / 1214 1.9 / 1859 3.8
26 TU	0056 1.8 / 0730 3.6 / 1315 1.8 / 1954 3.9
27 W	0151 1.2 / 0826 3.8 / 1409 1.7 / 2043 4.0
28 TH	0239 1.5 / 0913 3.9 / 1457 1.5 / 2126 4.1
29 F	0323 1.3 / 0955 4.1 / 1541 1.4 / 2206 4.2
30 SA	0404 1.1 / 1034 4.2 / 1624 1.3 / 2245 4.3

JULY

Day	Readings (Time, m)
1 SU	0445 1.0 / 1112 4.3 / 1705 1.2 / 2324 4.3
2 M	0525 0.9 / 1151 4.3 / 1746 1.1
3 TU	0004 4.4 / 0605 0.8 / 1232 4.4 / 1826 1.1
4 W	0045 4.3 / 0645 0.8 / 1314 4.4 / 1908 1.1
5 TH	0128 4.3 / 0727 0.9 / 1358 4.3 / 1952 1.1
6 F	0213 4.3 / 0812 0.9 / 1446 4.3 / 2039 1.2
7 SA	0302 4.2 / 0900 1.1 / 1538 4.2 / 2132 1.3
8 SU	0357 4.1 / 0955 1.3 / 1637 4.1 / 2233 1.5
9 M	0500 4.0 / 1059 1.4 / 1742 4.1 / 2342 1.5
10 TU	0611 3.9 / 1210 1.5 / 1852 4.1
11 W	0055 1.5 / 0725 3.9 / 1324 1.5 / 2000 4.1
12 TH	0205 1.3 / 0835 4.0 / 1431 1.4 / 2103 4.2
13 F	0307 1.1 / 0936 4.2 / 1532 1.2 / 2158 4.3
14 SA	0402 0.9 / 1030 4.3 / 1625 1.1 / 2248 4.4
15 SU	0452 0.8 / 1118 4.4 / 1714 1.0 / 2332 4.4
16 M	0537 0.7 / 1202 4.4 / 1759 0.9
17 TU	0014 4.4 / 0618 0.6 / 1243 4.4 / 1839 0.9
18 W	0053 4.3 / 0655 0.7 / 1321 4.4 / 1916 1.0
19 TH	0131 4.2 / 0729 0.9 / 1358 4.3 / 1951 1.1
20 F	0207 4.1 / 0801 1.1 / 1434 4.1 / 2025 1.3
21 SA	0245 3.9 / 0833 1.3 / 1512 4.0 / 2101 1.6
22 SU	0325 3.8 / 0910 1.6 / 1554 3.9 / 2144 1.8
23 M	0413 3.6 / 0958 1.9 / 1646 3.7 / 2244 2.0
24 TU	0516 3.5 / 1105 2.1 / 1752 3.7 / 2359 2.0
25 W	0636 3.5 / 1227 2.1 / 1908 3.7
26 TH	0113 1.9 / 0753 3.6 / 1339 2.0 / 2013 3.9
27 F	0213 1.7 / 0852 3.8 / 1436 1.8 / 2106 4.0
28 SA	0303 1.4 / 0938 4.0 / 1525 1.5 / 2150 4.2
29 SU	0349 1.1 / 1019 4.2 / 1610 1.2 / 2230 4.3
30 M	0431 0.9 / 1057 4.4 / 1652 1.0 / 2309 4.4
31 TU	0513 0.7 / 1135 4.5 / 1734 0.9 / 2348 4.5

AUGUST

Day	Readings (Time, m)
1 W	0553 0.5 / 1214 4.5 / 1814 0.8
2 TH	0027 4.5 / 0633 0.5 / 1255 4.6 / 1853 0.7
3 F	0108 4.5 / 0712 0.5 / 1336 4.5 / 1934 0.8
4 SA	0151 4.4 / 0752 0.7 / 1420 4.5 / 2016 1.0
5 SU ◐	0236 4.3 / 0835 0.9 / 1508 4.3 / 2103 1.2
6 M	0327 4.1 / 0925 1.3 / 1603 4.1 / 2201 1.5
7 TU	0429 3.9 / 1028 1.6 / 1711 3.9 / 2316 1.7
8 W	0549 3.8 / 1151 1.8 / 1835 3.9
9 TH	0045 1.8 / 0721 3.8 / 1320 1.8 / 1958 4.0
10 F	0205 1.6 / 0840 4.0 / 1434 1.6 / 2104 4.1
11 SA	0308 1.3 / 0939 4.2 / 1532 1.4 / 2156 4.3
12 SU ●	0358 1.0 / 1027 4.3 / 1620 1.1 / 2240 4.4
13 M	0441 0.8 / 1107 4.4 / 1702 0.9 / 2318 4.4
14 TU	0521 0.6 / 1143 4.5 / 1740 0.8 / 2352 4.4
15 W	0557 0.6 / 1216 4.5 / 1815 0.8
16 TH	0025 4.4 / 0629 0.6 / 1248 4.4 / 1847 1.0
17 F	0057 4.3 / 0657 0.8 / 1319 4.3 / 1915 1.0
18 SA	0129 4.2 / 0723 1.0 / 1350 4.2 / 1941 1.2
19 SU	0201 4.1 / 0748 1.3 / 1422 4.1 / 2009 1.5
20 M ◐	0236 3.9 / 0818 1.6 / 1458 3.9 / 2043 1.9
21 TU	0317 3.9 / 0857 1.9 / 1543 3.7 / 2133 2.0
22 W	0414 3.5 / 0958 2.2 / 1649 3.6 / 2257 2.2
23 TH	0543 3.5 / 1142 2.3 / 1821 3.6
24 F	0039 2.1 / 0720 3.6 / 1316 2.2 / 1944 3.8
25 SA	0151 1.8 / 0828 3.8 / 1418 1.9 / 2043 4.0
26 SU	0244 1.5 / 0916 4.1 / 1507 1.5 / 2128 4.2
27 M	0329 1.1 / 0956 4.3 / 1551 1.1 / 2208 4.4
28 TU ○	0412 0.7 / 1034 4.5 / 1633 0.8 / 2246 4.6
29 W	0453 0.4 / 1111 4.7 / 1714 0.6 / 2325 4.7
30 TH	0534 0.3 / 1150 4.7 / 1753 0.5
31 F	0004 4.7 / 0612 0.3 / 1230 4.8 / 1832 0.5

Chart Datum: 2·74 metres below Ordnance Datum (Newlyn)

TIME ZONE (UT)
For Summer Time add ONE hour in **non-shaded areas**

Dates in amber are **SPRINGS**
Dates in yellow are **NEAPS**

2007

SEPTEMBER

Date	Time m	Time m	Time m	Time m
1 SA	0045 4.7	0651 0.4	1311 4.7	1911 0.6
2 SU	0126 4.6	0729 0.6	1354 4.5	1952 0.9
3 M	0211 4.4	0811 1.0	1441 4.3	2038 1.2
4 TU	0303 4.1	0900 1.4	1537 4.0	◑ 2137 1.6
5 W	0410 3.8	1008 1.8	1653 3.8	2304 1.9
6 TH	0546 3.7	1148 2.1	1834 3.8	
7 F	0047 1.9	0729 3.8	1326 2.0	2000 3.9
8 SA	0206 1.7	0840 4.0	1434 1.7	2100 4.2
9 SU	0300 1.3	0930 4.3	1522 1.3	2145 4.4
10 M	0342 1.0	1010 4.4	1602 1.1	2222 4.4
11 TU	0419 0.8	1045 4.5	1638 0.8	● 2254 4.5
12 W	0454 0.6	1115 4.5	1712 0.7	2324 4.5
13 TH	0527 0.6	1144 4.5	1744 0.7	2352 4.4
14 F	0557 0.6	1211 4.4	1813 0.8	
15 SA	0021 4.4	0623 0.8	1240 4.4	1837 1.0
16 SU	0052 4.3	0646 1.0	1309 4.3	1900 1.2
17 M	0123 4.1	0709 1.3	1340 4.1	1926 1.4
18 TU	0155 4.0	0737 1.6	1413 4.0	1958 1.7
19 W	0234 3.8	0814 1.9	1455 3.8	◑ 2044 2.0
20 TH	0329 3.6	0912 2.3	1601 3.6	2203 2.2
21 F	0459 3.5	1101 2.4	1738 3.6	
22 SA	0001 2.2	0642 3.6	1247 2.2	1909 3.7
23 SU	0121 1.9	0754 3.9	1350 1.8	2012 4.0
24 M	0215 1.4	0844 4.2	1440 1.4	2059 4.3
25 TU	0301 1.0	0926 4.5	1524 1.0	2140 4.6
26 W	0345 0.6	1005 4.7	1606 0.7	○ 2219 4.7
27 TH	0427 0.3	1044 4.8	1648 0.4	2259 4.8
28 F	0508 0.2	1123 4.9	1729 0.3	2340 4.9
29 SA	0548 0.2	1204 4.9	1809 0.4	
30 SU	0021 4.8	0627 0.4	1246 4.8	1849 0.6

OCTOBER

Date	Time m	Time m	Time m	Time m
1 M	0105 4.6	0708 0.7	1331 4.6	1931 0.9
2 TU	0153 4.4	0751 1.2	1420 4.3	2020 1.3
3 W	0249 4.1	0845 1.6	1520 4.0	◑ 2123 1.7
4 TH	0404 3.8	1001 2.0	1644 3.8	2256 2.0
5 F	0547 3.7	1147 2.1	1827 3.8	
6 SA	0036 1.9	0719 3.9	1316 2.0	1945 4.0
7 SU	0146 1.7	0821 4.2	1413 1.7	2039 4.2
8 M	0234 1.4	0906 4.4	1456 1.4	2120 4.3
9 TU	0312 1.1	0942 4.5	1532 1.1	2154 4.4
10 W	0347 0.9	1014 4.5	1606 0.9	2224 4.4
11 TH	0420 0.8	1042 4.5	1639 0.8	● 2252 4.4
12 F	0452 0.7	1109 4.5	1710 0.8	2320 4.4
13 SA	0522 0.8	1136 4.4	1738 0.9	2350 4.4
14 SU	0549 1.0	1205 4.4	1804 1.0	
15 M	0020 4.3	0614 1.2	1236 4.3	1828 1.2
16 TU	0053 4.2	0639 1.4	1308 4.2	1856 1.4
17 W	0128 4.1	0710 1.7	1344 4.0	1930 1.7
18 TH	0209 3.9	0750 1.9	1428 3.9	2018 1.9
19 F	0306 3.8	0850 2.2	1532 3.7	◑ 2131 2.1
20 SA	0428 3.7	1027 2.3	1700 3.7	2315 2.1
21 SU	0600 3.8	1204 2.1	1827 3.8	
22 M	0037 1.8	0712 4.0	1312 1.8	1933 4.1
23 TU	0137 1.4	0806 4.3	1404 1.4	2024 4.3
24 W	0226 1.0	0852 4.6	1451 1.0	2109 4.6
25 TH	0312 0.7	0935 4.8	1536 0.7	2152 4.8
26 F	0357 0.4	1016 4.9	1621 0.5	○ 2235 4.9
27 SA	0440 0.4	1059 4.9	1704 0.4	2318 4.9
28 SU	0523 0.4	1142 4.9	1747 0.5	
29 M	0003 4.8	0606 0.6	1227 4.7	1830 0.7
30 TU	0051 4.6	0650 0.9	1314 4.5	1916 1.0
31 W	0143 4.4	0738 1.3	1407 4.3	2007 1.3

NOVEMBER

Date	Time m	Time m	Time m	Time m
1 TH	0243 4.1	0835 1.7	1508 4.0	◑ 2110 1.7
2 F	0357 3.9	0950 2.0	1625 3.8	2231 1.9
3 SA	0523 3.9	1119 2.1	1752 3.8	2356 1.9
4 SU	0643 4.0	1237 2.0	1907 3.9	
5 M	0102 1.7	0742 4.1	1334 1.7	2002 4.1
6 TU	0152 1.5	0828 4.3	1418 1.5	2045 4.2
7 W	0232 1.3	0906 4.4	1456 1.3	2121 4.3
8 TH	0309 1.2	0939 4.4	1531 1.1	2153 4.3
9 F	0344 1.1	1009 4.5	● 1605 1.0	2224 4.4
10 SA	0418 1.0	1038 4.5	1638 1.0	2254 4.4
11 SU	0451 1.0	1108 4.5	1709 1.0	2326 4.4
12 M	0522 1.1	1140 4.4	1739 1.1	
13 TU	0000 4.3	0551 1.3	1214 4.4	1807 1.2
14 W	0036 4.3	0622 1.4	1249 4.3	1839 1.4
15 TH	0114 4.2	0657 1.6	1328 4.1	1918 1.5
16 F	0159 4.1	0741 1.8	1414 4.0	2006 1.7
17 SA	0253 4.0	0838 2.0	1512 3.9	2109 1.8
18 SU	0400 3.9	0953 2.1	1623 3.8	2228 1.8
19 M	0516 4.0	1114 2.0	1739 3.9	2345 1.7
20 TU	0626 4.1	1225 1.7	1849 4.1	
21 W	0051 1.4	0726 4.3	1325 1.4	1948 4.3
22 TH	0148 1.1	0818 4.6	1418 1.1	2040 4.5
23 F	0240 0.9	0907 4.7	1508 0.8	2129 4.6
24 SA	0329 0.7	0953 4.8	1557 0.6	○ 2216 4.7
25 SU	0417 0.7	1039 4.8	1645 0.6	2304 4.7
26 M	0504 0.7	1126 4.8	1732 0.6	2353 4.7
27 TU	0552 0.8	1214 4.7	1819 0.7	
28 W	0043 4.6	0639 1.0	1303 4.5	1906 0.9
29 TH	0136 4.4	0729 1.3	1354 4.3	1955 1.2
30 F	0231 4.2	0822 1.6	1449 4.1	2048 1.4

DECEMBER

Date	Time m	Time m	Time m	Time m
1 SA	0331 4.1	0921 1.8	1548 3.9	◑ 2147 1.7
2 SU	0435 4.0	1028 1.9	1654 3.8	2254 1.8
3 M	0543 4.0	1137 1.9	1804 3.8	2359 1.8
4 TU	0646 4.0	1238 1.9	1908 3.8	
5 W	0057 1.8	0739 4.1	1331 1.7	2002 3.9
6 TH	0147 1.6	0825 4.2	1417 1.5	2047 4.1
7 F	0231 1.5	0905 4.3	1458 1.4	2126 4.2
8 SA	0311 1.4	0941 4.4	1537 1.2	2202 4.3
9 SU	0350 1.3	1015 4.4	1614 1.1	2237 4.3
10 M	0428 1.2	1049 4.4	1649 1.1	2312 4.4
11 TU	0504 1.2	1124 4.4	1724 1.1	2347 4.4
12 W	0539 1.3	1200 4.4	1758 1.1	
13 TH	0025 4.3	0613 1.3	1238 4.3	1832 1.2
14 F	0105 4.3	0651 1.4	1318 4.3	1911 1.2
15 SA	0148 4.2	0733 1.5	1401 4.2	1955 1.3
16 SU	0235 4.2	0822 1.6		◑ 2046 1.4
17 M	0329 4.1	0919 1.7	1546 4.0	2146 1.5
18 TU	0431 4.1	1025 1.7	1652 4.0	2254 1.6
19 W	0539 4.1	1136 1.7	1803 4.0	
20 TH	0005 1.5	0645 4.2	1246 1.5	1912 4.1
21 F	0112 1.4	0747 4.4	1350 1.3	2015 4.2
22 SA	0213 1.2	0845 4.5	1449 1.1	2113 4.4
23 SU	0310 1.1	0938 4.6	1544 0.9	2207 4.5
24 M	0404 0.9	1029 4.7	1635 0.7	○ 2258 4.6
25 TU	0455 0.9	1118 4.7	1725 0.6	2347 4.6
26 W	0544 0.9	1205 4.6	1811 0.6	
27 TH	0035 4.6	0630 0.9	1251 4.5	1855 0.9
28 F	0122 4.5	0715 1.1	1336 4.4	1936 0.9
29 SA	0207 4.4	0759 1.2	1419 4.2	2017 1.1
30 SU	0252 4.2	0843 1.4	1504 4.0	2059 1.4
31 M	0340 4.1	0930 1.6	1552 3.9	◑ 2146 1.6

TIDES

Chart Datum: 2·74 metres below Ordnance Datum (Newlyn)

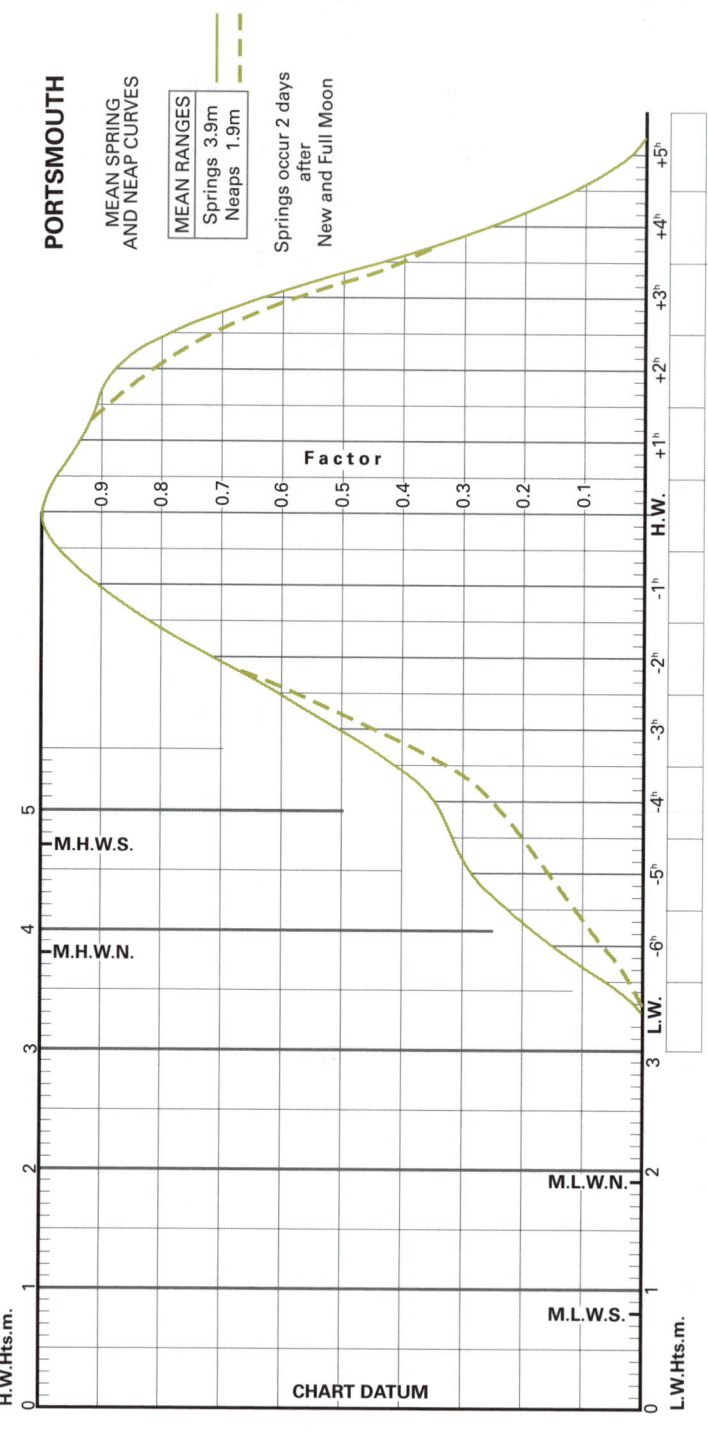

PORTSMOUTH

MEAN SPRING
AND NEAP CURVES

MEAN RANGES
Springs 3.9m
Neaps 1.9m

Springs occur 2 days
after
New and Full Moon

242

ENGLAND – PORTSMOUTH

LAT 50°48'N   LONG 1°07'W

TIMES AND HEIGHTS OF HIGH AND LOW WATERS

Dates in amber are **SPRINGS**
Dates in yellow are **NEAPS**

2007

JANUARY

#	Time	m	#	Time	m
1 M	0214 / 0907 / 1453 / 2140	1.5 / 4.5 / 1.3 / 4.3	16 TU	0208 / 0855 / 1442 / 2130	1.9 / 4.1 / 1.6 / 4.1
2 TU	0312 / 1002 / 1546 / 2235	1.4 / 4.6 / 1.2 / 4.5	17 W	0301 / 0945 / 1529 / 2219	1.6 / 4.3 / 1.4 / 4.3
3 W	0404 / 1051 / 1634 / 2325 ○	1.3 / 4.6 / 1.0 / 4.6	18 TH	0347 / 1030 / 1613 / 2303	1.4 / 4.5 / 1.1 / 4.5
4 TH	0450 / 1136 / 1719	1.2 / 4.6 / 1.0	19 F	0431 / 1113 / 1657 / 2347 ●	1.2 / 4.6 / 0.9 / 4.6
5 F	0010 / 0533 / 1218 / 1759	4.6 / 1.2 / 4.6 / 0.9	20 SA	0514 / 1156 / 1740	1.0 / 4.6 / 0.7
6 SA	0051 / 0613 / 1257 / 1837	4.6 / 1.2 / 4.5 / 1.0	21 SU	0030 / 0557 / 1240 / 1822	4.7 / 0.9 / 4.6 / 0.6
7 SU	0130 / 0652 / 1334 / 1913	4.5 / 1.3 / 4.4 / 1.1	22 M	0114 / 0640 / 1324 / 1905	4.7 / 0.8 / 4.6 / 0.6
8 M	0207 / 0729 / 1411 / 1948	4.4 / 1.4 / 4.2 / 1.2	23 TU	0158 / 0724 / 1408 / 1948	4.7 / 0.9 / 4.6 / 0.7
9 TU	0243 / 0805 / 1448 / 2022	4.3 / 1.5 / 4.1 / 1.4	24 W	0242 / 0809 / 1454 / 2032	4.7 / 0.9 / 4.5 / 0.8
10 W	0321 / 0843 / 1526 / 2058	4.2 / 1.7 / 4.0 / 1.5	25 TH	0328 / 0857 / 1541 / 2120 ◑	4.6 / 1.1 / 4.3 / 1.1
11 TH	0401 / 0924 / 1608 / 2141 ◑	4.1 / 1.8 / 3.8 / 1.7	26 F	0417 / 0951 / 1634 / 2215	4.4 / 1.4 / 4.1 / 1.4
12 F	0446 / 1015 / 1657 / 2235	4.0 / 2.0 / 3.7 / 1.9	27 SA	0514 / 1056 / 1739 / 2325	4.2 / 1.6 / 3.9 / 1.7
13 SA	0541 / 1122 / 1802 / 2346	3.9 / 2.1 / 3.6 / 2.1	28 SU	0624 / 1218 / 1903	4.0 / 1.8 / 3.8
14 SU	0648 / 1240 / 1921	3.9 / 2.1 / 3.7	29 M	0049 / 0745 / 1340 / 2031	1.8 / 4.0 / 1.7 / 3.9
15 M	0104 / 0756 / 1348 / 2032	2.0 / 4.0 / 1.9 / 3.9	30 TU	0208 / 0858 / 1447 / 2140	1.7 / 4.2 / 1.5 / 4.1
			31 W	0310 / 0957 / 1541 / 2234	1.6 / 4.3 / 1.3 / 4.4

FEBRUARY

#	Time	m	#	Time	m
1 TH	0400 / 1046 / 1626 / 2319	1.3 / 4.4 / 1.1 / 4.5	16 F	0334 / 1012 / 1558 / 2247	1.3 / 4.4 / 1.0 / 4.5
2 F	0443 / 1128 / 1707 / 2359 ○	1.2 / 4.5 / 0.9 / 4.4	17 SA	0418 / 1057 / 1642 / 2330 ●	1.0 / 4.5 / 0.7 / 4.7
3 SA	0522 / 1205 / 1744	1.1 / 4.5 / 0.8	18 SU	0500 / 1141 / 1724	0.7 / 4.7 / 0.5
4 SU	0034 / 0557 / 1240 / 1817	4.6 / 1.0 / 4.5 / 0.8	19 M	0013 / 0542 / 1226 / 1805	4.8 / 0.6 / 4.7 / 0.4
5 M	0107 / 0630 / 1313 / 1848	4.5 / 1.0 / 4.4 / 0.9	20 TU	0055 / 0623 / 1309 / 1846	4.9 / 0.5 / 4.8 / 0.4
6 TU	0137 / 0701 / 1345 / 1917	4.5 / 1.1 / 4.3 / 1.0	21 W	0137 / 0705 / 1352 / 1927	4.9 / 0.5 / 4.7 / 0.5
7 W	0208 / 0729 / 1417 / 1944	4.4 / 1.2 / 4.2 / 1.1	22 TH	0218 / 0746 / 1435 / 2008	4.8 / 0.7 / 4.6 / 0.7
8 TH	0239 / 0757 / 1449 / 2011	4.3 / 1.4 / 4.1 / 1.3	23 F	0259 / 0830 / 1520 / 2052	4.6 / 0.9 / 4.4 / 1.1
9 F	0310 / 0828 / 1522 / 2045	4.2 / 1.5 / 4.0 / 1.6	24 SA	0344 / 0920 / 1611 / 2147 ◑	4.3 / 1.3 / 4.1 / 1.5
10 SA	0346 / 0907 / 1603 / 2128 ◑	4.0 / 1.8 / 3.8 / 1.8	25 SU	0438 / 1026 / 1716 / 2303	4.0 / 1.7 / 3.8 / 1.9
11 SU	0433 / 1001 / 1702 / 2235	3.8 / 2.0 / 3.6 / 2.1	26 M	0552 / 1158 / 1853	3.8 / 1.9 / 3.7
12 M	0543 / 1129 / 1830	3.7 / 2.1 / 3.6	27 TU	0041 / 0735 / 1331 / 2031	2.0 / 3.7 / 1.8 / 3.9
13 TU	0022 / 0710 / 1317 / 2002	2.2 / 3.7 / 2.0 / 3.7	28 W	0208 / 0855 / 1440 / 2135	1.9 / 3.9 / 1.6 / 4.1
14 W	0150 / 0826 / 1423 / 2110	2.0 / 3.9 / 1.7 / 4.0			
15 TH	0247 / 0924 / 1513 / 2201	1.7 / 4.2 / 1.3 / 4.3			

MARCH

#	Time	m	#	Time	m
1 TH	0307 / 0951 / 1529 / 2223	1.6 / 4.2 / 1.3 / 4.4	16 F	0228 / 0859 / 1450 / 2137	1.6 / 4.1 / 1.2 / 4.3
2 F	0351 / 1035 / 1610 / 2303	1.3 / 4.3 / 1.0 / 4.5	17 SA	0315 / 0949 / 1535 / 2222	1.2 / 4.3 / 0.8 / 4.6
3 SA	0428 / 1112 / 1646 / 2338 ○	1.1 / 4.4 / 0.9 / 4.6	18 SU	0357 / 1035 / 1618 / 2306	0.8 / 4.6 / 0.5 / 4.8
4 SU	0502 / 1146 / 1720	0.9 / 4.4 / 0.8	19 M	0439 / 1120 / 1701 / 2348 ●	0.5 / 4.7 / 0.3 / 4.9
5 M	0009 / 0534 / 1218 / 1751	4.6 / 0.8 / 4.4 / 0.7	20 TU	0521 / 1205 / 1743	0.3 / 4.8 / 0.3
6 TU	0038 / 0604 / 1247 / 1820	4.5 / 0.8 / 4.4 / 0.8	21 W	0031 / 0602 / 1250 / 1823	5.0 / 0.3 / 4.9 / 0.3
7 W	0105 / 0631 / 1317 / 1845	4.5 / 0.9 / 4.4 / 0.9	22 TH	0112 / 0643 / 1333 / 1904	4.9 / 0.4 / 4.8 / 0.5
8 TH	0133 / 0655 / 1348 / 1909	4.5 / 1.0 / 4.3 / 1.0	23 F	0153 / 0724 / 1417 / 1945	4.8 / 0.6 / 4.6 / 0.8
9 F	0201 / 0719 / 1418 / 1935	4.4 / 1.1 / 4.2 / 1.2	24 SA	0234 / 0807 / 1503 / 2030	4.6 / 0.9 / 4.4 / 1.2
10 SA	0229 / 0748 / 1449 / 2006	4.2 / 1.3 / 4.1 / 1.5	25 SU	0318 / 0857 / 1556 / 2127 ◑	4.3 / 1.3 / 4.1 / 1.6
11 SU	0300 / 0824 / 1528 / 2048	4.1 / 1.6 / 3.9 / 1.8	26 M	0412 / 1005 / 1705 / 2249	3.9 / 1.7 / 3.8 / 2.0
12 M	0343 / 0914 / 1626 / 2151 ◑	3.8 / 1.9 / 3.7 / 2.1	27 TU	0531 / 1139 / 1848	3.6 / 1.9 / 3.7
13 TU	0452 / 1037 / 1755 / 2351	3.6 / 2.1 / 3.6 / 2.3	28 W	0029 / 0723 / 1313 / 2016	2.1 / 3.6 / 1.8 / 3.9
14 W	0627 / 1246 / 1933	3.6 / 2.0 / 3.7	29 TH	0155 / 0839 / 1419 / 2113	1.9 / 3.9 / 1.6 / 4.2
15 TH	0130 / 0755 / 1359 / 2044	2.0 / 3.8 / 1.6 / 4.0	30 F	0249 / 0930 / 1504 / 2158	1.5 / 4.1 / 1.3 / 4.4
			31 SA	0328 / 1011 / 1542 / 2235	1.3 / 4.2 / 1.1 / 4.5

APRIL

#	Time	m	#	Time	m
1 SU	0402 / 1047 / 1616 / 2308	1.0 / 4.3 / 0.9 / 4.5	16 M	0329 / 1007 / 1549 / 2237	0.8 / 4.6 / 0.5 / 4.8
2 M	0435 / 1119 / 1649 / 2337	0.9 / 4.4 / 0.8 / 4.5	17 TU	0413 / 1055 / 1633 / 2322 ●	0.5 / 4.7 / 0.4 / 4.9
3 TU	0506 / 1149 / 1721	0.8 / 4.4 / 0.8	18 W	0457 / 1142 / 1717	0.4 / 4.8 / 0.4
4 W	0004 / 0535 / 1219 / 1749	4.5 / 0.8 / 4.4 / 0.9	19 TH	0006 / 0539 / 1229 / 1800	5.0 / 0.3 / 4.9 / 0.5
5 TH	0033 / 0601 / 1250 / 1815	4.5 / 0.9 / 4.4 / 1.0	20 F	0049 / 0622 / 1315 / 1843	4.9 / 0.4 / 4.8 / 0.7
6 F	0101 / 0624 / 1321 / 1840	4.5 / 1.0 / 4.4 / 1.1	21 SA	0131 / 0705 / 1402 / 1927	4.8 / 0.6 / 4.6 / 0.9
7 SA	0129 / 0650 / 1353 / 1907	4.4 / 1.1 / 4.3 / 1.3	22 SU	0214 / 0750 / 1450 / 2015	4.5 / 1.0 / 4.4 / 1.3
8 SU	0158 / 0720 / 1427 / 1941	4.3 / 1.3 / 4.2 / 1.5	23 M	0301 / 0842 / 1546 / 2114	4.2 / 1.3 / 4.1 / 1.7
9 M	0231 / 0759 / 1509 / 2026	4.1 / 1.5 / 4.0 / 1.8	24 TU	0356 / 0947 / 1656 / 2229 ◑	3.9 / 1.6 / 3.9 / 2.1
10 TU	0315 / 0851 / 1609 / 2132	3.9 / 1.8 / 3.8 / 2.1	25 W	0513 / 1110 / 1823 / 2357	3.7 / 1.8 / 3.9 / 2.0
11 W	0423 / 1013 / 1730 / 2318	3.7 / 2.0 / 3.7 / 2.2	26 TH	0650 / 1234 / 1939	3.6 / 1.8 / 4.0
12 TH	0551 / 1205 / 1859	3.6 / 1.9 / 3.8	27 F	0116 / 0802 / 1338 / 2035	1.9 / 3.8 / 1.6 / 4.2
13 F	0054 / 0717 / 1323 / 2009	1.9 / 3.8 / 1.5 / 4.1	28 SA	0211 / 0854 / 1425 / 2119	1.6 / 4.0 / 1.4 / 4.3
14 SA	0156 / 0824 / 1417 / 2103	1.5 / 4.1 / 1.1 / 4.4	29 SU	0252 / 0936 / 1503 / 2157	1.2 / 4.1 / 1.2 / 4.4
15 SU	0245 / 0918 / 1504 / 2151	1.1 / 4.4 / 0.8 / 4.7	30 M	0327 / 1012 / 1539 / 2230	1.2 / 4.2 / 1.1 / 4.4

Chart Datum: 2·73 metres below Ordnance Datum (Newlyn)

TIDES

TIME ZONE (UT)
For Summer Time add ONE hour in **non-shaded areas**

ENGLAND – PORTSMOUTH
LAT 50°48′N   LONG 1°07′W
TIMES AND HEIGHTS OF HIGH AND LOW WATERS

Dates in amber are **SPRINGS**
Dates in yellow are **NEAPS**

2007

MAY

Day	Time m	Time m	Time m	Time m		Day	Time m	Time m	Time m	Time m
1 TU	0401 1.0	1045 4.3	1614 1.0	2301 4.5		16 W	0347 0.7	1032 4.7	1607 0.6	2258 4.9
2 W	0434 1.0	1118 4.3	1647 1.0	2331 4.5		17 TH	0435 0.6	1123 4.8	1654 0.6	2344 4.9
3 TH	0505 1.0	1151 4.4	1719 1.0			18 F	0522 0.5	1212 4.8	1741 0.7	
4 F	0002 4.5	0533 1.0	1225 4.4	1748 1.1		19 SA	0030 4.8	0607 0.6	1301 4.7	1827 0.9
5 SA	0034 4.5	0600 1.0	1259 4.4	1817 1.2		20 SU	0115 4.7	0653 0.8	1350 4.6	1913 1.1
6 SU	0105 4.4	0630 1.1	1334 4.3	1850 1.4		21 M	0200 4.5	0739 1.0	1440 4.4	2002 1.3
7 M	0138 4.3	0706 1.2	1413 4.2	1930 1.5		22 TU	0248 4.2	0828 1.3	1534 4.2	2056 1.6
8 TU	0216 4.1	0749 1.4	1459 4.1	2019 1.7		23 W	0340 4.0	0923 1.5	1633 4.1	2157 1.8
9 W	0304 4.0	0845 1.6	1558 4.0	2124 1.9		24 TH	0441 3.8	1026 1.7	1737 4.0	2305 1.9
10 TH	0407 3.9	0957 1.7	1707 3.9	2244 1.9		25 F	0551 3.7	1133 1.7	1841 4.0	
11 F	0521 3.8	1119 1.6	1822 4.0			26 SA	0015 1.9	0700 3.7	1237 1.7	1938 4.0
12 SA	0005 1.7	0637 3.9	1234 1.4	1929 4.2		27 SU	0116 1.8	0758 3.8	1330 1.6	2027 4.1
13 SU	0112 1.4	0746 4.1	1336 1.2	2027 4.5		28 M	0204 1.6	0847 3.9	1416 1.5	2110 4.2
14 M	0208 1.1	0845 4.4	1429 0.9	2120 4.7		29 TU	0246 1.4	0930 4.0	1458 1.4	2148 4.3
15 TU	0259 0.9	0939 4.5	1518 0.7	2209 4.8		30 W	0324 1.3	1010 4.2	1538 1.3	2225 4.4
						31 TH	0401 1.2	1048 4.3	1616 1.2	2301 4.4

JUNE

Day	Time m	Time m	Time m	Time m		Day	Time m	Time m	Time m	Time m
1 F	0437 1.1	1126 4.4	1653 1.2	2337 4.4		16 SA	0510 0.8	1202 4.7	1729 0.9	
2 SA	0511 1.1	1203 4.4	1728 1.2			17 SU	0016 4.7	0557 0.8	1252 4.7	1815 1.0
3 SU	0012 4.4	0545 1.1	1241 4.4	1804 1.3		18 M	0102 4.6	0642 0.8	1339 4.6	1900 1.1
4 M	0048 4.4	0621 1.1	1321 4.4	1842 1.3		19 TU	0147 4.4	0725 1.0	1426 4.5	1945 1.3
5 TU	0125 4.3	0701 1.1	1403 4.4	1926 1.4		20 W	0231 4.3	0807 1.1	1511 4.4	2029 1.4
6 W	0207 4.3	0747 1.2	1451 4.3	2015 1.5		21 TH	0315 4.1	0850 1.3	1555 4.2	2116 1.6
7 TH	0256 4.2	0839 1.3	1544 4.2	2110 1.5		22 F	0359 3.9	0936 1.5	1640 4.1	2207 1.8
8 F	0351 4.1	0937 1.3	1642 4.2	2213 1.6		23 SA	0448 3.8	1027 1.7	1729 4.0	2304 1.9
9 SA	0453 4.0	1041 1.4	1745 4.2	2320 1.5		24 SU	0542 3.7	1124 1.8	1823 3.9	
10 SU	0600 4.1	1148 1.3	1850 4.3			25 M	0007 1.9	0644 3.7	1227 1.8	1921 3.9
11 M	0029 1.4	0709 4.1	1255 1.3	1953 4.4		26 TU	0109 1.8	0750 3.7	1327 1.8	2018 4.0
12 TU	0134 1.3	0816 4.3	1357 1.2	2052 4.5		27 W	0203 1.7	0849 3.9	1420 1.7	2109 4.1
13 W	0234 1.1	0918 4.4	1454 1.1	2147 4.6		28 TH	0251 1.5	0939 4.1	1508 1.6	2154 4.3
14 TH	0329 1.0	1016 4.5	1549 1.0	2239 4.7		29 F	0335 1.4	1024 4.2	1552 1.4	2236 4.4
15 F	0421 0.8	1111 4.6	1640 0.9	2329 4.7		30 SA	0416 1.2	1106 4.3	1634 1.3	2316 4.4

JULY

Day	Time m	Time m	Time m	Time m		Day	Time m	Time m	Time m	Time m
1 SU	0456 1.1	1147 4.4	1714 1.2	2355 4.4		16 M	0005 4.6	0546 0.8	1241 4.6	1802 1.0
2 M	0535 1.0	1228 4.5	1754 1.1			17 TU	0048 4.5	0626 0.8	1322 4.6	1843 1.0
3 TU	0034 4.5	0615 0.9	1310 4.5	1835 1.1		18 W	0127 4.4	0704 0.9	1401 4.5	1920 1.1
4 W	0115 4.4	0656 0.9	1353 4.5	1917 1.1		19 TH	0204 4.3	0739 1.0	1437 4.5	1956 1.2
5 TH	0158 4.4	0739 0.9	1437 4.5	2002 1.1		20 F	0240 4.2	0812 1.2	1511 4.3	2032 1.4
6 F	0244 4.4	0824 1.0	1524 4.5	2051 1.2		21 SA	0317 4.1	0847 1.4	1546 4.2	2110 1.6
7 SA	0332 4.3	0914 1.1	1613 4.4	2144 1.3		22 SU	0355 3.9	0925 1.6	1625 4.1	2154 1.8
8 SU	0426 4.2	1009 1.2	1709 4.3	2245 1.4		23 M	0440 3.8	1013 1.8	1713 3.9	2253 2.0
9 M	0527 4.1	1111 1.4	1812 4.2	2355 1.5		24 TU	0539 3.6	1120 2.0	1815 3.8	
10 TU	0640 4.0	1223 1.5	1923 4.2			25 W	0012 2.0	0655 3.6	1242 2.1	1928 3.8
11 W	0111 1.5	0757 4.1	1337 1.5	2032 4.3		26 TH	0128 1.9	0815 3.8	1352 2.0	2035 4.0
12 TH	0221 1.4	0909 4.2	1444 1.4	2134 4.4		27 F	0227 1.7	0917 4.0	1447 1.8	2129 4.2
13 F	0321 1.2	1011 4.4	1541 1.3	2229 4.5		28 SA	0316 1.4	1006 4.2	1534 1.5	2215 4.3
14 SA	0414 1.0	1106 4.5	1633 1.1	2319 4.6		29 SU	0359 1.2	1050 4.4	1618 1.3	2257 4.4
15 SU	0502 0.9	1155 4.6	1720 1.1			30 M	0441 0.9	1132 4.5	1659 1.1	2338 4.5
						31 TU	0521 0.8	1213 4.6	1740 0.9	

AUGUST

Day	Time m	Time m	Time m	Time m		Day	Time m	Time m	Time m	Time m
1 W	0019 4.6	0601 0.7	1254 4.7	1820 0.8		16 TH	0100 4.5	0635 0.8	1328 4.6	1850 0.8
2 TH	0101 4.6	0641 0.6	1335 4.7	1901 0.8		17 F	0132 4.4	0705 0.9	1357 4.5	1919 1.1
3 F	0143 4.6	0722 0.6	1416 4.7	1943 0.8		18 SA	0204 4.3	0732 1.1	1427 4.4	1948 1.3
4 SA	0226 4.5	0803 0.8	1458 4.6	2027 1.0		19 SU	0236 4.2	0800 1.3	1458 4.3	2018 1.5
5 SU	0311 4.4	0848 1.0	1543 4.5	2116 1.2		20 M	0310 4.0	0832 1.6	1532 4.1	2054 1.7
6 M	0401 4.2	0940 1.3	1635 4.3	2216 1.5		21 TU	0350 3.8	0913 1.9	1614 3.9	2145 2.0
7 TU	0501 4.0	1044 1.6	1739 4.1	2333 1.7		22 W	0446 3.7	1016 2.2	1715 3.7	2311 2.2
8 W	0621 3.8	1208 1.8	1903 4.0			23 TH	0610 3.6	1207 2.3	1842 3.7	
9 TH	0102 1.7	0755 3.9	1334 1.8	2026 4.1		24 F	0101 2.1	0747 3.6	1333 2.1	2007 3.9
10 F	0219 1.5	0913 4.1	1444 1.6	2132 4.3		25 SA	0208 1.8	0857 4.0	1431 1.8	2107 4.1
11 SA	0318 1.3	1011 4.4	1539 1.4	2224 4.4		26 SU	0257 1.4	0946 4.3	1516 1.5	2154 4.3
12 SU	0407 1.0	1100 4.6	1624 1.2	2309 4.5		27 M	0340 1.1	1029 4.5	1558 1.2	2236 4.5
13 M	0449 0.8	1143 4.6	1705 1.0	2350 4.5		28 TU	0420 0.8	1109 4.6	1638 0.9	2317 4.6
14 TU	0528 0.7	1221 4.7	1743 0.9			29 W	0500 0.6	1150 4.8	1718 0.6	2359 4.7
15 W	0026 4.5	0603 0.7	1256 4.6	1818 0.9		30 TH	0540 0.5	1230 4.8	1759 0.6	
						31 F	0041 4.8	0619 0.5	1311 4.9	1839 0.6

Chart Datum: 2·73 metres below Ordnance Datum (Newlyn)

TIME ZONE (UT)
For Summer Time add ONE hour in **non-shaded areas**

ENGLAND – PORTSMOUTH

LAT 50°48′N   LONG 1°07′W

TIMES AND HEIGHTS OF HIGH AND LOW WATERS

Dates in amber are **SPRINGS**
Dates in yellow are **NEAPS**

2007

SEPTEMBER

Time	m		Time	m
1 SA 0123 / 0659 / 1351 / 1920	4.7 / 0.5 / 4.8 / 0.7		**16** SU 0130 / 0655 / 1347 / 1908	4.4 / 1.1 / 4.5 / 1.2
2 SU 0206 / 0739 / 1432 / 2003	4.7 / 0.8 / 4.7 / 0.9		**17** M 0201 / 0721 / 1416 / 1936	4.3 / 1.3 / 4.3 / 1.4
3 M 0250 / 0823 / 1515 / 2051	4.5 / 1.1 / 4.5 / 1.3		**18** TU 0233 / 0751 / 1447 / 2010	4.2 / 1.6 / 4.1 / 1.7
4 TU 0340 / 0916 / 1607 / 2153	4.2 / 1.5 / 4.0 / 1.6		**19** W 0311 / 0830 / 1527 / 2058	3.9 / 2.0 / 3.9 / 1.9
5 W 0444 / 1029 / 1716 / 2321	3.9 / 1.9 / 3.9 / 1.9		**20** TH 0408 / 0932 / 1629 / 2220	3.7 / 2.3 / 3.7 / 2.2
6 TH 0617 / 1205 / 1858	3.8 / 2.1 / 3.8		**21** F 0533 / 1136 / 1759	3.6 / 2.4 / 3.6
7 F 0059 / 0801 / 1336 / 2027	1.9 / 3.9 / 2.0 / 4.0		**22** SA 0030 / 0714 / 1310 / 1933	2.2 / 3.7 / 2.2 / 3.8
8 SA 0215 / 0910 / 1441 / 2127	1.6 / 4.2 / 1.7 / 4.3		**23** SU 0141 / 0827 / 1406 / 2038	1.8 / 4.0 / 1.8 / 4.1
9 SU 0308 / 1000 / 1528 / 2212	1.0 / 4.5 / 1.4 / 4.4		**24** M 0230 / 0916 / 1451 / 2126	1.4 / 4.3 / 1.4 / 4.4
10 M 0350 / 1042 / 1607 / 2252	1.0 / 4.6 / 1.1 / 4.6		**25** TU 0312 / 0959 / 1531 / 2209	1.0 / 4.6 / 1.0 / 4.6
11 TU 0427 / 1120 / 1643 / 2327 ●	0.8 / 4.7 / 1.0 / 4.6		**26** W 0352 / 1040 / 1611 / 2252 ○	0.7 / 4.8 / 0.8 / 4.8
12 W 0502 / 1153 / 1717 / 2359	0.7 / 4.7 / 0.9 / 4.6		**27** TH 0433 / 1121 / 1652 / 2335	0.5 / 4.9 / 0.6 / 4.9
13 TH 0534 / 1223 / 1748	0.7 / 4.6 / 0.9		**28** F 0513 / 1203 / 1733	0.4 / 5.0 / 0.5
14 F 0029 / 0603 / 1251 / 1816	4.5 / 0.8 / 4.6 / 1.0		**29** SA 0018 / 0553 / 1244 / 1814	4.9 / 0.5 / 5.0 / 0.5
15 SA 0100 / 0631 / 1319 / 1843	4.5 / 0.9 / 4.5 / 1.1		**30** SU 0102 / 0634 / 1326 / 1856	4.9 / 0.6 / 4.9 / 0.7

OCTOBER

Time	m		Time	m
1 M 0146 / 0717 / 1408 / 1941	4.7 / 0.9 / 4.7 / 1.0		**16** TU 0133 / 0651 / 1343 / 1905	4.4 / 1.5 / 4.3 / 1.5
2 TU 0233 / 0804 / 1453 / 2032	4.5 / 1.2 / 4.4 / 1.3		**17** W 0207 / 0723 / 1415 / 1941	4.3 / 1.7 / 4.2 / 1.7
3 W 0327 / 0902 / 1548 / 2138 ◑	4.0 / 1.7 / 4.1 / 1.7		**18** TH 0247 / 0805 / 1456 / 2030	4.1 / 2.0 / 4.0 / 1.9
4 TH 0437 / 1021 / 1704 / 2308	3.9 / 2.0 / 3.8 / 2.0		**19** F 0344 / 0907 / 1558 / 2146 ◑	3.9 / 2.3 / 3.8 / 2.1
5 F 0617 / 1157 / 1853	3.8 / 2.1 / 3.8		**20** SA 0502 / 1051 / 1720 / 2336	3.8 / 2.4 / 3.7 / 2.1
6 SA 0044 / 0748 / 1324 / 2013	1.9 / 4.0 / 2.0 / 4.0		**21** SU 0631 / 1227 / 1847	3.9 / 2.2 / 3.8
7 SU 0156 / 0849 / 1422 / 2107	1.7 / 4.3 / 1.7 / 4.3		**22** M 0056 / 0744 / 1328 / 1957	1.8 / 4.1 / 1.8 / 4.1
8 M 0244 / 0935 / 1504 / 2149	1.4 / 4.5 / 1.4 / 4.4		**23** TU 0151 / 0838 / 1415 / 2050	1.4 / 4.4 / 1.4 / 4.4
9 TU 0322 / 1014 / 1540 / 2226	1.1 / 4.6 / 1.2 / 4.5		**24** W 0236 / 0924 / 1459 / 2138	1.1 / 4.7 / 1.0 / 4.6
10 W 0357 / 1049 / 1614 / 2259	1.0 / 4.7 / 1.0 / 4.5		**25** TH 0319 / 1008 / 1542 / 2225	0.8 / 4.9 / 0.8 / 4.8
11 TH 0430 / 1119 / 1646 / 2329 ●	0.9 / 4.7 / 1.0 / 4.6		**26** F 0402 / 1052 / 1625 / 2311 ○	0.6 / 5.0 / 0.6 / 4.9
12 F 0502 / 1147 / 1716 / 2359	0.9 / 4.6 / 1.0 / 4.6		**27** SA 0446 / 1136 / 1709 / 2358	0.6 / 5.0 / 0.6 / 5.0
13 SA 0532 / 1215 / 1745	1.0 / 4.6 / 1.0		**28** SU 0530 / 1220 / 1754	0.6 / 5.0 / 0.6
14 SU 0029 / 0559 / 1244 / 1810	4.6 / 1.1 / 4.6 / 1.1		**29** M 0044 / 0614 / 1305 / 1839	4.9 / 0.8 / 4.9 / 0.8
15 M 0101 / 0624 / 1314 / 1836	4.5 / 1.3 / 4.5 / 1.3		**30** TU 0132 / 0700 / 1350 / 1926	4.8 / 1.0 / 4.7 / 1.0
			31 W 0223 / 0751 / 1439 / 2019	4.6 / 1.4 / 4.4 / 1.4

NOVEMBER

Time	m		Time	m
1 TH 0320 / 0851 / 1536 / 2123 ◑	4.3 / 1.7 / 4.1 / 1.7		**16** F 0233 / 0753 / 1438 / 2017	4.2 / 1.9 / 4.1 / 1.7
2 F 0430 / 1004 / 1650 / 2241	4.1 / 2.0 / 3.9 / 1.9		**17** SA 0327 / 0851 / 1535 / 2122	4.1 / 2.0 / 3.9 / 1.8
3 SA 0555 / 1129 / 1822	4.0 / 2.1 / 3.8		**18** SU 0433 / 1006 / 1643 / 2239	4.0 / 2.1 / 3.9 / 1.8
4 SU 0005 / 0712 / 1248 / 1937	1.9 / 4.1 / 2.0 / 3.9		**19** M 0546 / 1127 / 1758 / 2355	4.0 / 2.0 / 3.9 / 1.7
5 M 0114 / 0811 / 1346 / 2032	1.7 / 4.3 / 1.7 / 4.1		**20** TU 0656 / 1236 / 1910	4.2 / 1.8 / 4.1
6 TU 0205 / 0858 / 1430 / 2116	1.5 / 4.4 / 1.5 / 4.2		**21** W 0100 / 0756 / 1335 / 2012	1.5 / 4.4 / 1.5 / 4.3
7 W 0245 / 0937 / 1507 / 2154	1.4 / 4.5 / 1.3 / 4.4		**22** TH 0156 / 0849 / 1427 / 2109	1.2 / 4.7 / 1.2 / 4.6
8 TH 0321 / 1012 / 1541 / 2228	1.2 / 4.6 / 1.2 / 4.4		**23** F 0247 / 0939 / 1516 / 2202	1.0 / 4.8 / 0.9 / 4.7
9 F 0355 / 1043 / 1615 / 2300	1.2 / 4.6 / 1.1 / 4.5		**24** SA 0336 / 1028 / 1604 / 2253 ○	0.9 / 5.0 / 0.8 / 4.8
10 SA 0429 / 1114 / 1647 / 2332 ●	1.1 / 4.6 / 1.1 / 4.5		**25** SU 0424 / 1116 / 1653 / 2344	0.8 / 5.0 / 0.7 / 4.9
11 SU 0502 / 1144 / 1718	1.2 / 4.6 / 1.1		**26** M 0512 / 1203 / 1741	0.8 / 4.9 / 0.7
12 M 0004 / 0532 / 1216 / 1746	4.6 / 1.3 / 4.6 / 1.2		**27** TU 0033 / 0600 / 1250 / 1829	4.9 / 1.0 / 4.8 / 0.8
13 TU 0038 / 0601 / 1247 / 1815	4.5 / 1.4 / 4.6 / 1.3		**28** W 0124 / 0649 / 1338 / 1917	4.8 / 1.1 / 4.6 / 1.0
14 W 0113 / 0632 / 1320 / 1848	4.5 / 1.5 / 4.6 / 1.4		**29** TH 0215 / 0740 / 1427 / 2007	4.6 / 1.4 / 4.4 / 1.2
15 TH 0150 / 0708 / 1355 / 1927	4.3 / 1.7 / 4.2 / 1.6		**30** F 0310 / 0834 / 1521 / 2101	4.4 / 1.6 / 4.2 / 1.5

DECEMBER

Time	m		Time	m
1 SA 0409 / 0934 / 1620 / 2200 ◑	4.3 / 1.8 / 4.0 / 1.7		**16** SU 0309 / 0834 / 1515 / 2059	4.3 / 1.7 / 4.2 / 1.6
2 SU 0511 / 1040 / 1725 / 2304	4.2 / 1.8 / 3.8 / 1.8		**17** M 0403 / 0931 / 1611 / 2157	4.2 / 1.7 / 4.1 / 1.5
3 M 0615 / 1150 / 1834	4.1 / 2.0 / 3.8		**18** TU 0503 / 1036 / 1714 / 2303	4.2 / 1.8 / 4.0 / 1.5
4 TU 0009 / 0714 / 1253 / 1937	1.8 / 4.1 / 1.9 / 3.9		**19** W 0609 / 1146 / 1825	4.3 / 1.7 / 4.1
5 W 0109 / 0807 / 1345 / 2031	1.8 / 4.2 / 1.8 / 4.0		**20** TH 0012 / 0716 / 1257 / 1938	1.5 / 4.4 / 1.6 / 4.2
6 TH 0159 / 0853 / 1429 / 2116	1.7 / 4.3 / 1.6 / 4.1		**21** F 0121 / 0819 / 1402 / 2046	1.4 / 4.5 / 1.4 / 4.3
7 F 0242 / 0933 / 1509 / 2157	1.6 / 4.4 / 1.5 / 4.2		**22** SA 0223 / 0917 / 1500 / 2147	1.3 / 4.7 / 1.2 / 4.5
8 SA 0323 / 1010 / 1547 / 2234	1.5 / 4.5 / 1.4 / 4.3		**23** SU 0320 / 1011 / 1554 / 2244	1.2 / 4.8 / 1.0 / 4.7
9 SU 0402 / 1045 / 1624 / 2310	1.4 / 4.6 / 1.3 / 4.4		**24** M 0414 / 1103 / 1646 / 2337 ○	1.1 / 4.9 / 0.8 / 4.8
10 M 0439 / 1120 / 1659 / 2346 ●	1.4 / 4.5 / 1.2 / 4.5		**25** TU 0504 / 1152 / 1735	1.0 / 4.8 / 0.8
11 TU 0514 / 1154 / 1733	1.4 / 4.5 / 1.2		**26** W 0027 / 0552 / 1240 / 1821	4.8 / 1.0 / 4.8 / 0.8
12 W 0022 / 0547 / 1229 / 1806	4.5 / 1.4 / 4.5 / 1.2		**27** TH 0116 / 0639 / 1326 / 1906	4.8 / 1.1 / 4.6 / 0.9
13 TH 0100 / 0622 / 1305 / 1842	4.5 / 1.4 / 4.4 / 1.2		**28** F 0203 / 0724 / 1412 / 1948	4.7 / 1.2 / 4.5 / 1.0
14 F 0139 / 0700 / 1343 / 1922	4.4 / 1.5 / 4.3 / 1.3		**29** SA 0249 / 0809 / 1456 / 2030	4.5 / 1.4 / 4.3 / 1.2
15 SA 0222 / 0744 / 1426 / 2007	4.4 / 1.6 / 4.2 / 1.3		**30** SU 0333 / 0854 / 1540 / 2113	4.4 / 1.6 / 4.1 / 1.4
			31 M 0417 / 0943 / 1625 / 2201 ◑	4.2 / 1.8 / 3.9 / 1.6

Chart Datum: 2·73 metres below Ordnance Datum (Newlyn)

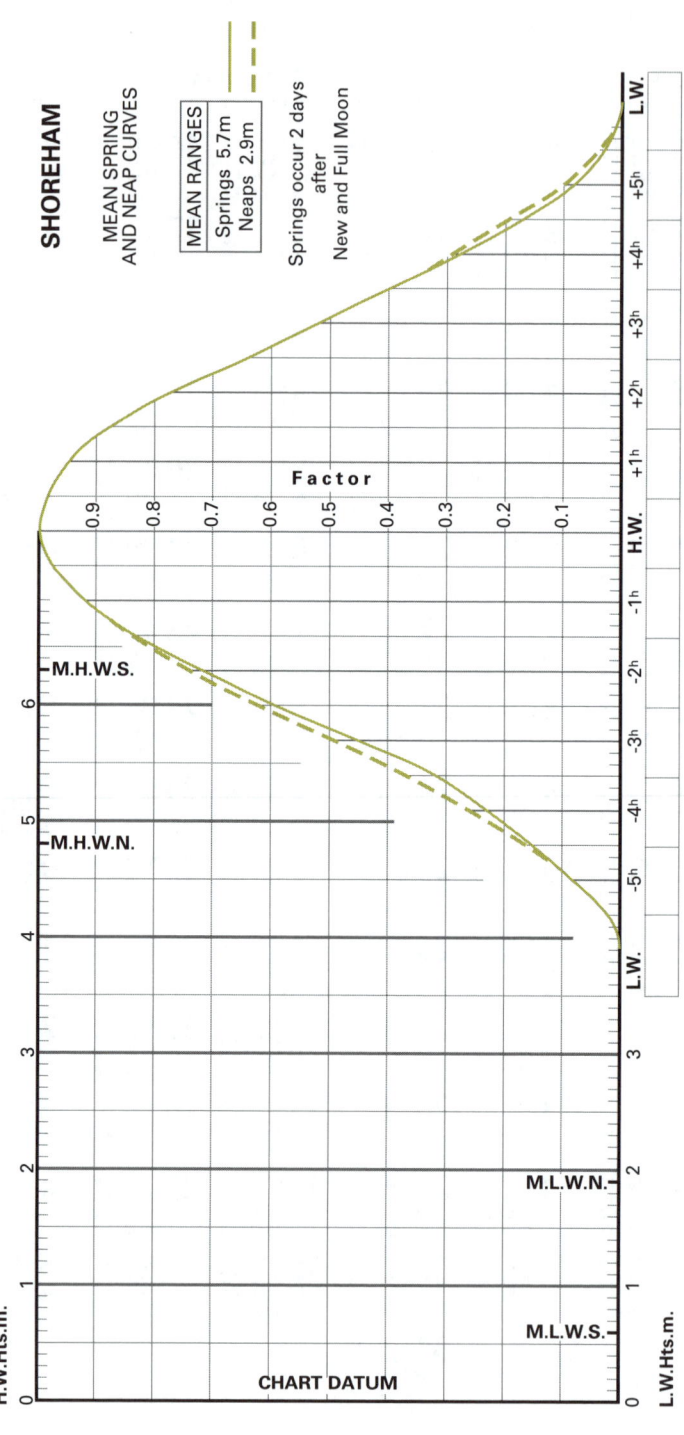

SHOREHAM

MEAN SPRING
AND NEAP CURVES

MEAN RANGES
Springs 5.7m
Neaps 2.9m

Springs occur 2 days
after
New and Full Moon

Factor

0.9 0.8 0.7 0.6 0.5 0.4 0.3 0.2 0.1

M.H.W.S.

M.H.W.N.

M.L.W.N.

M.L.W.S.

CHART DATUM

H.W.Hts.m.

L.W.Hts.m.

L.W. +5ʰ +4ʰ +3ʰ +2ʰ +1ʰ H.W. -1ʰ -2ʰ -3ʰ -4ʰ -5ʰ L.W.

ENGLAND – SHOREHAM

LAT 50°50'N   LONG 0°15'W

TIMES AND HEIGHTS OF HIGH AND LOW WATERS

Dates in amber are SPRINGS
Dates in yellow are NEAPS

2007

JANUARY

Day	Time	m	Time	m	Time	m	Time	m
1 M	0251	1.4	0906	5.7	1523	1.2	2140	5.6
2 TU	0348	1.3	1001	5.9	1616	1.0	2234	5.8
3 W ○	0438	1.1	1050	6.0	1704	0.9	2323	6.0
4 TH	0524	1.1	1136	6.0	1749	0.9		
5 F	0007	6.1	0607	1.1	1219	6.0	1831	0.9
6 SA	0048	6.1	0648	1.1	1258	5.9	1910	1.0
7 SU	0127	6.0	0726	1.2	1335	5.8	1947	1.1
8 M	0203	5.9	0803	1.3	1410	5.6	2023	1.2
9 TU	0238	5.7	0840	1.4	1444	5.4	2100	1.4
10 W	0311	5.5	0920	1.6	1520	5.2	2140	1.6
11 TH ◔	0347	5.3	1004	1.8	1602	4.9	2224	1.8
12 F	0433	5.0	1056	2.0	1658	4.7	2318	2.0
13 SA	0536	4.9	1156	2.1	1812	4.6		
14 SU	0023	2.2	0646	4.8	1306	2.1	1921	4.7
15 M	0137	2.2	0751	5.0	1419	1.9	2025	4.9
16 TU	0247	2.0	0849	5.2	1518	1.6	2120	5.3
17 W	0341	1.7	0939	5.5	1606	1.3	2210	5.6
18 TH	0426	1.4	1025	5.8	1649	1.1	2255	5.9
19 F ●	0508	1.2	1109	6.1	1731	0.8	2339	6.1
20 SA	0550	1.0	1152	6.2	1813	0.7		
21 SU	0022	6.3	0631	0.8	1235	6.3	1855	0.6
22 M	0105	6.4	0714	0.8	1318	6.3	1938	0.6
23 TU	0147	6.4	0759	0.8	1401	6.2	2022	0.6
24 W	0229	6.3	0844	0.9	1446	6.1	2108	0.8
25 TH ◑	0315	6.1	0933	1.0	1534	5.8	2157	1.1
26 F	0405	5.8	1028	1.3	1629	5.4	2254	1.4
27 SA	0504	5.4	1135	1.6	1737	5.1		
28 SU	0007	1.7	0616	5.1	1254	1.8	1900	4.9
29 M	0129	1.9	0741	5.1	1411	1.7	2030	5.0
30 TU	0242	1.7	0859	5.2	1516	1.5	2139	5.3
31 W	0342	1.5	0958	5.5	1610	1.2	2232	5.6

FEBRUARY

Day	Time	m	Time	m	Time	m	Time	m
1 TH	0431	1.3	1047	5.8	1656	1.0	2317	5.9
2 F ○	0514	1.1	1130	5.9	1737	0.9	2357	6.1
3 SA	0554	1.0	1208	6.0	1814	0.8		
4 SU	0033	6.1	0629	0.9	1243	6.0	1849	0.8
5 M	0107	6.1	0703	1.0	1314	5.9	1921	0.9
6 TU	0135	6.0	0735	1.0	1340	5.8	1953	1.0
7 W	0159	5.9	0806	1.1	1404	5.7	2023	1.1
8 TH	0221	5.7	0838	1.3	1432	5.5	2053	1.3
9 F	0250	5.5	0911	1.5	1505	5.2	2126	1.6
10 SA ◑	0326	5.2	0950	1.8	1547	4.9	2208	1.8
11 SU	0414	4.9	1046	2.1	1646	4.6	2313	2.2
12 M	0530	4.6	1206	2.2	1834	4.5		
13 TU	0045	2.3	0712	4.6	1337	2.1	1955	4.7
14 W	0219	2.1	0823	5.0	1454	1.7	2059	5.1
15 TH	0322	1.7	0920	5.4	1547	1.3	2153	5.6
16 F	0409	1.3	1009	5.8	1631	0.9	2240	6.0
17 SA ●	0451	0.9	1055	6.1	1713	0.6	2324	6.3
18 SU	0533	0.7	1138	6.4	1755	0.4		
19 M	0007	6.5	0614	0.5	1222	6.5	1837	0.3
20 TU	0048	6.6	0657	0.4	1303	6.6	1919	0.3
21 W	0128	6.6	0739	0.4	1344	6.5	2001	0.3
22 TH	0208	6.5	0822	0.6	1425	6.3	2043	0.4
23 F	0249	6.2	0907	0.9	1509	5.9	2129	1.0
24 SA ◑	0334	5.8	0956	1.3	1601	5.4	2222	1.5
25 SU	0430	5.2	1101	1.7	1709	4.9	2339	2.0
26 M	0546	4.8	1234	2.0	1843	4.6		
27 TU ◑	0117	2.1	0729	4.7	1402	1.9	2029	4.8
28 W	0235	1.9	0857	5.0	1508	1.6	2134	5.2

MARCH

Day	Time	m	Time	m	Time	m	Time	m
1 TH	0334	1.6	0953	5.4	1559	1.3	2221	5.6
2 F	0419	1.2	1036	5.7	1640	1.0	2301	5.9
3 SA ○	0458	1.0	1115	5.9	1716	0.8	2337	6.1
4 SU	0532	0.9	1150	6.0	1750	0.7		
5 M	0010	6.1	0605	0.8	1221	6.0	1822	0.7
6 TU	0039	6.1	0636	0.8	1247	6.0	1852	0.8
7 W	0102	6.0	0705	0.9	1308	5.9	1921	0.9
8 TH	0121	5.9	0733	0.9	1331	5.8	1948	1.0
9 F	0143	5.8	0800	1.1	1358	5.7	2013	1.2
10 SA	0212	5.6	0828	1.3	1429	5.4	2043	1.5
11 SU	0246	5.3	0904	1.6	1508	5.1	2125	1.8
12 M ◑	0329	4.9	0956	1.9	1601	4.7	2228	2.2
13 TU	0435	4.5	1115	2.2	1751	4.4		
14 W	0006	2.4	0640	4.5	1301	2.1	1928	4.7
15 TH	0152	2.1	0758	4.8	1427	1.7	2037	5.1
16 F	0258	1.6	0859	5.3	1521	1.2	2131	5.7
17 SA	0345	1.1	0949	5.8	1606	0.8	2218	6.1
18 SU	0428	0.7	1035	6.2	1648	0.5	2302	6.5
19 M ●	0510	0.4	1119	6.5	1731	0.2	2344	6.7
20 TU	0552	0.3	1202	6.6	1813	0.2		
21 W	0026	6.8	0634	0.2	1244	6.6	1855	0.2
22 TH	0106	6.7	0717	0.3	1325	6.5	1938	0.4
23 F	0145	6.5	0800	0.5	1406	6.2	2020	0.7
24 SA ◑	0225	6.1	0844	0.8	1447	5.8	2106	1.1
25 SU ◑	0310	5.6	0932	1.3	1544	5.3	2200	1.7
26 M	0408	5.0	1037	1.8	1654	4.8	2320	2.1
27 TU ◑	0526	4.6	1218	2.1	1830	4.6		
28 W	0105	2.2	0716	4.5	1345	1.9	2013	4.8
29 TH	0240	1.8	0840	4.8	1448	1.6	2112	5.3
30 F	0315	1.5	0931	5.3	1535	1.3	2155	5.6
31 SA	0356	1.2	1012	5.6	1613	1.0	2233	5.9

APRIL

Day	Time	m	Time	m	Time	m	Time	m
1 SU	0432	1.0	1049	5.8	1647	0.9	2308	6.0
2 M ○	0504	0.9	1122	5.9	1720	0.8	2339	6.1
3 TU	0536	0.8	1152	5.9	1752	0.8		
4 W	0006	6.0	0607	0.8	1217	5.9	1823	0.8
5 TH	0027	6.0	0636	0.8	1239	5.9	1852	0.9
6 F	0048	5.9	0704	0.9	1304	5.8	1918	1.0
7 SA	0114	5.8	0730	1.0	1332	5.7	1945	1.2
8 SU	0144	5.6	0800	1.2	1405	5.5	2018	1.5
9 M	0219	5.3	0839	1.5	1445	5.2	2104	1.8
10 TU	0303	5.0	0933	1.8	1542	4.8	2209	2.1
11 W	0410	4.6	1048	2.0	1724	4.6	2339	2.2
12 TH	0609	4.5	1225	2.0	1859	4.8		
13 F	0117	1.9	0729	4.9	1351	1.6	2007	5.3
14 SA	0225	1.3	0830	5.4	1448	1.1	2102	5.8
15 SU	0315	1.0	0922	5.8	1535	0.7	2150	6.2
16 M	0359	0.6	1010	6.2	1620	0.4	2235	6.5
17 TU ●	0443	0.4	1055	6.4	1704	0.3	2319	6.7
18 W	0527	0.2	1140	6.6	1748	0.3		
19 TH	0001	6.7	0611	0.2	1225	6.5	1833	0.3
20 F	0043	6.6	0656	0.3	1308	6.4	1917	0.5
21 SA	0124	6.3	0740	0.6	1352	6.1	2002	0.8
22 SU	0207	6.0	0826	0.9	1440	5.7	2050	1.3
23 M	0255	5.5	0917	1.3	1534	5.3	2146	1.7
24 TU ◑	0354	5.0	1019	1.7	1640	4.9	2302	2.1
25 W	0506	4.6	1150	2.0	1801	4.8		
26 TH	0037	2.1	0639	4.5	1311	1.9	1931	4.9
27 F	0147	1.9	0801	4.8	1411	1.7	2032	5.2
28 SA	0240	1.6	0854	5.1	1458	1.4	2118	5.5
29 SU	0322	1.3	0937	5.4	1538	1.2	2157	5.7
30 M	0358	1.1	1015	5.6	1614	1.1	2232	5.8

Chart Datum: 3·27 metres below Ordnance Datum (Newlyn)

TIDES

TIME ZONE (UT)
For Summer Time add ONE hour in **non-shaded areas**

ENGLAND – SHOREHAM
LAT 50°50'N   LONG 0°15'W
TIMES AND HEIGHTS OF HIGH AND LOW WATERS

Dates in amber are **SPRINGS**
Dates in yellow are **NEAPS**

2007

MAY

	Time	m		Time	m
1 TU	0433 / 1048 / 1649 / 2303	1.0 / 5.7 / 1.0 / 5.9	**16** W	0418 / 1032 / 1640 / 2254	0.5 / 6.2 / 0.5 / 6.5
2 W	0506 / 1118 / 1723 / ○2329	0.9 / 5.8 / 1.0 / 5.9	**17** TH	0505 / 1121 / 1728 / 2340	0.4 / 6.3 / 0.5 / 6.5
3 TH	0539 / 1146 / 1756 / 2355	0.9 / 5.8 / 1.0 / 5.9	**18** F	0553 / 1208 / 1815	0.4 / 6.3 / 0.6
4 F	0611 / 1214 / 1827	0.9 / 5.8 / 1.1	**19** SA	0025 / 0639 / 1256 / 1901	6.3 / 0.5 / 6.2 / 0.8
5 SA	0023 / 0641 / 1245 / 1856	5.8 / 1.0 / 5.8 / 1.1	**20** SU	0110 / 0726 / 1343 / 1948	6.1 / 0.7 / 6.0 / 1.0
6 SU	0054 / 0712 / 1317 / 1928	5.7 / 1.1 / 5.7 / 1.3	**21** M	0156 / 0813 / 1431 / 2037	5.8 / 1.0 / 5.8 / 1.3
7 M	0127 / 0746 / 1354 / 2007	5.6 / 1.2 / 5.5 / 1.4	**22** TU	0244 / 0902 / 1522 / 2129	5.5 / 1.3 / 5.5 / 1.6
8 TU	0206 / 0829 / 1439 / 2055	5.4 / 1.4 / 5.3 / 1.7	**23** W	0338 / 0958 / 1617 / ☽2231	5.1 / 1.6 / 5.2 / 1.8
9 W	0255 / 0923 / 1538 / 2158	5.1 / 1.6 / 5.0 / 1.9	**24** TH	0437 / 1103 / 1718 / 2345	4.8 / 1.8 / 5.0 / 2.0
10 TH	0402 / 1031 / 1658 / ☽2316	4.8 / 1.7 / 4.9 / 1.9	**25** F	0543 / 1215 / 1825	4.7 / 1.8 / 5.0
11 F	0533 / 1151 / 1822	4.8 / 1.7 / 5.1	**26** SA	0055 / 0655 / 1318 / 1930	1.9 / 4.7 / 1.8 / 5.1
12 SA	0038 / 0651 / 1308 / 1929	1.7 / 5.0 / 1.4 / 5.4	**27** SU	0152 / 0759 / 1411 / 2025	1.7 / 4.9 / 1.7 / 5.2
13 SU	0146 / 0755 / 1410 / 2027	1.4 / 5.4 / 1.1 / 5.8	**28** M	0239 / 0849 / 1457 / 2109	1.6 / 5.1 / 1.5 / 5.4
14 M	0241 / 0851 / 1503 / 2118	1.0 / 5.7 / 0.8 / 6.1	**29** TU	0321 / 0931 / 1538 / 2148	1.4 / 5.3 / 1.4 / 5.5
15 TU	0330 / 0942 / 1552 / 2207	0.7 / 6.0 / 0.6 / 6.3	**30** W	0400 / 1008 / 1618 / 2223	1.2 / 5.4 / 1.4 / 5.7
			31 TH	0438 / 1044 / 1656 / 2256	1.1 / 5.6 / 1.2 / 5.7

JUNE

	Time	m		Time	m
1 F	0514 / 1120 / 1732 / ○2330	1.1 / 5.7 / 1.2 / 5.8	**16** SA	0540 / 1159 / 1803	0.7 / 6.1 / 0.8
2 SA	0551 / 1155 / 1808	1.0 / 5.8 / 1.2	**17** SU	0014 / 0627 / 1247 / 1849	6.1 / 0.7 / 6.1 / 0.9
3 SU	0004 / 0626 / 1232 / 1843	5.8 / 1.0 / 5.8 / 1.2	**18** M	0100 / 0714 / 1333 / 1935	6.0 / 0.8 / 6.0 / 1.0
4 M	0041 / 0701 / 1309 / 1920	5.7 / 1.0 / 5.8 / 1.2	**19** TU	0145 / 0758 / 1417 / 2020	5.8 / 0.9 / 5.9 / 1.2
5 TU	0120 / 0739 / 1350 / 2001	5.7 / 1.1 / 5.7 / 1.3	**20** W	0229 / 0842 / 1501 / 2105	5.6 / 1.1 / 5.7 / 1.4
6 W	0202 / 0823 / 1436 / 2048	5.5 / 1.2 / 5.6 / 1.4	**21** TH	0313 / 0926 / 1545 / 2151	5.3 / 1.4 / 5.5 / 1.6
7 TH	0251 / 0913 / 1529 / 2145	5.4 / 1.3 / 5.4 / 1.5	**22** F	0400 / 1012 / 1632 / ☽2241	5.1 / 1.5 / 5.3 / 1.8
8 F	0349 / 1012 / 1630 / ☽2250	5.2 / 1.4 / 5.4 / 1.5	**23** SA	0451 / 1102 / 1722 / 2337	4.8 / 1.7 / 5.1 / 1.9
9 SA	0456 / 1118 / 1738	5.2 / 1.4 / 5.4	**24** SU	0546 / 1159 / 1817	4.7 / 1.9 / 5.0
10 SU	0000 / 0607 / 1228 / 1845	1.5 / 5.2 / 1.4 / 5.5	**25** M	0039 / 0645 / 1304 / 1915	1.9 / 4.7 / 1.9 / 5.0
11 M	0108 / 0716 / 1335 / 1950	1.3 / 5.3 / 1.2 / 5.7	**26** TU	0144 / 0745 / 1408 / 2012	1.8 / 4.8 / 1.9 / 5.1
12 TU	0210 / 0820 / 1435 / 2049	1.1 / 5.5 / 1.1 / 5.9	**27** W	0241 / 0842 / 1503 / 2103	1.7 / 5.0 / 1.7 / 5.2
13 W	0306 / 0919 / 1531 / 2144	0.9 / 5.8 / 0.9 / 6.0	**28** TH	0329 / 0932 / 1551 / 2149	1.5 / 5.2 / 1.6 / 5.4
14 TH	0359 / 1015 / 1623 / 2236	0.8 / 5.9 / 0.8 / 6.1	**29** F	0413 / 1017 / 1633 / 2231	1.3 / 5.5 / 1.4 / 5.6
15 F	0450 / 1108 / 1714 / ●2326	0.7 / 6.1 / 0.8 / 6.2	**30** SA	0454 / 1059 / 1714 / ○2311	1.2 / 5.7 / 1.3 / 5.8

JULY

	Time	m		Time	m
1 SU	0533 / 1140 / 1753 / 2350	1.0 / 5.8 / 1.2 / 5.8	**16** M	0007 / 0615 / 1237 / 1835	6.0 / 0.8 / 6.2 / 0.9
2 M	0612 / 1220 / 1831	0.9 / 5.9 / 1.1	**17** TU	0049 / 0657 / 1318 / 1916	6.0 / 0.8 / 6.1 / 1.0
3 TU	0030 / 0651 / 1300 / 1910	5.9 / 0.9 / 6.0 / 1.0	**18** W	0129 / 0736 / 1356 / 1955	5.9 / 0.9 / 6.0 / 1.1
4 W	0111 / 0731 / 1341 / 1952	5.9 / 0.9 / 6.0 / 1.0	**19** TH	0205 / 0813 / 1431 / 2031	5.7 / 1.0 / 5.9 / 1.2
5 TH	0154 / 0813 / 1424 / 2037	5.9 / 0.9 / 6.0 / 1.1	**20** F	0239 / 0848 / 1505 / 2108	5.5 / 1.2 / 5.7 / 1.4
6 F	0238 / 0858 / 1510 / 2126	5.8 / 0.9 / 5.9 / 1.1	**21** SA	0313 / 0925 / 1539 / 2148	5.3 / 1.4 / 5.4 / 1.6
7 SA	0327 / 0949 / 1601 / ☽2221	5.6 / 1.1 / 5.7 / 1.3	**22** SU	0351 / 1006 / 1618 / ☽2233	5.1 / 1.6 / 5.2 / 1.8
8 SU	0423 / 1046 / 1658 / 2325	5.4 / 1.2 / 5.6 / 1.4	**23** M	0439 / 1054 / 1710 / 2329	4.8 / 1.9 / 4.9 / 2.0
9 M	0527 / 1153 / 1805	5.3 / 1.4 / 5.4	**24** TU	0545 / 1154 / 1818	4.6 / 2.1 / 4.7
10 TU	0035 / 0640 / 1306 / 1917	1.5 / 5.2 / 1.5 / 5.4	**25** W	0036 / 0656 / 1310 / 1926	2.1 / 4.6 / 2.2 / 4.8
11 W	0147 / 0758 / 1417 / 2030	1.4 / 5.2 / 1.5 / 5.5	**26** TH	0157 / 0804 / 1431 / 2029	2.0 / 4.8 / 2.0 / 5.0
12 TH	0252 / 0909 / 1520 / 2134	1.3 / 5.4 / 1.3 / 5.7	**27** F	0304 / 0905 / 1529 / 2124	1.7 / 5.1 / 1.8 / 5.3
13 F	0350 / 1011 / 1615 / 2230	1.1 / 5.7 / 1.1 / 5.8	**28** SA	0353 / 0956 / 1614 / 2211	1.4 / 5.4 / 1.5 / 5.6
14 SA	0443 / 1104 / 1706 / ●2320	0.9 / 5.9 / 1.0 / 6.0	**29** SU	0435 / 1041 / 1655 / 2254	1.1 / 5.7 / 1.2 / 5.8
15 SU	0531 / 1153 / 1752	0.9 / 6.1 / 0.9	**30** M	0515 / 1123 / 1735 / ○2335	0.9 / 6.0 / 1.0 / 6.0
			31 TU	0555 / 1204 / 1815	0.8 / 6.2 / 0.9

AUGUST

	Time	m		Time	m
1 W	0016 / 0634 / 1245 / 1855	6.2 / 0.6 / 6.3 / 0.8	**16** TH	0105 / 0707 / 1327 / 1923	6.0 / 0.8 / 6.1 / 1.0
2 TH	0057 / 0714 / 1325 / 1936	6.2 / 0.6 / 6.3 / 0.7	**17** F	0134 / 0738 / 1354 / 1955	5.9 / 0.9 / 6.0 / 1.1
3 F	0138 / 0755 / 1405 / 2018	6.2 / 0.6 / 6.3 / 0.8	**18** SA	0159 / 0809 / 1417 / 2026	5.7 / 1.1 / 5.8 / 1.2
4 SA	0219 / 0838 / 1447 / 2103	6.1 / 0.7 / 6.2 / 0.9	**19** SU	0224 / 0840 / 1441 / 2059	5.5 / 1.3 / 5.6 / 1.5
5 SU	0304 / 0923 / 1533 / ☽2153	5.9 / 0.9 / 5.9 / 1.2	**20** M	0253 / 0914 / 1513 / ☽2138	5.3 / 1.6 / 5.3 / 1.7
6 M	0354 / 1016 / 1626 / 2254	5.5 / 1.3 / 5.5 / 1.5	**21** TU	0332 / 0955 / 1557 / 2229	4.9 / 1.9 / 4.9 / 2.0
7 TU	0457 / 1124 / 1734	5.2 / 1.6 / 5.2	**22** W	0429 / 1056 / 1710 / 2343	4.6 / 2.3 / 4.6 / 2.3
8 W	0011 / 0618 / 1249 / 1858	1.7 / 4.9 / 1.9 / 5.0	**23** TH	0615 / 1223 / 1851	4.4 / 2.4 / 4.6
9 TH	0136 / 0754 / 1410 / 2027	1.8 / 4.9 / 1.8 / 5.1	**24** F	0117 / 0735 / 1404 / 2003	2.2 / 4.6 / 2.2 / 4.8
10 F	0248 / 0913 / 1516 / 2135	1.5 / 5.2 / 1.5 / 5.4	**25** SA	0241 / 0842 / 1508 / 2102	1.9 / 5.0 / 1.8 / 5.3
11 SA	0346 / 1011 / 1610 / 2228	1.2 / 5.6 / 1.3 / 5.7	**26** SU	0331 / 0935 / 1553 / 2151	1.4 / 5.5 / 1.4 / 5.7
12 SU	0435 / 1058 / 1655 / ●2313	1.0 / 6.0 / 1.0 / 6.0	**27** M	0413 / 1020 / 1633 / 2234	1.1 / 5.9 / 1.0 / 6.0
13 M	0518 / 1140 / 1737 / 2354	0.8 / 6.2 / 0.9 / 6.1	**28** TU	0452 / 1102 / 1712 / ○2316	0.7 / 6.2 / 0.8 / 6.3
14 TU	0557 / 1219 / 1815	0.7 / 6.2 / 0.9	**29** W	0531 / 1143 / 1752 / 2357	0.6 / 6.7 / 0.6 / 6.4
15 W	0031 / 0633 / 1255 / 1850	6.1 / 0.8 / 6.2 / 0.9	**30** TH	0611 / 1223 / 1833	0.4 / 6.6 / 0.5
			31 F	0037 / 0651 / 1302 / 1913	6.5 / 0.4 / 6.6 / 0.5

Chart Datum: 3·27 metres below Ordnance Datum (Newlyn)

ENGLAND – SHOREHAM

LAT 50°50′N   LONG 0°15′W

2007

TIMES AND HEIGHTS OF HIGH AND LOW WATERS

SEPTEMBER

Time	m		Time	m
1 0117	6.4	**16** 0120	5.8
0732	0.5	0732	1.1
SA 1341	6.5	SU 1332	5.8
1955	0.6	1948	1.2
2 0158	6.3	**17** 0145	5.7
0814	0.7	0800	1.3
SU 1422	6.3	M 1358	5.6
2039	0.9	2017	1.4
3 0241	6.0	**18** 0214	5.4
0859	1.0	0831	1.6
M 1506	5.9	TU 1430	5.3
2128	1.3	2052	1.7
4 0331	5.5	**19** 0250	5.1
0952	1.5	0911	2.0
TU 1601	5.4	W 1511	5.0
◑ 2229	1.7	◐ 2141	2.1
5 0438	5.0	**20** 0342	4.7
1105	1.9	1013	2.3
W 1715	4.9	TH 1615	4.6
2357	2.0	2257	2.3
6 0611	4.7	**21** 0538	4.4
1242	2.2	1147	2.5
TH 1854	4.7	F 1821	4.5
7 0132	2.0	**22** 0039	2.3
0759	4.8	0708	4.7
F 1408	2.0	SA 1334	2.3
2030	5.0	1937	4.8
8 0244	1.7	**23** 0210	1.9
0910	5.3	0815	5.1
SA 1511	1.6	SU 1440	1.8
2130	5.4	2037	5.3
9 0337	1.3	**24** 0302	1.4
0959	5.7	0908	5.7
SU 1558	1.3	M 1525	1.3
2216	5.8	2126	5.8
10 0420	1.0	**25** 0344	1.0
1040	6.1	0953	6.1
M 1638	1.0	TU 1605	0.9
2256	6.0	2210	6.2
11 0457	0.8	**26** 0424	0.7
1118	6.2	1035	6.4
TU 1714	0.9	W 1645	0.6
● 2332	6.1	○ 2252	6.4
12 0531	0.8	**27** 0503	0.5
1152	6.3	1116	6.7
W 1748	0.8	TH 1725	0.5
		2334	6.6
13 0006	6.1	**28** 0544	0.4
0603	0.8	1157	6.7
TH 1225	6.2	F 1807	0.4
1820	0.9		
14 0035	6.1	**29** 0015	6.6
0635	0.8	0626	0.4
F 1251	6.1	SA 1237	6.7
1850	0.9	1849	0.5
15 0059	6.0	**30** 0056	6.5
0704	0.9	0709	0.5
SA 1312	6.0	SU 1317	6.5
1919	1.0	1933	0.6

OCTOBER

Time	m		Time	m
1 0138	6.3	**16** 0117	5.7
0753	0.8	0731	1.4
M 1359	6.2	TU 1328	5.7
2018	0.9	1947	1.4
2 0223	5.9	**17** 0147	5.5
0840	1.2	0804	1.6
TU 1445	5.8	W 1401	5.4
2109	1.4	2024	1.7
3 0318	5.4	**18** 0225	5.2
0936	1.7	0847	2.0
W 1544	5.2	TH 1443	5.0
◑ 2213	1.8	2114	2.0
4 0430	5.0	**19** 0318	4.9
1053	2.1	0949	2.3
TH 1704	4.8	F 1547	4.7
2347	2.1	◐ 2225	2.2
5 0604	4.8	**20** 0457	4.6
1234	2.2	1114	2.4
F 1847	4.7	SA 1745	4.6
		2357	2.2
6 0118	2.0	**21** 0633	4.8
0744	5.0	1249	2.2
SA 1354	2.0	SU 1904	4.9
2014	5.0		
7 0225	1.7	**22** 0124	1.9
0847	5.4	0740	5.2
SU 1452	1.6	M 1400	1.7
2108	5.4	2004	5.4
8 0315	1.4	**23** 0223	1.5
0932	5.8	0834	5.7
M 1536	1.3	TU 1450	1.3
2151	5.8	2055	5.8
9 0354	1.1	**24** 0310	1.0
1012	6.1	0921	6.2
TU 1612	1.0	W 1533	0.9
2229	6.0	2141	6.4
10 0429	0.9	**25** 0352	0.7
1047	6.2	1005	6.5
W 1646	0.9	TH 1616	0.6
2304	6.1	2226	6.5
11 0502	0.9	**26** 0435	0.5
1120	6.2	1048	6.7
TH 1718	0.9	F 1659	0.5
● 2335	6.1	○ 2310	6.6
12 0534	0.9	**27** 0519	0.5
1150	6.2	1130	6.7
F 1750	0.9	SA 1744	0.4
		2354	6.6
13 0002	6.0	**28** 0604	0.5
0604	1.0	1213	6.6
SA 1214	6.1	SU 1829	0.5
1820	1.0		
14 0026	6.0	**29** 0038	6.5
0634	1.1	0649	0.7
SU 1235	6.0	M 1257	6.5
1849	1.1	1915	0.7
15 0050	5.9	**30** 0125	6.3
0702	1.2	0737	1.0
M 1300	5.8	TU 1342	6.1
1918	1.2	2003	1.0
		31 0214	5.9
		0827	1.3
		W 1433	5.7
		2056	1.4

NOVEMBER

Time	m		Time	m
1 0311	5.5	**16** 0215	5.4
0924	1.7	0833	1.8
TH 1533	5.2	F 1431	5.2
◑ 2158	1.8	2058	1.8
2 0419	5.2	**17** 0307	5.2
1037	2.1	0929	2.0
F 1647	4.9	SA 1530	4.9
2322	2.0	◑ 2159	1.9
3 0539	5.0	**18** 0418	5.0
1208	2.1	1041	2.1
SA 1815	4.8	SU 1653	4.8
		2313	2.0
4 0044	2.0	**19** 0545	5.1
0703	5.1	1200	2.0
SU 1321	2.0	M 1818	5.0
1934	5.0		
5 0148	1.8	**20** 0030	1.8
0806	5.4	0655	5.3
M 1417	1.7	TU 1311	1.7
2031	5.3	1923	5.3
6 0238	1.5	**21** 0137	1.5
0855	5.6	0754	5.7
TU 1502	1.4	W 1410	1.3
2116	5.5	2020	5.7
7 0320	1.3	**22** 0233	1.2
0936	5.9	0847	6.1
W 1540	1.2	TH 1501	1.0
2156	5.7	2112	6.0
8 0357	1.2	**23** 0323	0.9
1012	6.0	0935	6.3
TH 1616	1.1	F 1550	0.7
2231	5.9	2201	6.3
9 0432	1.1	**24** 0411	0.8
1045	6.0	1023	6.5
F 1650	1.0	SA 1638	0.6
● 2303	5.9	○ 2250	6.4
10 0506	1.1	**25** 0500	0.7
1114	6.0	1110	6.6
SA 1724	1.0	SU 1726	0.6
2332	6.0	2339	6.4
11 0539	1.1	**26** 0548	0.7
1141	6.0	1157	6.5
SU 1756	1.1	M 1815	0.6
12 0000	5.9	**27** 0028	6.4
0611	1.2	0636	0.8
M 1209	5.9	TU 1244	6.3
1828	1.1	1903	0.8
13 0030	5.9	**28** 0118	6.2
0641	1.3	0725	1.0
TU 1238	5.8	W 1333	6.1
1859	1.2	1952	1.0
14 0100	5.8	**29** 0208	6.0
0713	1.4	0815	1.3
W 1310	5.7	TH 1423	5.7
1931	1.4	2043	1.2
15 0134	5.6	**30** 0300	5.7
0749	1.6	0908	1.6
TH 1347	5.4	F 1517	5.4
2010	1.6	2137	1.5

DECEMBER

Time	m		Time	m
1 0356	5.5	**16** 0253	5.6
1009	1.8	0909	1.6
SA 1617	5.1	SU 1515	5.4
◑ 2239	1.8	2133	1.5
2 0456	5.3	**17** 0346	5.4
1118	2.0	1006	1.7
SU 1721	4.9	M 1609	5.2
2348	1.9	◑ 2232	1.6
3 0601	5.2	**18** 0449	5.4
1228	2.0	1113	1.7
M 1830	4.9	TU 1719	5.2
		2340	1.6
4 0053	1.9	**19** 0601	5.4
0706	5.2	1225	1.6
TU 1328	1.9	W 1834	5.2
1936	5.0		
5 0150	1.8	**20** 0053	1.6
0803	5.3	0711	5.5
W 1420	1.7	TH 1333	1.5
2031	5.1	1943	5.4
6 0240	1.7	**21** 0200	1.4
0851	5.5	0815	5.7
TH 1506	1.5	F 1435	1.2
2117	5.3	2047	5.7
7 0324	1.6	**22** 0301	1.2
0933	5.6	0913	6.0
F 1547	1.4	SA 1532	1.0
2157	5.5	2146	5.9
8 0405	1.4	**23** 0357	1.0
1010	5.8	1007	6.2
SA 1626	1.2	SU 1625	0.8
2233	5.7	2241	6.1
9 0443	1.4	**24** 0449	0.9
1044	5.8	1059	6.3
SU 1703	1.2	M 1716	0.7
● 2308	5.8	○ 2334	6.3
10 0520	1.3	**25** 0539	0.8
1117	5.9	1149	6.3
M 1739	1.1	TU 1806	0.7
2342	5.9		
11 0555	1.3	**26** 0023	6.3
1150	5.9	0626	0.9
TU 1814	1.1	W 1238	6.3
		1853	0.7
12 0015	5.9	**27** 0111	6.3
0628	1.3	0713	0.9
W 1224	5.8	TH 1324	6.1
1848	1.2	1939	0.8
13 0050	5.8	**28** 0156	6.2
0702	1.4	0759	1.1
TH 1300	5.8	F 1409	5.9
1922	1.2	2024	1.0
14 0127	5.8	**29** 0240	6.0
0738	1.4	0844	1.3
F 1339	5.7	SA 1453	5.7
2000	1.3	2107	1.2
15 0207	5.7	**30** 0324	5.8
0820	1.5	0930	1.5
SA 1422	5.5	SU 1538	5.4
2043	1.4	2151	1.5
		31 0409	5.5
		1017	1.7
		M 1626	5.1
		◑ 2238	1.7

Chart Datum: 3·27 metres below Ordnance Datum (Newlyn)

TIDES

249

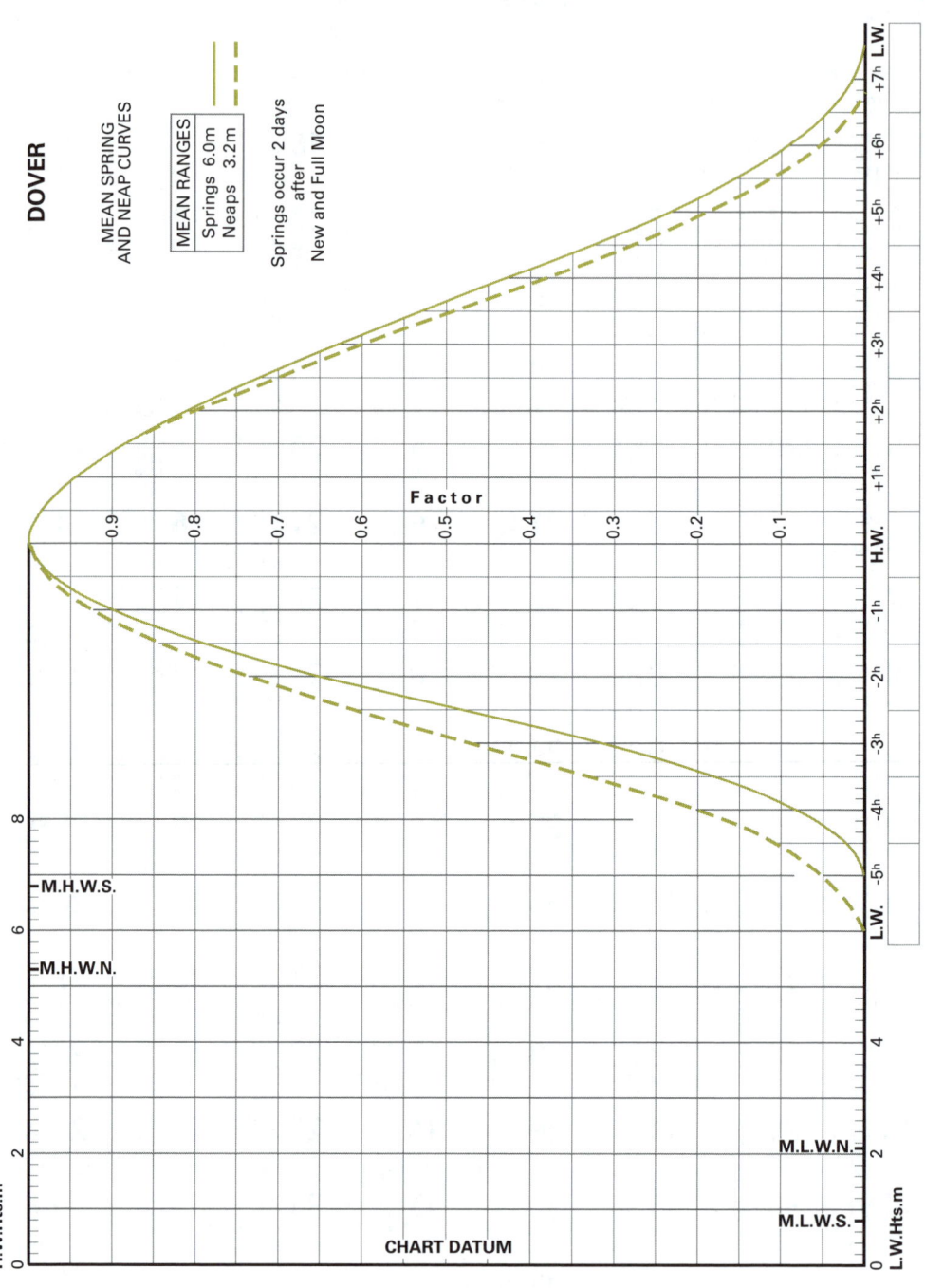

TIME ZONE (UT)
For Summer Time add ONE hour in **non-shaded areas**

Dates in amber are SPRINGS
Dates in yellow are NEAPS

2007

JANUARY

Day	Time	m	Time	m	Day	Time	m	Time	m
1 M	0333 / 0859	1.7 / 6.1	1614 / 2134	1.5 / 6.0	16 TU	0332 / 0845	2.1 / 5.6	1559 / 2119	1.8 / 5.7
2 TU	0441 / 0956	1.5 / 6.2	1719 / 2225	1.4 / 6.2	17 W	0428 / 0935	1.8 / 5.9	1652 / 2204	1.5 / 6.0
3 W ○	0539 / 1047	1.3 / 6.3	1812 / 2309	1.3 / 6.4	18 TH	0518 / 1020	1.5 / 6.1	1741 / 2245	1.3 / 6.3
4 TH	0630 / 1132	1.2 / 6.4	1858 / 2351	1.3 / 6.5	19 F ●	0606 / 1103	1.2 / 6.4	1829 / 2326	1.2 / 6.5
5 F	0717 / 1213	1.2 / 6.3	1939	1.3	20 SA	0653 / 1145	1.0 / 6.5	1915	1.1
6 SA	0031 / 0758	6.5 / 1.2	1252 / 2015	6.3 / 1.4	21 SU	0006 / 0739	6.7 / 0.9	1227 / 1958	6.6 / 1.0
7 SU	0110 / 0836	6.5 / 1.2	1330 / 2048	6.1 / 1.6	22 M	0048 / 0824	6.8 / 0.8	1308 / 2039	6.6 / 0.9
8 M	0148 / 0910	6.4 / 1.4	1408 / 2116	6.0 / 1.6	23 TU	0130 / 0906	6.8 / 0.8	1351 / 2118	6.5 / 1.0
9 TU	0225 / 0940	6.2 / 1.5	1445 / 2143	5.8 / 1.7	24 W	0215 / 0947	6.8 / 0.8	1432 / 2158	6.4 / 1.1
10 W	0300 / 1011	6.0 / 1.6	1525 / 2216	5.6 / 1.9	25 TH ◑	0302 / 1029	6.6 / 1.1	1528 / 2241	6.1 / 1.4
11 TH ◔	0339 / 1048	5.8 / 1.8	1611 / 2257	5.3 / 2.1	26 F	0354 / 1115	6.3 / 1.4	1627 / 2331	5.8 / 1.7
12 F	0426 / 1135	5.5 / 2.0	1712 / 2350	5.2 / 2.3	27 SA	0455 / 1211	5.9 / 1.7	1740	5.5
13 SA	0530 / 1236	5.3 / 2.2	1824	5.1	28 SU	0035 / 0611	2.0 / 5.6	1320 / 1903	2.0 / 5.3
14 SU	0104 / 0642	2.4 / 5.2	1349 / 1930	2.2 / 5.2	29 M	0152 / 0737	2.2 / 5.5	1437 / 2023	2.2 / 5.4
15 M	0225 / 0748	2.4 / 5.4	1458 / 2028	2.0 / 5.4	30 TU	0314 / 0858	2.0 / 5.6	1607 / 2132	1.9 / 5.7
					31 W	0436 / 1003	1.7 / 5.9	1721 / 2223	1.6 / 6.0

FEBRUARY

Day	Time	m	Time	m	Day	Time	m	Time	m
1 TH	0539 / 1051	1.4 / 6.1	1813 / 2304	1.4 / 6.3	16 F	0459 / 1007	1.4 / 6.2	1725 / 2229	1.3 / 6.4
2 F ○	0629 / 1130	1.2 / 6.2	1855 / 2341	1.2 / 6.5	17 SA ●	0551 / 1050	1.0 / 6.5	1816 / 2310	1.0 / 6.7
3 SA	0712 / 1204	1.0 / 6.3	1931	1.2	18 SU	0641 / 1131	0.8 / 6.7	1903 / 2350	0.8 / 6.9
4 SU	0017 / 0747	6.6 / 1.0	1237 / 2000	6.3 / 1.2	19 M	0729 / 1210	0.5 / 6.8	1946	0.7
5 M	0051 / 0818	6.6 / 1.0	1308 / 2025	6.2 / 1.2	20 TU	0029 / 0811	7.1 / 0.4	1249 / 2023	6.8 / 0.6
6 TU	0123 / 0842	6.5 / 1.1	1337 / 2045	6.1 / 1.3	21 W	0110 / 0849	7.1 / 0.4	1330 / 2059	6.8 / 0.7
7 W	0150 / 0905	6.4 / 1.2	1403 / 2109	6.0 / 1.4	22 TH	0152 / 0926	7.0 / 0.6	1413 / 2135	6.6 / 0.9
8 TH	0214 / 0931	6.2 / 1.4	1427 / 2137	5.9 / 1.6	23 F	0236 / 1003	6.7 / 0.9	1500 / 2215	6.2 / 1.2
9 F	0240 / 1002	6.0 / 1.6	1455 / 2211	5.7 / 1.8	24 SA ◑	0325 / 1046	6.3 / 1.4	1556 / 2302	5.8 / 1.7
10 SA ◔	0316 / 1039	5.8 / 1.9	1535 / 2253	5.4 / 2.1	25 SU	0426 / 1140	5.8 / 1.9	1708	5.3
11 SU	0405 / 1128	5.4 / 2.2	1637 / 2351	5.0 / 2.4	26 M	0006 / 0545	2.1 / 5.3	1255 / 1838	2.3 / 5.1
12 M	0537 / 1248	1.0 / 2.4	1846	4.9	27 TU	0133 / 0730	2.4 / 5.2	1425 / 2017	2.3 / 5.2
13 TU	0133 / 0715	2.5 / 5.1	1423 / 2000	2.3 / 5.6	28 W	0310 / 0905	2.2 / 5.4	1614 / 2128	2.0 / 5.6
14 W	0300 / 0824	2.2 / 5.4	1533 / 2058	2.0 / 5.6					
15 TH	0403 / 0920	1.8 / 5.8	1632 / 2146	1.6 / 6.0					

MARCH

Day	Time	m	Time	m	Day	Time	m	Time	m
1 TH	0440 / 1002	1.7 / 5.8	1716 / 2214	1.6 / 6.0	16 F	0337 / 0900	1.7 / 5.8	1608 / 2123	1.6 / 6.1
2 F	0535 / 1043	1.3 / 6.1	1801 / 2250	1.3 / 6.3	17 SA	0434 / 0948	1.3 / 6.3	1702 / 2207	1.2 / 6.5
3 SA ○	0619 / 1116	1.0 / 6.2	1839 / 2324	1.1 / 6.5	18 SU	0529 / 1030	0.9 / 6.6	1754 / 2248	0.9 / 6.8
4 SU	0656 / 1145	0.9 / 6.3	1910 / 2356	1.1 / 6.6	19 M ●	0621 / 1110	0.6 / 6.8	1841 / 2327	0.6 / 7.1
5 M	0726 / 1213	0.9 / 6.3	1935	1.1	20 TU	0708 / 1148	0.4 / 6.9	1923	0.5
6 TU	0027 / 0749	6.6 / 1.0	1241 / 1954	6.3 / 1.1	21 W	0007 / 0749	7.2 / 0.3	1227 / 2000	6.9 / 0.5
7 W	0054 / 0809	6.5 / 1.0	1305 / 2013	6.3 / 1.1	22 TH	0048 / 0827	7.2 / 0.4	1308 / 2036	6.8 / 0.6
8 TH	0115 / 0830	6.4 / 1.1	1324 / 2037	6.2 / 1.2	23 F	0129 / 0902	7.0 / 0.6	1351 / 2113	6.6 / 0.8
9 F	0133 / 0855	6.3 / 1.2	1343 / 2105	6.1 / 1.4	24 SA	0214 / 0940	6.7 / 1.0	1439 / 2153	6.2 / 1.3
10 SA	0158 / 0925	6.2 / 1.5	1412 / 2137	6.0 / 1.7	25 SU ◑	0304 / 1022	6.2 / 1.5	1536 / 2242	5.7 / 1.8
11 SU	0232 / 0959	5.9 / 1.8	1451 / 2215	5.7 / 2.0	26 M	0407 / 1118	5.6 / 2.1	1646 / 2350	5.3 / 2.2
12 M ◔	0316 / 1044	5.5 / 2.1	1542 / 2308	5.2 / 2.4	27 TU	0528 / 1240	5.1 / 2.5	1814	5.0
13 TU	0427 / 1151	5.0 / 2.5	1805	4.9	28 W	0123 / 0727	2.4 / 5.1	1418 / 2000	2.4 / 5.2
14 W	0044 / 0650	2.6 / 5.0	1351 / 1931	2.4 / 5.1	29 TH	0305 / 0853	2.1 / 5.4	1551 / 2105	2.0 / 5.6
15 TH	0230 / 0803	2.3 / 5.4	1508 / 2033	2.0 / 5.6	30 F	0420 / 0941	1.6 / 5.7	1647 / 2148	1.6 / 6.0
					31 SA	0510 / 1018	1.3 / 6.0	1731 / 2224	1.3 / 6.3

APRIL

Day	Time	m	Time	m	Day	Time	m	Time	m
1 SU	0551 / 1048	1.0 / 6.2	1807 / 2257	1.2 / 6.4	16 M	0500 / 1004	0.8 / 6.6	1723 / 2221	0.9 / 6.9
2 M ○	0625 / 1117	1.0 / 6.3	1837 / 2329	1.0 / 6.5	17 TU ●	0554 / 1045	0.5 / 6.8	1812 / 2303	0.7 / 7.1
3 TU	0651 / 1144	1.0 / 6.3	1900 / 2358	1.1 / 6.5	18 W	0642 / 1125	0.4 / 6.9	1857 / 2344	0.6 / 7.1
4 W	0713 / 1211	1.0 / 6.3	1920	1.1	19 TH	0726 / 1205	0.4 / 6.9	1938	0.6
5 TH	0022 / 0734	6.4 / 1.1	1234 / 1943	6.3 / 1.1	20 F	0026 / 0805	7.0 / 0.5	1249 / 2017	6.8 / 0.7
6 F	0041 / 0759	6.3 / 1.1	1251 / 2010	6.2 / 1.2	21 SA	0110 / 0843	6.8 / 0.6	1334 / 2057	6.5 / 1.0
7 SA	0100 / 0827	6.3 / 1.2	1313 / 2039	6.2 / 1.4	22 SU	0157 / 0922	6.5 / 1.2	1425 / 2140	6.2 / 1.4
8 SU	0127 / 0857	6.2 / 1.5	1345 / 2112	6.1 / 1.6	23 M	0251 / 1007	6.0 / 1.7	1521 / 2232	5.8 / 1.8
9 M	0203 / 0933	5.9 / 1.7	1426 / 2152	5.8 / 1.9	24 TU ◑	0354 / 1107	5.5 / 2.1	1626 / 2343	5.4 / 2.1
10 TU	0250 / 1018	5.6 / 2.1	1522 / 2246	5.4 / 2.2	25 W	0508 / 1226	5.2 / 2.4	1741	5.2
11 W	0407 / 1122	5.1 / 2.4	1729	5.1	26 TH	0106 / 0653	2.2 / 5.1	1348 / 1914	2.3 / 5.3
12 TH	0014 / 0625	2.4 / 5.1	1318 / 1857	2.3 / 5.3	27 F	0227 / 0814	2.0 / 5.3	1500 / 2023	2.0 / 5.6
13 F	0158 / 0736	2.1 / 5.5	1437 / 2001	2.0 / 5.7	28 SA	0333 / 0902	1.7 / 5.6	1558 / 2110	1.7 / 5.9
14 SA	0305 / 0833	1.6 / 5.9	1537 / 2053	1.5 / 6.1	29 SU	0425 / 0940	1.4 / 5.8	1644 / 2149	1.5 / 6.1
15 SU	0404 / 0921	1.2 / 6.3	1631 / 2138	1.1 / 6.6	30 M	0506 / 1012	1.3 / 6.0	1723 / 2224	1.3 / 6.2

Chart Datum: 3·67 metres below Ordnance Datum (Newlyn)

TIDES

TIME ZONE (UT)
For Summer Time add ONE hour in **non-shaded areas**

ENGLAND – DOVER

LAT 51°07'N   LONG 1°19'E

TIMES AND HEIGHTS OF HIGH AND LOW WATERS

Dates in amber are **SPRINGS**
Dates in yellow are **NEAPS**

2007

MAY

Day	Time m	Day	Time m
1 TU	0540 1.2 / 1042 6.1 / 1745 1.3 / 2256 6.3	**16**	0524 0.8 / 1021 6.6 / 1745 0.8 / ● 2240 6.8
2 W	0609 1.2 / 1112 6.2 / 1823 1.2 / ○ 2325 6.3	**17** TH	0618 0.7 / 1105 6.7 / 1834 0.8 / 2326 6.8
3 TH	0636 1.2 / 1141 6.2 / 1850 1.2 / 2351 6.2	**18** F	0705 0.7 / 1150 6.7 / 1920 0.8
4 F	0705 1.2 / 1206 6.2 / 1919 1.2	**19** SA	0012 6.7 / 0749 0.8 / 1236 6.6 / 2004 0.9
5 SA	0013 6.2 / 0735 1.2 / 1229 6.2 / 1950 1.3	**20** SU	0059 6.6 / 0831 1.1 / 1323 6.5 / 2049 1.1
6 SU	0039 6.2 / 0806 1.3 / 1257 6.2 / 2023 1.4	**21** M	0148 6.3 / 0914 1.4 / 1413 6.2 / 2135 1.4
7 M	0111 6.1 / 0840 1.5 / 1333 6.1 / 2059 1.6	**22** TU	0240 5.9 / 1001 1.7 / 1505 6.0 / 2227 1.6
8 TU	0152 5.9 / 0918 1.7 / 1420 5.8 / 2142 1.8	**23** W	0337 5.6 / 1054 2.0 / 1600 5.7 / ● 2326 1.9
9 W	0246 5.6 / 1005 1.9 / 1524 5.6 / 2238 2.0	**24** TH	0439 5.3 / 1156 2.2 / 1702 5.5
10 TH	0412 5.4 / 1108 2.1 / 1654 5.4 / ◑ 2357 2.0	**25** F	0030 2.0 / 0552 5.2 / 1300 2.2 / 1812 5.4
11 F	0551 5.4 / 1241 2.1 / 1815 5.5	**26** SA	0132 1.9 / 0708 5.3 / 1401 2.1 / 1923 5.5
12 SA	0122 1.8 / 0701 5.6 / 1358 1.8 / 1921 5.8	**27** SU	0229 1.8 / 0805 5.4 / 1458 2.0 / 2020 5.7
13 SU	0229 1.5 / 0759 5.9 / 1459 1.5 / 2017 6.2	**28** M	0321 1.7 / 0851 5.6 / 1549 1.8 / 2106 5.8
14 M	0328 1.2 / 0850 6.2 / 1555 1.2 / 2107 6.5	**29** TU	0408 1.5 / 0930 5.8 / 1634 1.6 / 2145 6.0
15 TU	0426 0.9 / 0937 6.4 / 1651 1.0 / 2154 6.7	**30** W	0450 1.4 / 1006 6.0 / 1714 1.5 / 2221 6.0
		31 TH	0528 1.3 / 1041 6.1 / 1750 1.4 / 2254 6.1

JUNE

Day	Time m	Day	Time m
1 F	0606 1.3 / 1114 6.2 / 1825 1.3 / ○ 2326 6.1	**16** SA	0653 1.0 / 1143 6.5 / 1910 1.0
2 SA	0642 1.3 / 1146 6.2 / 1902 1.3 / 2358 6.1	**17** SU	0007 6.5 / 0740 1.1 / 1228 6.5 / 1958 1.0
3 SU	0719 1.3 / 1219 6.2 / 1939 1.3	**18** M	0054 6.4 / 0825 1.2 / 1313 6.5 / 2044 1.1
4 M	0032 6.1 / 0755 1.3 / 1254 6.2 / 2016 1.3	**19** TU	0139 6.2 / 0907 1.3 / 1358 6.4 / 2128 1.2
5 TU	0110 6.1 / 0833 1.4 / 1335 6.2 / 2057 1.4	**20** W	0224 6.0 / 0948 1.5 / 1443 6.2 / 2211 1.4
6 W	0155 6.0 / 0914 1.5 / 1423 6.1 / 2142 1.5	**21** TH	0311 5.8 / 1027 1.7 / 1529 6.0 / 2253 1.6
7 TH	0248 5.8 / 1001 1.7 / 1519 6.0 / 2234 1.6	**22** F	0401 5.6 / 1108 1.9 / 1618 5.8 / ◑ 2338 1.8
8 F	0352 5.7 / 1056 1.8 / 1621 5.9 / ◑ 2337 1.6	**23** SA	0456 5.4 / 1154 2.1 / 1713 5.6
9 SA	0505 5.7 / 1203 1.8 / 1729 5.9	**24** SU	0027 1.9 / 0557 5.2 / 1250 2.2 / 1813 5.4
10 SU	0044 1.6 / 0616 5.7 / 1313 1.8 / 1836 5.9	**25** M	0123 2.0 / 0700 5.3 / 1352 2.2 / 1917 5.4
11 M	0149 1.5 / 0721 5.8 / 1418 1.6 / 1940 6.1	**26** TU	0220 2.0 / 0758 5.4 / 1453 2.1 / 2015 5.5
12 TU	0251 1.4 / 0819 6.0 / 1521 1.5 / 2039 6.2	**27** W	0316 1.8 / 0849 5.5 / 1549 1.9 / 2105 5.7
13 W	0355 1.2 / 0914 6.1 / 1623 1.3 / 2135 6.4	**28** TH	0409 1.7 / 0934 5.8 / 1638 1.7 / 2149 5.8
14 TH	0500 1.1 / 1006 6.3 / 1724 1.1 / 2229 6.5	**29** F	0457 1.5 / 1015 5.9 / 1723 1.5 / 2230 6.0
15 F	0600 1.0 / 1056 6.4 / 1819 1.0 / ○ 2319 6.5	**30** SA	0542 1.4 / 1054 6.1 / 1806 1.3 / ○ 2309 6.1

JULY

Day	Time m	Day	Time m
1 SU	0626 1.3 / 1131 6.2 / 1848 1.2 / 2347 6.2	**16** M	0005 6.4 / 0735 1.1 / 1219 6.6 / 1952 0.9
2 M	0708 1.3 / 1208 6.3 / 1931 1.2	**17** TU	0045 6.3 / 0815 1.2 / 1258 6.6 / 2033 1.0
3 TU	0026 6.2 / 0750 1.2 / 1247 6.4 / 2013 1.1	**18** W	0123 6.3 / 0851 1.2 / 1337 6.5 / 2109 1.1
4 W	0106 6.2 / 0831 1.2 / 1328 6.5 / 2056 1.1	**19** TH	0200 6.1 / 0921 1.4 / 1415 6.4 / 2140 1.2
5 TH	0147 6.2 / 0911 1.3 / 1411 6.5 / 2138 1.1	**20** F	0237 6.0 / 0947 1.5 / 1453 6.2 / 2209 1.4
6 F	0233 6.2 / 0952 1.3 / 1459 6.4 / 2222 1.2	**21** SA	0316 5.8 / 1012 1.7 / 1530 6.0 / 2238 1.6
7 SA	0324 6.0 / 1037 1.4 / 1551 6.3 / ◑ 2311 1.3	**22** SU	0359 5.5 / 1045 1.9 / 1613 5.7 / ◑ 2317 1.9
8 SU	0422 5.9 / 1129 1.6 / 1650 6.1	**23** M	0452 5.3 / 1130 2.2 / 1709 5.4
9 M	0007 1.5 / 0529 5.7 / 1231 1.8 / 1757 5.9	**24** TU	0010 2.1 / 0559 5.1 / 1236 2.4 / 1818 5.2
10 TU	0112 1.7 / 0645 5.6 / 1341 1.9 / 1911 5.8	**25** W	0124 2.2 / 0710 5.1 / 1401 2.4 / 1929 5.3
11 W	0221 1.7 / 0758 5.6 / 1453 1.8 / 2024 5.9	**26** TH	0237 2.2 / 0814 5.3 / 1512 2.2 / 2033 5.4
12 TH	0333 1.6 / 0904 5.8 / 1605 1.6 / 2132 6.0	**27** F	0339 1.9 / 0908 5.6 / 1610 1.8 / 2126 5.7
13 F	0449 1.5 / 1003 6.0 / 1714 1.4 / 2232 6.2	**28** SA	0434 1.7 / 0954 5.9 / 1701 1.5 / 2211 6.0
14 SA	0555 1.3 / 1053 6.3 / 1814 1.2 / ● 2322 6.3	**29** SU	0523 1.4 / 1034 6.2 / 1748 1.3 / 2252 6.2
15 SU	0649 1.2 / 1137 6.5 / 1906 1.0	**30** M	0610 1.3 / 1112 6.4 / 1835 1.1 / ○ 2331 6.4
		31 TU	0656 1.1 / 1151 6.6 / 1920 1.0

AUGUST

Day	Time m	Day	Time m
1 W	0010 6.5 / 0739 1.1 / 1230 6.7 / 2003 0.8	**16** TH	0058 6.4 / 0822 1.2 / 1312 6.6 / 2038 1.0
2 TH	0048 6.5 / 0819 1.0 / 1309 6.8 / 2044 0.8	**17** F	0129 6.3 / 0843 1.3 / 1343 6.5 / 2100 1.2
3 F	0127 6.5 / 0856 1.0 / 1350 6.8 / 2122 0.8	**18** SA	0158 6.1 / 0902 1.4 / 1411 6.3 / 2121 1.5
4 SA	0209 6.5 / 0933 1.1 / 1434 6.7 / 2200 1.0	**19** SU	0224 5.9 / 0926 1.5 / 1437 6.1 / 2147 1.6
5 SU	0255 6.3 / 1012 1.3 / 1522 6.4 / ◑ 2242 1.3	**20** M	0250 5.7 / 0957 1.8 / 1508 5.8 / ◑ 2221 1.9
6 M	0349 6.0 / 1058 1.6 / 1619 6.1 / 2334 1.7	**21** TU	0326 5.4 / 1036 2.1 / 1556 5.4 / 2306 2.2
7 TU	0456 5.6 / 1157 1.9 / 1729 5.7	**22** W	0440 5.1 / 1129 2.5 / 1729 5.1
8 W	0041 2.0 / 0621 5.4 / 1315 2.2 / 1856 5.5	**23** TH	0019 2.5 / 0630 5.0 / 1310 2.6 / 1857 5.1
9 TH	0202 2.1 / 0749 5.4 / 1439 2.1 / 2027 5.6	**24** F	0203 2.5 / 0743 5.2 / 1442 2.4 / 2008 5.3
10 F	0331 2.0 / 0905 5.6 / 1605 1.8 / 2141 5.8	**25** SA	0315 2.1 / 0843 5.5 / 1545 1.9 / 2105 5.7
11 SA	0456 1.7 / 1004 6.0 / 1717 1.4 / 2236 6.1	**26** SU	0412 1.7 / 0930 6.0 / 1638 1.5 / 2151 6.1
12 SU	0555 1.4 / 1048 6.3 / 1812 1.1 / ● 2318 6.3	**27** M	0503 1.4 / 1010 6.3 / 1728 1.2 / 2231 6.4
13 M	0642 1.2 / 1126 6.5 / 1859 0.9 / 2354 6.4	**28** TU	0551 1.2 / 1049 6.6 / 1816 0.9 / ○ 2309 6.6
14 TU	0722 1.1 / 1202 6.7 / 1938 0.9	**29** W	0636 1.0 / 1127 6.9 / 1902 0.7 / 2346 6.8
15 W	0026 6.4 / 0755 1.1 / 1238 6.7 / 2011 0.9	**30** TH	0719 0.9 / 1205 7.0 / 1944 0.7
		31 F	0023 6.8 / 0756 0.8 / 1245 7.1 / 2022 0.6

Chart Datum: 3·67 metres below Ordnance Datum (Newlyn)

TIME ZONE (UT)	ENGLAND – DOVER	Dates in amber are **SPRINGS**
For Summer Time add ONE hour in **non-shaded areas**	**LAT 51°07'N LONG 1°19'E** TIMES AND HEIGHTS OF HIGH AND LOW WATERS	Dates in yellow are **NEAPS** **2007**

SEPTEMBER

Day	Time	m	Day	Time	m
1 SA	0102 / 0832 / 1325 / 2058	6.8 / 0.8 / 7.0 / 0.7	16 SU	0118 / 0822 / 1327 / 2039	6.2 / 1.4 / 6.3 / 1.3
2 SU	0144 / 0908 / 1408 / 2134	6.6 / 1.0 / 6.8 / 1.0	17 M	0135 / 0849 / 1347 / 2107	6.1 / 1.5 / 6.1 / 1.6
3 M	0229 / 0947 / 1457 / 2215	6.4 / 1.2 / 6.4 / 1.4	18 TU	0158 / 0920 / 1417 / 2141	5.9 / 1.8 / 5.9 / 1.9
4 TU	0324 / 1033 / 1556 / 2307	5.9 / 1.7 / 6.0 / 1.9	19 W	0232 / 0958 / 1458 / 2224	5.7 / 2.1 / 5.5 / 2.3
5 W	0436 / 1134 / 1714	5.5 / 2.1 / 5.5	20 TH	0322 / 1048 / 1626 / 2324	5.2 / 2.5 / 5.0 / 2.6
6 TH	0020 / 0606 / 1301 / 1853	2.3 / 5.2 / 2.4 / 5.3	21 F	0553 / 1214 / 1832	4.9 / 2.7 / 5.0
7 F	0158 / 0745 / 1442 / 2037	2.4 / 5.3 / 2.2 / 5.5	22 SA	0128 / 0711 / 1410 / 1942	2.6 / 5.2 / 2.5 / 5.3
8 SA	0346 / 0903 / 1613 / 2140	2.1 / 5.7 / 1.8 / 5.9	23 SU	0248 / 0812 / 1516 / 2038	2.2 / 5.6 / 1.9 / 5.8
9 SU	0451 / 0953 / 1712 / 2225	1.7 / 1.6 / 1.3 / 6.2	24 M	0346 / 0900 / 1610 / 2124	1.8 / 6.1 / 1.5 / 6.2
10 M	0540 / 1031 / 1759 / 2300	1.3 / 6.4 / 1.0 / 6.4	25 TU	0436 / 0941 / 1701 / 2204	1.4 / 6.5 / 1.1 / 6.6
11 TU ●	0621 / 1105 / 1839 / 2330	1.1 / 6.6 / 0.9 / 6.5	26 W ○	0524 / 1021 / 1749 / 2242	1.1 / 6.8 / 0.8 / 6.8
12 W	0655 / 1138 / 1912 / 2359	1.1 / 6.7 / 0.9 / 6.5	27 TH	0609 / 1059 / 1835 / 2319	0.9 / 7.1 / 0.6 / 6.9
13 TH	0723 / 1211 / 1938	1.1 / 6.7 / 1.0	28 F	0651 / 1138 / 1917 / 2357	0.8 / 7.2 / 0.6 / 7.0
14 F	0028 / 0745 / 1242 / 1958	6.5 / 1.2 / 6.6 / 1.1	29 SA	0730 / 1218 / 1956	0.7 / 7.2 / 0.6
15 SA	0056 / 0802 / 1308 / 2017	6.4 / 1.3 / 6.5 / 1.2	30 SU	0037 / 0808 / 1300 / 2033	6.9 / 0.8 / 7.1 / 0.8

OCTOBER

Day	Time	m	Day	Time	m
1 M	0121 / 0846 / 1345 / 2111	6.7 / 1.0 / 6.6 / 1.1	16 TU	0100 / 0822 / 1313 / 2038	6.2 / 1.5 / 6.1 / 1.6
2 TU	0209 / 0928 / 1437 / 2154	6.4 / 1.4 / 6.3 / 1.6	17 W	0127 / 0855 / 1345 / 2113	6.1 / 1.8 / 5.9 / 1.9
3 W	0308 / 1016 / 1543 / 2249	5.9 / 1.8 / 5.8 / 2.1	18 TH	0205 / 0933 / 1428 / 2156	5.8 / 2.1 / 5.5 / 2.2
4 TH	0421 / 1023 / 1705	5.5 / 2.4 / 5.4	19 F	0257 / 1023 / 1540 / 2252	5.4 / 2.4 / 5.1 / 2.5
5 F	0012 / 0547 / 1258 / 1851	2.5 / 5.2 / 2.4 / 5.2	20 SA	0506 / 1138 / 1801	5.1 / 2.6 / 5.1
6 SA	0157 / 0729 / 1441 / 2025	2.5 / 5.4 / 2.1 / 5.5	21 SU	0039 / 0630 / 1330 / 1909	2.6 / 5.3 / 2.3 / 5.4
7 SU	0327 / 0840 / 1554 / 2119	2.1 / 5.8 / 1.7 / 5.9	22 M	0211 / 0733 / 1440 / 2005	2.3 / 5.7 / 1.9 / 5.8
8 M	0424 / 0926 / 1646 / 2159	1.7 / 6.1 / 1.3 / 6.1	23 TU	0311 / 0824 / 1535 / 2052	1.8 / 6.1 / 1.4 / 6.2
9 TU	0509 / 1003 / 1730 / 2231	1.4 / 6.4 / 1.1 / 6.3	24 W	0402 / 0908 / 1627 / 2134	1.4 / 6.6 / 1.1 / 6.6
10 W	0547 / 0950 / 1806 / 2259	1.2 / 6.6 / 1.0 / 6.4	25 TH	0451 / 0950 / 1718 / 2213	1.1 / 6.9 / 0.8 / 6.8
11 TH ●	0619 / 1110 / 1835 / 2328	1.1 / 6.7 / 1.1 / 6.5	26 F ○	0538 / 1031 / 1807 / 2253	0.9 / 7.1 / 0.7 / 7.0
12 F	0645 / 1141 / 1858 / 2356	1.2 / 6.6 / 1.1 / 6.5	27 SA	0624 / 1112 / 1852 / 2334	0.8 / 7.2 / 0.7 / 7.0
13 SA	0706 / 1209 / 1918	1.3 / 6.5 / 1.2	28 SU	0707 / 1155 / 1934	0.8 / 7.1 / 0.8
14 SU	0023 / 0727 / 1250 / 1941	6.4 / 1.3 / 6.3 / 1.3	29 M	0017 / 0748 / 1240 / 2014	6.9 / 0.9 / 6.9 / 1.0
15 M	0043 / 0753 / 1250 / 2008	6.3 / 1.4 / 6.3 / 1.4	30 TU	0105 / 0831 / 1329 / 2056	6.7 / 1.1 / 6.6 / 1.3
			31 W	0157 / 0917 / 1426 / 2143	6.4 / 1.4 / 6.2 / 1.7

NOVEMBER

Day	Time	m	Day	Time	m
1 TH ◑	0256 / 1011 / 1532 / 2241	6.0 / 1.8 / 5.7 / 2.2	16 F	0156 / 0920 / 1419 / 2139	6.0 / 1.9 / 5.7 / 2.1
2 F	0402 / 1120 / 1648	5.7 / 2.1 / 5.4	17 SA ●	0250 / 1010 / 1527 / 2232	5.7 / 2.1 / 5.4 / 2.3
3 SA	0000 / 0516 / 1243 / 1822	2.4 / 5.4 / 2.2 / 5.3	18 SU	0409 / 1115 / 1713 / 2347	5.5 / 2.2 / 5.3 / 2.3
4 SU	0125 / 0644 / 1404 / 1946	2.4 / 5.5 / 2.0 / 5.4	19 M	0537 / 1241 / 1826	5.5 / 2.1 / 5.5
5 M	0239 / 0757 / 1511 / 2040	2.2 / 5.7 / 1.7 / 5.7	20 TU	0118 / 0646 / 1354 / 1926	2.2 / 5.8 / 1.8 / 5.8
6 TU	0338 / 0847 / 1604 / 2120	1.9 / 6.0 / 1.5 / 6.0	21 W	0225 / 0743 / 1454 / 2017	1.9 / 6.1 / 1.5 / 6.1
7 W	0425 / 0928 / 1647 / 2154	1.6 / 6.2 / 1.3 / 6.1	22 TH	0323 / 0834 / 1551 / 2104	1.6 / 6.4 / 1.2 / 6.4
8 TH	0505 / 1004 / 1723 / 2225	1.5 / 6.4 / 1.3 / 6.3	23 F	0418 / 0921 / 1648 / 2149	1.3 / 6.7 / 1.0 / 6.6
9 F ●	0539 / 1038 / 1753 / 2257	1.4 / 6.4 / 1.3 / 6.4	24 SA ○	0511 / 1008 / 1742 / 2234	1.1 / 6.9 / 0.9 / 6.8
10 SA	0608 / 1110 / 1819 / 2327	1.3 / 6.4 / 1.3 / 6.4	25 SU	0602 / 1054 / 1833 / 2320	0.9 / 6.9 / 0.9 / 6.8
11 SU	0634 / 1139 / 1847 / 2355	1.3 / 6.4 / 1.3 / 6.4	26 M	0651 / 1142 / 1920	0.9 / 6.9 / 0.9
12 M	0702 / 1204 / 1916	1.4 / 6.3 / 1.4	27 TU	0007 / 0739 / 1231 / 2005	6.8 / 1.0 / 6.7 / 1.1
13 TU	0019 / 0733 / 1228 / 1947	6.3 / 1.4 / 6.2 / 1.5	28 W	0056 / 0827 / 1322 / 2051	6.7 / 1.1 / 6.5 / 1.4
14 W	0043 / 0805 / 1256 / 2020	6.3 / 1.6 / 6.1 / 1.6	29 TH	0147 / 0916 / 1416 / 2139	6.5 / 1.3 / 6.1 / 1.7
15 TH	0115 / 0840 / 1332 / 2057	6.1 / 1.7 / 5.9 / 1.8	30 F	0240 / 1008 / 1514 / 2231	6.2 / 1.6 / 5.8 / 1.9

DECEMBER

Day	Time	m	Day	Time	m
1 SA ◑	0336 / 1105 / 1617 / 2329	5.9 / 1.8 / 5.5 / 2.2	16 SU	0240 / 1001 / 1505 / 2216	6.1 / 1.7 / 5.8 / 1.8
2 SU	0437 / 1205 / 1727	5.7 / 1.9 / 5.4	17 M ●	0335 / 1053 / 1608 / 2312	6.0 / 1.7 / 5.7 / 1.9
3 M	0031 / 0544 / 1307 / 1839	2.3 / 5.6 / 2.0 / 5.3	18 TU	0440 / 1155 / 1723	5.9 / 1.8 / 5.6
4 TU	0135 / 0655 / 1406 / 1941	2.4 / 5.6 / 1.9 / 5.4	19 W	0020 / 0551 / 1304 / 1838	2.0 / 5.9 / 1.8 / 5.7
5 W	0235 / 0756 / 1502 / 2031	2.1 / 5.7 / 1.8 / 5.6	20 TH	0134 / 0701 / 1411 / 1943	2.0 / 6.0 / 1.6 / 5.8
6 TH	0331 / 0846 / 1552 / 2114	2.0 / 5.9 / 1.7 / 5.8	21 F	0243 / 0804 / 1517 / 2042	1.8 / 6.1 / 1.5 / 6.0
7 F	0419 / 0929 / 1635 / 2153	1.8 / 6.0 / 1.6 / 6.0	22 SA	0349 / 0903 / 1624 / 2137	1.6 / 6.3 / 1.3 / 6.3
8 SA	0500 / 1008 / 1713 / 2229	1.6 / 6.1 / 1.5 / 6.2	23 SU	0452 / 0959 / 1728 / 2229	1.3 / 6.5 / 1.2 / 6.5
9 SU ●	0536 / 1043 / 1749 / 2304	1.5 / 6.2 / 1.4 / 6.2	24 M ○	0551 / 1051 / 1825 / 2318	1.1 / 6.6 / 1.1 / 6.6
10 M	0610 / 1116 / 1824 / 2336	1.4 / 6.2 / 1.4 / 6.3	25 TU	0646 / 1141 / 1917	1.0 / 6.6 / 1.0
11 TU	0645 / 1148 / 1900	1.4 / 6.2 / 1.4	26 W	0004 / 0737 / 1229 / 2005	6.7 / 0.9 / 6.5 / 1.1
12 W	0007 / 0721 / 1220 / 1936	6.3 / 1.4 / 6.1 / 1.4	27 TH	0049 / 0826 / 1315 / 2048	6.7 / 1.0 / 6.4 / 1.2
13 TH	0038 / 0757 / 1253 / 2012	6.3 / 1.4 / 6.1 / 1.5	28 F	0134 / 0911 / 1400 / 2129	6.6 / 1.1 / 6.2 / 1.4
14 F	0113 / 0835 / 1352 / 2049	6.3 / 1.5 / 6.0 / 1.6	29 SA	0219 / 0954 / 1447 / 2207	6.4 / 1.2 / 6.0 / 1.6
15 SA	0153 / 0916 / 1413 / 2130	6.2 / 1.6 / 5.9 / 1.7	30 SU	0305 / 1034 / 1535 / 2245	6.2 / 1.4 / 5.7 / 1.8
			31 M ◑	0353 / 1115 / 1628 / 2325	6.0 / 1.7 / 5.5 / 2.1

Chart Datum: 3·67 metres below Ordnance Datum (Newlyn)

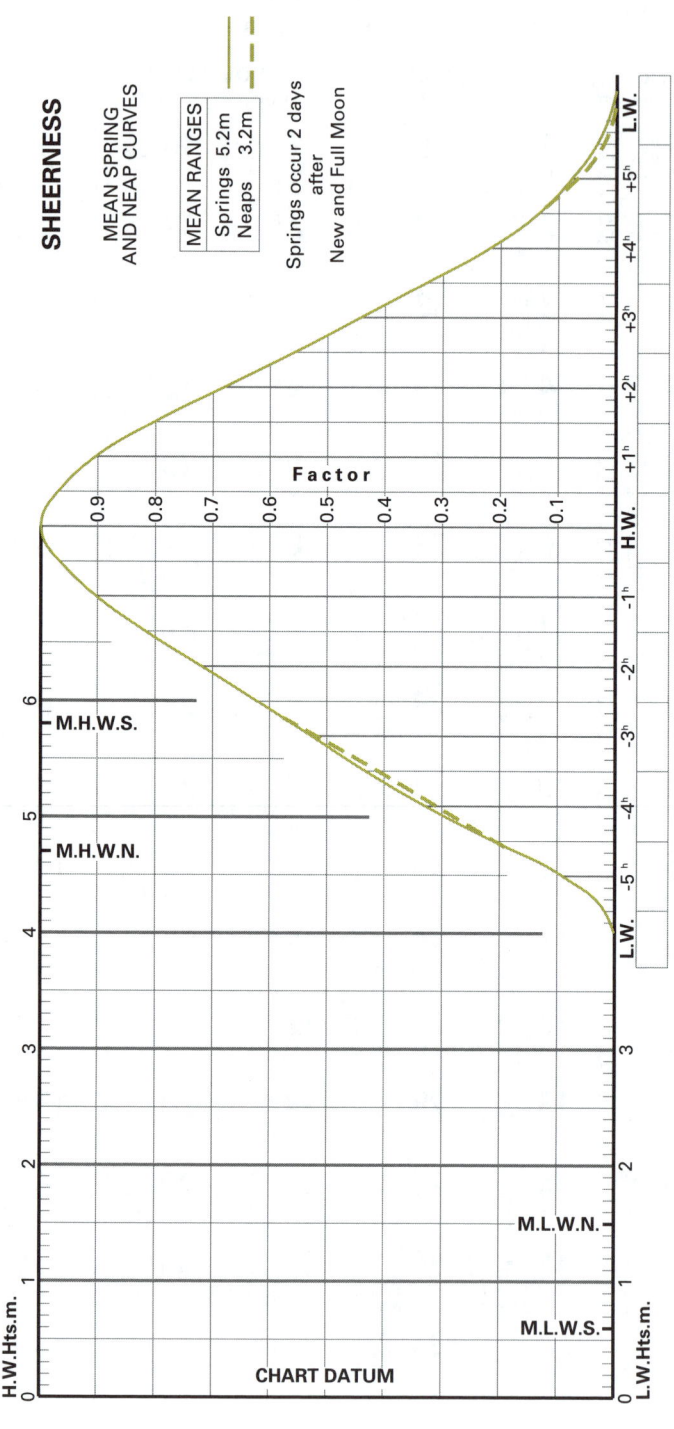

SHEERNESS

MEAN SPRING
AND NEAP CURVES

MEAN RANGES

Springs 5.2m
Neaps   3.2m

Springs occur 2 days
after
New and Full Moon

Factor

0.9
0.8
0.7
0.6
0.5
0.4
0.3
0.2
0.1

H.W.   -1ʰ   -2ʰ   -3ʰ   -4ʰ   -5ʰ   L.W.

L.W.   +5ʰ   +4ʰ   +3ʰ   +2ʰ   +1ʰ   H.W.

M.H.W.S.

M.H.W.N.

L.W.

M.L.W.N.

M.L.W.S.

H.W.Hts.m.

L.W.Hts.m.

CHART DATUM

ENGLAND – SHEERNESS

LAT 51°27'N   LONG 0°45'E

TIMES AND HEIGHTS OF HIGH AND LOW WATERS

Dates in amber are SPRINGS
Dates in yellow are NEAPS

2007

JANUARY

Time	m	Time	m
1 0353 / 1013 / M 1640 / 2253	1.3 / 5.2 / 1.1 / 5.3	**16** 0354 / 1012 / TU 1627 / 2240	1.6 / 4.8 / 1.4 / 5.0
2 0502 / 1114 / TU 1736 / 2347	1.1 / 5.4 / 1.1 / 5.4	**17** 0452 / 1109 / W 1718 / 2332	1.3 / 5.1 / 1.2 / 5.2
3 0603 / 1209 / W 1824 ○	0.9 / 5.5 / 1.1	**18** 0544 / 1159 / TH 1804	1.1 / 5.4 / 1.1
4 0035 / 0656 / TH 1300 / 1906	5.4 / 0.8 / 5.6 / 1.1	**19** 0018 / 0634 / F 1245 / ● 1848	5.4 / 0.9 / 5.6 / 0.9
5 0119 / 0744 / F 1345 / 1945	5.5 / 0.7 / 5.6 / 1.1	**20** 0102 / 0722 / SA 1329 / 1932	5.5 / 0.7 / 5.7 / 0.8
6 0159 / 0826 / SA 1427 / 2020	5.4 / 0.7 / 5.5 / 1.2	**21** 0143 / 0810 / SU 1413 / 2015	5.6 / 0.5 / 5.9 / 0.8
7 0237 / 0904 / SU 1506 / 2052	5.4 / 0.8 / 5.4 / 1.2	**22** 0223 / 0856 / M 1456 / 2057	5.7 / 0.4 / 5.9 / 0.8
8 0312 / 0936 / M 1543 / 2122	5.3 / 0.9 / 5.3 / 1.3	**23** 0304 / 0939 / TU 1539 / 2136	5.7 / 0.4 / 5.8 / 0.8
9 0346 / 1004 / TU 1619 / 2153	5.2 / 1.0 / 5.2 / 1.4	**24** 0345 / 1018 / W 1624 / 2214	5.7 / 0.5 / 5.6 / 0.9
10 0421 / 1033 / W 1657 / 2229	5.1 / 1.1 / 5.1 / 1.5	**25** 0427 / 1055 / TH 1710 / ◑ 2255	5.6 / 0.6 / 5.4 / 1.1
11 0500 / 1109 / TH 1738 / ◑ 2312	5.0 / 1.2 / 4.8 / 1.6	**26** 0515 / 1135 / F 1803 / 2344	5.4 / 0.9 / 5.1 / 1.2
12 0545 / 1154 / F 1827	4.8 / 1.4 / 4.6	**27** 0612 / 1227 / SA 1905	5.2 / 1.1 / 4.9
13 0005 / 0642 / SA 1255 / 1926	1.8 / 4.6 / 1.5 / 4.5	**28** 0049 / 0723 / SU 1343 / 2018	1.4 / 5.0 / 1.4 / 4.8
14 0116 / 0752 / SU 1415 / 2034	1.9 / 4.5 / 1.6 / 4.6	**29** 0215 / 0846 / M 1510 / 2134	1.5 / 4.9 / 1.5 / 4.8
15 0243 / 0906 / M 1528 / 2141	1.8 / 4.6 / 1.5 / 4.8	**30** 0343 / 1006 / TU 1628 / 2243	1.4 / 5.0 / 1.4 / 5.0
		31 0503 / 1114 / W 1730 / 2340	1.1 / 5.2 / 1.3 / 5.2

FEBRUARY

Time	m	Time	m
1 0605 / 1209 / TH 1818	0.9 / 5.4 / 1.2	**16** 0530 / 1142 / F 1749	1.0 / 5.4 / 1.0
2 0028 / 0654 / F 1255 / ○ 1856	5.3 / 0.7 / 5.5 / 1.1	**17** 0000 / 0623 / SA 1230 / ● 1835	5.4 / 0.7 / 5.7 / 0.8
3 0109 / 0735 / SA 1334 / 1931	5.4 / 0.7 / 5.6 / 1.1	**18** 0045 / 0712 / SU 1314 / 1919	5.6 / 0.4 / 5.9 / 0.7
4 0145 / 0811 / SU 1410 / 2002	5.5 / 0.6 / 5.6 / 1.0	**19** 0125 / 0758 / M 1356 / 2001	5.8 / 0.2 / 6.0 / 0.6
5 0217 / 0842 / M 1443 / 2031	5.5 / 0.6 / 5.5 / 1.0	**20** 0204 / 0840 / TU 1437 / 2040	6.0 / 0.1 / 6.0 / 0.6
6 0248 / 0909 / TU 1513 / 2059	5.5 / 0.7 / 5.4 / 1.1	**21** 0243 / 0919 / W 1517 / 2117	6.0 / 0.1 / 5.9 / 0.6
7 0317 / 0934 / W 1543 / 2125	5.4 / 0.8 / 5.3 / 1.1	**22** 0323 / 0954 / TH 1558 / 2152	6.0 / 0.3 / 5.7 / 0.7
8 0347 / 0958 / TH 1614 / 2153	5.3 / 0.9 / 5.2 / 1.2	**23** 0404 / 1026 / F 1641 / 2229	5.8 / 0.6 / 5.4 / 0.9
9 0418 / 1026 / F 1648 / 2225	5.2 / 1.0 / 5.0 / 1.4	**24** 0450 / 1101 / SA 1730 / ◑ 2315	5.5 / 0.9 / 5.1 / 1.1
10 0455 / 1059 / SA 1728 / ◑ 2306	4.9 / 1.3 / 4.8 / 1.6	**25** 0546 / 1151 / SU 1831	5.2 / 1.3 / 4.7
11 0541 / 1146 / SU 1821	4.7 / 1.5 / 4.5	**26** 0021 / 0702 / M 1312 / 1951	1.4 / 4.8 / 1.6 / 4.5
12 0005 / 0647 / M 1301 / 1934	1.8 / 4.4 / 1.7 / 4.4	**27** 0202 / 0836 / TU 1455 / 2119	1.5 / 4.7 / 1.7 / 4.6
13 0139 / 0815 / TU 1446 / 2059	1.9 / 4.4 / 1.7 / 4.6	**28** 0345 / 1004 / W 1621 / 2233	1.3 / 4.9 / 1.6 / 4.9
14 0320 / 0941 / W 1600 / 2213	1.6 / 4.7 / 1.5 / 4.8		
15 0430 / 1048 / TH 1658 / 2311	1.3 / 5.1 / 1.2 / 5.1		

MARCH

Time	m	Time	m
1 0503 / 1109 / TH 1722 / 2329	1.0 / 5.2 / 1.3 / 5.2	**16** 0406 / 1023 / F 1633 / 2245	1.2 / 5.1 / 1.2 / 5.1
2 0557 / 1158 / F 1805	0.8 / 5.4 / 1.2	**17** 0509 / 1119 / SA 1726 / 2334	0.8 / 5.5 / 0.9 / 5.5
3 0013 / 0639 / SA 1239 / ○ 1838	5.3 / 0.7 / 5.6 / 1.1	**18** 0604 / 1206 / SU 1813	0.5 / 5.8 / 0.8
4 0050 / 0713 / SU 1314 / 1909	5.5 / 0.6 / 5.6 / 1.0	**19** 0018 / 0651 / M 1250 / ● 1857	5.8 / 0.3 / 6.0 / 0.6
5 0122 / 0743 / M 1345 / 1938	5.5 / 0.6 / 5.6 / 0.9	**20** 0100 / 0736 / TU 1332 / 1939	6.0 / 0.2 / 6.1 / 0.5
6 0151 / 0811 / TU 1413 / 2007	5.6 / 0.6 / 5.6 / 0.8	**21** 0139 / 0816 / W 1412 / 2019	6.1 / 0.1 / 6.1 / 0.5
7 0219 / 0838 / W 1440 / 2035	5.6 / 0.6 / 5.5 / 0.9	**22** 0219 / 0854 / TH 1452 / 2057	6.1 / 0.2 / 5.9 / 0.5
8 0247 / 0903 / TH 1508 / 2100	5.5 / 0.7 / 5.5 / 1.0	**23** 0300 / 0927 / F 1532 / 2133	6.1 / 0.4 / 5.7 / 0.6
9 0315 / 0926 / F 1536 / 2124	5.4 / 0.8 / 5.3 / 1.1	**24** 0343 / 0959 / SA 1614 / 2211	5.8 / 0.7 / 5.4 / 0.8
10 0345 / 0949 / SA 1607 / 2149	5.3 / 1.0 / 5.1 / 1.2	**25** 0432 / 1035 / SU 1702 / ◑ 2259	5.5 / 1.1 / 5.0 / 1.1
11 0420 / 1016 / SU 1644 / 2224	5.1 / 1.2 / 4.9 / 1.4	**26** 0531 / 1127 / M 1804	5.1 / 1.5 / 4.7
12 0504 / 1057 / M 1733 / ◑ 2319	4.8 / 1.5 / 4.6 / 1.6	**27** 0009 / 0650 / TU 1252 / 1928	1.4 / 4.7 / 1.8 / 4.4
13 0605 / 1208 / TU 1843	4.5 / 1.8 / 4.4	**28** 0159 / 0824 / W 1438 / 2058	1.4 / 4.7 / 1.8 / 4.6
14 0049 / 0733 / W 1405 / 2018	1.7 / 4.4 / 1.8 / 4.4	**29** 0334 / 0948 / TH 1600 / 2210	1.2 / 4.9 / 1.6 / 4.9
15 0248 / 0910 / TH 1530 / 2142	1.6 / 4.7 / 1.5 / 4.7	**30** 0443 / 1048 / F 1657 / 2304	0.9 / 5.3 / 1.4 / 5.2
		31 0532 / 1135 / SA 1737 / 2346	0.8 / 5.5 / 1.2 / 5.4

APRIL

Time	m	Time	m
1 0609 / 1213 / SU 1810	0.7 / 5.5 / 1.0	**16** 0535 / 1138 / M 1744 / 2347	0.5 / 5.8 / 0.8 / 5.8
2 0021 / 0640 / M 1245 / ○ 1840	5.5 / 0.7 / 5.6 / 0.9	**17** 0624 / 1222 / TU 1831 ●	0.3 / 6.0 / 0.6
3 0052 / 0709 / TU 1314 / 1910	5.5 / 0.6 / 5.6 / 0.8	**18** 0031 / 0708 / W 1305 / 1915	6.0 / 0.3 / 6.0 / 0.5
4 0121 / 0737 / W 1340 / 1941	5.6 / 0.6 / 5.6 / 0.8	**19** 0114 / 0749 / TH 1347 / 1959	6.1 / 0.3 / 6.0 / 0.5
5 0150 / 0805 / TH 1407 / 2010	5.6 / 0.7 / 5.6 / 0.8	**20** 0158 / 0828 / F 1427 / 2040	6.1 / 0.4 / 5.9 / 0.5
6 0219 / 0832 / F 1435 / 2037	5.5 / 0.8 / 5.5 / 0.9	**21** 0242 / 0903 / SA 1509 / 2121	6.0 / 0.6 / 5.6 / 0.6
7 0249 / 0857 / SA 1505 / 2102	5.4 / 0.9 / 5.4 / 1.0	**22** 0329 / 0939 / SU 1552 / 2203	5.8 / 1.0 / 5.3 / 0.8
8 0321 / 0922 / SU 1537 / 2129	5.3 / 1.1 / 5.2 / 1.1	**23** 0421 / 1018 / M 1642 / 2253	5.4 / 1.3 / 5.0 / 1.1
9 0358 / 0950 / M 1614 / 2205	5.1 / 1.3 / 5.0 / 1.3	**24** 0522 / 1110 / TU 1744 ◑	5.1 / 1.6 / 4.7
10 0443 / 1034 / TU 1703 / ◑ 2301	4.9 / 1.5 / 4.8 / 1.4	**25** 0005 / 0634 / W 1229 / 1901	1.3 / 4.8 / 1.9 / 4.5
11 0545 / 1145 / W 1812	4.7 / 1.7 / 4.5	**26** 0141 / 0756 / TH 1402 / 2022	1.3 / 4.7 / 1.9 / 4.6
12 0028 / 0707 / TH 1329 / 1942	1.5 / 4.6 / 1.8 / 4.4	**27** 0300 / 0913 / F 1516 / 2132	1.2 / 4.9 / 1.7 / 4.8
13 0217 / 0838 / F 1454 / 2106	1.4 / 4.8 / 1.5 / 4.8	**28** 0402 / 1013 / SA 1613 / 2226	1.0 / 5.2 / 1.4 / 5.1
14 0334 / 0951 / SA 1558 / 2209	1.0 / 5.2 / 1.2 / 5.2	**29** 0450 / 1059 / SU 1657 / 2310	0.8 / 5.3 / 1.3 / 5.3
15 0439 / 1049 / SU 1653 / 2301	0.7 / 5.6 / 1.0 / 5.5	**30** 0528 / 1137 / M 1734 / 2346	0.6 / 5.4 / 1.1 / 5.4

Chart Datum: 2·90 metres below Ordnance Datum (Newlyn)

TIDES

255

TIDES

TIME ZONE (UT)
For Summer Time add ONE hour in **non-shaded areas**

ENGLAND – SHEERNESS

LAT 51°27'N   LONG 0°45'E

TIMES AND HEIGHTS OF HIGH AND LOW WATERS

Dates in amber are **SPRINGS**
Dates in yellow are **NEAPS**

2007

MAY

Time	m		Time	m
1 TU	0601 0.8 / 1210 5.5 / 1808 1.0	**16** W	0553 0.5 / 1155 5.8 / 1805 0.7 ●
2 W ○	0019 5.5 / 0631 0.8 / 1240 5.5 / 1841 0.9	**17** TH	0007 5.9 / 0640 0.5 / 1241 5.9 / 1855 0.6
3 TH	0051 5.5 / 0702 0.8 / 1309 5.6 / 1914 0.9	**18** F	0055 6.0 / 0724 0.5 / 1325 5.8 / 1944 0.5
4 F	0123 5.5 / 0733 0.8 / 1338 5.6 / 1947 0.9	**19** SA	0143 6.0 / 0806 0.7 / 1409 5.7 / 2031 0.5
5 SA	0155 5.5 / 0804 0.9 / 1409 5.5 / 2019 0.9	**20** SU	0231 5.9 / 0846 0.9 / 1453 5.5 / 2116 0.6
6 SU	0229 5.4 / 0835 1.0 / 1441 5.4 / 2051 1.0	**21** M	0321 5.6 / 0924 1.1 / 1538 5.3 / 2202 0.8
7 M	0305 5.3 / 0906 1.1 / 1516 5.3 / 2125 1.1	**22** TU	0412 5.4 / 1004 1.4 / 1627 5.1 / 2251 1.0
8 TU	0346 5.2 / 0942 1.3 / 1557 5.1 / 2206 1.2	**23** W ◐	0508 5.1 / 1052 1.6 / 1722 4.9 / 2351 1.1
9 W	0435 5.1 / 1029 1.5 / 1648 4.9 / 2303 1.2	**24** TH	0608 4.9 / 1152 1.8 / 1824 4.7
10 TH ◑	0535 4.9 / 1134 1.6 / 1753 4.8	**25** F	0101 1.2 / 0713 4.8 / 1307 1.8 / 1932 4.7
11 F	0018 1.3 / 0648 4.9 / 1256 1.6 / 1909 4.8	**26** SA	0207 1.2 / 0820 4.8 / 1417 1.7 / 2038 4.8
12 SA	0144 1.1 / 0806 5.0 / 1412 1.4 / 2025 5.0	**27** SU	0306 1.1 / 0921 4.9 / 1517 1.6 / 2137 4.9
13 SU	0257 0.9 / 0916 5.3 / 1517 1.2 / 2131 5.3	**28** M	0356 1.1 / 1012 5.1 / 1609 1.4 / 2226 5.1
14 M	0401 0.7 / 1015 5.5 / 1615 1.0 / 2227 5.5	**29** TU	0440 1.0 / 1055 5.2 / 1654 1.2 / 2309 5.2
15 TU	0500 0.6 / 1108 5.7 / 1711 0.9 / 2318 5.7	**30** W	0519 1.0 / 1132 5.3 / 1735 1.1 / 2348 5.3
		31 TH	0556 1.0 / 1207 5.4 / 1814 1.0

JUNE

Time	m		Time	m
1 F ○	0025 5.4 / 0632 0.9 / 1242 5.5 / 1851 0.9	**16** SA	0044 5.8 / 0706 0.8 / 1312 5.6 / 1937 0.9
2 SA	0102 5.4 / 0707 1.0 / 1317 5.5 / 1929 0.9	**17** SU	0136 5.8 / 0751 0.9 / 1357 5.6 / 2027 0.9
3 SU	0139 5.4 / 0743 1.0 / 1352 5.5 / 2008 0.9	**18** M	0225 5.7 / 0832 1.0 / 1442 5.5 / 2113 0.6
4 M	0217 5.4 / 0820 1.0 / 1428 5.4 / 2048 0.9	**19** TU	0312 5.6 / 0911 1.2 / 1525 5.4 / 2156 0.7
5 TU	0258 5.4 / 0859 1.1 / 1507 5.3 / 2130 0.9	**20** W	0358 5.4 / 0948 1.3 / 1608 5.2 / 2237 0.9
6 W	0342 5.4 / 0940 1.2 / 1550 5.2 / 2215 0.9	**21** TH	0444 5.2 / 1026 1.5 / 1652 5.1 / 2317 1.0
7 TH	0430 5.3 / 1026 1.3 / 1639 5.1 / 2306 1.0	**22** F ◑	0531 5.0 / 1108 1.6 / 1739 4.9
8 F ◑	0525 5.2 / 1120 1.4 / 1734 5.1	**23** SA ◖	0002 1.1 / 0620 4.9 / 1200 1.7 / 1832 4.8
9 SA	0003 1.0 / 0626 5.1 / 1222 1.4 / 1837 5.1	**24** SU	0056 1.2 / 0715 4.7 / 1303 1.8 / 1933 4.7
10 SU	0109 1.0 / 0733 5.1 / 1329 1.4 / 1946 5.1	**25** M	0157 1.3 / 0814 4.7 / 1414 1.7 / 2036 4.7
11 M	0216 0.9 / 0840 5.2 / 1436 1.3 / 2054 5.2	**26** TU	0258 1.3 / 0913 4.8 / 1519 1.6 / 2137 4.8
12 TU	0323 0.9 / 0943 5.3 / 1541 1.2 / 2157 5.4	**27** W	0353 1.3 / 1008 5.0 / 1615 1.4 / 2232 5.0
13 W	0427 0.8 / 1041 5.6 / 1645 1.0 / 2256 5.5	**28** TH	0443 1.2 / 1057 5.1 / 1706 1.3 / 2321 5.1
14 TH	0526 0.8 / 1134 5.6 / 1747 0.8 / 2351 5.7	**29** F	0527 1.1 / 1141 5.3 / 1752 1.1
15 F ●	0619 0.8 / 1224 5.6 / 1844 0.7	**30** SA ○	0006 5.3 / 0608 1.1 / 1223 5.4 / 1835 1.0

JULY

Time	m		Time	m
1 SU	0048 5.4 / 0648 1.0 / 1303 5.5 / 1918 0.9	**16** M	0131 5.7 / 0739 1.0 / 1348 5.6 / 2020 0.5
2 M	0129 5.5 / 0729 1.0 / 1342 5.5 / 2003 0.7	**17** TU	0215 5.7 / 0818 1.1 / 1428 5.5 / 2100 0.6
3 TU	0210 5.6 / 0811 0.9 / 1421 5.5 / 2048 0.7	**18** W	0256 5.6 / 0853 1.1 / 1505 5.5 / 2136 0.6
4 W	0251 5.6 / 0853 0.9 / 1500 5.5 / 2132 0.6	**19** TH	0335 5.5 / 0925 1.2 / 1541 5.4 / 2207 0.8
5 TH	0334 5.6 / 0934 1.0 / 1541 5.5 / 2214 0.6	**20** F	0411 5.3 / 0954 1.3 / 1615 5.3 / 2235 0.9
6 F	0419 5.5 / 1015 1.1 / 1624 5.4 / 2256 0.7	**21** SA	0447 5.2 / 1026 1.4 / 1652 5.1 / 2304 1.1
7 SA ◖	0507 5.4 / 1058 1.2 / 1711 5.4 / 2339 0.8	**22** SU ◖	0526 5.0 / 1103 1.5 / 1734 4.9 / 2343 1.3
8 SU	0600 5.2 / 1147 1.3 / 1806 5.3	**23** M	0610 4.8 / 1151 1.7 / 1825 4.7
9 M	0030 1.0 / 0659 5.1 / 1248 1.4 / 1910 5.2	**24** TU	0036 1.5 / 0704 4.6 / 1257 1.8 / 1931 4.5
10 TU	0136 1.1 / 0807 5.0 / 1400 1.4 / 2024 5.1	**25** W	0153 1.6 / 0811 4.6 / 1424 1.8 / 2047 4.5
11 W	0252 1.2 / 0916 5.1 / 1518 1.3 / 2138 5.2	**26** TH	0310 1.6 / 0922 4.7 / 1540 1.6 / 2158 4.7
12 TH	0406 1.2 / 1022 5.2 / 1634 1.1 / 2247 5.3	**27** F	0412 1.4 / 1025 4.9 / 1641 1.4 / 2258 5.0
13 F	0512 1.1 / 1123 5.3 / 1743 0.9 / 2348 5.5	**28** SA	0505 1.3 / 1119 5.2 / 1734 1.1 / 2348 5.3
14 SA ●	0609 1.1 / 1216 5.4 / 1843 0.7	**29** SU	0551 1.1 / 1206 5.4 / 1822 0.9
15 SU	0043 5.6 / 0656 1.0 / 1304 5.5 / 1934 0.6	**30** M ○	0033 5.5 / 0634 1.0 / 1248 5.5 / 1908 0.7
		31 TU	0115 5.7 / 0716 0.9 / 1328 5.7 / 1954 0.6

AUGUST

Time	m		Time	m
1 W	0156 5.8 / 0758 0.8 / 1406 5.8 / 2038 0.4	**16** TH	0232 5.7 / 0827 1.0 / 1438 5.6 / 2104 0.4
2 TH	0237 5.9 / 0840 0.8 / 1444 5.8 / 2120 0.4	**17** F	0303 5.6 / 0856 1.1 / 1508 5.6 / 2130 0.7
3 F	0318 5.8 / 0919 0.8 / 1522 5.8 / 2158 0.5	**18** SA	0333 5.5 / 0922 1.2 / 1538 5.5 / 2153 0.7
4 SA	0359 5.7 / 0955 0.9 / 1602 5.7 / 2233 0.6	**19** SU	0403 5.3 / 0948 1.3 / 1609 5.3 / 2218 1.0
5 SU ◖	0442 5.5 / 1032 1.1 / 1645 5.6 / 2308 0.8	**20** M ◖	0435 5.1 / 1017 1.4 / 1645 5.0 / 2250 1.3
6 M	0530 5.3 / 1116 1.2 / 1737 5.3 / 2352 1.1	**21** TU	0513 4.9 / 1056 1.6 / 1729 4.8 / 2334 1.6
7 TU	0627 5.0 / 1214 1.4 / 1843 5.1	**22** W	0602 4.6 / 1151 1.8 / 1830 4.6
8 W	0100 1.4 / 0738 4.8 / 1337 1.5 / 2006 4.9	**23** TH	0043 1.8 / 0710 4.5 / 1322 1.9 / 1956 4.4
9 TH	0233 1.5 / 0857 4.8 / 1512 1.4 / 2133 5.0	**24** F	0227 1.9 / 0837 4.5 / 1506 1.7 / 2125 4.6
10 F	0358 1.5 / 1014 5.0 / 1638 1.2 / 2249 5.2	**25** SA	0344 1.6 / 0955 4.8 / 1617 1.4 / 2233 5.0
11 SA	0509 1.3 / 1117 5.2 / 1746 0.9 / 2348 5.5	**26** SU	0442 1.4 / 1054 5.2 / 1714 1.1 / 2326 5.4
12 SU ●	0603 1.2 / 1209 5.4 / 1839 0.7	**27** M	0531 1.1 / 1143 5.5 / 1805 0.8
13 M	0037 5.7 / 0645 1.1 / 1253 5.6 / 1923 0.6	**28** TU ○	0012 5.7 / 0615 1.0 / 1226 5.7 / 1851 0.6
14 TU	0120 5.7 / 0723 1.1 / 1331 5.6 / 2001 0.5	**29** W	0054 5.9 / 0657 0.8 / 1305 5.8 / 1935 0.4
15 W	0157 5.7 / 0756 1.0 / 1406 5.6 / 2034 0.6	**30** TH	0135 6.0 / 0739 0.7 / 1343 6.0 / 2017 0.3
		31 F	0214 6.0 / 0819 0.7 / 1420 6.0 / 2057 0.3

Chart Datum: 2·90 metres below Ordnance Datum (Newlyn)

REEDS PBO ALMANAC UPDATES

Get your updates from January–June:

- **Available in PBO magazine, monthly.**

- **FREE by email:**

Register online @ **www.reedsalmanac.co.uk/updates** to receive an email reminder when the new updates are available to download.

OR

- **by post:**

Please fill in the form overleaf and return this card with an A4 stamped addressed envelope for 150 grams (70p 1st class, 52p 2nd class) **AND include a cheque for £2.00** for admin costs. Cheques payable to: Adlard Coles Nautical.

www.reedsalmanac.co.uk

• Updates are available FREE electronically (see overleaf for details)

UPDATES BY POST

Please fill in the form below and return this card with an A4 S.A.E for 150 grams and a cheque for £2 payable to Adlard Coles Nautical.

TITLE _____ INITIAL _____ SURNAME _____

ADDRESS _____

_____ POSTCODE _____ TEL _____

ALMANAC PRODUCT UPDATES & OFFERS

Please notify me when the new editions are available for: (please tick)

☐ Reeds Nautical Almanac   ☐ Looseleaf Almanac

☐ Channel Almanac ☐ Eastern Almanac ☐ Western Almanac ☐ PBO Small Craft Almanac

We would also like to keep you informed of new publications and offers from Adlard Coles Nautical. *Our promise: we will never pass on your details to third parties and we will only contact you from time to time with information we think is of interest to you.*

☐ Tick here if you do **not** wish to be informed of interesting new publications and offers, including notification when the new REEDS range is available.

What improvements would you like to see in our products or services?

Checklist: 1. A4 stamped addressed envelope (150grams) 2. Cheque 3. This reply card
Send to: **Adlard Coles Nautical, 38 Soho Square, London W1D 3HB.**

TIME ZONE (UT)
For Summer Time add ONE hour in **non-shaded areas**

ENGLAND – SHEERNESS

LAT 51°27'N   LONG 0°45'E

TIMES AND HEIGHTS OF HIGH AND LOW WATERS

Dates in amber are SPRINGS
Dates in yellow are NEAPS

2007

SEPTEMBER

Time	m		Time	m
1 0253	6.0	**16** 0255	5.5
0857	0.7	0851	1.1
SA 1458	6.0	SU 1503	5.5
2132	0.5	2115	0.9
2 0333	5.8	**17** 0323	5.4
0932	0.9	0915	1.2
SU 1538	5.9	M 1534	5.3
2204	0.7	2139	1.2
3 0414	5.5	**18** 0353	5.2
1008	1.0	0940	1.3
M 1623	5.6	TU 1608	5.1
2238	1.0	2206	1.4
4 0500	5.2	**19** 0428	5.0
1052	1.2	1014	1.5
TU 1716	5.3	W 1650	4.8
2323	1.3	2245	1.7
5 0558	4.9	**20** 0513	4.7
1153	1.4	1106	1.7
W 1828	4.9	TH 1747	4.6
		2350	1.9
6 0038	1.7	**21** 0618	4.5
0715	4.7	1229	1.9
TH 1332	1.6	F 1910	4.4
1959	4.8		
7 0224	1.8	**22** 0138	2.0
0844	4.7	0751	4.5
F 1516	1.4	SA 1429	1.7
2132	5.0	2047	4.6
8 0354	1.6	**23** 0308	1.7
1004	5.0	0918	4.8
SA 1639	1.1	SU 1546	1.3
2244	5.3	2201	5.1
9 0500	1.4	**24** 0410	1.4
1105	5.3	1021	5.2
SU 1737	0.9	M 1646	1.0
2337	5.6	2256	5.5
10 0548	1.2	**25** 0501	1.1
1152	5.5	1111	5.5
M 1822	0.6	TU 1738	0.7
		2343	5.8
11 0021	5.7	**26** 0547	0.9
0624	1.1	1825	5.8
TU 1232	5.6	W 1825	0.5
● 1858	0.6	○	
12 0058	5.7	**27** 0026	6.0
0656	1.0	0631	0.8
W 1306	5.7	TH 1235	6.0
1930	0.6	1909	0.4
13 0130	5.7	**28** 0107	6.1
0727	1.0	0713	0.7
TH 1337	5.7	F 1314	6.1
1959	0.6	1950	0.3
14 0200	5.7	**29** 0147	6.1
0757	1.0	0754	0.7
F 1406	5.7	SA 1354	6.2
2026	0.7	2029	0.4
15 0228	5.6	**30** 0226	6.0
0825	1.0	0834	0.7
SA 1434	5.7	SU 1435	6.1
2052	0.8	2104	0.6

OCTOBER

Time	m		Time	m
1 0306	5.8	**16** 0249	5.5
0912	0.8	0849	1.2
M 1519	5.9	TU 1507	5.4
2138	0.9	2107	1.2
2 0349	5.5	**17** 0320	5.3
0952	1.0	0916	1.3
TU 1607	5.6	W 1543	5.2
2214	1.2	2136	1.4
3 0436	5.2	**18** 0355	5.1
1039	1.2	0950	1.4
W 1705	5.2	TH 1626	5.0
2304	1.6	2216	1.7
4 0537	4.8	**19** 0441	4.9
1147	1.4	1041	1.6
TH 1820	4.9	F 1722	4.7
		2318	1.9
5 0023	1.9	**20** 0543	4.6
0657	4.6	1158	1.7
F 1333	1.5	SA 1837	4.6
1950	4.8		
6 0208	1.9	**21** 0050	2.0
0825	4.7	0707	4.6
SA 1508	1.3	SU 1344	1.6
2117	5.0	2005	4.8
7 0332	1.7	**22** 0221	1.8
0942	5.0	0833	4.8
SU 1619	1.0	M 1505	1.3
2223	5.4	2120	5.2
8 0434	1.5	**23** 0327	1.4
1039	5.3	0939	5.2
M 1743	0.8	TU 1607	1.0
2313	5.6	2220	5.5
9 0518	1.3	**24** 0422	1.2
1125	5.5	1033	5.5
TU 1752	0.7	W 1702	0.7
2353	5.7	2310	5.8
10 0553	1.2	**25** 0512	1.0
1202	5.6	1120	5.8
W 1824	0.7	TH 1752	0.6
		2355	6.0
11 0028	5.7	**26** 0600	0.9
0624	1.1	1204	6.0
TH 1235	5.7	F 1838	0.5
● 1852	0.7	○	
12 0058	5.7	**27** 0038	6.0
0654	1.0	0646	0.7
F 1305	5.7	SA 1248	6.1
1920	0.7	1921	0.5
13 0125	5.7	**28** 0121	6.0
0725	0.9	0732	0.7
SA 1335	5.7	SU 1332	6.2
1948	0.8	2001	0.6
14 0152	5.7	**29** 0202	5.9
0755	1.0	0816	0.7
SU 1404	5.6	M 1418	6.1
2015	0.9	2040	0.8
15 0220	5.6	**30** 0245	5.7
0823	1.1	0900	0.8
M 1435	5.5	TU 1506	5.9
2041	1.0	2118	1.1
		31 0329	5.5
		0945	0.9
		W 1558	5.6
		2159	1.4

NOVEMBER

Time	m		Time	m
1 0420	5.2	**16** 0336	5.2
1036	1.1	0944	1.3
TH 1658	5.2	F 1613	5.1
◗ 2250	1.7	2203	1.5
2 0520	4.9	**17** 0421	5.0
1146	1.3	1034	1.4
F 1807	5.0	SA 1707	5.0
		◗ 2258	1.7
3 0001	1.9	**18** 0518	4.9
0633	4.7	1138	1.4
SA 1316	1.4	SU 1812	4.9
1925	4.9		
4 0130	2.0	**19** 0010	1.8
0751	4.8	0628	4.8
SU 1434	1.2	M 1258	1.4
2041	5.0	1925	5.0
5 0247	1.8	**20** 0128	1.7
0903	5.0	0743	4.9
M 1539	1.1	TU 1415	1.2
2146	5.2	2037	5.2
6 0348	1.6	**21** 0238	1.5
1002	5.2	0853	5.2
TU 1630	1.0	W 1521	1.0
2237	5.4	2140	5.4
7 0436	1.4	**22** 0339	1.3
1049	5.4	0953	5.5
W 1710	0.9	TH 1622	0.8
2318	5.5	2236	5.6
8 0514	1.2	**23** 0436	1.1
1128	5.5	1047	5.7
TH 1741	0.9	F 1718	0.7
2353	5.5	2326	5.8
9 0550	1.1	**24** 0532	0.9
1203	5.5	1138	5.9
F 1813	1.0	SA 1809	0.7
●		○	
10 0024	5.6	**25** 0014	5.8
0623	1.0	0625	0.8
SA 1236	5.6	SU 1229	6.0
1843	0.9	1856	0.7
11 0053	5.6	**26** 0100	5.8
0657	1.0	0717	0.7
SU 1308	5.6	M 1318	6.0
1914	0.9	1940	0.8
12 0122	5.6	**27** 0145	5.8
0729	1.0	0807	0.6
M 1341	5.5	TU 1408	6.0
1944	1.0	2023	0.9
13 0152	5.6	**28** 0230	5.6
0801	1.0	0856	0.7
TU 1414	5.5	W 1459	5.8
2015	1.1	2104	1.2
14 0224	5.5	**29** 0317	5.4
0832	1.1	0944	0.8
W 1449	5.4	TH 1551	5.6
2046	1.2	2146	1.4
15 0258	5.3	**30** 0406	5.2
0906	1.2	1034	1.0
TH 1528	5.2	F 1645	5.3
2120	1.4	2231	1.6

DECEMBER

Time	m		Time	m
1 0459	5.0	**16** 0408	5.2
1130	1.1	1029	1.1
SA 1743	5.1	SU 1651	5.2
◗ 2326	1.8	2239	1.4
2 0558	4.9	**17** 0456	5.1
1233	1.2	1117	1.1
SU 1845	4.9	M 1745	5.1
		◗ 2332	1.5
3 0032	1.9	**18** 0552	5.1
0703	4.8	1212	1.1
M 1339	1.3	TU 1847	5.0
1950	4.9		
4 0145	1.9	**19** 0035	1.5
0809	4.8	0657	5.1
TU 1440	1.3	W 1320	1.1
2054	4.9	1955	5.1
5 0249	1.7	**20** 0146	1.5
0912	4.9	0808	5.1
W 1533	1.2	TH 1433	1.1
2150	5.0	2103	5.2
6 0346	1.6	**21** 0258	1.4
1006	5.1	0918	5.3
TH 1620	1.2	F 1545	1.0
2237	5.2	2206	5.3
7 0434	1.4	**22** 0407	1.2
1053	5.2	1023	5.5
F 1700	1.1	SA 1651	1.0
2317	5.3	2304	5.5
8 0517	1.4	**23** 0514	1.0
1134	5.3	1123	5.6
SA 1738	1.1	SU 1749	0.9
2353	5.4	2357	5.6
9 0557	1.1	**24** 0616	0.8
1212	5.4	1219	5.8
SU 1813	1.1	M 1841	0.9
●		○	
10 0027	5.5	**25** 0047	5.6
0634	1.0	0712	0.6
M 1249	5.4	TU 1313	5.8
1847	1.1	1928	0.9
11 0101	5.5	**26** 0135	5.6
0710	1.0	0805	0.6
TU 1325	5.5	W 1403	5.8
1922	1.0	2012	1.0
12 0135	5.6	**27** 0221	5.6
0747	0.9	0853	0.5
W 1402	5.5	TH 1451	5.8
1957	1.1	2053	1.1
13 0210	5.5	**28** 0305	5.5
0826	0.9	0938	0.6
TH 1440	5.4	F 1537	5.6
2034	1.1	2130	1.2
14 0246	5.4	**29** 0348	5.4
0905	1.0	1018	0.8
F 1520	5.4	SA 1622	5.4
2113	1.2	2206	1.4
15 0325	5.3	**30** 0431	5.3
0946	1.0	1056	0.9
SA 1603	5.3	SU 1708	5.2
2154	1.3	2244	1.5
		31 0515	5.1
		1135	1.1
		M 1755	5.0
		◗ 2329	1.6

Chart Datum: 2·90 metres below Ordnance Datum (Newlyn)

257

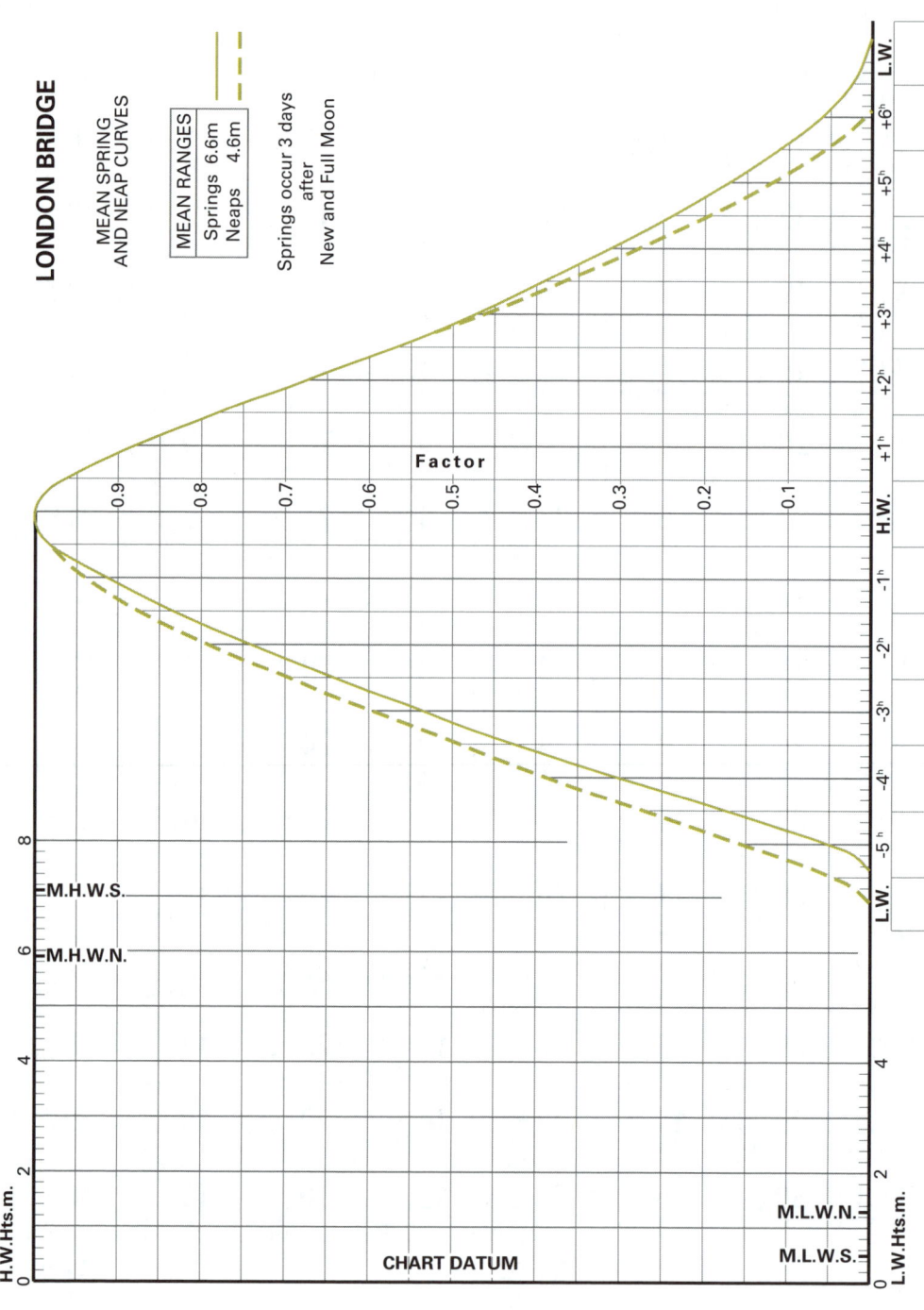

LONDON BRIDGE

MEAN SPRING
AND NEAP CURVES

MEAN RANGES	
Springs	6.6m
Neaps	4.6m

Springs occur 3 days
after
New and Full Moon

ENGLAND – LONDON BRIDGE

LAT 51°30′N LONG 0°05′W

TIMES AND HEIGHTS OF HIGH AND LOW WATERS

Dates in amber are **SPRINGS**
Dates in yellow are **NEAPS**

2007

JANUARY

Day	Time m	Time m	Day	Time m	Time m
1 M	0537 1.4	1131 6.3	16 TU	0501 1.6	1128 5.8
	1816 1.2			1744 1.3	2356 6.1
2 TU	0010 6.3	0645 1.2	17 W	0606 1.3	1226 6.2
	1231 6.5	1910 1.1		1841 1.1	
3 W	0104 6.4	0742 0.9	18 TH	0048 6.4	0707 1.0
	1326 6.7	2000 1.0 ○		1316 6.6	1933 1.0
4 TH	0153 6.5	0835 0.8	19 F	0136 6.6	0805 0.8
	1416 6.8	2047 1.1		1403 6.8	2023 0.9 ●
5 F	0237 6.6	0923 0.7	20 SA	0219 6.7	0901 0.7
	1504 6.8	2130 1.1		1448 6.9	2112 0.9
6 SA	0317 6.5	1007 0.7	21 SU	0302 6.8	0953 0.6
	1547 6.7	2208 1.2		1533 7.0	2158 1.0
7 SU	0353 6.4	1045 0.8	22 M	0343 6.8	1039 0.6
	1626 6.6	2240 1.3		1618 7.0	2241 0.9
8 M	0426 6.4	1117 1.0	23 TU	0425 6.8	1120 0.5
	1702 6.5	2304 1.4		1703 6.9	2320 0.9
9 TU	0459 6.4	1143 1.0	24 W	0507 6.8	1156 0.6
	1736 6.4	2328 1.4		1748 6.8	2356 0.9
10 W	0534 6.3	1208 1.1	25 TH	0550 6.8	1229 0.7
	1812 6.3	2359 1.4		1835 6.6 ◑	
11 TH	0614 6.2	1240 1.2	26 F	0034 1.0	0635 6.6
	1853 6.1 ◐			1305 0.9	1923 6.3
12 F	0038 1.4	0659 5.9	27 SA	0117 1.2	0727 6.3
	1322 1.4	1938 5.9		1350 1.2	2020 5.9
13 SA	0127 1.6	0753 5.7	28 SU	0210 1.5	0834 6.0
	1419 1.6	2032 5.7		1451 1.6	2131 5.6
14 SU	0232 1.8	0859 5.5	29 M	0322 1.8	0959 5.7
	1529 1.7	2139 5.6		1625 1.8	2247 5.6
15 M	0350 1.8	1016 5.5	30 TU	0516 1.8	1118 5.9
	1640 1.6	2252 5.8		1757 1.7	2355 5.8
			31 W	0640 1.4	1224 6.2
				1858 1.4	

FEBRUARY

Day	Time m	Time m	Day	Time m	Time m
1 TH	0052 6.2	0737 0.9	16 F	0028 6.3	0657 1.0
	1319 6.5	1948 1.2		1259 6.6	1919 1.0
2 F	0142 6.4	0827 0.7	17 SA	0117 6.6	0800 0.7
	1408 6.8	2035 1.0 ○		1347 6.9	2014 0.9 ●
3 SA	0225 6.6	0912 0.5	18 SU	0202 6.8	0854 0.4
	1451 6.8	2118 1.0		1432 7.1	2104 0.8
4 SU	0303 6.6	0953 0.6	19 M	0244 6.9	0943 0.3
	1530 6.7	2157 1.1		1516 7.2	2149 0.7
5 M	0336 6.5	1029 0.7	20 TU	0325 7.0	1025 0.3
	1602 6.7	2228 1.2		1559 7.2	2229 0.7
6 TU	0404 6.5	1057 0.8	21 W	0405 7.1	1102 0.3
	1632 6.6	2246 1.2		1641 7.1	2305 0.6
7 W	0433 6.5	1116 0.9	22 TH	0445 7.1	1132 0.4
	1701 6.5	2300 1.1		1722 6.9	2336 0.7
8 TH	0505 6.5	1128 1.0	23 F	0526 7.0	1158 0.6
	1734 6.5	2324 1.0		1804 6.6	
9 F	0540 6.4	1151 1.0	24 SA	0007 0.8	0608 6.8
	1810 6.4	2357 1.1		1229 0.9	1846 6.2 ◐
10 SA	0620 6.2	1224 1.1	25 SU	0045 1.1	0657 6.5
	1852 6.1 ◑			1311 1.3	1936 5.7 ○
11 SU	0036 1.3	0706 5.9	26 M	0134 1.5	0804 5.7
	1310 1.4	1941 5.8		1410 1.8	2055 5.3
12 M	0130 1.6	0805 5.5	27 TU	0248 1.9	0946 5.5
	1424 1.8	2041 5.5		1546 2.1	2228 5.3
13 TU	0259 1.9	0918 5.4	28 W	0520 1.8	1110 5.7
	1557 1.8	2201 5.5		1743 1.9	2338 5.7
14 W	0426 1.7	1050 5.6			
	1713 1.6	2326 5.8			
15 TH	0543 1.4	1205 6.1			
	1820 1.2				

MARCH

Day	Time m	Time m	Day	Time m	Time m
1 TH	0631 1.2	1213 6.2	16 F	0526 1.4	1141 6.1
	1843 1.4			1800 1.3	
2 F	0035 6.2	0722 0.7	17 SA	0001 6.2	0645 0.9
	1305 6.6	1931 1.1		1237 6.6	1902 1.0
3 SA	0123 6.5	0807 0.4	18 SU	0052 6.6	0744 0.5
	1350 6.9	2016 0.9 ○		1325 7.0	1955 0.7
4 SU	0205 6.7	0849 0.4	19 M	0136 6.9	0834 0.3
	1430 6.9	2058 0.8		1409 7.2	2044 0.6 ●
5 M	0241 6.7	0928 0.5	20 TU	0218 7.1	0920 0.2
	1504 6.8	2136 0.9		1452 7.3	2129 0.5
6 TU	0312 6.6	1002 0.6	21 W	0300 7.3	1000 0.2
	1533 6.6	2207 1.1		1534 7.2	2209 0.5
7 W	0338 6.5	1029 0.9	22 TH	0342 7.3	1035 0.3
	1559 6.6	2223 1.1		1615 7.1	2244 0.5
8 TH	0406 6.5	1044 1.0	23 F	0423 7.3	1103 0.4
	1627 6.6	2233 1.0		1655 6.9	2315 0.6
9 F	0436 6.6	1052 0.9	24 SA	0505 7.1	1130 0.7
	1659 6.6	2254 0.9		1734 6.6	2345 0.8
10 SA	0510 6.5	1114 0.9	25 SU	0550 6.7	1201 1.0
	1735 6.5	2324 0.9 ◑		1815 6.1 ◑	
11 SU	0549 6.3	1145 1.0	26 M	0022 1.1	0642 6.1
	1815 6.3	2359 1.0		1244 1.5	1903 5.6
12 M	0635 6.0	1225 1.3	27 TU	0116 1.5	0758 5.6
	1902 5.9			1347 2.0	2035 5.2
13 TU	0046 1.4	0731 5.6	28 W	0236 1.9	0937 5.5
	1327 1.7	2000 5.5		1525 2.2	2206 5.3
14 W	0207 1.8	0840 5.4	29 TH	0504 1.6	1050 5.8
	1514 2.0	2114 5.4		1718 1.9	2313 5.8
15 TH	0357 1.7	1013 5.5	30 F	0605 1.1	1149 6.3
	1646 1.7	2252 5.6		1816 1.4	
			31 SA	0007 6.3	0652 0.6
				1239 6.7	1904 1.0

APRIL

Day	Time m	Time m	Day	Time m	Time m
1 SU	0055 6.6	0735 0.4	16 M	0019 6.7	0716 0.4
	1323 6.9	1948 0.8		1257 7.1	1929 0.7
2 M	0136 6.7	0816 0.4	17 TU	0106 7.0	0805 0.2
	1401 6.9	2030 0.8 ○		1342 7.3	2018 0.5 ●
3 TU	0212 6.7	0855 0.5	18 W	0151 7.2	0850 0.2
	1433 6.7	2107 0.9		1426 7.3	2104 0.4
4 W	0244 6.5	0929 0.7	19 TH	0236 7.4	0931 0.2
	1501 6.6	2138 1.0		1508 7.2	2146 0.3
5 TH	0312 6.4	0956 0.9	20 F	0320 7.4	1006 0.2
	1527 6.5	2156 1.1		1550 7.0	2224 0.4
6 F	0340 6.4	1011 1.0	21 SA	0405 7.2	1038 0.6
	1556 6.6	2209 1.0		1631 6.8	2258 0.6
7 SA	0411 6.5	1024 1.0	22 SU	0451 7.0	1108 0.8
	1629 6.6	2232 0.8		1711 6.4	2333 0.8
8 SU	0446 6.5	1048 0.9	23 M	0541 6.6	1144 1.2
	1705 6.5	2301 0.8		1755 6.0	
9 M	0526 6.4	1122 1.0	24 TU	0014 1.1	0638 6.1
	1746 6.3	2338 1.0		1230 1.6	1849 5.6 ◑
10 TU	0614 6.1	1204 1.3	25 W	0112 1.4	0755 5.7
	1834 5.9			1332 2.0	2017 5.4
11 W	0026 1.3	0709 5.8	26 TH	0227 1.6	0914 5.7
	1303 1.7	1931 5.6		1455 2.1	2135 5.5
12 TH	0141 1.6	0818 5.6	27 F	0413 1.4	1019 6.0
	1435 1.9	2043 5.5		1631 1.8	2237 5.9
13 F	0330 1.6	0945 5.7	28 SA	0521 1.1	1115 6.3
	1614 1.8	2213 5.7		1737 1.4	2331 6.2
14 SA	0503 1.3	1109 6.2	29 SU	0611 0.8	1204 6.6
	1732 1.4	2325 6.2		1828 1.1	
15 SU	0619 0.8	1208 6.7	30 M	0019 6.5	0655 0.6
	1835 1.0			1248 6.7	1913 0.9

Chart Datum: 2·90 metres below Ordnance Datum (Newlyn)

TIDES

TIME ZONE (UT)
For Summer Time add ONE hour in **non-shaded areas**

ENGLAND – LONDON BRIDGE
LAT 51°30′N   LONG 0°05′W
TIMES AND HEIGHTS OF HIGH AND LOW WATERS

Dates in amber are SPRINGS
Dates in yellow are NEAPS

2007

MAY

Day	Time m	Time m	Time m	Time m
1 TU	0102 6.6	0737 0.6	1326 6.7	1955 0.9
2 W	0141 6.6	0816 0.7	1359 6.6	○ 2033 0.9
3 TH	0215 6.5	0851 0.9	1430 6.5	2104 1.0
4 F	0246 6.4	0920 1.0	1459 6.5	2129 1.0
5 SA	0318 6.4	0941 1.0	1531 6.5	2152 0.9
6 SU	0352 6.4	1004 1.0	1606 6.5	2219 0.9
7 M	0430 6.4	1034 1.0	1643 6.4	2253 0.9
8 TU	0513 6.4	1112 1.1	1725 6.3	2333 1.0
9 W	0602 6.2	1157 1.3	1814 6.1	
10 TH	0025 1.1	0658 6.0	1256 1.5	◑ 1911 5.8
11 F	0137 1.3	0804 5.8	1411 1.7	2021 5.8
12 SA	0303 1.3	0921 5.9	1537 1.6	2139 5.9
13 SU	0428 1.1	1035 6.3	1655 1.4	2248 6.3
14 M	0543 0.8	1136 6.6	1802 1.0	2346 6.7
15 TU	0642 0.5	1228 6.9	1900 0.7	
16 W	0038 7.0	0733 0.4	1317 7.1	● 1952 0.5
17 TH	0128 7.2	0820 0.3	1402 7.1	2041 0.4
18 F	0217 7.2	0903 0.4	1447 7.0	2127 0.4
19 SA	0305 7.2	0943 0.6	1530 6.9	2209 0.4
20 SU	0353 7.0	1020 0.8	1613 6.7	2250 0.6
21 M	0443 6.8	1056 1.0	1657 6.4	2330 0.8
22 TU	0534 6.5	1134 1.3	1742 6.1	
23 W	0013 1.0	0629 6.2	1219 1.5	◑ 1835 5.9
24 TH	0103 1.2	0731 6.0	1311 1.7	1942 5.7
25 F	0200 1.3	0835 5.9	1412 1.9	2050 5.7
26 SA	0303 1.3	0936 6.0	1519 1.8	2152 5.8
27 SU	0409 1.2	1031 6.1	1628 1.7	2248 6.0
28 M	0512 1.1	1122 6.3	1733 1.4	2339 6.2
29 TU	0605 1.0	1207 6.4	1827 1.2	
30 W	0026 6.3	0651 0.9	1249 6.5	1912 1.0
31 TH	0109 6.4	0733 0.9	1327 6.5	1953 1.0

JUNE

Day	Time m	Time m	Time m	Time m
1 F	0148 6.4	0811 0.9	1403 6.5	○ 2030 0.9
2 SA	0225 6.4	0846 1.0	1438 6.5	2106 0.9
3 SU	0302 6.4	0919 1.0	1514 6.5	2142 0.9
4 M	0340 6.5	0952 1.0	1551 6.5	2218 0.9
5 TU	0421 6.5	1029 1.0	1630 6.4	2258 0.8
6 W	0506 6.4	1111 1.1	1713 6.4	2342 0.9
7 TH	0555 6.4	1157 1.2	1801 6.3	
8 F	0031 0.9	0649 6.2	1250 1.3	◑ 1855 6.2
9 SA	0128 1.0	0749 6.1	1349 1.4	1958 6.1
10 SU	0231 1.0	0855 6.1	1457 1.4	2106 6.1
11 M	0345 1.1	1002 6.2	1612 1.4	2214 6.3
12 TU	0503 1.0	1105 6.4	1728 1.2	2318 6.5
13 W	0609 0.8	1202 6.6	1834 1.0	
14 TH	0017 6.7	0705 0.7	1255 6.8	1932 0.7
15 F	0112 6.9	0755 0.7	1345 6.8	● 2025 0.5
16 SA	0204 7.0	0843 0.7	1432 6.8	2116 0.5
17 SU	0255 7.0	0927 0.8	1517 6.7	2203 0.5
18 M	0345 6.9	1009 0.9	1601 6.6	2247 0.5
19 TU	0433 6.8	1049 1.1	1644 6.5	2327 0.6
20 W	0520 6.6	1125 1.2	1725 6.4	
21 TH	0004 0.8	0605 6.4	1202 1.3	1806 6.2
22 F	0041 0.9	0651 6.2	1240 1.5	◑ 1852 6.1
23 SA	0121 1.0	0739 6.0	1324 1.6	1945 5.9
24 SU	0208 1.2	0831 5.8	1416 1.7	2045 5.7
25 M	0301 1.3	0928 5.8	1515 1.7	2150 5.7
26 TU	0401 1.3	1027 5.8	1619 1.7	2253 5.8
27 W	0504 1.3	1123 6.0	1724 1.5	2350 6.0
28 TH	0602 1.1	1214 6.2	1823 1.2	
29 F	0040 6.2	0652 1.0	1300 6.5	1916 1.0
30 SA	0125 6.4	0738 0.9	1342 6.6	○ 2005 0.8

JULY

Day	Time m	Time m	Time m	Time m
1 SU	0207 6.6	0822 0.9	1422 6.6	2053 0.8
2 M	0249 6.6	0904 1.0	1502 6.6	2140 0.8
3 TU	0330 6.6	0947 1.0	1541 6.6	2224 0.7
4 W	0413 6.7	1029 1.0	1621 6.6	2306 0.7
5 TH	0458 6.6	1110 1.0	1703 6.6	2345 0.7
6 F	0544 6.6	1152 1.0	1747 6.6	
7 SA	0025 0.7	0632 6.5	1236 1.1	◑ 1834 6.5
8 SU	0107 0.8	0725 6.3	1324 1.2	1928 6.4
9 M	0156 1.0	0824 6.1	1419 1.4	2031 6.2
10 TU	0256 1.2	0930 6.0	1528 1.5	2142 6.1
11 W	0419 1.3	1038 6.0	1654 1.5	2256 6.1
12 TH	0542 1.3	1142 6.1	1817 1.3	
13 F	0004 6.3	0645 1.1	1241 6.4	1922 0.9
14 SA	0104 6.6	0740 0.9	1415 6.6	● 2018 0.6
15 SU	0158 6.8	0831 0.9	1422 6.7	2110 0.4
16 M	0248 6.9	0917 0.9	1506 6.7	2156 0.3
17 TU	0334 6.9	1000 0.9	1547 6.7	2237 0.4
18 W	0417 6.8	1039 1.0	1624 6.6	2313 0.5
19 TH	0455 6.7	1111 1.1	1657 6.6	2343 0.6
20 F	0530 6.6	1137 1.2	1731 6.5	
21 SA	0008 0.8	0604 6.4	1203 1.2	1806 6.4
22 SU	0036 0.9	0641 6.2	1235 1.3	◑ 1848 6.1
23 M	0110 1.1	0723 6.0	1317 1.5	1937 5.8
24 TU	0200 1.4	0814 5.7	1416 1.7	2038 5.5
25 W	0305 1.6	0919 5.6	1528 1.8	2155 5.4
26 TH	0415 1.6	1035 5.7	1639 1.6	2315 5.7
27 F	0522 1.3	1142 6.0	1746 1.3	
28 SA	0016 6.1	0621 1.1	1237 6.4	1850 1.0
29 SU	0106 6.5	0714 0.9	1415 6.5	1951 0.8
30 M	0151 6.7	0805 0.9	1407 6.7	○ 2046 0.6
31 TU	0233 6.9	0855 0.9	1447 6.8	2136 0.6

AUGUST

Day	Time m	Time m	Time m	Time m
1 W	0316 6.9	0941 0.9	1527 6.8	2221 0.5
2 TH	0358 6.9	1024 0.9	1606 6.8	2300 0.5
3 F	0440 6.9	1102 0.9	1645 6.9	2334 0.5
4 SA	0523 6.8	1138 0.9	1725 6.9	
5 SU	0004 0.6	0606 6.6	1215 0.9	◑ 1808 6.8
6 M	0037 0.8	0653 6.3	1254 1.1	1856 6.5
7 TU	0117 1.1	0747 5.9	1344 1.4	1956 6.1
8 W	0213 1.5	0855 5.6	1451 1.4	2117 5.7
9 TH	0337 1.8	1016 5.5	1632 1.8	2246 5.8
10 F	0526 1.7	1129 5.8	1815 1.4	2359 6.1
11 SA	0635 1.4	1231 6.2	1917 0.8	
12 SU	0058 6.6	0729 1.0	1323 6.6	● 2008 0.4
13 M	0149 6.9	0817 0.8	1408 6.8	2055 0.2
14 TU	0234 7.0	0902 0.8	1449 6.9	2138 0.2
15 W	0316 7.0	0944 0.8	1526 6.8	2216 0.3
16 TH	0352 6.9	1020 0.9	1557 6.7	2249 0.5
17 F	0422 6.7	1049 1.0	1625 6.7	2314 0.7
18 SA	0450 6.6	1107 1.1	1655 6.6	2329 0.8
19 SU	0520 6.5	1123 1.1	1728 6.5	2344 0.9
20 M	0554 6.4	1148 1.1	1806 6.3	●
21 TU	0010 1.1	0633 6.1	1225 1.3	1850 5.9
22 W	0051 1.4	0720 5.8	1317 1.6	1945 5.5
23 TH	0202 1.8	0819 5.5	1444 1.9	2056 5.3
24 F	0334 1.9	0941 5.4	1606 1.8	2237 5.5
25 SA	0450 1.6	1113 5.7	1720 1.4	2352 6.5
26 SU	0557 1.3	1213 6.2	1835 1.0	
27 M	0044 6.5	0656 1.0	1301 6.6	1938 0.7
28 TU	0130 6.6	0750 0.8	1344 6.8	○ 2032 0.5
29 W	0212 7.1	0840 0.8	1424 6.9	2120 0.4
30 TH	0254 7.1	0926 0.8	1503 7.0	2203 0.4
31 F	0335 7.1	1008 0.8	1541 7.1	2240 0.4

Chart Datum: 2·90 metres below Ordnance Datum (Newlyn)

ENGLAND – LONDON BRIDGE

LAT 51°30'N   LONG 0°05'W

TIMES AND HEIGHTS OF HIGH AND LOW WATERS

Dates in amber are SPRINGS
Dates in yellow are NEAPS

2007

SEPTEMBER

Day	Time m	Time m	Time m	Time m
1 SA	0415 7.0	1045 0.7	SA 1621 7.1	2310 0.5
2 SU	0456 6.9	1119 0.8	SU 1701 7.1	2336 0.7
3 M	0537 6.6	1150 0.9	M 1744 6.9	
4 TU	0004 0.9	0619 6.2	TU 1227 1.1	☽ 1831 6.4
5 W	0043 1.3	0708 5.8	W 1316 1.5	1933 5.9
6 TH	0139 1.8	0825 5.3	TH 1430 1.9	2110 5.5
7 F	0314 2.1	1002 5.3	F 1645 1.8	2241 5.7
8 SA	0516 1.9	1115 5.8	SA 1805 1.0	2348 6.2
9 SU	0619 1.4	1213 6.3	SU 1900 0.6	
10 M	0043 6.8	0709 0.9	M 1303 6.7	1946 0.3
11 TU	0130 7.1	0755 0.7	TU 1346 6.9	● 2029 0.1
12 W	0212 7.1	0839 0.6	W 1424 7.0	2110 0.2
13 TH	0249 7.0	0919 0.7	TH 1458 6.8	2146 0.4
14 F	0320 6.8	0955 0.9	F 1527 6.6	2217 0.7
15 SA	0346 6.7	1021 1.0	SA 1554 6.6	2239 0.9
16 SU	0411 6.6	1034 1.1	SU 1622 6.6	2246 1.0
17 M	0441 6.6	1046 1.0	M 1655 6.5	2259 1.0
18 TU	0514 6.5	1111 1.0	TU 1732 6.3	2326 1.1
19 W	0552 6.3	1144 1.2	W 1815 6.0	☾
20 TH	0003 1.3	0636 5.9	TH 1230 1.5	1908 5.6
21 F	0100 1.8	0733 5.5	F 1353 1.9	2014 5.4
22 SA	0246 2.1	0847 5.3	SA 1535 1.8	2147 5.4
23 SU	0417 1.9	1032 5.6	SU 1655 1.4	2321 6.0
24 M	0530 1.5	1140 6.1	M 1813 1.0	
25 TU	0016 6.6	0632 1.1	TU 1230 6.6	1914 0.6
26 W	0102 7.0	0726 0.8	W 1313 6.9	○ 2006 0.4
27 TH	0145 7.2	0816 0.7	TH 1354 7.1	2053 0.3
28 F	0226 7.3	0902 0.6	F 1434 7.2	2135 0.3
29 SA	0307 7.2	0945 0.6	SA 1516 7.3	2211 0.4
30 SU	0348 7.1	1023 0.6	SU 1558 7.3	2241 0.6

OCTOBER

Day	Time m	Time m	Time m	Time m
1 M	0428 6.9	1058 0.7	M 1641 7.1	2308 0.8
2 TU	0509 6.6	1131 0.9	TU 1727 6.8	2338 1.1
3 W	0551 6.2	1209 1.2	W 1819 6.3	☽
4 TH	0019 1.5	0640 5.7	TH 1304 1.5	1930 5.7
5 F	0121 2.0	0812 5.3	F 1428 1.8	2107 5.6
6 SA	0302 2.3	0943 5.4	SA 1632 1.6	2223 5.9
7 SU	0450 1.9	1049 5.9	SU 1738 1.0	2325 6.4
8 M	0551 1.4	1145 6.4	M 1829 0.6	
9 TU	0017 6.8	0640 0.9	TU 1233 6.8	1913 0.3
10 W	0103 7.1	0726 0.6	W 1316 6.9	1955 0.3
11 TH	0143 7.1	0809 0.6	TH 1354 6.9	● 2035 0.4
12 F	0217 6.9	0849 0.8	F 1428 6.7	2111 0.6
13 SA	0246 6.7	0923 0.9	SA 1457 6.6	2141 0.9
14 SU	0311 6.6	0949 1.1	SU 1525 6.5	2200 1.1
15 M	0337 6.6	1001 1.1	M 1555 6.5	2208 1.1
16 TU	0407 6.6	1017 1.1	TU 1629 6.5	2229 1.0
17 W	0441 6.5	1045 1.0	W 1707 6.4	2259 1.1
18 TH	0520 6.3	1120 1.1	TH 1751 6.1	2339 1.3
19 F	0604 6.0	1205 1.4	F 1844 5.8	☾
20 SA	0032 1.7	0659 5.7	SA 1317 1.7	1947 5.6
21 SU	0154 2.0	0808 5.5	SU 1501 1.7	2107 5.6
22 M	0336 1.9	0938 5.6	M 1624 1.4	2236 6.0
23 TU	0454 1.6	1055 6.1	TU 1740 1.0	2339 6.5
24 W	0600 1.2	1151 6.6	W 1842 0.7	
25 TH	0029 7.0	0656 0.9	TH 1239 7.0	1933 0.4
26 F	0115 7.2	0748 0.7	F 1324 7.2	○ 2020 0.4
27 SA	0159 7.3	0836 0.5	SA 1409 7.4	2103 0.4
28 SU	0242 7.2	0920 0.5	SU 1454 7.4	2141 0.5
29 M	0324 7.1	1002 0.6	M 1541 7.3	2216 0.7
30 TU	0406 6.8	1042 0.7	TU 1628 7.0	2248 0.9
31 W	0448 6.5	1121 0.9	W 1719 6.7	2324 1.3

NOVEMBER

Day	Time m	Time m	Time m	Time m
1 TH	0533 6.1	1206 1.2	TH 1817 6.2	☽
2 F	0009 1.6	0629 5.7	F 1304 1.4	1927 5.9
3 SA	0110 2.0	0754 5.5	SA 1420 1.5	2045 5.8
4 SU	0232 2.1	0912 5.6	SU 1549 1.4	2152 6.0
5 M	0402 1.9	1014 6.0	M 1655 1.1	2250 6.4
6 TU	0510 1.4	1109 6.3	TU 1747 0.8	2341 6.6
7 W	0604 1.2	1158 6.6	W 1833 0.6	
8 TH	0027 6.8	0651 1.0	TH 1242 6.7	1916 0.6
9 F	0108 6.8	0734 0.9	F 1323 6.7	● 1956 0.7
10 SA	0143 6.7	0813 0.9	SA 1359 6.6	2032 0.9
11 SU	0213 6.6	0848 1.0	SU 1431 6.5	2102 1.0
12 M	0241 6.5	0914 1.1	M 1502 6.4	2124 1.1
13 TU	0310 6.5	0935 1.1	TU 1534 6.4	2143 1.1
14 W	0342 6.5	1000 1.1	W 1611 6.4	2211 1.1
15 TH	0418 6.5	1032 1.0	TH 1651 6.4	2246 1.1
16 F	0457 6.4	1111 1.1	F 1736 6.3	2328 1.3
17 SA	0542 6.2	1159 1.2	SA 1828 6.1	☾
18 SU	0020 1.5	0634 6.0	SU 1302 1.4	1927 5.9
19 M	0126 1.7	0738 5.8	M 1421 1.4	2037 5.9
20 TU	0246 1.8	0854 5.9	TU 1541 1.3	2153 6.1
21 W	0409 1.6	1010 6.1	W 1659 1.1	2300 6.4
22 TH	0522 1.3	1113 6.5	TH 1805 0.8	2357 6.8
23 F	0625 1.0	1208 6.9	F 1901 0.6	
24 SA	0047 7.0	0721 0.7	SA 1300 7.1	○ 1950 0.6
25 SU	0135 7.1	0813 0.6	SU 1350 7.3	2036 0.6
26 M	0221 7.1	0902 0.5	M 1440 7.3	2119 0.7
27 TU	0306 6.9	0949 0.6	TU 1530 7.1	2200 0.9
28 W	0350 6.8	1035 0.7	W 1620 7.0	2239 1.1
29 TH	0435 6.5	1119 0.8	TH 1712 6.7	2318 1.3
30 F	0522 6.3	1205 1.0	F 1807 6.4	

DECEMBER

Day	Time m	Time m	Time m	Time m
1 SA	0001 1.5	0614 6.0	SA 1254 1.1	☽ 1904 6.2
2 SU	0050 1.8	0717 5.8	SU 1347 1.2	2006 6.0
3 M	0147 1.9	0824 5.8	M 1444 1.3	2107 6.0
4 TU	0250 1.9	0927 5.9	TU 1546 1.3	2204 6.0
5 W	0358 1.8	1025 6.0	W 1647 1.2	2258 6.2
6 TH	0506 1.6	1118 6.2	TH 1742 1.1	2347 6.3
7 F	0604 1.4	1207 6.3	F 1830 1.0	
8 SA	0031 6.4	0652 1.2	SA 1252 6.4	1913 1.0
9 SU	0111 6.5	0733 1.1	SU 1333 6.5	● 1952 1.1
10 M	0146 6.5	0811 1.0	M 1410 6.5	2027 1.1
11 TU	0220 6.5	0846 1.0	TU 1445 6.5	2058 1.1
12 W	0253 6.5	0920 1.0	W 1522 6.5	2129 1.2
13 TH	0327 6.5	0955 1.0	TH 1600 6.5	2203 1.2
14 F	0403 6.5	1032 1.0	F 1641 6.5	2242 1.2
15 SA	0442 6.5	1113 1.0	SA 1725 6.5	2324 1.2
16 SU	0526 6.4	1157 1.0	SU 1814 6.4	
17 M	0010 1.3	0614 6.3	M 1247 1.1	☾ 1907 6.2
18 TU	0103 1.4	0710 6.2	TU 1342 1.2	2006 6.1
19 W	0203 1.5	0816 6.1	W 1447 1.3	2114 6.0
20 TH	0316 1.6	0928 6.1	TH 1608 1.3	2223 6.1
21 F	0440 1.5	1040 6.3	F 1729 1.2	2328 6.3
22 SA	0557 1.3	1144 6.5	SA 1834 1.0	
23 SU	0025 6.6	0701 1.0	SU 1244 6.8	1929 0.9
24 M	0118 6.7	0759 0.7	M 1338 7.0	○ 2019 0.8
25 TU	0207 6.8	0853 0.6	TU 1431 7.1	2107 0.9
26 W	0254 6.8	0944 0.5	W 1522 7.0	2152 1.0
27 TH	0339 6.7	1032 0.5	TH 1611 7.0	2234 1.1
28 F	0423 6.6	1114 0.6	F 1658 6.8	2311 1.2
29 SA	0504 6.5	1153 0.7	SA 1743 6.7	2346 1.3
30 SU	0545 6.4	1227 0.9	SU 1827 6.4	
31 M	0020 1.4	0627 6.2	M 1303 1.1	☽ 1910 6.2

Chart Datum: 2·90 metres below Ordnance Datum (Newlyn)

TIDES

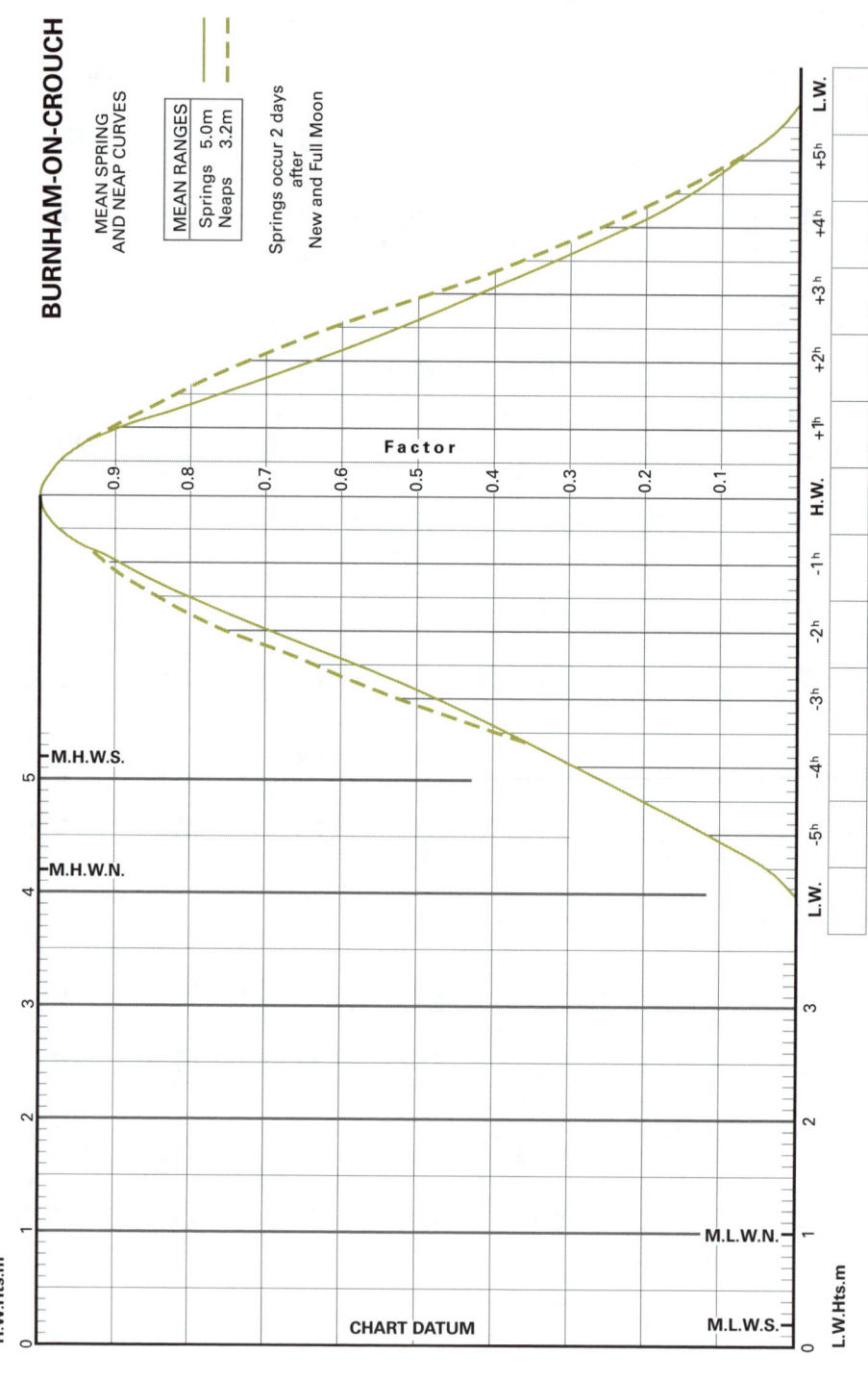

BURNHAM-ON-CROUCH

MEAN SPRING
AND NEAP CURVES

MEAN RANGES	
Springs	5.0m
Neaps	3.2m

Springs occur 2 days
after
New and Full Moon

Factor

0.9
0.8
0.7
0.6
0.5
0.4
0.3
0.2
0.1

M.H.W.S.

M.H.W.N.

M.L.W.N.

M.L.W.S.

CHART DATUM

H.W.Hts.m

L.W.Hts.m

L.W.

+5ʰ +4ʰ +3ʰ +2ʰ +1ʰ H.W. -1ʰ -2ʰ -3ʰ -4ʰ -5ʰ L.W.

ENGLAND – BURNHAM-ON-CROUCH

LAT 51°37'N   LONG 0°48'E

TIMES AND HEIGHTS OF HIGH AND LOW WATERS

Dates in amber are **SPRINGS**
Dates in yellow are **NEAPS**

2007

JANUARY

Day	Time	m		Day	Time	m
1 M	0412 / 1004 / 1658 / 2245	0.8 / 4.7 / 0.7 / 4.7		**16** TU	0405 / 1005 / 1643 / 2234	1.1 / 4.3 / 0.9 / 4.5
2 TU	0520 / 1106 / 1752 / 2340	0.7 / 4.8 / 0.7 / 4.8		**17** W	0510 / 1101 / 1737 / 2325	0.9 / 4.6 / 0.8 / 4.7
3 W ○	0619 / 1202 / 1836	0.4 / 5.0 / 0.7		**18** TH	0604 / 1150 / 1822	0.7 / 4.8 / 0.7
4 TH	0029 / 0707 / 1254 / 1917	4.8 / 0.3 / 5.0 / 0.8		**19** F ●	0011 / 0649 / 1238 / 1902	4.8 / 0.4 / 5.1 / 0.7
5 F	0114 / 0751 / 1338 / 1953	5.0 / 0.3 / 5.0 / 0.8		**20** SA	0056 / 0731 / 1322 / 1938	5.0 / 0.3 / 5.2 / 0.7
6 SA	0154 / 0833 / 1419 / 2028	5.0 / 0.3 / 5.0 / 0.9		**21** SU	0136 / 0812 / 1404 / 2015	5.1 / 0.2 / 5.2 / 0.5
7 SU	0230 / 0910 / 1457 / 2101	4.8 / 0.3 / 4.8 / 0.9		**22** M	0216 / 0851 / 1446 / 2054	5.1 / 0.2 / 5.2 / 0.5
8 M	0303 / 0943 / 1531 / 2131	4.8 / 0.4 / 4.7 / 1.0		**23** TU	0256 / 0930 / 1528 / 2131	5.1 / 0.1 / 5.2 / 0.5
9 TU	0336 / 1015 / 1606 / 2203	4.8 / 0.4 / 4.6 / 1.0		**24** W	0335 / 1008 / 1611 / 2211	5.1 / 0.1 / 5.1 / 0.5
10 W	0411 / 1048 / 1641 / 2239	4.7 / 0.5 / 4.5 / 1.1		**25** TH ◑	0416 / 1051 / 1657 / 2256	5.1 / 0.2 / 4.8 / 0.7
11 TH ◑	0450 / 1129 / 1722 / 2324	4.6 / 0.7 / 4.3 / 1.1		**26** F	0503 / 1140 / 1748 / 2348	4.8 / 0.4 / 4.6 / 0.9
12 F	0536 / 1221 / 1808	4.3 / 0.9 / 4.2		**27** SA	0558 / 1245 / 1848	4.6 / 0.7 / 4.2
13 SA	0023 / 0631 / 1323 / 1909	1.2 / 4.2 / 1.0 / 4.1		**28** SU	0101 / 0709 / 1406 / 2003	1.0 / 4.3 / 0.9 / 4.1
14 SU	0133 / 0741 / 1432 / 2020	1.3 / 4.1 / 1.0 / 4.1		**29** M	0231 / 0836 / 1534 / 2125	1.0 / 4.3 / 1.0 / 4.2
15 M	0250 / 0857 / 1541 / 2134	1.2 / 4.1 / 1.0 / 4.2		**30** TU	0405 / 1000 / 1646 / 2235	0.9 / 4.5 / 1.0 / 4.3
				31 W	0520 / 1106 / 1742 / 2331	0.7 / 4.7 / 0.9 / 4.6

FEBRUARY

Day	Time	m		Day	Time	m
1 TH	0618 / 1200 / 1827	0.4 / 4.8 / 0.9		**16** F	0549 / 1135 / 1805 / 2353	0.5 / 5.0 / 0.7 / 4.8
2 F ○	0020 / 0702 / 1248 / 1904	4.8 / 0.3 / 5.0 / 0.8		**17** SA ●	0636 / 1223 / 1845	0.3 / 5.2 / 0.5
3 SA	0104 / 0741 / 1329 / 1938	5.0 / 0.2 / 5.0 / 0.8		**18** SU	0039 / 0717 / 1307 / 1921	5.1 / 0.1 / 5.3 / 0.4
4 SU	0140 / 0816 / 1404 / 2010	5.0 / 0.2 / 5.0 / 0.8		**19** M	0120 / 0756 / 1349 / 1959	5.2 / 0.0 / 5.5 / 0.4
5 M	0213 / 0847 / 1435 / 2038	5.0 / 0.3 / 4.8 / 0.8		**20** TU	0159 / 0833 / 1429 / 2036	5.3 / -0.1 / 5.5 / 0.4
6 TU	0240 / 0913 / 1501 / 2104	5.0 / 0.3 / 4.8 / 0.8		**21** W	0237 / 0909 / 1507 / 2113	5.5 / -0.1 / 5.3 / 0.3
7 W	0307 / 0938 / 1528 / 2131	4.8 / 0.3 / 4.7 / 0.7		**22** TH	0315 / 0945 / 1548 / 2151	5.5 / 0.0 / 5.1 / 0.3
8 TH	0336 / 1005 / 1559 / 2202	4.8 / 0.4 / 4.7 / 0.8		**23** F	0354 / 1022 / 1629 / 2232	5.3 / 0.2 / 4.8 / 0.5
9 F	0410 / 1038 / 1634 / 2238	4.7 / 0.5 / 4.6 / 0.9		**24** SA ◑	0437 / 1106 / 1714 / 2320	5.0 / 0.5 / 4.5 / 0.8
10 SA ◑	0449 / 1119 / 1718 / 2326	4.6 / 0.8 / 4.3 / 1.0		**25** SU	0531 / 1206 / 1811	4.6 / 0.9 / 4.1
11 SU	0538 / 1140 / 1810	4.2 / 1.2 / 4.1		**26** M	0033 / 0648 / 1336 / 1935	1.0 / 4.2 / 1.2 / 3.8
12 M	0034 / 0641 / 1339 / 1921	1.2 / 4.2 / 1.1 / 4.0		**27** TU	0220 / 0831 / 1519 / 2109	1.1 / 4.1 / 1.2 / 4.0
13 TU	0158 / 0808 / 1502 / 2048	1.2 / 4.0 / 1.1 / 4.0		**28** W	0404 / 0957 / 1636 / 2222	0.9 / 4.3 / 1.1 / 4.3
14 W	0330 / 0938 / 1618 / 2207	1.1 / 4.0 / 1.0 / 4.2				
15 TH	0450 / 1043 / 1716 / 2305	0.9 / 4.6 / 0.9 / 4.6				

MARCH

Day	Time	m		Day	Time	m
1 TH	0514 / 1059 / 1729 / 2317	0.5 / 4.7 / 1.0 / 4.6		**16** F	0426 / 1021 / 1651 / 2237	0.8 / 4.6 / 0.9 / 4.6
2 F	0606 / 1149 / 1812	0.3 / 5.0 / 0.9		**17** SA	0526 / 1114 / 1739 / 2327	0.4 / 5.0 / 0.7 / 4.8
3 SA ○	0002 / 0647 / 1231 / 1847	4.8 / 0.2 / 5.1 / 0.8		**18** SU	0615 / 1201 / 1822	0.1 / 5.2 / 0.4
4 SU	0044 / 0720 / 1309 / 1918	5.0 / 0.2 / 5.0 / 0.7		**19** M ●	0013 / 0655 / 1246 / 1900	5.1 / -0.1 / 5.5 / 0.3
5 M	0119 / 0750 / 1341 / 1946	5.0 / 0.2 / 5.0 / 0.7		**20** TU	0057 / 0733 / 1328 / 1938	5.3 / -0.3 / 5.5 / 0.2
6 TU	0148 / 0816 / 1407 / 2013	5.0 / 0.3 / 4.8 / 0.7		**21** W	0137 / 0811 / 1407 / 2016	5.5 / -0.3 / 5.5 / 0.1
7 W	0214 / 0841 / 1430 / 2038	5.0 / 0.3 / 4.8 / 0.5		**22** TH	0216 / 0847 / 1445 / 2055	5.6 / -0.1 / 5.3 / 0.1
8 TH	0238 / 0905 / 1455 / 2105	5.0 / 0.3 / 4.8 / 0.5		**23** F	0255 / 0922 / 1524 / 2133	5.5 / 0.0 / 5.1 / 0.2
9 F	0306 / 0930 / 1524 / 2133	5.0 / 0.4 / 4.8 / 0.5		**24** SA	0335 / 0959 / 1603 / 2214	5.3 / 0.3 / 4.8 / 0.4
10 SA	0338 / 0958 / 1558 / 2206	4.8 / 0.5 / 4.7 / 0.7		**25** SU ◑	0420 / 1041 / 1647 / 2304	5.0 / 0.7 / 4.5 / 0.7
11 SU	0415 / 1033 / 1639 / 2248	4.6 / 0.8 / 4.5 / 0.9		**26** M	0517 / 1140 / 1746	4.5 / 1.1 / 4.0
12 M ◑	0500 / 1125 / 1731 / 2349	4.3 / 1.0 / 4.1 / 1.1		**27** TU	0024 / 0638 / 1316 / 1912	0.9 / 4.1 / 1.5 / 3.8
13 TU	0603 / 1252 / 1837	4.0 / 1.2 / 3.8		**28** W	0215 / 0818 / 1457 / 2043	1.0 / 4.1 / 1.5 / 4.0
14 W	0121 / 0729 / 1427 / 2007	1.2 / 4.0 / 1.2 / 3.8		**29** TH	0348 / 0939 / 1611 / 2154	0.8 / 4.3 / 1.2 / 4.2
15 TH	0301 / 0910 / 1550 / 2136	1.1 / 4.1 / 1.1 / 4.1		**30** F	0452 / 1036 / 1704 / 2248	0.5 / 4.7 / 1.0 / 4.6
				31 SA	0541 / 1123 / 1746 / 2334	0.3 / 5.0 / 0.9 / 4.8

APRIL

Day	Time	m		Day	Time	m
1 SU	0620 / 1205 / 1822	0.2 / 5.0 / 0.7		**16** M	0545 / 1132 / 1754 / 2341	0.0 / 5.2 / 0.4 / 5.2
2 M ○	0014 / 0651 / 1241 / 1853	5.0 / 0.2 / 5.0 / 0.7		**17** TU ●	0630 / 1218 / 1837	-0.1 / 5.3 / 0.2
3 TU	0050 / 0718 / 1312 / 1920	4.8 / 0.3 / 4.8 / 0.5		**18** W	0028 / 0709 / 1303 / 1918	5.3 / -0.1 / 5.3 / 0.1
4 W	0119 / 0744 / 1336 / 1946	4.8 / 0.3 / 4.8 / 0.5		**19** TH	0112 / 0747 / 1343 / 1959	5.5 / -0.1 / 5.4 / 0.1
5 TH	0145 / 0809 / 1359 / 2014	4.8 / 0.4 / 4.8 / 0.4		**20** F	0156 / 0826 / 1423 / 2040	5.5 / 0.0 / 5.2 / 0.1
6 F	0212 / 0835 / 1425 / 2042	4.8 / 0.4 / 4.8 / 0.4		**21** SA	0237 / 0903 / 1502 / 2121	5.5 / 0.2 / 5.0 / 0.2
7 SA	0241 / 0902 / 1456 / 2112	4.8 / 0.4 / 4.8 / 0.4		**22** SU	0322 / 0941 / 1544 / 2206	5.2 / 0.5 / 4.7 / 0.3
8 SU	0314 / 0930 / 1530 / 2146	4.8 / 0.5 / 4.7 / 0.5		**23** M	0411 / 1025 / 1630 / 2302	4.8 / 0.9 / 4.5 / 0.5
9 M	0352 / 1005 / 1611 / 2228	4.6 / 0.8 / 4.5 / 0.8		**24** TU ◑	0511 / 1124 / 1729	4.5 / 1.2 / 4.1
10 TU ◑	0439 / 1054 / 1702 / 2329	4.3 / 1.1 / 4.1 / 1.0		**25** W	0023 / 0625 / 1251 / 1843	0.8 / 4.2 / 1.5 / 4.0
11 W	0542 / 1216 / 1809	4.1 / 1.3 / 4.0		**26** TH	0153 / 0746 / 1418 / 2002	0.8 / 4.2 / 1.5 / 4.1
12 TH	0057 / 0703 / 1353 / 1933	1.0 / 4.0 / 1.3 / 4.0		**27** F	0312 / 0859 / 1530 / 2110	0.7 / 4.3 / 1.2 / 4.2
13 F	0233 / 0836 / 1513 / 2054	0.9 / 4.2 / 1.1 / 4.2		**28** SA	0413 / 0959 / 1626 / 2207	0.5 / 4.6 / 1.0 / 4.5
14 SA	0354 / 0948 / 1616 / 2159	0.5 / 4.6 / 0.9 / 4.6		**29** SU	0501 / 1046 / 1712 / 2254	0.4 / 4.8 / 0.9 / 4.7
15 SU	0455 / 1043 / 1707 / 2251	0.3 / 5.0 / 0.7 / 4.8		**30** M	0542 / 1128 / 1752 / 2338	0.4 / 4.8 / 0.7 / 4.7

Chart Datum: 2·35 metres below Ordnance Datum (Newlyn)

TIDES

TIME ZONE (UT)
For Summer Time add ONE hour in **non-shaded areas**

ENGLAND – BURNHAM-ON-CROUCH
LAT 51°37'N   LONG 0°48'E
TIMES AND HEIGHTS OF HIGH AND LOW WATERS

Dates in amber are **SPRINGS**
Dates in yellow are **NEAPS**

2007

MAY

Day	Time m	Time m	Time m	Time m		Day	Time m	Time m	Time m	Time m
1 TU	0617 0.4	1206 4.8	1826 0.7			16 W	0603 0.0	1151 5.2	1816 0.3	
2 W	0015 4.8	0645 0.4	1238 4.8	1855 0.5		17 TH	0001 5.2	0647 0.1	1239 5.2	1902 0.2
3 TH	0049 4.7	0713 0.4	1305 4.8	1924 0.5		18 F	0052 5.3	0727 0.1	1323 5.2	1946 0.2
4 F	0119 4.7	0742 0.5	1333 4.8	1954 0.4		19 SA	0140 5.3	0808 0.3	1406 5.1	2032 0.2
5 SA	0150 4.7	0812 0.5	1401 4.8	2026 0.4		20 SU	0226 5.2	0848 0.5	1448 5.0	2118 0.2
6 SU	0222 4.8	0842 0.7	1435 4.7	2100 0.4		21 M	0313 5.1	0929 0.8	1531 4.7	2205 0.3
7 M	0259 4.7	0913 0.8	1511 4.6	2137 0.5		22 TU	0403 4.8	1012 1.0	1618 4.6	2300 0.4
8 TU	0340 4.6	0951 0.9	1554 4.5	2221 0.7		23 W	0458 4.6	1104 1.2	1711 4.3	
9 W	0430 4.5	1040 1.1	1646 4.2	2320 0.8		24 TH	0002 0.5	0558 4.3	1210 1.3	1809 4.2
10 TH	0531 4.3	1148 1.2	1750 4.1			25 F	0111 0.7	0700 4.3	1325 1.5	1912 4.2
11 F	0038 0.8	0641 4.2	1312 1.2	1901 4.2		26 SA	0216 0.7	0806 4.3	1435 1.3	2015 4.2
12 SA	0159 0.7	0759 4.5	1428 1.1	2012 4.3		27 SU	0318 0.7	0906 4.3	1537 1.1	2116 4.3
13 SU	0316 0.4	0908 4.7	1534 0.9	2117 4.6		28 M	0410 0.7	1001 4.6	1630 1.0	2209 4.5
14 M	0419 0.2	1008 5.0	1633 0.7	2215 4.8		29 TU	0456 0.5	1046 4.7	1716 0.8	2257 4.6
15 TU	0514 0.1	1101 5.1	1725 0.4	2309 5.1		30 W	0536 0.5	1127 4.7	1756 0.7	2344 4.7
						31 TH	0614 0.5	1205 4.8	1832 0.7	

JUNE

Day	Time m	Time m	Time m	Time m		Day	Time m	Time m	Time m	Time m
1 F	0019 4.7	0647 0.5	1239 4.8	1905 0.5		16 SA	0040 5.1	0713 0.4	1309 5.0	1942 0.2
2 SA	0057 4.7	0720 0.7	1312 4.8	1940 0.5		17 SU	0131 5.2	0755 0.5	1355 5.0	2029 0.2
3 SU	0133 4.7	0754 0.7	1346 4.7	2016 0.4		18 M	0218 5.1	0835 0.7	1436 5.0	2114 0.2
4 M	0210 4.8	0828 0.7	1422 4.7	2055 0.4		19 TU	0304 5.1	0914 0.9	1519 4.8	2157 0.3
5 TU	0250 4.7	0904 0.8	1501 4.7	2134 0.4		20 W	0350 4.8	0952 1.0	1600 4.7	2241 0.3
6 W	0333 4.6	0942 0.9	1545 4.6	2218 0.5		21 TH	0433 4.7	1033 1.1	1643 4.6	2325 0.5
7 TH	0422 4.6	1028 1.0	1634 4.5	2310 0.5		22 F	0520 4.5	1120 1.2	1729 4.5	
8 F	0518 4.6	1124 1.0	1730 4.5			23 SA	0013 0.7	0608 4.3	1216 1.3	1819 4.3
9 SA	0011 0.5	0618 4.5	1231 1.1	1829 4.5		24 SU	0108 0.8	0702 4.2	1322 1.3	1916 4.2
10 SU	0122 0.4	0722 4.6	1342 1.0	1934 4.6		25 M	0206 0.8	0803 4.2	1429 1.2	2019 4.2
11 M	0234 0.4	0829 4.6	1453 0.9	2040 4.6		26 TU	0306 0.9	0905 4.3	1537 1.1	2122 4.6
12 TU	0342 0.3	0935 4.7	1600 0.8	2145 4.8		27 W	0405 0.8	1003 4.5	1637 1.0	2219 4.8
13 W	0444 0.3	1034 4.8	1702 0.5	2246 5.0		28 TH	0457 0.8	1052 4.6	1727 0.9	2310 4.6
14 TH	0540 0.3	1128 5.0	1801 0.4	2344 5.1		29 F	0545 0.7	1136 4.7	1813 0.7	2357 4.7
15 F	0629 0.3	1221 5.0	1852 0.3			30 SA	0627 0.7	1218 4.8	1851 0.5	

JULY

Day	Time m	Time m	Time m	Time m		Day	Time m	Time m	Time m	Time m
1 SU	0041 4.8	0704 0.7	1258 4.8	1931 0.5		16 M	0126 5.1	0742 0.8	1344 5.1	2021 0.2
2 M	0121 4.8	0740 0.7	1336 4.8	2009 0.4		17 TU	0210 5.1	0819 0.8	1423 5.1	2101 0.2
3 TU	0201 5.0	0815 0.8	1415 4.8	2048 0.3		18 W	0249 5.0	0855 0.9	1459 5.0	2136 0.2
4 W	0241 5.0	0852 0.8	1453 4.8	2126 0.3		19 TH	0327 5.0	0929 0.9	1533 5.0	2208 0.3
5 TH	0325 5.0	0930 0.8	1533 4.8	2205 0.3		20 F	0401 4.8	0959 0.9	1607 4.8	2240 0.4
6 F	0409 4.8	1011 0.8	1616 4.8	2249 0.3		21 SA	0434 4.6	1033 1.0	1642 4.7	2315 0.7
7 SA	0456 4.8	1057 0.9	1704 4.8	2338 0.4		22 SU	0511 4.5	1114 1.1	1724 4.5	2359 0.8
8 SU	0549 4.7	1151 0.9	1758 4.7			23 M	0554 4.3	1207 1.2	1815 4.4	
9 M	0040 0.4	0648 4.5	1259 1.0	1859 4.6		24 TU	0058 0.9	0648 4.1	1317 1.3	1919 4.1
10 TU	0152 0.7	0755 4.5	1416 1.0	2010 4.6		25 W	0206 1.0	0800 4.1	1436 1.3	2035 4.1
11 W	0310 0.7	0907 4.5	1537 0.9	2125 4.6		26 TH	0317 1.1	0918 4.2	1556 1.1	2149 4.3
12 TH	0424 0.7	1016 4.6	1652 0.6	2236 4.7		27 F	0425 1.0	1016 4.4	1704 1.0	2248 4.7
13 F	0526 0.7	1117 4.7	1758 0.5	2340 5.0		28 SA	0522 0.9	1114 4.7	1756 0.8	2340 4.8
14 SA	0619 0.7	1212 5.0	1851 0.3			29 SU	0609 0.8	1200 4.8	1839 0.5	
15 SU	0037 5.1	0702 0.7	1301 5.0	1938 0.2		30 M	0025 5.0	0648 0.8	1243 5.0	1918 0.4
						31 TU	0108 5.1	0723 0.7	1323 5.1	1956 0.3

AUGUST

Day	Time m	Time m	Time m	Time m		Day	Time m	Time m	Time m	Time m
1 W	0149 5.2	0800 0.7	1400 5.1	2033 0.2		16 TH	0226 5.0	0830 0.8	1434 5.1	2105 0.3
2 TH	0228 5.2	0835 0.7	1437 5.2	2109 0.1		17 F	0256 5.0	0858 0.8	1500 5.0	2130 0.4
3 F	0307 5.2	0912 0.5	1515 5.2	2145 0.1		18 SA	0322 4.8	0925 0.8	1528 5.0	2156 0.4
4 SA	0348 5.1	0950 0.5	1553 5.2	2222 0.2		19 SU	0350 4.8	0954 0.8	1559 4.6	2226 0.7
5 SU	0430 5.0	1032 0.7	1635 5.0	2305 0.4		20 M	0421 4.6	1029 1.0	1636 4.6	2303 1.0
6 M	0519 4.7	1120 0.9	1726 4.8			21 TU	0500 1.1	1115 1.1	1723 4.3	2356 1.0
7 TU	0000 0.5	0614 4.5	1225 1.0	1829 4.5		22 W	0550 4.2	1221 1.3	1823 4.1	
8 W	0117 0.9	0724 4.2	1353 1.1	1954 4.3		23 TH	0114 1.2	0657 4.0	1348 1.3	1948 4.0
9 TH	0250 1.1	0851 4.2	1533 1.0	2124 4.3		24 F	0237 1.3	0832 4.1	1521 1.2	2122 4.2
10 F	0416 1.0	1009 4.5	1655 0.8	2239 4.7		25 SA	0355 1.2	0954 4.3	1639 1.0	2228 4.6
11 SA	0518 0.9	1110 4.7	1758 0.6	2340 5.0		26 SU	0457 1.0	1050 4.7	1734 0.7	2320 4.8
12 SU	0609 0.9	1201 5.0	1846 0.3			27 M	0545 0.9	1136 5.0	1820 0.4	
13 M	0030 5.1	0649 0.8	1248 5.1	1927 0.2		28 TU	0006 5.1	0626 0.7	1219 5.1	1858 0.1
14 TU	0114 5.2	0724 0.8	1329 5.2	2003 0.2		29 W	0048 5.3	0703 0.7	1300 5.2	1935 0.1
15 W	0153 5.1	0759 0.8	1403 5.1	2036 0.2		30 TH	0128 5.3	0738 0.5	1338 5.3	2011 0.0
						31 F	0207 5.3	0814 0.6	1415 5.5	2046 0.0

Chart Datum: 2·35 metres below Ordnance Datum (Newlyn)

ENGLAND – BURNHAM-ON-CROUCH

LAT 51°37′N LONG 0°48′E

TIMES AND HEIGHTS OF HIGH AND LOW WATERS

Dates in amber are **SPRINGS**
Dates in yellow are **NEAPS**

2007

SEPTEMBER

Day	Time m	Time m	Time m	Time m	Day	Time m	Time m	Time m	Time m
1 SA	0245 5.3	0852 0.4	1452 5.5	2120 0.1	**16** SU	0243 4.8	0856 0.7	1454 5.0	2119 0.5
2 SU	0324 5.2	0930 0.4	1529 5.3	2156 0.2	**17** M	0309 4.8	0924 0.8	1525 4.8	2145 0.7
3 M	0403 5.0	1009 0.5	1611 5.1	2236 0.5	**18** TU	0341 4.8	0957 0.9	1600 4.7	2218 0.9
4 TU ◑	0448 4.7	1058 0.8	1703 4.7	2329 0.9	**19** W ◑	0420 4.6	1038 1.0	1644 4.3	2303 1.1
5 W	0544 4.3	1205 1.0	1814 4.3		**20** TH	0508 4.2	1140 1.2	1743 4.1	
6 TH	0053 1.2	0702 4.1	1349 1.1	1954 4.2	**21** F	0024 1.3	0613 4.0	1311 1.3	1907 4.0
7 F	0238 1.3	0839 4.1	1536 1.0	2126 4.3	**22** SA	0158 1.5	0744 4.0	1447 1.2	2048 4.1
8 SA	0406 1.2	0956 4.5	1650 0.7	2234 4.7	**23** SU	0321 1.3	0915 4.2	1606 0.9	2200 4.6
9 SU	0506 1.1	1053 4.8	1745 0.3	2326 5.1	**24** M	0425 1.1	1015 4.6	1704 0.5	2251 5.0
10 M	0550 0.9	1143 5.1	1829 0.2		**25** TU	0514 0.9	1103 5.0	1750 0.3	2336 5.2
11 TU ●	0012 5.2	0629 0.9	1225 5.2	1904 0.2	**26** W ○	0558 0.7	1148 5.2	1832 0.1	
12 W	0053 5.2	0703 0.8	1304 5.2	1935 0.3	**27** TH	0020 5.3	0637 0.5	1230 5.3	1909 0.0
13 TH	0128 5.1	0734 0.8	1335 5.1	2004 0.3	**28** F	0102 5.5	0715 0.4	1311 5.5	1946 0.0
14 F	0157 5.0	0803 0.8	1402 5.1	2029 0.4	**29** SA	0142 5.5	0753 0.3	1351 5.6	2022 0.0
15 SA	0221 5.0	0829 0.7	1427 5.0	2054 0.4	**30** SU	0220 5.3	0833 0.3	1430 5.6	2057 0.2

OCTOBER

Day	Time m	Time m	Time m	Time m	Day	Time m	Time m	Time m	Time m
1 M	0259 5.2	0913 0.3	1511 5.4	2134 0.4	**16** TU	0237 5.0	0902 0.7	1458 4.8	2115 0.8
2 TU	0339 5.0	0954 0.5	1556 5.1	2215 0.8	**17** W	0311 4.8	0935 0.8	1535 4.7	2147 0.9
3 W ◑	0423 4.6	1046 0.8	1652 4.6	2309 1.2	**18** TH	0350 4.6	1017 0.9	1619 4.5	2230 1.2
4 TH	0522 4.2	1203 1.0	1810 4.3		**19** F	0437 4.3	1115 1.1	1718 4.2	2339 1.5
5 F	0038 1.5	0644 4.1	1349 1.4	1946 4.2	**20** SA	0541 4.1	1240 1.2	1832 4.1	
6 SA	0220 1.6	0815 4.1	1520 0.8	2108 4.5	**21** SU	0114 1.5	0701 4.1	1408 1.0	2003 4.2
7 SU	0340 1.3	0928 4.5	1627 0.5	2210 4.8	**22** M	0235 1.3	0823 4.2	1524 0.8	2117 4.6
8 M	0438 1.1	1024 4.8	1718 0.3	2300 5.1	**23** TU	0341 1.1	0929 4.6	1625 0.5	2213 5.0
9 TU	0523 1.0	1112 5.0	1800 0.3	2343 5.1	**24** W	0436 0.9	1022 5.0	1716 0.2	2302 5.2
10 W	0603 0.8	1154 5.1	1834 0.3		**25** TH	0525 0.7	1111 5.2	1802 0.1	2349 5.3
11 TH ●	0022 5.1	0637 0.8	1231 5.1	1903 0.4	**26** F ○	0612 0.4	1158 5.3	1843 0.1	
12 F	0056 5.1	0707 0.7	1304 5.0	1930 0.4	**27** SA	0033 5.5	0653 0.3	1245 5.5	1922 0.1
13 SA	0124 5.0	0736 0.7	1332 5.0	1955 0.5	**28** SU	0116 5.3	0736 0.4	1329 5.6	2000 0.2
14 SU	0146 4.8	0803 0.7	1357 5.0	2021 0.5	**29** M	0158 5.3	0818 0.2	1413 5.6	2039 0.3
15 M	0210 5.0	0831 0.7	1426 4.8	2047 0.7	**30** TU	0238 5.1	0902 0.3	1459 5.3	2119 0.7
					31 W	0322 5.0	0949 0.5	1548 5.0	2202 1.0

NOVEMBER

Day	Time m	Time m	Time m	Time m	Day	Time m	Time m	Time m	Time m
1 TH ◑	0408 4.6	1046 0.7	1647 4.6	2257 1.3	**16** F	0329 4.6	1005 0.8	1605 4.5	2212 1.1
2 F	0507 4.3	1201 0.8	1759 4.3		**17** SA ◑	0416 4.5	1057 0.9	1659 4.3	2309 1.2
3 SA	0016 1.6	0620 4.2	1327 0.8	1917 4.3	**18** SU	0514 4.2	1205 0.9	1805 4.3	
4 SU	0142 1.6	0736 4.2	1444 0.8	2029 4.5	**19** M	0023 1.3	0623 4.2	1323 0.8	1917 4.3
5 M	0258 1.5	0844 4.5	1548 0.5	2131 4.6	**20** TU	0140 1.2	0735 4.3	1436 0.7	2028 4.6
6 TU	0358 1.2	0943 4.7	1639 0.4	2222 4.8	**21** W	0251 1.1	0841 4.6	1542 0.5	2131 4.8
7 W	0448 1.0	1034 4.8	1721 0.4	2306 5.0	**22** TH	0354 0.9	0943 4.8	1640 0.3	2227 5.0
8 TH	0531 0.9	1117 5.0	1758 0.4	2346 5.0	**23** F	0452 0.7	1039 5.1	1732 0.2	2319 5.1
9 F ●	0611 0.8	1156 5.0	1829 0.5		**24** SA ○	0546 0.4	1132 5.3	1821 0.1	
10 SA	0020 5.0	0643 0.7	1232 4.8	1858 0.5	**25** SU	0009 5.2	0636 0.3	1223 5.5	1903 0.3
11 SU	0051 4.8	0712 0.7	1304 4.8	1926 0.7	**26** M	0056 5.2	0723 0.3	1314 5.5	1944 0.4
12 M	0117 4.8	0742 0.7	1334 4.8	1955 0.7	**27** TU	0141 5.2	0811 0.2	1402 5.3	2026 0.5
13 TU	0144 4.8	0814 0.7	1406 4.8	2025 0.8	**28** W	0225 5.1	0858 0.2	1450 5.2	2108 0.8
14 W	0216 4.8	0847 0.7	1440 4.8	2056 0.9	**29** TH	0309 5.0	0947 0.3	1540 5.0	2151 1.0
15 TH	0250 4.8	0923 0.7	1520 4.7	2130 1.0	**30** F	0356 4.7	1040 0.4	1633 4.7	2239 1.2

DECEMBER

Day	Time m	Time m	Time m	Time m	Day	Time m	Time m	Time m	Time m
1 SA	0447 4.6	1139 0.5	1731 4.6	2337 1.3	**16** SU	0359 4.6	1037 0.5	1641 4.6	2244 1.0
2 SU	0545 4.5	1244 0.7	1831 4.3		**17** M ◑	0449 4.6	1129 0.7	1736 4.5	2339 1.1
3 M	0048 1.5	0646 4.3	1349 0.8	1936 4.3	**18** TU	0546 4.5	1233 0.7	1836 4.5	
4 TU	0158 1.5	0750 4.3	1452 0.8	2038 4.3	**19** W	0048 1.1	0649 4.5	1344 0.7	1944 4.3
5 W	0306 1.2	0853 4.6	1547 0.8	2136 4.5	**20** TH	0200 1.0	0759 4.6	1458 0.5	2052 4.6
6 TH	0406 1.1	0950 4.6	1636 0.8	2224 4.6	**21** F	0315 0.9	0908 4.7	1607 0.5	2157 4.7
7 F	0456 0.9	1040 4.7	1718 0.7	2308 4.7	**22** SA	0425 0.8	1015 4.8	1709 0.4	2257 4.8
8 SA	0541 0.8	1125 4.7	1757 0.7	2348 4.8	**23** SU	0530 0.5	1115 5.1	1803 0.4	2351 5.0
9 SU ●	0621 0.7	1206 4.8	1832 0.7		**24** M ○	0628 0.4	1213 5.2	1850 0.5	
10 M	0023 4.8	0654 0.7	1244 4.8	1904 0.8	**25** TU	0043 5.1	0719 0.2	1306 5.3	1933 0.5
11 TU	0056 4.8	0727 0.5	1318 4.8	1936 0.8	**26** W	0130 5.1	0808 0.2	1356 5.3	2015 0.7
12 W	0129 4.8	0802 0.5	1353 4.8	2010 0.8	**27** TH	0215 5.1	0855 0.1	1442 5.2	2056 0.8
13 TH	0202 4.8	0838 0.5	1429 4.8	2042 0.9	**28** F	0257 5.1	0938 0.2	1527 5.1	2133 0.9
14 F	0237 4.8	0915 0.5	1508 4.8	2119 0.9	**29** SA	0338 5.0	1019 0.3	1610 4.8	2211 1.0
15 SA	0316 4.7	0953 0.5	1552 4.7	2158 1.0	**30** SU	0419 4.8	1102 0.4	1654 4.6	2252 1.1
					31 M ◑	0502 4.7	1147 0.5	1740 4.5	2339 1.2

Chart Datum: 2·35 metres below Ordnance Datum (Newlyn)

TIDES

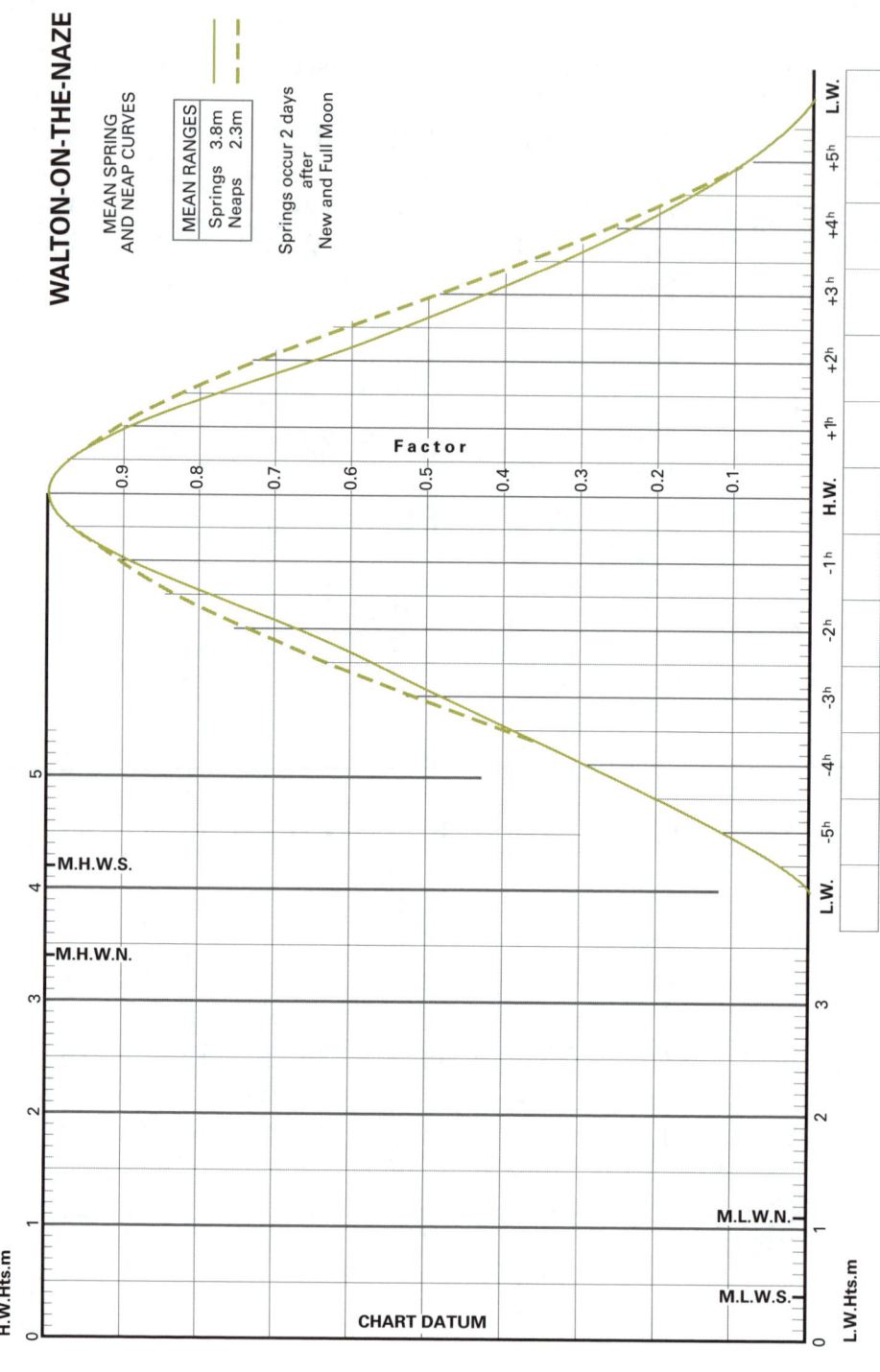

WALTON-ON-THE-NAZE

MEAN SPRING
AND NEAP CURVES

MEAN RANGES
Springs 3.8m
Neaps 2.3m

Springs occur 2 days
after
New and Full Moon

Factor

0.9
0.8
0.7
0.6
0.5
0.4
0.3
0.2
0.1

H.W.   -1ʰ   -2ʰ   -3ʰ   -4ʰ   -5ʰ   L.W.

+1ʰ   +2ʰ   +3ʰ   +4ʰ   +5ʰ   L.W.

H.W.Hts.m

5

M.H.W.S.

4

M.H.W.N.

3

2

1

M.L.W.N.

M.L.W.S.

CHART DATUM

0

L.W.Hts.m

3

2

1

0

TIME ZONE (UT)
For Summer Time add ONE hour in **non-shaded areas**

Dates in amber are **SPRINGS**
Dates in yellow are **NEAPS**

2007

JANUARY

Time m / Time m

1 M	0305 0.9 / 0920 3.8 / 1548 0.8 / 2200 3.8	16 TU	0258 1.2 / 0921 3.5 / 1534 1.0 / 2149 3.6
2 TU	0408 0.8 / 1020 3.9 / 1638 0.8 / 2252 3.9	17 W	0359 1.0 / 1015 3.7 / 1624 0.9 / 2238 3.8
3 W	0504 0.6 / 1114 4.0 / 1723 0.8 / ○2340 3.9	18 TH	0450 0.8 / 1102 3.9 / 1708 0.8 / 2322 3.9
4 TH	0556 0.5 / 1204 4.0 / 1806 0.9	19 F	0536 0.6 / 1148 4.1 / 1750 0.8 ●
5 F	0025 4.0 / 0643 0.5 / 1250 4.0 / 1845 0.9	20 SA	0006 4.0 / 0621 0.5 / 1233 4.2 / 1829 0.8
6 SA	0106 4.0 / 0728 0.5 / 1333 4.0 / 1923 1.0	21 SU	0048 4.1 / 0705 0.4 / 1317 4.2 / 1909 0.7
7 SU	0144 3.9 / 0808 0.5 / 1412 3.9 / 1958 1.0	22 M	0130 4.1 / 0747 0.3 / 1401 4.2 / 1950 0.7
8 M	0219 3.9 / 0844 0.6 / 1448 3.8 / 2031 1.1	23 TU	0211 4.1 / 0829 0.3 / 1444 4.2 / 2031 0.7
9 TU	0253 3.9 / 0918 0.6 / 1524 3.7 / 2105 1.1	24 W	0252 4.1 / 0911 0.3 / 1530 4.1 / 2114 0.7
10 W	0329 3.8 / 0954 0.7 / 1601 3.6 / 2144 1.2	25 TH	0335 4.1 / 0957 0.4 / 1618 3.9 / ◐2202 0.8
11 TH	0410 3.7 / 1037 0.8 / 1643 3.5 / ◐2232 1.2	26 F	0424 3.9 / 1049 0.6 / 1711 3.7 / 2258 1.0
12 F	0458 3.5 / 1129 1.0 / 1732 3.4 / 2331 1.3	27 SA	0521 3.7 / 1152 0.8 / 1812 3.4
13 SA	0556 3.4 / 1227 1.1 / 1832 3.3	28 SU	0007 1.1 / 0632 3.5 / 1307 1.0 / 1924 3.3
14 SU	0037 1.4 / 0703 3.3 / 1331 1.1 / 1941 3.3	29 M	0130 1.3 / 0756 3.5 / 1429 1.1 / 2043 3.4
15 M	0148 1.3 / 0816 3.3 / 1436 1.1 / 2051 3.4	30 TU	0258 1.0 / 0916 3.6 / 1537 1.1 / 2219 3.7
		31 W	0408 0.8 / 1020 3.8 / 1629 1.0 / 2244 3.7

FEBRUARY

Time m / Time m

1 TH	0503 0.6 / 1112 3.9 / 1713 1.0 / 2331 3.9	16 F	0436 0.7 / 1048 4.0 / 1651 0.8 / 2305 3.9
2 F	0550 0.5 / 1158 4.0 / 1752 0.9 ○	17 SA	0522 0.5 / 1134 4.2 / 1732 0.7 / ●2349 4.1
3 SA	0014 4.0 / 0632 0.4 / 1240 4.0 / 1829 0.9	18 SU	0606 0.3 / 1218 4.3 / 1811 0.6
4 SU	0052 4.0 / 0710 0.4 / 1317 4.0 / 1903 0.9	19 M	0031 4.2 / 0648 0.2 / 1301 4.4 / 1851 0.6
5 M	0126 4.0 / 0743 0.5 / 1349 3.9 / 1933 0.9	20 TU	0112 4.3 / 0728 0.1 / 1343 4.4 / 1931 0.6
6 TU	0155 4.0 / 0811 0.5 / 1417 3.9 / 2001 0.9	21 W	0152 4.4 / 0807 0.1 / 1423 4.3 / 2011 0.6
7 W	0223 3.9 / 0838 0.5 / 1445 3.8 / 2031 0.8	22 TH	0231 4.4 / 0846 0.2 / 1505 4.1 / 2052 0.5
8 TH	0253 3.9 / 0908 0.6 / 1517 3.8 / 2104 0.9	23 F	0312 4.3 / 0926 0.4 / 1548 3.9 / 2136 0.7
9 F	0328 3.8 / 0943 0.7 / 1554 3.7 / 2143 1.0	24 SA	0357 4.0 / 1013 0.7 / 1635 3.6 / ◑2228 0.9
10 SA	0409 3.7 / 1027 0.9 / 1639 3.5 / ◑2234 1.1	25 SU	0453 3.7 / 1115 1.0 / 1735 3.3 / 2340 1.1
11 SU	0500 3.4 / 1128 1.1 / 1734 3.3 / 2341 1.3	26 M	0612 3.4 / 1239 1.3 / 1857 3.1
12 M	0606 3.2 / 1242 1.2 / 1844 3.2	27 TU	0120 1.2 / 0751 3.3 / 1415 1.3 / 2028 3.2
13 TU	0100 1.3 / 0729 3.2 / 1359 1.2 / 2008 3.2	28 W	0257 1.0 / 0914 3.5 / 1527 1.2 / 2138 3.5
14 W	0225 1.2 / 0855 3.4 / 1510 1.1 / 2123 3.4		
15 TH	0340 1.0 / 0958 3.7 / 1605 1.0 / 2219 3.7		

MARCH

Time m / Time m

1 TH	0403 0.7 / 1013 3.8 / 1617 1.1 / 2230 3.7	16 F	0318 0.9 / 0937 3.7 / 1541 1.0 / 2152 3.7
2 F	0452 0.5 / 1101 4.0 / 1657 1.0 / 2314 3.9	17 SA	0414 0.6 / 1028 4.0 / 1626 0.8 / 2240 3.9
3 SA	0534 0.4 / 1142 4.1 / 1734 0.9 / ○2354 4.0	18 SU	0500 0.3 / 1113 4.2 / 1708 0.6 / 2324 4.1
4 SU	0610 0.4 / 1220 4.0 / 1808 0.8	19 M	0543 0.1 / 1156 4.4 / 1748 0.5 ●
5 M	0030 4.0 / 0642 0.4 / 1253 4.0 / 1838 0.8	20 TU	0007 4.3 / 0624 0.0 / 1239 4.4 / 1829 0.4
6 TU	0100 4.0 / 0710 0.5 / 1320 3.9 / 1906 0.8	21 W	0049 4.4 / 0704 0.0 / 1320 4.4 / 1910 0.3
7 W	0127 4.0 / 0736 0.5 / 1344 3.9 / 1933 0.7	22 TH	0129 4.5 / 0743 0.1 / 1400 4.3 / 1951 0.3
8 TH	0153 4.0 / 0802 0.5 / 1410 3.9 / 2002 0.7	23 F	0210 4.4 / 0821 0.2 / 1440 4.1 / 2033 0.4
9 F	0222 4.0 / 0830 0.6 / 1440 3.9 / 2033 0.7	24 SA	0252 4.3 / 0901 0.5 / 1521 3.9 / 2117 0.6
10 SA	0255 3.9 / 0900 0.7 / 1516 3.8 / 2109 0.8	25 SU	0339 4.0 / 0946 0.8 / 1607 3.6 / ◑2211 0.8
11 SU	0334 3.7 / 0937 0.9 / 1559 3.6 / 2154 1.0	26 M	0438 3.6 / 1049 1.2 / 1708 3.2 / 2332 1.0
12 M	0421 3.5 / 1033 1.1 / 1653 3.3 / ◑2259 1.2	27 TU	0603 3.3 / 1221 1.5 / 1835 3.1
13 TU	0526 3.2 / 1158 1.3 / 1802 3.1	28 W	0116 1.1 / 0739 3.3 / 1354 1.5 / 2003 3.2
14 W	0025 1.3 / 0651 3.2 / 1327 1.3 / 1928 3.1	29 TH	0242 0.9 / 0856 3.5 / 1504 1.3 / 2111 3.4
15 TH	0158 1.2 / 0829 3.3 / 1444 1.2 / 2053 3.3	30 F	0345 0.7 / 0951 3.8 / 1553 1.1 / 2203 3.7
		31 SA	0428 0.5 / 1036 4.0 / 1633 1.0 / 2247 3.9

APRIL

Time m / Time m

1 SU	0505 0.4 / 1116 4.0 / 1708 0.8 / 2325 4.0	16 M	0432 0.2 / 1045 4.2 / 1640 0.6 / 2253 4.2
2 M	0539 0.4 / 1151 4.0 / 1741 0.8 ○	17 TU	0516 0.1 / 1129 4.3 / 1724 0.4 / ●2339 4.3
3 TU	0000 3.9 / 0608 0.5 / 1223 3.9 / 1810 0.7	18 W	0558 0.1 / 1213 4.3 / 1807 0.3
4 W	0030 3.9 / 0635 0.5 / 1248 3.9 / 1838 0.7	19 TH	0023 4.4 / 0639 0.1 / 1255 4.3 / 1851 0.3
5 TH	0057 3.9 / 0702 0.6 / 1312 3.9 / 1907 0.6	20 F	0108 4.4 / 0720 0.2 / 1337 4.2 / 1935 0.3
6 F	0125 3.9 / 0730 0.6 / 1339 3.9 / 1938 0.6	21 SA	0152 4.4 / 0800 0.2 / 1418 4.0 / 2020 0.4
7 SA	0156 3.9 / 0759 0.6 / 1411 3.9 / 2010 0.6	22 SU	0238 4.2 / 0842 0.7 / 1501 3.8 / 2109 0.5
8 SU	0230 3.9 / 0830 0.7 / 1447 3.8 / 2047 0.7	23 M	0330 3.9 / 0929 1.0 / 1550 3.6 / 2209 0.7
9 M	0310 3.7 / 0907 0.9 / 1530 3.6 / 2132 0.9	24 TU	0432 3.6 / 1032 1.3 / 1651 3.3 / ◑2331 0.9
10 TU	0359 3.5 / 1000 1.2 / 1623 3.3 / ◑2237 1.1	25 W	0549 3.4 / 1157 1.5 / 1808 3.2
11 W	0504 3.3 / 1124 1.4 / 1733 3.2	26 TH	0055 0.9 / 0708 3.4 / 1318 1.5 / 1923 3.3
12 TH	0003 1.1 / 0627 3.2 / 1255 1.4 / 1855 3.2	27 F	0208 0.8 / 0818 3.5 / 1425 1.3 / 2029 3.4
13 F	0132 1.0 / 0756 3.4 / 1409 1.2 / 2013 3.4	28 SA	0306 0.7 / 0915 3.7 / 1518 1.1 / 2123 3.6
14 SA	0248 0.7 / 0905 3.7 / 1508 1.0 / 2115 3.7	29 SU	0351 0.6 / 1001 3.9 / 1601 1.0 / 2209 3.8
15 SU	0345 0.5 / 0958 4.0 / 1556 0.8 / 2206 3.9	30 M	0429 0.6 / 1041 3.9 / 1638 0.8 / 2250 3.8

TIDES

Chart Datum: 2·16 metres below Ordnance Datum (Newlyn)

TIME ZONE (UT)
For Summer Time add ONE hour in **non-shaded areas**

ENGLAND – WALTON-ON-THE-NAZE

LAT 51°51′N   LONG 1°17′E

TIMES AND HEIGHTS OF HIGH AND LOW WATERS

Dates in amber are **SPRINGS**
Dates in yellow are **NEAPS**

2007

MAY

Day	Time m	Time m	Time m	Time m
1 TU	0502 0.6	1117 3.9	1712 0.8	2326 3.9
16 W	0449 0.2	1103 4.2	1701 0.5	● 2313 4.2
2 W	0532 0.6	1148 3.9	1743 0.7	○ 2359 3.8
17 TH	0534 0.3	1149 4.2	1750 0.4	
3 TH	0602 0.6	1216 3.9	1814 0.7	
18 F	0002 4.3	0617 0.3	1234 4.2	1838 0.4
4 F	0030 3.8	0633 0.7	1244 3.9	1846 0.6
19 SA	0052 4.3	0701 0.5	1319 4.1	1927 0.4
5 SA	0102 3.8	0705 0.7	1314 3.9	1920 0.6
20 SU	0140 4.2	0744 0.7	1403 4.0	2016 0.4
6 SU	0136 3.9	0737 0.8	1349 3.8	1957 0.6
21 M	0229 4.1	0828 0.9	1448 3.8	2108 0.5
7 M	0214 3.8	0811 0.8	1427 3.7	2037 0.7
22 TU	0321 3.9	0915 1.1	1537 3.7	2206 0.6
8 TU	0257 3.7	0852 1.0	1512 3.6	2125 0.8
23 W	0419 3.7	1011 1.3	1632 3.5	◑ 2311 0.7
9 W	0349 3.6	0945 1.2	1606 3.4	2228 0.9
24 TH	0521 3.5	1119 1.4	1733 3.4	
10 TH	0453 3.5	1058 1.3	1713 3.3	◑ 2345 0.9
25 F	0016 0.8	0624 3.5	1229 1.5	1835 3.4
11 F	0606 3.4	1217 1.3	1825 3.4	
26 SA	0117 0.8	0727 3.5	1334 1.4	1936 3.4
12 SA	0101 0.8	0720 3.6	1328 1.2	1933 3.5
27 SU	0214 0.8	0825 3.5	1432 1.2	2034 3.5
13 SU	0212 0.6	0827 3.8	1429 1.0	2035 3.7
28 M	0303 0.8	0917 3.7	1522 1.1	2125 3.6
14 M	0311 0.4	0924 4.0	1524 0.8	2131 3.9
29 TU	0346 0.7	1001 3.8	1605 0.9	2211 3.7
15 TU	0403 0.3	1015 4.1	1613 0.6	2223 4.1
30 W	0423 0.7	1040 3.8	1642 0.8	2252 3.8
31 TH	0459 0.7	1116 3.9	1718 0.8	2330 3.8

JUNE

Day	Time m	Time m	Time m	Time m
1 F	0534 0.7	1149 3.9	1754 0.7	○
16 SA	0602 0.6	1220 4.0	1833 0.4	
2 SA	0007 3.8	0610 0.8	1223 3.9	1831 0.9
17 SU	0042 4.2	0647 0.7	1307 4.0	1924 0.4
3 SU	0045 3.8	0646 0.8	1258 3.8	1910 0.6
18 M	0132 4.1	0730 0.8	1351 4.0	2012 0.4
4 M	0123 3.9	0722 0.8	1336 3.8	1951 0.6
19 TU	0220 4.1	0812 1.0	1435 3.9	2059 0.5
5 TU	0205 3.8	0801 0.9	1417 3.8	2034 0.6
20 W	0307 3.9	0854 1.1	1518 3.8	2146 0.5
6 W	0250 3.8	0843 1.0	1502 3.7	2121 0.7
21 TH	0353 3.8	0938 1.2	1603 3.7	2233 0.7
7 TH	0341 3.7	0932 1.1	1554 3.6	2217 0.7
22 F	0441 3.6	1028 1.3	1651 3.6	◑ 2322 0.8
8 F	0439 3.7	1032 1.1	1652 3.6	◑ 2320 0.7
23 SA	0532 3.5	1124 1.4	1743 3.5	
9 SA	0542 3.6	1138 1.2	1754 3.6	
24 SU	0013 0.9	0626 3.4	1226 1.4	1839 3.4
10 SU	0026 0.6	0645 3.7	1245 1.1	1856 3.7
25 M	0107 0.9	0724 3.4	1329 1.3	1940 3.4
11 M	0133 0.6	0749 3.7	1351 1.0	2000 3.7
26 TU	0203 1.0	0824 3.5	1432 1.2	2040 3.5
12 TU	0237 0.5	0852 3.8	1453 0.9	2102 3.9
27 W	0258 0.9	0919 3.6	1528 1.1	2135 3.6
13 W	0335 0.5	0949 3.9	1552 0.7	2201 4.0
28 TH	0347 0.9	1007 3.7	1615 1.0	2224 3.7
14 TH	0427 0.5	1041 4.0	1647 0.6	2256 4.1
29 F	0432 0.9	1049 3.8	1658 0.8	2309 3.8
15 F	0515 0.5	1132 4.0	1740 0.5	● 2350 4.1
30 SA	0513 0.8	1129 3.9	1739 0.7	○ 2351 3.9

JULY

Day	Time m	Time m	Time m	Time m
1 SU	0552 0.8	1208 3.9	1821 0.7	
16 M	0037 4.1	0633 0.9	1256 4.1	1915 0.4
2 M	0032 3.9	0631 0.8	1248 3.9	1902 0.6
17 TU	0123 4.1	0713 0.9	1337 4.1	1958 0.4
3 TU	0114 4.0	0709 0.9	1328 3.9	1944 0.5
18 W	0204 4.0	0751 1.0	1415 4.0	2036 0.4
4 W	0156 4.0	0748 0.9	1408 3.9	2025 0.5
19 TH	0243 4.0	0827 1.0	1450 4.0	2111 0.5
5 TH	0241 4.0	0829 0.9	1450 3.9	2108 0.5
20 F	0319 3.9	0901 1.0	1525 3.9	2145 0.6
6 F	0327 3.9	0914 0.9	1535 3.9	2155 0.5
21 SA	0354 3.7	0937 1.1	1602 3.8	2222 0.8
7 SA	0417 3.9	1003 1.0	1625 3.9	◑ 2247 0.6
22 SU	0432 3.6	1021 1.2	1646 3.6	◑ 2308 0.9
8 SU	0512 3.8	1101 1.0	1721 3.8	2347 0.6
23 M	0517 3.5	1116 1.3	1739 3.5	
9 M	0612 3.6	1205 1.1	1823 3.7	
24 TU	0004 1.0	0612 3.3	1222 1.4	1842 3.3
10 TU	0054 0.8	0716 3.6	1317 1.1	1931 3.7
25 W	0107 1.1	0721 3.3	1335 1.4	1955 3.3
11 W	0207 0.8	0826 3.6	1432 1.0	2043 3.7
26 TH	0213 1.2	0836 3.4	1450 1.2	2106 3.5
12 TH	0316 0.8	0932 3.7	1542 0.9	2151 3.8
27 F	0317 1.1	0938 3.6	1553 1.1	2203 3.7
13 F	0414 0.8	1030 3.8	1644 0.7	2252 4.0
28 SA	0410 1.0	1028 3.8	1642 0.9	2252 3.9
14 SA	0504 0.8	1123 4.0	1739 0.5	● 2347 4.1
29 SU	0454 0.9	1112 3.9	1726 0.7	2336 4.0
15 SU	0550 0.9	1211 4.0	1829 0.4	
30 M	0535 0.9	1153 4.0	1808 0.6	○
31 TU	0019 4.1	0613 0.8	1234 4.1	1848 0.5

AUGUST

Day	Time m	Time m	Time m	Time m
1 W	0101 4.2	0652 0.8	1313 4.1	1928 0.4
16 TH	0140 4.0	0725 0.9	1348 4.1	2002 0.5
2 TH	0142 4.2	0730 0.8	1352 4.2	2007 0.3
17 F	0211 4.0	0755 0.9	1416 4.0	2030 0.6
3 F	0223 4.2	0810 0.7	1431 4.2	2046 0.3
18 SA	0238 3.9	0824 0.9	1445 4.0	2058 0.6
4 SA	0305 4.1	0851 0.7	1511 4.2	2126 0.4
19 SU	0307 3.8	0856 0.9	1517 3.9	2130 0.8
5 SU	0350 4.0	0936 0.8	1555 4.0	◑ 2212 0.6
20 M	0340 3.7	0933 1.1	1556 3.7	◑ 2210 0.9
6 M	0440 3.8	1028 1.0	1648 3.9	2309 0.8
21 TU	0421 3.6	1022 1.2	1644 3.5	2306 1.1
7 TU	0538 3.6	1133 1.1	1754 3.6	
22 W	0513 3.4	1130 1.4	1747 3.3	
8 W	0022 1.0	0647 3.4	1255 1.2	1915 3.5
23 TH	0019 1.3	0621 3.2	1251 1.4	1910 3.2
9 TH	0148 1.2	0810 3.4	1428 1.1	2042 3.5
24 F	0136 1.4	0752 3.3	1417 1.3	2040 3.4
10 F	0308 1.1	0925 3.6	1545 0.9	2154 3.8
25 SA	0249 1.3	0911 3.5	1530 1.1	2144 3.7
11 SA	0407 1.0	1024 3.8	1644 0.6	2252 4.0
26 SU	0347 1.1	1005 3.8	1622 0.8	2233 3.9
12 SU	0454 1.0	1113 4.0	1733 0.5	● 2341 4.1
27 M	0432 1.0	1049 4.0	1705 0.6	2317 4.1
13 M	0536 0.9	1158 4.1	1817 0.4	
28 TU	0512 0.8	1130 4.1	1746 0.4	○ 2358 4.3
14 TU	0025 4.2	0614 0.9	1240 4.2	1856 0.4
29 W	0551 0.8	1210 4.2	1826 0.3	
15 W	0105 4.1	0651 0.9	1316 4.1	1931 0.4
30 TH	0039 4.3	0629 0.7	1250 4.3	1904 0.2
31 F	0120 4.3	0708 0.6	1328 4.4	1942 0.2

Chart Datum: 2·16 metres below Ordnance Datum (Newlyn)

TIME ZONE (UT)
For Summer Time add ONE hour in **non-shaded areas**

Dates in amber are **SPRINGS**
Dates in yellow are **NEAPS**

2007

SEPTEMBER

Date	Time m	Date	Time m
1 SA	0200 4.3, 0748 0.6, 1407 4.4, 2019 0.3	16 SU	0158 3.9, 0753 0.8, 1409 4.0, 2017 0.7
2 SU	0240 4.2, 0829 0.6, 1446 4.3, 2058 0.4	17 M	0225 3.9, 0823 0.9, 1441 3.9, 2046 0.8
3 M	0321 4.0, 0912 0.7, 1530 4.1, 2141 0.7	18 TU	0258 3.9, 0859 1.0, 1518 4.0, 2121 1.0
4 TU	0408 3.8, 1004 0.9, 1624 3.8, ◑ 2237 1.0	19 W	0339 3.7, 0943 1.1, 1604 3.5, ◐ 2210 1.2
5 W	0506 3.5, 1114 1.1, 1738 3.5, 2359 1.3	20 TH	0429 3.4, 1049 1.3, 1705 3.3, 2332 1.4
6 TH	0626 3.3, 1252 1.2, 1915 3.4	21 F	0537 3.2, 1216 1.4, 1830 3.2
7 F	0137 1.4, 0759 3.3, 1431 1.1, 2044 3.5	22 SA	0100 1.5, 0706 3.2, 1345 1.3, 2008 3.3
8 SA	0259 1.3, 0913 3.6, 1540 0.8, 2149 3.8	23 SU	0217 1.4, 0833 3.4, 1459 1.0, 2116 3.7
9 SU	0355 1.2, 1008 3.9, 1632 0.5, 2239 4.1	24 M	0317 1.2, 0931 3.7, 1553 0.7, 2206 4.0
10 M	0437 1.0, 1055 4.1, 1715 0.4, 2323 4.2	25 TU	0403 1.0, 1017 4.0, 1637 0.5, 2249 4.2
11 TU	0515 1.0, 1136 4.2, 1752 0.4 ●	26 W	0444 0.8, 1100 4.2, 1718 0.3, ○ 2331 4.3
12 W	0003 4.2, 0551 0.9, 1214 4.2, 1826 0.5	27 TH	0524 0.7, 1141 4.3, 1758 0.2
13 TH	0039 4.1, 0625 0.9, 1247 4.1, 1857 0.5	28 F	0012 4.4, 0604 0.6, 1222 4.4, 1837 0.2
14 F	0109 4.0, 0656 0.9, 1315 4.1, 1924 0.6	29 SA	0054 4.4, 0645 0.6, 1303 4.5, 1916 0.2
15 SA	0135 4.0, 0724 0.8, 1341 4.0, 1950 0.6	30 SU	0134 4.5, 0728 0.5, 1344 4.5, 1954 0.4

OCTOBER

Date	Time m	Date	Time m
1 M	0214 4.2, 0811 0.5, 1427 4.3, 2034 0.6	16 TU	0152 4.0, 0759 0.8, 1413 3.9, 2013 0.9
2 TU	0256 4.0, 0856 0.7, 1514 4.1, 2118 0.9	17 W	0227 3.9, 0835 0.9, 1452 3.8, 2048 1.0
3 W	0342 3.7, 0951 0.9, 1612 3.7, 2216 1.3	18 TH	0307 3.7, 0920 1.0, 1538 3.6, 2134 1.3
4 TH	0443 3.4, 1112 1.1, 1734 3.5, 2345 1.5	19 F	0357 3.5, 1022 1.2, 1639 3.4, ◐ 2248 1.5
5 F	0609 3.3, 1252 1.1, 1908 3.4	20 SA	0503 3.3, 1147 1.3, 1757 3.3
6 SA	0120 1.6, 0736 3.3, 1416 0.9, 2027 3.6	21 SU	0019 1.5, 0625 3.3, 1309 1.1, 1924 3.4
7 SU	0235 1.4, 0846 3.6, 1519 0.7, 2126 3.9	22 M	0134 1.4, 0744 3.4, 1420 0.9, 2035 3.7
8 M	0329 1.2, 0940 3.9, 1607 0.5, 2214 4.1	23 TU	0236 1.2, 0847 3.7, 1517 0.7, 2129 4.0
9 TU	0411 1.1, 1026 4.0, 1646 0.5, 2255 4.1	24 W	0327 1.0, 0938 4.0, 1605 0.4, 2216 4.2
10 W	0449 0.9, 1106 4.1, 1720 0.5, 2333 4.1	25 TH	0413 0.8, 1025 4.2, 1648 0.3, 2301 4.3
11 TH	0524 0.9, 1142 4.1, 1751 0.6 ●	26 F	0457 0.6, 1110 4.3, 1730 0.3, ○ 2344 4.4
12 F	0006 4.1, 0556 0.9, 1214 4.0, 1820 0.6	27 SA	0541 0.5, 1155 4.4, 1812 0.3
13 SA	0035 4.0, 0627 0.8, 1243 4.0, 1847 0.7	28 SU	0027 4.3, 0626 0.5, 1240 4.5, 1853 0.4
14 SU	0058 3.9, 0656 0.8, 1310 4.0, 1915 0.7	29 M	0111 4.3, 0712 0.4, 1326 4.4, 1934 0.5
15 M	0123 4.0, 0726 0.8, 1340 3.9, 1943 0.8	30 TU	0153 4.1, 0759 0.5, 1414 4.3, 2017 0.8
		31 W	0238 4.0, 0850 0.6, 1505 4.0, 2104 1.1

NOVEMBER

Date	Time m	Date	Time m
1 TH	0326 3.7, 0951 0.8, 1607 3.7, ◐ 2203 1.4	16 F	0246 3.7, 0907 0.9, 1523 3.6, 2115 1.2
2 F	0428 3.5, 1110 0.9, 1722 3.5, 2324 1.6	17 SA	0335 3.6, 1003 1.0, 1620 3.5, ◐ 2216 1.3
3 SA	0544 3.4, 1231 0.9, 1840 3.5	18 SU	0435 3.4, 1114 1.0, 1728 3.5, 2331 1.4
4 SU	0045 1.6, 0658 3.4, 1342 0.9, 1949 3.6	19 M	0547 3.4, 1227 0.9, 1840 3.5
5 M	0155 1.5, 0804 3.6, 1442 0.7, 2049 3.7	20 TU	0043 1.3, 0657 3.5, 1335 0.8, 1948 3.7
6 TU	0252 1.3, 0900 3.8, 1530 0.6, 2138 3.9	21 W	0149 1.2, 0801 3.7, 1437 0.7, 2049 3.9
7 W	0338 1.1, 0949 3.9, 1609 0.6, 2220 4.0	22 TH	0248 1.0, 0900 3.9, 1531 0.5, 2143 4.0
8 TH	0419 1.0, 1030 4.0, 1644 0.6, 2258 4.0	23 F	0342 0.8, 0954 4.1, 1620 0.4, 2232 4.1
9 F	0456 0.9, 1108 4.0, 1715 0.7, 2331 4.0	24 SA	0433 0.6, 1045 4.3, 1706 0.4, ○ 2320 4.2
10 SA	0530 0.8, 1143 3.9, 1746 0.7	25 SU	0523 0.5, 1134 4.4, 1751 0.5
11 SU	0001 3.9, 0608 0.8, 1215 3.9, 1816 0.8	26 M	0006 4.2, 0613 0.5, 1225 4.4, 1835 0.6
12 M	0028 3.9, 0633 0.8, 1246 3.9, 1847 0.8	27 TU	0053 4.2, 0704 0.4, 1315 4.3, 1920 0.7
13 TU	0056 3.9, 0707 0.8, 1319 3.9, 1919 0.9	28 W	0139 4.1, 0755 0.4, 1405 4.2, 2005 0.9
14 W	0129 3.9, 0743 0.8, 1355 3.9, 1952 1.0	29 TH	0225 4.0, 0848 0.5, 1457 4.0, 2052 1.1
15 TH	0205 3.9, 0822 0.8, 1436 3.8, 2029 1.1	30 F	0314 3.8, 0945 0.6, 1553 3.8, 2144 1.3

DECEMBER

Date	Time m	Date	Time m
1 SA	0407 3.7, 1048 0.7, 1653 3.7, 2246 1.4	16 SU	0317 3.7, 0942 0.7, 1601 3.7, ◐ 2149 1.1
2 SU	0507 3.6, 1151 0.8, 1756 3.5, 2354 1.5	17 M	0409 3.7, 1038 0.8, 1658 3.6, ◐ 2248 1.2
3 M	0610 3.5, 1252 0.9, 1858 3.5	18 TU	0508 3.6, 1140 0.8, 1801 3.6, 2354 1.2
4 TU	0100 1.5, 0712 3.5, 1350 0.9, 1958 3.5	19 W	0613 3.6, 1247 0.8, 1906 3.6
5 W	0203 1.3, 0812 3.6, 1441 0.9, 2053 3.6	20 TH	0102 1.1, 0720 3.7, 1355 0.7, 2011 3.7
6 TH	0259 1.2, 0907 3.7, 1527 0.9, 2140 3.7	21 F	0211 1.0, 0827 3.8, 1500 0.7, 2114 3.8
7 F	0346 1.0, 0955 3.8, 1607 0.8, 2222 3.8	22 SA	0317 0.9, 0931 3.9, 1558 0.6, 2211 3.9
8 SA	0428 0.9, 1038 3.8, 1643 0.8, 2300 3.9	23 SU	0418 0.7, 1029 4.1, 1649 0.6, 2303 4.0
9 SU	0506 0.8, 1117 3.9, 1718 0.8, 2334 3.9	24 M	0514 0.6, 1124 4.2, 1738 0.7, ○ 2353 4.1
10 M	0542 0.8, 1154 3.9, 1753 0.6	25 TU	0609 0.4, 1217 4.3, 1824 0.7
11 TU	0006 3.9, 0617 0.7, 1229 3.9, 1827 0.9	26 W	0041 4.1, 0701 0.4, 1308 4.3, 1909 0.8
12 W	0040 3.9, 0655 0.7, 1305 3.9, 1903 0.9	27 TH	0128 4.1, 0751 0.3, 1357 4.2, 1952 0.9
13 TH	0115 3.9, 0733 0.7, 1343 3.9, 1938 1.0	28 F	0212 4.1, 0838 0.4, 1443 4.1, 2033 1.0
14 F	0152 3.9, 0813 0.7, 1424 3.9, 2017 1.0	29 SA	0255 4.0, 0923 0.5, 1528 3.9, 2114 1.1
15 SA	0232 3.8, 0855 0.7, 1510 3.8, 2100 1.1	30 SU	0338 3.8, 1009 0.6, 1614 3.7, 2158 1.2
		31 M	0423 3.8, 1057 0.7, 1702 3.6, ◐ 2248 1.3

Chart Datum: 2·16 metres below Ordnance Datum (Newlyn)

TIDES

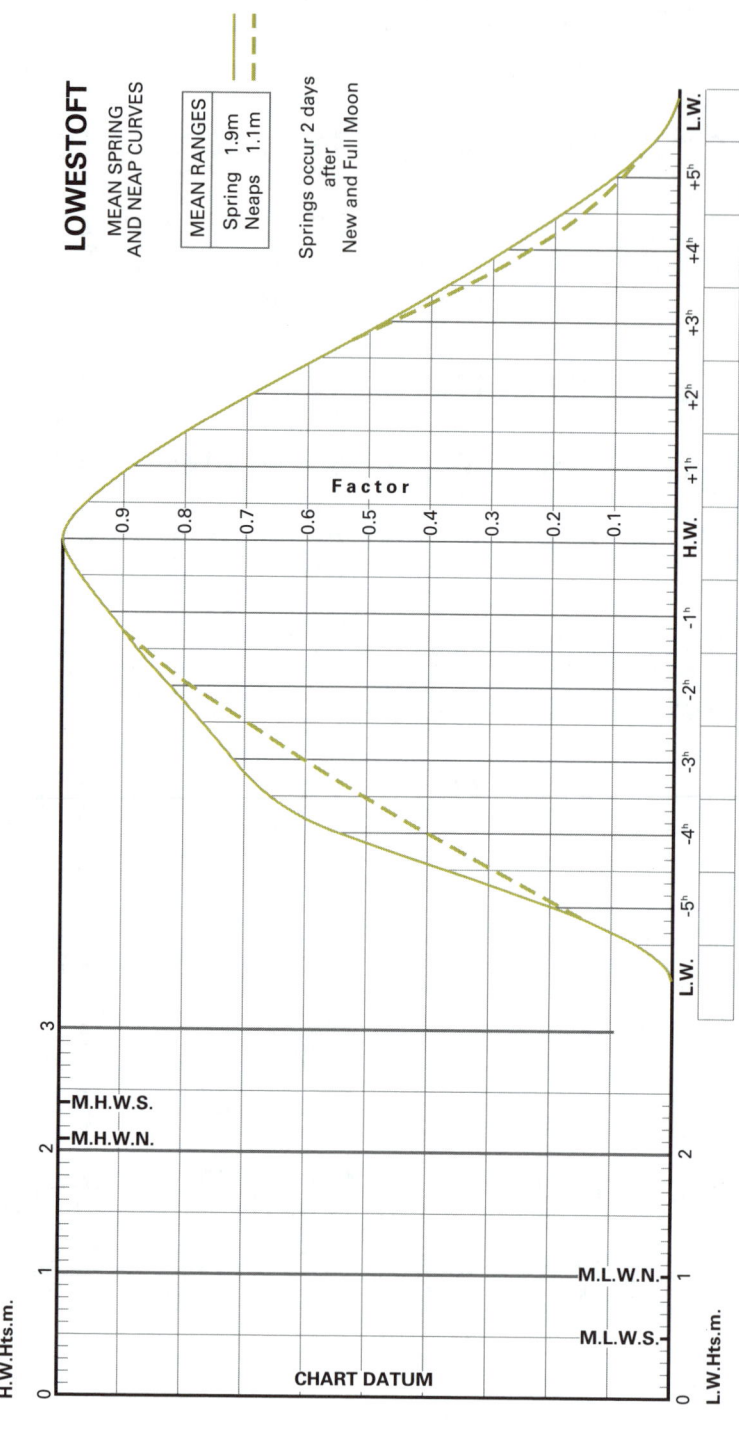

LOWESTOFT

MEAN SPRING
AND NEAP CURVES

MEAN RANGES

Spring 1.9m
Neaps 1.1m

Springs occur 2 days
after
New and Full Moon

ENGLAND – LOWESTOFT

LAT 52°28'N   LONG 1°45'E

TIMES AND HEIGHTS OF HIGH AND LOW WATERS

Dates in amber are SPRINGS
Dates in yellow are NEAPS

2007

JANUARY

Day	Time	m	Time	m	Time	m	Time	m
1 M	0051	1.0	0655	2.4	1328	0.8	1945	2.3
16 TU	0053	1.2	0703	2.1	1313	1.0	1940	2.2
2 TU	0155	0.8	0759	2.4	1421	0.8	2030	2.4
17 W	0144	1.0	0800	2.2	1358	1.0	2020	2.3
3 W ○	0252	0.7	0901	2.4	1510	0.9	2113	2.5
18 TH	0233	0.9	0850	2.3	1443	1.0	2059	2.4
4 TH	0344	0.6	0955	2.4	1553	0.9	2155	2.5
19 F ●	0322	0.7	0936	2.3	1529	0.8	2139	2.5
5 F	0431	0.5	1043	2.4	1633	0.9	2237	2.5
20 SA	0410	0.5	1020	2.4	1614	0.8	2220	2.5
6 SA	0514	0.5	1128	2.3	1709	1.0	2316	2.5
21 SU	0457	0.4	1103	2.4	1657	0.8	2301	2.6
7 SU	0555	0.5	1211	2.2	1741	1.0	2353	2.5
22 M	0543	0.3	1146	2.3	1738	0.8	2343	2.6
8 M	0634	0.6	1251	2.1	1812	1.1		
23 TU	0626	0.3	1229	2.3	1817	0.8		
9 TU	0030	2.5	0711	0.6	1330	2.1	1844	1.1
24 W	0025	2.6	0709	0.4	1314	2.2	1857	0.9
10 W	0109	2.4	0749	0.7	1411	2.0	1921	1.2
25 TH ☽	0109	2.6	0754	0.5	1403	2.1	1941	1.0
11 TH ☽	0151	2.3	0831	0.8	1504	2.0	2006	1.3
26 F	0158	2.5	0845	0.6	1506	2.0	2034	1.0
12 F	0239	2.3	0921	0.9	1616	2.0	2100	1.3
27 SA	0257	2.4	0949	0.8	1630	2.0	2144	1.1
13 SA	0339	2.2	1027	1.0	1717	2.0	2217	1.4
28 SU	0422	2.3	1107	0.9	1736	2.1	2324	1.1
14 SU	0454	2.1	1132	1.0	1810	2.1	2353	1.3
29 M	0547	2.2	1219	1.0	1836	2.1		
15 M	0603	2.1	1226	1.0	1857	2.2		
30 TU	0048	0.9	0707	2.2	1325	1.0	1931	2.2
31 W	0157	0.8	0818	2.3	1421	1.0	2020	2.2

FEBRUARY

Day	Time	m	Time	m	Time	m	Time	m
1 TH	0252	0.6	0910	2.3	1507	1.0	2102	2.4
16 F	0217	0.7	0842	2.3	1430	0.9	2037	2.3
2 F ○	0338	0.5	0952	2.3	1545	0.9	2141	2.5
17 SA ●	0307	0.5	0924	2.4	1516	0.8	2118	2.5
3 SA	0418	0.4	1030	2.3	1619	0.9	2218	2.5
18 SU	0355	0.3	1004	2.4	1600	0.7	2159	2.6
4 SU	0456	0.4	1106	2.3	1649	0.9	2253	2.5
19 M	0439	0.2	1043	2.4	1640	0.6	2240	2.7
5 M	0530	0.4	1139	2.2	1717	0.9	2327	2.5
20 TU	0522	0.1	1123	2.4	1719	0.6	2321	2.7
6 TU	0602	0.5	1209	2.2	1744	0.9		
21 W	0603	0.2	1203	2.3	1757	0.6		
7 W	0001	2.4	0632	0.6	1239	2.1	1813	0.9
22 TH	0004	2.7	0642	0.3	1245	2.2	1836	0.7
8 TH	0037	2.4	0702	0.7	1312	2.1	1847	1.0
23 F	0049	2.6	0723	0.5	1329	2.1	1920	0.8
9 F	0116	2.3	0735	0.8	1350	2.0	1928	1.1
24 SA ☽	0140	2.5	0810	0.7	1421	2.0	2014	0.9
10 SA ☽	0159	2.2	0815	0.9	1438	2.0	2017	1.2
25 SU	0247	2.3	0912	1.0	1538	2.0	2131	1.0
11 SU	0253	2.1	0908	1.1	1549	2.0	2122	1.3
26 M	0429	2.2	1052	1.1	1701	2.0	2323	0.9
12 M	0411	2.0	1031	1.2	1714	2.0	2310	1.2
27 TU	0602	2.1	1218	1.2	1811	2.1		
13 TU	0541	2.0	1154	1.2	1816	2.1		
28 W	0046	0.8	0727	2.2	1327	1.1	1917	2.2
14 W	0027	1.4	0652	2.1	1252	1.1	1909	2.4
15 TH	0124	0.9	0754	2.2	1342	1.0	1955	2.2

MARCH

Day	Time	m	Time	m	Time	m	Time	m
1 TH	0151	0.7	0822	2.2	1416	1.1	2007	2.2
16 F	0100	0.8	0737	2.2	1322	1.0	1922	2.2
2 F	0239	0.5	0902	2.3	1455	1.0	2046	2.3
17 SA	0153	0.6	0822	2.3	1410	0.9	2008	2.3
3 SA ○	0319	0.5	0936	2.3	1527	0.9	2121	2.4
18 SU	0243	0.4	0902	2.4	1455	0.7	2050	2.5
4 SU	0355	0.4	1007	2.3	1557	0.8	2154	2.5
19 M ●	0330	0.2	0940	2.4	1537	0.6	2133	2.6
5 M	0428	0.4	1036	2.2	1624	0.8	2227	2.5
20 TU	0414	0.1	1018	2.4	1618	0.5	2216	2.7
6 TU	0458	0.4	1104	2.2	1650	0.7	2300	2.5
21 W	0455	0.1	1057	2.4	1658	0.5	2300	2.8
7 W	0526	0.5	1131	2.2	1717	0.8	2333	2.4
22 TH	0535	0.2	1136	2.3	1738	0.5	2345	2.7
8 TH	0553	0.6	1200	2.2	1746	0.8		
23 F	0615	0.4	1217	2.3	1820	0.6		
9 F	0008	2.4	0620	0.7	1232	2.2	1818	0.9
24 SA	0034	2.5	0655	0.6	1301	2.2	1907	0.6
10 SA	0045	2.3	0650	0.8	1309	2.1	1857	0.9
25 SU ☽	0132	2.4	0741	0.9	1351	2.1	2006	0.7
11 SU	0127	2.2	0727	0.9	1353	2.1	1944	1.0
26 M	0257	2.2	0842	1.2	1459	2.0	2133	0.8
12 M ☽	0219	2.1	0816	1.1	1448	2.0	2046	1.1
27 TU	0436	2.1	1038	1.3	1623	2.0	2314	0.8
13 TU	0335	2.0	0928	1.2	1605	2.0	2234	1.1
28 W	0604	2.1	1205	1.3	1739	2.1		
14 W	0526	2.0	1122	1.2	1730	2.0		
29 TH	0026	0.7	0717	2.2	1309	1.2	1849	2.1
15 TH	0001	1.0	0640	2.1	1230	1.1	1831	2.1
30 F	0125	0.6	0804	2.2	1354	1.1	1941	2.0
31 SA	0211	0.5	0840	2.2	1430	1.0	2019	2.3

APRIL

Day	Time	m	Time	m	Time	m	Time	m
1 SU	0249	0.5	0910	2.2	1501	0.9	2053	2.3
16 M	0213	0.3	0834	2.4	1426	0.7	2020	2.5
2 M ○	0322	0.5	0938	2.3	1529	0.8	2126	2.4
17 TU ●	0301	0.2	0913	2.4	1511	0.6	2107	2.7
3 TU	0353	0.5	1004	2.3	1557	0.7	2159	2.4
18 W	0346	0.1	0952	2.4	1555	0.5	2154	2.7
4 W	0422	0.5	1030	2.3	1624	0.7	2233	2.4
19 TH	0428	0.2	1031	2.4	1639	0.4	2243	2.7
5 TH	0449	0.6	1057	2.3	1652	0.7	2307	2.4
20 F	0509	0.4	1112	2.4	1723	0.4	2333	2.6
6 F	0516	0.6	1127	2.3	1723	0.7	2342	2.3
21 SA	0550	0.6	1154	2.3	1810	0.5		
7 SA	0544	0.7	1200	2.2	1757	0.8		
22 SU	0028	2.4	0632	0.8	1239	2.3	1901	0.5
8 SU	0020	2.2	0616	0.8	1237	2.2	1835	0.8
23 M	0135	2.3	0718	1.1	1330	2.2	2004	0.6
9 M	0103	2.1	0655	1.0	1321	2.1	1923	0.9
24 TU ☽	0302	2.1	0817	1.3	1432	2.1	2126	0.7
10 TU	0157	2.0	0745	1.1	1414	2.1	2027	1.0
25 W	0424	2.1	1001	1.4	1545	2.1	2247	0.7
11 W	0314	2.0	0852	1.3	1519	2.0	2207	1.0
26 TH	0539	2.1	1128	1.3	1657	2.1	2351	0.6
12 TH	0510	2.0	1038	1.3	1636	2.0	2330	0.8
27 F	0645	2.2	1230	1.2	1803	2.1		
13 F	0617	2.1	1155	1.2	1747	2.1		
28 SA	0046	0.6	0732	2.2	1318	1.1	1859	2.2
14 SA	0028	0.6	0710	2.2	1251	1.0	1843	2.2
29 SU	0132	0.6	0810	2.2	1356	1.0	1943	2.2
15 SU	0123	0.5	0754	2.3	1340	0.9	1933	2.4
30 M	0211	0.6	0841	2.2	1429	0.9	2021	2.3

Chart Datum: 1·50 metres below Ordnance Datum (Newlyn)

TIDES

TIDES

TIME ZONE (UT)
For Summer Time add ONE hour in **non-shaded areas**

ENGLAND – LOWESTOFT
LAT 52°28'N   LONG 1°45'E
TIMES AND HEIGHTS OF HIGH AND LOW WATERS

Dates in amber are **SPRINGS**
Dates in yellow are **NEAPS**

2007

MAY

Day	Time m	Day	Time m
1 TU	0245 0.6 / 0908 2.3 / 1459 0.8 / 2057 2.3	16 W	0232 0.3 / 0846 2.4 / 1448 0.6 / ● 2046 2.6
2 W	0316 0.6 / 0933 2.3 / 1529 0.8 / ○ 2133 2.3	17 TH	0319 0.3 / 0927 2.4 / 1537 0.5 / 2139 2.6
3 TH	0345 0.6 / 0959 2.3 / 1559 0.7 / 2208 2.3	18 F	0404 0.4 / 1009 2.4 / 1626 0.4 / 2233 2.5
4 F	0414 0.7 / 1028 2.3 / 1632 0.7 / 2245 2.3	19 SA	0448 0.6 / 1052 2.4 / 1715 0.4 / 2328 2.4
5 SA	0444 0.7 / 1100 2.3 / 1707 0.7 / 2322 2.2	20 SU	0531 0.8 / 1136 2.4 / 1804 0.4
6 SU	0517 0.8 / 1135 2.3 / 1744 0.7	21 M	0026 2.3 / 0613 0.9 / 1222 2.4 / 1856 0.4
7 M	0003 2.2 / 0553 0.9 / 1214 2.3 / 1826 0.8	22 TU	0131 2.2 / 0658 1.1 / 1311 2.3 / 1954 0.5
8 TU	0050 2.1 / 0636 1.0 / 1259 2.2 / 1917 0.8	23 W	0244 2.1 / 0748 1.3 / 1408 2.2 / ◑ 2100 0.6
9 W	0145 2.1 / 0727 1.1 / 1351 2.2 / 2021 0.8	24 TH	0355 2.1 / 0852 1.4 / 1503 2.2 / 2208 0.6
10 TH	0258 2.0 / 0829 1.2 / 1448 2.1 / ◑ 2142 0.8	25 F	0500 2.1 / 1023 1.4 / 1606 2.1 / 2308 0.7
11 F	0441 2.1 / 0948 1.2 / 1552 2.1 / 2255 0.7	26 SA	0601 2.1 / 1135 1.3 / 1710 2.1
12 SA	0545 2.2 / 1108 1.2 / 1702 2.2 / 2355 0.5	27 SU	0001 0.7 / 0652 2.1 / 1231 1.2 / 1807 2.1
13 SU	0638 2.2 / 1210 1.1 / 1805 2.3	28 M	0049 0.7 / 0734 2.2 / 1315 1.1 / 1859 2.2
14 M	0050 0.4 / 0724 2.3 / 1305 0.9 / 1901 2.4	29 TU	0130 0.7 / 0808 2.2 / 1353 1.0 / 1946 2.2
15 TU	0142 0.3 / 0806 2.3 / 1358 0.8 / 1954 2.5	30 W	0206 0.7 / 0836 2.3 / 1428 0.9 / 2030 2.2
		31 TH	0239 0.7 / 0902 2.3 / 1503 0.8 / 2110 2.2

JUNE

Day	Time m	Day	Time m
1 F	0311 0.8 / 0931 2.4 / 1539 0.8 / ○ 2150 2.2	16 SA	0348 0.7 / 0952 2.5 / 1620 0.4 / 2231 2.4
2 SA	0346 0.8 / 1003 2.4 / 1617 0.7 / 2230 2.2	17 SU	0433 0.8 / 1037 2.5 / 1710 0.4 / 2325 2.4
3 SU	0422 0.8 / 1039 2.4 / 1658 0.7 / 2311 2.2	18 M	0516 0.9 / 1121 2.5 / 1757 0.3
4 M	0500 0.8 / 1117 2.4 / 1741 0.7 / 2355 2.2	19 TU	0018 2.3 / 0556 1.0 / 1205 2.5 / 1844 0.4
5 TU	0541 0.9 / 1158 2.4 / 1827 0.7	20 W	0111 2.2 / 0635 1.1 / 1248 2.4 / 1931 0.5
6 W	0042 2.2 / 0625 1.0 / 1243 2.3 / 1917 0.6	21 TH	0208 2.1 / 0713 1.2 / 1332 2.4 / 2021 0.6
7 TH	0134 2.1 / 0713 1.1 / 1331 2.3 / 2012 0.6	22 F	0309 2.0 / 0754 1.2 / 1418 2.3 / ◑ 2115 0.7
8 F	0234 2.1 / 0806 1.1 / 1421 2.3 / ◑ 2114 0.6	23 SA	0410 2.0 / 0842 1.3 / 1509 2.2 / 2214 0.8
9 SA	0357 2.1 / 0907 1.2 / 1516 2.3 / 2219 0.6	24 SU	0507 2.0 / 0948 1.4 / 1612 2.2 / 2312 0.8
10 SU	0509 2.1 / 1017 1.2 / 1622 2.3 / 2321 0.5	25 M	0600 2.1 / 1126 1.3 / 1719 2.1
11 M	0604 2.2 / 1129 1.1 / 1733 2.4	26 TU	0003 0.9 / 0647 2.1 / 1229 1.2 / 1819 2.1
12 TU	0020 0.5 / 0653 2.3 / 1235 1.0 / 1836 2.4	27 W	0049 0.9 / 0728 2.2 / 1318 1.1 / 1917 2.1
13 W	0116 0.5 / 0739 2.3 / 1336 0.8 / 1936 2.4	28 TH	0129 0.9 / 0802 2.2 / 1401 1.0 / 2010 2.2
14 TH	0209 0.6 / 0824 2.4 / 1434 0.7 / 2035 2.5	29 F	0208 0.9 / 0835 2.3 / 1442 0.9 / 2057 2.2
15 F	0300 0.6 / 0908 2.4 / 1528 0.5 / ● 2134 2.5	30 SA	0246 0.9 / 0908 2.4 / 1524 0.8 / ○ 2140 2.2

JULY

Day	Time m	Day	Time m
1 SU	0326 0.9 / 0944 2.4 / 1608 0.7 / 2221 2.3	16 M	0421 0.9 / 1021 2.5 / 1700 0.5 / 2313 2.3
2 M	0408 0.8 / 1023 2.5 / 1652 0.6 / 2303 2.3	17 TU	0500 0.9 / 1103 2.6 / 1741 0.3 / 2356 2.3
3 TU	0450 0.8 / 1103 2.5 / 1737 0.5 / 2345 2.3	18 W	0535 0.9 / 1142 2.6 / 1821 0.4
4 W	0532 0.9 / 1144 2.5 / 1821 0.5	19 TH	0037 2.2 / 0606 1.0 / 1220 2.5 / 1858 0.5
5 TH	0028 2.3 / 0613 0.9 / 1226 2.5 / 1905 0.5	20 F	0117 2.1 / 0638 1.0 / 1257 2.5 / 1935 0.6
6 F	0114 2.2 / 0655 1.0 / 1308 2.5 / 1951 0.5	21 SA	0157 2.1 / 0712 1.1 / 1337 2.4 / 2014 0.7
7 SA	0203 2.1 / 0740 1.0 / 1354 2.5 / ◑ 2042 0.5	22 SU	0243 2.0 / 0752 1.2 / 1423 2.3 / ◑ 2059 0.9
8 SU	0304 2.1 / 0832 1.1 / 1446 2.4 / 2141 0.6	23 M	0346 2.0 / 0843 1.3 / 1520 2.2 / 2159 1.0
9 M	0426 2.1 / 0933 1.1 / 1551 2.4 / 2249 0.7	24 TU	0451 2.0 / 0954 1.3 / 1636 2.1 / 2312 1.1
10 TU	0530 2.1 / 1055 1.1 / 1713 2.3 / 2356 0.7	25 W	0547 2.1 / 1141 1.3 / 1750 2.1
11 W	0626 2.2 / 1216 1.0 / 1825 2.3	26 TH	0011 1.1 / 0639 2.1 / 1246 1.2 / 1858 2.1
12 TH	0058 0.8 / 0717 2.3 / 1327 0.8 / 1934 2.3	27 F	0100 1.1 / 0726 2.2 / 1337 1.0 / 2001 2.2
13 F	0157 0.8 / 0806 2.3 / 1430 0.7 / 2041 2.4	28 SA	0145 1.0 / 0808 2.3 / 1424 0.9 / 2049 2.2
14 SA	0251 0.9 / 0853 2.4 / 1526 0.5 / ● 2138 2.4	29 SU	0229 1.0 / 0847 2.4 / 1510 0.7 / 2129 2.3
15 SU	0339 0.9 / 0938 2.5 / 1615 0.4 / ○ 2227 2.4	30 M	0312 0.9 / 0925 2.5 / 1555 0.6 / ○ 2208 2.4
		31 TU	0356 0.8 / 1004 2.6 / 1639 0.4 / 2247 2.4

AUGUST

Day	Time m	Day	Time m
1 W	0438 0.8 / 1043 2.6 / 1722 0.3 / 2326 2.4	16 TH	0508 0.9 / 1114 2.6 / 1748 0.4 / 2357 2.3
2 TH	0518 0.8 / 1123 2.7 / 1803 0.3	17 F	0536 0.9 / 1148 2.6 / 1819 0.3
3 F	0005 2.3 / 0555 0.8 / 1203 2.7 / 1843 0.4	18 SA	0028 2.2 / 0604 0.9 / 1224 2.5 / 1849 0.5
4 SA	0047 2.3 / 0634 0.8 / 1244 2.6 / 1924 0.4	19 SU	0100 2.1 / 0636 1.0 / 1302 2.4 / 1920 0.8
5 SU	0131 2.2 / 0715 0.9 / 1330 2.6 / ◐ 2009 0.6	20 M	0136 2.1 / 0715 1.1 / 1345 2.3 / ◐ 1957 1.0
6 M	0222 2.1 / 0804 1.0 / 1423 2.5 / 2103 0.8	21 TU	0221 2.1 / 0802 1.2 / 1439 2.2 / 2044 1.1
7 TU	0333 2.1 / 0906 1.1 / 1538 2.3 / 2220 0.9	22 W	0323 2.1 / 0905 1.3 / 1557 2.1 / 2158 1.3
8 W	0454 2.1 / 1040 1.1 / 1712 2.3 / 2343 1.0	23 TH	0446 2.1 / 1057 1.3 / 1730 2.1 / 2336 1.3
9 TH	0559 2.2 / 1213 1.0 / 1835 2.3	24 F	0553 2.1 / 1218 1.1 / 1845 2.1
10 F	0054 1.1 / 0658 2.3 / 1328 0.8 / 1953 2.3	25 SA	0036 1.2 / 0649 2.2 / 1312 1.0 / 1946 2.2
11 SA	0157 1.0 / 0753 2.4 / 1429 0.6 / 2050 2.4	26 SU	0125 1.1 / 0737 2.3 / 1401 0.8 / 2030 2.3
12 SU	0247 1.0 / 0840 2.4 / 1518 0.5 / ● 2134 2.4	27 M	0211 1.0 / 0819 2.4 / 1448 0.6 / 2108 2.4
13 M	0328 0.9 / 0921 2.5 / 1600 0.4 / 2213 2.4	28 TU	0254 0.9 / 0858 2.5 / 1533 0.5 / ○ 2145 2.4
14 TU	0405 0.8 / 1001 2.6 / 1639 0.4 / 2250 2.3	29 W	0336 0.8 / 0937 2.5 / 1616 0.3 / 2222 2.5
15 W	0438 0.8 / 1038 2.6 / 1715 0.4 / 2325 2.3	30 TH	0417 0.7 / 1017 2.7 / 1657 0.2 / 2300 2.5
		31 F	0456 0.7 / 1057 2.8 / 1737 0.2 / 2338 2.4

Chart Datum: 1·50 metres below Ordnance Datum (Newlyn)

TIME ZONE (UT)	ENGLAND – LOWESTOFT	Dates in amber are SPRINGS
For Summer Time add ONE hour in **non-shaded areas**	LAT 52°28'N LONG 1°45'E	Dates in yellow are NEAPS
	TIMES AND HEIGHTS OF HIGH AND LOW WATERS	**2007**

SEPTEMBER

Time	m		Time	m
1 0534	0.7	**16**	0534	0.9
1139	2.8		1153	2.5
SA 1815	0.4	SU	1805	0.8
2 0018	2.4	**17**	0018	2.3
0612	0.8		0606	1.0
SU 1223	2.7	M	1230	2.4
1854	0.5		1833	0.9
3 0101	2.3	**18**	0054	2.3
0655	0.8		0644	1.0
M 1311	2.6	TU	1312	2.3
1938	0.7		1909	1.0
4 0149	2.2	**19**	0137	2.2
0747	0.9		0800	1.1
TU 1413	2.4	W	1404	2.1
☽ 2031	1.0	☾	1954	1.2
5 0253	2.2	**20**	0229	2.2
0856	1.0		0831	1.2
W 1548	2.3	TH	1521	2.1
2158	1.2		2057	1.4
6 0418	2.1	**21**	0339	2.1
1044	1.0		1015	1.2
TH 1725	2.2	F	1713	2.1
2339	1.3		2248	1.4
7 0532	2.2	**22**	0503	2.2
1211	0.8		1145	1.1
F 1854	2.3	SA	1824	2.2
8 0053	1.2	**23**	0006	1.3
0639	2.3		0607	2.2
SA 1320	0.7	SU	1241	0.9
1957	2.3		1919	2.3
9 0150	1.1	**24**	0057	1.2
0736	2.4		0658	2.3
SU 1414	0.6	M	1330	0.7
2041	2.4		2002	2.4
10 0233	1.1	**25**	0143	1.0
0820	2.5		0742	2.5
M 1457	0.5	TU	1417	0.5
2116	2.4		2040	2.5
11 0308	1.0	**26**	0227	0.9
0858	2.5		0824	2.6
TU 1535	0.4	W	1503	0.4
● 2148	2.4	○	2116	2.5
12 0340	0.9	**27**	0310	0.8
0934	2.6		0906	2.7
W 1610	0.4	TH	1546	0.3
2220	2.4		2153	2.5
13 0410	0.8	**28**	0351	0.7
1009	2.6		0949	2.8
TH 1642	0.5	F	1628	0.2
2249	2.4		2231	2.5
14 0438	0.8	**29**	0432	0.6
1044	2.6		1033	2.9
F 1711	0.5	SA	1708	0.3
2318	2.3		2310	2.3
15 0506	0.9	**30**	0513	0.6
1118	2.6		1118	2.8
SA 1738	0.6	SU	1748	0.5
2346	2.3		2351	2.4

OCTOBER

Time	m		Time	m
1 0556	0.7	**16**	0542	0.9
1207	2.7		1203	2.3
M 1828	0.7	TU	1757	1.0
2 0034	2.4	**17**	0019	2.4
0644	0.7		0620	1.0
TU 1303	2.5	W	1246	2.2
1912	1.0		1834	1.1
3 0124	2.3	**18**	0102	2.3
0741	0.8		0707	1.1
W 1418	2.3	TH	1338	2.1
☽ 2008	1.2		1921	1.2
4 0226	2.2	**19**	0153	2.2
0900	0.9		0808	1.1
TH 1602	2.2	F	1450	2.1
2141	1.4	☾	2022	1.4
5 0345	2.2	**20**	0254	2.2
1039	0.8		0939	1.1
F 1728	2.3	SA	1647	2.1
2324	1.4		2147	1.4
6 0501	2.2	**21**	0405	2.2
1153	0.7		1104	1.0
SA 1845	2.3	SU	1753	2.2
			2319	1.3
7 0032	1.3	**22**	0517	2.3
0610	2.3		1202	0.8
SU 1255	0.7	M	1845	2.3
1938	2.4			
8 0125	1.2	**23**	0017	1.2
0708	2.4		0614	2.4
M 1346	0.6	TU	1254	0.6
2017	2.4		1929	2.4
9 0206	1.1	**24**	0107	1.1
0752	2.4		0704	2.5
TU 1427	0.6	W	1343	0.5
2050	2.4		2008	2.5
10 0240	1.0	**25**	0155	0.9
0829	2.5		0751	2.6
W 1502	0.6	TH	1430	0.4
2119	2.4		2046	2.5
11 0311	0.9	**26**	0241	0.8
0905	2.6		0838	2.8
TH 1535	0.6	F	1516	0.3
● 2147	2.4	○	2125	2.6
12 0341	0.9	**27**	0326	0.7
0940	2.6		0925	2.8
F 1605	0.6	SA	1559	0.3
2215	2.4		2205	2.6
13 0410	0.8	**28**	0412	0.6
1015	2.5		1014	2.8
SA 1632	0.7	SU	1642	0.5
2242	2.4		2246	2.6
14 0439	0.9	**29**	0458	0.6
1050	2.5		1105	2.7
SU 1658	0.8	M	1724	0.7
2311	2.4		2328	2.5
15 0509	0.9	**30**	0547	0.6
1125	2.4		1200	2.6
M 1726	0.9	TU	1807	0.9
2343	2.4			
		31	0014	2.5
			0639	0.6
		W	1304	2.4
			1853	1.1

NOVEMBER

Time	m		Time	m
1 0105	2.4	**16**	0037	2.4
0740	0.7		0657	0.9
TH 1424	2.3	F	1321	2.2
☽ 1948	1.3		1900	1.2
2 0204	2.3	**17**	0127	2.3
0855	0.7		0756	1.0
F 1552	2.2	SA	1422	2.1
2107	1.5	☾	1957	1.3
3 0313	2.3	**18**	0221	2.3
1014	0.7		0907	0.9
SA 1707	2.2	SU	1559	2.1
2244	1.5		2103	1.3
4 0425	2.3	**19**	0319	2.3
1121	0.7		1020	0.8
SU 1814	2.3	M	1714	2.2
2352	1.4		2220	1.3
5 0532	2.3	**20**	0424	2.3
1218	0.7		1122	0.7
M 1907	2.3	TU	1807	2.3
			2330	1.2
6 0047	1.3	**21**	0531	2.4
0629	2.3		1218	0.6
TU 1308	0.7	W	1854	2.3
1947	2.3			
7 0131	1.2	**22**	0029	1.1
0717	2.4		0629	2.5
W 1349	0.7	TH	1310	0.5
2021	2.3		1937	2.4
8 0208	1.1	**23**	0124	1.0
0758	2.4		0723	2.6
TH 1425	0.7	F	1401	0.5
2050	2.4		2019	2.5
9 0241	1.0	**24**	0217	0.8
0837	2.5		0816	2.7
F 1458	0.7	SA	1449	0.5
● 2116	2.4	○	2100	2.5
10 0313	0.9	**25**	0308	0.7
0914	2.5		0909	2.7
SA 1527	0.8	SU	1536	0.5
2142	2.5		2142	2.6
11 0345	0.9	**26**	0400	0.6
0951	2.4		1004	2.7
SU 1556	0.8	M	1622	0.7
2210	2.5		2226	2.6
12 0417	0.8	**27**	0451	0.5
1027	2.4		1100	2.6
M 1625	0.9	TU	1707	0.8
2241	2.5		2311	2.6
13 0451	0.9	**28**	0542	0.5
1105	2.3		1158	2.5
TU 1657	1.0	W	1752	1.0
2316	2.5		2358	2.5
14 0528	0.9	**29**	0635	0.5
1145	2.3		1300	2.3
W 1733	1.0	TH	1837	1.1
2354	2.4			
15 0609	0.9	**30**	0047	2.5
1229	2.2		0731	0.6
TH 1814	1.1	F	1409	2.2
			1924	1.3

DECEMBER

Time	m		Time	m
1 0139	2.4	**16**	0104	2.4
0831	0.6		0740	0.8
SA 1523	2.2	SU	1354	2.1
☽ 2019	1.4		1932	1.2
2 0236	2.4	**17**	0150	2.4
0936	0.7		0834	0.7
SU 1630	2.2	M	1454	2.1
2130	1.4	☾	2026	1.2
3 0338	2.3	**18**	0241	2.4
1039	0.7		0936	0.7
M 1732	2.2	TU	1621	2.1
2254	1.4		2128	1.2
4 0444	2.3	**19**	0339	2.4
1136	0.8		1041	0.7
TU 1827	2.3	W	1728	2.2
2359	1.4		2241	1.2
5 0545	2.3	**20**	0452	2.4
1226	0.8		1144	0.7
W 1913	2.3	TH	1821	2.3
			2355	1.1
6 0052	1.2	**21**	0603	2.4
0639	2.3		1243	0.7
TH 1310	0.9	F	1909	2.3
1950	2.3			
7 0136	1.1	**22**	0101	1.0
0730	2.3		0704	2.5
F 1349	0.9	SA	1338	0.7
2021	2.3		1955	2.4
8 0214	1.0	**23**	0202	0.8
0815	2.3		0805	2.5
SA 1423	0.9	SU	1431	0.7
2047	2.4		2040	2.5
9 0250	0.9	**24**	0300	0.6
0857	2.3		0905	2.5
SU 1455	0.9	M	1522	0.7
2115	2.4	○	2125	2.5
10 0326	0.9	**25**	0355	0.5
0936	2.3		1004	2.5
M 1527	0.9	TU	1610	0.8
2145	2.5		2211	2.6
11 0403	0.8	**26**	0447	0.4
1015	2.3		1058	2.5
TU 1602	0.9	W	1655	0.9
2219	2.5		2257	2.6
12 0442	0.8	**27**	0536	0.3
1054	2.3		1150	2.4
W 1639	0.9	TH	1737	1.0
2257	2.5		2342	2.6
13 0523	0.8	**28**	0623	0.4
1135	2.3		1241	2.3
TH 1719	1.0	F	1816	1.1
2337	2.5			
14 0606	0.8	**29**	0026	2.5
1218	2.2		0709	0.4
F 1800	1.0	SA	1335	2.2
			1854	1.1
15 0019	2.4	**30**	0110	2.5
0652	0.8		0756	0.6
SA 1304	2.2	SU	1433	2.1
1844	1.1		1933	1.2
		31	0155	2.4
			0846	0.7
		M	1547	2.0
		☽	2017	1.3

Chart Datum: 1·50 metres below Ordnance Datum (Newlyn)

TIDES

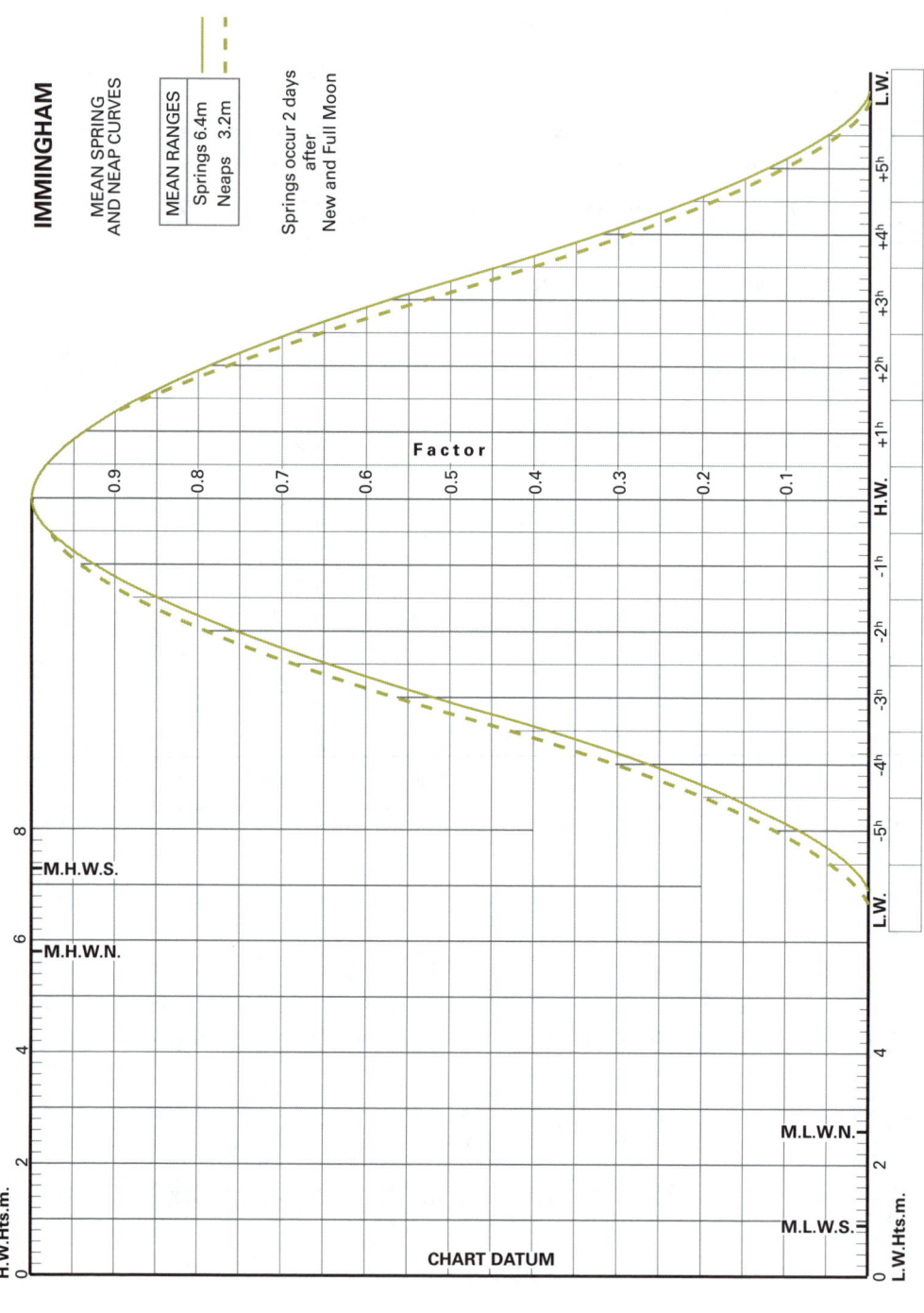

IMMINGHAM

MEAN SPRING
AND NEAP CURVES

MEAN RANGES
Springs 6.4m
Neaps   3.2m

Springs occur 2 days
after
New and Full Moon

Factor

0.9 0.8 0.7 0.6 0.5 0.4 0.3 0.2 0.1

+5ʰ +4ʰ +3ʰ +2ʰ +1ʰ H.W. -1ʰ -2ʰ -3ʰ -4ʰ -5ʰ L.W.

L.W.

H.W.Hts.m.

M.H.W.S.

M.H.W.N.

8

6

4

2

0

M.L.W.N.

M.L.W.S.

CHART DATUM

L.W.Hts.m.

4

2

0

ENGLAND–IMMINGHAM

LAT 53°38'N   LONG 0°11'W

TIMES AND HEIGHTS OF HIGH AND LOW WATERS

2007

JANUARY

Time m | Time m

1 0326 6.5 / 0956 1.9 / M 1610 6.4 / 2227 1.9
16 0323 5.9 / 0939 2.3 / TU 1558 6.1 / 2207 2.3

2 0432 6.6 / 1052 1.8 / TU 1701 6.7 / 2324 1.6
17 0422 6.2 / 1034 2.1 / W 1645 6.5 / 2304 1.9

3 0530 6.7 / 1141 1.7 / W 1746 6.9 / O
18 0513 6.5 / 1124 1.8 / TH 1728 6.8 / 2356 1.6

4 0015 1.3 / 0620 6.8 / TH 1227 1.7 / 1826 7.0
19 0601 6.7 / 1210 1.6 / F 1809 7.0 / ●

5 0102 1.2 / 0705 6.9 / F 1307 1.7 / 1905 7.1
20 0044 1.2 / 0645 6.9 / SA 1254 1.5 / 1849 7.3

6 0145 1.2 / 0745 6.8 / SA 1344 1.7 / 1941 7.1
21 0129 1.0 / 0728 7.0 / SU 1335 1.4 / 1928 7.4

7 0223 1.3 / 0822 6.6 / SU 1417 1.9 / 2016 7.0
22 0211 0.8 / 0809 7.1 / M 1415 1.3 / 2008 7.5

8 0258 1.5 / 0856 6.4 / M 1448 2.0 / 2050 6.8
23 0253 0.8 / 0851 7.0 / TU 1455 1.4 / 2050 7.4

9 0332 1.7 / 0930 6.2 / TU 1520 2.2 / 2126 6.5
24 0333 0.9 / 0933 6.8 / W 1536 1.6 / 2135 7.3

10 0406 1.9 / 1006 6.0 / W 1556 2.4 / 2206 6.3
25 0415 1.2 / 1019 6.5 / TH 1621 1.8 / ◗ 2225 6.9

11 0446 2.2 / 1048 5.8 / TH 1640 2.6 / ◗ 2254 6.0
26 0502 1.6 / 1112 6.2 / F 1713 2.2 / 2324 6.5

12 0533 2.4 / 1142 5.6 / F 1735 2.8 / 2354 5.8
27 0558 2.0 / 1216 5.9 / SA 1820 2.5

13 0630 2.6 / 1249 5.5 / SA 1842 2.9
28 0036 6.2 / 0708 2.4 / SU 1330 5.7 / 1945 2.6

14 0105 5.7 / 0733 2.6 / SU 1400 5.6 / 1952 2.9
29 0158 6.0 / 0829 2.5 / M 1445 5.8 / 2112 2.4

15 0218 5.7 / 0838 2.5 / M 1503 5.8 / 2101 2.6
30 0322 6.0 / 0943 2.4 / TU 1554 6.1 / 2223 2.0

31 0438 6.2 / 1043 2.2 / W 1651 6.4 / 2320 1.6

FEBRUARY

Time m | Time m

1 0536 6.5 / 1133 2.0 / TH 1736 6.7
16 0503 6.5 / 1110 1.9 / F 1709 6.8 / 2344 1.3

2 0008 1.3 / 0619 6.7 / F 1217 1.7 / O 1815 7.0
17 0550 6.9 / 1156 1.5 / SA 1751 7.2 / ●

3 0052 1.1 / 0656 6.8 / SA 1255 1.6 / 1850 7.1
18 0031 0.9 / 0632 7.1 / SU 1240 1.2 / 1831 7.5

4 0130 1.0 / 0728 6.8 / SU 1329 1.6 / 1924 7.1
19 0114 0.6 / 0711 7.3 / M 1320 1.0 / 1910 7.7

5 0204 1.1 / 0757 6.7 / M 1359 1.6 / 1955 7.1
20 0155 0.4 / 0749 7.3 / TU 1359 0.9 / 1950 7.8

6 0233 1.2 / 0823 6.6 / TU 1425 1.7 / 2024 7.0
21 0233 0.5 / 0826 7.2 / W 1437 1.0 / 2030 7.7

7 0259 1.4 / 0849 6.5 / W 1450 1.8 / 2052 6.7
22 0309 0.7 / 0904 7.0 / TH 1515 1.2 / 2113 7.4

8 0325 1.4 / 0916 6.3 / TH 1518 2.0 / 2123 6.5
23 0346 1.2 / 0945 6.6 / F 1555 1.6 / 2201 6.9

9 0354 2.0 / 0949 6.1 / F 1550 2.2 / 2159 6.2
24 0427 1.7 / 1032 6.2 / SA 1643 2.1 / ◗ 2300 6.3

10 0429 2.3 / 1029 5.8 / SA 1633 2.6 / 2245 5.8
25 0518 2.3 / 1134 5.7 / SU 1750 2.5

11 0522 2.6 / 1125 5.5 / SU 1739 2.9 / 2353 5.5
26 0020 5.8 / 0635 2.8 / M 1259 5.5 / 1933 2.7

12 0635 2.8 / 1257 5.4 / M 1901 3.0
27 0155 5.6 / 0817 2.9 / TU 1425 5.6 / 2110 2.4

13 0137 5.4 / 0754 2.8 / TU 1427 5.5 / 2023 2.8
28 0329 5.8 / 0935 2.7 / W 1541 5.9 / 2215 2.0

14 0304 5.7 / 0909 2.6 / W 1532 5.9 / 2144 2.4

15 0409 6.1 / 1016 2.2 / TH 1624 6.4 / 2251 1.8

MARCH

Time m | Time m

1 0442 6.1 / 1031 2.3 / TH 1637 6.3 / 2307 1.6
16 0352 6.1 / 0953 2.3 / F 1557 6.4 / 2230 1.6

2 0529 6.4 / 1118 2.0 / F 1720 6.7 / 2351 1.2
17 0444 6.6 / 1047 1.8 / SA 1643 6.9 / 2322 1.0

3 0605 6.6 / 1158 1.7 / SA 1756 6.9 / O
18 0529 7.0 / 1134 1.3 / SU 1726 7.3

4 0030 1.0 / 0635 6.8 / SU 1235 1.5 / 1829 7.1
19 0008 0.6 / 0609 7.3 / M 1218 1.0 / ● 1807 7.7

5 0106 1.0 / 0702 6.8 / M 1308 1.4 / 1900 7.1
20 0051 0.3 / 0647 7.4 / TU 1259 0.7 / 1848 7.9

6 0136 1.0 / 0726 6.8 / TU 1335 1.4 / 1928 7.1
21 0130 0.3 / 0723 7.4 / W 1339 0.6 / 1929 7.9

7 0203 1.2 / 0749 6.8 / W 1359 1.4 / 1955 7.0
22 0208 0.4 / 0759 7.3 / TH 1417 0.7 / 2010 7.7

8 0226 1.1 / 0812 6.7 / TH 1422 1.5 / 2020 6.8
23 0244 0.8 / 0835 7.0 / F 1455 1.1 / 2055 7.3

9 0248 1.6 / 0837 6.5 / F 1446 1.7 / 2048 6.5
24 0320 1.3 / 0915 6.6 / SA 1536 1.5 / 2145 6.7

10 0311 1.8 / 0906 6.3 / SA 1514 2.0 / 2120 6.2
25 0359 2.0 / 1001 6.1 / SU 1625 2.0 / ◗ 2249 6.0

11 0340 2.2 / 0941 6.0 / SU 1551 2.3 / 2202 5.8
26 0451 2.6 / 1105 5.7 / M 1738 2.5

12 0426 2.6 / 1028 5.6 / M 1653 2.7 / ◗ 2305 5.4
27 0020 5.6 / 0613 3.1 / TU 1238 5.5 / 1931 2.6

13 0544 3.0 / 1145 5.3 / TU 1824 2.9
28 0154 5.5 / 0800 3.1 / W 1405 5.6 / 2055 2.3

14 0110 5.3 / 0717 3.0 / W 1351 5.4 / 1955 2.7
29 0319 5.8 / 0914 2.8 / TH 1516 5.9 / 2153 1.9

15 0248 5.6 / 0842 2.7 / TH 1503 5.8 / 2123 2.2
30 0421 6.1 / 1007 2.4 / F 1611 6.3 / 2240 1.5

31 0502 6.4 / 1051 2.0 / SA 1653 6.6 / 2321 1.3

APRIL

Time m | Time m

1 0535 6.6 / 1131 1.7 / SU 1730 6.8 / 2358 1.1
16 0501 7.0 / 1106 1.3 / M 1658 7.4 / 2338 0.6

2 0604 6.7 / 1208 1.5 / M 1803 6.9 / O
17 0542 7.3 / 1152 0.9 / TU 1743 7.7 / ●

3 0032 1.1 / 0630 6.8 / TU 1240 1.4 / 1832 7.0
18 0022 0.4 / 0620 7.4 / W 1237 0.6 / 1826 7.8

4 0103 1.1 / 0653 6.8 / W 1309 1.3 / 1900 6.9
19 0104 0.4 / 0657 7.4 / TH 1319 0.6 / 1910 7.7

5 0130 1.2 / 0717 6.8 / TH 1334 1.4 / 1927 6.9
20 0143 0.6 / 0734 7.3 / F 1400 0.7 / 1955 7.4

6 0155 1.4 / 0741 6.8 / F 1358 1.5 / 1954 6.7
21 0221 1.0 / 0813 7.0 / SA 1441 1.0 / 2043 7.0

7 0218 1.6 / 0806 6.6 / SA 1423 1.6 / 2022 6.5
22 0259 1.6 / 0854 6.6 / SU 1526 1.5 / 2137 6.4

8 0243 1.8 / 0835 6.4 / SU 1452 1.9 / 2056 6.2
23 0341 2.1 / 0941 6.2 / M 1620 2.0 / 2247 5.9

9 0314 2.2 / 0911 6.1 / M 1532 2.2 / 2142 5.8
24 0435 2.7 / 1045 5.8 / TU 1735 2.3 / ◗

10 0401 2.6 / 0959 5.8 / TU 1636 2.5 / ◗ 2250 5.5
25 0014 5.6 / 0551 3.0 / W 1213 5.6 / 1906 2.3

11 0515 2.9 / 1111 5.5 / W 1804 2.6
26 0131 5.6 / 0722 3.1 / TH 1332 5.7 / 2018 2.1

12 0054 5.4 / 0646 3.0 / TH 1306 5.5 / 1931 2.4
27 0241 5.7 / 0834 2.8 / F 1439 5.9 / 2114 1.9

13 0222 5.7 / 0809 2.7 / F 1424 6.0 / 2052 1.9
28 0338 6.0 / 0929 2.4 / SA 1534 6.2 / 2200 1.6

14 0324 6.2 / 0919 2.2 / SA 1521 6.5 / 2156 1.4
29 0421 6.3 / 1015 2.1 / SU 1619 6.4 / 2241 1.5

15 0416 6.6 / 1016 1.7 / SU 1611 7.0 / 2250 0.9
30 0457 6.4 / 1057 1.8 / M 1657 6.6 / 2319 1.4

TIDES

Chart Datum: 3·90 metres below Ordnance Datum (Newlyn)

TIME ZONE (UT)
For Summer Time add ONE hour in **non-shaded areas**

ENGLAND – IMMINGHAM

LAT 53°38'N   LONG 0°11'W

TIMES AND HEIGHTS OF HIGH AND LOW WATERS

Dates in amber are **SPRINGS**
Dates in yellow are **NEAPS**

2007

MAY

Day	Time m	Time m	Time m	Time m		Day	Time m	Time m	Time m	Time m
1 TU	0527 6.6	1135 1.6	1731 6.7	2355 1.3		**16** W	0514 7.1	1128 1.0	1722 7.4	● 2355 0.7
2 W	0555 6.7	1209 1.5	1803 6.7 ○			**17** TH	0556 7.2	1216 0.8	1811 7.5	
3 TH	0028 1.3	0621 6.8	1241 1.4	1834 6.7		**18** F	0039 0.8	0636 7.2	1303 0.7	1859 7.4
4 F	0059 1.4	0649 6.8	1310 1.4	1905 6.7		**19** SA	0122 1.0	0717 7.2	1348 0.8	1947 7.1
5 SA	0128 1.5	0717 6.8	1339 1.5	1937 6.6		**20** SU	0203 1.3	0757 7.0	1434 1.1	2037 6.8
6 SU	0156 1.7	0746 6.7	1410 1.6	2011 6.4		**21** M	0245 1.7	0840 6.7	1522 1.4	2133 6.3
7 M	0227 1.9	0819 6.5	1445 1.8	2050 6.2		**22** TU	0328 2.2	0927 6.4	1615 1.7	2237 6.0
8 TU	0305 2.2	0858 6.3	1531 2.0	2142 5.9		**23** W	0418 2.6	1025 6.1	1717 2.0	◗ 2345 5.7
9 W	0354 2.5	0948 6.0	1634 2.2	2253 5.7		**24** TH	0519 2.8	1134 5.8	1822 2.1	
10 TH	0501 2.7	1057 5.8	1749 2.2 ◐			**25** F	0050 5.6	0626 2.9	1309 5.8	1924 2.1
11 F	0028 5.7	0617 2.7	1224 5.9	1904 2.0		**26** SA	0150 5.7	0735 2.8	1349 5.9	2019 2.1
12 SA	0145 5.9	0732 2.5	1340 6.2	2015 1.7		**27** SU	0244 5.8	0836 2.6	1446 6.0	2109 1.9
13 SU	0247 6.2	0840 2.1	1443 6.5	2119 1.3		**28** M	0331 6.0	0929 2.3	1536 6.1	2154 1.8
14 M	0341 6.6	0941 1.7	1539 6.9	2216 1.0		**29** TU	0412 6.2	1016 2.1	1619 6.3	2237 1.7
15 TU	0429 6.8	1037 1.3	1631 7.2	2307 0.8		**30** W	0447 6.4	1059 1.9	1659 6.4	2318 1.6
						31 TH	0521 6.6	1139 1.7	1736 6.5	2356 1.6

JUNE

Day	Time m	Time m	Time m	Time m		Day	Time m	Time m	Time m	Time m
1 F	0554 6.7	1217 1.6	1814 6.6 ○			**16** SA	0023 1.3	0622 7.0	1255 0.9	1856 7.0
2 SA	0033 1.6	0628 6.8	1253 1.5	1851 6.6		**17** SU	0108 1.3	0705 7.1	1342 0.9	1945 6.9
3 SU	0108 1.6	0702 6.8	1329 1.5	1930 6.5		**18** M	0151 1.5	0746 7.0	1429 1.0	2032 6.7
4 M	0142 1.7	0737 6.7	1514 1.2	2010 6.4		**19** TU	0232 1.7	0828 6.9	1514 1.2	2120 6.4
5 TU	0219 1.8	0813 6.6	1448 1.6	2054 6.3		**20** W	0313 2.0	0911 6.6	1558 1.5	2208 6.1
6 W	0301 2.0	0855 6.5	1535 1.6	2145 6.2		**21** TH	0354 2.3	0956 6.4	1643 1.8	2258 5.9
7 TH	0349 2.2	0944 6.4	1629 1.7	2246 6.0		**22** F	0438 2.5	1047 6.1	1730 2.0	◗ 2350 5.7
8 F	0445 2.3	1042 6.3	1730 1.7	◗ 2354 6.0		**23** SA	0527 2.7	1144 5.9	1820 2.2	
9 SA	0548 2.3	1149 6.3	1834 1.7			**24** SU	0044 5.6	0623 2.8	1245 5.8	1913 2.3
10 SU	0102 6.0	0655 2.3	1259 6.0	1939 1.6		**25** M	0139 5.6	0724 2.8	1347 5.8	2009 2.3
11 M	0206 6.2	0803 2.1	1406 6.5	2044 1.5		**26** TU	0233 5.8	0828 2.6	1446 5.8	2104 2.2
12 TU	0305 6.3	0910 1.9	1511 6.7	2145 1.4		**27** W	0323 6.0	0930 2.4	1541 6.0	2156 2.1
13 W	0400 6.6	1012 1.6	1612 6.8	2242 1.3		**28** TH	0410 6.2	1024 2.2	1631 6.1	2245 1.9
14 TH	0451 6.8	1110 1.3	1711 7.0	2334 1.2		**29** F	0452 6.4	1114 1.9	1717 6.3	2331 1.8
15 F	0539 6.9	1204 1.1	1805 7.1 ●			**30** SA	0533 6.6	1200 1.7	1801 6.5 ○	

JULY

Day	Time m	Time m	Time m	Time m		Day	Time m	Time m	Time m	Time m
1 SU	0013 1.7	0612 6.8	1244 1.5	1842 6.6		**16** M	0058 1.5	0654 7.1	1335 0.9	1938 6.9
2 M	0054 1.7	0650 6.9	1326 1.3	1924 6.7		**17** TU	0139 1.5	0733 7.1	1417 0.9	2017 6.8
3 TU	0134 1.6	0728 7.0	1407 1.2	2006 6.7		**18** W	0216 1.6	0811 7.1	1454 1.0	2053 6.6
4 W	0213 1.6	0807 7.0	1448 1.2	2049 6.6		**19** TH	0250 1.8	0847 6.9	1529 1.3	2127 6.4
5 TH	0253 1.7	0848 7.0	1530 1.2	2134 6.5		**20** F	0322 2.0	0922 6.7	1601 1.6	2200 6.1
6 F	0336 1.8	0932 6.9	1615 1.3	2223 6.4		**21** SA	0354 2.2	1000 6.4	1636 1.9	2238 5.9
7 SA	0424 1.9	1022 6.8	1704 1.5	◗ 2318 6.2		**22** SU	0432 2.4	1043 6.1	1717 2.2	◗ 2326 5.7
8 SU	0517 2.1	1119 6.6	1800 1.7			**23** M	0520 2.7	1137 5.8	1809 2.5	
9 M	0020 6.1	0619 2.2	1225 6.4	1904 1.9		**24** TU	0028 5.6	0619 2.8	1247 5.6	1910 2.6
10 TU	0127 6.1	0730 2.3	1338 6.3	2015 2.0		**25** W	0138 5.6	0728 2.9	1403 5.6	2017 2.6
11 W	0233 6.1	0847 2.2	1454 6.3	2124 2.0		**26** TH	0243 5.8	0842 2.7	1512 5.7	2123 2.4
12 TH	0338 6.2	0959 1.9	1607 6.4	2227 1.8		**27** F	0340 6.0	0956 2.4	1612 6.0	2221 2.2
13 F	0437 6.5	1057 1.6	1713 6.6	2323 1.7		**28** SA	0429 6.3	1057 2.0	1704 6.3	2313 2.0
14 SA	0528 6.7	1159 1.2	1809 6.8 ●			**29** SU	0514 6.6	1148 1.6	1749 6.6	2359 1.7
15 SU	0013 1.6	0613 7.0	1249 1.0	1856 6.9 ○		**30** M	0555 6.9	1234 1.3	1832 6.8	
						31 TU	0041 1.5	0634 7.1	1317 1.0	1912 7.0

AUGUST

Day	Time m	Time m	Time m	Time m		Day	Time m	Time m	Time m	Time m
1 W	0122 1.4	0713 7.3	1357 0.8	1952 7.0		**16** TH	0153 1.5	0746 7.2	1425 1.0	2017 6.8
2 TH	0200 1.3	0751 7.4	1436 0.8	2030 7.0		**17** F	0221 1.6	0817 7.1	1453 1.3	2042 6.6
3 F	0238 1.3	0831 7.4	1513 0.9	2110 6.8		**18** SA	0247 1.6	0846 6.8	1518 1.6	2108 6.4
4 SA	0317 1.4	0912 7.3	1551 1.1	2152 6.6		**19** SU	0313 2.0	0916 6.5	1544 1.9	2137 6.2
5 SU	0359 1.7	0958 7.0	1633 1.5	◗ 2241 6.3		**20** M	0344 2.2	0950 6.2	1617 2.3	◗ 2216 5.9
6 M	0447 2.0	1053 6.6	1724 1.9	2340 6.0		**21** TU	0425 2.5	1034 5.8	1705 2.6	2311 5.6
7 TU	0548 2.3	1201 6.2	1833 2.3			**22** W	0525 2.9	1145 5.4	1816 2.9	
8 W	0054 5.8	0708 2.5	1325 5.9	1957 2.5		**23** TH	0046 5.4	0642 3.0	1331 5.4	1936 3.0
9 TH	0212 5.8	0840 2.4	1453 5.9	2116 2.5		**24** F	0211 5.6	0806 2.9	1453 5.6	2057 2.7
10 F	0325 6.0	0958 2.0	1617 6.2	2221 2.2		**25** SA	0314 5.9	0937 2.4	1556 6.0	2203 2.4
11 SA	0428 6.4	1100 1.6	1720 6.5	2315 1.9		**26** SU	0406 6.4	1040 1.9	1648 6.4	2255 2.0
12 SU	0518 6.7	1151 1.2	1807 6.8 ●			**27** M	0451 6.8	1130 1.4	1732 6.8	2340 1.6
13 M	0001 1.7	0600 7.0	1237 0.9	1845 6.9		**28** TU	0532 7.6	1215 1.0	1813 7.1 ○	
14 TU	0043 1.5	0637 7.2	1318 0.8	1919 6.9		**29** W	0022 1.4	0611 7.4	1257 0.7	1851 7.2
15 W	0120 1.4	0713 7.2	1354 0.9	1949 6.9		**30** TH	0102 1.1	0650 7.5	1335 0.6	1927 7.3
						31 F	0140 1.0	0728 7.8	1412 0.6	2003 7.2

Chart Datum: 3·90 metres below Ordnance Datum (Newlyn)

ENGLAND – IMMINGHAM

LAT 53°38'N   LONG 0°11'W

TIMES AND HEIGHTS OF HIGH AND LOW WATERS

Dates in amber are **SPRINGS**
Dates in yellow are **NEAPS**

2007

SEPTEMBER

Day	Time	m	Day	Time	m
1 SA	0217 / 0808 / 1448 / 2040	1.1 / 7.7 / 0.8 / 7.0	16 SU	0214 / 0811 / 1437 / 2025	1.6 / 6.9 / 1.6 / 6.6
2 SU	0255 / 0850 / 1523 / 2120	1.2 / 7.5 / 1.2 / 6.7	17 M	0238 / 0838 / 1500 / 2052	1.8 / 6.6 / 1.9 / 6.4
3 M	0335 / 0937 / 1601 / 2206	1.6 / 7.0 / 1.7 / 6.3	18 TU	0306 / 0909 / 1528 / 2125	2.1 / 6.2 / 2.3 / 6.1
4 TU	0422 / 1033 / 1651 / 2306	2.0 / 6.5 / 2.3 / 5.9	19 W	0342 / 0949 / 1610 / 2212	2.4 / 5.8 / 2.7 / 5.7
5 W	0527 / 1150 / 1808	2.4 / 5.9 / 2.8	20 TH	0441 / 1053 / 1723 / 2337	2.8 / 5.4 / 3.1 / 5.4
6 TH	0031 / 0703 / 1328 / 1950	5.7 / 2.7 / 5.7 / 2.9	21 F	0607 / 1306 / 1858	3.0 / 5.3 / 3.2
7 F	0158 / 0842 / 1502 / 2111	5.7 / 2.4 / 5.9 / 2.7	22 SA	0137 / 0738 / 1431 / 2027	5.5 / 2.8 / 5.6 / 2.9
8 SA	0314 / 0952 / 1619 / 2210	6.0 / 1.9 / 6.2 / 2.3	23 SU	0243 / 0909 / 1533 / 2136	5.9 / 2.3 / 6.1 / 2.5
9 SU	0414 / 1046 / 1710 / 2258	6.5 / 1.5 / 6.6 / 2.0	24 M	0335 / 1011 / 1623 / 2227	6.4 / 1.8 / 6.6 / 2.0
10 M	0459 / 1132 / 1748 / 2340	6.8 / 1.1 / 6.8 / 1.7	25 TU	0420 / 1101 / 1706 / 2312	6.9 / 1.3 / 7.0 / 1.6
11 TU ●	0538 / 1213 / 1820	7.1 / 0.9 / 6.9	26 W ○	0502 / 1145 / 1746 / 2355	7.3 / 0.8 / 7.2 / 1.2
12 W	0019 / 0613 / 1250 / 1849	1.5 / 7.2 / 0.9 / 7.0	27 TH	0543 / 1227 / 1823	7.7 / 0.6 / 7.4
13 TH	0054 / 0646 / 1322 / 1915	1.4 / 7.3 / 1.0 / 7.0	28 F	0036 / 0623 / 1307 / 1859	1.0 / 7.9 / 0.5 / 7.5
14 F	0124 / 0717 / 1351 / 1939	1.4 / 7.2 / 1.1 / 6.9	29 SA	0116 / 0704 / 1344 / 1934	0.9 / 7.9 / 0.6 / 7.4
15 SA	0150 / 0745 / 1415 / 2001	1.5 / 7.1 / 1.4 / 6.8	30 SU	0155 / 0746 / 1420 / 2011	0.9 / 7.8 / 0.9 / 7.2

OCTOBER

Day	Time	m	Day	Time	m
1 M	0234 / 0831 / 1457 / 2051	1.1 / 7.4 / 1.4 / 6.8	16 TU	0211 / 0811 / 1428 / 2020	1.8 / 6.5 / 2.0 / 6.5
2 TU	0316 / 0921 / 1536 / 2138	1.5 / 6.9 / 2.0 / 6.4	17 W	0240 / 0843 / 1457 / 2054	2.0 / 6.2 / 2.3 / 6.2
3 W	0407 / 1024 / 1627 / 2241	2.0 / 6.2 / 2.6 / 5.9	18 TH	0318 / 0926 / 1539 / 2139	2.3 / 5.9 / 2.7 / 5.9
4 TH	0521 / 1153 / 1750	2.5 / 5.8 / 3.1	19 F	0417 / 1031 / 1646 / 2249	2.7 / 5.5 / 3.1 / 5.6
5 F	0013 / 0703 / 1326 / 1934	5.7 / 2.6 / 5.7 / 3.1	20 SA	0540 / 1233 / 1817	2.8 / 5.4 / 3.2
6 SA	0139 / 0828 / 1450 / 2049	5.8 / 2.3 / 5.9 / 2.8	21 SU	0045 / 0705 / 1357 / 1942	5.6 / 2.6 / 5.7 / 2.9
7 SU	0250 / 0929 / 1556 / 2144	6.1 / 1.9 / 6.3 / 2.4	22 M	0200 / 0824 / 1459 / 2052	6.0 / 2.2 / 6.1 / 2.5
8 M	0346 / 1018 / 1641 / 2230	6.5 / 1.6 / 6.6 / 2.0	23 TU	0255 / 0929 / 1550 / 2148	6.5 / 1.7 / 6.6 / 2.0
9 TU	0431 / 1101 / 1716 / 2311	6.8 / 1.3 / 6.8 / 1.7	24 W	0344 / 1022 / 1634 / 2238	7.0 / 1.2 / 7.0 / 1.6
10 W	0510 / 1139 / 1747 / 2349	7.0 / 1.1 / 6.9 / 1.5	25 TH	0430 / 1110 / 1715 / 2325	7.4 / 0.9 / 7.2 / 1.2
11 TH ●	0545 / 1214 / 1815	7.1 / 1.1 / 7.0	26 F ○	0515 / 1155 / 1754	7.7 / 0.7 / 7.4
12 F	0023 / 0617 / 1247 / 1840	1.4 / 7.1 / 1.2 / 7.0	27 SA	0010 / 0559 / 1237 / 1832	0.9 / 7.8 / 0.6 / 7.5
13 SA	0054 / 0647 / 1315 / 1904	1.4 / 7.1 / 1.3 / 7.0	28 SU	0054 / 0644 / 1318 / 1910	0.8 / 7.8 / 0.8 / 7.4
14 SU	0120 / 0716 / 1340 / 1928	1.5 / 7.0 / 1.5 / 6.9	29 M	0137 / 0730 / 1357 / 1949	0.9 / 7.6 / 1.1 / 7.2
15 M	0145 / 0743 / 1403 / 1952	1.6 / 6.8 / 1.7 / 6.8	30 TU	0220 / 0819 / 1436 / 2031	1.1 / 7.2 / 1.6 / 6.9
			31 W	0307 / 0913 / 1519 / 2119	1.5 / 6.7 / 2.1 / 6.5

NOVEMBER

Day	Time	m	Day	Time	m
1 TH ☽	0402 / 1021 / 1612 / 2222	1.9 / 6.2 / 2.7 / 6.1	16 F	0309 / 0920 / 1525 / 2123	2.1 / 6.0 / 2.5 / 6.2
2 F	0515 / 1145 / 1726 / 2346	2.2 / 5.8 / 3.1 / 5.9	17 SA	0404 / 1021 / 1623 / 2224	2.3 / 5.8 / 2.8 / 6.0
3 SA	0639 / 1302 / 1855	2.3 / 5.8 / 3.1	18 SU	0514 / 1146 / 1736 / 2344	2.4 / 5.7 / 2.9 / 6.0
4 SU	0104 / 0751 / 1412 / 2008	5.9 / 2.2 / 5.9 / 2.9	19 M	0628 / 1308 / 1854	2.3 / 5.8 / 2.8
5 M	0211 / 0849 / 1512 / 2105	6.1 / 1.9 / 6.1 / 2.6	20 TU	0103 / 0738 / 1413 / 2004	6.2 / 2.0 / 6.1 / 2.5
6 TU	0308 / 0938 / 1559 / 2153	6.4 / 1.7 / 6.4 / 2.2	21 W	0208 / 0843 / 1509 / 2107	6.5 / 1.7 / 6.4 / 2.1
7 W	0356 / 1021 / 1637 / 2236	6.6 / 1.6 / 6.6 / 2.0	22 TH	0306 / 0942 / 1600 / 2205	6.9 / 1.4 / 6.8 / 1.7
8 TH	0437 / 1100 / 1710 / 2316	6.8 / 1.5 / 6.7 / 1.7	23 F	0400 / 1036 / 1646 / 2258	7.2 / 1.2 / 7.0 / 1.4
9 F	0514 / 1136 / 1740 / 2352	6.9 / 1.5 / 6.9 / 1.6	24 SA ○	0452 / 1126 / 1729 / 2348	7.4 / 1.0 / 7.2 / 1.1
10 SA	0548 / 1210 / 1808	6.9 / 1.5 / 7.0	25 SU	0543 / 1212 / 1811	7.5 / 1.0 / 7.3
11 SU	0024 / 0621 / 1242 / 1835	1.6 / 6.9 / 1.5 / 7.0	26 M	0037 / 0633 / 1257 / 1853	0.9 / 7.5 / 1.1 / 7.3
12 M	0055 / 0653 / 1310 / 1903	1.6 / 6.8 / 1.6 / 6.9	27 TU	0125 / 0723 / 1340 / 1935	0.9 / 7.3 / 1.3 / 7.2
13 TU	0124 / 0725 / 1338 / 1932	1.6 / 6.7 / 1.8 / 6.8	28 W	0213 / 0813 / 1422 / 2018	1.1 / 7.0 / 1.7 / 7.0
14 W	0154 / 0758 / 1408 / 2002	1.8 / 6.5 / 2.0 / 6.7	29 TH	0302 / 0908 / 1506 / 2106	1.3 / 6.7 / 2.1 / 6.7
15 TH	0228 / 0835 / 1442 / 2038	1.9 / 6.3 / 2.2 / 6.4	30 F	0355 / 1009 / 1554 / 2200	1.6 / 6.3 / 2.5 / 6.4

DECEMBER

Day	Time	m	Day	Time	m
1 SA ☽	0454 / 1114 / 1651 / 2306	1.9 / 6.0 / 2.8 / 6.2	16 SU	0352 / 1004 / 1602 / 2203	1.8 / 6.1 / 2.4 / 6.5
2 SU	0556 / 1218 / 1757	2.1 / 5.8 / 3.0	17 M	0446 / 1103 / 1659 / 2303	1.9 / 6.0 / 2.5 / 6.4
3 M	0015 / 0657 / 1319 / 1906	6.0 / 2.2 / 5.8 / 3.0	18 TU	0546 / 1211 / 1806	2.0 / 5.9 / 2.6
4 TU	0120 / 0755 / 1416 / 2011	6.0 / 2.2 / 5.9 / 2.8	19 W	0010 / 0651 / 1321 / 1917	6.4 / 2.0 / 6.0 / 2.5
5 W	0220 / 0847 / 1508 / 2108	6.1 / 2.1 / 6.0 / 2.6	20 TH	0122 / 0800 / 1426 / 2029	6.4 / 1.9 / 6.2 / 2.3
6 TH	0314 / 0934 / 1553 / 2158	6.2 / 2.0 / 6.3 / 2.3	21 F	0231 / 0907 / 1527 / 2137	6.6 / 1.8 / 6.4 / 2.0
7 F	0402 / 1018 / 1632 / 2242	6.4 / 1.9 / 6.5 / 2.1	22 SA	0338 / 1009 / 1622 / 2239	6.8 / 1.6 / 6.7 / 1.6
8 SA	0444 / 1059 / 1708 / 2323	6.5 / 1.8 / 6.7 / 1.9	23 SU	0440 / 1105 / 1713 / 2336	7.0 / 1.6 / 7.0 / 1.3
9 SU ●	0524 / 1138 / 1741	6.6 / 1.7 / 6.8	24 M ○	0539 / 1157 / 1759	7.1 / 1.4 / 7.2
10 M	0001 / 0601 / 1215 / 1814	1.7 / 6.6 / 1.7 / 6.9	25 TU	0029 / 0632 / 1245 / 1843	1.6 / 7.2 / 1.4 / 7.3
11 TU	0038 / 0638 / 1249 / 1848	1.7 / 6.7 / 1.7 / 6.9	26 W	0120 / 0722 / 1329 / 1925	0.9 / 7.2 / 1.4 / 7.3
12 W	0113 / 0715 / 1322 / 1921	1.6 / 6.6 / 1.8 / 6.9	27 TH	0207 / 0810 / 1411 / 2007	0.9 / 7.0 / 1.6 / 7.2
13 TH	0148 / 0753 / 1356 / 1954	1.7 / 6.5 / 1.9 / 6.8	28 F	0253 / 0856 / 1451 / 2049	1.0 / 6.8 / 1.8 / 7.0
14 F	0225 / 0832 / 1432 / 2031	1.7 / 6.4 / 2.0 / 6.7	29 SA	0337 / 0941 / 1530 / 2133	1.3 / 6.5 / 2.1 / 6.8
15 SA	0306 / 0915 / 1514 / 2113	1.8 / 6.3 / 2.2 / 6.6	30 SU	0419 / 1027 / 1609 / 2220	1.6 / 6.2 / 2.4 / 6.5
			31 M ☽	0503 / 1116 / 1654 / 2313	1.9 / 5.9 / 2.7 / 6.2

Chart Datum: 3·90 metres below Ordnance Datum (Newlyn)

TIDES

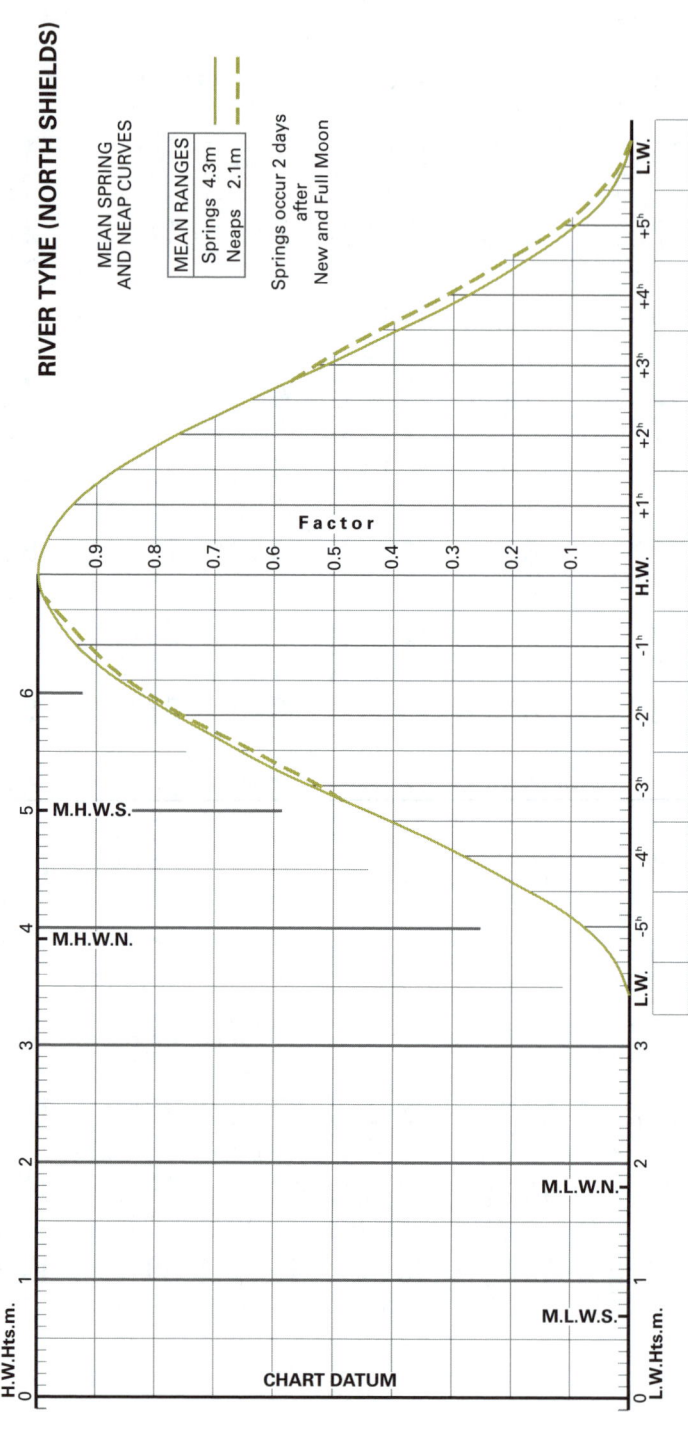

RIVER TYNE (NORTH SHIELDS)

MEAN SPRING
AND NEAP CURVES

MEAN RANGES
Springs 4.3m
Neaps 2.1m

Springs occur 2 days
after
New and Full Moon

Factor

0.9
0.8
0.7
0.6
0.5
0.4
0.3
0.2
0.1

M.H.W.S.

M.H.W.N.

M.L.W.N.

M.L.W.S.

CHART DATUM

H.W.Hts.m.

L.W.Hts.m.

H.W.

L.W.

L.W.

ENGLAND – NORTH SHIELDS

LAT 55°01'N   LONG 1°26'W

TIMES AND HEIGHTS OF HIGH AND LOW WATERS

Dates in amber are **SPRINGS**
Dates in yellow are **NEAPS**

2007

JANUARY

Time	m		Time	m
1 M 0058 / 0730 / 1336 / 1958	4.6 / 1.4 / 4.6 / 1.3		**16** TU 0104 / 0724 / 1330 / 1955	4.1 / 1.8 / 4.3 / 1.7
2 TU 0159 / 0824 / 1425 / 2052	4.7 / 1.3 / 4.8 / 1.1		**17** W 0159 / 0813 / 1415 / 2041	4.3 / 1.6 / 4.5 / 1.4
3 W 0253 / 0911 / 1510 / ○2141	4.8 / 1.3 / 4.9 / 0.9		**18** TH 0245 / 0856 / 1455 / 2124	4.5 / 1.4 / 4.7 / 1.1
4 TH 0341 / 0954 / 1552 / 2226	4.9 / 1.3 / 5.0 / 0.8		**19** F 0328 / 0938 / 1534 / ●2207	4.8 / 1.2 / 4.9 / 0.8
5 F 0425 / 1033 / 1631 / 2308	4.8 / 1.3 / 5.0 / 0.8		**20** SA 0410 / 1018 / 1613 / 2249	4.9 / 1.1 / 5.1 / 0.5
6 SA 0507 / 1109 / 1709 / 2346	4.8 / 1.4 / 5.0 / 0.9		**21** SU 0451 / 1059 / 1652 / 2332	5.0 / 1.0 / 5.2 / 0.5
7 SU 0546 / 1143 / 1747	4.6 / 1.5 / 4.9		**22** M 0534 / 1139 / 1734	5.0 / 1.0 / 5.3
8 M 0023 / 0624 / 1217 / 1824	1.0 / 4.5 / 1.6 / 4.8		**23** TU 0014 / 0617 / 1219 / 1817	0.6 / 4.9 / 1.1 / 5.2
9 TU 0059 / 0703 / 1251 / 1904	1.2 / 4.3 / 1.7 / 4.6		**24** W 0058 / 0703 / 1301 / 1904	0.6 / 4.7 / 1.2 / 5.1
10 W 0137 / 0745 / 1329 / 1948	1.4 / 4.2 / 1.9 / 4.4		**25** TH 0144 / 0752 / 1348 / ◑1956	0.8 / 4.5 / 1.4 / 4.9
11 TH 0219 / 0831 / 1414 / ◑2037	1.6 / 4.0 / 2.0 / 4.2		**26** F 0234 / 0847 / 1444 / 2057	1.1 / 4.3 / 1.6 / 4.6
12 F 0309 / 0924 / 1513 / 2135	1.8 / 3.9 / 2.2 / 4.0		**27** SA 0335 / 0953 / 1556 / 2212	1.5 / 4.1 / 1.8 / 4.3
13 SA 0409 / 1026 / 1630 / 2244	1.9 / 3.8 / 2.3 / 3.9		**28** SU 0451 / 1107 / 1726 / 2338	1.7 / 4.1 / 1.9 / 4.2
14 SU 0519 / 1133 / 1753 / 2358	2.0 / 3.9 / 2.2 / 4.0		**29** M 0615 / 1223 / 1852	1.8 / 4.3 / 1.7
15 M 0627 / 1236 / 1901	1.9 / 4.0 / 2.0		**30** TU 0059 / 0726 / 1329 / 1959	4.3 / 1.7 / 4.4 / 1.4
			31 W 0204 / 0822 / 1422 / 2053	4.4 / 1.6 / 4.6 / 1.1

FEBRUARY

Time	m		Time	m
1 TH 0255 / 0907 / 1505 / 2137	4.6 / 1.5 / 4.6 / 0.9		**16** F 0229 / 0841 / 1436 / 2108	4.5 / 1.3 / 4.7 / 0.9
2 F 0337 / 0945 / 1543 / ○2216	4.7 / 1.3 / 4.9 / 0.8		**17** SA 0312 / 0922 / 1515 / ●2150	4.8 / 1.1 / 5.0 / 0.5
3 SA 0414 / 1019 / 1617 / 2251	4.8 / 1.3 / 5.0 / 0.7		**18** SU 0352 / 1002 / 1553 / 2232	5.1 / 0.8 / 5.3 / 0.3
4 SU 0448 / 1050 / 1650 / 2322	4.8 / 1.2 / 5.0 / 0.7		**19** M 0432 / 1040 / 1632 / 2313	5.2 / 0.7 / 5.4 / 0.1
5 M 0520 / 1119 / 1722 / 2352	4.7 / 1.2 / 5.0 / 0.8		**20** TU 0512 / 1119 / 1713 / 2353	5.2 / 0.7 / 5.5 / 0.2
6 TU 0551 / 1147 / 1754	4.6 / 1.3 / 4.9		**21** W 0552 / 1157 / 1756	5.0 / 0.7 / 5.4
7 W 0022 / 0623 / 1217 / 1827	1.0 / 4.5 / 1.4 / 4.7		**22** TH 0033 / 0634 / 1237 / 1841	0.4 / 4.8 / 0.9 / 5.2
8 TH 0053 / 0657 / 1248 / 1903	1.2 / 4.3 / 1.5 / 4.5		**23** F 0115 / 0720 / 1322 / 1933	0.8 / 4.6 / 1.2 / 4.8
9 F 0127 / 0735 / 1323 / 1944	1.4 / 4.2 / 1.8 / 4.3		**24** SA 0202 / 0813 / 1417 / ◑2036	1.2 / 4.3 / 1.5 / 4.4
10 SA 0207 / 0819 / 1409 / ◑2035	1.7 / 4.0 / 2.0 / 4.0		**25** SU 0303 / 0919 / 1534 / 2159	1.7 / 4.0 / 1.8 / 4.1
11 SU 0259 / 0915 / 1514 / 2143	2.0 / 3.8 / 2.2 / 3.8		**26** M 0430 / 1043 / 1720 / 2337	2.0 / 3.9 / 1.8 / 4.0
12 M 0413 / 1029 / 1652 / 2312	2.1 / 3.7 / 2.3 / 3.8		**27** TU 0611 / 1212 / 1853	2.1 / 4.0 / 1.6
13 TU 0547 / 1153 / 1830	2.1 / 3.8 / 2.1		**28** W 0103 / 0724 / 1322 / 1956	4.1 / 1.9 / 4.2 / 1.3
14 W 0039 / 0702 / 1302 / 1934	3.9 / 1.9 / 4.1 / 1.7			
15 TH 0142 / 0756 / 1354 / 2024	4.2 / 1.7 / 4.4 / 1.3			

MARCH

Time	m		Time	m
1 TH 0203 / 0816 / 1413 / 2044	4.3 / 1.7 / 4.5 / 1.0		**16** F 0118 / 0733 / 1325 / 1959	4.2 / 1.6 / 4.4 / 1.1
2 F 0246 / 0855 / 1453 / 2122	4.5 / 1.4 / 4.7 / 0.9		**17** SA 0205 / 0817 / 1409 / 2043	4.6 / 1.2 / 4.8 / 0.6
3 SA 0321 / 0928 / 1526 / ○2155	4.6 / 1.3 / 4.9 / 0.7		**18** SU 0247 / 0858 / 1449 / 2126	4.9 / 0.9 / 5.1 / 0.3
4 SU 0353 / 0957 / 1557 / 2224	4.7 / 1.1 / 5.0 / 0.7		**19** M 0327 / 0937 / 1528 / ●2207	5.1 / 0.7 / 5.4 / 0.1
5 M 0421 / 1025 / 1625 / 2252	4.7 / 1.0 / 5.0 / 0.7		**20** TU 0406 / 1016 / 1608 / 2248	5.2 / 0.5 / 5.5 / 0.0
6 TU 0449 / 1052 / 1654 / 2319	4.7 / 1.0 / 5.0 / 0.8		**21** W 0445 / 1055 / 1651 / 2327	5.2 / 0.5 / 5.5 / 0.2
7 W 0517 / 1119 / 1724 / 2347	4.7 / 1.1 / 4.9 / 0.9		**22** TH 0525 / 1135 / 1736	5.1 / 0.5 / 5.4
8 TH 0546 / 1146 / 1755	4.6 / 1.2 / 4.7		**23** F 0007 / 0607 / 1218 / 1824	0.5 / 4.9 / 0.7 / 5.1
9 F 0015 / 0616 / 1216 / 1828	1.1 / 4.5 / 1.3 / 4.5		**24** SA 0049 / 0652 / 1305 / 1919	1.0 / 4.6 / 1.0 / 4.6
10 SA 0045 / 0650 / 1249 / 1906	1.3 / 4.3 / 1.5 / 4.3		**25** SU 0137 / 0745 / 1405 / ◑2027	1.5 / 4.3 / 1.4 / 4.2
11 SU 0119 / 0730 / 1330 / 1955	1.6 / 4.1 / 1.8 / 4.0		**26** M 0240 / 0853 / 1527 / 2153	1.9 / 4.0 / 1.7 / 3.9
12 M 0206 / 0822 / 1431 / ◑2104	1.9 / 3.9 / 2.0 / 3.8		**27** TU 0416 / 1022 / 1713 / 2330	2.2 / 3.8 / 1.7 / 3.9
13 TU 0321 / 0937 / 1607 / 2238	2.1 / 3.7 / 2.1 / 3.7		**28** W 0559 / 1153 / 1839	2.2 / 4.0 / 1.5
14 W 0510 / 1110 / 1756	2.2 / 3.7 / 1.9		**29** TH 0049 / 0707 / 1301 / 1936	4.0 / 1.9 / 4.2 / 1.2
15 TH 0013 / 0637 / 1230 / 1907	3.9 / 2.0 / 4.0 / 1.5		**30** F 0143 / 0753 / 1350 / 2019	4.3 / 1.7 / 4.4 / 1.0
			31 SA 0222 / 0830 / 1428 / 2053	4.4 / 1.4 / 4.6 / 0.9

APRIL

Time	m		Time	m
1 SU 0254 / 0901 / 1500 / 2123	4.6 / 1.2 / 4.8 / 0.8		**16** M 0217 / 0828 / 1418 / 2056	4.9 / 0.9 / 5.1 / 0.3
2 M 0323 / 0929 / 1529 / ○2151	4.7 / 1.1 / 4.8 / 0.7		**17** TU 0257 / 0910 / 1501 / ●2139	5.1 / 0.6 / 5.4 / 0.1
3 TU 0351 / 0958 / 1558 / 2219	4.7 / 1.0 / 4.9 / 0.7		**18** W 0338 / 0952 / 1545 / 2221	5.2 / 0.5 / 5.5 / 0.2
4 W 0418 / 1025 / 1627 / 2247	4.7 / 1.0 / 4.8 / 0.8		**19** TH 0418 / 1035 / 1632 / 2303	5.2 / 0.4 / 5.4 / 0.4
5 TH 0445 / 1053 / 1657 / 2314	4.7 / 1.0 / 4.8 / 0.9		**20** F 0500 / 1119 / 1721 / 2345	5.1 / 0.5 / 5.2 / 0.8
6 F 0514 / 1122 / 1729 / 2342	4.6 / 1.1 / 4.6 / 1.1		**21** SA 0544 / 1206 / 1814	4.9 / 0.7 / 4.9
7 SA 0544 / 1153 / 1804	4.5 / 1.2 / 4.4		**22** SU 0029 / 0631 / 1258 / 1912	1.2 / 4.6 / 1.0 / 4.5
8 SU 0012 / 0617 / 1228 / 1844	1.4 / 4.4 / 1.4 / 4.2		**23** M 0119 / 0725 / 1400 / 2019	1.6 / 4.3 / 1.3 / 4.1
9 M 0048 / 0658 / 1312 / 1936	1.6 / 4.2 / 1.6 / 4.0		**24** TU 0223 / 0832 / 1517 / ◑2137	2.0 / 4.1 / 1.5 / 3.9
10 TU 0136 / 0751 / 1415 / ◑2045	1.9 / 4.0 / 1.8 / 3.8		**25** W 0350 / 0953 / 1646 / 2301	2.2 / 3.9 / 1.6 / 3.9
11 W 0252 / 0904 / 1543 / 2214	2.2 / 3.8 / 1.9 / 3.8		**26** TH 0521 / 1116 / 1802	2.2 / 4.0 / 1.4
12 TH 0436 / 1031 / 1719 / 2340	2.2 / 3.8 / 1.7 / 4.0		**27** F 0012 / 0628 / 1223 / 1857	4.0 / 2.0 / 4.1 / 1.3
13 F 0600 / 1149 / 1831	1.9 / 4.1 / 1.3		**28** SA 0105 / 0715 / 1313 / 1940	4.1 / 1.7 / 4.3 / 1.2
14 SA 0044 / 0658 / 1248 / 1925	4.3 / 1.6 / 4.4 / 0.9		**29** SU 0145 / 0753 / 1352 / 2015	4.3 / 1.5 / 4.5 / 1.0
15 SU 0134 / 0745 / 1335 / 2012	4.6 / 1.2 / 4.8 / 0.5		**30** M 0219 / 0827 / 1427 / 2046	4.5 / 1.3 / 4.6 / 1.0

Chart Datum: 2·60 metres below Ordnance Datum (Newlyn)

TIDES

TIME ZONE (UT)
For Summer Time add ONE hour in **non-shaded areas**

ENGLAND – NORTH SHIELDS
LAT 55°01'N   LONG 1°26'W
TIMES AND HEIGHTS OF HIGH AND LOW WATERS

Dates in amber are **SPRINGS**
Dates in yellow are **NEAPS**

2007

MAY

Day	Time m	Time m	Day	Time m	Time m
1 TU	0249 4.6 / 0859 1.2 / 1459 4.7 / 2117 0.9		16 W	0230 5.0 / 0846 0.7 / 1440 5.2 / 2114 0.5 ●	
2 W	0319 4.7 / 0930 1.1 / 1531 4.7 / 2147 0.9 ○		17 TH	0313 5.1 / 0933 0.6 / 1529 5.2 / 2159 0.5	
3 TH	0348 4.7 / 1001 1.0 / 1603 4.7 / 2217 1.0		18 F	0356 5.1 / 1021 0.5 / 1620 5.2 / 2244 0.8	
4 F	0417 4.7 / 1032 1.0 / 1637 4.6 / 2247 1.1		19 SA	0441 5.0 / 1110 0.5 / 1712 5.0 / 2329 1.0	
5 SA	0448 4.7 / 1104 1.0 / 1712 4.5 / 2318 1.2		20 SU	0527 4.9 / 1159 0.7 / 1806 4.7	
6 SU	0521 4.6 / 1139 1.2 / 1750 4.4 / 2353 1.4		21 M	0014 1.3 / 0615 4.7 / 1252 0.9 / 1902 4.4	
7 M	0558 4.4 / 1219 1.3 / 1835 4.2		22 TU	0103 1.7 / 0707 4.5 / 1348 1.1 / 2001 4.2	
8 TU	0033 1.6 / 0641 4.3 / 1308 1.4 / 1928 4.1		23 W	0158 1.9 / 0806 4.3 / 1450 1.3 / 2104 4.0 ☽	
9 W	0125 1.8 / 0735 4.1 / 1410 1.5 / 2033 4.0		24 TH	0304 2.1 / 0912 4.1 / 1557 1.5 / 2211 3.9	
10 TH	0235 2.0 / 0841 4.0 / 1524 1.5 / 2148 4.0 ☽		25 F	0418 2.1 / 1022 4.0 / 1703 1.5 / 2316 3.9	
11 F	0358 2.0 / 0955 4.1 / 1641 1.4 / 2302 4.1		26 SA	0527 2.0 / 1127 4.1 / 1801 1.5	
12 SA	0514 1.8 / 1106 4.3 / 1750 1.1		27 SU	0012 4.1 / 0623 1.9 / 1223 4.2 / 1849 1.4	
13 SU	0005 4.3 / 0616 1.5 / 1208 4.5 / 1847 0.8		28 M	0059 4.1 / 0710 1.7 / 1311 4.3 / 1930 1.3	
14 M	0059 4.6 / 0709 1.2 / 1301 4.8 / 1939 0.6		29 TU	0139 4.3 / 0751 1.5 / 1352 4.4 / 2008 1.2	
15 TU	0146 4.8 / 0758 1.0 / 1351 5.1 / 2028 0.5		30 W	0215 4.4 / 0829 1.4 / 1431 4.4 / 2044 1.2	
			31 TH	0249 4.5 / 0905 1.2 / 1508 4.5 / 2119 1.1	

JUNE

Day	Time m	Time m	Day	Time m	Time m
1 F	0322 4.6 / 0941 1.1 / 1545 4.6 / 2153 1.2 ○		16 SA	0342 5.0 / 1015 0.6 / 1615 4.9 / 2232 1.0	
2 SA	0355 4.7 / 1017 1.1 / 1622 4.6 / 2228 1.2		17 SU	0428 5.0 / 1104 0.6 / 1706 4.8 / 2316 1.2	
3 SU	0429 4.7 / 1054 1.0 / 1701 4.5 / 2304 1.3		18 M	0513 4.9 / 1151 0.6 / 1754 4.7 / 2358 1.3	
4 M	0505 4.7 / 1133 1.0 / 1743 4.5 / 2343 1.4		19 TU	0558 4.8 / 1237 0.8 / 1842 4.5	
5 TU	0545 4.6 / 1217 1.0 / 1828 4.4		20 W	0040 1.5 / 0644 4.7 / 1323 1.0 / 1930 4.3	
6 W	0026 1.5 / 0629 4.5 / 1305 1.1 / 1918 4.3		21 TH	0123 1.7 / 0732 4.5 / 1410 1.2 / 2020 4.1	
7 TH	0116 1.6 / 0720 4.5 / 1359 1.1 / 2015 4.2		22 F	0210 1.9 / 0823 4.3 / 1459 1.4 / 2112 3.9 ☽	
8 F	0214 1.7 / 0817 4.4 / 1459 1.2 / 2118 4.2 ☽		23 SA	0304 2.0 / 0920 4.1 / 1553 1.5 / 2209 3.9	
9 SA	0319 1.7 / 0920 4.4 / 1604 1.2 / 2223 4.2		24 SU	0409 2.1 / 1021 4.0 / 1652 1.6 / 2308 3.9	
10 SU	0427 1.7 / 1026 4.4 / 1709 1.1 / 2327 4.3		25 M	0518 2.0 / 1125 4.0 / 1752 1.7	
11 M	0534 1.6 / 1132 4.6 / 1812 1.0		26 TU	0005 4.0 / 0621 1.9 / 1226 4.1 / 1846 1.6	
12 TU	0025 4.5 / 0636 1.4 / 1234 4.7 / 1911 0.9		27 W	0058 4.1 / 0718 1.6 / 1320 4.2 / 1934 1.5	
13 W	0119 4.6 / 0735 1.1 / 1333 4.8 / 2006 0.9		28 TH	0143 4.3 / 0803 1.4 / 1408 4.3 / 2018 1.4	
14 TH	0209 4.8 / 0830 0.9 / 1429 4.9 / 2057 0.9		29 F	0224 4.4 / 0845 1.1 / 1450 4.4 / 2058 1.3	
15 F	0256 4.9 / 0923 0.7 / 1523 5.0 / 2146 0.9 ●		30 SA	0301 4.6 / 0925 1.2 / 1531 4.5 / 2137 1.3 ○	

JULY

Day	Time m	Time m	Day	Time m	Time m
1 SU	0337 4.7 / 1005 1.0 / 1610 4.6 / 2215 1.2		16 M	0416 5.0 / 1054 0.5 / 1653 4.8 / 2259 1.2	
2 M	0414 4.8 / 1045 0.8 / 1650 4.7 / 2254 1.2		17 TU	0456 5.0 / 1134 0.6 / 1734 4.7 / 2335 1.2	
3 TU	0452 4.9 / 1126 0.8 / 1731 4.7 / 2334 1.2		18 W	0535 4.9 / 1212 0.7 / 1813 4.6	
4 W	0532 4.9 / 1208 0.7 / 1815 4.6		19 TH	0009 1.3 / 0613 4.8 / 1249 0.9 / 1851 4.4	
5 TH	0015 1.2 / 0613 4.9 / 1253 0.7 / 1900 4.6		20 F	0043 1.5 / 0653 4.7 / 1324 1.1 / 1930 4.3	
6 F	0059 1.3 / 0659 4.8 / 1339 0.8 / 1950 4.4		21 SA	0119 1.6 / 0734 4.5 / 1403 1.3 / 2013 4.1	
7 SA	0147 1.4 / 0750 4.7 / 1430 1.0 / 2044 4.3 ☽		22 SU	0201 1.8 / 0821 4.2 / 1448 1.6 / 2102 3.9 ☽	
8 SU	0241 1.5 / 0848 4.6 / 1528 1.1 / 2145 4.2		23 M	0254 2.0 / 0917 4.0 / 1543 1.8 / 2200 3.8	
9 M	0346 1.6 / 0953 4.5 / 1633 1.3 / 2251 4.2		24 TU	0404 2.1 / 1024 3.9 / 1651 1.9 / 2307 3.8	
10 TU	0459 1.6 / 1106 4.4 / 1745 1.3 / 2359 4.3		25 W	0529 2.1 / 1140 3.9 / 1804 1.9	
11 W	0616 1.5 / 1220 4.5 / 1855 1.4		26 TH	0015 3.9 / 0644 2.0 / 1252 4.0 / 1907 1.8	
12 TH	0102 4.4 / 0726 1.3 / 1329 4.6 / 1956 1.3		27 F	0114 4.1 / 0742 1.7 / 1348 4.2 / 1958 1.6	
13 F	0159 4.6 / 0827 1.0 / 1430 4.7 / 2050 1.2		28 SA	0201 4.4 / 0828 1.4 / 1434 4.4 / 2042 1.4	
14 SA	0248 4.8 / 0921 0.8 / 1522 4.8 / 2138 1.2 ●		29 SU	0242 4.6 / 0910 1.1 / 1515 4.6 / 2122 1.2	
15 SU	0334 4.9 / 1010 0.6 / 1610 4.8 / 2220 1.2		30 M	0319 4.8 / 0950 0.8 / 1554 4.8 / 2200 1.1 ○	
			31 TU	0356 5.0 / 1030 0.6 / 1633 4.9 / 2239 0.9	

AUGUST

Day	Time m	Time m	Day	Time m	Time m
1 W	0433 5.1 / 1110 0.4 / 1712 5.0 / 2317 0.9		16 TH	0507 5.1 / 1139 0.7 / 1737 4.7 / 2336 1.2	
2 TH	0511 5.2 / 1150 0.4 / 1753 4.9 / 2355 0.9		17 F	0540 4.9 / 1209 0.9 / 1810 4.6	
3 F	0552 5.2 / 1231 0.5 / 1835 4.8		18 SA	0005 1.3 / 0613 4.8 / 1239 1.1 / 1843 4.4	
4 SA	0035 1.0 / 0635 5.1 / 1313 0.7 / 1920 4.6		19 SU	0037 1.5 / 0650 4.6 / 1312 1.3 / 1920 4.2	
5 SU	0119 1.2 / 0724 4.9 / 1359 1.0 / 2011 4.4 ☽		20 M	0112 1.7 / 0732 4.3 / 1350 1.6 / 2004 4.1 ☽	
6 M	0210 1.4 / 0821 4.7 / 1455 1.3 / 2111 4.2		21 TU	0157 1.9 / 0823 4.0 / 1440 1.9 / 2058 3.9	
7 TU	0315 1.6 / 0931 4.4 / 1605 1.6 / 2224 4.1		22 W	0301 2.2 / 0931 3.8 / 1551 2.2 / 2209 3.8	
8 W	0441 1.8 / 1056 4.2 / 1732 1.8 / 2343 4.1		23 TH	0436 2.2 / 1058 3.7 / 1726 2.2 / 2333 3.8	
9 TH	0614 1.6 / 1224 4.3 / 1853 1.7		24 F	0615 2.1 / 1226 3.9 / 1844 2.0	
10 F	0056 4.3 / 0729 1.3 / 1336 4.4 / 1955 1.6		25 SA	0044 4.1 / 0719 1.7 / 1328 4.2 / 1938 1.7	
11 SA	0155 4.6 / 0827 1.0 / 1432 4.6 / 2045 1.4		26 SU	0136 4.4 / 0807 1.3 / 1413 4.5 / 2022 1.4	
12 SU	0242 4.8 / 0916 0.8 / 1517 4.8 / 2127 1.3 ●		27 M	0217 4.7 / 0849 0.9 / 1453 4.8 / 2101 1.2	
13 M	0323 5.0 / 0957 0.6 / 1556 4.8 / 2203 1.1		28 TU	0255 5.0 / 0928 0.6 / 1530 5.0 / 2139 0.9 ○	
14 TU	0359 5.1 / 1034 0.5 / 1632 4.8 / 2236 1.1		29 W	0331 5.3 / 1007 0.3 / 1608 5.1 / 2216 0.7	
15 W	0434 5.1 / 1108 0.6 / 1705 4.8 / 2307 1.1		30 TH	0408 5.4 / 1046 0.2 / 1646 5.2 / 2253 0.7	
			31 F	0446 5.5 / 1125 0.2 / 1725 5.1 / 2331 0.7	

Chart Datum: 2·60 metres below Ordnance Datum (Newlyn)

ENGLAND – NORTH SHIELDS

LAT 55°01'N   LONG 1°26'W

TIMES AND HEIGHTS OF HIGH AND LOW WATERS

TIME ZONE (UT)
For Summer Time add ONE hour in **non-shaded areas**

Dates in amber are **SPRINGS**
Dates in yellow are **NEAPS**

2007

SEPTEMBER

Day	Time m	Time m	Time m	Time m		Day	Time m	Time m	Time m	Time m
1 SA	0528 5.5	1204 0.4	1806 5.0			16 SU	0540 4.8	1158 1.1	1801 4.6	
2 SU	0011 0.9	0612 5.3	1246 0.7	1850 4.7		17 M	0003 1.4	0614 4.6	1228 1.4	1835 4.4
3 M	0055 1.1	0703 5.0	1331 1.2	1940 4.5		18 TU	0037 1.6	0654 4.3	1303 1.7	1916 4.2
4 TU	0148 1.4	0804 4.6	1428 1.6	◑ 2043 4.2		19 W	0119 1.9	0744 4.0	1349 2.0	◐ 2008 4.0
5 W	0301 1.7	0923 4.2	1550 2.0	2205 4.0		20 TH	0220 2.1	0852 3.8	1500 2.3	2120 3.8
6 TH	0441 1.8	1100 4.1	1732 2.1	2335 4.1		21 F	0353 2.2	1023 3.7	1647 2.4	2249 3.8
7 F	0618 1.6	1230 4.2	1853 1.9			22 SA	0539 2.0	1155 3.9	1815 2.1	
8 SA	0050 4.3	0727 1.3	1336 4.4	1949 1.6		23 SU	0008 4.1	0648 1.6	1258 4.2	1910 1.8
9 SU	0146 4.6	0818 1.0	1423 4.6	2032 1.5		24 M	0103 4.4	0737 1.2	1344 4.6	1954 1.4
10 M	0229 4.9	0900 0.8	1500 4.8	2107 1.3		25 TU	0146 4.8	0819 0.8	1424 4.9	2033 1.1
11 TU	0304 5.0	0935 0.7	1533 4.9	● 2139 1.1		26 W	0224 5.2	0859 0.5	1501 5.2	○ 2111 0.8
12 W	0336 5.1	1006 0.6	1603 4.9	2208 1.1		27 TH	0302 5.4	0939 0.3	1539 5.3	2149 0.7
13 TH	0406 5.1	1035 0.7	1632 4.9	2236 1.0		28 F	0341 5.6	1019 0.2	1617 5.3	2228 0.6
14 F	0436 5.1	1103 0.8	1701 4.8	2304 1.1		29 SA	0422 5.6	1058 0.3	1656 5.2	2309 0.6
15 SA	0507 5.0	1130 0.9	1730 4.7	2333 1.2		30 SU	0506 5.5	1139 0.6	1738 5.1	2352 0.8

OCTOBER

Day	Time m	Time m	Time m	Time m		Day	Time m	Time m	Time m	Time m
1 M	0555 5.2	1221 1.0	1824 4.8			16 TU	0549 4.5	1155 1.5	1802 4.5	
2 TU	0040 1.1	0650 4.8	1309 1.3	1916 4.5		17 W	0014 1.6	0630 4.3	1230 1.8	1841 4.3
3 W	0139 1.4	0757 4.4	1411 1.9	◑ 2023 4.2		18 TH	0058 1.8	0721 4.1	1316 2.1	1933 4.1
4 TH	0259 1.7	0921 4.1	1541 2.2	2149 4.1		19 F	0158 2.0	0827 3.9	1425 2.3	◑ 2041 4.0
5 F	0439 1.7	1057 4.0	1723 2.2	2320 4.2		20 SA	0322 2.0	0950 3.8	1604 2.4	2204 4.0
6 SA	0607 1.5	1219 4.2	1837 2.0			21 SU	0454 1.9	1114 4.0	1731 2.1	2321 4.2
7 SU	0031 4.4	0709 1.3	1317 4.4	1927 1.6		22 M	0605 1.5	1218 4.3	1831 1.8	
8 M	0124 4.6	0755 1.1	1359 4.6	2007 1.5		23 TU	0021 4.5	0658 1.1	1308 4.7	1918 1.5
9 TU	0204 4.8	0832 0.9	1433 4.7	2040 1.3		24 W	0109 4.9	0744 0.8	1351 4.9	2000 1.1
10 W	0238 5.0	0904 0.9	1500 4.8	2110 1.2		25 TH	0151 5.2	0828 0.5	1431 5.2	2042 0.9
11 TH	0309 5.0	0932 0.8	1532 4.9	● 2139 1.1		26 F	0234 5.5	0910 0.4	1510 5.3	○ 2124 0.7
12 F	0339 5.0	1000 0.8	1600 4.9	2208 1.1		27 SA	0317 5.6	0952 0.4	1550 5.3	2208 0.6
13 SA	0409 5.0	1028 0.9	1628 4.9	2237 1.1		28 SU	0403 5.6	1035 0.6	1632 5.3	2253 0.6
14 SU	0440 4.9	1056 1.1	1657 4.8	2307 1.2		29 M	0452 5.4	1118 0.9	1716 5.1	2341 0.8
15 M	0513 4.7	1124 1.3	1728 4.7	2338 1.4		30 TU	0546 5.1	1203 1.2	1805 4.9	
						31 W	0034 1.0	0645 4.7	1255 1.7	1859 4.6

NOVEMBER

Day	Time m	Time m	Time m	Time m		Day	Time m	Time m	Time m	Time m
1 TH	0137 1.3	0752 4.4	1357 2.0	◑ 2005 4.4		16 F	0049 1.6	0706 4.2	1259 2.0	◑ 1910 4.3
2 F	0251 1.5	0909 4.1	1518 2.3	2124 4.2		17 SA	0144 1.7	0805 4.1	1400 2.1	◐ 2010 4.2
3 SA	0416 1.6	1031 4.1	1648 2.3	2246 4.2		18 SU	0252 1.7	0915 4.0	1517 2.2	2120 4.2
4 SU	0534 1.5	1144 4.1	1759 2.1	2355 4.4		19 M	0406 1.7	1027 4.1	1635 2.1	2231 4.3
5 M	0634 1.4	1240 4.3	1852 1.9			20 TU	0516 1.4	1133 4.3	1742 1.9	2335 4.6
6 TU	0049 4.5	0719 1.3	1324 4.5	1933 1.7		21 W	0616 1.2	1228 4.6	1838 1.6	
7 W	0132 4.7	0756 1.2	1400 4.6	2008 1.5		22 TH	0031 4.8	0709 0.9	1318 4.8	1929 1.3
8 TH	0208 4.8	0828 1.1	1432 4.7	2042 1.4		23 F	0123 5.1	0758 0.8	1403 5.0	2018 1.0
9 F	0242 4.8	0859 1.1	1502 4.8	● 2114 1.3		24 SA	0212 5.3	0846 0.7	1447 5.2	○ 2106 0.8
10 SA	0315 4.9	0929 1.1	1532 4.9	2146 1.2		25 SU	0302 5.4	0933 0.7	1531 5.2	2156 0.7
11 SU	0348 4.8	0959 1.2	1601 4.9	2217 1.2		26 M	0354 5.4	1019 0.9	1615 5.2	2246 0.7
12 M	0422 4.8	1030 1.3	1632 4.8	2250 1.3		27 TU	0447 5.2	1105 1.1	1702 5.1	2337 0.7
13 TU	0457 4.7	1101 1.4	1704 4.8	2324 1.3		28 W	0541 5.0	1152 1.4	1750 5.0	
14 W	0535 4.5	1134 1.6	1740 4.6			29 TH	0030 0.9	0636 4.7	1241 1.7	1842 4.8
15 TH	0003 1.5	0616 4.4	1212 1.8	1820 4.5		30 F	0126 1.1	0735 4.4	1334 1.9	1940 4.6

DECEMBER

Day	Time m	Time m	Time m	Time m		Day	Time m	Time m	Time m	Time m
1 SA	0226 1.3	0837 4.2	1435 2.1	◑ 2044 4.4		16 SU	0128 1.3	0740 4.3	1335 1.8	◑ 1941 4.6
2 SU	0330 1.5	0943 4.1	1545 2.2	2154 4.3		17 M	0221 1.4	0837 4.2	1433 1.9	◐ 2039 4.5
3 M	0437 1.6	1049 4.0	1658 2.2	2302 4.3		18 TU	0322 1.4	0941 4.2	1540 1.9	2143 4.5
4 TU	0539 1.6	1148 4.1	1801 2.1			19 W	0427 1.4	1046 4.3	1651 1.9	2251 4.6
5 W	0002 4.3	0631 1.6	1240 4.2	1852 1.9		20 TH	0534 1.3	1150 4.4	1800 1.7	2359 4.7
6 TH	0054 4.4	0715 1.5	1323 4.4	1936 1.8		21 F	0639 1.2	1249 4.6	1905 1.5	
7 F	0139 4.5	0754 1.5	1402 4.5	2016 1.6		22 SA	0103 4.8	0737 1.2	1343 4.8	2004 1.2
8 SA	0219 4.6	0830 1.4	1437 4.7	2054 1.4		23 SU	0203 5.0	0832 1.1	1433 5.0	2059 0.9
9 SU	0257 4.6	0905 1.4	1510 4.8	● 2129 1.3		24 M	0259 5.1	0923 1.1	1510 5.1	○ 2152 0.7
10 M	0334 4.7	0939 1.4	1542 4.8	2204 1.2		25 TU	0352 5.1	1011 1.1	1606 5.2	2243 0.6
11 TU	0410 4.7	1013 1.4	1615 4.8	2240 1.2		26 W	0443 5.1	1056 1.2	1651 5.2	2331 0.6
12 W	0446 4.7	1047 1.4	1649 4.8	2317 1.2		27 TH	0532 4.9	1139 1.3	1736 5.1	
13 TH	0525 4.6	1123 1.5	1726 4.8	2357 1.2		28 F	0017 0.7	0619 4.8	1220 1.5	1821 5.0
14 F	0606 4.5	1202 1.6	1806 4.7			29 SA	0103 0.9	0706 4.5	1301 1.7	1908 4.8
15 SA	0040 1.3	0650 4.4	1246 1.7	1850 4.6		30 SU	0148 1.2	0754 4.3	1344 1.8	1958 4.6
						31 M	0235 1.4	0845 4.1	1434 2.0	◑ 2052 4.3

Chart Datum: 2·60 metres below Ordnance Datum (Newlyn)

TIDES

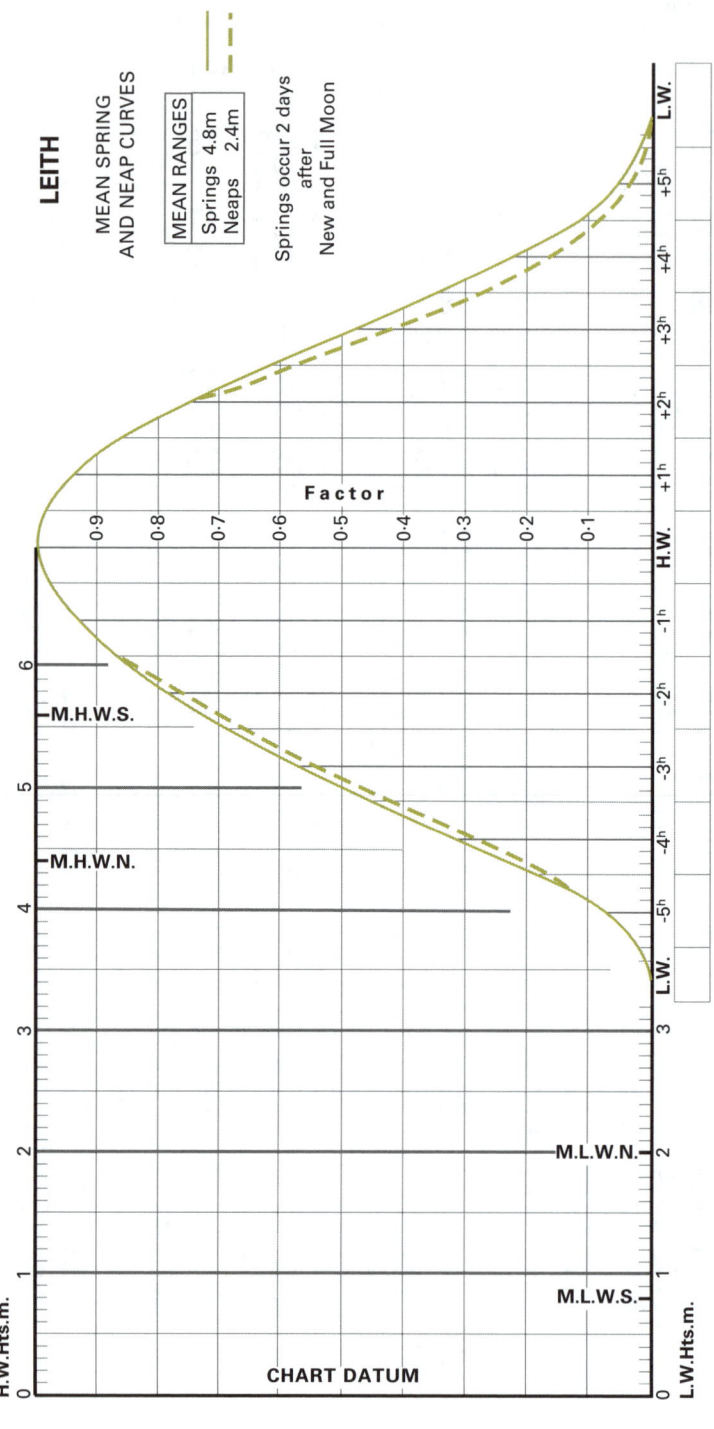

LEITH

MEAN SPRING
AND NEAP CURVES

MEAN RANGES
Springs 4.8m
Neaps   2.4m

Springs occur 2 days
after
New and Full Moon

SCOTLAND – LEITH

LAT 55°59'N   LONG 3°11'W

TIMES AND HEIGHTS OF HIGH AND LOW WATERS

Dates in amber are SPRINGS
Dates in yellow are NEAPS

2007

JANUARY

Time	m		Time	m
1 M 0003	5.0		**16** TU 0008	4.5
0622	1.5		0611	1.9
1239	5.0		1230	4.6
1846	1.4		1837	1.8
2 TU 0104	5.2		**17** W 0106	4.7
0716	1.5		0658	1.7
1331	5.2		1322	4.9
1944	1.1		1924	1.5
3 W 0158	5.3		**18** TH 0154	5.0
0803	1.4		0742	1.5
1419	5.3		1406	5.1
○ 2035	0.9		2009	1.2
4 TH 0247	5.3		**19** F 0237	5.3
0846	1.4		0825	1.3
1503	5.4		1446	5.3
2122	0.8		● 2055	0.9
5 F 0332	5.3		**20** SA 0317	5.5
0924	1.4		0908	1.1
1546	5.4		1524	5.5
2203	0.8		2140	0.6
6 SA 0414	5.3		**21** SU 0357	5.6
0957	1.4		0951	1.0
1627	5.3		1603	5.6
2239	0.9		2225	0.5
7 SU 0454	5.1		**22** M 0439	5.6
1025	1.5		1033	1.0
1707	5.2		1644	5.7
2308	1.1		2307	0.5
8 M 0533	5.0		**23** TU 0522	5.5
1051	1.6		1111	1.1
1745	5.1		1727	5.6
2334	1.3		2347	0.6
9 TU 0612	4.8		**24** W 0608	5.3
1122	1.7		1148	1.2
1825	4.9		1812	5.5
10 W 0005	1.5		**25** TH 0026	0.9
0652	4.6		0656	5.1
1159	1.9		1227	1.5
1908	4.7		◐ 1902	5.3
11 TH 0044	1.7		**26** F 0107	1.3
0737	4.4		0751	4.8
1244	2.1		1318	1.7
◐ 1958	4.5		2003	5.0
12 F 0132	1.9		**27** SA 0202	1.6
0828	4.3		0855	4.6
1344	2.4		1434	2.0
2054	4.4		2119	4.7
13 SA 0236	2.1		**28** SU 0327	1.9
0924	4.3		1008	4.5
1510	2.5			
2156	4.3		2241	4.6
14 SU 0402	2.2		**29** M 0504	2.0
1025	4.3		1122	4.6
1642	2.4		1741	1.8
2302	4.3			
15 M 0516	2.1		**30** TU 0000	4.7
1128	4.4		0620	1.9
1746	2.1		1232	4.8
			1853	1.5
			31 W 0108	4.9
			0716	1.8
			1329	5.0
			1949	1.2

FEBRUARY

Time	m		Time	m
1 TH 0200	5.1		**16** F 0135	5.0
0759	1.6		0729	1.4
1415	5.2		1347	5.1
2034	0.9		2000	1.0
2 F 0243	5.2		**17** SA 0218	5.4
0836	1.4		0812	1.1
1456	5.3		1427	5.5
○ 2113	0.8		● 2044	0.6
3 SA 0320	5.2		**18** SU 0258	5.6
0908	1.3		0854	0.8
1533	5.4		1504	5.7
2146	0.7		2127	0.3
4 SU 0355	5.2		**19** M 0337	5.8
0937	1.2		0935	0.6
1607	5.4		1543	5.9
2215	0.8		2208	0.1
5 M 0428	5.2		**20** TU 0417	5.8
1002	1.2		1013	0.5
1640	5.3		1623	6.0
2239	0.9		2248	0.2
6 TU 0500	5.1		**21** W 0459	5.6
1026	1.2		1050	0.7
1712	5.2		1706	5.9
2301	1.0		2324	0.4
7 W 0534	4.9		**22** TH 0542	5.4
1050	1.4		1122	0.9
1746	5.1		1751	5.6
2325	1.2		2356	0.9
8 TH 0610	4.8		**23** F 0628	5.1
1116	1.6		1157	1.2
1822	4.8		1842	5.3
2353	1.5			
9 F 0649	4.6		**24** SA 0030	1.3
1148	1.7		0720	4.7
1904	4.6		1245	1.6
			◐ 1943	4.8
10 SA 0027	1.8		**25** SU 0121	1.9
0733	4.4		0826	4.4
1227	2.1		1406	1.9
◐ 1954	4.3		2104	4.5
11 SU 0116	2.1		**26** M 0302	2.3
0828	4.2		0945	4.3
1332	2.4		1614	2.0
2100	4.1		2233	4.4
12 M 0239	2.4		**27** TU 0506	2.3
0933	4.1		1110	4.4
1540	2.5		1752	1.8
2217	4.1			
13 TU 0442	2.3		**28** W 0002	4.5
1046	4.2		0621	2.1
1722	2.2		1226	4.6
2336	4.3		1856	1.4
14 W 0552	2.1			
1200	4.4			
1823	1.8			
15 TH 0044	4.6			
0644	1.8			
1301	4.8			
1913	1.4			

MARCH

Time	m		Time	m
1 TH 0108	4.8		**16** F 0016	4.7
0710	1.8		0622	1.7
1322	4.9		1232	4.8
1942	1.1		1853	1.2
2 F 0154	5.0		**17** SA 0109	5.1
0746	1.6		0707	1.3
1404	5.2		1319	5.2
2020	0.9		1939	0.7
3 SA 0230	5.1		**18** SU 0152	5.5
0816	1.3		0749	0.9
1440	5.3		1359	5.6
○ 2052	0.8		2023	0.3
4 SU 0301	5.2		**19** M 0232	5.7
0844	1.1		0830	0.6
1512	5.4		1438	5.9
2119	0.7		● 2105	0.1
5 M 0330	5.2		**20** TU 0311	5.8
0911	1.0		0911	0.4
1542	5.4		1519	6.1
2144	0.7		2145	0.0
6 TU 0358	5.2		**21** W 0352	5.8
0937	1.0		0951	0.4
1611	5.4		1601	6.1
2207	0.7		2223	0.2
7 W 0428	5.1		**22** TH 0433	5.7
1000	1.0		1029	0.5
1642	5.2		1647	5.9
2228	0.9		2259	0.5
8 TH 0459	5.0		**23** F 0517	5.4
1021	1.2		1104	0.7
1714	5.1		1735	5.6
2247	1.1		2331	1.0
9 F 0533	4.9		**24** SA 0604	5.1
1041	1.3		1142	1.1
1749	4.9		1829	5.1
2307	1.4			
10 SA 0609	4.7		**25** SU 0004	1.6
1106	1.6		0657	4.7
1828	4.6		1235	1.5
2332	1.7		◐ 1934	4.7
11 SU 0650	4.5		**26** M 0100	2.1
1140	1.8		0806	4.4
1916	4.3		1409	1.9
			2055	4.4
12 M 0010	2.1		**27** TU 0300	2.5
0740	4.2		0928	4.3
1234	2.2		1618	1.9
◐ 2018	4.1		2221	4.3
13 TU 0129	2.4		**28** W 0453	2.4
0846	4.1		1051	4.3
1435	2.4		1740	1.6
2139	4.1		2349	4.5
14 W 0412	2.5		**29** TH 0559	2.1
1008	4.1		1205	4.6
1656	2.1		1837	1.4
2303	4.3			
15 TH 0530	2.1		**30** F 0049	4.7
1129	4.4		0644	1.8
1802	1.7		1258	4.9
			1918	1.2
			31 SA 0131	4.9
			0717	1.6
			1339	5.1
			1952	1.0

APRIL

Time	m		Time	m
1 SU 0205	5.0		**16** M 0121	5.5
0745	1.3		0718	0.9
1413	5.2		1328	5.6
2020	0.8		1953	0.3
2 M 0234	5.1		**17** TU 0203	5.7
0814	1.1		0802	0.6
1444	5.3		1411	5.9
○ 2045	0.8		● 2037	0.2
3 TU 0300	5.1		**18** W 0244	5.8
0843	1.0		0843	0.4
1514	5.3		1456	6.0
2109	0.7		2119	0.2
4 W 0327	5.2		**19** TH 0326	5.7
0911	0.9		0931	0.3
1544	5.3		1542	6.0
2134	0.8		2200	0.4
5 TH 0357	5.1		**20** F 0410	5.6
0936	1.0		1014	0.5
1615	5.2		1631	5.7
2156	1.0		2238	0.8
6 F 0428	5.0		**21** SA 0456	5.4
0957	1.1		1057	0.7
1649	5.0		1723	5.4
2214	1.2		2314	1.3
7 SA 0501	4.9		**22** SU 0545	5.1
1018	1.3		1142	1.1
1725	4.8		1820	5.0
2233	1.4		2353	1.8
8 SU 0537	4.7		**23** M 0642	4.7
1043	1.4		1240	1.4
1806	4.6		1926	4.6
2258	1.7			
9 M 0618	4.5		**24** TU 0053	2.2
1120	1.7		0751	4.5
1854	4.4		1412	1.7
2338	2.1		◐ 2037	4.4
10 TU 0707	4.3		**25** W 0238	2.4
1219	2.0		0906	4.4
1954	4.0		1553	1.7
○			2152	4.3
11 W 0107	2.4		**26** TH 0409	2.4
0811	4.2		1019	4.4
1415	2.1		1703	1.6
2109	4.2		2309	4.4
12 TH 0336	2.4		**27** F 0511	2.2
0933	4.2		1127	4.6
1619	1.9		1757	1.5
2230	4.4			
13 F 0454	2.1		**28** SA 0011	4.6
1052	4.5		0556	1.9
1728	1.5		1222	4.8
2340	4.8		1838	1.3
14 SA 0548	1.7		**29** SU 0055	4.7
1155	4.9		0634	1.6
1821	1.0		1305	4.9
			1911	1.2
15 SU 0035	5.1		**30** M 0130	4.9
0634	1.3		0707	1.4
1245	5.3		1341	5.0
1908	0.6		1938	1.0

Chart Datum: 2·90 metres below Ordnance Datum (Newlyn)

TIME ZONE (UT)	SCOTLAND – LEITH	Dates in amber are SPRINGS
For Summer Time add ONE hour in **non-shaded areas**	LAT 55°59'N LONG 3°11'W	Dates in yellow are NEAPS
	TIMES AND HEIGHTS OF HIGH AND LOW WATERS	**2007**

MAY

Day	Time m	Time m	Time m	Time m		Day	Time m	Time m	Time m	Time m
1 TU	0200 5.0	0741 1.2	1414 5.1	2006 1.0		16 W ●	0135 5.5	0736 0.7	1349 5.7	2010 0.5
2 W ○	0228 5.1	0813 1.1	1446 5.1	2034 0.9		17 TH	0220 5.6	0827 0.5	1439 5.8	2057 0.6
3 TH	0257 5.1	0845 1.0	1519 5.1	2102 1.0		18 F	0305 5.6	0917 0.4	1529 5.7	2141 0.8
4 F	0329 5.1	0915 1.0	1553 5.1	2130 1.1		19 SA	0352 5.5	1006 0.5	1621 5.5	2224 1.1
5 SA	0402 5.1	0944 1.1	1630 5.0	2155 1.3		20 SU	0440 5.3	1053 0.7	1714 5.3	2304 1.4
6 SU	0436 5.0	1012 1.2	1708 4.9	2221 1.5		21 M	0532 5.1	1142 1.0	1809 5.0	2345 1.8
7 M	0514 4.8	1045 1.4	1751 4.7	2253 1.8		22 TU	0628 4.9	1235 1.3	1907 4.7	
8 TU	0556 4.7	1129 1.6	1839 4.6	2345 2.0		23 W ☾	0033 2.1	0729 4.7	1342 1.5	2007 4.5
9 W	0646 4.5	1236 1.7	1936 4.5			24 TH	0142 2.3	0833 4.5	1459 1.7	2108 4.3
10 TH ☽	0118 2.2	0746 4.4	1403 1.8	2043 4.5		25 F	0302 2.3	0935 4.5	1605 1.7	2210 4.3
11 F	0255 2.2	0859 4.5	1535 1.6	2156 4.6		26 SA	0407 2.2	1035 4.5	1658 1.7	2311 4.4
12 SA	0410 2.0	1013 4.7	1644 1.3	2302 4.8		27 SU	0500 2.0	1132 4.6	1742 1.6	
13 SU	0507 1.6	1116 5.0	1741 1.0			28 M	0004 4.5	0547 1.8	1222 4.7	1820 1.4
14 M	0000 5.1	0557 1.3	1211 5.3	1832 0.7		29 TU	0047 4.7	0629 1.6	1305 4.8	1854 1.3
15 TU	0050 5.3	0646 1.0	1301 5.5	1922 0.6		30 W	0123 4.8	0709 1.4	1344 4.9	1928 1.2
						31 TH	0157 4.9	0746 1.3	1422 5.0	2003 1.2

JUNE

Day	Time m	Time m	Time m	Time m		Day	Time m	Time m	Time m	Time m
1 F ○	0231 5.0	0823 1.1	1459 5.0	2037 1.2		16 SA	0251 5.4	0910 0.6	1521 5.5	2128 1.1
2 SA	0306 5.1	0859 1.1	1536 5.0	2113 1.3		17 SU	0339 5.4	1000 0.6	1611 5.4	2211 1.2
3 SU	0342 5.1	0937 1.1	1614 5.0	2150 1.3		18 M	0428 5.3	1047 0.7	1701 5.2	2250 1.4
4 M	0419 5.1	1016 1.1	1654 5.0	2228 1.5		19 TU	0516 5.2	1130 0.9	1749 5.0	2324 1.6
5 TU	0458 5.0	1058 1.2	1737 4.9	2311 1.6		20 W	0606 5.1	1210 1.1	1837 4.8	2357 1.8
6 W	0541 4.9	1145 1.3	1824 4.9			21 TH	0656 4.9	1249 1.4	1926 4.6	
7 TH	0001 1.8	0628 4.9	1239 1.3	1916 4.8		22 F ●	0039 2.0	0748 4.7	1333 1.6	2015 4.4
8 F ☽	0102 1.9	0722 4.8	1340 1.4	2016 4.7		23 SA	0134 2.1	0841 4.5	1429 1.8	2106 4.3
9 SA	0211 1.9	0824 4.8	1449 1.4	2121 4.7		24 SU	0245 2.2	0935 4.4	1537 1.9	2200 4.3
10 SU	0321 1.8	0934 4.8	1558 1.3	2226 4.8		25 M	0400 2.2	1032 4.4	1640 1.8	2256 4.3
11 M	0425 1.7	1041 5.0	1702 1.2	2326 5.0		26 TU	0503 2.1	1130 4.4	1733 1.8	2352 4.5
12 TU	0525 1.4	1142 5.1	1801 1.1			27 W	0556 1.9	1227 4.5	1819 1.7	
13 W	0022 5.1	0622 1.2	1241 5.3	1858 1.0		28 TH	0044 4.6	0642 1.6	1317 4.7	1900 1.5
14 TH	0114 5.3	0721 0.9	1336 5.4	1951 1.0		29 F	0130 4.8	0725 1.4	1401 4.9	1940 1.4
15 F	0203 5.4	0817 0.7	1429 5.5	2041 1.0		30 SA ○	0211 5.0	0806 1.2	1441 5.0	2021 1.3

JULY

Day	Time m	Time m	Time m	Time m		Day	Time m	Time m	Time m	Time m
1 SU	0249 5.1	0848 1.0	1520 5.1	2102 1.2		16 M	0329 5.4	0951 0.5	1558 5.4	2153 1.2
2 M	0326 5.2	0930 0.9	1559 5.2	2144 1.2		17 TU	0412 5.4	1031 0.6	1640 5.3	2226 1.2
3 TU	0404 5.3	1014 0.8	1639 5.3	2226 1.2		18 W	0454 5.4	1105 0.7	1720 5.1	2252 1.3
4 W	0443 5.3	1057 0.8	1721 5.2	2307 1.3		19 TH	0534 5.2	1130 0.9	1800 4.9	2318 1.5
5 TH	0524 5.3	1140 0.8	1805 5.1	2349 1.4		20 F	0615 5.0	1158 1.2	1839 4.7	2350 1.7
6 F	0609 5.2	1224 1.0	1853 5.0			21 SA	0657 4.8	1229 1.4	1922 4.5	
7 SA	0032 1.5	0657 5.1	1310 1.1	1946 4.9		22 SU ☽	0029 1.9	0742 4.6	1311 1.7	2008 4.4
8 SU	0125 1.7	0752 5.0	1404 1.3	2047 4.7		23 M	0123 2.1	0836 4.4	1408 2.0	2101 4.3
9 M	0231 1.8	0859 4.9	1512 1.5	2153 4.7		24 TU	0242 2.3	0935 4.2	1532 2.1	2200 4.2
10 TU	0349 1.8	1013 4.8	1631 1.6	2259 4.7		25 W	0420 2.3	1041 4.2	1655 2.1	2304 4.3
11 W	0505 1.6	1126 4.9	1744 1.5			26 TH	0530 2.1	1150 4.3	1754 2.0	
12 TH	0003 4.9	0615 1.4	1234 5.0	1848 1.4		27 F	0009 4.5	0623 1.8	1253 4.6	1841 1.8
13 F	0103 5.1	0719 1.1	1334 5.2	1943 1.3		28 SA	0106 4.7	0710 1.5	1341 4.9	1925 1.5
14 SA ●	0155 5.2	0816 0.8	1426 5.3	2032 1.2		29 SU	0152 5.0	0754 1.2	1423 5.1	2007 1.3
15 SU	0243 5.4	0906 0.6	1514 5.4	2115 1.2		30 M ○	0232 5.2	0837 0.9	1502 5.3	2049 1.1
						31 TU	0308 5.4	0920 0.6	1540 5.5	2130 0.9

AUGUST

Day	Time m	Time m	Time m	Time m		Day	Time m	Time m	Time m	Time m
1 W	0345 5.6	1003 0.4	1619 5.5	2211 0.9		16 TH	0425 5.5	1031 0.7	1647 5.2	2219 1.1
2 TH	0423 5.7	1044 0.4	1659 5.5	2249 0.9		17 F	0459 5.3	1052 0.9	1720 5.0	2241 1.3
3 F	0503 5.7	1122 0.5	1742 5.4	2325 1.1		18 SA	0534 5.1	1113 1.1	1756 4.9	2306 1.5
4 SA	0546 5.6	1159 0.7	1827 5.2			19 SU	0611 4.9	1139 1.4	1835 4.7	2336 1.7
5 SU ☽	0000 1.3	0633 5.4	1236 1.1	1916 4.9		20 M ☽	0654 4.6	1212 1.7	1919 4.5	
6 M	0046 1.5	0727 5.1	1323 1.5	2015 4.7		21 TU	0016 2.0	0744 4.4	1259 2.1	2011 4.3
7 TU	0152 1.8	0836 4.8	1436 1.8	2126 4.5		22 W	0122 2.3	0847 4.2	1423 2.4	2114 4.2
8 W	0330 1.9	1000 4.6	1620 2.0	2242 4.6		23 TH	0330 2.5	0958 4.1	1624 2.4	2224 4.2
9 TH	0506 1.8	1123 4.7	1746 1.9	2356 4.7		24 F	0511 2.2	1115 4.3	1735 2.2	2338 4.4
10 F	0624 1.4	1237 4.9	1850 1.7			25 SA	0609 1.9	1226 4.6	1825 1.9	
11 SA	0100 5.0	0724 1.1	1336 5.1	1938 1.5		26 SU	0041 4.8	0656 1.5	1318 5.0	1908 1.5
12 SU ●	0151 5.3	0813 0.8	1422 5.3	2019 1.3		27 M	0128 5.1	0739 1.1	1400 5.3	1949 1.2
13 M	0234 5.4	0855 0.6	1501 5.4	2055 1.1		28 TU ○	0207 5.4	0821 0.7	1438 5.6	2029 0.9
14 TU	0313 5.5	0932 0.5	1538 5.3	2127 1.1		29 W	0243 5.7	0902 0.4	1515 5.7	2109 0.7
15 W	0350 5.5	1004 0.6	1613 5.3	2155 1.1		30 TH	0320 5.9	0942 0.2	1553 5.8	2148 0.6
						31 F	0358 6.0	1021 0.2	1633 5.7	2225 0.7

Chart Datum: 2·90 metres below Ordnance Datum (Newlyn)

SCOTLAND – LEITH

LAT 55°59'N   LONG 3°11'W

TIMES AND HEIGHTS OF HIGH AND LOW WATERS

Dates in amber are SPRINGS
Dates in yellow are NEAPS

2007

SEPTEMBER

Day	Time m				Day	Time m			
1 SA	0440 5.9	1057 0.4	1715 5.5	2259 0.9	16 SU	0500 5.2	1107 1.0	1717 5.0	2230 1.4
2 SU	0525 5.7	1131 0.8	1800 5.3	2334 1.1	17 M	0536 4.9	1052 1.4	1754 4.8	2255 1.6
3 M	0614 5.4	1205 1.3	1850 5.0		18 TU	0618 4.7	1118 1.8	1836 4.6	2330 1.9
4 TU	0021 1.5	0711 5.0	1253 1.8	1951 4.6 ◐	19 W	0706 4.4	1155 2.2	1926 4.4 ◑	
5 W	0137 1.6	0827 4.6	1423 2.2	2110 4.5	20 TH	0025 2.3	0807 4.2	1319 2.5	2031 4.2
6 TH	0339 2.0	0957 4.5	1628 2.3	2233 4.5	21 F	0232 2.5	0921 4.1	1551 2.6	2148 4.2
7 F	0519 1.7	1126 4.6	1748 2.1	2351 4.8	22 SA	0445 2.2	1040 4.3	1710 2.3	2304 4.5
8 SA	0627 1.4	1238 4.9	1842 1.8		23 SU	0545 1.8	1152 4.7	1800 1.9	
9 SU	0052 5.1	0717 1.1	1329 5.1	1923 1.6	24 M	0008 4.8	0631 1.4	1246 5.1	1842 1.5
10 M	0138 5.3	0758 0.8	1408 5.3	1956 1.3	25 TU	0056 5.2	0714 0.9	1329 5.4	1922 1.1
11 TU	0216 5.5	0833 0.7	1441 5.3	2027 1.1 ●	26 W	0136 5.6	0755 0.5	1408 5.7	2002 0.8 ○
12 W	0250 5.6	0903 0.6	1512 5.3	2056 1.0	27 TH	0213 5.9	0835 0.3	1446 5.9	2042 0.6
13 TH	0322 5.5	0929 0.6	1541 5.1	2123 1.0	28 F	0252 6.1	0915 0.2	1526 5.9	2122 0.5
14 F	0354 5.5	0952 0.8	1612 5.2	2147 1.1	29 SA	0334 6.1	0954 0.3	1607 5.8	2202 0.6
15 SA	0426 5.3	1012 0.9	1643 5.1	2208 1.2	30 SU	0419 6.0	1031 0.6	1650 5.6	2241 0.8

OCTOBER

Day	Time m				Day	Time m			
1 M	0507 5.7	1107 1.0	1737 5.3	2323 1.1	16 TU	0511 4.9	1019 1.6	1720 4.9	2233 1.6
2 TU	0601 5.3	1143 1.6	1829 5.0		17 W	0552 4.7	1044 1.9	1801 4.7	2309 1.9
3 W	0017 1.5	0704 4.9	1240 2.1	1936 4.6 ◑	18 TH	0640 4.5	1121 2.2	1850 4.5	
4 TH	0146 1.9	0824 4.6	1427 2.5	2059 4.5	19 F	0007 2.1	0736 4.3	1241 2.5	1952 4.4 ●
5 F	0346 1.9	0949 4.5	1618 2.4	2220 4.6	20 SA	0154 2.3	0846 4.3	1503 2.6	2109 4.4
6 SA	0509 1.6	1114 4.6	1727 2.2	2333 4.8	21 SU	0356 2.1	1002 4.4	1628 2.3	2225 4.6
7 SU	0609 1.4	1220 4.9	1817 1.9		22 M	0505 1.7	1112 4.8	1722 1.9	2327 4.9
8 M	0030 5.1	0654 1.1	1307 5.1	1854 1.7	23 TU	0554 1.3	1208 5.1	1807 1.5	
9 TU	0114 5.3	0731 1.0	1343 5.2	1925 1.4	24 W	0018 5.3	0639 0.9	1255 5.5	1849 1.2
10 W	0150 5.4	0800 0.9	1414 5.3	1954 1.2	25 TH	0102 5.7	0722 0.6	1337 5.7	1932 0.9
11 TH	0223 5.5	0826 0.8	1442 5.3	2024 1.1 ●	26 F	0145 5.9	0805 0.4	1418 5.9	2016 0.6 ○
12 F	0254 5.5	0851 0.8	1510 5.3	2053 1.1	27 SA	0229 6.1	0847 0.4	1500 5.9	2101 0.5
13 SA	0326 5.4	0914 0.9	1539 5.3	2120 1.1	28 SU	0315 6.1	0930 0.5	1543 5.8	2147 0.6
14 SU	0358 5.3	0937 1.1	1610 5.2	2144 1.2	29 M	0404 5.9	1012 0.9	1629 5.6	2234 0.8
15 M	0433 5.1	0958 1.3	1644 5.1	2206 1.4	30 TU	0456 5.6	1053 1.3	1718 5.3	2324 1.1
					31 W	0553 5.3	1137 1.8	1815 5.0	

NOVEMBER

Day	Time m				Day	Time m			
1 TH	0024 1.4	0658 4.9	1236 2.2	1925 4.8 ◑	16 F	0619 4.7	1119 2.1	1823 4.7	
2 F	0146 1.7	0811 4.6	1407 2.5	2040 4.7	17 SA	0010 1.9	0711 4.6	1232 2.3	1918 4.6 ●
3 SA	0322 1.8	0925 4.5	1537 2.5	2152 4.7	18 SU	0126 2.0	0813 4.5	1410 2.4	2025 4.6
4 SU	0436 1.7	1039 4.6	1643 2.3	2259 4.8	19 M	0253 1.9	0922 4.6	1532 2.3	2138 4.7
5 M	0534 1.5	1143 4.7	1734 2.1	2355 5.0	20 TU	0410 1.6	1030 4.8	1635 2.0	2244 5.0
6 TU	0619 1.4	1232 4.9	1814 1.9		21 W	0509 1.3	1129 5.1	1728 1.7	2340 5.3
7 W	0042 5.1	0653 1.3	1311 5.0	1849 1.6	22 TH	0601 1.1	1221 5.3	1818 1.3	
8 TH	0121 5.2	0721 1.2	1343 5.1	1923 1.4	23 F	0032 5.5	0650 0.9	1309 5.6	1907 1.0
9 F	0156 5.3	0747 1.1	1413 5.2	1956 1.1 ●	24 SA	0122 5.8	0738 0.8	1354 5.7	1958 0.8 ○
10 SA	0230 5.3	0814 1.1	1441 5.3	2028 1.2	25 SU	0212 5.9	0827 0.8	1439 5.7	2050 0.6
11 SU	0303 5.2	0843 1.2	1512 5.3	2059 1.2	26 M	0303 5.9	0915 0.9	1526 5.7	2142 0.6
12 M	0337 5.2	0911 1.3	1544 5.2	2129 1.3	27 TU	0354 5.8	1001 1.1	1614 5.6	2233 0.7
13 TU	0414 5.1	0939 1.5	1619 5.1	2159 1.4	28 W	0448 5.6	1045 1.4	1706 5.4	2324 1.0
14 W	0452 5.0	1007 1.7	1655 5.0	2232 1.5	29 TH	0543 5.3	1129 1.8	1802 5.2	
15 TH	0533 4.8	1038 1.9	1736 4.8	2313 1.7	30 F	0017 1.2	0641 5.0	1216 2.1	1904 5.0

DECEMBER

Day	Time m				Day	Time m			
1 SA	0118 1.5	0742 4.7	1313 2.3	2008 4.8 ◐	16 SU	0003 1.5	0647 4.8	1211 2.0	1848 4.9
2 SU	0229 1.7	0844 4.5	1427 2.4	2111 4.7	17 M	0055 1.5	0740 4.7	1313 2.1	1943 4.9
3 M	0338 1.8	0946 4.5	1538 2.4	2211 4.7	18 TU	0156 1.6	0841 4.7	1427 2.1	2048 4.9
4 TU	0437 1.8	1047 4.5	1638 2.2	2310 4.7	19 W	0307 1.6	0947 4.8	1542 2.0	2200 4.9
5 W	0526 1.8	1144 4.6	1730 2.1		20 TH	0420 1.5	1052 4.9	1650 1.8	2308 5.1
6 TH	0003 4.8	0605 1.7	1232 4.8	1814 1.8	21 F	0527 1.4	1151 5.1	1753 1.5	
7 F	0050 4.9	0640 1.6	1311 4.9	1855 1.6	22 SA	0011 5.3	0627 1.3	1247 5.3	1853 1.2
8 SA	0132 5.0	0713 1.5	1346 5.0	1933 1.5	23 SU	0110 5.4	0724 1.2	1338 5.4	1952 0.9
9 SU	0210 5.0	0746 1.4	1419 5.1	2009 1.4 ●	24 M	0204 5.6	0817 1.1	1427 5.6	2048 0.7 ○
10 M	0246 5.1	0821 1.4	1452 5.2	2045 1.3	25 TU	0257 5.7	0906 1.1	1516 5.6	2140 0.6
11 TU	0322 5.1	0855 1.4	1527 5.2	2121 1.2	26 W	0347 5.6	0952 1.2	1604 5.6	2228 0.6
12 W	0359 5.1	0931 1.5	1602 5.2	2158 1.2	27 TH	0437 5.5	1033 1.3	1652 5.5	2313 0.7
13 TH	0436 5.1	1007 1.6	1639 5.2	2237 1.3	28 F	0525 5.3	1109 1.5	1741 5.4	2354 1.0
14 F	0516 5.0	1044 1.7	1718 5.1	2318 1.4	29 SA	0614 5.0	1140 1.7	1832 5.2	
15 SA	0600 4.9	1123 1.8	1801 5.0		30 SU	0031 1.3	0702 4.8	1213 1.9	1923 4.9
					31 M	0108 1.6	0751 4.6	1259 2.1	2017 4.7 ◐

TIDES

Chart Datum: 2·90 metres below Ordnance Datum (Newlyn)

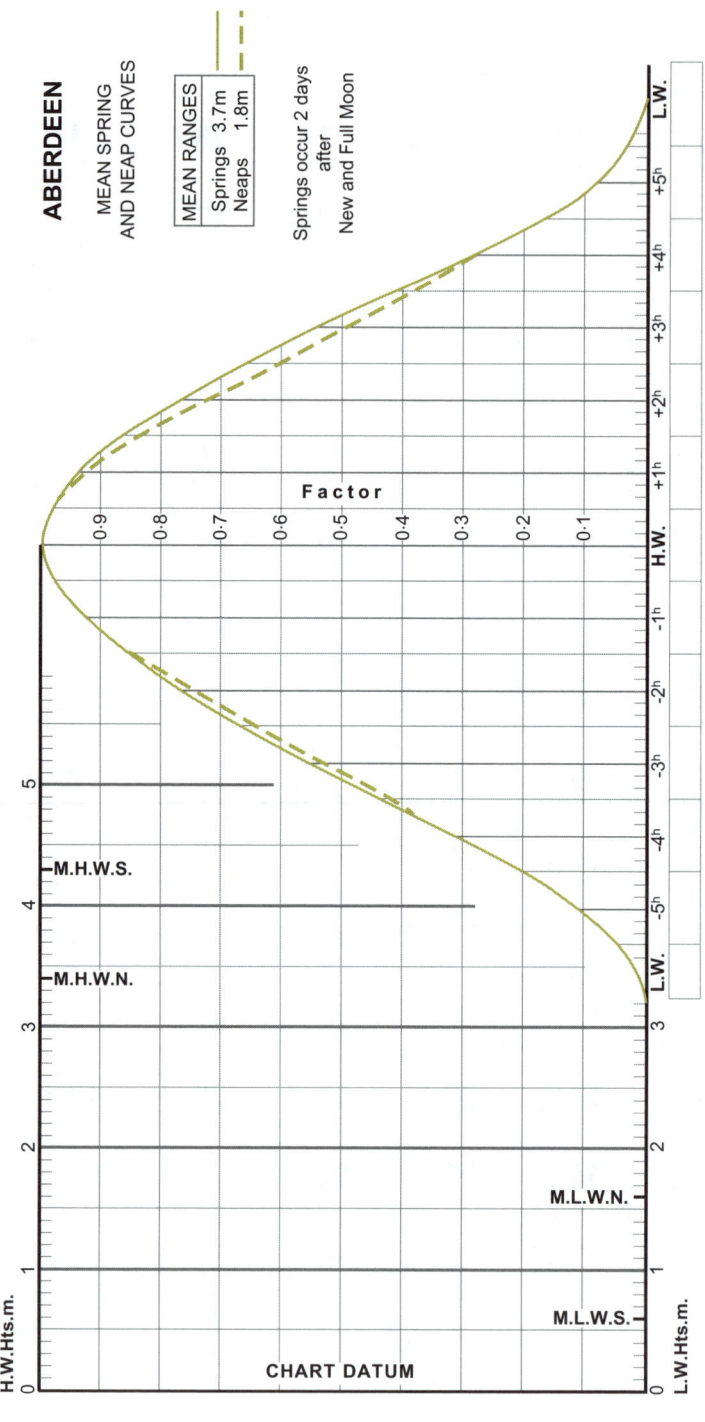

ABERDEEN

MEAN SPRING
AND NEAP CURVES

MEAN RANGES	
Springs	3.7m
Neaps	1.8m

Springs occur 2 days
after
New and Full Moon

Factor

0·9   0·8   0·7   0·6   0·5   0·4   0·3   0·2   0·1

H.W.   -1ʰ   -2ʰ   -3ʰ   -4ʰ   -5ʰ   L.W.

L.W.   +5ʰ   +4ʰ   +3ʰ   +2ʰ   +1ʰ   H.W.

5

M.H.W.S.

4

M.H.W.N.

3

2

M.L.W.N.

1

H.W.Hts.m.

M.L.W.S.

CHART DATUM

L.W.Hts.m.

SCOTLAND – ABERDEEN

LAT 57°09'N   LONG 2°05'W

TIMES AND HEIGHTS OF HIGH AND LOW WATERS

Dates in amber are **SPRINGS**
Dates in yellow are **NEAPS**

2007

JANUARY

Day				
1 M	0510 1.3	1129 4.0	1738 1.3	2353 4.0
2 TU	0603 1.3	1218 4.1	1830 1.1	
3 W ○	0047 4.1	0649 1.2	1303 4.2	1917 0.9
4 TH	0136 4.1	0731 1.2	1345 4.3	2001 0.8
5 F	0221 4.1	0810 1.2	1425 4.3	2042 0.8
6 SA	0303 4.1	0847 1.3	1503 4.2	2121 0.8
7 SU	0343 3.9	0922 1.4	1541 4.1	2159 0.9
8 M	0421 3.8	0956 1.4	1619 4.1	2236 1.1
9 TU	0500 3.7	1031 1.6	1659 3.9	2315 1.2
10 W	0541 3.5	1110 1.7	1742 3.8	2358 1.4
11 TH ◑	0627 3.4	1157 1.9	1832 3.6	
12 F	0049 1.6	0719 3.3	1258 2.0	1930 3.5
13 SA	0149 1.7	0820 3.3	1413 2.1	2039 3.4
14 SU	0257 1.8	0928 3.4	1533 2.0	2154 3.4
15 M	0406 1.8	1031 3.5	1642 1.8	2259 3.5
16 TU	0503 1.6	1122 3.7	1734 1.6	2352 3.7
17 W	0550 1.5	1207 3.9	1818 1.3	
18 TH	0038 3.9	0632 1.3	1247 4.0	1859 1.0
19 F ●	0122 4.1	0713 1.2	1326 4.2	1941 0.8
20 SA	0204 4.2	0754 1.0	1405 4.4	2023 0.6
21 SU	0246 4.3	0834 1.0	1445 4.4	2106 0.5
22 M	0328 4.2	0915 1.0	1526 4.5	2148 0.5
23 TU	0411 4.0	0956 1.0	1610 4.4	2233 0.6
24 W	0457 4.0	1039 1.1	1657 4.3	2320 0.8
25 TH ◐	0546 3.8	1127 1.3	1749 4.1	
26 F	0012 1.1	0641 3.7	1227 1.5	1851 3.9
27 SA	0114 1.3	0746 3.5	1339 1.6	2006 3.7
28 SU	0228 1.6	0901 3.5	1506 1.7	2133 3.6
29 M	0355 1.6	1017 3.6	1633 1.5	2254 3.7
30 TU	0507 1.6	1121 3.7	1738 1.3	2358 3.8
31 W	0600 1.5	1213 3.9	1829 1.1	

FEBRUARY

Day				
1 TH	0049 3.9	0643 1.4	1257 4.1	1911 0.9
2 F ○	0132 4.0	0720 1.2	1335 4.2	1950 0.7
3 SA	0208 4.0	0755 1.2	1410 4.3	2025 0.7
4 SU	0242 4.0	0815 0.9	1443 4.3	2057 0.7
5 M	0314 4.0	0856 1.1	1515 4.2	2128 0.8
6 TU	0345 3.9	0925 1.2	1547 4.1	2159 0.9
7 W	0417 3.8	0954 1.3	1620 4.0	2230 1.1
8 TH	0451 3.7	1026 1.4	1657 3.8	2304 1.3
9 F	0530 3.5	1103 1.6	1739 3.6	2344 1.5
10 SA	0616 3.4	1149 1.8	1832 3.4	
11 SU	0037 1.8	0714 3.3	1257 2.0	1942 3.3
12 M	0151 1.9	0826 3.2	1433 2.0	2109 3.2
13 TU	0323 1.9	0947 3.3	1611 1.9	2234 3.4
14 W	0441 1.8	1054 3.5	1714 1.5	2335 3.6
15 TH	0534 1.5	1145 3.7	1800 1.2	
16 F	0023 3.9	0617 1.3	1228 4.0	1842 0.8
17 SA ●	0105 4.1	0657 1.0	1307 4.3	1924 0.5
18 SU	0145 4.3	0737 0.8	1346 4.5	2005 0.3
19 M	0225 4.4	0815 0.7	1425 4.6	2045 0.2
20 TU	0305 4.4	0854 0.6	1506 4.7	2126 0.2
21 W	0345 4.3	0933 0.7	1548 4.6	2207 0.4
22 TH	0427 4.1	1014 0.9	1635 4.4	2251 0.8
23 F	0513 3.9	1100 1.1	1727 4.1	2340 1.1
24 SA ◐	0607 3.6	1158 1.4	1832 3.8	
25 SU	0042 1.5	0713 3.4	1316 1.6	1954 3.5
26 M	0207 1.8	0837 3.3	1501 1.7	2134 3.4
27 TU	0353 1.9	1006 3.4	1634 1.5	2259 3.5
28 W	0503 1.7	1114 3.6	1733 1.2	2357 3.7

MARCH

Day				
1 TH	0551 1.5	1203 3.8	1818 1.0	
2 F	0040 3.8	0629 1.3	1243 4.0	1855 0.8
3 SA ○	0115 3.9	0702 1.2	1317 4.1	1928 0.7
4 SU	0146 4.0	0733 1.0	1348 4.2	1959 0.6
5 M	0214 4.0	0801 0.9	1417 4.2	2028 0.6
6 TU	0242 4.0	0829 0.9	1446 4.2	2055 0.7
7 W	0309 3.9	0855 1.0	1516 4.1	2122 0.8
8 TH	0338 3.9	0923 1.1	1548 4.0	2150 1.0
9 F	0409 3.8	0952 1.2	1622 3.8	2220 1.2
10 SA	0444 3.6	1026 1.4	1702 3.6	2256 1.5
11 SU	0525 3.4	1108 1.6	1753 3.4	2343 1.7
12 M ◑	0620 3.3	1209 1.8	1905 3.2	
13 TU	0059 2.0	0735 3.2	1347 1.9	2034 3.1
14 W	0247 2.0	0902 3.2	1537 1.7	2207 3.3
15 TH	0416 1.8	1021 3.4	1647 1.4	2312 3.6
16 F	0511 1.5	1117 3.7	1735 1.0	2359 3.9
17 SA	0554 1.2	1201 4.0	1818 0.6	
18 SU	0040 4.1	0633 0.9	1241 4.3	1859 0.3
19 M ●	0120 4.3	0712 0.6	1321 4.6	1940 0.1
20 TU	0158 4.4	0751 0.5	1402 4.7	2020 0.1
21 W	0237 4.4	0830 0.4	1444 4.7	2100 0.2
22 TH	0317 4.3	0910 0.5	1529 4.6	2141 0.5
23 F	0359 4.1	0953 0.7	1618 4.3	2225 0.9
24 SA	0445 3.9	1043 1.0	1714 3.9	2315 1.3
25 SU ◐	0539 3.6	1144 1.2	1824 3.6	
26 M	0020 1.7	0649 3.4	1308 1.5	1949 3.3
27 TU	0153 2.0	0815 3.3	1456 1.5	2130 3.3
28 W	0341 1.9	0946 3.4	1620 1.3	2248 3.4
29 TH	0445 1.7	1053 3.6	1713 1.1	2339 3.6
30 F	0529 1.5	1140 3.7	1754 0.9	
31 SA	0016 3.7	0604 1.3	1218 3.9	1827 0.8

APRIL

Day				
1 SU	0047 3.8	0636 1.1	1250 4.0	1858 0.7
2 M ○	0115 3.9	0706 1.0	1320 4.1	1928 0.7
3 TU	0142 4.0	0734 0.9	1350 4.1	1955 0.7
4 W	0209 4.0	0802 0.9	1419 4.1	2022 0.8
5 TH	0237 3.9	0829 0.9	1450 4.0	2049 0.9
6 F	0306 3.9	0857 1.0	1523 3.9	2117 1.0
7 SA	0336 3.8	0928 1.1	1559 3.7	2148 1.2
8 SU	0411 3.7	1003 1.2	1640 3.5	2224 1.5
9 M	0451 3.5	1048 1.4	1733 3.4	2314 1.7
10 TU	0545 3.3	1152 1.6	1845 3.2	
11 W	0031 1.9	0700 3.2	1323 1.6	2009 3.2
12 TH	0215 1.9	0823 3.2	1459 1.5	2134 3.4
13 F	0339 1.7	0940 3.4	1610 1.2	2239 3.6
14 SA	0437 1.4	1040 3.7	1702 0.8	2328 3.9
15 SU	0523 1.1	1128 4.0	1748 0.5	
16 M	0010 4.1	0605 0.8	1213 4.3	1831 0.2
17 TU ●	0051 4.3	0646 0.6	1256 4.5	1913 0.2
18 W	0131 4.4	0727 0.4	1340 4.6	1955 0.2
19 TH	0211 4.4	0809 0.4	1426 4.6	2037 0.4
20 F	0252 4.3	0854 0.5	1514 4.4	2120 0.7
21 SA	0336 4.1	0941 0.8	1608 4.1	2205 1.1
22 SU	0424 3.9	1034 0.9	1708 3.8	2257 1.5
23 M	0520 3.6	1138 1.1	1817 3.5	
24 TU ◐	0002 1.8	0628 3.4	1257 1.3	1934 3.3
25 W	0128 2.0	0746 3.3	1427 1.4	2100 3.3
26 TH	0301 1.9	0909 3.4	1544 1.3	2212 3.3
27 F	0407 1.7	1015 3.5	1637 1.1	2302 3.5
28 SA	0453 1.5	1104 3.6	1718 1.0	2340 3.6
29 SU	0531 1.3	1143 3.7	1753 0.9	
30 M	0012 3.7	0605 1.2	1218 3.8	1824 0.9

Chart Datum: 2·25 metres below Ordnance Datum (Newlyn)

TIDES

TIME ZONE (UT)
For Summer Time add ONE hour in **non-shaded areas**

SCOTLAND – ABERDEEN
LAT 57°09'N   LONG 2°05'W
TIMES AND HEIGHTS OF HIGH AND LOW WATERS

Dates in amber are **SPRINGS**
Dates in yellow are **NEAPS**

2007

MAY

Day	Time	m	Time	m	Time	m	Time	m
1 TU	0041	3.8	0637	1.0	1251	3.9	1855	0.8
2 W ○	0110	3.9	0708	1.0	1323	3.9	1924	0.8
3 TH	0139	3.9	0738	0.9	1356	3.9	1953	0.9
4 F	0209	3.9	0808	0.9	1430	3.9	2023	1.0
5 SA	0240	3.9	0840	1.0	1506	3.8	2054	1.1
6 SU	0313	3.8	0915	1.0	1545	3.7	2129	1.3
7 M	0349	3.7	0955	1.1	1630	3.5	2211	1.5
8 TU	0433	3.6	1044	1.2	1725	3.4	2304	1.6
9 W	0527	3.5	1146	1.3	1831	3.3		
10 TH ◐	0015	1.8	0634	3.4	1303	1.3	1943	3.3
11 F	0139	1.8	0747	3.4	1420	1.2	2055	3.4
12 SA	0254	1.6	0858	3.5	1528	1.0	2200	3.6
13 SU	0356	1.4	1001	3.8	1625	0.8	2253	3.8
14 M	0448	1.1	1056	4.0	1716	0.6	2340	4.0
15 TU	0537	0.9	1146	4.2	1804	0.4		
16 W ●	0023	4.2	0623	0.7	1235	4.4	1849	0.4
17 TH	0106	4.2	0709	0.5	1324	4.4	1934	0.5
18 F	0149	4.3	0756	0.5	1414	4.3	2019	0.7
19 SA	0233	4.2	0844	0.5	1507	4.2	2104	0.9
20 SU	0319	4.1	0934	0.6	1602	4.0	2151	1.2
21 M	0409	3.9	1027	0.8	1700	3.7	2241	1.5
22 TU	0503	3.7	1125	1.0	1759	3.5	2338	1.7
23 W ◐	0603	3.6	1229	1.1	1901	3.3		
24 TH	0044	1.8	0706	3.5	1337	1.3	2007	3.2
25 F	0156	1.9	0814	3.4	1444	1.3	2114	3.3
26 SA	0306	1.8	0921	3.4	1544	1.3	2209	3.3
27 SU	0404	1.7	1017	3.5	1632	1.2	2254	3.5
28 M	0451	1.5	1104	3.6	1713	1.2	2332	3.6
29 TU	0532	1.3	1145	3.7	1750	1.1		
30 W	0007	3.7	0609	1.2	1224	3.7	1824	1.1
31 TH	0041	3.8	0644	1.1	1302	3.8	1857	1.1

JUNE

Day	Time	m	Time	m	Time	m	Time	m
1 F ○	0114	3.9	0719	1.0	1339	3.8	1931	1.1
2 SA	0147	3.9	0754	1.0	1416	3.8	2006	1.1
3 SU	0221	3.9	0831	0.9	1456	3.8	2042	1.2
4 M	0257	3.9	0910	0.9	1537	3.7	2122	1.2
5 TU	0337	3.9	0953	0.9	1624	3.7	2205	1.3
6 W	0421	3.8	1041	1.0	1715	3.6	2255	1.4
7 TH	0512	3.7	1135	1.0	1812	3.5	2354	1.5
8 F ◐	0610	3.7	1237	1.0	1913	3.5		
9 SA	0101	1.6	0713	3.7	1343	1.0	2016	3.5
10 SU	0209	1.5	0819	3.7	1447	1.0	2121	3.6
11 M	0315	1.4	0926	3.8	1550	0.9	2220	3.7
12 TU	0417	1.2	1029	3.9	1650	0.8	2313	3.9
13 W	0515	1.0	1128	4.1	1744	0.8		
14 TH	0002	4.0	0609	0.8	1224	4.2	1835	0.8
15 F ●	0050	4.1	0700	0.7	1317	4.2	1922	0.9
16 SA	0135	4.2	0750	0.5	1410	4.2	2008	1.0
17 SU	0221	4.2	0838	0.5	1501	4.1	2052	1.1
18 M	0306	4.1	0926	0.6	1551	3.9	2135	1.2
19 TU	0353	4.0	1013	0.7	1640	3.8	2218	1.4
20 W	0440	3.9	1100	0.8	1728	3.6	2303	1.5
21 TH	0529	3.8	1149	1.0	1817	3.4	2352	1.6
22 F ◐	0620	3.6	1240	1.2	1908	3.3		
23 SA	0048	1.7	0714	3.5	1335	1.4	2003	3.2
24 SU	0152	1.8	0814	3.4	1434	1.5	2103	3.3
25 M	0300	1.8	0920	3.4	1534	1.5	2201	3.3
26 TU	0406	1.7	1021	3.4	1630	1.4	2251	3.5
27 W	0500	1.6	1114	3.5	1717	1.4	2336	3.6
28 TH	0545	1.4	1201	3.6	1759	1.3		
29 F	0016	3.7	0625	1.2	1245	3.7	1837	1.2
30 SA ○	0054	3.9	0703	1.1	1325	3.8	1915	1.2

JULY

Day	Time	m	Time	m	Time	m	Time	m
1 SU	0130	4.0	0742	0.9	1405	3.9	1953	1.1
2 M	0207	4.0	0821	0.8	1446	3.9	2032	1.1
3 TU	0245	4.1	0902	0.7	1527	3.9	2112	1.1
4 W	0324	4.1	0944	0.7	1610	3.9	2153	1.1
5 TH	0406	4.1	1028	0.7	1656	3.8	2237	1.2
6 F	0452	4.0	1115	0.8	1745	3.7	2326	1.3
7 SA ◐	0544	3.9	1208	0.9	1839	3.6		
8 SU	0024	1.4	0641	3.9	1307	1.0	1939	3.6
9 M	0130	1.5	0747	3.8	1412	1.1	2045	3.6
10 TU	0241	1.5	0900	3.7	1523	1.0	2153	3.6
11 W	0357	1.4	1016	3.8	1635	1.0	2256	3.7
12 TH	0507	1.2	1124	3.9	1737	1.2	2352	3.9
13 F	0606	0.9	1224	4.0	1829	1.1		
14 SA ●	0041	4.0	0658	0.7	1318	4.0	1915	1.1
15 SU	0127	4.2	0745	0.6	1406	4.1	1957	1.1
16 M	0210	4.2	0828	0.5	1449	4.0	2036	1.1
17 TU	0250	4.2	0909	0.5	1530	4.0	2112	1.1
18 W	0330	4.2	0948	0.6	1609	3.8	2148	1.2
19 TH	0409	4.1	1025	0.8	1648	3.7	2223	1.3
20 F	0448	3.9	1103	1.0	1727	3.6	2300	1.5
21 SA	0530	3.7	1143	1.2	1809	3.4	2343	1.6
22 SU ◐	0617	3.6	1229	1.4	1858	3.3		
23 M	0038	1.8	0712	3.4	1325	1.6	1955	3.3
24 TU	0150	1.9	0819	3.3	1432	1.7	2102	3.3
25 W	0313	1.9	0937	3.3	1546	1.7	2210	3.4
26 TH	0431	1.7	1047	3.4	1651	1.7	2307	3.5
27 F	0525	1.5	1143	3.5	1739	1.5	2353	3.7
28 SA	0608	1.3	1229	3.7	1821	1.3		
29 SU	0034	3.9	0647	1.0	1310	3.9	1859	1.2
30 M ○	0112	4.1	0726	0.7	1349	4.0	1937	1.0
31 TU	0149	4.2	0805	0.5	1428	4.1	2016	0.9

AUGUST

Day	Time	m	Time	m	Time	m	Time	m
1 W	0226	4.3	0845	0.4	1507	4.2	2054	0.8
2 TH	0305	4.4	0925	0.4	1547	4.1	2133	0.9
3 F	0346	4.4	1006	0.5	1629	4.0	2213	1.0
4 SA	0429	4.3	1049	0.6	1715	3.9	2258	1.1
5 SU	0518	4.1	1137	0.9	1806	3.7	2351	1.3
6 M ◐	0616	3.9	1234	1.2	1907	3.6		
7 TU	0059	1.5	0726	3.7	1345	1.4	2018	3.5
8 W	0223	1.6	0851	3.6	1511	1.6	2137	3.5
9 TH	0357	1.5	1019	3.6	1635	1.6	2249	3.7
10 F	0510	1.2	1132	3.8	1736	1.4	2347	3.9
11 SA	0606	0.9	1227	3.9	1823	1.3		
12 SU ●	0035	4.1	0651	0.7	1313	4.0	1903	1.2
13 M	0116	4.2	0732	0.6	1352	4.1	1939	1.1
14 TU	0152	4.3	0809	0.5	1427	4.1	2013	1.0
15 W	0227	4.3	0843	0.5	1500	4.0	2044	1.0
16 TH	0301	4.3	0915	0.6	1532	3.9	2114	1.1
17 F	0334	4.2	0946	0.8	1604	3.8	2144	1.2
18 SA	0408	4.0	1016	1.0	1637	3.7	2215	1.4
19 SU	0445	3.8	1049	1.2	1715	3.5	2252	1.5
20 M ◐	0528	3.6	1128	1.5	1800	3.4	2338	1.7
21 TU	0621	3.4	1219	1.7	1856	3.3		
22 W	0044	1.9	0729	3.2	1332	1.9	2006	3.2
23 TH	0221	2.0	0855	3.2	1506	2.0	2126	3.3
24 F	0403	1.8	1021	3.3	1627	1.8	2237	3.5
25 SA	0503	1.5	1122	3.5	1719	1.6	2328	3.7
26 SU	0546	1.2	1208	3.8	1800	1.3		
27 M	0010	4.0	0625	0.9	1248	4.0	1838	1.1
28 TU ○	0048	4.2	0703	0.6	1325	4.2	1915	0.9
29 W	0125	4.4	0742	0.3	1403	4.3	1952	0.7
30 TH	0202	4.6	0821	0.2	1440	4.4	2030	0.7
31 F	0241	4.6	0900	0.2	1519	4.4	2108	0.7

Chart Datum: 2·25 metres below Ordnance Datum (Newlyn)

TIME ZONE (UT)
For Summer Time add ONE hour in **non-shaded areas**

Dates in amber are **SPRINGS**
Dates in yellow are **NEAPS**

2007

SEPTEMBER

Day	Time	m	Day	Time	m
1 SA	0322	4.6	**16** SU	0333	4.0
	0939	0.4		0935	1.1
	1600	4.2		1554	3.9
	2148	0.8		2140	1.3
2 SU	0407	4.4	**17** M	0409	3.9
	1021	0.7		1005	1.3
	1644	4.0		1629	3.7
	2233	1.0		2214	1.5
3 M	0458	4.2	**18** TU	0450	3.6
	1109	1.1		1040	1.6
	1736	3.8		1711	3.6
	2329	1.3		2258	1.7
4 TU	0600	3.9	**19** W	0543	3.4
	1208	1.5		1127	1.8
	1840	3.6 ◐		1806	3.4 ◐
5 W	0044	1.5	**20** TH	0000	1.9
	0719	3.6		0653	3.2
	1329	1.8		1240	2.1
	1959	3.4		1919	3.3
6 TH	0223	1.6	**21** F	0137	2.0
	0856	3.5		0820	3.2
	1513	1.6		1427	2.1
	2129	3.5		2042	3.3
7 F	0402	1.4	**22** SA	0324	1.8
	1028	3.6		0950	3.3
	1634	1.8		1557	1.9
	2243	3.7		2200	3.5
8 SA	0507	1.2	**23** SU	0431	1.5
	1132	3.8		1053	3.6
	1727	1.5		1650	1.6
	2337	3.9		2255	3.8
9 SU	0555	0.9	**24** M	0516	1.1
	1218	3.9		1139	3.9
	1808	1.3		1732	1.3
				2339	4.1
10 M	0020	4.1	**25** TU	0556	0.8
	0635	0.7		1218	4.1
	1255	4.0		1810	1.0
	1843	1.2			
11 TU	0056	4.2	**26** W	0018	4.3
	0709	0.6		0635	0.5
	1327	4.1		1256	4.4
	1915	1.0 ●		1848	0.8 ○
12 W	0128	4.3	**27** TH	0056	4.6
	0741	0.6		0714	0.3
	1357	4.1		1333	4.5
	1945	1.0		1926	0.6
13 TH	0159	4.3	**28** F	0136	4.7
	0811	0.6		0753	0.2
	1425	4.1		1411	4.5
	2014	1.0		2004	0.6
14 F	0230	4.3	**29** SA	0218	4.8
	0839	0.7		0833	0.3
	1454	4.0		1450	4.4
	2042	1.0		2045	0.6
15 SA	0301	4.2	**30** SU	0302	4.7
	0907	0.9		0913	0.6
	1523	4.0		1532	4.3
	2110	1.1		2128	0.8

OCTOBER

Day	Time	m	Day	Time	m
1 M	0350	4.4	**16** TU	0344	3.8
	0957	0.9		0932	1.4
	1618	4.1		1555	3.8
	2218	1.0		2151	1.4
2 TU	0446	4.1	**17** W	0426	3.7
	1047	1.3		1008	1.6
	1712	3.8		1635	3.7
	2319	1.3		2236	1.6
3 W	0555	3.8	**18** TH	0519	3.5
	1151	1.7		1055	1.9
	1820	3.6		1728	3.5
				2337	1.8 ◐
4 TH	0040	1.5	**19** F	0628	3.3
	0718	3.5		1206	2.1
	1319	2.0		1840	3.4 ◐
	1943	3.5			
5 F	0222	1.5	**20** SA	0102	1.8
	0856	3.5		0747	3.3
	1504	2.0		1345	2.1
	2113	3.6		1958	3.4
6 SA	0350	1.4	**21** SU	0235	1.7
	1019	3.6		0908	3.4
	1616	1.8		1511	1.9
	2224	3.7		2113	3.6
7 SU	0448	1.2	**22** M	0345	1.4
	1114	3.8		1014	3.7
	1705	1.6		1610	1.7
	2315	3.9		2214	3.8
8 M	0532	1.0	**23** TU	0437	1.1
	1154	3.9		1103	4.0
	1743	1.4		1657	1.4
	2355	4.1		2302	4.1
9 TU	0608	0.9	**24** W	0522	0.8
	1227	4.0		1145	4.2
	1817	1.2		1739	1.1
				2346	4.4
10 W	0029	4.2	**25** TH	0604	0.5
	0645	0.6		1225	4.4
	1257	4.1		1820	0.8
	1847	1.1			
11 TH	0101	4.3	**26** F	0029	4.6
	0709	0.8		0645	0.4
	1324	4.1		1305	4.5
	1917	1.0 ●		1901	0.7 ○
12 F	0131	4.3	**27** SA	0113	4.7
	0738	0.8		0727	0.4
	1352	4.1		1345	4.5
	1946	1.0		1943	0.6
13 SA	0202	4.2	**28** SU	0159	4.7
	0806	0.9		0810	0.6
	1420	4.1		1426	4.5
	2015	1.1		2028	0.6
14 SU	0234	4.1	**29** M	0248	4.6
	0833	1.0		0853	0.8
	1449	4.1		1510	4.3
	2044	1.2		2117	0.8
15 M	0307	4.0	**30** TU	0341	4.3
	0901	1.2		0940	1.2
	1520	4.0		1558	4.1
	2115	1.3		2211	1.0
			31 W	0442	4.0
				1032	1.5
				1654	3.9
				2314	1.2

NOVEMBER

Day	Time	m	Day	Time	m
1 TH	0551	3.8	**16** F	0504	3.6
	1136	1.9		1040	1.8
	1802	3.7 ◐		1703	3.7
				2322	1.5
2 F	0030	1.4	**17** SA	0605	3.5
	0705	3.5		1141	1.9
	1257	2.1		1805	3.6 ◑
	1918	3.6			
3 SA	0156	1.4	**18** SU	0030	1.6
	0829	3.5		0712	3.5
	1425	2.1		1259	2.0
	2038	3.6		1914	3.6
4 SU	0315	1.4	**19** M	0146	1.5
	0944	3.5		0821	3.5
	1537	1.9		1417	1.9
	2148	3.7		2023	3.7
5 M	0413	1.3	**20** TU	0254	1.3
	1039	3.7		0927	3.7
	1630	1.7		1522	1.7
	2241	3.8		2128	3.9
6 TU	0458	1.2	**21** W	0353	1.1
	1120	3.8		1024	3.9
	1711	1.6		1617	1.5
	2323	4.0		2226	4.1
7 W	0535	1.1	**22** TH	0446	0.9
	1154	3.9		1113	4.1
	1747	1.4		1708	1.2
				2318	4.3
8 TH	0000	4.0	**23** F	0535	0.7
	0607	1.1		1157	4.3
	1225	4.0		1756	1.0
	1820	1.3			
9 F	0034	4.1	**24** SA	0008	4.5
	0638	1.0		0622	0.7
	1254	4.1		1241	4.4
	1853	1.2 ●		1843	0.8 ○
10 SA	0107	4.1	**25** SU	0058	4.6
	0708	1.0		0708	0.7
	1323	4.1		1324	4.5
	1924	1.1		1931	0.7
11 SU	0141	4.1	**26** M	0149	4.6
	0738	1.1		0754	0.9
	1353	4.1		1408	4.5
	1955	1.1		2021	0.6
12 M	0215	4.1	**27** TU	0241	4.5
	0808	1.2		0841	1.1
	1424	4.1		1455	4.4
	2027	1.2		2112	0.7
13 TU	0251	4.0	**28** W	0337	4.3
	0839	1.3		0928	1.3
	1456	4.0		1544	4.2
	2102	1.2		2205	0.8
14 W	0329	3.8	**29** TH	0434	4.0
	0913	1.5		1018	1.5
	1532	4.0		1638	4.1
	2141	1.3		2302	1.0
15 TH	0413	3.7	**30** F	0533	3.8
	0952	1.6		1112	1.8
	1613	3.8		1737	3.9
	2226	1.4			

DECEMBER

Day	Time	m	Day	Time	m
1 SA	0003	1.2	**16** SU	0538	3.7
	0634	3.6		1115	1.7
	1215	1.9		1734	3.9
	1839	3.8 ◑		2358	1.3
2 SU	0109	1.4	**17** M	0634	3.6
	0739	3.5		1214	1.7
	1323	2.0		1833	3.8 ◐
	1946	3.7			
3 M	0215	1.5	**18** TU	0100	1.3
	0846	3.4		0735	3.6
	1434	2.0		1323	1.8
	2055	3.6		1937	3.8
4 TU	0319	1.5	**19** W	0206	1.3
	0947	3.5		0841	3.7
	1540	1.9		1433	1.7
	2156	3.7		2045	3.9
5 W	0413	1.5	**20** TH	0311	1.2
	1036	3.6		0945	3.8
	1633	1.8		1540	1.6
	2247	3.7		2154	4.0
6 TH	0457	1.4	**21** F	0415	1.2
	1117	3.7		1044	3.9
	1718	1.6		1644	1.4
	2331	3.8		2258	4.1
7 F	0536	1.4	**22** SA	0516	1.1
	1154	3.9		1136	4.1
	1757	1.5		1743	1.1
				2357	4.3
8 SA	0011	3.9	**23** SU	0610	1.0
	0611	1.3		1225	4.3
	1228	4.0		1837	0.9
	1833	1.3			
9 SU	0050	3.9	**24** M	0053	4.4
	0645	1.3		0659	1.0
	1301	4.1		1312	4.4
	1908	1.2 ●		1927	0.7 ○
10 M	0127	4.0	**25** TU	0146	4.4
	0718	1.3		0746	1.1
	1334	4.1		1358	4.4
	1943	1.2		2017	0.6
11 TU	0204	4.0	**26** W	0238	4.3
	0752	1.3		0831	1.1
	1407	4.1		1444	4.4
	2018	1.1		2105	0.6
12 W	0241	4.0	**27** TH	0328	4.2
	0827	1.3		0914	1.2
	1441	4.1		1530	4.4
	2055	1.1		2152	0.7
13 TH	0320	3.9	**28** F	0416	4.1
	0903	1.4		0956	1.4
	1518	4.1		1616	4.2
	2134	1.1		2238	0.8
14 F	0401	3.8	**29** SA	0503	3.9
	0942	1.5		1039	1.5
	1557	4.0		1704	4.1
	2216	1.2		2325	1.1
15 SA	0447	3.8	**30** SU	0551	3.7
	1025	1.6		1125	1.7
	1642	3.9		1754	3.9
	2304	1.2			
			31 M	0014	1.3
				0641	3.5
				1217	1.8
				1847	3.7 ◑

Chart Datum: 2·25 metres below Ordnance Datum (Newlyn)

TIDES

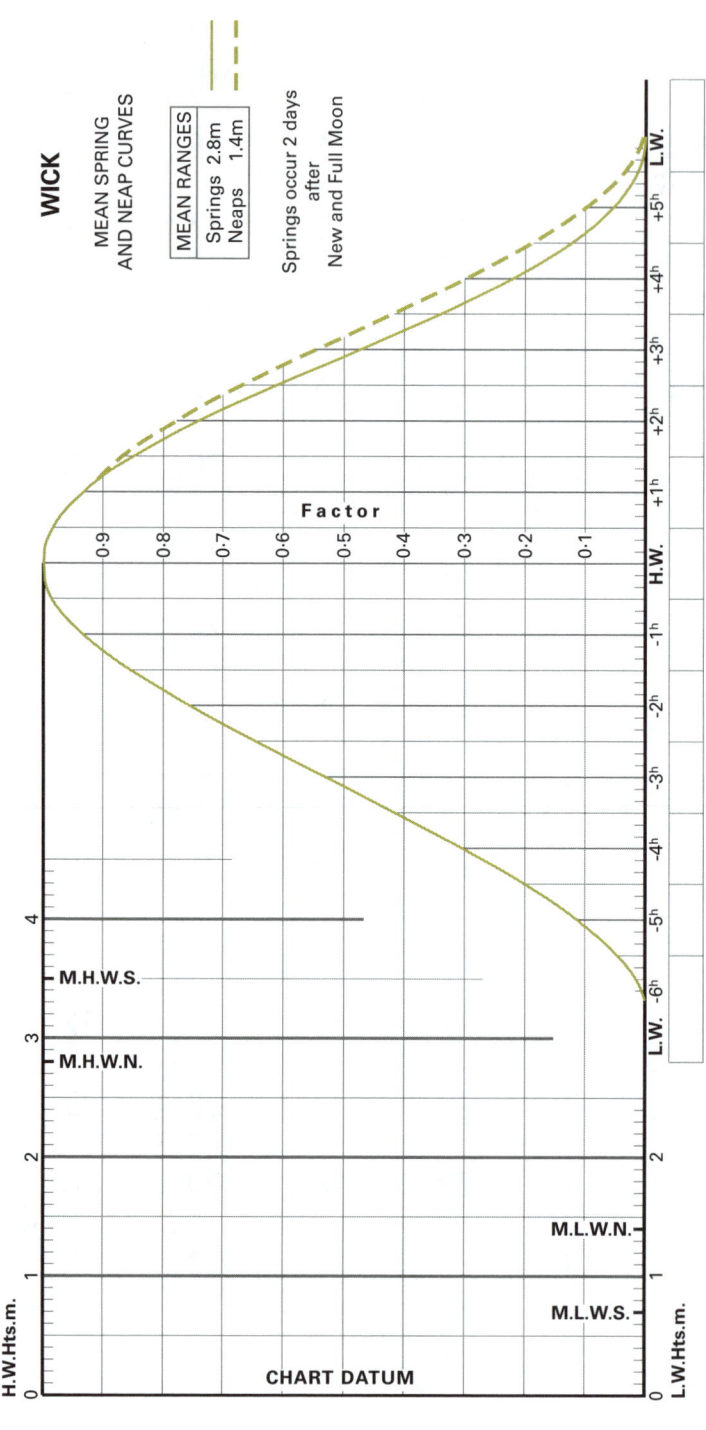

WICK

MEAN SPRING
AND NEAP CURVES

MEAN RANGES	
Springs	2.8m
Neaps	1.4m

Springs occur 2 days
after
New and Full Moon

TIME ZONE (UT)
For Summer Time add ONE hour in **non-shaded areas**

SCOTLAND – WICK
LAT 58°26'N   LONG 3°05'W
TIMES AND HEIGHTS OF HIGH AND LOW WATERS

Dates in amber are SPRINGS
Dates in yellow are NEAPS
2007

JANUARY

Day	Time	m	Time	m	Time	m	Time	m
1 M	0300	1.1	0920	3.2	1528	1.1	2145	3.3
16 TU	0256	1.4	0909	3.0	1529	1.3	2141	3.0
2 TU	0351	1.1	1011	3.4	1620	1.0	2239	3.3
17 W	0341	1.3	0955	3.2	1612	1.1	2228	3.1
3 W	0435	1.1	1057	3.5	1707	0.8	○2329	3.4
18 TH	0421	1.2	1038	3.3	1652	0.9	2313	3.3
4 TH	0517	1.1	1141	3.5	1751	0.7		
19 F	0500	1.1	1120	3.5	1731	0.7	●2356	3.4
5 F	0013	3.3	0555	1.1	1222	3.6	1832	0.7
20 SA	0540	1.0	1201	3.6	1812	0.6		
6 SA	0056	3.3	0631	1.2	1301	3.5	1911	0.6
21 SU	0039	3.4	0619	0.9	1243	3.7	1853	0.5
7 SU	0135	3.2	0705	1.2	1338	3.5	1948	0.8
22 M	0123	3.4	0659	0.9	1325	3.7	1935	0.5
8 M	0213	3.1	0738	1.3	1415	3.3	2024	1.0
23 TU	0207	3.3	0739	0.9	1408	3.6	2019	0.6
9 TU	0250	2.9	0810	1.4	1452	3.2	2101	1.1
24 W	0251	3.2	0820	1.0	1453	3.5	2106	0.7
10 W	0330	2.8	0845	1.6	1533	3.1	2144	1.2
25 TH	0339	3.1	0906	1.2	1544	3.4	◑2200	1.0
11 TH	0415	2.7	0928	1.6	1620	2.9	◐2238	1.4
26 F	0432	2.9	1001	1.3	1643	3.2	2308	1.2
12 F	0507	2.7	1029	1.7	1718	2.8	2344	1.5
27 SA	0534	2.8	1128	1.4	1754	3.0		
13 SA	0608	2.7	1202	1.7	1827	2.7		
28 SU	0027	1.3	0645	2.8	1304	1.4	1917	2.9
14 SU	0055	1.5	0713	2.7	1330	1.7	1939	2.8
29 M	0150	1.4	0802	2.9	1429	1.3	2041	3.0
15 M	0201	1.5	0816	2.8	1439	1.5	2046	2.9
30 TU	0258	1.4	0909	3.1	1532	1.1	2147	3.1
31 W	0348	1.3	1003	3.2	1620	0.9	2238	3.2

FEBRUARY

Day	Time	m	Time	m	Time	m	Time	m
1 TH	0430	1.2	1049	3.4	1702	0.8	2322	3.2
16 F	0407	1.1	1018	3.3	1635	0.7	2257	3.3
2 F	0506	1.1	1130	3.5	1739	0.7	○	
17 SA	0445	0.9	1101	3.5	1714	0.5	●2340	3.5
3 SA	0001	3.3	0539	1.1	1208	3.5	1812	0.6
18 SU	0523	0.8	1143	3.7	1754	0.3		
4 SU	0036	3.3	0610	1.0	1242	3.5	1845	0.6
19 M	0021	3.5	0600	0.6	1225	3.8	1833	0.2
5 M	0109	3.3	0640	1.0	1314	3.5	1916	0.7
20 TU	0103	3.6	0638	0.6	1306	3.8	1913	0.3
6 TU	0140	3.1	0709	1.0	1345	3.4	1945	0.8
21 W	0143	3.4	0717	0.7	1348	3.7	1953	0.4
7 W	0210	3.0	0736	1.1	1415	3.3	2014	0.9
22 TH	0224	3.3	0756	0.8	1432	3.6	2035	0.7
8 TH	0241	2.9	0806	1.2	1447	3.1	2046	1.1
23 F	0307	3.1	0839	1.0	1522	3.3	2122	1.0
9 F	0316	2.8	0839	1.3	1525	2.9	2123	1.3
24 SA	0357	2.9	0934	1.2	1622	3.0	◑2228	1.3
10 SA	0358	2.7	0921	1.5	1614	2.8	◐2216	1.5
25 SU	0458	2.8	1110	1.4	1739	2.8		
11 SU	0454	2.6	1028	1.7	1723	2.6	2346	1.6
26 M	0005	1.6	0616	2.7	1304	1.4	1916	2.7
12 M	0606	2.6	1239	1.7	1852	2.6		
27 TU	0147	1.6	0746	2.8	1430	1.2	2045	2.8
13 TU	0121	1.6	0726	2.7	1414	1.5	2019	2.7
28 W	0255	1.5	0858	3.0	1526	1.0	2143	2.9
14 W	0234	1.5	0837	2.8	1511	1.3	2123	2.9
15 TH	0325	1.3	0932	3.1	1555	1.0	2213	3.1

MARCH

Day	Time	m	Time	m	Time	m	Time	m
1 TH	0341	1.3	0951	3.1	1609	0.8	2227	3.1
16 F	0302	1.2	0903	3.0	1529	0.8	2151	3.1
2 F	0416	1.2	1034	3.3	1644	0.7	2305	3.2
17 SA	0343	1.0	0952	3.2	1610	0.5	2235	3.3
3 SA	0447	1.0	1111	3.4	1716	0.6	○2338	3.2
18 SU	0421	0.8	1037	3.5	1649	0.3	2316	3.5
4 SU	0517	0.9	1145	3.5	1745	0.6		
19 M	0459	0.6	1120	3.7	1729	0.1	●2357	3.5
5 M	0009	3.2	0545	0.8	1217	3.5	1814	0.6
20 TU	0537	0.5	1202	3.8	1808	0.1		
6 TU	0039	3.2	0613	0.8	1247	3.4	1842	0.6
21 W	0037	3.5	0615	0.4	1245	3.8	1847	0.2
7 W	0106	3.2	0640	0.8	1314	3.3	1909	0.7
22 TH	0116	3.4	0655	0.5	1328	3.7	1927	0.5
8 TH	0133	3.1	0707	0.9	1343	3.2	1935	0.9
23 F	0156	3.3	0737	0.6	1414	3.5	2008	0.8
9 F	0201	3.0	0734	1.0	1413	3.1	2003	1.0
24 SA	0238	3.1	0823	0.8	1506	3.2	2054	1.2
10 SA	0232	2.9	0805	1.2	1449	2.9	2034	1.2
25 SU	0328	2.9	0926	1.1	1610	2.8	◑2201	1.5
11 SU	0311	2.8	0843	1.3	1535	2.7	2116	1.4
26 M	0431	2.7	1110	1.2	1733	2.6	2349	1.7
12 M	0400	2.7	0938	1.5	1640	2.5	◐2233	1.6
27 TU	0554	2.7	1257	1.2	1913	2.6		
13 TU	0511	2.6	1156	1.6	1817	2.5		
28 W	0134	1.6	0724	2.7	1415	1.0	2031	2.7
14 W	0046	1.6	0640	2.6	1342	1.4	1954	2.6
29 TH	0237	1.5	0835	2.9	1505	0.9	2123	2.9
15 TH	0209	1.5	0801	2.7	1444	1.1	2101	2.8
30 F	0319	1.3	0926	3.0	1544	0.8	2203	3.0
31 SA	0352	1.1	1008	3.2	1616	0.7	2237	3.1

APRIL

Day	Time	m	Time	m	Time	m	Time	m
1 SU	0421	1.0	1044	3.3	1645	0.6	2309	3.1
16 M	0353	0.7	1008	3.5	1621	0.2	2248	3.4
2 M	0450	0.8	1118	3.3	1714	0.6	○2338	3.2
17 TU	0433	0.5	1054	3.6	1702	0.1	●2330	3.5
3 TU	0518	0.8	1148	3.3	1742	0.6		
18 W	0514	0.4	1140	3.7	1743	0.2		
4 W	0006	3.2	0546	0.7	1218	3.3	1809	0.6
19 TH	0010	3.5	0556	0.4	1226	3.7	1823	0.4
5 TH	0034	3.2	0614	0.8	1247	3.2	1835	0.7
20 F	0051	3.4	0639	0.4	1313	3.5	1905	0.7
6 F	0101	3.1	0642	0.8	1317	3.1	1902	0.9
21 SA	0132	3.3	0726	0.6	1402	3.3	1948	1.0
7 SA	0129	3.1	0711	0.9	1349	3.0	1930	1.0
22 SU	0217	3.1	0820	0.8	1457	3.0	2036	1.3
8 SU	0201	3.0	0744	1.0	1427	2.8	2003	1.2
23 M	0308	3.0	0931	0.9	1602	2.7	2144	1.5
9 M	0240	2.8	0825	1.2	1515	2.7	2047	1.4
24 TU	0411	2.8	1059	1.1	1719	2.6	◑2319	1.6
10 TU	0329	2.7	0924	1.3	1622	2.5	◐2203	1.6
25 W	0528	2.7	1227	1.1	1843	2.5		
11 W	0436	2.6	1128	1.3	1753	2.5		
26 TH	0053	1.6	0647	2.7	1339	1.0	1955	2.6
12 TH	0012	1.6	0603	2.6	1303	1.2	1922	2.6
27 F	0159	1.5	0756	2.8	1429	0.9	2046	2.7
13 F	0132	1.4	0722	2.7	1407	0.9	2029	2.8
28 SA	0244	1.3	0850	2.9	1508	0.8	2127	2.8
14 SA	0228	1.2	0827	3.0	1457	0.6	2121	3.1
29 SU	0319	1.1	0934	3.0	1541	0.7	2203	3.0
15 SU	0312	0.9	0920	3.2	1540	0.4	2206	3.3
30 M	0351	1.0	1012	3.1	1611	0.7	2235	3.0

Chart Datum: 1·71 metres below Ordnance Datum (Newlyn)

TIME ZONE (UT)
For Summer Time add ONE hour in **non-shaded areas**

SCOTLAND – WICK
LAT 58°26′N   LONG 3°05′W
TIMES AND HEIGHTS OF HIGH AND LOW WATERS

Dates in amber are SPRINGS
Dates in yellow are NEAPS

2007

MAY

Day	Time m	Time m	Time m	Time m
1 TU	0422 0.9	1047 3.1	1641 0.7	2306 3.1
2 W	0453 0.8	1120 3.2	1711 0.7	○ 2336 3.1
3 TH	0524 0.8	1152 3.1	1740 0.8	
4 F	0005 3.2	0554 0.8	1225 3.1	1808 0.8
5 SA	0035 3.1	0625 0.8	1259 3.0	1838 1.0
6 SU	0107 3.1	0659 0.9	1335 2.9	1911 1.1
7 M	0142 3.0	0737 0.9	1417 2.8	1950 1.2
8 TU	0223 2.9	0824 1.0	1507 2.7	2040 1.3
9 W	0313 2.8	0929 1.1	1612 2.6	2153 1.5
10 TH	0416 2.7	1102 1.1	1730 2.6	◑ 2331 1.4
11 F	0531 2.7	1222 1.0	1845 2.7	
12 SA	0046 1.3	0644 2.8	1326 0.8	1950 2.8
13 SU	0147 1.1	0748 3.0	1421 0.6	2046 3.0
14 M	0238 1.0	0847 3.2	1509 0.4	2135 3.2
15 TU	0325 0.8	0941 3.4	1554 0.4	2220 3.3
16 W	0410 0.6	1032 3.5	1638 0.4	● 2304 3.4
17 TH	0456 0.5	1122 3.5	1722 0.5	2348 3.4
18 F	0544 0.4	1212 3.5	1806 0.6	
19 SA	0031 3.4	0632 0.4	1302 3.3	1849 0.9
20 SU	0115 3.3	0723 0.5	1353 3.1	1934 1.1
21 M	0201 3.2	0818 0.7	1447 2.9	2022 1.3
22 TU	0252 3.0	0920 0.8	1546 2.7	2118 1.4
23 W	0349 2.9	1027 0.9	1648 2.6	◐ 2227 1.5
24 TH	0453 2.8	1135 1.0	1753 2.5	2342 1.5
25 F	0559 2.7	1241 1.0	1857 2.6	
26 SA	0055 1.5	0703 2.7	1337 1.0	1954 2.6
27 SU	0154 1.4	0802 2.8	1423 1.0	2042 2.7
28 M	0239 1.2	0853 2.8	1502 0.9	2123 2.8
29 TU	0319 1.1	0937 2.9	1537 0.9	2200 3.0
30 W	0356 1.0	1017 3.0	1612 0.9	2235 3.1
31 TH	0432 0.9	1055 3.0	1645 0.9	2308 3.1

JUNE

Day	Time m	Time m	Time m	Time m
1 F	0507 0.9	1132 3.0	1717 0.9	○ 2342 3.2
2 SA	0542 0.8	1209 3.0	1750 0.9	
3 SU	0016 3.2	0617 0.8	1247 3.0	1825 1.0
4 M	0052 3.2	0656 0.8	1328 2.9	1904 1.1
5 TU	0131 3.1	0738 0.8	1412 2.9	1946 1.1
6 W	0213 3.1	0826 0.8	1501 2.8	2035 1.2
7 TH	0301 3.0	0923 0.8	1558 2.7	2134 1.3
8 F	0357 2.9	1031 0.9	1702 2.7	◑ 2246 1.3
9 SA	0501 2.9	1141 0.8	1807 2.7	2359 1.3
10 SU	0608 2.9	1246 0.8	1910 2.8	
11 M	0106 1.2	0713 3.0	1347 0.7	2010 2.9
12 TU	0207 1.0	0819 3.1	1442 0.7	2106 3.1
13 W	0304 0.9	0921 3.2	1534 0.7	2157 3.2
14 TH	0358 0.7	1019 3.3	1622 0.7	2246 3.3
15 F	0449 0.6	1113 3.3	1709 0.8	● 2332 3.4
16 SA	0540 0.5	1205 3.3	1754 0.9	
17 SU	0018 3.4	0628 0.5	1255 3.2	1837 1.0
18 M	0103 3.4	0717 0.5	1343 3.1	1919 1.1
19 TU	0147 3.3	0804 0.6	1430 3.0	2000 1.2
20 W	0232 3.2	0851 0.7	1517 2.8	2041 1.3
21 TH	0319 3.1	0940 0.9	1605 2.7	2126 1.4
22 F	0410 3.0	1032 1.0	1657 2.6	◐ 2223 1.5
23 SA	0504 2.8	1129 1.1	1751 2.5	2333 1.5
24 SU	0603 2.7	1228 1.2	1850 2.6	
25 M	0047 1.5	0705 2.7	1308 1.2	1947 2.6
26 TU	0156 1.4	0807 2.7	1421 1.2	2040 2.8
27 W	0251 1.3	0903 2.8	1507 1.1	2126 2.9
28 TH	0337 1.2	0951 2.8	1548 1.1	2207 3.0
29 F	0417 1.0	1035 2.9	1625 1.1	2245 3.1
30 SA	0455 0.9	1116 3.0	1702 1.0	○ 2323 3.2

JULY

Day	Time m	Time m	Time m	Time m
1 SU	0533 0.8	1156 3.1	1739 1.0	
2 M	0001 3.3	0610 0.7	1237 3.1	1816 0.9
3 TU	0040 3.3	0649 0.6	1319 3.1	1855 0.9
4 W	0120 3.3	0731 0.6	1402 3.1	1936 0.9
5 TH	0202 3.3	0814 0.6	1447 3.0	2019 1.0
6 F	0246 3.2	0902 0.6	1536 2.9	2106 1.1
7 SA	0335 3.2	0956 0.7	1630 2.8	◐ 2202 1.2
8 SU	0432 3.1	1100 0.8	1729 2.8	2315 1.3
9 M	0537 3.0	1210 0.9	1833 2.8	
10 TU	0034 1.3	0647 3.0	1320 1.0	1940 2.8
11 W	0151 1.2	0803 3.0	1427 1.0	2046 3.0
12 TH	0300 1.0	0915 3.0	1526 1.0	2144 3.1
13 F	0358 0.8	1017 3.1	1616 1.0	2235 3.3
14 SA	0449 0.6	1110 3.2	1701 1.0	● 2322 3.4
15 SU	0535 0.5	1158 3.2	1742 0.9	
16 M	0006 3.5	0618 0.4	1243 3.2	1820 0.9
17 TU	0048 3.5	0658 0.5	1323 3.1	1856 1.0
18 W	0128 3.4	0736 0.5	1402 3.0	1930 1.0
19 TH	0205 3.3	0812 0.7	1439 2.9	2002 1.1
20 F	0243 3.2	0848 0.8	1517 2.8	2036 1.2
21 SA	0322 3.0	0927 1.0	1558 2.7	2115 1.3
22 SU	0406 2.9	1013 1.2	1646 2.6	◐ 2209 1.5
23 M	0500 2.7	1114 1.3	1742 2.6	2336 1.6
24 TU	0606 2.6	1227 1.4	1847 2.6	
25 W	0111 1.5	0721 2.6	1340 1.4	1954 2.7
26 TH	0228 1.4	0833 2.7	1442 1.3	2052 2.8
27 F	0320 1.2	0931 2.8	1529 1.3	2141 3.0
28 SA	0403 1.0	1018 2.9	1610 1.1	2224 3.1
29 SU	0441 0.8	1100 3.1	1647 1.0	2304 3.3
30 M	0518 0.7	1141 3.2	1723 0.9	○ 2344 3.4
31 TU	0555 0.5	1221 3.3	1801 0.8	

AUGUST

Day	Time m	Time m	Time m	Time m
1 W	0023 3.5	0633 0.4	1302 3.3	1838 0.7
2 TH	0104 3.6	0712 0.3	1343 3.3	1916 0.8
3 F	0144 3.6	0752 0.4	1424 3.2	1955 0.8
4 SA	0226 3.5	0834 0.6	1508 3.1	2037 1.0
5 SU	0313 3.3	0922 0.8	1557 2.9	◑ 2128 1.1
6 M	0407 3.1	1022 1.0	1654 2.8	2242 1.3
7 TU	0515 3.0	1141 1.2	1803 2.8	
8 W	0021 1.3	0635 2.8	1308 1.3	1920 2.8
9 TH	0155 1.2	0806 2.8	1427 1.3	2036 2.9
10 F	0305 1.0	0920 3.0	1525 1.2	2137 3.1
11 SA	0358 0.8	1016 3.1	1610 1.1	2226 3.3
12 SU	0442 0.6	1103 3.2	1649 1.0	● 2310 3.4
13 M	0521 0.5	1144 3.2	1723 0.9	2350 3.5
14 TU	0557 0.5	1221 3.2	1756 0.9	
15 W	0026 3.5	0630 0.5	1256 3.2	1827 0.9
16 TH	0101 3.5	0701 0.5	1327 3.1	1857 0.9
17 F	0133 3.4	0732 0.7	1358 3.0	1926 1.0
18 SA	0204 3.3	0801 0.8	1429 2.9	1955 1.1
19 SU	0237 3.1	0834 1.0	1503 2.8	2028 1.3
20 M	0314 2.9	0907 1.2	1544 2.7	◑ 2110 1.4
21 TU	0402 2.7	0956 1.4	1637 2.6	2218 1.6
22 W	0510 2.6	1124 1.6	1746 2.6	
23 TH	0031 1.6	0639 2.5	1303 1.6	1906 2.6
24 F	0204 1.5	0808 2.6	1419 1.5	2018 2.8
25 SA	0259 1.2	0910 2.8	1509 1.3	2114 3.0
26 SU	0341 1.0	0957 3.0	1549 1.2	2159 3.2
27 M	0418 0.7	1039 3.2	1626 1.0	2241 3.4
28 TU	0454 0.5	1119 3.4	1701 0.8	○ 2321 3.6
29 W	0531 0.3	1158 3.5	1737 0.7	
30 TH	0001 3.7	0608 0.2	1238 3.5	1814 0.6
31 F	0041 3.8	0646 0.2	1317 3.4	1852 0.6

Chart Datum: 1·71 metres below Ordnance Datum (Newlyn)

TIME ZONE (UT)	Dates in amber are SPRINGS
For Summer Time add ONE hour in non-shaded areas	Dates in yellow are NEAPS

SCOTLAND – WICK

LAT 58°26'N   LONG 3°05'W

2007

TIMES AND HEIGHTS OF HIGH AND LOW WATERS

SEPTEMBER

Time	m	Time	m
1 0122	3.7	**16** 0129	3.3
0725	0.4	0720	0.9
SA 1357	3.3	SU 1347	3.1
1931	0.7	1922	1.1
2 0205	3.6	**17** 0201	3.1
0806	0.6	0747	1.1
SU 1439	3.2	M 1419	3.0
2014	0.9	1953	1.2
3 0253	3.4	**18** 0237	2.9
0851	0.9	0818	1.3
M 1527	3.0	TU 1457	2.9
2106	1.1	2032	1.4
4 0351	3.1	**19** 0323	2.7
0950	1.3	0859	1.5
TU 1626	2.9	W 1545	2.8
☽ 2234	1.3	☽ 2130	1.6
5 0506	2.9	**20** 0428	2.6
1126	1.6	1014	1.7
W 1741	2.8	TH 1654	2.7
		2353	1.6
6 0027	1.3	**21** 0603	2.5
0639	2.7	1227	1.7
TH 1310	1.6	F 1821	2.7
1908	2.8		
7 0200	1.4	**22** 0128	1.5
0814	2.8	0737	2.6
F 1427	1.5	SA 1348	1.6
2027	3.0	1940	2.8
8 0302	1.0	**23** 0227	1.2
0918	3.0	0842	2.9
SA 1517	1.3	SU 1440	1.4
2124	3.2	2040	3.0
9 0347	0.8	**24** 0310	0.9
1005	3.1	0929	3.1
SU 1556	1.2	M 1521	1.1
2210	3.4	2128	3.3
10 0424	0.6	**25** 0348	0.6
1045	3.2	1011	3.3
M 1628	1.0	TU 1558	0.9
2250	3.5	2211	3.5
11 0457	0.6	**26** 0425	0.4
1120	3.3	1051	3.5
TU 1658	0.9	W 1634	0.7
● 2326	3.5	○ 2253	3.7
12 0528	0.5	**27** 0503	0.3
1152	3.3	1131	3.6
W 1728	0.9	TH 1711	0.6
2359	3.5	2335	3.9
13 0557	0.7	**28** 0541	0.2
1222	3.3	1210	3.6
TH 1757	0.8	F 1750	0.5
14 0030	3.5	**29** 0017	3.9
0625	0.6	0620	0.3
F 1251	3.2	SA 1250	3.6
1826	0.9	1830	0.6
15 0100	3.4	**30** 0102	3.8
0653	0.8	0659	0.5
SA 1319	3.2	SU 1330	3.5
1854	1.0	1912	0.7

OCTOBER

Time	m	Time	m
1 0148	3.6	**16** 0135	3.1
0741	0.8	0714	1.2
M 1413	3.3	TU 1346	3.1
1959	0.9	1931	1.2
2 0240	3.3	**17** 0213	2.9
0827	1.2	0746	1.4
TU 1502	3.1	W 1424	3.0
2101	1.1	2012	1.4
3 0343	3.0	**18** 0300	2.8
0931	1.5	0828	1.6
W 1604	2.9	TH 1511	2.9
☽ 2242	1.3	2111	1.5
4 0504	2.8	**19** 0403	2.6
1117	1.7	0935	1.7
TH 1724	2.9	F 1615	2.8
		● 2310	1.5
5 0025	1.3	**20** 0531	2.6
0639	2.7	1142	1.8
F 1300	1.7	SA 1738	2.8
1851	2.9		
6 0147	1.1	**21** 0041	1.4
0803	2.9	0656	2.7
SA 1410	1.6	SU 1304	1.6
2005	3.1	1855	2.9
7 0242	0.9	**22** 0144	1.1
0858	3.0	0803	2.9
SU 1456	1.4	M 1401	1.4
2101	3.2	1959	3.1
8 0323	0.8	**23** 0233	0.9
0940	3.1	0854	3.1
M 1531	1.2	TU 1446	1.2
2145	3.3	2052	3.3
9 0357	0.7	**24** 0315	0.6
1017	3.2	0939	3.4
TU 1602	1.0	W 1527	1.0
2223	3.4	2140	3.6
10 0427	0.7	**25** 0355	0.5
1021	3.3	1021	3.5
W 1631	1.0	TH 1607	0.8
2258	3.5	2226	3.8
11 0455	0.7	**26** 0435	0.4
1102	3.6	1102	3.6
TH 1701	0.9	F 1648	0.6
● 2330	3.5	○ 2311	3.9
12 0524	0.7	**27** 0515	0.4
1149	3.3	1143	3.7
F 1730	0.9	SA 1730	0.6
		2358	3.9
13 0001	3.4	**28** 0557	0.5
0551	0.8	1225	3.6
SA 1217	3.3	SU 1815	0.6
1759	0.9		
14 0031	3.4	**29** 0046	3.7
0619	0.9	0639	0.8
SU 1245	3.3	M 1308	3.5
1828	1.0	1902	0.7
15 0102	3.2	**30** 0137	3.5
0646	1.1	0723	1.1
M 1314	3.2	TU 1353	3.4
1858	1.1	1956	0.9
		31 0232	3.3
		0813	1.4
		W 1445	3.2
		2106	1.1

NOVEMBER

Time	m	Time	m
1 0337	3.0	**16** 0246	2.9
0918	1.6	0815	1.5
TH 1547	3.1	F 1450	3.0
☽ 2232	1.2	2103	1.3
2 0452	2.8	**17** 0344	2.8
1048	1.8	0915	1.6
F 1701	3.0	SA 1547	3.0
2358	1.2	● 2225	1.3
3 0613	2.8	**18** 0456	2.7
1219	1.8	1044	1.7
SA 1818	3.0	SU 1657	2.9
		2348	1.3
4 0113	1.1	**19** 0611	2.8
0726	2.8	1209	1.6
SU 1332	1.6	M 1810	3.0
1928	3.1		
5 0208	1.0	**20** 0055	1.1
0822	2.9	0717	2.9
M 1422	1.5	TU 1314	1.5
2025	3.2	1915	3.1
6 0250	1.0	**21** 0151	0.9
0906	3.1	0814	3.1
TU 1500	1.3	W 1408	1.3
2112	3.2	2014	3.3
7 0324	0.9	**22** 0241	0.8
0943	3.2	0905	3.3
W 1533	1.2	TH 1457	1.1
2152	3.3	2110	3.5
8 0354	0.9	**23** 0327	0.7
1017	3.3	0952	3.5
TH 1605	1.1	F 1544	0.9
2229	3.3	2203	3.7
9 0424	0.9	**24** 0411	0.6
1049	3.3	1037	3.6
F 1638	1.0	SA 1631	0.7
● 2303	3.4	○ 2255	3.7
10 0454	0.9	**25** 0456	0.7
1119	3.4	1122	3.7
SA 1710	1.0	SU 1719	0.6
2337	3.3	2346	3.7
11 0524	1.0	**26** 0541	0.8
1149	3.4	1206	3.7
SU 1741	1.0	M 1809	0.6
12 0010	3.3	**27** 0037	3.6
0553	1.1	0626	1.0
M 1219	3.4	TU 1252	3.6
1813	1.0	1900	0.7
13 0044	3.2	**28** 0130	3.5
0622	1.2	0712	1.2
TU 1251	3.3	W 1340	3.5
1846	1.1	1955	0.8
14 0119	3.1	**29** 0224	3.2
0654	1.3	0800	1.4
W 1325	3.3	TH 1430	3.4
1923	1.2	2055	0.9
15 0159	3.0	**30** 0322	3.0
0730	1.4	0853	1.6
TH 1403	3.2	F 1526	3.2
2006	1.2	2201	1.1

DECEMBER

Time	m	Time	m
1 0422	2.9	**16** 0323	2.9
0955	1.7	0852	1.4
SA 1628	3.1	SU 1522	3.2
☽ 2308	1.2	2144	1.1
2 0525	2.8	**17** 0421	2.9
1109	1.7	0951	1.5
SU 1732	3.0	M 1620	3.1
		2254	1.1
3 0015	1.2	**18** 0525	2.9
0628	2.8	1107	1.5
M 1225	1.7	TU 1726	3.1
1837	3.0		
4 0116	1.2	**19** 0005	1.1
0729	2.8	0630	2.9
TU 1332	1.6	W 1225	1.5
1939	3.0	1834	3.2
5 0206	1.2	**20** 0110	1.1
0822	2.9	0733	3.0
W 1424	1.5	TH 1333	1.4
2034	3.1	1942	3.2
6 0247	1.2	**21** 0211	1.0
0906	3.0	0834	3.2
TH 1507	1.4	F 1435	1.2
2121	3.1	2049	3.3
7 0324	1.2	**22** 0307	1.0
0945	3.2	0929	3.3
F 1545	1.3	SA 1533	1.0
2203	3.2	2151	3.5
8 0358	1.1	**23** 0358	1.0
1021	3.3	1020	3.5
SA 1622	1.2	SU 1626	0.8
2242	3.2	2248	3.5
9 0432	1.1	**24** 0446	1.0
1055	3.3	1109	3.6
SU 1657	1.1	M 1717	0.7
● 2319	3.2	○ 2341	3.6
10 0505	1.2	**25** 0533	1.0
1128	3.4	1155	3.7
M 1732	1.0	TU 1807	0.6
2355	3.2		
11 0537	1.2	**26** 0032	3.5
1201	3.4	0616	1.1
TU 1806	1.0	W 1242	3.7
		1855	0.6
12 0032	3.2	**27** 0121	3.4
0609	1.2	0659	1.2
W 1236	3.4	TH 1327	3.6
1841	1.0	1942	0.6
13 0110	3.2	**28** 0208	3.3
0644	1.2	0739	1.2
TH 1312	3.4	F 1412	3.5
1919	1.0	2028	0.8
14 0150	3.1	**29** 0254	3.1
0723	1.3	0819	1.4
F 1350	3.3	SA 1458	3.4
2001	1.0	2115	1.0
15 0233	3.0	**30** 0341	2.9
0805	1.4	0859	1.5
SA 1433	3.3	SU 1546	3.2
2048	1.1	2205	1.1
		31 0430	2.8
		0948	1.6
		M 1639	3.1
		☽ 2300	1.3

Chart Datum: 1·71 metres below Ordnance Datum (Newlyn)

TIDES

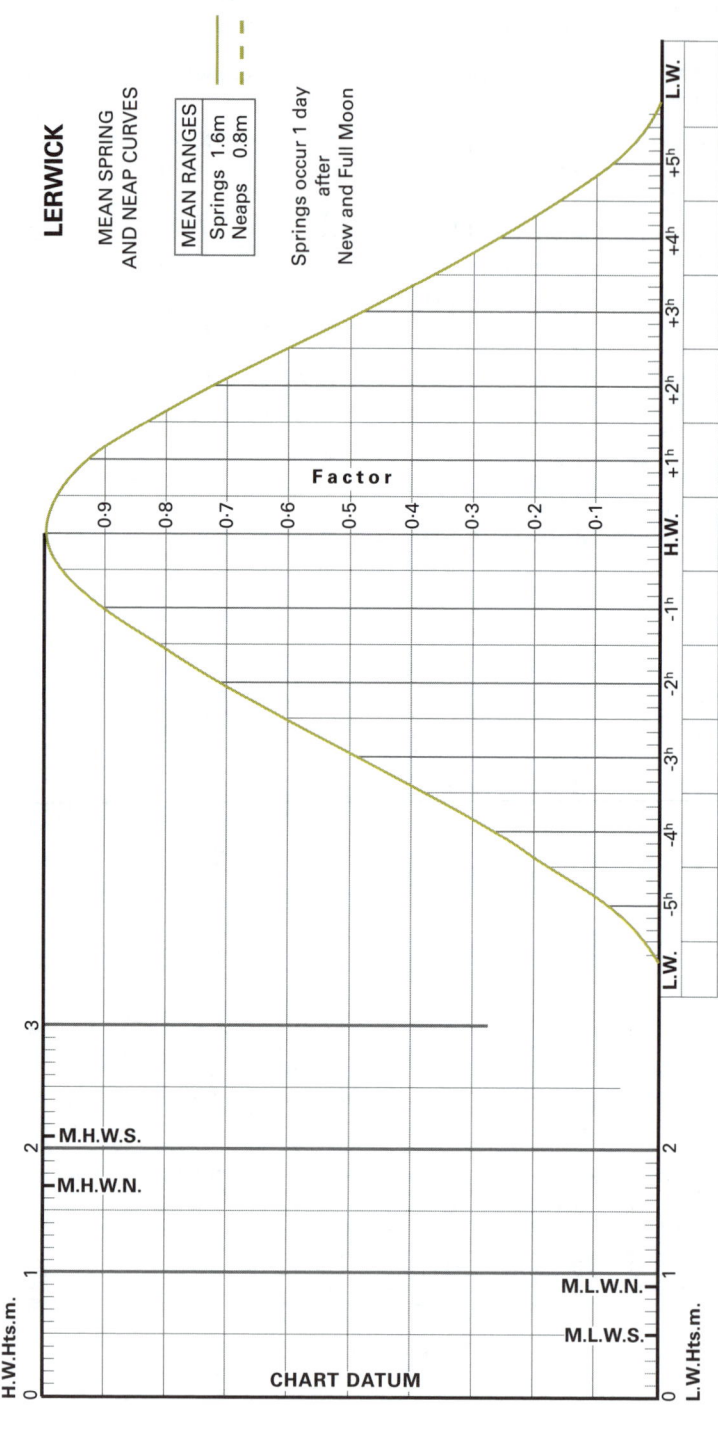

LERWICK

MEAN SPRING
AND NEAP CURVES

MEAN RANGES
Springs 1.6m
Neaps 0.8m

Springs occur 1 day
after
New and Full Moon

Factor

0·9
0·8
0·7
0·6
0·5
0·4
0·3
0·2
0·1

H.W.   -1ʰ   -2ʰ   -3ʰ   -4ʰ   -5ʰ   L.W.
+5ʰ   +4ʰ   +3ʰ   +2ʰ   +1ʰ

M.H.W.S.
M.H.W.N.

M.L.W.N.
M.L.W.S.

CHART DATUM

H.W.Hts.m.
L.W.Hts.m.

3
2
2

SCOTLAND – LERWICK

LAT 60°09'N   LONG 1°08'W

TIMES AND HEIGHTS OF HIGH AND LOW WATERS

Dates in amber are **SPRINGS**
Dates in yellow are **NEAPS**

2007

JANUARY

Day	Time m	Day	Time m
1 M	0242 0.8 / 0856 2.0 / 1510 0.8 / 2127 2.0	16 TU	0229 1.0 / 0845 1.9 / 1507 0.9 / 2118 1.9
2 TU	0332 0.8 / 0946 2.1 / 1601 0.7 / 2222 2.1	17 W	0316 0.9 / 0929 2.0 / 1550 0.8 / 2205 2.0
3 W	0418 0.8 / 1032 2.2 / 1647 0.6 / 2311 2.1	18 TH	0400 0.9 / 1011 2.1 / 1632 0.6 / 2250 2.1
4 TH	0500 0.8 / 1116 2.3 / 1731 0.5 / 2355 2.1	19 F	0443 0.8 / 1054 2.2 / 1714 0.5 / 2335 2.1
5 F	0541 0.8 / 1157 2.3 / 1814 0.5	20 SA	0524 0.7 / 1136 2.3 / 1755 0.4
6 SA	0036 2.0 / 0619 0.8 / 1237 2.2 / 1854 0.5	21 SU	0019 2.1 / 0604 0.6 / 1218 2.3 / 1836 0.3
7 SU	0115 2.0 / 0656 0.9 / 1315 2.2 / 1933 0.6	22 M	0103 2.1 / 0644 0.6 / 1300 2.3 / 1918 0.3
8 M	0152 1.9 / 0730 0.9 / 1352 2.1 / 2011 0.7	23 TU	0146 2.1 / 0726 0.7 / 1343 2.3 / 2002 0.4
9 TU	0228 1.8 / 0804 0.9 / 1429 2.0 / 2049 0.7	24 W	0230 2.0 / 0809 0.7 / 1429 2.2 / 2049 0.5
10 W	0305 1.7 / 0840 1.0 / 1508 1.9 / 2131 0.8	25 TH	0317 1.9 / 0857 0.8 / 1521 2.1 / 2141 0.7
11 TH	0347 1.7 / 0925 1.0 / 1554 1.8 / 2223 0.9	26 F	0409 1.8 / 0954 0.9 / 1621 1.9 / 2247 0.8
12 F	0435 1.7 / 1031 1.1 / 1649 1.7 / 2328 1.0	27 SA	0511 1.7 / 1115 1.0 / 1736 1.8
13 SA	0536 1.7 / 1205 1.2 / 1801 1.7	28 SU	0015 0.9 / 0626 1.7 / 1256 0.9 / 1906 1.8
14 SU	0037 1.0 / 0652 1.7 / 1320 1.1 / 1926 1.7	29 M	0135 1.0 / 0743 1.8 / 1412 0.9 / 2028 1.8
15 M	0137 1.0 / 0755 1.8 / 1419 1.0 / 2028 1.8	30 TU	0239 1.0 / 0849 1.9 / 1512 0.7 / 2133 1.9
		31 W	0330 0.9 / 0942 2.0 / 1601 0.6 / 2222 2.0

FEBRUARY

Day	Time m	Day	Time m
1 TH	0412 0.8 / 1027 2.1 / 1642 0.5 / 2304 2.1	16 F	0346 0.8 / 0953 2.0 / 1615 0.5 / 2234 2.0
2 F	0450 0.8 / 1107 2.2 / 1719 0.4 / 2341 2.0	17 SA	0427 0.6 / 1037 2.2 / 1656 0.3 / 2317 2.1
3 SA	0525 0.7 / 1144 2.2 / 1755 0.4	18 SU	0507 0.5 / 1119 2.3 / 1735 0.2 / 2359 2.2
4 SU	0015 2.0 / 0558 0.7 / 1219 2.2 / 1828 0.4	19 M	0545 0.4 / 1200 2.4 / 1815 0.1
5 M	0048 2.0 / 0629 0.7 / 1251 2.2 / 1900 0.5	20 TU	0040 2.1 / 0624 0.4 / 1241 2.4 / 1855 0.2
6 TU	0118 1.9 / 0658 0.7 / 1321 2.1 / 1931 0.5	21 W	0120 2.1 / 0703 0.4 / 1323 2.3 / 1937 0.3
7 W	0147 1.9 / 0727 0.8 / 1351 2.0 / 2003 0.6	22 TH	0200 2.0 / 0746 0.5 / 1408 2.2 / 2020 0.5
8 TH	0217 1.8 / 0758 0.8 / 1425 1.9 / 2037 0.8	23 F	0243 1.9 / 0832 0.6 / 1459 2.0 / 2109 0.7
9 F	0253 1.7 / 0834 0.9 / 1505 1.8 / 2116 0.9	24 SA	0332 1.8 / 0929 0.8 / 1600 1.8 / 2212 0.9
10 SA	0335 1.7 / 0920 1.0 / 1555 1.7 / 2207 1.0	25 SU	0433 1.7 / 1059 0.9 / 1721 1.7 / 2358 1.0
11 SU	0428 1.6 / 1036 1.1 / 1658 1.6 / 2334 1.1	26 M	0557 1.6 / 1252 0.9 / 1911 1.6
12 M	0534 1.6 / 1238 1.1 / 1829 1.6	27 TU	0130 1.1 / 0731 1.7 / 1411 0.8 / 2035 1.7
13 TU	0102 1.1 / 0704 1.6 / 1352 1.0 / 2005 1.6	28 W	0235 1.0 / 0840 1.8 / 1507 0.6 / 2128 1.8
14 W	0208 1.0 / 0816 1.8 / 1448 0.8 / 2102 1.8		
15 TH	0301 0.9 / 0908 1.9 / 1533 0.7 / 2150 1.9		

MARCH

Day	Time m	Day	Time m
1 TH	0321 0.9 / 0930 1.9 / 1549 0.5 / 2209 1.8	16 F	0239 0.8 / 0841 1.8 / 1507 0.5 / 2127 1.9
2 F	0358 0.8 / 1011 2.0 / 1624 0.4 / 2244 1.9	17 SA	0323 0.7 / 0928 2.0 / 1550 0.3 / 2210 2.0
3 SA	0431 0.7 / 1048 2.1 / 1657 0.4 / 2316 1.9	18 SU	0404 0.5 / 1012 2.2 / 1630 0.1 / 2252 2.1
4 SU	0503 0.6 / 1121 2.1 / 1728 0.4 / 2346 2.0	19 M	0443 0.4 / 1055 2.3 / 1710 0.0 / 2332 2.1
5 M	0532 0.5 / 1153 2.1 / 1757 0.4	20 TU	0522 0.3 / 1137 2.3 / 1750 0.0
6 TU	0014 1.9 / 0600 0.5 / 1222 2.1 / 1825 0.4	21 W	0011 2.1 / 0601 0.3 / 1220 2.3 / 1830 0.1
7 W	0041 1.9 / 0627 0.6 / 1249 2.0 / 1853 0.5	22 TH	0050 2.1 / 0642 0.3 / 1304 2.2 / 1911 0.3
8 TH	0106 1.9 / 0656 0.6 / 1317 2.0 / 1923 0.6	23 F	0130 2.0 / 0726 0.4 / 1352 2.1 / 1955 0.5
9 F	0134 1.8 / 0727 0.7 / 1350 1.9 / 1954 0.7	24 SA	0212 1.9 / 0816 0.5 / 1446 1.9 / 2044 0.8
10 SA	0206 1.7 / 0802 0.8 / 1428 1.8 / 2029 0.9	25 SU	0302 1.8 / 0918 0.7 / 1549 1.7 / 2148 1.0
11 SU	0245 1.7 / 0845 0.9 / 1516 1.6 / 2112 1.0	26 M	0403 1.7 / 1058 0.8 / 1714 1.5 / 2343 1.1
12 M	0335 1.6 / 0948 1.0 / 1622 1.5 / 2225 1.1	27 TU	0530 1.6 / 1239 0.8 / 1910 1.5
13 TU	0442 1.6 / 1155 1.0 / 1749 1.5	28 W	0113 1.1 / 0709 1.6 / 1354 0.7 / 2021 1.6
14 W	0031 1.1 / 0608 1.6 / 1321 0.9 / 1941 1.6	29 TH	0215 1.0 / 0815 1.7 / 1445 0.6 / 2105 1.7
15 TH	0145 1.0 / 0743 1.7 / 1420 0.7 / 2040 1.7	30 F	0259 0.8 / 0904 1.8 / 1524 0.5 / 2141 1.8
		31 SA	0334 0.7 / 0944 1.9 / 1556 0.4 / 2213 1.8

APRIL

Day	Time m	Day	Time m
1 SU	0406 0.6 / 1020 2.0 / 1627 0.4 / 2244 1.9	16 M	0336 0.4 / 0944 2.1 / 1602 0.1 / 2222 2.1
2 M	0435 0.5 / 1053 2.0 / 1656 0.4 / 2313 1.9	17 TU	0417 0.3 / 1029 2.2 / 1643 0.1 / 2303 2.1
3 TU	0504 0.5 / 1123 2.0 / 1723 0.4 / 2339 1.9	18 W	0458 0.2 / 1114 2.3 / 1725 0.1 / 2342 2.1
4 W	0532 0.5 / 1152 2.0 / 1751 0.4	19 TH	0541 0.2 / 1200 2.2 / 1807 0.3
5 TH	0005 1.9 / 0600 0.5 / 1220 2.0 / 1819 0.5	20 F	0022 2.1 / 0625 0.2 / 1249 2.1 / 1849 0.4
6 F	0031 1.9 / 0631 0.5 / 1250 1.9 / 1849 0.6	21 SA	0104 2.0 / 0713 0.5 / 1342 2.0 / 1935 0.7
7 SA	0100 1.9 / 0705 0.6 / 1325 1.8 / 1921 0.7	22 SU	0150 1.9 / 0807 0.5 / 1438 1.8 / 2026 0.9
8 SU	0132 1.8 / 0742 0.7 / 1405 1.7 / 1957 0.8	23 M	0241 1.8 / 0914 0.6 / 1540 1.6 / 2133 1.0
9 M	0210 1.7 / 0828 0.8 / 1457 1.6 / 2043 1.0	24 TU	0342 1.7 / 1042 0.7 / 1658 1.5 / 2308 1.1
10 TU	0300 1.6 / 0932 0.8 / 1604 1.5 / 2156 1.0	25 W	0459 1.6 / 1207 0.7 / 1832 1.5
11 W	0408 1.6 / 1112 0.8 / 1727 1.5 / 2355 1.0	26 TH	0034 1.0 / 0629 1.6 / 1317 0.6 / 1937 1.5
12 TH	0531 1.5 / 1242 0.7 / 1906 1.5	27 F	0138 0.9 / 0736 1.7 / 1408 0.6 / 2023 1.6
13 F	0112 0.9 / 0702 1.6 / 1344 0.6 / 2008 1.7	28 SA	0225 0.8 / 0826 1.8 / 1448 0.5 / 2100 1.7
14 SA	0208 0.6 / 0807 1.8 / 1434 0.4 / 2056 1.8	29 SU	0302 0.8 / 0908 1.8 / 1521 0.5 / 2135 1.8
15 SU	0254 0.6 / 0858 1.9 / 1519 0.2 / 2140 2.0	30 M	0336 0.6 / 0946 1.8 / 1552 0.5 / 2207 1.8

Chart Datum: 1·22 metres below Ordnance Datum (Local)

TIDES

TIME ZONE (UT)
For Summer Time add ONE hour in **non-shaded areas**

SCOTLAND – LERWICK
LAT 60°09'N LONG 1°08'W
TIMES AND HEIGHTS OF HIGH AND LOW WATERS

Dates in amber are **SPRINGS**
Dates in yellow are **NEAPS**

2007

MAY

Day	Time m	Time m	Time m	Time m	Day	Time m	Time m	Time m	Time m
1 TU	0406 0.6	1021 1.9	1621 0.4	2238 1.9	16 W	0354 0.3	1008 2.1	1619 0.3	2235 2.1
2 W	0436 0.5	1054 1.9	1650 0.5	○2306 1.9	17 TH	0440 0.3	1058 2.1	1703 0.3	2318 2.1
3 TH	0507 0.5	1126 1.9	1720 0.5	2334 1.9	18 F	0526 0.2	1149 2.1	1748 0.4	
4 F	0539 0.5	1158 1.9	1751 0.6		19 SA	0002 2.1	0614 0.2	1242 2.0	1833 0.6
5 SA	0003 1.9	0613 0.5	1233 1.8	1824 0.7	20 SU	0048 2.0	0705 0.3	1335 1.9	1921 0.7
6 SU	0035 1.9	0650 0.6	1311 1.8	1900 0.7	21 M	0136 2.0	0800 0.4	1428 1.7	2011 0.9
7 M	0111 1.8	0733 0.6	1356 1.7	1941 0.8	22 TU	0227 1.9	0900 0.5	1522 1.6	2108 0.9
8 TU	0152 1.8	0822 0.7	1450 1.6	2033 0.9	23 W	0321 1.8	1006 0.6	1621 1.5	◑2215 1.0
9 W	0244 1.7	0923 0.7	1553 1.5	2140 0.9	24 TH	0421 1.7	1114 0.6	1729 1.5	2330 1.0
10 TH	0349 1.6	1038 0.7	1705 1.5	◐2308 0.9	25 F	0534 1.6	1219 0.7	1835 1.5	
11 F	0502 1.6	1159 0.6	1824 1.6		26 SA	0041 0.9	0644 1.6	1316 0.6	1928 1.5
12 SA	0029 0.9	0621 1.7	1304 0.5	1929 1.7	27 SU	0139 0.8	0741 1.6	1401 0.6	2013 1.6
13 SU	0130 0.7	0730 1.8	1400 0.4	2021 1.8	28 M	0224 0.8	0829 1.7	1440 0.6	2054 1.7
14 M	0221 0.6	0826 1.9	1449 0.3	2108 1.9	29 TU	0303 0.7	0912 1.7	1515 0.6	2131 1.8
15 TU	0309 0.5	0918 2.0	1535 0.2	2152 2.0	30 W	0338 0.6	0952 1.8	1548 0.6	2205 1.9
					31 TH	0412 0.6	1029 1.8	1622 0.6	2238 1.9

JUNE

Day	Time m	Time m	Time m	Time m	Day	Time m	Time m	Time m	Time m
1 F	0447 0.6	1106 1.8	1656 0.6	○2310 1.9	16 SA	0518 0.3	1145 2.0	1736 0.6	2350 2.1
2 SA	0523 0.5	1144 1.8	1732 0.7	2345 2.0	17 SU	0607 0.3	1235 1.9	1821 0.7	
3 SU	0602 0.5	1223 1.8	1810 0.7		18 M	0036 2.1	0655 0.3	1323 1.9	1905 0.7
4 M	0021 1.9	0643 0.5	1306 1.8	1850 0.7	19 TU	0123 2.0	0744 0.4	1408 1.8	1949 0.7
5 TU	0101 1.9	0727 0.5	1352 1.7	1934 0.8	20 W	0208 1.9	0832 0.4	1452 1.7	2033 0.8
6 W	0144 1.9	0815 0.5	1443 1.7	2024 0.8	21 TH	0253 1.8	0920 0.5	1537 1.6	2119 0.9
7 TH	0234 1.8	0907 0.5	1538 1.6	2119 0.8	22 F	0340 1.7	1011 0.6	1625 1.5	◑2215 0.9
8 F	0332 1.8	1007 0.5	1638 1.6	◑2224 0.8	23 SA	0432 1.7	1106 0.7	1721 1.5	2324 0.9
9 SA	0436 1.7	1115 0.5	1743 1.6	2339 0.8	24 SU	0536 1.6	1206 0.8	1825 1.5	
10 SU	0545 1.7	1224 0.5	1849 1.7		25 M	0038 0.9	0647 1.6	1304 0.8	1923 1.6
11 M	0051 0.7	0656 1.8	1327 0.5	1947 1.7	26 TU	0141 0.9	0749 1.6	1355 0.8	2014 1.7
12 TU	0153 0.7	0800 1.9	1423 0.5	2040 1.8	27 W	0231 0.8	0841 1.7	1440 0.8	2058 1.8
13 W	0248 0.5	0900 1.9	1514 0.5	2129 1.9	28 TH	0315 0.8	0927 1.7	1521 0.8	2137 1.8
14 TH	0339 0.4	0956 2.0	1603 0.5	2217 2.0	29 F	0354 0.7	1010 1.8	1601 0.7	2215 1.9
15 F	0429 0.4	1052 2.0	1650 0.5	●2304 2.1	30 SA	0433 0.6	1051 1.8	1641 0.7	○2253 2.0

JULY

Day	Time m	Time m	Time m	Time m	Day	Time m	Time m	Time m	Time m
1 SU	0512 0.5	1133 1.9	1720 0.7	2332 2.0	16 M	0556 0.3	1221 2.0	1805 0.6	
2 M	0553 0.4	1215 1.9	1801 0.7		17 TU	0023 2.1	0637 0.3	1301 1.9	1843 0.7
3 TU	0012 2.0	0633 0.4	1258 1.9	1840 0.6	18 W	0103 2.1	0717 0.3	1339 1.8	1919 0.7
4 W	0053 2.0	0715 0.4	1341 1.8	1922 0.6	19 TH	0141 2.0	0755 0.4	1415 1.8	1954 0.7
5 TH	0135 2.0	0758 0.4	1426 1.8	2006 0.7	20 F	0218 1.9	0832 0.6	1450 1.7	2029 0.8
6 F	0220 2.0	0845 0.4	1514 1.7	2054 0.7	21 SA	0256 1.8	0911 0.7	1528 1.6	2110 0.9
7 SA	0311 1.9	0936 0.5	1607 1.7	◑2148 0.8	22 SU	0339 1.7	0957 0.8	1612 1.6	◑2206 1.0
8 SU	0409 1.8	1036 0.6	1705 1.7	2257 0.8	23 M	0429 1.6	1056 0.9	1706 1.6	2335 1.0
9 M	0515 1.8	1148 0.6	1811 1.7		24 TU	0535 1.6	1208 0.9	1818 1.6	
10 TU	0020 0.8	0631 1.8	1303 0.7	1919 1.7	25 W	0058 1.0	0706 1.5	1315 1.0	1933 1.6
11 W	0136 0.7	0747 1.8	1408 0.7	2021 1.8	26 TH	0204 0.9	0815 1.6	1412 0.9	2028 1.7
12 TH	0240 0.6	0856 1.8	1505 0.7	2117 1.9	27 F	0256 0.8	0908 1.7	1502 0.9	2114 1.8
13 F	0336 0.5	0958 1.9	1556 0.7	2209 2.0	28 SA	0339 0.7	0953 1.8	1546 0.8	2156 1.9
14 SA	0426 0.4	1052 2.0	1642 0.7	●2257 2.1	29 SU	0418 0.6	1036 1.9	1627 0.7	2237 2.0
15 SU	0512 0.3	1139 2.0	1724 0.7	2341 2.1	30 M	0457 0.4	1117 2.0	1706 0.6	○2318 2.1
					31 TU	0536 0.3	1159 2.0	1745 0.6	2357 2.2

AUGUST

Day	Time m	Time m	Time m	Time m	Day	Time m	Time m	Time m	Time m
1 W	0615 0.3	1239 2.0	1823 0.5		16 TH	0036 2.2	0644 0.4	1303 1.9	1845 0.6
2 TH	0037 2.2	0654 0.2	1320 2.0	1902 0.5	17 F	0108 2.1	0715 0.5	1332 1.9	1915 0.7
3 F	0118 2.2	0735 0.3	1401 1.9	1943 0.6	18 SA	0139 2.0	0747 0.6	1402 1.8	1947 0.8
4 SA	0200 2.1	0818 0.4	1444 1.9	2028 0.6	19 SU	0213 1.9	0819 0.7	1436 1.7	2023 0.9
5 SU	0249 2.0	0906 0.5	1533 1.8	◑2120 0.7	20 M	0252 1.8	0857 0.9	1517 1.7	◑2109 1.0
6 M	0345 1.9	1003 0.7	1630 1.7	2228 0.8	21 TU	0341 1.7	0946 1.0	1607 1.6	2226 1.1
7 TU	0454 1.8	1121 0.8	1739 1.7		22 W	0442 1.6	1111 1.1	1709 1.6	
8 W	0009 0.9	0621 1.7	1254 0.9	1901 1.7	23 TH	0023 1.1	0612 1.5	1243 1.1	1838 1.6
9 TH	0136 0.8	0752 1.7	1407 0.9	2014 1.8	24 F	0139 1.0	0755 1.6	1351 1.0	1959 1.7
10 F	0243 0.7	0904 1.8	1504 0.9	2114 1.9	25 SA	0234 0.8	0849 1.7	1443 0.9	2050 1.9
11 SA	0336 0.5	0959 1.9	1550 0.8	2203 2.1	26 SU	0317 0.7	0933 1.8	1527 0.8	2133 2.0
12 SU	0419 0.4	1043 2.0	1630 0.7	●2246 2.1	27 M	0356 0.5	1014 2.0	1606 0.7	2215 2.1
13 M	0458 0.3	1122 2.0	1706 0.6	2325 2.2	28 TU	0434 0.3	1054 2.1	1644 0.6	○2255 2.2
14 TU	0535 0.3	1158 2.0	1741 0.6		29 W	0512 0.2	1134 2.1	1722 0.5	2335 2.3
15 W	0001 2.2	0610 0.3	1232 2.0	1814 0.6	30 TH	0550 0.2	1213 2.1	1800 0.4	
					31 F	0015 2.4	0629 0.2	1252 2.1	1839 0.4

Chart Datum: 1·22 metres below Ordnance Datum (Local)

SCOTLAND – LERWICK

LAT 60°09'N   LONG 1°08'W

TIMES AND HEIGHTS OF HIGH AND LOW WATERS

Dates in amber are **SPRINGS**
Dates in yellow are **NEAPS**

2007

SEPTEMBER

Day	Time	m	Day	Time	m
1 SA	0056 / 0709 / 1331 / 1920	2.3 / 0.3 / 2.1 / 0.5	16 SU	0103 / 0705 / 1318 / 1914	2.0 / 0.7 / 1.9 / 0.8
2 SU	0139 / 0752 / 1413 / 2006	2.2 / 0.5 / 2.0 / 0.6	17 M	0136 / 0736 / 1350 / 1950	1.9 / 0.8 / 1.9 / 0.9
3 M	0229 / 0839 / 1501 / 2100	2.1 / 0.7 / 1.9 / 0.8	18 TU	0215 / 0811 / 1429 / 2034	1.8 / 0.9 / 1.8 / 1.0
4 TU	0330 / 0936 / 1559 / 2218 ◑	1.9 / 0.9 / 1.8 / 0.9	19 W	0304 / 0854 / 1519 / 2140	1.7 / 1.1 / 1.7 / 1.1
5 W	0445 / 1110 / 1716	1.7 / 1.1 / 1.7	20 TH	0408 / 1007 / 1623 / 2348	1.6 / 1.2 / 1.7 / 1.1
6 TH	0014 / 0629 / 1254 / 1852	0.9 / 1.7 / 1.1 / 1.8	21 F	0531 / 1214 / 1744	1.5 / 1.2 / 1.7
7 F	0138 / 0803 / 1404 / 2008	0.8 / 1.7 / 1.0 / 1.9	22 SA	0106 / 0727 / 1325 / 1921	1.0 / 1.6 / 1.1 / 1.7
8 SA	0239 / 0902 / 1455 / 2102	0.7 / 1.8 / 0.9 / 2.0	23 SU	0202 / 0822 / 1417 / 2019	0.8 / 1.8 / 1.0 / 1.9
9 SU	0325 / 0945 / 1535 / 2147	0.5 / 1.9 / 0.8 / 2.1	24 M	0246 / 0905 / 1500 / 2104	0.6 / 1.9 / 0.8 / 2.0
10 M	0402 / 1022 / 1610 / 2226	0.5 / 2.0 / 0.7 / 2.2	25 TU	0326 / 0945 / 1539 / 2147	0.5 / 2.0 / 0.7 / 2.2
11 TU	0436 / 1056 / 1642 / 2301 ●	0.4 / 2.0 / 0.6 / 2.2	26 W	0405 / 1025 / 1618 / 2228 ○	0.3 / 2.2 / 0.5 / 2.3
12 W	0508 / 1127 / 1714 / 2334	0.4 / 2.0 / 0.6 / 2.2	27 TH	0444 / 1104 / 1657 / 2309	0.2 / 2.2 / 0.4 / 2.4
13 TH	0539 / 1156 / 1744	0.4 / 2.0 / 0.6	28 F	0524 / 1143 / 1736 / 2351	0.2 / 2.3 / 0.4 / 2.4
14 F	0005 / 0608 / 1224 / 1813	2.2 / 0.5 / 2.0 / 0.6	29 SA	0604 / 1222 / 1817	0.3 / 2.2 / 0.4
15 SA	0034 / 0636 / 1251 / 1842	2.1 / 0.6 / 2.0 / 0.7	30 SU	0035 / 0644 / 1302 / 1901	2.4 / 0.4 / 2.2 / 0.5

OCTOBER

Day	Time	m	Day	Time	m
1 M	0123 / 0728 / 1345 / 1951	2.2 / 0.6 / 2.1 / 0.6	16 TU	0110 / 0703 / 1316 / 1928	2.0 / 0.9 / 2.0 / 0.9
2 TU	0219 / 0817 / 1435 / 2051	2.1 / 0.9 / 2.0 / 0.8	17 W	0150 / 0738 / 1354 / 2015	1.8 / 1.0 / 1.9 / 1.0
3 W	0323 / 0918 / 1537 / 2222 ◑	1.9 / 1.1 / 1.8 / 0.9	18 TH	0241 / 0823 / 1443 / 2118	1.7 / 1.1 / 1.8 / 1.0
4 TH	0443 / 1105 / 1658	1.7 / 1.2 / 1.8	19 F	0346 / 0932 / 1549 / 2259 ◑	1.6 / 1.2 / 1.7 / 1.0
5 F	0007 / 0632 / 1240 / 1836	0.8 / 1.7 / 1.2 / 1.8	20 SA	0502 / 1130 / 1706	1.6 / 1.2 / 1.7
6 SA	0124 / 0750 / 1346 / 1946	0.8 / 1.7 / 1.1 / 1.9	21 SU	0023 / 0638 / 1247 / 1831	0.9 / 1.7 / 1.1 / 1.8
7 SU	0220 / 0839 / 1433 / 2038	0.7 / 1.8 / 1.0 / 2.0	22 M	0121 / 0743 / 1342 / 1940	0.8 / 1.8 / 1.0 / 1.9
8 M	0301 / 0918 / 1511 / 2121	0.6 / 1.9 / 0.8 / 2.1	23 TU	0210 / 0830 / 1428 / 2031	0.6 / 1.9 / 0.8 / 2.1
9 TU	0336 / 0952 / 1545 / 2158	0.5 / 2.0 / 0.7 / 2.1	24 W	0254 / 0912 / 1510 / 2117	0.5 / 2.1 / 0.7 / 2.2
10 W	0407 / 1023 / 1616 / 2233	0.5 / 2.0 / 0.7 / 2.2	25 TH	0336 / 0954 / 1551 / 2202	0.4 / 2.2 / 0.6 / 2.4
11 TH	0437 / 1053 / 1646 / 2305 ●	0.5 / 2.1 / 0.6 / 2.2	26 F	0417 / 1035 / 1633 / 2247 ○	0.3 / 2.3 / 0.5 / 2.4
12 F	0506 / 1121 / 1716 / 2335	0.5 / 2.1 / 0.6 / 2.2	27 SA	0459 / 1115 / 1716 / 2333	0.3 / 2.3 / 0.4 / 2.4
13 SA	0534 / 1148 / 1745	0.6 / 2.1 / 0.7	28 SU	0541 / 1156 / 1801	0.4 / 2.3 / 0.4
14 SU	0004 / 0602 / 1215 / 1816	2.1 / 0.7 / 2.1 / 0.7	29 M	0022 / 0624 / 1239 / 1849	2.3 / 0.6 / 2.2 / 0.5
15 M	0035 / 0631 / 1244 / 1850	2.0 / 0.8 / 2.0 / 0.8	30 TU	0116 / 0711 / 1326 / 1943	2.2 / 0.8 / 2.2 / 0.6
			31 W	0214 / 0802 / 1419 / 2047	2.0 / 1.0 / 2.1 / 0.7

NOVEMBER

Day	Time	m	Day	Time	m
1 TH	0317 / 0905 / 1521 / 2210 ◑	1.9 / 1.2 / 1.9 / 0.8	16 F	0229 / 0808 / 1423 / 2100	1.8 / 1.1 / 1.9 / 0.9
2 F	0429 / 1033 / 1634 / 2338	1.7 / 1.2 / 1.9 / 0.8	17 SA	0328 / 0909 / 1523 / 2208 ◑	1.7 / 1.1 / 1.9 / 0.9
3 SA	0557 / 1202 / 1759	1.7 / 1.2 / 1.9	18 SU	0433 / 1026 / 1632 / 2327	1.7 / 1.2 / 1.8 / 0.9
4 SU	0050 / 0708 / 1311 / 1909	0.8 / 1.7 / 1.1 / 1.9	19 M	0546 / 1153 / 1745	1.7 / 1.1 / 1.9
5 M	0146 / 0759 / 1402 / 2003	0.8 / 1.8 / 1.0 / 2.0	20 TU	0034 / 0656 / 1259 / 1856	0.8 / 1.8 / 1.0 / 1.9
6 TU	0228 / 0839 / 1442 / 2048	0.7 / 1.9 / 0.9 / 2.0	21 W	0131 / 0751 / 1353 / 1956	0.7 / 1.9 / 0.9 / 2.1
7 W	0304 / 0915 / 1518 / 2127	0.7 / 2.0 / 0.8 / 2.1	22 TH	0221 / 0840 / 1442 / 2050	0.6 / 2.1 / 0.7 / 2.2
8 TH	0335 / 0949 / 1551 / 2204	0.7 / 2.0 / 0.8 / 2.1	23 F	0308 / 0925 / 1529 / 2141	0.5 / 2.2 / 0.6 / 2.3
9 F	0406 / 1020 / 1622 / 2239	0.7 / 2.1 / 0.7 / 2.1	24 SA	0354 / 1009 / 1615 / 2231 ○	0.5 / 2.3 / 0.5 / 2.4
10 SA	0435 / 1051 / 1653 / 2312	0.7 / 2.1 / 0.7 / 2.1	25 SU	0439 / 1053 / 1703 / 2323	0.5 / 2.3 / 0.5 / 2.3
11 SU	0505 / 1119 / 1725 / 2344	0.7 / 2.1 / 0.7 / 2.1	26 M	0525 / 1138 / 1752	0.6 / 2.3 / 0.6
12 M	0535 / 1148 / 1759	0.8 / 2.1 / 0.8	27 TU	0017 / 0611 / 1225 / 1842	2.3 / 0.8 / 2.3 / 0.5
13 TU	0018 / 0608 / 1220 / 1836	2.0 / 0.9 / 2.1 / 0.8	28 W	0112 / 0658 / 1315 / 1936	2.2 / 0.9 / 2.2 / 0.5
14 W	0056 / 0643 / 1255 / 1917	2.0 / 1.0 / 2.1 / 0.8	29 TH	0206 / 0748 / 1407 / 2034	2.0 / 1.0 / 2.2 / 0.6
15 TH	0139 / 0721 / 1335 / 2004	1.9 / 1.0 / 2.0 / 0.9	30 F	0300 / 0842 / 1501 / 2137	1.9 / 1.1 / 2.1 / 0.7

DECEMBER

Day	Time	m	Day	Time	m
1 SA	0357 / 0943 / 1600 / 2246 ◑	1.8 / 1.2 / 2.0 / 0.8	16 SU	0306 / 0845 / 1459 / 2131	1.8 / 1.0 / 2.0 / 0.8
2 SU	0500 / 1056 / 1707 / 2355	1.7 / 1.2 / 1.9 / 0.9	17 M	0401 / 0942 / 1558 / 2232	1.8 / 1.0 / 1.9 / 0.8
3 M	0606 / 1214 / 1818	1.7 / 1.1 / 1.8	18 TU	0502 / 1051 / 1704 / 2343	1.8 / 1.1 / 1.9 / 0.8
4 TU	0056 / 0704 / 1319 / 1919	0.9 / 1.7 / 1.1 / 1.9	19 W	0609 / 1211 / 1816	1.8 / 1.0 / 1.9
5 W	0146 / 0754 / 1410 / 2011	0.9 / 1.8 / 1.0 / 1.9	20 TH	0053 / 0714 / 1321 / 1927	0.8 / 1.9 / 0.9 / 2.0
6 TH	0227 / 0837 / 1452 / 2057	0.9 / 1.9 / 0.9 / 1.9	21 F	0154 / 0811 / 1421 / 2031	0.7 / 2.0 / 0.8 / 2.1
7 F	0304 / 0917 / 1529 / 2139	0.9 / 2.0 / 0.9 / 2.0	22 SA	0249 / 0904 / 1516 / 2130	0.7 / 2.1 / 0.7 / 2.2
8 SA	0338 / 0953 / 1604 / 2218	0.8 / 2.1 / 0.8 / 2.0	23 SU	0340 / 0954 / 1607 / 2228	0.7 / 2.2 / 0.6 / 2.2
9 SU	0411 / 1027 / 1639 / 2256	0.9 / 2.1 / 0.8 / 2.0	24 M	0428 / 1042 / 1657 / 2322 ○	0.7 / 2.3 / 0.5 / 2.2
10 M	0444 / 1100 / 1713 / 2332	0.9 / 2.2 / 0.8 / 2.0	25 TU	0515 / 1130 / 1746	0.7 / 2.3 / 0.4
11 TU	0519 / 1133 / 1750	0.9 / 2.2 / 0.7	26 W	0013 / 0600 / 1217 / 1834	2.2 / 0.8 / 2.3 / 0.4
12 W	0010 / 0554 / 1208 / 1828	2.0 / 0.9 / 2.2 / 0.7	27 TH	0102 / 0644 / 1303 / 1921	2.1 / 0.8 / 2.3 / 0.4
13 TH	0050 / 0632 / 1244 / 1909	2.0 / 0.9 / 2.1 / 0.7	28 F	0147 / 0728 / 1349 / 2008	2.0 / 0.9 / 2.2 / 0.5
14 F	0131 / 0712 / 1324 / 1952	1.9 / 0.9 / 2.1 / 0.7	29 SA	0231 / 0810 / 1434 / 2055	1.9 / 1.0 / 2.1 / 0.7
15 SA	0216 / 0756 / 1408 / 2039	1.9 / 1.0 / 2.0 / 0.7	30 SU	0315 / 0854 / 1520 / 2144	1.8 / 1.0 / 2.0 / 0.8
			31 M	0401 / 0943 / 1609 / 2239 ◑	1.7 / 1.1 / 1.9 / 0.9

Chart Datum: 1·22 metres below Ordnance Datum (Local)

TIDES

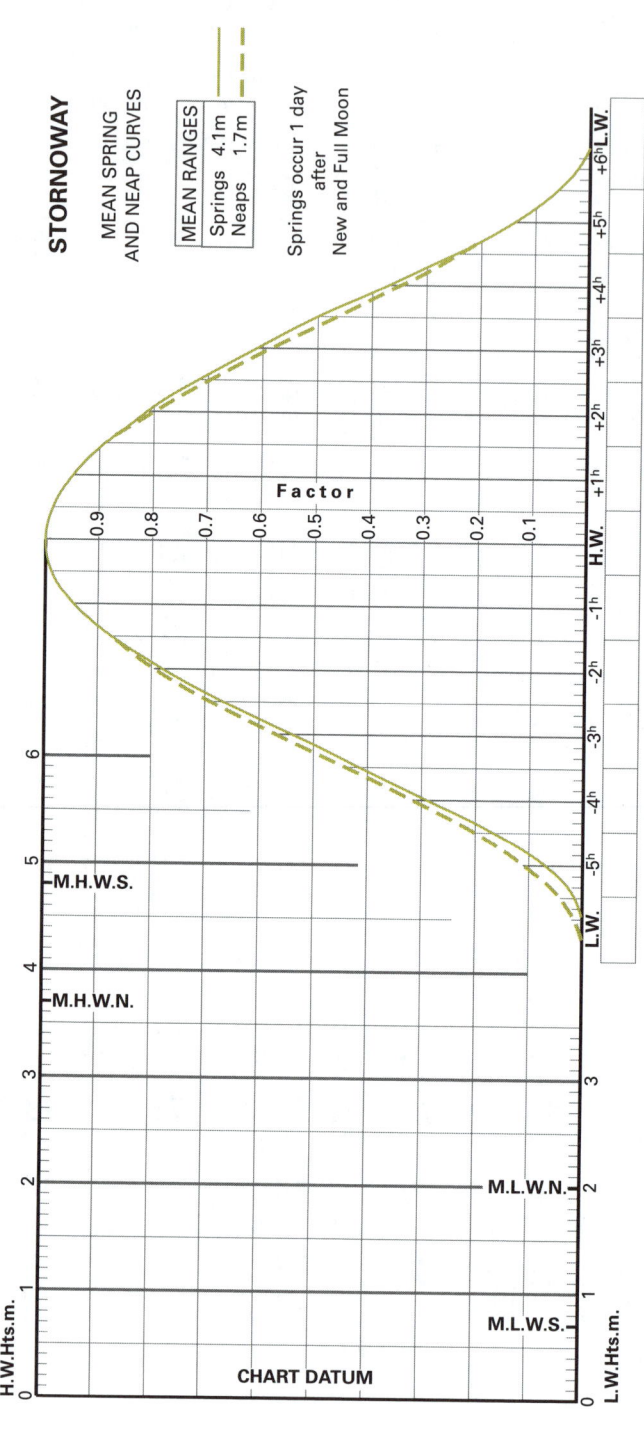

STORNOWAY

MEAN SPRING
AND NEAP CURVES

MEAN RANGES
Springs 4.1m
Neaps   1.7m

Springs occur 1 day
after
New and Full Moon

SCOTLAND – STORNOWAY

LAT 58°12'N   LONG 6°23'W

TIMES AND HEIGHTS OF HIGH AND LOW WATERS

2007

JANUARY

Day	Time	m	Time	m
1 M	0458 / 1116 / 1717 / 2333	4.2 / 1.4 / 4.1 / 1.3	16 TU 0452 / 1107 / 1721 / 2333	4.0 / 1.8 / 3.8 / 1.6
2 TU	0546 / 1210 / 1807	4.4 / 1.2 / 4.3	17 W 0534 / 1156 / 1804	4.2 / 1.5 / 4.1
3 W ○	0021 / 0629 / 1300 / 1852	1.2 / 4.6 / 1.1 / 4.4	18 TH 0016 / 0613 / 1241 / 1844	1.4 / 4.5 / 1.2 / 4.3
4 TH	0105 / 0709 / 1345 / 1933	1.1 / 4.7 / 1.0 / 4.4	19 F ● 0057 / 0652 / 1323 / 1922	1.1 / 4.7 / 0.9 / 4.4
5 F	0145 / 0748 / 1426 / 2012	1.1 / 4.7 / 0.9 / 4.3	20 SA 0137 / 0730 / 1404 / 2000	0.9 / 4.9 / 0.6 / 4.5
6 SA	0224 / 0825 / 1504 / 2050	1.1 / 4.7 / 0.9 / 4.2	21 SU 0215 / 0809 / 1444 / 2037	0.8 / 5.0 / 0.5 / 4.5
7 SU	0301 / 0902 / 1542 / 2127	1.2 / 4.6 / 1.0 / 4.1	22 M 0254 / 0849 / 1525 / 2117	0.7 / 5.0 / 0.4 / 4.4
8 M	0337 / 0939 / 1619 / 2205	1.3 / 4.5 / 1.2 / 3.9	23 TU 0334 / 0931 / 1607 / 2200	0.8 / 4.9 / 0.6 / 4.2
9 TU	0415 / 1018 / 1658 / 2249	1.5 / 4.2 / 1.4 / 3.7	24 W 0416 / 1020 / 1652 / 2251	1.0 / 4.6 / 0.8 / 4.0
10 W	0455 / 1103 / 1740 / 2340	1.7 / 4.0 / 1.6 / 3.6	25 TH ☽ 0503 / 1118 / 1741 / 2357	1.2 / 4.4 / 1.1 / 3.7
11 TH ☾	0540 / 1155 / 1827	1.9 / 3.8 / 1.8	26 F 0558 / 1227 / 1838	1.5 / 4.1 / 1.4
12 F	0041 / 0633 / 1255 / 1923	3.5 / 2.1 / 3.6 / 2.0	27 SA 0116 / 0707 / 1346 / 1947	3.6 / 1.8 / 3.8 / 1.7
13 SA	0152 / 0737 / 1406 / 2032	3.5 / 2.2 / 3.5 / 2.0	28 SU 0239 / 0839 / 1506 / 2116	3.6 / 1.9 / 3.7 / 1.8
14 SU	0306 / 0853 / 1527 / 2146	3.6 / 2.2 / 3.6 / 2.0	29 M 0354 / 1013 / 1619 / 2236	3.7 / 1.7 / 3.8 / 1.7
15 M	0405 / 1008 / 1631 / 2245	3.7 / 2.1 / 3.7 / 1.8	30 TU 0455 / 1120 / 1718 / 2333	3.9 / 1.5 / 3.9 / 1.5
			31 W 0543 / 1213 / 1805	4.2 / 1.2 / 4.0

FEBRUARY

Day	Time	m	Time	m
1 TH	0018 / 0623 / 1257 / 1844	1.3 / 4.4 / 1.0 / 4.2	16 F 0000 / 0556 / 1226 / 1827	1.3 / 4.5 / 1.0 / 4.4
2 F ○	0058 / 0658 / 1335 / 1918	1.1 / 4.6 / 0.8 / 4.3	17 SA ● 0041 / 0634 / 1306 / 1904	1.0 / 4.9 / 0.6 / 4.6
3 SA	0134 / 0730 / 1409 / 1949	0.9 / 4.7 / 0.7 / 4.3	18 SU 0120 / 0711 / 1345 / 1939	0.7 / 5.1 / 0.3 / 4.8
4 SU	0207 / 0801 / 1441 / 2020	0.8 / 4.7 / 0.7 / 4.3	19 M 0157 / 0748 / 1423 / 2013	0.4 / 5.3 / 0.1 / 4.8
5 M	0240 / 0830 / 1512 / 2049	0.8 / 4.7 / 0.8 / 4.2	20 TU 0235 / 0826 / 1502 / 2049	0.4 / 5.3 / 0.1 / 4.7
6 TU	0311 / 0900 / 1543 / 2120	0.9 / 4.5 / 0.9 / 4.1	21 W 0313 / 0906 / 1541 / 2128	0.4 / 5.1 / 0.3 / 4.5
7 W	0343 / 0931 / 1615 / 2155	1.1 / 4.3 / 1.1 / 3.9	22 TH 0353 / 0951 / 1622 / 2213	0.7 / 4.8 / 0.7 / 4.1
8 TH	0416 / 1005 / 1650 / 2235	1.4 / 4.0 / 1.4 / 3.7	23 F 0437 / 1046 / 1707 / 2314	1.0 / 4.3 / 1.1 / 3.8
9 F	0453 / 1045 / 1730 / 2328	1.6 / 3.8 / 1.7 / 3.5	24 SA ☾ 0528 / 1203 / 1800	1.4 / 3.9 / 1.6
10 SA	0537 / 1140 / 1818	1.9 / 3.5 / 1.9	25 SU ☾ 0049 / 0637 / 1335 / 1912	3.5 / 1.8 / 3.6 / 2.0
11 SU	0037 / 0630 / 1259 / 1921	3.4 / 2.1 / 3.4 / 2.1	26 M 0224 / 0836 / 1505 / 2111	3.5 / 2.0 / 3.5 / 2.1
12 M	0158 / 0746 / 1440 / 2054	3.4 / 2.2 / 3.3 / 2.2	27 TU 0347 / 1020 / 1622 / 2237	3.6 / 1.8 / 3.6 / 1.9
13 TU	0323 / 0933 / 1612 / 2222	3.5 / 2.2 / 3.5 / 2.0	28 W 0450 / 1120 / 1717 / 2327	3.9 / 1.4 / 3.8 / 1.6
14 W	0427 / 1050 / 1707 / 2316	3.8 / 1.9 / 3.7 / 1.7		
15 TH	0515 / 1142 / 1750	4.1 / 1.4 / 4.1		

MARCH

Day	Time	m	Time	m
1 TH	0535 / 1204 / 1756	4.2 / 1.1 / 4.0	16 F 0448 / 1118 / 1726 / 2336	4.2 / 1.3 / 4.2 / 1.3
2 F	0006 / 0609 / 1241 / 1827	1.3 / 4.4 / 0.9 / 4.1	17 SA 0531 / 1201 / 1804	4.6 / 0.8 / 4.5
3 SA ○	0041 / 0639 / 1314 / 1855	1.0 / 4.6 / 0.7 / 4.3	18 SU 0016 / 0610 / 1241 / 1839	0.9 / 5.0 / 0.4 / 4.8
4 SU	0114 / 0707 / 1343 / 1922	0.8 / 4.7 / 0.6 / 4.4	19 M ● 0055 / 0647 / 1320 / 1913	0.5 / 5.3 / 0.1 / 5.0
5 M	0144 / 0733 / 1412 / 1948	0.7 / 4.7 / 0.6 / 4.4	20 TU 0134 / 0725 / 1357 / 1948	0.3 / 5.4 / 0.0 / 5.0
6 TU	0214 / 0758 / 1439 / 2014	0.7 / 4.6 / 0.7 / 4.4	21 W 0212 / 0803 / 1435 / 2024	0.3 / 5.4 / 0.1 / 4.9
7 W	0243 / 0824 / 1507 / 2042	0.8 / 4.5 / 0.8 / 4.3	22 TH 0251 / 0844 / 1514 / 2103	0.4 / 5.1 / 0.4 / 4.6
8 TH	0312 / 0851 / 1536 / 2112	0.9 / 4.3 / 1.0 / 4.1	23 F 0332 / 0930 / 1554 / 2148	0.6 / 4.7 / 0.8 / 4.3
9 F	0342 / 0919 / 1608 / 2144	1.2 / 4.0 / 1.3 / 3.9	24 SA 0417 / 1029 / 1638 / 2252	1.0 / 4.2 / 1.3 / 3.9
10 SA	0416 / 0949 / 1644 / 2226	1.5 / 3.8 / 1.6 / 3.6	25 SU ☾ 0510 / 1155 / 1730	1.5 / 3.8 / 1.8
11 SU	0454 / 1030 / 1726 / 2340	1.8 / 3.5 / 1.9 / 3.4	26 M 0035 / 0628 / 1329 / 1848	3.6 / 1.9 / 3.5 / 2.2
12 M ☾	0543 / 1215 / 1827	2.0 / 3.3 / 2.2	27 TU 0207 / 0834 / 1458 / 2059	3.6 / 2.0 / 3.4 / 2.2
13 TU	0112 / 0659 / 1414 / 2009	3.4 / 2.2 / 3.2 / 2.3	28 W 0329 / 1009 / 1604 / 2218	3.7 / 1.7 / 3.6 / 2.0
14 W	0243 / 0904 / 1548 / 2155	3.5 / 2.1 / 3.5 / 2.1	29 TH 0431 / 1101 / 1704 / 2304	3.9 / 1.4 / 3.7 / 1.7
15 TH	0356 / 1028 / 1643 / 2252	3.8 / 1.7 / 3.8 / 1.7	30 F 0514 / 1140 / 1736 / 2341	4.2 / 1.2 / 3.9 / 1.4
			31 SA 0546 / 1213 / 1803	4.3 / 1.0 / 4.1

APRIL

Day	Time	m	Time	m
1 SU	0015 / 0614 / 1244 / 1828	1.1 / 4.5 / 0.8 / 4.3	16 M 0543 / 1211 / 1812	5.0 / 0.4 / 4.9
2 M ○	0047 / 0639 / 1313 / 1853	0.9 / 4.6 / 0.7 / 4.4	17 TU ● 0028 / 0622 / 1251 / 1848	0.6 / 5.3 / 0.2 / 5.0
3 TU	0117 / 0704 / 1339 / 1917	0.8 / 4.6 / 0.7 / 4.5	18 W 0109 / 0703 / 1331 / 1925	0.5 / 5.3 / 0.2 / 5.0
4 W	0146 / 0728 / 1406 / 1943	0.8 / 4.5 / 0.7 / 4.5	19 TH 0151 / 0744 / 1410 / 2004	0.4 / 5.2 / 0.2 / 4.9
5 TH	0214 / 0754 / 1433 / 2011	0.8 / 4.4 / 0.9 / 4.4	20 F 0233 / 0829 / 1451 / 2046	0.5 / 4.9 / 0.6 / 4.7
6 F	0243 / 0822 / 1503 / 2041	1.0 / 4.2 / 1.1 / 4.2	21 SA 0318 / 0920 / 1532 / 2137	0.8 / 4.5 / 1.1 / 4.4
7 SA	0314 / 0851 / 1534 / 2114	1.2 / 4.0 / 1.3 / 4.0	22 SU 0407 / 1024 / 1617 / 2248	1.2 / 4.1 / 1.5 / 4.1
8 SU	0348 / 0925 / 1609 / 2156	1.4 / 3.7 / 1.6 / 3.8	23 M 0505 / 1146 / 1710	1.5 / 3.7 / 1.9
9 M	0427 / 1017 / 1651 / 2311	1.7 / 3.5 / 1.9 / 3.6	24 TU ☾ 0015 / 0625 / 1307 / 1828	3.8 / 1.8 / 3.5 / 2.2
10 TU ☾	0519 / 1208 / 1752	1.9 / 3.3 / 2.2	25 W 0136 / 0803 / 1429 / 2015	3.8 / 1.9 / 3.4 / 2.3
11 W	0044 / 0641 / 1351 / 1936	3.5 / 2.0 / 3.3 / 2.3	26 TH 0251 / 0927 / 1542 / 2133	3.8 / 1.7 / 3.5 / 2.1
12 TH	0208 / 0832 / 1514 / 2115	3.6 / 1.9 / 3.5 / 2.1	27 F 0353 / 1022 / 1631 / 2225	3.9 / 1.5 / 3.7 / 1.8
13 F	0319 / 0951 / 1612 / 2216	3.9 / 1.5 / 3.9 / 1.7	28 SA 0439 / 1102 / 1705 / 2306	4.1 / 1.3 / 3.9 / 1.6
14 SA	0415 / 1044 / 1656 / 2303	4.3 / 1.1 / 4.3 / 1.3	29 SU 0514 / 1137 / 1733 / 2342	4.2 / 1.2 / 4.1 / 1.4
15 SU	0501 / 1129 / 1735 / 2346	4.7 / 0.7 / 4.6 / 0.9	30 M 0545 / 1209 / 1800	4.3 / 1.1 / 4.3

Chart Datum: 2·71 metres below Ordnance Datum (Newlyn)

TIDES

TIME ZONE (UT)	SCOTLAND – STORNOWAY	Dates in amber are SPRINGS
For Summer Time add ONE hour in **non-shaded areas**	**LAT 58°12'N LONG 6°23'W**	Dates in yellow are NEAPS
	TIMES AND HEIGHTS OF HIGH AND LOW WATERS	**2007**

MAY

Time	m		Time	m
1 TU	0016 1.2 / 0611 4.3 / 1240 1.0 / 1825 4.4	**16** W ●	0002 0.9 / 0600 5.0 / 1225 0.5 / 1826 4.8
2 W ○	0048 1.1 / 0637 4.4 / 1308 0.9 / 1851 4.5	**17** TH	0049 0.7 / 0646 5.0 / 1309 0.6 / 1908 4.9
3 TH	0119 1.0 / 0704 4.3 / 1337 0.9 / 1919 4.5	**18** F	0136 0.7 / 0733 4.8 / 1351 0.7 / 1951 4.8
4 F	0150 1.0 / 0734 4.2 / 1406 1.0 / 1951 4.4	**19** SA	0223 0.8 / 0822 4.6 / 1434 0.9 / 2038 4.7
5 SA	0222 1.1 / 0807 4.1 / 1438 1.2 / 2025 4.3	**20** SU	0312 0.9 / 0916 4.3 / 1518 1.2 / 2131 4.5
6 SU	0256 1.2 / 0843 3.9 / 1512 1.4 / 2103 4.1	**21** M	0403 1.1 / 1014 4.0 / 1604 1.5 / 2232 4.3
7 M	0334 1.4 / 0928 3.7 / 1549 1.6 / 2153 3.9	**22** TU	0500 1.4 / 1119 3.8 / 1655 1.8 / 2340 4.1
8 TU	0419 1.5 / 1034 3.5 / 1634 1.8 / 2303 3.8	**23** W ◑	0603 1.6 / 1226 3.6 / 1759 2.1
9 W	0517 1.7 / 1159 3.4 / 1738 2.0	**24** TH	0048 3.9 / 0713 1.7 / 1337 3.4 / 1916 2.2
10 TH ◑	0020 3.7 / 0633 1.7 / 1319 3.4 / 1905 2.1	**25** F	0157 3.8 / 0823 1.8 / 1447 3.5 / 2032 2.1
11 F	0132 3.8 / 0755 1.6 / 1432 3.6 / 2028 1.9	**26** SA	0301 3.8 / 0925 1.7 / 1544 3.6 / 2133 2.0
12 SA	0238 4.0 / 0907 1.4 / 1533 3.9 / 2133 1.7	**27** SU	0354 3.9 / 1015 1.6 / 1626 3.8 / 2223 1.8
13 SU	0337 4.3 / 1005 1.1 / 1622 4.2 / 2226 1.4	**28** M	0437 3.9 / 1056 1.5 / 1701 3.9 / 2306 1.6
14 M	0429 4.6 / 1054 0.8 / 1706 4.5 / 2315 1.1	**29** TU	0514 4.0 / 1134 1.4 / 1732 4.1 / 2344 1.5
15 TU	0516 4.8 / 1141 0.6 / 1746 4.7	**30** W	0547 4.0 / 1208 1.3 / 1801 4.3
		31 TH	0021 1.4 / 0618 4.1 / 1242 1.2 / 1831 4.4

JUNE

Time	m		Time	m
1 F ○	0057 1.2 / 0651 4.1 / 1315 1.1 / 1903 4.4	**16** SA	0131 0.8 / 0727 4.5 / 1341 0.9 / 1943 4.7
2 SA	0133 1.2 / 0726 4.1 / 1349 1.1 / 1939 4.4	**17** SU	0220 0.8 / 0816 4.4 / 1424 1.0 / 2028 4.7
3 SU	0210 1.1 / 0804 4.0 / 1424 1.2 / 2017 4.4	**18** M	0307 0.8 / 0903 4.3 / 1507 1.0 / 2114 4.6
4 M	0249 1.1 / 0846 3.9 / 1501 1.3 / 2059 4.3	**19** TU	0352 1.0 / 0950 4.1 / 1549 1.4 / 2201 4.4
5 TU	0330 1.2 / 0933 3.8 / 1541 1.4 / 2147 4.1	**20** W	0439 1.1 / 1039 3.9 / 1633 1.6 / 2252 4.2
6 W	0417 1.2 / 1029 3.7 / 1627 1.6 / 2245 4.0	**21** TH	0526 1.4 / 1131 3.7 / 1721 1.8 / 2347 4.0
7 TH	0511 1.3 / 1133 3.6 / 1724 1.7 / 2349 4.0	**22** F ◐	0617 1.6 / 1230 3.5 / 1815 2.0
8 F ◐	0612 1.4 / 1240 3.6 / 1831 1.8	**23** SA	0048 3.8 / 0712 1.7 / 1337 3.4 / 1917 2.1
9 SA	0054 4.0 / 0716 1.3 / 1347 3.6 / 1941 1.8	**24** SU	0154 3.7 / 0815 1.8 / 1445 3.5 / 2027 2.1
10 SU	0159 4.1 / 0821 1.3 / 1451 3.8 / 2049 1.6	**25** M	0301 3.6 / 0918 1.8 / 1542 3.6 / 2134 2.0
11 M	0301 4.2 / 0924 1.2 / 1548 4.0 / 2152 1.5	**26** TU	0359 3.6 / 1013 1.8 / 1627 3.8 / 2229 1.9
12 TU	0400 4.3 / 1023 1.1 / 1640 4.2 / 2251 1.3	**27** W	0447 3.7 / 1101 1.7 / 1706 3.9 / 2317 1.7
13 W	0455 4.4 / 1117 1.0 / 1727 4.4 / 2346 1.1	**28** TH	0529 3.8 / 1143 1.5 / 1741 4.1
14 TH	0547 4.5 / 1207 0.9 / 1813 4.6	**29** F	0000 1.6 / 0608 3.9 / 1223 1.4 / 1816 4.3
15 F ●	0040 0.9 / 0638 4.5 / 1255 0.9 / 1858 4.7	**30** SA	0042 1.4 / 0645 4.0 / 1300 1.2 / 1852 4.4

JULY

Time	m		Time	m
1 SU	0122 1.2 / 0723 4.1 / 1337 1.1 / 1928 4.5	**16** M	0211 0.7 / 0800 4.4 / 1412 1.0 / 2009 4.8
2 M	0201 1.0 / 0801 4.1 / 1414 1.1 / 2006 4.6	**17** TU	0251 0.7 / 0839 4.3 / 1450 1.0 / 2046 4.7
3 TU	0241 0.9 / 0839 4.1 / 1452 1.1 / 2045 4.5	**18** W	0329 0.8 / 0916 4.2 / 1526 1.1 / 2123 4.5
4 W	0322 0.8 / 0920 4.1 / 1531 1.1 / 2128 4.5	**19** TH	0406 0.9 / 0954 4.0 / 1603 1.3 / 2201 4.3
5 TH	0405 0.8 / 1005 4.0 / 1613 1.2 / 2217 4.4	**20** F	0443 1.2 / 1034 3.8 / 1641 1.5 / 2243 4.0
6 F	0451 0.9 / 1057 3.8 / 1700 1.4 / 2314 4.2	**21** SA	0522 1.4 / 1120 3.6 / 1722 1.8 / 2333 3.8
7 SA	0541 1.0 / 1157 3.7 / 1756 1.5 ◐	**22** SU ◐	0605 1.7 / 1216 3.5 / 1811 2.0
8 SU	0017 4.1 / 0637 1.2 / 1305 3.7 / 1859 1.6	**23** M	0032 3.6 / 0655 1.9 / 1325 3.4 / 1910 2.2
9 M	0125 4.0 / 0739 1.3 / 1414 3.7 / 2012 1.7	**24** TU	0148 3.4 / 0801 2.1 / 1445 3.5 / 2029 2.2
10 TU	0235 4.0 / 0849 1.4 / 1523 3.8 / 2132 1.6	**25** W	0319 3.4 / 0927 2.1 / 1552 3.6 / 2156 2.1
11 W	0345 4.0 / 1002 1.4 / 1625 4.0 / 2244 1.5	**26** TH	0426 3.5 / 1033 1.9 / 1642 3.8 / 2257 1.9
12 TH	0448 4.1 / 1107 1.3 / 1719 4.2 / 2346 1.2	**27** F	0515 3.7 / 1123 1.7 / 1723 4.0 / 2345 1.6
13 F	0545 4.2 / 1202 1.2 / 1807 4.5	**28** SA	0557 3.9 / 1206 1.5 / 1801 4.3
14 SA	0040 1.0 / 0635 4.3 / 1250 1.1 / 1850 4.6	**29** SU	0027 1.3 / 0634 4.1 / 1245 1.3 / 1836 4.6
15 SU	0128 0.8 / 0719 4.3 / 1333 1.0 / 1931 4.8	**30** M	0107 1.0 / 0709 4.3 / 1322 1.0 / 1912 4.8 ○
		31 TU	0146 0.7 / 0744 4.4 / 1358 0.8 / 1947 4.9

AUGUST

Time	m		Time	m
1 W	0223 0.5 / 0819 4.5 / 1435 0.7 / 2024 4.9	**16** TH	0256 0.7 / 0838 4.3 / 1458 1.0 / 2043 4.6
2 TH	0301 0.4 / 0855 4.4 / 1512 0.8 / 2103 4.9	**17** F	0327 0.9 / 0909 4.2 / 1529 1.1 / 2114 4.4
3 F	0341 0.5 / 0934 4.3 / 1551 0.9 / 2146 4.7	**18** SA	0359 1.1 / 0942 4.0 / 1602 1.4 / 2147 4.1
4 SA	0423 0.6 / 1020 4.1 / 1634 1.1 / 2239 4.4	**19** SU	0433 1.4 / 1022 3.8 / 1638 1.7 / 2227 3.8
5 SU	0508 0.9 / 1117 3.9 / 1723 1.4 / 2346 4.1 ◐	**20** M	0511 1.7 / 1113 3.6 / 1720 2.0 / 2324 3.5 ◐
6 M	0600 1.3 / 1231 3.7 / 1825 1.7	**21** TU	0556 2.0 / 1221 3.5 / 1813 2.2
7 TU	0105 3.9 / 0702 1.6 / 1353 3.6 / 1950 1.9	**22** W	0048 3.3 / 0655 2.2 / 1343 3.4 / 1927 2.4
8 W	0227 3.7 / 0827 1.8 / 1513 3.7 / 2137 1.8	**23** TH	0243 3.3 / 0832 2.3 / 1512 3.6 / 2129 2.3
9 TH	0346 3.8 / 1003 1.8 / 1623 3.9 / 2253 1.5	**24** F	0405 3.5 / 1010 2.2 / 1614 3.8 / 2241 2.0
10 F	0452 3.9 / 1109 1.6 / 1717 4.2 / 2349 1.2	**25** SA	0456 3.7 / 1103 1.9 / 1659 4.1 / 2326 1.6
11 SA	0545 4.1 / 1158 1.3 / 1801 4.5	**26** SU	0536 4.0 / 1144 1.6 / 1738 4.5
12 SU ●	0035 1.0 / 0627 4.2 / 1241 1.1 / 1838 4.7	**27** M	0006 1.2 / 0611 4.3 / 1223 1.2 / 1814 4.8
13 M	0116 0.7 / 0703 4.3 / 1318 1.0 / 1912 4.8	**28** TU ○	0044 0.8 / 0645 4.6 / 1259 0.9 / 1849 5.1
14 TU	0151 0.6 / 0736 4.4 / 1353 0.9 / 1944 4.8	**29** W	0121 0.5 / 0719 4.8 / 1335 0.7 / 1923 5.3
15 W	0225 0.4 / 0808 4.4 / 1426 0.9 / 2014 4.8	**30** TH	0158 0.3 / 0752 4.9 / 1411 0.5 / 1959 5.3
		31 F	0235 0.2 / 0827 4.8 / 1448 0.6 / 2037 5.2

Chart Datum: 2·71 metres below Ordnance Datum (Newlyn)

TIME ZONE (UT)
For Summer Time add ONE hour in **non-shaded areas**

Dates in amber are **SPRINGS**
Dates in yellow are **NEAPS**

SEPTEMBER

Time	m	Time	m
1 SA	0313 0.4 / 0905 4.6 / 1527 0.7 / 2120 4.9	**16** SU	0318 1.2 / 0859 4.2 / 1527 1.4 / 2102 4.1
2 SU	0353 0.7 / 0948 4.4 / 1609 1.0 / 2213 4.5	**17** M	0350 1.5 / 0934 4.0 / 1601 1.7 / 2133 3.8
3 M	0437 1.1 / 1046 4.0 / 1658 1.4 / 2329 4.1	**18** TU	0426 1.8 / 1021 3.8 / 1640 2.0 / 2217 3.6
4 TU	0528 1.5 / 1214 3.8 / 1804 1.8	**19** W	0509 2.1 / 1136 3.6 / 1730 2.3
5 W	0102 3.7 / 0633 2.0 / 1345 3.7 / 1956 2.0	**20** TH	0015 3.3 / 0608 2.4 / 1302 3.5 / 1847 2.4
6 TH	0231 3.6 / 0828 2.0 / 1511 3.8 / 2150 1.8	**21** F	0211 3.3 / 0746 2.5 / 1428 3.6 / 2055 2.3
7 F	0352 3.7 / 1008 2.0 / 1621 4.0 / 2254 1.5	**22** SA	0335 3.5 / 0940 2.3 / 1538 3.9 / 2212 1.9
8 SA	0453 3.9 / 1103 1.7 / 1711 4.3 / 2340 1.2	**23** SU	0427 3.6 / 1033 2.0 / 1628 4.3 / 2257 1.5
9 SU	0537 4.1 / 1145 1.4 / 1748 4.6	**24** M	0507 4.2 / 1114 1.6 / 1709 4.7 / 2336 1.1
10 M	0018 0.9 / 0610 4.3 / 1222 1.2 / 1819 4.7	**25** TU	0543 4.6 / 1153 1.2 / 1747 5.0
11 TU ●	0053 0.8 / 0640 4.4 / 1255 1.0 / 1848 4.8	**26** W ○	0014 0.7 / 0617 4.9 / 1231 0.9 / 1823 5.3
12 W	0123 0.7 / 0708 4.5 / 1327 0.9 / 1915 4.9	**27** TH	0052 0.4 / 0651 5.1 / 1308 0.6 / 1859 5.5
13 TH	0153 0.7 / 0735 4.5 / 1357 0.9 / 1941 4.8	**28** F	0129 0.2 / 0725 5.1 / 1346 0.5 / 1936 5.5
14 F	0221 0.8 / 0801 4.5 / 1427 1.0 / 2006 4.6	**29** SA	0207 0.3 / 0801 5.1 / 1425 0.6 / 2017 5.3
15 SA	0249 0.9 / 0829 4.4 / 1456 1.1 / 2033 4.4	**30** SU	0246 0.6 / 0841 4.9 / 1507 0.8 / 2102 4.9

OCTOBER

Time	m	Time	m
1 M	0327 0.9 / 0927 4.5 / 1551 1.2 / 2201 4.4	**16** TU	0317 1.5 / 0904 4.2 / 1534 1.7 / 2110 3.9
2 TU	0411 1.4 / 1033 4.2 / 1644 1.6 / 2327 4.0	**17** W	0352 1.8 / 0951 3.9 / 1614 1.9 / 2205 3.6
3 W ◐	0503 1.8 / 1207 3.9 / 1800 2.0	**18** TH	0435 2.1 / 1107 3.7 / 1706 2.2 / 2359 3.4
4 TH	0058 3.7 / 0616 2.3 / 1334 3.9 / 2001 2.1	**19** F ◐	0535 2.4 / 1230 3.7 / 1825 2.3
5 F	0225 3.7 / 0823 2.4 / 1456 4.0 / 2140 1.8	**20** SA	0133 3.5 / 0710 2.5 / 1345 3.8 / 2006 2.2
6 SA	0345 3.8 / 0951 2.1 / 1604 4.2 / 2236 1.5	**21** SU	0251 3.7 / 0849 2.3 / 1453 4.0 / 2125 1.9
7 SU	0441 4.0 / 1040 1.8 / 1651 4.4 / 2316 1.3	**22** M	0348 4.0 / 0951 2.0 / 1549 4.4 / 2217 1.4
8 M	0517 4.1 / 1119 1.6 / 1726 4.5 / 2351 1.1	**23** TU	0432 4.3 / 1037 1.6 / 1635 4.7 / 2300 1.1
9 TU	0546 4.3 / 1154 1.3 / 1756 4.7	**24** W	0511 4.7 / 1119 1.3 / 1717 5.1 / 2341 0.7
10 W	0022 1.0 / 0612 4.5 / 1227 1.2 / 1822 4.7	**25** TH	0548 4.9 / 1201 1.0 / 1757 5.3
11 TH ●	0051 0.9 / 0638 4.6 / 1258 1.1 / 1847 4.7	**26** F ○	0022 0.5 / 0624 5.1 / 1243 0.8 / 1837 5.4
12 F	0119 0.9 / 0703 4.6 / 1328 1.0 / 1911 4.7	**27** SA	0102 0.5 / 0702 5.2 / 1325 0.7 / 1919 5.4
13 SA	0147 1.0 / 0729 4.6 / 1358 1.1 / 1937 4.6	**28** SU	0143 0.5 / 0742 5.1 / 1408 0.7 / 2004 5.1
14 SU	0215 1.1 / 0757 4.5 / 1428 1.2 / 2005 4.4	**29** M	0224 0.8 / 0826 4.9 / 1454 0.9 / 2055 4.8
15 M	0244 1.3 / 0829 4.4 / 1500 1.4 / 2035 4.1	**30** TU	0307 1.1 / 0918 4.7 / 1543 1.4 / 2159 4.4
		31 W	0353 1.6 / 1027 4.4 / 1642 1.6 / 2318 4.0

NOVEMBER

Time	m	Time	m
1 TH ◐	0447 2.0 / 1149 4.2 / 1758 1.9	**16** F	0417 2.0 / 1044 3.9 / 1657 1.9 / 2333 3.6
2 F	0038 3.8 / 0601 2.3 / 1306 4.1 / 1930 2.0	**17** SA ◐	0515 2.2 / 1155 3.9 / 1805 1.9
3 SA	0156 3.7 / 0741 2.4 / 1420 4.1 / 2057 1.9	**18** SU	0050 3.6 / 0632 2.3 / 1302 3.9 / 1920 1.9
4 SU	0312 3.7 / 0905 2.2 / 1527 4.1 / 2156 1.7	**19** M	0200 3.7 / 0752 2.2 / 1406 4.1 / 2031 1.7
5 M	0408 3.9 / 1001 2.0 / 1618 4.3 / 2239 1.5	**20** TU	0301 3.9 / 0900 2.0 / 1506 4.3 / 2131 1.4
6 TU	0446 4.1 / 1045 1.8 / 1657 4.4 / 2315 1.4	**21** W	0353 4.2 / 0956 1.7 / 1559 4.6 / 2223 1.1
7 W	0517 4.2 / 1122 1.6 / 1729 4.4 / 2348 1.3	**22** TH	0438 4.5 / 1046 1.4 / 1648 4.8 / 2310 0.9
8 TH	0545 4.4 / 1158 1.4 / 1757 4.5	**23** F	0521 4.6 / 1135 1.1 / 1735 5.0 / 2356 0.8
9 F ●	0019 1.2 / 0612 4.5 / 1231 1.3 / 1824 4.5	**24** SA ○	0603 5.0 / 1223 1.0 / 1822 5.1
10 SA	0049 1.2 / 0638 4.6 / 1303 1.3 / 1850 4.5	**25** SU	0041 0.8 / 0646 5.1 / 1312 0.9 / 1909 5.0
11 SU	0119 1.2 / 0707 4.6 / 1336 1.3 / 1920 4.4	**26** M	0126 0.8 / 0731 5.0 / 1401 0.9 / 1959 4.9
12 M	0149 1.2 / 0738 4.6 / 1409 1.3 / 1952 4.3	**27** TU	0210 1.0 / 0819 5.0 / 1450 1.0 / 2052 4.6
13 TU	0221 1.3 / 0813 4.5 / 1443 1.4 / 2029 4.1	**28** W	0255 1.2 / 0911 4.8 / 1541 1.1 / 2149 4.3
14 W	0256 1.5 / 0852 4.3 / 1521 1.6 / 2112 3.9	**29** TH	0342 1.5 / 1009 4.6 / 1635 1.4 / 2251 4.1
15 TH	0333 1.8 / 0940 4.1 / 1603 1.7 / 2213 3.7	**30** F	0433 1.8 / 1113 4.4 / 1735 1.6 / 2357 3.8

DECEMBER

Time	m	Time	m
1 SA ◐	0532 2.1 / 1219 4.2 / 1840 1.8	**16** SU ◐	0454 1.8 / 1112 4.1 / 1737 1.5 / 2359 3.7
2 SU	0105 3.7 / 0642 2.2 / 1327 4.1 / 1950 1.9	**17** M ◐	0553 1.9 / 1215 4.1 / 1837 1.5
3 M	0216 3.6 / 0758 2.3 / 1434 4.0 / 2056 1.8	**18** TU	0106 3.7 / 0659 1.9 / 1320 4.1 / 1940 1.5
4 TU	0319 3.7 / 0907 2.2 / 1533 4.0 / 2151 1.8	**19** W	0212 3.8 / 0808 1.9 / 1424 4.2 / 2045 1.4
5 W	0407 3.9 / 1003 2.0 / 1622 4.0 / 2236 1.7	**20** TH	0314 4.0 / 0917 1.7 / 1527 4.3 / 2148 1.3
6 TH	0446 4.0 / 1049 1.8 / 1703 4.1 / 2316 1.6	**21** F	0410 4.2 / 1021 1.5 / 1627 4.4 / 2246 1.2
7 F	0521 4.2 / 1131 1.7 / 1738 4.1 / 2352 1.5	**22** SA	0502 4.5 / 1120 1.3 / 1723 4.6 / 2340 1.1
8 SA	0552 4.4 / 1209 1.5 / 1811 4.2	**23** SU	0551 4.7 / 1216 1.1 / 1815 4.7
9 SU	0027 1.4 / 0623 4.5 / 1247 1.4 / 1842 4.2	**24** M ○	0030 1.0 / 0638 4.9 / 1309 0.9 / 1905 4.7
10 M ●	0101 1.3 / 0655 4.5 / 1323 1.3 / 1916 4.2	**25** TU	0118 1.0 / 0724 5.0 / 1359 0.8 / 1953 4.7
11 TU	0135 1.3 / 0729 4.6 / 1359 1.3 / 1951 4.2	**26** W	0203 1.0 / 0809 5.0 / 1445 0.8 / 2039 4.6
12 W	0209 1.3 / 0805 4.5 / 1436 1.3 / 2029 4.1	**27** TH	0246 1.1 / 0854 4.9 / 1530 0.8 / 2124 4.4
13 TH	0245 1.4 / 0843 4.5 / 1515 1.3 / 2110 4.0	**28** F	0328 1.2 / 0939 4.7 / 1614 1.0 / 2210 4.1
14 F	0323 1.5 / 0925 4.3 / 1557 1.3 / 2157 3.9	**29** SA	0411 1.4 / 1026 4.5 / 1700 1.3 / 2300 3.9
15 SA	0405 1.6 / 1014 4.2 / 1644 1.4 / 2254 3.7	**30** SU	0456 1.7 / 1118 4.2 / 1747 1.5 / 2357 3.7
		31 M ◐	0546 1.9 / 1217 4.0 / 1840 1.6

Chart Datum: 2·71 metres below Ordnance Datum (Newlyn)

TIDES

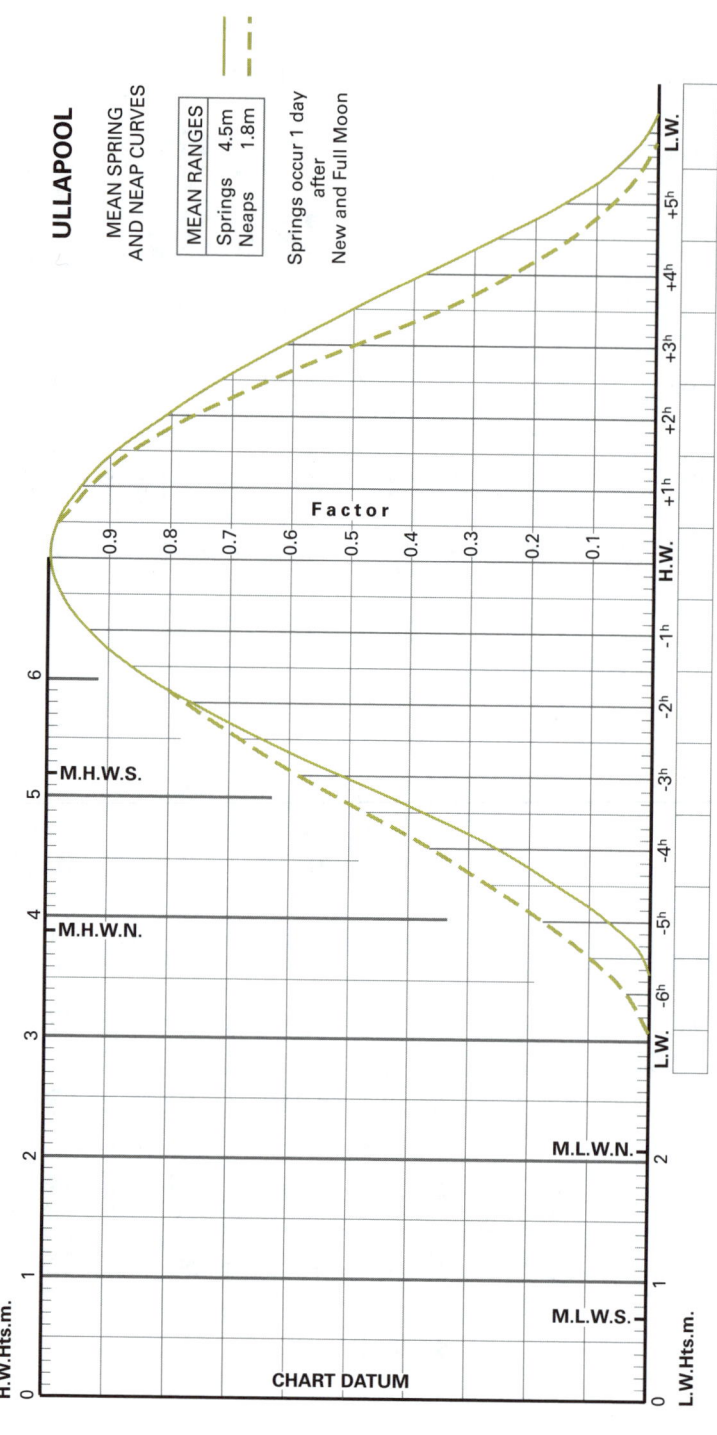

ULLAPOOL

MEAN SPRING
AND NEAP CURVES

MEAN RANGES	
Springs	4.5m
Neaps	1.8m

Springs occur 1 day
after
New and Full Moon

SCOTLAND – ULLAPOOL

LAT 57°54'N LONG 5°10'W

TIMES AND HEIGHTS OF HIGH AND LOW WATERS

Dates in amber are SPRINGS
Dates in yellow are NEAPS

2007

JANUARY

Day	Time m	Day	Time m
1 M	0507 4.7 / 1124 1.6 / 1729 4.8 / 2343 1.5	**16** TU	0503 4.4 / 1116 2.1 / 1726 4.3 / 2341 1.9
2 TU	0555 4.9 / 1217 1.4 / 1819 4.9	**17** W	0545 4.7 / 1203 1.8 / 1809 4.5
3 W ○	0031 1.4 / 0637 5.1 / 1306 1.3 / 1904 5.0	**18** TH	0023 1.6 / 0622 4.9 / 1247 1.4 / 1848 4.8
4 TH	0115 1.4 / 0716 5.2 / 1350 1.1 / 1945 5.0	**19** F ●	0104 1.4 / 0659 5.2 / 1329 1.1 / 1926 5.0
5 F	0155 1.3 / 0754 5.2 / 1431 1.1 / 2024 4.9	**20** SA	0144 1.2 / 0737 5.4 / 1410 0.9 / 2005 5.1
6 SA	0234 1.4 / 0830 5.2 / 1510 1.2 / 2101 4.8	**21** SU	0224 1.0 / 0816 5.5 / 1450 0.7 / 2046 5.1
7 SU	0311 1.4 / 0904 5.0 / 1548 1.3 / 2137 4.6	**22** M	0304 1.0 / 0857 5.5 / 1532 0.7 / 2127 5.0
8 M	0347 1.6 / 0939 4.9 / 1625 1.4 / 2214 4.4	**23** TU	0344 1.0 / 0940 5.4 / 1614 0.8 / 2213 4.8
9 TU	0424 1.7 / 1015 4.6 / 1703 1.6 / 2256 4.2	**24** W	0427 1.2 / 1028 5.2 / 1658 1.0 / 2304 4.6
10 W	0503 1.9 / 1055 4.4 / 1743 1.9 / 2346 4.0	**25** TH ◑	0514 1.5 / 1123 4.9 / 1746 1.4
11 TH ◐	0546 2.2 / 1147 4.2 / 1830 2.1	**26** F	0005 4.3 / 0608 1.8 / 1231 4.5 / 1842 1.7
12 F	0050 3.9 / 0637 2.4 / 1258 4.0 / 1927 2.3	**27** SA	0120 4.2 / 0717 2.1 / 1350 4.3 / 1954 2.0
13 SA	0203 3.9 / 0745 2.5 / 1417 3.9 / 2040 2.3	**28** SU	0243 4.1 / 0847 2.2 / 1515 4.2 / 2124 2.1
14 SU	0314 4.0 / 0907 2.5 / 1533 3.9 / 2154 2.3	**29** M	0404 4.2 / 1018 2.1 / 1634 4.3 / 2244 2.0
15 M	0414 4.1 / 1020 2.4 / 1636 4.1 / 2253 2.1	**30** TU	0506 4.5 / 1127 1.8 / 1733 4.5 / 2342 1.8
		31 W	0554 4.7 / 1219 1.5 / 1819 4.7

FEBRUARY

Day	Time m	Day	Time m
1 TH	0028 1.6 / 0633 5.0 / 1303 1.2 / 1857 4.8	**16** F	0009 1.6 / 0603 4.9 / 1232 1.2 / 1832 4.9
2 F ○	0108 1.4 / 0707 5.1 / 1341 1.0 / 1930 4.9	**17** SA ●	0049 1.2 / 0640 5.3 / 1312 0.8 / 1908 5.1
3 SA	0144 1.2 / 0738 5.2 / 1416 0.9 / 2001 5.0	**18** SU	0128 0.8 / 0717 5.6 / 1352 0.5 / 1945 5.3
4 SU	0217 1.1 / 0807 5.2 / 1449 0.9 / 2031 4.9	**19** M	0206 0.6 / 0755 5.7 / 1431 0.3 / 2022 5.4
5 M	0249 1.1 / 0835 5.1 / 1520 1.0 / 2100 4.8	**20** TU	0244 0.5 / 0834 5.7 / 1509 0.3 / 2101 5.2
6 TU	0320 1.2 / 0904 5.0 / 1550 1.1 / 2130 4.6	**21** W	0323 0.6 / 0915 5.5 / 1549 0.5 / 2142 5.0
7 W	0351 1.4 / 0933 4.8 / 1621 1.3 / 2202 4.4	**22** TH	0404 0.8 / 1001 5.2 / 1629 0.8 / 2228 4.7
8 TH	0423 1.6 / 1004 4.5 / 1653 1.6 / 2239 4.2	**23** F	0448 1.2 / 1055 4.8 / 1713 1.3 / 2326 4.3
9 F	0458 1.8 / 1041 4.3 / 1729 1.9 / 2328 4.0	**24** SA ◑	0540 1.7 / 1207 4.3 / 1806 1.8
10 SA ◐	0540 2.1 / 1130 4.0 / 1813 2.2	**25** SU	0048 4.0 / 0649 2.1 / 1338 4.0 / 1920 2.3
11 SU	0043 3.8 / 0634 2.4 / 1257 3.7 / 1917 2.4	**26** M	0227 3.9 / 0838 2.3 / 1515 3.9 / 2117 2.4
12 M	0215 3.8 / 0758 2.6 / 1447 3.7 / 2104 2.5	**27** TU	0357 4.1 / 1024 2.1 / 1634 4.1 / 2244 2.2
13 TU	0337 3.8 / 0947 2.5 / 1614 3.8 / 2232 2.3	**28** W	0500 4.3 / 1126 1.7 / 1728 4.3 / 2336 1.8
14 W	0439 4.2 / 1059 2.4 / 1712 4.1 / 2325 1.9		
15 TH	0525 4.5 / 1149 1.7 / 1755 4.5		

MARCH

Day	Time m	Day	Time m
1 TH	0544 4.6 / 1210 1.4 / 1807 4.5	**16** F	0456 4.5 / 1125 1.4 / 1730 4.5 / 2345 1.4
2 F	0016 1.5 / 0618 4.8 / 1247 1.1 / 1838 4.7	**17** SA	0536 4.9 / 1207 0.9 / 1807 4.9
3 SA ○	0052 1.3 / 0647 5.0 / 1321 0.9 / 1907 4.9	**18** SU	0025 0.9 / 0614 5.3 / 1247 0.5 / 1842 5.2
4 SU	0124 1.1 / 0714 5.1 / 1351 0.7 / 1933 4.9	**19** M ●	0104 0.6 / 0651 5.6 / 1326 0.2 / 1918 5.4
5 M	0154 1.0 / 0740 5.1 / 1420 0.8 / 1959 4.9	**20** TU	0142 0.3 / 0730 5.8 / 1405 0.0 / 1955 5.4
6 TU	0223 0.9 / 0805 5.1 / 1447 0.8 / 2025 4.9	**21** W	0221 0.3 / 0810 5.7 / 1443 0.1 / 2033 5.3
7 W	0251 1.0 / 0830 5.0 / 1515 1.0 / 2052 4.7	**22** TH	0301 0.4 / 0853 5.4 / 1522 0.4 / 2114 5.0
8 TH	0319 1.1 / 0858 4.8 / 1542 1.2 / 2121 4.6	**23** F	0342 0.7 / 0941 5.0 / 1603 0.9 / 2200 4.7
9 F	0350 1.3 / 0927 4.5 / 1612 1.4 / 2153 4.3	**24** SA	0428 1.1 / 1040 4.5 / 1646 1.4 / 2300 4.3
10 SA	0423 1.6 / 1001 4.2 / 1644 1.8 / 2234 4.1	**25** SU ◑	0521 1.6 / 1200 4.1 / 1739 2.0
11 SU	0501 1.9 / 1045 3.9 / 1722 2.1 / 2336 3.8	**26** M	0030 4.0 / 0636 2.0 / 1332 3.8 / 1859 2.4
12 M ◐	0550 2.2 / 1203 3.6 / 1818 2.4	**27** TU	0210 3.9 / 0835 2.2 / 1506 3.8 / 2106 2.4
13 TU	0123 3.7 / 0708 2.5 / 1413 3.6 / 2014 2.6	**28** W	0339 4.0 / 1010 1.9 / 1619 4.0 / 2225 2.1
14 W	0256 3.8 / 0915 2.4 / 1547 3.7 / 2207 2.3	**29** TH	0439 4.2 / 1104 1.6 / 1707 4.2 / 2313 1.8
15 TH	0406 4.1 / 1035 1.9 / 1647 4.1 / 2302 1.9	**30** F	0520 4.4 / 1144 1.3 / 1742 4.4 / 2351 1.5
		31 SA	0553 4.6 / 1219 1.1 / 1812 4.6

APRIL

Day	Time m	Day	Time m
1 SU	0025 1.2 / 0620 4.8 / 1251 0.9 / 1838 4.8	**16** M	0545 5.3 / 1217 0.4 / 1815 5.2
2 M ○	0056 1.1 / 0645 4.9 / 1320 0.8 / 1903 4.9	**17** TU ●	0036 0.5 / 0625 5.5 / 1258 0.2 / 1852 5.3
3 TU	0126 0.9 / 0710 4.9 / 1348 0.8 / 1929 4.9	**18** W	0118 0.3 / 0706 5.6 / 1338 0.1 / 1930 5.4
4 W	0154 0.9 / 0736 4.9 / 1415 0.8 / 1954 4.8	**19** TH	0159 0.3 / 0750 5.5 / 1419 0.3 / 2010 5.2
5 TH	0222 1.0 / 0802 4.8 / 1441 1.0 / 2021 4.8	**20** F	0242 0.4 / 0837 5.2 / 1459 0.6 / 2054 5.0
6 F	0251 1.1 / 0830 4.6 / 1509 1.2 / 2050 4.6	**21** SA	0326 0.7 / 0931 4.8 / 1541 1.1 / 2144 4.7
7 SA	0322 1.3 / 0902 4.4 / 1539 1.4 / 2124 4.4	**22** SU	0415 1.1 / 1037 4.3 / 1628 1.5 / 2248 4.3
8 SU	0357 1.5 / 0940 4.1 / 1612 1.7 / 2206 4.2	**23** M	0513 1.6 / 1153 4.0 / 1723 2.0
9 M	0436 1.8 / 1031 3.9 / 1652 2.0 / 2310 3.9	**24** TU ◑	0012 4.0 / 0628 1.9 / 1313 3.8 / 1841 2.1
10 TU ◐	0528 2.0 / 1201 3.6 / 1751 2.3	**25** W	0140 3.9 / 0806 2.0 / 1434 3.7 / 2024 2.3
11 W	0048 3.8 / 0646 2.2 / 1346 3.6 / 1940 2.4	**26** TH	0301 3.9 / 0928 1.8 / 1543 3.9 / 2143 2.1
12 TH	0216 3.8 / 0839 2.1 / 1510 3.8 / 2129 2.2	**27** F	0401 4.2 / 1023 1.6 / 1631 4.0 / 2234 1.8
13 F	0325 4.1 / 0958 1.7 / 1612 4.1 / 2227 1.7	**28** SA	0445 4.2 / 1106 1.4 / 1708 4.2 / 2315 1.4
14 SA	0419 4.5 / 1050 1.2 / 1658 4.5 / 2313 1.3	**29** SU	0519 4.4 / 1142 1.2 / 1739 4.4 / 2352 1.4
15 SU	0504 4.9 / 1135 0.8 / 1737 4.9 / 2355 0.9	**30** M	0549 4.5 / 1215 1.1 / 1808 4.6

Chart Datum: 2·75 metres below Ordnance Datum (Newlyn)

TIDES

TIME ZONE (UT)
For Summer Time add ONE hour in **non-shaded areas**

SCOTLAND – ULLAPOOL

LAT 57°54'N   LONG 5°10'W

TIMES AND HEIGHTS OF HIGH AND LOW WATERS

Dates in amber are **SPRINGS**
Dates in yellow are **NEAPS**

2007

MAY

Time	m		Time	m
1 0025	1.2	**16**	0011	0.7
0616	4.6		0604	5.2
TU 1247	1.0	W 1233	0.5
1834	4.7	● 1830	5.2
2 0057	1.1	**17**	0057	0.6
0644	4.7		0650	5.2
W 1316	1.0	TH 1316	0.5
○ 1901	4.8		1912	5.2
3 0127	1.1	**18**	0143	0.5
0712	4.7		0739	5.1
TH 1345	1.0	F 1359	0.6
1929	4.8		1956	5.1
4 0158	1.1	**19**	0230	0.6
0742	4.6		0831	4.9
F 1414	1.1	SA 1443	0.9
1959	4.7		2043	4.9
5 0230	1.1	**20**	0318	0.8
0815	4.5		0927	4.6
SA 1444	1.3	SU 1527	1.2
2031	4.6		2134	4.7
6 0304	1.3	**21**	0408	1.1
0852	4.3		1027	4.3
SU 1517	1.4	M 1615	1.5
2110	4.4		2234	4.4
7 0342	1.4	**22**	0504	1.4
0938	4.1		1130	4.0
M 1555	1.7	TU 1708	1.9
2158	4.3		2341	4.2
8 0425	1.6	**23**	0606	1.7
1039	3.9		1235	3.9
TU 1640	1.9	W 1811	2.1
2303	4.1	◑	
9 0520	1.8	**24**	0052	4.0
1157	3.8		0715	1.8
W 1743	2.1	TH 1342	3.8
			1925	2.2
10 0022	4.0	**25**	0204	3.9
0633	1.9		0825	1.8
TH 1317	3.8	F 1448	3.8
◑ 1911	2.2		2039	2.1
11 0137	4.0	**26**	0307	3.9
0759	1.8		0927	1.7
F 1429	3.9	SA 1543	3.9
2039	2.0		2141	2.0
12 0243	4.2	**27**	0358	4.0
0912	1.5		1018	1.6
SA 1532	4.1	SU 1627	4.1
2144	1.7		2232	1.8
13 0340	4.5	**28**	0440	4.1
1011	1.2		1101	1.5
SU 1623	4.5	M 1705	4.2
2237	1.3		2315	1.6
14 0431	4.8	**29**	0517	4.2
1101	0.8		1139	1.4
M 1708	4.8	TU 1738	4.4
2325	1.0		2353	1.5
15 0518	5.1	**30**	0551	4.3
1148	0.6		1214	1.3
TU 1749	5.0	W 1810	4.6
		31	0029	1.4
			0624	4.4
		TH 1248	1.2
			1840	4.7

JUNE

Time	m		Time	m
1 0105	1.3	**16**	0136	0.8
0657	4.5		0736	4.9
F 1321	1.2	SA 1348	1.0
○ 1912	4.7		1948	5.1
2 0140	1.2	**17**	0224	0.8
0733	4.5		0825	4.8
SA 1355	1.3	SU 1432	1.1
1946	4.7		2033	5.0
3 0216	1.2	**18**	0311	0.9
0811	4.4		0914	4.6
SU 1430	1.3	M 1516	1.2
2024	4.7		2119	4.8
4 0254	1.2	**19**	0357	1.0
0853	4.3		1002	4.4
M 1507	1.4	TU 1600	1.4
2106	4.6		2206	4.6
5 0335	1.3	**20**	0443	1.2
0940	4.2		1051	4.2
TU 1548	1.5	W 1645	1.6
2154	4.5		2256	4.4
6 0421	1.4	**21**	0530	1.4
1034	4.1		1142	4.0
W 1636	1.7	TH 1732	1.8
2250	4.4		2350	4.1
7 0513	1.4	**22**	0620	1.6
1136	4.0		1238	3.8
TH 1732	1.8	F 1825	2.0
2353	4.3	◐	
8 0613	1.6	**23**	0051	4.0
1242	4.0		0714	1.8
F 1839	1.9	SA 1340	3.8
◐			1925	2.1
9 0058	4.3	**24**	0157	3.8
0719	1.5		0815	1.9
SA 1349	4.0	SU 1443	3.8
1951	1.8		2033	2.2
10 0203	4.3	**25**	0301	3.8
0827	1.4		0918	1.9
SU 1453	4.1	M 1541	3.9
2101	1.7		2140	2.1
11 0306	4.4	**26**	0359	3.9
0931	1.3		1016	1.8
M 1552	4.3	TU 1630	4.1
2204	1.5		2237	2.0
12 0405	4.6	**27**	0449	4.0
1030	1.2		1105	1.7
TU 1644	4.6	W 1712	4.2
2301	1.3		2326	1.8
13 0501	4.7	**28**	0533	4.1
1124	1.0		1148	1.6
W 1733	4.8	TH 1750	4.4
2355	1.0		
14 0555	4.9	**29**	0008	1.6
1214	1.0		0612	4.3
TH 1819	5.0	F 1228	1.5
			1825	4.6
15 0046	0.9	**30**	0049	1.4
0646	4.9		0649	4.4
F 1302	0.9	SA 1305	1.4
● 1903	5.1	○ 1901	4.8

JULY

Time	m		Time	m
1 0128	1.2	**16**	0217	0.8
0727	4.5		0810	4.8
SU 1343	1.3	M 1421	1.1
1937	4.9		2017	5.1
2 0207	1.1	**17**	0257	0.8
0805	4.6		0848	4.7
M 1421	1.2	TU 1459	1.1
2015	4.9		2053	5.0
3 0247	1.0	**18**	0335	0.9
0845	4.6		0925	4.6
TU 1500	1.2	W 1536	1.2
2055	4.9		2129	4.8
4 0328	1.0	**19**	0412	1.0
0927	4.5		1003	4.4
W 1540	1.2	TH 1613	1.4
2138	4.9		2205	4.6
5 0410	1.0	**20**	0448	1.3
1013	4.4		1042	4.2
TH 1624	1.3	F 1651	1.6
2226	4.7		2243	4.3
6 0455	1.1	**21**	0527	1.5
1105	4.3		1129	4.0
F 1712	1.5	SA 1731	1.8
2320	4.6		2331	4.0
7 0545	1.2	**22**	0609	1.8
1205	4.2		1228	3.8
SA 1806	1.6	SU 1819	2.1
◐		◐	
8 0022	4.5	**23**	0036	3.8
0641	1.4		0659	2.0
SU 1311	4.1	M 1308	3.7
1910	1.8		1919	2.3
9 0130	4.3	**24**	0156	3.7
0745	1.5		0807	2.2
M 1420	4.1	TU 1450	3.8
2023	1.8		2040	2.4
10 0241	4.3	**25**	0317	3.7
0857	1.6		0930	2.2
TU 1530	4.2	W 1556	3.9
2141	1.8		2203	2.3
11 0354	4.3	**26**	0426	3.8
1010	1.6		1038	2.1
W 1634	4.4	TH 1649	4.1
2252	1.6		2305	2.0
12 0500	4.4	**27**	0519	4.0
1114	1.5		1129	1.9
TH 1728	4.6	F 1732	4.4
2353	1.3		2353	1.7
13 0557	4.6	**28**	0600	4.2
1208	1.3		1211	1.6
F 1816	4.8	SA 1810	4.6
14 0045	1.1	**29**	0035	1.4
0646	4.7		0637	4.5
SA 1257	1.2	SU 1251	1.4
● 1859	5.0		1845	4.9
15 0133	0.9	**30**	0115	1.1
0730	4.8		0712	4.7
SU 1340	1.1	M 1329	1.1
○ 1901	4.8	○ 1920	5.1
		31	0153	0.8
			0747	4.9
		TU 1407	1.0
			1956	5.3

AUGUST

Time	m		Time	m
1 0231	0.6	**16**	0304	0.8
0824	4.9		0846	4.8
W 1444	0.9	TH 1507	1.1
2034	5.3		2049	4.9
2 0310	0.6	**17**	0335	0.9
0902	4.9		0916	4.6
TH 1523	0.9	F 1538	1.2
2114	5.2		2118	4.7
3 0349	0.6	**18**	0406	1.2
0944	4.8		0948	4.4
F 1603	1.0	SA 1611	1.4
2158	5.1		2150	4.4
4 0430	0.8	**19**	0438	1.5
1031	4.6		1024	4.2
SA 1646	1.2	SU 1646	1.7
2249	4.8		2227	4.2
5 0514	1.1	**20**	0513	1.8
1127	4.3		1112	4.0
SU 1736	1.5	M 1726	2.0
◑ 2352	4.5	◑ 2316	3.9
6 0606	1.5	**21**	0555	2.1
1238	4.1		1229	3.8
M 1837	1.8	TU 1819	2.3
7 0109	4.2	**22**	0053	3.6
0709	1.8		0655	2.4
TU 1359	4.0	W 1400	3.7
2000	2.0		1940	2.5
8 0234	4.1	**23**	0240	3.6
0836	2.0		0842	2.5
W 1523	4.1	TH 1521	3.8
2139	2.0		2135	2.4
9 0400	4.1	**24**	0405	3.7
1008	2.0		1017	2.3
TH 1634	4.3	F 1623	4.1
2258	1.7		2247	2.1
10 0507	4.3	**25**	0500	4.0
1115	1.8		1111	2.0
F 1728	4.6	SA 1709	4.4
2355	1.4		2334	1.7
11 0557	4.5	**26**	0540	4.3
1205	1.5		1152	1.6
SA 1811	4.9	SU 1746	4.8
12 0042	1.1	**27**	0014	1.3
0638	4.7		0614	4.7
SU 1248	1.3	M 1231	1.3
● 1847	5.0		1820	5.1
13 0122	0.9	**28**	0053	0.9
0713	4.9		0647	5.0
M 1327	1.1	TU 1308	0.9
1920	5.2	○ 1855	5.4
14 0159	0.7	**29**	0130	0.5
0745	4.9		0721	5.2
TU 1402	1.0	W 1344	0.7
1951	5.2		1930	5.6
15 0233	0.7	**30**	0207	0.3
0816	4.9		0757	5.3
W 1435	1.0	TH 1421	0.6
2020	5.1		2007	5.6
		31	0244	0.3
			0833	5.2
		F 1459	0.6
			2047	5.5

Chart Datum: 2·75 metres below Ordnance Datum (Newlyn)

TIME ZONE (UT)	SCOTLAND – ULLAPOOL	Dates in amber are SPRINGS
For Summer Time add ONE hour in non-shaded areas	LAT 57°54'N LONG 5°10'W	Dates in yellow are NEAPS
	TIMES AND HEIGHTS OF HIGH AND LOW WATERS	2007

SEPTEMBER

Time m

Day		Day	
1 SA	0322 0.4 / 0913 5.0 / 1539 0.8 / 2131 5.2	16 SU	0327 1.2 / 0904 4.6 / 1536 1.4 / 2111 4.5
2 SU	0402 0.7 / 0957 4.8 / 1622 1.1 / 2223 4.8	17 M	0356 1.5 / 0937 4.4 / 1609 1.7 / 2145 4.2
3 M	0445 1.2 / 1053 4.4 / 1711 1.5 / 2334 4.4	18 TU	0429 1.8 / 1018 4.1 / 1648 2.0 / 2231 3.9
4 TU	0535 1.7 / 1214 4.1 / 1816 1.9	19 W	0507 2.2 / 1124 3.9 / 1737 2.3
5 W	0105 4.1 / 0643 2.2 / 1350 4.0 / 1957 2.2	20 TH	0005 3.6 / 0601 2.5 / 1314 3.8 / 1855 2.5
6 TH	0240 3.9 / 0833 2.4 / 1522 4.1 / 2151 2.0	21 F	0207 3.6 / 0755 2.7 / 1442 3.9 / 2103 2.4
7 F	0404 4.1 / 1012 2.2 / 1630 4.4 / 2258 1.7	22 SA	0334 3.8 / 0950 2.6 / 1548 4.1 / 2219 2.1
8 SA	0503 4.3 / 1110 1.9 / 1719 4.6 / 2345 1.3	23 SU	0431 4.1 / 1043 2.0 / 1636 4.5 / 2305 1.6
9 SU	0545 4.6 / 1153 1.5 / 1756 4.9	24 M	0511 4.5 / 1124 1.6 / 1715 4.9 / 2345 1.1
10 M	0025 1.1 / 0618 4.8 / 1230 1.3 / 1827 5.1	25 TU	0545 4.8 / 1202 1.2 / 1751 5.3
11 TU	0100 0.9 / 0648 4.9 / 1304 1.1 / 1855 5.2 ●	26 W	0023 0.7 / 0619 5.2 / 1240 0.8 / 1826 5.6 ○
12 W	0132 0.8 / 0715 5.0 / 1336 1.0 / 1921 5.2	27 TH	0101 0.4 / 0653 5.4 / 1317 0.6 / 1903 5.8
13 TH	0202 0.7 / 0742 5.0 / 1406 1.0 / 1947 5.1	28 F	0139 0.2 / 0728 5.5 / 1356 0.5 / 1942 5.8
14 F	0230 0.8 / 0808 4.9 / 1435 1.0 / 2014 5.0	29 SA	0217 0.3 / 0806 5.4 / 1435 0.5 / 2024 5.6
15 SA	0258 1.0 / 0836 4.8 / 1505 1.2 / 2041 4.8	30 SU	0256 0.5 / 0846 5.2 / 1517 0.8 / 2112 5.2

OCTOBER

Time m

Day		Day	
1 M	0337 0.9 / 0932 4.9 / 1603 1.2 / 2210 4.7	16 TU	0323 1.6 / 0907 4.6 / 1542 1.7 / 2123 4.3
2 TU	0421 1.4 / 1031 4.5 / 1656 1.6 / 2332 4.3	17 W	0357 1.9 / 0948 4.3 / 1622 2.0 / 2215 4.0
3 W	0514 2.0 / 1201 4.2 / 1809 2.0 ◑	18 TH	0436 2.2 / 1051 4.1 / 1713 2.2 / 2345 3.7
4 TH	0103 4.0 / 0629 2.4 / 1340 4.1 / 2000 2.2	19 F	0531 2.5 / 1230 3.9 / 1828 2.4 ◑
5 F	0235 4.0 / 0827 2.5 / 1508 4.2 / 2140 2.0	20 SA	0128 3.7 / 0711 2.6 / 1356 4.0 / 2015 2.3
6 SA	0352 4.1 / 0955 2.2 / 1612 4.4 / 2238 1.7	21 SU	0249 3.9 / 0902 2.4 / 1503 4.2 / 2134 2.0
7 SU	0444 4.3 / 1047 1.9 / 1657 4.6 / 2320 1.4	22 M	0350 4.2 / 1002 2.0 / 1556 4.6 / 2226 1.5
8 M	0522 4.6 / 1128 1.6 / 1732 4.8 / 2357 1.2	23 TU	0435 4.6 / 1048 1.6 / 1640 4.9 / 2309 1.1
9 TU	0553 4.8 / 1203 1.4 / 1801 5.0	24 W	0513 4.9 / 1129 1.2 / 1720 5.3 / 2351 0.7
10 W	0030 1.0 / 0620 4.9 / 1237 1.2 / 1827 5.1	25 TH	0550 5.2 / 1210 0.9 / 1800 5.6
11 TH	0101 0.9 / 0646 5.0 / 1307 1.1 / 1853 5.1 ●	26 F	0031 0.5 / 0626 5.5 / 1251 0.6 / 1840 5.7 ○
12 F	0129 0.9 / 0712 5.0 / 1337 1.1 / 1919 5.0	27 SA	0112 0.4 / 0704 5.6 / 1333 0.6 / 1923 5.7
13 SA	0157 1.0 / 0737 5.0 / 1406 1.2 / 1946 4.9	28 SU	0153 0.5 / 0745 5.5 / 1417 0.7 / 2010 5.4
14 SU	0225 1.1 / 0804 4.9 / 1436 1.3 / 2014 4.8	29 M	0234 0.8 / 0828 5.3 / 1502 0.9 / 2104 5.1
15 M	0253 1.4 / 0834 4.8 / 1508 1.5 / 2046 4.5	30 TU	0318 1.2 / 0918 5.0 / 1552 1.2 / 2208 4.7
		31 W	0405 1.6 / 1020 4.7 / 1650 1.6 / 2325 4.3

NOVEMBER

Time m

Day		Day	
1 TH	0500 2.1 / 1144 4.4 / 1803 2.0 ◑	16 F	0421 2.1 / 1035 4.3 / 1659 2.0 / 2323 4.0
2 F	0045 4.1 / 0614 2.4 / 1312 4.2 / 1934 2.1	17 SA	0516 2.3 / 1149 4.2 / 1804 2.1 ◑
3 SA	0206 4.0 / 0750 2.5 / 1434 4.0 / 2058 2.0	18 SU	0043 3.9 / 0632 2.4 / 1306 4.2 / 1923 2.1
4 SU	0318 4.1 / 0912 2.3 / 1538 4.4 / 2159 1.8	19 M	0158 4.0 / 0801 2.3 / 1413 4.4 / 2038 1.9
5 M	0411 4.3 / 1009 2.1 / 1625 4.5 / 2244 1.6	20 TU	0302 4.2 / 0912 2.1 / 1512 4.6 / 2140 1.6
6 TU	0451 4.5 / 1054 1.8 / 1702 4.6 / 2322 1.4	21 W	0356 4.5 / 1008 1.8 / 1604 4.9 / 2232 1.3
7 W	0523 4.7 / 1132 1.6 / 1734 4.8 / 2357 1.3	22 TH	0443 4.9 / 1057 1.4 / 1652 5.2 / 2320 1.0
8 TH	0553 4.8 / 1207 1.5 / 1803 4.8	23 F	0525 5.2 / 1145 1.1 / 1739 5.4
9 F	0029 1.2 / 0620 4.9 / 1241 1.4 / 1831 4.9 ●	24 SA	0006 0.8 / 0606 5.4 / 1232 0.9 / 1826 5.5 ○
10 SA	0100 1.2 / 0648 5.0 / 1312 1.3 / 1859 4.9	25 SU	0051 0.8 / 0649 5.5 / 1319 0.8 / 1915 5.5
11 SU	0129 1.3 / 0716 5.0 / 1344 1.4 / 1929 4.8	26 M	0136 0.9 / 0733 5.5 / 1406 0.8 / 2006 5.3
12 M	0159 1.4 / 0745 5.0 / 1416 1.4 / 2001 4.7	27 TU	0220 1.0 / 0820 5.4 / 1455 1.0 / 2100 5.0
13 TU	0230 1.5 / 0817 4.9 / 1450 1.5 / 2037 4.5	28 W	0306 1.3 / 0910 5.1 / 1547 1.2 / 2158 4.7
14 W	0302 1.7 / 0853 4.7 / 1527 1.7 / 2120 4.3	29 TH	0354 1.6 / 1007 4.9 / 1641 1.5 / 2300 4.5
15 TH	0338 1.9 / 0938 4.5 / 1609 1.9 / 2213 4.1	30 F	0446 1.9 / 1111 4.6 / 1741 1.7

DECEMBER

Time m

Day		Day	
1 SA	0005 4.2 / 0545 2.2 / 1223 4.4 / 1846 1.9 ◑	16 SU	0459 2.0 / 1111 4.6 / 1737 1.7 / 2356 4.2
2 SU	0113 4.1 / 0653 2.3 / 1336 4.3 / 1954 2.0	17 M	0557 2.1 / 1215 4.5 / 1837 1.8
3 M	0223 4.0 / 0807 2.4 / 1445 4.2 / 2100 2.0	18 TU	0106 4.2 / 0705 2.2 / 1323 4.5 / 1944 1.8
4 TU	0324 4.1 / 0915 2.3 / 1542 4.3 / 2157 1.9	19 W	0215 4.2 / 0818 2.1 / 1430 4.5 / 2053 1.7
5 W	0413 4.3 / 1012 2.2 / 1629 4.3 / 2244 1.8	20 TH	0319 4.4 / 0928 2.0 / 1534 4.7 / 2158 1.6
6 TH	0453 4.5 / 1059 2.0 / 1708 4.5 / 2325 1.7	21 F	0417 4.7 / 1032 1.7 / 1634 4.9 / 2257 1.4
7 F	0529 4.6 / 1141 1.8 / 1744 4.6	22 SA	0510 4.9 / 1129 1.4 / 1731 5.0 / 2350 1.3
8 SA	0002 1.6 / 0601 4.8 / 1219 1.7 / 1817 4.6	23 SU	0558 5.2 / 1223 1.2 / 1824 5.2
9 SU	0037 1.6 / 0632 4.9 / 1255 1.6 / 1850 4.7 ●	24 M	0040 1.2 / 0643 5.4 / 1314 1.0 / 1914 5.2 ○
10 M	0110 1.5 / 0703 5.0 / 1329 1.5 / 1924 4.7	25 TU	0127 1.1 / 0728 5.5 / 1403 0.9 / 2002 5.2
11 TU	0143 1.5 / 0736 5.0 / 1404 1.5 / 1959 4.7	26 W	0212 1.1 / 0813 5.4 / 1450 0.9 / 2049 5.1
12 W	0217 1.6 / 0810 5.0 / 1441 1.5 / 2035 4.6	27 TH	0256 1.2 / 0857 5.3 / 1536 1.0 / 2135 4.9
13 TH	0252 1.6 / 0847 4.9 / 1519 1.5 / 2115 4.5	28 F	0340 1.4 / 0942 5.1 / 1621 1.2 / 2222 4.6
14 F	0329 1.7 / 0928 4.8 / 1600 1.6 / 2201 4.4	29 SA	0423 1.6 / 1028 4.8 / 1706 1.5 / 2311 4.4
15 SA	0411 1.8 / 1016 4.7 / 1645 1.7 / 2254 4.3	30 SU	0508 1.8 / 1119 4.5 / 1753 1.7
		31 M	0006 4.1 / 0556 2.1 / 1219 4.3 / 1844 2.0 ◑

Chart Datum: 2·75 metres below Ordnance Datum (Newlyn)

TIDES

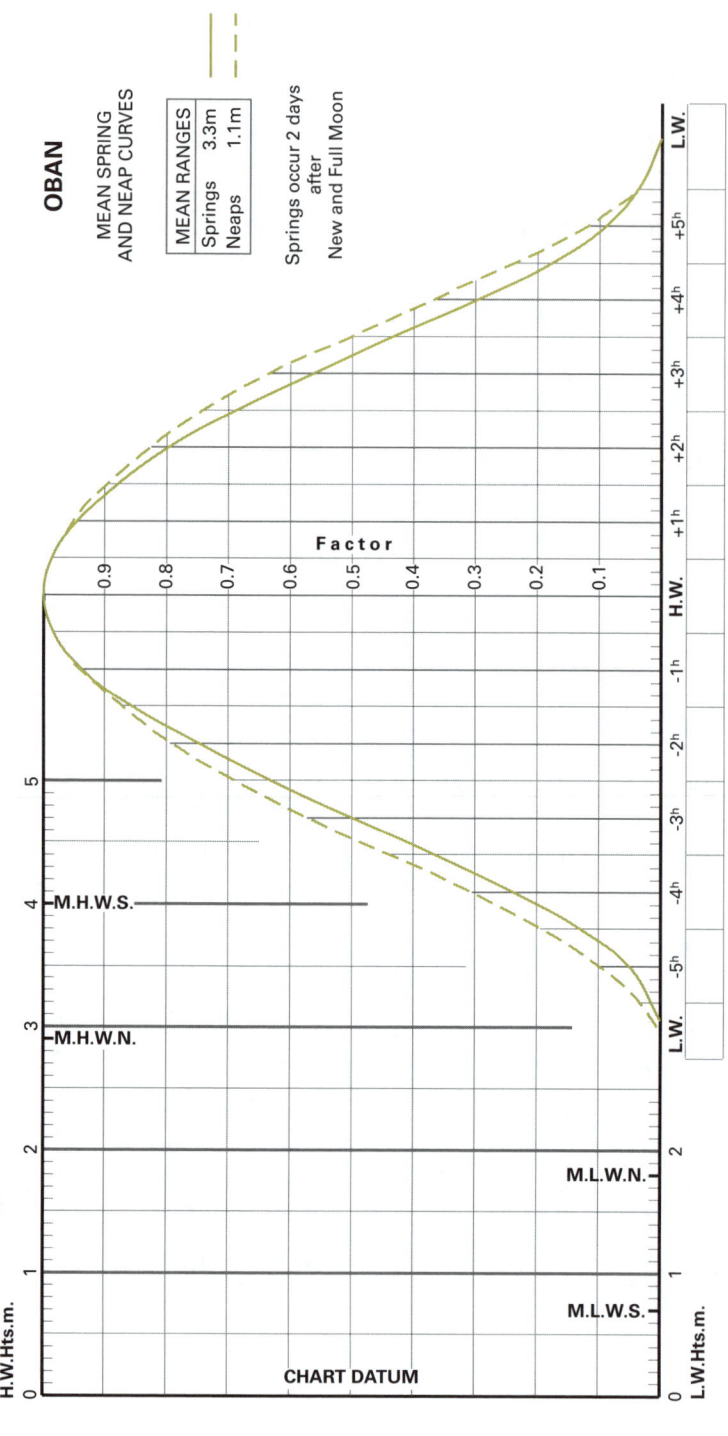

OBAN

MEAN SPRING
AND NEAP CURVES

MEAN RANGES	
Springs	3.3m
Neaps	1.1m

Springs occur 2 days
after
New and Full Moon

SCOTLAND – OBAN

LAT 56°25′N   LONG 5°29′W

TIMES AND HEIGHTS OF HIGH AND LOW WATERS

Dates in amber are **SPRINGS**
Dates in yellow are **NEAPS**

2007

JANUARY

Time	m		Time	m
1 0341	3.4	**16**	0349	3.2
1008	1.3		0934	1.7
M 1624	3.6	TU	1610	3.3
2218	1.3		2221	1.6
2 0430	3.6	**17**	0435	3.5
1104	1.2		1034	1.5
TU 1709	3.7	W	1654	3.5
2305	1.2		2302	1.3
3 0513	3.8	**18**	0516	3.7
1153	1.2		1123	1.3
W 1749	3.8	TH	1733	3.7
○ 2349	1.1		2341	1.1
4 0554	3.9	**19**	0556	3.9
1238	1.2		1208	1.0
TH 1826	3.8	F	1810	3.8
		●		
5 0032	1.0	**20**	0019	0.9
0633	4.0		0633	4.0
F 1320	1.2	SA	1250	0.9
1902	3.8		1844	3.8
6 0113	1.0	**21**	0059	0.7
0711	4.0		0710	4.1
SA 1400	1.3	SU	1331	0.8
1937	3.7		1919	3.8
7 0152	1.0	**22**	0139	0.6
0748	3.9		0748	4.1
SU 1438	1.4	M	1412	0.8
2011	3.6		1956	3.7
8 0231	1.1	**23**	0221	0.6
0823	3.8		0827	4.0
M 1514	1.6	TU	1453	0.9
2045	3.5		2035	3.6
9 0309	1.3	**24**	0305	0.8
0859	3.6		0910	3.8
TU 1550	1.7	W	1538	1.1
2120	3.3		2117	3.4
10 0348	1.4	**25**	0353	1.0
0935	3.5		0958	3.6
W 1630	1.9	TH	1628	1.3
2159	3.2	◑	2204	3.2
11 0430	1.6	**26**	0449	1.2
1015	3.3		1057	3.3
TH 1718	2.0	F	1726	1.5
◑ 2246	3.1		2305	3.0
12 0517	1.8	**27**	0557	1.5
1104	3.1		1226	3.1
F 1815	2.1	SA	1835	1.7
2351	2.9			
13 0612	1.9	**28**	0038	2.9
1216	3.0		0719	1.6
SA 1922	2.1	SU	1417	3.0
			1952	1.7
14 0135	2.9	**29**	0229	3.0
0715	2.0		0858	1.6
SU 1403	3.0	M	1543	3.2
2032	2.0		2109	1.6
15 0254	3.0	**30**	0353	3.2
0824	1.9		1021	1.5
M 1517	3.2	TU	1639	3.3
2133	1.8		2211	1.4
		31	0439	3.5
			1114	1.3
		W	1718	3.5
			2300	1.2

FEBRUARY

Time	m		Time	m
1 0514	3.7	**16**	0504	3.7
1155	1.2		1116	1.1
TH 1750	3.6	F	1723	3.6
2342	1.0		2326	0.8
2 0549	3.9	**17**	0542	4.0
1232	1.1		1157	0.8
F 1820	3.8	SA	1756	3.6
○		●		
3 0021	0.9	**18**	0004	0.6
0622	4.0		0618	4.2
SA 1307	1.1	SU	1235	0.6
1849	3.8		1828	3.9
4 0058	0.8	**19**	0043	0.3
0655	4.0		0653	4.3
SU 1340	1.1	M	1313	0.5
1918	3.8		1900	4.0
5 0133	0.8	**20**	0122	0.3
0727	4.0		0729	4.3
M 1410	1.2	TU	1350	0.5
1947	3.8		1934	3.9
6 0205	0.9	**21**	0203	0.3
0756	3.9		0805	4.1
TU 1439	1.3	W	1429	0.6
2014	3.7		2010	3.8
7 0236	1.1	**22**	0246	0.5
0825	3.8		0844	3.8
W 1506	1.5	TH	1510	0.8
2042	3.6		2049	3.6
8 0307	1.3	**23**	0332	0.8
0852	3.6		0927	3.5
TH 1534	1.7	F	1557	1.1
2113	3.4		2131	3.3
9 0339	1.5	**24**	0426	1.2
0921	3.4		1019	3.1
F 1607	1.8	SA	1653	1.4
2148	3.2	◑	2224	3.0
10 0418	1.7	**25**	0534	1.5
0955	3.2		1153	2.8
SA 1659	2.0	SU	1803	1.7
◑ 2232	3.0			
11 0512	1.9	**26**	0006	2.8
1042	2.9		0705	1.7
SU 1816	2.1	M	1428	2.7
2343	2.8		1927	1.8
12 0628	2.1	**27**	0302	2.9
1227	2.8		0924	1.7
M 1940	2.1	TU	1557	2.9
		◑	2100	1.6
13 0234	2.9	**28**	0422	3.1
0754	2.0		1029	1.5
TU 1517	2.9	W	1642	3.1
2104	1.9		2204	1.4
14 0341	3.1			
0925	1.8			
W 1608	3.2			
2204	1.6			
15 0425	3.4			
1030	1.6			
TH 1648	3.4			
2248	1.2			

MARCH

Time	m		Time	m
1 0442	3.4	**16**	0402	3.5
1110	1.3		1011	1.3
TH 1708	3.4	F	1627	3.3
2249	1.1		2221	1.0
2 0501	3.6	**17**	0441	3.8
1143	1.1		1055	0.9
F 1731	3.6	SA	1700	3.6
2327	0.9		2302	0.7
3 0530	3.8	**18**	0517	4.1
1213	1.0		1134	0.6
SA 1757	3.7	SU	1731	3.8
○			2342	0.3
4 0002	0.7	**19**	0554	4.3
0601	3.9		1211	0.3
SU 1242	0.9	M	1803	4.0
1824	3.9	●		
5 0036	0.7	**20**	0021	0.1
0631	4.0		0629	4.4
M 1310	0.9	TU	1248	0.3
1852	3.9		1835	4.0
6 0107	0.7	**21**	0103	0.1
0659	4.0		0705	4.3
TU 1337	1.0	W	1325	0.3
1917	3.9		1910	4.0
7 0136	0.8	**22**	0144	0.2
0726	3.9		0742	4.1
W 1402	1.1	TH	1404	0.5
1942	3.8		1947	3.8
8 0202	1.0	**23**	0228	0.5
0751	3.8		0820	3.7
TH 1424	1.3	F	1446	0.7
2008	3.7		2025	3.6
9 0227	1.2	**24**	0316	0.8
0814	3.6		0902	3.3
F 1443	1.5	SA	1533	1.1
2036	3.5		2108	3.3
10 0253	1.4	**25**	0412	1.2
0839	3.4		0954	2.9
SA 1506	1.7	SU	1629	1.4
2108	3.2	◑	2202	3.0
11 0325	1.7	**26**	0522	1.6
0910	3.2		1149	2.6
SU 1543	1.9	M	1739	1.6
2147	3.0		2352	2.7
12 0414	1.9	**27**	0712	1.8
0951	2.9		1424	2.6
M 1712	2.1	TU	1905	1.7
◑ 2250	2.8			
13 0555	2.1	**28**	0312	2.8
1114	2.6		0920	1.6
TU 1858	2.0	W	1539	2.8
			2039	1.6
14 0213	2.8	**29**	0407	3.1
0739	2.0		1011	1.4
W 1503	2.8	TH	1617	3.0
2029	1.8		2140	1.3
15 0319	3.1	**30**	0414	3.3
0914	1.7		1046	1.2
TH 1550	3.1	F	1637	3.3
2135	1.5		2224	1.1
		31	0433	3.5
			1115	1.1
		SA	1658	3.5
			2301	0.9

APRIL

Time	m		Time	m
1 0501	3.7	**16**	0448	4.1
1143	1.0		1104	0.5
SU 1725	3.7	M	1700	3.8
2334	0.8		2316	0.4
2 0531	3.8	**17**	0526	4.2
1209	0.9		1142	0.4
M 1754	3.8	TU	1735	4.0
○		●		
3 0006	0.7	**18**	0000	0.2
0601	3.9		0604	4.3
TU 1236	0.9	W	1221	0.3
1821	3.9		1811	4.0
4 0036	0.8	**19**	0044	0.1
0629	3.9		0642	4.2
W 1302	0.9	TH	1300	0.4
1847	3.9		1849	4.0
5 0104	0.9	**20**	0128	0.4
0655	3.8		0721	3.9
TH 1328	1.1	F	1342	0.5
1913	3.8		1929	3.8
6 0131	1.0	**21**	0215	0.6
0720	3.7		0802	3.6
F 1349	1.2	SA	1426	0.8
1940	3.7		2010	3.6
7 0155	1.2	**22**	0305	1.0
0744	3.5		0847	3.2
SA 1409	1.4	SU	1514	1.1
2009	3.5		2056	3.3
8 0222	1.4	**23**	0402	1.3
0811	3.3		0942	2.9
SU 1437	1.6	M	1610	1.3
2042	3.3		2154	3.0
9 0258	1.6	**24**	0514	1.6
0844	3.1		1144	2.6
M 1518	1.7	TU	1715	1.5
2125	3.1	◑	2329	2.7
10 0354	1.8	**25**	0702	1.8
0932	2.8		1342	2.6
TU 1633	1.9	W	1832	1.6
◑ 2235	2.9			
11 0540	1.9	**26**	0152	2.9
1111	2.6		0841	1.7
W 1817	1.9	TH	1449	2.8
			1956	1.5
12 0123	2.9	**27**	0300	3.0
0722	1.8		0932	1.5
TH 1425	2.7	F	1527	3.0
1944	1.7		2100	1.4
13 0240	2.8	**28**	0327	3.2
0843	1.5		1008	1.4
F 1516	3.0	SA	1553	3.2
2054	1.4		2147	1.2
14 0328	3.5	**29**	0355	3.4
0939	1.2		1039	1.2
SA 1554	3.3	SU	1620	3.4
2147	1.0		2226	1.1
15 0409	3.8	**30**	0426	3.5
1023	0.8		1106	1.0
SU 1627	3.6	M	1650	3.6
2233	0.6		2300	1.0

TIDES

Chart Datum: 2·10 metres below Ordnance Datum (Newlyn)

SCOTLAND – OBAN

LAT 56°25′N LONG 5°29′W

TIMES AND HEIGHTS OF HIGH AND LOW WATERS

2007

TIME ZONE (UT)
For Summer Time add ONE hour in **non-shaded areas**

Dates in amber are **SPRINGS**
Dates in yellow are **NEAPS**

MAY

Date	Time m	Time m	Time m	Time m
1 TU	0458 3.7	1133 1.0	1721 3.7	2332 0.9
2 W	0530 3.7	1200 1.0	1751 3.8	○
3 TH	0003 1.0	0600 3.7	1230 1.0	1820 3.8
4 F	0035 1.0	0630 3.7	1258 1.1	1849 3.7
5 SA	0107 1.1	0658 3.6	1325 1.2	1920 3.6
6 SU	0138 1.3	0728 3.4	1354 1.3	1954 3.5
7 M	0212 1.4	0801 3.3	1429 1.4	2034 3.3
8 TU	0257 1.6	0844 3.1	1516 1.6	2124 3.2
9 W	0400 1.7	0942 2.9	1620 1.7	2233 3.1
10 TH	0525 1.7	1106 2.7	1739 1.7	◐
11 F	0011 3.1	0650 1.6	1313 2.8	1857 1.5
12 SA	0147 3.3	0802 1.4	1425 3.0	2009 1.3
13 SU	0246 3.5	0900 1.2	1511 3.3	2110 1.0
14 M	0334 3.8	0948 0.9	1552 3.5	2204 0.8
15 TU	0419 3.9	1033 0.7	1631 3.7	2253 0.6
16 W	0502 4.0	1115 0.6	1712 3.9	● 2341 0.5
17 TH	0544 4.0	1157 0.5	1753 4.0	
18 F	0029 0.5	0626 3.9	1241 0.6	1835 3.9
19 SA	0117 0.6	0709 3.7	1324 0.7	1918 3.8
20 SU	0206 0.9	0753 3.5	1410 0.8	2002 3.6
21 M	0257 1.1	0840 3.2	1458 1.0	2049 3.4
22 TU	0352 1.4	0933 2.9	1550 1.2	2142 3.2
23 W	0455 1.6	1050 2.8	1645 1.4	◐ 2246 3.0
24 TH	0612 1.7	1234 2.7	1747 1.5	
25 F	0013 2.9	0734 1.7	1339 2.8	1852 1.6
26 SA	0137 3.0	0836 1.7	1427 2.9	1958 1.5
27 SU	0229 3.0	0920 1.6	1505 3.1	2053 1.5
28 M	0310 3.2	0956 1.5	1540 3.2	2139 1.4
29 TU	0348 3.3	1027 1.4	1616 3.4	2219 1.3
30 W	0426 3.4	1058 1.2	1651 3.5	2257 1.2
31 TH	0503 3.5	1130 1.2	1727 3.6	2335 1.2

JUNE

Date	Time m	Time m	Time m	Time m
1 F	0540 3.6	1203 1.1	1802 3.7	○
2 SA	0013 1.2	0615 3.6	1237 1.1	1836 3.9
3 SU	0053 1.2	0649 3.5	1311 1.1	1912 3.6
4 M	0133 1.2	0725 3.4	1346 1.2	1950 3.6
5 TU	0215 1.3	0803 3.3	1426 1.3	2033 3.5
6 W	0301 1.4	0848 3.2	1511 1.3	2121 3.4
7 TH	0356 1.4	0940 3.0	1604 1.4	2219 3.3
8 F	0459 1.5	1042 2.9	1706 1.4	◐ 2328 3.3
9 SA	0608 1.5	1156 2.9	1815 1.4	
10 SU	0048 3.3	0716 1.4	1318 3.0	1927 1.3
11 M	0204 3.4	0819 1.3	1428 3.2	2037 1.2
12 TU	0306 3.6	0916 1.1	1524 3.4	2141 1.0
13 W	0400 3.7	1007 1.0	1613 3.6	2238 0.9
14 TH	0450 3.7	1056 0.9	1659 3.8	2332 0.8
15 F	0537 3.8	1142 0.8	1744 3.9	●
16 SA	0023 0.8	0621 3.7	1228 0.7	1828 3.9
17 SU	0112 0.9	0705 3.6	1312 0.8	1911 3.9
18 M	0200 1.0	0748 3.5	1356 0.8	1954 3.8
19 TU	0247 1.2	0830 3.3	1440 1.0	2036 3.6
20 W	0333 1.4	0912 3.2	1525 1.1	2118 3.4
21 TH	0421 1.5	0957 3.0	1610 1.3	2203 3.2
22 F	0510 1.7	1048 2.9	1658 1.5	◐ 2252 3.1
23 SA	0605 1.8	1154 2.8	1748 1.6	2352 3.0
24 SU	0706 1.8	1308 2.9	1843 1.7	
25 M	0103 2.9	0808 1.8	1410 2.9	1941 1.7
26 TU	0214 3.0	0904 1.7	1502 3.1	2041 1.7
27 W	0313 3.1	0950 1.6	1549 3.2	2138 1.4
28 TH	0403 3.2	1031 1.4	1632 3.4	2230 1.1
29 F	0448 3.4	1109 1.3	1714 3.5	2317 1.3
30 SA	0531 3.5	1146 1.2	1753 3.6	○

JULY

Date	Time m	Time m	Time m	Time m
1 SU	0002 1.2	0610 3.5	1222 1.0	1831 3.7
2 M	0045 1.1	0646 3.6	1259 1.0	1908 3.8
3 TU	0127 1.0	0721 3.5	1336 0.9	1945 3.8
4 W	0209 1.0	0757 3.5	1415 0.9	2024 3.7
5 TH	0251 1.1	0836 3.4	1457 1.0	2107 3.7
6 F	0336 1.1	0920 3.3	1544 1.0	2155 3.5
7 SA	0428 1.3	1010 3.1	1638 1.2	◐ 2252 3.4
8 SU	0527 1.4	1111 3.0	1742 1.3	
9 M	0004 3.3	0633 1.4	1229 3.0	1855 1.4
10 TU	0133 3.2	0743 1.5	1400 3.0	2014 1.4
11 W	0255 3.3	0851 1.4	1515 3.2	2132 1.3
12 TH	0402 3.4	0953 1.2	1614 3.4	2239 1.2
13 F	0457 3.6	1046 1.1	1702 3.7	2334 1.1
14 SA	0543 3.6	1134 0.9	1744 3.8	●
15 SU	0022 1.0	0623 3.7	1219 0.8	1824 3.9
16 M	0106 1.0	0700 3.7	1301 0.7	1902 4.0
17 TU	0147 1.0	0735 3.6	1340 0.8	1938 3.9
18 W	0226 1.1	0808 3.6	1418 0.8	2013 3.8
19 TH	0302 1.3	0839 3.4	1455 1.0	2046 3.6
20 F	0337 1.4	0911 3.3	1532 1.2	2120 3.4
21 SA	0414 1.6	0946 3.2	1611 1.4	2156 3.3
22 SU	0457 1.8	1028 3.0	1655 1.6	◐ 2236 3.1
23 M	0549 1.9	1126 2.9	1747 1.8	2331 2.9
24 TU	0654 2.0	1305 2.8	1848 1.9	
25 W	0116 2.8	0809 1.9	1437 2.9	1957 1.9
26 TH	0255 2.9	0923 1.8	1537 3.1	2112 1.8
27 F	0357 3.1	1016 1.5	1624 3.3	2220 1.6
28 SA	0443 3.3	1057 1.3	1705 3.5	2311 1.3
29 SU	0524 3.5	1133 1.1	1744 3.8	2354 1.1
30 M	0602 3.6	1208 0.8	1821 3.9	○
31 TU	0034 0.9	0635 3.7	1243 0.7	1856 4.0

AUGUST

Date	Time m	Time m	Time m	Time m
1 W	0114 0.7	0706 3.7	1320 0.6	1930 4.1
2 TH	0151 0.7	0738 3.7	1358 0.6	2006 4.0
3 F	0230 0.8	0813 3.6	1438 0.7	2045 3.8
4 SA	0311 0.9	0853 3.5	1523 0.8	2128 3.6
5 SU	0357 1.1	0937 3.3	1614 1.1	◑ 2219 3.4
6 M	0452 1.3	1032 3.1	1717 1.4	2329 3.1
7 TU	0600 1.5	1155 2.9	1836 1.6	
8 W	0127 2.9	0718 1.6	1402 2.9	2010 1.6
9 TH	0309 3.0	0839 1.5	1537 3.2	2152 1.5
10 F	0417 3.1	0949 1.3	1630 3.4	2252 1.3
11 SA	0503 3.4	1042 1.1	1705 3.7	2336 1.1
12 SU	0538 3.6	1126 0.9	1737 3.9	●
13 M	0014 1.0	0609 3.7	1206 0.7	1809 4.0
14 TU	0050 0.9	0639 3.8	1243 0.7	1842 4.1
15 W	0123 0.9	0708 3.8	1318 0.7	1912 4.0
16 TH	0155 1.0	0736 3.8	1351 0.8	1942 3.9
17 F	0225 1.1	0803 3.7	1422 1.0	2010 3.8
18 SA	0254 1.3	0830 3.6	1453 1.2	2038 3.4
19 SU	0325 1.5	0900 3.4	1527 1.4	2105 3.4
20 M	0401 1.7	0935 3.2	1607 1.7	◑ 2136 3.2
21 TU	0452 1.9	1020 3.0	1700 1.9	2216 2.9
22 W	0604 2.1	1143 2.8	1812 2.1	2334 2.7
23 TH	0730 2.0	1432 2.9	1935 2.1	
24 F	0302 2.9	0902 1.9	1531 3.1	2110 1.9
25 SA	0354 3.1	0959 1.6	1613 3.4	2216 1.5
26 SU	0432 3.3	1039 1.2	1649 3.7	2259 1.2
27 M	0508 3.5	1113 0.9	1725 3.9	2337 0.9
28 TU	0541 3.7	1147 0.6	1759 4.2	○
29 W	0014 0.6	0611 3.8	1222 0.4	1833 4.3
30 TH	0050 0.5	0640 3.9	1259 0.3	1906 4.3
31 F	0126 0.5	0712 3.9	1338 0.4	1941 4.2

Chart Datum: 2·10 metres below Ordnance Datum (Newlyn)

SCOTLAND – OBAN

LAT 56°25'N   LONG 5°29'W

TIMES AND HEIGHTS OF HIGH AND LOW WATERS

Dates in amber are **SPRINGS**
Dates in yellow are **NEAPS**

2007

SEPTEMBER

Time	m		Time	m
1 SA	0204 0.6 / 0747 3.8 / 1419 0.5 / 2018 3.9	**16** SU	0214 1.3 / 0754 3.7 / 1417 1.3 / 1959 3.7	
2 SU	0244 0.8 / 0825 3.6 / 1504 0.8 / 2059 3.6	**17** M	0239 1.5 / 0823 3.5 / 1446 1.6 / 2023 3.4	
3 M	0330 1.0 / 0908 3.4 / 1557 1.1 / 2149 3.2	**18** TU	0306 1.7 / 0857 3.3 / 1520 1.8 / 2051 3.2	
4 TU	0426 1.3 / 1001 3.1 / 1704 1.5 / 2305 2.9	**19** W	0346 1.9 / 0939 3.0 / 1614 2.1 / 2128 2.9	
5 W	0536 1.6 / 1140 2.8 / 1830 1.7	**20** TH	0517 2.1 / 1049 2.8 / 1747 2.2 / 2240 2.7	
6 TH	0143 2.8 / 0700 1.7 / 1430 2.9 / 2046 1.7	**21** F	0652 2.1 / 1415 2.9 / 1925 2.1	
7 F	0322 2.9 / 0833 1.6 / 1550 3.2 / 2204 1.5	**22** SA	0247 2.8 / 0825 1.9 / 1508 3.2 / 2058 1.8	
8 SA	0416 3.1 / 0940 1.3 / 1626 3.5 / 2247 1.3	**23** SU	0332 3.1 / 0925 1.6 / 1547 3.5 / 2152 1.5	
9 SU	0450 3.4 / 1028 1.1 / 1648 3.7 / 2321 1.1	**24** M	0408 3.3 / 1007 1.2 / 1622 3.8 / 2232 1.1	
10 M	0514 3.6 / 1107 0.9 / 1714 3.9 / 2352 1.0	**25** TU	0440 3.6 / 1043 0.8 / 1656 4.1 / 2310 0.8	
11 TU ●	0541 3.8 / 1144 0.7 / 1743 4.0	**26** W ○	0510 3.8 / 1119 0.6 / 1730 4.3 / 2345 0.5	
12 W	0021 0.9 / 0608 3.9 / 1218 0.7 / 1812 4.1	**27** TH	0540 4.0 / 1157 0.4 / 1805 4.4	
13 TH	0050 0.9 / 0636 4.0 / 1250 0.7 / 1841 4.1	**28** F	0021 0.4 / 0611 4.1 / 1236 0.3 / 1839 4.4	
14 F	0119 1.0 / 0702 3.9 / 1320 0.8 / 1908 4.0	**29** SA	0059 0.4 / 0645 4.1 / 1318 0.4 / 1915 4.2	
15 SA	0147 1.1 / 0727 3.9 / 1348 1.0 / 1934 3.9	**30** SU	0138 0.5 / 0722 3.9 / 1402 0.6 / 1954 3.9	

OCTOBER

Time	m		Time	m
1 M	0220 0.7 / 0802 3.7 / 1450 0.9 / 2036 3.5	**16** TU	0205 1.5 / 0757 3.6 / 1416 1.7 / 1955 3.4	
2 TU	0308 1.0 / 0847 3.4 / 1546 1.3 / 2127 3.1	**17** W	0232 1.7 / 0832 3.4 / 1452 1.9 / 2026 3.2	
3 W	0405 1.4 / 0945 3.1 / 1657 1.6 / 2258 2.8	**18** TH	0311 1.9 / 0916 3.2 / 1550 2.1 / 2108 3.0	
4 TH	0515 1.6 / 1146 2.9 / 1835 1.8	**19** F	0426 2.1 / 1028 3.0 / 1728 2.2 / 2232 2.7	
5 F	0145 2.7 / 0640 1.7 / 1430 3.0 / 2047 1.7	**20** SA	0601 2.1 / 1329 3.0 / 1903 2.1	
6 SA	0307 2.9 / 0811 1.6 / 1534 3.3 / 2146 1.5	**21** SU	0206 2.8 / 0727 1.9 / 1428 3.3 / 2021 1.8	
7 SU	0353 3.1 / 0916 1.4 / 1600 3.5 / 2222 1.3	**22** M	0255 3.1 / 0835 1.6 / 1510 3.6 / 2114 1.5	
8 M	0419 3.3 / 1002 1.1 / 1617 3.7 / 2253 1.2	**23** TU	0333 3.3 / 0925 1.3 / 1548 3.9 / 2158 1.1	
9 TU	0440 3.6 / 1041 1.0 / 1643 3.8 / 2321 1.0	**24** W	0405 3.6 / 1009 0.9 / 1624 4.2 / 2237 0.8	
10 W	0506 3.8 / 1116 0.9 / 1711 4.0 / 2347 0.9	**25** TH	0436 3.9 / 1051 0.7 / 1700 4.3 / 2315 0.6	
11 TH ●	0535 3.9 / 1148 0.8 / 1740 4.0	**26** F ○	0510 4.0 / 1133 0.5 / 1737 4.4 / 2353 0.5	
12 F	0015 1.0 / 0602 4.0 / 1220 0.9 / 1808 4.0	**27** SA	0546 4.1 / 1216 0.5 / 1816 4.3	
13 SA	0043 1.0 / 0630 4.0 / 1249 1.0 / 1837 4.0	**28** SU	0033 0.5 / 0624 4.1 / 1302 0.6 / 1855 4.1	
14 SU	0112 1.1 / 0657 3.9 / 1318 1.2 / 1904 3.8	**29** M	0116 0.6 / 0705 4.0 / 1349 0.8 / 1936 3.8	
15 M	0140 1.3 / 0726 3.8 / 1347 1.4 / 1929 3.7	**30** TU	0201 0.8 / 0749 3.8 / 1440 1.1 / 2022 3.4	
		31 W	0251 1.1 / 0837 3.5 / 1538 1.4 / 2115 3.1	

NOVEMBER

Time	m		Time	m
1 TH ◖	0347 1.3 / 0937 3.3 / 1648 1.7 / 2245 2.8	**16** F	0259 1.8 / 0908 3.4 / 1541 2.0 / 2111 3.1	
2 F	0451 1.5 / 1117 3.1 / 1824 1.9	**17** SA ◗	0354 1.9 / 1010 3.2 / 1657 2.0 / 2221 2.9	
3 SA	0109 2.8 / 0607 1.6 / 1341 3.1 / 2008 1.8	**18** SU	0506 1.9 / 1139 3.2 / 1818 2.0	
4 SU	0223 2.9 / 0729 1.6 / 1447 3.3 / 2107 1.7	**19** M	0001 2.9 / 0622 1.8 / 1324 3.4 / 1930 1.8	
5 M	0309 3.1 / 0836 1.5 / 1517 3.4 / 2146 1.5	**20** TU	0152 3.0 / 0736 1.6 / 1423 3.6 / 2029 1.5	
6 TU	0336 3.3 / 0927 1.3 / 1541 3.5 / 2218 1.4	**21** W	0243 3.3 / 0840 1.4 / 1510 3.8 / 2119 1.3	
7 W	0402 3.5 / 1008 1.2 / 1609 3.7 / 2246 1.3	**22** TH	0325 3.5 / 0935 1.1 / 1554 4.0 / 2204 1.0	
8 TH	0432 3.7 / 1044 1.2 / 1639 3.8 / 2313 1.2	**23** F	0406 3.8 / 1026 0.9 / 1636 4.2 / 2248 0.8	
9 F ●	0503 3.8 / 1117 1.1 / 1710 3.9 / 2342 1.2	**24** SA ○	0447 4.0 / 1115 0.8 / 1718 4.2 / 2331 0.7	
10 SA	0534 3.9 / 1149 1.2 / 1742 3.9	**25** SU	0529 4.1 / 1204 0.7 / 1801 4.2	
11 SU	0013 1.2 / 0605 4.0 / 1223 1.3 / 1813 3.9	**26** M	0015 0.7 / 0612 4.1 / 1253 0.8 / 1844 4.0	
12 M	0045 1.2 / 0636 3.9 / 1256 1.4 / 1844 3.8	**27** TU	0101 0.7 / 0657 4.1 / 1343 1.0 / 1928 3.8	
13 TU	0116 1.3 / 0709 3.8 / 1329 1.5 / 1914 3.6	**28** W	0147 0.8 / 0742 3.9 / 1434 1.2 / 2014 3.5	
14 W	0147 1.5 / 0743 3.7 / 1404 1.7 / 1945 3.4	**29** TH	0236 1.0 / 0831 3.7 / 1528 1.4 / 2104 3.2	
15 TH	0219 1.6 / 0821 3.5 / 1445 1.9 / 2022 3.3	**30** F	0327 1.2 / 0923 3.5 / 1628 1.7 / 2205 3.0	

DECEMBER

Time	m		Time	m
1 SA ◖	0422 1.4 / 1025 3.3 / 1737 1.8 / 2340 2.9	**16** SU	0331 1.5 / 0946 3.5 / 1618 1.7 / 2155 3.2	
2 SU	0522 1.6 / 1152 3.2 / 1855 1.9	**17** M ◗	0424 1.6 / 1045 3.4 / 1722 1.8 / 2257 3.1	
3 M	0106 2.9 / 0627 1.6 / 1325 3.2 / 2006 1.9	**18** TU	0529 1.6 / 1200 3.4 / 1831 1.7	
4 TU	0203 3.0 / 0734 1.7 / 1420 3.2 / 2058 1.8	**19** W	0013 3.1 / 0643 1.6 / 1326 3.5 / 1938 1.6	
5 W	0246 3.1 / 0836 1.6 / 1500 3.3 / 2137 1.7	**20** TH	0140 3.2 / 0758 1.5 / 1437 3.6 / 2040 1.5	
6 TH	0324 3.3 / 0927 1.6 / 1535 3.4 / 2211 1.6	**21** F	0251 3.4 / 0909 1.4 / 1535 3.7 / 2137 1.3	
7 F	0401 3.5 / 1010 1.5 / 1611 3.6 / 2243 1.5	**22** SA	0347 3.6 / 1013 1.2 / 1627 3.9 / 2229 1.1	
8 SA	0437 3.7 / 1049 1.5 / 1648 3.7 / 2316 1.4	**23** SU	0437 3.8 / 1109 1.0 / 1714 3.9 / 2318 0.9	
9 SU ●	0514 3.8 / 1126 1.4 / 1726 3.7 / 2351 1.4	**24** M ○	0524 4.0 / 1201 0.9 / 1759 4.0	
10 M	0551 3.8 / 1204 1.4 / 1802 3.8	**25** TU	0004 0.8 / 0609 4.1 / 1251 0.9 / 1841 3.9	
11 TU	0026 1.3 / 0626 3.9 / 1243 1.4 / 1837 3.7	**26** W	0051 0.8 / 0653 4.1 / 1339 1.0 / 1923 3.8	
12 W	0101 1.3 / 0702 3.8 / 1322 1.5 / 1910 3.6	**27** TH	0136 0.8 / 0735 4.0 / 1424 1.1 / 2004 3.6	
13 TH	0134 1.3 / 0737 3.8 / 1400 1.5 / 1944 3.5	**28** F	0220 0.9 / 0817 3.9 / 1509 1.3 / 2044 3.5	
14 F	0208 1.4 / 0815 3.7 / 1439 1.6 / 2021 3.4	**29** SA	0304 1.0 / 0859 3.7 / 1554 1.5 / 2124 3.3	
15 SA	0246 1.5 / 0857 3.6 / 1524 1.7 / 2104 3.3	**30** SU	0348 1.2 / 0941 3.5 / 1640 1.7 / 2208 3.1	
		31 M ◖	0434 1.4 / 1027 3.3 / 1730 1.9 / 2301 3.0	

Chart Datum: 2·10 metres below Ordnance Datum (Newlyn)

TIDES

309

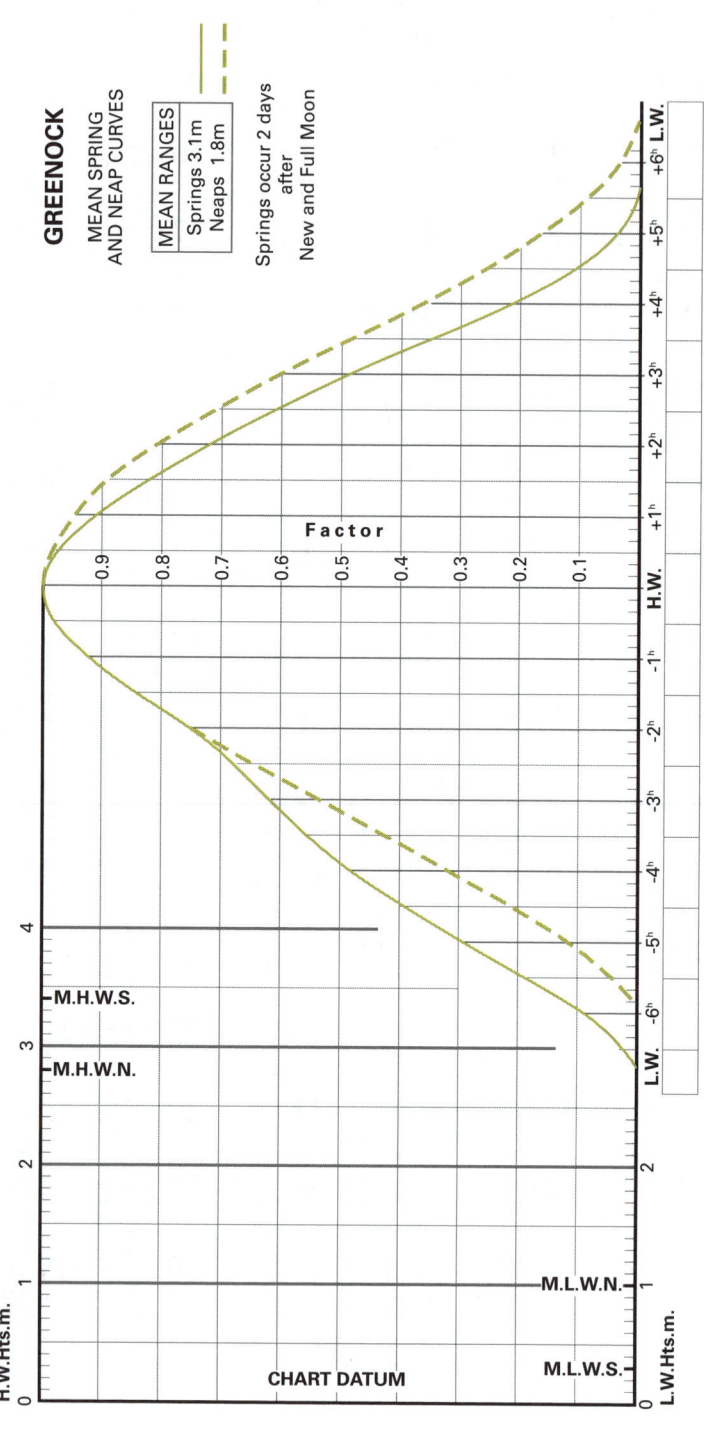

GREENOCK

MEAN SPRING
AND NEAP CURVES

MEAN RANGES
Springs 3.1m
Neaps 1.8m

Springs occur 2 days
after
New and Full Moon

Factor

0.9
0.8
0.7
0.6
0.5
0.4
0.3
0.2
0.1

H.W. −1ʰ −2ʰ −3ʰ −4ʰ −5ʰ −6ʰ L.W.

H.W. +1ʰ +2ʰ +3ʰ +4ʰ +5ʰ +6ʰ L.W.

H.W.Hts.m.

M.H.W.S.
M.H.W.N.

M.L.W.N.
M.L.W.S.

CHART DATUM

L.W.Hts.m.

SCOTLAND – GREENOCK
LAT 55°57'N   LONG 4°46'W
TIMES AND HEIGHTS OF HIGH AND LOW WATERS

Dates in amber are SPRINGS
Dates in yellow are NEAPS

2007

JANUARY

Day	Time m	Time m	Day	Time m	Time m
1 M	0333 0.7 / 1027 3.2	1603 0.8 / 2303 3.2	**16** TU	0327 1.1 / 1038 3.0	1613 0.9 / 2233 2.9
2 TU	0428 0.7 / 1119 3.3	1655 0.6 / 2358 3.3	**17** W	0416 0.9 / 1124 3.2	1656 0.7 / 2328 3.0
3 W ○	0517 0.7 / 1205 3.5	1741 0.5	**18** TH	0500 0.8 / 1204 3.3	1736 0.5
4 TH	0050 3.3 / 0603 0.7	1249 3.6 / 1824 0.5	**19** F ●	0017 3.1 / 0541 0.7	1242 3.4 / 1815 0.3
5 F	0138 3.3 / 0648 0.7	1330 3.7 / 1905 0.5	**20** SA	0104 3.2 / 0623 0.6	1322 3.6 / 1855 0.2
6 SA	0221 3.2 / 0730 0.8	1410 3.7 / 1945 0.5	**21** SU	0150 3.2 / 0706 0.5	1402 3.6 / 1938 0.1
7 SU	0301 3.2 / 0811 0.8	1449 3.7 / 2025 0.6	**22** M	0234 3.2 / 0750 0.5	1443 3.7 / 2022 0.1
8 M	0338 3.2 / 0851 0.8	1526 3.7 / 2105 0.6	**23** TU	0316 3.2 / 0835 0.5	1525 3.7 / 2108 0.1
9 TU	0415 3.1 / 0931 0.9	1604 3.6 / 2147 0.8	**24** W	0356 3.2 / 0922 0.5	1607 3.7 / 2158 0.3
10 W	0454 3.1 / 1013 1.0	1642 3.4 / 2232 0.9	**25** TH ◑	0437 3.2 / 1011 0.6	1651 3.5 / 2253 0.4
11 TH ◑	0534 3.0 / 1101 1.1	1724 3.3 / 2323 1.0	**26** F	0520 3.1 / 1106 0.8	1740 3.3 / 2355 0.6
12 F	0618 2.9 / 1156 1.3	1810 3.1	**27** SA	0607 3.0 / 1211 1.0	1836 3.1
13 SA	0021 1.1 / 0707 2.8	1301 1.3 / 1903 3.0	**28** SU	0105 0.8 / 0704 2.9	1330 1.0 / 2001 2.9
14 SU	0125 1.1 / 0810 2.8	1415 1.3 / 2007 2.9	**29** M	0219 0.9 / 0833 2.9	1455 1.0 / 2159 2.9
15 M	0230 1.1 / 0933 2.9	1521 1.1 / 2124 2.9	**30** TU	0327 0.9 / 1013 3.0	1601 0.8 / 2306 3.0
			31 W	0424 0.8 / 1110 3.2	1652 0.6

FEBRUARY

Day	Time m	Time m	Day	Time m	Time m
1 TH	0000 3.1 / 0512 0.7	1158 3.4 / 1734 0.5	**16** F	0443 0.8 / 1142 3.2	1717 0.3
2 F ○	0048 3.1 / 0554 0.6	1240 3.5 / 1813 0.4	**17** SA ●	0005 3.1 / 0524 0.6	1223 3.4 / 1755 0.1
3 SA	0132 3.1 / 0633 0.6	1319 3.6 / 1848 0.4	**18** SU	0052 3.1 / 0605 0.4	1305 3.6 / 1834 0.0
4 SU	0209 3.1 / 0709 0.6	1356 3.6 / 1922 0.4	**19** M	0135 3.2 / 0645 0.3	1346 3.7 / 1915 -0.1
5 M	0241 3.1 / 0743 0.6	1430 3.6 / 1956 0.4	**20** TU	0215 3.3 / 0727 0.2	1427 3.8 / 1957 -0.1
6 TU	0311 3.1 / 0817 0.6	1503 3.6 / 2029 0.5	**21** W	0252 3.3 / 0810 0.2	1507 3.8 / 2041 0.0
7 W	0341 3.1 / 0851 0.6	1535 3.5 / 2104 0.6	**22** TH	0328 3.4 / 0854 0.3	1547 3.7 / 2128 0.2
8 TH	0411 3.1 / 0927 0.7	1608 3.4 / 2141 0.7	**23** F	0404 3.3 / 0941 0.4	1627 3.5 / 2219 0.5
9 F	0444 3.0 / 1007 0.9	1645 3.3 / 2222 0.8	**24** SA ◑	0444 3.2 / 1033 0.7	1711 3.2 / 2322 0.8
10 SA	0522 2.9 / 1054 1.0	1727 3.1 / 2312 1.0	**25** SU	0529 3.1 / 1141 0.9	1804 2.9
11 SU	0607 2.8 / 1153 1.2	1817 2.9	**26** M	0044 1.0 / 0623 2.9	1319 1.0 / 1925 2.6
12 M	0014 1.1 / 0706 2.7	1307 1.3 / 1920 2.7	**27** TU ◑	0210 1.1 / 0743 2.7	1450 0.9 / 2205 2.7
13 TU	0127 1.2 / 0827 2.6	1447 1.2 / 2043 2.7	**28** W	0319 1.0 / 1003 2.9	1552 0.7 / 2304 2.9
14 W	0254 1.1 / 1003 2.8	1551 0.9 / 2212 2.8			
15 TH	0357 1.0 / 1059 3.0	1637 0.6 / 2316 2.9			

MARCH

Day	Time m	Time m	Day	Time m	Time m
1 TH	0414 0.8 / 1058 3.1	1639 0.5 / 2351 3.0	**16** F	0330 0.9 / 1027 3.0	1608 0.4 / 2257 2.9
2 F	0459 0.7 / 1143 3.3	1719 0.4	**17** SA	0419 0.7 / 1114 3.2	1650 0.1 / 2345 3.0
3 SA ○	0033 3.1 / 0537 0.5	1224 3.4 / 1753 0.3	**18** SU	0501 0.4 / 1158 3.4	1729 -0.1
4 SU ○	0112 3.1 / 0611 0.5	1301 3.4 / 1824 0.3	**19** M ●	0028 3.2 / 0541 0.2	1242 3.6 / 1808 -0.2
5 M	0144 3.1 / 0642 0.4	1335 3.4 / 1853 0.4	**20** TU	0110 3.3 / 0621 0.1	1325 3.7 / 1849 -0.2
6 TU	0213 3.1 / 0711 0.4	1405 3.4 / 1922 0.4	**21** W	0148 3.3 / 0702 0.0	1407 3.8 / 1931 -0.1
7 W	0238 3.1 / 0741 0.4	1435 3.4 / 1953 0.4	**22** TH	0224 3.4 / 0744 0.1	1447 3.7 / 2015 0.0
8 TH	0304 3.1 / 0813 0.4	1505 3.4 / 2025 0.5	**23** F	0259 3.5 / 0829 0.2	1527 3.6 / 2102 0.3
9 F	0331 3.1 / 0848 0.5	1537 3.3 / 2100 0.5	**24** SA	0336 3.4 / 0915 0.3	1608 3.4 / 2153 0.6
10 SA	0401 3.1 / 0926 0.6	1613 3.2 / 2140 0.7	**25** SU ◑	0416 3.3 / 1009 0.6	1653 3.1 / 2257 0.9
11 SU	0435 2.9 / 1011 0.8	1652 3.0 / 2228 0.9	**26** M	0501 3.1 / 1123 0.9	1750 2.7
12 M ◑	0516 2.8 / 1109 1.0	1741 2.8 / 2329 1.1	**27** TU	0028 1.2 / 0558 2.9	1311 1.0 / 2025 2.5
13 TU	0613 2.6 / 1221 1.1	1847 2.6	**28** W	0151 1.2 / 0724 2.7	1430 0.8 / 2153 2.7
14 W	0042 1.2 / 0739 2.5	1402 1.0 / 2016 2.6	**29** TH	0258 1.1 / 0940 2.9	1528 0.7 / 2245 2.9
15 TH	0215 1.2 / 0922 2.7	1520 0.7 / 2153 2.7	**30** F	0352 0.8 / 1034 3.1	1614 0.5 / 2328 3.0
			31 SA	0436 0.6 / 1118 3.2	1652 0.4

APRIL

Day	Time m	Time m	Day	Time m	Time m
1 SU	0006 3.0 / 0512 0.5	1158 3.3 / 1725 0.3	**16** M	0433 0.4 / 1130 3.4	1700 -0.1 / 2359 3.2
2 M ○	0041 3.1 / 0544 0.4	1234 3.3 / 1754 0.3	**17** TU ●	0516 0.2 / 1216 3.5	1742 -0.2
3 TU	0112 3.1 / 0613 0.4	1306 3.2 / 1822 0.4	**18** W	0040 3.3 / 0557 0.0	1302 3.6 / 1824 -0.1
4 W	0139 3.1 / 0640 0.4	1335 3.2 / 1849 0.4	**19** TH	0120 3.4 / 0639 0.0	1347 3.6 / 1908 0.0
5 TH	0204 3.1 / 0709 0.3	1405 3.2 / 1920 0.4	**20** F	0158 3.5 / 0723 0.0	1430 3.6 / 1954 0.0
6 F	0229 3.2 / 0741 0.3	1436 3.2 / 1953 0.4	**21** SA	0236 3.5 / 0809 0.1	1513 3.5 / 2044 0.4
7 SA	0257 3.2 / 0817 0.4	1511 3.2 / 2031 0.5	**22** SU	0315 3.5 / 0859 0.3	1557 3.2 / 2138 0.7
8 SU	0327 3.1 / 0857 0.5	1547 3.1 / 2113 0.6	**23** M	0356 3.4 / 0957 0.6	1648 2.9 / 2243 1.0
9 M	0400 3.0 / 0944 0.7	1628 2.9 / 2203 0.8	**24** TU ◑	0444 3.2 / 1113 0.8	1755 2.7
10 TU	0437 2.8 / 1044 0.8	1719 2.7 / 2304 1.0	**25** W ◑	0001 1.2 / 0543 2.9	1244 0.8 / 1955 2.6
11 W	0532 2.6 / 1157 0.9	1830 2.6	**26** TH	0116 1.2 / 0706 2.8	1354 0.8 / 2117 2.7
12 TH	0015 1.1 / 0703 2.6	1324 0.8 / 1956 2.6	**27** F	0222 1.1 / 0856 2.9	1451 0.6 / 2208 2.8
13 F	0138 1.1 / 0840 2.7	1439 0.5 / 2124 2.7	**28** SA	0318 0.9 / 0957 3.0	1538 0.5 / 2251 3.0
14 SA	0253 0.9 / 0951 3.0	1533 0.2 / 2227 2.9	**29** SU	0404 0.7 / 1044 3.1	1618 0.4 / 2329 3.0
15 SU	0348 0.6 / 1043 3.2	1618 0.0 / 2315 3.1	**30** M	0443 0.5 / 1124 3.2	1652 0.4

Chart Datum: 1·62 metres below Ordnance Datum (Newlyn)

TIDES

SCOTLAND – GREENOCK

LAT 55°57'N   LONG 4°46'W

TIMES AND HEIGHTS OF HIGH AND LOW WATERS

TIME ZONE (UT)
For Summer Time add ONE hour in **non-shaded areas**

Dates in amber are **SPRINGS**
Dates in yellow are **NEAPS**

2007

MAY

Time	m	Time	m
1 TU 0004	3.0	**16** W 0453	0.2
0516	0.4	1152	3.4
1200	3.1	1718	0.0
1723	0.4		
2 W 0037	3.1	**17** TH 0014	3.3
0546	0.4	0538	0.1
1232	3.1	1242	3.5
○ 1752	0.5	1804	0.1
3 TH 0106	3.1	**18** F 0057	3.4
0614	0.4	0622	0.1
1303	3.1	1330	3.4
1821	0.5	1851	0.2
4 F 0132	3.1	**19** SA 0138	3.5
0644	0.4	0709	0.1
1336	3.1	1418	3.4
1854	0.5	1941	0.4
5 SA 0200	3.2	**20** SU 0219	3.6
0718	0.3	0757	0.2
1412	3.1	1506	3.3
1931	0.5	2033	0.6
6 SU 0230	3.2	**21** M 0300	3.5
0756	0.4	0849	0.3
1450	3.0	1555	3.1
2013	0.5	2127	0.7
7 M 0303	3.2	**22** TU 0344	3.4
0840	0.4	0945	0.5
1530	3.0	1649	2.9
2059	0.6	2223	0.9
8 TU 0338	3.1	**23** W 0432	3.3
0931	0.5	1050	0.6
1616	2.8	1750	2.8
2151	0.8	☽ 2325	1.0
9 W 0418	2.9	**24** TH 0528	3.1
1031	0.6	1202	0.7
1712	2.7	1857	2.7
2249	0.9		
10 TH 0515	2.8	**25** F 0029	1.1
1140	0.6	0633	2.9
1820	2.6	1308	0.7
☽ 2355	0.9	2007	2.7
11 F 0636	2.7	**26** SA 0134	1.1
1253	0.5	0747	2.9
1933	2.7	1406	0.7
		2110	2.7
12 SA 0105	0.9	**27** SU 0235	0.9
0801	2.8	0900	2.9
1359	0.3	1456	0.6
2045	2.8	2201	2.8
13 SU 0214	0.9	**28** M 0327	0.8
0913	3.0	0957	2.9
1456	0.2	1540	0.6
2149	2.9	2246	2.9
14 M 0315	0.6	**29** TU 0411	0.7
1011	3.2	1043	2.9
1546	0.0	1619	0.6
2243	3.0	2327	3.1
15 TU 0406	0.4	**30** W 0449	0.6
1103	3.3	1122	2.9
1633	0.0	1654	0.6
2330	3.2		
		31 TH 0004	3.0
		0523	0.5
		1158	2.9
		1727	0.6

JUNE

Time	m	Time	m
1 F 0037	3.1	**16** SA 0041	3.4
0555	0.4	0613	0.2
1233	3.0	1323	3.2
○ 1800	0.6	1841	0.4
2 SA 0107	3.2	**17** SU 0125	3.5
0628	0.4	0700	0.2
1312	3.0	1414	3.2
1837	0.6	1931	0.5
3 SU 0138	3.2	**18** M 0208	3.5
0705	0.3	0747	0.2
1353	3.0	1503	3.1
1918	0.6	2020	0.6
4 M 0212	3.2	**19** TU 0250	3.5
0745	0.3	0835	0.3
1436	2.9	1550	3.0
2003	0.6	2107	0.7
5 TU 0248	3.2	**20** W 0332	3.5
0831	0.3	0923	0.4
1522	2.9	1636	3.0
2050	0.6	2154	0.7
6 W 0327	3.2	**21** TH 0416	3.4
0922	0.3	1015	0.6
1610	2.9	1722	2.9
2141	0.6	2243	0.8
7 TH 0411	3.1	**22** F 0502	3.2
1018	0.4	1112	0.7
1704	2.8	1808	2.8
2234	0.7	☽ 2337	0.9
8 F 0504	3.0	**23** SA 0552	3.1
1120	0.4	1213	0.8
1801	2.8	1856	2.8
2332	0.7		
9 SA 0609	2.9	**24** SU 0036	1.0
1223	0.3	0644	2.9
1859	2.8	1314	0.8
		1947	2.7
10 SU 0034	0.8	**25** M 0141	1.0
0721	2.9	0742	2.8
1325	0.3	1410	0.8
2000	2.8	2051	2.7
11 M 0139	0.7	**26** TU 0245	1.0
0835	3.0	0848	2.8
1424	0.2	1501	0.8
2107	2.8	2158	2.8
12 TU 0244	0.6	**27** W 0340	0.8
0943	3.1	0953	2.8
1519	0.2	1548	0.8
2211	3.0	2252	2.9
13 W 0344	0.5	**28** TH 0426	0.7
1041	3.1	1045	2.8
1612	0.2	1630	0.7
2306	3.1	2335	3.0
14 TH 0437	0.3	**29** F 0506	0.6
1136	3.2	1129	2.9
1702	0.3	1708	0.7
2355	3.2		
15 F 0526	0.2	**30** SA 0012	3.1
1229	3.3	0542	0.5
● 1752	0.3	1212	2.9
		○ 1746	0.6

JULY

Time	m	Time	m
1 SU 0047	3.2	**16** M 0116	3.4
0618	0.4	0650	0.2
1256	2.9	1410	3.1
1825	0.6	1916	0.5
2 M 0121	3.3	**17** TU 0157	3.5
0655	0.3	0731	0.2
1341	2.9	1453	3.1
1907	0.6	1958	0.6
3 TU 0158	3.3	**18** W 0236	3.5
0736	0.2	0811	0.3
1427	2.9	1531	3.1
1951	0.6	2039	0.6
4 W 0237	3.3	**19** TH 0314	3.5
0819	0.2	0851	0.4
1513	3.0	1607	3.0
2036	0.5	2118	0.6
5 TH 0317	3.3	**20** F 0351	3.4
0905	0.2	0932	0.5
1558	3.0	1643	3.0
2123	0.5	2158	0.7
6 F 0359	3.3	**21** SA 0428	3.3
0956	0.2	1016	0.7
1643	3.0	1720	3.0
2211	0.5	2242	0.8
7 SA 0446	3.2	**22** SU 0508	3.2
1052	0.2	1102	0.8
1730	2.9	1800	2.9
2304	0.6	☽ 2331	1.0
8 SU 0538	3.1	**23** M 0552	3.0
1152	0.3	1203	1.0
1818	2.9	1844	2.8
9 M 0002	0.7	**24** TU 0031	1.1
0639	3.0	0643	2.8
1255	0.4	1310	1.1
1911	2.8	1937	2.7
10 TU 0107	0.8	**25** W 0151	1.1
0755	2.9	0746	2.7
1358	0.5	1419	1.1
2020	2.8	2051	2.7
11 W 0219	0.8	**26** TH 0310	1.0
0922	2.9	0901	2.7
1501	0.5	1520	1.0
2146	2.9	2217	2.8
12 TH 0332	0.7	**27** F 0405	0.8
1034	3.0	1017	2.7
1601	0.5	1610	0.9
2251	3.0	2310	3.0
13 F 0432	0.5	**28** SA 0449	0.6
1134	3.1	1114	2.8
1656	0.5	1653	0.8
2344	3.2	2350	3.1
14 SA 0522	0.3	**29** SU 0527	0.4
1229	3.1	1200	2.9
● 1746	0.5	1731	0.7
15 SU 0031	3.3	**30** M 0027	3.2
0607	0.2	0603	0.3
1322	3.1	1246	3.0
1832	0.5	○ 1809	0.6
		31 TU 0104	3.3
		0639	0.1
		1330	3.0
		1849	0.5

AUGUST

Time	m	Time	m
1 W 0143	3.4	**16** TH 0216	3.5
0717	0.0	0739	0.4
1414	3.1	1500	3.1
1930	0.4	2003	0.5
2 TH 0222	3.5	**17** F 0249	3.5
0757	0.0	0813	0.5
1455	3.1	1529	3.1
2013	0.3	2037	0.6
3 F 0301	3.5	**18** SA 0321	3.5
0840	0.0	0847	0.6
1534	3.1	1600	3.1
2057	0.3	2113	0.6
4 SA 0341	3.5	**19** SU 0353	3.4
0927	0.1	0923	0.7
1612	3.1	1632	3.1
2143	0.4	2152	0.8
5 SU 0422	3.4	**20** M 0428	3.2
1019	0.3	1003	0.9
1652	3.1	1708	3.0
◑ 2233	0.6	◑ 2236	0.9
6 M 0508	3.2	**21** TU 0509	3.0
1119	0.5	1052	1.1
1737	3.0	1752	2.8
2331	0.7	2331	1.0
7 TU 0602	3.0	**22** W 0559	2.8
1228	0.7	1155	1.2
1829	2.9	1846	2.7
8 W 0041	0.9	**23** TH 0044	1.2
0716	2.8	0704	2.6
1344	0.8	1321	1.3
1935	2.8	1956	2.7
9 TH 0211	0.9	**24** F 0240	1.2
0927	2.7	0826	2.6
1457	0.8	1453	1.2
2136	2.8	2136	2.8
10 F 0334	0.8	**25** SA 0341	0.9
1042	2.9	1001	2.7
1559	0.8	1548	1.0
2245	3.0	2241	3.0
11 SA 0431	0.6	**26** SU 0425	0.6
1138	3.0	1102	2.9
1651	0.7	1631	0.8
2336	3.2	2324	3.2
12 SU 0516	0.4	**27** M 0503	0.3
1227	3.1	1147	3.0
1736	0.6	1709	0.7
●			
13 M 0021	3.4	**28** TU 0003	3.5
0555	0.3	0538	0.1
1314	3.1	1230	3.1
1816	0.5	○ 1745	0.5
14 TU 0103	3.5	**29** W 0042	3.5
0632	0.3	0613	0.0
1354	3.1	1311	3.2
1853	0.5	1823	0.4
15 W 0141	3.5	**30** TH 0122	3.6
0706	0.3	0650	-0.1
1429	3.1	1350	3.2
1929	0.5	1903	0.3
		31 F 0202	3.6
		0730	0.0
		1427	3.3
		1945	0.3

Chart Datum: 1·62 metres below Ordnance Datum (Newlyn)

SCOTLAND – GREENOCK

LAT 55°57′N   LONG 4°46′W

TIMES AND HEIGHTS OF HIGH AND LOW WATERS

Dates in amber are **SPRINGS**
Dates in yellow are **NEAPS**

2007

SEPTEMBER

Time	m		Time	m
1 0241	3.7	**16**	0249	3.4
0812	0.1		0806	0.6
SA 1503	3.4	SU	1518	3.3
2028	0.3		2033	0.6
2 0320	3.6	**17**	0321	3.4
0857	0.2		0840	0.7
SU 1540	3.4	M	1549	3.2
2114	0.4		2111	0.8
3 0359	3.5	**18**	0355	3.2
0947	0.5		0918	0.9
M 1619	3.3	TU	1624	3.1
2204	0.6		2154	0.9
4 0443	3.2	**19**	0434	3.0
1048	0.8		1004	1.1
TU 1703	3.2	W	1706	2.9
◔ 2306	0.9	◔	2249	1.1
5 0535	2.9	**20**	0524	2.8
1210	1.1		1106	1.3
W 1756	3.0	TH	1801	2.8
6 0031	1.0	**21**	0001	1.3
0658	2.6		0633	2.6
TH 1340	1.2	F	1227	1.4
1907	2.8		1915	2.7
7 0217	1.0	**22**	0155	1.2
0942	2.7		0801	2.6
F 1452	1.1	SA	1411	1.4
2131	2.9		2049	2.8
8 0328	0.8	**23**	0305	0.9
1042	3.0		0939	2.8
SA 1550	0.9	SU	1515	1.1
2233	3.2		2204	3.0
9 0419	0.6	**24**	0351	0.6
1130	3.1		1040	3.0
SU 1637	0.8	M	1600	0.9
2321	3.3		2252	3.3
10 0500	0.4	**25**	0431	0.3
1212	3.2		1123	3.2
M 1717	0.6	TU	1640	0.7
			2334	3.4
11 0003	3.5	**26**	0508	0.1
0534	0.3		1204	3.3
TU 1252	3.2	W	1718	0.5
● 1753	0.6	○		
12 0042	3.5	**27**	0016	3.6
0606	0.4		0544	0.0
W 1326	3.2	TH	1243	3.4
1826	0.5		1756	0.4
13 0118	3.5	**28**	0058	3.7
0636	0.4		0622	0.0
TH 1356	3.2	F	1321	3.4
1856	0.5		1836	0.3
14 0149	3.5	**29**	0140	3.8
0705	0.5		0703	0.0
F 1423	3.2	SA	1358	3.5
1926	0.6		1918	0.3
15 0219	3.5	**30**	0221	3.8
0735	0.5		0746	0.2
SA 1450	3.3	SU	1435	3.6
1958	0.6		2003	0.3

OCTOBER

Time	m		Time	m
1 0301	3.7	**16**	0254	3.3
0832	0.4		0810	0.8
M 1512	3.6	TU	1515	3.4
2050	0.5		2041	0.8
2 0342	3.5	**17**	0330	3.2
0924	0.8		0850	0.9
TU 1553	3.5	W	1550	3.3
2144	0.7		2127	0.9
3 0427	3.2	**18**	0410	3.0
1027	1.1		0938	1.1
W 1638	3.3	TH	1629	3.1
◑ 2252	1.0		2223	1.1
4 0525	2.9	**19**	0500	2.9
1159	1.3		1039	1.3
TH 1735	3.1	F	1723	2.9
		◑	2334	1.2
5 0033	1.1	**20**	0611	2.7
0756	2.7		1154	1.4
F 1324	1.4	SA	1839	2.8
1855	3.0			
6 0200	1.0	**21**	0059	1.4
0931	2.9		0736	2.7
SA 1431	1.2	SU	1319	1.4
2108	3.0		2004	2.9
7 0303	0.8	**22**	0215	0.8
1024	3.1		0901	2.9
SU 1527	1.0	M	1429	1.2
2209	3.3		2120	3.1
8 0353	0.6	**23**	0309	0.6
1107	3.2		1004	3.1
M 1613	0.8	TU	1523	0.9
2255	3.4		2216	3.3
9 0432	0.5	**24**	0354	0.3
1145	3.3		1051	3.2
TU 1653	0.7	W	1608	0.7
2337	3.5		2304	3.5
10 0507	0.5	**25**	0435	0.1
1220	3.3		1133	3.4
W 1727	0.6	TH	1650	0.5
			2349	3.7
11 0014	3.5	**26**	0516	0.1
0537	0.5		1214	3.5
TH 1252	3.3	F	1732	0.4
● 1757	0.6	○		
12 0049	3.4	**27**	0035	3.7
0607	0.6		0557	0.1
F 1321	3.3	SA	1254	3.6
1826	0.6		1814	0.4
13 0119	3.4	**28**	0120	3.8
0633	0.6		0640	0.2
SA 1348	3.4	SU	1333	3.7
1855	0.6		1858	0.4
14 0149	3.4	**29**	0204	3.7
0702	0.7		0727	0.4
SU 1415	3.4	M	1413	3.8
1926	0.6		1945	0.4
15 0220	3.4	**30**	0248	3.6
0734	0.7		0816	0.7
M 1444	3.4	TU	1453	3.8
2002	0.7		2036	0.6
		31	0334	3.4
			0911	1.0
		W	1536	3.7
			2133	0.7

NOVEMBER

Time	m		Time	m
1 0425	3.2	**16**	0356	3.1
1016	1.2		0925	1.1
TH 1624	3.5	F	1607	3.2
◑ 2243	0.9		2206	0.9
2 0534	2.9	**17**	0447	2.9
1134	1.4		1021	1.2
F 1723	3.3	SA	1657	3.1
		◑	2310	0.9
3 0009	1.0	**18**	0551	2.9
0729	2.8		1127	1.3
SA 1250	1.4	SU	1803	3.0
1839	3.1			
4 0125	1.0	**19**	0019	0.9
0854	2.9		0701	2.9
SU 1356	1.3	M	1237	1.3
2020	3.2		1918	3.1
5 0225	0.9	**20**	0126	0.7
0948	3.1		0812	2.9
M 1453	1.2	TU	1344	1.2
2130	3.3		2034	3.2
6 0316	0.8	**21**	0225	0.6
1031	3.2		0919	3.1
TU 1542	1.0	W	1444	1.0
2221	3.4		2139	3.3
7 0359	0.7	**22**	0318	0.4
1109	3.3		1015	3.2
W 1624	0.8	TH	1538	0.8
2304	3.4		2235	3.5
8 0436	0.7	**23**	0406	0.3
1145	3.4		1104	3.4
TH 1701	0.7	F	1626	0.6
2343	3.4		2326	3.6
9 0508	0.7	**24**	0452	0.3
1218	3.4		1149	3.5
F 1733	0.7	SA	1713	0.4
●		○		
10 0018	3.3	**25**	0016	3.6
0538	0.7		0538	0.3
SA 1250	3.4	SU	1233	3.7
1802	0.7		1758	0.4
11 0050	3.3	**26**	0106	3.6
0607	0.8		0625	0.5
SU 1319	3.5	M	1316	3.8
1832	0.7		1845	0.4
12 0122	3.3	**27**	0155	3.6
0638	0.8		0714	0.6
M 1347	3.5	TU	1358	3.8
1905	0.7		1935	0.4
13 0156	3.3	**28**	0244	3.5
0712	0.8		0806	0.8
TU 1418	3.5	W	1441	3.8
1941	0.7		2026	0.5
14 0233	3.3	**29**	0334	3.4
0752	0.9		0900	1.0
W 1451	3.5	TH	1526	3.8
2023	0.8		2121	0.7
15 0312	3.2	**30**	0427	3.2
0835	1.0		0957	1.1
TH 1527	3.4	F	1614	3.6
2110	0.8		2221	0.8

DECEMBER

Time	m		Time	m
1 0526	3.1	**16**	0432	3.0
1059	1.3		1001	1.0
SA 1707	3.5	SU	1638	3.3
◑ 2329	0.9	◑	2242	0.6
2 0632	3.0	**17**	0522	3.0
1204	1.3		1057	1.0
SU 1808	3.3	M	1730	3.2
		◑	2343	0.6
3 0037	1.0	**18**	0617	3.0
0741	3.0		1158	1.1
M 1310	1.3	TU	1832	3.2
1914	3.2			
4 0140	1.0	**19**	0045	0.6
0847	3.0		0716	3.0
TU 1412	1.2	W	1303	1.1
2027	3.2		1942	3.1
5 0234	0.9	**20**	0147	0.6
0942	3.1		0820	3.0
W 1507	1.1	TH	1408	1.0
2134	3.2		2101	3.2
6 0322	0.9	**21**	0246	0.6
1029	3.2		0938	3.1
TH 1555	0.9	F	1512	0.9
2227	3.2		2211	3.3
7 0405	0.9	**22**	0343	0.5
1111	3.3		1039	3.3
F 1637	0.8	SA	1609	0.7
2312	3.2		2311	3.4
8 0443	0.9	**23**	0436	0.5
1149	3.4		1131	3.4
SA 1714	0.8	SU	1701	0.5
2350	3.2			
9 0517	0.9	**24**	0006	3.4
1224	3.4		0526	0.6
SU 1748	0.7	M	1219	3.6
●		○	1750	0.4
10 0025	3.2	**25**	0101	3.4
0549	0.9		0616	0.6
M 1256	3.5	TU	1304	3.7
1819	0.7		1838	0.4
11 0101	3.2	**26**	0153	3.4
0623	0.9		0705	0.7
TU 1326	3.5	W	1349	3.8
1853	0.7		1925	0.4
12 0139	3.2	**27**	0242	3.4
0700	0.8		0754	0.7
W 1359	3.5	TH	1433	3.9
1930	0.6		2012	0.4
13 0219	3.2	**28**	0329	3.3
0741	0.8		0841	0.8
TH 1434	3.5	F	1516	3.8
2011	0.6		2100	0.5
14 0301	3.1	**29**	0413	3.2
0824	0.9		0929	0.9
F 1512	3.5	SA	1559	3.7
2057	0.6		2148	0.6
15 0345	3.1	**30**	0456	3.2
0911	0.9		1018	1.0
SA 1553	3.4	SU	1643	3.6
2147	0.6		2241	0.8
		31	0541	3.1
			1112	1.1
		M	1729	3.4
		◔	2340	1.0

TIDES

Chart Datum: 1·62 metres below Ordnance Datum (Newlyn)

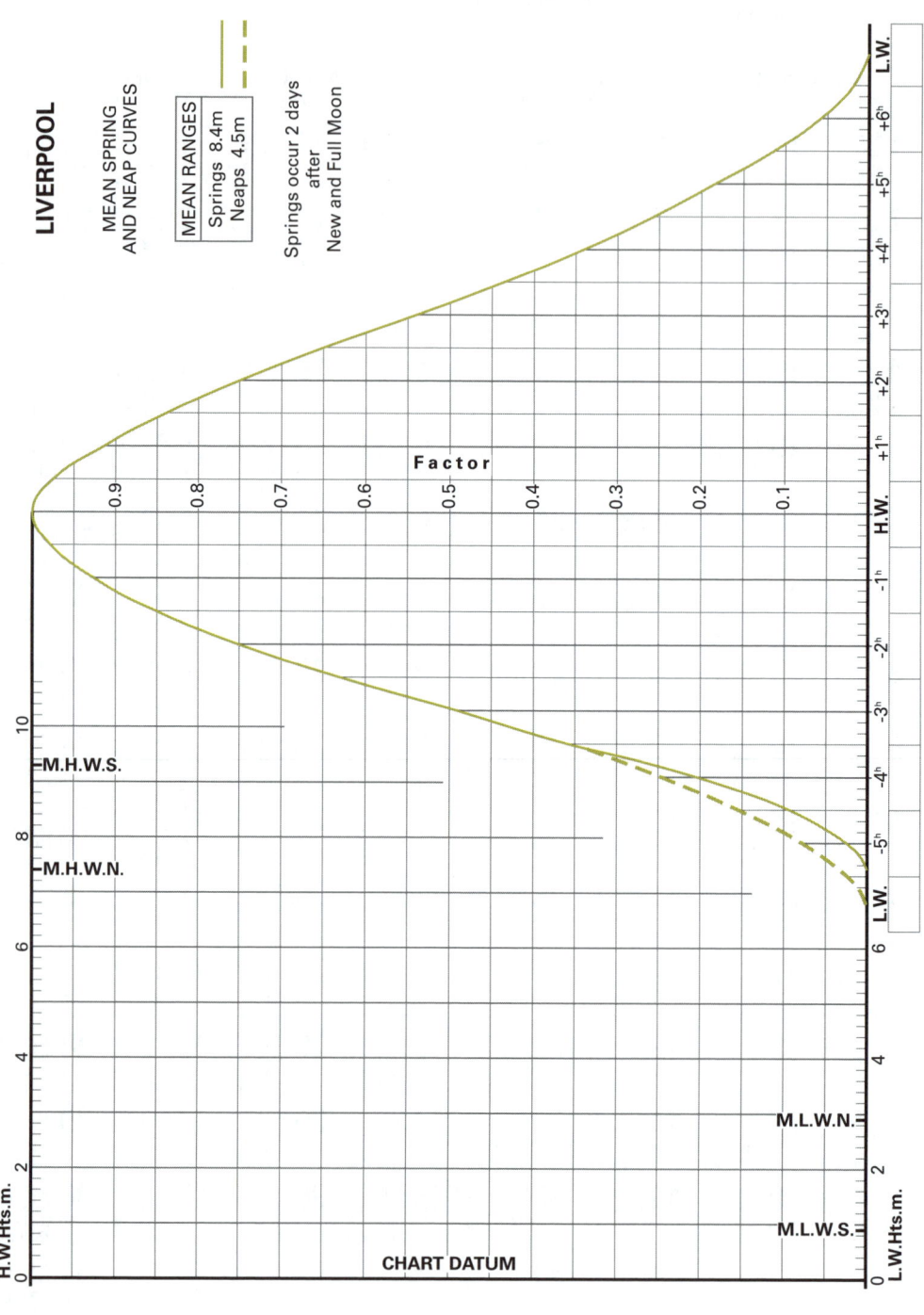

LIVERPOOL

MEAN SPRING
AND NEAP CURVES

MEAN RANGES
Springs 8.4m
Neaps 4.5m

Springs occur 2 days
after
New and Full Moon

Factor

0.9
0.8
0.7
0.6
0.5
0.4
0.3
0.2
0.1

L.W.
+6ʰ
+5ʰ
+4ʰ
+3ʰ
+2ʰ
+1ʰ
H.W.
-1ʰ
-2ʰ
-3ʰ
-4ʰ
-5ʰ
L.W.

M.H.W.S.
M.H.W.N.

M.L.W.N.
M.L.W.S.

H.W.Hts.m.
L.W.Hts.m.

CHART DATUM

TIME ZONE (UT)	ENGLAND – LIVERPOOL (ALFRED DK)	Dates in amber are SPRINGS
For Summer Time add ONE hour in **non-shaded areas**	LAT 53°24'N LONG 3°01'W	Dates in yellow are NEAPS
	TIMES AND HEIGHTS OF HIGH AND LOW WATERS	**2007**

JANUARY

Day	Time m	Time m	Time m	Time m
1 M	0322 2.1	0910 8.4	1555 2.1	2136 8.7
2 TU	0418 1.9	1003 8.8	1651 1.7	2229 8.9
3 W ○	0507 1.7	1050 9.0	1741 1.5	2317 9.0
4 TH	0551 1.6	1134 9.2	1828 1.4	
5 F	0000 9.0	0633 1.7	1215 9.2	1911 1.4
6 SA	0041 8.9	0712 1.8	1255 9.2	1951 1.5
7 SU	0119 8.7	0750 1.9	1333 9.0	2029 1.7
8 M	0156 8.5	0825 2.1	1410 8.8	2104 1.9
9 TU	0232 8.3	0857 2.4	1448 8.5	2138 2.2
10 W	0311 8.0	0930 2.7	1527 8.2	2213 2.6
11 TH ◑	0353 7.7	1011 3.0	1612 7.8	2257 2.9
12 F	0443 7.4	1104 3.3	1705 7.5	2354 3.2
13 SA	0545 7.1	1210 3.4	1809 7.3	
14 SU	0100 3.2	0657 7.2	1322 3.4	1920 7.3
15 M	0207 3.1	0806 7.5	1431 3.1	2028 7.5
16 TU	0308 2.8	0903 7.9	1532 2.7	2125 7.9
17 W	0401 2.3	0951 8.4	1626 2.2	2214 8.4
18 TH	0449 2.0	1035 8.8	1716 1.7	2259 8.7
19 F ●	0535 1.6	1118 9.2	1804 1.4	2342 9.0
20 SA	0620 1.4	1201 9.5	1850 1.1	
21 SU	0026 9.2	0703 1.2	1244 9.7	1934 0.9
22 M	0110 9.3	0745 1.2	1328 9.8	2015 0.8
23 TU	0153 9.3	0825 1.2	1412 9.7	2056 1.0
24 W	0236 9.1	0906 1.4	1457 9.5	2136 1.3
25 TH ◑	0322 8.8	0949 1.8	1545 9.1	2220 1.8
26 F	0411 8.3	1039 2.2	1638 8.5	2313 2.3
27 SA	0511 7.8	1143 2.7	1743 8.0	
28 SU	0021 2.8	0626 7.5	1304 3.0	1903 7.7
29 M	0145 3.0	0752 7.6	1437 2.9	2028 7.8
30 TU	0311 2.8	0903 8.0	1554 2.4	2134 8.1
31 W	0415 2.4	0958 8.5	1651 1.9	2226 8.5

FEBRUARY

Day	Time m	Time m	Time m	Time m
1 TH	0504 2.0	1044 8.9	1738 1.5	2310 8.8
2 F ○	0546 1.7	1125 9.1	1820 1.2	2349 8.9
3 SA	0624 1.6	1202 9.3	1857 1.4	
4 SU	0024 9.0	0659 1.5	1237 9.3	1932 1.2
5 M	0057 8.9	0731 1.6	1310 9.2	2003 1.4
6 TU	0128 8.8	0759 1.7	1342 9.0	2030 1.6
7 W	0200 8.6	0822 1.9	1414 8.8	2053 1.9
8 TH	0232 8.4	0849 2.2	1448 8.5	2119 2.3
9 F	0306 8.1	0924 2.5	1525 8.1	2154 2.7
10 SA ◑	0346 7.7	1009 3.0	1610 7.6	2245 3.2
11 SU	0439 7.2	1111 3.4	1709 7.1	
12 M	0000 3.5	0550 6.9	1234 3.6	1826 6.9
13 TU	0124 3.5	0719 7.1	1356 3.3	1954 7.1
14 W	0238 3.1	0835 7.6	1509 2.8	2106 7.7
15 TH	0341 2.5	0931 8.2	1610 2.1	2158 8.3
16 F	0434 1.9	1017 8.9	1703 1.4	2243 8.9
17 SA ●	0522 1.4	1101 9.4	1751 0.9	2326 9.3
18 SU	0607 1.0	1143 9.8	1835 0.5	
19 M	0008 9.6	0649 0.7	1226 10.1	1917 0.3
20 TU	0050 9.7	0729 0.5	1309 10.2	1956 0.3
21 W	0132 9.7	0807 0.6	1351 10.0	2032 0.6
22 TH	0213 9.4	0845 0.9	1434 9.6	2109 1.1
23 F	0255 9.0	0925 1.4	1519 9.0	2149 1.7
24 SA ◑	0341 8.4	1013 2.1	1611 8.3	2239 2.5
25 SU	0438 7.7	1116 2.8	1719 7.5	2349 3.2
26 M	0601 7.2	1248 3.2	1854 7.1	
27 TU	0127 3.4	0741 7.2	1438 3.0	2024 7.4
28 W	0310 3.1	0853 7.8	1551 2.3	2125 7.9

MARCH

Day	Time m	Time m	Time m	Time m
1 TH	0411 2.5	0946 8.4	1642 1.7	2213 8.4
2 F	0455 2.0	1029 8.8	1724 1.3	2253 8.8
3 SA ○	0532 1.6	1107 9.1	1800 1.1	2328 8.9
4 SU	0607 1.4	1141 9.2	1834 1.0	2359 9.0
5 M	0638 1.3	1212 9.2	1904 1.1	
6 TU	0029 9.1	0706 1.3	1243 9.2	1930 1.3
7 W	0058 8.9	0729 1.4	1312 9.0	1951 1.5
8 TH	0127 8.6	0750 1.6	1342 8.8	2011 1.7
9 F	0157 8.6	0817 1.9	1413 8.5	2038 2.1
10 SA	0228 8.3	0849 2.3	1447 8.1	2110 2.6
11 SU	0304 7.9	0929 2.8	1529 7.6	2153 3.1
12 M ◑	0352 7.4	1025 3.3	1628 7.1	2306 3.6
13 TU	0502 6.9	1154 3.5	1748 6.8	
14 W	0045 3.7	0635 6.9	1326 3.3	1925 7.0
15 TH	0209 3.3	0804 7.5	1444 2.7	2042 7.6
16 F	0317 2.6	0904 8.2	1548 1.9	2135 8.4
17 SA	0412 1.8	0952 9.0	1641 1.1	2220 9.0
18 SU	0501 1.1	1036 9.6	1728 0.5	2302 9.5
19 M ●	0545 0.6	1119 10.1	1811 0.1	2344 9.8
20 TU	0628 0.3	1202 10.3	1852 0.0	
21 W	0026 9.9	0707 0.2	1246 10.2	1930 0.1
22 TH	0107 9.8	0746 0.4	1329 10.0	2006 0.5
23 F	0148 9.5	0825 0.8	1412 9.5	2043 1.1
24 SA	0230 9.0	0906 1.4	1458 8.8	2123 1.9
25 SU ◑	0316 8.3	0956 2.1	1552 7.9	2215 2.7
26 M	0415 7.6	1104 2.8	1706 7.2	2328 3.4
27 TU	0545 7.1	1242 3.1	1844 6.9	
28 W	0114 3.6	0719 7.2	1423 2.8	2004 7.3
29 TH	0251 3.1	0828 7.7	1529 2.2	2101 7.8
30 F	0347 2.5	0920 8.3	1617 1.7	2146 8.3
31 SA	0430 2.0	1002 8.7	1656 1.3	2224 8.7

APRIL

Day	Time m	Time m	Time m	Time m
1 SU	0506 1.6	1039 8.9	1730 1.2	2258 8.9
2 M ○	0539 1.4	1113 9.0	1801 1.1	2329 8.9
3 TU	0609 1.3	1144 9.0	1829 1.2	2358 8.9
4 W	0635 1.3	1213 9.0	1852 1.3	
5 TH	0027 8.9	0657 1.4	1242 8.8	1913 1.5
6 F	0056 8.7	0722 1.5	1312 8.7	1938 1.7
7 SA	0126 8.7	0751 1.8	1344 8.5	2007 2.1
8 SU	0158 8.4	0825 2.1	1420 8.1	2041 2.5
9 M	0236 8.0	0905 2.6	1504 7.6	2123 3.0
10 TU ◑	0326 7.6	1001 3.0	1603 7.2	2233 3.5
11 W	0434 7.2	1126 3.2	1722 6.9	
12 TH	0009 3.5	0601 7.2	1255 3.0	1854 7.1
13 F	0134 3.1	0726 7.6	1412 2.4	2009 7.8
14 SA	0244 2.4	0829 8.4	1517 1.6	2104 8.5
15 SU	0342 1.7	0921 9.1	1611 0.9	2150 9.1
16 M	0432 1.0	1008 9.6	1659 0.4	2234 9.6
17 TU ●	0518 0.6	1053 10.0	1743 0.2	2317 9.8
18 W	0603 0.3	1138 10.1	1824 0.1	
19 TH	0000 9.8	0645 0.3	1223 10.0	1903 0.4
20 F	0043 9.7	0727 0.5	1308 9.7	1941 0.8
21 SA	0126 9.3	0810 0.9	1354 9.1	2021 1.4
22 SU	0211 8.9	0855 1.4	1443 8.5	2105 2.1
23 M	0300 8.3	0949 2.1	1539 7.8	2158 2.8
24 TU ◑	0401 7.7	1057 2.6	1652 7.2	2309 3.3
25 W	0523 7.3	1220 2.8	1814 7.0	
26 TH	0040 3.5	0642 7.3	1343 2.7	1926 7.2
27 F	0206 3.2	0748 7.6	1448 2.3	2023 7.6
28 SA	0306 2.7	0841 8.0	1537 2.0	2109 8.1
29 SU	0351 2.3	0926 8.4	1617 1.7	2148 8.4
30 M	0429 1.9	1006 8.6	1652 1.5	2224 8.7

TIDES

Chart Datum: 4·93 metres below Ordnance Datum (Newlyn)

ENGLAND – LIVERPOOL (ALFRED DK)

TIME ZONE (UT)
For Summer Time add ONE hour in **non-shaded areas**

LAT 53°24'N   LONG 3°01'W
TIMES AND HEIGHTS OF HIGH AND LOW WATERS

Dates in amber are **SPRINGS**
Dates in yellow are **NEAPS**

2007

MAY

Day	Time m	Day	Time m
1 TU	0503 1.7 / 1041 8.7 / 1722 1.4 / 2257 8.8	16 W	0452 0.8 / 1029 9.7 / 1715 0.6 / 2253 9.6
2 W	0533 1.6 / 1113 8.7 / 1749 1.4 / 2327 8.8	17 TH	0540 0.6 / 1117 9.7 / 1758 0.6 / 2338 9.6
3 TH	0601 1.5 / 1144 8.7 / 1815 1.5 / 2358 8.8	18 F	0627 0.6 / 1205 9.6 / 1841 0.8
4 F	0629 1.5 / 1215 8.6 / 1844 1.6	19 SA	0023 9.4 / 0713 0.7 / 1253 9.3 / 1922 1.2
5 SA	0029 8.7 / 0700 1.6 / 1249 8.5 / 1914 1.8	20 SU	0110 9.2 / 0800 1.0 / 1341 8.9 / 2005 1.7
6 SU	0103 8.6 / 0735 1.8 / 1325 8.4 / 1948 2.1	21 M	0157 8.8 / 0849 1.4 / 1430 8.4 / 2051 2.2
7 M	0140 8.4 / 0813 2.0 / 1405 8.1 / 2026 2.4	22 TU	0246 8.4 / 0941 1.9 / 1523 7.9 / 2142 2.7
8 TU	0222 8.2 / 0857 2.3 / 1452 7.8 / 2113 2.8	23 W	0342 8.0 / 1038 2.3 / 1623 7.4 / 2241 3.1
9 W	0314 7.9 / 0954 2.6 / 1549 7.5 / 2218 3.1	24 TH	0446 7.6 / 1139 2.6 / 1729 7.2 / 2347 3.3
10 TH	0418 7.6 / 1105 2.7 / 1700 7.3 / 2336 3.1	25 F	0554 7.5 / 1242 2.7 / 1835 7.2
11 F	0532 7.7 / 1220 2.5 / 1819 7.5	26 SA	0055 3.2 / 0658 7.5 / 1345 2.6 / 1933 7.4
12 SA	0052 2.8 / 0646 8.0 / 1333 2.1 / 1929 7.9	27 SU	0201 3.0 / 0755 7.7 / 1440 2.4 / 2024 7.7
13 SU	0203 2.3 / 0751 8.5 / 1439 1.6 / 2028 8.5	28 M	0256 2.7 / 0844 7.9 / 1526 2.2 / 2109 8.1
14 M	0306 1.8 / 0848 9.0 / 1537 1.1 / 2120 9.0	29 TU	0341 2.3 / 0928 8.1 / 1605 2.0 / 2148 8.3
15 TU	0401 1.2 / 0940 9.4 / 1628 0.8 / 2207 9.4	30 W	0420 2.1 / 1008 8.3 / 1640 1.8 / 2225 8.5
		31 TH	0456 1.9 / 1044 8.4 / 1713 1.7 / 2300 8.7

JUNE

Day	Time m	Day	Time m
1 F	0531 1.7 / 1119 8.4 / 1747 1.7 / 2334 8.7	16 SA	0616 1.0 / 1154 9.1 / 1826 1.3
2 SA	0608 1.7 / 1155 8.5 / 1823 1.7	17 SU	0010 9.2 / 0705 1.0 / 1242 9.0 / 1910 1.5
3 SU	0010 8.7 / 0647 1.7 / 1233 8.5 / 1859 1.8	18 M	0056 9.1 / 0753 1.1 / 1328 8.8 / 1953 1.8
4 M	0048 8.7 / 0727 1.7 / 1314 8.4 / 1938 2.0	19 TU	0142 8.9 / 0839 1.3 / 1413 8.5 / 2036 2.1
5 TU	0130 8.6 / 0810 1.8 / 1357 8.3 / 2021 2.2	20 W	0227 8.6 / 0923 1.6 / 1457 8.2 / 2119 2.4
6 W	0215 8.5 / 0856 1.9 / 1444 8.2 / 2108 2.4	21 TH	0312 8.3 / 1006 2.0 / 1542 7.8 / 2204 2.7
7 TH	0305 8.4 / 0946 2.0 / 1536 8.0 / 2202 2.5	22 F	0359 8.0 / 1051 2.3 / 1631 7.5 / 2253 3.0
8 F	0401 8.3 / 1043 2.1 / 1635 7.8 / 2305 2.6	23 SA	0452 7.7 / 1139 2.6 / 1728 7.3 / 2348 3.1
9 SA	0503 8.2 / 1145 2.2 / 1741 7.8	24 SU	0551 7.4 / 1232 2.8 / 1830 7.2
10 SU	0011 2.6 / 0608 8.3 / 1251 2.1 / 1849 8.0	25 M	0048 3.2 / 0654 7.4 / 1329 2.9 / 1931 7.4
11 M	0121 2.4 / 0714 8.4 / 1359 1.9 / 1953 8.3	26 TU	0149 3.0 / 0754 7.5 / 1426 2.7 / 2026 7.7
12 TU	0230 2.0 / 0817 8.7 / 1504 1.6 / 2052 8.6	27 W	0247 2.6 / 0849 7.7 / 1518 2.5 / 2114 8.0
13 W	0334 1.7 / 0917 8.9 / 1602 1.4 / 2145 8.9	28 TH	0339 2.5 / 0937 7.9 / 1604 2.2 / 2157 8.3
14 TH	0431 1.3 / 1012 9.1 / 1653 1.2 / 2235 9.2	29 F	0426 2.2 / 1020 8.1 / 1647 2.0 / 2237 8.5
15 F	0525 1.1 / 1104 9.2 / 1741 1.2 / 2323 9.2	30 SA	0511 1.9 / 1101 8.3 / 1728 1.8 / 2317 8.7

JULY

Day	Time m	Day	Time m
1 SU	0555 1.7 / 1141 8.5 / 1809 1.7 / 2356 8.9	16 M	0657 1.0 / 1229 8.9 / 1900 1.5
2 M	0639 1.7 / 1222 8.6 / 1851 1.7	17 TU	0041 9.2 / 0739 1.0 / 1310 8.8 / 1939 1.6
3 TU	0037 9.0 / 0722 1.4 / 1304 8.7 / 1932 1.7	18 W	0121 9.1 / 0818 1.2 / 1348 8.7 / 2015 1.8
4 W	0120 9.0 / 0805 1.4 / 1347 8.7 / 2013 1.7	19 TH	0159 8.9 / 0854 1.5 / 1423 8.4 / 2048 2.1
5 TH	0204 9.1 / 0848 1.4 / 1431 8.7 / 2056 1.8	20 F	0236 8.6 / 0928 1.8 / 1459 8.2 / 2120 2.4
6 F	0250 9.0 / 0931 1.5 / 1517 8.5 / 2142 2.0	21 SA	0314 8.3 / 1001 2.2 / 1537 7.8 / 2156 2.7
7 SA	0339 8.8 / 1017 1.7 / 1608 8.3 / 2233 2.2	22 SU	0355 7.9 / 1038 2.6 / 1621 7.5 / 2243 3.1
8 SU	0433 8.6 / 1110 2.0 / 1705 8.0 / 2334 2.5	23 M	0443 7.5 / 1128 3.0 / 1717 7.2 / 2346 3.3
9 M	0534 8.3 / 1212 2.3 / 1811 7.8	24 TU	0543 7.2 / 1230 3.2 / 1827 7.1
10 TU	0045 2.6 / 0641 8.1 / 1324 2.4 / 1923 7.9	25 W	0057 3.4 / 0655 7.1 / 1338 3.2 / 1942 7.3
11 W	0204 2.5 / 0755 8.1 / 1439 2.3 / 2033 8.1	26 TH	0207 3.2 / 0811 7.2 / 1441 2.9 / 2045 7.7
12 TH	0319 2.2 / 0905 8.3 / 1546 2.0 / 2134 8.5	27 F	0310 2.8 / 0912 7.6 / 1538 2.6 / 2136 8.1
13 F	0424 1.8 / 1005 8.6 / 1643 1.8 / 2227 8.9	28 SA	0406 2.3 / 1002 8.0 / 1628 2.2 / 2219 8.6
14 SA	0520 1.4 / 1058 8.8 / 1733 1.6 / 2315 9.1	29 SU	0456 1.9 / 1046 8.4 / 1714 1.8 / 2300 8.9
15 SU	0611 1.1 / 1145 8.9 / 1818 1.5 / 2359 9.2	30 M	0543 1.5 / 1127 8.7 / 1758 1.5 / 2341 9.2
		31 TU	0628 1.2 / 1208 8.9 / 1840 1.3

AUGUST

Day	Time m	Day	Time m
1 W	0021 9.4 / 0711 0.9 / 1249 9.1 / 1920 1.2	16 TH	0054 9.2 / 0749 1.1 / 1316 8.8 / 1947 1.6
2 TH	0103 9.5 / 0751 0.8 / 1330 9.1 / 1959 1.2	17 F	0127 9.0 / 0819 1.4 / 1347 8.6 / 2012 1.8
3 F	0146 9.6 / 0830 0.9 / 1411 9.1 / 2038 1.3	18 SA	0159 8.8 / 0844 1.8 / 1419 8.4 / 2036 2.3
4 SA	0229 9.4 / 0908 1.1 / 1453 8.9 / 2118 1.6	19 SU	0232 8.7 / 0907 2.2 / 1452 8.1 / 2106 2.5
5 SU	0314 9.1 / 0948 1.5 / 1539 8.5 / 2204 2.0	20 M	0308 8.0 / 0938 2.6 / 1529 7.7 / 2148 2.9
6 M	0405 8.6 / 1036 2.1 / 1633 8.0 / 2303 2.5	21 TU	0351 7.5 / 1024 3.1 / 1618 7.3 / 2248 3.4
7 TU	0505 8.0 / 1138 2.6 / 1741 7.6	22 W	0448 7.1 / 1135 3.5 / 1724 7.0
8 W	0022 2.9 / 0621 7.6 / 1259 3.0 / 1906 7.5	23 TH	0013 3.6 / 0603 6.8 / 1258 3.6 / 1856 7.0
9 TH	0157 2.6 / 0750 7.6 / 1431 2.9 / 2029 7.8	24 F	0136 3.4 / 0739 6.9 / 1413 3.3 / 2019 7.5
10 F	0322 2.4 / 0905 7.9 / 1546 2.5 / 2131 8.3	25 SA	0247 2.9 / 0852 7.5 / 1517 2.7 / 2114 8.1
11 SA	0425 1.8 / 1002 8.4 / 1641 2.0 / 2221 8.8	26 SU	0348 2.2 / 0943 8.1 / 1610 2.2 / 2158 8.7
12 SU	0516 1.4 / 1050 8.7 / 1727 1.7 / 2304 9.2	27 M	0439 1.6 / 1025 8.6 / 1657 1.6 / 2239 9.2
13 M	0600 1.0 / 1132 8.9 / 1807 1.5 / 2344 9.3	28 TU	0525 1.1 / 1105 9.0 / 1740 1.2 / 2319 9.6
14 TU	0640 0.9 / 1210 9.0 / 1843 1.4	29 W	0609 0.7 / 1145 9.2 / 1822 0.9 / 2359 9.9
15 W	0020 9.3 / 0716 1.0 / 1244 8.9 / 1917 1.5	30 TH	0650 0.5 / 1225 9.5 / 1901 0.7
		31 F	0040 10.0 / 0728 0.5 / 1306 9.5 / 1939 0.8

Chart Datum: 4·93 metres below Ordnance Datum (Newlyn)

ENGLAND – LIVERPOOL (ALFRED DK)

LAT 53°24'N   LONG 3°01'W

TIMES AND HEIGHTS OF HIGH AND LOW WATERS

Dates in amber are SPRINGS
Dates in yellow are NEAPS

2007

SEPTEMBER

Day	Time m	Time m	Time m	Time m
1 SA	0122 9.9	0805 0.6	1346 9.4	2017 1.0
16 SU	0123 8.8	0758 1.8	1341 8.6	2000 2.0
2 SU	0205 9.6	0841 1.0	1427 9.0	2056 1.4
17 M	0155 8.5	0822 2.2	1412 8.3	2031 2.4
3 M	0250 9.1	0921 1.6	1512 8.5	2142 2.0
18 TU	0230 8.1	0854 2.6	1449 7.9	2109 2.9
4 TU	0341 8.4	1008 2.4	1606 7.9	2243 2.7
19 W	0311 7.6	0935 3.2	1535 7.4	2204 3.4
5 W	0446 7.6	1114 3.1	1722 7.4	
20 TH	0407 7.0	1044 3.7	1640 7.0	2336 3.7
6 TH	0015 3.1	0617 7.2	1249 3.4	1903 7.3
21 F	0524 6.7	1221 3.8	1810 6.9	
7 F	0204 3.0	0752 7.4	1435 3.1	2023 7.8
22 SA	0106 3.5	0708 6.9	1343 3.4	1944 7.4
8 SA	0322 2.3	0858 7.9	1543 2.6	2120 8.4
23 SU	0221 2.8	0824 7.5	1450 2.8	2043 8.2
9 SU	0416 1.7	0949 8.4	1631 2.0	2205 8.9
24 M	0322 2.1	0914 8.2	1545 2.1	2128 8.9
10 M	0501 1.2	1032 8.8	1711 1.6	2245 9.2
25 TU	0414 1.4	0957 8.8	1632 1.5	2210 9.5
11 TU	0539 1.0	1109 9.0	1746 1.4	2321 9.3
26 ○	0459 0.8	1037 9.3	1716 1.0	2252 9.9
12 W	0614 0.9	1142 9.2	1819 1.3	2353 9.3
27 TH	0542 0.4	1117 9.6	1758 0.6	2333 10.1
13 TH	0646 1.0	1213 9.0	1849 1.4	
28 F	0623 0.3	1158 9.6	1839 0.5	
14 F	0023 9.2	0714 1.2	1242 8.9	1914 1.5
29 SA	0015 10.1	0701 0.4	1240 9.7	1918 0.6
15 SA	0053 9.0	0738 1.5	1311 8.8	1936 1.7
30 SU	0059 9.9	0739 0.7	1321 9.5	1957 0.9

OCTOBER

Day	Time m	Time m	Time m	Time m
1 M	0143 9.5	0817 1.2	1404 9.1	2040 1.4
16 TU	0126 8.4	0751 2.2	1343 8.4	2007 2.3
2 TU	0231 8.8	0858 1.9	1451 8.5	2130 2.1
17 W	0202 8.1	0824 2.7	1420 8.1	2045 2.8
3 W	0325 8.1	0949 2.7	1549 7.8	2238 2.8
18 TH	0245 7.6	0906 3.2	1507 7.7	2139 3.2
4 TH	0438 7.4	1100 3.3	1713 7.3	
19 F	0340 7.2	1010 3.6	1610 7.3	2303 3.5
5 F	0016 3.1	0613 7.1	1245 3.5	1848 7.4
20 SA	0454 6.9	1143 3.7	1730 7.2	
6 SA	0154 2.8	0735 7.4	1420 3.2	2000 7.8
21 SU	0030 3.3	0625 7.0	1305 3.4	1855 7.6
7 SU	0302 2.2	0836 7.9	1521 2.6	2055 8.4
22 M	0145 2.7	0743 7.6	1413 2.8	2001 8.2
8 M	0352 1.7	0923 8.4	1606 2.1	2139 8.8
23 TU	0247 2.0	0837 8.3	1511 2.1	2052 8.9
9 TU	0433 1.3	1004 8.8	1644 1.7	2218 9.1
24 W	0341 1.3	0923 9.0	1602 1.5	2139 9.5
10 W	0509 1.2	1039 9.0	1718 1.5	2253 9.2
25 TH	0429 0.8	1007 9.4	1649 1.0	2224 9.9
11 TH	0541 1.2	1111 9.0	1749 1.4	2324 9.2
26 F	0513 0.5	1049 9.7	1734 0.6	2308 10.1
12 F	0610 1.3	1141 9.0	1817 1.5	2353 9.0
27 SA	0556 0.4	1132 9.8	1817 0.6	2353 10.0
13 SA	0636 1.4	1209 9.0	1842 1.6	
28 SU	0636 0.6	1216 9.7	1901 0.7	
14 SU	0022 8.9	0658 1.6	1239 8.8	1906 1.7
29 M	0039 9.8	0716 0.9	1301 9.5	1945 1.0
15 M	0053 8.7	0723 1.9	1309 8.7	1934 2.0
30 TU	0127 9.3	0758 1.5	1347 9.1	2032 1.5
31 W	0218 8.7	0844 2.1	1438 8.6	2127 2.1

NOVEMBER

Day	Time m	Time m	Time m	Time m
1 TH	0315 8.0	0938 2.8	1538 8.0	2235 2.5
16 F	0230 7.9	0853 2.9	1452 8.0	2129 2.8
2 F	0426 7.5	1047 3.3	1654 7.6	2356 2.8
17 SA	0322 7.6	0951 3.2	1549 7.8	2235 3.0
3 SA	0547 7.2	1213 3.4	1814 7.6	
18 SU	0426 7.3	1103 3.4	1656 7.7	2349 2.9
4 SU	0117 2.7	0700 7.2	1338 3.2	1922 7.8
19 M	0540 7.4	1218 3.2	1808 7.9	
5 M	0223 2.4	0759 7.8	1441 2.8	2018 8.2
20 TU	0059 2.6	0653 7.7	1327 2.8	1915 8.3
6 TU	0315 2.0	0848 8.2	1530 2.4	2105 8.5
21 W	0206 2.1	0756 8.3	1432 2.3	2014 8.8
7 W	0357 1.8	0930 8.5	1610 2.1	2146 8.8
22 TH	0306 1.6	0850 8.8	1530 1.7	2109 9.3
8 TH	0433 1.6	1007 8.8	1645 1.8	2223 8.9
23 F	0359 1.2	0939 9.3	1623 1.2	2159 9.6
9 F	0504 1.6	1040 8.9	1716 1.7	2256 8.9
24 SA	0447 0.9	1026 9.6	1713 0.9	2249 9.8
10 SA	0533 1.6	1111 8.9	1746 1.7	2326 8.8
25 SU	0533 0.8	1112 9.7	1802 0.8	2338 9.7
11 SU	0601 1.7	1142 8.9	1815 1.7	2357 8.7
26 M	0618 0.9	1159 9.7	1850 0.9	
12 M	0629 1.8	1213 8.9	1846 1.8	
27 TU	0027 9.5	0702 1.2	1247 9.5	1939 1.1
13 TU	0030 8.6	0659 2.0	1248 8.7	1919 2.0
28 W	0117 9.2	0747 1.6	1336 9.2	2029 1.4
14 W	0106 8.4	0732 2.2	1324 8.5	1955 2.2
29 TH	0207 8.7	0835 2.1	1426 8.8	2121 1.8
15 TH	0145 8.2	0809 2.6	1404 8.3	2037 2.5
30 F	0300 8.2	0925 2.5	1519 8.4	2217 2.2

DECEMBER

Day	Time m	Time m	Time m	Time m
1 SA	0358 7.8	1021 2.9	1619 8.0	2316 2.5
16 SU	0305 8.1	0932 2.6	1528 8.5	2208 2.4
2 SU	0501 7.5	1122 3.2	1724 7.8	
17 M	0358 7.9	1027 2.8	1624 8.3	2306 2.5
3 M	0017 2.7	0608 7.4	1228 3.3	1830 7.7
18 TU	0459 7.8	1130 2.9	1726 8.3	
4 TU	0121 2.7	0711 7.5	1335 3.2	1932 7.8
19 W	0011 2.5	0606 7.8	1239 2.8	1832 8.3
5 W	0220 2.6	0806 7.8	1436 2.9	2026 8.0
20 TH	0121 2.4	0714 8.0	1352 2.6	1939 8.5
6 TH	0309 2.4	0853 8.1	1526 2.6	2112 8.2
21 F	0231 2.1	0819 8.4	1502 2.2	2044 8.8
7 F	0351 2.2	0935 8.4	1607 2.3	2154 8.4
22 SA	0333 1.8	0917 8.8	1605 1.7	2143 9.1
8 SA	0427 2.0	1013 8.6	1645 2.1	2231 8.5
23 SU	0429 1.5	1011 9.2	1701 1.3	2238 9.3
9 SU	0502 1.9	1048 8.8	1721 2.0	2306 8.6
24 ○	0520 1.3	1101 9.4	1754 1.0	2329 9.4
10 M	0536 1.9	1122 8.9	1757 1.9	2340 8.6
25 TU	0608 1.2	1149 9.6	1845 0.9	
11 TU	0610 1.9	1157 8.9	1834 1.9	
26 W	0018 9.4	0654 1.3	1237 9.5	1934 0.9
12 W	0016 8.6	0646 2.0	1234 8.8	1912 1.9
27 TH	0106 9.2	0739 1.5	1323 9.4	2020 1.1
13 TH	0055 8.5	0723 2.1	1313 8.8	1952 2.0
28 F	0151 8.9	0823 1.8	1408 9.2	2104 1.4
14 F	0135 8.4	0803 2.2	1354 8.7	2034 2.1
29 SA	0235 8.6	0905 2.1	1454 8.9	2147 1.8
15 SA	0218 8.3	0845 2.4	1438 8.6	2118 2.2
30 SU	0319 8.2	0948 2.5	1536 8.5	2230 2.2
31 M	0405 7.8	1033 2.8	1624 8.0	2317 2.6

Chart Datum: 4·93 metres below Ordnance Datum (Newlyn)

TIDES

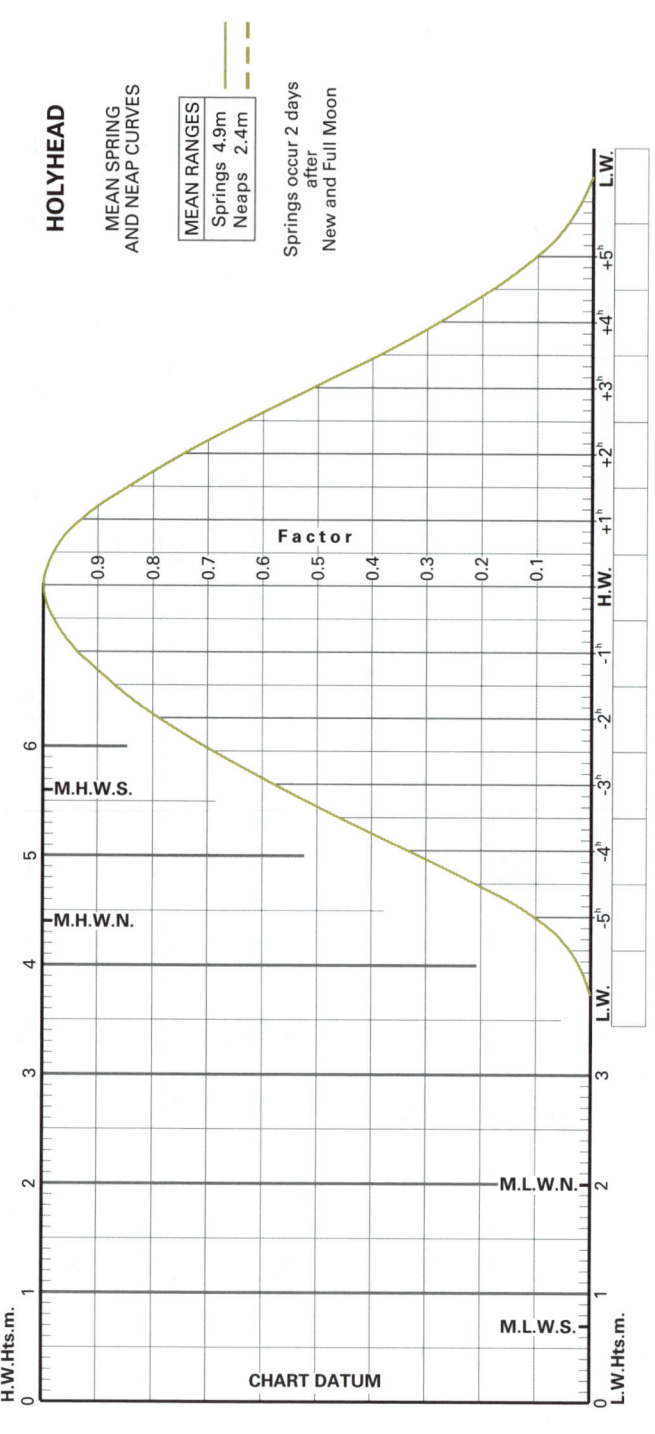

HOLYHEAD

MEAN SPRING
AND NEAP CURVES

MEAN RANGES	
Springs	4.9m
Neaps	2.4m

Springs occur 2 days
after
New and Full Moon

WALES – HOLYHEAD

LAT 53°19′N   LONG 4°37′W

TIMES AND HEIGHTS OF HIGH AND LOW WATERS

Dates in amber are **SPRINGS**
Dates in yellow are **NEAPS**

2007

JANUARY

Day	Time m	Time m	Time m	Time m		Day	Time m	Time m	Time m	Time m
1 M	0156 1.4	0820 5.1	1428 1.4	2042 5.2		16 TU	0158 1.9	0817 4.8	1424 1.9	2041 4.7
2 TU	0251 1.4	0910 5.3	1522 1.2	2135 5.3		17 W	0246 1.7	0901 5.0	1511 1.5	2126 5.0
3 W ○	0340 1.3	0956 5.5	1612 1.1	2223 5.4		18 TH	0329 1.4	0942 5.3	1554 1.2	2207 5.2
4 TH	0424 1.2	1039 5.6	1657 1.0	2307 5.3		19 F ●	0409 1.2	1021 5.5	1635 0.9	2248 5.4
5 F	0505 1.2	1120 5.6	1739 1.0	2348 5.3		20 SA	0449 1.0	1101 5.7	1716 0.7	2328 5.5
6 SA	0544 1.3	1159 5.6	1818 1.0			21 SU	0529 0.9	1142 5.9	1758 0.6	
7 SU	0027 5.2	0621 1.3	1237 5.5	1856 1.2		22 M	0010 5.5	0610 0.8	1224 5.9	1840 0.6
8 M	0104 5.0	0658 1.5	1314 5.3	1935 1.3		23 TU	0053 5.4	0653 0.9	1308 5.8	1925 0.7
9 TU	0142 4.8	0736 1.7	1352 5.1	2014 1.5		24 W	0138 5.3	0739 1.0	1354 5.7	2012 0.9
10 W	0221 4.7	0817 1.8	1432 4.9	2057 1.8		25 TH ◑	0226 5.1	0829 1.3	1445 5.4	2105 1.2
11 TH ◑	0305 4.5	0904 2.1	1518 4.7	2147 2.0		26 F	0320 4.8	0927 1.6	1544 5.1	2207 1.5
12 F	0400 4.4	0959 2.3	1616 4.5	2247 2.1		27 SA	0427 4.6	1038 1.8	1657 4.8	2321 1.8
13 SA	0507 4.3	1108 2.4	1728 4.4	2355 2.2		28 SU	0548 4.6	1200 1.9	1822 4.7	
14 SU	0619 4.3	1222 2.4	1843 4.4			29 M	0039 1.9	0709 4.7	1321 1.8	1943 4.8
15 M	0101 2.1	0724 4.5	1329 2.2	1948 4.5		30 TU	0152 1.8	0816 4.9	1430 1.5	2047 4.9
						31 W	0251 1.6	0909 5.2	1524 1.3	2137 5.1

FEBRUARY

Day	Time m	Time m	Time m	Time m		Day	Time m	Time m	Time m	Time m
1 TH	0337 1.4	0952 5.4	1608 1.0	2219 5.2		16 F	0312 1.4	0923 5.3	1536 1.0	2152 5.2
2 F ○	0416 1.2	1030 5.5	1646 0.9	2255 5.3		17 SA ●	0352 1.0	1002 5.6	1616 0.6	2230 5.5
3 SA	0452 1.1	1105 5.6	1721 0.8	2328 5.3		18 SU	0430 0.7	1041 5.9	1655 0.3	2309 5.7
4 SU	0524 1.0	1138 5.6	1754 0.9			19 M	0509 0.5	1121 6.1	1735 0.2	2348 5.7
5 M	0000 5.2	0556 1.1	1211 5.5	1825 0.9		20 TU	0549 0.4	1202 6.2	1816 0.2	
6 TU	0031 5.2	0627 1.1	1242 5.4	1856 1.1		21 W	0028 5.6	0630 0.5	1245 6.0	1858 0.4
7 W	0102 5.0	0700 1.3	1314 5.2	1929 1.3		22 TH	0111 5.5	0714 0.7	1330 5.8	1943 0.8
8 TH	0135 4.9	0734 1.6	1347 5.0	2004 1.5		23 F	0155 5.2	0802 1.0	1419 5.4	2033 1.2
9 F	0211 4.7	0812 1.8	1424 4.8	2043 1.8		24 SA ◑	0246 4.9	0900 1.5	1518 4.9	2135 1.7
10 SA ◑	0253 4.5	0858 2.1	1510 4.5	2134 2.1		25 SU	0352 4.6	1016 1.8	1639 4.5	2257 2.1
11 SU	0351 4.3	1001 2.3	1618 4.2	2246 2.3		26 M	0525 4.4	1150 2.0	1822 4.4	
12 M	0514 4.2	1127 2.4	1756 4.1			27 TU	0030 2.2	0701 4.5	1320 1.8	1949 4.5
13 TU	0015 2.4	0642 4.3	1256 2.2	1924 4.3		28 W	0150 2.0	0811 4.8	1427 1.5	2048 4.8
14 W	0131 2.1	0750 4.6	1403 1.9	2026 4.6						
15 TH	0227 1.8	0841 4.9	1453 1.4	2112 4.9						

MARCH

Day	Time m	Time m	Time m	Time m		Day	Time m	Time m	Time m	Time m
1 TH	0245 1.7	0901 5.1	1515 1.2	2130 5.0		16 F	0201 1.7	0812 4.9	1426 1.2	2048 5.0
2 F	0326 1.4	0939 5.3	1553 1.0	2203 5.1		17 SA	0246 1.2	0856 5.3	1510 0.7	2127 5.3
3 SA ○	0400 1.2	1012 5.4	1625 0.8	2233 5.2		18 SU	0326 0.8	0936 5.7	1550 0.4	2205 5.6
4 SU	0431 1.0	1042 5.5	1655 0.8	2301 5.3		19 M ●	0405 0.5	1016 6.0	1629 0.1	2243 5.8
5 M	0459 0.9	1112 5.5	1724 0.8	2329 5.3		20 TU	0444 0.2	1057 6.2	1709 0.0	2322 5.8
6 TU	0528 0.9	1141 5.5	1752 0.8	2357 5.3		21 W	0525 0.2	1139 6.2	1750 0.2	
7 W	0557 1.0	1210 5.4	1820 1.0			22 TH	0003 5.7	0607 0.3	1223 6.0	1832 0.4
8 TH	0027 5.2	0627 1.1	1240 5.2	1849 1.2		23 F	0046 5.5	0652 0.6	1310 5.7	1918 0.9
9 F	0058 5.0	0658 1.3	1311 5.0	1921 1.4		24 SA	0131 5.3	0743 1.0	1401 5.2	2008 1.4
10 SA	0130 4.9	0734 1.6	1345 4.8	1957 1.7		25 SU ◑	0222 4.9	0844 1.4	1503 4.7	2112 1.9
11 SU	0208 4.6	0816 1.9	1428 4.5	2043 2.1		26 M	0330 4.6	1005 1.8	1633 4.3	2239 2.3
12 M ◑	0259 4.4	0916 2.2	1530 4.2	2154 2.4		27 TU ◐	0507 4.4	1140 1.9	1819 4.3	2154 2.4
13 TU	0417 4.2	1044 2.3	1718 4.0	2334 2.4		28 W	0015 2.3	0643 4.5	1306 1.7	1938 4.5
14 W	0601 4.2	1222 2.1	1900 4.2			29 TH	0132 2.0	0751 4.7	1407 1.5	2030 4.7
15 TH	0101 2.2	0718 4.5	1335 1.7	2003 4.6		30 F	0224 1.7	0838 5.0	1451 1.2	2107 4.9
						31 SA	0303 1.4	0914 5.2	1526 1.0	2137 5.1

APRIL

Day	Time m	Time m	Time m	Time m		Day	Time m	Time m	Time m	Time m
1 SU	0335 1.2	0945 5.3	1556 0.9	2204 5.2		16 M	0256 0.8	0906 5.7	1520 0.3	2137 5.6
2 M ○	0403 1.0	1014 5.4	1624 0.8	2231 5.3		17 TU ●	0338 0.4	0949 6.0	1601 0.2	2217 5.7
3 TU	0431 0.9	1043 5.4	1651 0.8	2258 5.3		18 W	0420 0.3	1033 6.1	1644 0.2	2258 5.8
4 W	0459 0.9	1112 5.4	1719 0.9	2327 5.3		19 TH	0504 0.2	1119 6.0	1727 0.3	2341 5.7
5 TH	0529 1.0	1142 5.3	1748 1.0	2357 5.2		20 F	0550 0.4	1206 5.8	1812 0.7	
6 F	0600 1.1	1212 5.1	1818 1.2			21 SA	0026 5.5	0638 0.6	1256 5.4	1859 1.1
7 SA	0028 5.1	0632 1.3	1245 5.0	1849 1.4		22 SU	0114 5.3	0732 1.0	1350 5.0	1951 1.5
8 SU	0102 4.9	0709 1.5	1321 4.7	1927 1.7		23 M	0208 5.0	0836 1.4	1456 4.6	2055 2.0
9 M	0141 4.7	0754 1.7	1406 4.5	2015 2.0		24 TU ◐	0315 4.7	0952 1.7	1619 4.4	2216 2.2
10 TU ◑	0233 4.5	0854 2.0	1511 4.2	2126 2.3		25 W	0439 4.5	1115 1.8	1750 4.3	2341 2.3
11 W	0346 4.3	1018 2.1	1651 4.1	2301 2.3		26 TH	0604 4.5	1229 1.7	1902 4.4	
12 TH	0521 4.3	1148 1.9	1826 4.3			27 F	0053 2.1	0711 4.6	1329 1.5	1953 4.6
13 F	0025 2.1	0638 4.6	1258 1.5	1929 4.6		28 SA	0147 1.8	0800 4.8	1414 1.3	2031 4.8
14 SA	0125 1.6	0736 5.0	1352 1.0	2016 5.0		29 SU	0228 1.6	0838 5.0	1451 1.2	2103 4.9
15 SU	0213 1.2	0823 5.4	1438 0.6	2057 5.3		30 M	0302 1.4	0911 5.1	1522 1.1	2132 5.1

Chart Datum: 3·05 metres below Ordnance Datum (Newlyn)

TIDES

TIME ZONE (UT)
For Summer Time add ONE hour in **non-shaded areas**

WALES – HOLYHEAD
LAT 53°19'N   LONG 4°37'W
TIMES AND HEIGHTS OF HIGH AND LOW WATERS

Dates in amber are **SPRINGS**
Dates in yellow are **NEAPS**

2007

MAY

Date	Time m	Time m	Time m	Time m		Date	Time m	Time m	Time m	Time m
1 TU	0333 1.2	0943 5.2	1552 1.0	2201 5.2		16 W	0313 0.6	0926 5.8	1537 0.5	●2154 5.6
2 W	0403 1.1	1014 5.2	1621 1.0	○2230 5.2		17 TH	0400 0.5	1015 5.8	1623 0.5	2239 5.7
3 TH	0433 1.1	1045 5.2	1650 1.1	2301 5.3		18 F	0449 0.5	1104 5.7	1709 0.7	2325 5.6
4 F	0505 1.1	1118 5.1	1722 1.2	2333 5.2		19 SA	0539 0.6	1154 5.5	1756 0.9	
5 SA	0539 1.2	1152 5.0	1755 1.3			20 SU	0012 5.5	0630 0.7	1246 5.2	1845 1.4
6 SU	0007 5.1	0615 1.3	1229 4.9	1830 1.5		21 M	0102 5.3	0724 1.0	1341 4.9	1936 1.5
7 M	0045 5.0	0656 1.4	1310 4.7	1912 1.7		22 TU	0154 5.1	0822 1.3	1440 4.6	2033 1.8
8 TU	0128 4.9	0745 1.6	1359 4.5	2004 1.9		23 W	0252 4.8	0925 1.5	1546 4.4	●2138 2.1
9 W	0221 4.7	0844 1.7	1503 4.3	2110 2.1		24 TH	0358 4.6	1032 1.7	1656 4.3	2249 2.2
10 TH	0328 4.6	0956 1.7	1625 4.3	○2229 2.1		25 F	0507 4.5	1137 1.7	1804 4.3	2356 2.1
11 F	0445 4.6	1112 1.6	1745 4.4	2343 1.9		26 SA	0612 4.5	1236 1.7	1900 4.4	
12 SA	0556 4.8	1218 1.3	1848 4.7			27 SU	0054 2.0	0708 4.6	1326 1.6	1945 4.6
13 SU	0045 1.6	0656 5.1	1315 1.0	1940 5.0		28 M	0143 1.8	0755 4.7	1409 1.5	2024 4.8
14 M	0138 1.2	0749 5.4	1405 0.7	2026 5.2		29 TU	0225 1.6	0836 4.8	1446 1.4	2059 4.9
15 TU	0227 0.9	0838 5.6	1452 0.5	2110 5.5		30 W	0302 1.5	0913 4.9	1521 1.3	2132 5.0
						31 TH	0337 1.3	0949 5.0	1554 1.3	2206 5.1

JUNE

Date	Time m	Time m	Time m	Time m		Date	Time m	Time m	Time m	Time m
1 F	0412 1.2	1024 5.0	1628 1.2	○2239 5.2		16 SA	0442 0.7	1056 5.4	1658 0.9	2314 5.6
2 SA	0449 1.2	1100 5.0	1703 1.3	2315 5.2		17 SU	0532 0.7	1146 5.3	1745 1.0	
3 SU	0526 1.2	1138 5.0	1740 1.3	2353 5.2		18 M	0001 5.5	0620 0.8	1235 5.1	1830 1.2
4 M	0606 1.2	1219 4.9	1820 1.4			19 TU	0047 5.4	0708 0.9	1322 4.9	1916 1.4
5 TU	0034 5.2	0649 1.2	1303 4.8	1904 1.5		20 W	0133 5.2	0757 1.1	1409 4.7	2002 1.6
6 W	0119 5.1	0737 1.3	1352 4.7	1954 1.6		21 TH	0220 5.0	0846 1.4	1458 4.5	2052 1.8
7 TH	0210 5.0	0831 1.3	1448 4.6	2051 1.7		22 F	0309 4.8	0938 1.6	1551 4.4	●2147 2.0
8 F	0306 4.9	0931 1.4	1553 4.5	○2155 1.8		23 SA	0403 4.6	1034 1.8	1650 4.3	2248 2.1
9 SA	0409 4.9	1035 1.3	1701 4.6	2302 1.7		24 SU	0503 4.5	1133 1.9	1752 4.3	2352 2.2
10 SU	0515 5.0	1139 1.3	1807 4.7			25 M	0607 4.4	1231 1.9	1851 4.4	
11 M	0006 1.6	0619 5.1	1240 1.1	1906 4.9		26 TU	0053 2.1	0707 4.5	1324 1.8	1943 4.6
12 TU	0107 1.3	0720 5.2	1337 1.0	2000 5.1		27 W	0148 1.9	0802 4.6	1412 1.7	2028 4.7
13 W	0204 1.1	0817 5.3	1430 0.9	2050 5.3		28 TH	0235 1.7	0848 4.7	1454 1.6	2108 4.9
14 TH	0258 0.9	0912 5.4	1521 0.9	2139 5.4		29 F	0317 1.5	0930 4.8	1533 1.5	2146 5.1
15 F	0351 0.8	1005 5.5	1610 0.9	●2227 5.5		30 SA	0357 1.3	1009 4.9	1611 1.3	○2223 5.2

JULY

Date	Time m	Time m	Time m	Time m		Date	Time m	Time m	Time m	Time m
1 SU	0436 1.2	1047 5.0	1649 1.2	2301 5.3		16 M	0522 0.7	1133 5.3	1730 1.0	2345 5.6
2 M	0515 1.0	1127 5.1	1728 1.1	2340 5.4		17 TU	0603 0.7	1214 5.2	1809 1.1	
3 TU	0555 0.9	1208 5.1	1808 1.1			18 W	0025 5.5	0643 0.9	1253 5.0	1847 1.2
4 W	0021 5.4	0637 0.9	1251 5.1	1850 1.2		19 TH	0103 5.3	0721 1.0	1330 4.9	1925 1.4
5 TH	0105 5.4	0721 0.9	1336 5.0	1936 1.2		20 F	0141 5.2	0800 1.3	1408 4.7	2004 1.6
6 F	0151 5.4	0809 1.0	1424 4.9	2025 1.4		21 SA	0219 4.6	0841 1.5	1449 4.5	2048 1.9
7 SA	0240 5.2	0901 1.1	1517 4.7	●2121 1.5		22 SU	0302 4.7	0927 1.8	1538 4.4	●2139 2.1
8 SU	0336 5.1	0959 1.3	1619 4.7	2225 1.6		23 M	0355 4.4	1022 2.0	1639 4.3	2244 2.3
9 M	0440 5.0	1104 1.4	1729 4.6	2335 1.7		24 TU	0502 4.3	1129 2.2	1751 4.2	
10 TU	0551 4.9	1212 1.5	1840 4.7			25 W	0000 2.3	0620 4.2	1240 2.2	1902 4.4
11 W	0046 1.6	0704 4.9	1319 1.4	1944 4.9		26 TH	0113 2.2	0733 4.3	1342 2.0	2000 4.6
12 TH	0154 1.4	0811 5.0	1421 1.3	2042 5.1		27 F	0212 1.9	0830 4.5	1433 1.8	2047 4.9
13 F	0256 1.2	0911 5.1	1516 1.2	2133 5.3		28 SA	0300 1.6	0915 4.7	1516 1.5	2127 5.1
14 SA	0350 0.9	1003 5.2	1604 1.1	●2220 5.5		29 SU	0341 1.3	0954 5.0	1554 1.3	2205 5.3
15 SU	0438 0.8	1050 5.3	1648 1.0	2303 5.6		30 M	0419 1.0	1032 5.1	1632 1.0	○2243 5.6
						31 TU	0458 0.7	1109 5.3	1710 0.9	2321 5.7

AUGUST

Date	Time m	Time m	Time m	Time m		Date	Time m	Time m	Time m	Time m
1 W	0536 0.6	1148 5.4	1749 0.8			16 TH	0610 0.8	1217 5.2	1814 1.1	
2 TH	0001 5.8	0616 0.5	1229 5.4	1828 0.8		17 F	0028 5.4	0642 1.0	1249 5.1	1846 1.2
3 F	0043 5.8	0657 0.6	1310 5.3	1911 0.9		18 SA	0101 5.2	0714 1.2	1321 4.9	1920 1.5
4 SA	0126 5.6	0741 0.8	1355 5.1	1957 1.1		19 SU	0134 5.0	0749 1.5	1357 4.7	1958 1.8
5 SU	0213 5.4	0829 1.0	1444 4.9	●2050 1.4		20 M	0210 4.8	0828 1.8	1438 4.5	●2044 2.1
6 M	0306 5.2	0926 1.4	1544 4.7	2156 1.7		21 TU	0255 4.5	0916 2.1	1533 4.3	2145 2.3
7 TU	0413 4.9	1036 1.7	1701 4.6	2317 1.8		22 W	0400 4.2	1025 2.4	1652 4.2	2309 2.5
8 W	0538 4.6	1156 1.9	1827 4.6			23 TH	0537 4.1	1155 2.4	1821 4.3	
9 TH	0042 1.8	0706 4.7	1316 1.8	1942 4.8		24 F	0040 2.3	0710 4.2	1314 2.2	1932 4.6
10 F	0158 1.5	0819 4.8	1422 1.6	2041 5.1		25 SA	0148 1.9	0812 4.5	1410 1.9	2023 4.9
11 SA	0258 1.2	0914 5.0	1513 1.4	2129 5.3		26 SU	0237 1.5	0856 4.8	1454 1.5	2104 5.2
12 SU	0346 1.0	0958 5.2	1556 1.2	●2209 5.5		27 M	0318 1.1	0933 5.1	1532 1.2	2141 5.5
13 M	0426 0.8	1036 5.3	1633 1.0	2247 5.6		28 TU	0355 0.8	1009 5.4	1608 0.8	○2218 5.8
14 TU	0503 0.7	1111 5.3	1708 1.0	2322 5.6		29 W	0432 0.5	1045 5.5	1645 0.6	2256 6.0
15 W	0537 0.7	1145 5.3	1741 1.0	2355 5.6		30 TH	0510 0.3	1122 5.6	1723 0.5	2336 6.1
						31 F	0549 0.3	1202 5.6	1803 0.6	

Chart Datum: 3·05 metres below Ordnance Datum (Newlyn)

WALES – HOLYHEAD

LAT 53°19'N   LONG 4°37'W

TIMES AND HEIGHTS OF HIGH AND LOW WATERS

Dates in amber are **SPRINGS**
Dates in yellow are **NEAPS**

2007

SEPTEMBER		OCTOBER		NOVEMBER		DECEMBER	
Time m	Time m	Time m	Time m	Time m	Time m	Time m	Time m

SEPTEMBER

1 0017 6.0 / 0629 0.5 / SA 1243 5.5 / 1845 0.7
16 0024 5.3 / 0633 1.3 / SU 1242 5.1 / 1844 1.5

2 0101 5.8 / 0713 0.8 / SU 1327 5.3 / 1932 1.0
17 0056 5.0 / 0705 1.6 / M 1316 4.9 / 1920 1.7

3 0149 5.5 / 0801 1.2 / M 1416 5.0 / 2028 1.4
18 0131 4.8 / 0742 1.9 / TU 1355 4.7 / 2003 2.0

4 0245 5.0 / 0900 1.6 / TU 1518 4.7 / 2140 1.8
19 0213 4.5 / 0828 2.2 / W 1445 4.5 / 2103 2.3

5 0402 4.6 / 1018 2.0 / W 1646 4.5 / 2314 2.0
20 0316 4.2 / 0935 2.5 / TH 1601 4.3 / 2228 2.5

6 0544 4.5 / 1152 2.2 / TH 1824 4.6
21 0501 4.0 / 1112 2.6 / F 1740 4.3

7 0045 1.8 / 0716 4.6 / F 1316 2.0 / 1940 4.9
22 0006 2.3 / 0642 4.2 / SA 1241 2.3 / 1857 4.6

8 0158 1.5 / 0821 4.8 / SA 1417 1.8 / 2034 5.2
23 0116 1.9 / 0744 4.6 / SU 1339 1.9 / 1950 5.0

9 0250 1.2 / 0907 5.0 / SU 1502 1.5 / 2116 5.4
24 0206 1.4 / 0828 4.9 / M 1424 1.5 / 2033 5.4

10 0331 1.0 / 0943 5.2 / M 1539 1.2 / 2151 5.5
25 0247 1.0 / 0905 5.3 / TU 1502 1.1 / 2111 5.7

11 0405 0.9 / 1014 5.3 / TU 1611 1.1 / ● 2223 5.6
26 0325 0.6 / 0941 5.6 / W 1540 0.7 / ○ 2150 6.0

12 0437 0.8 / 1043 5.3 / W 1641 1.0 / 2253 5.6
27 0403 0.3 / 1017 5.8 / TH 1617 0.5 / 2229 6.2

13 0506 0.9 / 1112 5.4 / TH 1710 1.0 / 2324 5.6
28 0442 0.2 / 1055 5.8 / F 1657 0.4 / 2311 6.2

14 0535 0.9 / 1141 5.3 / F 1740 1.1 / 2354 5.4
29 0522 0.3 / 1135 5.8 / SA 1739 0.5 / 2354 6.1

15 0604 1.1 / 1211 5.2 / SA 1811 1.2
30 0604 0.5 / 1218 5.7 / SU 1825 0.7

OCTOBER

1 0041 5.8 / 0649 0.9 / M 1304 5.4 / 1915 1.1
16 0028 5.0 / 0633 1.6 / TU 1247 5.1 / 1854 1.7

2 0133 5.4 / 0740 1.4 / TU 1356 5.1 / 2016 1.5
17 0105 4.8 / 0711 1.9 / W 1326 4.9 / 1939 2.0

3 0235 4.9 / 0843 1.9 / W 1504 4.8 / ◑ 2136 1.8
18 0150 4.5 / 0758 2.2 / TH 1417 4.7 / 2038 2.2

4 0402 4.5 / 1007 2.3 / TH 1636 4.6 / 2309 1.9
19 0252 4.3 / 0904 2.5 / F 1526 4.5 / ◑ 2157 2.3

5 0545 4.4 / 1141 2.3 / F 1811 4.7
20 0427 4.2 / 1033 2.5 / SA 1656 4.5 / 2324 2.1

6 0035 1.8 / 0708 4.6 / SA 1300 2.1 / 1922 4.9
21 0601 4.3 / 1157 2.3 / SU 1813 4.7

7 0140 1.5 / 0804 4.9 / SU 1357 1.8 / 2013 5.2
22 0034 1.8 / 0704 4.7 / M 1259 1.9 / 1910 5.1

8 0228 1.3 / 0845 5.1 / M 1439 1.6 / 2051 5.4
23 0127 1.3 / 0751 5.0 / TU 1347 1.5 / 1957 5.4

9 0305 1.1 / 0917 5.2 / TU 1514 1.3 / 2124 5.5
24 0212 0.9 / 0832 5.4 / W 1430 1.1 / 2040 5.8

10 0337 1.0 / 0946 5.3 / W 1544 1.2 / 2154 5.5
25 0253 0.6 / 0911 5.6 / TH 1511 0.8 / 2122 6.0

11 0406 1.0 / 1013 5.4 / TH 1613 1.1 / ● 2224 5.5
26 0334 0.4 / 0950 5.8 / F 1552 0.6 / ○ 2205 6.2

12 0434 1.0 / 1041 5.4 / F 1642 1.1 / 2254 5.5
27 0416 0.4 / 1031 5.9 / SA 1636 0.5 / 2250 6.1

13 0502 1.1 / 1110 5.4 / SA 1712 1.2 / 2324 5.4
28 0459 0.6 / 1114 5.9 / SU 1722 0.6 / 2338 6.0

14 0531 1.2 / 1140 5.3 / SU 1744 1.3 / 2355 5.2
29 0545 0.8 / 1200 5.8 / M 1812 0.8

15 0601 1.4 / 1212 5.2 / M 1817 1.5
30 0029 5.6 / 0632 1.2 / TU 1249 5.5 / 1907 1.1

31 0125 5.2 / 0726 1.6 / W 1344 5.2 / 2011 1.5

NOVEMBER

1 0230 4.8 / 0829 2.0 / TH 1451 5.0 / ◑ 2125 1.7
16 0138 4.7 / 0741 2.1 / F 1359 4.9 / 2021 1.9

2 0352 4.6 / 0947 2.3 / F 1613 4.8 / 2247 1.8
17 0236 4.5 / 0841 2.2 / SA 1459 4.8 / ● 2127 2.0

3 0519 4.5 / 1110 2.3 / SA 1736 4.8
18 0350 4.4 / 0953 2.3 / SU 1611 4.8 / 2239 1.9

4 0002 1.8 / 0634 4.6 / SU 1224 2.2 / 1844 4.9
19 0510 4.5 / 1108 2.2 / M 1723 4.9 / 2347 1.6

5 0104 1.6 / 0730 4.8 / M 1322 2.0 / 1937 5.0
20 0617 4.7 / 1213 1.9 / TU 1826 5.1

6 0153 1.5 / 0811 4.9 / TU 1407 1.8 / 2019 5.2
21 0045 1.4 / 0712 5.0 / W 1309 1.6 / 1920 5.4

7 0232 1.4 / 0845 5.1 / W 1444 1.6 / 2054 5.3
22 0137 1.1 / 0759 5.3 / TH 1359 1.2 / 2010 5.7

8 0305 1.3 / 0916 5.2 / TH 1517 1.4 / 2126 5.3
23 0225 0.8 / 0844 5.5 / F 1447 1.0 / 2059 5.9

9 0336 1.2 / 0945 5.3 / F 1548 1.3 / ● 2158 5.4
24 0311 0.7 / 0929 5.7 / SA 1535 0.8 / ○ 2148 5.9

10 0405 1.2 / 1015 5.4 / SA 1619 1.3 / 2230 5.3
25 0357 0.7 / 1014 5.9 / SU 1623 0.7 / 2238 5.9

11 0435 1.3 / 1045 5.4 / SU 1651 1.3 / 2302 5.3
26 0444 0.8 / 1100 5.9 / M 1714 0.7 / 2329 5.8

12 0506 1.4 / 1117 5.4 / M 1725 1.4 / 2336 5.2
27 0532 1.0 / 1148 5.8 / TU 1806 0.8

13 0539 1.5 / 1151 5.3 / TU 1801 1.5
28 0021 5.5 / 0621 1.2 / W 1239 5.6 / 1900 1.0

14 0012 5.0 / 0614 1.7 / W 1229 5.2 / 1840 1.6
29 0117 5.2 / 0713 1.5 / TH 1332 5.4 / 1958 1.3

15 0052 4.8 / 0654 1.9 / TH 1310 5.1 / 1926 1.8
30 0215 4.9 / 0809 1.8 / F 1429 5.2 / 2059 1.5

DECEMBER

1 0319 4.7 / 0911 2.1 / SA 1533 5.0 / ◑ 2205 1.7
16 0215 4.8 / 0817 1.8 / SU 1432 5.1 / 2055 1.6

2 0428 4.5 / 1020 2.2 / SU 1641 4.8 / 2311 1.8
17 0311 4.7 / 0914 1.9 / M 1529 5.0 / ● 2155 1.6

3 0537 4.5 / 1129 2.3 / M 1748 4.8
18 0417 4.6 / 1019 1.9 / TU 1634 5.0 / 2259 1.6

4 0013 1.8 / 0638 4.6 / TU 1232 2.2 / 1848 4.8
19 0526 4.7 / 1127 1.9 / W 1742 5.1

5 0107 1.8 / 0728 4.7 / W 1326 2.0 / 1939 4.9
20 0004 1.5 / 0632 4.9 / TH 1234 1.7 / 1847 5.2

6 0153 1.7 / 0810 4.9 / TH 1411 1.9 / 2023 5.0
21 0106 1.3 / 0731 5.1 / F 1335 1.5 / 1949 5.4

7 0234 1.6 / 0847 5.1 / F 1451 1.7 / 2102 5.0
22 0203 1.2 / 0825 5.3 / SA 1433 1.2 / 2047 5.5

8 0310 1.5 / 0922 5.2 / SA 1528 1.6 / 2138 5.1
23 0257 1.1 / 0916 5.6 / SU 1527 1.0 / 2142 5.6

9 0343 1.5 / 0955 5.3 / SU 1603 1.5 / ● 2213 5.1
24 0347 1.0 / 1005 5.7 / M 1619 0.8 / ○ 2233 5.6

10 0416 1.4 / 1028 5.4 / M 1638 1.4 / 2248 5.2
25 0436 1.0 / 1052 5.8 / TU 1710 0.7 / 2323 5.6

11 0450 1.4 / 1100 5.4 / TU 1714 1.4 / 2324 5.1
26 0523 1.0 / 1139 5.8 / W 1759 0.7

12 0525 1.4 / 1138 5.4 / W 1751 1.3
27 0012 5.5 / 0608 1.1 / TH 1226 5.8 / 1846 0.8

13 0001 5.1 / 0602 1.5 / TH 1216 5.4 / 1831 1.4
28 0059 5.3 / 0654 1.3 / F 1312 5.6 / 1934 1.1

14 0042 5.0 / 0642 1.6 / F 1257 5.3 / 1914 1.4
29 0146 5.0 / 0739 1.5 / SA 1358 5.4 / 2022 1.3

15 0126 4.9 / 0727 1.7 / SA 1342 5.2 / 2001 1.5
30 0233 4.8 / 0827 1.8 / SU 1445 5.1 / 2112 1.6

31 0324 4.6 / 0919 2.0 / M 1537 4.8 / ◑ 2207 1.8

Chart Datum: 3·05 metres below Ordnance Datum (Newlyn)

TIDES

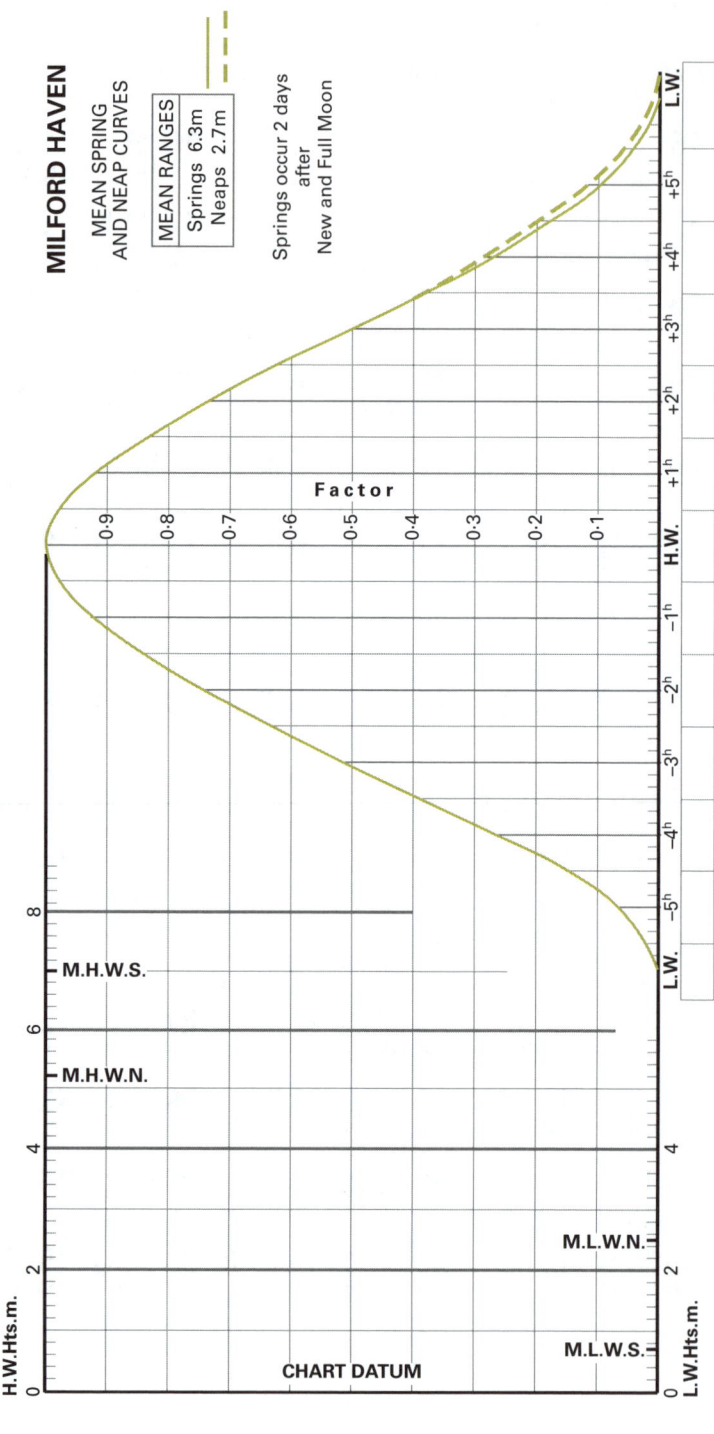

MILFORD HAVEN

MEAN SPRING
AND NEAP CURVES

MEAN RANGES
Springs 6.3m
Neaps 2.7m

Springs occur 2 days
after
New and Full Moon

Factor

0·9 0·8 0·7 0·6 0·5 0·4 0·3 0·2 0·1

L.W.   +5h   +4h   +3h   +2h   +1h   H.W.   -1h   -2h   -3h   -4h   -5h   L.W.

H.W.Hts.m.

8

M.H.W.S.

6

M.H.W.N.

4

2

0

CHART DATUM

M.L.W.N.

M.L.W.S.

L.W.Hts.m.

4

2

TIME ZONE (UT)	WALES – MILFORD HAVEN	Dates in amber are SPRINGS
For Summer Time add ONE hour in non-shaded areas	LAT 51°42'N LONG 5°03'W	Dates in yellow are NEAPS
	TIMES AND HEIGHTS OF HIGH AND LOW WATERS	2007

JANUARY

Day	Time m	Time m	Time m	Time m
1 M	0359 6.1	1026 1.7	1630 6.2	2251 1.6
2 TU	0457 6.4	1122 1.5	1725 6.4	2341 1.4
3 W ○	0547 6.6	1212 1.3	1814 6.5	
4 TH	0027 1.3	0633 6.8	1258 1.2	1858 6.6
5 F	0110 1.2	0715 6.8	1339 1.1	1938 6.5
6 SA	0149 1.2	0754 6.7	1417 1.2	2016 6.4
7 SU	0225 1.3	0831 6.6	1453 1.4	2052 6.3
8 M	0300 1.5	0907 6.4	1527 1.6	2127 6.0
9 TU	0334 1.7	0942 6.2	1600 1.8	2202 5.8
10 W	0408 2.0	1019 5.9	1636 2.1	2241 5.5
11 TH ◑	0448 2.2	1059 5.6	1719 2.3	2326 5.3
12 F	0537 2.5	1149 5.3	1815 2.6	
13 SA	0023 5.1	0643 2.7	1253 5.1	1926 2.7
14 SU	0139 5.0	0801 2.7	1411 5.1	2043 2.6
15 M	0255 5.2	0915 2.5	1522 5.3	2149 2.3
16 TU	0355 5.6	1016 2.2	1620 5.7	2242 2.0
17 W	0446 6.0	1107 1.8	1709 6.0	2328 1.6
18 TH	0531 6.4	1153 1.4	1755 6.4	
19 F ●	0011 1.3	0614 6.7	1236 1.0	1837 6.6
20 SA	0054 1.0	0657 7.0	1319 0.8	1920 6.8
21 SU	0135 0.8	0739 7.2	1401 0.6	2002 6.9
22 M	0217 0.7	0822 7.2	1443 0.6	2044 6.9
23 TU	0258 0.8	0905 7.1	1526 0.8	2126 6.7
24 W	0340 1.0	0948 6.9	1609 1.0	2210 6.4
25 TH ☾	0424 1.3	1036 6.6	1655 1.4	2258 6.1
26 F	0514 1.7	1128 6.1	1748 1.9	2355 5.7
27 SA	0617 2.1	1232 5.7	1857 2.2	
28 SU	0107 5.4	0739 2.3	1352 5.5	2022 2.3
29 M	0233 5.4	0910 2.3	1516 5.5	2143 2.2
30 TU	0353 5.7	1024 2.0	1628 5.8	2246 1.9
31 W	0454 6.1	1122 1.6	1722 6.1	2337 1.5

FEBRUARY

Day	Time m	Time m	Time m	Time m
1 TH	0543 6.4	1209 1.3	1807 6.4	
2 F ○	0020 1.3	0624 6.7	1249 1.1	1846 6.6
3 SA	0057 1.1	0701 6.8	1324 1.0	1921 6.6
4 SU	0132 1.0	0735 6.8	1356 1.0	1953 6.5
5 M	0203 1.0	0807 6.8	1426 1.1	2024 6.5
6 TU	0233 1.1	0837 6.6	1454 1.2	2053 6.3
7 W	0301 1.3	0907 6.4	1521 1.4	2123 6.1
8 TH	0329 1.6	0937 6.2	1549 1.7	2153 5.8
9 F	0400 1.9	1009 5.8	1621 2.1	2228 5.5
10 SA ☽	0437 2.2	1047 5.5	1701 2.4	2313 5.2
11 SU	0527 2.6	1139 5.1	1801 2.7	
12 M	0020 4.9	0649 2.8	1259 4.8	1943 2.9
13 TU	0200 4.9	0834 2.7	1444 4.9	2117 2.6
14 W	0326 5.3	0952 2.3	1559 5.4	2221 2.1
15 TH	0425 5.8	1049 1.7	1653 5.9	2311 1.6
16 F	0514 6.4	1136 1.2	1739 6.4	2355 1.1
17 SA ●	0558 6.9	1220 0.7	1821 6.9	
18 SU	0037 0.7	0640 7.3	1302 0.3	1902 7.2
19 M	0119 0.4	0721 7.5	1343 0.2	1943 7.3
20 TU	0159 0.3	0803 7.6	1423 0.2	2023 7.2
21 W	0238 0.3	0844 7.5	1502 0.4	2102 7.0
22 TH	0318 0.6	0925 7.1	1542 0.8	2143 6.6
23 F	0358 1.1	1008 6.6	1623 1.4	2227 6.1
24 SA ☾	0444 1.6	1057 6.0	1711 1.9	2320 5.6
25 SU	0544 2.2	1200 5.4	1821 2.5	
26 M	0037 5.2	0719 2.5	1333 5.0	2006 2.6
27 TU	0222 5.1	0908 2.4	1514 5.2	2138 2.4
28 W	0349 5.6	1023 2.0	1623 5.6	2240 1.9

MARCH

Day	Time m	Time m	Time m	Time m
1 TH	0446 6.0	1115 1.6	1712 6.0	2326 1.5
2 F	0529 6.4	1155 1.2	1751 6.4	
3 SA ○	0003 1.2	0606 6.7	1229 1.0	1825 6.6
4 SU	0037 1.0	0639 6.8	1259 0.9	1856 6.7
5 M	0107 0.9	0709 6.9	1327 0.8	1925 6.7
6 TU	0135 0.9	0738 6.8	1354 0.9	1953 6.7
7 W	0203 0.9	0806 6.7	1420 1.0	2020 6.5
8 TH	0230 1.1	0833 6.5	1446 1.2	2047 6.3
9 F	0257 1.3	0900 6.3	1512 1.5	2114 6.0
10 SA ☽	0325 1.7	0929 5.9	1540 1.9	2145 5.7
11 SU	0358 2.1	1003 5.5	1613 2.3	2225 5.3
12 M	0442 2.5	1050 5.1	1704 2.7	◑ 2327 5.0
13 TU	0555 2.8	1208 4.8	1844 2.9	
14 W	0109 4.8	0757 2.7	1407 4.8	2044 2.6
15 TH	0254 5.2	0924 2.2	1534 5.3	2155 2.1
16 F	0358 5.8	1023 1.6	1629 6.0	2246 1.4
17 SA	0448 6.5	1112 1.0	1714 6.6	2331 0.9
18 SU	0533 7.1	1156 0.5	1757 7.0	
19 M ●	0014 0.4	0616 7.5	1238 0.1	1838 7.4
20 TU	0056 0.1	0658 7.7	1319 0.0	1918 7.5
21 W	0136 0.1	0739 7.7	1359 0.1	1958 7.4
22 TH	0216 0.2	0820 7.4	1438 0.4	2037 7.1
23 F	0256 0.6	0901 7.0	1516 0.9	2118 6.7
24 SA	0337 1.1	0945 6.4	1557 1.5	2202 6.1
25 SU ☾	0423 1.7	1034 5.8	1646 2.1	2257 5.5
26 M	0527 2.3	1140 5.1	1759 2.6	
27 TU	0018 5.1	0710 2.6	1319 4.9	1951 2.7
28 W	0207 5.1	0856 2.4	1459 5.1	2121 2.4
29 TH	0329 5.5	1004 2.0	1602 5.5	2218 1.9
30 F	0422 6.0	1050 1.6	1647 6.0	2301 1.5
31 SA	0503 6.3	1126 1.3	1723 6.3	2336 1.2

APRIL

Day	Time m	Time m	Time m	Time m
1 SU	0538 6.6	1158 1.1	1756 6.5	
2 M ○	0007 1.0	0609 6.7	1228 0.9	1825 6.6
3 TU	0037 0.9	0639 6.7	1255 0.9	1854 6.7
4 W	0106 0.9	0707 6.7	1322 0.9	1921 6.7
5 TH	0133 0.9	0734 6.6	1349 1.0	1948 6.6
6 F	0201 1.1	0802 6.5	1415 1.2	2016 6.4
7 SA	0230 1.3	0830 6.2	1443 1.5	2045 6.1
8 SU	0300 1.6	0901 5.9	1512 1.8	2118 5.8
9 M	0335 2.0	0937 5.6	1548 2.2	2200 5.5
10 TU	0422 2.3	1028 5.2	1642 2.5	◑ 2304 5.1
11 W	0535 2.6	1146 4.9	1814 2.8	
12 TH	0038 5.0	0724 2.5	1333 4.9	2007 2.5
13 F	0215 5.4	0848 2.0	1457 5.4	2119 2.0
14 SA	0323 6.0	0949 1.4	1555 6.0	2214 1.4
15 SU	0416 6.6	1040 0.9	1643 6.6	2302 0.8
16 M	0503 7.1	1126 0.5	1728 7.0	2346 0.4
17 TU ●	0548 7.4	1210 0.2	1811 7.3	
18 W	0030 0.2	0632 7.5	1253 0.1	1852 7.4
19 TH	0113 0.2	0715 7.5	1335 0.3	1934 7.3
20 F	0156 0.4	0759 7.2	1416 0.6	2016 7.0
21 SA	0238 0.7	0842 6.9	1457 1.1	2059 6.6
22 SU	0323 1.2	0928 6.2	1540 1.6	2147 6.1
23 M	0413 1.8	1020 5.6	1631 2.1	2244 5.6
24 TU ☾	0519 2.2	1125 5.1	1743 2.5	2359 5.3
25 W	0649 2.5	1252 4.9	1918 2.6	
26 TH	0131 5.2	0817 2.3	1419 5.1	2040 2.4
27 F	0246 5.5	0922 2.0	1522 5.4	2138 2.0
28 SA	0341 5.8	1009 1.7	1608 5.8	2222 1.7
29 SU	0425 6.1	1047 1.5	1647 6.1	2259 1.5
30 M	0502 6.3	1121 1.3	1721 6.3	2333 1.3

Chart Datum: 3·71 metres below Ordnance Datum (Newlyn)

TIDES

TIME ZONE (UT)
For Summer Time add ONE hour in **non-shaded areas**

WALES – MILFORD HAVEN
LAT 51°42'N   LONG 5°03'W
TIMES AND HEIGHTS OF HIGH AND LOW WATERS

Dates in amber are SPRINGS
Dates in yellow are NEAPS

2007

MAY

Day	Time	m	Time	m	Day	Time	m	Time	m
1 TU	0535	6.4	1152	1.2	16 W	0522	7.1	1144	0.6
	1752	6.5				1745	7.0 ●		
2 W	0005	1.2	0606	6.5	17 TH	0007	0.5	0609	7.2
	1223	1.1	1822	6.5 ○		1230	0.5	1830	7.1
3 TH	0036	1.1	0637	6.5	18 F	0055	0.5	0657	7.1
	1253	1.1	1852	6.6		1315	0.6	1916	7.1
4 F	0107	1.1	0707	6.4	19 SA	0141	0.7	0743	6.8
	1322	1.2	1922	6.5		1359	0.9	2002	6.8
5 SA	0139	1.2	0738	6.3	20 SU	0227	0.9	0830	6.5
	1352	1.3	1954	6.4		1443	1.2	2048	6.5
6 SU	0212	1.4	0810	6.1	21 M	0315	1.3	0917	6.1
	1424	1.5	2027	6.2		1529	1.6	2136	6.2
7 M	0247	1.6	0846	5.9	22 TU	0405	1.7	1007	5.7
	1459	1.8	2106	5.9		1618	2.0	2229	5.8
8 TU	0328	1.8	0929	5.6	23 W	0502	2.0	1103	5.3
	1542	2.1	2154	5.7		1717	2.3	2329	5.5 ◐
9 W	0419	2.1	1024	5.3	24 TH	0607	2.2	1208	5.1
	1639	2.3	2258	5.5		1827	2.5		
10 TH	0528	2.2	1135	5.2	25 F	0038	5.4	0716	2.3
	1758	2.4 ◐				1320	5.1	1937	2.4
11 F	0015	5.4	0651	2.1	26 SA	0148	5.4	0820	2.2
	1258	5.3	1926	2.2		1424	5.3	2040	2.3
12 SA	0135	5.7	0807	1.8	27 SU	0247	5.5	0915	2.0
	1415	5.6	2037	1.9		1518	5.5	2132	2.0
13 SU	0243	6.1	0910	1.4	28 M	0337	5.7	1000	1.8
	1516	6.0	2137	1.4		1603	5.8	2217	1.8
14 M	0340	6.5	1005	1.0	29 TU	0420	5.9	1041	1.6
	1609	6.5	2229	1.0		1643	6.0	2257	1.6
15 TU	0432	6.8	1056	0.7	30 W	0500	6.1	1118	1.5
	1658	6.8	2319	0.7		1720	6.2	2334	1.5
					31 TH	0536	6.2	1153	1.4
						1755	6.3		

JUNE

Day	Time	m	Time	m	Day	Time	m	Time	m
1 F	0011	1.4	0611	6.2	16 SA	0043	0.9	0646	6.7
	1228	1.3	1829	6.4 ○		1302	1.0	1905	6.8
2 SA	0047	1.3	0647	6.3	17 SU	0132	0.9	0733	6.6
	1302	1.3	1904	6.4		1347	1.0	1952	6.8
3 SU	0123	1.3	0723	6.2	18 M	0218	1.0	0819	6.4
	1338	1.4	1941	6.4		1431	1.2	2036	6.6
4 M	0201	1.3	0801	6.2	19 TU	0303	1.2	0902	6.2
	1415	1.5	2020	6.3		1514	1.5	2120	6.3
5 TU	0242	1.4	0842	6.0	20 W	0346	1.5	0945	5.9
	1455	1.6	2103	6.2		1556	1.7	2204	6.1
6 W	0326	1.5	0927	5.9	21 TH	0430	1.8	1029	5.6
	1541	1.7	2152	6.0		1640	2.0	2249	5.8
7 TH	0416	1.7	1019	5.7	22 F	0515	2.0	1116	5.4
	1634	1.9	2248	5.8		1729	2.2	2339	5.5
8 F	0513	1.8	1118	5.6	23 SA	0606	2.2	1210	5.2
	1734	2.0	2350	5.9 ◐		1825	2.4		
9	0618	1.8	1224	5.6	24 SU	0036	5.4	0704	2.3
SA	1846	2.0				1314	5.1	1927	2.4
10	0057	5.9	0725	1.7	25 M	0141	5.3	0806	2.3
SU	1333	5.7	1955	1.8		1418	5.2	2032	2.4
11 M	0204	6.0	0831	1.6	26 TU	0243	5.3	0907	2.2
	1438	5.9	2101	1.6		1516	5.4	2131	2.2
12 TU	0307	6.2	0933	1.4	27 W	0339	5.5	1001	2.0
	1538	6.2	2202	1.4		1607	5.7	2223	2.0
13 W	0407	6.4	1030	1.2	28 TH	0428	5.7	1047	1.8
	1634	6.4	2259	1.1		1652	5.9	2309	1.7
14 TH	0503	6.6	1123	1.0	29 F	0512	5.9	1129	1.6
	1727	6.7	2352	1.0		1733	6.2	2351	1.5
15 F	0556	6.7	1213	1.0	30 SA	0553	6.1	1209	1.5
	1818	6.8 ●				1813	6.4 ○		

JULY

Day	Time	m	Time	m	Day	Time	m	Time	m
1 SU	0032	1.3	0633	6.2	16 M	0123	0.9	0722	6.6
	1248	1.3	1851	6.5		1334	1.0	1939	6.8
2 M	0112	1.2	0713	6.3	17 TU	0204	0.9	0802	6.5
	1327	1.2	1932	6.6		1413	1.1	2018	6.7
3 TU	0153	1.1	0753	6.4	18 W	0241	1.1	0839	6.4
	1407	1.2	2013	6.6		1449	1.2	2054	6.5
4 W	0234	1.0	0835	6.4	19 TH	0316	1.3	0914	6.2
	1448	1.2	2056	6.4		1524	1.4	2130	6.3
5 TH	0317	1.1	0918	6.3	20 F	0349	1.5	0949	5.9
	1531	1.3	2141	6.5		1557	1.7	2205	6.0
6 F	0401	1.2	1004	6.1	21 SA	0423	1.8	1025	5.7
	1617	1.4	2229	6.4		1633	2.0	2243	5.7
7 SA	0449	1.4	1053	5.9	22 SU	0500	2.1	1106	5.4
	1708	1.6	2322	6.1 ◐		1716	2.3	2327	5.4
8 SU	0543	1.6	1149	5.8	23 M	0547	2.4	1157	5.1
	1807	1.8				1813	2.5		
9 M	0022	5.9	0645	1.8	24 TU	0023	5.1	0652	2.6
	1254	5.6	1917	2.0		1306	5.0	1928	2.7
10 TU	0131	5.8	0757	1.9	25 W	0140	5.0	0811	2.6
	1406	5.6	2034	1.9		1428	5.1	2048	2.6
11 W	0243	5.8	0910	1.8	26 TH	0300	5.1	0925	2.4
	1518	5.8	2147	1.8		1536	5.4	2156	2.3
12 TH	0353	5.9	1016	1.7	27 F	0403	5.4	1023	2.1
	1623	6.1	2251	1.5		1630	5.7	2249	1.9
13 F	0456	6.2	1114	1.4	28 SA	0454	5.7	1110	1.7
	1721	6.4	2347	1.2		1715	6.1	2335	1.5
14 SA	0551	6.4	1205	1.2	29 SU	0538	6.1	1152	1.4
	1812	6.7 ●				1757	6.5		
15 SU	0037	1.0	0638	6.5	30 M	0017	1.2	0618	6.4
	1252	1.1	1857	6.8		1233	1.1	1837	6.8 ○
					31 TU	0058	0.9	0659	6.6
						1313	0.9	1917	7.0

AUGUST

Day	Time	m	Time	m	Day	Time	m	Time	m
1 W	0138	0.7	0738	6.8	16 TH	0211	0.9	0808	6.6
	1353	0.8	1958	7.1		1418	1.0	2022	6.7
2 TH	0218	0.6	0818	6.8	17 F	0240	1.1	0839	6.4
	1432	0.7	2039	7.1		1447	1.2	2052	6.5
3 F	0258	0.7	0859	6.7	18 SA	0307	1.4	0908	6.2
	1512	0.9	2120	6.9		1516	1.5	2122	6.2
4 SA	0339	0.9	0940	6.5	19 SU	0335	1.7	0938	5.9
	1554	1.1	2204	6.6		1546	1.8	2153	5.9
5 SU	0421	1.2	1024	6.2	20 M	0405	2.0	1012	5.6
	1639	1.5	2252	6.2 ◑		1621	2.2	2230	5.5 ◑
6 M	0509	1.7	1116	5.8	21 TU	0442	2.4	1055	5.2
	1734	1.9	2350	5.8		1708	2.6	2318	5.1
7 TU	0611	2.1	1221	5.5	22 W	0537	2.7	1157	4.9
	1850	2.2				1826	2.7		
8 W	0105	5.4	0733	2.3	23 TH	0033	4.8	0716	2.9
	1347	5.3	2025	2.3		1336	4.8	2012	2.8
9 TH	0234	5.4	0903	2.2	24 F	0225	4.8	0855	2.7
	1514	5.5	2149	2.0		1509	5.2	2133	2.4
10 F	0355	5.6	1015	1.9	25 SA	0342	5.2	1001	2.2
	1624	6.0	2254	1.6		1608	5.7	2229	1.9
11 SA	0456	6.0	1111	1.5	26 SU	0434	5.8	1050	1.7
	1718	6.4	2345	1.3		1654	6.3	2314	1.4
12 SU	0545	6.3	1158	1.2	27 M	0518	6.3	1132	1.2
	1803	6.7 ●				1735	6.7	2356	0.9
13 M	0028	1.0	0626	6.6	28 TU	0558	6.7	1212	0.8
	1238	1.0	1842	6.9		1816	7.1 ○		
14 TU	0106	0.9	0703	6.7	29 W	0036	0.5	0637	7.0
	1314	0.9	1918	6.9		1252	0.6	1855	7.4
15 W	0139	0.9	0737	6.7	30 TH	0116	0.3	0716	7.2
	1347	0.9	1951	6.9		1332	0.4	1935	7.5
					31 F	0156	0.3	0755	7.2
						1411	0.5	2015	7.4

Chart Datum: 3·71 metres below Ordnance Datum (Newlyn)

TIME ZONE (UT)
For Summer Time add ONE hour in **non-shaded areas**

Dates in amber are **SPRINGS**
Dates in yellow are **NEAPS**

2007

SEPTEMBER

Time	m		Time	m
1 0234	0.5	**16** 0229	1.3
0834	7.0	0830	6.4
SA 1450	1.2	SU 1440	1.5
2056	7.1	2044	6.3
2 0313	0.8	**17** 0255	1.6
0914	6.7	0859	6.1
SU 1530	1.1	M 1509	1.8
2139	6.7	2112	5.9
3 0354	1.3	**18** 0323	2.0
0957	6.3	0929	5.7
M 1614	1.6	TU 1542	2.0
2226	6.1	2146	5.5
4 0441	1.9	**19** 0356	2.4
1049	5.8	1008	5.4
TU 1711	2.1	W 1625	2.6
◑ 2327	5.5	◑ 2231	5.1
5 0545	2.4	**20** 0445	2.8
1200	5.3	1107	5.0
W 1841	2.5	TH 1737	2.9
		2345	4.7
6 0053	5.1	**21** 0621	3.1
0727	2.6	1247	4.8
TH 1343	5.2	F 1939	2.9
2032	2.5		
7 0238	5.2	**22** 0146	4.8
0905	2.4	0823	2.8
F 1517	5.6	SA 1436	5.2
2154	2.1	2104	2.4
8 0355	5.6	**23** 0314	5.3
1013	2.0	0932	2.3
SA 1619	6.1	SU 1538	5.8
2249	1.6	2201	1.8
9 0447	6.1	**24** 0406	5.9
1102	1.5	1022	1.7
SU 1705	6.5	M 1625	6.4
2332	1.2	2247	1.2
10 0528	6.4	**25** 0450	6.5
1141	1.2	1105	1.1
M 1745	6.8	TU 1708	7.0
		2329	0.7
11 0008	1.0	**26** 0531	6.9
0604	6.7	1147	0.7
TU 1216	1.0	W 1749	7.4
● 1819	6.9	○	
12 0040	0.9	**27** 0010	0.4
0637	6.6	0610	7.3
W 1248	0.9	TH 1227	0.4
1851	7.0	1829	7.6
13 0109	0.9	**28** 0051	0.2
0707	6.8	0650	7.4
TH 1317	0.9	F 1308	0.3
1920	6.9	1911	7.7
14 0137	1.0	**29** 0131	0.3
0735	6.7	0730	7.4
F 1346	1.0	SA 1348	0.4
1948	6.8	1952	7.5
15 0203	1.1	**30** 0210	0.5
0803	6.6	0810	7.2
SA 1413	1.2	SU 1429	0.7
2016	6.6	2034	7.1

OCTOBER

Time	m		Time	m
1 0250	0.9	**16** 0226	1.7
0851	6.8	0829	6.2
M 1511	1.2	TU 1444	1.8
2118	6.6	2044	6.0
2 0333	1.5	**17** 0255	2.0
0937	6.3	0902	5.9
TU 1559	1.7	W 1519	2.2
2209	5.9	2120	5.6
3 0422	2.1	**18** 0331	2.4
1033	5.7	0943	5.7
W 1703	2.3	TH 1605	2.5
◑ 2314	5.3	2207	5.2
4 0534	2.6	**19** 0421	2.7
1151	5.3	1042	5.2
TH 1844	2.6	F 1714	2.8
		◑ 2320	4.9
5 0047	5.0	**20** 0547	3.0
0722	2.8	1211	5.1
F 1336	5.3	SA 1900	2.8
2028	2.5		
6 0229	5.2	**21** 0102	4.9
0854	2.5	0741	2.8
SA 1501	5.7	SU 1349	5.3
2138	2.0	2023	2.3
7 0337	5.7	**22** 0231	5.4
0954	2.0	0853	2.3
SU 1557	6.1	M 1457	5.9
2227	1.6	2123	1.8
8 0424	6.1	**23** 0329	6.0
1038	1.6	0947	1.7
M 1641	6.5	TU 1549	6.5
2305	1.3	2213	1.2
9 0502	6.4	**24** 0416	6.5
1115	1.3	1034	1.2
TU 1717	6.7	W 1636	7.0
2338	1.1	2259	0.8
10 0536	6.6	**25** 0500	7.0
1147	1.1	1118	0.8
W 1750	6.8	TH 1720	7.4
		2342	0.5
11 0008	1.1	**26** 0543	7.3
0606	6.8	1202	0.5
TH 1218	1.1	F 1805	7.6
● 1820	6.9	○	
12 0037	1.0	**27** 0025	0.4
0636	6.6	0625	7.4
F 1247	1.1	SA 1246	0.4
1849	6.8	1848	7.6
13 0104	1.1	**28** 0107	0.5
0704	6.8	0708	7.4
SA 1316	1.1	SU 1330	0.6
1917	6.7	1933	7.3
14 0131	1.2	**29** 0151	0.7
0732	6.6	0751	7.2
SU 1344	1.3	M 1415	0.9
1945	6.3	2018	6.9
15 0158	1.4	**30** 0234	1.1
0800	6.5	0837	6.8
M 1413	1.5	TU 1502	1.3
2014	6.3	2106	6.4
		31 0320	1.6
		0926	6.3
		W 1554	1.8
		2200	5.9

NOVEMBER

Time	m		Time	m
1 0413	2.2	**16** 0323	2.2
1024	5.9	0934	5.8
TH 1700	2.2	F 1558	2.3
◐ 2304	5.4	2200	5.5
2 0523	2.6	**17** 0414	2.5
1137	5.5	1031	5.6
F 1827	2.5	SA 1659	2.4
		◐ 2304	5.3
3 0025	5.2	**18** 0523	2.6
0654	2.7	1142	5.5
SA 1304	5.5	SU 1818	2.4
1953	2.4		
4 0151	5.3	**19** 0021	5.3
0816	2.5	0650	2.5
SU 1421	5.7	M 1300	5.6
2100	2.1	1935	2.2
5 0258	5.6	**20** 0139	5.5
0916	2.2	0805	2.2
M 1519	6.0	TU 1411	6.0
2149	1.9	2040	1.8
6 0348	5.9	**21** 0245	5.9
1003	1.9	0907	1.8
TU 1605	6.2	W 1510	6.4
2229	1.6	2137	1.4
7 0428	6.2	**22** 0340	6.4
1041	1.6	1001	1.4
W 1644	6.4	TH 1604	6.8
2304	1.5	2229	1.1
8 0504	6.4	**23** 0430	6.8
1116	1.4	1052	1.1
TH 1719	6.5	F 1655	7.1
2336	1.4	2318	0.9
9 0536	6.6	**24** 0519	7.1
1149	1.4	1142	0.8
F 1751	6.6	SA 1744	7.2
		○	
10 0007	1.3	**25** 0005	0.7
0607	6.6	0606	7.2
SA 1221	1.3	SU 1231	0.7
1822	6.6	1833	7.2
11 0037	1.3	**26** 0052	0.8
0638	6.7	0653	7.2
SU 1252	1.3	M 1319	0.8
1853	6.5	1921	7.1
12 0107	1.4	**27** 0138	0.9
0708	6.6	0741	7.1
M 1323	1.4	TU 1407	0.9
1923	6.4	2010	6.8
13 0137	1.5	**28** 0224	1.2
0739	6.5	0829	6.9
TU 1356	1.6	W 1456	1.2
1955	6.2	2058	6.4
14 0208	1.7	**29** 0311	1.6
0812	6.3	0918	6.5
W 1431	1.8	TH 1548	1.6
2030	6.0	2149	6.0
15 0242	2.0	**30** 0401	1.9
0849	6.1	1011	6.2
TH 1510	2.0	F 1643	2.0
2110	5.7	2242	5.7

DECEMBER

Time	m		Time	m
1 0458	2.3	**16** 0404	2.0
1108	5.8	1017	6.1
SA 1746	2.2	SU 1639	1.9
◐ 2343	5.4	◐ 2243	5.7
2 0604	2.5	**17** 0457	2.1
1213	5.6	1113	5.9
SU 1853	2.4	M 1737	2.0
		◐ 2342	5.6
3 0052	5.3	**18** 0601	2.2
0713	2.5	1216	5.9
M 1322	5.6	TU 1844	2.0
1958	2.4		
4 0159	5.4	**19** 0050	5.6
0819	2.4	0713	2.2
TU 1425	5.6	W 1325	5.9
2057	2.2	1954	2.0
5 0258	5.6	**20** 0201	5.7
0916	2.2	0825	2.0
W 1520	5.8	TH 1433	6.1
2146	2.1	2102	1.8
6 0348	5.8	**21** 0307	6.0
1003	2.0	0933	1.7
TH 1607	6.0	F 1538	6.3
2228	1.9	2204	1.5
7 0430	6.1	**22** 0408	6.4
1045	1.8	1034	1.4
F 1648	6.1	SA 1638	6.6
2307	1.7	2301	1.3
8 0509	6.3	**23** 0504	6.7
1124	1.7	1130	1.1
SA 1727	6.2	SU 1734	6.8
2343	1.6	2353	1.1
9 0545	6.4	**24** 0557	6.9
1201	1.6	1223	0.9
SU 1803	6.3	M 1826	6.9
●		○	
10 0017	1.5	**25** 0042	0.9
0619	6.5	0647	7.1
M 1236	1.5	TU 1314	0.8
1837	6.4	1915	6.9
11 0051	1.5	**26** 0130	0.9
0654	6.6	0734	7.1
TU 1311	1.5	W 1401	0.9
1911	6.3	2001	6.8
12 0125	1.5	**27** 0215	1.1
0729	6.5	0820	7.0
W 1347	1.5	TH 1447	1.0
1947	6.3	2045	6.6
13 0200	1.6	**28** 0258	1.3
0805	6.5	0903	6.8
TH 1425	1.5	F 1530	1.3
2024	6.2	2128	6.3
14 0237	1.7	**29** 0340	1.5
0844	6.4	0946	6.5
F 1505	1.6	SA 1612	1.6
2105	6.0	2210	6.0
15 0318	1.8	**30** 0422	1.8
0928	6.2	1030	6.1
SA 1549	1.8	SU 1655	1.9
2151	5.9	2254	5.7
		31 0507	2.1
		1116	5.8
		M 1742	2.2
		◐ 2344	5.4

Chart Datum: 3·71 metres below Ordnance Datum (Newlyn)

TIDES

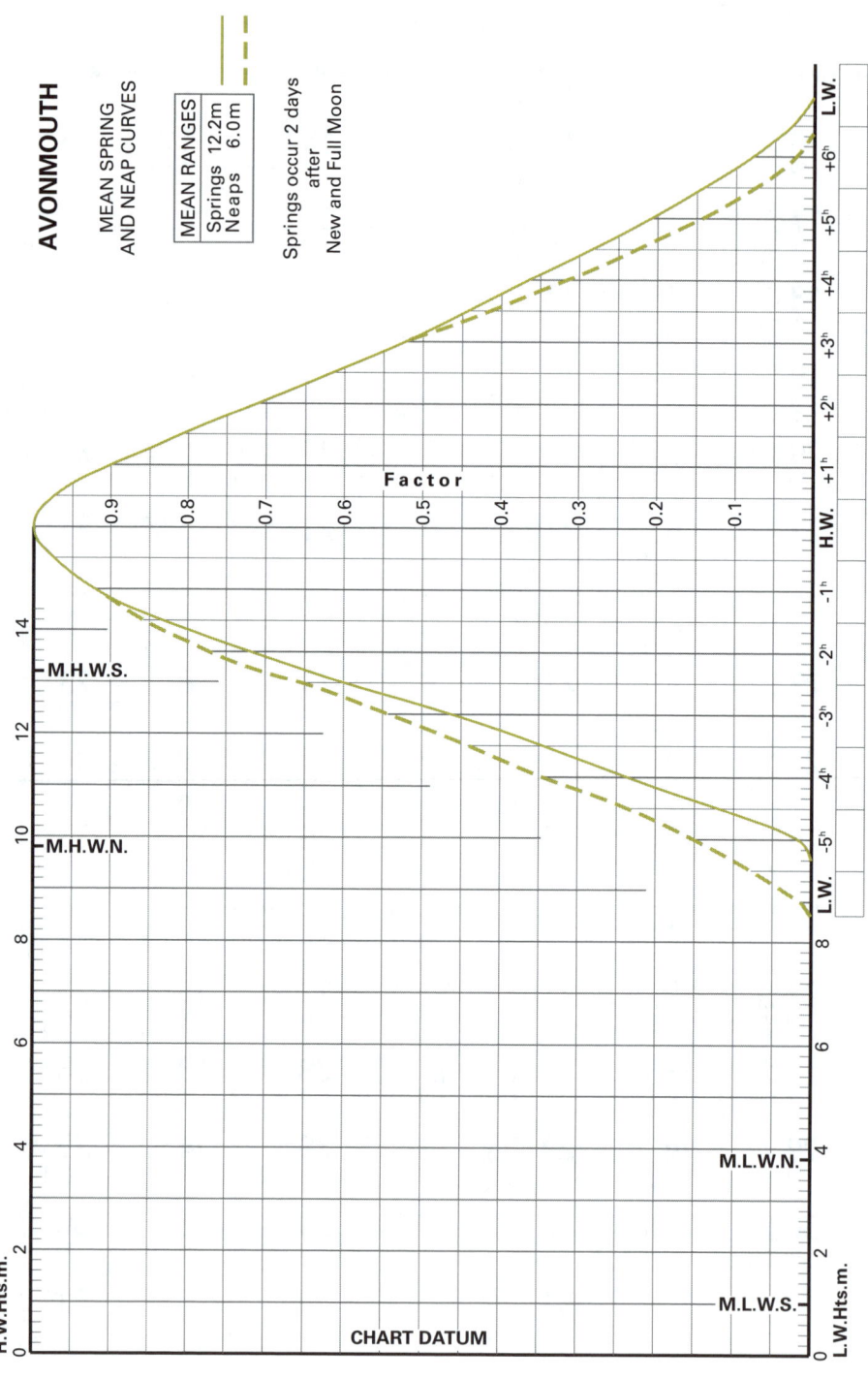

AVONMOUTH

MEAN SPRING
AND NEAP CURVES

MEAN RANGES
Springs 12.2m
Neaps 6.0m

Springs occur 2 days
after
New and Full Moon

Factor

0.9
0.8
0.7
0.6
0.5
0.4
0.3
0.2
0.1

H.W. -1ʰ -2ʰ -3ʰ -4ʰ -5ʰ L.W.

+1ʰ +2ʰ +3ʰ +4ʰ +5ʰ +6ʰ L.W.

M.H.W.S.

M.H.W.N.

M.L.W.N.

M.L.W.S.

H.W.Hts.m.

L.W.Hts.m.

CHART DATUM

TIME ZONE (UT)
For Summer Time add ONE hour in **non-shaded areas**

Dates in amber are **SPRINGS**
Dates in yellow are **NEAPS**

2007

JANUARY

Day	Time m	Day	Time m
1 M	0452 11.3 / 1133 2.8 / 1724 11.7	16 TU	0439 10.5 / 1106 3.1 / 1706 10.8 / 2339 2.9
2 TU	0000 2.5 / 0548 11.9 / 1818 12.1	17 W	0535 11.4 / 1206 2.5 / 1800 11.5
3 W	0055 2.0 / 0639 12.3 / 1325 2.0 / 1908 12.4 ○	18 TH	0036 2.4 / 0624 12.1 / 1303 2.1 / 1850 12.2
4 TH	0146 1.8 / 0726 12.6 / 1416 1.8 / 1955 12.5	19 F	0130 2.0 / 0711 12.7 / 1357 1.7 / 1937 12.6 ●
5 F	0234 1.7 / 0810 12.7 / 1502 1.8 / 2039 12.4	20 SA	0222 1.8 / 0756 13.0 / 1449 1.5 / 2023 12.9
6 SA	0316 1.8 / 0852 12.6 / 1542 2.0 / 2118 12.2	21 SU	0310 1.6 / 0841 13.3 / 1536 1.3 / 2106 13.1
7 SU	0351 2.0 / 0929 12.4 / 1613 2.3 / 2152 11.9	22 M	0351 1.5 / 0923 13.4 / 1616 1.2 / 2147 13.1
8 M	0417 2.1 / 1003 12.0 / 1637 2.5 / 2222 11.6	23 TU	0427 1.4 / 1004 13.3 / 1651 1.3 / 2226 13.0
9 TU	0441 2.5 / 1034 11.6 / 1700 2.7 / 2252 11.2	24 W	0500 1.6 / 1045 13.0 / 1723 1.5 / 2305 12.5
10 W	0509 2.7 / 1106 11.2 / 1730 2.8 / 2324 10.7	25 TH	0532 1.9 / 1127 12.5 / 1757 1.9 / 2347 11.9 ◑
11 TH	0543 2.9 / 1142 10.7 / 1806 3.1 ◑	26 F	0608 2.4 / 1214 11.6 / 1836 2.6
12 F	0004 10.3 / 0625 3.3 / 1229 10.2 / 1852 3.5	27 SA	0035 11.0 / 0652 3.1 / 1315 10.8 / 1927 3.4
13 SA	0057 9.8 / 0720 3.8 / 1330 9.8 / 1953 3.9	28 SU	0143 10.3 / 0756 3.8 / 1438 10.2 / 2051 3.9
14 SU	0208 9.6 / 0834 4.0 / 1447 9.8 / 2113 4.0	29 M	0315 10.0 / 0955 4.1 / 1603 10.2 / 2234 3.8
15 M	0330 9.9 / 0955 3.8 / 1602 10.2 / 2233 3.6	30 TU	0434 10.4 / 1117 3.5 / 1713 10.8 / 2344 3.1
		31 W	0538 11.2 / 1219 2.7 / 1811 11.5

FEBRUARY

Day	Time m	Day	Time m
1 TH	0041 2.3 / 0630 12.0 / 1314 2.1 / 1900 12.1	16 F	0020 2.5 / 0607 12.1 / 1250 2.0 / 1835 12.3
2 F	0134 1.8 / 0717 12.6 / 1404 1.7 / 1945 12.5 ○	17 SA	0119 1.9 / 0656 12.9 / 1347 1.4 / 1922 13.0 ●
3 SA	0222 1.5 / 0759 12.9 / 1450 1.5 / 2025 12.7	18 SU	0213 1.4 / 0741 13.6 / 1439 1.0 / 2007 13.5
4 SU	0304 1.4 / 0837 12.9 / 1529 1.5 / 2100 12.6	19 M	0300 1.0 / 0825 13.9 / 1524 0.7 / 2049 13.8
5 M	0339 1.5 / 0910 12.7 / 1600 1.8 / 2129 12.4	20 TU	0341 0.8 / 0906 14.1 / 1603 0.6 / 2127 13.8
6 TU	0405 1.9 / 0938 12.5 / 1620 2.1 / 2154 12.1	21 W	0415 0.8 / 0945 14.0 / 1634 0.8 / 2204 13.5
7 W	0422 2.0 / 1004 12.1 / 1634 2.2 / 2219 11.7	22 TH	0443 1.1 / 1023 13.5 / 1700 1.2 / 2240 12.9
8 TH	0440 2.1 / 1030 11.7 / 1653 2.3 / 2244 11.4	23 F	0508 1.6 / 1101 12.6 / 1726 1.8 / 2317 12.0
9 F	0505 2.3 / 1057 11.2 / 1723 2.5 / 2315 10.9	24 SA	0536 2.2 / 1142 11.5 / 1758 2.7 / 2359 10.9 ◑
10 SA	0537 2.8 / 1132 10.6 / 1756 3.1 / 2355 10.2	25 SU	0613 3.2 / 1236 10.3 / 1843 3.7
11 SU	0620 3.4 / 1221 10.0 / 1845 3.8	26 M	0101 9.8 / 0709 4.2 / 1415 9.4 / 2001 4.5
12 M	0054 9.6 / 0725 4.1 / 1335 9.4 / 2004 4.3	27 TU	0257 9.4 / 0943 4.6 / 1552 9.6 / 2222 4.2
13 TU	0225 9.4 / 0906 4.2 / 1518 9.5 / 2151 4.1	28 W	0422 9.9 / 1108 3.7 / 1702 10.4 / 2330 3.2
14 W	0406 9.6 / 1035 3.6 / 1643 10.3 / 2314 3.3		
15 TH	0514 11.0 / 1148 2.7 / 1744 11.4		

MARCH

Day	Time m	Day	Time m
1 TH	0526 11.0 / 1204 2.6 / 1758 11.4	16 F	0451 10.9 / 1130 2.7 / 1724 11.4
2 F	0024 2.2 / 0616 12.0 / 1255 1.8 / 1843 12.2	17 SA	0002 2.5 / 0546 12.2 / 1233 1.7 / 1814 12.5
3 SA	0113 1.5 / 0659 12.7 / 1342 1.3 / 1924 12.7 ○	18 SU	0100 1.6 / 0634 13.2 / 1328 1.1 / 1900 13.4
4 SU	0159 1.1 / 0738 13.0 / 1426 1.1 / 2001 12.9	19 M	0152 1.0 / 0719 13.9 / 1417 0.6 / 1943 13.9 ●
5 M	0241 1.0 / 0813 13.0 / 1505 1.2 / 2032 12.8	20 TU	0239 0.6 / 0802 14.3 / 1501 0.3 / 2024 14.1
6 TU	0317 1.2 / 0843 12.8 / 1535 1.6 / 2059 12.5	21 W	0319 0.5 / 0844 14.3 / 1539 0.4 / 2103 14.1
7 W	0343 1.6 / 0909 12.5 / 1554 1.9 / 2123 12.2	22 TH	0353 0.6 / 0923 14.0 / 1609 0.7 / 2140 13.6
8 TH	0357 1.9 / 0933 12.2 / 1603 2.1 / 2145 12.0	23 F	0420 1.0 / 1000 13.4 / 1633 1.3 / 2215 12.9
9 F	0410 2.0 / 0955 11.9 / 1618 2.1 / 2208 11.6	24 SA	0444 1.6 / 1038 12.4 / 1657 2.0 / 2251 11.9
10 SA	0431 2.1 / 1021 11.5 / 1642 2.3 / 2236 11.2	25 SU	0510 2.4 / 1118 11.1 / 1728 2.9 / 2332 10.6 ◑
11 SU	0500 2.4 / 1055 10.9 / 1714 2.8 / 2314 10.5	26 M	0547 3.4 / 1212 9.8 / 1813 4.0
12 M	0537 3.1 / 1141 10.1 / 1756 3.5 ◑	27 TU	0039 9.5 / 0647 4.4 / 1405 9.0 / 1939 4.8 ◑
13 TU	0009 9.7 / 0632 3.9 / 1250 9.4 / 1904 4.3	28 W	0244 9.2 / 0933 4.6 / 1533 9.4 / 2203 4.2
14 W	0134 9.2 / 0817 4.3 / 1439 9.3 / 2112 4.4	29 TH	0400 9.9 / 1045 3.5 / 1638 10.3 / 2305 3.1
15 TH	0335 9.7 / 1010 3.7 / 1621 10.2 / 2254 3.5	30 F	0500 11.0 / 1137 2.5 / 1731 11.3 / 2355 2.1
		31 SA	0549 11.9 / 1225 1.7 / 1815 12.2

APRIL

Day	Time m	Day	Time m
1 SU	0042 1.4 / 0630 12.5 / 1310 1.3 / 1853 12.6	16 M	0029 1.5 / 0607 13.2 / 1257 1.0 / 1832 13.4
2 M	0128 1.1 / 0707 12.8 / 1353 1.2 / 1927 12.8 ○	17 TU	0121 1.0 / 0653 13.8 / 1347 0.6 / 1916 13.9 ●
3 TU	0209 1.1 / 0741 12.8 / 1431 1.3 / 1958 12.7	18 W	0209 0.6 / 0737 14.1 / 1431 0.4 / 1958 14.1
4 W	0245 1.3 / 0811 12.6 / 1503 1.6 / 2026 12.4	19 TH	0252 0.5 / 0820 14.1 / 1510 0.5 / 2038 13.9
5 TH	0313 1.6 / 0838 12.3 / 1523 2.0 / 2051 12.2	20 F	0328 0.7 / 0901 13.7 / 1543 1.0 / 2117 13.4
6 F	0330 1.9 / 0902 12.1 / 1533 2.1 / 2114 12.0	21 SA	0400 1.2 / 0942 12.9 / 1611 1.6 / 2155 12.6
7 SA	0343 2.0 / 0926 11.8 / 1549 2.1 / 2139 11.7	22 SU	0427 1.8 / 1022 11.9 / 1638 2.3 / 2234 11.6
8 SU	0405 2.0 / 0955 11.5 / 1615 2.2 / 2210 11.3	23 M	0457 2.6 / 1105 10.8 / 1711 3.1 / 2319 10.5
9 M	0435 2.3 / 1032 11.0 / 1648 2.6 / 2251 10.7	24 TU	0537 3.5 / 1203 9.7 / 1759 4.0 ◑
10 TU	0513 2.9 / 1120 10.3 / 1730 3.3 / 2347 10.0	25 W	0033 9.6 / 0641 4.2 / 1341 9.2 / 1921 4.5
11 W	0608 3.6 / 1227 9.6 / 1836 4.1	26 TH	0216 9.5 / 0842 4.3 / 1459 9.5 / 2120 4.1
12 TH	0108 9.5 / 0745 4.0 / 1407 9.5 / 2036 4.2	27 F	0324 10.0 / 1003 3.6 / 1555 10.2 / 2225 3.2
13 F	0301 9.9 / 0938 3.5 / 1549 10.3 / 2223 3.4	28 SA	0421 10.8 / 1057 2.7 / 1651 11.1 / 2316 2.4
14 SA	0419 11.0 / 1100 2.5 / 1655 11.5 / 2332 2.4	29 SU	0509 11.5 / 1145 2.1 / 1736 11.7
15 SU	0517 12.2 / 1202 1.6 / 1747 12.6	30 M	0004 1.8 / 0551 12.0 / 1230 1.7 / 1814 12.2

Chart Datum: 6·50 metres below Ordnance Datum (Newlyn)

TIDES

TIME ZONE (UT)
For Summer Time add ONE hour in **non-shaded areas**

ENGLAND – AVONMOUTH

LAT 51°30'N   LONG 2°44'W

TIMES AND HEIGHTS OF HIGH AND LOW WATERS

Dates in amber are **SPRINGS**
Dates in yellow are **NEAPS**

2007

MAY

Day	Time m	Day	Time m
1 TU	0049 1.5 / 0630 12.3 / 1313 1.6 / 1850 12.4	16 W	0048 1.2 / 0626 13.3 / 1314 1.0 / 1849 13.4 ●
2 W	0131 1.4 / 0705 12.3 / 1352 1.6 / 1923 12.4 ○	17 TH	0139 1.0 / 0713 13.5 / 1402 0.9 / 1934 13.5
3 TH	0208 1.5 / 0738 12.2 / 1426 1.8 / 1954 12.3	18 F	0226 0.9 / 0800 13.4 / 1445 1.0 / 2018 13.4
4 F	0240 1.7 / 0809 12.1 / 1453 2.0 / 2023 12.1	19 SA	0308 1.1 / 0845 13.0 / 1524 1.3 / 2101 12.9
5 SA	0305 1.9 / 0839 11.9 / 1512 2.1 / 2051 11.9	20 SU	0346 1.5 / 0929 12.5 / 1558 1.8 / 2143 12.3
6 SU	0326 2.0 / 0909 11.7 / 1533 2.2 / 2121 11.7	21 M	0420 2.1 / 1013 11.7 / 1630 2.4 / 2225 11.6
7 M	0353 2.1 / 0943 11.5 / 1602 2.3 / 2158 11.4	22 TU	0454 2.6 / 1057 10.9 / 1705 3.0 / 2312 10.8
8 TU	0426 2.3 / 1023 11.1 / 1638 2.6 / 2242 10.9	23 W	0534 3.2 / 1148 10.2 / 1750 3.5 ◑
9 W	0509 2.7 / 1114 10.6 / 1725 3.1 / 2339 10.4	24 TH	0012 10.2 / 0625 3.6 / 1255 9.7 / 1849 3.9
10 TH	0607 3.2 / 1217 10.1 / 1830 3.6 ◑	25 F	0128 9.9 / 0729 3.8 / 1406 9.7 / 2000 3.9
11 F	0053 10.2 / 0728 3.4 / 1339 10.1 / 2004 3.7	26 SA	0234 10.1 / 0839 3.6 / 1507 10.0 / 2114 3.5
12 SA	0222 10.5 / 0858 3.1 / 1506 10.6 / 2139 3.2	27 SU	0330 10.4 / 0949 3.3 / 1601 10.5 / 2219 3.0
13 SU	0340 11.2 / 1018 2.5 / 1616 11.4 / 2253 2.4	28 M	0421 10.9 / 1050 2.8 / 1649 11.1 / 2315 2.5
14 M	0443 12.1 / 1124 1.8 / 1714 12.3 / 2353 1.7	29 TU	0508 11.3 / 1142 2.4 / 1733 11.5
15 TU	0537 12.8 / 1222 1.3 / 1804 13.0	30 W	0004 2.1 / 0551 11.6 / 1229 2.1 / 1813 11.9
		31 TH	0049 1.9 / 0630 11.8 / 1313 2.0 / 1851 12.1

JUNE

Day	Time m	Day	Time m
1 F	0132 1.8 / 0709 11.9 / 1353 2.0 / 1928 12.1 ○	16 SA	0208 1.4 / 0746 12.7 / 1429 1.4 / 2004 12.9 ○
2 SA	0211 1.9 / 0747 11.9 / 1428 2.1 / 2004 12.1	17 SU	0257 1.5 / 0834 12.6 / 1514 1.6 / 2050 12.7
3 SU	0247 2.0 / 0824 11.8 / 1500 2.1 / 2040 12.0	18 M	0341 1.7 / 0920 12.3 / 1553 1.9 / 2134 12.4
4 M	0321 2.1 / 0902 11.7 / 1530 2.2 / 2117 11.9	19 TU	0419 2.0 / 1003 11.9 / 1627 2.2 / 2215 11.9
5 TU	0355 2.1 / 0942 11.6 / 1604 2.3 / 2157 11.7	20 W	0452 2.3 / 1042 11.4 / 1658 2.5 / 2255 11.4
6 W	0432 2.2 / 1024 11.5 / 1643 2.5 / 2242 11.5	21 TH	0522 2.6 / 1120 10.9 / 1732 2.8 / 2336 10.9
7 TH	0516 2.4 / 1111 11.2 / 1729 2.7 / 2334 11.2	22 F	0558 2.9 / 1201 10.5 / 1812 3.1 ◑
8 F	0608 2.6 / 1205 11.0 / 1825 3.0 ◑	23 SA	0023 10.4 / 0640 3.1 / 1250 10.1 / 1901 3.4
9 SA	0035 11.0 / 0708 2.7 / 1309 10.8 / 1933 3.1	24 SU	0120 10.1 / 0730 3.4 / 1349 9.9 / 2000 3.6
10 SU	0146 11.0 / 0817 2.7 / 1422 10.8 / 2053 3.0	25 M	0221 10.1 / 0848 3.1 / 1454 10.0 / 2106 3.5
11 M	0300 11.2 / 0933 2.6 / 1535 11.2 / 2212 2.7	26 TU	0322 10.2 / 0938 3.4 / 1556 10.3 / 2216 3.1
12 TU	0408 11.6 / 1047 2.4 / 1641 11.7 / 2321 2.3	27 W	0420 10.5 / 1047 3.1 / 1651 10.8 / 2318 2.7
13 W	0509 12.0 / 1151 2.0 / 1737 12.2	28 TH	0513 11.0 / 1146 2.6 / 1740 11.4
14 TH	0020 1.8 / 0604 12.4 / 1248 1.8 / 1828 12.7	29 F	0012 2.3 / 0601 11.4 / 1238 2.3 / 1825 11.8 ●
15 F	0116 1.6 / 0656 12.7 / 1340 1.5 / 1917 12.9 ●	30 SA	0102 2.0 / 0647 11.7 / 1327 2.1 / 1909 12.1 ○

JULY

Day	Time m	Day	Time m
1 SU	0151 1.9 / 0731 11.9 / 1413 2.1 / 1951 12.3	16 M	0249 1.5 / 0825 12.5 / 1506 1.4 / 2039 12.8
2 M	0238 1.9 / 0815 12.0 / 1457 2.1 / 2033 12.3	17 TU	0334 1.4 / 0907 12.5 / 1547 1.5 / 2120 12.7
3 TU	0322 1.9 / 0858 12.1 / 1536 2.1 / 2114 12.4	18 W	0411 1.6 / 0945 12.3 / 1619 1.8 / 2155 12.4
4 W	0402 1.8 / 0939 12.2 / 1612 2.0 / 2154 12.4	19 TH	0439 2.0 / 1017 11.9 / 1643 2.1 / 2227 12.0
5 TH	0440 1.8 / 1019 12.2 / 1648 2.0 / 2236 12.3	20 F	0500 2.2 / 1046 11.5 / 1705 2.3 / 2257 11.5
6 F	0517 1.8 / 1101 12.0 / 1726 2.1 / 2321 12.0	21 SA	0523 2.5 / 1115 11.1 / 1734 2.6 / 2329 10.9
7 SA	0556 2.0 / 1146 11.7 / 1809 2.4 ◑	22 SU	0554 2.7 / 1150 10.6 / 1810 3.0 ◑
8 SU	0011 11.6 / 0641 2.3 / 1238 11.2 / 1859 2.8	23 M	0009 10.4 / 0633 3.1 / 1236 10.0 / 1858 3.5
9 M	0111 11.2 / 0736 2.7 / 1341 10.8 / 2004 3.2	24 TU	0105 9.8 / 0726 3.6 / 1340 9.6 / 2005 3.9
10 TU	0223 10.8 / 0848 3.1 / 1458 10.6 / 2136 3.4	25 W	0218 9.6 / 0839 3.9 / 1501 9.7 / 2126 3.8
11 W	0340 10.8 / 1016 3.1 / 1614 10.9 / 2258 3.0	26 TH	0336 9.8 / 1000 3.7 / 1615 10.2 / 2241 3.3
12 TH	0451 11.1 / 1129 2.7 / 1720 11.4 / 2345 2.6	27 F	0443 10.4 / 1113 3.1 / 1715 11.0 / 2345 2.6
13 F	0004 2.5 / 0552 11.6 / 1231 2.2 / 1816 12.0	28 SA	0540 11.1 / 1214 2.5 / 1806 11.7
14 SA	0103 2.0 / 0647 12.1 / 1327 1.8 / 1907 12.5 ●	29 SU	0042 2.1 / 0630 11.7 / 1310 2.2 / 1853 12.3
15 SU	0158 1.6 / 0738 12.4 / 1419 1.5 / 1955 12.8	30 M	0138 1.8 / 0717 12.2 / 1404 1.9 / 1938 12.7 ○
		31 TU	0231 1.6 / 0803 12.5 / 1453 1.7 / 2021 13.0

AUGUST

Day	Time m	Day	Time m
1 W	0319 1.4 / 0845 12.8 / 1536 1.6 / 2102 13.1	16 TH	0351 1.4 / 0918 12.6 / 1600 1.5 / 2127 12.7
2 TH	0400 1.4 / 0925 12.9 / 1612 1.5 / 2141 13.2	17 F	0416 1.8 / 0945 12.2 / 1619 1.9 / 2154 12.2
3 F	0434 1.3 / 1003 12.9 / 1642 1.6 / 2220 13.0	18 SA	0431 2.2 / 1009 11.8 / 1634 2.2 / 2218 11.8
4 SA	0504 1.5 / 1041 12.6 / 1711 1.8 / 2300 12.5	19 SU	0445 2.3 / 1033 11.4 / 1654 2.4 / 2243 11.2
5 SU	0534 1.8 / 1112 12.1 / 1743 2.2 / 2344 11.8 ◐	20 M	0507 2.6 / 1101 10.9 / 1722 2.8 / 2314 10.6 ◐
6 M	0609 2.4 / 1205 11.3 / 1823 2.9	21 TU	0538 3.0 / 1137 10.2 / 1800 3.5 / 2357 9.8
7 TU	0037 10.9 / 0654 3.1 / 1305 10.5 / 1918 3.7	22 W	0622 3.7 / 1230 9.5 / 1859 4.2
8 W	0154 10.1 / 0804 3.8 / 1433 9.9 / 2115 4.2	23 TH	0109 9.2 / 0735 4.4 / 1406 9.2 / 2042 4.4
9 TH	0327 10.0 / 1001 3.9 / 1602 10.2 / 2251 3.6	24 F	0300 9.2 / 0923 4.3 / 1547 9.7 / 2215 3.8
10 F	0444 10.5 / 1119 3.2 / 1713 11.0 / 2357 2.7	25 SA	0422 10.1 / 1051 3.5 / 1654 10.8 / 2329 2.8
11 SA	0547 11.3 / 1220 2.4 / 1810 11.9	26 SU	0522 11.1 / 1158 2.7 / 1747 11.8
12 SU	0053 1.9 / 0639 12.1 / 1315 1.7 / 1858 12.6 ●	27 M	0029 2.1 / 0613 12.0 / 1257 2.1 / 1834 12.7
13 M	0146 1.4 / 0726 12.6 / 1405 1.3 / 1942 13.0	28 TU	0125 1.6 / 0659 12.7 / 1350 1.6 / 1918 13.3 ○
14 TU	0234 1.1 / 0808 12.8 / 1450 1.1 / 2022 13.2	29 W	0217 1.2 / 0743 13.2 / 1439 1.3 / 2001 13.6
15 W	0316 1.1 / 0846 12.8 / 1529 1.2 / 2057 13.0	30 TH	0303 1.0 / 0824 13.4 / 1521 1.1 / 2042 13.8
		31 F	0343 0.9 / 0903 13.5 / 1556 1.2 / 2121 13.7

Chart Datum: 6·50 metres below Ordnance Datum (Newlyn)

ENGLAND – AVONMOUTH

LAT 51°30'N   LONG 2°44'W

TIMES AND HEIGHTS OF HIGH AND LOW WATERS

Dates in amber are SPRINGS
Dates in yellow are NEAPS

2007

SEPTEMBER

Time m	Time m
1 0415 1.1 0940 13.3 SA 1625 1.4 2158 13.4	**16** 0357 2.2 0932 11.9 SU 1601 2.2 2141 11.8
2 0441 1.4 1017 12.9 SU 1649 1.8 2236 12.6	**17** 0406 2.4 0954 11.5 M 1618 2.4 2204 11.4
3 0506 1.9 1054 12.1 M 1716 2.4 2317 11.6	**18** 0427 2.5 1019 11.0 TU 1643 2.7 2233 10.7
4 0536 2.7 1136 11.1 TU 1751 3.2 ◑	**19** 0455 2.9 1054 10.4 W 1716 3.3 ◑ 2315 10.0
5 0009 10.4 0617 3.6 W 1236 10.0 1843 4.2	**20** 0533 3.7 1144 9.6 TH 1805 4.3
6 0142 9.4 0732 4.5 TH 1428 9.4 2123 4.6	**21** 0020 9.2 0634 4.5 F 1310 9.0 1952 4.7
7 0325 9.5 0959 4.3 F 1556 10.0 2247 3.7	**22** 0221 9.0 0844 4.7 SA 1520 9.6 2151 4.1
8 0437 10.4 1109 3.2 SA 1703 11.0 2344 2.5	**23** 0359 9.9 1031 3.8 SU 1630 10.7 2310 2.9
9 0534 11.4 1203 2.2 SU 1755 12.1	**24** 0500 11.2 1138 2.7 M 1723 12.0
10 0034 1.6 0621 12.3 M 1253 1.4 1839 12.9	**25** 0008 2.0 0549 12.3 TU 1234 2.0 1809 13.0
11 0122 1.1 0703 12.9 TU 1340 1.0 ● 1919 13.3	**26** 0101 1.3 0634 13.1 W 1325 1.4 ○ 1853 13.7
12 0207 0.9 0741 13.1 W 1423 0.9 1955 13.3	**27** 0151 0.9 0716 13.6 TH 1413 1.1 1936 14.1
13 0248 1.0 0815 13.0 TH 1501 1.1 2027 13.1	**28** 0236 0.7 0758 13.9 F 1455 0.9 2017 14.1
14 0322 1.3 0844 12.7 F 1532 1.5 2055 12.7	**29** 0316 0.8 0837 13.8 SA 1532 1.0 2057 13.9
15 0346 1.9 0909 12.3 SA 1550 2.0 2119 12.3	**30** 0349 1.0 0916 13.5 SU 1602 1.3 2137 13.4

OCTOBER

Time m	Time m
1 0416 1.5 0953 12.9 M 1628 1.9 2216 12.3	**16** 0336 2.4 0923 11.6 TU 1551 2.5 2136 11.4
2 0441 2.2 1032 12.0 TU 1655 2.6 2258 11.3	**17** 0359 2.5 0951 11.2 W 1618 2.7 2209 10.9
3 0511 3.0 1115 10.8 W 1731 3.6 ◑ 2353 10.0	**18** 0429 2.9 1029 10.6 TH 1653 3.2 2253 10.2
4 0555 4.0 1224 9.7 TH 1831 4.6	**19** 0508 3.5 1121 9.9 F 1742 3.9 ◑ 2356 9.5
5 0142 9.2 0725 4.8 F 1423 9.5 2117 4.6	**20** 0606 4.3 1237 9.4 SA 1909 4.5
6 0310 9.6 0944 4.2 SA 1537 10.2 2225 3.6	**21** 0133 9.2 0753 4.6 SU 1436 9.7 2109 4.0
7 0414 10.5 1044 3.1 SU 1637 11.2 2317 2.5	**22** 0322 10.0 0949 3.9 M 1553 10.8 2233 3.0
8 0507 11.5 1135 2.1 M 1727 12.2	**23** 0426 11.2 1102 2.9 TU 1650 11.9 2335 2.1
9 0004 1.6 0552 12.3 TU 1222 1.4 1809 12.8	**24** 0518 12.3 1200 2.0 W 1740 12.9
10 0049 1.2 0632 12.8 W 1307 1.1 1847 13.1	**25** 0028 1.4 0604 13.1 TH 1252 1.4 1826 13.6
11 0132 1.0 0708 13.0 TH 1349 1.0 ● 1922 13.1	**26** 0118 1.0 0648 13.7 F 1341 1.1 ○ 1910 14.0
12 0212 1.2 0740 13.0 F 1427 1.3 1954 12.9	**27** 0205 0.8 0731 13.9 SA 1426 1.0 1954 14.0
13 0246 1.5 0810 12.6 SA 1458 1.7 2023 12.5	**28** 0246 0.8 0813 13.8 SU 1506 1.1 2037 13.7
14 0311 2.0 0836 12.3 SU 1519 2.1 2048 12.1	**29** 0323 1.2 0854 13.5 M 1542 1.4 2120 13.1
15 0324 2.3 0859 11.9 M 1532 2.3 2111 11.8	**30** 0356 1.7 0936 12.8 TU 1614 2.0 2203 12.2
	31 0426 2.4 1018 11.9 W 1647 2.8 2248 11.2

NOVEMBER

Time m	Time m
1 0501 3.2 1107 10.9 TH 1728 3.6 ◑ 2347 10.1	**16** 0419 2.8 1020 10.9 F 1648 3.0 2246 10.6
2 0547 4.0 1219 10.0 F 1831 4.3	**17** 0501 3.3 1111 10.5 SA 1738 3.5 ◑ 2343 10.2
3 0118 9.5 0707 4.5 SA 1355 9.9 2029 4.4	**18** 0557 3.8 1217 10.2 SU 1848 3.8
4 0236 9.8 0900 4.2 SU 1503 10.3 2143 3.7	**19** 0056 10.0 0714 4.0 M 1341 10.3 2016 3.7
5 0337 10.4 1004 3.4 M 1559 11.0 2237 2.9	**20** 0224 10.2 0851 3.8 TU 1504 10.9 2141 3.2
6 0429 11.2 1056 2.6 TU 1649 11.7 2325 2.2	**21** 0342 11.0 1014 3.1 W 1611 11.7 2252 2.5
7 0515 11.9 1143 2.0 W 1733 12.3	**22** 0443 11.9 1121 2.4 TH 1708 12.5 2352 1.8
8 0010 1.8 0555 12.3 TH 1228 1.6 1812 12.6	**23** 0535 12.7 1218 1.8 F 1800 13.1
9 0053 1.5 0632 12.6 F 1311 1.5 1849 12.6	**24** 0046 1.4 0623 13.3 SA 1311 1.4 ○ 1848 13.5
10 0133 1.6 0706 12.6 SA 1350 1.6 1923 12.5	**25** 0136 1.1 0709 13.6 SU 1400 1.2 1935 13.6
11 0209 1.8 0739 12.4 SU 1424 1.9 1955 12.3	**26** 0223 1.1 0755 13.6 M 1447 1.3 2022 13.3
12 0239 2.1 0809 12.2 M 1452 2.1 2025 12.0	**27** 0306 1.3 0840 13.3 TU 1530 1.6 2109 12.9
13 0300 2.3 0838 11.9 TU 1515 2.4 2054 11.7	**28** 0345 1.7 0925 12.8 W 1610 2.0 2155 12.3
14 0320 2.5 0906 11.7 W 1539 2.5 2124 11.4	**29** 0421 2.3 1011 12.1 TH 1648 2.5 2241 11.5
15 0346 2.6 0939 11.3 TH 1609 2.7 2201 11.1	**30** 0457 2.8 1058 11.4 F 1727 3.1 2331 10.8

DECEMBER

Time m	Time m
1 0539 3.4 1154 10.8 SA 1813 3.5 ◑	**16** 0502 2.8 1103 11.4 SU 1735 2.8 2330 11.1
2 0031 10.2 0630 3.8 SU 1259 10.4 1909 3.8	**17** 0549 3.0 1156 11.1 M 1827 3.0 ◑
3 0142 10.0 0734 3.9 M 1411 10.3 2015 3.8	**18** 0025 10.8 0644 3.3 TU 1300 10.9 1927 3.2
4 0245 10.1 0846 3.8 TU 1510 10.6 2127 3.6	**19** 0132 10.6 0753 3.5 W 1413 10.9 2043 3.3
5 0341 10.5 0956 3.4 W 1603 10.9 2231 3.2	**20** 0250 10.7 0922 3.4 TH 1530 11.2 2209 3.0
6 0431 11.0 1054 2.9 TH 1652 11.3 2324 2.7	**21** 0406 11.2 1045 3.0 F 1639 11.7 2321 2.5
7 0517 11.5 1145 2.4 F 1736 11.7	**22** 0509 11.9 1152 2.4 SA 1739 12.2
8 0011 2.3 0558 11.9 SA 1231 2.1 1817 11.9	**23** 0021 2.0 0604 12.5 SU 1250 1.9 1833 12.7
9 0056 2.0 0637 12.2 SU 1314 2.0 ● 1856 12.0	**24** 0116 1.6 0654 13.0 M 1346 1.6 ○ 1924 13.0
10 0137 2.0 0715 12.3 M 1355 2.0 1934 12.0	**25** 0208 1.4 0743 13.2 TU 1438 1.4 2014 13.1
11 0214 2.1 0751 12.2 TU 1433 2.1 2011 11.9	**26** 0257 1.4 0831 13.2 W 1526 1.4 2101 12.9
12 0247 2.3 0827 12.1 W 1508 2.3 2047 11.8	**27** 0341 1.5 0917 13.1 TH 1608 1.6 2145 12.6
13 0316 2.4 0902 11.9 TH 1540 2.4 2123 11.7	**28** 0418 1.8 0959 12.7 F 1644 2.0 2225 12.2
14 0346 2.5 0938 11.8 F 1613 2.5 2201 11.6	**29** 0450 2.2 1039 12.2 SA 1713 2.4 2303 11.6
15 0421 2.6 1018 11.6 SA 1651 2.6 2242 11.4	**30** 0519 2.5 1118 11.6 SU 1742 2.7 2340 11.0
	31 0553 2.9 1159 11.0 M 1818 3.1 ◑

Chart Datum: 6·50 metres below Ordnance Datum (Newlyn)

TIDES

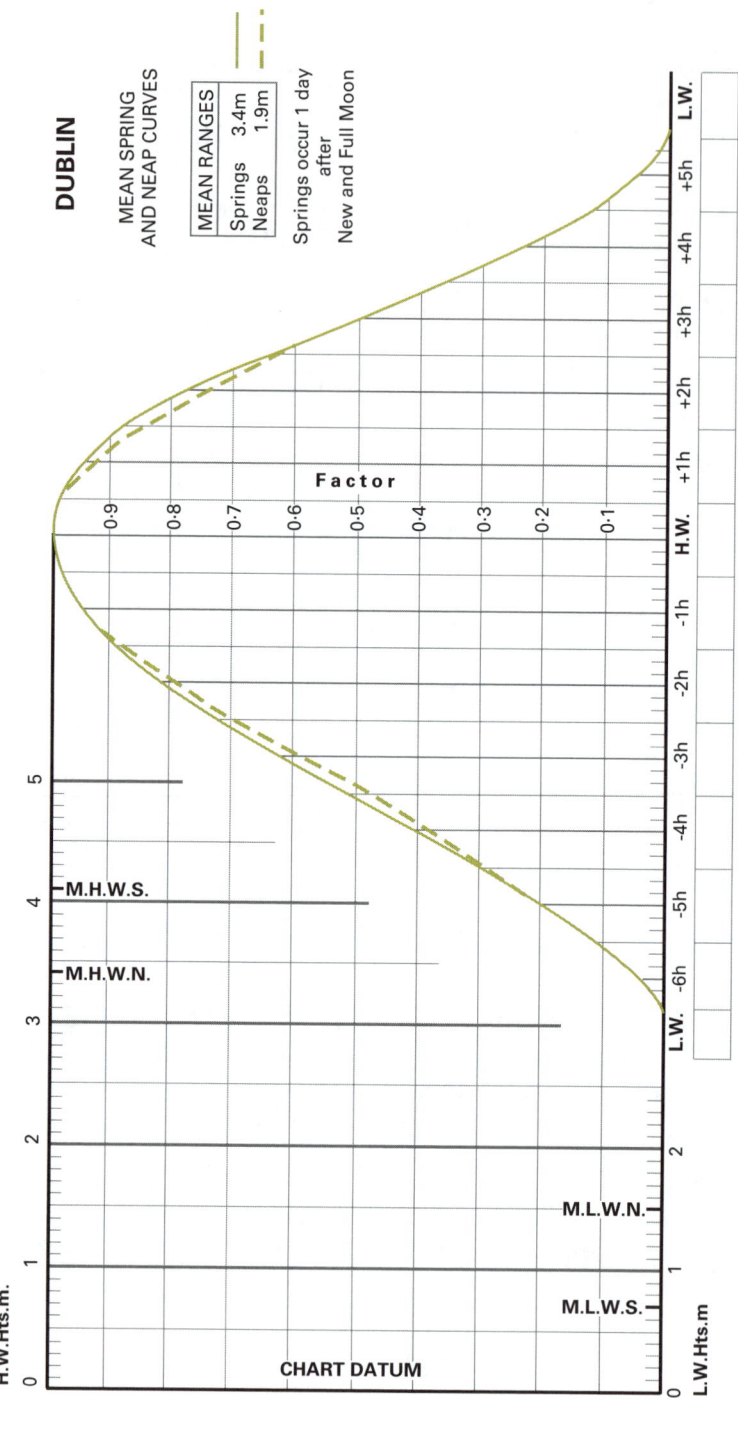

DUBLIN

MEAN SPRING
AND NEAP CURVES

MEAN RANGES	
Springs	3.4m
Neaps	1.9m

Springs occur 1 day
after
New and Full Moon

Factor

0·9 0·8 0·7 0·6 0·5 0·4 0·3 0·2 0·1

M.H.W.S.
M.H.W.N.

M.L.W.N.
M.L.W.S.

CHART DATUM

H.W.Hts.m.
L.W.Hts.m

L.W.

+5h +4h +3h +2h +1h H.W. -1h -2h -3h -4h -5h -6h L.W.

TIME ZONE (UT)
For Summer Time add ONE hour in **non-shaded areas**

LAT 53°21'N   LONG 6°13'W

TIMES AND HEIGHTS OF HIGH AND LOW WATERS

Dates in amber are **SPRINGS**
Dates in yellow are **NEAPS**

2007

JANUARY

Time	m		Time	m
1 0301	1.1		**16** 0252	1.5
0941	3.8		0930	3.6
M 1526	1.1		TU 1520	1.4
2202	3.8		2158	3.5
2 0355	1.0		**17** 0337	1.3
1032	4.0		1012	3.8
TU 1619	1.0		W 1602	1.2
2257	3.9		2242	3.7
3 0441	1.0		**18** 0417	1.1
1118	4.0		1051	3.9
W 1707	0.8		TH 1641	0.9
○ 2343	3.9		2322	3.8
4 0522	1.0		**19** 0454	1.0
1159	4.1		1129	4.1
TH 1750	0.7		F 1720	0.7
			●	
5 0024	3.8		**20** 0001	3.9
0559	1.0		0532	0.8
F 1237	4.1		SA 1209	4.2
1831	0.7		1759	0.5
6 0103	3.8		**21** 0042	3.9
0636	1.0		0611	0.7
SA 1315	4.1		SU 1250	4.3
1912	0.7		1842	0.4
7 0141	3.7		**22** 0125	4.0
0713	1.1		0654	0.7
SU 1354	4.0		M 1335	4.3
1953	0.8		1928	0.4
8 0221	3.6		**23** 0211	3.9
0754	1.2		0740	0.8
M 1435	3.9		TU 1423	4.3
2035	0.9		2017	0.5
9 0304	3.5		**24** 0259	3.8
0837	1.3		0831	0.9
TU 1518	3.8		W 1513	4.2
2119	1.0		2109	0.6
10 0349	3.4		**25** 0351	3.7
0925	1.4		0926	1.0
W 1604	3.6		TH 1606	4.0
2206	1.2		☽ 2205	0.9
11 0440	3.3		**26** 0450	3.6
1019	1.5		1027	1.2
TH 1655	3.5		F 1706	3.8
☽ 2256	1.4		2307	1.1
12 0539	3.2		**27** 0558	3.5
1119	1.7		1137	1.3
F 1756	3.3		SA 1818	3.6
2353	1.5			
13 0644	3.2		**28** 0019	1.3
1223	1.7		0712	3.5
SA 1906	3.3		SU 1256	1.4
			1939	3.5
14 0055	1.6		**29** 0141	1.4
0746	3.3		0825	3.6
SU 1328	1.7		M 1416	1.4
2011	3.3		2056	3.5
15 0157	1.6		**30** 0255	1.4
0841	3.4		0930	3.7
M 1429	1.6		TU 1525	1.2
2109	3.4		2203	3.6
			31 0351	1.2
			1026	3.8
			W 1617	1.0
			2258	3.7

FEBRUARY

Time	m		Time	m
1 0435	1.1		**16** 0400	1.0
1113	4.0		1030	3.9
TH 1701	0.8		F 1623	0.7
2341	3.7		2304	3.8
2 0512	1.0		**17** 0437	0.8
1151	4.0		1109	4.1
F 1739	0.7		SA 1701	0.4
○			● 2341	4.0
3 0014	3.7		**18** 0513	0.5
0545	0.9		1147	4.3
SA 1222	4.0		SU 1740	0.2
1814	0.6			
4 0042	3.7		**19** 0018	4.0
0616	0.9		0551	0.4
SU 1252	4.0		M 1228	4.4
1847	0.6		1820	0.1
5 0110	3.6		**20** 0058	4.1
0648	0.9		0631	0.4
M 1324	4.0		TU 1311	4.4
1921	0.6		1903	0.2
6 0142	3.6		**21** 0141	4.0
0720	0.9		0715	0.4
TU 1359	3.9		W 1357	4.3
1955	0.8		1949	0.3
7 0217	3.5		**22** 0226	3.9
0754	1.0		0804	0.6
W 1436	3.8		TH 1446	4.2
2029	0.9		2039	0.6
8 0255	3.5		**23** 0316	3.8
0831	1.1		0859	0.8
TH 1516	3.6		F 1540	3.9
2106	1.1		2133	0.9
9 0336	3.4		**24** 0413	3.6
0912	1.3		1001	1.1
F 1600	3.5		SA 1642	3.7
2147	1.3		☽ 2234	1.2
10 0424	3.3		**25** 0524	3.4
1000	1.5		1113	1.3
SA 1652	3.3		SU 1804	3.4
☽ 2238	1.5		2350	1.5
11 0524	3.1		**26** 0649	3.4
1108	1.7		1241	1.4
SU 1800	3.1		M 1933	3.3
2352	1.7			
12 0646	3.1		**27** 0128	1.6
1236	1.7		0809	3.4
M 1931	3.1		TU 1412	1.3
			2055	3.4
13 0113	1.7		**28** 0249	1.5
0803	3.2		0920	3.6
TU 1355	1.6		W 1518	1.1
2043	3.2		2201	3.5
14 0226	1.6			
0901	3.4			
W 1458	1.3			
2139	3.4			
15 0319	1.3			
0949	3.7			
TH 1544	1.0			
2224	3.6			

MARCH

Time	m		Time	m
1 0341	1.3		**16** 0254	1.2
1016	3.8		0921	3.6
TH 1606	0.9		F 1519	0.8
2250	3.6		2201	3.7
2 0421	1.1		**17** 0336	0.9
1101	3.9		1004	3.9
F 1644	0.7		SA 1600	0.6
2328	3.6		2239	3.9
3 0455	0.9		**18** 0414	0.6
1136	4.0		1044	4.2
SA 1718	0.6		SU 1638	0.1
○ 2355	3.6		2316	4.0
4 0526	0.8		**19** 0451	0.3
1203	4.0		1124	4.3
SU 1749	0.6		M 1717	0.0
			● 2352	4.1
5 0015	3.6		**20** 0529	0.2
0554	0.7		1205	4.4
M 1228	3.9		TU 1757	0.0
1818	0.6			
6 0038	3.7		**21** 0031	4.1
0621	0.7		0609	0.2
TU 1256	3.9		W 1249	4.4
1846	0.7		1838	0.1
7 0106	3.7		**22** 0113	4.1
0648	0.7		0654	0.3
W 1327	3.8		TH 1336	4.2
1914	0.7		1923	0.4
8 0138	3.7		**23** 0158	3.9
0718	0.8		0744	0.5
TH 1403	3.7		F 1427	4.0
1945	0.9		2012	0.7
9 0215	3.6		**24** 0248	3.8
0752	0.9		0840	0.7
F 1442	3.6		SA 1523	3.8
2020	1.0		2107	1.0
10 0255	3.5		**25** 0345	3.6
0831	1.1		0945	1.0
SA 1525	3.4		SU 1631	3.5
2100	1.2		☽ 2210	1.4
11 0341	3.3		**26** 0459	3.4
0917	1.3		1058	1.2
SU 1615	3.2		M 1755	3.3
2149	1.5		2325	1.6
12 0435	3.2		**27** 0627	3.3
1017	1.5		1226	1.3
M 1719	3.0		TU 1923	3.2
☽ 2300	1.7			
13 0548	3.0		**28** 0105	1.7
1153	1.6		0748	3.4
TU 1856	3.0		W 1354	1.2
			2043	3.3
14 0037	1.7		**29** 0225	1.5
0721	3.1		0859	3.6
W 1323	1.5		TH 1446	1.0
2017	3.1		2144	3.4
15 0157	1.5		**30** 0317	1.3
0830	3.3		0954	3.7
TH 1431	1.1		F 1541	0.8
2115	3.4		2228	3.5
			31 0356	1.1
			1037	3.8
			SA 1618	0.7
			2302	3.6

APRIL

Time	m		Time	m
1 0430	0.9		**16** 0347	0.5
1111	3.9		1018	4.1
SU 1650	0.6		M 1613	0.1
2327	3.6		2249	4.0
2 0500	0.8		**17** 0427	0.3
1138	3.8		1101	4.3
M 1720	0.6		TU 1654	0.0
○ 2346	3.6		● 2328	4.1
3 0529	0.7		**18** 0508	0.2
1203	3.8		1146	4.3
TU 1748	0.7		W 1735	0.1
4 0008	3.7		**19** 0008	4.1
0555	0.7		0551	0.2
W 1230	3.8		TH 1233	4.3
1813	0.7		1817	0.3
5 0035	3.7		**20** 0052	4.1
0620	0.7		0638	0.3
TH 1301	3.7		F 1322	4.1
1839	0.8		1903	0.5
6 0108	3.7		**21** 0139	4.0
0649	0.8		0731	0.5
F 1337	3.7		SA 1416	3.9
1911	0.9		1953	0.8
7 0145	3.7		**22** 0230	3.8
0725	0.9		0830	0.7
SA 1417	3.6		SU 1515	3.7
1948	1.0		2049	1.1
8 0227	3.6		**23** 0329	3.7
0806	1.0		0933	0.9
SU 1502	3.4		M 1623	3.4
2032	1.2		2150	1.4
9 0313	3.4		**24** 0442	3.5
0856	1.2		1042	1.0
M 1553	3.2		TU 1739	3.2
2125	1.4		☽ 2300	1.6
10 0408	3.3		**25** 0601	3.4
1001	1.3		1200	1.1
TU 1659	3.1		W 1857	3.2
☽ 2237	1.6			
11 0516	3.2		**26** 0022	1.7
1127	1.4		0716	3.5
W 1824	3.1		TH 1317	1.1
			2010	3.3
12 0004	1.6		**27** 0141	1.5
0638	3.2		0823	3.5
TH 1250	1.2		F 1418	1.0
1942	3.2		2108	3.4
13 0121	1.4		**28** 0238	1.4
0750	3.4		0918	3.6
F 1356	0.9		SA 1506	0.9
2042	3.4		2151	3.5
14 0219	1.2		**29** 0322	1.2
0846	3.7		1002	3.7
SA 1448	0.6		SU 1545	0.8
2129	3.7		2225	3.5
15 0305	0.8		**30** 0359	1.0
0934	3.9		1038	3.7
SU 1532	0.3		M 1618	0.8
2210	3.9		2252	3.6

Chart Datum: 0·20 metres above Ordnance Datum (Dublin)

TIDES

TIME ZONE (UT)
For Summer Time add ONE hour in **non-shaded areas**

IRELAND – DUBLIN (NORTH WALL)
LAT 53°21'N   LONG 6°13'W
TIMES AND HEIGHTS OF HIGH AND LOW WATERS

Dates in amber are **SPRINGS**
Dates in yellow are **NEAPS**

2007

MAY

Time	m		Time	m
1 TU	0432 0.9 / 1109 3.7 / 1649 0.8 / 2316 3.7		**16** W	0406 0.5 / 1044 4.2 / 1634 0.3 / ● 2309 4.0
2 W	0502 0.9 / 1138 3.7 / 1717 0.8 / ○ 2340 3.7		**17** TH	0452 0.4 / 1133 4.2 / 1718 0.4 / 2352 4.1
3 TH	0530 0.9 / 1207 3.7 / 1743 0.9		**18** F	0540 0.4 / 1222 4.1 / 1802 0.5
4 F	0009 3.7 / 0556 0.9 / 1240 3.6 / 1812 0.9		**19** SA	0037 4.1 / 0629 0.4 / 1314 4.0 / 1848 0.7
5 SA	0044 3.8 / 0629 0.9 / 1318 3.6 / 1847 1.0		**20** SU	0126 4.0 / 0723 0.5 / 1407 3.8 / 1937 1.0
6 SU	0124 3.7 / 0707 0.9 / 1400 3.5 / 1928 1.1		**21** M	0217 3.9 / 0819 0.7 / 1504 3.6 / 2030 1.2
7 M	0208 3.7 / 0754 1.0 / 1448 3.4 / 2016 1.2		**22** TU	0314 3.8 / 0918 0.8 / 1605 3.4 / 2127 1.4
8 TU	0256 3.6 / 0848 1.1 / 1541 3.3 / 2112 1.4		**23** W	0418 3.6 / 1019 1.0 / 1710 3.3 / ● 2229 1.5
9 W	0351 3.5 / 0953 1.1 / 1643 3.3 / 2218 1.5		**24** TH	0526 3.5 / 1123 1.1 / 1816 3.2 / 2334 1.6
10 TH	0454 3.4 / 1104 1.0 / 1752 3.3 / ○ 2330 1.5		**25** F	0633 3.5 / 1228 1.1 / 1919 3.2
11 F	0602 3.5 / 1215 1.0 / 1901 3.4		**26** SA	0043 1.6 / 0735 3.5 / 1329 1.1 / 2014 3.3
12 SA	0039 1.3 / 0709 3.6 / 1319 0.8 / 2001 3.5		**27** SU	0147 1.5 / 0830 3.5 / 1421 1.1 / 2100 3.4
13 SU	0139 1.1 / 0808 3.8 / 1414 0.6 / 2053 3.7		**28** M	0240 1.3 / 0918 3.6 / 1505 1.1 / 2140 3.5
14 M	0231 0.9 / 0903 3.9 / 1504 0.4 / 2141 3.9		**29** TU	0323 1.2 / 1000 3.6 / 1543 1.0 / 2215 3.6
15 TU	0320 0.7 / 0954 4.1 / 1550 0.3 / 2225 4.0		**30** W	0401 1.1 / 1038 3.6 / 1617 1.0 / 2246 3.7
			31 TH	0435 1.1 / 1113 3.6 / 1648 1.0 / 2316 3.7

JUNE

Time	m		Time	m
1 F	0507 1.0 / 1147 3.6 / 1719 1.0 / ○ 2348 3.8		**16** SA	0534 0.6 / 1215 3.9 / 1751 0.8
2 SA	0538 1.0 / 1222 3.6 / 1752 1.0		**17** SU	0026 4.1 / 0623 0.6 / 1304 3.9 / 1834 0.9
3 SU	0025 3.8 / 0614 1.0 / 1302 3.6 / 1829 1.0		**18** M	0112 4.0 / 0712 0.6 / 1352 3.7 / 1919 1.0
4 M	0107 3.8 / 0656 0.9 / 1346 3.6 / 1912 1.1		**19** TU	0159 4.0 / 0802 0.7 / 1442 3.6 / 2006 1.1
5 TU	0152 3.8 / 0744 0.9 / 1434 3.6 / 2001 1.1		**20** W	0249 3.9 / 0854 0.8 / 1532 3.5 / 2056 1.2
6 W	0241 3.8 / 0838 0.9 / 1525 3.5 / 2055 1.2		**21** TH	0342 3.8 / 0946 0.9 / 1625 3.3 / 2150 1.4
7 TH	0334 3.8 / 0936 0.9 / 1620 3.5 / 2153 1.2		**22** F	0439 3.6 / 1039 1.1 / 1722 3.3 / ○ 2247 1.5
8 F	0430 3.7 / 1037 0.9 / 1720 3.5 / ○ 2255 1.3		**23** SA	0540 3.5 / 1134 1.2 / 1820 3.2 / 2347 1.6
9 SA	0530 3.7 / 1140 0.9 / 1822 3.5 / 2358 1.2		**24** SU	0641 3.4 / 1230 1.3 / 1916 3.3
10 SU	0633 3.8 / 1242 0.8 / 1923 3.6		**25** M	0048 1.6 / 0740 3.4 / 1328 1.3 / 2009 3.3
11 M	0100 1.2 / 0736 3.8 / 1342 0.8 / 2021 3.7		**26** TU	0150 1.5 / 0835 3.4 / 1421 1.3 / 2057 3.4
12 TU	0201 1.0 / 0838 3.9 / 1439 0.7 / 2116 3.8		**27** W	0245 1.4 / 0925 3.5 / 1507 1.3 / 2141 3.6
13 W	0258 0.9 / 0937 3.9 / 1532 0.7 / 2208 3.9		**28** TH	0332 1.3 / 1010 3.5 / 1548 1.2 / 2219 3.7
14 TH	0353 0.8 / 1033 4.0 / 1621 0.7 / 2256 4.0		**29** F	0411 1.2 / 1051 3.6 / 1624 1.1 / 2255 3.8
15 F	0444 0.6 / 1126 4.0 / 1707 0.7 / ● 2342 4.0		**30** SA	0447 1.1 / 1129 3.6 / 1659 1.1 / ○ 2330 3.9

JULY

Time	m		Time	m
1 SU	0522 1.0 / 1206 3.7 / 1734 1.0		**16** M	0014 4.1 / 0612 0.6 / 1250 3.8 / 1818 0.9
2 M	0007 3.9 / 0559 0.9 / 1245 3.7 / 1812 1.0		**17** TU	0053 4.1 / 0655 0.6 / 1328 3.7 / 1855 0.9
3 TU	0048 4.0 / 0640 0.8 / 1328 3.7 / 1854 0.9		**18** W	0132 4.0 / 0737 0.7 / 1407 3.6 / 1935 1.0
4 W	0132 4.0 / 0726 0.7 / 1413 3.7 / 1939 0.9		**19** TH	0214 3.9 / 0820 0.8 / 1448 3.5 / 2018 1.1
5 TH	0219 4.0 / 0816 0.7 / 1501 3.7 / 2029 1.0		**20** F	0257 3.8 / 0904 0.9 / 1530 3.4 / 2104 1.2
6 F	0309 4.0 / 0910 0.7 / 1551 3.7 / 2123 1.0		**21** SA	0343 3.7 / 0951 1.1 / 1617 3.3 / 2155 1.4
7 SA	0402 4.0 / 1006 0.8 / 1646 3.6 / ○ 2220 1.1		**22** SU	0435 3.5 / 1040 1.3 / 1711 3.3 / ● 2251 1.5
8 SU	0458 3.9 / 1105 0.9 / 1746 3.6 / 2322 1.2		**23** M	0537 3.3 / 1133 1.4 / 1814 3.2 / 2354 1.6
9 M	0602 3.8 / 1209 1.0 / 1851 3.5		**24** TU	0649 3.2 / 1233 1.5 / 1920 3.2
10 TU	0029 1.3 / 0712 3.7 / 1316 1.1 / 1958 3.6		**25** W	0101 1.7 / 0756 3.2 / 1336 1.6 / 2020 3.3
11 W	0140 1.2 / 0824 3.7 / 1422 1.1 / 2102 3.7		**26** TH	0210 1.6 / 0856 3.3 / 1436 1.5 / 2111 3.5
12 TH	0249 1.1 / 0932 3.8 / 1523 1.1 / 2159 3.8		**27** F	0308 1.4 / 0947 3.4 / 1525 1.4 / 2156 3.7
13 F	0350 1.0 / 1031 3.8 / 1615 1.0 / 2249 4.0		**28** SA	0352 1.2 / 1031 3.6 / 1604 1.2 / 2234 3.8
14 SA	0443 0.8 / 1123 3.8 / 1700 0.9 / ● 2334 4.0		**29** SU	0428 1.0 / 1110 3.7 / 1640 1.0 / 2310 4.0
15 SU	0530 0.7 / 1208 3.8 / 1740 0.9		**30** M	0503 0.8 / 1146 3.8 / 1715 0.9 / ○ 2346 4.1
			31 TU	0540 0.6 / 1223 3.9 / 1751 0.7

AUGUST

Time	m		Time	m
1 W	0025 4.2 / 0618 0.5 / 1303 3.9 / 1830 0.7		**16** TH	0102 4.0 / 0704 0.7 / 1328 3.6 / 1902 0.9
2 TH	0107 4.3 / 0701 0.4 / 1345 3.9 / 1913 0.7		**17** F	0137 4.0 / 0740 0.8 / 1403 3.6 / 1938 1.0
3 F	0151 4.2 / 0748 0.5 / 1430 3.9 / 2000 0.8		**18** SA	0215 3.8 / 0817 0.9 / 1440 3.5 / 2017 1.1
4 SA	0240 4.2 / 0838 0.6 / 1518 3.8 / 2052 0.9		**19** SU	0256 3.7 / 0856 1.1 / 1521 3.5 / 2059 1.3
5 SU	0331 4.0 / 0933 0.8 / 1611 3.7 / ○ 2149 1.1		**20** M	0341 3.5 / 0941 1.3 / 1607 3.3 / ● 2149 1.5
6 M	0429 3.9 / 1032 1.0 / 1712 3.5 / 2254 1.2		**21** TU	0435 3.3 / 1035 1.5 / 1705 3.2 / 2258 1.7
7 TU	0537 3.7 / 1140 1.2 / 1826 3.5		**22** W	0551 3.1 / 1144 1.7 / 1826 3.2
8 W	0010 1.4 / 0701 3.5 / 1258 1.4 / 1944 3.5		**23** TH	0020 1.7 / 0723 3.1 / 1259 1.7 / 1945 3.2
9 TH	0134 1.4 / 0823 3.5 / 1416 1.4 / 2054 3.6		**24** F	0140 1.6 / 0833 3.2 / 1410 1.6 / 2044 3.4
10 F	0251 1.2 / 0935 3.6 / 1520 1.3 / 2155 3.8		**25** SA	0247 1.4 / 0928 3.4 / 1504 1.4 / 2132 3.7
11 SA	0351 1.0 / 1033 3.7 / 1609 1.1 / 2245 4.0		**26** SU	0331 1.1 / 1011 3.6 / 1543 1.1 / 2211 3.9
12 SU	0438 0.8 / 1120 3.8 / 1649 1.0 / ● 2326 4.1		**27** M	0407 0.8 / 1048 3.8 / 1618 0.9 / 2247 4.1
13 M	0518 0.6 / 1159 3.8 / 1725 0.9 / 2359 4.1		**28** TU	0440 0.6 / 1123 3.9 / 1652 0.6 / ○ 2322 4.3
14 TU	0555 0.6 / 1229 3.7 / 1757 0.8		**29** W	0516 0.5 / 1157 4.0 / 1727 0.5 / 2359 4.4
15 W	0029 4.1 / 0630 0.6 / 1257 3.7 / 1829 0.8		**30** TH	0554 0.2 / 1234 4.0 / 1805 0.4
			31 F	0039 4.4 / 0634 0.6 / 1315 4.0 / 1847 0.5

Chart Datum: 0·20 metres above Ordnance Datum (Dublin)

IRELAND – DUBLIN (NORTH WALL)

LAT 53°21'N   LONG 6°13'W

TIMES AND HEIGHTS OF HIGH AND LOW WATERS

Dates in amber are **SPRINGS**
Dates in yellow are **NEAPS**

2007

SEPTEMBER

Day	Time m	Time m	Time m	Time m	Day	Time m	Time m	Time m	Time m
1 SA	0123 4.4	0718 0.4	1359 4.0	1933 0.6	**16** SU	0142 3.8	0731 0.9	1402 3.7	1939 1.0
2 SU	0212 4.2	0807 0.6	1447 3.9	2025 0.8	**17** M	0221 3.7	0807 1.1	1442 3.6	2018 1.2
3 M	0305 4.0	0902 0.9	1540 3.9	2126 1.0	**18** TU	0305 3.5	0849 1.3	1527 3.4	2105 1.4
4 TU	0406 3.7	1005 1.2	1645 3.5	◑ 2237 1.3	**19** W	0357 3.3	0943 1.6	1621 3.3	◐ 2209 1.6
5 W	0526 3.5	1118 1.5	1809 3.4		**20** TH	0507 3.1	1101 1.8	1732 3.2	2344 1.7
6 TH	0001 1.4	0701 3.4	1247 1.6	1933 3.5	**21** F	0650 3.0	1226 1.8	1904 3.2	
7 F	0135 1.4	0826 3.4	1411 1.5	2046 3.7	**22** SA	0109 1.6	0807 3.2	1341 1.7	2011 3.4
8 SA	0249 1.1	0934 3.6	1510 1.4	2146 3.9	**23** SU	0216 1.3	0902 3.4	1435 1.4	2101 3.7
9 SU	0341 0.9	1027 3.7	1554 1.2	2234 4.0	**24** M	0302 0.9	0945 3.7	1515 1.1	2142 4.0
10 M	0422 0.7	1108 3.7	1631 1.0	2311 4.1	**25** TU	0339 0.6	1021 3.9	1551 0.8	2219 4.2
11 TU	0458 0.6	1140 3.7	1704 0.9	● 2340 4.1	**26** W	0414 0.3	1055 4.0	1627 0.5	○ 2256 4.4
12 W	0531 0.6	1204 3.7	1734 0.8		**27** TH	0451 0.1	1130 4.1	1703 0.4	2334 4.5
13 TH	0005 4.0	0601 0.6	1226 3.7	1803 0.8	**28** F	0528 0.1	1207 4.2	1742 0.3	
14 F	0034 4.0	0630 0.7	1254 3.7	1833 0.8	**29** SA	0015 4.5	0608 0.2	1248 4.2	1825 0.4
15 SA	0106 3.9	0700 0.8	1326 3.7	1904 0.9	**30** SU	0102 4.3	0652 0.4	1333 4.1	1913 0.5

OCTOBER

Day	Time m	Time m	Time m	Time m	Day	Time m	Time m	Time m	Time m
1 M	0152 4.2	0742 0.7	1422 3.9	2008 0.8	**16** TU	0157 3.6	0733 1.2	1415 3.7	1953 1.2
2 TU	0249 3.9	0838 1.1	1519 3.8	2113 1.0	**17** W	0242 3.5	0817 1.4	1501 3.6	2042 1.4
3 W	0357 3.6	0944 1.4	1628 3.6	◐ 2226 1.3	**18** TH	0335 3.3	0911 1.6	1553 3.4	2145 1.5
4 TH	0525 3.4	1100 1.6	1753 3.5	2351 1.3	**19** F	0442 3.1	1026 1.8	1657 3.3	◐ 2309 1.6
5 F	0654 3.3	1229 1.7	1915 3.6		**20** SA	0609 3.1	1149 1.8	1815 3.3	
6 SA	0121 1.3	0816 3.4	1350 1.6	2027 3.7	**21** SU	0029 1.4	0727 3.3	1300 1.6	1924 3.6
7 SU	0229 1.1	0918 3.6	1446 1.4	2125 3.9	**22** M	0134 1.2	0824 3.5	1356 1.4	2020 3.7
8 M	0318 0.9	1006 3.7	1530 1.2	2212 4.0	**23** TU	0225 0.8	0910 3.7	1441 1.1	2107 4.0
9 TU	0358 0.6	1044 3.8	1607 1.0	2249 4.0	**24** W	0308 0.5	0949 3.9	1522 0.8	2150 4.2
10 W	0432 0.7	1114 3.8	1641 0.9	2317 4.0	**25** TH	0347 0.3	1027 4.1	1602 0.5	2232 4.4
11 TH	0504 0.7	1137 3.8	1712 0.9	● 2343 4.0	**26** F	0427 0.2	1105 4.2	1642 0.4	○ 2315 4.4
12 F	0533 0.7	1159 3.8	1741 0.9		**27** SA	0507 0.2	1145 4.2	1725 0.4	
13 SA	0010 3.9	0559 0.8	1226 3.8	1809 0.9	**28** SU	0000 4.4	0548 0.6	1228 4.2	1811 0.4
14 SU	0042 3.9	0627 0.9	1257 3.8	1839 1.0	**29** M	0050 4.3	0634 0.6	1315 4.1	1902 0.6
15 M	0117 3.8	0657 1.0	1334 3.8	1913 1.1	**30** TU	0143 4.1	0724 0.9	1408 4.0	2000 0.8
					31 W	0244 3.8	0821 1.2	1507 3.9	2103 1.0

NOVEMBER

Day	Time m	Time m	Time m	Time m	Day	Time m	Time m	Time m	Time m
1 TH	0354 3.6	0925 1.5	1615 3.7	◑ 2212 1.1	**16** F	0318 3.4	0849 1.5	1532 3.6	2125 1.3
2 F	0512 3.4	1036 1.7	1731 3.7	2328 1.2	**17** SA	0418 3.3	0953 1.6	1629 3.6	◐ 2232 1.3
3 SA	0631 3.4	1155 1.7	1845 3.7		**18** SU	0525 3.3	1104 1.6	1731 3.6	2342 1.2
4 SU	0047 1.2	0744 3.4	1312 1.6	1952 3.7	**19** M	0634 3.4	1212 1.6	1835 3.6	
5 M	0153 1.1	0845 3.6	1412 1.5	2051 3.8	**20** TU	0047 1.1	0735 3.5	1312 1.4	1935 3.8
6 TU	0245 1.0	0933 3.7	1500 1.3	2139 3.9	**21** W	0145 0.9	0828 3.7	1405 1.2	2030 4.0
7 W	0327 0.9	1011 3.7	1541 1.2	2219 3.9	**22** TH	0236 0.7	0916 3.9	1454 0.9	2123 4.1
8 TH	0404 0.9	1042 3.8	1617 1.1	2252 3.9	**23** F	0323 0.6	1001 4.1	1541 0.7	2213 4.2
9 F	0436 0.9	1109 3.8	1650 1.0	2322 3.9	**24** SA	0407 0.5	1046 4.2	1628 0.6	○ 2303 4.3
10 SA	0506 0.9	1135 3.9	1722 1.0	2352 3.8	**25** SU	0452 0.5	1130 4.2	1715 0.5	2353 4.2
11 SU	0534 1.0	1203 3.9	1752 1.0		**26** M	0536 0.6	1216 4.3	1804 0.5	
12 M	0024 3.8	0602 1.1	1236 3.9	1822 1.1	**27** TU	0044 4.1	0621 0.8	1305 4.2	1856 0.6
13 TU	0100 3.7	0633 1.2	1313 3.9	1857 1.1	**28** W	0139 4.0	0710 1.0	1357 4.1	1950 0.7
14 W	0141 3.6	0711 1.3	1355 3.8	1939 1.2	**29** TH	0236 3.8	0803 1.2	1453 4.0	2048 0.8
15 TH	0227 3.5	0756 1.4	1441 3.7	2028 1.3	**30** F	0338 3.6	0902 1.4	1553 3.9	2149 1.0

DECEMBER

Day	Time m	Time m	Time m	Time m	Day	Time m	Time m	Time m	Time m
1 SA	0443 3.5	1004 1.6	1657 3.8	◑ 2252 1.1	**16** SU	0349 3.6	0919 1.4	1559 3.8	2155 1.0
2 SU	0550 3.4	1110 1.7	1803 3.7	2358 1.2	**17** M	0445 3.5	1018 1.4	1653 3.8	◐ 2255 1.0
3 M	0655 3.4	1220 1.7	1907 3.7		**18** TU	0545 3.5	1121 1.4	1752 3.8	2359 1.1
4 TU	0104 1.3	0754 3.5	1327 1.6	2006 3.7	**19** W	0648 3.6	1226 1.4	1855 3.8	
5 W	0204 1.2	0845 3.6	1425 1.5	2059 3.7	**20** TH	0104 1.0	0750 3.7	1330 1.3	2000 3.8
6 TH	0253 1.2	0928 3.7	1513 1.4	2145 3.7	**21** F	0207 1.0	0848 3.8	1431 1.1	2104 3.9
7 F	0334 1.2	1006 3.8	1555 1.3	2225 3.7	**22** SA	0304 0.9	0943 4.0	1528 0.9	2204 4.0
8 SA	0410 1.2	1041 3.8	1632 1.2	2302 3.7	**23** SU	0356 0.8	1034 4.1	1622 0.7	2259 4.1
9 SU	0443 1.2	1114 3.9	1706 1.2	2336 3.7	**24** M	0444 0.8	1122 4.2	1712 0.6	○ 2350 4.1
10 M	0513 1.1	1145 3.9	1738 1.1		**25** TU	0529 0.8	1208 4.3	1800 0.5	
11 TU	0010 3.7	0543 1.2	1218 3.9	1809 1.1	**26** W	0039 4.0	0611 0.8	1254 4.3	1847 0.5
12 W	0046 3.7	0616 1.2	1255 3.9	1843 1.1	**27** TH	0127 3.9	0655 0.9	1341 4.2	1935 0.6
13 TH	0125 3.7	0654 1.2	1336 3.9	1924 1.0	**28** F	0216 3.8	0741 1.1	1430 4.1	2025 0.7
14 F	0209 3.6	0737 1.2	1421 3.9	2010 1.0	**29** SA	0307 3.6	0831 1.2	1520 4.0	2115 0.9
15 SA	0257 3.6	0825 1.3	1509 3.9	2100 1.0	**30** SU	0359 3.5	0924 1.4	1613 3.8	2208 1.1
					31 M	0455 3.4	1022 1.5	1711 3.6	◑ 2303 1.2

Chart Datum: 0·20 metres above Ordnance Datum (Dublin)

TIDES

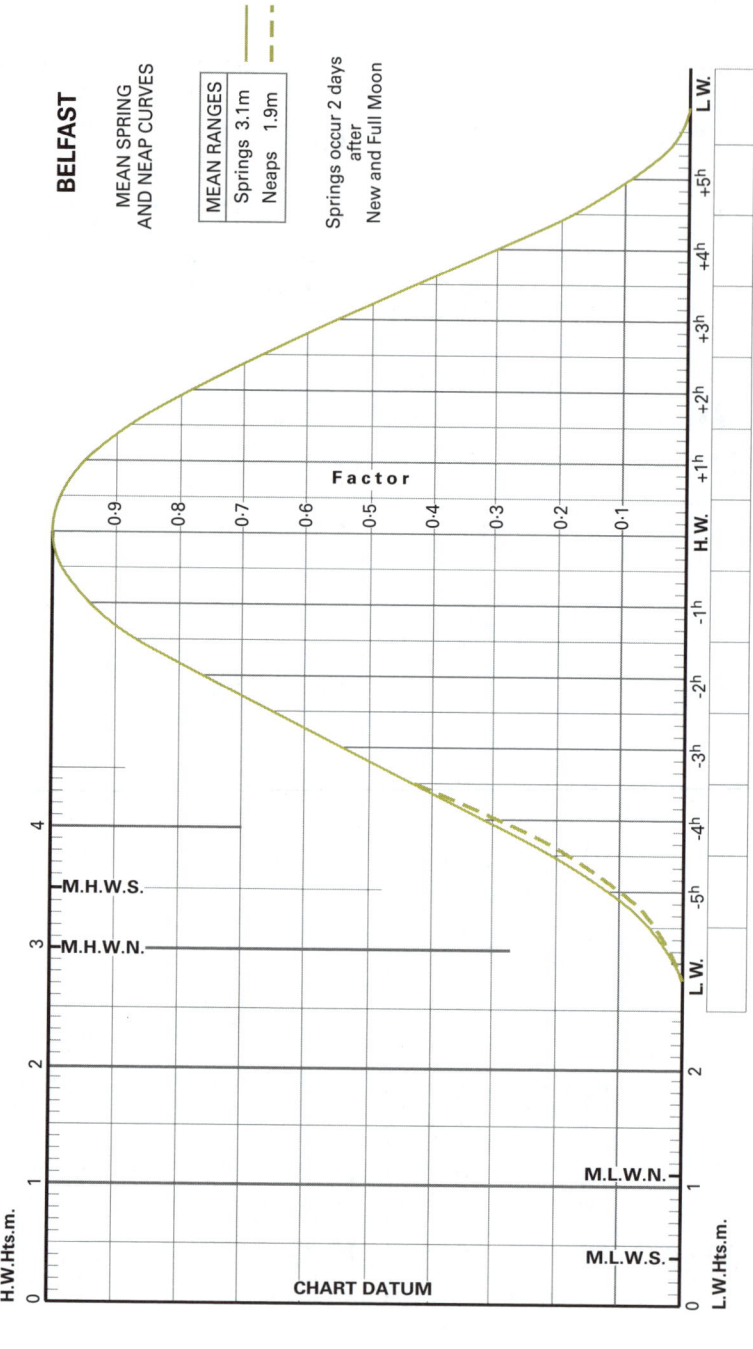

BELFAST

MEAN SPRING
AND NEAP CURVES

MEAN RANGES
Springs 3.1m
Neaps 1.9m

Springs occur 2 days
after
New and Full Moon

NORTHERN IRELAND – BELFAST

LAT 54°36'N   LONG 5°55'W

TIMES AND HEIGHTS OF HIGH AND LOW WATERS

Dates in amber are SPRINGS
Dates in yellow are NEAPS

2007

JANUARY

Day	Time	m	Time	m	Time	m	Time	m
1 M	0240	0.8	0857	3.3	1504	0.9	2126	3.3
2 TU	0334	0.8	0951	3.4	1600	0.9	2220	3.3
3 W ○	0424	0.8	1040	3.6	1650	0.7	2309	3.3
4 TH	0510	0.8	1125	3.6	1736	0.6	2354	3.2
5 F	0554	0.9	1208	3.7	1818	0.6		
6 SA	0037	3.2	0634	0.9	1250	3.7	1857	0.6
7 SU	0118	3.1	0713	0.8	1330	3.6	1935	0.7
8 M	0159	3.0	0750	1.0	1411	3.6	2013	0.7
9 TU	0241	3.0	0829	1.0	1453	3.5	2053	0.8
10 W	0324	2.9	0911	1.1	1536	3.3	2136	0.9
11 TH ◑	0409	2.9	0957	1.1	1622	3.2	2225	1.0
12 F	0458	2.9	1051	1.2	1714	3.1	2322	1.1
13 SA	0552	2.8	1159	1.3	1812	3.0		
14 SU	0029	1.1	0652	2.8	1313	1.3	1915	2.9
15 M	0136	1.1	0800	2.9	1417	1.2	2023	3.0
16 TU	0233	1.0	0903	3.0	1511	1.0	2123	3.1
17 W	0323	0.9	0953	3.2	1559	0.8	2211	3.2
18 TH	0408	0.8	1033	3.3	1641	0.7	2252	3.2
19 F ●	0450	0.7	1109	3.4	1722	0.5	2330	3.3
20 SA	0530	0.7	1144	3.5	1801	0.4		
21 SU	0009	3.3	0609	0.6	1222	3.6	1841	0.3
22 M	0052	3.3	0651	0.6	1305	3.6	1923	0.3
23 TU	0138	3.2	0734	0.6	1350	3.6	2008	0.3
24 W	0227	3.2	0820	0.6	1440	3.6	2057	0.4
25 TH ◑	0318	3.1	0909	0.7	1533	3.5	2151	0.6
26 F	0412	3.1	1004	0.8	1632	3.4	2255	0.8
27 SA	0512	3.0	1111	1.0	1739	3.2		
28 SU	0012	0.9	0620	3.0	1236	1.1	1858	3.0
29 M	0128	1.0	0737	3.0	1355	1.0	2020	3.0
30 TU	0233	1.0	0847	3.2	1504	0.9	2126	3.1
31 W	0329	0.9	0944	3.3	1601	0.7	2218	3.1

FEBRUARY

Day	Time	m	Time	m	Time	m	Time	m
1 TH	0418	0.8	1032	3.5	1648	0.6	2303	3.1
2 F ○	0501	0.8	1114	3.6	1728	0.5	2343	3.1
3 SA	0539	0.8	1153	3.6	1803	0.6		
4 SU	0020	3.0	0612	0.8	1231	3.6	1833	0.6
5 M	0054	3.0	0643	0.8	1307	3.5	1902	0.6
6 TU	0128	3.0	0715	0.8	1342	3.5	1934	0.6
7 W	0202	3.0	0749	0.8	1418	3.4	2009	0.7
8 TH	0238	3.0	0827	0.8	1455	3.3	2047	0.8
9 F	0317	3.0	0908	0.9	1535	3.2	2129	0.9
10 SA ◑	0401	2.9	0956	1.1	1623	3.0	2220	1.0
11 SU	0454	2.8	1108	1.3	1723	2.9	2328	1.2
12 M	0558	2.7	1203	1.3	1833	2.8		
13 TU	0104	1.2	0710	2.7	1353	1.2	1948	2.8
14 W	0213	1.1	0830	2.9	1452	0.9	2102	2.9
15 TH	0306	0.9	0927	3.1	1541	0.7	2152	3.1
16 F	0352	0.8	1007	3.3	1623	0.6	2231	3.2
17 SA ●	0433	0.6	1043	3.4	1703	0.3	2309	3.2
18 SU	0511	0.5	1121	3.5	1741	0.2	2348	3.3
19 M	0550	0.4	1201	3.6	1820	0.1		
20 TU	0030	3.3	0629	0.4	1246	3.7	1900	0.1
21 W	0115	3.3	0715	0.6	1333	3.7	1943	0.6
22 TH	0201	3.3	0755	0.6	1422	3.6	2029	0.4
23 F	0250	3.2	0842	0.5	1514	3.5	2120	0.6
24 SA ◐	0341	3.1	0936	0.7	1611	3.2	2223	0.9
25 SU ◑	0439	3.0	1046	0.9	1720	3.0	2353	1.1
26 M	0552	2.9	1226	1.0	1853	2.8		
27 TU ◑	0116	1.1	0723	2.9	1352	0.9	2021	2.8
28 W	0225	1.1	0836	3.1	1504	0.8	2121	2.9

MARCH

Day	Time	m	Time	m	Time	m	Time	m
1 TH	0323	0.9	0931	3.3	1557	0.6	2209	3.0
2 F	0409	0.8	1016	3.4	1638	0.5	2249	3.0
3 SA ○	0447	0.7	1056	3.5	1711	0.5	2324	3.0
4 SU	0519	0.7	1132	3.5	1738	0.5	2356	3.0
5 M	0547	0.7	1206	3.5	1803	0.6		
6 TU	0025	3.0	0614	0.7	1238	3.4	1829	0.6
7 W	0052	3.0	0643	0.7	1308	3.4	1858	0.6
8 TH	0121	3.1	0715	0.7	1340	3.3	1931	0.6
9 F	0153	3.1	0751	0.7	1414	3.3	2007	0.7
10 SA	0228	3.1	0830	0.8	1453	3.1	2048	0.9
11 SU	0308	3.0	0916	1.0	1542	3.0	2137	1.0
12 M ◑	0359	2.9	1014	1.2	1648	2.8	2239	1.2
13 TU	0509	2.7	1204	1.2	1801	2.7		
14 W	0031	1.3	0626	2.7	1329	1.1	1916	2.7
15 TH	0150	1.1	0743	2.8	1428	0.8	2030	2.9
16 F	0244	0.9	0846	3.0	1516	0.5	2121	3.0
17 SA	0329	0.7	0932	3.2	1559	0.3	2202	3.2
18 SU	0410	0.5	1014	3.4	1638	0.1	2242	3.3
19 M ●	0448	0.4	1056	3.6	1716	0.1	2324	3.3
20 TU	0526	0.3	1140	3.6	1754	0.1		
21 W	0007	3.4	0605	0.3	1227	3.7	1835	0.1
22 TH	0053	3.4	0648	0.3	1316	3.6	1918	0.3
23 F	0139	3.4	0733	0.3	1407	3.5	2005	0.5
24 SA	0227	3.3	0822	0.4	1500	3.3	2057	0.7
25 SU ◑	0318	3.2	0919	0.6	1558	3.1	2202	1.0
26 M	0415	3.0	1036	0.8	1710	2.8	2334	1.2
27 TU	0530	2.9	1215	0.9	1853	2.7		
28 W	0056	1.2	0703	2.9	1339	0.8	2009	2.7
29 TH	0207	1.1	0814	3.0	1447	0.7	2103	2.9
30 F	0304	0.9	0907	3.2	1536	0.5	2147	2.9
31 SA	0349	0.8	0951	3.3	1613	0.5	2224	3.0

APRIL

Day	Time	m	Time	m	Time	m	Time	m
1 SU	0425	0.7	1030	3.4	1642	0.5	2257	3.1
2 M ○	0455	0.7	1105	3.3	1706	0.6	2326	3.0
3 TU	0521	0.7	1136	3.3	1731	0.6	2352	3.1
4 W	0548	0.7	1205	3.3	1758	0.6		
5 TH	0017	3.1	0616	0.7	1234	3.3	1826	0.7
6 F	0045	3.2	0647	0.7	1306	3.3	1859	0.7
7 SA	0117	3.2	0723	0.7	1342	3.2	1936	0.8
8 SU	0153	3.2	0802	0.8	1425	3.1	2018	0.9
9 M	0234	3.1	0849	0.9	1518	2.9	2109	1.1
10 TU ◑	0324	3.0	0949	1.0	1625	2.8	2211	1.2
11 W	0432	2.8	1126	1.1	1737	2.7	2338	1.3
12 TH	0551	2.8	1257	0.9	1847	2.7		
13 F	0113	1.2	0704	2.9	1356	0.7	1953	2.9
14 SA	0211	1.0	0807	3.1	1445	0.4	2046	3.1
15 SU	0258	0.7	0859	3.3	1528	0.2	2131	3.2
16 M	0340	0.6	0946	3.5	1608	0.1	2215	3.3
17 TU ●	0421	0.4	1032	3.6	1648	0.1	2300	3.4
18 W	0502	0.3	1118	3.7	1729	0.2	2346	3.5
19 TH	0545	0.3	1210	3.6	1813	0.3		
20 F	0033	3.5	0630	0.3	1301	3.5	1859	0.4
21 SA	0121	3.5	0718	0.3	1353	3.4	1948	0.6
22 SU	0209	3.4	0810	0.5	1448	3.2	2044	0.9
23 M	0259	3.3	0911	0.6	1547	2.9	2151	1.1
24 TU ◑	0356	3.2	1029	0.8	1701	2.7	2309	1.2
25 W	0505	3.0	1150	0.9	1832	2.7		
26 TH	0023	1.2	0629	3.0	1305	0.8	1939	2.7
27 F	0130	1.1	0738	3.0	1409	0.7	2031	2.8
28 SA	0228	1.0	0832	3.1	1457	0.6	2113	2.9
29 SU	0315	0.9	0918	3.2	1534	0.6	2150	3.0
30 M	0353	0.8	0957	3.2	1604	0.6	2223	3.0

TIDES

Chart Datum: 2·01 metres below Ordnance Datum (Belfast)

TIME ZONE (UT)
For Summer Time add ONE hour in **non-shaded areas**

NORTHERN IRELAND – BELFAST
LAT 54°36′N   LONG 5°55′W
TIMES AND HEIGHTS OF HIGH AND LOW WATERS

Dates in amber are **SPRINGS**
Dates in yellow are **NEAPS**

2007

MAY

Time	m		Time	m
1 0425	0.8	**16** 0356	0.5
1032	3.2	1012	3.5
TU 1631	0.7	W 1623	0.3
2253	3.1	● 2238	3.5
2 0454	0.8	**17** 0443	0.4
1104	3.2	1104	3.6
W 1700	0.7	TH 1709	0.4
○ 2321	3.2	2327	3.5
3 0524	0.7	**18** 0531	0.4
1135	3.3	1155	3.5
TH 1729	0.7	F 1757	0.5
2349	3.2		
4 0555	0.7	**19** 0015	3.6
1207	3.2	0619	0.4
F 1801	0.8	SA 1247	3.4
		1846	0.6
5 0020	3.3	**20** 0104	3.6
0627	0.7	0709	0.4
SA 1242	3.2	SU 1340	3.3
1836	0.8	1938	0.8
6 0055	3.3	**21** 0152	3.5
0704	0.7	0803	0.5
SU 1322	3.2	M 1434	3.1
1915	0.9	2034	0.9
7 0132	3.3	**22** 0242	3.4
0746	0.8	0903	0.6
M 1408	3.1	TU 1531	2.9
2001	0.9	2134	1.1
8 0215	3.2	**23** 0335	3.3
0834	0.8	1008	0.7
TU 1503	2.9	W 1636	2.8
2053	1.1	◐ 2237	1.1
9 0306	3.1	**24** 0433	3.2
0934	0.9	1126	0.7
W 1607	2.8	TH 1747	2.7
2154	1.1	2339	1.2
10 0407	3.0	**25** 0538	3.1
1051	0.9	1216	0.8
TH 1713	2.8	F 1850	2.7
◐ 2303	1.2		
11 0519	3.0	**26** 0039	1.2
1212	0.8	0644	3.0
F 1818	2.9	SA 1313	0.8
		1942	2.8
12 0019	1.1	**27** 0136	1.1
0629	3.1	0744	3.0
SA 1314	0.6	SU 1403	0.8
1918	3.0	2027	2.8
13 0124	1.0	**28** 0227	1.0
0733	3.2	0834	3.1
SU 1406	0.4	M 1445	0.8
2012	3.1	2107	2.9
14 0219	0.8	**29** 0313	1.0
0829	3.4	0919	3.1
M 1453	0.3	TU 1522	0.8
2102	3.3	2144	3.0
15 0308	0.6	**30** 0352	0.9
0921	3.5	0959	3.2
TU 1538	0.3	W 1557	0.8
2150	3.4	2220	3.1
		31 0428	0.8
		1037	3.2
		TH 1632	0.8
		2255	3.2

JUNE

Time	m		Time	m
1 0503	0.8	**16** 0524	0.5
1112	3.2	1143	3.3
F 1707	0.8	SA 1746	0.7
○ 2329	3.3		
2 0539	0.8	**17** 0000	3.6
1148	3.2	0613	0.4
SA 1744	0.8	SU 1234	3.3
		1835	0.8
3 0003	3.4	**18** 0047	3.6
0615	0.7	0702	0.4
SU 1225	3.2	M 1324	3.1
1822	0.8	1925	0.8
4 0038	3.4	**19** 0134	3.6
0653	0.7	0751	0.5
M 1306	3.2	TU 1414	3.0
1903	0.9	2014	0.9
5 0117	3.4	**20** 0221	3.5
0735	0.7	0840	0.6
TU 1353	3.1	W 1504	2.9
1949	0.9	2103	1.0
6 0200	3.3	**21** 0308	3.4
0823	0.7	0930	0.6
W 1445	3.0	TH 1554	2.8
2039	0.9	2153	1.0
7 0249	3.3	**22** 0357	3.3
0918	0.7	1022	0.7
TH 1544	2.9	F 1644	2.8
2134	1.0	◑ 2245	1.1
8 0344	3.2	**23** 0448	3.1
1020	0.7	1116	0.8
F 1645	2.9	SA 1735	2.8
◑ 2232	1.0	2340	1.1
9 0447	3.2	**24** 0543	3.0
1126	0.7	1211	0.9
SA 1745	3.0	SU 1828	2.8
2335	1.0		
10 0554	3.2	**25** 0038	1.2
1230	0.6	0641	3.0
SU 1843	3.0	M 1306	1.0
		1922	2.8
11 0041	0.9	**26** 0137	1.2
0700	3.3	0742	2.9
M 1330	0.5	TU 1357	1.0
1940	3.1	2017	2.9
12 0146	0.8	**27** 0232	1.1
0803	3.3	0840	3.0
TU 1425	0.5	W 1445	0.9
2035	3.2	2108	3.0
13 0245	0.7	**28** 0322	1.0
0903	3.4	0931	3.1
W 1517	0.5	TH 1529	0.9
2129	3.4	2153	3.2
14 0341	0.6	**29** 0406	0.9
0959	3.4	1015	3.1
TH 1607	0.5	F 1610	0.8
2221	3.5	2234	3.3
15 0433	0.5	**30** 0446	0.8
1052	3.4	1055	3.2
F 1657	0.6	SA 1650	0.8
● 2311	3.5	○ 2310	3.3

JULY

Time	m		Time	m
1 0524	0.7	**16** 0605	0.5
1131	3.2	1219	3.1
SU 1729	0.8	M 1820	0.8
2343	3.4		
2 0602	0.6	**17** 0028	3.6
1208	3.2	0646	0.5
M 1809	0.8	TU 1303	3.0
		1901	0.8
3 0018	3.4	**18** 0112	3.6
0640	0.5	0725	0.5
TU 1248	3.2	W 1346	3.0
1849	0.8	1941	0.9
4 0057	3.5	**19** 0154	3.5
0721	0.5	0801	0.6
W 1332	3.1	TH 1427	2.9
1932	0.8	2019	0.9
5 0140	3.5	**20** 0236	3.4
0804	0.5	0838	0.7
TH 1421	3.1	F 1509	2.9
2018	0.8	2058	1.0
6 0228	3.5	**21** 0318	3.3
0853	0.5	0918	0.8
F 1514	3.1	SA 1552	2.9
2107	0.8	2141	1.0
7 0319	3.4	**22** 0403	3.2
0946	0.6	1003	0.9
SA 1610	3.0	SU 1638	2.9
● 2200	0.8	◑ 2231	1.1
8 0417	3.3	**23** 0452	3.0
1047	0.6	1056	1.0
SU 1708	3.0	M 1728	2.8
2300	0.9	2335	1.2
9 0521	3.3	**24** 0548	2.9
1154	0.7	1203	1.1
M 1808	3.0	TU 1825	2.8
10 0009	1.0	**25** 0050	1.2
0632	3.2	0652	2.8
TU 1304	0.8	W 1315	1.1
1911	3.1	1929	2.9
11 0126	0.9	**26** 0159	1.2
0745	3.2	0804	2.8
W 1409	0.8	TH 1415	1.1
2015	3.2	2035	3.0
12 0235	0.8	**27** 0257	1.0
0854	3.2	0910	2.9
TH 1507	0.7	F 1506	1.0
2115	3.3	2129	3.1
13 0336	0.7	**28** 0346	0.8
0954	3.2	0958	3.1
F 1600	0.7	SA 1551	0.9
2209	3.4	2211	3.2
14 0431	0.6	**29** 0428	0.6
1046	3.2	1037	3.2
SA 1649	0.7	SU 1632	0.8
● 2259	3.5	2245	3.4
15 0520	0.5	**30** 0506	0.5
1134	3.2	1112	3.2
SU 1735	0.8	M 1711	0.7
2344	3.6	○ 2317	3.4
		31 0543	0.4
		1146	3.2
		TU 1749	0.7
		2353	3.5

AUGUST

Time	m		Time	m
1 0620	0.3	**16** 0045	3.5
1224	3.2	0649	0.6
W 1828	0.6	TH 1311	3.0
		1901	0.8
2 0033	3.6	**17** 0122	3.5
0658	0.3	0718	0.6
TH 1307	3.2	F 1346	3.0
1908	0.6	1934	0.8
3 0117	3.6	**18** 0159	3.4
0739	0.3	0751	0.7
F 1353	3.2	SA 1423	3.0
1952	0.6	2011	0.9
4 0204	3.6	**19** 0236	3.3
0823	0.4	0827	0.8
SA 1443	3.2	SU 1502	3.0
2038	0.7	2052	1.0
5 0255	3.5	**20** 0316	3.2
0913	0.5	0908	0.9
SU 1536	3.1	M 1546	3.0
◑ 2129	0.8	◐ 2138	1.1
6 0350	3.4	**21** 0403	3.0
1010	0.7	0956	1.1
M 1633	3.1	TU 1637	2.9
2228	0.9	2237	1.2
7 0456	3.2	**22** 0502	2.8
1123	0.9	1108	1.2
TU 1737	3.0	W 1736	2.8
2348	1.0		
8 0613	3.0	**23** 0011	1.3
1250	1.0	0610	2.7
W 1851	3.0	TH 1236	1.3
		1843	2.8
9 0120	1.0	**24** 0132	1.3
0742	2.9	0728	2.7
TH 1402	1.0	F 1350	1.2
2006	3.1	1957	2.9
10 0236	0.9	**25** 0233	1.0
0857	3.0	0848	2.9
F 1502	0.9	SA 1445	1.0
2109	3.3	2058	3.1
11 0338	0.7	**26** 0322	0.7
0953	3.1	0936	3.0
SA 1554	0.8	SU 1530	0.9
2201	3.4	2139	3.2
12 0429	0.5	**27** 0405	0.5
1040	3.1	1012	3.2
SU 1639	0.8	M 1610	0.7
● 2246	3.5	2214	3.4
13 0512	0.5	**28** 0443	0.4
1122	3.1	1045	3.2
M 1720	0.8	TU 1647	0.6
2327	3.6	○ 2249	3.5
14 0549	0.5	**29** 0518	0.3
1200	3.1	1120	3.3
TU 1757	0.8	W 1724	0.6
		2327	3.6
15 0007	3.6	**30** 0554	0.2
0621	0.5	1158	3.3
W 1237	3.0	TH 1802	0.5
1829	0.8		
		31 0009	3.7
		0631	0.2
		F 1241	3.3
		1841	0.5

Chart Datum: 2·01 metres below Ordnance Datum (Belfast)

NORTHERN IRELAND – BELFAST

LAT 54°36'N   LONG 5°55'W

TIMES AND HEIGHTS OF HIGH AND LOW WATERS

Dates in amber are **SPRINGS**
Dates in yellow are **NEAPS**

2007

SEPTEMBER

Day	Time m	Time m	Day	Time m	Time m
1 SA	0055 3.7 / 0711 0.3	1327 3.3 / 1925 0.5	16 SU	0119 3.4 / 0711 0.8	1337 3.2 / 1933 0.9
2 SU	0143 3.6 / 0755 0.4	1415 3.3 / 2012 0.6	17 M	0155 3.3 / 0746 0.8	1414 3.2 / 2013 0.9
3 M	0235 3.5 / 0844 0.6	1507 3.2 / 2104 0.7	18 TU	0234 3.2 / 0826 0.9	1456 3.1 / 2058 1.1
4 TU	0333 3.3 / 0940 0.9	1606 3.1 / 2206 0.9 ◑	19 W	0322 3.0 / 0913 1.1	1547 3.0 / 2155 1.2 ◑
5 W	0441 3.0 / 1100 1.2	1715 3.0 / 2343 1.1	20 TH	0425 2.8 / 1013 1.3	1652 2.9 / 2330 1.3
6 TH	0608 2.8 / 1242 1.2	1839 3.0	21 F	0537 2.7 / 1146 1.4	1804 2.8
7 F	0119 1.0 / 0749 2.8	1356 1.2 / 1959 3.1	22 SA	0103 1.2 / 0652 2.7	1322 1.3 / 1915 2.9
8 SA	0236 0.8 / 0855 2.9	1456 1.0 / 2059 3.3	23 SU	0204 0.9 / 0809 2.9	1418 1.1 / 2016 3.1
9 SU	0334 0.6 / 0944 3.1	1545 0.9 / 2146 3.5	24 M	0253 0.7 / 0900 3.1	1503 0.9 / 2102 3.3
10 M	0419 0.5 / 1025 3.1	1625 0.8 / 2228 3.5	25 TU	0335 0.5 / 0939 3.2	1542 0.7 / 2142 3.5
11 TU	0455 0.5 / 1102 3.1	1700 0.8 / 2306 3.5 ●	26 W	0413 0.3 / 1016 3.3	1619 0.6 / 2222 3.6 ○
12 W	0524 0.5 / 1136 3.1	1730 0.8 / 2341 3.5	27 TH	0448 0.2 / 1054 3.4	1656 0.5 / 2304 3.7
13 TH	0548 0.6 / 1206 3.1	1757 0.8	28 F	0525 0.2 / 1135 3.5	1735 0.5 / 2349 3.7
14 F	0014 3.5 / 0612 0.7	1234 3.1 / 1825 0.8	29 SA	0604 0.3 / 1219 3.5	1818 0.4
15 SA	0046 3.4 / 0639 0.7	1304 3.2 / 1857 0.8	30 SU	0038 3.7 / 0646 0.4	1305 3.5 / 1903 0.5

OCTOBER

Day	Time m	Time m	Day	Time m	Time m
1 M	0129 3.6 / 0732 0.6	1354 3.4 / 1952 0.6	16 TU	0123 3.3 / 0715 0.9	1339 3.3 / 1944 1.0
2 TU	0224 3.4 / 0823 0.8	1447 3.3 / 2047 0.7	17 W	0204 3.2 / 0756 1.0	1419 3.3 / 2031 1.1
3 W	0325 3.2 / 0923 1.1	1546 3.2 / 2157 0.9 ◑	18 TH	0255 3.0 / 0845 1.2	1508 3.1 / 2127 1.2
4 TH	0436 2.9 / 1052 1.3	1658 3.1 / 2338 1.0	19 F	0359 2.9 / 1101 1.4	1611 3.0 / 2246 1.2 ◑
5 F	0612 2.8 / 1225 1.4	1825 3.0	20 SA	0510 2.8 / 1101 1.4	1725 2.9
6 SA	0106 1.0 / 0739 2.8	1338 1.2 / 1940 3.2	21 SU	0022 1.1 / 0620 2.8	1235 1.3 / 1835 3.0
7 SU	0220 0.8 / 0837 2.9	1438 1.1 / 2037 3.3	22 M	0125 0.9 / 0725 3.0	1338 1.2 / 1936 3.2
8 M	0313 0.7 / 0922 3.1	1525 0.9 / 2123 3.4	23 TU	0215 0.7 / 0820 3.1	1426 1.0 / 2028 3.4
9 TU	0354 0.6 / 1001 3.1	1604 0.9 / 2204 3.5	24 W	0258 0.5 / 0905 3.3	1508 0.8 / 2114 3.5
10 W	0427 0.6 / 1036 3.2	1635 0.8 / 2241 3.5	25 TH	0338 0.4 / 0948 3.4	1549 0.6 / 2200 3.7
11 TH	0451 0.7 / 1107 3.2	1702 0.8 / 2314 3.5 ●	26 F	0417 0.3 / 1031 3.5	1630 0.5 / 2247 3.7 ○
12 F	0514 0.8 / 1137 3.2	1729 0.8 / 2344 3.4	27 SA	0458 0.4 / 1115 3.6	1714 0.5 / 2336 3.7
13 SA	0539 0.8 / 1201 3.2	1757 0.9	28 SU	0542 0.5 / 1202 3.6	1800 0.5
14 SU	0014 3.4 / 0606 0.8	1230 3.3 / 1829 0.9	29 M	0028 3.6 / 0628 0.6	1251 3.6 / 1848 0.5
15 M	0047 3.4 / 0638 0.8	1303 3.4 / 1904 0.9	30 TU	0122 3.5 / 0717 0.8	1340 3.6 / 1940 0.6
			31 W	0218 3.3 / 0812 1.0	1433 3.5 / 2039 0.7

NOVEMBER

Day	Time m	Time m	Day	Time m	Time m
1 TH	0318 3.1 / 0916 1.2	1531 3.3 / 2152 0.9 ◑	16 F	0236 3.1 / 0827 1.2	1444 3.3 / 2107 1.0
2 F	0429 2.9 / 1036 1.3	1639 3.2 / 2316 0.9	17 SA	0336 3.0 / 0924 1.3	1539 3.2 / 2212 1.0 ●
3 SA	0555 2.8 / 1153 1.4	1756 3.1	18 SU	0441 2.9 / 1027 1.3	1645 3.1 / 2325 1.0
4 SU	0032 0.9 / 0708 2.8	1302 1.3 / 1906 3.2	19 M	0545 2.9 / 1136 1.3	1754 3.2
5 M	0140 0.9 / 0804 2.9	1402 1.2 / 2004 3.3	20 TU	0032 0.9 / 0646 3.0	1244 1.2 / 1858 3.3
6 TU	0234 0.8 / 0850 3.0	1452 1.1 / 2053 3.3	21 W	0129 0.7 / 0742 3.2	1343 1.0 / 1956 3.4
7 W	0316 0.8 / 0930 3.1	1533 1.0 / 2135 3.4	22 TH	0219 0.6 / 0833 3.3	1435 0.9 / 2050 3.5
8 TH	0348 0.8 / 1006 3.2	1607 0.9 / 2213 3.4	23 F	0306 0.5 / 0923 3.5	1525 0.7 / 2142 3.6
9 F	0416 0.9 / 1038 3.3	1637 0.9 / 2248 3.4 ●	24 SA	0353 0.5 / 1012 3.6	1613 0.6 / 2234 3.6 ○
10 SA	0443 0.9 / 1108 3.3	1707 0.9 / 2320 3.4	25 SU	0440 0.6 / 1100 3.7	1701 0.5 / 2327 3.6
11 SU	0512 0.9 / 1138 3.4	1738 0.9 / 2352 3.4	26 M	0528 0.6 / 1149 3.7	1750 0.6
12 M	0543 0.9 / 1209 3.5	1811 0.9	27 TU	0019 3.5 / 0617 0.8	1239 3.7 / 1841 0.6
13 TU	0026 3.3 / 0617 1.0	1243 3.5 / 1847 0.9	28 W	0113 3.4 / 0709 0.9	1328 3.7 / 1934 0.5
14 W	0104 3.3 / 0655 1.0	1318 3.4 / 1927 0.9	29 TH	0208 3.3 / 0804 0.9	1419 3.6 / 2031 0.6
15 TH	0146 3.2 / 0738 1.1	1358 3.4 / 2013 1.0	30 F	0306 3.1 / 0903 1.1	1513 3.5 / 2135 0.7

DECEMBER

Day	Time m	Time m	Day	Time m	Time m
1 SA	0408 2.9 / 1006 1.2	1611 3.4 / 2240 0.8 ◑	16 SU	0307 3.1 / 0900 1.1	1512 3.4 / 2140 0.8
2 SU	0516 2.9 / 1110 1.3	1713 3.3 / 2344 0.9	17 M	0404 3.0 / 0954 1.1	1608 3.3 / 2240 0.8 ●
3 M	0620 2.8 / 1212 1.3	1817 3.2	18 TU	0504 3.0 / 1053 1.1	1711 3.3 / 2344 0.8
4 TU	0044 0.9 / 0717 2.9	1311 1.2 / 1918 3.2	19 W	0604 3.1 / 1158 1.1	1819 3.3
5 W	0139 1.0 / 0808 3.0	1406 1.2 / 2013 3.2	20 TH	0049 0.8 / 0704 3.1	1308 1.1 / 1926 3.3
6 TH	0226 1.0 / 0853 3.1	1456 1.1 / 2102 3.2	21 F	0150 0.7 / 0805 3.2	1412 0.9 / 2030 3.4
7 F	0307 1.0 / 0934 3.2	1538 1.0 / 2146 3.3	22 SA	0247 0.7 / 0903 3.4	1511 0.8 / 2130 3.4
8 SA	0344 1.0 / 1012 3.3	1616 1.0 / 2226 3.3	23 SU	0341 0.7 / 0958 3.5	1606 0.7 / 2226 3.5
9 SU	0419 1.0 / 1049 3.4	1650 0.9 / 2303 3.3 ●	24 M	0432 0.7 / 1049 3.6	1657 0.5 / 2320 3.4 ○
10 M	0454 1.0 / 1123 3.5	1725 0.9 / 2338 3.3	25 TU	0521 0.7 / 1139 3.7	1747 0.5
11 TU	0529 0.9 / 1156 3.5	1800 0.8	26 W	0011 3.4 / 0610 0.8	1227 3.8 / 1835 0.5
12 W	0012 3.3 / 0605 0.9	1228 3.5 / 1837 0.8	27 TH	0102 3.3 / 0658 0.8	1315 3.8 / 1924 0.5
13 TH	0049 3.3 / 0644 1.0	1302 3.5 / 1916 0.8	28 F	0153 3.2 / 0747 0.9	1402 3.7 / 2012 0.5
14 F	0129 3.2 / 0725 1.0	1340 3.5 / 1958 0.8	29 SA	0243 3.1 / 0835 1.0	1450 3.6 / 2102 0.6
15 SA	0215 3.1 / 0810 1.0	1423 3.4 / 2046 0.8	30 SU	0332 3.0 / 0925 1.0	1508 3.6 / 2152 0.8
			31 M	0421 2.9 / 1016 1.1	1628 3.3 / 2246 0.9 ◑

TIDES

Chart Datum: 2·01 metres below Ordnance Datum (Belfast)

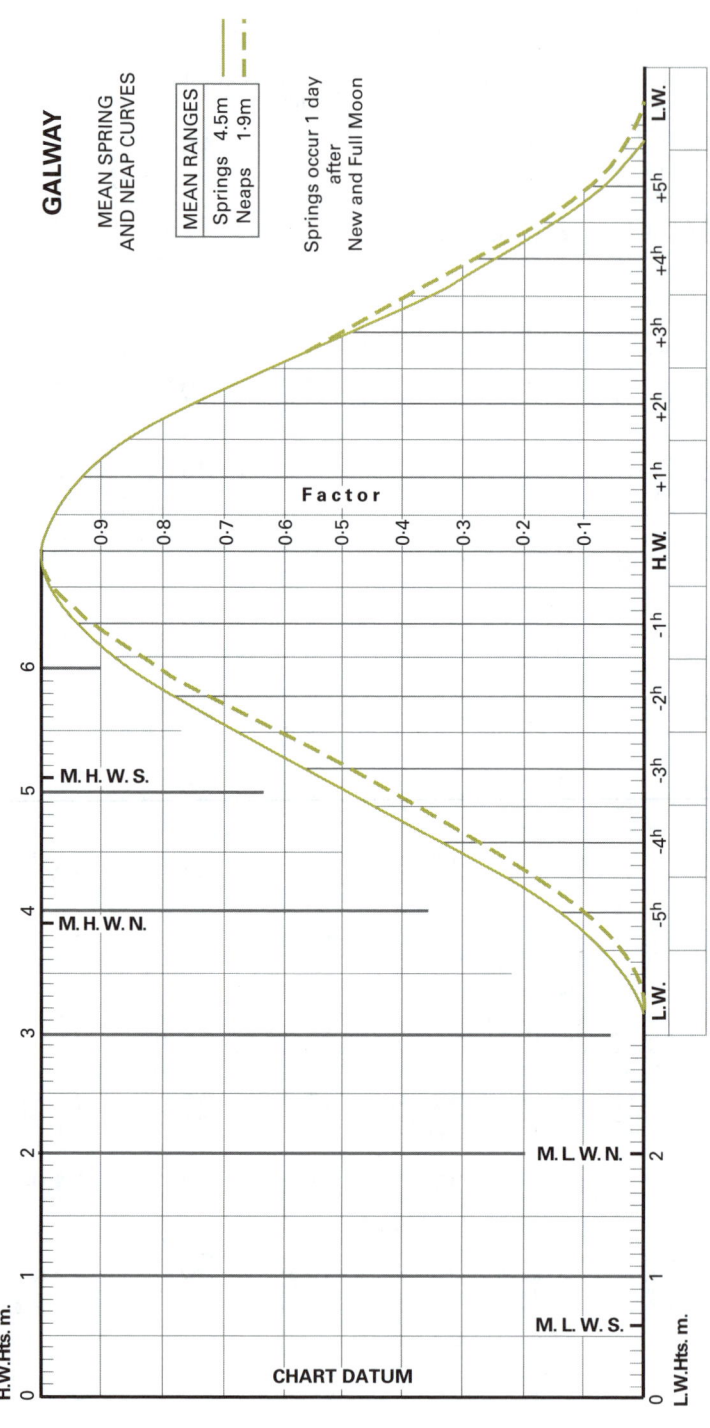

GALWAY

MEAN SPRING
AND NEAP CURVES

MEAN RANGES	
Springs	4.5m
Neaps	1.9m

Springs occur 1 day
after
New and Full Moon

Factor

0·9
0·8
0·7
0·6
0·5
0·4
0·3
0·2
0·1

H.W. -1h -2h -3h -4h -5h L.W. +5h +4h +3h +2h +1h H.W. L.W.

H.W.Hts. m.

M. H. W. S.

M. H. W. N.

M. L. W. N.

M. L. W. S.

CHART DATUM

L.W.Hts. m.

TIME ZONE (UT)	IRELAND – GALWAY	Dates in amber are SPRINGS
For Summer Time add ONE hour in non-shaded areas	LAT 53°16'N LONG 9°03'W	Dates in yellow are NEAPS
	TIMES AND HEIGHTS OF HIGH AND LOW WATERS	2007

JANUARY

Day	Time	m	Day	Time	m
1 M	0258 / 0902 / 1523 / 2122	4.6 / 1.4 / 4.6 / 1.4	16 TU	0254 / 0903 / 1526 / 2124	4.1 / 1.7 / 4.0 / 1.6
2 TU	0348 / 0952 / 1614 / 2207	4.8 / 1.2 / 4.7 / 1.2	17 W	0341 / 0949 / 1612 / 2206	4.3 / 1.4 / 4.2 / 1.3
3 W	0435 / 1039 / 1702 / ○2251	4.9 / 1.0 / 4.8 / 1.2	18 TH	0425 / 1032 / 1655 / 2247	4.6 / 1.0 / 4.5 / 1.1
4 TH	0521 / 1124 / 1748 / 2333	4.9 / 0.9 / 4.8 / 1.1	19 F	0508 / 1112 / 1737 / ●2327	4.8 / 0.7 / 4.7 / 0.9
5 F	0605 / 1206 / 1831	5.0 / 0.8 / 4.7	20 SA	0551 / 1151 / 1819	5.0 / 0.5 / 4.9
6 SA	0014 / 0646 / 1245 / 1912	1.1 / 4.9 / 0.8 / 4.6	21 SU	0007 / 0633 / 1231 / 1859	0.7 / 5.1 / 0.3 / 4.9
7 SU	0054 / 0727 / 1322 / 1953	1.2 / 4.8 / 0.9 / 4.5	22 M	0047 / 0714 / 1310 / 1941	0.7 / 5.2 / 0.3 / 4.8
8 M	0133 / 0806 / 1400 / 2035	1.3 / 4.7 / 1.1 / 4.4	23 TU	0128 / 0756 / 1350 / 2024	0.7 / 5.1 / 0.6 / 4.7
9 TU	0212 / 0845 / 1438 / 2119	1.5 / 4.5 / 1.3 / 4.2	24 W	0212 / 0841 / 1434 / 2112	0.9 / 4.9 / 0.8 / 4.5
10 W	0255 / 0925 / 1520 / 2206	1.7 / 4.2 / 1.5 / 4.0	25 TH	0300 / 0932 / 1522 / ☽2209	1.2 / 4.6 / 1.1 / 4.3
11 TH	0343 / 1007 / 1607 / ☽2255	1.9 / 4.0 / 1.8 / 3.9	26 F	0357 / 1031 / 1620 / 2314	1.5 / 4.3 / 1.5 / 4.1
12 F	0441 / 1053 / 1703 / 2348	2.1 / 3.8 / 2.0 / 3.8	27 SA	0508 / 1139 / 1733	1.8 / 4.1 / 1.8
13 SA	0549 / 1147 / 1816	2.2 / 3.7 / 2.1	28 SU	0027 / 0634 / 1258 / 1910	4.0 / 1.8 / 4.0 / 1.8
14 SU	0048 / 0703 / 1259 / 1935	3.8 / 2.2 / 3.6 / 2.0	29 M	0147 / 0757 / 1418 / 2027	4.1 / 1.7 / 4.1 / 1.6
15 M	0156 / 0810 / 1427 / 2036	3.9 / 2.0 / 3.7 / 1.9	30 TU	0254 / 0901 / 1521 / 2119	4.3 / 1.5 / 4.2 / 1.6
			31 W	0346 / 0951 / 1611 / 2202	4.5 / 1.2 / 4.4 / 1.3

FEBRUARY

Day	Time	m	Day	Time	m
1 TH	0431 / 1034 / 1655 / 2242	4.7 / 1.0 / 4.6 / 1.1	16 F	0412 / 1017 / 1642 / 2233	4.5 / 0.8 / 4.5 / 0.8
2 F	0514 / 1112 / 1736 / ○2320	4.8 / 0.8 / 4.7 / 1.0	17 SA	0454 / 1055 / 1721 / ●2312	4.9 / 0.4 / 4.8 / 0.5
3 SA	0554 / 1149 / 1815 / 2356	4.9 / 0.6 / 4.7 / 0.9	18 SU	0535 / 1133 / 1800 / 2350	5.1 / 0.1 / 5.0 / 0.3
4 SU	0632 / 1223 / 1852	4.9 / 0.6 / 4.7	19 M	0616 / 1210 / 1839	5.3 / 0.0 / 5.1
5 M	0031 / 0707 / 1256 / 1928	0.8 / 4.9 / 0.7 / 4.7	20 TU	0028 / 0656 / 1249 / 1917	0.2 / 5.3 / 0.0 / 5.1
6 TU	0106 / 0741 / 1327 / 2003	0.9 / 4.7 / 0.8 / 4.5	21 W	0108 / 0736 / 1327 / 1956	0.3 / 5.2 / 0.2 / 4.9
7 W	0139 / 0814 / 1400 / 2038	1.1 / 4.6 / 1.0 / 4.3	22 TH	0149 / 0817 / 1408 / 2038	0.6 / 5.0 / 0.6 / 4.6
8 TH	0214 / 0845 / 1433 / 2114	1.3 / 4.3 / 1.3 / 4.1	23 F	0234 / 0904 / 1452 / 2128	0.9 / 4.6 / 1.1 / 4.2
9 F	0251 / 0918 / 1508 / 2155	1.6 / 4.1 / 1.6 / 3.9	24 SA	0327 / 1002 / 1546 / ☽2236	1.4 / 4.2 / 1.6 / 3.9
10 SA	0332 / 1002 / 1550 / ☽2246	1.9 / 3.8 / 1.9 / 3.7	25 SU	0439 / 1116 / 1704	1.8 / 3.8 / 2.0
11 SU	0427 / 1058 / 1646 / 2346	2.1 / 3.6 / 2.2 / 3.6	26 M	0005 / 0615 / 1247 / 1859	3.7 / 1.9 / 3.7 / 2.1
12 M	0611 / 1249 / 1904	2.3 / 3.4 / 2.2	27 TU	0139 / 0757 / 1416 / 2028	3.8 / 1.7 / 3.8 / 1.9
13 TU	0101 / 0749 / 1357 / 2023	3.6 / 2.1 / 3.5 / 2.0	28 W	0247 / 0903 / 1515 / 2114	4.1 / 1.4 / 4.1 / 1.6
14 W	0233 / 0850 / 1518 / 2112	3.8 / 1.7 / 3.8 / 1.6			
15 TH	0328 / 0936 / 1602 / 2154	4.2 / 1.5 / 4.2 / 1.2			

MARCH

Day	Time	m	Day	Time	m
1 TH	0335 / 0944 / 1559 / 2149	4.3 / 1.2 / 4.3 / 1.3	16 F	0306 / 0911 / 1540 / 2130	4.2 / 1.1 / 4.3 / 1.1
2 F	0417 / 1018 / 1639 / 2224	4.6 / 0.9 / 4.6 / 1.0	17 SA	0349 / 0951 / 1618 / 2209	4.6 / 0.6 / 4.7 / 0.6
3 SA	0457 / 1051 / 1716 / 2259	4.8 / 0.7 / 4.7 / 0.8	18 SU	0430 / 1030 / 1656 / 2248	5.0 / 0.2 / 5.0 / 0.3
4 SU	0534 / 1124 / 1752 / 2333	4.9 / 0.6 / 4.8 / 0.7	19 M	0512 / 1108 / 1734 / ●2327	5.3 / 0.0 / 5.2 / 0.1
5 M	0610 / 1155 / 1826	4.9 / 0.5 / 4.8	20 TU	0553 / 1145 / 1813	5.4 / -0.1 / 5.3
6 TU	0005 / 0643 / 1225 / 1859	0.7 / 4.9 / 0.6 / 4.8	21 W	0006 / 0633 / 1224 / 1850	0.0 / 5.4 / 0.0 / 5.2
7 W	0037 / 0714 / 1254 / 1930	0.7 / 4.7 / 0.7 / 4.6	22 TH	0046 / 0714 / 1303 / 1929	0.1 / 5.3 / 0.2 / 5.0
8 TH	0108 / 0744 / 1323 / 2000	0.9 / 4.6 / 1.0 / 4.4	23 F	0128 / 0756 / 1343 / 2010	0.4 / 4.9 / 0.7 / 4.7
9 F	0139 / 0811 / 1353 / 2030	1.1 / 4.3 / 1.2 / 4.2	24 SA	0213 / 0843 / 1427 / 2058	0.8 / 4.5 / 1.2 / 4.3
10 SA	0213 / 0842 / 1426 / 2108	1.4 / 4.1 / 1.6 / 4.0	25 SU	0307 / 0941 / 1522 / ☽2206	1.3 / 4.1 / 1.8 / 3.9
11 SU	0252 / 0926 / 1506 / 2201	1.7 / 3.8 / 1.9 / 3.7	26 M	0423 / 1101 / 1650 / 2350	1.7 / 3.7 / 2.1 / 3.7
12 M	0341 / 1027 / 1600 / ☽2306	2.0 / 3.5 / 2.2 / 3.6	27 TU	0600 / 1236 / 1841	1.8 / 3.6 / 2.2
13 TU	0456 / 1138 / 1844	2.2 / 3.2 / 2.4	28 W	0121 / 0743 / 1402 / 2014	3.8 / 1.7 / 3.8 / 1.9
14 W	0019 / 0725 / 1329 / 2000	3.5 / 2.0 / 3.5 / 2.0	29 TH	0226 / 0846 / 1455 / 2054	4.0 / 1.4 / 4.1 / 1.6
15 TH	0206 / 0825 / 1500 / 2049	3.8 / 1.6 / 3.9 / 1.6	30 F	0313 / 0920 / 1536 / 2125	4.3 / 1.2 / 4.4 / 1.1
			31 SA	0354 / 0951 / 1613 / 2159	4.5 / 0.9 / 4.6 / 1.0

APRIL

Day	Time	m	Day	Time	m
1 SU	0432 / 1022 / 1649 / 2233	4.7 / 0.8 / 4.7 / 0.8	16 M	0401 / 1000 / 1625 / 2221	5.0 / 0.3 / 5.1 / 0.3
2 M	0508 / 1054 / 1723 / ○2306	4.8 / 0.7 / 4.8 / 0.7	17 TU	0444 / 1040 / 1705 / ●2302	5.3 / 0.1 / 5.3 / 0.1
3 TU	0543 / 1124 / 1756 / 2337	4.8 / 0.7 / 4.8 / 0.7	18 W	0528 / 1119 / 1745 / 2344	5.4 / 0.1 / 5.4 / 0.1
4 W	0616 / 1153 / 1828	4.7 / 0.8 / 4.8	19 TH	0612 / 1200 / 1826	5.4 / 0.2 / 5.3
5 TH	0008 / 0646 / 1221 / 1858	0.8 / 4.6 / 0.9 / 4.7	20 F	0026 / 0655 / 1241 / 1907	0.2 / 5.2 / 0.5 / 5.1
6 F	0038 / 0716 / 1249 / 1928	0.9 / 4.5 / 1.1 / 4.5	21 SA	0111 / 0740 / 1323 / 1951	0.5 / 4.9 / 0.9 / 4.7
7 SA	0110 / 0747 / 1321 / 1959	1.2 / 4.3 / 1.3 / 4.3	22 SU	0159 / 0828 / 1409 / 2042	0.9 / 4.5 / 1.4 / 4.3
8 SU	0146 / 0821 / 1356 / 2037	1.4 / 4.1 / 1.6 / 4.1	23 M	0255 / 0928 / 1507 / 2150	1.3 / 4.1 / 1.8 / 4.0
9 M	0227 / 0906 / 1439 / 2132	1.7 / 3.8 / 1.9 / 3.8	24 TU	0409 / 1044 / 1633 / ☽2326	1.6 / 3.8 / 2.1 / 3.8
10 TU	0319 / 1009 / 1536 / 2239	1.9 / 3.6 / 2.2 / 3.7	25 W	0533 / 1210 / 1804	1.7 / 3.7 / 2.1
11 W	0432 / 1119 / 1808 / 2350	2.0 / 3.5 / 2.3 / 3.7	26 TH	0048 / 0652 / 1327 / 1920	3.8 / 1.7 / 3.8 / 2.0
12 TH	0648 / 1244 / 1924	1.9 / 3.6 / 2.0	27 F	0152 / 0758 / 1423 / 2014	4.0 / 1.5 / 4.1 / 1.7
13 F	0114 / 0748 / 1418 / 2015	3.9 / 1.5 / 4.0 / 1.6	28 SA	0241 / 0841 / 1505 / 2053	4.2 / 1.3 / 4.3 / 1.4
14 SA	0227 / 0837 / 1505 / 2100	4.3 / 1.1 / 4.4 / 1.1	29 SU	0323 / 0917 / 1542 / 2129	4.4 / 1.1 / 4.5 / 1.2
15 SU	0317 / 0920 / 1545 / 2141	4.7 / 0.6 / 4.8 / 0.6	30 M	0402 / 0950 / 1617 / 2203	4.5 / 1.0 / 4.6 / 1.0

Chart Datum: 0·20 metres above Ordnance Datum (Dublin)

TIDES

TIME ZONE (UT)	IRELAND – GALWAY	Dates in amber are SPRINGS
For Summer Time add ONE hour in **non-shaded areas**	LAT 53°16′N LONG 9°03′W	Dates in yellow are NEAPS

TIMES AND HEIGHTS OF HIGH AND LOW WATERS

2007

MAY

Time m	Time m
1 0438 4.6 / 1022 1.0 / TU 1650 4.7 / 2237 0.9	**16** 0419 5.1 / 1014 0.5 / W 1638 5.2 / 2240 0.4
2 0513 4.6 / 1052 1.0 / W 1723 4.7 / ○ 2309 0.9	**17** 0506 5.2 / 1056 0.5 / TH 1722 5.3 / 2325 0.4
3 0546 4.6 / 1121 1.0 / TH 1756 4.7 / 2341 1.0	**18** 0553 5.2 / 1140 0.6 / F 1807 5.2
4 0620 4.5 / 1151 1.1 / F 1829 4.7	**19** 0012 0.4 / 0640 5.0 / SA 1224 0.8 / 1852 5.0
5 0014 1.1 / 0653 4.4 / SA 1223 1.3 / 1903 4.5	**20** 0059 0.6 / 0727 4.8 / SU 1309 1.1 / 1939 4.7
6 0050 1.2 / 0729 4.3 / SU 1259 1.4 / 1939 4.4	**21** 0148 0.9 / 0816 4.5 / M 1356 1.4 / 2030 4.4
7 0129 1.3 / 0809 4.1 / M 1339 1.6 / 2021 4.2	**22** 0241 1.2 / 0912 4.2 / TU 1451 1.7 / 2132 4.1
8 0214 1.5 / 0856 4.0 / TU 1426 1.9 / 2115 4.1	**23** 0343 1.4 / 1016 3.9 / W 1559 2.0 / ● 2247 4.0
9 0308 1.7 / 0955 3.8 / W 1525 2.1 / 2219 4.0	**24** 0452 1.6 / 1125 3.8 / TH 1716 2.1 / 2357 3.9
10 0417 1.7 / 1100 3.8 / TH 1654 2.1 / ◑ 2325 4.0	**25** 0557 1.7 / 1231 3.8 / F 1824 2.0
11 0552 1.7 / 1209 3.9 / F 1839 1.9	**26** 0101 3.9 / 0657 1.6 / SA 1333 4.0 / 1923 1.8
12 0034 4.2 / 0704 1.4 / SA 1323 4.2 / 1937 1.5	**27** 0158 4.0 / 0752 1.6 / SU 1424 4.1 / 2014 1.6
13 0143 4.4 / 0800 1.1 / SU 1423 4.5 / 2027 1.2	**28** 0246 4.1 / 0837 1.5 / M 1505 4.3 / 2056 1.5
14 0241 4.7 / 0848 0.8 / M 1511 4.8 / 2112 0.8	**29** 0327 4.2 / 0915 1.4 / TU 1542 4.4 / 2134 1.3
15 0331 5.0 / 0932 0.6 / TU 1555 5.1 / 2156 0.5	**30** 0406 4.3 / 0951 1.3 / W 1617 4.5 / 2211 1.2
	31 0443 4.3 / 1024 1.3 / TH 1651 4.6 / 2247 1.1

JUNE

Time m	Time m
1 0520 4.4 / 1058 1.2 / F 1727 4.6 / ○ 2323 1.1	**16** 0541 4.9 / 1126 0.9 / SA 1754 5.0
2 0558 4.4 / 1132 1.3 / SA 1805 4.6	**17** 0001 0.6 / 0628 4.8 / SU 1211 1.0 / 1841 4.9
3 0000 1.1 / 0636 4.4 / SU 1208 1.3 / 1844 4.6	**18** 0048 0.6 / 0715 4.7 / M 1255 1.1 / 1927 4.8
4 0040 1.1 / 0716 4.4 / M 1248 1.3 / 1924 4.5	**19** 0133 0.8 / 0801 4.5 / TU 1339 1.3 / 2014 4.6
5 0121 1.1 / 0757 4.3 / TU 1330 1.5 / 2008 4.4	**20** 0218 1.0 / 0848 4.3 / W 1424 1.5 / 2104 4.3
6 0206 1.2 / 0843 4.2 / W 1418 1.6 / 2059 4.3	**21** 0306 1.2 / 0939 4.1 / TH 1515 1.7 / 2159 4.1
7 0256 1.3 / 0936 4.1 / TH 1513 1.7 / 2157 4.3	**22** 0358 1.4 / 1032 3.9 / F 1615 1.9 / ● 2256 3.9
8 0354 1.4 / 1035 4.1 / F 1621 1.8 / ◑ 2259 4.3	**23** 0455 1.6 / 1127 3.8 / SA 1722 2.0 / 2353 3.8
9 0459 1.4 / 1136 4.1 / SA 1741 1.8	**24** 0554 1.8 / 1224 3.8 / SU 1828 2.0
10 0001 4.3 / 0609 1.4 / SU 1241 4.2 / 1855 1.6	**25** 0054 3.7 / 0654 1.8 / M 1325 3.9 / 1929 1.9
11 0107 4.4 / 0718 1.3 / M 1345 4.4 / 1956 1.3	**26** 0157 3.7 / 0752 1.8 / TU 1421 4.0 / 2024 1.7
12 0211 4.6 / 0817 1.2 / TU 1442 4.7 / 2049 1.1	**27** 0251 3.8 / 0842 1.7 / W 1507 4.1 / 2110 1.5
13 0308 4.7 / 0907 1.0 / W 1532 4.9 / 2138 0.8	**28** 0338 4.0 / 0926 1.6 / TH 1548 4.3 / 2152 1.3
14 0400 4.6 / 0954 0.9 / TH 1619 5.0 / 2225 0.7	**29** 0420 4.1 / 1006 1.4 / F 1627 4.5 / 2232 1.1
15 0451 4.9 / 1040 0.9 / F 1706 5.1 / ● 2314 0.6	**30** 0501 4.3 / 1045 1.3 / SA 1707 4.6 / ○ 2312 1.0

JULY

Time m	Time m
1 0542 4.4 / 1123 1.2 / SU 1748 4.7 / 2352 0.8	**16** 0616 4.7 / 1156 0.9 / M 1829 4.9
2 0623 4.5 / 1201 1.1 / M 1829 4.7	**17** 0030 0.5 / 0658 4.7 / TU 1236 0.9 / 1910 4.8
3 0030 0.7 / 0702 4.6 / TU 1241 1.0 / 1910 4.8	**18** 0109 0.6 / 0738 4.6 / W 1314 1.0 / 1951 4.7
4 0110 0.7 / 0742 4.5 / W 1321 1.1 / 1952 4.7	**19** 0147 0.8 / 0819 4.5 / TH 1353 1.2 / 2031 4.5
5 0151 0.7 / 0824 4.5 / TH 1404 1.2 / 2038 4.6	**20** 0225 1.0 / 0900 4.3 / F 1433 1.4 / 2113 4.2
6 0236 0.9 / 0911 4.4 / F 1452 1.3 / 2130 4.5	**21** 0306 1.3 / 0942 4.1 / SA 1517 1.7 / 2158 4.0
7 0325 1.1 / 1003 4.3 / SA 1549 1.5 / ○ 2230 4.4	**22** 0351 1.6 / 1027 3.9 / SU 1611 1.9 / ● 2246 3.7
8 0421 1.4 / 1102 4.2 / SU 1656 1.6 / 2332 4.3	**23** 0444 1.9 / 1115 3.8 / M 1723 2.1 / 2340 3.6
9 0525 1.5 / 1205 4.1 / M 1815 1.7	**24** 0552 2.0 / 1212 3.7 / TU 1847 2.1
10 0039 4.2 / 0639 1.6 / TU 1316 4.2 / 1933 1.5	**25** 0051 3.5 / 0711 2.1 / W 1327 3.7 / 1958 1.9
11 0150 4.3 / 0754 1.5 / W 1424 4.4 / 2036 1.3	**26** 0221 3.5 / 0818 1.9 / TH 1439 3.9 / 2053 1.7
12 0255 4.4 / 0853 1.4 / TH 1521 4.6 / 2130 1.0	**27** 0322 3.8 / 0909 1.7 / F 1529 4.1 / 2138 1.3
13 0351 4.5 / 0944 1.2 / F 1611 4.7 / 2219 0.8	**28** 0407 4.0 / 0952 1.4 / SA 1611 4.4 / 2218 1.0
14 0443 4.6 / 1030 1.1 / SA 1659 4.9 / ● 2305 0.7	**29** 0447 4.3 / 1032 1.1 / SU 1652 4.6 / 2258 0.7
15 0531 4.7 / 1114 1.0 / SU 1745 4.9 / 2349 0.6	**30** 0527 4.5 / 1111 0.9 / M 1732 4.8 / ○ 2335 0.5
	31 0606 4.7 / 1148 0.7 / TU 1812 5.0

AUGUST

Time m	Time m
1 0013 0.3 / 0643 4.8 / W 1225 0.6 / 1851 5.0	**16** 0039 0.5 / 0711 4.7 / TH 1246 0.8 / 1923 4.8
2 0050 0.3 / 0721 4.8 / TH 1303 0.6 / 1931 5.0	**17** 0112 0.7 / 0747 4.6 / F 1319 1.0 / 1957 4.6
3 0129 0.4 / 0759 4.7 / F 1343 0.8 / 2012 4.8	**18** 0145 1.0 / 0821 4.4 / SA 1353 1.2 / 2031 4.3
4 0210 0.6 / 0839 4.6 / SA 1427 1.0 / 2059 4.6	**19** 0219 1.3 / 0856 4.2 / SU 1428 1.5 / 2107 4.0
5 0255 1.0 / 0926 4.3 / SU 1517 1.3 / ◑ 2158 4.3	**20** 0255 1.6 / 0934 4.0 / M 1508 1.9 / ● 2153 3.7
6 0348 1.3 / 1024 4.1 / M 1621 1.6 / 2306 4.1	**21** 0336 1.9 / 1021 3.8 / TU 1602 2.1 / 2250 3.5
7 0452 1.7 / 1134 4.0 / TU 1747 1.8	**22** 0436 2.2 / 1116 3.6 / W 1812 2.3 / 2358 3.4
8 0021 3.9 / 0616 1.9 / W 1259 4.0 / 1927 1.7	**23** 0647 2.3 / 1225 3.6 / TH 1940 2.1
9 0143 4.0 / 0745 1.8 / TH 1421 4.1 / 2038 1.4	**24** 0208 3.4 / 0759 2.1 / F 1421 3.8 / 2035 1.7
10 0253 4.2 / 0848 1.6 / F 1519 4.4 / 2129 1.1	**25** 0312 3.7 / 0850 1.8 / SA 1515 4.1 / 2118 1.3
11 0347 4.4 / 0935 1.3 / SA 1606 4.7 / 2212 0.8	**26** 0351 4.1 / 0932 1.4 / SU 1555 4.4 / 2156 0.8
12 0433 4.6 / 1018 1.1 / SU 1650 4.8 / ● 2251 0.6	**27** 0427 4.4 / 1011 1.0 / M 1632 4.8 / 2234 0.5
13 0516 4.7 / 1057 0.9 / M 1731 4.9 / 2329 0.5	**28** 0504 4.7 / 1049 0.6 / TU 1710 5.0 / ○ 2310 0.2
14 0557 4.8 / 1135 0.8 / TU 1810 5.0	**29** 0541 4.9 / 1125 0.4 / W 1749 5.2 / 2347 0.1
15 0005 0.5 / 0634 4.8 / W 1211 0.7 / 1847 4.9	**30** 0618 5.1 / 1202 0.2 / TH 1828 5.3
	31 0024 0.1 / 0653 5.3 / F 1240 0.3 / 1906 5.2

Chart Datum: 0·20 metres above Ordnance Datum (Dublin)

IRELAND – GALWAY

LAT 53°16′N   LONG 9°03′W

TIMES AND HEIGHTS OF HIGH AND LOW WATERS

Dates in amber are **SPRINGS**
Dates in yellow are **NEAPS**

2007

SEPTEMBER

#	Day	Time	m	#	Day	Time	m
1	SA	0102 / 0730 / 1319 / 1946	0.2 / 5.0 / 0.5 / 5.0	16	SU	0106 / 0745 / 1318 / 1955	1.1 / 4.5 / 1.2 / 4.4
2	SU	0142 / 0808 / 1401 / 2031	0.6 / 4.7 / 0.9 / 4.7	17	M	0137 / 0817 / 1350 / 2030	1.4 / 4.3 / 1.5 / 4.1
3	M	0226 / 0851 / 1450 / 2129	1.0 / 4.4 / 1.3 / 4.3	18	TU	0210 / 0853 / 1427 / 2116	1.7 / 4.1 / 1.8 / 3.8
4	TU	0318 / 0948 / 1555 / 2245	1.5 / 4.1 / 1.7 / 3.9	19	W	0249 / 0941 / 1515 / 2218	2.1 / 3.9 / 2.2 / 3.5
5	W	0429 / 1110 / 1736	2.0 / 3.8 / 1.9	20	TH	0343 / 1040 / 1634 / 2328	2.4 / 3.7 / 2.4 / 3.4
6	TH	0013 / 0612 / 1255 / 1935	3.8 / 2.1 / 3.8 / 1.8	21	F	0628 / 1147 / 1910	2.4 / 3.6 / 2.1
7	F	0142 / 0741 / 1416 / 2041	3.9 / 2.0 / 4.1 / 1.4	22	SA	0143 / 0732 / 1334 / 2005	3.5 / 2.2 / 3.8 / 1.7
8	SA	0247 / 0838 / 1509 / 2121	4.2 / 1.7 / 4.4 / 1.1	23	SU	0245 / 0822 / 1445 / 2048	3.9 / 1.8 / 4.2 / 1.3
9	SU	0334 / 0920 / 1552 / 2154	4.4 / 1.4 / 4.7 / 0.8	24	M	0322 / 0904 / 1526 / 2127	4.3 / 1.3 / 4.6 / 0.8
10	M	0415 / 0958 / 1632 / 2228	4.6 / 1.1 / 4.9 / 0.6	25	TU	0357 / 0944 / 1604 / 2204	4.6 / 0.9 / 5.0 / 0.4
11	TU	0453 / 1034 / 1709 / 2302	4.8 / 0.9 / 5.0 / 0.5	26	W	0432 / 1021 / 1642 / 2241	5.0 / 0.6 / 5.3 / 0.2
12	W	0531 / 1109 / 1746 / 2335	4.9 / 0.7 / 5.0 / 0.6	27	TH	0509 / 1059 / 1721 / 2318	5.2 / 0.3 / 5.4 / 0.1
13	TH	0606 / 1143 / 1820	4.9 / 0.7 / 5.0	28	F	0547 / 1137 / 1802 / 2356	5.3 / 0.2 / 5.5 / 0.1
14	F	0006 / 0640 / 1215 / 1853	0.7 / 4.8 / 0.8 / 4.8	29	SA	0625 / 1216 / 1843	5.3 / 0.3 / 5.4
15	SA	0036 / 0713 / 1246 / 1924	0.8 / 4.7 / 1.0 / 4.6	30	SU	0036 / 0703 / 1258 / 1925	0.4 / 5.2 / 0.5 / 5.1

OCTOBER

#	Day	Time	m	#	Day	Time	m
1	M	0118 / 0743 / 1341 / 2013	0.8 / 4.9 / 0.9 / 4.7	16	TU	0103 / 0747 / 1323 / 2005	1.6 / 4.4 / 1.6 / 4.1
2	TU	0203 / 0829 / 1431 / 2112	1.3 / 4.5 / 1.3 / 4.2	17	W	0139 / 0824 / 1403 / 2052	1.9 / 4.2 / 1.8 / 3.9
3	W	0257 / 0927 / 1539 / 2232	1.8 / 4.1 / 1.8 / 3.9	18	TH	0221 / 0912 / 1451 / 2154	2.2 / 4.0 / 2.1 / 3.7
4	TH	0419 / 1058 / 1728	2.2 / 3.9 / 2.0	19	F	0317 / 1012 / 1559 / 2303	2.4 / 3.9 / 2.2 / 3.6
5	F	0004 / 0604 / 1242 / 1925	3.8 / 2.2 / 3.9 / 1.8	20	SA	0551 / 1117 / 1826	2.5 / 3.9 / 2.1
6	SA	0129 / 0723 / 1355 / 2024	4.0 / 2.0 / 4.2 / 1.5	21	SU	0022 / 0655 / 1228 / 1924	3.7 / 2.2 / 4.0 / 1.7
7	SU	0228 / 0816 / 1447 / 2059	4.3 / 1.7 / 4.5 / 1.2	22	M	0150 / 0747 / 1350 / 2012	4.1 / 1.8 / 4.3 / 1.3
8	M	0311 / 0856 / 1529 / 2129	4.5 / 1.4 / 4.7 / 1.0	23	TU	0238 / 0832 / 1446 / 2054	4.4 / 1.4 / 4.7 / 0.9
9	TU	0349 / 0933 / 1607 / 2200	4.7 / 1.2 / 4.9 / 0.8	24	W	0318 / 0913 / 1530 / 2133	4.8 / 1.0 / 5.1 / 0.6
10	W	0426 / 1008 / 1644 / 2232	4.9 / 1.0 / 5.0 / 0.8	25	TH	0357 / 0953 / 1612 / 2212	5.1 / 0.6 / 5.3 / 0.4
11	TH	0501 / 1043 / 1718 / 2303	4.9 / 0.9 / 5.0 / 0.8	26	F	0436 / 1033 / 1655 / 2251	5.4 / 0.4 / 5.5 / 0.3
12	F	0535 / 1115 / 1751 / 2333	4.9 / 0.9 / 4.9 / 0.9	27	SA	0517 / 1114 / 1740 / 2332	5.5 / 0.3 / 5.5 / 0.4
13	SA	0608 / 1145 / 1824	4.9 / 1.0 / 4.8	28	SU	0600 / 1157 / 1825	5.4 / 0.4 / 5.4
14	SU	0001 / 0641 / 1217 / 1855	1.1 / 4.8 / 1.1 / 4.6	29	M	0014 / 0642 / 1242 / 1911	0.6 / 5.3 / 0.6 / 5.1
15	M	0031 / 0713 / 1249 / 1928	1.3 / 4.6 / 1.3 / 4.4	30	TU	0059 / 0727 / 1328 / 2001	1.0 / 5.0 / 0.9 / 4.9
				31	W	0147 / 0816 / 1421 / 2101	1.4 / 4.7 / 1.3 / 4.3

NOVEMBER

#	Day	Time	m	#	Day	Time	m
1	TH	0245 / 0916 / 1526 / 2217	1.9 / 4.3 / 1.7 / 4.0	16	F	0208 / 0851 / 1439 / 2133	2.1 / 4.3 / 1.8 / 4.0
2	F	0403 / 1040 / 1659 / 2340	2.2 / 4.1 / 1.9 / 4.0	17	SA	0304 / 0946 / 1539 / 2236	2.3 / 4.2 / 1.9 / 3.9
3	SA	0534 / 1207 / 1835	2.2 / 4.0 / 1.8	18	SU	0422 / 1047 / 1659 / 2341	2.3 / 4.2 / 1.9 / 4.0
4	SU	0055 / 0645 / 1319 / 1943	4.1 / 2.2 / 4.2 / 1.6	19	M	0602 / 1150 / 1828	2.2 / 4.3 / 1.7
5	M	0155 / 0742 / 1415 / 2025	4.3 / 1.9 / 4.4 / 1.5	20	TU	0047 / 0704 / 1257 / 1928	4.2 / 1.9 / 4.4 / 1.5
6	TU	0240 / 0827 / 1500 / 2059	4.5 / 1.6 / 4.5 / 1.3	21	W	0149 / 0756 / 1403 / 2018	4.5 / 1.5 / 4.7 / 1.2
7	W	0319 / 0906 / 1539 / 2131	4.7 / 1.4 / 4.7 / 1.2	22	TH	0240 / 0843 / 1458 / 2103	4.8 / 1.2 / 5.0 / 0.9
8	TH	0355 / 0942 / 1615 / 2203	4.8 / 1.3 / 4.7 / 1.2	23	F	0326 / 0928 / 1547 / 2146	5.1 / 0.9 / 5.2 / 0.7
9	F	0429 / 1017 / 1650 / 2234	4.9 / 1.2 / 4.8 / 1.2	24	SA	0410 / 1012 / 1635 / 2229	5.3 / 0.7 / 5.3 / 0.7
10	SA	0503 / 1050 / 1724 / 2303	4.9 / 1.2 / 4.7 / 1.3	25	SU	0456 / 1058 / 1723 / 2314	5.4 / 0.5 / 5.3 / 0.7
11	SU	0538 / 1124 / 1758 / 2333	4.9 / 1.3 / 4.7 / 1.4	26	M	0542 / 1144 / 1812	5.4 / 0.5 / 5.2
12	M	0613 / 1159 / 1833	4.8 / 1.3 / 4.6	27	TU	0000 / 0629 / 1232 / 1901	0.9 / 5.3 / 0.7 / 5.0
13	TU	0006 / 0648 / 1230 / 1910	1.5 / 4.7 / 1.4 / 4.4	28	W	0047 / 0717 / 1319 / 1951	1.1 / 5.1 / 0.9 / 4.8
14	W	0042 / 0725 / 1308 / 1950	1.7 / 4.6 / 1.5 / 4.3	29	TH	0136 / 0807 / 1409 / 2046	1.4 / 4.8 / 1.1 / 4.4
15	TH	0122 / 0805 / 1350 / 2036	1.9 / 4.4 / 1.7 / 4.1	30	F	0229 / 0902 / 1504 / 2149	1.7 / 4.5 / 1.4 / 4.2

DECEMBER

#	Day	Time	m	#	Day	Time	m
1	SA	0331 / 1008 / 1611 / 2258	2.0 / 4.3 / 1.7 / 4.1	16	SU	0248 / 0920 / 1515 / 2204	1.8 / 4.5 / 1.5 / 4.2
2	SU	0445 / 1117 / 1727	2.1 / 4.1 / 1.8	17	M	0346 / 1015 / 1612 / 2303	1.9 / 4.4 / 1.6 / 4.2
3	M	0003 / 0554 / 1225 / 1837	4.0 / 2.1 / 4.1 / 1.8	18	TU	0453 / 1115 / 1718	2.0 / 4.4 / 1.6
4	TU	0105 / 0655 / 1328 / 1937	4.1 / 2.0 / 4.1 / 1.8	19	W	0004 / 0608 / 1219 / 1831	4.3 / 1.9 / 4.4 / 1.6
5	W	0159 / 0750 / 1423 / 2024	4.3 / 1.9 / 4.2 / 1.7	20	TH	0109 / 0718 / 1329 / 1942	4.4 / 1.7 / 4.5 / 1.7
6	TH	0245 / 0837 / 1508 / 2102	4.4 / 1.7 / 4.3 / 1.6	21	F	0210 / 0818 / 1434 / 2039	4.6 / 1.4 / 4.7 / 1.5
7	F	0324 / 0918 / 1548 / 2137	4.5 / 1.6 / 4.4 / 1.5	22	SA	0305 / 0911 / 1531 / 2129	4.9 / 1.1 / 4.9 / 1.1
8	SA	0401 / 0956 / 1625 / 2211	4.6 / 1.4 / 4.4 / 1.5	23	SU	0355 / 1001 / 1623 / 2217	5.1 / 0.9 / 5.0 / 1.0
9	SU	0437 / 1033 / 1702 / 2245	4.7 / 1.3 / 4.5 / 1.4	24	M	0444 / 1050 / 1714 / 2304	5.2 / 0.7 / 5.1 / 0.9
10	M	0514 / 1109 / 1739 / 2320	4.7 / 1.3 / 4.5 / 1.4	25	TU	0534 / 1137 / 1804 / 2350	5.2 / 0.6 / 5.1 / 0.9
11	TU	0552 / 1146 / 1818 / 2356	4.8 / 1.2 / 4.5 / 1.5	26	W	0622 / 1223 / 1851	5.2 / 0.6 / 5.0
12	W	0631 / 1223 / 1857	4.8 / 1.2 / 4.5	27	TH	0036 / 0708 / 1307 / 1937	1.0 / 5.1 / 0.7 / 4.8
13	TH	0034 / 0710 / 1301 / 1936	1.5 / 4.7 / 1.2 / 4.4	28	F	0120 / 0753 / 1350 / 2024	1.1 / 4.9 / 0.8 / 4.6
14	F	0115 / 0749 / 1341 / 2019	1.6 / 4.6 / 1.2 / 4.3	29	SA	0253 / 0840 / 1434 / 2114	1.6 / 4.7 / 1.1 / 4.3
15	SA	0159 / 0832 / 1425 / 2108	1.7 / 4.6 / 1.3 / 4.2	30	SU	0253 / 0929 / 1521 / 2208	1.6 / 4.4 / 1.4 / 4.1
				31	M	0347 / 1022 / 1616 / 2304	1.7 / 4.1 / 1.7 / 4.0

Chart Datum: 0·20 metres above Ordnance Datum (Dublin)

TIDES

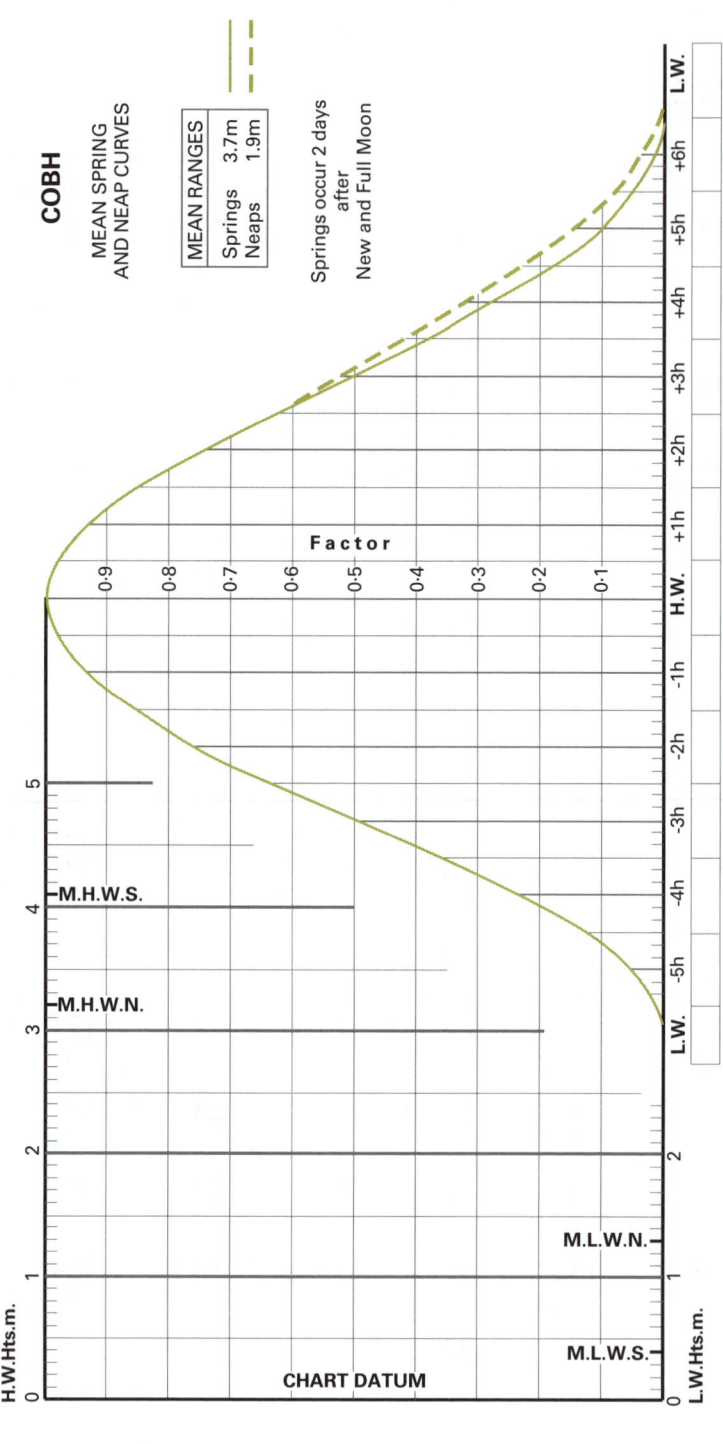

COBH

MEAN SPRING
AND NEAP CURVES

MEAN RANGES

Springs 3.7m
Neaps 1.9m

Springs occur 2 days
after
New and Full Moon

Factor

0·9 0·8 0·7 0·6 0·5 0·4 0·3 0·2 0·1

L.W. +6h +5h +4h +3h +2h +1h H.W. -1h -2h -3h -4h -5h L.W.

H.W.Hts.m.

M.H.W.S.

M.H.W.N.

M.L.W.N.

M.L.W.S.

CHART DATUM

L.W.Hts.m.

IRELAND – COBH

LAT 51°51'N   LONG 8°18'W

TIMES AND HEIGHTS OF HIGH AND LOW WATERS

2007

TIME ZONE (UT)
For Summer Time add ONE hour in **non-shaded areas**

JANUARY

Day	Time m	Time m	Time m	Time m
1 M	0301 3.7	0944 0.9	1535 3.7	2208 0.9
2 TU	0404 3.8	1043 0.8	1631 3.8	2302 0.8
3 W	0459 4.0	1133 0.7	1720 3.9	○ 2349 0.7
4 TH	0545 4.1	1218 0.7	1804 4.0	
5 F	0031 0.6	0627 4.1	1258 0.7	1842 3.9
6 SA	0110 0.7	0706 4.0	1336 0.8	1919 3.9
7 SU	0147 0.7	0743 4.0	1412 0.9	1954 3.8
8 M	0224 0.8	0821 3.8	1449 1.0	2030 3.7
9 TU	0302 1.0	0859 3.7	1526 1.1	2109 3.6
10 W	0341 1.1	0938 3.6	1606 1.2	2150 3.5
11 TH	0424 1.2	1020 3.5	1652 1.4	◑ 2237 3.4
12 F	0515 1.3	1108 3.4	1747 1.5	2332 3.3
13 SA	0616 1.4	1206 3.3	1852 1.5	
14 SU	0038 3.3	0722 1.5	1314 3.3	1957 1.4
15 M	0149 3.4	0827 1.4	1424 3.4	2100 1.3
16 TU	0256 3.5	0929 1.2	1527 3.5	2158 1.1
17 W	0355 3.7	1024 1.0	1621 3.7	2248 0.9
18 TH	0446 3.9	1113 0.8	1707 3.9	2332 0.7
19 F	0530 4.1	1156 0.6	1749 4.0 ●	
20 SA	0013 0.6	0612 4.2	1237 0.5	1828 4.0
21 SU	0054 0.5	0653 4.2	1317 0.5	1909 4.1
22 M	0135 0.4	0735 4.2	1358 0.5	1950 4.0
23 TU	0218 0.5	0818 4.1	1441 0.6	2033 4.0
24 W	0302 0.6	0903 4.0	1525 0.7	2118 3.9
25 TH	0349 0.7	0949 3.9	1612 0.9	◑ 2206 3.7
26 F	0441 0.9	1040 3.7	1705 1.1	2300 3.6
27 SA	0540 1.1	1139 3.5	1809 1.2	
28 SU	0005 3.4	0652 1.2	1252 3.3	1926 1.3
29 M	0126 3.3	0816 1.3	1412 3.3	2050 1.2
30 TU	0250 3.4	0937 1.1	1525 3.5	2203 1.0
31 W	0359 3.7	1039 0.9	1624 3.7	2259 0.8

FEBRUARY

Day	Time m	Time m	Time m	Time m
1 TH	0452 3.9	1128 0.7	1712 3.8	2343 0.6
2 F	0535 4.0	1208 0.6	1752 3.9 ○	
3 SA	0020 0.6	0613 4.1	1243 0.6	1827 4.0
4 SU	0053 0.5	0647 4.1	1315 0.6	1859 3.9
5 M	0123 0.6	0720 4.0	1344 0.7	1929 3.9
6 TU	0153 0.7	0751 3.9	1413 0.9	2000 3.8
7 W	0223 0.8	0822 3.8	1444 0.9	2032 3.8
8 TH	0255 0.9	0855 3.7	1516 1.1	2108 3.7
9 F	0331 1.1	0930 3.6	1554 1.2	2147 3.5
10 SA	0414 1.3	1011 3.5	1640 1.4	◑ 2236 3.4
11 SU	0510 1.4	1104 3.4	1746 1.5	2339 3.2
12 M	0627 1.5	1213 3.1	1909 1.6	
13 TU	0059 3.2	0748 1.5	1340 3.1	2027 1.4
14 W	0226 3.3	0901 1.3	1503 3.3	2133 1.2
15 TH	0334 3.6	1004 1.0	1603 3.6	2228 0.8
16 F	0426 3.8	1054 0.7	1650 3.8	2313 0.6
17 SA	0511 4.1	1138 0.4	1732 4.0	● 2354 0.3
18 SU	0553 4.2	1218 0.3	1811 4.1	
19 M	0034 0.2	0633 4.3	1257 0.2	1849 4.2
20 TU	0114 0.2	0713 4.3	1336 0.2	1929 4.2
21 W	0155 0.2	0754 4.2	1417 0.3	2009 4.1
22 TH	0238 0.3	0836 4.1	1458 0.5	2051 4.0
23 F	0323 0.5	0920 3.9	1542 0.7	2135 3.8
24 SA	0411 0.8	1007 3.6	1632 1.0	◑ 2227 3.5
25 SU	0509 1.1	1105 3.3	1735 1.2	2334 3.2
26 M	0624 1.3	1226 3.1	1900 1.4	
27 TU	0111 3.1	0804 1.3	1401 3.1	2043 1.3
28 W	0245 3.3	0933 1.1	1517 3.3	2159 1.0

MARCH

Day	Time m	Time m	Time m	Time m
1 TH	0350 3.6	1031 0.8	1613 3.6	2250 0.7
2 F	0438 3.8	1115 0.6	1657 3.8	2330 0.5
3 SA	0517 4.0	1151 0.5	1734 3.9 ○	
4 SU	0002 0.5	0551 4.0	1222 0.5	1806 4.0
5 M	0030 0.5	0623 4.0	1248 0.5	1835 4.0
6 TU	0055 0.5	0651 4.0	1313 0.6	1901 3.9
7 W	0120 0.6	0718 3.9	1338 0.7	1929 3.9
8 TH	0147 0.7	0745 3.8	1406 0.8	1958 3.8
9 F	0217 0.8	0815 3.8	1436 0.9	2030 3.7
10 SA	0251 1.0	0848 3.6	1510 1.1	2107 3.6
11 SU	0331 1.2	0927 3.5	1552 1.3	2152 3.4
12 M	0425 1.4	1019 3.2	1654 1.5	◑ 2254 3.2
13 TU	0542 1.5	1130 3.0	1825 1.6	
14 W	0018 3.1	0711 1.5	1301 3.0	1951 1.4
15 TH	0153 3.2	0830 1.2	1434 3.2	2102 1.1
16 F	0306 3.5	0935 0.9	1536 3.5	2159 0.7
17 SA	0359 3.8	1027 0.6	1624 3.8	2247 0.4
18 SU	0444 4.1	1112 0.3	1706 4.0	2330 0.2
19 M	0527 4.2	1153 0.1	1746 4.2 ●	
20 TU	0011 0.0	0607 4.3	1233 0.1	1826 4.3
21 W	0052 0.0	0648 4.3	1313 0.1	1905 4.2
22 TH	0134 0.1	0729 4.2	1354 0.2	1946 4.1
23 F	0217 0.2	0811 4.0	1437 0.4	2028 4.0
24 SA	0302 0.5	0855 3.8	1522 0.6	2113 3.8
25 SU	0352 0.8	0943 3.5	1613 0.9	◑ 2206 3.4
26 M	0451 1.1	1043 3.1	1718 1.2	2317 3.1
27 TU	0608 1.3	1210 2.9	1846 1.3	
28 W	0102 3.0	0751 1.3	1347 3.0	2030 1.2
29 TH	0228 3.2	0913 1.0	1458 3.2	2138 0.9
30 F	0326 3.5	1006 0.8	1549 3.5	2226 0.7
31 SA	0411 3.7	1048 0.6	1631 3.7	2304 0.5

APRIL

Day	Time m	Time m	Time m	Time m
1 SU	0450 3.9	1123 0.5	1707 3.8	2335 0.5
2 M	0524 3.9	1153 0.5	1739 3.9 ○	
3 TU	0001 0.5	0554 3.9	1218 0.5	1806 3.9
4 W	0024 0.5	0621 3.9	1241 0.6	1833 3.9
5 TH	0048 0.6	0646 3.9	1307 0.7	1900 3.9
6 F	0116 0.7	0713 3.8	1335 0.8	1929 3.8
7 SA	0148 0.8	0743 3.7	1407 0.9	2002 3.7
8 SU	0224 1.0	0818 3.6	1443 1.1	2040 3.6
9 M	0307 1.1	0900 3.4	1528 1.2	2127 3.4
10 TU	0402 1.3	0954 3.2	1631 1.4	◑ 2229 3.2
11 W	0515 1.4	1104 3.1	1754 1.4	2349 3.2
12 TH	0639 1.3	1229 3.1	1917 1.4	
13 F	0117 3.3	0755 1.1	1354 3.3	2026 1.0
14 SA	0229 3.5	0859 0.8	1458 3.6	2125 0.7
15 SU	0324 3.8	0953 0.5	1550 3.8	2216 0.4
16 M	0413 4.1	1042 0.3	1636 4.1	2303 0.2
17 TU	0459 4.2	1127 0.1	1720 4.2	● 2348 0.0
18 W	0543 4.3	1210 0.1	1803 4.2	
19 TH	0032 0.0	0626 4.2	1254 0.1	1845 4.2
20 F	0117 0.1	0709 4.1	1337 0.2	1928 4.1
21 SA	0202 0.3	0753 3.9	1423 0.4	2012 3.9
22 SU	0250 0.5	0839 3.7	1511 0.6	2100 3.6
23 M	0342 0.8	0929 3.4	1604 0.9	2155 3.4
24 TU	0441 1.0	1030 3.1	1709 1.1	◑ 2307 3.1
25 W	0554 1.2	1149 3.0	1829 1.2	
26 TH	0036 3.1	0719 1.2	1315 3.0	1953 1.1
27 F	0152 3.2	0831 1.0	1421 3.2	2057 0.9
28 SA	0248 3.4	0924 0.9	1512 3.4	2145 0.8
29 SU	0334 3.6	1008 0.7	1555 3.6	2225 0.7
30 M	0414 3.7	1045 0.6	1632 3.7	2258 0.6

TIDES

Chart Datum: 0·13 metres above Ordnance Datum (Dublin)

TIME ZONE (UT)
For Summer Time add ONE hour in **non-shaded areas**

IRELAND – COBH
LAT 51°51'N   LONG 8°18'W
TIMES AND HEIGHTS OF HIGH AND LOW WATERS

Dates in amber are **SPRINGS**
Dates in yellow are **NEAPS**

2007

MAY

Day	Time m	Time m	Time m	Time m		Day	Time m	Time m	Time m	Time m
1 TU	0450 3.8	1117 0.6	1706 3.8	2327 0.6		16 W	0433 4.1	1104 0.3	1656 4.1	●2329 0.2
2 W	0522 3.8	1145 0.6	1737 3.8	○2353 0.7		17 TH	0522 4.1	1152 0.2	1744 4.1	
3 TH	0551 3.8	1212 0.7	1806 3.8			18 F	0017 0.2	0608 4.1	1239 0.3	1830 4.1
4 F	0021 0.7	0619 3.8	1242 0.7	1836 3.8		19 SA	0104 0.3	0654 4.0	1326 0.3	1915 4.0
5 SA	0054 0.7	0649 3.7	1315 0.8	1909 3.8		20 SU	0151 0.4	0740 3.8	1413 0.5	2002 3.9
6 SU	0130 0.8	0723 3.7	1351 0.9	1946 3.7		21 M	0240 0.6	0827 3.6	1502 0.7	2050 3.7
7 M	0210 0.9	0802 3.6	1433 1.0	2027 3.6		22 TU	0331 0.8	0916 3.4	1554 0.8	2143 3.5
8 TU	0256 1.0	0848 3.5	1522 1.1	2117 3.5		23 W	0426 1.0	1010 3.2	1651 1.0	◑2243 3.3
9 W	0352 1.1	0943 3.3	1621 1.2	2217 3.4		24 TH	0527 1.1	1113 3.1	1756 1.1	2351 3.2
10 TH	0457 1.2	1048 3.3	1731 1.2	◑2327 3.4		25 F	0633 1.1	1221 3.1	1901 1.1	
11 F	0610 1.1	1201 3.3	1844 1.1			26 SA	0059 3.2	0734 1.1	1326 3.2	1959 1.0
12 SA	0042 3.5	0720 1.0	1314 3.4	1951 0.9		27 SU	0156 3.3	0828 1.0	1420 3.3	2050 1.0
13 SU	0150 3.6	0822 0.8	1418 3.6	2051 0.6		28 M	0246 3.4	0915 0.9	1507 3.5	2135 0.9
14 M	0248 3.8	0919 0.6	1514 3.8	2146 0.4		29 TU	0330 3.6	0958 0.8	1551 3.6	2215 0.8
15 TU	0342 4.0	1013 0.4	1606 4.0	2239 0.3		30 W	0412 3.6	1038 0.8	1631 3.7	2252 0.8
						31 TH	0450 3.7	1114 0.8	1709 3.8	2327 0.8

JUNE

Day	Time m	Time m	Time m	Time m		Day	Time m	Time m	Time m	Time m
1 F	0525 3.7	1149 0.8	1745 3.8	○		16 SA	0006 0.4	0556 3.9	1228 0.4	1819 4.0
2 SA	0003 0.7	0559 3.7	1225 0.8	1820 3.8		17 SU	0054 0.4	0643 3.9	1315 0.4	1905 4.0
3 SU	0040 0.8	0634 3.7	1303 0.8	1857 3.8		18 M	0140 0.5	0727 3.8	1400 0.5	1949 3.9
4 M	0119 0.8	0712 3.7	1343 0.8	1937 3.8		19 TU	0225 0.6	0811 3.7	1446 0.6	2034 3.7
5 TU	0202 0.8	0755 3.6	1427 0.8	2021 3.7		20 W	0311 0.8	0855 3.6	1532 0.8	2119 3.6
6 W	0249 0.8	0842 3.6	1515 0.9	2110 3.7		21 TH	0357 0.9	0940 3.4	1618 0.9	2206 3.5
7 TH	0340 0.9	0934 3.5	1608 0.9	2204 3.6		22 F	0446 1.0	1027 3.3	1708 1.0	◑2256 3.3
8 F	0436 1.0	1031 3.5	1707 1.0	◑2304 3.6		23 SA	0538 1.1	1119 3.3	1801 1.1	2352 3.3
9 SA	0538 1.0	1132 3.5	1810 0.9			24 SU	0632 1.2	1216 3.2	1856 1.2	
10 SU	0008 3.6	0643 0.9	1236 3.5	1915 0.9		25 M	0051 3.3	0727 1.2	1317 3.3	1950 1.2
11 M	0113 3.6	0747 0.9	1340 3.6	2019 0.8		26 TU	0150 3.3	0821 1.2	1415 3.3	2044 1.1
12 TU	0215 3.7	0848 0.8	1442 3.7	2120 0.7		27 W	0244 3.4	0913 1.1	1509 3.5	2135 1.0
13 W	0314 3.8	0949 0.6	1542 3.8	2220 0.5		28 TH	0336 3.5	1004 1.0	1600 3.6	2223 0.9
14 TH	0412 3.9	1046 0.6	1639 3.9	2315 0.4		29 F	0423 3.6	1050 0.9	1646 3.7	2307 0.8
15 F	0506 3.9	1139 0.4	1731 4.0	●		30 SA	0506 3.7	1132 0.8	1728 3.8	○2348 0.7

JULY

Day	Time m	Time m	Time m	Time m		Day	Time m	Time m	Time m	Time m
1 SU	0546 3.7	1211 0.7	1808 3.9			16 M	0041 0.5	0629 3.9	1300 0.4	1850 4.0
2 M	0028 0.7	0625 3.8	1251 0.6	1847 3.9		17 TU	0122 0.5	0709 3.8	1340 0.5	1930 3.9
3 TU	0109 0.6	0704 3.8	1331 0.6	1928 3.9		18 W	0201 0.6	0747 3.8	1419 0.6	2008 3.8
4 W	0150 0.6	0746 3.8	1414 0.6	2010 3.9		19 TH	0239 0.7	0824 3.7	1456 0.7	2045 3.7
5 TH	0234 0.7	0830 3.8	1459 0.7	2056 3.9		20 F	0317 0.8	0902 3.6	1533 0.8	2123 3.6
6 F	0320 0.7	0917 3.7	1546 0.7	2144 3.8		21 SA	0355 1.0	0940 3.5	1612 1.0	2202 3.5
7 SA	0409 0.8	1006 3.7	1637 0.8	◑2235 3.7		22 SU	0436 1.1	1021 3.4	1656 1.1	◑2246 3.4
8 SU	0503 0.9	1100 3.6	1734 0.9	2333 3.6		23 M	0525 1.2	1112 3.3	1749 1.2	2339 3.3
9 M	0603 1.0	1200 3.5	1839 1.0			24 TU	0625 1.3	1213 3.2	1853 1.3	
10 TU	0037 3.5	0711 1.0	1307 3.5	1949 1.0		25 W	0045 3.2	0730 1.4	1324 3.2	1959 1.3
11 W	0147 3.5	0822 1.0	1418 3.5	2102 0.9		26 TH	0159 3.2	0835 1.3	1435 3.3	2102 1.2
12 TH	0256 3.6	0932 0.9	1528 3.7	2209 0.8		27 F	0306 3.3	0936 1.1	1536 3.5	2200 1.0
13 F	0400 3.7	1036 0.7	1631 3.8	2307 0.6		28 SA	0402 3.5	1029 0.9	1627 3.7	2249 0.8
14 SA	0457 3.8	1130 0.6	1724 3.9	●2357 0.5		29 SU	0449 3.7	1114 0.7	1711 3.9	2332 0.6
15 SU	0546 3.9	1217 0.5	1809 4.0			30 M	0531 3.8	1154 0.6	1752 4.0	○
						31 TU	0012 0.5	0609 3.9	1233 0.5	1830 4.1

AUGUST

Day	Time m	Time m	Time m	Time m		Day	Time m	Time m	Time m	Time m
1 W	0051 0.5	0648 3.9	1312 0.4	1909 4.1		16 TH	0130 0.6	0718 3.9	1344 0.6	1935 3.9
2 TH	0130 0.4	0727 3.9	1352 0.4	1950 4.1		17 F	0200 0.7	0749 3.8	1414 0.7	2006 3.8
3 F	0211 0.5	0808 3.9	1434 0.5	2032 4.0		18 SA	0230 0.8	0821 3.7	1444 0.8	2038 3.7
4 SA	0254 0.6	0851 3.9	1519 0.6	2116 3.9		19 SU	0302 1.0	0856 3.6	1518 1.0	2113 3.6
5 SU	0339 0.7	0937 3.8	1606 0.7	◑2204 3.7		20 M	0338 1.1	0937 3.4	1557 1.2	◑2152 3.4
6 M	0429 0.9	1027 3.6	1700 0.9	2259 3.5		21 TU	0422 1.3	1020 3.3	1648 1.4	2240 3.3
7 TU	0528 1.1	1128 3.4	1807 1.1			22 W	0523 1.5	1119 3.2	1758 1.5	2346 3.1
8 W	0007 3.3	0641 1.2	1244 3.3	1927 1.2		23 TH	0644 1.5	1237 3.1	1919 1.5	
9 TH	0129 3.3	0806 1.2	1410 3.4	2055 1.1		24 F	0113 3.1	0802 1.4	1406 3.2	2032 1.3
10 F	0249 3.4	0928 1.0	1527 3.5	2208 0.9		25 SA	0241 3.2	0909 1.2	1513 3.4	2135 1.0
11 SA	0355 3.6	1033 0.8	1626 3.8	2302 0.7		26 SU	0340 3.5	1004 0.9	1604 3.7	2226 0.8
12 SU	0448 3.7	1122 0.5	1713 3.9	●2346 0.5		27 M	0427 3.7	1050 0.6	1648 3.9	2309 0.5
13 M	0532 3.9	1204 0.4	1754 4.0			28 TU	0508 3.9	1129 0.4	1728 4.1	○2348 0.4
14 TU	0024 0.5	0610 3.9	1240 0.4	1829 4.0		29 W	0546 4.0	1210 0.2	1806 4.2	
15 W	0058 0.5	0645 3.9	1313 0.5	1903 4.0		30 TH	0026 0.3	0623 4.1	1247 0.2	1844 4.2
						31 F	0105 0.3	0702 4.1	1327 0.2	1924 4.2

a

Chart Datum: 0·13 metres above Ordnance Datum (Dublin)

IRELAND – COBH

LAT 51°51'N   LONG 8°18'W

TIMES AND HEIGHTS OF HIGH AND LOW WATERS

Dates in amber are **SPRINGS**
Dates in yellow are **NEAPS**

2007

SEPTEMBER

Time	m		Time	m
1 SA 0145 0742 1409 2005	0.3 4.0 0.3 4.1	**16** SU 0148 0743 1401 1957	0.8 3.8 0.9 3.8
2 SU 0228 0824 1453 2049	0.5 3.9 0.5 3.9	**17** M 0218 0816 1434 2029	1.0 3.7 1.0 3.7
3 M 0313 0910 1541 2136	0.7 3.8 0.7 3.7	**18** TU 0253 0853 1513 2108	1.1 3.5 1.2 3.5
4 TU 0403 1001 1636 ☽2232	0.9 3.5 1.0 3.4	**19** W 0336 0938 1603 ☽2157	1.3 3.4 1.4 3.3
5 W 0504 1105 1746 2347	1.1 3.3 1.2 3.1	**20** TH 0436 1037 1715 2303	1.5 3.2 1.6 3.1
6 TH 0625 1236 1920	1.3 3.2 1.3	**21** F 0602 1157 1843	1.6 3.1 1.6
7 F 0124 0806 1414 2058	3.1 1.2 3.3 1.1	**22** SA 0031 0727 1332 2001	3.0 1.5 3.2 1.4
8 SA 0246 0928 1523 2202	3.3 1.0 3.5 0.9	**23** SU 0207 0836 1443 2104	3.2 1.2 3.5 1.0
9 SU 0345 1024 1614 2249	3.6 0.7 3.8 0.6	**24** M 0309 0932 1534 2156	3.5 0.8 3.8 0.7
10 M 0432 1108 1655 2328	3.8 0.5 4.0 0.5	**25** TU 0356 1019 1618 2240	3.8 0.5 4.0 0.5
11 TU 0512 1144 1732 ●	3.9 0.4 4.1	**26** W 0438 1101 1659 ○2321	4.0 0.3 4.2 0.3
12 W 0001 0547 1215 1804	0.5 4.0 0.4 4.1	**27** TH 0518 1142 1739	4.2 0.2 4.3
13 TH 0030 0618 1241 1833	0.5 4.0 0.5 4.0	**28** F 0001 0557 1223 1819	0.2 4.2 0.1 4.3
14 F 0055 0646 1306 1900	0.6 3.9 0.6 3.9	**29** SA 0042 0637 1305 1900	0.2 4.2 0.2 4.2
15 SA 0120 0714 1332 1928	0.7 3.8 0.7 3.9	**30** SU 0123 0719 1349 1942	0.3 4.1 0.3 4.1

OCTOBER

Time	m		Time	m
1 M 0207 0803 1435 2027	0.5 4.0 0.5 3.9	**16** TU 0146 0746 1404 1957	1.0 3.7 1.1 3.7
2 TU 0255 0851 1525 2117	0.7 3.8 0.8 3.6	**17** W 0223 0825 1446 2038	1.2 3.6 1.3 3.5
3 W 0348 0946 1624 ☽2216	1.0 3.5 1.1 3.3	**18** TH 0309 0911 1538 2129	1.3 3.5 1.4 3.4
4 TH 0454 1057 1738 2338	1.2 3.2 1.3 3.1	**19** F 0410 1011 1647 ☽2235	1.5 3.3 1.5 3.2
5 F 0620 1235 1919	1.3 3.2 1.3	**20** SA 0529 1125 1809 2356	1.5 3.2 1.5 3.2
6 SA 0116 0801 1403 2043	3.1 1.2 3.3 1.1	**21** SU 0650 1250 1926	1.4 3.3 1.3
7 SU 0230 0911 1503 2139	3.3 0.9 3.6 0.9	**22** M 0121 0759 1402 2029	3.3 1.2 3.6 1.0
8 M 0324 1001 1549 2223	3.6 0.7 3.8 0.7	**23** TU 0227 0856 1456 2122	3.6 0.9 3.9 0.7
9 TU 0408 1042 1629 2300	3.8 0.6 4.0 0.6	**24** W 0319 0947 1544 2210	3.9 0.6 4.1 0.5
10 W 0446 1116 1704 2331	3.9 0.5 4.0 0.6	**25** TH 0406 1034 1630 2255	4.1 0.4 4.3 0.3
11 TH 0519 1145 1735 ●2358	4.0 0.6 4.0 0.6	**26** F 0450 1119 1714 ○2339	4.2 0.3 4.3 0.3
12 F 0549 1204 1803	4.0 0.2 4.0	**27** SA 0534 1204 1758	4.3 0.2 4.3
13 SA 0021 0616 1233 1828	0.7 3.9 0.7 3.9	**28** SU 0023 0618 1250 1842	0.3 4.3 0.3 4.2
14 SU 0046 0643 1259 1854	0.8 3.9 0.8 3.9	**29** M 0108 0703 1336 1927	0.4 4.2 0.4 4.1
15 M 0114 0713 1330 1924	1.0 3.8 1.0 3.8	**30** TU 0155 0750 1425 2014	0.5 4.0 0.6 3.8
		31 W 0246 0841 1518 2105	0.7 3.8 0.9 3.6

NOVEMBER

Time	m		Time	m
1 TH 0342 0939 1618 ☽2205	1.0 3.5 1.1 3.3	**16** F 0257 0858 1525 2114	1.2 3.6 1.3 3.5
2 F 0447 1048 1729 2320	1.2 3.3 1.3 3.1	**17** SA 0354 0954 1626 ☽2215	1.3 3.5 1.4 3.4
3 SA 0607 1212 1854	1.2 3.3 1.3	**18** SU 0500 1059 1735 2324	1.4 3.5 1.4 3.4
4 SU 0045 0730 1329 2006	3.2 1.2 3.4 1.2	**19** M 0612 1209 1846	1.3 3.5 1.3
5 M 0156 0834 1427 2101	3.3 1.0 3.6 1.0	**20** TU 0036 0719 1317 1951	3.5 1.1 3.7 1.1
6 TU 0249 0924 1513 2146	3.5 0.9 3.7 0.9	**21** W 0143 0821 1417 2049	3.7 0.9 3.9 0.9
7 W 0333 1006 1554 2224	3.7 0.8 3.8 0.8	**22** TH 0241 0917 1512 2143	3.9 0.7 4.0 0.7
8 TH 0413 1042 1631 2258	3.9 0.7 3.9 0.8	**23** F 0336 1011 1604 2234	4.1 0.6 4.2 0.5
9 F 0448 1113 1705 ●2327	3.9 0.8 3.9 0.8	**24** SA 0428 1103 1654 ○2324	4.2 0.5 4.2 0.4
10 SA 0521 1140 1735 2354	4.0 0.8 3.9 0.8	**25** SU 0518 1153 1743	4.3 0.4 4.2
11 SU 0551 1207 1803	4.0 0.9 3.9	**26** M 0012 0606 1241 1830	0.4 4.3 0.4 4.2
12 M 0022 0621 1238 1831	0.9 3.9 0.9 3.9	**27** TU 0059 0654 1329 1917	0.5 4.2 0.5 4.0
13 TU 0053 0654 1312 1903	0.9 3.9 1.0 3.8	**28** W 0147 0743 1418 2004	0.6 4.1 0.7 3.8
14 W 0129 0729 1350 1940	1.0 3.8 1.1 3.7	**29** TH 0237 0833 1509 2053	0.7 3.9 0.9 3.6
15 TH 0209 0810 1434 2022	1.1 3.7 1.2 3.6	**30** F 0330 0926 1603 2146	0.9 3.7 1.1 3.5

DECEMBER

Time	m		Time	m
1 SA 0428 1024 1703 ☽2245	1.1 3.5 1.2 3.3	**16** SU 0335 0936 1602 2153	1.1 3.8 1.2 3.6
2 SU 0531 1127 1808 2351	1.2 3.4 1.3 3.3	**17** M 0430 1030 1658 ☽2251	1.2 3.7 1.2 3.6
3 M 0638 1233 1912	1.2 3.4 1.3	**18** TU 0531 1130 1802 2354	1.2 3.7 1.2 3.6
4 TU 0059 0739 1334 2008	3.3 1.2 3.4 1.2	**19** W 0637 1234 1909	1.2 3.7 1.2
5 W 0158 0833 1426 2058	3.4 1.1 3.5 1.1	**20** TH 0100 0744 1339 2015	3.6 1.1 3.7 1.1
6 TH 0249 0921 1513 2143	3.6 1.1 3.7 1.1	**21** F 0207 0851 1443 2119	3.7 1.0 3.8 0.9
7 F 0335 1004 1557 2224	3.7 1.0 3.8 1.0	**22** SA 0312 0954 1545 2219	3.9 0.8 3.9 0.8
8 SA 0417 1042 1637 2300	3.8 1.0 3.8 0.9	**23** SU 0413 1053 1642 2314	4.0 0.7 4.0 0.6
9 SU 0457 1118 1713 ●2334	3.9 0.9 3.9 0.9	**24** M 0510 1145 1734 ○	4.1 0.7 4.1
10 M 0534 1152 1747	4.0 0.9 3.9	**25** TU 0004 0600 1234 1821	0.5 4.2 0.5 4.1
11 TU 0008 0608 1227 1819	0.9 4.0 0.9 3.9	**26** W 0051 0647 1321 1906	0.5 4.2 0.5 4.0
12 W 0043 0644 1303 1853	0.9 4.0 1.0 3.9	**27** TH 0137 0732 1406 1950	0.5 4.1 0.6 3.9
13 TH 0120 0721 1342 1931	0.9 3.9 1.0 3.8	**28** F 0222 0817 1451 2033	0.6 4.0 0.8 3.8
14 F 0201 0801 1425 2013	1.0 3.9 1.1 3.8	**29** SA 0307 0901 1535 2116	0.8 3.8 0.9 3.6
15 SA 0246 0846 1511 2100	1.0 3.8 1.1 3.7	**30** SU 0354 0946 1621 2200	0.9 3.7 1.1 3.5
		31 M 0442 1034 1711 ☽2249	1.1 3.5 1.2 3.4

TIDES

Chart Datum: 0·13 metres above Ordnance Datum (Dublin)

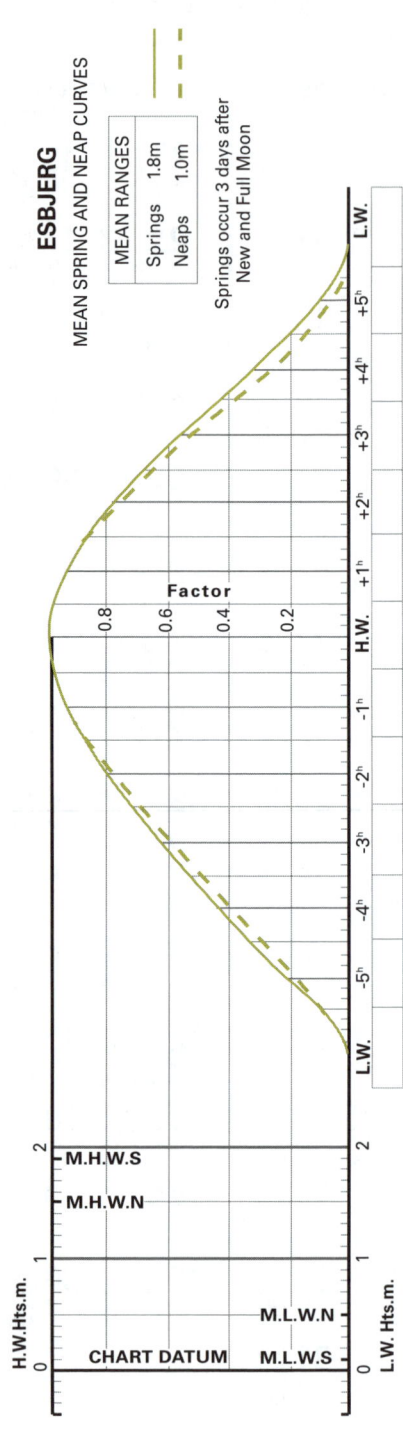

ESBJERG

MEAN SPRING AND NEAP CURVES

MEAN RANGES

Springs 1.8m
Neaps   1.0m

Springs occur 3 days after
New and Full Moon

TIME ZONE -0100
(Danish Standard Time)
Subtract 1 hour for UT
For Danish Summer Time add
ONE hour in **non-shaded areas**

DENMARK – ESBJERG

LAT 55°28'N   LONG 8°26'E

TIMES AND HEIGHTS OF HIGH AND LOW WATERS

Dates in amber are **SPRINGS**
Dates in yellow are **NEAPS**

2007

JANUARY

Time	m		Time	m
1 0013	1.5		**16** 0006	1.5
0604	0.2		0604	0.3
M 1244	1.7		TU 1235	1.5
1842	0.2		1835	0.3
2 0112	1.6		**17** 0107	1.5
0709	0.1		0709	0.3
TU 1346	1.7		W 1336	1.5
1937	0.2		1930	0.2
3 0207	1.7		**18** 0201	1.6
0806	0.1		0802	0.2
W 1442	1.6		TH 1431	1.5
○ 2027	0.2		2017	0.2
4 0257	1.7		**19** 0249	1.6
0858	0.0		0848	0.1
TH 1532	1.6		F 1520	1.4
2112	0.2		● 2100	0.1
5 0342	1.7		**20** 0333	1.7
0946	0.0		0933	0.0
F 1615	1.5		SA 1604	1.6
2154	0.2		2142	0.1
6 0423	1.8		**21** 0413	1.8
1030	0.1		1015	-0.1
SA 1654	1.5		SU 1646	1.6
2234	0.2		2224	0.0
7 0500	1.7		**22** 0453	1.8
1111	0.1		1057	-0.1
SU 1730	1.4		M 1726	1.5
2312	0.2		2306	0.0
8 0535	1.7		**23** 0533	1.8
1149	0.1		1140	-0.2
M 1803	1.4		TU 1806	1.5
2348	0.2		2349	-0.1
9 0609	1.7		**24** 0615	1.8
1226	0.2		1224	-0.1
TU 1836	1.4		W 1848	1.5
10 0026	0.2		**25** 0034	-0.1
0645	1.7		0701	1.8
W 1304	0.2		TH 1311	-0.1
1912	1.4		◑ 1934	1.5
11 0106	0.2		**26** 0123	0.0
0725	1.7		0753	1.7
TH 1344	0.3		F 1402	0.0
◑ 1957	1.4		2026	1.4
12 0151	0.2		**27** 0216	0.0
0812	1.6		0852	1.7
F 1429	0.3		SA 1457	0.1
2048	1.4		2127	1.4
13 0242	0.3		**28** 0318	0.1
0909	1.6		1003	1.6
SA 1521	0.3		SU 1603	0.2
2150	1.4		2237	1.4
14 0340	0.3		**29** 0432	0.2
1014	1.5		1120	1.5
SU 1622	0.3		M 1716	0.3
2259	1.4		2349	1.4
15 0450	0.4		**30** 0551	0.1
1126	1.5		1233	1.5
M 1730	0.3		TU 1826	0.4
			31 0055	1.5
			0702	0.1
			W 1337	1.5
			1924	0.2

FEBRUARY

Time	m		Time	m
1 0154	1.6		**16** 0131	1.5
0800	0.0		0740	0.0
TH 1433	1.5		F 1409	1.4
2015	0.1		1954	0.1
2 0246	1.7		**17** 0224	1.6
0850	-0.1		0829	-0.1
F 1521	1.5		SA 1500	1.5
○ 2100	0.1		● 2040	0.0
3 0331	1.7		**18** 0311	1.7
0934	-0.1		0912	-0.2
SA 1602	1.4		SU 1545	1.5
2139	0.1		2122	-0.1
4 0410	1.7		**19** 0354	1.8
1013	0.0		0954	-0.3
SU 1636	1.4		M 1625	1.5
2215	0.0		2204	-0.2
5 0444	1.7		**20** 0434	1.8
1048	0.0		1036	-0.3
M 1706	1.4		TU 1704	1.5
2249	0.0		2245	-0.2
6 0513	1.7		**21** 0515	1.8
1121	0.0		1117	-0.3
TU 1732	1.4		W 1742	1.5
2321	0.0		2327	-0.3
7 0541	1.6		**22** 0557	1.8
1151	0.1		1159	-0.2
W 1758	1.4		TH 1821	1.4
2354	0.0			
8 0609	1.6		**23** 0012	-0.2
1222	0.1		0641	1.7
TH 1827	1.4		F 1243	-0.1
			1903	1.4
9 0030	0.0		**24** 0059	-0.2
0643	1.6		0731	1.6
F 1257	0.1		SA 1331	0.0
1904	1.4		◑ 1952	1.4
10 0109	0.1		**25** 0151	-0.1
0724	1.5		0831	1.5
SA 1336	0.1		SU 1425	0.1
◑ 1950	1.4		2053	1.3
11 0154	0.1		**26** 0254	0.0
0815	1.5		0945	1.4
SU 1423	0.2		M 1533	0.2
2044	1.4		2209	1.3
12 0248	0.2		**27** 0417	0.1
0916	1.4		1107	1.3
M 1520	0.3		TU 1657	0.3
2151	1.3		2329	1.4
13 0355	0.3		**28** 0546	0.1
1035	1.3		1221	1.3
TU 1633	0.3		W 1812	0.2
2313	1.4			
14 0521	0.3			
1200	1.3			
W 1756	0.3			
15 0030	1.4			
0642	0.2			
TH 1311	1.4			
1903	0.2			

MARCH

Time	m		Time	m
1 0039	1.4		**16** 0612	0.0
0654	0.0		1244	1.3
TH 1324	1.4		F 1832	0.1
1910	0.1			
2 0138	1.5		**17** 0059	1.5
0748	-0.1		0713	-0.1
F 1418	1.4		SA 1342	1.4
1958	0.0		1927	0.0
3 0229	1.6		**18** 0155	1.6
0833	-0.2		0802	-0.2
SA 1502	1.4		SU 1433	1.4
2041	0.0		2014	-0.2
4 0313	1.6		**19** 0244	1.7
0914	-0.2		0847	-0.3
SU 1539	1.4		M 1518	1.5
○ 2118	-0.1		● 2058	-0.3
5 0350	1.6		**20** 0329	1.7
0949	-0.2		0929	-0.4
M 1611	1.4		TU 1559	1.5
2153	-0.1		2140	-0.3
6 0421	1.6		**21** 0412	1.7
1020	-0.1		1010	-0.4
TU 1638	1.4		W 1637	1.5
2224	-0.1		2222	-0.4
7 0448	1.6		**22** 0454	1.7
1048	-0.1		1051	-0.3
W 1701	1.4		TH 1715	1.5
2253	-0.1		2305	-0.4
8 0512	1.5		**23** 0536	1.6
1115	0.0		1133	-0.2
TH 1724	1.4		F 1754	1.4
2324	-0.1		2349	-0.3
9 0537	1.5		**24** 0621	1.5
1145	0.0		1216	-0.1
F 1750	1.4		SA 1834	1.4
2357	-0.1			
10 0608	1.5		**25** 0037	-0.2
1218	0.0		0712	1.4
SA 1824	1.4		SU 1303	0.0
			◑ 1923	1.3
11 0036	-0.1		**26** 0131	-0.1
0648	1.4		0813	1.3
SU 1257	0.0		M 1357	0.1
1906	1.4		2025	1.3
12 0119	0.0		**27** 0238	0.0
0736	1.4		0930	1.2
M 1342	0.1		TU 1506	0.2
◑ 1957	1.3		2145	1.3
13 0212	0.1		**28** 0409	0.0
0837	1.3		1051	1.2
TU 1438	0.2		W 1636	0.2
2100	1.3		2306	1.3
14 0318	0.1		**29** 0533	0.0
0957	1.2		1201	1.2
W 1550	0.2		TH 1750	0.0
2223	1.3			
15 0448	0.1		**30** 0015	1.4
1130	1.2		0634	-0.1
TH 1719	0.2		F 1300	1.3
2351	1.4		1846	0.0
			31 0113	1.5
			0725	-0.2
			SA 1351	1.3
			1934	-0.1

APRIL

Time	m		Time	m
1 0203	1.6		**16** 0123	1.5
0809	-0.2		0732	-0.3
SU 1434	1.4		M 1403	1.4
2016	-0.2		1945	-0.2
2 0247	1.6		**17** 0215	1.6
0847	-0.2		0818	-0.4
M 1511	1.4		TU 1448	1.5
○ 2054	-0.2		● 2031	-0.3
3 0324	1.5		**18** 0303	1.6
0921	-0.2		0902	-0.4
TU 1543	1.4		W 1530	1.5
2127	-0.2		2116	-0.4
4 0354	1.5		**19** 0349	1.6
0949	-0.2		0944	-0.4
W 1610	1.4		TH 1610	1.5
2157	-0.2		2200	-0.4
5 0421	1.4		**20** 0433	1.6
1015	-0.1		1026	-0.3
TH 1633	1.4		F 1649	1.4
2226	-0.2		2245	-0.3
6 0445	1.4		**21** 0518	1.5
1042	-0.1		1108	-0.2
F 1656	1.4		SA 1728	1.4
2257	-0.2		2331	-0.3
7 0511	1.4		**22** 0603	1.4
1112	-0.1		1151	-0.1
SA 1721	1.4		SU 1811	1.4
2331	-0.2			
8 0542	1.4		**23** 0021	-0.2
1147	-0.1		0655	1.3
SU 1754	1.4		M 1238	0.0
			1900	1.4
9 0010	-0.2		**24** 0116	-0.1
0621	1.3		0757	1.1
M 1227	0.0		TU 1332	0.1
1835	1.4		◑ 2003	1.3
10 0056	-0.1		**25** 0225	0.0
0711	1.3		0909	1.1
TU 1314	0.0		W 1439	0.2
◑ 1926	1.4		2118	1.3
11 0150	0.0		**26** 0349	0.0
0812	1.2		1023	1.1
W 1410	0.1		TH 1602	0.2
2027	1.3		2235	1.3
12 0257	0.0		**27** 0505	0.0
0932	1.1		1128	1.1
TH 1521	0.2		F 1715	0.1
2145	1.3		2341	1.4
13 0421	0.0		**28** 0604	-0.1
1100	1.2		1225	1.2
F 1644	0.1		SA 1813	0.0
2312	1.4			
14 0539	-0.1		**29** 0039	1.5
1212	1.2		0654	-0.2
SA 1757	0.0		SU 1315	1.3
			1903	-0.1
15 0024	1.4		**30** 0130	1.5
0641	-0.2		0737	-0.2
SU 1312	1.3		M 1359	1.4
1854	-0.1		1947	-0.2

Chart Datum: 0·69 metres below Dansk Normal Null

TIDES

TIDES

DENMARK – ESBJERG

LAT 55°28′N   LONG 8°26′E

TIMES AND HEIGHTS OF HIGH AND LOW WATERS

TIME ZONE -0100
(Danish Standard Time)
Subtract 1 hour for UT
For Danish Summer Time add
ONE hour in **non-shaded areas**

Dates in amber are **SPRINGS**
Dates in yellow are **NEAPS**

2007

MAY

Day	Time m	Day	Time m
1 TU	0214 1.5 / 0815 -0.2 / 1439 1.4 / 2026 -0.2	**16** W ●	0149 1.6 / 0750 -0.3 / 1420 1.4 / 2007 -0.3
2 W ○	0253 1.5 / 0849 -0.2 / 1513 1.4 / 2100 -0.2	**17** TH	0241 1.5 / 0836 -0.3 / 1505 1.4 / 2056 -0.4
3 TH	0327 1.4 / 0918 -0.2 / 1544 1.4 / 2132 -0.2	**18** F	0330 1.5 / 0921 -0.3 / 1548 1.5 / 2143 -0.4
4 F	0357 1.4 / 0946 -0.1 / 1610 1.4 / 2203 -0.2	**19** SA	0418 1.4 / 1004 -0.2 / 1630 1.5 / 2230 -0.3
5 SA	0425 1.3 / 1015 -0.1 / 1636 1.4 / 2236 -0.2	**20** SU	0503 1.3 / 1048 -0.1 / 1711 1.4 / 2318 -0.3
6 SU	0454 1.3 / 1048 -0.1 / 1703 1.4 / 2312 -0.2	**21** M	0551 1.3 / 1132 0.0 / 1755 1.4
7 M	0527 1.3 / 1125 -0.1 / 1736 1.4 / 2354 -0.2	**22** TU	0009 -0.2 / 0639 1.2 / 1218 0.0 / 1843 1.4
8 TU	0608 1.2 / 1208 -0.1 / 1817 1.4	**23** W ◑	0103 -0.1 / 0734 1.1 / 1309 0.1 / 1939 1.4
9 W	0042 -0.2 / 0658 1.2 / 1256 0.0 / 1906 1.4	**24** TH	0203 0.0 / 0835 1.1 / 1408 0.1 / 2043 1.4
10 TH ◑	0136 -0.1 / 0758 1.2 / 1352 0.0 / 2006 1.4	**25** F	0312 0.0 / 0939 1.1 / 1515 0.1 / 2151 1.4
11 F	0240 -0.1 / 0910 1.1 / 1457 0.1 / 2118 1.4	**26** SA	0420 0.0 / 1041 1.1 / 1626 0.1 / 2256 1.4
12 SA	0353 -0.1 / 1027 1.2 / 1610 0.1 / 2237 1.4	**27** SU	0521 0.0 / 1139 1.2 / 1730 0.1 / 2355 1.4
13 SU	0504 -0.2 / 1137 1.2 / 1720 0.0 / 2349 1.5	**28** M	0613 -0.1 / 1231 1.3 / 1824 0.0
14 M	0606 -0.2 / 1237 1.3 / 1821 -0.1	**29** TU	0048 1.4 / 0700 -0.1 / 1320 1.3 / 1913 0.0
15 TU	0052 1.5 / 0700 -0.3 / 1331 1.4 / 1916 -0.2	**30** W	0137 1.4 / 0741 -0.1 / 1404 1.4 / 1957 -0.1
		31 TH	0221 1.4 / 0817 -0.1 / 1444 1.4 / 2035 -0.1

JUNE

Day	Time m	Day	Time m
1 F ○	0301 1.4 / 0851 -0.1 / 1520 1.4 / 2111 -0.1	**16** SA ○	0318 1.4 / 0903 -0.1 / 1533 1.5 / 2133 -0.3
2 SA	0337 1.3 / 0923 -0.1 / 1552 1.4 / 2146 -0.1	**17** SU	0408 1.4 / 0948 -0.1 / 1617 1.5 / 2221 -0.2
3 SU	0412 1.3 / 0956 -0.1 / 1622 1.4 / 2222 -0.1	**18** M	0454 1.3 / 1032 0.0 / 1700 1.5 / 2309 -0.2
4 M	0446 1.3 / 1032 -0.1 / 1653 1.4 / 2302 -0.2	**19** TU	0537 1.2 / 1115 0.0 / 1742 1.5 / 2355 -0.1
5 TU	0523 1.3 / 1112 -0.1 / 1728 1.5 / 2345 -0.2	**20** W	0619 1.2 / 1158 0.0 / 1824 1.5
6 W	0603 1.3 / 1155 -0.1 / 1809 1.5	**21** TH	0042 -0.1 / 0703 1.2 / 1243 0.0 / 1910 1.5
7 TH	0032 -0.2 / 0651 1.2 / 1242 -0.1 / 1856 1.5	**22** F ◑	0130 0.0 / 0750 1.1 / 1331 0.1 / 2000 1.5
8 F	0124 -0.2 / 0745 1.2 / 1335 0.0 / 1951 1.5	**23** SA	0221 0.1 / 0842 1.2 / 1424 0.1 / 2057 1.4
9 SA	0220 -0.2 / 0845 1.2 / 1433 0.0 / 2055 1.5	**24** SU	0316 0.1 / 0939 1.2 / 1523 0.1 / 2157 1.4
10 SU	0322 -0.1 / 0952 1.2 / 1537 0.0 / 2206 1.5	**25** M	0416 0.1 / 1040 1.2 / 1628 0.2 / 2300 1.4
11 M	0427 -0.1 / 1059 1.2 / 1645 0.0 / 2318 1.5	**26** TU	0517 0.1 / 1139 1.3 / 1735 0.1
12 TU	0531 -0.1 / 1203 1.3 / 1751 0.0	**27** W	0001 1.4 / 0613 0.1 / 1236 1.3 / 1836 0.1
13 W	0026 1.5 / 0631 -0.1 / 1302 1.3 / 1852 -0.2	**28** TH	0057 1.4 / 0703 0.1 / 1327 1.4 / 1927 0.1
14 TH	0128 1.5 / 0726 -0.1 / 1356 1.4 / 1949 -0.2	**29** F	0150 1.4 / 0747 0.1 / 1415 1.4 / 2013 0.0
15 F ●	0225 1.5 / 0816 -0.1 / 1446 1.5 / 2042 -0.2	**30** SA ●	0237 1.4 / 0827 0.0 / 1457 1.5 / 2054 0.0

JULY

Day	Time m	Day	Time m
1 SU	0321 1.4 / 0903 0.0 / 1535 1.5 / 2133 -0.1	**16** M	0359 1.4 / 0936 0.0 / 1608 1.6 / 2212 -0.2
2 M	0400 1.4 / 0941 0.0 / 1611 1.5 / 2211 -0.1	**17** TU	0441 1.4 / 1018 0.0 / 1648 1.6 / 2254 -0.1
3 TU	0439 1.4 / 1019 0.0 / 1645 1.6 / 2251 -0.2	**18** W	0518 1.3 / 1057 0.0 / 1725 1.6 / 2333 -0.1
4 W	0517 1.4 / 1100 -0.1 / 1721 1.6 / 2333 -0.2	**19** TH	0552 1.3 / 1135 0.0 / 1800 1.6
5 TH	0556 1.4 / 1142 -0.1 / 1801 1.6	**20** F	0012 0.0 / 0626 1.3 / 1213 0.0 / 1836 1.6
6 F	0018 -0.2 / 0638 1.3 / 1227 -0.1 / 1845 1.7	**21** SA	0049 0.1 / 0701 1.3 / 1253 0.1 / 1915 1.6
7 SA	0104 -0.2 / 0724 1.3 / 1315 -0.1 / 1935 1.6	**22** SU ◑	0128 0.1 / 0741 1.3 / 1335 0.1 / 1959 1.5
8 SU	0155 -0.1 / 0816 1.3 / 1408 -0.1 / 2033 1.6	**23** M	0210 0.2 / 0829 1.3 / 1423 0.2 / 2051 1.4
9 M	0251 -0.1 / 0915 1.3 / 1506 0.0 / 2139 1.5	**24** TU	0259 0.2 / 0927 1.3 / 1519 0.2 / 2154 1.4
10 TU	0352 0.0 / 1022 1.3 / 1613 0.0 / 2253 1.5	**25** W	0358 0.3 / 1035 1.3 / 1629 0.3 / 2306 1.4
11 W	0459 0.1 / 1132 1.3 / 1726 0.0	**26** TH	0509 0.3 / 1145 1.4 / 1750 0.3
12 TH	0008 1.5 / 0606 0.1 / 1239 1.4 / 1837 0.0	**27** F	0017 1.4 / 0620 0.3 / 1248 1.4 / 1857 0.2
13 F	0116 1.4 / 0708 0.1 / 1339 1.5 / 1940 -0.1	**28** SA	0119 1.4 / 0716 0.2 / 1344 1.5 / 1951 0.1
14 SA ●	0218 1.4 / 0803 0.1 / 1434 1.5 / 2036 -0.1	**29** SU	0214 1.4 / 0803 0.1 / 1432 1.6 / 2035 0.0
15 SU	0312 1.4 / 0851 0.0 / 1524 1.6 / 2126 -0.2	**30** M ○	0302 1.5 / 0845 0.1 / 1515 1.6 / 2116 -0.1
		31 TU	0345 1.5 / 0924 0.0 / 1554 1.7 / 2155 -0.1

AUGUST

Day	Time m	Day	Time m
1 W	0424 1.5 / 1003 0.0 / 1631 1.7 / 2234 -0.2	**16** TH	0453 1.5 / 1035 0.0 / 1703 1.7 / 2306 0.0
2 TH	0502 1.5 / 1043 -0.1 / 1709 1.8 / 2315 -0.2	**17** F	0521 1.5 / 1109 0.0 / 1733 1.7 / 2337 0.1
3 F	0539 1.5 / 1124 -0.1 / 1748 1.8 / 2357 -0.2	**18** SA	0548 1.5 / 1142 0.0 / 1801 1.7
4 SA	0618 1.5 / 1207 -0.1 / 1830 1.8	**19** SU	0009 0.1 / 0616 1.5 / 1216 0.1 / 1833 1.6
5 SU ◑	0040 -0.1 / 0659 1.5 / 1253 -0.1 / 1917 1.7	**20** M ◑	0041 0.2 / 0649 1.5 / 1254 0.1 / 1910 1.5
6 M	0127 0.0 / 0745 1.4 / 1342 0.0 / 2012 1.7	**21** TU	0118 0.2 / 0730 1.5 / 1336 0.2 / 1957 1.5
7 TU	0219 0.1 / 0841 1.4 / 1439 0.1 / 2118 1.6	**22** W	0201 0.3 / 0821 1.5 / 1427 0.3 / 2055 1.5
8 W	0319 0.2 / 0949 1.4 / 1548 0.1 / 2238 1.5	**23** TH	0254 0.4 / 0925 1.4 / 1530 0.4 / 2210 1.4
9 TH	0433 0.3 / 1109 1.4 / 1712 0.2 / 2359 1.4	**24** F	0403 0.4 / 1045 1.4 / 1659 0.4 / 2336 1.4
10 F	0551 0.3 / 1223 1.5 / 1831 0.1	**25** SA	0531 0.4 / 1205 1.5 / 1824 0.3
11 SA	0110 1.5 / 0657 0.3 / 1327 1.6 / 1935 0.0	**26** SU	0048 1.5 / 0642 0.3 / 1309 1.6 / 1923 0.2
12 SU	0210 1.5 / 0751 0.2 / 1424 1.7 / 2027 0.0	**27** M	0147 1.5 / 0735 0.2 / 1402 1.7 / 2009 0.1
13 M ●	0302 1.5 / 0838 0.1 / 1512 1.7 / 2113 -0.1	**28** TU ○	0237 1.6 / 0820 0.1 / 1449 1.8 / 2052 0.0
14 TU	0345 1.5 / 0920 0.1 / 1554 1.8 / 2154 -0.1	**29** W	0321 1.6 / 0901 0.0 / 1531 1.9 / 2132 -0.1
15 W	0421 1.5 / 0959 0.0 / 1630 1.8 / 2232 0.0	**30** TH	0402 1.7 / 0942 0.0 / 1611 1.9 / 2212 -0.2
		31 F	0439 1.7 / 1021 0.0 / 1650 1.9 / 2251 -0.2

Chart Datum: 0·69 metres below Dansk Normal Null

TIME ZONE -0100
(Danish Standard Time)
Subtract 1 hour for UT
For Danish Summer Time add
ONE hour in **non-shaded areas**

DENMARK – ESBJERG

LAT 55°28'N   LONG 8°26'E

TIMES AND HEIGHTS OF HIGH AND LOW WATERS

Dates in amber are SPRINGS
Dates in yellow are NEAPS

2007

SEPTEMBER

Day	Time m	Day	Time m
1 SA	0516 1.7 / 1103 -0.1 / 1730 1.9 / 2332 -0.1	**16** SU	0514 1.6 / 1112 0.1 / 1728 1.7 / 2330 0.2
2 SU	0553 1.6 / 1145 -0.1 / 1812 1.8	**17** M	0538 1.6 / 1144 0.1 / 1756 1.7
3 M	0015 0.0 / 0632 1.6 / 1230 -0.1 / 1859 1.8	**18** TU	0001 0.2 / 0609 1.7 / 1220 0.2 / 1832 1.6
4 TU	0100 0.1 / 0717 1.6 / 1321 0.0 / 1955 1.6	**19** W	0037 0.3 / 0648 1.6 / 1301 0.2 / 1917 1.6
5 W	0151 0.3 / 0812 1.5 / 1419 0.2 / 2106 1.5	**20** TH	0120 0.3 / 0736 1.6 / 1351 0.3 / 2013 1.5
6 TH	0252 0.4 / 0925 1.5 / 1535 0.3 / 2231 1.5	**21** F	0212 0.4 / 0834 1.6 / 1452 0.4 / 2127 1.5
7 F	0413 0.5 / 1052 1.5 / 1709 1.0 / 2352 1.5	**22** SA	0318 0.5 / 0950 1.6 / 1616 0.4 / 2257 1.5
8 SA	0538 0.4 / 1209 1.6 / 1824 0.2	**23** SU	0445 0.5 / 1118 1.6 / 1745 0.3
9 SU	0059 1.5 / 0642 0.3 / 1312 1.7 / 1922 0.1	**24** M	0014 1.5 / 0603 0.4 / 1230 1.7 / 1848 0.2
10 M	0155 1.6 / 0734 0.2 / 1406 1.8 / 2011 0.0	**25** TU	0115 1.6 / 0701 0.3 / 1327 1.8 / 1938 0.1
11 TU ●	0242 1.6 / 0819 0.1 / 1454 1.9 / 2053 0.0	**26** W ○	0207 1.7 / 0750 0.2 / 1418 1.9 / 2022 0.0
12 W	0322 1.6 / 0900 0.1 / 1533 1.9 / 2131 0.0	**27** TH	0252 1.7 / 0834 0.1 / 1504 2.0 / 2104 -0.1
13 TH	0356 1.6 / 0936 0.1 / 1608 1.8 / 2204 0.1	**28** F	0333 1.8 / 0916 0.0 / 1547 2.0 / 2145 -0.1
14 F	0425 1.6 / 1010 0.1 / 1637 1.6 / 2234 0.1	**29** SA	0412 1.8 / 0958 -0.1 / 1629 2.0 / 2226 0.0
15 SA	0451 1.6 / 1041 0.1 / 1703 1.7 / 2302 0.2	**30** SU	0450 1.8 / 1041 -0.1 / 1711 1.9 / 2307 0.0

OCTOBER

Day	Time m	Day	Time m
1 M	0528 1.7 / 1125 -0.1 / 1755 1.8 / 2350 0.1	**16** TU	0509 1.7 / 1118 0.2 / 1729 1.7 / 2330 0.3
2 TU	0608 1.7 / 1212 0.0 / 1845 1.7	**17** W	0539 1.7 / 1154 0.2 / 1805 1.7
3 W ◑	0036 0.3 / 0654 1.7 / 1304 0.1 / 1943 1.6	**18** TH	0008 0.3 / 0617 1.7 / 1237 0.3 / 1850 1.6
4 TH	0127 0.4 / 0753 1.6 / 1406 0.3 / 2058 1.5	**19** F ◑	0051 0.4 / 0704 1.7 / 1327 0.3 / 1946 1.5
5 F	0231 0.5 / 0909 1.6 / 1529 0.3 / 2221 1.5	**20** SA	0144 0.4 / 0800 1.7 / 1428 0.3 / 2056 1.5
6 SA	0354 0.6 / 1033 1.6 / 1658 0.3 / 2334 1.5	**21** SU	0248 0.5 / 0909 1.7 / 1544 0.4 / 2220 1.5
7 SU	0515 0.5 / 1146 1.7 / 1806 0.2	**22** M	0406 0.5 / 1032 1.7 / 1703 0.3 / 2336 1.6
8 M	0036 1.6 / 0618 0.4 / 1248 1.8 / 1900 0.1	**23** TU	0521 0.4 / 1148 1.8 / 1809 0.2
9 TU	0128 1.6 / 0709 0.3 / 1341 1.9 / 1945 0.1	**24** W	0039 1.6 / 0624 0.3 / 1251 1.9 / 1903 0.1
10 W	0214 1.7 / 0754 0.2 / 1427 1.9 / 2027 0.1	**25** TH	0133 1.7 / 0717 0.2 / 1346 1.9 / 1951 0.0
11 TH ●	0253 1.7 / 0835 0.1 / 1507 1.9 / 2103 0.1	**26** F ○	0221 1.8 / 0806 0.1 / 1436 2.0 / 2036 0.0
12 F	0327 1.7 / 0912 0.1 / 1542 1.8 / 2135 0.2	**27** SA	0305 1.8 / 0851 0.0 / 1524 2.0 / 2119 0.0
13 SA	0357 1.7 / 0945 0.1 / 1612 1.8 / 2203 0.2	**28** SU	0346 1.8 / 0937 0.0 / 1609 1.9 / 2202 0.1
14 SU	0423 1.7 / 1015 0.2 / 1637 1.7 / 2230 0.2	**29** M	0427 1.8 / 1022 0.0 / 1655 1.8 / 2245 0.2
15 M	0446 1.7 / 1045 0.2 / 1701 1.7 / 2258 0.3	**30** TU	0507 1.8 / 1109 0.0 / 1742 1.7 / 2329 0.2
		31 W	0551 1.8 / 1158 0.1 / 1834 1.6

NOVEMBER

Day	Time m	Day	Time m
1 TH ◑	0015 0.4 / 0639 1.8 / 1253 0.2 / 1933 1.5	**16** F	0558 1.8 / 1221 0.2 / 1835 1.6
2 F	0108 0.4 / 0739 1.7 / 1357 0.3 / 2043 1.5	**17** SA ●	0033 0.3 / 0643 1.8 / 1312 0.2 / 1928 1.6
3 SA	0211 0.5 / 0850 1.7 / 1514 0.3 / 2155 1.5	**18** SU	0125 0.4 / 0737 1.8 / 1409 0.2 / 2031 1.5
4 SU	0326 0.5 / 1006 1.7 / 1631 0.4 / 2302 1.5	**19** M	0224 0.4 / 0840 1.8 / 1515 0.3 / 2142 1.5
5 M	0441 0.5 / 1114 1.8 / 1735 0.2	**20** TU	0331 0.4 / 0953 1.8 / 1623 0.2 / 2254 1.6
6 TU	0000 1.6 / 0545 0.4 / 1214 1.8 / 1828 0.2	**21** W	0440 0.4 / 1108 1.8 / 1729 0.2
7 W	0052 1.7 / 0639 0.3 / 1308 1.9 / 1915 0.2	**22** TH	0000 1.7 / 0546 0.3 / 1215 1.8 / 1827 0.1
8 TH	0139 1.7 / 0726 0.2 / 1355 1.9 / 1957 0.2	**23** F	0058 1.7 / 0645 0.2 / 1317 1.9 / 1921 0.1
9 F	0221 1.8 / 0809 0.2 / 1438 1.8 / 2033 0.2	**24** SA ○	0151 1.7 / 0740 0.1 / 1413 1.9 / 2010 0.1
10 SA ●	0258 1.8 / 0848 0.2 / 1515 1.8 / 2106 0.2	**25** SU	0239 1.8 / 0831 0.0 / 1506 1.8 / 2057 0.1
11 SU	0331 1.8 / 0921 0.2 / 1548 1.7 / 2136 0.3	**26** M	0325 1.8 / 0921 0.0 / 1556 1.8 / 2142 0.2
12 M	0400 1.8 / 0954 0.2 / 1616 1.7 / 2203 0.3	**27** TU	0409 1.8 / 1009 0.0 / 1645 1.7 / 2227 0.2
13 TU	0426 1.8 / 1025 0.2 / 1644 1.6 / 2234 0.3	**28** W	0454 1.8 / 1058 0.1 / 1733 1.6 / 2312 0.3
14 W	0451 1.8 / 1100 0.2 / 1714 1.6 / 2309 0.3	**29** TH	0539 1.8 / 1149 0.1 / 1823 1.5 / 2359 0.3
15 TH	0521 1.8 / 1138 0.2 / 1750 1.6 / 2348 0.3	**30** F	0627 1.8 / 1242 0.2 / 1915 1.5

DECEMBER

Day	Time m	Day	Time m
1 SA ◑	0049 0.4 / 0721 1.8 / 1339 0.2 / 2013 1.5	**16** SU	0018 0.2 / 0630 1.8 / 1256 0.1 / 1912 1.5
2 SU	0145 0.4 / 0821 1.8 / 1442 0.3 / 2114 1.5	**17** M ●	0107 0.2 / 0719 1.8 / 1348 0.1 / 2005 1.5
3 M	0247 0.4 / 0926 1.7 / 1548 0.3 / 2215 1.5	**18** TU	0200 0.3 / 0815 1.8 / 1444 0.1 / 2106 1.5
4 TU	0354 0.4 / 1031 1.7 / 1651 0.3 / 2314 1.5	**19** W	0259 0.2 / 0920 1.8 / 1545 0.2 / 2212 1.5
5 W	0501 0.4 / 1132 1.7 / 1748 0.3	**20** TH	0403 0.3 / 1033 1.7 / 1651 0.3 / 2321 1.5
6 TH	0009 1.6 / 0601 0.3 / 1228 1.7 / 1839 0.3	**21** F	0512 0.2 / 1146 1.7 / 1754 0.2
7 F	0100 1.7 / 0655 0.3 / 1319 1.7 / 1924 0.2	**22** SA	0026 1.6 / 0618 0.2 / 1255 1.7 / 1855 0.2
8 SA	0146 1.7 / 0743 0.2 / 1406 1.7 / 2004 0.2	**23** SU	0126 1.6 / 0721 0.1 / 1358 1.7 / 1950 0.2
9 SU ●	0229 1.7 / 0825 0.2 / 1448 1.7 / 2040 0.3	**24** M ○	0221 1.7 / 0818 0.1 / 1455 1.7 / 2040 0.2
10 M	0307 1.7 / 0903 0.2 / 1527 1.6 / 2112 0.3	**25** TU	0312 1.7 / 0911 0.0 / 1548 1.6 / 2128 0.2
11 TU	0341 1.7 / 0937 0.2 / 1601 1.6 / 2145 0.3	**26** W	0359 1.8 / 1001 0.0 / 1636 1.6 / 2213 0.2
12 W	0412 1.7 / 1012 0.2 / 1633 1.6 / 2218 0.3	**27** TH	0444 1.8 / 1049 0.0 / 1721 1.5 / 2257 0.2
13 TH	0440 1.8 / 1048 0.2 / 1706 1.6 / 2254 0.2	**28** F	0527 1.8 / 1136 0.0 / 1804 1.5 / 2341 0.2
14 F	0512 1.8 / 1127 0.1 / 1743 1.6 / 2334 0.2	**29** SA	0611 1.8 / 1222 0.1 / 1848 1.5
15 SA	0548 1.8 / 1209 0.1 / 1824 1.6	**30** SU	0026 0.2 / 0656 1.8 / 1309 0.2 / 1933 1.4
		31 M ◑	0112 0.2 / 0745 1.7 / 1358 0.2 / 2021 1.4

Chart Datum: 0·69 metres below Dansk Normal Null

TIDES

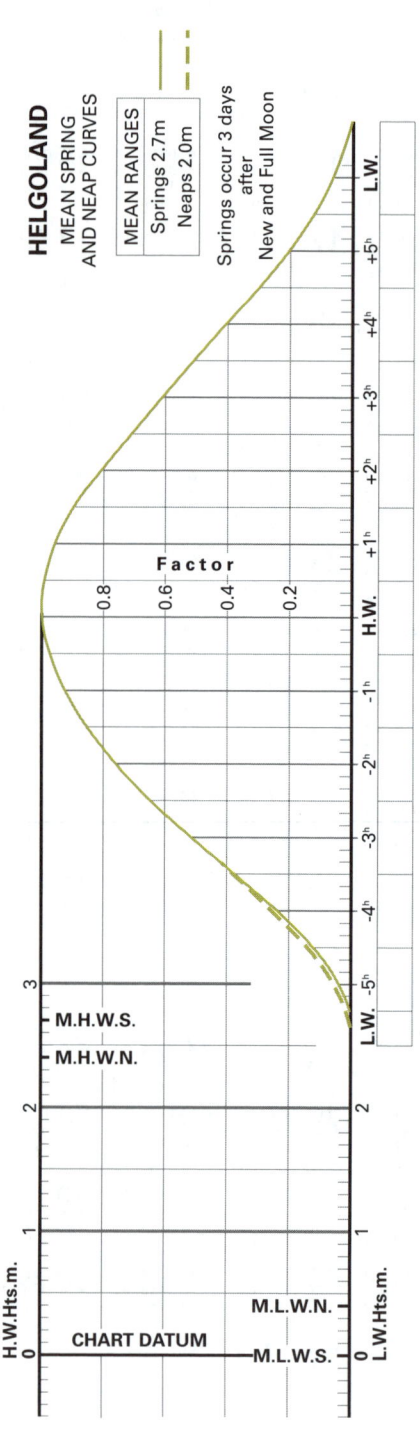

HELGOLAND
MEAN SPRING
AND NEAP CURVES

MEAN RANGES
Springs 2.7m
Neaps 2.0m

Springs occur 3 days
after
New and Full Moon

TIME ZONE -0100
(German Standard Time)
Subtract 1 hour for UT
For German Summer Time add
ONE hour in **non-shaded areas**

GERMANY – HELGOLAND

LAT 54°11'N   LONG 7°53'E

TIMES AND HEIGHTS OF HIGH AND LOW WATERS

Dates in amber are **SPRINGS**
Dates in yellow are **NEAPS**

2007

JANUARY

Day	Time m	Time m	Time m	Time m
1 M	0351 0.7	0935 3.0	1624 0.7	2207 3.0
16 TU	0335 1.0	0923 2.9	1603 0.9	2149 3.0
2 TU	0457 0.6	1040 3.0	1724 0.7	2305 3.1
17 W	0439 0.9	1023 3.0	1700 0.9	2244 3.1
3 W	0557 0.6	1137 3.1	1816 0.7	○2355 3.2
18 TH	0537 0.8	1115 3.1	1753 0.8	2335 3.2
4 TH	0647 0.6	1226 3.1	1900 0.7	
19 F	0630 0.7	1203 3.1	1843 0.7 ●	
5 F	0039 3.3	0732 0.6	1308 3.0	1940 0.7
20 SA	0021 3.3	0718 0.5	1252 3.1	1931 0.6
6 SA	0121 3.3	0815 0.6	1349 3.0	2020 0.7
21 SU	0105 3.3	0804 0.4	1338 3.1	2015 0.6
7 SU	0201 3.3	0856 0.6	1428 3.0	2057 0.6
22 M	0147 3.4	0846 0.3	1420 3.0	2054 0.5
8 M	0238 3.3	0931 0.5	1504 2.9	2130 0.6
23 TU	0228 3.4	0925 0.3	1458 3.0	2131 0.5
9 TU	0311 3.2	1001 0.5	1538 2.9	2202 0.7
24 W	0309 3.3	1006 0.4	1539 3.0	2211 0.5
10 W	0344 3.2	1032 0.7	1612 2.8	2235 0.8
25 TH	0354 3.3	1048 0.5	1623 2.8	◑2255 0.6
11 TH	0419 3.1	1105 0.8	1649 2.8	◑2312 0.9
26 F	0442 3.3	1130 0.7	1709 2.9	2343 0.7
12 F	0458 3.0	1143 0.9	1733 2.8	
27 SA	0534 3.1	1219 0.8	1804 2.9	
13 SA	0000 1.0	0550 2.9	1237 1.0	1830 2.7
28 SU	0046 0.8	0639 3.0	1326 0.9	1914 2.9
14 SU	0106 1.1	0658 2.9	1346 1.0	1938 2.8
29 M	0207 0.8	0759 2.9	1448 0.9	2036 2.9
15 M	0222 1.0	0813 2.9	1458 1.0	2047 2.9
30 TU	0334 0.7	0922 2.9	1608 0.8	2153 3.0
31 W	0450 0.7	1035 2.9	1714 0.8	2257 3.1

FEBRUARY

Day	Time m	Time m	Time m	Time m
1 TH	0551 0.6	1133 3.0	1807 0.8	2348 3.2
16 F	0521 0.7	1100 3.0	1739 0.8	2319 3.2
2 F	0641 0.6	1219 3.0	1852 0.7 ○	
17 SA	0618 0.5	1150 3.1	1831 0.6 ●	
3 SA	0030 3.3	0723 0.6	1258 3.0	1930 0.6
18 SU	0005 3.3	0706 0.3	1236 3.1	1917 0.4
4 SU	0108 3.3	0801 0.5	1332 3.0	2005 0.6
19 M	0048 3.4	0749 0.2	1320 3.0	1959 0.3
5 M	0144 3.3	0835 0.5	1403 3.0	2037 0.5
20 TU	0129 3.4	0829 0.2	1401 3.0	2037 0.3
6 TU	0215 3.3	0904 0.5	1433 3.0	2105 0.5
21 W	0210 3.4	0907 0.2	1438 3.0	2114 0.3
7 W	0244 3.2	0929 0.5	1502 2.9	2133 0.5
22 TH	0251 3.3	0944 0.4	1515 3.0	2153 0.4
8 TH	0312 3.1	0955 0.5	1532 2.9	2201 0.6
23 F	0333 3.3	1022 0.5	1555 3.0	2234 0.5
9 F	0339 3.1	1020 0.6	1600 2.9	2227 0.7
24 SA	0418 3.2	1100 0.7	1638 3.0	◑2319 0.6
10 SA	0407 3.0	1045 0.8	1631 2.8	◑2300 0.8
25 SU	0508 3.0	1147 0.8	1731 2.9	
11 SU	0446 2.8	1125 0.9	1717 2.7	2357 0.9
26 M	0021 0.7	0614 2.8	1255 0.9	1845 2.8
12 M	0548 2.7	1233 1.0	1829 2.7	
27 TU	0146 0.7	0740 2.7	1425 1.0	2016 2.8
13 TU	0120 1.0	0714 2.7	1359 1.0	1955 2.7
28 W	0323 0.7	0912 2.7	1556 0.9	2143 3.0
14 W	0252 0.9	0844 2.7	1525 1.0	2116 2.9
15 TH	0414 0.8	1001 2.9	1638 0.9	2224 3.1

MARCH

Day	Time m	Time m	Time m	Time m
1 TH	0445 0.6	1029 2.8	1706 0.9	2249 3.1
16 F	0348 0.6	0936 2.7	1614 0.8	2158 3.0
2 F	0544 0.6	1123 2.9	1756 0.7	2335 3.2
17 SA	0500 0.5	1040 2.9	1718 0.6	2254 3.2
3 SA	0627 0.5	1204 3.0	1837 0.6	
18 SU	0556 0.3	1129 3.0	1810 0.4	2341 3.3
4 SU	0013 3.2	0705 0.4	1237 3.0	○1913 0.5
19 M	0643 0.2	1213 3.0	1855 0.3 ●	
5 M	0048 3.2	0738 0.4	1307 3.0	1944 0.4
20 TU	0023 3.3	0725 0.1	1254 3.0	1935 0.2
6 TU	0120 3.2	0806 0.4	1334 3.0	2012 0.4
21 W	0105 3.3	0804 0.1	1333 3.0	2015 0.2
7 W	0148 3.2	0831 0.4	1400 3.0	2038 0.4
22 TH	0147 3.3	0842 0.2	1412 3.1	2055 0.2
8 TH	0213 3.1	0855 0.4	1426 3.0	2104 0.4
23 F	0229 3.2	0918 0.3	1450 3.1	2135 0.3
9 F	0239 3.1	0919 0.4	1454 2.9	2131 0.4
24 SA	0312 3.1	0955 0.5	1530 3.1	2217 0.4
10 SA	0306 3.0	0942 0.5	1520 2.9	2155 0.5
25 SU	0358 3.0	1035 0.6	1614 3.0	◑2304 0.5
11 SU	0331 2.9	1003 0.5	1547 2.8	2222 0.6
26 M	0450 2.8	1123 0.7	1709 2.9	
12 M	0404 2.7	1036 0.7	1628 2.7	◑2311 0.7
27 TU	0005 0.6	0556 2.6	1232 0.8	1823 2.8
13 TU	0502 2.6	1140 0.9	1738 2.6	
28 W	0129 0.6	0721 2.5	1402 0.9	1955 2.8
14 W	0035 0.8	0630 2.5	1314 1.0	1912 2.7
29 TH	0305 0.6	0854 2.6	1536 0.8	2123 2.9
15 TH	0216 0.7	0810 2.6	1452 0.9	2044 2.8
30 F	0428 0.5	1010 2.7	1647 0.7	2228 3.0
31 SA	0524 0.4	1100 2.8	1733 0.6	2310 3.1

APRIL

Day	Time m	Time m	Time m	Time m
1 SU	0600 0.4	1135 2.9	1810 0.5	2344 3.1
16 M	0523 0.2	1059 2.9	1740 0.3	2311 3.2
2 M	0633 0.4	1206 3.0	1845 0.4 ○	
17 TU	0613 0.1	1144 3.0	1828 0.2	●2356 3.3
3 TU	0019 3.1	0704 0.3	1236 3.0	1917 0.3
18 W	0656 0.1	1225 3.0	1911 0.1	
4 W	0050 3.1	0732 0.3	1302 3.0	1943 0.3
19 TH	0039 3.3	0735 0.1	1305 3.1	1953 0.1
5 TH	0117 3.1	0757 0.3	1326 3.0	2010 0.3
20 F	0123 3.2	0815 0.2	1346 3.1	2037 0.2
6 F	0142 3.0	0822 0.3	1353 3.0	2038 0.3
21 SA	0209 3.1	0855 0.3	1429 3.1	2121 0.2
7 SA	0210 2.9	0848 0.3	1422 2.9	2107 0.3
22 SU	0257 2.9	0935 0.4	1512 3.0	2206 0.2
8 SU	0239 2.9	0914 0.4	1452 2.9	2136 0.3
23 M	0345 2.8	1017 0.5	1559 3.0	2254 0.4
9 M	0311 2.8	0940 0.5	1524 2.8	2207 0.4
24 TU	0437 2.6	1107 0.6	1653 2.9	◑2352 0.5
10 TU	0348 2.6	1015 0.6	1606 2.7	◑2254 0.5
25 W	0539 2.5	1210 0.7	1801 2.8	
11 W	0442 2.5	1115 0.7	1711 2.6	
26 TH	0106 0.5	0655 2.4	1331 0.7	1922 2.8
12 TH	0010 0.6	0603 2.4	1244 0.8	1839 2.7
27 F	0231 0.5	0818 2.5	1458 0.7	2044 2.9
13 F	0147 0.5	0739 2.5	1421 0.8	2009 2.8
28 SA	0349 0.4	0931 2.6	1608 0.6	2148 2.9
14 SA	0318 0.4	0904 2.6	1543 0.6	2124 3.0
29 SU	0443 0.4	1021 2.7	1655 0.5	2231 3.0
15 SU	0428 0.3	1009 2.8	1647 0.5	2222 3.1
30 M	0519 0.3	1056 2.9	1732 0.5	2307 3.0

Chart Datum: 1·68 metres below Normal Null (German reference level)

TIDES

TIME ZONE -0100
(German Standard Time)
Subtract 1 hour for UT
For German Summer Time add
ONE hour in **non-shaded areas**

GERMANY – HELGOLAND

LAT 54°11'N   LONG 7°53'E
TIMES AND HEIGHTS OF HIGH AND LOW WATERS

Dates in amber are **SPRINGS**
Dates in yellow are **NEAPS**

2007

MAY

Day	Time m	Time m	Time m	Time m		Day	Time m	Time m	Time m	Time m
1 TU	0552 0.4	1128 3.0	1809 0.4	2343 3.0		16 W	0538 0.2	1113 3.0	1801 0.2	● 2332 3.2
2 W	0626 0.4	1201 3.0	1844 0.4	○		17 TH	0627 0.2	1158 3.1	1849 0.1	
3 TH	0017 3.0	0657 0.4	1230 3.0	1915 0.3		18 F	0020 3.1	0711 0.2	1241 3.1	1935 0.1
4 F	0047 3.0	0725 0.4	1257 3.0	1944 0.3		19 SA	0107 3.1	0753 0.2	1326 3.1	2023 0.2
5 SA	0116 3.0	0755 0.4	1327 3.0	2017 0.3		20 SU	0156 3.0	0837 0.3	1413 3.1	2111 0.3
6 SU	0148 2.9	0826 0.4	1400 3.0	2051 0.3		21 M	0246 2.8	0921 0.4	1459 3.0	2157 0.2
7 M	0225 2.8	0858 0.4	1437 2.9	2127 0.3		22 TU	0334 2.7	1004 0.4	1546 3.0	2244 0.3
8 TU	0304 2.7	0933 0.5	1516 2.9	2207 0.3		23 W	0423 2.6	1050 0.5	1635 3.0	● 2334 0.4
9 W	0347 2.6	1014 0.5	1601 2.8	2255 0.3		24 TH	0516 2.5	1144 0.6	1731 2.9	
10 TH	0440 2.5	1110 0.6	1659 2.8	◐ 2359 0.4		25 F	0032 0.5	0617 2.6	1248 0.6	1836 2.9
11 F	0548 2.5	1224 0.7	1813 2.8			26 SA	0138 0.5	0725 2.5	1400 0.6	1947 2.8
12 SA	0120 0.4	0708 2.5	1348 0.7	1933 2.9		27 SU	0247 0.5	0832 2.5	1509 0.6	2051 2.9
13 SU	0241 0.3	0825 2.6	1504 0.5	2045 3.0		28 M	0345 0.4	0927 2.7	1604 0.6	2143 2.9
14 M	0348 0.3	0930 2.8	1609 0.4	2145 3.1		29 TU	0430 0.4	1009 2.8	1647 0.5	2226 3.0
15 TU	0445 0.2	1024 2.9	1707 0.3	2239 3.2		30 W	0509 0.5	1046 3.0	1729 0.5	2307 3.0
						31 TH	0548 0.5	1124 3.0	1811 0.5	2345 3.0

JUNE

Day	Time m	Time m	Time m	Time m		Day	Time m	Time m	Time m	Time m
1 F	0625 0.5	1200 3.1	1849 0.4	○		16 SA	0009 3.0	0654 0.3	1227 3.2	1924 0.2
2 SA	0022 3.0	0700 0.5	1235 3.1	1926 0.4		17 SU	0058 3.0	0739 0.4	1313 3.2	2013 0.2
3 SU	0058 3.0	0737 0.5	1311 3.1	2005 0.4		18 M	0146 2.9	0824 0.4	1400 3.2	2101 0.2
4 M	0138 2.9	0815 0.5	1350 3.1	2045 0.4		19 TU	0234 2.8	0908 0.4	1446 3.2	2145 0.2
5 TU	0218 2.8	0852 0.4	1429 3.0	2125 0.3		20 W	0319 2.7	0948 0.4	1528 3.1	2226 0.3
6 W	0301 2.8	0932 0.4	1511 3.0	2208 0.3		21 TH	0401 2.7	1027 0.5	1610 3.1	2306 0.4
7 TH	0346 2.7	1016 0.5	1558 3.0	2256 0.2		22 F	0444 2.7	1109 0.6	1654 3.0	◐ 2348 0.5
8 F	0437 2.6	1106 0.5	1650 3.0	◐ 2350 0.3		23 SA	0530 2.6	1156 0.6	1743 2.9	
9 SA	0533 2.6	1204 0.5	1751 3.0			24 SU	0036 0.6	0622 2.6	1252 0.7	1840 2.9
10 SU	0052 0.3	0637 2.6	1312 0.6	1858 3.0		25 M	0133 0.6	0721 2.7	1357 0.8	1943 2.9
11 M	0200 0.4	0744 2.7	1424 0.5	2007 3.1		26 TU	0236 0.7	0822 2.8	1502 0.7	2047 2.9
12 TU	0307 0.4	0849 2.8	1533 0.4	2112 3.1		27 W	0334 0.6	0917 2.8	1600 0.7	2143 2.9
13 W	0409 0.4	0949 2.9	1638 0.4	2215 3.1		28 TH	0426 0.6	1005 2.9	1652 0.6	2234 3.0
14 TH	0509 0.3	1047 3.0	1739 0.3	2315 3.1		29 F	0513 0.6	1052 3.1	1743 0.6	2320 3.0
15 F	0605 0.3	1139 3.1	1835 0.2	●		30 SA	0558 0.6	1137 3.1	1830 0.6	○

JULY

Day	Time m	Time m	Time m	Time m		Day	Time m	Time m	Time m	Time m
1 SU	0004 3.0	0642 0.6	1220 3.2	1915 0.5		16 M	0052 3.0	0728 0.5	1304 3.3	2003 0.4
2 M	0047 3.0	0726 0.6	1301 3.2	1958 0.4		17 TU	0135 2.9	0811 0.5	1347 3.3	2046 0.4
3 TU	0131 3.0	0809 0.5	1342 3.2	2039 0.3		18 W	0216 2.9	0851 0.4	1427 3.3	2124 0.3
4 W	0212 2.9	0847 0.4	1421 3.2	2119 0.2		19 TH	0254 2.9	0925 0.4	1503 3.2	2157 0.4
5 TH	0251 2.8	0925 0.4	1501 3.2	2201 0.2		20 F	0329 2.8	0957 0.5	1538 3.2	2228 0.5
6 F	0335 2.8	1008 0.4	1548 3.1	2247 0.3		21 SA	0403 2.8	1030 0.6	1613 3.1	2300 0.6
7 SA	0423 2.8	1053 0.5	1647 3.1	◐ 2333 0.4		22 SU	0439 2.8	1105 0.7	1650 3.0	◐ 2333 0.7
8 SU	0512 2.8	1142 0.5	1728 3.1			23 M	0518 2.8	1146 0.8	1734 2.9	
9 M	0021 0.5	0604 2.8	1239 0.6	1827 3.1		24 TU	0018 0.8	0607 2.7	1244 0.9	1834 2.8
10 TU	0121 0.6	0705 2.8	1350 0.6	1937 3.0		25 W	0122 0.9	0712 2.7	1358 0.9	1947 2.8
11 W	0231 0.5	0815 2.9	1507 0.6	2051 3.0		26 TH	0235 0.9	0823 2.8	1514 0.8	2102 2.8
12 TH	0343 0.6	0926 3.0	1622 0.5	2203 3.0		27 F	0344 0.8	0929 2.9	1622 0.7	2207 2.9
13 F	0450 0.5	1032 3.1	1729 0.4	2308 3.0		28 SA	0444 0.8	1027 3.0	1721 0.7	2301 3.0
14 SA	0551 0.5	1130 3.2	1827 0.4	●		29 SU	0538 0.8	1119 3.2	1815 0.6	2349 3.0
15 SU	0005 3.0	0643 0.5	1219 3.2	1917 0.4 ○		30 M	0628 0.7	1205 3.2	1903 0.5	
						31 TU	0035 3.1	0715 0.6	1248 3.3	1946 0.4

AUGUST

Day	Time m	Time m	Time m	Time m		Day	Time m	Time m	Time m	Time m
1 W	0118 3.1	0757 0.5	1328 3.4	2026 0.3		16 TH	0150 3.0	0827 0.5	1402 3.3	2053 0.4
2 TH	0157 3.0	0834 0.4	1406 3.3	2103 0.3		17 F	0221 3.0	0856 0.4	1432 3.2	2119 0.5
3 F	0234 3.0	0910 0.4	1445 3.3	2142 0.3		18 SA	0250 3.0	0923 0.5	1501 3.2	2146 0.5
4 SA	0313 2.9	0949 0.4	1529 3.3	2224 0.4		19 SU	0320 2.9	0951 0.6	1532 3.1	2212 0.7
5 SU	0357 2.9	1032 0.5	1616 3.2	◐ 2305 0.6		20 M	0350 2.9	1020 0.7	1602 3.0	◐ 2238 0.8
6 M	0443 2.9	1117 0.6	1704 3.2	2348 0.7		21 TU	0421 2.9	1051 0.8	1637 2.9	2313 0.9
7 TU	0532 2.9	1211 0.7	1802 3.0			22 W	0503 2.8	1141 0.9	1733 2.8	
8 W	0047 0.8	0634 2.9	1326 0.7	1918 2.9		23 TH	0013 1.0	0609 2.7	1259 1.0	1853 2.7
9 TH	0206 0.9	0754 2.9	1455 0.7	2043 2.9		24 F	0138 1.0	0733 2.7	1431 0.9	2024 2.7
10 F	0331 0.8	0916 3.0	1619 0.6	2202 2.9		25 SA	0305 1.0	0856 2.9	1555 0.8	2142 2.8
11 SA	0444 0.8	1027 3.1	1726 0.6	2306 3.0		26 SU	0419 0.9	1004 3.0	1702 0.7	2243 2.9
12 SU	0543 0.7	1123 3.2	1820 0.5	2357 3.0		27 M	0519 0.8	1059 3.2	1756 0.6	2331 3.0
13 M	0632 0.7	1210 3.3	1906 0.5	●		28 TU	0610 0.7	1145 3.3	1843 0.6	○
14 TU	0040 3.0	0715 0.6	1251 3.3	1946 0.5		29 W	0015 3.1	0655 0.6	1226 3.4	1925 0.4
15 W	0117 3.0	0753 0.5	1328 3.3	2022 0.4 ○		30 TH	0056 3.1	0736 0.5	1306 3.4	2003 0.3
						31 F	0134 3.1	0813 0.4	1345 3.2	2040 0.4

Chart Datum: 1·68 metres below Normal Null (German reference level)

GERMANY – HELGOLAND

LAT 54°11′N   LONG 7°53′E

TIMES AND HEIGHTS OF HIGH AND LOW WATERS

Dates in amber are **SPRINGS**
Dates in yellow are **NEAPS**

2007

SEPTEMBER

Day	Wk	Time	m	Time	m	Time	m	Time	m
1	SA	0210	3.1	0849	0.4	1425	3.4	2116	0.4
2	SU	0247	3.1	0927	0.4	1507	3.3	2154	0.6
3	M	0328	3.1	1009	0.5	1552	3.2	2234	0.7
4	TU	0412	3.1	1055	0.6	1642	3.1	2319	0.9
5	W	0504	3.0	1152	0.7	1745	2.9		
6	TH	0022	1.0	0613	2.9	1312	0.7	1906	2.7
7	F	0148	1.1	0741	2.9	1448	0.8	2039	2.8
8	SA	0322	1.0	0911	3.0	1618	0.7	2202	2.8
9	SU	0440	0.9	1023	3.2	1722	0.6	2300	2.9
10	M	0533	0.8	1113	3.3	1807	0.6	2342	3.0
11	TU	0615	0.7	1152	3.3	1844	0.5		
12	W	0017	3.1	0653	0.6	1229	3.3	1919	0.5
13	TH	0050	3.1	0728	0.5	1303	3.3	1950	0.6
14	F	0119	3.1	0757	0.5	1333	3.3	2016	0.5
15	SA	0146	3.1	0824	0.5	1359	3.2	2040	0.6
16	SU	0212	3.1	0850	0.5	1425	3.1	2105	0.6
17	M	0239	3.0	0917	0.6	1453	3.0	2129	0.7
18	TU	0308	3.0	0944	0.7	1523	3.0	2154	0.8
19	W	0338	2.9	1013	0.8	1557	2.8	2226	1.0
20	TH	0418	2.8	1057	0.9	1650	2.7	2323	1.1
21	F	0521	2.7	1213	1.0	1810	2.6		
22	SA	0050	1.1	0649	2.7	1351	0.9	1947	2.6
23	SU	0228	1.1	0821	2.8	1524	0.8	2114	2.7
24	M	0351	0.9	0936	3.0	1635	0.6	2218	2.9
25	TU	0453	0.8	1031	3.2	1728	0.5	2306	3.0
26	W	0544	0.6	1116	3.3	1814	0.4	2348	3.1
27	TH	0628	0.5	1158	3.4	1855	0.4		
28	F	0028	3.1	0709	0.5	1239	3.4	1933	0.4
29	SA	0106	3.2	0748	0.4	1320	3.4	2011	0.5
30	SU	0144	3.2	0829	0.5	1403	3.4	2049	0.6

OCTOBER

Day	Wk	Time	m	Time	m	Time	m	Time	m
1	M	0222	3.2	0909	0.5	1447	3.2	2128	0.7
2	TU	0303	3.2	0952	0.5	1534	3.1	2209	0.8
3	W	0349	3.1	1040	0.7	1627	2.9	2258	1.0
4	TH	0444	3.0	1139	0.8	1731	2.7		
5	F	0002	1.1	0556	2.9	1258	0.8	1852	2.6
6	SA	0129	1.1	0725	2.9	1433	0.9	2024	2.6
7	SU	0304	1.1	0856	3.0	1602	0.8	2146	2.8
8	M	0422	0.9	1006	3.2	1703	0.6	2241	2.9
9	TU	0512	0.8	1051	3.2	1741	0.6	2316	3.0
10	W	0548	0.7	1043	3.3	1811	0.6	2346	3.1
11	TH	0623	0.6	1159	3.2	1843	0.6		
12	F	0018	3.1	0657	0.6	1233	3.2	1913	0.6
13	SA	0047	3.1	0726	0.6	1303	3.2	1940	0.6
14	SU	0112	3.1	0753	0.6	1329	3.1	2005	0.6
15	M	0138	3.1	0821	0.5	1355	3.1	2031	0.6
16	TU	0206	3.1	0850	0.6	1424	3.0	2057	0.7
17	W	0237	3.0	0919	0.7	1457	2.9	2125	0.8
18	TH	0311	3.0	0952	0.8	1535	2.8	2200	0.9
19	F	0352	2.9	1035	0.8	1626	2.6	2254	1.1
20	SA	0451	2.8	1143	0.9	1739	2.5		
21	SU	0014	1.1	0611	2.8	1314	0.8	1909	2.6
22	M	0148	1.1	0740	2.9	1445	0.7	2035	2.7
23	TU	0312	0.9	0857	3.1	1557	0.6	2142	2.8
24	W	0416	0.8	0955	3.2	1651	0.5	2233	3.0
25	TH	0509	0.6	1043	3.3	1739	0.4	2316	3.1
26	F	0557	0.5	1128	3.4	1822	0.4	2358	3.2
27	SA	0642	0.5	1212	3.4	1903	0.5		
28	SU	0038	3.2	0726	0.5	1257	3.3	1944	0.5
29	M	0120	3.3	0811	0.5	1345	3.3	2027	0.6
30	TU	0204	3.3	0857	0.5	1434	3.1	2110	0.7
31	W	0248	3.2	0943	0.6	1523	3.0	2153	0.8

NOVEMBER

Day	Wk	Time	m	Time	m	Time	m	Time	m
1	TH	0334	3.2	1031	0.6	1615	2.8	2242	0.9
2	F	0428	3.1	1127	0.7	1715	2.7	2343	1.0
3	SA	0534	3.0	1237	0.8	1828	2.6		
4	SU	0059	1.0	0654	2.9	1359	0.8	1950	2.6
5	M	0225	1.0	0817	3.0	1521	0.8	2107	2.7
6	TU	0342	0.9	0927	3.1	1622	0.7	2203	2.9
7	W	0435	0.8	1015	3.1	1701	0.6	2240	3.0
8	TH	0512	0.8	1051	3.2	1733	0.7	2311	3.1
9	F	0548	0.7	1126	3.2	1806	0.7	2344	3.2
10	SA	0625	0.7	1202	3.2	1839	0.7		
11	SU	0015	3.2	0657	0.6	1234	3.1	1909	0.7
12	M	0044	3.2	0728	0.6	1304	3.1	1938	0.7
13	TU	0114	3.2	0800	0.6	1335	3.0	2008	0.7
14	W	0146	3.1	0834	0.6	1409	2.9	2039	0.7
15	TH	0221	3.1	0908	0.6	1445	2.9	2113	0.8
16	F	0257	3.0	0944	0.7	1525	2.8	2151	0.9
17	SA	0339	3.0	1028	0.7	1614	2.7	2240	0.9
18	SU	0431	2.9	1124	0.7	1715	2.6	2345	1.0
19	M	0538	2.9	1237	0.7	1830	2.6		
20	TU	0104	1.0	0656	3.0	1358	0.7	1948	2.7
21	W	0224	0.9	0811	3.1	1509	0.7	2057	2.8
22	TH	0332	0.8	0914	3.2	1609	0.6	2153	3.0
23	F	0432	0.6	1009	3.2	1703	0.5	2244	3.1
24	SA	0528	0.5	1102	3.3	1754	0.5	2331	3.2
25	SU	0620	0.5	1153	3.2	1840	0.5		
26	M	0017	3.2	0709	0.5	1243	3.2	1925	0.6
27	TU	0103	3.3	0759	0.5	1334	3.1	2012	0.6
28	W	0152	3.3	0849	0.5	1426	3.0	2059	0.6
29	TH	0239	3.3	0936	0.5	1515	2.9	2142	0.7
30	F	0323	3.2	1022	0.5	1602	2.8	2227	0.8

DECEMBER

Day	Wk	Time	m	Time	m	Time	m	Time	m
1	SA	0410	3.2	1110	0.6	1653	2.7	2318	0.8
2	SU	0504	3.1	1204	0.7	1751	2.6		
3	M	0017	0.9	0608	3.0	1306	0.8	1856	2.6
4	TU	0126	0.9	0719	2.9	1415	0.8	2005	2.7
5	W	0238	1.0	0828	3.0	1519	0.8	2107	2.8
6	TH	0341	0.9	0926	3.0	1611	0.8	2155	3.0
7	F	0430	0.9	1013	3.1	1653	0.8	2234	3.1
8	SA	0513	0.8	1055	3.1	1732	0.8	2312	3.2
9	SU	0555	0.8	1134	3.1	1810	0.8	2349	3.2
10	M	0635	0.7	1211	3.1	1845	0.7		
11	TU	0024	3.2	0711	0.7	1248	3.1	1921	0.7
12	W	0059	3.2	0749	0.6	1325	3.0	1958	0.7
13	TH	0136	3.2	0827	0.6	1403	3.0	2033	0.7
14	F	0211	3.2	0903	0.5	1439	2.9	2108	0.7
15	SA	0248	3.1	0940	0.5	1518	2.8	2146	0.7
16	SU	0329	3.1	1022	0.5	1602	2.8	2230	0.7
17	M	0416	3.1	1108	0.6	1652	2.7	2320	0.8
18	TU	0509	3.1	1203	0.7	1751	2.7		
19	W	0022	0.9	0613	3.1	1308	0.7	1858	2.8
20	TH	0134	0.9	0724	3.1	1419	0.8	2008	2.9
21	F	0249	0.8	0835	3.1	1528	0.7	2114	3.0
22	SA	0400	0.7	0943	3.2	1633	0.6	2216	3.1
23	SU	0507	0.6	1047	3.1	1733	0.6	2313	3.2
24	M	0607	0.5	1145	3.1	1827	0.6		
25	TU	0004	3.2	0701	0.5	1237	3.1	1914	0.6
26	W	0053	3.3	0751	0.5	1326	3.0	2002	0.6
27	TH	0142	3.3	0841	0.5	1415	3.0	2049	0.6
28	F	0228	3.3	0927	0.4	1501	2.9	2130	0.5
29	SA	0309	3.3	1006	0.4	1542	2.8	2208	0.6
30	SU	0348	3.2	1043	0.5	1622	2.8	2246	0.7
31	M	0429	3.2	1122	0.6	1704	2.8	2329	0.8

Chart Datum: 1·68 metres below Normal Null (German reference level)

TIDES

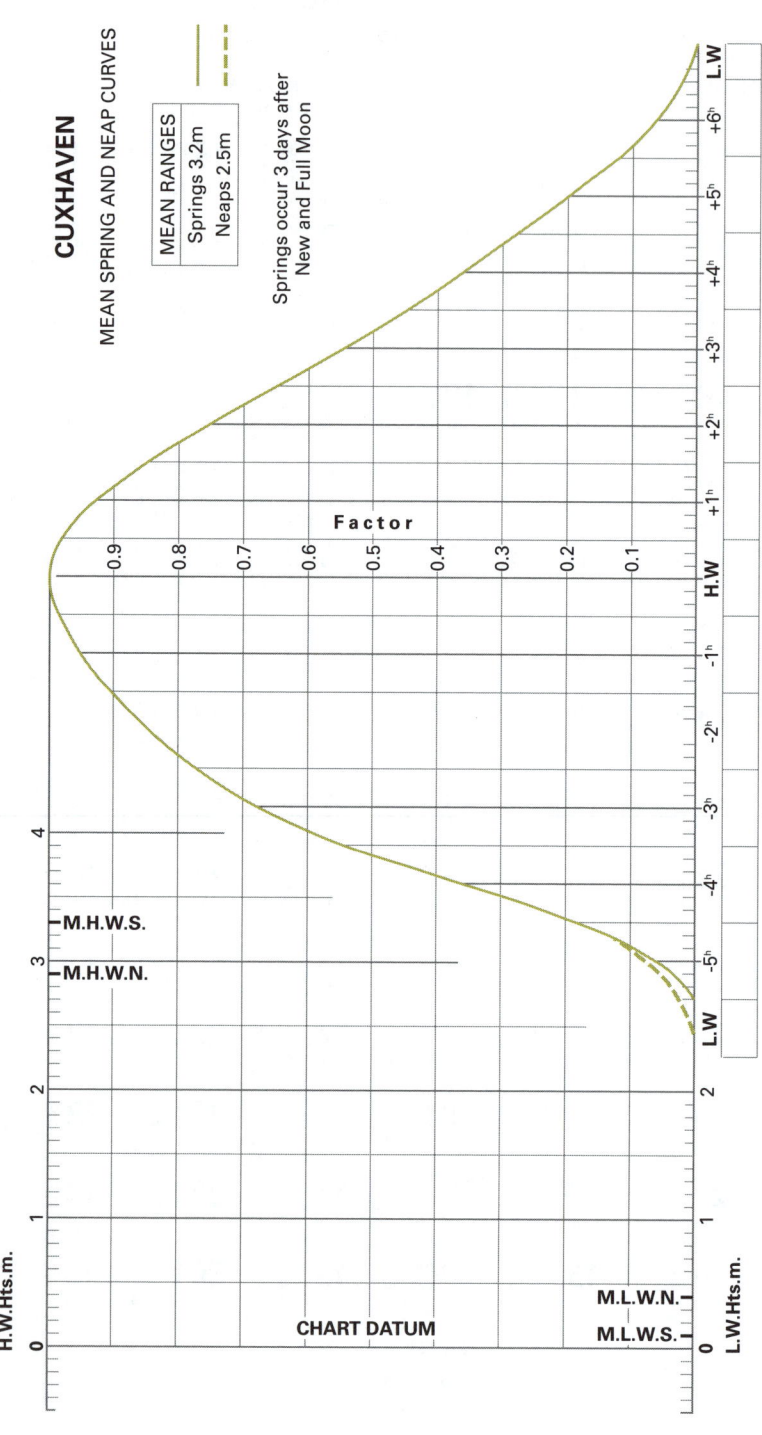

CUXHAVEN

MEAN SPRING AND NEAP CURVES

MEAN RANGES
Springs 3.2m
Neaps 2.5m

Springs occur 3 days after
New and Full Moon

TIME ZONE -0100
(German Standard Time)
Subtract 1 hour for UT
For German Summer Time add
ONE hour in **non-shaded areas**

GERMANY – CUXHAVEN

LAT 53°52'N   LONG 8°43'E

TIMES AND HEIGHTS OF HIGH AND LOW WATERS

Dates in amber are SPRINGS
Dates in yellow are NEAPS

2007

JANUARY

Day	Time m	Time m	Time m	Time m
1 M	0511 0.7	1048 3.6	1746 0.7	2321 3.6
2 TU	0619 0.6	1154 3.6	1849 0.7	
3 W	0020 3.7	0720 0.6	1252 3.6	1943 0.7
4 TH	0109 3.8	0812 0.6	1340 3.6	2028 0.7
5 F	0152 3.9	0856 0.6	1422 3.6	2108 0.7
6 SA	0233 0.6	0939 0.6	1502 3.6	2148 0.7
7 SU	0313 3.9	1019 0.6	1542 3.5	2224 0.6
8 M	0349 3.9	1054 0.5	1618 3.4	2255 0.6
9 TU	0423 3.8	1123 0.5	1652 3.4	2324 0.7
10 W	0457 3.7	1152 3.3	1727 3.3	2354 0.8
11 TH	0532 3.7	1223 0.8	1803 3.3	
12 F	0028 0.9	0611 3.5	1258 0.9	1847 3.2
13 SA	0113 1.0	0703 3.5	1350 1.0	1944 3.3
14 SU	0217 1.1	0809 3.4	1459 1.0	2052 3.3
15 M	0334 1.1	0923 3.5	1614 1.0	2201 3.4
16 TU	0450 0.9	1032 3.5	1723 0.9	2303 3.5
17 W	0557 0.8	1134 3.6	1823 0.9	2358 3.7
18 TH	0657 0.7	1230 3.7	1918 0.8	
19 F	0047 3.8	0751 0.6	1321 3.7	2009 0.7
20 SA	0134 3.9	0840 0.5	1410 3.7	2057 0.6
21 SU	0219 4.0	0928 0.5	1455 3.7	2142 0.6
22 M	0301 4.1	1011 0.4	1536 3.6	2220 0.5
23 TU	0340 4.0	1049 0.3	1615 3.6	2255 0.5
24 W	0420 4.0	1128 0.4	1656 3.6	2334 0.6
25 TH	0504 4.0	1210 0.5	1740 3.6	
26 F	0018 0.7	0551 3.9	1251 0.7	1825 3.5
27 SA	0105 0.7	0643 3.7	1338 0.8	1918 3.4
28 SU	0203 0.8	0749 3.5	1443 0.9	2028 3.4
29 M	0321 0.8	0910 3.4	1604 0.9	2149 3.4
30 TU	0449 0.8	1034 3.4	1727 0.8	2306 3.5
31 W	0609 0.7	1148 3.5	1838 0.8	

FEBRUARY

Day	Time m	Time m	Time m	Time m
1 TH	0009 3.7	0713 0.6	1247 3.5	1934 0.8
2 F	0100 3.9	0804 0.5	1333 3.6	2018 0.7
3 SA	0142 4.0	0847 0.5	1411 3.6	2057 0.6
4 SU	0219 4.0	0925 0.5	1445 3.6	2132 0.6
5 M	0254 4.0	0959 0.5	1517 3.6	2204 0.5
6 TU	0326 3.9	1028 0.5	1547 3.5	2230 0.4
7 W	0354 3.8	1052 0.6	1617 3.7	2255 0.5
8 TH	0424 3.7	1117 0.5	1647 3.7	2321 0.6
9 F	0453 3.7	1140 0.6	1715 3.4	2344 0.7
10 SA	0521 3.6	1202 0.8	1745 3.3	
11 SU	0012 0.8	0559 3.4	1237 0.9	1832 3.2
12 M	0104 0.9	0700 3.3	1341 1.0	1943 3.2
13 TU	0225 1.0	0824 3.3	1510 1.0	2107 3.3
14 W	0400 0.9	0952 3.3	1641 1.0	2227 3.4
15 TH	0527 0.8	1110 3.5	1800 0.9	2334 3.7
16 F	0639 0.6	1214 3.6	1904 0.8	
17 SA	0030 3.8	0738 0.5	1308 3.7	1957 0.6
18 SU	0118 4.0	0828 0.4	1355 3.7	2043 0.4
19 M	0201 4.0	0913 0.3	1437 3.7	2125 0.4
20 TU	0243 4.1	0954 0.2	1516 3.7	2204 0.3
21 W	0322 4.1	1031 0.3	1553 3.7	2239 0.3
22 TH	0401 4.0	1107 0.4	1631 3.7	2316 0.4
23 F	0444 3.9	1144 0.5	1711 3.7	2355 0.6
24 SA	0528 3.8	1221 0.7	1753 3.6	
25 SU	0037 0.6	0618 3.6	1303 0.8	1845 3.4
26 M	0132 0.7	0724 3.3	1407 0.9	1958 3.3
27 TU	0254 0.7	0851 3.2	1537 0.9	2128 3.4
28 W	0432 0.7	1025 3.2	1711 0.9	2254 3.5

MARCH

Day	Time m	Time m	Time m	Time m
1 TH	0600 0.6	1143 3.4	1827 0.8	2359 3.7
2 F	0704 0.5	1239 3.5	1921 0.7	
3 SA	0046 3.9	0749 0.5	1319 3.6	2002 0.5
4 SU	0124 3.9	0826 0.5	1351 3.6	2038 0.5
5 M	0159 3.9	0900 0.4	1420 3.6	2110 0.4
6 TU	0230 3.9	0929 0.4	1447 3.6	2138 0.4
7 W	0257 3.8	0955 0.4	1513 3.6	2202 0.3
8 TH	0323 3.7	1018 0.4	1540 3.6	2226 0.4
9 F	0351 3.7	1041 0.4	1609 3.5	2250 0.4
10 SA	0419 3.6	1103 0.5	1636 3.5	2311 0.5
11 SU	0445 3.5	1121 0.6	1702 3.4	2333 0.6
12 M	0517 3.3	1147 0.7	1742 3.2	
13 TU	0016 0.7	0614 3.1	1246 0.9	1851 3.1
14 W	0136 0.8	0740 3.1	1420 1.0	2023 3.2
15 TH	0320 0.7	0919 3.2	1605 0.9	2154 3.4
16 F	0458 0.6	1045 3.3	1734 0.8	2308 3.6
17 SA	0616 0.5	1152 3.5	1842 0.6	
18 SU	0005 3.8	0716 0.3	1245 3.6	1935 0.4
19 M	0053 4.0	0806 0.2	1330 3.7	2019 0.3
20 TU	0137 4.0	0848 0.1	1410 3.7	2100 0.2
21 W	0218 4.1	0928 0.2	1449 3.7	2139 0.2
22 TH	0300 4.1	1006 0.3	1526 3.8	2219 0.2
23 F	0342 4.0	1042 0.4	1605 3.7	2257 0.3
24 SA	0425 3.8	1118 0.5	1645 3.7	2335 0.4
25 SU	0511 3.6	1155 0.6	1729 3.5	
26 M	0017 0.5	0602 3.4	1238 0.7	1822 3.4
27 TU	0111 0.6	0708 3.1	1341 0.8	1935 3.3
28 W	0231 0.6	0834 3.0	1510 0.9	2106 3.4
29 TH	0411 0.6	1008 3.1	1648 0.8	2234 3.5
30 F	0541 0.5	1126 3.3	1806 0.7	2338 3.6
31 SA	0642 0.4	1217 3.4	1856 0.6	

APRIL

Day	Time m	Time m	Time m	Time m
1 SU	0021 3.7	0720 0.4	1250 3.5	1934 0.5
2 M	0055 3.8	0752 0.4	1320 3.6	2009 0.4
3 TU	0129 3.8	0825 0.3	1348 3.6	2041 0.3
4 W	0200 3.8	0854 0.3	1414 3.6	2108 0.3
5 TH	0227 3.7	0920 0.3	1439 3.6	2132 0.3
6 F	0253 3.7	0944 0.3	1506 3.6	2157 0.3
7 SA	0322 3.6	1009 0.3	1536 3.5	2224 0.3
8 SU	0353 3.5	1033 0.4	1607 3.5	
9 M	0424 3.4	1057 0.5	1638 3.4	2318 0.4
10 TU	0500 3.2	1128 0.6	1719 3.3	
11 W	0000 0.5	0555 3.0	1223 0.7	1823 3.2
12 TH	0113 0.5	0716 3.0	1350 0.8	1951 3.3
13 F	0250 0.5	0850 3.1	1532 0.8	2121 3.4
14 SA	0427 0.4	1015 3.2	1700 0.7	2235 3.6
15 SU	0544 0.3	1121 3.4	1808 0.5	2333 3.8
16 M	0644 0.2	1214 3.5	1903 0.3	
17 TU	0023 3.9	0734 0.1	1300 3.6	1950 0.2
18 W	0110 4.0	0818 0.1	1341 3.7	2033 0.1
19 TH	0154 4.0	0858 0.2	1421 3.8	2114 0.1
20 F	0239 3.9	0938 0.2	1501 3.8	2157 0.2
21 SA	0325 3.8	1018 0.3	1543 3.7	2240 0.2
22 SU	0411 3.6	1057 0.4	1626 3.6	2322 0.3
23 M	0459 3.4	1136 0.5	1712 3.6	
24 TU	0005 0.4	0551 3.2	1221 0.7	1805 3.5
25 W	0058 0.5	0653 3.0	1319 0.7	1912 3.4
26 TH	0209 0.5	0810 2.9	1438 0.8	2034 3.4
27 F	0336 0.5	0934 3.0	1607 0.7	2156 3.5
28 SA	0459 0.4	1047 3.2	1723 0.6	2259 3.6
29 SU	0559 0.3	1137 3.4	1815 0.5	2342 3.6
30 M	0637 0.3	1210 3.5	1853 0.5	

TIDES

Chart Datum: 1·66 metres below Normal Null (German reference level)

TIME ZONE -0100
(German Standard Time)
Subtract 1 hour for UT
For German Summer Time add ONE hour in **non-shaded areas**

GERMANY – CUXHAVEN

LAT 53°52'N   LONG 8°43'E

TIMES AND HEIGHTS OF HIGH AND LOW WATERS

Dates in amber are SPRINGS
Dates in yellow are NEAPS

2007

MAY

Day	Time	m	Day	Time	m
1 TU	0018 / 0711 / 1241 / 1931	3.7 / 0.3 / 3.6 / 0.4	16 W	0659 / 1228 / 1922	0.2 / 3.6 / 0.2
2 W ○	0054 / 0746 / 1313 / 2007	3.7 / 0.4 / 3.6 / 0.4	17 TH	0046 / 0749 / 1315 / 2009	3.9 / 0.2 / 3.7 / 0.1
3 TH	0128 / 0818 / 1343 / 2037	3.7 / 0.4 / 3.7 / 0.3	18 F	0136 / 0833 / 1358 / 2054	3.8 / 0.2 / 3.8 / 0.1
4 F	0158 / 0847 / 1410 / 2105	3.7 / 0.4 / 3.7 / 0.3	19 SA	0224 / 0915 / 1442 / 2140	3.7 / 0.3 / 3.8 / 0.2
5 SA	0228 / 0915 / 1440 / 2135	3.6 / 0.4 / 3.6 / 0.3	20 SU	0312 / 0959 / 1527 / 2228	3.6 / 0.4 / 3.8 / 0.2
6 SU	0302 / 0945 / 1514 / 2207	3.5 / 0.4 / 3.6 / 0.3	21 M	0401 / 1042 / 1612 / 2313	3.5 / 0.4 / 3.7 / 0.2
7 M	0339 / 1016 / 1551 / 2242	3.4 / 0.4 / 3.6 / 0.3	22 TU	0448 / 1123 / 1657 / 2356	3.3 / 0.5 / 3.6 / 0.3
8 TU	0418 / 1049 / 1630 / 2319	3.3 / 0.5 / 3.5 / 0.3	23 W ☽	0538 / 1205 / 1747	3.2 / 0.6 / 3.6
9 W	0501 / 1128 / 1715	3.2 / 0.6 / 3.4	24 TH	0043 / 0632 / 1255 / 1843	0.4 / 3.1 / 0.6 / 3.5
10 TH ☽	0004 / 0553 / 1221 / 1812	0.3 / 3.1 / 0.6 / 3.4	25 F	0139 / 0733 / 1356 / 1949	0.5 / 3.0 / 0.7 / 3.4
11 F	0106 / 0702 / 1333 / 1926	0.4 / 3.0 / 0.7 / 3.4	26 SA	0245 / 0841 / 1509 / 2059	0.5 / 3.0 / 0.7 / 3.4
12 SA	0227 / 0823 / 1459 / 2046	0.4 / 3.1 / 0.7 / 3.6	27 SU	0356 / 0948 / 1621 / 2204	0.5 / 3.2 / 0.7 / 3.5
13 SU	0351 / 0939 / 1620 / 2157	0.4 / 3.2 / 0.6 / 3.7	28 M	0459 / 1041 / 1719 / 2254	0.4 / 3.3 / 0.6 / 3.6
14 M	0504 / 1043 / 1728 / 2257	0.3 / 3.4 / 0.4 / 3.8	29 TU	0546 / 1123 / 1806 / 2337	0.4 / 3.5 / 0.5 / 3.6
15 TU	0604 / 1138 / 1827 / 2353	0.2 / 3.5 / 0.3 / 3.8	30 W	0626 / 1201 / 1850	0.4 / 3.6 / 0.5

JUNE

Day	Time	m	Day	Time	m
1 F ○	0058 / 0745 / 1315 / 2009	3.7 / 0.5 / 3.7 / 0.4	16 SA	0125 / 0816 / 1343 / 2043	3.7 / 0.4 / 3.8 / 0.2
2 SA	0135 / 0820 / 1349 / 2045	3.7 / 0.5 / 3.7 / 0.4	17 SU	0214 / 0901 / 1429 / 2130	3.6 / 0.4 / 3.9 / 0.3
3 SU	0213 / 0857 / 1425 / 2123	3.6 / 0.5 / 3.8 / 0.4	18 M	0302 / 0946 / 1514 / 2218	3.6 / 0.4 / 3.9 / 0.3
4 M	0253 / 0934 / 1504 / 2202	3.6 / 0.5 / 3.8 / 0.3	19 TU	0349 / 1029 / 1558 / 2302	3.5 / 0.4 / 3.8 / 0.3
5 TU	0334 / 1010 / 1544 / 2240	3.5 / 0.4 / 3.7 / 0.3	20 W	0434 / 1108 / 1640 / 2342	3.3 / 0.4 / 3.7 / 0.3
6 W	0416 / 1048 / 1626 / 2322	3.4 / 0.5 / 3.7 / 0.3	21 TH	0517 / 1145 / 1722	3.3 / 0.5 / 3.7
7 TH	0502 / 1131 / 1713	3.3 / 0.5 / 3.6	22 F ☽	0020 / 0600 / 1224 / 1807	0.4 / 3.2 / 0.6 / 3.6
8 F ☽	0009 / 0552 / 1221 / 1804	0.3 / 3.2 / 0.5 / 3.6	23 SA	0100 / 0646 / 1308 / 1856	0.5 / 3.2 / 0.7 / 3.5
9 SA	0102 / 0649 / 1319 / 1905	0.3 / 3.2 / 0.6 / 3.6	24 SU	0146 / 0738 / 1401 / 1954	0.6 / 3.2 / 0.7 / 3.5
10 SU	0204 / 0753 / 1427 / 2012	0.4 / 3.2 / 0.6 / 3.7	25 M	0242 / 0836 / 1506 / 2058	0.6 / 3.2 / 0.8 / 3.5
11 M	0314 / 0900 / 1539 / 2120	0.4 / 3.3 / 0.6 / 3.7	26 TU	0346 / 0937 / 1614 / 2200	0.7 / 3.3 / 0.8 / 3.5
12 TU	0422 / 1004 / 1649 / 2225	0.4 / 3.4 / 0.5 / 3.7	27 W	0448 / 1032 / 1715 / 2255	0.6 / 3.4 / 0.7 / 3.5
13 W	0526 / 1104 / 1755 / 2329	0.4 / 3.5 / 0.4 / 3.7	28 TH	0542 / 1122 / 1810 / 2346	0.6 / 3.5 / 0.6 / 3.6
14 TH	0629 / 1202 / 1858	0.4 / 3.6 / 0.3	29 F	0631 / 1208 / 1901	0.6 / 3.7 / 0.6
15 F ●	0030 / 0726 / 1256 / 1954	3.7 / 0.4 / 3.7 / 0.2	30 SA ○	0034 / 0718 / 1252 / 1948	3.6 / 0.6 / 3.8 / 0.5

JULY

Day	Time	m	Day	Time	m
1 SU	0120 / 0803 / 1334 / 2033	3.7 / 0.6 / 3.8 / 0.5	16 M	0208 / 0852 / 1419 / 2123	3.6 / 0.5 / 4.0 / 0.4
2 M	0205 / 0847 / 1416 / 2117	3.7 / 0.6 / 3.9 / 0.5	17 TU	0251 / 0934 / 1501 / 2206	3.6 / 0.5 / 4.0 / 0.4
3 TU	0249 / 0930 / 1457 / 2158	3.7 / 0.5 / 3.9 / 0.4	18 W	0332 / 1014 / 1541 / 2244	3.5 / 0.4 / 3.9 / 0.4
4 W	0330 / 1008 / 1536 / 2237	3.6 / 0.5 / 3.9 / 0.3	19 TH	0410 / 1047 / 1616 / 2315	3.5 / 0.4 / 3.8 / 0.3
5 TH	0409 / 1043 / 1616 / 2317	3.5 / 0.4 / 3.8 / 0.3	20 F	0445 / 1117 / 1651 / 2346	3.4 / 0.5 / 3.8 / 0.5
6 F	0453 / 1125 / 1702	3.4 / 0.5 / 3.8	21 SA	0520 / 1149 / 1727	3.4 / 0.6 / 3.7
7 SA ☽	0003 / 0540 / 1217 / 1750	0.3 / 3.4 / 0.4 / 3.8	22 SU ☽	0017 / 0556 / 1220 / 1804	0.6 / 3.4 / 0.7 / 3.6
8 SU	0049 / 0628 / 1302 / 1842	0.4 / 3.4 / 0.6 / 3.8	23 M	0048 / 0634 / 1257 / 1848	0.7 / 3.3 / 0.8 / 3.5
9 M	0138 / 0721 / 1357 / 1941	0.5 / 3.4 / 0.6 / 3.7	24 TU	0129 / 0724 / 1352 / 1949	0.8 / 3.3 / 0.9 / 3.4
10 TU	0236 / 0822 / 1505 / 2051	0.6 / 3.4 / 0.7 / 3.7	25 W	0230 / 0828 / 1505 / 2102	0.9 / 3.3 / 0.9 / 3.4
11 W	0346 / 0932 / 1621 / 2205	0.6 / 3.5 / 0.6 / 3.6	26 TH	0345 / 0939 / 1624 / 2215	0.9 / 3.4 / 0.8 / 3.4
12 TH	0500 / 1042 / 1737 / 2317	0.6 / 3.5 / 0.5 / 3.6	27 F	0458 / 1045 / 1735 / 2320	0.8 / 3.5 / 0.7 / 3.5
13 F	0610 / 1148 / 1846	0.5 / 3.7 / 0.4	28 SA	0603 / 1143 / 1838	0.8 / 3.6 / 0.6
14 SA ●	0023 / 0713 / 1245 / 1947	3.6 / 0.5 / 3.8 / 0.4	29 SU	0016 / 0659 / 1234 / 1933	3.6 / 0.8 / 3.8 / 0.6
15 SU	0120 / 0806 / 1334 / 2037	3.6 / 0.5 / 3.9 / 0.4	30 M ○	0108 / 0751 / 1320 / 2022	3.7 / 0.7 / 3.9 / 0.5
			31 TU	0155 / 0838 / 1404 / 2108	3.7 / 0.6 / 4.0 / 0.5

AUGUST

Day	Time	m	Day	Time	m
1 W	0238 / 0921 / 1443 / 2148	3.7 / 0.5 / 4.1 / 0.4	16 TH	0307 / 0952 / 1517 / 2215	3.6 / 0.5 / 3.9 / 0.5
2 TH	0316 / 0957 / 1520 / 2224	3.7 / 0.5 / 4.1 / 0.3	17 F	0337 / 1020 / 1547 / 2241	3.6 / 0.4 / 3.9 / 0.5
3 F	0352 / 1031 / 1558 / 2301	3.6 / 0.4 / 4.0 / 0.3	18 SA	0407 / 1045 / 1616 / 2306	3.5 / 0.5 / 3.8 / 0.5
4 SA	0432 / 1110 / 1641 / 2343	3.6 / 0.5 / 4.0 / 0.5	19 SU	0437 / 1112 / 1647 / 2332	3.5 / 0.6 / 3.7 / 0.7
5 SU ☽	0516 / 1154 / 1728	3.6 / 0.6 / 3.9	20 M ☽	0507 / 1137 / 1717 / 2356	3.5 / 0.8 / 3.6 / 0.9
6 M	0025 / 0600 / 1239 / 1818	0.6 / 3.6 / 0.7 / 3.8	21 TU	0538 / 1204 / 1752	3.4 / 0.9 / 3.6
7 TU	0107 / 0648 / 1330 / 1916	0.7 / 3.5 / 0.7 / 3.6	22 W	0026 / 0620 / 1249 / 1848	1.0 / 3.3 / 1.0 / 3.3
8 W	0203 / 0751 / 1439 / 2032	0.8 / 3.4 / 0.7 / 3.5	23 TH	0121 / 0725 / 1403 / 2008	1.0 / 3.3 / 1.0 / 3.2
9 TH	0320 / 0911 / 1606 / 2157	0.9 / 3.5 / 0.7 / 3.4	24 F	0246 / 0848 / 1537 / 2137	1.1 / 3.3 / 0.9 / 3.3
10 F	0447 / 1033 / 1732 / 2318	0.8 / 3.6 / 0.6 / 3.5	25 SA	0419 / 1011 / 1706 / 2256	1.0 / 3.4 / 0.7 / 3.4
11 SA	0604 / 1143 / 1844	0.7 / 3.7 / 0.6	26 SU	0539 / 1119 / 1818 / 2359	0.9 / 3.6 / 0.6 / 3.5
12 SU	0023 / 0707 / 1239 / 1941	3.6 / 0.7 / 3.9 / 0.5	27 M	0643 / 1213 / 1916	0.8 / 3.8 / 0.5
13 M ●	0114 / 0757 / 1324 / 2028	3.6 / 0.7 / 4.0 / 0.6	28 TU ○	0051 / 0736 / 1300 / 2005	3.6 / 0.7 / 4.0 / 0.6
14 TU	0157 / 0840 / 1405 / 2109	3.6 / 0.6 / 4.0 / 0.5	29 W	0136 / 0821 / 1342 / 2048	3.7 / 0.6 / 4.1 / 0.4
15 W	0234 / 0918 / 1443 / 2145	3.6 / 0.5 / 4.0 / 0.5	30 TH	0216 / 0901 / 1421 / 2127	3.7 / 0.5 / 4.1 / 0.4
			31 F	0253 / 0938 / 1458 / 2203	3.8 / 0.5 / 4.0 / 0.4

Chart Datum: 1·66 metres below Normal Null (German reference level)

GERMANY – CUXHAVEN

TIME ZONE -0100
(German Standard Time)
Subtract 1 hour for UT
For German Summer Time add
ONE hour in **non-shaded areas**

LAT 53°52′N   LONG 8°43′E

TIMES AND HEIGHTS OF HIGH AND LOW WATERS

Dates in amber are **SPRINGS**
Dates in yellow are **NEAPS**

2007

SEPTEMBER

Day	Time m	Day	Time m
1 SA	0328 3.8 / 1014 0.5 / 1537 4.1 / 2238 0.5	16 SU	0328 3.7 / 1013 0.5 / 1541 3.7 / 2227 0.6
2 SU	0405 3.8 / 1051 0.5 / 1619 4.0 / 2316 0.6	17 M	0356 3.6 / 1037 0.6 / 1610 3.6 / 2251 0.7
3 M	0446 3.7 / 1132 0.6 / 1706 3.9 / 2356 0.8	18 TU	0425 3.5 / 1102 0.7 / 1639 3.5 / 2313 0.9
4 TU ◐	0530 3.6 / 1216 0.7 / 1757 3.7	19 W ◑	0455 3.5 / 1127 0.9 / 1712 3.4 / 2341 1.0
5 W	0039 0.9 / 0620 3.5 / 1308 0.8 / 1859 3.4	20 TH	0533 3.4 / 1207 0.9 / 1803 3.2
6 TH	0137 1.0 / 0728 3.4 / 1422 0.8 / 2021 3.3	21 F	0033 1.1 / 0636 3.2 / 1318 1.0 / 1924 3.1
7 F	0301 1.1 / 0857 3.5 / 1558 0.8 / 2155 3.3	22 SA	0159 1.2 / 0803 3.3 / 1456 0.9 / 2100 3.1
8 SA	0438 1.0 / 1027 3.6 / 1732 0.8 / 2319 3.4	23 SU	0341 1.1 / 0935 3.4 / 1635 0.7 / 2227 3.3
9 SU	0601 0.9 / 1138 3.8 / 1841 0.6	24 M	0511 0.9 / 1049 3.6 / 1752 0.6 / 2334 3.4
10 M	0019 3.5 / 0659 0.8 / 1228 3.9 / 1929 0.6	25 TU	0618 0.8 / 1145 3.8 / 1851 0.5
11 TU ●	0101 3.6 / 0741 0.7 / 1307 4.0 / 2007 0.5	26 W ○	0025 3.6 / 0710 0.7 / 1231 4.0 / 1939 0.4
12 W	0135 3.7 / 0819 0.6 / 1343 4.0 / 2043 0.5	27 TH	0108 3.7 / 0755 0.6 / 1313 4.1 / 2021 0.4
13 TH	0206 3.7 / 0854 0.6 / 1417 3.9 / 2114 0.5	28 F	0147 3.8 / 0835 0.5 / 1354 4.1 / 2100 0.4
14 F	0235 3.7 / 0924 0.5 / 1447 3.9 / 2141 0.6	29 SA	0224 3.8 / 0914 0.5 / 1435 4.2 / 2137 0.5
15 SA	0301 3.7 / 0950 0.5 / 1514 3.8 / 2204 0.6	30 SU	0302 3.9 / 0954 0.5 / 1517 4.1 / 2214 0.6

OCTOBER

Day	Time m	Day	Time m
1 M	0340 3.9 / 1033 0.5 / 1601 3.9 / 2252 0.7	16 TU	0323 3.6 / 1010 0.6 / 1541 3.5 / 2219 0.7
2 TU	0422 3.8 / 1113 0.6 / 1649 3.7 / 2332 0.8	17 W	0354 3.6 / 1038 0.7 / 1614 3.4 / 2245 0.8
3 W ◑	0507 3.7 / 1158 0.7 / 1742 3.5	18 TH	0427 3.5 / 1108 0.8 / 1650 3.3 / 2317 1.0
4 TH ◑	0017 1.0 / 0600 3.5 / 1252 0.8 / 1846 3.3	19 F ◑	0506 3.4 / 1148 0.9 / 1739 3.1
5 F	0117 1.1 / 0709 3.4 / 1407 0.8 / 2008 3.1	20 SA	0007 1.1 / 0604 3.3 / 1251 0.9 / 1852 3.0
6 SA	0242 1.1 / 0838 3.5 / 1543 0.9 / 2142 3.2	21 SU	0126 1.1 / 0725 3.3 / 1422 0.8 / 2022 3.1
7 SU	0420 1.1 / 1009 3.6 / 1717 0.8 / 2305 3.3	22 M	0303 1.1 / 0854 3.5 / 1557 0.7 / 2149 3.2
8 M	0544 0.9 / 1120 3.7 / 1824 0.7	23 TU	0432 0.9 / 1010 3.6 / 1715 0.6 / 2257 3.4
9 TU	0000 3.5 / 0638 0.8 / 1206 3.8 / 1904 0.6	24 W	0541 0.8 / 1109 3.8 / 1815 0.5 / 2349 3.6
10 W	0034 3.6 / 0714 0.7 / 1239 3.9 / 1935 0.6	25 TH	0636 0.7 / 1157 3.9 / 1905 0.5
11 TH ●	0102 3.7 / 0749 0.7 / 1313 3.9 / 2008 0.6	26 F ○	0035 3.7 / 0724 0.6 / 1244 4.0 / 1950 0.4
12 F	0132 3.7 / 0824 0.6 / 1346 3.8 / 2040 0.6	27 SA	0116 3.8 / 0808 0.5 / 1329 4.0 / 2031 0.5
13 SA	0201 3.7 / 0854 0.6 / 1414 4.0 / 2107 0.6	28 SU	0156 3.9 / 0851 0.5 / 1414 4.0 / 2112 0.6
14 SU	0227 3.7 / 0920 0.6 / 1443 3.7 / 2131 0.6	29 M	0238 3.9 / 0935 0.5 / 1501 3.9 / 2154 0.7
15 M	0253 3.7 / 0945 0.5 / 1511 3.6 / 2154 0.6	30 TU	0321 3.9 / 1020 0.5 / 1550 3.8 / 2236 0.7
		31 W	0405 3.8 / 1104 0.5 / 1638 3.5 / 2317 0.8

NOVEMBER

Day	Time m	Day	Time m
1 TH ◑	0451 3.7 / 1148 0.6 / 1730 3.4	16 F	0413 3.6 / 1102 0.7 / 1641 3.3 / 2310 0.9
2 F	0002 0.9 / 0543 3.6 / 1240 0.7 / 1831 3.2	17 SA	0453 3.6 / 1143 0.7 / 1728 3.2 / 2357 1.0 ●
3 SA	0058 1.0 / 0647 3.5 / 1347 0.8 / 1944 3.0	18 SU	0544 3.5 / 1237 0.7 / 1829 3.1
4 SU	0212 1.0 / 0806 3.5 / 1511 0.8 / 2108 3.1	19 M	0101 1.0 / 0651 3.5 / 1350 0.7 / 1944 3.1
5 M	0340 1.0 / 0930 3.5 / 1636 0.8 / 2225 3.3	20 TU	0222 1.0 / 0809 3.6 / 1513 0.7 / 2102 3.2
6 TU	0501 1.0 / 1040 3.6 / 1743 0.7 / 2320 3.4	21 W	0344 1.0 / 0923 3.7 / 1629 0.7 / 2211 3.4
7 W	0559 0.8 / 1128 3.7 / 1825 0.7 / 2356 3.6	22 TH	0456 0.8 / 1027 3.8 / 1732 0.6 / 2308 3.6
8 TH	0638 0.7 / 1204 3.8 / 1857 0.7	23 F	0558 0.7 / 1124 3.9 / 1828 0.5
9 F	0025 3.7 / 0714 0.7 / 1240 3.8 / 1931 0.7	24 SA ○	0000 3.7 / 0654 0.6 / 1218 3.9 / 1921 0.5
10 SA ●	0057 3.7 / 0751 0.7 / 1315 3.8 / 2006 0.7	25 SU	0049 3.8 / 0746 0.5 / 1309 3.9 / 2008 0.5
11 SU	0129 3.7 / 0824 0.6 / 1347 3.7 / 2036 0.7	26 M	0134 3.9 / 0833 0.5 / 1359 3.8 / 2053 0.6
12 M	0158 3.7 / 0854 0.6 / 1418 3.7 / 2105 0.7	27 TU	0219 3.9 / 0922 0.5 / 1450 3.8 / 2140 0.7
13 TU	0228 3.7 / 0924 0.6 / 1451 3.6 / 2133 0.7	28 W	0306 3.9 / 1012 0.5 / 1541 3.6 / 2225 0.7
14 W	0301 3.7 / 0955 0.6 / 1525 3.5 / 2202 0.7	29 TH	0352 3.9 / 1059 0.5 / 1629 3.5 / 2307 0.7
15 TH	0336 3.7 / 1027 0.6 / 1602 3.4 / 2233 0.8	30 F	0438 3.8 / 1141 0.5 / 1717 3.3 / 2348 0.8

DECEMBER

Day	Time m	Day	Time m
1 SA ◑	0525 3.7 / 1226 0.6 / 1808 3.2	16 SU ◑	0443 3.7 / 1140 0.6 / 1718 3.3 / 2349 0.8
2 SU	0035 0.8 / 0618 3.6 / 1318 0.7 / 1906 3.1	17 M ◐	0528 3.7 / 1225 0.6 / 1807 3.3
3 M	0132 0.9 / 0720 3.5 / 1420 0.8 / 2012 3.1	18 TU	0040 0.9 / 0621 3.6 / 1319 0.7 / 1905 3.3
4 TU	0240 1.0 / 0830 3.5 / 1530 0.8 / 2121 3.2	19 W	0142 0.9 / 0725 3.7 / 1425 0.8 / 2012 3.3
5 W	0354 1.0 / 0939 3.5 / 1638 0.8 / 2221 3.4	20 TH	0255 1.0 / 0836 3.8 / 1538 0.8 / 2121 3.4
6 TH	0500 1.0 / 1037 3.6 / 1733 0.8 / 2308 3.5	21 F	0410 0.9 / 0947 3.9 / 1649 0.7 / 2228 3.5
7 F	0553 0.9 / 1124 3.7 / 1816 0.8 / 2347 3.6	22 SA	0522 0.7 / 1055 3.7 / 1756 0.7 / 2331 3.6
8 SA	0638 0.8 / 1207 3.7 / 1856 0.8	23 SU	0630 0.6 / 1200 3.7 / 1859 0.6
9 SU ●	0025 3.7 / 0721 0.8 / 1247 3.7 / 1935 0.8	24 M ○	0029 3.8 / 0731 0.5 / 1259 3.7 / 1954 0.6
10 M	0102 3.8 / 0759 0.7 / 1325 3.7 / 2012 0.7	25 TU	0120 3.9 / 0824 0.4 / 1351 3.7 / 2042 0.6
11 TU	0137 3.8 / 0836 0.7 / 1402 3.6 / 2048 0.7	26 W	0207 3.9 / 0914 0.5 / 1441 3.6 / 2129 0.6
12 W	0213 3.8 / 0913 0.6 / 1441 3.6 / 2124 0.7	27 TH	0254 4.0 / 1005 0.5 / 1530 3.6 / 2215 0.6
13 TH	0250 3.8 / 0950 0.6 / 1519 3.5 / 2158 0.7	28 F	0340 3.9 / 1051 0.4 / 1615 3.5 / 2255 0.6
14 F	0326 3.8 / 1024 0.5 / 1556 3.5 / 2230 0.7	29 SA	0422 3.9 / 1129 0.4 / 1656 3.4 / 2330 0.6
15 SA	0403 3.7 / 1100 0.5 / 1635 3.4 / 2306 0.7	30 SU	0502 3.8 / 1204 0.5 / 1737 3.3
		31 M ◑	0006 0.7 / 0543 3.7 / 1240 0.6 / 1819 3.2

Chart Datum: 1·66 metres below Normal Null (German reference level)

TIDES

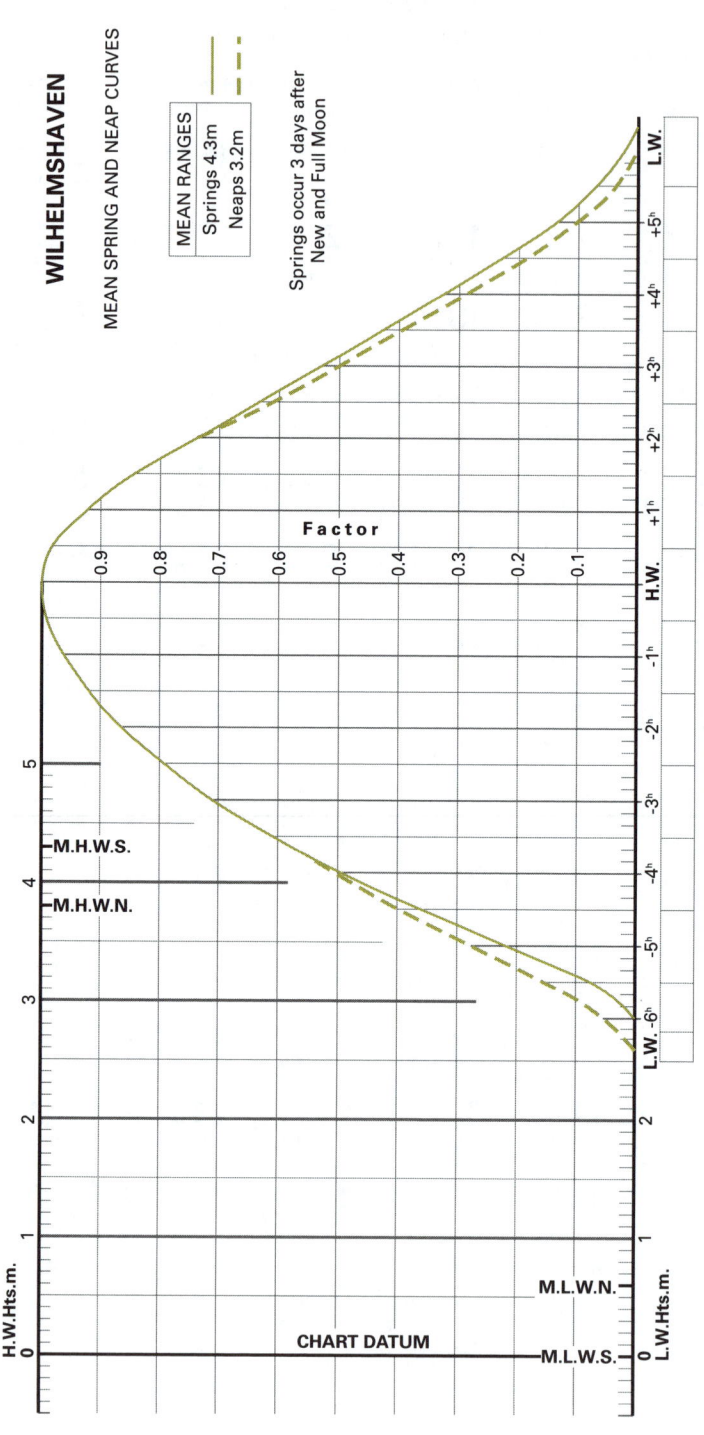

WILHELMSHAVEN

MEAN SPRING AND NEAP CURVES

MEAN RANGES
Springs 4.3m
Neaps 3.2m

Springs occur 3 days after
New and Full Moon

Factor

0.9 0.8 0.7 0.6 0.5 0.4 0.3 0.2 0.1

H.W.Hts.m.

M.H.W.S.

M.H.W.N.

CHART DATUM

M.L.W.N.

M.L.W.S.

L.W.Hts.m.

H.W.

L.W.

TIME ZONE -0100
(German Standard Time)
Subtract 1 hour for UT
For German Summer Time add
ONE hour in **non-shaded areas**

GERMANY – WILHELMSHAVEN

LAT 53°31'N   LONG 8°09'E

TIMES AND HEIGHTS OF HIGH AND LOW WATERS

Dates in amber are **SPRINGS**
Dates in yellow are **NEAPS**

2007

JANUARY

Day	Time	m	Day	Time	m
1 M	0410 / 1034 / 1648 / 2304	0.9 / 4.6 / 0.9 / 4.5	16 TU	0353 / 1013 / 1628 / 2243	1.3 / 4.4 / 1.2 / 4.5
2 TU	0520 / 1140 / 1751	0.8 / 4.6 / 0.9	17 W	0501 / 1116 / 1730 / 2339	1.1 / 4.5 / 1.1 / 4.7
3 W ○	0003 / 0624 / 1238 / 1847	4.7 / 0.8 / 4.6 / 0.9	18 TH	0601 / 1214 / 1826	1.0 / 4.6 / 1.0
4 TH	0054 / 0717 / 1327 / 1934	4.8 / 0.7 / 4.6 / 0.9	19 F ●	0031 / 0655 / 1307 / 1918	4.8 / 0.9 / 4.7 / 0.9
5 F	0139 / 0802 / 1410 / 2015	4.9 / 0.7 / 4.6 / 0.9	20 SA	0119 / 0747 / 1358 / 2008	4.9 / 0.7 / 4.7 / 0.8
6 SA	0220 / 0846 / 1450 / 2056	5.0 / 0.7 / 4.6 / 0.8	21 SU	0206 / 0836 / 1446 / 2053	5.0 / 0.6 / 4.6 / 0.7
7 SU	0301 / 0927 / 1529 / 2132	5.0 / 0.7 / 4.5 / 0.7	22 M	0249 / 0920 / 1528 / 2129	5.0 / 0.4 / 4.6 / 0.6
8 M	0338 / 1001 / 1604 / 2203	4.9 / 0.6 / 4.4 / 0.7	23 TU	0331 / 0958 / 1606 / 2203	5.0 / 0.4 / 4.5 / 0.6
9 TU	0411 / 1030 / 1637 / 2232	4.8 / 0.6 / 4.4 / 0.8	24 W	0412 / 1037 / 1646 / 2241	5.0 / 0.4 / 4.5 / 0.7
10 W	0443 / 1100 / 1709 / 2303	4.8 / 0.6 / 4.3 / 0.9	25 TH ◑	0456 / 1118 / 1726 / 2323	5.0 / 0.6 / 4.5 / 0.8
11 TH ◑	0517 / 1131 / 1743 / 2336	4.6 / 0.9 / 4.2 / 1.1	26 F	0540 / 1200 / 1809	4.9 / 0.8 / 4.4
12 F	0554 / 1207 / 1824	4.5 / 1.1 / 4.2	27 SA	0007 / 0629 / 1245 / 1900	0.9 / 4.7 / 1.0 / 4.4
13 SA	0020 / 0644 / 1257 / 1920	1.3 / 4.4 / 1.2 / 4.2	28 SU	0103 / 0733 / 1346 / 2009	1.0 / 4.5 / 1.1 / 4.4
14 SU	0123 / 0749 / 1405 / 2029	1.4 / 4.3 / 1.3 / 4.2	29 M	0219 / 0854 / 1505 / 2130	1.0 / 4.4 / 1.2 / 4.4
15 M	0238 / 0902 / 1519 / 2139	1.4 / 4.4 / 1.3 / 4.3	30 TU	0347 / 1019 / 1627 / 2248	1.0 / 4.4 / 1.1 / 4.5
			31 W	0509 / 1133 / 1739 / 2353	0.9 / 4.5 / 1.0 / 4.7

FEBRUARY

Day	Time	m	Day	Time	m
1 TH	0617 / 1232 / 1837	0.8 / 4.5 / 1.0	16 F	0540 / 1200 / 1810	0.9 / 4.6 / 1.0
2 F ○	0045 / 0711 / 1319 / 1925	4.9 / 0.8 / 4.6 / 0.9	17 SA ●	0015 / 0641 / 1257 / 1905	4.8 / 0.7 / 4.6 / 0.8
3 SA	0129 / 0754 / 1359 / 2005	5.0 / 0.7 / 4.6 / 0.8	18 SU	0106 / 0733 / 1346 / 1952	5.0 / 0.5 / 4.7 / 0.6
4 SU	0209 / 0832 / 1434 / 2042	5.0 / 0.7 / 4.6 / 0.7	19 M	0152 / 0820 / 1431 / 2035	5.0 / 0.3 / 4.7 / 0.5
5 M	0245 / 0908 / 1507 / 2113	5.0 / 0.6 / 4.6 / 0.6	20 TU	0235 / 0903 / 1511 / 2114	5.1 / 0.2 / 4.6 / 0.4
6 TU	0317 / 0937 / 1536 / 2140	4.9 / 0.6 / 4.6 / 0.6	21 W	0316 / 0942 / 1547 / 2148	5.1 / 0.3 / 4.6 / 0.4
7 W	0345 / 1002 / 1604 / 2205	4.9 / 0.6 / 4.5 / 0.6	22 TH	0356 / 1018 / 1623 / 2224	5.0 / 0.4 / 4.6 / 0.5
8 TH	0413 / 1027 / 1631 / 2230	4.8 / 0.6 / 4.4 / 0.7	23 F	0438 / 1055 / 1700 / 2301	4.9 / 0.6 / 4.6 / 0.6
9 F	0440 / 1051 / 1705 / 2254	4.7 / 0.8 / 4.3 / 0.9	24 SA ◑	0519 / 1130 / 1738 / 2340	4.8 / 0.8 / 4.5 / 0.7
10 SA ◑	0506 / 1113 / 1724 / 2322	4.5 / 0.9 / 4.3 / 1.0	25 SU	0606 / 1210 / 1828	4.6 / 1.0 / 4.4
11 SU	0541 / 1146 / 1809	4.3 / 1.0 / 4.1	26 M	0032 / 0710 / 1311 / 1940	0.9 / 4.3 / 1.2 / 4.3
12 M	0011 / 0641 / 1247 / 1920	1.2 / 4.2 / 1.3 / 4.1	27 TU	0152 / 0836 / 1437 / 2111	1.0 / 4.2 / 1.3 / 4.4
13 TU	0129 / 0804 / 1413 / 2046	1.3 / 4.1 / 1.4 / 4.2	28 W	0331 / 1010 / 1611 / 2238	1.0 / 4.2 / 1.2 / 4.5
14 W	0301 / 0934 / 1543 / 2208	1.2 / 4.2 / 1.3 / 4.4			
15 TH	0427 / 1054 / 1703 / 2317	1.1 / 4.4 / 1.1 / 4.6			

MARCH

Day	Time	m	Day	Time	m
1 TH	0502 / 1129 / 1729 / 2346	0.9 / 4.3 / 1.0 / 4.7	16 F	0356 / 1032 / 1634 / 2254	0.9 / 4.2 / 1.0 / 4.6
2 F	0608 / 1224 / 1825	0.7 / 4.5 / 0.9	17 SA	0515 / 1142 / 1745 / 2354	0.7 / 4.4 / 0.8 / 4.8
3 SA	0034 / 0656 / 1306 / 1909	4.8 / 0.7 / 4.6 / 0.8	18 SU	0618 / 1238 / 1842	0.5 / 4.6 / 0.6
4 SU ○	0115 / 0734 / 1341 / 1946	4.9 / 0.6 / 4.6 / 0.7	19 M ●	0046 / 0710 / 1326 / 1928	5.0 / 0.3 / 4.6 / 0.4
5 M	0151 / 0808 / 1412 / 2019	4.9 / 0.5 / 4.6 / 0.5	20 TU	0132 / 0756 / 1408 / 2010	5.0 / 0.2 / 4.7 / 0.3
6 TU	0223 / 0839 / 1440 / 2047	4.9 / 0.5 / 4.6 / 0.5	21 W	0215 / 0837 / 1447 / 2050	5.1 / 0.2 / 4.7 / 0.3
7 W	0251 / 0905 / 1505 / 2111	4.9 / 0.5 / 4.6 / 0.4	22 TH	0257 / 0917 / 1523 / 2128	5.1 / 0.2 / 4.7 / 0.3
8 TH	0317 / 0928 / 1530 / 2135	4.8 / 0.5 / 4.6 / 0.5	23 F	0339 / 0953 / 1559 / 2204	5.0 / 0.4 / 4.7 / 0.3
9 F	0343 / 0951 / 1557 / 2159	4.7 / 0.5 / 4.5 / 0.6	24 SA	0421 / 1028 / 1636 / 2241	4.8 / 0.5 / 4.6 / 0.5
10 SA	0408 / 1014 / 1620 / 2221	4.6 / 0.6 / 4.4 / 0.7	25 SU ◑	0503 / 1103 / 1716 / 2321	4.6 / 0.7 / 4.5 / 0.6
11 SU	0431 / 1032 / 1643 / 2242	4.5 / 0.7 / 4.3 / 0.8	26 M	0551 / 1144 / 1806	4.4 / 0.9 / 4.4
12 M ◑	0501 / 1057 / 1722 / 2323	4.2 / 0.9 / 4.1 / 1.0	27 TU ◑	0013 / 0655 / 1244 / 1919	0.7 / 4.1 / 1.1 / 4.3
13 TU	0556 / 1152 / 1831	4.0 / 1.2 / 4.0	28 W	0131 / 0821 / 1411 / 2051	0.9 / 4.0 / 1.2 / 4.3
14 W	0039 / 0723 / 1322 / 2005	1.1 / 4.0 / 1.3 / 4.1	29 TH	0311 / 0955 / 1549 / 2222	0.9 / 4.0 / 1.1 / 4.5
15 TH	0219 / 0903 / 1505 / 2138	1.1 / 4.0 / 1.3 / 4.3	30 F	0443 / 1114 / 1708 / 2329	0.8 / 4.2 / 0.9 / 4.6
			31 SA	0546 / 1205 / 1800	0.6 / 4.4 / 0.7

APRIL

Day	Time	m	Day	Time	m
1 SU	0013 / 0626 / 1240 / 1839	4.7 / 0.5 / 4.5 / 0.6	16 M	0546 / 1210 / 1809	0.3 / 4.5 / 0.5
2 M ○	0048 / 0700 / 1312 / 1916	4.8 / 0.5 / 4.6 / 0.5	17 TU ●	0020 / 0640 / 1258 / 1859	4.9 / 0.2 / 4.6 / 0.3
3 TU	0123 / 0734 / 1343 / 1949	4.8 / 0.4 / 4.6 / 0.4	18 W	0109 / 0726 / 1340 / 1943	5.0 / 0.1 / 4.7 / 0.2
4 W	0155 / 0804 / 1409 / 2017	4.8 / 0.4 / 4.6 / 0.4	19 TH	0154 / 0808 / 1420 / 2025	5.0 / 0.2 / 4.8 / 0.2
5 TH	0223 / 0831 / 1433 / 2041	4.8 / 0.4 / 4.7 / 0.4	20 F	0238 / 0848 / 1459 / 2106	4.9 / 0.3 / 4.8 / 0.2
6 F	0249 / 0854 / 1459 / 2106	4.7 / 0.4 / 4.6 / 0.4	21 SA	0323 / 0928 / 1538 / 2147	4.8 / 0.4 / 4.7 / 0.3
7 SA	0316 / 0918 / 1527 / 2132	4.6 / 0.4 / 4.5 / 0.4	22 SU	0408 / 1005 / 1619 / 2226	4.6 / 0.5 / 4.6 / 0.3
8 SU	0344 / 0943 / 1555 / 2158	4.5 / 0.5 / 4.5 / 0.5	23 M	0453 / 1043 / 1701 / 2309	4.4 / 0.6 / 4.6 / 0.5
9 M	0413 / 1007 / 1624 / 2225	4.3 / 0.6 / 4.4 / 0.6	24 TU ◑	0542 / 1126 / 1752	4.2 / 0.8 / 4.5
10 TU ◑	0447 / 1037 / 1703 / 2306	4.2 / 0.8 / 4.2 / 0.7	25 W	0001 / 0642 / 1223 / 1859	0.6 / 4.0 / 0.9 / 4.4
11 W	0540 / 1128 / 1808	4.0 / 1.0 / 4.1	26 TH	0110 / 0758 / 1341 / 2022	0.7 / 3.9 / 1.0 / 4.3
12 TH	0015 / 0701 / 1252 / 1937	0.8 / 3.9 / 1.1 / 4.2	27 F	0237 / 0923 / 1509 / 2146	0.7 / 4.0 / 0.9 / 4.4
13 F	0150 / 0837 / 1432 / 2108	0.8 / 4.0 / 1.1 / 4.4	28 SA	0401 / 1037 / 1626 / 2252	0.6 / 4.1 / 0.8 / 4.5
14 SA	0326 / 1005 / 1600 / 2225	0.7 / 4.2 / 0.9 / 4.6	29 SU	0503 / 1127 / 1719 / 2336	0.5 / 4.3 / 0.6 / 4.6
15 SU	0443 / 1114 / 1711 / 2326	0.5 / 4.4 / 0.7 / 4.8	30 M	0543 / 1202 / 1758	0.4 / 4.5 / 0.6

Chart Datum: 2·26 metres below Normal Null (German reference level)

TIDES

GERMANY – WILHELMSHAVEN

LAT 53°31'N LONG 8°09'E

TIMES AND HEIGHTS OF HIGH AND LOW WATERS

TIME ZONE –0100
(German Standard Time)
Subtract 1 hour for UT
For German Summer Time add
ONE hour in non-shaded areas

Dates in amber are SPRINGS
Dates in yellow are NEAPS

2007

MAY

Day	Time	m		Day	Time	m
1 TU	0012	4.7		16 W	0606	0.3
	0619	0.4			1226	4.6
	1234	4.6			1830	0.3 ●
	1837	0.5				
2 W	0048	4.7		17 TH	0046	4.9
	0655	0.5			0657	0.2
	1308	4.6			1313	4.7
○	1915	0.5			1919	0.2
3 TH	0123	4.7		18 F	0136	4.8
	0729	0.4			0742	0.3
	1338	4.7			1356	4.8
	1946	0.4			2003	0.2
4 F	0154	4.7		19 SA	0223	4.7
	0758	0.4			0824	0.3
	1405	4.7			1438	4.8
	2014	0.4			2049	0.2
5 SA	0224	4.6		20 SU	0310	4.6
	0826	0.4			0907	0.4
	1435	4.7			1522	4.8
	2044	0.4			2134	0.3
6 SU	0257	4.5		21 M	0358	4.4
	0854	0.5			0949	0.5
	1508	4.6			1606	4.7
	2115	0.4			2218	0.3
7 M	0332	4.4		22 TU	0443	4.3
	0925	0.5			1029	0.6
	1542	4.5			1650	4.6
	2149	0.4			2301	0.4
8 TU	0409	4.3		23 W	0530	4.1
	0959	0.6			1112	0.7
	1619	4.5			1737	4.6
	2225	0.4		☽	2348	0.5
9 W	0450	4.2		24 TH	0621	4.0
	1038	0.7			1201	0.8
	1703	4.4			1833	4.5
	2310	0.5				
10 TH	0542	4.0		25 F	0043	0.6
	1127	0.8			0721	4.0
☽	1801	4.3			1301	0.8
					1938	4.4
11 F	0010	0.5		26 SA	0149	0.6
	0650	4.0			0830	4.0
	1237	0.9			1413	0.8
	1916	4.3			2050	4.4
12 SA	0130	0.6		27 SU	0301	0.5
	0811	4.0			0937	4.1
	1401	0.9			1524	0.8
	2037	4.3			2155	4.5
13 SU	0253	0.5		28 M	0404	0.6
	0930	4.2			1032	4.3
	1521	0.8			1624	0.7
	2151	4.3			2247	4.5
14 M	0406	0.4		29 TU	0453	0.5
	1036	4.3			1114	4.4
	1630	0.6			1712	0.7
	2253	4.8			2330	4.6
15 TU	0508	0.3		30 W	0536	0.5
	1134	4.5			1152	4.6
	1732	0.4			1757	0.6
	2351	4.8				
				31 TH	0011	4.6
					0618	0.6
					1231	4.6
					1840	0.6

JUNE

Day	Time	m		Day	Time	m
1 F	0051	4.6		16 SA	0123	4.7
	0656	0.6			0725	0.4
	1308	4.7			1339	4.8
○	1918	0.4			1952	0.3
2 SA	0129	4.6		17 SU	0212	4.7
	0732	0.5			0810	0.5
	1343	4.7			1424	4.9
	1955	0.5			2040	0.3
3 SU	0207	4.6		18 M	0259	4.5
	0809	0.5			0855	0.5
	1420	4.8			1509	4.9
	2033	0.5			2127	0.3
4 M	0248	4.6		19 TU	0346	4.4
	0846	0.5			0938	0.5
	1458	4.8			1553	4.8
	2111	0.4			2210	0.3
5 TU	0328	4.4		20 W	0428	4.3
	0922	0.5			1017	0.5
	1537	4.7			1635	4.8
	2149	0.4			2249	0.3
6 W	0410	4.3		21 TH	0509	4.2
	0959	0.6			1054	0.5
	1618	4.6			1715	4.7
	2230	0.3			2328	0.5
7 TH	0454	4.2		22 F	0549	4.2
	1041	0.6			1133	0.7
	1704	4.6			1758	4.6
	2317	0.3				
8 F	0543	4.2		23 SA	0008	0.6
	1129	0.7			0634	4.1
☽	1756	4.6			1216	0.8
				☽	1845	4.5
9 SA	0009	0.4		24 SU	0054	0.7
	0638	4.1			0724	4.1
	1225	0.7			1309	0.9
	1857	4.6			1942	4.4
10 SU	0111	0.4		25 M	0151	0.8
	0742	4.2			0823	4.2
	1331	0.8			1413	1.0
	2005	4.6			2046	4.4
11 M	0219	0.5		26 TU	0256	0.8
	0849	4.3			0924	4.3
	1443	0.7			1521	1.0
	2114	4.7			2149	4.5
12 TU	0327	0.5		27 W	0357	0.8
	0955	4.4			1020	4.4
	1552	0.6			1623	0.9
	2221	4.7			2245	4.5
13 W	0432	0.4		28 TH	0452	0.7
	1058	4.5			1110	4.5
	1700	0.5			1719	0.8
	2326	4.7			2336	4.5
14 TH	0535	0.4		29 F	0543	0.8
	1157	4.6			1157	4.6
	1805	0.4			1810	0.7
15 F	0028	4.7		30 SA	0025	4.6
	0634	0.4			0631	0.7
	1251	4.7			1243	4.7
●	1902	0.3		○	1858	0.7

JULY

Day	Time	m		Day	Time	m
1 SU	0111	4.6		16 M	0203	4.6
	0716	0.7			0802	0.6
	1327	4.8			1413	5.0
	1943	0.6			2033	0.4
2 M	0158	4.7		17 TU	0247	4.5
	0801	0.6			0845	0.6
	1409	4.9			1456	5.0
	2028	0.5			2117	0.4
3 TU	0242	4.6		18 W	0327	4.5
	0844	0.6			0925	0.5
	1450	4.9			1536	5.0
	2110	0.4			2155	0.4
4 W	0324	4.5		19 TH	0404	4.5
	0921	0.5			0959	0.4
	1530	4.9			1611	4.9
	2148	0.3			2226	0.4
5 TH	0404	4.4		20 F	0437	4.4
	0955	0.5			1029	0.5
	1611	4.8			1644	4.8
	2228	0.3			2257	0.5
6 F	0447	4.4		21 SA	0509	4.3
	1036	0.5			1100	0.6
	1656	4.8			1717	4.7
	2313	0.3			2329	0.7
7 SA	0532	4.3		22 SU	0542	4.3
	1122	0.6			1132	0.8
	1744	4.8			1752	4.6
☽	2359	0.4		☽		
8 SU	0617	4.3		23 M	0001	0.8
	1209	0.6			0617	4.3
	1833	4.7			1209	1.0
					1834	4.4
9 M	0048	0.5		24 TU	0042	1.0
	0707	4.3			0706	4.2
	1302	0.7			1302	1.1
	1932	4.7			1933	4.3
10 TU	0145	0.7		25 W	0142	1.1
	0808	4.4			0811	4.2
	1409	0.8			1414	1.2
	2042	4.6			2046	4.3
11 W	0253	0.7		26 TH	0256	1.1
	0918	4.4			0923	4.3
	1524	0.7			1532	1.1
	2158	4.6			2200	4.3
12 TH	0405	0.7		27 F	0408	1.0
	1031	4.5			1031	4.4
	1640	0.6			1644	0.9
	2311	4.6			2306	4.4
13 F	0517	0.7		28 SA	0513	0.9
	1138	4.6			1129	4.6
	1752	0.6			1746	0.8
14 SA	0017	4.6		29 SU	0005	4.5
	0621	0.7			0612	0.9
	1237	4.8			1222	4.8
●	1855	0.5			1842	0.7
15 SU	0114	4.6		30 M	0058	4.6
	0716	0.7			0704	0.8
	1327	4.9			1311	4.9
	1947	0.4		○	1933	0.6
				31 TU	0146	4.7
					0752	0.7
					1356	5.0
					2020	0.5

AUGUST

Day	Time	m		Day	Time	m
1 W	0231	4.7		16 TH	0301	4.6
	0836	0.6			0905	0.5
	1437	5.1			1511	5.0
	2102	0.4			2129	0.5
2 TH	0311	4.6		17 F	0331	4.6
	0912	0.5			0933	0.5
	1515	5.0			1540	4.9
	2139	0.3			2155	0.5
3 F	0348	4.6		18 SA	0358	4.5
	0944	0.4			0958	0.5
	1555	5.0			1608	4.8
	2215	0.3			2220	0.6
4 SA	0426	4.5		19 SU	0426	4.5
	1021	0.5			1025	0.7
	1638	4.9			1636	4.7
	2256	0.4			2246	0.8
5 SU	0507	4.5		20 M	0452	4.4
	1104	0.6			1051	0.8
	1722	4.9			1703	4.6
☽	2338	0.6		☽	2310	0.9
6 M	0547	4.5		21 TU	0519	4.4
	1147	0.7			1118	1.0
	1807	4.7			1735	4.4
					2340	1.1
7 TU	0019	0.8		22 W	0558	4.2
	0632	4.4			1200	1.2
	1235	0.8			1828	4.2
	1903	4.6				
8 W	0112	1.0		23 TH	0033	1.3
	0733	4.4			0704	4.2
	1343	0.9			1312	1.3
	2019	4.4			1947	4.1
9 TH	0226	1.1		24 F	0155	1.3
	0853	4.4			0829	4.2
	1509	0.9			1443	1.2
	2147	4.4			2117	4.2
10 F	0351	1.0		25 SA	0325	1.2
	1016	4.5			0953	4.3
	1636	0.8			1611	1.0
	2308	4.4			2239	4.3
11 SA	0510	0.9		26 SU	0446	1.1
	1129	4.7			1103	4.5
	1751	0.7			1724	0.8
					2345	4.5
12 SU	0013	4.5		27 M	0552	1.0
	0615	0.8			1200	4.8
	1227	4.9			1823	0.7
	1851	0.6				
13 M	0105	4.6		28 TU	0040	4.6
	0708	0.8			0647	0.8
	1316	5.0			1249	4.9
●	1939	0.6		○	1915	0.5
14 TU	0149	4.6		29 W	0127	4.7
	0752	0.7			0734	0.6
	1359	5.0			1334	5.0
	2021	0.5			2001	0.4
15 W	0227	4.6		30 TH	0210	4.7
	0832	0.6			0816	0.5
	1437	5.0			1415	5.1
	2058	0.5			2042	0.3
				31 F	0248	4.7
					0853	0.5
					1454	5.1
					2119	0.3

Chart Datum: 2·26 metres below Normal Null (German reference level)

TIME ZONE -0100
(German Standard Time)
Subtract 1 hour for UT
For German Summer Time add ONE hour in **non-shaded areas**

GERMANY – WILHELMSHAVEN

LAT 53°31'N   LONG 8°09'E

TIMES AND HEIGHTS OF HIGH AND LOW WATERS

Dates in amber are **SPRINGS**
Dates in yellow are **NEAPS**

2007

SEPTEMBER

Day	Time m	Day	Time m
1 SA	0323 4.7 / 0927 0.4 / 1533 5.1 / 2154 0.4	**16** SU	0318 4.6 / 0926 0.6 / 1531 4.7 / 2141 0.7
2 SU	0359 4.7 / 1002 0.5 / 1614 4.9 / 2231 0.6	**17** M	0344 4.5 / 0950 0.7 / 1557 4.6 / 2204 0.8
3 M	0437 4.7 / 1041 0.6 / 1657 4.8 / 2309 0.8	**18** TU	0409 4.5 / 1014 0.8 / 1623 4.5 / 2226 1.0
4 TU ◐	0516 4.6 / 1123 0.8 / 1744 4.6 / 2350 1.0	**19** W ◐	0435 4.4 / 1039 1.0 / 1653 4.3 / 2253 1.1
5 W	0603 4.5 / 1212 0.9 / 1843 4.4	**20** TH	0510 4.2 / 1117 1.1 / 1743 4.1 / 2342 1.3
6 TH	0045 1.2 / 0708 4.4 / 1324 1.0 / 2004 4.2	**21** F	0613 4.1 / 1225 1.3 / 1902 4.0
7 F	0206 1.3 / 0836 4.4 / 1500 1.1 / 2139 4.2	**22** SA	0105 1.5 / 0742 4.1 / 1400 1.2 / 2039 4.0
8 SA	0342 1.3 / 1008 4.6 / 1636 1.0 / 2305 1.0	**23** SU	0245 1.4 / 0915 4.3 / 1537 1.0 / 2209 4.2
9 SU	0506 1.1 / 1122 4.7 / 1749 0.8	**24** M	0414 1.2 / 1033 4.5 / 1655 0.8 / 2319 4.4
10 M	0005 4.5 / 0607 0.9 / 1215 4.9 / 1839 0.7	**25** TU	0524 0.9 / 1131 4.7 / 1756 0.6
11 TU ●	0048 4.6 / 0652 0.8 / 1257 4.9 / 1918 0.6	**26** W ○	0013 4.5 / 0619 0.8 / 1221 4.9 / 1847 0.5
12 W	0125 4.6 / 0732 0.7 / 1335 5.0 / 1955 0.6	**27** TH	0059 4.6 / 0706 0.7 / 1306 5.0 / 1932 0.4
13 TH	0158 4.6 / 0807 0.6 / 1410 4.9 / 2028 0.6	**28** F	0140 4.7 / 0749 0.5 / 1348 5.1 / 2014 0.4
14 F	0228 4.7 / 0838 0.6 / 1440 4.9 / 2056 0.6	**29** SA	0218 4.8 / 0829 0.5 / 1430 5.1 / 2053 0.5
15 SA	0253 4.7 / 0903 0.5 / 1506 4.8 / 2119 0.6	**30** SU	0255 4.8 / 0907 0.5 / 1512 5.0 / 2130 0.6

OCTOBER

Day	Time m	Day	Time m
1 M	0332 4.8 / 0944 0.5 / 1555 4.8 / 2206 0.7	**16** TU	0310 4.6 / 0921 0.7 / 1527 4.5 / 2129 0.8
2 TU	0410 4.7 / 1022 0.6 / 1639 4.6 / 2244 0.9	**17** W	0338 4.6 / 0948 0.8 / 1557 4.4 / 2156 1.0
3 W ◐	0452 4.6 / 1104 0.8 / 1728 4.4 / 2326 1.1	**18** TH	0408 4.5 / 1018 0.9 / 1631 4.2 / 2227 1.1
4 TH	0542 4.5 / 1156 0.9 / 1828 4.2	**19** F ◐	0445 4.3 / 1056 1.0 / 1719 4.0 / 2314 1.3
5 F	0023 1.3 / 0649 4.4 / 1309 1.1 / 1949 4.0	**20** SA	0542 4.2 / 1157 1.1 / 1831 3.9
6 SA	0145 1.4 / 0817 4.4 / 1444 1.1 / 2123 4.1	**21** SU	0029 1.4 / 0703 4.2 / 1324 1.1 / 2002 4.0
7 SU	0322 1.3 / 0950 4.5 / 1620 1.0 / 2248 4.3	**22** M	0204 1.4 / 0834 4.4 / 1457 1.0 / 2130 4.1
8 M	0447 1.1 / 1104 4.7 / 1730 0.8 / 2345 4.4	**23** TU	0333 1.2 / 0953 4.6 / 1616 0.8 / 2241 4.3
9 TU	0544 0.9 / 1152 4.8 / 1812 0.6	**24** W	0444 1.0 / 1055 4.7 / 1718 0.6 / 2336 4.5
10 W ●	0020 4.6 / 0623 0.8 / 1228 4.8 / 1845 0.7	**25** TH	0542 0.8 / 1147 4.9 / 1812 0.5
11 TH ●	0051 4.6 / 0659 0.6 / 1303 4.8 / 1919 0.7	**26** F ○	0024 4.6 / 0634 0.7 / 1236 5.0 / 1900 0.5
12 F	0122 4.7 / 0735 0.7 / 1337 4.8 / 1952 0.7	**27** SA	0108 4.8 / 0720 0.5 / 1322 5.0 / 1943 0.5
13 SA	0151 4.7 / 0806 0.6 / 1407 4.8 / 2020 0.7	**28** SU	0149 4.8 / 0803 0.5 / 1407 5.0 / 2025 0.6
14 SU	0216 4.7 / 0832 0.6 / 1433 4.7 / 2044 0.7	**29** M	0229 4.9 / 0847 0.5 / 1454 4.9 / 2107 0.7
15 M	0242 4.7 / 0856 0.6 / 1459 4.6 / 2106 0.7	**30** TU	0311 4.9 / 0929 0.6 / 1541 4.7 / 2147 0.8
		31 W	0353 4.8 / 1010 0.6 / 1627 4.5 / 2226 0.9

NOVEMBER

Day	Time m	Day	Time m
1 TH ◐	0436 4.7 / 1053 0.7 / 1716 4.3 / 2308 1.1	**16** F	0355 4.6 / 1010 0.8 / 1624 4.2 / 2219 1.0
2 F	0526 4.6 / 1143 0.9 / 1813 4.1	**17** SA ◐	0435 4.5 / 1050 0.9 / 1710 4.1 / 2303 1.2
3 SA	0003 1.2 / 0629 4.5 / 1248 1.0 / 1925 3.9	**18** SU	0525 4.4 / 1143 0.9 / 1810 4.0
4 SU	0115 1.3 / 0747 4.4 / 1411 1.0 / 2047 4.0	**19** M	0004 1.3 / 0632 4.4 / 1253 1.0 / 1925 4.0
5 M	0242 1.3 / 0912 4.5 / 1537 1.0 / 2206 4.2	**20** TU	0123 1.3 / 0750 4.5 / 1414 0.9 / 2043 4.2
6 TU	0403 1.2 / 1024 4.6 / 1646 0.9 / 2303 4.4	**21** W	0245 1.2 / 0907 4.6 / 1530 0.8 / 2154 4.3
7 W	0502 1.0 / 1113 4.7 / 1730 0.7 / 2340 4.5	**22** TH	0357 1.0 / 1013 4.7 / 1635 0.7 / 2254 4.5
8 TH	0543 0.9 / 1150 4.7 / 1805 0.8	**23** F	0501 0.8 / 1112 4.8 / 1734 0.6 / 2348 4.6
9 F	0011 4.6 / 0622 0.9 / 1227 4.8 / 1841 0.8	**24** SA ○	0600 0.7 / 1209 4.9 / 1829 0.6
10 SA ●	0044 4.7 / 0700 0.8 / 1303 4.7 / 1916 0.8	**25** SU	0038 4.8 / 0654 0.6 / 1301 4.9 / 1917 0.6
11 SU	0116 4.7 / 0734 0.7 / 1336 4.7 / 1947 0.8	**26** M	0124 4.9 / 0742 0.5 / 1351 4.8 / 2003 0.7
12 M	0145 4.7 / 0804 0.7 / 1407 4.6 / 2015 0.8	**27** TU	0209 4.9 / 0831 0.6 / 1441 4.7 / 2049 0.7
13 TU	0215 4.7 / 0833 0.7 / 1438 4.6 / 2044 0.8	**28** W	0255 4.9 / 0919 0.6 / 1531 4.6 / 2133 0.8
14 W	0247 4.7 / 0904 0.7 / 1511 4.5 / 2112 0.8	**29** TH	0341 4.9 / 1004 0.6 / 1618 4.4 / 2214 0.8
15 TH	0321 4.6 / 0936 0.8 / 1545 4.4 / 2143 0.9	**30** F	0425 4.8 / 1045 0.6 / 1703 4.2 / 2254 0.9

DECEMBER

Day	Time m	Day	Time m
1 SA ◐	0510 4.7 / 1129 0.7 / 1751 4.1 / 2340 1.0	**16** SU ◐	0428 4.7 / 1048 0.7 / 1702 4.2 / 2255 0.9
2 SU	0602 4.6 / 1220 0.9 / 1847 4.0	**17** M	0513 4.6 / 1132 0.7 / 1751 4.2 / 2344 1.0
3 SA	0036 1.1 / 0703 4.5 / 1321 1.0 / 1952 4.0	**18** TU	0605 4.6 / 1225 0.8 / 1847 4.2
4 TU	0143 1.2 / 0813 4.4 / 1431 1.0 / 2100 4.1	**19** W	0043 1.1 / 0708 4.6 / 1329 0.9 / 1953 4.3
5 W	0256 1.2 / 0922 4.5 / 1541 1.0 / 2202 4.3	**20** TH	0155 1.2 / 0819 4.7 / 1440 1.0 / 2103 4.4
6 TH	0402 1.2 / 1021 4.6 / 1638 1.0 / 2250 4.5	**21** F	0310 1.1 / 0932 4.7 / 1551 0.9 / 2212 4.5
7 F	0456 1.1 / 1108 4.6 / 1723 1.0 / 2330 4.6	**22** SA	0422 0.9 / 1042 4.7 / 1700 0.8 / 2316 4.6
8 SA	0543 1.0 / 1151 4.7 / 1806 1.0	**23** SU	0533 0.8 / 1149 4.7 / 1804 0.8
9 SU ●	0008 4.7 / 0627 0.9 / 1232 4.7 / 1845 0.9	**24** M ○	0016 4.8 / 0636 0.7 / 1249 4.6 / 1900 0.7
10 M	0046 4.7 / 0707 0.9 / 1311 4.6 / 1921 0.9	**25** TU	0108 4.9 / 0730 0.6 / 1342 4.7 / 1949 0.7
11 TU	0122 4.8 / 0744 0.8 / 1350 4.6 / 1958 0.8	**26** W	0156 4.9 / 0821 0.6 / 1431 4.6 / 2037 0.8
12 W	0159 4.8 / 0822 0.8 / 1428 4.6 / 2035 0.8	**27** TH	0244 5.0 / 0911 0.6 / 1520 4.6 / 2123 0.7
13 TH	0236 4.8 / 0859 0.7 / 1505 4.5 / 2108 0.8	**28** F	0330 5.0 / 0957 0.5 / 1604 4.5 / 2203 0.7
14 F	0312 4.8 / 0933 0.7 / 1541 4.4 / 2139 0.8	**29** SA	0411 4.9 / 1034 0.5 / 1643 4.3 / 2238 0.7
15 SA	0349 4.7 / 1008 0.7 / 1620 4.3 / 2214 0.9	**30** SU	0450 4.8 / 1109 0.6 / 1721 4.3 / 2313 0.8
		31 M ◐	0529 4.7 / 1145 0.6 / 1801 4.2 / 2351 0.9

Chart Datum: 2·26 metres below Normal Null (German reference level)

TIDES

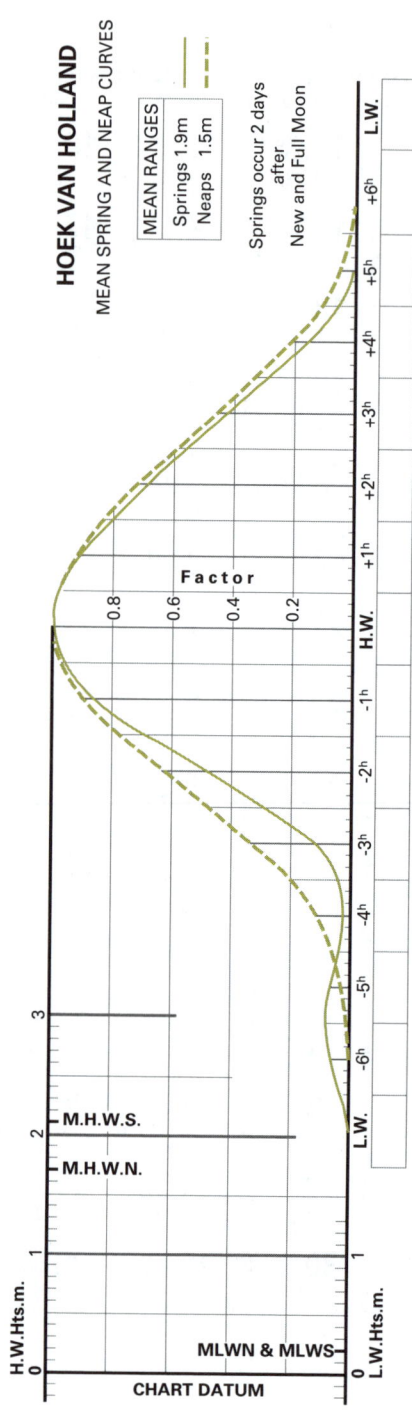

HOEK VAN HOLLAND

MEAN SPRING AND NEAP CURVES

MEAN RANGES	
Springs	1.9m
Neaps	1.5m

Springs occur 2 days
after
New and Full Moon

Factor

0.8
0.6
0.4
0.2

H.W. -1ʰ -2ʰ -3ʰ -4ʰ -5ʰ -6ʰ L.W.

+1ʰ +2ʰ +3ʰ +4ʰ +5ʰ +6ʰ

H.W.Hts.m.

3
M.H.W.S.
2
M.H.W.N.
1

0

MLWN & MLWS
CHART DATUM

L.W.Hts.m.

1

0

Note - Double LWs often occur.
The predictions are for the lower
LW which is usually the first.

TIME ZONE -0100
(Dutch Standard Time)
Subtract 1 hour for UT
For Dutch Summer Time add
ONE hour in non-shaded areas

NETHERLANDS – HOEK VAN HOLLAND

LAT 51°59'N   LONG 4°07'E

TIMES AND HEIGHTS OF HIGH AND LOW WATERS

Dates in amber are **SPRINGS**
Dates in yellow are **NEAPS**

2007

JANUARY

Day	Time m	Time m	Time m	Time m
1 M	0025 2.0	0600 0.5	1245 2.0	1825 0.3
2 TU	0125 2.0	0910 0.4	1335 2.1	1914 0.4
3 W	0218 2.0	0955 0.3	1428 2.1	○ 2230 0.4
4 TH	0303 2.0	1106 0.3	1515 2.2	2315 0.4
5 F	0355 2.0	0845 0.2	1605 2.2	
6 SA	0026 0.5	0435 2.0	0930 0.2	1646 2.2
7 SU	0105 0.5	0515 1.9	1005 0.1	1725 2.2
8 M	0145 0.5	0545 1.9	1049 0.1	1806 2.1
9 TU	0225 0.5	0625 1.9	1134 0.1	1845 2.0
10 W	0050 0.5	0659 1.9	1224 0.1	1930 2.0
11 TH	0140 0.5	0756 1.8	1324 0.1	◑ 2013 1.9
12 F	0215 0.4	0846 1.7	1415 0.2	2109 1.8
13 SA	0315 0.4	0947 0.3	1515 0.3	2215 1.7
14 SU	0450 0.4	1056 1.6	1730 0.3	2325 1.7
15 M	0550 0.4	1156 1.7	1830 0.4	
16 TU	0036 1.8	0640 0.4	1256 1.8	1930 0.4
17 W	0120 1.8	0720 0.4	1339 1.9	2120 0.4
18 TH	0206 1.9	0734 0.3	1425 2.0	2225 0.4
19 F	0245 2.0	0754 0.2	1506 2.2	● 2247 0.4
20 SA	0325 2.0	0836 0.2	1538 2.2	2315 0.4
21 SU	0407 2.0	0909 0.1	1621 2.3	
22 M	0004 0.4	0449 2.0	0944 0.0	1705 2.3
23 TU	0044 0.4	0528 2.0	1031 0.0	1747 2.2
24 W	0135 0.4	0616 1.9	1119 0.0	1840 2.2
25 TH	0210 0.5	0706 1.9	1225 0.0	◐ 1928 2.1
26 F	0220 0.5	0806 1.8	1335 0.0	2035 2.0
27 SA	0240 0.4	0905 1.9	1455 0.1	2139 1.8
28 SU	0324 0.4	1004 1.8	1555 0.2	2306 1.7
29 M	0434 0.4	1130 1.8	1720 0.3	
30 TU	0015 1.7	0549 0.4	1234 1.9	2040 0.3
31 W	0119 1.8	0910 0.3	1345 2.0	2205 0.3

FEBRUARY

Day	Time m	Time m	Time m	Time m
1 TH	0214 1.9	1010 0.2	1429 2.1	2250 0.4
2 F	0310 1.9	1055 0.2	1509 2.1	○ 2320 0.4
3 SA	0344 1.9	1125 0.2	1544 2.1	
4 SU	0000 0.4	0413 2.0	0905 0.1	1625 2.2
5 M	0046 0.5	0444 2.0	0934 0.1	1659 2.1
6 TU	0105 0.5	0519 2.0	1015 0.1	1736 2.1
7 W	0127 0.5	0555 2.0	1053 0.1	1810 2.0
8 TH	0000 0.4	0621 2.0	1145 0.1	1845 2.0
9 F	0040 0.4	0655 1.9	1224 0.1	1913 1.9
10 SA	0124 0.3	0746 1.9	1325 0.1	◐ 1959 1.8
11 SU	0205 0.3	0840 1.8	1435 0.2	2104 1.7
12 M	0304 0.4	0956 1.6	1620 0.3	2224 1.6
13 TU	0517 0.4	1115 1.6	1754 0.3	2355 1.6
14 W	0620 0.3	1236 1.7	1900 0.4	
15 TH	0054 1.7	0645 0.3	1319 1.9	2125 0.4
16 F	0150 1.8	0704 0.3	1406 2.0	2210 0.4
17 SA	0225 1.9	0736 0.2	1438 2.2	● 2235 0.4
18 SU	0306 2.0	0808 0.1	1518 2.3	2316 0.4
19 M	0345 2.0	0841 0.0	1601 2.3	2344 0.4
20 TU	0425 2.0	0925 0.0	1645 2.3	
21 W	0024 0.4	0505 2.1	1005 -0.1	1725 2.2
22 TH	0116 0.4	0549 2.1	1054 0.0	1815 2.1
23 F	0125 0.4	0635 2.1	1154 0.0	1906 2.0
24 SA	0134 0.3	0725 2.0	1355 0.0	◑ 2006 1.8
25 SU	0210 0.3	0830 1.9	1435 0.1	2114 1.6
26 M	0315 0.3	0840 1.8	1554 0.2	2245 1.5
27 TU	0425 0.3	0956 1.7	1705 0.3	
28 W	0016 1.6	0540 0.3	1235 1.8	2050 0.3

MARCH

Day	Time m	Time m	Time m	Time m
1 TH	0120 1.7	0915 0.2	1339 2.0	2204 0.3
2 F	0209 1.8	1005 0.1	1425 2.1	2250 0.3
3 SA	0244 1.9	1035 0.1	1455 2.1	2304 0.4
4 SU	0325 1.9	1114 0.1	1528 2.1	○ 2336 0.4
5 M	0349 2.0	0839 0.1	1559 2.1	2359 0.4
6 TU	0425 2.0	0909 0.1	1636 2.1	2130 0.4
7 W	0449 2.0	0945 0.1	1701 2.1	2205 0.3
8 TH	0515 2.0	1014 0.1	1736 2.0	2245 0.3
9 F	0545 2.0	1106 0.1	1759 2.0	2314 0.3
10 SA	0615 2.0	1134 0.1	1829 2.0	
11 SU	0004 0.2	0649 2.0	1240 0.2	1904 1.9
12 M	0126 0.2	0729 1.9	1416 0.2	◑ 2005 1.7
13 TU	0214 0.3	0850 1.7	1530 0.3	2145 1.5
14 W	0506 0.3	1046 1.6	1727 0.3	2315 1.5
15 TH	0554 0.3	1154 1.7	1900 0.3	
16 F	0025 1.6	0610 0.2	1253 1.9	2105 0.3
17 SA	0114 1.7	0915 0.2	1335 2.1	2200 0.3
18 SU	0158 1.8	0705 0.1	1418 2.2	2230 0.3
19 M	0239 1.9	0735 0.0	1456 2.3	● 2306 0.4
20 TU	0317 2.0	0815 -0.1	1535 2.3	2039 0.4
21 W	0359 2.1	0900 -0.1	1617 2.3	2126 0.3
22 TH	0438 2.2	0945 0.0	1705 2.2	2209 0.3
23 F	0522 2.2	1040 0.0	1747 2.0	2305 0.3
24 SA	0608 2.1	1310 0.1	1840 1.9	
25 SU	0030 0.2	0655 2.0	1340 0.1	◑ 1940 1.7
26 M	0135 0.2	0649 1.9	1440 0.2	2054 1.5
27 TU	0245 0.2	0935 1.7	1545 0.3	2245 1.4
28 W	0414 0.2	1115 1.7	1817 0.3	2354 1.5
29 TH	0515 0.2	1224 1.9	2030 0.3	
30 F	0055 1.7	0835 0.1	1314 2.0	2136 0.2
31 SA	0145 1.8	0945 0.1	1355 2.0	2204 0.2

APRIL

Day	Time m	Time m	Time m	Time m
1 SU	0226 1.8	1014 0.1	1425 2.0	2230 0.3
2 M	0256 1.9	1040 0.1	1455 2.1	○ 2306 0.3
3 TU	0325 2.0	1050 0.2	1529 2.1	2317 0.3
4 W	0345 2.0	1115 0.1	1559 2.1	2335 0.3
5 TH	0420 2.1	1155 0.1	1629 2.0	2140 0.3
6 F	0445 2.1	1234 0.1	1659 2.0	2210 0.2
7 SA	0515 2.1	1315 0.2	1725 2.0	2244 0.2
8 SU	0545 2.1	1116 0.2	1759 1.9	2330 0.1
9 M	0619 2.0	1330 0.2	1846 1.8	
10 TU	0030 0.1	0705 1.9	1410 0.2	◑ 1935 1.7
11 W	0145 0.1	0805 1.8	1505 0.3	2110 1.5
12 TH	0255 0.2	1015 1.7	1710 0.3	2235 1.4
13 F	0404 0.2	1125 1.8	1900 0.3	2355 1.5
14 SA	0504 0.2	1225 2.0	2046 0.3	
15 SU	0050 1.7	0544 0.1	1310 2.1	2136 0.3
16 M	0132 1.8	0636 0.0	1345 2.2	2155 0.3
17 TU	0211 2.0	0709 0.0	1429 2.3	● 1940 0.3
18 W	0255 2.1	0751 0.0	1512 2.2	2018 0.3
19 TH	0336 2.2	0836 0.0	1557 2.2	2059 0.2
20 F	0417 2.2	0926 0.1	1640 2.1	2145 0.2
21 SA	0501 2.2	1320 0.1	1725 1.9	2234 0.1
22 SU	0547 2.2	1347 0.1	1814 1.8	2354 0.1
23 M	0645 2.0	1340 0.2	1925 1.6	
24 TU	0114 0.1	0745 1.9	1425 0.2	◑ 2034 1.5
25 W	0230 0.1	0705 1.8	1620 0.3	2215 1.4
26 TH	0350 0.1	1044 1.8	1755 0.3	2325 1.5
27 F	0445 0.1	1155 1.9	1924 0.3	
28 SA	0026 1.6	0534 0.1	1246 2.0	2025 0.2
29 SU	0110 1.7	0835 0.1	1326 2.0	2115 0.2
30 M	0145 1.8	0920 0.1	1355 2.0	2145 0.2

Chart Datum: 0·84 metres below NAP Datum

TIDES

TIME ZONE -0100
(Dutch Standard Time)
Subtract 1 hour for UT
For Dutch Summer Time add
ONE hour in **non-shaded areas**

NETHERLANDS – HOEK VAN HOLLAND

LAT 51°59'N   LONG 4°07'E

TIMES AND HEIGHTS OF HIGH AND LOW WATERS

Dates in amber are **SPRINGS**
Dates in yellow are **NEAPS**

2007

MAY

Time	m	Time	m
1 0215	1.9	**16** 0146	2.0
0930	0.2	0649	0.0
TU 1425	2.0	W 1407	2.2
2236	0.2	● 1920	0.3
2 0250	1.9	**17** 0229	2.1
1000	0.2	0735	0.1
W 1459	2.0	TH 1455	2.1
○ 2250	0.2	1959	0.2
3 0315	2.0	**18** 0316	2.2
1050	0.2	0826	0.1
TH 1531	2.0	F 1539	2.0
2310	0.2	2045	0.2
4 0349	2.0	**19** 0358	2.2
1125	0.2	1215	0.2
F 1605	2.0	SA 1625	1.9
2354	0.2	2136	0.1
5 0418	2.1	**20** 0446	2.2
1204	0.2	1321	0.2
SA 1635	2.0	SU 1719	1.8
		2224	0.1
6 0024	0.1	**21** 0536	2.1
0451	2.1	1354	0.2
SU 1256	0.2	M 1815	1.7
1705	1.9	2324	0.0
7 0104	0.1	**22** 0636	2.0
0525	2.1	1456	0.3
M 1324	0.2	TU 1903	1.6
1746	1.8		
8 0150	0.1	**23** 0035	0.0
0601	2.0	0735	1.9
TU 1357	0.2	W 1527	0.3
1830	1.8	● 2009	1.6
9 0005	0.1	**24** 0150	0.0
0649	2.0	0856	1.8
W 1450	0.3	TH 1617	0.3
1925	1.6	2114	1.5
10 0120	0.0	**25** 0305	0.0
0805	1.8	1005	1.8
TH 1547	0.3	F 1730	0.3
☽ 2050	1.5	2246	1.5
11 0225	0.1	**26** 0404	0.1
0936	1.8	1116	1.8
F 1657	0.3	SA 1835	0.3
2206	1.5	2346	1.6
12 0336	0.1	**27** 0504	0.1
1050	1.9	1206	1.9
SA 1840	0.3	SU 1945	0.3
2315	1.6		
13 0425	0.1	**28** 0030	1.7
1145	2.0	0555	0.1
SU 2005	0.3	M 1245	1.9
		2030	0.3
14 0016	1.7	**29** 0105	1.7
0515	0.0	0700	0.2
M 1240	2.1	TU 1326	1.9
2056	0.3	2126	0.2
15 0059	1.9	**30** 0139	1.8
0606	0.0	0810	0.2
TU 1325	2.2	W 1354	1.9
2135	0.3	2205	0.2
		31 0216	1.9
		0930	0.2
		TH 1429	1.9
		2004	0.2

JUNE

Time	m	Time	m
1 0249	2.0	**16** 0258	2.1
1017	0.3	1125	0.3
F 1508	2.0	SA 1531	1.9
○ 2250	0.2	2040	0.1
2 0326	2.0	**17** 0345	2.2
1115	0.3	1205	0.3
SA 1546	1.9	SU 1625	1.9
2325	0.1	2125	0.1
3 0359	2.0	**18** 0435	2.2
1150	0.3	1305	0.3
SU 1615	1.9	M 1715	1.8
2140	0.1	2209	0.0
4 0435	2.1	**19** 0525	2.1
1230	0.3	1355	0.3
M 1656	1.8	TU 1800	1.8
2215	0.1	2254	0.0
5 0511	2.1	**20** 0615	2.1
1304	0.3	1435	0.4
TU 1735	1.8	W 1844	1.7
2300	0.0	2354	0.0
6 0555	2.0	**21** 0710	2.0
1355	0.3	1520	0.4
W 1819	1.7	TH 1930	1.7
2344	0.0		
7 0646	2.0	**22** 0104	0.0
1434	0.3	0805	1.9
TH 1920	1.6	F 1430	0.4
		☽ 2015	1.6
8 0050	0.0	**23** 0220	0.0
0744	1.9	0900	1.8
F 1535	0.4	SA 1515	0.4
☽ 2025	1.6	2114	1.6
9 0149	0.0	**24** 0327	0.1
0854	1.9	1005	1.8
SA 1630	0.4	SU 1620	0.3
2135	1.6	2230	1.6
10 0245	0.0	**25** 0435	0.1
1004	2.0	1116	1.9
SU 1740	0.4	M 1705	0.3
2246	1.7	2336	1.6
11 0344	0.0	**26** 0534	0.2
1116	2.0	1205	1.8
M 1904	0.4	TU 1755	0.3
2340	1.8		
12 0444	0.0	**27** 0036	1.7
1209	2.0	0625	0.2
TU 2000	0.3	W 1249	1.8
		1850	0.3
13 0031	1.9	**28** 0104	1.7
0544	0.1	0730	0.3
W 1305	2.0	TH 1336	1.8
1824	0.3	1914	0.2
14 0125	2.0	**29** 0149	1.8
0646	0.1	0840	0.3
TH 1350	2.0	F 1405	1.9
1904	0.3	1954	0.2
15 0215	2.1	**30** 0229	1.9
0736	0.2	0954	0.4
F 1445	2.0	SA 1445	1.9
● 1956	0.2	○ 2015	0.2

JULY

Time	m	Time	m
1 0305	2.0	**16** 0338	2.2
1050	0.4	1154	0.4
SU 1530	1.9	M 1615	1.9
2056	0.2	2106	0.1
2 0340	2.1	**17** 0425	2.2
1130	0.4	1235	0.4
M 1605	1.9	TU 1655	1.9
2115	0.1	2146	0.1
3 0425	2.1	**18** 0505	2.1
1210	0.4	1324	0.4
TU 1645	1.8	W 1735	1.9
2155	0.1	2229	0.0
4 0506	2.1	**19** 0549	2.1
1255	0.3	1415	0.4
W 1730	1.8	TH 1815	1.9
2235	0.0	2320	0.0
5 0545	2.1	**20** 0624	2.0
1346	0.4	1455	0.4
TH 1809	1.8	F 1850	1.9
2314	0.0		
6 0631	2.1	**21** 0005	0.1
1414	0.4	0716	2.0
F 1859	1.7	SA 1330	0.4
		1929	1.8
7 0015	0.0	**22** 0120	0.1
0730	2.0	0805	1.9
SA 1505	0.4	SU 1420	0.4
☽ 1955	1.7	☽ 2025	1.7
8 0120	0.0	**23** 0205	0.1
0829	2.0	0844	1.8
SU 1520	0.4	M 1520	0.4
2106	1.8	2120	1.7
9 0224	0.0	**24** 0400	0.2
0935	2.0	0949	1.7
M 1524	0.4	TU 1634	0.3
2206	1.8	2236	1.6
10 0346	0.0	**25** 0516	0.3
1046	1.9	1105	1.6
TU 1625	0.4	W 1746	0.3
2309	1.8	2346	1.6
11 0435	0.1	**26** 0555	0.3
1156	1.9	1226	1.7
W 1724	0.4	TH 1814	0.3
12 0015	1.9	**27** 0034	1.7
0545	0.2	0700	0.4
TH 1256	1.9	F 1310	1.7
1836	0.3	1910	0.3
13 0115	2.0	**28** 0129	1.8
0644	0.3	0740	0.4
F 1349	1.9	SA 1406	1.8
1904	0.3	1924	0.3
14 0205	2.0	**29** 0209	2.0
1026	0.3	1006	0.4
SA 1438	1.9	SU 1436	1.9
● 1943	0.2	1945	0.2
15 0255	2.1	**30** 0249	2.2
1105	0.4	1034	0.4
SU 1536	1.9	M 1515	1.9
2026	0.2	○ 2019	0.2
		31 0325	2.2
		1116	0.5
		TU 1549	1.9
		2055	0.1

AUGUST

Time	m	Time	m
1 0405	2.2	**16** 0446	2.2
1156	0.4	1254	0.5
W 1629	1.9	TH 1706	2.0
2125	0.0	2156	0.1
2 0446	2.2	**17** 0515	2.1
1224	0.4	1334	0.5
TH 1707	1.9	F 1735	2.0
2205	0.0	2240	0.1
3 0526	2.2	**18** 0555	2.1
1310	0.4	1104	0.5
F 1749	1.9	SA 1804	2.0
2251	0.0	2314	0.2
4 0608	2.2	**19** 0624	2.0
1350	0.4	1204	0.4
SA 1835	1.9	SU 1846	2.0
2345	0.0		
5 0659	2.1	**20** 0004	0.2
1417	0.5	0706	1.9
SU 1921	1.9	M 1304	0.4
☽		☽ 1926	1.9
6 0044	0.0	**21** 0126	0.2
0755	2.0	0735	1.8
M 1430	0.4	TU 1354	0.4
2019	1.9	2026	1.8
7 0215	0.1	**22** 0220	0.3
0906	1.9	0834	1.7
TU 1510	0.4	W 1616	0.4
2136	1.8	2124	1.6
8 0324	0.2	**23** 0440	0.4
1025	1.8	1006	1.6
W 1610	0.4	TH 1716	0.4
2250	1.8	2245	1.6
9 0435	0.3	**24** 0535	0.4
1146	1.7	1125	1.6
TH 1724	0.4	F 1816	0.3
10 0005	1.9	**25** 0015	1.7
0544	0.3	0625	0.4
F 1256	1.8	SA 1250	1.7
1814	0.3	1850	0.3
11 0116	2.0	**26** 0105	1.9
0915	0.4	0750	0.5
SA 1356	1.8	SU 1329	1.8
2146	0.2	1854	0.3
12 0203	2.1	**27** 0155	2.0
1020	0.4	0950	0.5
SU 1439	1.9	M 1415	1.9
2230	0.2	1914	0.2
13 0249	2.1	**28** 0225	2.2
1055	0.5	1030	0.5
M 1526	1.9	TU 1445	2.0
● 2005	0.2	○ 1950	0.1
14 0325	2.2	**29** 0301	2.3
1140	0.5	1044	0.5
TU 1555	2.0	W 1525	2.0
2045	0.1	2026	0.1
15 0406	2.2	**30** 0338	2.3
1220	0.5	1114	0.5
W 1629	2.0	TH 1600	2.1
2115	0.1	2059	0.0
		31 0418	2.3
		1210	0.5
		F 1641	2.1
		2142	0.0

Chart Datum: 0·84 metres below NAP Datum

TIME ZONE -0100 (Dutch Standard Time)
Subtract 1 hour for UT
For Dutch Summer Time add ONE hour in **non-shaded areas**

NETHERLANDS – HOEK VAN HOLLAND
LAT 51°59'N   LONG 4°07'E
TIMES AND HEIGHTS OF HIGH AND LOW WATERS

Dates in amber are **SPRINGS**
Dates in yellow are **NEAPS**

2007

SEPTEMBER

Day	Time m	Time m	Time m	Time m
1 SA	0459 2.3	1256 0.5	1721 2.1	2225 0.0
2 SU	0545 2.2	1330 0.5	1805 2.1	2325 0.1
3 M	0628 2.1	1350 0.5	1856 2.1	
4 TU	0130 0.1	0725 1.9	1340 0.4	1949 2.0
5 W	0226 0.2	0834 1.8	1440 0.4	2116 1.9
6 TH	0324 0.3	1016 1.6	1600 0.4	2246 1.8
7 F	0440 0.4	1140 1.6	1710 0.4	
8 SA	0003 1.9	0800 0.4	1243 1.7	2017 0.3
9 SU	0120 2.1	0930 0.4	1334 1.9	2136 0.2
10 M	0153 2.1	1027 0.4	1425 1.9	2226 0.2
11 TU	0231 2.2	1040 0.5	1454 2.0	2254 0.2
12 W	0305 2.2	1104 0.5	1535 2.0	2015 0.2
13 TH	0339 2.2	1145 0.5	1558 2.1	2044 0.2
14 F	0411 2.2	1220 0.5	1636 2.1	2126 0.2
15 SA	0445 2.2	0943 0.5	1705 2.1	2154 0.2
16 SU	0515 2.1	1024 0.4	1736 2.1	2233 0.3
17 M	0545 2.1	1105 0.4	1759 2.1	2315 0.3
18 TU	0616 2.0	1156 0.3	1835 2.0	
19 W	0005 0.3	0649 2.0	1250 0.3	1909 1.9
20 TH	0135 0.4	0735 1.8	1405 0.4	2004 1.7
21 F	0416 0.5	0916 1.6	1651 0.4	2210 1.7
22 SA	0515 0.5	1034 1.5	1745 0.4	2340 1.8
23 SU	0610 0.5	1204 1.6	1830 0.3	
24 M	0040 2.0	0830 0.5	1305 1.8	1815 0.3
25 TU	0119 2.2	0925 0.4	1339 1.9	1845 0.2
26 W	0155 2.3	1010 0.5	1416 2.0	1920 0.1
27 TH	0235 2.4	0748 0.5	1455 2.2	1955 0.2
28 F	0315 2.4	0815 0.5	1535 2.2	2035 0.0
29 SA	0356 0.4	0855 0.5	1615 2.3	2115 0.1
30 SU	0435 2.3	0939 0.4	1657 2.3	2205 0.1

OCTOBER

Day	Time m	Time m	Time m	Time m
1 M	0521 2.2	1029 0.4	1739 2.3	2305 0.2
2 TU	0607 2.2	1124 0.4	1826 2.2	
3 W	0117 0.3	0706 1.9	1257 0.3	1925 2.0
4 TH	0216 0.3	0814 1.7	1420 0.4	2045 1.9
5 F	0315 0.4	1005 1.6	1535 0.4	2240 1.9
6 SA	0604 0.5	1135 1.6	1814 0.3	2354 2.0
7 SU	0750 0.4	1230 1.8	1955 0.3	
8 M	0055 2.1	0857 0.4	1315 1.9	2116 0.4
9 TU	0135 2.2	0944 0.4	1355 2.0	2154 0.2
10 W	0205 2.2	1010 0.5	1429 2.0	2220 0.3
11 TH	0239 2.2	1025 0.5	1505 2.1	1953 0.3
12 F	0311 2.2	0758 0.4	1528 2.2	2025 0.3
13 SA	0342 2.2	0843 0.5	1601 2.2	2335 0.3
14 SU	0416 2.2	0926 0.4	1636 2.2	2135 0.3
15 M	0446 2.1	0954 0.4	1701 2.2	2205 0.3
16 TU	0516 2.1	1029 0.3	1729 2.2	2250 0.4
17 W	0546 2.0	1115 0.3	1801 2.1	2334 0.4
18 TH	0619 2.0	1154 0.3	1841 2.1	
19 F	0130 0.5	0710 1.8	1320 0.3	1933 1.9
20 SA	0310 0.5	0824 1.6	1435 0.3	2124 1.8
21 SU	0450 0.5	1006 1.6	1534 0.4	2254 1.9
22 M	0610 0.5	1126 1.6	1644 0.3	
23 TU	0000 2.1	0816 0.5	1225 1.8	1723 0.3
24 W	0045 2.2	0855 0.5	1306 2.0	1809 0.2
25 TH	0126 2.3	0935 0.5	1345 2.1	1850 0.1
26 F	0207 2.4	0719 0.5	1427 2.2	1929 0.1
27 SA	0250 2.4	0758 0.4	1508 2.3	2011 0.1
28 SU	0332 2.4	0835 0.4	1552 2.4	2059 0.2
29 M	0417 2.2	0926 0.3	1636 2.4	2149 0.3
30 TU	0506 2.1	1011 0.3	1725 2.3	2205 0.3
31 W	0110 0.4	0555 2.0	1115 0.3	1811 2.2

NOVEMBER

Day	Time m	Time m	Time m	Time m
1 TH	0110 0.4	0655 1.8	1225 0.3	1915 2.1
2 F	0145 0.5	0815 1.7	1340 0.3	2045 1.9
3 SA	0425 0.5	0924 1.6	1510 0.3	2215 1.9
4 SU	0544 0.5	1056 1.6	1754 0.3	2336 2.0
5 M	0655 0.5	1156 1.8	1905 0.3	
6 TU	0014 2.1	0810 0.4	1246 1.9	2024 0.2
7 W	0106 2.1	0900 0.4	1325 2.0	2100 0.3
8 TH	0139 2.2	0925 0.4	1359 2.0	1927 0.3
9 F	0215 2.2	1016 0.4	1429 2.1	2130 0.3
10 SA	0248 2.2	0804 0.4	1501 2.1	2205 0.4
11 SU	0315 2.1	0834 0.4	1535 2.2	2255 0.4
12 M	0355 2.1	0904 0.4	1610 2.2	2335 0.4
13 TU	0426 2.1	0935 0.3	1639 2.2	
14 W	0015 0.4	0455 2.0	1014 0.3	1709 2.2
15 TH	0057 0.5	0525 2.0	1055 0.2	1746 2.1
16 F	0146 0.5	0608 1.9	1145 0.2	1825 2.1
17 SA	0210 0.5	0655 1.8	1235 0.2	1925 2.0
18 SU	0300 0.5	0816 1.7	1356 0.2	2055 1.9
19 M	0410 0.6	0936 1.7	1455 0.2	2210 2.0
20 TU	0530 0.6	1040 1.7	1555 0.2	2320 2.1
21 W	0717 0.5	1139 1.8	1645 0.1	
22 TH	0009 2.2	0824 0.5	1236 2.0	1745 0.2
23 F	0058 2.3	0620 0.5	1319 2.1	1830 0.2
24 SA	0145 2.3	0654 0.4	1406 2.2	1915 0.2
25 SU	0228 2.3	0735 0.4	1452 2.3	2005 0.3
26 M	0317 2.2	0825 0.3	1535 2.4	2049 0.3
27 TU	0405 2.1	0904 0.3	1620 2.3	
28 W	0045 0.4	0455 2.0	1005 0.2	1715 2.3
29 TH	0125 0.4	0549 1.9	1053 0.2	1805 2.2
30 F	0225 0.5	0645 1.8	1154 0.2	1910 2.1

DECEMBER

Day	Time m	Time m	Time m	Time m
1 SA	0305 0.5	0755 1.8	1305 0.2	2009 2.0
2 SU	0405 0.5	0856 1.7	1420 0.2	2125 1.9
3 M	0515 0.5	1006 1.7	1535 0.2	2235 1.9
4 TU	0605 0.5	1110 1.7	1634 0.3	2345 2.0
5 W	0715 0.5	1205 1.8	1735 0.3	
6 TH	0024 2.0	0807 0.4	1256 1.9	1900 0.3
7 F	0109 2.0	0905 0.4	1330 1.9	1950 0.3
8 SA	0144 2.0	0734 0.4	1406 2.0	2037 0.4
9 SU	0225 2.0	0805 0.4	1439 2.1	2140 0.4
10 M	0300 2.0	0850 0.3	1516 2.1	2227 0.4
11 TU	0332 2.0	0855 0.3	1545 2.1	2320 0.5
12 W	0405 2.0	0924 0.3	1621 2.2	
13 TH	0005 0.5	0441 2.0	0954 0.2	1659 2.2
14 F	0056 0.5	0519 1.9	1035 0.2	1735 2.2
15 SA	0136 0.5	0554 1.9	1119 0.1	1815 2.1
16 SU	0215 0.5	0645 1.8	1203 0.1	1908 2.1
17 M	0254 0.5	0745 1.8	1304 0.1	2014 2.1
18 TU	0310 0.6	0855 1.8	1415 0.1	2130 2.0
19 W	0330 0.6	1000 1.8	1515 0.1	2235 2.1
20 TH	0415 0.5	1105 1.9	1620 0.1	2340 2.1
21 F	0504 0.5	1206 2.0	1714 0.2	
22 SA	0035 2.1	0555 0.5	1255 2.1	1820 0.2
23 SU	0129 2.1	0645 0.4	1347 2.2	1904 0.3
24 M	0222 2.1	0735 0.3	1435 2.2	2000 0.3
25 TU	0316 2.0	0815 0.3	1525 2.3	2335 0.4
26 W	0358 2.0	0859 0.2	1615 2.3	
27 TH	0024 0.5	0449 2.0	0945 0.1	1701 2.3
28 F	0136 0.5	0540 2.0	1031 0.1	1744 2.2
29 SA	0204 0.5	0626 1.9	1130 0.1	1839 2.1
30 SU	0254 0.5	0710 1.9	1236 0.1	1936 2.0
31 M	0134 0.5	0755 1.8	1324 0.1	2025 1.9

Chart Datum: 0·84 metres below NAP Datum

TIDES

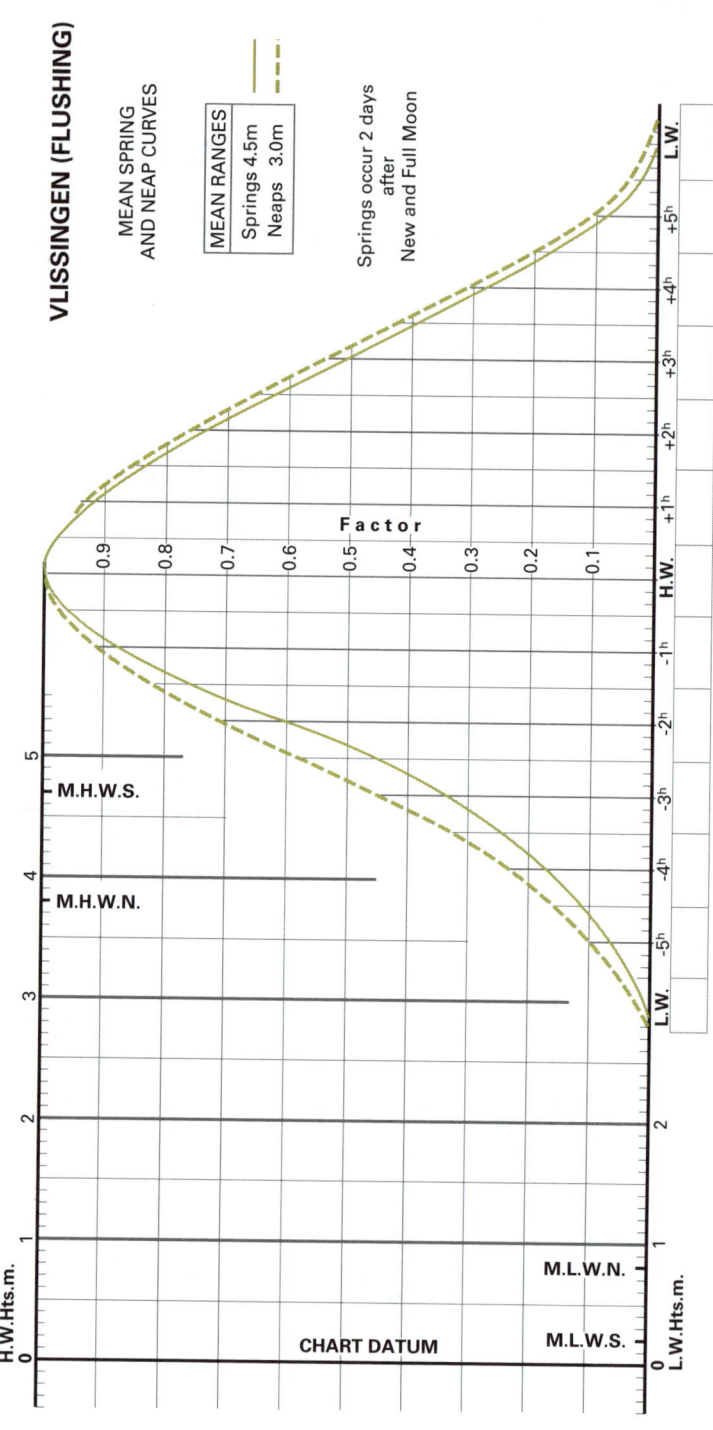

VLISSINGEN (FLUSHING)

MEAN SPRING
AND NEAP CURVES

MEAN RANGES		
Springs	4.5m	
Neaps	3.0m	

Springs occur 2 days
after
New and Full Moon

Factor

TIME ZONE -0100
(Dutch Standard Time)
Subtract 1 hour for UT
For Dutch Summer Time add
ONE hour in **non-shaded areas**

NETHERLANDS – VLISSINGEN

LAT 51°27'N   LONG 3°36'E

TIMES AND HEIGHTS OF HIGH AND LOW WATERS

Dates in amber are SPRINGS
Dates in yellow are NEAPS

2007

JANUARY

Day	Time m	Time m	Time m	Time m
1 M	0606 0.8	1159 4.4	1836 0.5	
2 TU	0035 4.4	0700 0.6	1256 4.4	1926 0.5
3 W	0129 4.5	0749 0.4	1349 4.7	2010 0.5
4 TH	0216 4.5	0841 0.3	1436 4.7	2052 0.6
5 F	0258 4.6	0922 0.3	1517 4.8	2129 0.7
6 SA	0337 4.5	1006 0.3	1559 4.7	2205 0.7
7 SU	0419 4.5	1039 0.4	1639 4.6	2242 0.8
8 M	0456 4.4	1115 0.4	1718 4.5	2321 0.8
9 TU	0536 4.3	1156 0.4	1756 4.3	2356 0.9
10 W	0616 4.2	1236 0.5	1835 4.2	
11 TH	0035 0.9	0656 4.1	1310 0.6	1922 4.0
12 F	0126 1.0	0746 3.9	1354 0.8	2014 3.8
13 SA	0214 1.1	0846 3.7	1515 0.9	2126 3.7
14 SU	0340 1.2	0956 3.7	1626 1.0	2225 3.7
15 M	0444 1.1	1106 3.8	1726 0.9	2338 3.9
16 TU	0549 1.0	1159 4.0	1826 0.8	
17 W	0030 4.1	0646 0.8	1252 4.2	1910 0.7
18 TH	0115 4.3	0735 0.6	1335 4.5	1949 0.6
19 F	0158 4.5	0820 0.4	1415 4.7	2036 0.5
20 SA	0235 4.6	0902 0.2	1455 4.8	2116 0.5
21 SU	0317 4.7	0951 0.1	1537 4.9	2200 0.5
22 M	0359 4.7	1035 0.0	1619 4.9	2242 0.5
23 TU	0440 4.7	1118 0.0	1702 4.8	2328 0.6
24 W	0525 4.6	1201 0.1	1751 4.7	
25 TH	0012 0.6	0612 4.5	1250 0.2	1845 4.5
26 F	0055 0.7	0705 4.3	1335 0.3	1948 4.2
27 SA	0156 0.8	0812 4.2	1435 0.6	2055 4.2
28 SU	0302 1.0	0921 4.0	1555 0.7	2216 3.9
29 M	0424 1.0	1046 4.0	1715 0.8	2325 3.9
30 TU	0550 0.8	1200 4.1	1821 0.7	
31 W	0031 4.1	0651 0.6	1259 4.4	1918 0.6

FEBRUARY

Day	Time m	Time m	Time m	Time m
1 TH	0128 4.3	0748 0.4	1344 4.6	1959 0.6
2 F	0208 4.5	0829 0.3	1428 4.7	2040 0.5
3 SA	0246 4.5	0910 0.2	1506 4.7	2116 0.6
4 SU	0320 4.6	0946 0.2	1539 4.7	2146 0.6
5 M	0356 4.6	1021 0.2	1616 4.7	2215 0.6
6 TU	0427 4.6	1049 0.3	1646 4.6	2250 0.6
7 W	0459 4.5	1114 0.3	1719 4.5	2320 0.6
8 TH	0531 4.5	1145 0.4	1752 4.4	2346 0.7
9 F	0606 4.3	1221 0.5	1826 4.2	
10 SA	0019 0.7	0639 4.1	1256 0.6	1916 4.0
11 SU	0108 0.9	0856 3.9	1350 0.8	2016 3.7
12 M	0205 1.1	0856 3.6	1505 1.0	2136 3.6
13 TU	0354 1.2	1014 3.6	1650 1.0	2305 3.6
14 W	0526 1.0	1135 3.8	1801 0.9	
15 TH	0005 3.9	0626 0.8	1235 4.2	1850 0.7
16 F	0056 4.2	0720 0.5	1319 4.5	1935 0.6
17 SA	0137 4.4	0801 0.3	1357 4.7	2015 0.5
18 SU	0217 4.6	0848 0.1	1437 4.9	2055 0.4
19 M	0256 4.8	0930 -0.1	1516 5.0	2139 0.3
20 TU	0336 4.9	1016 -0.2	1557 5.0	2221 0.3
21 W	0416 4.9	1056 -0.2	1641 4.9	2306 0.3
22 TH	0459 4.9	1138 -0.1	1726 4.8	2348 0.4
23 F	0545 4.7	1222 0.1	1818 4.5	
24 SA	0036 0.5	0636 4.5	1310 0.3	1915 4.2
25 SU	0136 0.7	0746 4.2	1416 0.6	2030 3.8
26 M	0234 0.9	0906 3.9	1523 0.9	2155 3.6
27 TU	0416 0.9	1038 3.8	1716 0.9	2326 3.7
28 W	0545 0.8	1200 4.1	1826 0.8	

MARCH

Day	Time m	Time m	Time m	Time m
1 TH	0026 4.0	0645 0.5	1256 4.4	1915 0.7
2 F	0116 4.3	0738 0.3	1338 4.6	1949 0.6
3 SA	0156 4.4	0815 0.2	1416 4.6	2019 0.6
4 SU	0228 4.5	0851 0.2	1445 4.7	2052 0.6
5 M	0257 4.6	0920 0.2	1516 4.7	2119 0.5
6 TU	0326 4.7	0949 0.2	1546 4.7	2156 0.5
7 W	0357 4.7	1022 0.2	1612 4.7	2222 0.5
8 TH	0426 4.7	1045 0.3	1643 4.6	2246 0.5
9 F	0456 4.6	1109 0.3	1708 4.5	2316 0.5
10 SA	0526 4.5	1135 0.4	1738 4.3	2345 0.5
11 SU	0558 4.3	1216 0.5	1820 4.1	
12 M	0025 0.6	0635 4.1	1306 0.8	1916 3.8
13 TU	0125 0.9	0756 3.7	1425 1.0	2045 3.5
14 W	0310 1.1	0946 3.6	1620 1.1	2226 3.5
15 TH	0456 0.9	1109 3.8	1724 0.9	2339 3.8
16 F	0559 0.7	1209 4.2	1830 0.7	
17 SA	0031 4.1	0656 0.4	1256 4.5	1916 0.5
18 SU	0116 4.4	0742 0.1	1335 4.8	1955 0.4
19 M	0150 4.7	0826 0.0	1412 5.0	2037 0.3
20 TU	0229 4.9	0905 -0.2	1451 5.1	2118 0.2
21 W	0312 5.0	0950 -0.2	1533 5.1	2200 0.2
22 TH	0353 5.1	1030 -0.2	1616 4.9	2245 0.2
23 F	0435 5.0	1115 0.0	1702 4.7	2326 0.2
24 SA	0521 4.8	1155 0.2	1751 4.4	
25 SU	0015 0.4	0612 4.5	1245 0.4	1849 4.0
26 M	0110 0.6	0719 4.1	1345 0.8	2005 3.7
27 TU	0223 0.8	0844 3.8	1526 1.0	2146 3.5
28 W	0359 0.8	1031 3.8	1701 1.0	2306 3.7
29 TH	0530 0.7	1146 4.1	1806 0.8	
30 F	0006 4.0	0630 0.4	1235 4.4	1856 0.7
31 SA	0056 4.2	0715 0.3	1315 4.5	1930 0.7

APRIL

Day	Time m	Time m	Time m	Time m
1 SU	0128 4.4	0750 0.2	1345 4.6	1958 0.5
2 M	0157 4.5	0820 0.2	1416 4.6	2026 0.5
3 TU	0225 4.6	0850 0.2	1445 4.7	2055 0.4
4 W	0255 4.7	0926 0.2	1512 4.7	2128 0.4
5 TH	0327 4.7	0950 0.2	1540 4.6	2155 0.4
6 F	0356 4.7	1015 0.3	1612 4.6	2222 0.4
7 SA	0422 4.6	1046 0.4	1642 4.5	2245 0.4
8 SU	0453 4.5	1116 0.5	1713 4.4	2319 0.4
9 M	0527 4.4	1150 0.6	1748 4.2	
10 TU	0005 0.5	0615 4.2	1246 0.8	1846 3.8
11 W	0110 0.7	0726 3.8	1355 1.0	2020 3.5
12 TH	0245 0.9	0915 3.7	1555 1.1	2149 3.5
13 F	0414 0.7	1035 3.9	1705 0.9	2305 3.8
14 SA	0524 0.5	1135 4.3	1800 0.7	
15 SU	0000 4.2	0630 0.3	1226 4.6	1849 0.5
16 M	0041 4.5	0715 0.1	1306 4.8	1930 0.4
17 TU	0123 4.7	0758 -0.1	1346 5.0	2016 0.2
18 W	0206 4.9	0842 -0.1	1428 5.0	2055 0.2
19 TH	0246 5.0	0925 -0.1	1512 5.0	2138 0.1
20 F	0330 5.1	1007 0.0	1556 4.8	2226 0.1
21 SA	0415 5.0	1050 0.1	1645 4.6	2308 0.2
22 SU	0502 4.7	1136 0.3	1732 4.3	
23 M	0000 0.3	0559 4.4	1226 0.6	1836 4.0
24 TU	0055 0.5	0710 4.0	1325 0.9	1945 3.7
25 W	0209 0.6	0829 3.9	1455 1.0	2115 3.5
26 TH	0345 0.7	0955 3.9	1625 1.0	2236 3.7
27 F	0506 0.6	1110 4.1	1725 0.9	2329 3.9
28 SA	0556 0.5	1159 4.3	1820 0.7	
29 SU	0018 4.1	0640 0.4	1239 4.4	1855 0.6
30 M	0051 4.3	0716 0.3	1311 4.5	1926 0.6

Chart Datum: 2·32 metres below NAP Datum

TIDES

TIME ZONE -0100
(Dutch Standard Time)
Subtract 1 hour for UT
For Dutch Summer Time add
ONE hour in **non-shaded areas**

NETHERLANDS – VLISSINGEN

LAT 51°27'N   LONG 3°36'E
TIMES AND HEIGHTS OF HIGH AND LOW WATERS

Dates in amber are **SPRINGS**
Dates in yellow are **NEAPS**

2007

MAY

Time	m		Time	m
1 0126	4.4		**16** 0056	4.7
0746	0.3		0736	0.0
TU 1342	4.5		W 1326	4.9
1959	0.5		1952	0.2
2 0155	4.5		**17** 0143	4.9
0816	0.3		0820	0.0
W 1412	4.6		TH 1409	4.9
○ 2031	0.4		2038	0.2
3 0227	4.6		**18** 0228	4.9
0850	0.3		0906	0.1
TH 1446	4.6		F 1456	4.8
2106	0.4		2123	0.1
4 0257	4.6		**19** 0313	4.9
0919	0.3		0945	0.2
F 1516	4.6		SA 1542	4.6
2136	0.4		2209	0.1
5 0329	4.6		**20** 0402	4.8
0952	0.4		1030	0.3
SA 1546	4.5		SU 1630	4.5
2206	0.4		2301	0.2
6 0401	4.6		**21** 0452	4.7
1026	0.5		1116	0.5
SU 1619	4.4		M 1725	4.3
2241	0.4		2345	0.3
7 0435	4.5		**22** 0549	4.4
1056	0.6		1205	0.7
M 1656	4.3		TU 1820	4.0
2316	0.4			
8 0515	4.4		**23** 0046	0.4
1140	0.7		0649	4.2
TU 1739	4.1		W 1254	0.9
			◑ 1926	3.8
9 0006	0.5		**24** 0145	0.5
0606	4.2		0755	4.0
W 1230	0.8		TH 1410	1.0
1840	3.9		2030	3.7
10 0106	0.6		**25** 0245	0.6
0720	4.0		0915	3.9
TH 1346	1.0		F 1520	1.0
◑ 2000	3.7		2139	3.7
11 0236	0.6		**26** 0400	0.6
0845	3.9		1020	4.0
F 1510	1.0		SA 1624	1.0
2116	3.7		2246	3.8
12 0346	0.5		**27** 0505	0.6
0958	4.1		1115	4.1
SA 1627	0.9		SU 1725	0.8
2226	3.9		2336	3.9
13 0456	0.4		**28** 0556	0.5
1059	4.3		1200	4.2
SU 1725	0.7		M 1809	0.7
2326	4.2			
14 0556	0.3		**29** 0015	4.1
1156	4.6		0635	0.5
M 1816	0.6		TU 1240	4.3
			1844	0.6
15 0011	4.5		**30** 0052	4.2
0646	0.1		0716	0.5
TU 1237	4.8		W 1311	4.4
1906	0.4		1926	0.6
			31 0125	4.3
			0746	0.5
			TH 1346	4.4
			2002	0.5

JUNE

Time	m		Time	m
1 0158	4.4		**16** 0217	4.8
0819	0.4		0848	0.3
F 1419	4.5		SA 1447	4.6
○ 2040	0.4		2115	0.1
2 0236	4.5		**17** 0307	4.8
0856	0.5		0930	0.4
SA 1455	4.5		SU 1537	4.6
2118	0.4		2159	0.1
3 0311	4.5		**18** 0355	4.7
0936	0.5		1011	0.5
SU 1529	4.4		M 1620	4.5
2155	0.4		2246	0.2
4 0347	4.5		**19** 0445	4.7
1010	0.6		1058	0.7
M 1607	4.4		TU 1710	4.4
2236	0.3		2336	0.2
5 0425	4.5		**20** 0535	4.5
1050	0.6		1134	0.8
TU 1647	4.3		W 1756	4.2
2315	0.3			
6 0507	4.4		**21** 0015	0.3
1136	0.7		0619	4.3
W 1736	4.1		TH 1226	0.9
			1839	4.1
7 0010	0.4		**22** 0106	0.4
0559	4.3		0716	4.2
TH 1226	0.8		F 1320	0.9
1829	4.0		◑ 1936	3.9
8 0106	0.4		**23** 0200	0.5
0706	4.2		0804	4.0
F 1319	0.9		SA 1420	1.0
◑ 1935	3.9		2030	3.8
9 0205	0.4		**24** 0256	0.6
0815	4.2		0916	3.9
SA 1430	0.9		SU 1519	1.0
2046	3.9		2146	3.7
10 0305	0.4		**25** 0356	0.7
0919	4.2		1015	3.9
SU 1535	0.9		M 1626	1.0
2145	4.0		2240	3.8
11 0416	0.4		**26** 0455	0.7
1026	4.3		1116	3.9
M 1646	0.8		TU 1714	0.9
2250	4.2		2336	3.9
12 0526	0.3		**27** 0555	0.7
1126	4.4		1159	4.0
TU 1751	0.6		W 1816	0.8
2345	4.4			
13 0622	0.3		**28** 0020	4.0
1217	4.6		0635	0.7
W 1846	0.5		TH 1246	4.2
			1859	0.7
14 0037	4.6		**29** 0105	4.2
0716	0.2		0720	0.6
TH 1308	4.6		F 1326	4.3
1935	0.3		1939	0.6
15 0130	4.7		**30** 0138	4.3
0802	0.2		0758	0.6
F 1359	4.6		SA 1401	4.4
● 2027	0.2		○ 2019	0.5

JULY

Time	m		Time	m
1 0218	4.5		**16** 0301	4.8
0836	0.6		0916	0.6
SU 1439	4.4		M 1525	4.6
2102	0.4		2150	0.2
2 0255	4.6		**17** 0346	4.8
0918	0.6		0955	0.7
M 1519	4.5		TU 1606	4.6
2148	0.3		2229	0.2
3 0337	4.6		**18** 0425	4.7
1001	0.6		1035	0.7
TU 1559	4.4		W 1646	4.5
2235	0.2		2311	0.2
4 0417	4.6		**19** 0505	4.6
1042	0.6		1114	0.7
W 1637	4.4		TH 1721	4.4
2316	0.2		2346	0.3
5 0458	4.6		**20** 0546	4.5
1126	0.7		1148	0.8
TH 1722	4.3		F 1759	4.3
6 0002	0.2		**21** 0025	0.4
0548	4.5		0625	4.3
F 1209	0.7		SA 1225	0.8
1812	4.3		1839	4.2
7 0044	0.2		**22** 0105	0.5
0641	4.4		0709	4.1
SA 1259	0.8		SU 1315	0.9
◑ 1906	4.2		◑ 1931	4.0
8 0140	0.4		**23** 0144	0.7
0746	4.3		0806	3.9
SU 1356	0.8		M 1404	1.1
2005	4.1		2026	3.8
9 0236	0.4		**24** 0250	0.8
0848	4.2		0859	3.7
M 1506	0.9		TU 1525	1.1
2116	4.1		2136	3.6
10 0346	0.5		**25** 0406	0.9
0955	4.2		1016	3.7
TU 1610	0.8		W 1633	1.1
2221	4.1		2256	3.7
11 0456	0.5		**26** 0515	0.9
1106	4.2		1126	3.8
W 1731	0.7		TH 1739	1.0
2328	4.3		2356	3.8
12 0606	0.5		**27** 0605	0.9
1205	4.3		1226	4.0
TH 1835	0.6		F 1835	0.8
13 0032	4.4		**28** 0045	4.1
0700	0.4		0658	0.8
F 1306	4.4		SA 1305	4.2
1925	0.4		1926	0.6
14 0125	4.6		**29** 0130	4.3
0750	0.5		0734	0.7
SA 1356	4.5		SU 1348	4.4
● 2015	0.2		2010	0.5
15 0215	4.7		**30** 0208	4.5
0836	0.5		0820	0.6
SU 1441	4.6		M 1422	4.5
2106	0.2		○ 2048	0.3
			31 0240	4.7
			0900	0.6
			TU 1501	4.6
			2132	0.2

AUGUST

Time	m		Time	m
1 0321	4.8		**16** 0357	4.8
0942	0.5		1005	0.7
W 1539	4.7		TH 1612	4.7
2216	0.1		2238	0.3
2 0359	4.9		**17** 0432	4.7
1025	0.5		1035	0.7
TH 1619	4.7		F 1648	4.6
2255	0.0		2310	0.3
3 0439	4.8		**18** 0505	4.5
1108	0.6		1110	0.7
F 1659	4.6		SA 1719	4.5
2342	0.1		2340	0.4
4 0526	4.7		**19** 0542	4.4
1150	0.6		1140	0.8
SA 1746	4.6		SU 1756	4.4
5 0026	0.1		**20** 0010	0.6
0616	4.6		0615	4.2
SU 1235	0.7		M 1209	0.8
◑ 1836	4.4		◑ 1829	4.3
6 0112	0.3		**21** 0039	0.7
0712	4.4		0655	4.0
M 1326	0.8		TU 1255	1.0
1936	4.3		1926	3.9
7 0208	0.5		**22** 0130	0.9
0815	4.1		0756	3.7
TU 1436	0.9		W 1350	1.2
2046	4.1		2025	3.6
8 0316	0.7		**23** 0255	1.2
0932	4.0		0904	3.5
W 1545	0.9		TH 1606	1.2
2206	4.0		2159	3.5
9 0440	0.8		**24** 0446	1.2
1056	3.9		1034	3.5
TH 1715	0.8		F 1705	1.1
2325	4.1		2326	3.7
10 0556	0.7		**25** 0539	1.0
1205	4.1		1201	3.8
F 1825	0.6		SA 1816	0.9
11 0036	4.4		**26** 0026	4.1
0655	0.6		0636	0.9
SA 1305	4.3		SU 1246	4.1
1926	0.4		1906	0.6
12 0125	4.6		**27** 0105	4.4
0739	0.6		0715	0.7
SU 1345	4.5		M 1326	4.4
2009	0.3		1948	0.4
13 0208	4.7		**28** 0146	4.7
0826	0.6		0758	0.6
M 1427	4.6		TU 1358	4.6
● 2051	0.2		○ 2028	0.2
14 0247	4.8		**29** 0217	4.9
0900	0.7		0838	0.5
TU 1505	4.6		W 1436	4.8
2129	0.2		2105	0.1
15 0326	4.8		**30** 0255	5.0
0936	0.7		0921	0.5
W 1538	4.7		TH 1516	4.9
2206	0.2		2150	0.0
			31 0335	5.1
			1000	0.4
			F 1553	4.9
			2236	0.0

Chart Datum: 2·32 metres below NAP Datum

TIME ZONE -0100
(Dutch Standard Time)
Subtract 1 hour for UT
For Dutch Summer Time add
ONE hour in **non-shaded areas**

NETHERLANDS – VLISSINGEN

LAT 51°27'N   LONG 3°36'E

TIMES AND HEIGHTS OF HIGH AND LOW WATERS

Dates in amber are **SPRINGS**
Dates in yellow are **NEAPS**

2007

SEPTEMBER

Date	Time m	Time m	Time m	Time m		Date	Time m	Time m	Time m	Time m
1 SA	0416 5.0	1046 0.5	1633 4.9	2316 0.0		**16** SU	0432 4.6	1036 0.7	1645 4.6	2300 0.3
2 SU	0459 4.8	1126 0.5	1717 4.8	2356 0.2		**17** M	0500 4.5	1106 0.7	1712 4.5	2326 0.6
3 M	0546 4.6	1210 0.6	1807 4.6			**18** TU	0530 4.3	1124 0.8	1741 4.3	2356 0.8
4 TU	0046 0.4	0638 4.3	1259 0.7	1905 4.3		**19** W	0605 4.1	1216 0.9	1819 4.1	
5 W	0140 0.7	0749 4.0	1410 0.9	2028 4.0		**20** TH	0040 1.0	0650 3.8	1259 1.1	1914 3.7
6 TH	0255 0.9	0921 3.7	1533 1.0	2155 3.9		**21** F	0149 1.3	0821 3.5	1500 1.3	2115 3.6
7 F	0425 1.0	1045 3.8	1709 0.8	2325 4.1		**22** SA	0405 1.3	1000 3.5	1640 1.1	2256 3.8
8 SA	0555 0.9	1154 4.1	1826 0.6			**23** SU	0515 1.1	1125 3.8	1739 0.8	2356 4.2
9 SU	0029 4.4	0650 0.7	1256 4.3	1915 0.4		**24** M	0610 0.9	1216 4.2	1835 0.6	
10 M	0115 4.7	0729 0.7	1331 4.5	1956 0.3		**25** TU	0040 4.5	0652 0.7	1256 4.5	1920 0.3
11 TU	0156 4.8	0806 0.7	1408 4.6	2032 0.2		**26** W	0112 4.8	0732 0.6	1332 4.7	2000 0.1
12 W	0226 4.8	0838 0.7	1437 4.7	2106 0.3		**27** TH	0150 5.0	0812 0.5	1406 5.0	2042 0.0
13 TH	0257 4.8	0906 0.6	1509 4.8	2135 0.3		**28** F	0228 5.2	0856 0.4	1446 5.1	2126 0.0
14 F	0330 4.8	0935 0.6	1541 4.8	2206 0.3		**29** SA	0309 5.2	0936 0.4	1527 5.1	2205 0.0
15 SA	0358 4.7	1004 0.6	1610 4.7	2235 0.4		**30** SU	0353 5.1	1018 0.4	1609 5.1	2248 0.1

OCTOBER

Date	Time m	Time m	Time m	Time m		Date	Time m	Time m	Time m	Time m
1 M	0436 4.9	1102 0.4	1653 4.9	2332 0.3		**16** TU	0426 4.5	1036 0.7	1642 4.5	2256 0.7
2 TU	0525 4.6	1148 0.5	1746 4.6			**17** W	0455 4.4	1105 0.7	1711 4.4	2326 0.8
3 W	0015 0.6	0619 4.2	1241 0.7	1845 4.3		**18** TH	0536 4.2	1145 0.8	1752 4.2	
4 TH	0115 0.9	0736 3.8	1355 0.9	2016 4.0		**19** F	0015 1.0	0627 3.9	1234 0.9	1850 3.9
5 F	0235 1.1	0902 3.7	1530 0.9	2156 3.9		**20** SA	0120 1.2	0747 3.6	1404 1.1	2040 3.7
6 SA	0425 1.1	1036 3.8	1654 0.6	2315 4.2		**21** SU	0325 1.3	0915 3.6	1556 1.0	2210 3.9
7 SU	0534 1.0	1139 4.1	1806 0.5			**22** M	0436 1.2	1035 3.8	1706 0.8	2316 4.2
8 M	0016 4.5	0636 0.8	1230 4.3	1856 0.4		**23** TU	0524 1.0	1131 4.2	1806 0.5	
9 TU	0055 4.6	0716 0.7	1306 4.5	1932 0.3		**24** W	0006 4.6	0620 0.8	1217 4.5	1850 0.3
10 W	0125 4.7	0739 0.7	1339 4.6	2006 0.3		**25** TH	0043 4.9	0702 0.6	1256 4.8	1935 0.2
11 TH	0157 4.7	0810 0.6	1408 4.7	2036 0.3		**26** F	0123 5.1	0746 0.5	1339 5.0	2016 0.1
12 F	0227 4.8	0830 0.4	1438 4.8	2106 0.4		**27** SA	0205 5.1	0830 0.4	1423 5.2	2058 0.1
13 SA	0257 4.8	0916 0.4	1512 4.8	2138 0.4		**28** SU	0246 5.1	0916 0.3	1505 5.2	2142 0.1
14 SU	0330 4.7	0946 0.6	1541 4.8	2206 0.5		**29** M	0331 5.0	1001 0.3	1550 5.1	2225 0.3
15 M	0357 4.6	1005 0.6	1612 4.7	2230 0.6		**30** TU	0418 4.8	1045 0.4	1636 4.9	2308 0.5
						31 W	0507 4.5	1136 0.5	1731 4.6	2358 0.6

NOVEMBER

Date	Time m	Time m	Time m	Time m		Date	Time m	Time m	Time m	Time m
1 TH	0605 4.2	1236 0.6	1840 4.3			**16** F	0517 4.2	1136 0.7	1739 4.3	2355 1.0
2 F	0055 1.0	0715 3.9	1346 0.8	1955 4.1		**17** SA	0605 4.0	1235 0.8	1835 4.1	
3 SA	0214 1.2	0841 3.7	1515 0.8	2119 4.0		**18** SU	0054 1.2	0715 3.8	1346 0.8	2006 4.0
4 SU	0355 1.2	1000 3.8	1635 0.7	2240 4.1		**19** M	0214 1.2	0841 3.8	1454 0.8	2119 4.1
5 M	0515 1.1	1105 4.0	1736 0.6	2336 4.3		**20** TU	0340 1.1	0949 3.9	1616 0.7	2225 4.3
6 TU	0559 0.9	1155 4.2	1822 0.5			**21** W	0446 1.0	1052 4.2	1726 0.5	2325 4.5
7 W	0019 4.5	0640 0.8	1236 4.4	1900 0.5		**22** TH	0546 0.8	1146 4.5	1816 0.4	
8 TH	0058 4.6	0716 0.7	1309 4.5	1936 0.5		**23** F	0012 4.8	0636 0.6	1230 4.8	1905 0.2
9 F	0129 4.6	0746 0.7	1338 4.6	2006 0.5		**24** SA	0059 4.9	0723 0.5	1316 4.9	1956 0.2
10 SA	0158 4.6	0816 0.6	1411 4.7	2036 0.5		**25** SU	0145 5.0	0812 0.3	1406 5.1	2038 0.2
11 SU	0228 4.6	0851 0.6	1446 4.7	2106 0.5		**26** M	0230 4.9	0858 0.3	1450 5.1	2122 0.3
12 M	0303 4.6	0920 0.6	1517 4.7	2138 0.6		**27** TU	0319 4.8	0945 0.3	1536 5.0	2205 0.5
13 TU	0332 4.6	0956 0.6	1550 4.6	2205 0.7		**28** W	0407 4.6	1036 0.3	1629 4.8	2249 0.6
14 W	0406 4.5	1020 0.6	1618 4.5	2236 0.8		**29** TH	0459 4.5	1126 0.4	1721 4.6	2338 0.8
15 TH	0440 4.4	1056 0.7	1658 4.4	2309 0.9		**30** F	0551 4.3	1215 0.5	1821 4.4	

DECEMBER

Date	Time m	Time m	Time m	Time m		Date	Time m	Time m	Time m	Time m
1 SA	0029 1.0	0649 4.1	1326 0.6	1925 4.2		**16** SU	0556 4.2	1225 0.5	1826 4.3	
2 SU	0129 1.1	0755 3.9	1420 0.7	2036 4.0		**17** M	0040 1.0	0651 4.1	1314 0.6	1924 4.2
3 M	0245 1.2	0906 3.8	1536 0.8	2145 4.0		**18** TU	0134 1.0	0800 4.0	1425 0.6	2040 4.2
4 TU	0354 1.2	1016 3.9	1645 0.8	2249 4.1		**19** W	0256 1.0	0908 4.1	1530 0.6	2148 4.3
5 W	0516 1.1	1109 4.0	1746 0.7	2345 4.2		**20** TH	0355 1.0	1016 4.2	1640 0.6	2252 4.2
6 TH	0600 1.0	1158 4.1	1820 0.7			**21** F	0506 0.9	1115 4.4	1745 0.5	2347 4.5
7 F	0026 4.3	0646 0.9	1238 4.2	1901 0.7		**22** SA	0612 0.7	1212 4.6	1846 0.4	
8 SA	0101 4.3	0716 0.8	1316 4.3	1936 0.6		**23** SU	0042 4.6	0708 0.5	1302 4.7	1935 0.4
9 SU	0136 4.4	0756 0.7	1349 4.5	2011 0.6		**24** M	0136 4.7	0759 0.4	1355 4.9	2026 0.4
10 M	0209 4.5	0831 0.6	1426 4.5	2046 0.6		**25** TU	0225 4.7	0850 0.2	1442 4.9	2108 0.5
11 TU	0242 4.5	0901 0.6	1459 4.6	2115 0.7		**26** W	0316 4.7	0936 0.2	1532 4.9	2152 0.6
12 W	0320 4.5	0940 0.5	1532 4.6	2150 0.7		**27** TH	0357 4.6	1026 0.2	1619 4.8	2236 0.7
13 TH	0352 4.5	1016 0.5	1608 4.6	2228 0.8		**28** F	0445 4.5	1110 0.2	1706 4.7	2315 0.8
14 F	0429 4.4	1055 0.5	1647 4.5	2306 0.8		**29** SA	0529 4.4	1151 0.3	1755 4.5	2355 0.9
15 SA	0512 4.3	1146 0.5	1731 4.4	2350 0.9		**30** SU	0615 4.3	1235 0.4	1845 4.3	
						31 M	0046 1.0	0705 4.1	1325 0.6	1935 4.1

Chart Datum: 2·32 metres below NAP Datum

TIDES

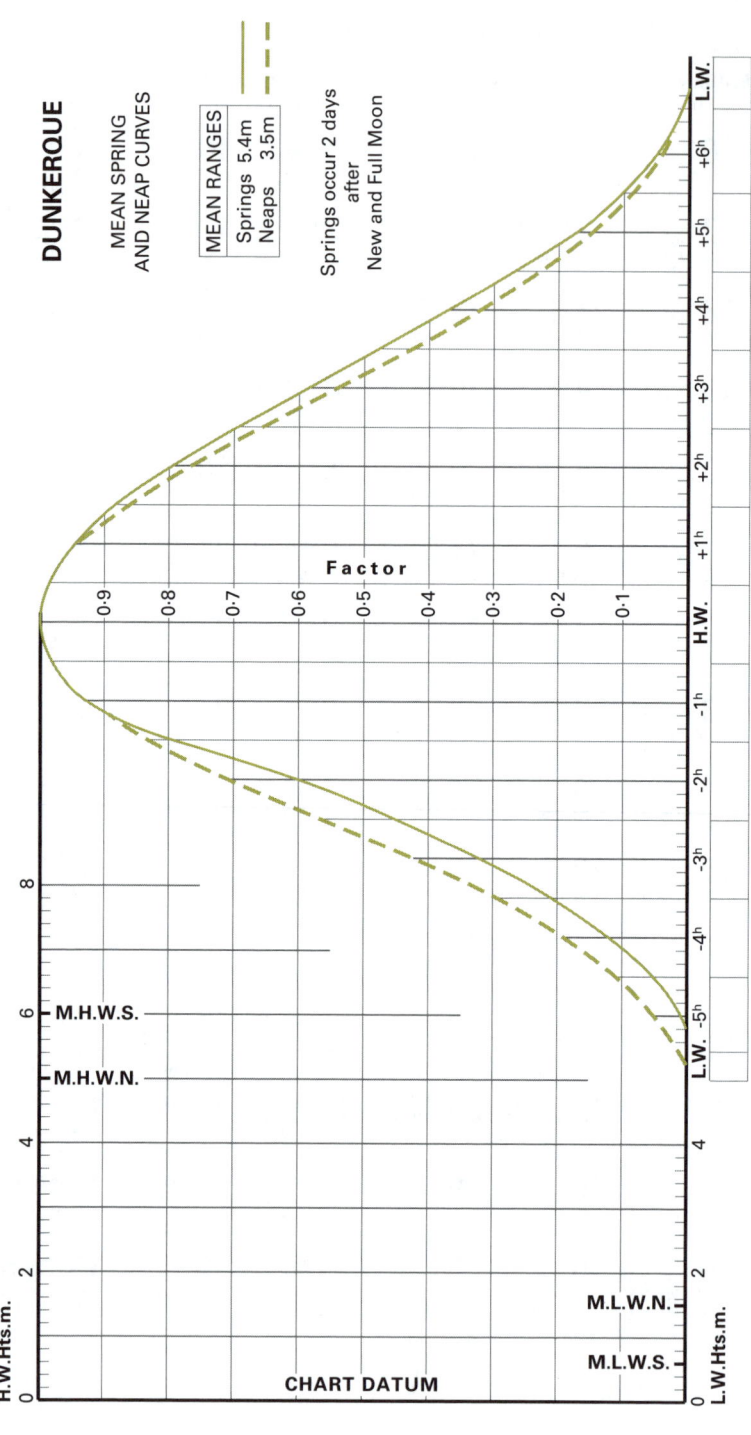

DUNKERQUE

MEAN SPRING
AND NEAP CURVES

MEAN RANGES	
Springs	5.4m
Neaps	3.5m

Springs occur 2 days
after
New and Full Moon

Factor

0·9
0·8
0·7
0·6
0·5
0·4
0·3
0·2
0·1

+6ʰ +5ʰ +4ʰ +3ʰ +2ʰ +1ʰ H.W. -1ʰ -2ʰ -3ʰ -4ʰ -5ʰ -6ʰ

L.W.

L.W.

8

6 M.H.W.S.

M.H.W.N.

4

2

M.L.W.N.

M.L.W.S.

H.W.Hts.m.

L.W.Hts.m.

CHART DATUM

TIME ZONE -0100
(French Standard Time)
Subtract 1 hour for UT
For French Summer Time add
ONE hour in **non-shaded areas**

FRANCE – DUNKERQUE

LAT 51°03'N   LONG 2°22'E

TIMES AND HEIGHTS OF HIGH AND LOW WATERS

Dates in amber are **SPRINGS**
Dates in yellow are **NEAPS**

2007

JANUARY

Day	Time m	Day	Time m
1 M	0514 1.3 / 1042 5.4 / 1748 1.1 / 2325 5.5	16 TU	0502 1.7 / 1044 5.0 / 1729 1.5 / 2312 5.1
2 TU	0614 1.1 / 1140 5.6 / 1843 1.0	17 W	0559 1.4 / 1135 5.3 / 1821 1.3 / 2358 5.4
3 W	0013 5.6 / 0706 1.0 / 1231 5.7 / 1930 1.0 ○	18 TH	0648 1.1 / 1219 5.5 / 1908 1.1
4 TH	0058 5.7 / 0752 0.8 / 1318 5.8 / 2013 1.0	19 F	0037 5.6 / 0733 0.9 / 1300 5.8 / 1951 1.0 ●
5 F	0141 5.7 / 0834 0.7 / 1402 5.9 / 2053 1.0	20 SA	0117 5.8 / 0817 0.7 / 1341 6.0 / 2034 0.8
6 SA	0221 5.7 / 0915 0.7 / 1443 5.8 / 2131 1.0	21 SU	0157 5.9 / 0900 0.5 / 1423 6.0 / 2116 0.7
7 SU	0259 5.7 / 0952 0.8 / 1522 5.7 / 2206 1.1	22 M	0238 5.9 / 0943 0.4 / 1506 6.0 / 2158 0.7
8 M	0334 5.6 / 1028 0.9 / 1558 5.6 / 2240 1.3	23 TU	0319 5.9 / 1026 0.5 / 1549 5.9 / 2239 0.8
9 TU	0409 5.5 / 1103 1.0 / 1634 5.4 / 2315 1.4	24 W	0401 5.9 / 1109 0.5 / 1635 5.8 / 2322 1.0
10 W	0447 5.3 / 1138 1.1 / 1712 5.2 / 2352 1.5	25 TH	0448 5.7 / 1154 0.7 / 1725 5.6 ◑
11 TH	0529 5.2 / 1218 1.3 / 1757 5.0 ◐	26 F	0010 1.2 / 0541 5.6 / 1247 1.0 / 1823 5.3
12 F	0036 1.7 / 0619 5.0 / 1308 1.5 / 1851 4.8	27 SA	0108 1.4 / 0644 5.3 / 1351 1.2 / 1934 5.0
13 SA	0133 1.9 / 0718 4.8 / 1413 1.7 / 1956 4.7	28 SU	0220 1.6 / 0800 5.1 / 1506 1.4 / 2056 4.9
14 SU	0247 1.9 / 0829 4.7 / 1524 1.7 / 2109 4.7	29 M	0340 1.6 / 0925 5.0 / 1629 1.5 / 2216 4.9
15 M	0358 1.9 / 0942 4.8 / 1629 1.6 / 2216 4.8	30 TU	0505 1.5 / 1042 5.2 / 1744 1.3 / 2323 5.2
		31 W	0611 1.2 / 1144 5.4 / 1837 1.1

FEBRUARY

Day	Time m	Day	Time m
1 TH	0012 5.4 / 0700 0.9 / 1233 5.6 / 1921 1.0	16 F	0633 1.0 / 1204 5.6 / 1853 1.0
2 F	0053 5.6 / 0743 0.7 / 1313 5.8 / 2000 0.9 ○	17 SA	0020 5.6 / 0718 0.7 / 1245 5.7 / 1936 0.7 ●
3 SA	0130 5.7 / 0821 0.6 / 1350 5.8 / 2036 0.9	18 SU	0059 5.8 / 0801 0.4 / 1324 6.1 / 2016 0.6
4 SU	0204 5.8 / 0857 0.6 / 1424 5.8 / 2109 0.9	19 M	0137 6.0 / 0843 0.3 / 1404 6.2 / 2057 0.5
5 M	0235 5.8 / 0930 0.6 / 1456 5.8 / 2140 0.9	20 TU	0216 6.1 / 0924 0.2 / 1444 6.2 / 2137 0.5
6 TU	0305 5.8 / 1001 0.7 / 1526 5.7 / 2210 1.0	21 W	0255 6.1 / 1005 0.2 / 1525 6.1 / 2217 0.6
7 W	0335 5.7 / 1029 0.8 / 1555 5.6 / 2238 1.1	22 TH	0337 6.1 / 1046 0.4 / 1608 5.9 / 2257 0.8
8 TH	0406 5.6 / 1058 0.9 / 1626 5.4 / 2307 1.2	23 F	0422 5.9 / 1129 0.6 / 1656 5.6 / 2341 1.0
9 F	0439 5.4 / 1129 1.1 / 1702 5.2 / 2340 1.4	24 SA	0514 5.6 / 1218 1.0 / 1753 5.2 ◐
10 SA	0517 5.2 / 1207 1.4 / 1747 4.9	25 SU	0036 1.3 / 0617 5.2 / 1322 1.4 / 1905 4.8
11 SU	0023 1.7 / 0611 4.8 / 1259 1.7 / 1851 4.6	26 M	0151 1.6 / 0741 4.9 / 1446 1.7 / 2039 4.6
12 M	0125 1.9 / 0726 4.6 / 1417 1.9 / 2011 4.4	27 TU	0325 1.7 / 0919 4.8 / 1622 1.7 / 2210 4.7
13 TU	0257 2.0 / 0856 4.5 / 1545 1.8 / 2140 4.5	28 W	0459 1.5 / 1041 5.0 / 1735 1.4 / 2316 5.0
14 W	0425 1.9 / 1018 4.8 / 1703 1.6 / 2250 4.9		
15 TH	0538 1.4 / 1117 5.2 / 1805 1.3 / 2341 5.3		

MARCH

Day	Time m	Day	Time m
1 TH	0600 1.1 / 1140 5.3 / 1825 1.1	16 F	0512 1.3 / 1054 5.2 / 1742 1.2 / 2317 5.3
2 F	0004 5.3 / 0646 0.8 / 1222 5.6 / 1904 1.0	17 SA	0609 0.9 / 1141 5.6 / 1830 0.9 / 2359 5.6 ●
3 SA	0036 5.6 / 0725 0.6 / 1257 5.7 / 1939 0.9	18 SU	0655 0.5 / 1222 5.9 / 1912 0.6
4 SU	0109 5.7 / 0759 0.6 / 1328 5.8 / 2011 0.8 ○	19 M	0033 5.9 / 0738 0.3 / 1259 6.1 / 1952 0.5 ●
5 M	0139 5.8 / 0831 0.5 / 1358 5.8 / 2041 0.8	20 TU	0110 6.1 / 0819 0.2 / 1338 6.2 / 2032 0.4
6 TU	0207 5.8 / 0901 0.5 / 1426 5.8 / 2110 0.8	21 W	0150 6.2 / 0900 0.1 / 1418 6.2 / 2112 0.4
7 W	0233 5.6 / 0929 0.6 / 1451 5.8 / 2138 0.8	22 TH	0230 6.3 / 0941 0.2 / 1500 6.1 / 2153 0.5
8 TH	0300 5.8 / 0956 0.7 / 1517 5.7 / 2205 0.9	23 F	0314 6.2 / 1023 0.4 / 1544 5.9 / 2234 0.7
9 F	0327 5.7 / 1022 0.8 / 1544 5.5 / 2231 1.0	24 SA	0401 6.0 / 1106 0.7 / 1633 5.5 / 2319 0.9
10 SA	0354 5.5 / 1050 1.0 / 1612 5.3 / 2301 1.2	25 SU	0455 5.6 / 1155 1.2 / 1731 5.1 ◑
11 SU	0424 5.3 / 1125 1.3 / 1647 5.0 / 2339 1.5	26 M	0016 1.3 / 0601 5.1 / 1302 1.6 / 1845 4.7
12 M	0509 5.0 / 1213 1.6 / 1748 4.6 ◐	27 TU	0132 1.6 / 0727 4.7 / 1432 1.8 / 2023 4.5
13 TU	0038 1.8 / 0633 4.6 / 1326 1.9 / 1929 4.4	28 W	0311 1.7 / 0908 4.7 / 1605 1.7 / 2151 4.6
14 W	0208 2.0 / 0819 4.5 / 1505 1.9 / 2106 4.4	29 TH	0439 1.4 / 1024 5.0 / 1713 1.4 / 2252 5.0
15 TH	0349 1.8 / 0950 4.7 / 1636 1.6 / 2224 4.8	30 F	0538 1.1 / 1118 5.3 / 1801 1.2 / 2337 5.3
		31 SA	0622 0.8 / 1157 5.5 / 1839 1.0

APRIL

Day	Time m	Day	Time m
1 SU	0009 5.5 / 0658 0.7 / 1229 5.7 / 1911 0.9	16 M	0626 0.5 / 1151 5.9 / 1843 0.7
2 M	0039 5.7 / 0729 0.6 / 1259 5.7 / 1941 0.8 ○	17 TU	0004 5.9 / 0710 0.3 / 1230 6.1 / 1925 0.5 ●
3 TU	0109 5.8 / 0758 0.6 / 1327 5.8 / 2009 0.8	18 W	0043 6.1 / 0753 0.2 / 1310 6.1 / 2007 0.5
4 W	0135 5.8 / 0827 0.6 / 1353 5.8 / 2039 0.7	19 TH	0125 6.2 / 0835 0.3 / 1353 6.1 / 2049 0.5
5 TH	0202 5.8 / 0857 0.6 / 1417 5.7 / 2108 0.8	20 F	0209 6.2 / 0918 0.4 / 1438 6.0 / 2132 0.5
6 F	0229 5.8 / 0925 0.7 / 1444 5.7 / 2136 0.9	21 SA	0257 6.1 / 1002 0.6 / 1527 5.7 / 2217 0.7
7 SA	0256 5.7 / 0952 0.9 / 1512 5.6 / 2204 1.0	22 SU	0348 5.9 / 1048 0.9 / 1619 5.4 / 2305 0.9
8 SU	0324 5.5 / 1022 1.0 / 1541 5.3 / 2236 1.2	23 M	0444 5.5 / 1140 1.3 / 1717 5.1
9 M	0357 5.3 / 1059 1.3 / 1617 5.0 / 2317 1.4	24 TU	0001 1.2 / 0548 5.1 / 1245 1.6 / 1826 4.7 ◑
10 TU	0444 5.0 / 1149 1.6 / 1719 4.7 ○	25 W	0116 1.5 / 0708 4.8 / 1408 1.8 / 1955 4.5
11 W	0018 1.6 / 0612 4.7 / 1302 1.8 / 1902 4.4	26 TH	0243 1.5 / 0839 4.7 / 1528 1.7 / 2113 4.7
12 TH	0142 1.7 / 0748 4.6 / 1433 1.8 / 2031 4.5	27 F	0400 1.4 / 0947 4.9 / 1634 1.5 / 2210 4.9
13 F	0317 1.6 / 0917 4.9 / 1602 1.5 / 2149 4.9	28 SA	0500 1.1 / 1038 5.2 / 1723 1.2 / 2255 5.2
14 SA	0438 1.2 / 1022 5.3 / 1708 1.1 / 2244 5.3	29 SU	0545 0.9 / 1119 5.4 / 1803 1.1 / 2333 5.4
15 SU	0538 0.8 / 1110 5.7 / 1759 0.8 / 2328 5.6	30 M	0621 0.8 / 1154 5.5 / 1837 1.0

Chart Datum: 2·69 metres below IGN Datum

TIDES

FRANCE – DUNKERQUE

LAT 51°03'N   LONG 2°22'E

TIMES AND HEIGHTS OF HIGH AND LOW WATERS

TIME ZONE -0100
(French Standard Time)
Subtract 1 hour for UT
For French Summer Time add
ONE hour in **non-shaded areas**

Dates in amber are **SPRINGS**
Dates in yellow are **NEAPS**

2007

MAY

Day	Time	m	Day	Time	m
1 TU	0005	5.6	**16** W	0643	0.5
	0653	0.8		1204	5.9
	1226	5.6		1900 ●	0.7
	1907	0.9			
2 W	0037	5.6	**17** TH	0020	6.0
	0723	0.8		0730	0.5
	1255	5.6		1249	6.0
	1938 ○	0.9		1946	0.6
3 TH	0105	5.7	**18** F	0107	6.1
	0755	0.8		0815	0.5
	1322	5.7		1336	5.9
	2010	0.8		2032	0.5
4 F	0134	5.7	**19** SA	0156	6.1
	0828	0.8		0901	0.6
	1350	5.7		1427	5.8
	2043	0.8		2118	0.6
5 SA	0205	5.7	**20** SU	0248	6.0
	0900	0.9		0948	0.8
	1421	5.6		1519	5.6
	2115	0.9		2206	0.7
6 SU	0238	5.6	**21** M	0341	5.8
	0932	1.0		1035	1.1
	1455	5.5		1610	5.4
	2149	1.0		2254	0.9
7 M	0313	5.5	**22** TU	0434	5.5
	1007	1.1		1124	1.3
	1532	5.3		1701	5.2
	2226	1.1		2347	1.1
8 TU	0354	5.3	**23** W	0530	5.2
	1049	1.3		1220	1.6
	1619	5.0		1758 ◐	4.9
	2311	1.3			
9 W	0451	5.1	**24** TH	0049	1.3
	1142	1.5		0635	4.9
	1728	4.8		1325	1.7
				1908	4.8
10 TH	0011	1.4	**25** F	0157	1.4
	0605	4.9		0751	4.8
	1247	1.6		1434	1.7
	1839 ◐	4.7		2019	4.8
11 F	0125	1.4	**26** SA	0304	1.3
	0718	4.9		0856	4.9
	1405	1.6		1536	1.6
	1953	4.8		2118	4.9
12 SA	0245	1.3	**27** SU	0403	1.2
	0835	5.1		0949	5.0
	1523	1.4		1631	1.4
	2106	5.0		2208	5.1
13 SU	0400	1.0	**28** M	0454	1.1
	0942	5.4		1035	5.2
	1629	1.1		1718	1.3
	2205	5.3		2252	5.2
14 M	0502	0.8	**29** TU	0537	1.1
	1034	5.6		1116	5.3
	1724	0.9		1759	1.2
	2253	5.6		2333	5.3
15 TU	0555	0.6	**30** W	0615	1.0
	1120	5.8		1153	5.4
	1814	0.8		1835	1.1
	2338	5.8			
			31 TH	0008	5.4
				0652	1.0
				1226	5.5
				1911	1.0

JUNE

Day	Time	m	Day	Time	m
1 F	0041	5.5	**16** SA	0100	5.9
	0729	1.0		0805	0.7
	1258	5.5		1333	5.7
	1947 ○	0.9		2023	0.6
2 SA	0115	5.6	**17** SU	0152	5.9
	0806	1.0		0851	0.8
	1332	5.6		1423	5.7
	2025	0.9		2110	0.6
3 SU	0152	5.6	**18** M	0242	5.9
	0844	1.0		0937	0.9
	1410	5.6		1510	5.6
	2103	0.9		2156	0.6
4 M	0231	5.6	**19** TU	0331	5.7
	0922	1.0		1020	1.1
	1452	5.5		1554	5.5
	2143	0.9		2240	0.7
5 TU	0314	5.6	**20** W	0417	5.5
	1003	1.1		1103	1.2
	1536	5.4		1637	5.4
	2224	0.9		2324	0.9
6 W	0359	5.4	**21** TH	0502	5.3
	1047	1.2		1146	1.4
	1623	5.2		1720	5.2
	2310	1.0			
7 TH	0450	5.3	**22** F	0011	1.1
	1135	1.3		0549	5.1
	1715	5.1		1234	1.5
				1809 ◐	5.0
8 F	0001	1.1	**23** SA	0103	1.2
	0547	5.2		0643	5.0
	1230	1.4		1329	1.6
	1811 ◐	5.1		1907	4.9
9 SA	0105	1.1	**24** SU	0200	1.3
	0648	5.2		0744	4.8
	1334	1.4		1430	1.7
	1913	5.1		2012	4.8
10 SU	0213	1.1	**25** M	0300	1.4
	0754	5.2		0847	4.8
	1444	1.3		1530	1.6
	2020	5.2		2114	4.9
11 M	0323	1.0	**26** TU	0357	1.4
	0901	5.3		0945	4.9
	1551	1.2		1628	1.5
	2126	5.3		2210	5.0
12 TU	0428	0.9	**27** W	0452	1.4
	1002	5.5		1037	5.0
	1653	1.1		1721	1.4
	2224	5.5		2301	5.1
13 W	0528	0.8	**28** TH	0542	1.3
	1057	5.6		1123	5.1
	1750	0.9		1809	1.3
	2319	5.7		2346	5.3
14 TH	0624	0.7	**29** F	0627	1.2
	1150	5.7		1205	5.3
	1844	0.8		1851	1.1
15 F	0008	5.9	**30** SA	0024	5.4
	0716	0.7		0710	1.1
	1241	5.7		1243	5.4
	1935 ●	0.7		1932 ○	1.0

JULY

Day	Time	m	Day	Time	m
1 SU	0102	5.6	**16** M	0146	5.9
	0751	1.0		0840	0.9
	1321	5.6		1412	5.7
	2012	0.8		2059	0.5
2 M	0141	5.7	**17** TU	0230	5.9
	0833	0.9		0920	0.9
	1400	5.6		1451	5.7
	2054	0.7		2140	0.5
3 TU	0222	5.8	**18** W	0311	5.8
	0914	0.9		0958	1.0
	1442	5.7		1528	5.7
	2136	0.7		2218	0.6
4 W	0304	5.8	**19** TH	0349	5.7
	0956	0.9		1033	1.1
	1524	5.6		1603	5.6
	2218	0.7		2254	0.8
5 TH	0347	5.7	**20** F	0425	5.5
	1037	1.0		1108	1.2
	1605	5.5		1637	5.4
	2300	0.7		2329	0.9
6 F	0432	5.6	**21** SA	0502	5.3
	1120	1.0		1144	1.3
	1649	5.5		1716	5.3
	2345	0.8			
7 SA	0522	5.5	**22** SU	0008	1.1
	1207	1.1		0544	5.1
	1739 ◐	5.4		1225	1.5
				1801 ◐	5.1
8 SU	0040	0.9	**23** M	0053	1.4
	0617	5.4		0633	4.9
	1302	1.3		1318	1.7
	1836	5.3		1857	4.8
9 M	0141	1.0	**24** TU	0152	1.6
	0719	5.3		0733	4.7
	1408	1.4		1427	1.9
	1943	5.2		2008	4.7
10 TU	0251	1.1	**25** W	0301	1.7
	0829	5.2		0846	4.6
	1520	1.4		1538	1.9
	2057	5.2		2125	4.7
11 W	0402	1.1	**26** TH	0410	1.7
	0943	5.2		0958	4.7
	1631	1.3		1646	1.7
	2211	5.3		2233	4.9
12 TH	0514	1.1	**27** F	0514	1.6
	1051	5.3		1058	4.9
	1740	1.1		1747	1.5
	2317	5.5		2327	5.1
13 F	0618	1.0	**28** SA	0610	1.3
	1151	5.5		1147	5.2
	1839	0.9		1836	1.2
14 SA	0011	5.7	**29** SU	0010	5.4
	0711	0.9		0655	1.1
	1243	5.6		1228	5.4
	1930 ●	0.7		1918	0.9
15 SU	0100	5.8	**30** M	0048	5.7
	0758	0.9		0737	1.0
	1330	5.7		1306	5.6
	2016	0.6		1959 ○	0.7
			31 TU	0126	5.8
				0818	0.8
				1343	5.8
				2039	0.6

AUGUST

Day	Time	m	Day	Time	m
1 W	0205	6.0	**16** TH	0242	5.9
	0859	0.8		0929	0.9
	1421	5.8		1454	5.8
	2120	0.5		2148	0.6
2 TH	0244	6.0	**17** F	0314	5.8
	0939	0.7		0959	1.0
	1458	5.9		1524	5.8
	2201	0.4		2218	0.7
3 F	0324	6.0	**18** SA	0344	5.7
	1018	0.8		1029	1.1
	1536	5.8		1554	5.6
	2241	0.5		2248	0.9
4 SA	0406	5.9	**19** SU	0416	5.5
	1058	0.9		1059	1.2
	1618	5.8		1627	5.4
	2323	0.6		2319	1.1
5 SU	0454	5.7	**20** M	0451	5.3
	1140	1.0		1131	1.4
	1706 ◑	5.6		1706	5.2
				2355 ◑	1.4
6 M	0011	0.8	**21** TU	0534	5.0
	0548	5.5		1211	1.7
	1231	1.3		1758	4.9
	1805	5.4			
7 TU	0111	1.1	**22** W	0045	1.7
	0651	5.2		0635	4.7
	1338	1.5		1312	2.0
	1916	5.2		1911	4.6
8 W	0226	1.4	**23** TH	0200	2.0
	0809	5.0		0754	4.4
	1458	1.6		1443	2.1
	2046	5.0		2040	4.5
9 TH	0350	1.5	**24** F	0328	2.0
	0937	4.9		0922	4.5
	1623	1.5		1611	1.9
	2212	5.1		2206	4.7
10 F	0514	1.4	**25** SA	0449	1.7
	1053	5.1		1034	4.8
	1739	1.2		1725	1.5
	2320	5.4		2306	5.1
11 SA	0615	1.2	**26** SU	0551	1.4
	1151	5.4		1126	5.2
	1834	0.9		1817	1.1
				2352	5.5
12 SU	0011	5.7	**27** M	0637	1.1
	0703	1.0		1207	5.5
	1238	5.6		1859	0.8
	1920	0.7			
13 M	0053	5.8	**28** TU	0027	5.8
	0744	0.9		0717	0.9
	1315	5.7		1243	5.8
	2001 ●	0.5		1938 ○	0.6
14 TU	0132	5.9	**29** W	0102	6.0
	0821	0.9		0756	0.7
	1349	5.8		1317	5.9
	2040	0.5		2017	0.4
15 W	0208	5.9	**30** TH	0139	6.1
	0856	0.9		0835	0.6
	1422	5.9		1351	6.1
	2115	0.5		2057	0.3
			31 F	0217	6.2
				0914	0.6
				1428	6.1
				2137	0.3

Chart Datum: 2·69 metres below IGN Datum

TIME ZONE -0100
(French Standard Time)
Subtract 1 hour for UT
For French Summer Time add ONE hour in **non-shaded areas**

FRANCE – DUNKERQUE

LAT 51°03'N   LONG 2°22'E

TIMES AND HEIGHTS OF HIGH AND LOW WATERS

Dates in amber are **SPRINGS**
Dates in yellow are **NEAPS**

2007

SEPTEMBER

Day	Time	m	Time	m	Day	Time	m	Time	m
1 SA	0256	6.1	1506	6.1	16 SU	0303	5.8	1513	5.7
	0953	0.7	2217	0.4		0953	1.1	2210	1.0
2 SU	0338	6.0	1549	6.0	17 M	0331	5.6	1543	5.5
	1033	0.8	2258	0.7		1019	1.2	2238	1.2
3 M	0426	5.8	1640	5.7	18 TU	0400	5.4	1614	5.3
	1115	1.0	2344	1.0		1049	1.4	2311	1.5
4 TU	0523	5.4	1743	5.4	19 W	0434	5.1	1657	4.9
	1206	1.3				1127	1.7	2356	1.8
5 W	0047	1.4	1317	1.6	20 TH	0531	4.7	1828	4.5
	0631	5.0	1903	5.0		1222	2.0		
6 TH	0212	1.7	1449	1.7	21 F	0109	2.1	1348	2.1
	0759	4.7	2045	4.9		0713	4.4	2001	4.4
7 F	0350	1.7	1622	1.5	22 SA	0245	2.1	1532	2.0
	0935	4.8	2213	5.1		0844	4.5	2133	4.7
8 SA	0510	1.5	1732	1.1	23 SU	0417	1.8	1653	1.5
	1048	5.1	2316	5.4		1003	4.8	2237	5.2
9 SU	0604	1.2	1822	0.8	24 M	0523	1.4	1747	1.1
	1141	5.4				1057	5.3	2323	5.6
10 M	0002	5.7	1220	5.7	25 TU	0610	1.1	1831	0.7
	0646	1.0	1903	0.6		1137	5.6		
11 TU	0036	5.8	1251	5.8	26 W	0002	5.9	1211	5.9
	0722	0.9	1939	0.6		0650	0.8	1911	0.5
12 W	0109	5.9	1320	5.9	27 TH	0033	6.2	1244	6.1
	0755	0.9	2013	0.6		0729	0.7	1951	0.4
13 TH	0140	5.9	1350	5.9	28 F	0110	6.3	1320	6.2
	0826	0.9	2044	0.6		0808	0.6	2030	0.3
14 F	0209	5.9	1418	5.9	29 SA	0149	6.3	1359	6.3
	0856	0.9	2114	0.7		0848	0.6	2111	0.4
15 SA	0236	5.9	1446	5.8	30 SU	0230	6.2	1441	6.2
	0925	1.0	2142	0.8		0929	0.7	2152	0.5

OCTOBER

Day	Time	m	Time	m	Day	Time	m	Time	m
1 M	0315	6.0	1528	6.0	16 TU	0258	5.6	1512	5.6
	1010	0.8	2236	0.8		0950	1.2	2207	1.3
2 TU	0405	5.7	1623	5.7	17 W	0327	5.4	1544	5.3
	1055	1.1	2325	1.2		1022	1.4	2241	1.5
3 W	0504	5.3	1731	5.3	18 TH	0402	5.1	1626	5.0
	1150	1.4				1101	1.6	2328	1.8
4 TH	0033	1.7	1306	1.7	19 F	0455	4.8	1759	4.7
	0615	4.9	1856	4.9		1157	1.8		
5 F	0205	1.9	1440	1.7	20 SA	0038	2.0	1314	2.0
	0747	4.7	2039	4.9		0636	4.5	1924	4.6
6 SA	0339	1.8	1607	1.5	21 SU	0205	2.1	1446	1.8
	0920	4.8	2159	5.1		0800	4.6	2050	4.9
7 SU	0451	1.5	1712	1.1	22 M	0334	1.8	1610	1.5
	1026	5.1	2256	5.4		0919	4.9	2158	5.3
8 M	0542	1.3	1800	0.8	23 TU	0443	1.4	1710	1.0
	1114	5.4	2339	5.7		1025	5.4	2248	5.7
9 TU	0621	1.1	1838	0.7	24 W	0535	1.1	1758	0.7
	1150	5.7				1058	5.7	2329	6.0
10 W	0010	5.8	1220	5.8	25 TH	0619	0.9	1842	0.5
	0655	1.0	1911	0.7		1136	6.0		
11 TH	0040	5.9	1252	5.9	26 F	0005	6.2	1213	6.2
	0725	1.0	1942	0.7		0701	0.8	1923	0.4
12 F	0108	5.9	1319	5.9	27 SA	0043	6.3	1254	6.3
	0754	0.9	2011	0.8		0742	0.7	2005	0.4
13 SA	0134	5.9	1345	5.9	28 SU	0125	6.3	1338	6.3
	0824	0.9	2040	0.8		0825	0.7	2049	0.5
14 SU	0201	5.9	1412	5.9	29 M	0210	6.1	1425	6.2
	0854	1.0	2110	0.9		0909	0.7	2133	0.7
15 M	0229	5.8	1441	5.7	30 TU	0259	5.9	1517	6.0
	0923	1.1	2138	1.1		0955	0.8	2220	1.1
					31 W	0352	5.6	1617	5.7
						1044	1.0	2313	1.4

NOVEMBER

Day	Time	m	Time	m	Day	Time	m	Time	m
1 TH	0450	5.3	1722	5.3	16 F	0354	5.2	1628	5.1
	1141	1.3				1052	1.4	2315	1.7
2 F	0021	1.7	1252	1.5	17 SA	0448	5.0	1737	5.0
	0556	5.0	1841	5.0		1145	1.6		
3 SA	0142	1.9	1415	1.6	18 SU	0017	1.8	1248	1.6
	0721	4.8	2013	4.9		0600	4.8	1847	4.9
4 SU	0304	1.9	1533	1.4	19 M	0127	1.8	1403	1.6
	0844	4.8	2123	5.1		0711	4.8	1959	5.0
5 M	0412	1.7	1636	1.2	20 TU	0245	1.7	1522	1.4
	0945	5.1	2218	5.3		0821	5.0	2110	5.3
6 TU	0505	1.4	1726	1.0	21 W	0356	1.5	1628	1.1
	1033	5.3	2302	5.5		0925	5.3	2207	5.6
7 W	0547	1.3	1806	0.9	22 TH	0455	1.2	1723	0.8
	1113	5.5	2338	5.6		1017	5.6	2256	5.8
8 TH	0622	1.2	1840	0.9	23 F	0547	1.0	1813	0.7
	1148	5.7				1104	5.9	2341	6.0
9 F	0007	5.7	1221	5.7	24 SA	0635	0.9	1901	0.6
	0654	1.1	1910	0.9		1150	6.1		
10 SA	0038	5.8	1240	5.8	25 SU	0023	6.1	1237	6.2
	0725	1.0	1940	1.0		0722	0.8	1948	0.6
11 SU	0106	5.8	1320	5.8	26 M	0110	6.1	1327	6.2
	0757	1.0	2012	1.0		0810	0.7	2034	0.7
12 M	0134	5.8	1349	5.8	27 TU	0159	6.0	1419	6.1
	0830	1.0	2045	1.1		0857	0.7	2122	0.9
13 TU	0206	5.7	1422	5.7	28 W	0250	5.9	1514	6.0
	0902	1.1	2117	1.2		0946	0.8	2210	1.1
14 W	0239	5.6	1459	5.6	29 TH	0341	5.6	1609	5.7
	0934	1.2	2151	1.3		1036	0.9	2300	1.4
15 TH	0315	5.4	1538	5.4	30 F	0433	5.4	1706	5.4
	1010	1.3	2228	1.5		1128	1.1	2354	1.6

DECEMBER

Day	Time	m	Time	m	Day	Time	m	Time	m
1 SA	0528	5.1	1809	5.1	16 SU	0433	5.3	1710	5.3
	1226	1.3				1132	1.2	2351	1.5
2 SU	0059	1.8	1331	1.4	17 M	0526	5.2	1808	5.2
	0632	4.9	1923	5.0		1223	1.3		
3 M	0206	1.9	1437	1.5	18 TU	0050	1.5	1324	1.3
	0746	4.9	2030	4.9		0626	5.2	1911	5.2
4 TU	0311	1.8	1540	1.4	19 W	0156	1.6	1436	1.3
	0851	4.9	2127	5.0		0731	5.2	2019	5.2
5 W	0410	1.7	1636	1.3	20 TH	0309	1.5	1547	1.2
	0945	5.1	2216	5.2		0838	5.3	2128	5.4
6 TH	0502	1.5	1725	1.1	21 F	0418	1.4	1652	1.0
	1033	5.2	2300	5.3		0944	5.5	2231	5.5
7 F	0547	1.4	1807	1.2	22 SA	0521	1.2	1753	0.9
	1117	5.4	2340	5.4		1045	5.7	2328	5.7
8 SA	0625	1.3	1843	1.2	23 SU	0620	1.0	1849	0.8
	1157	5.5				1141	5.9		
9 SU	0014	5.5	1232	5.6	24 M	0015	5.8	1235	6.0
	0701	1.2	1917	1.1		0714	0.9	1940	0.8
10 M	0046	5.6	1304	5.7	25 TU	0106	5.9	1327	6.1
	0737	1.1	1952	1.1		0804	0.7	2028	0.8
11 TU	0118	5.7	1337	5.7	26 W	0154	5.9	1418	6.1
	0814	1.0	2028	1.1		0852	0.6	2114	0.9
12 W	0153	5.7	1414	5.7	27 TH	0241	5.9	1507	6.0
	0850	1.0	2105	1.1		0938	0.6	2158	1.0
13 TH	0231	5.7	1454	5.7	28 F	0325	5.7	1553	5.8
	0927	1.0	2143	1.2		1023	0.7	2240	1.2
14 F	0309	5.6	1536	5.6	29 SA	0408	5.6	1638	5.5
	1005	1.1	2222	1.3		1106	0.9	2322	1.4
15 SA	0348	5.4	1620	5.4	30 SU	0451	5.4	1723	5.3
	1046	1.1	2304	1.4		1150	1.0		
					31 M	0006	1.5	1237	1.2
						0537	5.2	1814	5.1

Chart Datum: 2·69 metres below IGN Datum

TIDES

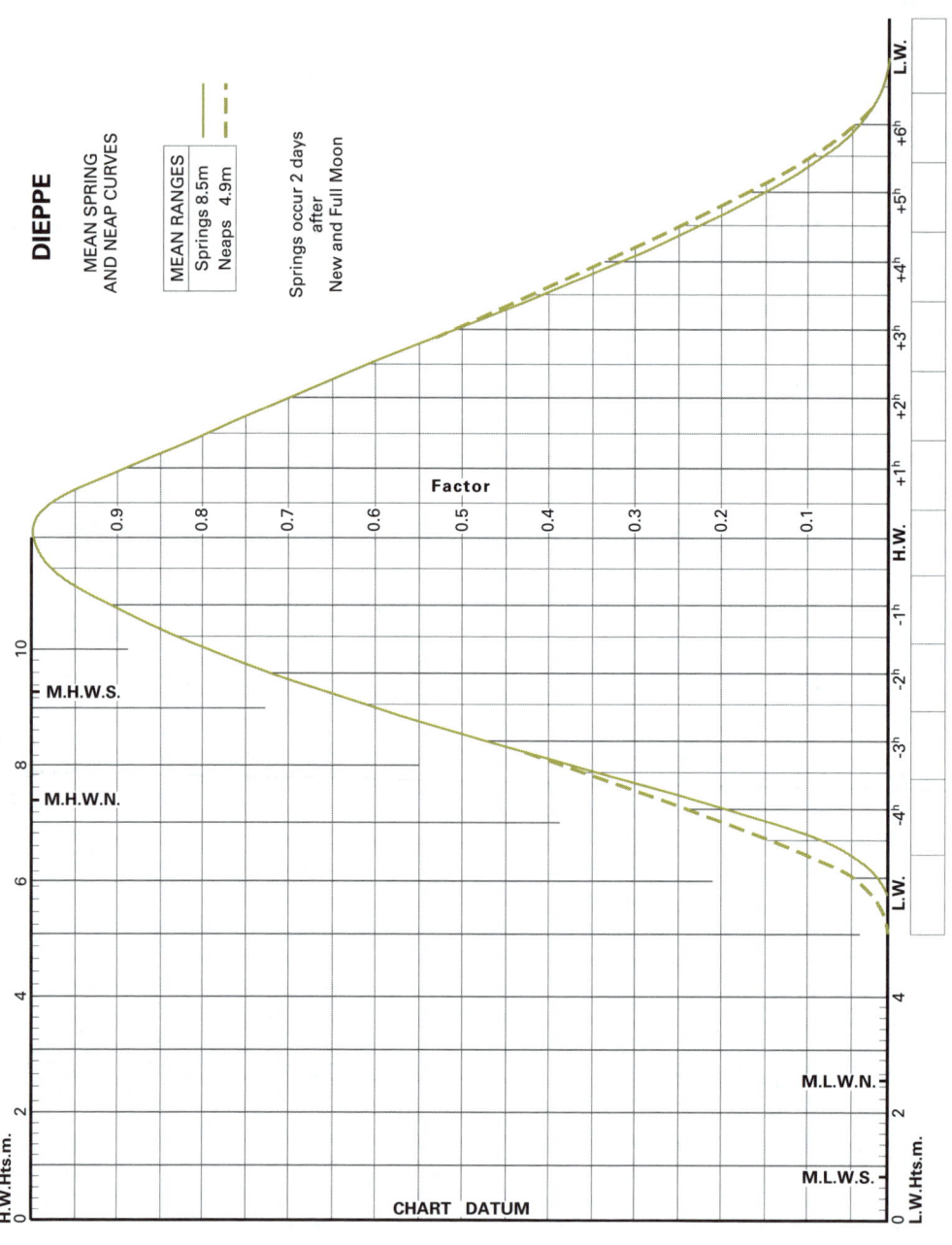

DIEPPE

MEAN SPRING
AND NEAP CURVES

MEAN RANGES
Springs 8.5m
Neaps 4.9m

Springs occur 2 days
after
New and Full Moon

Factor

0.9 0.8 0.7 0.6 0.5 0.4 0.3 0.2 0.1

M.H.W.S.

M.H.W.N.

L.W.

M.L.W.N.

M.L.W.S.

CHART DATUM

H.W.Hts.m.

L.W.Hts.m.

TIME ZONE -0100
(French Standard Time)
Subtract 1 hour for UT
For French Summer Time add
ONE hour in **non-shaded areas**

FRANCE – DIEPPE

LAT 49°56'N   LONG 1°05'E

TIMES AND HEIGHTS OF HIGH AND LOW WATERS

Dates in amber are **SPRINGS**
Dates in yellow are **NEAPS**

2007

JANUARY

Day	Time m	Time m	Time m	Time m
1 M	0357 2.0	0938 8.3	1633 1.7	2206 8.2
2 TU	0457 1.8	1033 8.5	1729 1.4	2300 8.5
3	0550 1.6	1122 8.7	1820 1.2	○ 2348 8.7
4 TH	0638 1.5	1207 8.9	1906 1.1	
5 F	0035 8.8	0722 1.4	1249 8.9	1948 1.1
6 SA	0115 8.8	0803 1.4	1328 8.9	2027 1.2
7 SU	0153 8.7	0840 1.5	1405 8.7	2102 1.4
8 M	0229 8.5	0913 1.7	1442 8.5	2133 1.6
9 TU	0304 8.3	0944 2.0	1517 8.2	2203 1.9
10 W	0338 8.0	1016 2.2	1552 7.8	2235 2.2
11 TH	0414 7.7	1054 2.5	1631 7.4	☽ 2314 2.5
12 F	0457 7.3	1141 2.8	1720 7.0	
13 SA	0003 2.9	0555 7.0	1238 3.0	1827 6.8
14 SU	0107 3.1	0712 6.9	1351 3.0	1949 6.8
15 M	0228 3.1	0828 7.1	1511 2.8	2059 7.1
16 TU	0344 2.7	0928 7.5	1615 2.3	2155 7.6
17 W	0442 2.3	1019 8.0	1709 1.9	2244 8.1
18 TH	0533 1.9	1106 8.4	1759 1.5	2330 8.5
19 F	0622 1.5	1150 8.8	1848 1.1	
20 SA	0017 8.8	0709 1.3	1233 9.1	1935 0.9
21 SU	0100 9.1	0755 1.1	1316 9.3	2020 0.7
22 M	0143 9.2	0839 1.0	1359 9.3	2102 0.7
23 TU	0225 9.2	0921 1.0	1442 9.2	2142 0.8
24 W	0307 9.0	1001 1.2	1525 8.9	2222 1.1
25 TH	0349 8.7	1042 1.5	1610 8.5	☽ 2303 1.5
26 F	0435 8.3	1129 1.9	1651 8.0	2351 2.0
27 SA	0533 7.8	1227 2.3	1808 7.5	
28 SU	0054 2.5	0649 7.4	1344 2.5	1932 7.2
29 M	0218 2.7	0816 7.4	1510 2.4	2056 7.4
30 TU	0343 2.5	0932 7.7	1624 2.0	2205 7.8
31 W	0452 2.1	1032 8.2	1726 1.6	2259 8.3

FEBRUARY

Day	Time m	Time m	Time m	Time m
1 TH	0548 1.7	1119 8.5	1816 1.3	2343 8.6
2 F	0634 1.5	1200 8.8	1859 1.1	○
3 SA	0024 8.8	0713 1.3	1237 9.0	1936 1.0
4 SU	0058 8.9	0748 1.2	1310 9.0	2009 1.0
5 M	0131 8.9	0820 1.1	1342 9.0	2038 1.1
6 TU	0201 8.9	0847 1.3	1413 8.8	2104 1.2
7 W	0230 8.7	0912 1.5	1442 8.6	2127 1.5
8 TH	0257 8.4	0937 1.8	1509 8.2	2152 1.8
9 F	0324 8.1	1008 2.1	1539 7.8	2222 2.2
10 SA	0357 7.7	1045 2.5	1616 7.3	☽ 2302 2.7
11 SU	0441 7.2	1135 2.9	1710 6.8	2358 3.2
12 M	0549 6.7	1243 3.2	1839 6.4	
13 TU	0122 3.4	0737 6.6	1419 3.1	2024 6.7
14 W	0306 3.1	0901 7.1	1545 2.6	2134 7.3
15 TH	0419 2.4	1000 7.8	1648 1.9	2228 8.0
16 F	0517 1.8	1050 8.4	1744 1.3	2315 8.6
17 SA	0610 1.3	1136 9.0	1836 0.8	● 2359 9.1
18 SU	0659 0.9	1219 9.4	1924 0.5	
19 M	0044 9.4	0745 0.6	1301 9.7	2007 0.2
20 TU	0125 9.6	0827 0.5	1342 9.7	2047 0.1
21 W	0205 9.6	0906 0.6	1422 9.6	2124 0.4
22 TH	0244 9.3	0942 0.8	1503 9.2	2159 0.9
23 F	0322 8.9	1019 1.2	1544 8.7	2236 1.5
24 SA	0404 8.3	1101 1.8	1633 7.9	☽ 2321 2.1
25 SU	0458 7.6	1157 2.4	1740 7.2	
26 M	0024 2.8	0620 7.0	1319 2.8	1918 6.8
27 TU	0201 3.1	0809 7.0	1500 2.7	2056 7.1
28 W	0341 2.7	0930 7.5	1622 2.1	2201 7.7

MARCH

Day	Time m	Time m	Time m	Time m
1 TH	0452 2.1	1024 8.1	1720 1.6	2247 8.3
2 F	0542 1.6	1107 8.5	1805 1.2	2327 8.7
3 SA	0621 1.3	1143 8.8	1842 1.0	
4 SU	0001 8.9	0654 1.1	1215 9.0	○ 1914 0.9
5 M	0033 9.0	0724 1.1	1245 9.1	1942 0.9
6 TU	0102 9.0	0752 1.0	1314 9.1	2008 0.9
7 W	0130 9.0	0818 1.1	1342 9.0	2032 1.1
8 TH	0156 8.9	0841 1.3	1408 8.7	2054 1.3
9 F	0221 8.6	0905 1.5	1434 8.4	2117 1.7
10 SA	0247 8.3	0932 1.8	1502 8.0	2144 2.1
11 SU	0317 7.9	1005 2.3	1538 7.5	2220 2.6
12 M	0356 7.3	1050 2.8	1627 6.9	☽ 2314 3.1
13 TU	0457 6.7	1158 3.2	1748 6.4	
14 W	0038 3.4	0649 6.4	1337 3.2	1952 6.6
15 TH	0233 3.1	0832 7.0	1515 2.6	2109 7.3
16 F	0353 2.4	0936 7.8	1623 1.8	2204 8.1
17 SA	0454 1.7	1027 8.5	1721 1.1	2252 8.8
18 SU	0548 1.1	1113 9.1	1814 0.6	2336 9.3
19 M	0639 0.7	1157 9.6	1902 0.3	●
20 TU	0021 9.6	0725 0.4	1239 9.8	1945 0.1
21 W	0101 9.7	0806 0.3	1320 9.8	2024 0.2
22 TH	0140 9.7	0844 0.4	1400 9.7	2101 0.5
23 F	0219 9.4	0920 0.7	1440 9.2	2136 1.0
24 SA	0257 8.9	0957 1.2	1523 8.5	2213 1.6
25 SU	0339 8.2	1040 1.8	1612 7.7	☽ 2259 2.4
26 M	0434 7.4	1136 2.5	1722 7.0	
27 TU	0006 3.0	0602 6.8	1301 2.9	1906 6.7
28 W	0147 3.2	0755 6.8	1443 2.7	2040 7.1
29 TH	0325 2.7	0911 7.4	1601 2.1	2138 7.7
30 F	0429 2.1	1001 8.0	1655 1.6	2222 8.3
31 SA	0515 1.6	1041 8.4	1736 1.3	2259 8.6

APRIL

Day	Time m	Time m	Time m	Time m
1 SU	0551 1.3	1115 8.7	1811 1.1	2331 8.8
2 M	0623 1.2	1146 8.9	1841 1.0	○
3 TU	0001 8.9	0653 1.1	1215 8.9	1909 1.0
4 W	0030 9.0	0721 1.1	1244 8.9	1936 1.0
5 TH	0058 9.0	0748 1.1	1312 8.9	2001 1.2
6 F	0124 8.9	0813 1.2	1339 8.7	2025 1.4
7 SA	0151 8.7	0839 1.4	1408 8.4	2050 1.7
8 SU	0219 8.4	0907 1.7	1439 8.0	2119 2.1
9 M	0252 7.9	0941 2.1	1517 7.6	2158 2.6
10 TU	0333 7.4	1027 2.6	1607 7.0	☽ 2254 3.0
11 W	0435 6.8	1135 2.9	1727 6.6	
12 TH	0015 3.2	0618 6.6	1309 2.9	1916 6.8
13 F	0201 2.9	0755 7.1	1442 2.4	2034 7.5
14 SA	0320 2.2	0902 7.9	1551 1.7	2131 8.2
15 SU	0422 1.5	0956 8.6	1650 1.1	2221 8.9
16 M	0518 1.0	1045 9.1	1744 0.6	2306 9.3
17 TU	0610 0.7	1130 9.5	1833 0.4	● 2350 9.6
18 W	0658 0.5	1214 9.7	1918 0.3	
19 TH	0035 9.6	0741 0.4	1257 9.7	1959 0.4
20 F	0116 9.5	0822 0.5	1339 9.4	2038 0.7
21 SA	0156 9.2	0900 0.8	1422 9.0	2115 1.2
22 SU	0238 8.7	0940 1.3	1507 8.4	2156 1.8
23 M	0323 8.1	1025 1.9	1559 7.7	2245 2.4
24 TU	0420 7.4	1122 2.4	1708 7.1	☽ 2351 2.9
25 W	0540 6.9	1238 2.7	1834 6.9	
26 TH	0117 3.0	0712 6.8	1401 2.6	1957 7.1
27 F	0237 2.7	0829 7.2	1512 2.3	2058 7.6
28 SA	0339 2.2	0915 7.7	1607 1.9	2143 8.0
29 SU	0428 1.8	1004 8.1	1651 1.6	2221 8.4
30 M	0508 1.6	1039 8.4	1729 1.4	2255 8.6

TIDES

Chart Datum: 4·45 metres below IGN Datum

TIME ZONE -0100
(French Standard Time)
Subtract 1 hour for UT
For French Summer Time add
ONE hour in **non-shaded areas**

FRANCE – DIEPPE
LAT 49°56'N   LONG 1°05'E
TIMES AND HEIGHTS OF HIGH AND LOW WATERS

Dates in amber are **SPRINGS**
Dates in yellow are **NEAPS**

2007

MAY

Day	Time m	Time m	Time m	Time m	Day	Time m	Time m	Time m	Time m
1 TU	0544 1.4	1113 8.6	1803 1.3	2327 8.7	16 W	0539 0.9	1104 9.2	1803 0.8	2323 9.3
2 W	0618 1.3	1144 8.6	1835 1.3	○ 2357 8.8	17 TH	0630 0.7	1151 9.3	1851 0.7	
3 TH	0650 1.3	1215 8.7	1906 1.3		18 F	0010 9.3	0717 0.7	1237 9.3	1936 0.8
4 F	0028 8.8	0720 1.3	1246 8.7	1935 1.4	19 SA	0056 9.3	0802 0.7	1323 9.1	2018 1.0
5 SA	0058 8.7	0750 1.3	1317 8.6	2004 1.6	20 SU	0140 9.0	0845 1.0	1409 8.8	2100 1.4
6 SU	0129 8.6	0821 1.5	1350 8.4	2034 1.8	21 M	0225 8.6	0934 1.3	1456 8.4	2144 1.8
7 M	0203 8.3	0854 1.7	1427 8.1	2109 2.1	22 TU	0312 8.1	1013 1.8	1547 7.9	2232 2.2
8 TU	0241 8.0	0933 2.0	1509 7.7	2153 2.4	23 W	0406 7.6	1103 2.2	1643 7.5	◐ 2328 2.6
9 W	0327 7.5	1022 2.3	1603 7.3	2249 2.7	24 TH	0506 7.2	1202 2.5	1746 7.2	
10 TH ◑	0430 7.2	1125 2.5	1716 7.1		25 F	0031 2.7	0613 7.0	1305 2.5	1853 7.2
11 F	0001 2.8	0553 7.1	1245 2.5	1840 7.3	26 SA	0135 2.6	0722 7.1	1407 2.4	1957 7.4
12 SA	0126 2.5	0714 7.4	1405 2.1	1952 7.7	27 SU	0235 2.4	0824 7.3	1505 2.2	2051 7.7
13 SU	0241 2.0	0822 8.0	1513 1.6	2053 8.3	28 M	0330 2.2	0915 7.6	1557 2.0	2136 8.0
14 M	0345 1.5	0921 8.5	1614 1.2	2147 8.8	29 TU	0420 1.9	0959 7.9	1643 1.8	2216 8.2
15 TU	0444 1.2	1015 8.9	1711 0.9	2236 9.1	30 W	0504 1.7	1038 8.1	1725 1.6	2253 8.4
					31 TH	0544 1.6	1116 8.3	1803 1.6	2329 8.5

JUNE

Day	Time m	Time m	Time m	Time m	Day	Time m	Time m	Time m	Time m
1 F ○	0621 1.5	1152 8.4	1840 1.6		16 SA	0659 0.9	1226 9.0	1918 1.1	
2 SA	0004 8.5	0657 1.4	1227 8.5	1914 1.6	17 SU	0043 9.0	0748 0.9	1313 8.9	2004 1.2
3 SU	0040 8.6	0734 1.4	1303 8.5	1950 1.6	18 M	0129 8.9	0833 1.0	1358 8.8	2049 1.4
4 M	0116 8.5	0811 1.4	1342 8.4	2027 1.7	19 TU	0213 8.7	0916 1.2	1442 8.5	2130 1.6
5 TU	0156 8.4	0851 1.5	1423 8.3	2108 1.9	20 W	0257 8.4	0956 1.5	1525 8.2	2211 1.9
6 W	0239 8.2	0934 1.7	1509 8.0	2153 2.0	21 TH	0340 8.0	1035 1.8	1609 7.9	2252 2.2
7 TH	0327 8.0	1022 1.9	1600 7.8	2245 2.2	22 F	0425 7.7	1116 2.1	1655 7.6	◑ 2337 2.4
8 F	0422 7.8	1116 2.0	1658 7.7	◑ 2344 2.2	23 SA	0515 7.3	1203 2.4	1747 7.3	
9 SA	0525 7.7	1218 2.0	1803 7.7		24 SU	0028 2.6	0611 7.1	1257 2.6	1846 7.2
10 SU	0051 2.2	0634 7.7	1325 1.9	1910 7.9	25 M	0127 2.7	0716 7.0	1359 2.6	1950 7.2
11 M	0200 2.0	0744 7.9	1434 1.7	2015 8.2	26 TU	0231 2.6	0821 7.1	1503 2.5	2049 7.5
12 TU	0308 1.7	0849 8.2	1540 1.5	2116 8.5	27 W	0333 2.4	0919 7.4	1602 2.3	2140 7.7
13 W	0413 1.4	0949 8.5	1641 1.3	2211 8.7	28 TH	0427 2.1	1008 7.7	1653 2.1	2225 8.0
14 TH	0512 1.2	1044 8.7	1737 1.2	2303 8.9	29 F	0515 1.9	1053 8.0	1738 1.9	2307 8.2
15 F	0608 1.0	1136 8.9	1829 1.1	● 2353 9.0	30 SA	0559 1.6	1134 8.2	1820 1.7	○ 2347 8.4

JULY

Day	Time m	Time m	Time m	Time m	Day	Time m	Time m	Time m	Time m
1 SU	0642 1.5	1214 8.5	1901 1.6		16 M	0035 8.9	0738 1.0	1303 8.9	1953 1.2
2 M	0029 8.6	0725 1.3	1255 8.6	1943 1.5	17 TU	0117 8.9	0820 1.0	1342 8.9	2033 1.2
3 TU	0110 8.7	0808 1.2	1336 8.7	2025 1.4	18 W	0156 8.9	0857 1.1	1420 8.8	2108 1.4
4 W	0152 8.7	0851 1.1	1418 8.7	2107 1.4	19 TH	0232 8.7	0929 1.3	1455 8.6	2140 1.6
5 TH	0234 8.7	0933 1.2	1501 8.6	2150 1.5	20 F	0307 8.4	0957 1.6	1530 8.3	2210 1.9
6 F	0318 8.5	1015 1.3	1545 8.4	2234 1.6	21 SA	0341 8.0	1027 1.9	1604 7.9	2243 2.2
7 SA	0404 8.3	1059 1.5	1633 8.2	◑ 2322 1.8	22 SU	0417 7.6	1102 2.3	1643 7.5	◑ 2323 2.5
8 SU	0456 8.1	1148 1.7	1727 8.0		23 M	0500 7.2	1146 2.7	1732 7.1	
9 M	0017 2.0	0558 7.9	1248 2.0	1832 7.9	24 TU	0016 2.9	0600 6.8	1245 3.0	1842 6.9
10 TU	0124 2.1	0711 7.7	1359 2.1	1944 7.8	25 W	0125 3.0	0724 6.7	1405 3.1	2003 6.9
11 W	0240 2.0	0826 7.8	1514 2.0	2055 8.0	26 TH	0247 2.9	0843 6.9	1525 2.9	2109 7.3
12 TH	0352 1.8	0936 8.0	1622 1.8	2159 8.3	27 F	0356 2.5	0944 7.4	1626 2.4	2203 7.7
13 F	0457 1.5	1038 8.3	1723 1.6	2256 8.6	28 SA	0452 2.0	1034 7.9	1717 2.0	2250 8.2
14 SA	0556 1.3	1132 8.6	1818 1.4	● 2347 8.8	29 SU	0543 1.7	1119 8.3	1805 1.6	2333 8.5
15 SU	0650 1.1	1219 8.8	1908 1.2		30 M ○	0631 1.3	1201 8.7	1851 1.4	
					31 TU	0017 8.9	0717 1.0	1242 8.9	1935 1.1

AUGUST

Day	Time m	Time m	Time m	Time m	Day	Time m	Time m	Time m	Time m
1 W	0058 9.1	0801 0.8	1323 9.1	2017 1.0	16 TH	0130 9.0	0828 1.0	1350 9.0	2038 1.2
2 TH	0139 9.2	0842 0.7	1402 9.2	2057 0.9	17 F	0201 8.9	0855 1.2	1420 8.8	2104 1.4
3 F	0219 9.2	0920 0.8	1442 9.1	2136 1.0	18 SA	0230 8.6	0918 1.5	1449 8.5	2128 1.7
4 SA	0259 9.0	0957 1.0	1522 8.9	2215 1.3	19 SU	0258 8.3	0941 1.8	1516 8.2	2155 2.1
5 SU	0341 8.7	1035 1.3	1604 8.5	◑ 2258 1.6	20 M	0326 7.8	1010 2.2	1546 7.7	◑ 2230 2.3
6 M	0428 8.2	1119 1.8	1654 8.1	2349 2.0	21 TU	0402 7.3	1048 2.8	1625 7.2	2315 2.9
7 TU	0527 7.7	1216 2.3	1800 7.6		22 W	0453 6.8	1142 3.3	1727 6.7	
8 W	0057 2.4	0648 7.3	1335 2.6	1926 7.4	23 TH	0022 3.3	0619 6.4	1305 3.5	1915 6.5
9 TH	0225 2.4	0820 7.3	1503 2.5	2051 7.6	24 F	0200 3.3	0812 6.6	1452 3.2	2043 6.9
10 F	0347 2.1	0939 7.8	1619 2.1	2201 8.0	25 SA	0330 2.7	0922 7.2	1602 2.6	2142 7.6
11 SA	0457 1.7	1039 8.3	1722 1.7	2255 8.5	26 SU	0431 2.1	1014 7.9	1656 1.9	2230 8.2
12 SU	0556 1.3	1127 8.7	1815 1.4	2340 8.8	27 M	0524 1.5	1059 8.5	1746 1.4	2313 8.8
13 M ●	0643 1.1	1208 9.0	1858 1.2		28 TU	0614 1.1	1141 9.0	1833 1.1	○ 2355 9.2
14 TU	0021 9.0	0723 0.9	1245 9.1	1936 1.1	29 W	0701 0.7	1221 9.3	1918 0.8	
15 W	0057 9.1	0758 0.9	1318 9.1	2009 1.1	30 TH	0038 9.5	0743 0.5	1301 9.5	2000 0.7
					31 F	0118 9.6	0823 0.5	1339 9.6	2039 0.7

Chart Datum: 4·45 metres below IGN Datum

TIME ZONE -0100
(French Standard Time)
Subtract 1 hour for UT
For French Summer Time add
ONE hour in **non-shaded areas**

FRANCE – DIEPPE

LAT 49°56'N   LONG 1°05'E

TIMES AND HEIGHTS OF HIGH AND LOW WATERS

Dates in amber are **SPRINGS**
Dates in yellow are **NEAPS**

2007

SEPTEMBER

Time	m		Time	m
1 0157	9.5	**16** 0155	8.7
0859	0.6	0840	1.5
SA 1418	9.4	SU 1410	8.6
2117	0.8	2052	1.7
2 0236	9.3	**17** 0220	8.4
0934	0.9	0903	1.9
SU 1456	9.1	M 1435	8.3
2154	1.2	2117	2.0
3 0317	8.8	**18** 0248	8.0
1011	1.4	0929	2.3
M 1538	8.6	TU 1503	7.8
2235	1.7	2149	2.4
4 0403	8.1	**19** 0322	7.4
1054	2.0	1004	2.8
TU 1627	7.9	W 1540	7.3
2326	2.2	2231	2.9
5 0505	7.4	**20** 0409	6.8
1155	2.7	1056	3.4
W 1739	7.3	TH 1637	6.7
		2334	3.3
6 0041	2.7	**21** 0529	6.4
0642	7.0	1219	3.7
TH 1326	3.0	F 1824	6.4
1922	7.0		
7 0223	2.7	**22** 0115	3.4
0826	7.2	0737	6.5
F 1505	2.7	SA 1415	3.4
2054	7.5	2011	6.8
8 0351	2.2	**23** 0258	2.8
0937	7.8	0852	7.3
SA 1620	2.1	SU 1532	2.6
2156	8.1	2113	7.6
9 0455	1.6	**24** 0403	2.1
1028	8.4	0945	8.1
SU 1716	1.6	M 1627	1.8
2242	8.6	2202	8.4
10 0544	1.2	**25** 0457	1.4
1109	8.9	1030	8.7
M 1800	1.2	TU 1718	1.3
2322	8.9	2246	9.0
11 0624	1.0	**26** 0547	0.9
1146	9.1	1113	9.2
TU 1838	1.1	W 1807	0.9
● 2357	9.1	○ 2328	9.4
12 0657	1.0	**27** 0634	0.6
1218	9.2	1154	9.5
W 1909	1.1	TH 1853	0.6
13 0030	9.1	**28** 0012	9.7
0727	1.0	0718	0.5
TH 1248	9.1	F 1234	9.7
1938	1.1	1936	0.5
14 0059	9.1	**29** 0053	9.7
0754	1.1	0758	0.6
F 1316	9.1	SA 1313	9.7
2004	1.2	2016	0.6
15 0128	8.9	**30** 0134	9.6
0819	1.2	0835	0.7
SA 1344	8.9	SU 1353	9.5
2029	1.4	2055	0.8

OCTOBER

Time	m		Time	m
1 0215	9.3	**16** 0152	8.4
0911	1.1	0834	2.0
M 1433	9.1	TU 1404	8.3
2134	1.2	2051	2.0
2 0257	8.7	**17** 0222	8.0
0950	1.7	0902	2.4
TU 1516	8.5	W 1435	7.9
2217	1.8	2123	2.4
3 0347	8.0	**18** 0258	7.6
1037	2.3	0938	2.8
W 1610	7.7	TH 1515	7.4
◐ 2311	2.4	2206	2.8
4 0455	7.2	**19** 0346	7.0
1143	2.9	1032	3.3
TH 1729	7.1	F 1612	6.8
		◐ 2307	3.2
5 0032	2.9	**20** 0502	6.6
0637	6.9	1150	3.5
F 1321	3.1	SA 1745	6.6
1913	7.0		
6 0215	2.7	**21** 0037	3.2
0812	7.3	0651	6.8
SA 1454	2.7	SU 1332	3.2
2037	7.5	1925	7.0
7 0334	2.2	**22** 0216	2.7
0916	7.9	0809	7.4
SU 1600	2.0	M 1452	2.5
2133	8.1	2031	7.7
8 0431	1.7	**23** 0325	2.0
1002	8.4	0906	8.1
M 1651	1.6	TU 1552	1.8
2217	8.5	2125	8.4
9 0516	1.4	**24** 0421	1.4
1041	8.8	0955	8.8
TU 1732	1.3	W 1645	1.3
2254	8.8	2213	9.0
10 0552	1.2	**25** 0514	1.0
1116	9.0	1041	9.3
W 1806	1.2	TH 1737	0.9
2328	9.0	2259	9.4
11 0623	1.2	**26** 0603	0.7
1146	9.1	1124	9.6
TH 1836	1.1	F 1825	0.7
● 2358	9.0	○ 2343	9.6
12 0652	1.2	**27** 0649	0.6
1218	9.1	1207	9.7
F 1905	1.2	SA 1911	0.6
13 0028	9.0	**28** 0030	9.7
0720	1.3	0732	0.7
SA 1243	9.0	SU 1249	9.7
1933	1.3	1954	0.6
14 0056	8.8	**29** 0113	9.5
0746	1.4	0812	0.9
SU 1310	8.9	M 1332	9.4
1959	1.4	2036	0.9
15 0124	8.7	**30** 0158	9.1
0810	1.7	0853	1.3
M 1337	8.6	TU 1415	9.0
2024	1.7	2118	1.3
		31 0244	8.6
		0935	1.8
		W 1503	8.4
		2204	1.8

NOVEMBER

Time	m		Time	m
1 0338	7.9	**16** 0248	7.8
1026	2.4	0930	2.6
TH 1600	7.7	F 1506	7.6
◐ 2300	2.4	2157	2.5
2 0445	7.4	**17** 0337	7.4
1133	2.9	1022	2.9
F 1713	7.2	SA 1601	7.3
		◐ 2253	2.7
3 0014	2.8	**18** 0443	7.1
0608	7.1	1128	3.0
SA 1256	3.0	SU 1713	7.1
1837	7.1		
4 0137	2.7	**19** 0003	2.8
0730	7.3	0603	7.2
SU 1414	2.7	M 1248	2.9
1955	7.3	1833	7.3
5 0249	2.4	**20** 0125	2.5
0836	7.7	0719	7.6
M 1517	2.3	TU 1405	2.5
2055	7.8	1944	7.7
6 0346	2.0	**21** 0238	2.1
0925	8.1	0822	8.1
TU 1609	1.9	W 1511	1.9
2141	8.2	2045	8.3
7 0432	1.8	**22** 0341	1.6
1005	8.5	0918	8.6
W 1651	1.6	TH 1611	1.4
2220	8.4	2140	8.8
8 0511	1.6	**23** 0439	1.3
1041	8.7	1009	9.1
TH 1728	1.5	F 1707	1.1
2255	8.6	2231	9.1
9 0546	1.5	**24** 0533	1.0
1113	8.8	1058	9.3
F 1802	1.4	SA 1759	0.9
2328	8.7	○ 2320	9.3
10 0619	1.5	**25** 0623	0.9
1116	9.0	1145	9.5
SA 1835	1.4	SU 1849	0.7
● 2359	8.7		
11 0650	1.5	**26** 0010	9.4
1214	8.8	0710	1.0
SU 1906	1.4	M 1231	9.5
		1937	0.8
12 0031	8.7	**27** 0100	9.3
0719	1.6	0756	1.1
M 1244	8.7	TU 1317	9.3
1936	1.5	2023	0.9
13 0102	8.6	**28** 0147	9.0
0748	1.8	0841	1.4
TU 1314	8.6	W 1404	9.0
2005	1.7	2108	1.2
14 0134	8.4	**29** 0236	8.6
0817	2.0	0927	1.8
W 1346	8.4	TH 1453	8.5
2037	1.9	2155	1.6
15 0208	8.1	**30** 0327	8.2
0850	2.3	1016	2.2
TH 1423	8.0	F 1545	8.0
2113	2.2	2245	2.1

DECEMBER

Time	m		Time	m
1 0422	7.7	**16** 0329	8.0
1110	2.5	1014	2.3
SA 1642	7.6	SU 1548	7.9
2339	2.4	◐ 2240	2.1
2 0521	7.4	**17** 0420	7.8
1210	2.7	1106	2.4
SU 1744	7.3	M 1643	7.7
		◐ 2333	2.2
3 0039	2.7	**18** 0519	7.7
0626	7.3	1207	2.4
M 1313	2.8	TU 1746	7.6
1851	7.2		
4 0143	2.7	**19** 0035	2.3
0733	7.4	0627	7.7
TU 1415	2.6	W 1316	2.4
1958	7.3	1857	7.7
5 0244	2.5	**20** 0147	2.2
0833	7.6	0738	7.9
W 1514	2.4	TH 1430	2.1
2055	7.6	2007	8.0
6 0341	2.3	**21** 0301	2.0
0922	7.9	0844	8.3
TH 1606	2.1	F 1540	1.8
2142	7.8	2112	8.3
7 0429	2.1	**22** 0409	1.7
1004	8.2	0944	8.6
F 1652	1.9	SA 1642	1.4
2224	8.1	2212	8.6
8 0512	1.9	**23** 0509	1.4
1042	8.4	1040	8.9
SA 1733	1.7	SU 1740	1.1
2301	8.3	2307	8.9
9 0551	1.8	**24** 0605	1.3
1118	8.5	1132	9.1
SU 1810	1.6	M 1834	0.9
◐ 2337	8.4	○ 2359	9.1
10 0627	1.8	**25** 0657	1.2
1153	8.6	1222	9.3
M 1846	1.5	TU 1926	0.8
11 0013	8.5	**26** 0052	9.1
0701	1.7	0747	1.2
TU 1227	8.6	W 1309	9.2
1920	1.5	2014	0.8
12 0049	8.5	**27** 0139	9.1
0735	1.8	0833	1.3
W 1302	8.6	TH 1355	9.1
1955	1.5	2059	1.0
13 0125	8.5	**28** 0223	8.9
0810	1.9	0916	1.5
TH 1339	8.5	F 1438	8.8
2032	1.6	2140	1.3
14 0203	8.4	**29** 0306	8.6
0848	2.0	0955	1.8
F 1418	8.4	SA 1521	8.4
2111	1.8	2218	1.7
15 0244	8.2	**30** 0348	8.2
0928	2.1	1033	2.1
SA 1501	8.1	SU 1604	8.0
2153	1.9	2255	2.1
		31 0431	7.8
		1114	2.4
		M 1649	7.6
		◐ 2336	2.4

TIDES

Chart Datum: 4·45 metres below IGN Datum

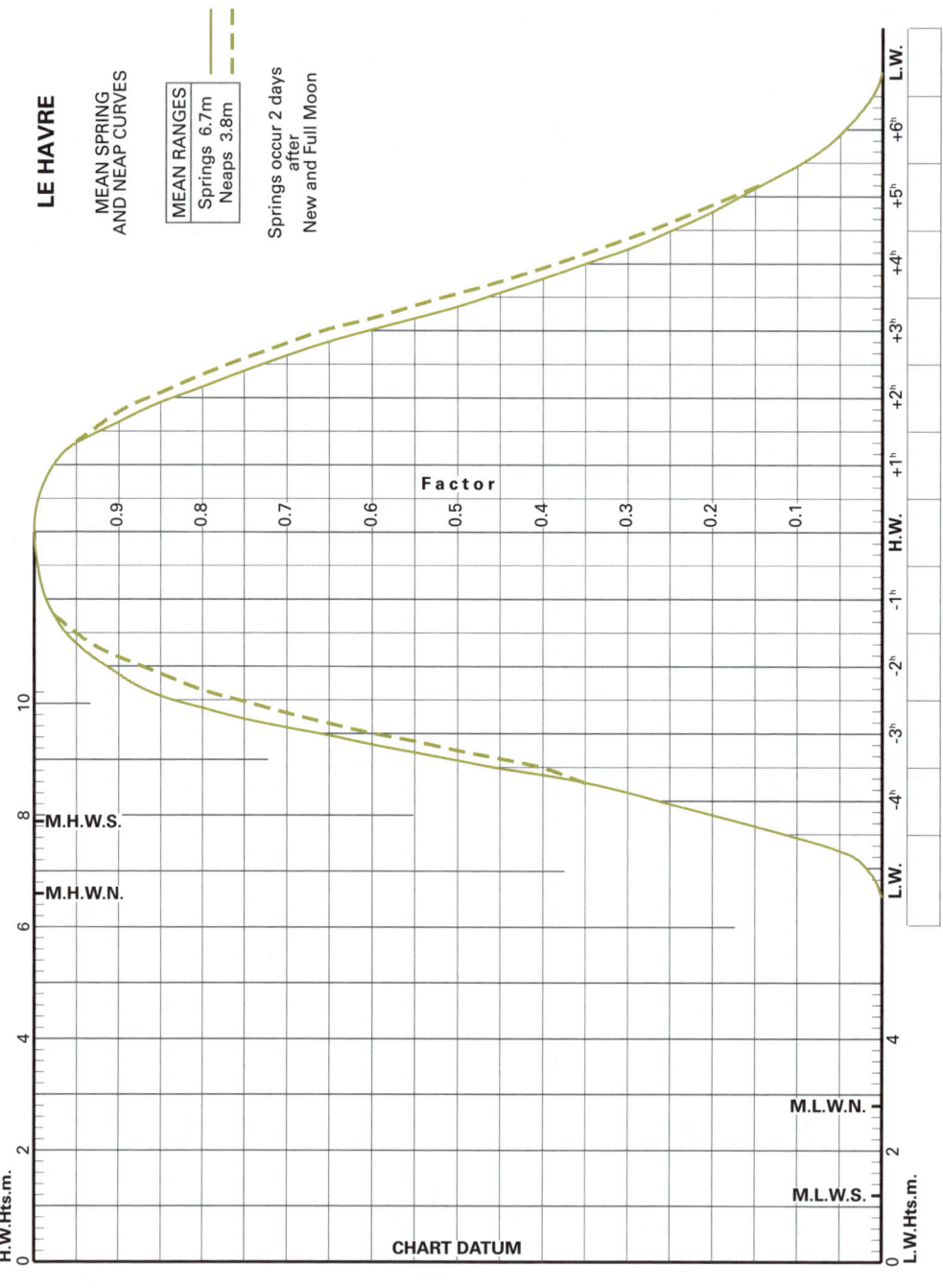

LE HAVRE

MEAN SPRING
AND NEAP CURVES

MEAN RANGES
Springs 6.7m
Neaps 3.8m

Springs occur 2 days
after
New and Full Moon

Factor

0.9
0.8
0.7
0.6
0.5
0.4
0.3
0.2
0.1

H.W.Hts.m.

10

M.H.W.S.

M.H.W.N.

8

6

4

2

0

CHART DATUM

L.W.Hts.m.

M.L.W.N.

M.L.W.S.

L.W.

H.W.

L.W.

+6ʰ
+5ʰ
+4ʰ
+3ʰ
+2ʰ
+1ʰ

−1ʰ
−2ʰ
−3ʰ
−4ʰ

4

2

0

TIME ZONE -0100
(French Standard Time)
Subtract 1 hour for UT
For French Summer Time add
ONE hour in **non-shaded areas**

FRANCE – LE HAVRE

LAT 49°29'N   LONG 0°07'E

TIMES AND HEIGHTS OF HIGH AND LOW WATERS

Dates in amber are **SPRINGS**
Dates in yellow are **NEAPS**

2007

JANUARY

Day	Time	m	Time	m	Day	Time	m	Time	m
1 M	0307 / 0842	2.3 / 7.3	1543 / 2115	2.1 / 7.3	16 TU	0251 / 0830	3.0 / 6.8	1524 / 2102	2.7 / 6.8
2 TU	0407 / 0936	2.1 / 7.5	1640 / 2209	1.8 / 7.5	17 W	0351 / 0920	2.6 / 7.1	1619 / 2150	2.2 / 7.1
3 W O	0501 / 1025	2.0 / 7.6	1732 / 2256	1.6 / 7.6	18 TH	0443 / 1004	2.2 / 7.4	1710 / 2234	1.8 / 7.4
4 TH	0549 / 1109	1.9 / 7.7	1817 / 2340	1.5 / 7.6	19 F ●	0532 / 1047	1.9 / 7.6	1800 / 2317	1.5 / 7.6
5 F	0633 / 1149	1.8 / 7.7	1859	1.5	20 SA	0621 / 1129	1.6 / 7.8	1847 / 2359	1.2 / 7.7
6 SA	0020 / 0712	7.6 / 1.8	1227 / 1936	7.7 / 1.5	21 SU	0707 / 1212	1.4 / 7.9	1931	1.0
7 SU	0057 / 0749	7.5 / 1.9	1304 / 2011	7.6 / 1.7	22 M	0042 / 0750	7.8 / 1.3	1256 / 2013	7.9 / 1.0
8 M	0133 / 0823	7.4 / 2.1	1340 / 2043	7.4 / 1.9	23 TU	0125 / 0831	7.8 / 1.4	1339 / 2052	7.9 / 1.2
9 TU	0209 / 0855	7.2 / 2.3	1414 / 2113	7.2 / 2.2	24 W	0209 / 0911	7.7 / 1.6	1423 / 2130	7.7 / 1.5
10 W	0244 / 0927	7.0 / 2.6	1449 / 2144	6.9 / 2.5	25 TH C	0252 / 0951	7.5 / 1.9	1509 / 2210	7.4 / 1.9
11 TH C	0320 / 1001	6.8 / 2.9	1528 / 2220	6.7 / 2.8	26 F	0340 / 1035	7.2 / 2.3	1603 / 2257	7.1 / 2.4
12 F	0405 / 1044	6.6 / 3.1	1619 / 2308	6.4 / 3.1	27 SA	0440 / 1131	6.9 / 2.6	1714	6.7
13 SA	0505 / 1140	6.5 / 3.3	1731	6.3	28 SU	0000 / 0557	2.8 / 6.7	1248 / 1843	2.9 / 6.6
14 SU	0009 / 0620	3.3 / 6.4	1251 / 1854	3.3 / 6.3	29 M	0127 / 0723	3.0 / 6.7	1418 / 2009	2.8 / 6.7
15 M	0129 / 0731	3.3 / 6.5	1415 / 2005	3.1 / 6.5	30 TU	0251 / 0837	2.8 / 6.9	1534 / 2115	2.4 / 7.0
					31 W	0402 / 0933	2.5 / 7.2	1639 / 2206	2.0 / 7.3

FEBRUARY

Day	Time	m	Time	m	Day	Time	m	Time	m
1 TH	0502 / 1019	2.1 / 7.4	1731 / 2248	1.7 / 7.5	16 F	0429 / 0949	2.2 / 7.3	1658 / 2219	1.7 / 7.4
2 F O	0548 / 1058	1.9 / 7.6	1812 / 2326	1.5 / 7.6	17 SA ●	0522 / 1032	1.7 / 7.7	1750 / 2301	1.2 / 7.7
3 SA	0625 / 1134	1.7 / 7.7	1847	1.4	18 SU	0611 / 1115	1.2 / 8.0	1836 / 2343	0.8 / 7.9
4 SU	0000 / 0658	7.7 / 1.6	1207 / 1918	7.8 / 1.3	19 M	0656 / 1157	0.9 / 8.2	1918	0.6
5 M	0032 / 0729	7.6 / 1.6	1239 / 1947	7.7 / 1.4	20 TU	0024 / 0737	8.1 / 0.8	1239 / 1957	8.2 / 0.6
6 TU	0103 / 0757	7.6 / 1.7	1310 / 2013	7.6 / 1.6	21 W	0105 / 0815	8.0 / 0.9	1321 / 2033	8.1 / 0.9
7 W	0133 / 0823	7.4 / 1.9	1338 / 2037	7.4 / 1.9	22 TH	0145 / 0851	7.9 / 1.2	1402 / 2108	7.8 / 1.3
8 TH	0200 / 0847	7.3 / 2.2	1405 / 2100	7.2 / 2.2	23 F	0225 / 0927	7.6 / 1.6	1445 / 2143	7.5 / 1.9
9 F	0227 / 0913	7.1 / 2.5	1436 / 2128	6.9 / 2.6	24 SA C	0307 / 1007	7.2 / 2.2	1535 / 2226	7.0 / 2.5
10 SA C	0301 / 0948	6.8 / 2.8	1516 / 2206	6.6 / 3.0	25 SU	0403 / 1100	6.8 / 2.7	1649 / 2329	6.5 / 3.1
11 SU	0347 / 1036	6.5 / 3.2	1614 / 2302	6.2 / 3.4	26 M	0530 / 1221	6.4 / 3.1	1837	6.3
12 M	0457 / 1145	6.2 / 3.5	1750	6.0	27 TU	0108 / 0716	3.3 / 6.4	1408 / 2009	3.0 / 6.5
13 TU	0025 / 0643	3.6 / 6.2	1323 / 1934	3.4 / 6.2	28 W	0251 / 0832	3.0 / 6.6	1537 / 2110	2.5 / 6.9
14 W	0215 / 0803	3.3 / 6.5	1455 / 2043	2.9 / 6.6					
15 TH	0330 / 0901	2.8 / 6.9	1600 / 2134	2.3 / 7.1					

MARCH

Day	Time	m	Time	m	Day	Time	m	Time	m
1 TH	0409 / 0924	2.5 / 7.0	1639 / 2154	2.0 / 7.2	16 F	0306 / 0836	2.7 / 6.9	1535 / 2110	2.1 / 7.1
2 F	0500 / 1004	2.0 / 7.3	1722 / 2230	1.6 / 7.4	17 SA	0406 / 0925	2.0 / 7.4	1635 / 2155	1.5 / 7.6
3 SA	0537 / 1039	1.7 / 7.5	1755 / 2302	1.4 / 7.6	18 SU	0501 / 1009	1.4 / 7.8	1728 / 2237	1.0 / 7.9
4 SU O	0607 / 1110	1.5 / 7.7	1824 / 2332	1.3 / 7.7	19 M ●	0550 / 1052	1.0 / 8.1	1814 / 2319	0.6 / 8.1
5 M	0635 / 1140	1.4 / 7.8	1852	1.3	20 TU	0635 / 1135	0.7 / 8.3	1856	0.5
6 TU	0001 / 0703	7.7 / 1.4	1210 / 1918	7.8 / 1.3	21 W	0000 / 0715	8.2 / 0.6	1218 / 1935	8.3 / 0.5
7 W	0030 / 0728	7.7 / 1.5	1239 / 1941	7.7 / 1.5	22 TH	0041 / 0754	8.1 / 0.7	1300 / 2010	8.1 / 0.9
8 TH	0057 / 0751	7.6 / 1.7	1306 / 2003	7.5 / 1.7	23 F	0120 / 0830	7.9 / 1.1	1342 / 2044	7.8 / 1.4
9 F	0122 / 0814	7.4 / 1.9	1331 / 2025	7.3 / 2.1	24 SA	0159 / 0906	7.5 / 1.6	1426 / 2119	7.3 / 2.0
10 SA	0147 / 0839	7.2 / 2.2	1400 / 2050	7.0 / 2.4	25 SU C	0242 / 0945	7.1 / 2.2	1518 / 2203	6.8 / 2.7
11 SU	0218 / 0909	6.9 / 2.6	1438 / 2124	6.6 / 2.9	26 M	0338 / 1039	6.6 / 2.8	1637 / 2310	6.3 / 3.3
12 M C	0300 / 0953	6.5 / 3.0	1534 / 2217	6.2 / 3.4	27 TU	0512 / 1204	6.2 / 3.1	1827	6.2
13 TU	0407 / 1059	6.1 / 3.4	1707 / 2341	5.9 / 3.7	28 W	0056 / 0658	3.4 / 6.2	1351 / 1952	3.0 / 6.4
14 W	0600 / 1245	6.0 / 3.4	1905	6.1	29 TH	0237 / 0812	3.0 / 6.5	1515 / 2048	2.5 / 6.8
15 TH	0146 / 0735	3.4 / 6.3	1427 / 2018	2.8 / 6.6	30 F	0345 / 0901	2.5 / 6.9	1610 / 2128	2.0 / 7.1
					31 SA	0431 / 0938	2.0 / 7.2	1650 / 2201	1.7 / 7.4

APRIL

Day	Time	m	Time	m	Day	Time	m	Time	m
1 SU	0505 / 1011	1.7 / 7.4	1722 / 2231	1.5 / 7.5	16 M	0430 / 0941	1.4 / 7.8	1656 / 2208	1.0 / 7.9
2 M O	0536 / 1041	1.5 / 7.6	1752 / 2259	1.4 / 7.6	17 TU ●	0522 / 1027	1.0 / 8.0	1745 / 2252	0.8 / 8.1
3 TU	0605 / 1110	1.4 / 7.7	1820 / 2328	1.4 / 7.7	18 W	0609 / 1115	0.7 / 8.1	1829 / 2334	0.7 / 8.1
4 W	0633 / 1140	1.4 / 7.6	1846 / 2357	1.4 / 7.6	19 TH	0652 / 1157	0.7 / 8.1	1910	0.8
5 TH	0658 / 1210	1.5 / 7.6	1910	1.6	20 F	0017 / 0733	8.0 / 0.8	1241 / 1948	8.0 / 1.1
6 F	0025 / 0722	7.6 / 1.6	1238 / 1934	7.4 / 1.8	21 SA	0058 / 0811	7.8 / 1.1	1326 / 2025	7.6 / 1.6
7 SA	0051 / 0748	7.4 / 1.8	1308 / 1959	7.2 / 2.1	22 SU	0140 / 0849	7.5 / 1.6	1414 / 2103	7.2 / 2.2
8 SU	0120 / 0816	7.2 / 2.1	1341 / 2027	6.9 / 2.4	23 M	0226 / 0931	7.1 / 2.2	1509 / 2150	6.7 / 2.8
9 M	0154 / 0847	6.9 / 2.4	1423 / 2102	6.6 / 2.9	24 TU C	0324 / 1026	6.6 / 2.7	1625 / 2259	6.4 / 3.2
10 TU	0240 / 0930	6.5 / 2.8	1520 / 2154	6.2 / 3.3	25 W	0448 / 1144	6.3 / 3.0	1754	6.3
11 W C	0346 / 1034	6.2 / 3.1	1647 / 2319	6.1 / 3.5	26 TH	0026 / 0618	3.3 / 6.2	1306 / 1912	2.9 / 6.4
12 TH	0528 / 1219	6.1 / 3.1	1833	6.3	27 F	0143 / 0731	3.0 / 6.5	1415 / 2009	2.6 / 6.7
13 F	0116 / 0700	3.2 / 6.4	1353 / 1943	2.6 / 6.7	28 SA	0247 / 0823	2.6 / 6.8	1512 / 2051	2.3 / 7.0
14 SA	0232 / 0802	2.5 / 6.9	1501 / 2038	2.0 / 7.2	29 SU	0338 / 0903	2.2 / 7.0	1558 / 2125	2.0 / 7.3
15 SU	0333 / 0854	1.9 / 7.4	1601 / 2124	1.4 / 7.6	30 M	0420 / 0937	1.9 / 7.3	1638 / 2155	1.8 / 7.4

Chart Datum: 4·38 metres below IGN Datum

TIDES

TIME ZONE -0100
(French Standard Time)
Subtract 1 hour for UT
For French Summer Time add
ONE hour in **non-shaded areas**

FRANCE – LE HAVRE

LAT 49°29'N   LONG 0°07'E

TIMES AND HEIGHTS OF HIGH AND LOW WATERS

Dates in amber are SPRINGS
Dates in yellow are NEAPS

2007

MAY

Day	Time	m	Day	Time	m
1 TU	0458 / 1009 / 1714 / 2226	1.8 / 7.4 / 1.7 / 7.5	**16** W	0451 / 1003 / 1714 / ● 2226	1.2 / 7.8 / 1.1 / 7.9
2 W	0531 / 1041 / 1745 / ○ 2257	1.7 / 7.4 / 1.7 / 7.6	**17** TH	0542 / 1052 / 1803 / 2312	1.0 / 7.9 / 1.1 / 7.9
3 TH	0601 / 1113 / 1814 / 2328	1.6 / 7.4 / 1.7 / 7.5	**18** F	0629 / 1140 / 1847 / 2357	0.9 / 7.9 / 1.2 / 7.9
4 F	0629 / 1146 / 1842 / 2358	1.6 / 7.4 / 1.8 / 7.5	**19** SA	0713 / 1228 / 1929	1.0 / 7.8 / 1.4
5 SA	0659 / 1218 / 1911	1.6 / 7.3 / 1.9	**20** SU	0042 / 0755 / 1315 / 2010	7.7 / 1.3 / 7.5 / 1.8
6 SU	0029 / 0729 / 1253 / 1942	7.4 / 1.8 / 7.2 / 2.1	**21** M	0127 / 0837 / 1404 / 2052	7.4 / 1.6 / 7.2 / 2.2
7 M	0105 / 0802 / 1333 / 2016	7.2 / 2.0 / 7.0 / 2.4	**22** TU	0214 / 0920 / 1456 / 2140	7.1 / 2.0 / 6.9 / 2.6
8 TU	0146 / 0838 / 1419 / 2056	7.0 / 2.3 / 6.6 / 2.7	**23** W	0308 / 1011 / 1556 / ◑ 2237	6.7 / 2.4 / 6.6 / 2.9
9 W	0235 / 0923 / 1516 / 2150	6.7 / 2.5 / 6.5 / 3.0	**24** TH	0411 / 1109 / 1702 / 2340	6.5 / 2.7 / 6.5 / 3.0
10 TH	0337 / 1027 / 1631 / ◑ 2311	6.5 / 2.8 / 6.4 / 3.1	**25** F	0520 / 1210 / 1808	6.4 / 2.8 / 6.5
11 F	0459 / 1154 / 1756	6.4 / 2.7 / 6.6	**26** SA	0043 / 0627 / 1310 / 1908	3.0 / 6.4 / 2.7 / 6.7
12 SA	0040 / 0620 / 1313 / 1903	2.9 / 6.7 / 2.4 / 6.9	**27** SU	0142 / 0727 / 1408 / 1959	2.7 / 6.6 / 2.6 / 6.9
13 SU	0151 / 0723 / 1420 / 2000	2.4 / 7.0 / 2.0 / 7.3	**28** M	0239 / 0817 / 1503 / 2041	2.5 / 6.8 / 2.4 / 7.1
14 M	0255 / 0820 / 1523 / 2051	1.9 / 7.4 / 1.6 / 7.6	**29** TU	0331 / 0859 / 1552 / 2118	2.3 / 7.0 / 2.2 / 7.2
15 TU	0356 / 0912 / 1622 / 2139	1.5 / 7.6 / 1.3 / 7.8	**30** W	0416 / 0938 / 1634 / 2154	2.1 / 7.1 / 2.1 / 7.3
			31 TH	0456 / 1015 / 1712 / 2229	2.0 / 7.2 / 2.0 / 7.4

JUNE

Day	Time	m	Day	Time	m
1 F	0531 / 1052 / 1746 / ○ 2304	1.8 / 7.3 / 2.0 / 7.4	**16** SA	0611 / 1131 / 1830 / 2345	1.2 / 7.7 / 1.5 / 7.7
2 SA	0606 / 1128 / 1821 / 2339	1.7 / 7.3 / 1.9 / 7.4	**17** SU	0658 / 1219 / 1916	1.2 / 7.6 / 1.6
3 SU	0642 / 1205 / 1857	1.7 / 7.3 / 2.0	**18** M	0030 / 0743 / 1304 / 1958	7.6 / 1.3 / 7.5 / 1.8
4 M	0016 / 0719 / 1245 / 1935	7.4 / 1.7 / 7.2 / 2.1	**19** TU	0114 / 0824 / 1349 / 2040	7.5 / 1.5 / 7.3 / 2.0
5 TU	0057 / 0758 / 1328 / 2015	7.3 / 1.8 / 7.1 / 2.2	**20** W	0157 / 0904 / 1432 / 2120	7.3 / 1.8 / 7.1 / 2.3
6 W	0141 / 0839 / 1415 / 2100	7.2 / 2.0 / 7.0 / 2.4	**21** TH	0241 / 0943 / 1517 / 2202	7.0 / 2.1 / 6.9 / 2.6
7 TH	0230 / 0926 / 1507 / 2153	7.0 / 2.1 / 6.9 / 2.5	**22** F	0327 / 1024 / 1605 / ◑ 2246	6.8 / 2.4 / 6.7 / 2.8
8 F	0324 / 1022 / 1607 / ◑ 2255	6.9 / 2.3 / 6.8 / 2.6	**23** SA	0419 / 1109 / 1700 / 2337	6.6 / 2.7 / 6.6 / 2.9
9 SA	0428 / 1125 / 1715	6.8 / 2.3 / 6.9	**24** SU	0518 / 1202 / 1759	6.4 / 2.9 / 6.5
10 SU	0002 / 0538 / 1232 / 1821	2.5 / 6.9 / 2.2 / 7.0	**25** M	0034 / 0622 / 1302 / 1859	3.0 / 6.4 / 2.9 / 6.6
11 M	0111 / 0646 / 1341 / 1923	2.4 / 7.0 / 2.1 / 7.2	**26** TU	0139 / 0725 / 1407 / 1955	2.9 / 6.4 / 2.9 / 6.7
12 TU	0220 / 0749 / 1449 / 2022	2.1 / 7.2 / 1.9 / 7.4	**27** W	0242 / 0822 / 1508 / 2044	2.7 / 6.6 / 2.7 / 6.9
13 W	0325 / 0850 / 1551 / 2117	1.8 / 7.4 / 1.7 / 7.6	**28** TH	0337 / 0911 / 1559 / 2128	2.5 / 6.8 / 2.5 / 7.1
14 TH	0425 / 0947 / 1648 / 2209	1.5 / 7.6 / 1.6 / 7.7	**29** F	0424 / 0955 / 1645 / 2209	2.2 / 7.0 / 2.3 / 7.3
15 F	0520 / 1040 / 1741 / ● 2258	1.3 / 7.7 / 1.5 / 7.7	**30** SA	0508 / 1036 / 1727 / ● 2248	2.0 / 7.2 / 2.1 / 7.4

JULY

Day	Time	m	Day	Time	m
1 SU	0550 / 1116 / 1809 / 2327	1.7 / 7.3 / 1.9 / 7.5	**16** M	0649 / 1206 / 1905	1.3 / 7.7 / 1.6
2 M	0633 / 1156 / 1852	1.6 / 7.4 / 1.8	**17** TU	0015 / 0730 / 1246 / 1943	7.7 / 1.3 / 7.6 / 1.6
3 TU	0007 / 0717 / 1237 / 1935	7.6 / 1.5 / 7.4 / 1.8	**18** W	0054 / 0805 / 1323 / 2017	7.7 / 1.4 / 7.5 / 1.8
4 W	0049 / 0759 / 1319 / 2018	7.6 / 1.4 / 7.4 / 1.8	**19** TH	0130 / 0837 / 1359 / 2049	7.5 / 1.6 / 7.4 / 2.0
5 TH	0132 / 0841 / 1404 / 2100	7.5 / 1.5 / 7.4 / 1.9	**20** F	0206 / 0906 / 1434 / 2118	7.3 / 1.9 / 7.2 / 2.3
6 F	0217 / 0922 / 1449 / 2144	7.4 / 1.7 / 7.3 / 2.0	**21** SA	0241 / 0934 / 1509 / 2149	7.1 / 2.2 / 6.9 / 2.6
7 SA	0305 / 1005 / 1539 / ○ 2231	7.3 / 1.8 / 7.2 / 2.2	**22** SU	0317 / 1006 / 1548 / ◑ 2227	6.8 / 2.6 / 6.7 / 2.9
8 SU	0358 / 1055 / 1635 / 2327	7.1 / 2.1 / 7.0 / 2.4	**23** M	0402 / 1047 / 1640 / 2318	6.5 / 3.0 / 6.5 / 3.2
9 M	0501 / 1154 / 1742	7.0 / 2.3 / 7.0	**24** TU	0506 / 1145 / 1752	6.2 / 3.3 / 6.3
10 TU	0034 / 0615 / 1306 / 1854	2.5 / 6.9 / 2.4 / 7.0	**25** W	0027 / 0632 / 1304 / 1910	3.3 / 6.1 / 3.4 / 6.4
11 W	0151 / 0731 / 1423 / 2004	2.4 / 6.9 / 2.4 / 7.1	**26** TH	0153 / 0750 / 1430 / 2015	3.2 / 6.3 / 3.1 / 6.6
12 TH	0304 / 0842 / 1531 / 2108	2.1 / 7.1 / 2.2 / 7.3	**27** F	0305 / 0851 / 1533 / 2107	2.8 / 6.6 / 2.8 / 6.9
13 F	0407 / 0944 / 1632 / 2202	1.9 / 7.3 / 2.0 / 7.5	**28** SA	0401 / 0939 / 1626 / 2152	2.3 / 6.9 / 2.4 / 7.2
14 SA	0507 / 1036 / 1730 / ● 2250	1.6 / 7.5 / 1.8 / 7.6	**29** SU	0452 / 1022 / 1715 / 2233	1.9 / 7.2 / 2.0 / 7.5
15 SU	0602 / 1123 / 1822 / 2334	1.4 / 7.6 / 1.7 / 7.7	**30** M	0541 / 1102 / 1802 / ○ 2313	1.6 / 7.4 / 1.7 / 7.7
			31 TU	0627 / 1142 / 1847 / 2354	1.3 / 7.6 / 1.5 / 7.8

AUGUST

Day	Time	m	Day	Time	m
1 W	0710 / 1222 / 1929	1.1 / 7.7 / 1.3	**16** TH	0026 / 0737 / 1251 / 1947	7.8 / 1.3 / 7.7 / 1.6
2 TH	0035 / 0750 / 1303 / 2009	7.9 / 1.0 / 7.8 / 1.3	**17** F	0058 / 0803 / 1322 / 2013	7.7 / 1.5 / 7.5 / 1.8
3 F	0116 / 0828 / 1344 / 2047	7.9 / 1.1 / 7.7 / 1.4	**18** SA	0129 / 0827 / 1351 / 2037	7.5 / 1.8 / 7.3 / 2.1
4 SA	0158 / 0905 / 1425 / 2125	7.7 / 1.3 / 7.6 / 1.7	**19** SU	0157 / 0849 / 1418 / 2102	7.2 / 2.2 / 7.1 / 2.4
5 SU	0241 / 0942 / 1508 / ◑ 2206	7.5 / 1.7 / 7.3 / 2.0	**20** M	0226 / 0914 / 1449 / ◑ 2133	6.9 / 2.5 / 6.8 / 2.8
6 M	0330 / 1025 / 1600 / 2256	7.2 / 2.1 / 7.1 / 2.4	**21** TU	0303 / 0949 / 1531 / 2218	6.6 / 3.0 / 6.5 / 3.2
7 TU	0432 / 1121 / 1710	6.8 / 2.6 / 6.8	**22** W	0358 / 1042 / 1637 / 2324	6.2 / 3.4 / 6.2 / 3.5
8 W	0004 / 0557 / 1240 / 1838	2.7 / 6.6 / 2.9 / 6.7	**23** TH	0534 / 1204 / 1826	5.9 / 3.7 / 6.1
9 TH	0135 / 0730 / 1411 / 2002	2.7 / 6.7 / 2.8 / 6.9	**24** F	0108 / 0722 / 1400 / 1949	3.5 / 6.1 / 3.4 / 6.4
10 F	0255 / 0847 / 1525 / 2107	2.4 / 7.0 / 2.5 / 7.2	**25** SA	0239 / 0830 / 1512 / 2046	3.0 / 6.5 / 2.9 / 6.8
11 SA	0406 / 0943 / 1635 / 2157	2.0 / 7.3 / 2.1 / 7.4	**26** SU	0340 / 0919 / 1608 / 2132	2.4 / 7.0 / 2.3 / 7.3
12 SU	0509 / 1028 / 1731 / 2239	1.7 / 7.5 / 1.8 / 7.6	**27** M	0434 / 1001 / 1659 / 2213	1.8 / 7.4 / 1.8 / 7.6
13 M	0557 / 1108 / 1813 / ● 2317	1.4 / 7.7 / 1.6 / 7.8	**28** TU	0524 / 1041 / 1746 / ○ 2253	1.4 / 7.7 / 1.4 / 7.9
14 TU	0635 / 1145 / 1848 / 2353	1.3 / 7.7 / 1.5 / 7.8	**29** W	0610 / 1120 / 1830 / 2333	1.0 / 7.9 / 1.2 / 8.1
15 W	0707 / 1218 / 1919	1.2 / 7.7 / 1.5	**30** TH	0652 / 1200 / 1911	0.8 / 8.0 / 1.0
			31 F	0014 / 0731 / 1240 / 1949	8.2 / 0.8 / 8.1 / 1.0

Chart Datum: 4·38 metres below IGN Datum

TIME ZONE -0100
(French Standard Time)
Subtract 1 hour for UT
For French Summer Time add
ONE hour in **non-shaded areas**

FRANCE – LE HAVRE

LAT 49°29'N   LONG 0°07'E
TIMES AND HEIGHTS OF HIGH AND LOW WATERS

Dates in amber are SPRINGS
Dates in yellow are NEAPS

2007

SEPTEMBER

Day	Time m	Day	Time m
1 SA	0055 8.1 / 0808 0.9 / 1320 7.9 / 2026 1.2	16 SU	0053 7.5 / 0750 1.9 / 1311 7.4 / 2001 2.0
2 SU	0137 7.9 / 0843 1.3 / 1359 7.7 / 2103 1.6	17 M	0119 7.3 / 0812 2.2 / 1335 7.2 / 2025 2.4
3 M	0219 7.5 / 0918 1.8 / 1441 7.4 / 2142 2.1	18 TU	0147 6.9 / 0837 2.6 / 1404 6.9 / 2055 2.7
4 TU	0308 7.1 / 0959 2.4 / 1532 7.0 / ◑ 2232 2.6	19 W	0223 6.5 / 0909 3.1 / 1445 6.5 / ◑ 2136 3.2
5 W	0415 6.6 / 1057 3.0 / 1651 6.6 / 2347 3.0	20 TH	0318 6.2 / 0958 3.5 / 1550 6.1 / 2238 3.5
6 TH	0558 6.4 / 1231 3.3 / 1837 6.5	21 F	0449 5.9 / 1118 3.8 / 1741 6.0
7 F	0133 2.9 / 0736 6.5 / 1414 3.0 / 2002 6.7	22 SA	0027 3.6 / 0651 6.1 / 1330 3.6 / 1917 6.3
8 SA	0259 2.5 / 0844 6.9 / 1534 2.5 / 2100 7.1	23 SU	0210 3.0 / 0800 6.6 / 1445 2.9 / 2017 6.8
9 SU	0408 2.0 / 0932 7.3 / 1634 2.0 / 2143 7.4	24 M	0312 2.3 / 0850 7.1 / 1540 2.2 / 2104 7.4
10 M	0459 1.6 / 1010 7.6 / 1717 1.7 / 2220 7.7	25 TU	0406 1.7 / 0932 7.5 / 1631 1.7 / 2146 7.8
11 TU	0537 1.4 / 1045 7.7 / 1751 1.5 / ● 2253 7.8	26 W	0456 1.2 / 1012 7.8 / 1720 1.3 / ○ 2227 8.1
12 W	0608 1.3 / 1116 7.7 / 1820 1.5 / 2324 7.9	27 TH	0543 0.9 / 1052 8.0 / 1805 1.0 / 2308 8.2
13 TH	0637 1.4 / 1146 7.8 / 1848 1.6 / 2355 7.8	28 F	0626 0.7 / 1133 8.2 / 1847 0.9 / 2350 8.3
14 F	0704 1.4 / 1215 7.7 / 1915 1.6	29 SA	0706 0.8 / 1213 8.1 / 1927 0.9
15 SA	0025 7.7 / 0728 1.6 / 1244 7.6 / 1938 1.8	30 SU	0033 8.1 / 0744 1.0 / 1254 8.0 / 2006 1.2

OCTOBER

Day	Time m	Day	Time m
1 M	0116 7.9 / 0821 1.4 / 1335 7.7 / 2043 1.6	16 TU	0051 7.2 / 0744 2.3 / 1303 7.2 / 2000 2.3
2 TU	0202 7.5 / 0858 2.0 / 1419 7.3 / 2124 2.2	17 W	0123 6.9 / 0812 2.7 / 1336 6.9 / 2031 2.7
3 W	0255 7.0 / 0941 2.7 / 1515 6.8 / ◑ 2216 2.7	18 TH	0204 6.6 / 0846 3.1 / 1421 6.6 / 2111 3.0
4 TH	0410 6.5 / 1046 3.2 / 1642 6.4 / 2340 3.1	19 F	0300 6.3 / 0934 3.5 / 1525 6.3 / ◑ 2210 3.3
5 F	0556 6.3 / 1231 3.4 / 1826 6.4	20 SA	0420 6.1 / 1050 3.7 / 1658 6.1 / 2349 3.4
6 SA	0126 2.9 / 0724 6.6 / 1406 3.0 / 1945 6.7	21 SU	0610 6.2 / 1248 3.5 / 1835 6.4
7 SU	0243 2.5 / 0825 7.0 / 1514 2.5 / 2039 7.1	22 M	0128 2.9 / 0719 6.7 / 1405 2.8 / 1937 6.9
8 M	0342 2.0 / 0907 7.3 / 1605 2.1 / 2119 7.4	23 TU	0234 2.3 / 0812 7.2 / 1504 2.2 / 2028 7.4
9 TU	0426 1.7 / 0943 7.5 / 1644 1.8 / 2153 7.6	24 W	0330 1.7 / 0857 7.6 / 1558 1.7 / 2114 7.8
10 W	0502 1.6 / 1014 7.7 / 1717 1.6 / 2224 7.7	25 TH	0423 1.3 / 0940 7.9 / 1649 1.3 / 2158 8.0
11 TH	0532 1.5 / 1043 7.8 / 1747 1.6 / ● 2254 7.8	26 F	0512 1.0 / 1023 8.1 / 1738 1.0 / ○ 2243 8.2
12 F	0602 1.5 / 1112 7.8 / 1816 1.6 / 2324 7.7	27 SA	0559 0.9 / 1106 8.2 / 1823 0.9 / 2329 8.2
13 SA	0630 1.6 / 1141 7.7 / 1843 1.6 / 2354 7.6	28 SU	0642 1.0 / 1149 8.1 / 1906 1.0
14 SU	0655 1.8 / 1209 7.6 / 1908 1.8	29 M	0015 8.1 / 0723 1.2 / 1233 7.9 / 1948 1.2
15 M	0023 7.4 / 0719 2.0 / 1235 7.5 / 1933 2.0	30 TU	0102 7.8 / 0803 1.7 / 1317 7.6 / 2029 1.6
		31 W	0151 7.4 / 0844 2.2 / 1405 7.3 / 2113 2.1

NOVEMBER

Day	Time m	Day	Time m
1 TH	0247 6.9 / 0932 2.8 / 1503 6.8 / ◑ 2208 2.6	16 F	0156 6.8 / 0836 2.9 / 1411 6.8 / 2101 2.7
2 F	0401 6.6 / 1040 3.2 / 1623 6.5 / 2325 2.9	17 SA	0249 6.6 / 0925 3.2 / 1508 6.6 / ◑ 2156 2.9
3 SA	0527 6.5 / 1207 3.3 / 1749 6.4	18 SU	0355 6.4 / 1033 3.3 / 1620 6.5 / 2313 3.0
4 SU	0048 2.9 / 0645 6.6 / 1324 3.0 / 1905 6.6	19 M	0518 6.5 / 1159 3.2 / 1743 6.6
5 M	0156 2.6 / 0747 6.9 / 1426 2.7 / 2003 6.9	20 TU	0035 2.8 / 0630 6.8 / 1316 2.8 / 1851 6.9
6 TU	0253 2.3 / 0831 7.2 / 1518 2.3 / 2046 7.2	21 W	0146 2.4 / 0728 7.2 / 1422 2.3 / 1949 7.3
7 W	0339 2.1 / 0908 7.4 / 1601 2.1 / 2122 7.4	22 TH	0250 2.0 / 0820 7.5 / 1523 1.9 / 2042 7.6
8 TH	0419 1.9 / 0940 7.5 / 1639 1.9 / 2155 7.5	23 F	0349 1.6 / 0909 7.8 / 1620 1.5 / 2134 7.8
9 F	0455 1.9 / 1011 7.6 / 1714 1.8 / 2227 7.5	24 SA	0443 1.4 / 0957 7.9 / 1713 1.2 / ○ 2224 8.0
10 SA	0529 1.8 / 1041 7.6 / 1746 1.8 / ● 2259 7.5	25 SU	0534 1.3 / 1048 8.0 / 1802 1.1 / 2314 8.0
11 SU	0559 1.9 / 1112 7.6 / 1815 1.8 / 2331 7.5	26 M	0621 1.3 / 1132 8.0 / 1849 1.1
12 M	0628 2.0 / 1142 7.6 / 1844 1.9	27 TU	0003 7.9 / 0707 1.5 / 1219 7.9 / 1935 1.3
13 TU	0002 7.4 / 0656 2.1 / 1212 7.5 / 1914 2.0	28 W	0053 7.7 / 0752 1.8 / 1306 7.7 / 2019 1.6
14 W	0035 7.2 / 0726 2.3 / 1245 7.3 / 1945 2.2	29 TH	0143 7.5 / 0837 2.1 / 1354 7.4 / 2105 1.9
15 TH	0113 7.0 / 0759 2.6 / 1325 7.1 / 2019 2.4	30 F	0235 7.1 / 0925 2.5 / 1447 7.0 / 2154 2.3

DECEMBER

Day	Time m	Day	Time m
1 SA	0332 6.8 / 1018 2.8 / 1546 6.7 / ◑ 2249 2.7	16 SU	0234 7.0 / 0922 2.6 / 1450 7.0 / 2147 2.4
2 SU	0435 6.7 / 1118 3.0 / 1652 6.6 / 2348 2.9	17 M	0326 6.9 / 1015 2.7 / 1544 6.9 / ◑ 2242 2.5
3 M	0541 6.6 / 1220 3.1 / 1800 6.5	18 TU	0427 6.8 / 1116 2.8 / 1650 6.9 / 2345 2.6
4 TU	0050 2.9 / 0645 6.7 / 1323 3.0 / 1906 6.6	19 W	0537 6.9 / 1224 2.7 / 1803 6.9
5 W	0151 2.8 / 0741 6.8 / 1423 2.8 / 2002 6.8	20 TH	0055 2.5 / 0644 7.0 / 1338 2.5 / 1913 7.0
6 TH	0248 2.6 / 0827 7.1 / 1516 2.5 / 2048 7.0	21 F	0211 2.3 / 0747 7.3 / 1452 2.2 / 2018 7.3
7 F	0338 2.4 / 0906 7.2 / 1603 2.3 / 2128 7.1	22 SA	0320 2.0 / 0846 7.5 / 1555 1.8 / 2119 7.5
8 SA	0421 2.3 / 0942 7.4 / 1644 2.1 / 2205 7.2	23 SU	0420 1.8 / 0941 7.7 / 1653 1.5 / 2215 7.7
9 SU	0500 2.2 / 1017 7.4 / 1720 2.0 / ● 2240 7.3	24 M	0516 1.6 / 1033 7.9 / 1748 1.3 / ○ 2307 7.8
10 M	0535 2.1 / 1051 7.5 / 1755 1.9 / 2315 7.4	25 TU	0609 1.5 / 1122 7.9 / 1839 1.2 / 2356 7.9
11 TU	0609 2.1 / 1125 7.5 / 1828 1.8 / 2350 7.4	26 W	0658 1.5 / 1209 7.9 / 1927 1.2
12 W	0643 2.1 / 1159 7.5 / 1904 1.8	27 TH	0043 7.8 / 0744 1.6 / 1254 7.8 / 2010 1.3
13 TH	0026 7.3 / 0719 2.2 / 1236 7.5 / 1940 1.9	28 F	0128 7.6 / 0826 1.8 / 1338 7.6 / 2050 1.6
14 F	0106 7.2 / 0757 2.3 / 1317 7.3 / 2019 2.1	29 SA	0211 7.4 / 0905 2.1 / 1420 7.3 / 2127 2.0
15 SA	0148 7.1 / 0837 2.5 / 1401 7.2 / 2100 2.2	30 SU	0254 7.1 / 0943 2.4 / 1503 7.0 / 2204 2.4
		31 M	0339 6.9 / 1022 2.8 / 1551 6.7 / ◑ 2243 2.7

Chart Datum: 4·38 metres below IGN Datum

TIDES

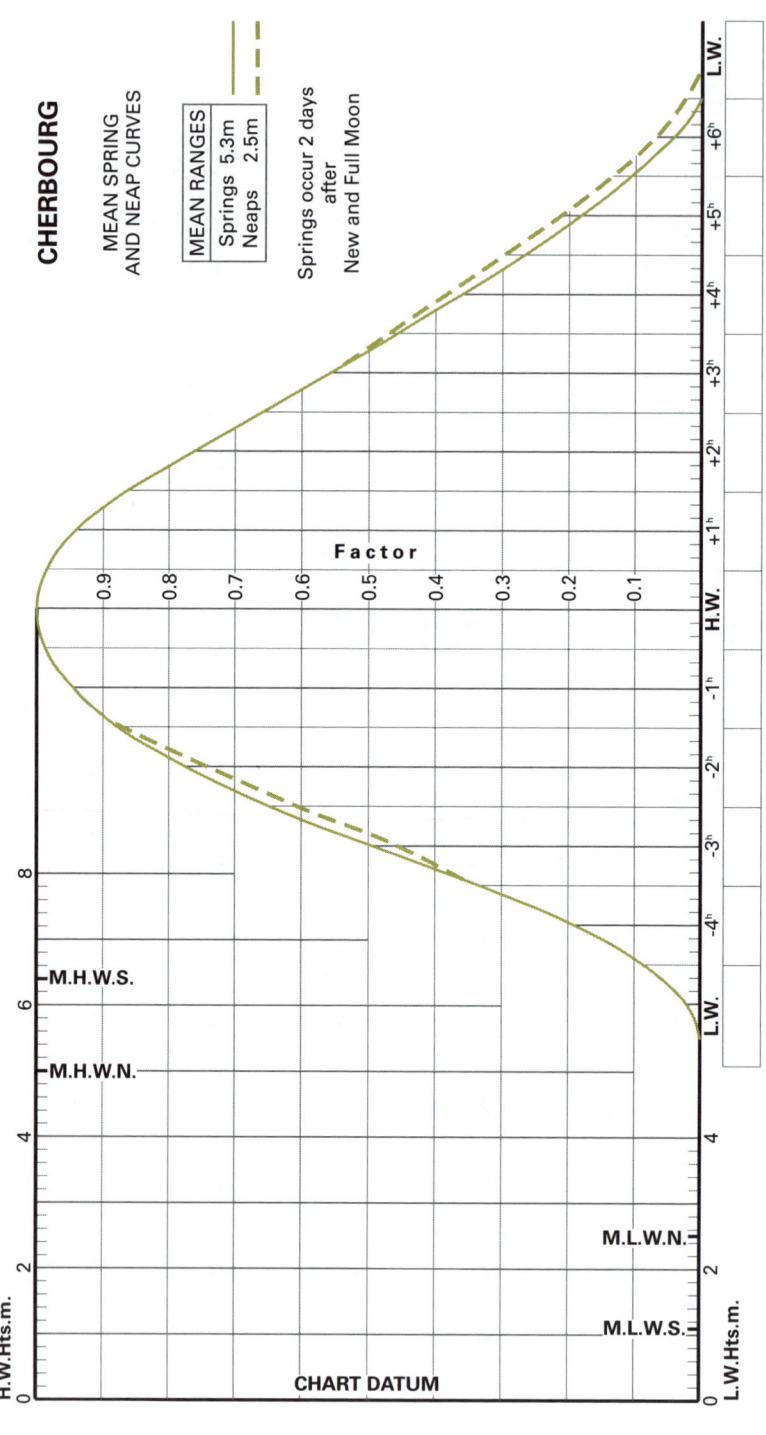

CHERBOURG

MEAN SPRING
AND NEAP CURVES

MEAN RANGES
Springs 5.3m
Neaps 2.5m

Springs occur 2 days
after
New and Full Moon

Factor

0.9
0.8
0.7
0.6
0.5
0.4
0.3
0.2
0.1

L.W.
+6ʰ
+5ʰ
+4ʰ
+3ʰ
+2ʰ
+1ʰ
H.W.
-1ʰ
-2ʰ
-3ʰ
-4ʰ
L.W.

M.H.W.S.
M.H.W.N.
M.L.W.N.
M.L.W.S.

8
6
4
2

H.W.Hts.m.
L.W.Hts.m.

CHART DATUM

TIME ZONE -0100
(French Standard Time)
Subtract 1 hour for UT
For French Summer Time add
ONE hour in **non-shaded areas**

FRANCE – CHERBOURG

LAT 49°39'N   LONG 1°38'W

TIMES AND HEIGHTS OF HIGH AND LOW WATERS

Dates in amber are **SPRINGS**
Dates in yellow are **NEAPS**

2007

JANUARY

Day	Time	m	Time	m	Time	m	Time	m
1 M	0100	2.0	0641	5.7	1335	1.8	1914	5.7
2 TU	0158	1.9	0736	5.9	1430	1.6	2009	5.9
3 W ○	0249	1.8	0825	6.1	1518	1.4	2058	6.0
4 TH	0336	1.7	0909	6.2	1603	1.3	2141	6.0
5 F	0418	1.6	0950	6.2	1643	1.3	2221	6.0
6 SA	0458	1.7	1029	6.2	1722	1.4	2258	5.8
7 SU	0535	1.7	1106	6.1	1758	1.6	2334	5.8
8 M	0610	1.9	1142	5.9	1832	1.7		
9 TU	0009	5.6	0645	2.1	1216	5.7	1906	1.9
10 W	0043	5.4	0720	2.2	1250	5.4	1941	2.2
11 TH ◑	0121	5.2	0800	2.5	1329	5.1	2021	2.5
12 F	0206	5.0	0848	2.7	1419	4.9	2113	2.7
13 SA	0305	4.8	0951	2.9	1526	4.9	2222	2.8
14 SU	0418	4.8	1108	2.8	1648	4.9	2340	2.8
15 M	0532	5.0	1221	2.6	1804	4.9		
16 TU	0050	2.6	0633	5.3	1320	2.3	1903	5.2
17 W	0145	2.3	0724	5.6	1411	1.9	1952	5.6
18 TH	0234	1.9	0809	5.9	1458	1.6	2037	5.8
19 F ●	0319	1.7	0853	6.2	1543	1.3	2121	6.1
20 SA	0403	1.4	0936	6.4	1627	1.0	2204	6.2
21 SU	0446	1.3	1019	6.5	1709	0.9	2246	6.3
22 M	0529	1.2	1101	6.5	1751	0.9	2329	6.2
23 TU	0611	1.3	1144	6.4	1833	1.0		
24 W	0011	6.1	0654	1.4	1226	6.2	1916	1.2
25 TH ◐	0052	5.9	0739	1.7	1311	5.9	2002	1.6
26 F	0139	5.6	0830	2.1	1402	5.5	2055	2.0
27 SA	0236	5.3	0933	2.4	1511	5.2	2203	2.4
28 SU	0353	5.1	1054	2.5	1640	5.0	2327	2.5
29 M	0520	5.1	1220	2.4	1807	5.1		
30 TU	0051	2.4	0635	5.4	1331	2.1	1916	5.4
31 W	0156	2.2	0734	5.6	1427	1.8	2010	5.7

FEBRUARY

Day	Time	m	Time	m	Time	m	Time	m
1 TH	0247	1.9	0822	5.9	1514	1.5	2054	5.9
2 F ○	0330	1.7	0903	6.1	1554	1.3	2131	6.0
3 SA	0408	1.5	0940	6.2	1630	1.2	2205	6.1
4 SU	0442	1.4	1013	6.3	1703	1.2	2237	6.1
5 M	0514	1.4	1045	6.2	1733	1.2	2307	6.0
6 TU	0543	1.5	1114	6.1	1801	1.4	2335	5.8
7 W	0612	1.7	1141	5.9	1828	1.6		
8 TH	0001	5.6	0641	1.9	1208	5.6	1856	1.9
9 F	0028	5.4	0712	2.2	1237	5.3	1926	2.2
10 SA ◑	0100	5.2	0749	2.5	1314	5.0	2005	2.6
11 SU	0146	4.9	0839	2.8	1410	4.7	2104	2.9
12 M	0259	4.7	0957	2.9	1545	4.5	2238	3.0
13 TU	0445	4.7	1136	2.8	1737	4.6		
14 W	0019	2.8	0609	5.0	1255	2.4	1847	5.1
15 TH	0126	2.4	0706	5.4	1353	1.9	1938	5.5
16 F	0219	1.9	0755	5.9	1442	1.4	2024	5.9
17 SA ●	0306	1.5	0840	6.3	1528	1.0	2107	6.2
18 SU	0349	1.1	0923	6.6	1611	0.7	2150	6.5
19 M	0432	0.9	1006	6.8	1653	0.5	2231	6.6
20 TU	0512	0.8	1047	6.8	1733	0.5	2310	6.6
21 W	0552	0.8	1127	6.7	1812	0.7	2348	6.4
22 TH	0632	1.1	1206	6.4	1852	1.1		
23 F	0024	6.0	0714	1.5	1246	5.9	1934	1.6
24 SA ◗	0105	5.6	0801	2.0	1333	5.4	2023	2.2
25 SU	0158	5.2	0902	2.4	1443	4.9	2132	2.7
26 M	0322	4.8	1034	2.7	1634	4.7	2315	2.9
27 TU	0511	4.8	1216	2.5	1814	4.9		
28 W	0052	2.6	0633	5.1	1328	2.1	1917	5.3

MARCH

Day	Time	m	Time	m	Time	m	Time	m
1 TH	0154	2.2	0729	5.5	1420	1.8	2001	5.6
2 F	0239	1.9	0811	5.9	1501	1.5	2037	5.9
3 SA	0316	1.6	0847	6.1	1536	1.2	2110	6.1
4 SU ○	0349	1.4	0920	6.2	1607	1.1	2140	6.1
5 M	0419	1.3	0950	6.2	1636	1.1	2209	6.2
6 TU	0447	1.3	1018	6.3	1703	1.1	2235	6.1
7 W	0514	1.3	1044	6.2	1728	1.3	2300	6.0
8 TH	0540	1.5	1108	6.0	1753	1.5	2323	5.8
9 F	0606	1.7	1132	5.7	1818	1.7	2347	5.6
10 SA	0635	1.9	1159	5.4	1846	2.1		
11 SU	0015	5.3	0709	2.3	1231	5.1	1922	2.5
12 M ◑	0053	5.0	0755	2.6	1321	4.7	2016	2.9
13 TU	0159	4.6	0908	2.9	1458	4.4	2152	3.1
14 W	0401	4.5	1057	2.8	1714	4.6	2345	2.9
15 TH	0542	4.9	1227	2.4	1825	5.0		
16 F	0103	2.3	0642	5.4	1328	1.8	1916	5.5
17 SA	0156	1.8	0732	5.9	1418	1.3	2001	6.0
18 SU	0243	1.3	0818	6.4	1504	0.8	2044	6.4
19 M ●	0327	0.9	0902	6.7	1548	0.5	2127	6.6
20 TU	0409	0.6	0945	6.9	1629	0.4	2207	6.7
21 W	0450	0.6	1026	6.9	1709	0.4	2246	6.7
22 TH	0530	0.7	1106	6.7	1748	0.7	2323	6.4
23 F	0610	1.0	1145	6.3	1827	1.2		
24 SA	0000	6.1	0652	1.4	1225	5.8	1909	1.8
25 SU ◑	0039	5.6	0739	2.0	1314	5.2	1959	2.4
26 M	0132	5.1	0841	2.5	1429	4.7	2114	2.9
27 TU ◗	0301	4.7	1018	2.7	1632	4.6	2305	3.0
28 W	0456	4.7	1159	2.5	1803	4.9		
29 TH	0035	2.7	0614	5.1	1306	2.2	1855	5.2
30 F	0131	2.2	0704	5.4	1354	1.8	1934	5.6
31 SA	0213	1.9	0744	5.7	1433	1.5	2008	5.8

APRIL

Day	Time	m	Time	m	Time	m	Time	m
1 SU	0249	1.6	0819	6.0	1506	1.3	2039	6.0
2 M ○	0320	1.4	0851	6.1	1536	1.2	2109	6.1
3 TU	0349	1.3	0921	6.2	1604	1.2	2137	6.1
4 W	0417	1.3	0948	6.1	1631	1.3	2203	6.1
5 TH	0444	1.3	1014	6.1	1657	1.4	2227	6.0
6 F	0511	1.4	1040	5.9	1723	1.6	2252	5.9
7 SA	0539	1.6	1107	5.7	1749	1.8	2319	5.7
8 SU	0609	1.8	1137	5.4	1820	2.2	2350	5.4
9 M	0645	2.1	1213	5.1	1859	2.5		
10 TU ◑	0031	5.1	0733	2.4	1307	4.7	1957	2.8
11 W	0137	4.7	0846	2.7	1441	4.5	2129	3.0
12 TH	0326	4.6	1025	2.6	1640	4.7	2312	2.8
13 F	0504	4.9	1151	2.2	1803	4.9		
14 SA	0029	2.3	0608	5.4	1254	1.7	1843	5.6
15 SU	0124	1.7	0700	5.9	1346	1.2	1930	6.1
16 M	0214	1.2	0749	6.3	1435	0.8	2015	6.4
17 TU ●	0300	0.9	0836	6.6	1520	0.6	2058	6.6
18 W	0344	0.7	0921	6.8	1603	0.5	2141	6.7
19 TH	0427	0.6	1004	6.7	1645	0.7	2221	6.6
20 F	0510	0.7	1046	6.5	1726	1.0	2300	6.4
21 SA	0552	1.0	1128	6.1	1808	1.5	2340	6.0
22 SU	0635	1.5	1212	5.6	1852	2.0		
23 M	0023	5.6	0725	2.0	1304	5.1	1946	2.5
24 TU ◑	0118	5.1	0827	2.4	1419	4.8	2100	2.9
25 W	0241	4.8	0952	2.6	1559	4.7	2233	2.9
26 TH	0415	4.8	1116	2.5	1718	4.9	2349	2.6
27 F	0527	5.0	1220	2.2	1811	5.1		
28 SA	0047	2.3	0620	5.3	1310	2.0	1852	5.4
29 SU	0132	1.7	0704	5.5	1351	1.7	1929	5.7
30 M	0211	1.8	0742	5.7	1427	1.6	2003	5.9

Chart Datum: 3·29 metres below IGN Datum

TIDES

TIME ZONE -0100
(French Standard Time)
Subtract 1 hour for UT
For French Summer Time add
ONE hour in **non-shaded areas**

FRANCE – CHERBOURG

LAT 49°39'N   LONG 1°38'W

TIMES AND HEIGHTS OF HIGH AND LOW WATERS

Dates in amber are **SPRINGS**
Dates in yellow are **NEAPS**

2007

MAY

Time m	Time m
1 TU 0245 1.6 / 0818 5.9 / 1500 1.5 / 2035 6.0	**16** W 0233 1.1 / 0809 6.4 / 1453 0.9 / ● 2031 6.4
2 W 0317 1.5 / 0850 5.9 / 1531 1.5 / ○ 2105 6.0	**17** TH 0322 0.9 / 0859 6.4 / 1540 0.9 / 2117 6.5
3 TH 0348 1.4 / 0920 5.9 / 1600 1.5 / 2133 6.0	**18** F 0408 0.9 / 0946 6.4 / 1625 1.1 / 2200 6.4
4 F 0418 1.4 / 0949 5.9 / 1630 1.6 / 2201 6.0	**19** SA 0454 1.0 / 1032 6.2 / 1709 1.3 / 2244 6.2
5 SA 0449 1.5 / 1020 5.8 / 1700 1.7 / 2232 5.9	**20** SU 0538 1.2 / 1117 5.9 / 1754 1.7 / 2327 6.0
6 SU 0521 1.6 / 1054 5.6 / 1732 1.9 / 2306 5.7	**21** M 0624 1.5 / 1204 5.6 / 1841 2.0
7 M 0555 1.8 / 1131 5.4 / 1808 2.1 / 2344 5.5	**22** TU 0013 5.6 / 0713 1.8 / 1254 5.3 / 1933 2.4
8 TU 0636 2.0 / 1215 5.1 / 1853 2.4	**23** W 0105 5.3 / 0807 2.1 / 1354 5.0 / ◑ 2034 2.6
9 W 0031 5.2 / 0728 2.2 / 1311 4.9 / 1954 2.6	**24** TH 0208 5.0 / 0910 2.3 / 1503 4.8 / 2142 2.7
10 TH 0134 5.0 / 0836 2.3 / 1429 4.8 / ◑ 2114 2.7	**25** F 0317 4.9 / 1016 2.4 / 1610 4.9 / 2248 2.6
11 F 0257 4.9 / 0956 2.3 / 1558 4.9 / 2236 2.5	**26** SA 0423 4.9 / 1118 2.3 / 1710 5.0 / 2348 2.5
12 SA 0419 5.1 / 1111 2.0 / 1708 5.2 / 2346 2.2	**27** SU 0523 5.0 / 1214 2.2 / 1800 5.2
13 SU 0526 5.5 / 1215 1.7 / 1804 5.6	**28** M 0042 2.3 / 0615 5.2 / 1302 2.1 / 1844 5.4
14 M 0049 1.7 / 0624 5.8 / 1312 1.3 / 1855 6.0	**29** TU 0128 2.1 / 0702 5.4 / 1346 1.9 / 1924 5.6
15 TU 0143 1.4 / 0718 6.2 / 1404 1.1 / 1944 6.3	**30** W 0208 1.9 / 0744 5.5 / 1424 1.8 / 2002 5.8
	31 TH 0246 1.7 / 0822 5.6 / 1500 1.8 / 2037 5.9

JUNE

Time m	Time m
1 F 0322 1.6 / 0858 5.7 / 1535 1.7 / ○ 2110 5.9	**16** SA 0356 1.1 / 0936 6.1 / 1612 1.4 / 2148 6.3
2 SA 0358 1.5 / 0933 5.7 / 1611 1.7 / 2145 5.9	**17** SU 0443 1.1 / 1023 6.0 / 1658 1.5 / 2233 6.2
3 SU 0435 1.5 / 1009 5.7 / 1647 1.8 / 2221 5.9	**18** M 0528 1.2 / 1108 5.9 / 1743 1.7 / 2317 6.0
4 M 0512 1.5 / 1048 5.7 / 1725 1.9 / 2301 5.8	**19** TU 0612 1.4 / 1151 5.7 / 1826 1.9
5 TU 0552 1.6 / 1130 5.5 / 1806 2.0 / 2344 5.7	**20** W 0000 5.8 / 0654 1.6 / 1233 5.5 / 1910 2.1
6 W 0635 1.7 / 1216 5.4 / 1854 2.1	**21** TH 0043 5.6 / 0737 1.9 / 1317 5.3 / 1955 2.3
7 TH 0031 5.5 / 0725 1.8 / 1308 5.3 / 1949 2.3	**22** F 0127 5.3 / 0821 2.1 / 1404 5.1 / ◑ 2045 2.5
8 F 0125 5.4 / 0821 1.9 / 1407 5.2 / ◑ 2052 2.3	**23** SA 0217 5.1 / 0911 2.3 / 1457 4.9 / 2141 2.6
9 SA 0228 5.3 / 0925 1.9 / 1514 5.2 / 2200 2.3	**24** SU 0313 4.9 / 1008 2.5 / 1557 4.9 / 2243 2.6
10 SU 0336 5.3 / 1032 1.9 / 1622 5.3 / 2308 2.1	**25** M 0416 4.8 / 1110 2.5 / 1659 5.0 / 2345 2.6
11 M 0445 5.4 / 1138 1.8 / 1726 5.5	**26** TU 0522 4.9 / 1211 2.5 / 1758 5.1
12 TU 0015 1.9 / 0551 5.6 / 1240 1.6 / 1824 5.8	**27** W 0044 2.4 / 0623 5.0 / 1306 2.3 / 1849 5.3
13 W 0116 1.6 / 0653 5.8 / 1339 1.5 / 1920 6.0	**28** TH 0135 2.2 / 0715 5.2 / 1353 2.2 / 1934 5.5
14 TH 0213 1.4 / 0752 6.0 / 1433 1.4 / 2012 6.2	**29** F 0220 1.9 / 0801 5.4 / 1437 2.0 / 2015 5.7
15 F 0306 1.2 / 0846 6.1 / 1524 1.4 / ● 2101 6.3	**30** SA 0303 1.7 / 0843 5.6 / 1518 1.8 / ○ 2055 5.9

JULY

Time m	Time m
1 SU 0344 1.5 / 0922 5.7 / 1558 1.7 / 2134 6.0	**16** M 0433 1.1 / 1013 6.0 / 1647 1.5 / 2222 6.3
2 M 0425 1.4 / 1002 5.8 / 1639 1.6 / 2214 6.1	**17** TU 0514 1.1 / 1052 6.0 / 1726 1.5 / 2300 6.2
3 TU 0505 1.3 / 1042 5.9 / 1720 1.6 / 2255 6.1	**18** W 0551 1.2 / 1128 5.9 / 1803 1.6 / 2336 6.0
4 W 0546 1.2 / 1124 5.8 / 1802 1.6 / 2338 6.0	**19** TH 0626 1.4 / 1202 5.7 / 1837 1.8
5 TH 0628 1.3 / 1207 5.8 / 1846 1.7	**20** F 0011 5.8 / 0658 1.6 / 1236 5.5 / 1912 2.0
6 F 0021 5.9 / 0712 1.4 / 1252 5.6 / 1933 1.8	**21** SA 0043 5.5 / 0732 1.9 / 1309 5.3 / 1949 2.3
7 SA 0107 5.8 / 0759 1.6 / 1339 5.5 / ◑ 2025 2.0	**22** SU 0119 5.2 / 0809 2.3 / 1347 5.1 / ◑ 2033 2.6
8 SU 0158 5.6 / 0853 1.8 / 1434 5.4 / 2126 2.2	**23** M 0202 4.9 / 0855 2.6 / 1438 4.9 / 2131 2.8
9 M 0259 5.4 / 0955 2.0 / 1540 5.3 / 2235 2.2	**24** TU 0301 4.7 / 0959 2.8 / 1548 4.8 / 2246 2.8
10 TU 0413 5.3 / 1106 2.1 / 1654 5.3 / 2348 2.1	**25** W 0425 4.6 / 1119 2.8 / 1712 4.8
11 W 0531 5.3 / 1218 2.1 / 1805 5.5	**26** TH 0003 2.7 / 0552 4.7 / 1232 2.7 / 1820 5.1
12 TH 0101 1.9 / 0644 5.5 / 1325 1.9 / 1908 5.7	**27** F 0108 2.4 / 0655 5.0 / 1330 2.4 / 1913 5.4
13 F 0203 1.6 / 0748 5.7 / 1424 1.8 / 2004 6.0	**28** SA 0200 2.0 / 0745 5.3 / 1419 2.1 / 1958 5.7
14 SA 0259 1.4 / 0843 5.9 / 1516 1.6 / ● 2055 6.1	**29** SU 0246 1.7 / 0829 5.6 / 1503 1.8 / 2041 6.0
15 SU 0348 1.2 / 0931 6.0 / 1604 1.5 / 2140 6.2	**30** M 0330 1.4 / 0910 5.9 / 1546 1.5 / ○ 2122 6.2
	31 TU 0411 1.1 / 0950 6.1 / 1627 1.3 / 2202 6.4

AUGUST

Time m	Time m
1 W 0452 0.9 / 1030 6.2 / 1707 1.2 / 2243 6.4	**16** TH 0522 1.2 / 1057 6.1 / 1732 1.4 / 2305 6.2
2 TH 0531 0.9 / 1110 6.2 / 1747 1.2 / 2323 6.4	**17** F 0551 1.3 / 1126 5.9 / 1801 1.6 / 2333 6.0
3 F 0610 0.9 / 1149 6.1 / 1828 1.3	**18** SA 0618 1.6 / 1152 5.7 / 1829 1.9
4 SA 0004 6.3 / 0650 1.1 / 1228 6.0 / 1910 1.5	**19** SU 0000 5.7 / 0645 1.9 / 1218 5.5 / 1859 2.2
5 SU 0044 6.0 / 0733 1.4 / 1309 5.7 / ◑ 1957 1.9	**20** M 0027 5.3 / 0715 2.3 / 1248 5.2 / ◑ 1935 2.5
6 M 0130 5.6 / 0822 1.9 / 1357 5.4 / 2055 2.2	**21** TU 0102 5.0 / 0751 2.6 / 1328 4.9 / 2024 2.8
7 TU 0230 5.3 / 0923 2.3 / 1505 5.2 / 2210 2.4	**22** W 0155 4.6 / 0847 3.0 / 1434 4.6 / 2141 3.0
8 W 0355 5.0 / 1045 2.5 / 1637 5.1 / 2338 2.4	**23** TH 0328 4.4 / 1024 3.1 / 1627 4.6 / 2324 2.9
9 TH 0531 5.0 / 1212 2.5 / 1802 5.3	**24** F 0530 4.6 / 1205 2.9 / 1757 4.9
10 F 0059 2.1 / 0650 5.3 / 1324 2.2 / 1909 5.6	**25** SA 0044 2.5 / 0637 5.0 / 1310 2.5 / 1853 5.3
11 SA 0202 1.8 / 0750 5.6 / 1422 1.9 / 2002 5.9	**26** SU 0139 2.0 / 0726 5.4 / 1359 2.1 / 1938 5.7
12 SU 0254 1.4 / 0838 5.9 / 1510 1.6 / 2047 6.2	**27** M 0225 1.6 / 0809 5.8 / 1444 1.6 / 2021 6.1
13 M 0338 1.2 / 0918 6.1 / 1551 1.4 / ● 2127 6.3	**28** TU 0308 1.2 / 0850 6.1 / 1526 1.3 / ○ 2102 6.4
14 TU 0416 1.1 / 0954 6.1 / 1628 1.4 / 2202 6.4	**29** W 0350 0.9 / 0930 6.4 / 1606 1.0 / 2142 6.7
15 W 0451 1.1 / 1027 6.1 / 1701 1.4 / 2235 6.3	**30** TH 0429 0.7 / 1009 6.5 / 1646 0.9 / 2222 6.7
	31 F 0508 0.6 / 1047 6.5 / 1725 0.9 / 2302 6.7

Chart Datum: 3·29 metres below IGN Datum

TIME ZONE -0100
(French Standard Time)
Subtract 1 hour for UT
For French Summer Time add
ONE hour in **non-shaded areas**

FRANCE – CHERBOURG

LAT 49°39'N   LONG 1°38'W

TIMES AND HEIGHTS OF HIGH AND LOW WATERS

Dates in amber are **SPRINGS**
Dates in yellow are **NEAPS**

2007

SEPTEMBER

Time	m		Time	m
1 0547	0.8	**16** 0540	1.7	
1124	6.4	1110	5.9	
SA 1805	1.1	SU 1751	1.8	
2341	6.4	2319	5.7	
2 0625	1.1	**17** 0605	2.0	
1200	6.2	1133	5.6	
SU 1846	1.4	M 1819	2.0	
		2345	5.4	
3 0020	6.0	**18** 0632	2.3	
0706	1.6	1200	5.3	
M 1239	5.8	TU 1852	2.4	
1932	1.9			
4 0107	5.5	**19** 0018	5.0	
0754	2.1	0705	2.7	
TU 1327	5.4	W 1237	5.0	
2031	2.3	1936	2.8	
5 0211	5.0	**20** 0107	4.7	
0900	2.6	0756	3.1	
W 1441	5.0	TH 1339	4.7	
2158	2.6	2048	3.0	
6 0356	4.8	**21** 0244	4.4	
1041	2.9	0935	3.3	
TH 1634	4.9	F 1541	4.5	
2339	2.5	2243	3.0	
7 0544	4.9	**22** 0503	4.6	
1216	2.7	1133	3.0	
F 1804	5.2	SA 1726	4.8	
8 0059	2.2	**23** 0013	2.6	
0653	5.3	0610	5.0	
SA 1323	2.3	SU 1242	2.5	
1904	5.6	1823	5.3	
9 0155	1.8	**24** 0109	2.0	
0740	5.7	0657	5.5	
SU 1413	1.9	M 1331	2.0	
1949	6.0	1909	5.8	
10 0239	1.4	**25** 0156	1.5	
0819	6.0	0739	5.9	
M 1454	1.6	TU 1416	1.5	
2028	6.2	1952	6.3	
11 0317	1.2	**26** 0239	1.1	
0854	6.2	0820	6.3	
TU 1529	1.4	W 1459	1.1	
● 2103	6.4	○ 2034	6.6	
12 0350	1.1	**27** 0321	0.7	
0925	6.2	0901	6.6	
W 1601	1.3	TH 1540	0.9	
2134	6.4	2116	6.8	
13 0420	1.1	**28** 0402	0.6	
0955	6.2	0940	6.7	
TH 1630	1.3	F 1621	0.8	
2203	6.3	2158	6.9	
14 0448	1.2	**29** 0442	0.6	
1022	6.2	1019	6.7	
F 1658	1.4	SA 1702	0.8	
2230	6.2	2238	6.7	
15 0514	1.4	**30** 0521	0.9	
1047	6.0	1056	6.5	
SA 1725	1.6	SU 1742	1.1	
2255	6.0	2319	6.4	

OCTOBER

Time	m		Time	m
1 0601	1.3	**16** 0534	2.1	
1134	6.2	1101	5.7	
M 1825	1.5	TU 1751	2.1	
		2318	5.4	
2 0003	5.9	**17** 0603	2.4	
0644	1.8	1132	5.4	
TU 1215	5.8	W 1825	2.3	
1913	2.0	2354	5.1	
3 0051	5.4	**18** 0639	2.7	
0735	2.4	1211	5.1	
W 1307	5.3	TH 1910	2.6	
◑ 2016	2.4			
4 0204	4.9	**19** 0047	4.8	
0849	2.9	0733	3.0	
TH 1430	4.9	F 1314	4.8	
2152	2.7	◑ 2018	2.9	
5 0400	4.7	**20** 0217	4.5	
1039	3.0	0901	3.2	
F 1626	4.9	SA 1458	4.7	
2330	2.5	2158	2.9	
6 0535	5.0	**21** 0415	4.7	
1205	2.7	1049	3.0	
SA 1748	5.2	SU 1638	4.9	
		2326	2.5	
7 0041	2.2	**22** 0527	5.1	
0632	5.3	1201	2.5	
SU 1303	2.3	M 1741	5.4	
1841	5.6			
8 0130	1.8	**23** 0030	2.0	
0713	5.7	0617	5.6	
M 1348	1.9	TU 1255	2.0	
1922	5.9	1831	5.8	
9 0211	1.6	**24** 0120	1.5	
0748	6.0	0702	6.0	
TU 1426	1.7	W 1343	1.5	
1959	6.1	1918	6.3	
10 0246	1.4	**25** 0207	1.1	
0821	6.1	0746	6.4	
W 1459	1.5	TH 1429	1.2	
2032	6.2	2004	6.6	
11 0318	1.3	**26** 0252	0.9	
0852	6.2	0828	6.6	
TH 1530	1.4	F 1514	0.9	
● 2103	6.3	○ 2049	6.8	
12 0347	1.3	**27** 0335	0.8	
0920	6.2	0911	6.7	
F 1559	1.4	SA 1558	0.8	
2131	6.2	2134	6.8	
13 0415	1.4	**28** 0418	0.9	
0946	6.2	0952	6.7	
SA 1627	1.5	SU 1641	0.9	
2158	6.1	2218	6.6	
14 0441	1.6	**29** 0500	1.1	
1010	6.1	1033	6.5	
SU 1654	1.6	M 1725	1.1	
2223	5.9	2303	6.3	
15 0507	1.8	**30** 0543	1.5	
1035	5.9	1115	6.2	
M 1722	1.8	TU 1811	1.5	
2249	5.7	2350	5.9	
		31 0630	2.0	
		1201	5.8	
		W 1902	1.9	

NOVEMBER

Time	m		Time	m
1 0043	5.4	**16** 0630	2.6	
0725	2.5	1206	5.3	
TH 1256	5.4	F 1900	2.4	
◑ 2005	2.4			
2 0155	5.0	**17** 0042	5.0	
0838	2.9	0724	2.8	
F 1413	5.0	SA 1304	5.1	
2129	2.6	◑ 2001	2.5	
3 0330	4.8	**18** 0152	4.9	
1010	2.9	0836	2.9	
SA 1547	5.0	SU 1419	5.0	
2253	2.5	2116	2.5	
4 0452	5.0	**19** 0317	4.9	
1127	2.7	0959	2.8	
SU 1703	5.1	M 1541	5.1	
2358	2.3	2234	2.4	
5 0548	5.3	**20** 0432	5.2	
1224	2.4	1113	2.5	
M 1759	5.4	TU 1651	5.4	
		2341	2.0	
6 0050	2.1	**21** 0531	5.5	
0632	5.5	1215	2.1	
TU 1311	2.1	W 1750	5.7	
1843	5.6			
7 0133	1.9	**22** 0042	1.7	
0709	5.8	0623	5.9	
W 1351	1.9	TH 1310	1.7	
1922	5.8	1844	6.1	
8 0210	1.7	**23** 0135	1.4	
0745	6.0	0712	6.3	
TH 1427	1.8	F 1402	1.3	
1959	6.0	1936	6.4	
9 0244	1.7	**24** 0225	1.2	
0817	6.1	0800	6.5	
F 1459	1.7	SA 1451	1.1	
2032	6.0	○ 2027	6.5	
10 0315	1.6	**25** 0313	1.1	
0848	6.1	0847	6.6	
SA 1531	1.6	SU 1540	1.0	
● 2103	6.0	2117	6.5	
11 0345	1.7	**26** 0400	1.2	
0916	6.1	0933	6.6	
SU 1601	1.6	M 1627	1.0	
2133	6.0	2205	6.4	
12 0415	1.8	**27** 0446	1.4	
0944	6.0	1018	6.5	
M 1632	1.7	TU 1714	1.2	
2202	5.8	2253	6.2	
13 0445	1.9	**28** 0533	1.7	
1013	5.9	1104	6.2	
TU 1703	1.8	W 1802	1.4	
2233	5.7	2342	5.9	
14 0515	2.1	**29** 0621	2.0	
1046	5.8	1152	5.9	
W 1736	2.0	TH 1852	1.8	
2309	5.5			
15 0549	2.3	**30** 0032	5.5	
1123	5.6	0712	2.3	
TH 1814	2.2	F 1243	5.6	
2350	5.2	1946	2.1	

DECEMBER

Time	m		Time	m
1 0130	5.2	**16** 0033	5.4	
0810	2.6	0715	2.3	
SA 1342	5.3	SU 1250	5.5	
◑ 2046	2.4	1943	2.0	
2 0234	5.0	**17** 0125	5.3	
0916	2.8	0810	2.4	
SU 1448	5.1	M 1345	5.4	
2151	2.5	● 2040	2.1	
3 0341	5.0	**18** 0226	5.2	
1024	2.8	0914	2.5	
M 1555	5.0	TU 1450	5.3	
2256	2.5	2145	2.2	
4 0444	5.1	**19** 0334	5.3	
1127	2.7	1025	2.4	
TU 1659	5.1	W 1601	5.3	
2354	2.4	2255	2.1	
5 0539	5.3	**20** 0443	5.4	
1223	2.5	1136	2.2	
W 1755	5.2	TH 1712	5.5	
6 0047	2.3	**21** 0004	2.0	
0626	5.5	0548	5.7	
TH 1312	2.3	F 1242	1.9	
1844	5.4	1818	5.8	
7 0132	2.1	**22** 0109	1.7	
0708	5.7	0648	6.0	
F 1354	2.1	SA 1342	1.6	
1928	5.6	1919	6.0	
8 0212	2.0	**23** 0206	1.6	
0747	5.8	0743	6.2	
SA 1433	1.9	SU 1438	1.3	
2007	5.7	2016	6.2	
9 0249	1.9	**24** 0300	1.4	
0822	5.9	0835	6.4	
SU 1508	1.8	M 1530	1.1	
● 2043	5.8	○ 2109	6.3	
10 0324	1.9	**25** 0350	1.4	
0855	6.0	0924	6.5	
M 1543	1.7	TU 1619	1.0	
2117	5.8	2158	6.3	
11 0358	1.9	**26** 0438	1.4	
0928	6.0	1011	6.4	
TU 1618	1.6	W 1706	1.1	
2151	5.8	2245	6.2	
12 0433	1.9	**27** 0524	1.5	
1003	6.0	1056	6.3	
W 1654	1.6	TH 1751	1.2	
2227	5.8	2329	6.0	
13 0508	2.0	**28** 0607	1.7	
1040	5.9	1139	6.1	
TH 1731	1.7	F 1833	1.3	
2305	5.7			
14 0546	2.1	**29** 0012	5.8	
1119	5.8	0649	1.9	
F 1810	1.8	SA 1220	5.9	
2347	5.5	1915	1.8	
15 0627	2.2	**30** 0053	5.5	
1202	5.7	0731	2.2	
SA 1853	1.9	SU 1302	5.6	
		1956	2.1	
		31 0136	5.3	
		0816	2.5	
		M 1347	5.3	
		◑ 2041	2.4	

Chart Datum: 3·29 metres below IGN Datum

TIDES

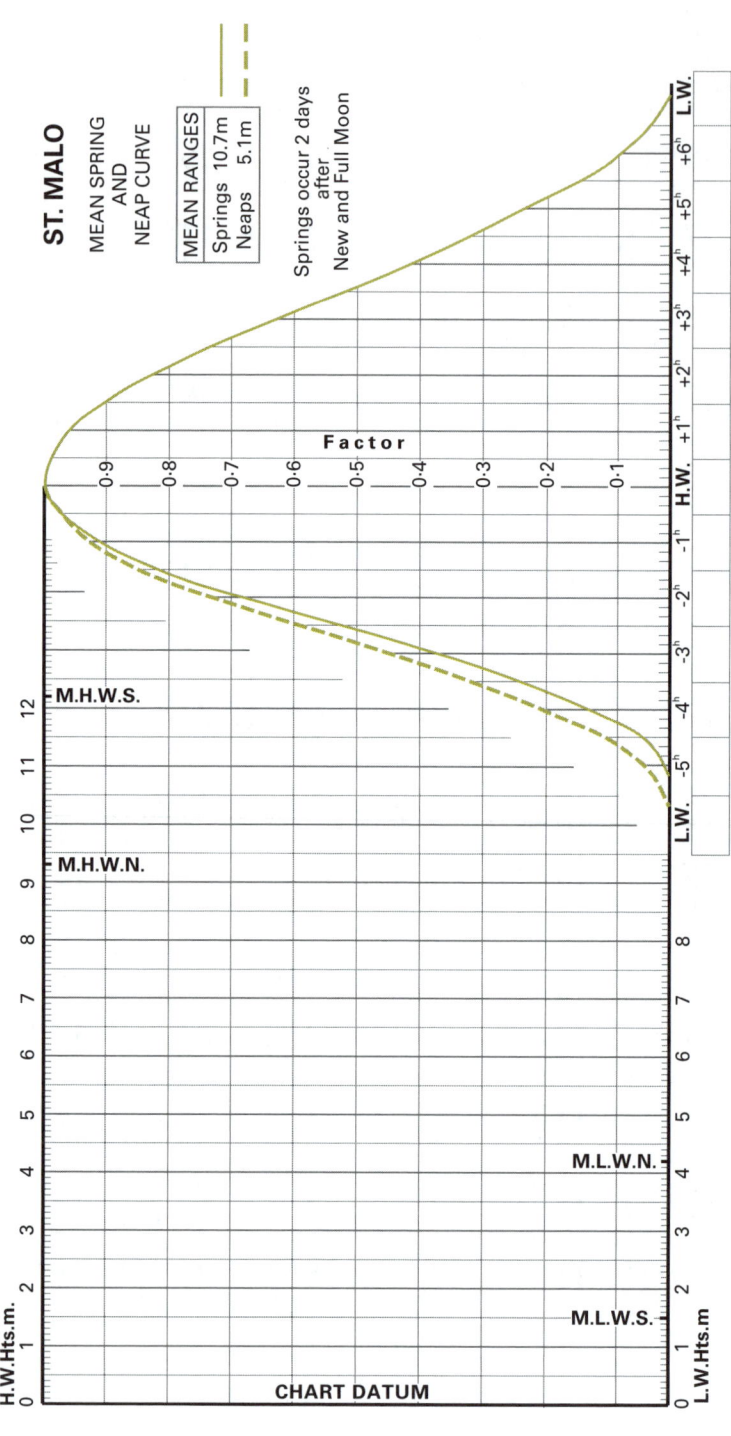

ST. MALO

MEAN SPRING
AND
NEAP CURVE

MEAN RANGES
Springs 10.7m   Neaps 5.1m

Springs occur 2 days
after
New and Full Moon

Factor

0·9 0·8 0·7 0·6 0·5 0·4 0·3 0·2 0·1

M.H.W.S.

M.H.W.N.

M.L.W.N.

M.L.W.S.

H.W.Hts.m.

L.W.Hts.m

CHART DATUM

H.W.   -1ʰ -2ʰ -3ʰ -4ʰ -5ʰ L.W.

L.W. +6ʰ +5ʰ +4ʰ +3ʰ +2ʰ +1ʰ H.W.

TIME ZONE -0100
(French Standard Time)
Subtract 1 hour for UT
For French Summer Time add
ONE hour in **non-shaded areas**

FRANCE – ST MALO

LAT 48°38'N   LONG 2°02'W

TIMES AND HEIGHTS OF HIGH AND LOW WATERS

Dates in amber are **SPRINGS**
Dates in yellow are **NEAPS**

2007

JANUARY

Time m	Time m
1 0458 10.4 / 1149 3.0 / M 1731 10.5	**16** 0447 9.5 / 1126 3.8 / TU 1712 9.6 / 2354 3.7
2 0016 2.9 / 0555 10.5 / TU 1247 2.5 / 1826 10.9	**17** 0540 10.2 / 1223 3.2 / W 1805 10.3
3 0110 2.6 / 0644 11.3 / W 1339 2.2 / ○ 1915 11.2	**18** 0050 3.1 / 0627 10.9 / TH 1315 2.5 / 1853 10.9
4 0158 2.4 / 0729 11.6 / TH 1425 2.0 / 1958 11.3	**19** 0139 2.5 / 0712 11.5 / F 1405 2.0 / ● 1938 11.4
5 0241 2.3 / 0810 11.6 / F 1507 2.0 / 2038 11.3	**20** 0228 2.0 / 0755 11.9 / SA 1454 1.6 / 2021 11.7
6 0320 2.3 / 0848 11.6 / SA 1545 2.1 / 2114 11.1	**21** 0314 1.7 / 0838 12.2 / SU 1540 1.3 / 2103 11.9
7 0357 2.4 / 0924 11.4 / SU 1621 2.4 / 2149 10.9	**22** 0358 1.5 / 0921 12.3 / M 1624 1.2 / 2144 11.9
8 0430 2.7 / 0958 11.0 / M 1653 2.7 / 2222 10.5	**23** 0440 1.6 / 1002 12.2 / TU 1705 1.5 / 2225 11.6
9 0501 3.1 / 1031 10.5 / TU 1723 3.2 / 2254 10.0	**24** 0520 2.0 / 1044 11.7 / W 1746 1.9 / 2306 11.1
10 0533 3.6 / 1103 10.0 / W 1753 3.6 / 2327 9.6	**25** 0600 2.5 / 1128 11.1 / TH 1827 2.6 / ◐ 2350 10.5
11 0607 4.0 / 1139 9.5 / TH 1829 4.1 / ◑	**26** 0644 3.2 / 1216 10.3 / F 1914 3.3
12 0006 9.1 / 0650 4.4 / F 1225 9.0 / 1915 4.5	**27** 0045 9.8 / 0740 3.8 / SA 1319 9.6 / 2014 3.9
13 0105 8.7 / 0747 4.7 / SA 1332 8.7 / 2019 4.7	**28** 0157 9.3 / 0855 4.2 / SU 1445 9.2 / 2132 4.2
14 0225 8.6 / 0902 4.8 / SU 1456 8.6 / 2140 4.7	**29** 0329 9.3 / 1021 4.1 / M 1618 9.3 / 2254 4.0
15 0344 8.9 / 1021 4.4 / M 1611 9.0 / 2254 4.3	**30** 0450 9.7 / 1139 3.5 / TU 1729 9.9
	31 0005 3.5 / 0550 10.4 / W 1242 2.9 / 1824 10.5

FEBRUARY

Time m	Time m
1 0104 2.9 / 0639 11.0 / TH 1333 2.4 / 1909 11.0	**16** 0035 3.1 / 0613 10.8 / F 1302 2.4 / 1840 10.9
2 0151 2.4 / 0721 11.4 / F 1417 2.0 / ○ 1948 11.3	**17** 0129 2.2 / 0700 11.7 / SA 1355 1.5 / ● 1925 11.7
3 0232 2.1 / 0758 11.7 / SA 1456 1.8 / 2023 11.5	**18** 0219 1.5 / 0744 12.4 / SU 1444 0.9 / 2008 12.3
4 0308 1.9 / 0832 11.8 / SU 1530 1.7 / 2055 11.5	**19** 0305 1.0 / 0826 12.8 / M 1529 0.5 / 2049 12.6
5 0341 1.9 / 0904 11.7 / M 1601 1.8 / 2125 11.4	**20** 0348 0.7 / 0907 13.0 / TU 1610 0.5 / 2127 12.5
6 0409 2.1 / 0934 11.5 / TU 1627 2.1 / 2153 11.1	**21** 0427 0.9 / 0946 12.8 / W 1649 0.8 / 2205 12.2
7 0434 2.4 / 1000 11.1 / W 1650 2.5 / 2218 10.7	**22** 0503 1.4 / 1024 12.2 / TH 1724 1.6 / 2241 11.6
8 0458 2.9 / 1025 10.6 / TH 1713 3.0 / 2243 10.2	**23** 0539 2.2 / 1103 11.3 / F 1800 2.5 / 2320 10.7
9 0524 3.4 / 1052 10.0 / F 1738 3.6 / 2309 9.6	**24** 0616 3.1 / 1145 10.2 / SA 1840 3.5 / ◑
10 0555 4.0 / 1123 9.4 / SA 1811 4.2 / ◑ 2345 9.0	**25** 0005 9.8 / 0706 4.0 / SU 1244 9.2 / 1937 4.4
11 0638 4.5 / 1209 8.7 / SU 1901 4.8	**26** 0120 8.9 / 0824 4.6 / M 1427 8.5 / 2107 4.8
12 0049 8.4 / 0745 5.0 / M 1338 8.2 / 2023 5.1	**27** 0316 8.8 / 1010 4.5 / TU 1617 8.8 / 2246 4.5
13 0249 8.3 / 0928 4.9 / TU 1535 8.4 / 2214 4.8	**28** 0444 9.4 / 1135 3.8 / W 1725 9.6 / 2359 3.7
14 0420 8.9 / 1058 4.2 / W 1653 9.1 / 2332 4.0	
15 0522 9.8 / 1204 3.3 / TH 1751 10.0	

MARCH

Time m	Time m
1 0541 10.2 / 1234 3.0 / TH 1813 10.4	**16** 0457 9.8 / 1142 3.2 / F 1728 10.1
2 0054 2.9 / 0625 10.9 / F 1320 2.4 / 1852 11.0	**17** 0013 3.0 / 0550 10.9 / SA 1241 2.2 / 1817 11.1
3 0136 2.3 / 0703 11.4 / SA 1359 2.0 / 1927 11.4	**18** 0109 2.0 / 0638 11.7 / SU 1334 1.2 / 1903 12.0
4 0213 1.9 / 0737 11.7 / SU 1434 1.7 / ○ 1958 11.6	**19** 0159 1.1 / 0723 12.7 / M 1423 0.6 / ● 1945 12.6
5 0246 1.7 / 0808 11.9 / M 1504 1.6 / 2028 11.7	**20** 0245 0.6 / 0805 13.2 / TU 1508 0.2 / 2026 12.9
6 0315 1.7 / 0838 11.9 / TU 1532 1.6 / 2055 11.7	**21** 0327 0.4 / 0846 13.2 / W 1548 0.3 / 2104 12.9
7 0341 1.8 / 0904 11.7 / W 1555 1.9 / 2120 11.5	**22** 0406 0.7 / 0924 12.9 / TH 1625 0.8 / 2140 12.4
8 0404 2.1 / 0929 11.4 / TH 1616 2.2 / 2143 11.1	**23** 0441 1.3 / 1002 12.1 / F 1659 1.7 / 2216 11.7
9 0426 2.5 / 0951 10.9 / F 1637 2.8 / 2205 10.6	**24** 0515 2.2 / 1039 11.1 / SA 1732 2.8 / 2253 10.8
10 0449 3.1 / 1015 10.3 / SA 1659 3.4 / 2228 10.0	**25** 0551 3.2 / 1122 10.0 / SU 1810 3.9 / ◑ 2338 9.7
11 0516 3.7 / 1042 9.6 / SU 1727 4.1 / 2257 9.3	**26** 0639 4.2 / 1222 8.9 / M 1908 4.8
12 0554 4.3 / 1121 8.9 / M 1810 4.7 / ◑ 2344 8.6	**27** 0057 8.8 / 0800 4.8 / TU 1416 8.4 / 2049 5.2
13 0655 4.9 / 1234 8.2 / TU 1926 5.3	**28** 0259 8.6 / 0955 4.7 / W 1602 8.8 / 2231 4.7
14 0150 8.2 / 0839 5.0 / W 1502 8.2 / 2136 5.1	**29** 0423 9.3 / 1115 4.0 / TH 1703 9.6 / 2337 3.8
15 0349 8.7 / 1030 4.3 / TH 1629 9.0 / 2307 4.2	**30** 0516 10.1 / 1208 3.2 / F 1746 10.3
	31 0027 3.0 / 0558 10.7 / SA 1251 2.6 / 1823 10.9

APRIL

Time m	Time m
1 0106 2.5 / 0634 11.2 / SU 1327 2.2 / 1856 11.4	**16** 0038 2.0 / 0609 11.9 / M 1305 1.3 / 1833 12.1
2 0142 2.1 / 0707 11.6 / M 1400 1.9 / ○ 1926 11.6	**17** 0131 1.2 / 0656 12.6 / TU 1355 0.8 / ● 1917 12.6
3 0213 1.9 / 0738 11.7 / TU 1430 1.8 / 1955 11.7	**18** 0219 0.8 / 0740 13.0 / W 1440 0.6 / 1959 12.8
4 0242 1.8 / 0807 11.8 / W 1457 1.8 / 2022 11.7	**19** 0302 0.7 / 0822 12.9 / TH 1521 0.7 / 2038 12.8
5 0308 1.9 / 0833 11.7 / TH 1521 2.0 / 2048 11.6	**20** 0342 1.0 / 0902 12.5 / F 1558 1.3 / 2116 12.3
6 0333 2.1 / 0858 11.4 / F 1544 2.3 / 2111 11.3	**21** 0419 1.6 / 0942 11.8 / SA 1634 2.1 / 2154 11.6
7 0358 2.4 / 0923 11.0 / SA 1607 2.8 / 2135 10.8	**22** 0455 2.4 / 1022 10.9 / SU 1709 3.1 / 2235 10.7
8 0424 2.9 / 0949 10.5 / SU 1632 3.4 / 2201 10.3	**23** 0533 3.3 / 1108 9.9 / M 1750 4.0 / 2324 9.8
9 0453 3.5 / 1020 9.8 / M 1702 4.0 / 2234 9.6	**24** 0622 4.2 / 1211 9.0 / TU 1849 4.8 / ◐
10 0533 4.1 / 1102 9.1 / TU 1748 4.7 / 2326 8.9	**25** 0041 9.0 / 0737 4.7 / W 1348 8.6 / 2020 5.1
11 0633 4.7 / 1218 8.4 / W 1904 5.2	**26** 0221 8.8 / 0914 4.7 / TH 1520 8.8 / 2150 4.7
12 0120 8.5 / 0810 4.8 / TH 1428 8.4 / 2103 5.0	**27** 0340 9.2 / 1029 4.2 / F 1621 9.5 / 2253 4.0
13 0311 9.0 / 0956 4.2 / F 1554 9.2 / 2233 4.0	**28** 0435 9.8 / 1123 3.5 / SA 1706 10.1 / 2341 3.4
14 0422 10.0 / 1110 3.1 / SA 1655 10.3 / 2338 2.9	**29** 0518 10.4 / 1206 3.0 / SU 1744 10.6
15 0519 11.0 / 1210 2.1 / SU 1747 11.3	**30** 0024 2.9 / 0556 10.8 / M 1245 2.6 / 1818 11.1

Chart Datum: 6·29 metres below IGN Datum

TIDES

TIDES

FRANCE – ST MALO

LAT 48°38'N   LONG 2°02'W

TIMES AND HEIGHTS OF HIGH AND LOW WATERS

Dates in amber are **SPRINGS**
Dates in yellow are **NEAPS**

2007

MAY

Date	Time m	Time m	Time m	Time m
1 TU	0101 2.6	0631 11.1	1320 2.4	1850 11.3
16 W	0059 1.7	0628 12.1	1324 1.4	1849 12.2 ●
2 W ○	0135 2.3	0704 11.3	1352 2.3	1921 11.5
17 TH	0150 1.4	0716 12.3	1412 1.3	1934 12.4
3 TH	0207 2.2	0735 11.4	1422 2.2	1951 11.6
18 F	0237 1.3	0801 12.3	1455 1.4	2017 12.4
4 F	0238 2.2	0805 11.4	1450 2.3	2019 11.5
19 SA	0320 1.4	0845 12.0	1536 1.8	2058 12.0
5 SA	0308 2.3	0834 11.2	1519 2.5	2046 11.3
20 SU	0401 1.9	0928 11.4	1615 2.4	2140 11.5
6 SU	0338 2.5	0904 11.0	1548 2.9	2116 11.0
21 M	0440 2.5	1012 10.8	1654 3.1	2224 10.8
7 M	0410 2.9	0937 10.5	1620 3.4	2151 10.5
22 TU	0522 3.2	1059 10.0	1738 3.8	2313 10.1
8 TU	0446 3.4	1017 10.0	1658 3.9	2233 9.9
23 W ◑	0608 3.8	1153 9.4	1830 4.4	
9 W	0530 3.8	1108 9.4	1748 4.4	2334 9.4
24 TH	0013 9.5	0706 4.3	1300 9.0	1936 4.7
10 TH ◑	0631 4.2	1221 9.0	1901 4.7	
25 F	0124 9.1	0814 4.5	1414 9.0	2047 4.6
11 F	0102 9.2	0752 4.2	1352 9.0	2033 4.5
26 SA	0236 9.2	0922 4.3	1520 9.2	2151 4.3
12 SA	0230 9.5	0919 3.8	1511 9.4	2154 3.8
27 SU	0337 9.4	1021 4.0	1613 9.7	2245 3.9
13 SU	0342 10.2	1031 3.1	1616 10.3	2300 3.0
28 M	0428 9.8	1112 3.6	1658 10.1	2333 3.5
14 M	0442 10.9	1134 2.3	1712 11.1	
29 TU	0513 10.2	1157 3.3	1738 10.5	
15 TU	0001 2.2	0537 11.6	1231 1.7	1802 11.8
30 W	0018 3.1	0554 10.5	1239 3.0	1815 10.9
31 TH	0058 2.8	0632 10.8	1317 2.8	1851 11.1

JUNE

Date	Time m	Time m	Time m	Time m
1 F ○	0136 2.6	0709 11.0	1353 2.7	1925 11.3
16 SA	0219 1.8	0750 11.6	1437 2.0	2004 11.9
2 SA	0213 2.5	0744 11.1	1428 2.6	1959 11.4
17 SU	0305 1.8	0836 11.5	1521 2.1	2048 11.8
3 SU	0250 2.4	0819 11.1	1503 2.7	2033 11.3
18 M	0349 2.0	0920 11.3	1603 2.4	2131 11.5
4 M	0328 2.5	0856 11.0	1541 2.9	2111 11.2
19 TU	0430 2.3	1002 10.9	1643 2.8	2212 11.1
5 TU	0407 2.7	0937 10.7	1620 3.1	2152 10.9
20 W	0509 2.8	1043 10.5	1723 3.3	2254 10.6
6 W	0449 2.9	1022 10.4	1704 3.4	2240 10.5
21 TH	0548 3.3	1124 10.0	1803 3.7	2337 10.0
7 TH	0536 3.2	1112 10.1	1754 3.7	2335 10.1
22 F ◑	0628 3.7	1208 9.6	1847 4.1	
8 F	0630 3.5	1210 9.8	1854 3.9	
23 SA	0025 9.5	0714 4.1	1300 9.2	1940 4.4
9 SA	0040 9.9	0733 3.6	1317 9.7	2003 3.9
24 SU	0121 9.2	0808 4.3	1402 9.1	2040 4.5
10 SU	0151 10.0	0842 3.5	1428 9.8	2115 3.7
25 M	0226 9.1	0911 4.4	1508 9.2	2144 4.4
11 M	0301 10.3	0952 3.2	1536 10.2	2224 3.2
26 TU	0331 9.2	1015 4.2	1609 9.5	2244 4.1
12 TU	0408 10.6	1059 2.8	1639 10.7	2329 2.7
27 W	0429 9.5	1113 3.9	1700 9.9	2338 3.7
13 W	0509 11.0	1200 2.4	1736 11.2	
28 TH	0520 9.9	1204 3.6	1746 10.4	
14 TH	0032 2.3	0607 11.3	1257 2.1	1829 11.6
29 F	0028 3.2	0607 10.3	1250 3.2	1829 10.8
15 F ●	0128 2.0	0700 11.6	1349 2.0	1918 11.9
30 SA ○	0113 2.9	0651 10.7	1333 2.9	1909 11.1

JULY

Date	Time m	Time m	Time m	Time m
1 SU	0157 2.6	0732 10.9	1949 11.4	
16 M	0256 1.9	0827 11.5	1511 2.1	2038 11.9
2 M	0241 2.3	0813 11.2	1458 2.5	2028 11.6
17 TU	0338 1.9	0906 11.5	1551 2.1	2116 11.8
3 TU	0325 2.1	0853 11.3	1540 2.4	2109 11.6
18 W	0415 2.0	0942 11.3	1627 2.3	2151 11.5
4 W	0408 2.1	0935 11.3	1623 2.4	2151 11.5
19 TH	0449 2.3	1016 11.0	1659 2.7	2225 11.1
5 TH	0451 2.2	1018 11.1	1706 2.6	2235 11.3
20 F	0518 2.8	1048 10.6	1729 3.2	2257 10.5
6 F	0534 2.4	1102 10.8	1750 2.9	2321 10.9
21 SA	0546 3.3	1120 10.1	1800 3.7	2331 9.9
7 SA ◑	0619 2.8	1149 10.5	1838 3.3	
22 SU ◑	0617 3.8	1156 9.5	1837 4.2	
8 SU	0013 10.5	0708 3.1	1243 10.1	1934 3.6
23 M	0012 9.3	0657 4.3	1243 9.1	1927 4.7
9 M	0114 10.1	0807 3.4	1347 9.9	2041 3.8
24 TU	0110 8.8	0753 4.7	1355 8.7	2038 4.9
10 TU	0226 9.9	0917 3.6	1502 9.9	2155 3.7
25 W	0231 8.6	0913 4.9	1520 8.8	2159 4.7
11 W	0343 10.0	1030 3.5	1617 10.2	2308 3.3
26 TH	0351 8.9	1034 4.6	1631 9.3	2308 4.2
12 TH	0456 10.3	1140 3.1	1724 10.7	
27 F	0456 9.4	1138 4.1	1726 9.9	
13 F	0017 2.8	0601 10.7	1242 2.8	1822 11.2
28 SA	0005 3.5	0550 10.0	1232 3.5	1813 10.6
14 SA ●	0117 2.4	0656 11.1	1338 2.4	1912 11.6
29 SU	0058 2.9	0638 10.6	1321 2.9	1857 11.2
15 SU	0210 2.0	0744 11.4	1427 2.2	1956 11.8
30 M ○	0147 2.3	0724 11.1	1408 2.4	1939 11.7
31 TU	0235 1.9	0803 11.6	1453 2.0	2019 12.1

AUGUST

Date	Time m	Time m	Time m	Time m
1 W	0320 1.5	0844 11.9	1536 1.7	2100 12.3
16 TH	0351 1.8	0914 11.7	1601 2.0	2123 11.8
2 TH	0402 1.4	0924 12.0	1617 1.6	2139 12.3
17 F	0418 2.0	0943 11.4	1627 2.3	2151 11.4
3 F	0442 1.4	1003 11.8	1656 1.8	2219 12.0
18 SA	0441 2.5	1009 11.0	1651 2.8	2217 10.8
4 SA	0520 1.8	1042 11.5	1735 2.3	2300 11.5
19 SU	0502 3.0	1034 10.4	1714 3.4	2242 10.2
5 SU ◑	0558 2.4	1123 10.9	1816 2.9	2344 10.8
20 M ◑	0526 3.6	1100 9.8	1743 4.1	2312 9.5
6 M	0640 3.1	1210 10.3	1905 3.6	
21 TU	0556 4.3	1133 9.2	1823 4.7	2354 8.8
7 TU	0042 10.0	0734 3.8	1312 9.7	2012 4.1
22 W	0641 4.9	1231 8.5	1926 5.2	
8 W	0200 9.4	0848 4.2	1440 9.4	2138 4.2
23 TH	0124 8.2	0758 5.4	1432 8.3	2112 5.2
9 TH	0337 9.3	1016 4.2	1613 9.7	2302 3.7
24 F	0321 8.4	1000 5.2	1606 8.9	2244 4.6
10 F	0459 9.8	1135 3.7	1724 10.4	
25 SA	0437 9.1	1118 4.4	1706 9.7	2346 3.7
11 SA	0015 3.1	0600 10.5	1239 3.0	1817 11.1
26 SU	0532 10.0	1214 3.5	1754 10.7	
12 SU	0112 2.5	0649 11.1	1332 2.4	1903 11.6
27 M	0042 2.7	0620 10.8	1305 2.6	1839 11.5
13 M ●	0201 2.0	0732 11.5	1416 2.0	1943 11.9
28 TU ○	0132 2.0	0703 11.5	1353 1.9	1921 12.2
14 TU	0243 1.8	0809 11.7	1456 1.8	2019 12.1
29 W	0220 1.4	0745 12.1	1438 1.4	2002 12.7
15 W	0319 1.7	0843 11.8	1530 1.8	2052 12.0
30 TH	0304 1.0	0824 12.5	1521 1.1	2041 12.9
31 F	0345 0.8	0903 12.6	1601 1.1	2120 12.8

Chart Datum: 6·29 metres below IGN Datum

FRANCE – ST MALO

LAT 48°38'N   LONG 2°02'W

TIMES AND HEIGHTS OF HIGH AND LOW WATERS

2007

SEPTEMBER		OCTOBER		NOVEMBER		DECEMBER	
Time m	Time m	Time m	Time m	Time m	Time m	Time m	Time m

SEPTEMBER

1 0423 1.1 / 0940 12.4 / SA 1638 1.5 / 2157 12.4
16 0402 2.5 / 0930 11.2 / SU 1613 2.7 / 2138 11.0

2 0458 1.6 / 1017 11.9 / SU 1714 2.1 / 2236 11.6
17 0422 3.0 / 0951 10.7 / M 1636 3.3 / 2201 10.4

3 0533 2.5 / 1055 11.1 / M 1752 3.0 / 2318 10.6
18 0443 3.6 / 1014 10.1 / TU 1702 4.0 / 2226 9.7

4 0612 3.4 / 1140 10.2 / TU 1839 3.9 ☽
19 0510 4.3 / 1041 9.4 / W 1737 4.6 / ☽ 2302 8.9

5 0015 9.6 / 0705 4.3 / W 1245 9.3 / 1951 4.6
20 0550 5.0 / 1126 8.7 / TH 1834 5.2

6 0150 8.9 / 0831 4.9 / TH 1434 9.0 / 2134 4.6
21 0018 8.2 / 0702 5.6 / F 1335 8.1 / 2018 5.4

7 0343 9.0 / 1017 4.6 / F 1613 9.5 / 2303 3.9
22 0249 8.2 / 0920 5.5 / SA 1533 8.7 / 2213 4.7

8 0457 9.8 / 1134 3.8 / SA 1716 10.4
23 0410 9.0 / 1050 4.5 / SU 1637 9.7 / 2319 3.7

9 0008 3.1 / 0549 10.6 / SU 1230 3.0 / 1804 11.1
24 0505 10.0 / 1148 3.4 / M 1727 10.8

10 0059 2.4 / 0631 11.2 / M 1315 2.3 / 1844 11.7
25 0016 2.6 / 0552 11.0 / TU 1239 2.4 / 1812 11.7

11 0141 2.0 / 0708 11.6 / TU 1355 2.0 / ● 1920 12.0
26 0107 1.7 / 0636 11.9 / W 1328 1.6 / ○ 1855 12.5

12 0217 1.8 / 0742 11.9 / W 1430 1.8 / 1952 12.1
27 0155 1.1 / 0718 12.5 / TH 1414 1.1 / 1937 13.0

13 0249 1.7 / 0812 11.9 / TH 1501 1.8 / 2022 12.1
28 0239 0.8 / 0758 12.8 / F 1458 0.9 / 2017 13.2

14 0317 1.8 / 0841 11.8 / F 1528 1.9 / 2050 11.9
29 0320 0.8 / 0837 12.9 / SA 1538 1.0 / 2056 12.9

15 0341 2.1 / 0906 11.6 / SA 1552 2.3 / 2115 11.5
30 0358 1.1 / 0914 12.6 / SU 1616 1.4 / 2135 12.4

OCTOBER

1 0433 1.8 / 0952 12.0 / M 1653 2.2 / 2214 11.5
16 0350 3.1 / 0917 10.9 / TU 1608 3.3 / 2131 10.5

2 0508 2.8 / 1031 11.1 / TU 1731 3.2 / 2257 10.4
17 0413 3.7 / 0943 10.3 / W 1636 3.8 / 2200 9.8

3 0547 3.8 / 1117 10.1 / W 1819 4.1 / ☽ 2357 9.3
18 0441 4.3 / 1014 9.7 / TH 1713 4.4 / 2239 9.1

4 0644 4.8 / 1230 9.2 / TH 1936 4.8
19 0523 4.9 / 1101 9.0 / F 1808 5.0 / ☽ 2348 8.4

5 0146 8.7 / 0821 5.2 / F 1426 8.9 / 2126 4.8
20 0634 5.4 / 1244 8.4 / SA 1938 5.2

6 0333 9.0 / 1007 4.7 / SA 1556 9.5 / 2248 4.0
21 0202 8.4 / 0831 5.3 / SU 1445 8.8 / 2127 4.7

7 0438 9.8 / 1115 3.9 / SU 1653 10.3 / 2344 3.2
22 0328 9.1 / 1007 4.5 / M 1555 9.7 / 2240 3.7

8 0524 10.6 / 1204 3.1 / M 1737 11.0
23 0427 10.1 / 1110 3.4 / TU 1650 10.7 / 2338 2.7

9 0031 2.6 / 0602 11.2 / TU 1246 2.4 / 1815 11.5
24 0517 11.1 / 1205 2.4 / W 1739 11.7

10 0109 2.2 / 0637 11.6 / W 1323 2.2 / 1849 11.8
25 0035 1.8 / 0604 11.9 / TH 1257 1.7 / 1825 12.4

11 0143 2.1 / 0709 11.6 / TH 1356 2.0 / ● 1920 11.9
26 0125 1.2 / 0648 12.5 / F 1346 1.2 / ○ 1910 12.8

12 0213 2.0 / 0738 11.9 / F 1426 2.0 / 1949 11.9
27 0211 1.0 / 0730 12.8 / SA 1432 1.0 / 1953 12.9

13 0240 2.1 / 0805 11.8 / SA 1453 2.1 / 2017 11.7
28 0254 1.1 / 0811 12.8 / SU 1515 1.2 / 2035 12.6

14 0304 2.3 / 0830 11.6 / SU 1518 2.4 / 2042 11.4
29 0333 1.5 / 0851 12.5 / M 1556 1.6 / 2116 12.1

15 0327 2.6 / 0854 11.3 / M 1542 2.8 / 2106 11.0
30 0411 2.2 / 0932 11.9 / TU 1635 2.3 / 2159 11.2

31 0449 3.1 / 1015 11.3 / W 1717 3.2 / 2247 10.2

NOVEMBER

1 0532 4.0 / 1105 10.1 / TH 1807 4.1 / ☽ 2348 9.3
16 0435 4.0 / 1010 10.0 / F 1707 4.0 / 2239 9.5

2 0630 4.7 / 1216 9.3 / F 1918 4.7
17 0520 4.5 / 1101 9.5 / SA 1801 4.4 / ☽ 2341 9.0

3 0120 8.8 / 0756 5.1 / SA 1352 9.0 / 2050 4.7
18 0624 4.8 / 1216 9.1 / SU 1913 4.5

4 0253 9.0 / 0927 4.8 / SU 1515 9.4 / 2207 4.3
19 0110 8.9 / 0750 4.8 / M 1348 9.2 / 2037 4.3

5 0358 9.6 / 1033 4.1 / M 1614 9.9 / 2303 3.7
20 0234 9.3 / 0916 4.3 / TU 1505 9.8 / 2153 3.6

6 0446 10.2 / 1123 3.5 / TU 1700 10.5 / 2348 3.1
21 0342 10.0 / 1027 3.5 / W 1608 10.5 / 2258 2.9

7 0525 10.7 / 1206 3.0 / W 1739 10.9
22 0439 10.8 / 1128 2.7 / TH 1704 11.3 / 2356 2.2

8 0028 2.8 / 0601 11.1 / TH 1244 2.7 / 1815 11.2
23 0531 11.5 / 1226 2.1 / F 1757 11.9

9 0104 2.6 / 0634 11.4 / F 1319 2.5 / 1848 11.4
24 0054 1.7 / 0620 12.1 / SA 1319 1.6 / ○ 1847 12.2

10 0136 2.5 / 0705 11.6 / SA 1351 2.4 / ● 1919 11.4
25 0144 1.5 / 0707 12.4 / SU 1410 1.4 / 1934 12.3

11 0206 2.5 / 0734 11.6 / SU 1422 2.4 / 1949 11.4
26 0231 1.5 / 0752 12.5 / M 1457 1.4 / 2021 12.1

12 0234 2.6 / 0802 11.5 / M 1451 2.5 / 2017 11.2
27 0315 1.8 / 0837 12.3 / TU 1541 1.7 / 2106 11.7

13 0302 2.9 / 0829 11.3 / TU 1521 2.8 / 2046 10.9
28 0357 2.3 / 0921 11.8 / W 1625 2.2 / 2152 11.1

14 0330 3.1 / 0858 11.0 / W 1552 3.1 / 2118 10.5
29 0439 2.9 / 1007 11.1 / TH 1709 2.9 / 2239 10.4

15 0400 3.6 / 0931 10.6 / TH 1626 3.6 / 2154 10.0
30 0523 3.6 / 1055 10.4 / F 1755 3.6 / 2331 9.7

DECEMBER

1 0613 4.2 / 1150 9.8 / SA 1849 4.1 / ☽
16 0522 3.7 / 1058 10.3 / SU 1756 3.5 / 2328 9.8

2 0033 9.2 / 0712 4.6 / SU 1255 9.3 / 1951 4.5
17 0613 3.9 / 1153 9.9 / M 1851 3.7 / ☽

3 0144 9.0 / 0820 4.7 / M 1409 9.2 / 2058 4.5
18 0028 9.5 / 0715 4.1 / TU 1259 9.7 / 1954 3.8

4 0255 9.1 / 0928 4.5 / TU 1516 9.3 / 2201 4.2
19 0139 9.5 / 0827 4.0 / W 1413 9.8 / 2106 3.7

5 0354 9.5 / 1027 4.1 / W 1612 9.7 / 2255 3.9
20 0254 9.8 / 0943 3.7 / TH 1527 10.1 / 2218 3.3

6 0442 10.0 / 1118 3.7 / TH 1659 10.1 / 2342 3.5
21 0403 10.3 / 1054 3.2 / F 1635 10.5 / 2325 2.8

7 0524 10.4 / 1204 3.3 / F 1741 10.4
22 0506 10.9 / 1200 2.6 / SA 1738 11.1

8 0026 3.2 / 0602 10.8 / SA 1245 3.0 / 1820 10.7
23 0029 2.3 / 0603 11.5 / SU 1300 2.0 / 1835 11.5

9 0104 3.0 / 0638 11.1 / SU 1323 2.8 / ● 1856 10.9
24 0126 2.0 / 0655 11.9 / M 1355 1.7 / ○ 1927 11.7

10 0140 2.8 / 0712 11.2 / M 1359 2.6 / 1931 11.0
25 0217 1.8 / 0744 12.1 / TU 1446 1.5 / 2016 11.8

11 0214 2.8 / 0745 11.3 / TU 1435 2.5 / 2005 11.0
26 0305 1.8 / 0830 12.1 / W 1533 1.6 / 2101 11.7

12 0248 2.8 / 0818 11.3 / W 1511 2.6 / 2039 11.0
27 0349 2.0 / 0914 11.9 / TH 1617 1.9 / 2143 11.4

13 0324 2.9 / 0853 11.2 / TH 1548 2.7 / 2116 10.8
28 0430 2.4 / 0956 11.5 / F 1658 2.3 / 2223 10.9

14 0400 3.1 / 0931 11.0 / F 1627 2.9 / 2155 10.5
29 0509 2.8 / 1036 11.0 / SA 1735 2.9 / 2302 10.3

15 0439 3.4 / 1012 10.6 / SA 1709 3.2 / 2238 10.1
30 0546 3.4 / 1116 10.4 / SU 1812 3.5 / 2342 9.8

31 0625 3.9 / 1158 9.7 / 1851 4.0 / ☽

Chart Datum: 6·29 metres below IGN Datum

TIDES

389

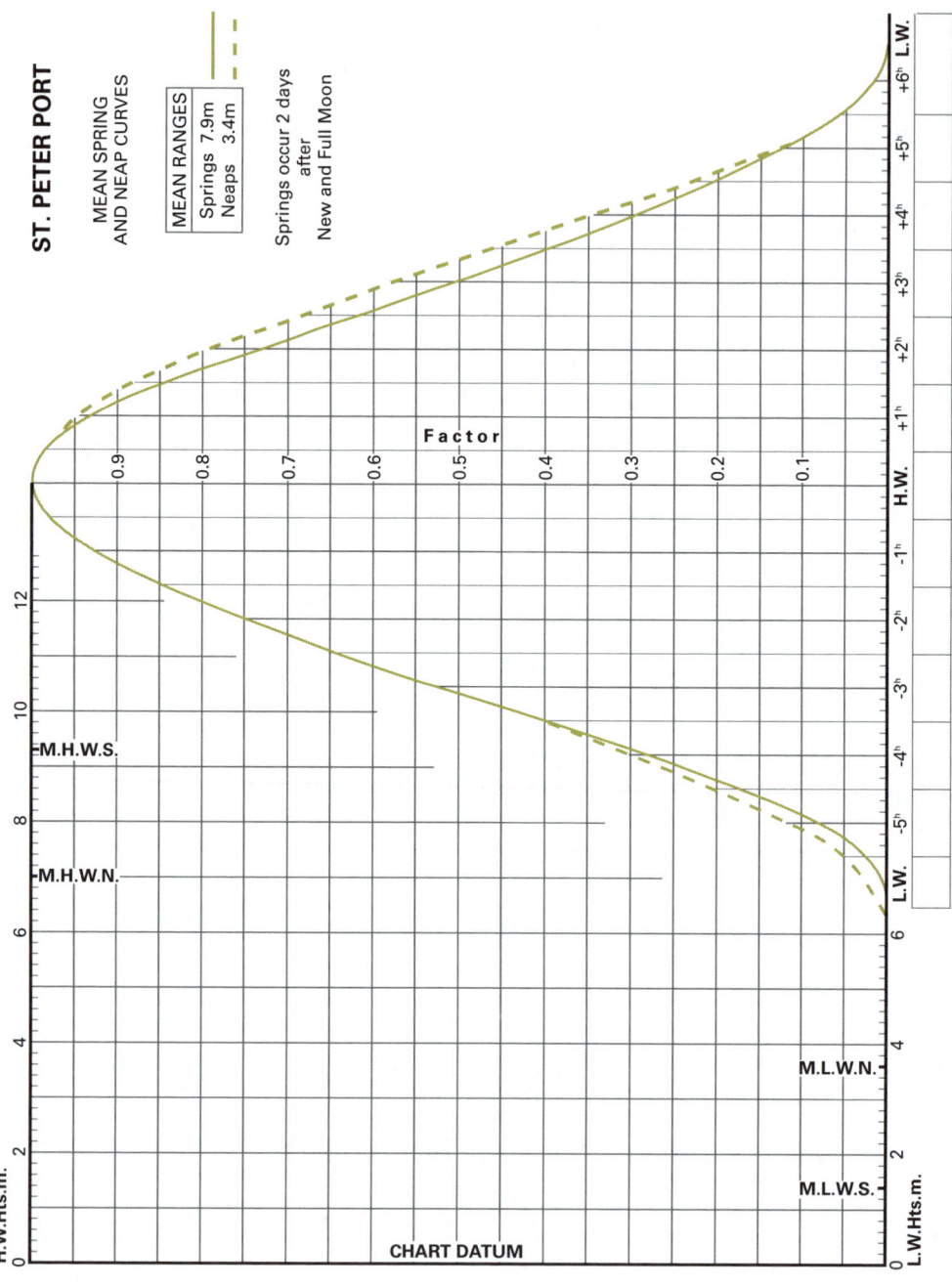

ST. PETER PORT

MEAN SPRING
AND NEAP CURVES

MEAN RANGES
Springs 7.9m
Neaps 3.4m

Springs occur 2 days
after
New and Full Moon

Factor

0.9 0.8 0.7 0.6 0.5 0.4 0.3 0.2 0.1

H.W.Hts.m.

M.H.W.S.

M.H.W.N.

CHART DATUM

L.W. +6ʰ +5ʰ +4ʰ +3ʰ +2ʰ +1ʰ H.W. -1ʰ -2ʰ -3ʰ -4ʰ -5ʰ L.W.

M.L.W.N.

M.L.W.S.

L.W.Hts.m.

TIME ZONE (UT)
For Summer Time add ONE hour in **non-shaded areas**

CHANNEL ISLES – ST PETER PORT

LAT 49°27'N   LONG 2°31'W

TIMES AND HEIGHTS OF HIGH AND LOW WATERS

Dates in amber are **SPRINGS**
Dates in yellow are **NEAPS**

2007

JANUARY

Day	Time	m	Day	Time	m
1 M	0419 / 1051 / 1650 / 2314	8.0 / 2.6 / 8.1 / 2.5	**16** TU	0405 / 1027 / 1631 / 2251	7.4 / 3.2 / 7.4 / 3.1
2 TU	0515 / 1146 / 1745	8.4 / 2.2 / 8.3	**17** W	0459 / 1122 / 1725 / 2344	7.9 / 2.7 / 7.8 / 2.6
3 W	0006 / 0604 / 1237 / 1835	2.2 / 8.7 / 1.9 / 8.5	**18** TH	0547 / 1213 / 1814	8.4 / 2.2 / 8.3
4 TH	0054 / 0650 / 1324 / 1920	2.0 / 8.9 / 1.7 / 8.7	**19** F	0032 / 0633 / 1301 / 1900	2.1 / 8.8 / 1.7 / 8.7
5 F	0138 / 0733 / 1406 / 2002	1.9 / 9.0 / 1.7 / 8.7	**20** SA	0118 / 0717 / 1346 / 1943	1.7 / 9.2 / 1.3 / 9.0
6 SA	0217 / 0812 / 1445 / 2039	1.9 / 8.9 / 1.8 / 8.5	**21** SU	0202 / 0800 / 1429 / 2025	1.5 / 9.4 / 1.1 / 9.1
7 SU	0253 / 0848 / 1520 / 2113	2.1 / 8.8 / 2.0 / 8.3	**22** M	0243 / 0841 / 1510 / 2105	1.3 / 9.5 / 1.1 / 9.1
8 M	0326 / 0922 / 1552 / 2145	2.4 / 8.5 / 2.3 / 8.0	**23** TU	0323 / 0922 / 1549 / 2144	1.4 / 9.4 / 1.2 / 8.9
9 TU	0357 / 0955 / 1623 / 2217	2.7 / 8.1 / 2.7 / 7.7	**24** W	0402 / 1003 / 1629 / 2225	1.7 / 9.0 / 1.6 / 8.5
10 W	0430 / 1029 / 1656 / 2252	3.0 / 7.7 / 3.1 / 7.3	**25** TH	0443 / 1047 / 1712 / 2310	2.1 / 8.5 / 2.2 / 8.0
11 TH	0506 / 1107 / 1733 / 2333	3.4 / 7.3 / 3.4 / 7.0	**26** F	0531 / 1138 / 1802	2.7 / 7.9 / 2.8
12 F	0553 / 1155 / 1823	3.7 / 7.0 / 3.7	**27** SA	0005 / 0630 / 1244 / 1907	7.5 / 3.2 / 7.3 / 3.3
13 SA	0029 / 0656 / 1300 / 1929	6.8 / 3.9 / 6.7 / 3.9	**28** SU	0120 / 0757 / 1411 / 2037	7.1 / 3.5 / 7.0 / 3.6
14 SU	0146 / 0812 / 1419 / 2043	6.7 / 3.9 / 6.7 / 3.8	**29** M	0253 / 0934 / 1540 / 2204	7.1 / 3.4 / 7.1 / 3.4
15 M	0302 / 0924 / 1530 / 2152	6.9 / 3.6 / 7.0 / 3.5	**30** TU	0412 / 1047 / 1648 / 2309	7.5 / 3.0 / 7.5 / 3.0
			31 W	0510 / 1144 / 1742	8.0 / 2.5 / 8.0

FEBRUARY

Day	Time	m	Day	Time	m
1 TH	0001 / 0558 / 1232 / 1827	2.5 / 8.4 / 2.0 / 8.4	**16** F	0533 / 1159 / 1801	8.3 / 2.0 / 8.4
2 F	0046 / 0641 / 1314 / 1908	2.1 / 8.8 / 1.7 / 8.7	**17** SA	0019 / 0619 / 1247 / 1846	1.9 / 9.0 / 1.3 / 9.0
3 SA	0126 / 0720 / 1352 / 1945	1.8 / 9.0 / 1.5 / 8.8	**18** SU	0105 / 0703 / 1331 / 1928	1.3 / 9.6 / 0.8 / 9.4
4 SU	0202 / 0756 / 1426 / 2018	1.6 / 9.1 / 1.4 / 8.8	**19** M	0148 / 0745 / 1412 / 2008	0.8 / 9.9 / 0.5 / 9.7
5 M	0233 / 0828 / 1456 / 2048	1.6 / 9.0 / 1.6 / 8.7	**20** TU	0228 / 0825 / 1451 / 2046	0.6 / 10.0 / 0.4 / 9.7
6 TU	0301 / 0857 / 1522 / 2115	1.8 / 8.8 / 1.8 / 8.4	**21** W	0306 / 0903 / 1528 / 2123	0.7 / 9.8 / 0.7 / 9.4
7 W	0328 / 0924 / 1547 / 2141	2.1 / 8.5 / 2.2 / 8.1	**22** TH	0342 / 0942 / 1604 / 2200	1.1 / 9.3 / 1.3 / 8.8
8 TH	0353 / 0951 / 1611 / 2207	2.5 / 8.0 / 2.6 / 7.7	**23** F	0419 / 1021 / 1642 / 2239	1.8 / 8.6 / 2.1 / 8.1
9 F	0419 / 1020 / 1637 / 2236	2.9 / 7.6 / 3.1 / 7.3	**24** SA	0500 / 1107 / 1727 / 2327	2.5 / 7.8 / 2.9 / 7.4
10 SA	0451 / 1055 / 1713 / 2316	3.3 / 7.1 / 3.5 / 6.9	**25** SU	0556 / 1210 / 1830	3.3 / 7.0 / 3.7
11 SU	0539 / 1146 / 1808	3.8 / 6.7 / 3.9	**26** M	0042 / 0731 / 1358 / 2020	6.8 / 3.9 / 6.5 / 4.0
12 M	0019 / 0700 / 1310 / 1941	6.6 / 4.1 / 6.4 / 4.1	**27** TU	0244 / 0934 / 1541 / 2202	6.7 / 3.7 / 6.8 / 3.7
13 TU	0204 / 0842 / 1455 / 2117	6.5 / 3.9 / 6.6 / 3.9	**28** W	0407 / 1044 / 1643 / 2302	7.2 / 3.1 / 7.3 / 3.1
14 W	0337 / 1002 / 1613 / 2230	7.0 / 3.4 / 7.1 / 3.3			
15 TH	0441 / 1105 / 1711 / 2329	7.6 / 2.7 / 7.7 / 2.6			

MARCH

Day	Time	m	Day	Time	m
1 TH	0500 / 1133 / 1729 / 2348	7.8 / 2.5 / 7.9 / 2.5	**16** F	0418 / 1043 / 1650 / 2307	7.7 / 2.5 / 7.9 / 2.4
2 F	0544 / 1215 / 1809	8.4 / 2.0 / 8.4	**17** SA	0510 / 1136 / 1738 / 2357	8.5 / 1.7 / 8.6 / 1.6
3 SA	0028 / 0622 / 1252 / 1845	2.0 / 8.8 / 1.6 / 8.8	**18** SU	0557 / 1223 / 1823	9.2 / 0.9 / 9.3
4 SU	0104 / 0658 / 1327 / 1919	1.6 / 9.1 / 1.3 / 9.0	**19** M	0042 / 0640 / 1307 / 1904	0.9 / 9.8 / 0.4 / 9.7
5 M	0137 / 0730 / 1358 / 1950	1.4 / 9.2 / 1.3 / 9.0	**20** TU	0126 / 0722 / 1348 / 1944	0.5 / 10.1 / 0.2 / 9.9
6 TU	0206 / 0800 / 1425 / 2018	1.4 / 9.1 / 1.4 / 8.9	**21** W	0206 / 0803 / 1427 / 2022	0.3 / 10.2 / 0.3 / 9.9
7 W	0232 / 0828 / 1449 / 2043	1.5 / 8.9 / 1.6 / 8.7	**22** TH	0244 / 0842 / 1504 / 2059	0.5 / 9.9 / 0.7 / 9.5
8 TH	0256 / 0853 / 1511 / 2106	1.8 / 8.6 / 2.0 / 8.4	**23** F	0321 / 0920 / 1540 / 2135	1.0 / 9.3 / 1.4 / 8.9
9 F	0319 / 0917 / 1532 / 2129	2.2 / 8.2 / 2.5 / 8.0	**24** SA	0358 / 0959 / 1617 / 2214	1.7 / 8.4 / 2.2 / 8.1
10 SA	0342 / 0942 / 1556 / 2155	2.4 / 7.8 / 2.9 / 7.6	**25** SU	0440 / 1045 / 1702 / 2301	2.6 / 7.5 / 3.2 / 7.3
11 SU	0410 / 1014 / 1627 / 2231	3.1 / 7.3 / 3.4 / 7.1	**26** M	0537 / 1151 / 1809	3.4 / 6.7 / 3.9
12 M	0452 / 1101 / 1717 / 2329	3.6 / 6.8 / 3.9 / 6.7	**27** TU	0019 / 0722 / 1353 / 2009	6.6 / 3.9 / 6.4 / 4.2
13 TU	0605 / 1223 / 1849	4.0 / 6.4 / 4.2	**28** W	0228 / 0921 / 1525 / 2145	6.6 / 3.7 / 6.7 / 3.7
14 W	0111 / 0809 / 1426 / 2049	6.5 / 4.0 / 6.5 / 4.0	**29** TH	0345 / 1022 / 1620 / 2239	7.1 / 3.1 / 7.3 / 3.1
15 TH	0308 / 0939 / 1553 / 2208	6.9 / 3.3 / 7.1 / 3.2	**30** F	0435 / 1107 / 1703 / 2321	7.7 / 2.5 / 7.9 / 2.5
			31 SA	0516 / 1145 / 1740 / 2358	8.2 / 2.0 / 8.4 / 2.0

APRIL

Day	Time	m	Day	Time	m
1 SU	0553 / 1220 / 1814	8.7 / 1.6 / 8.7	**16** M	0527 / 1153 / 1753	9.2 / 0.9 / 9.3
2 M	0033 / 0627 / 1254 / 1846	1.6 / 8.9 / 1.4 / 8.9	**17** TU	0015 / 0612 / 1239 / 1836	0.9 / 9.7 / 0.5 / 9.7
3 TU	0105 / 0659 / 1323 / 1917	1.4 / 9.0 / 1.4 / 9.0	**18** W	0100 / 0657 / 1322 / 1918	0.5 / 9.9 / 0.4 / 9.9
4 W	0134 / 0729 / 1350 / 1945	1.4 / 9.0 / 1.5 / 8.9	**19** TH	0143 / 0740 / 1403 / 1958	0.4 / 9.9 / 0.5 / 9.8
5 TH	0201 / 0757 / 1415 / 2011	1.5 / 8.8 / 1.7 / 8.7	**20** F	0224 / 0821 / 1443 / 2037	0.7 / 9.5 / 1.0 / 9.4
6 F	0226 / 0823 / 1439 / 2035	1.8 / 8.6 / 2.0 / 8.4	**21** SA	0303 / 0902 / 1521 / 2116	1.2 / 9.0 / 1.7 / 8.8
7 SA	0251 / 0848 / 1502 / 2100	2.1 / 8.2 / 2.5 / 8.1	**22** SU	0344 / 0945 / 1601 / 2158	1.9 / 8.2 / 2.5 / 8.1
8 SU	0316 / 0916 / 1528 / 2128	2.5 / 7.8 / 2.9 / 7.7	**23** M	0430 / 1034 / 1649 / 2248	2.7 / 7.4 / 3.3 / 7.4
9 M	0346 / 0951 / 1602 / 2207	3.0 / 7.3 / 3.4 / 7.3	**24** TU	0531 / 1141 / 1756	3.4 / 6.8 / 3.9
10 TU	0431 / 1042 / 1655 / 2309	3.5 / 6.8 / 3.8 / 6.9	**25** W	0001 / 0700 / 1322 / 1934	6.8 / 3.7 / 6.5 / 4.1
11 W	0545 / 1204 / 1825	3.8 / 6.5 / 4.1	**26** TH	0146 / 0838 / 1445 / 2102	6.7 / 3.6 / 6.6 / 3.8
12 TH	0043 / 0741 / 1354 / 2019	6.7 / 3.7 / 6.7 / 3.8	**27** F	0303 / 0940 / 1540 / 2158	7.0 / 3.2 / 7.2 / 3.2
13 F	0229 / 0908 / 1520 / 2137	7.1 / 3.1 / 7.3 / 3.1	**28** SA	0355 / 1026 / 1624 / 2242	7.5 / 2.7 / 7.7 / 2.7
14 SA	0342 / 1011 / 1618 / 2236	7.8 / 2.3 / 8.0 / 2.3	**29** SU	0438 / 1105 / 1701 / 2320	7.9 / 2.3 / 8.1 / 2.3
15 SU	0437 / 1104 / 1707 / 2327	8.5 / 1.5 / 8.7 / 1.5	**30** M	0516 / 1141 / 1737 / 2355	8.3 / 2.0 / 8.5 / 2.0

Chart Datum: 5·06 metres below Ordnance Datum (Local)

TIME ZONE (UT)
For Summer Time add ONE hour in **non-shaded areas**

CHANNEL ISLES – ST PETER PORT
LAT 49°27'N   LONG 2°31'W
TIMES AND HEIGHTS OF HIGH AND LOW WATERS

Dates in amber are **SPRINGS**
Dates in yellow are **NEAPS**

2007

MAY

Time	m		Time	m
1 TU	0551 8.5 / 1215 1.8 / 1811 8.7		**16** W ●	0546 9.2 / 1211 1.0 / 1810 9.4
2 W ○	0028 1.8 / 0625 8.7 / 1247 1.7 / 1843 8.8		**17** TH	0036 1.0 / 0634 9.4 / 1258 1.0 / 1855 9.5
3 TH	0100 1.7 / 0658 8.7 / 1316 1.8 / 1914 8.8		**18** F	0123 0.9 / 0721 9.4 / 1343 1.1 / 1939 9.4
4 F	0131 1.7 / 0729 8.6 / 1345 1.9 / 1943 8.6		**19** SA	0208 1.1 / 0807 9.1 / 1427 1.4 / 2022 9.2
5 SA	0201 1.9 / 0759 8.4 / 1414 2.2 / 2011 8.4		**20** SU	0252 1.4 / 0852 8.7 / 1509 1.9 / 2104 8.7
6 SU	0230 2.2 / 0829 8.1 / 1443 2.5 / 2041 8.2		**21** M	0337 1.9 / 0937 8.1 / 1553 2.5 / 2148 8.2
7 M	0302 2.5 / 0903 7.8 / 1515 2.9 / 2117 7.9		**22** TU	0424 2.5 / 1025 7.6 / 1640 3.1 / 2236 7.6
8 TU	0339 2.9 / 0945 7.4 / 1556 3.3 / 2203 7.5		**23** W ◑	0518 3.0 / 1121 7.1 / 1735 3.5 / 2334 7.2
9 W	0429 3.2 / 1040 7.1 / 1652 3.6 / 2305 7.2		**24** TH	0620 3.4 / 1228 6.8 / 1841 3.8
10 TH ◑	0541 3.4 / 1153 6.9 / 1812 3.7		**25** F	0044 6.9 / 0730 3.5 / 1340 6.8 / 1953 3.7
11 F	0023 7.2 / 0709 3.3 / 1317 7.0 / 1943 3.4		**26** SA	0157 6.9 / 0836 3.4 / 1442 7.0 / 2057 3.5
12 SA	0147 7.4 / 0828 2.8 / 1436 7.5 / 2058 2.9		**27** SU	0258 7.1 / 0930 3.1 / 1532 7.3 / 2149 3.1
13 SU	0300 7.9 / 0933 2.3 / 1538 8.1 / 2201 2.3		**28** M	0348 7.4 / 1015 2.8 / 1616 7.7 / 2233 2.8
14 M	0401 8.4 / 1030 1.7 / 1632 8.6 / 2256 1.7		**29** TU	0432 7.7 / 1056 2.6 / 1656 8.0 / 2313 2.5
15 TU	0455 8.9 / 1122 1.3 / 1722 9.1 / 2347 1.2		**30** W	0513 8.0 / 1134 2.4 / 1735 8.3 / 2352 2.2
			31 TH	0553 8.2 / 1211 2.2 / 1812 8.5

JUNE

Time	m		Time	m
1 F ○	0030 2.1 / 0630 8.3 / 1248 2.1 / 1848 8.5		**16** SA	0111 1.4 / 0711 8.9 / 1331 1.6 / 1927 9.4
2 SA	0107 2.0 / 0707 8.4 / 1324 2.2 / 1923 8.5		**17** SU	0159 1.4 / 0759 8.8 / 1417 1.7 / 2012 9.0
3 SU	0144 2.0 / 0744 8.3 / 1359 2.4 / 1958 8.5		**18** M	0245 1.5 / 0844 8.6 / 1500 1.9 / 2055 8.8
4 M	0221 2.1 / 0821 8.2 / 1436 2.4 / 2035 8.3		**19** TU	0328 1.8 / 0927 8.3 / 1541 2.3 / 2135 8.4
5 TU	0300 2.3 / 0901 8.0 / 1514 2.6 / 2115 8.2		**20** W	0409 2.2 / 1008 7.9 / 1621 2.7 / 2216 8.0
6 W	0342 2.5 / 0945 7.8 / 1558 2.9 / 2202 8.0		**21** TH	0451 2.6 / 1049 7.5 / 1702 3.0 / 2257 7.6
7 TH	0431 2.6 / 1036 7.6 / 1650 3.0 / 2257 7.8		**22** F ◑	0534 3.0 / 1133 7.2 / 1747 3.4 / 2345 7.2
8 F	0529 2.8 / 1134 7.5 / 1753 3.1 / 2359 7.7		**23** SA	0622 3.3 / 1225 7.0 / 1840 3.6
9 SA	0635 2.8 / 1240 7.5 / 1903 3.1		**24** SU	0040 6.9 / 0716 3.5 / 1324 6.9 / 1939 3.7
10 SU	0108 7.7 / 0745 2.7 / 1351 7.6 / 2016 2.9		**25** M	0144 6.9 / 0815 3.5 / 1427 7.0 / 2042 3.6
11 M	0220 7.8 / 0853 2.5 / 1459 7.9 / 2125 2.5		**26** TU	0248 7.0 / 0914 3.4 / 1525 7.2 / 2141 3.3
12 TU	0328 8.1 / 0957 2.2 / 1601 8.3 / 2228 2.2		**27** W	0346 7.2 / 1009 3.2 / 1616 7.5 / 2233 3.0
13 W	0429 8.4 / 1056 1.9 / 1657 8.6 / 2325 1.8		**28** TH	0438 7.5 / 1058 2.9 / 1703 7.9 / 2322 2.7
14 TH	0527 8.6 / 1150 1.7 / 1750 8.9		**29** F	0526 7.8 / 1144 2.6 / 1748 8.2
15 F ●	0019 1.5 / 0620 8.8 / 1243 1.6 / 1839 9.1		**30** SA ○	0007 2.3 / 0611 8.1 / 1229 2.4 / 1830 8.4

JULY

Time	m		Time	m
1 SU	0052 2.1 / 0654 8.3 / 1311 2.2 / 1911 8.6		**16** M	0151 1.4 / 0749 8.8 / 1407 1.6 / 2001 9.1
2 M	0135 1.9 / 0736 8.4 / 1353 2.1 / 1951 8.7		**17** TU	0233 1.4 / 0830 8.8 / 1446 1.7 / 2039 9.0
3 TU	0217 1.8 / 0817 8.5 / 1433 2.0 / 2031 8.8		**18** W	0310 1.5 / 0906 8.6 / 1521 1.9 / 2114 8.7
4 W	0258 1.7 / 0857 8.5 / 1513 2.1 / 2111 8.7		**19** TH	0344 1.8 / 0939 8.3 / 1553 2.2 / 2146 8.4
5 TH	0339 1.8 / 0938 8.4 / 1554 2.2 / 2154 8.6		**20** F	0415 2.3 / 1011 8.0 / 1624 2.6 / 2218 7.9
6 F	0422 2.0 / 1022 8.2 / 1637 2.4 / 2240 8.3		**21** SA	0446 2.7 / 1043 7.6 / 1656 3.0 / 2252 7.5
7 SA ◑	0508 2.3 / 1110 8.0 / 1727 2.7 / 2332 8.0		**22** SU ◑	0519 3.2 / 1119 7.2 / 1735 3.4 / 2332 7.1
8 SU	0600 2.5 / 1205 7.7 / 1825 2.9		**23** M	0601 3.6 / 1206 6.9 / 1827 3.8
9 M	0032 7.7 / 0702 2.8 / 1311 7.5 / 1936 3.1		**24** TU	0028 6.7 / 0701 3.9 / 1314 6.7 / 1938 3.9
10 TU	0146 7.5 / 0816 3.0 / 1426 7.5 / 2057 3.0		**25** W	0145 6.6 / 0815 3.9 / 1433 6.8 / 2054 3.8
11 W	0304 7.6 / 0933 2.9 / 1540 7.7 / 2212 2.7		**26** TH	0305 6.8 / 0928 3.7 / 1543 7.1 / 2202 3.4
12 TH	0417 7.8 / 1042 2.6 / 1644 8.1 / 2317 2.3		**27** F	0412 7.1 / 1031 3.3 / 1641 7.6 / 2301 2.9
13 F	0520 8.1 / 1141 2.3 / 1741 8.5		**28** SA	0508 7.6 / 1125 2.8 / 1731 8.1 / 2352 2.4
14 SA ●	0013 1.9 / 0615 8.4 / 1235 2.0 / 1832 8.8		**29** SU	0558 8.0 / 1214 2.4 / 1817 8.5
15 SU	0105 1.6 / 0705 8.7 / 1323 1.7 / 1918 9.0		**30** M ○	0040 1.9 / 0643 8.5 / 1301 1.9 / 1859 8.9
			31 TU	0125 1.5 / 0725 8.8 / 1343 1.6 / 1940 9.2

AUGUST

Time	m		Time	m
1 W	0207 1.2 / 0805 9.0 / 1423 1.4 / 2020 9.4		**16** TH	0243 1.4 / 0837 8.9 / 1453 1.6 / 2045 9.0
2 TH	0246 1.1 / 0844 9.1 / 1502 1.4 / 2058 9.4		**17** F	0311 1.7 / 0905 8.7 / 1519 1.9 / 2112 8.6
3 F	0324 1.2 / 0921 9.0 / 1539 1.5 / 2137 9.2		**18** SA	0335 2.1 / 0931 8.3 / 1544 2.3 / 2138 8.2
4 SA	0402 1.5 / 1000 8.7 / 1617 1.9 / 2217 8.7		**19** SU	0358 2.6 / 0956 7.9 / 1609 2.8 / 2205 7.7
5 SU ◑	0441 2.0 / 1042 8.3 / 1659 2.4 / 2303 8.2		**20** M ◑	0422 3.1 / 1024 7.4 / 1637 3.3 / 2236 7.2
6 M	0527 2.6 / 1131 7.8 / 1751 3.0		**21** TU	0452 3.6 / 1100 7.0 / 1717 3.8 / 2320 6.7
7 TU	0000 7.5 / 0626 3.2 / 1236 7.3 / 1903 3.5		**22** W	0543 4.1 / 1157 6.6 / 1831 4.2
8 W	0121 7.1 / 0751 3.6 / 1406 7.1 / 2047 3.5		**23** TH	0038 6.4 / 0719 4.3 / 1341 6.5 / 2016 4.1
9 TH	0301 7.0 / 0928 3.5 / 1536 7.3 / 2215 3.1		**24** F	0234 6.5 / 0858 4.1 / 1518 6.9 / 2140 3.7
10 F	0421 7.4 / 1042 3.0 / 1644 7.9 / 2318 2.6		**25** SA	0356 7.0 / 1012 3.5 / 1622 7.5 / 2244 3.0
11 SA	0520 8.0 / 1138 2.5 / 1736 8.4		**26** SU	0453 7.6 / 1109 2.8 / 1713 8.2 / 2336 2.3
12 SU ●	0009 2.0 / 0608 8.4 / 1227 2.0 / 1822 8.9		**27** M	0541 8.3 / 1157 2.2 / 1758 8.8
13 M	0054 1.6 / 0651 8.8 / 1310 1.7 / 1903 9.2		**28** TU ○	0022 1.6 / 0624 8.8 / 1243 1.6 / 1840 9.3
14 TU	0134 1.3 / 0730 9.0 / 1348 1.5 / 1941 9.3		**29** W	0106 1.1 / 0705 9.3 / 1325 1.1 / 1921 9.7
15 W	0210 1.2 / 0805 9.1 / 1422 1.4 / 2015 9.2		**30** TH	0147 0.7 / 0744 9.6 / 1404 0.9 / 2000 9.9
			31 F	0225 0.7 / 0822 9.6 / 1442 0.9 / 2038 9.8

Chart Datum: 5·06 metres below Ordnance Datum (Local)

CHANNEL ISLES – ST PETER PORT

LAT 49°27'N   LONG 2°31'W

TIMES AND HEIGHTS OF HIGH AND LOW WATERS

Dates in amber are **SPRINGS**
Dates in yellow are **NEAPS**

2007

SEPTEMBER

Day	Time	m		Day	Time	m
1 SA	0302	0.9		**16** SU	0256	2.1
	0858	9.4			0852	8.5
	1518	1.2			1507	2.3
	2115	9.5			2102	8.3
2 SU	0337	1.3		**17** M	0316	2.6
	0935	9.0			0915	8.1
	1554	1.7			1529	2.8
	2154	8.8			2126	7.8
3 M	0415	2.0		**18** TU	0337	3.1
	1014	8.4			0940	7.6
	1634	2.4			1554	3.3
	2237	8.0			2154	7.3
4 TU	0458	2.8		**19**	0405	3.6
	1101	7.7			1012	7.1
	1725	3.2			1631	3.8
	2335	7.2			2235	6.8
5 W	0559	3.6		**20** TH	0450	4.1
	1211	7.0			1100	6.7
	1850	3.8			1737	4.2
					2351	6.4
6 TH	0115	6.7		**21**	0624	4.5
	0746	4.0			1250	6.4
	1405	6.8			1944	4.3
	2057	3.8				
7 F	0311	6.9		**22** SA	0204	6.4
	0933	3.8			0831	4.3
	1538	7.3			1449	6.8
	2217	3.2			2116	3.7
8 SA	0419	7.5		**23** SU	0333	7.0
	1038	3.1			0948	3.6
	1636	7.9			1556	7.6
	2309	2.6			2219	2.9
9 SU	0508	8.1		**24** M	0428	7.8
	1126	2.5			1044	2.8
	1722	8.5			1646	8.3
	2352	2.0			2310	2.1
10 M	0549	8.6		**25** TU	0514	8.5
	1208	2.0			1132	2.0
	1802	9.0			1731	9.0
					2356	1.4
11 TU	0031	1.6		**26** W	0557	9.1
	0626	9.0			1216	1.3
	1246	1.6			1814	9.6
	1839	9.2				
12 W	0108	1.3		**27** TH	0039	0.9
	0701	9.2			0637	9.6
	1321	1.4			1259	0.9
	1913	9.4			1855	10.0
13 TH	0140	1.3		**28** F	0121	0.6
	0733	9.2			0717	9.9
	1352	1.4			1340	0.7
	1944	9.3			1936	10.1
14 F	0209	1.4		**29** SA	0200	0.6
	0802	9.1			0756	9.9
	1419	1.5			1419	0.7
	2012	9.1			2015	9.9
15 SA	0234	1.7		**30** SU	0238	0.9
	0828	8.8			0834	9.6
	1444	1.9			1457	1.1
	2038	8.7			2054	9.4

OCTOBER

Day	Time	m		Day	Time	m
1 M	0315	1.5		**16** TU	0244	2.7
	0912	9.1			0843	8.2
	1501	2.8			1501	2.4
	2134	8.7			2058	7.9
2 TU	0353	2.3		**17** W	0308	3.1
	0953	8.4			0910	7.8
	1617	2.6			1530	3.2
	2220	7.9			2129	7.4
3 W	0439	3.1		**18** TH	0339	3.6
	1042	7.6			0946	7.2
	1714	3.4			1609	3.7
	2323	7.0			2214	6.9
4 TH	0547	3.9		**19** F	0426	4.1
	1159	7.0			1043	6.9
	1851	4.0			1714	4.1
					2329	6.6
5 F	0118	6.6		**20** SA	0552	4.4
	0745	4.2			1215	6.7
	1358	6.9			1907	4.1
	2050	3.8				
6 SA	0259	6.9		**21** SU	0120	6.6
	0920	3.8			0754	4.2
	1519	7.3			1402	7.0
	2158	3.2			2039	3.6
7 SU	0358	7.5		**22** M	0253	7.2
	1017	3.1			0913	3.5
	1612	7.9			1515	7.7
	2244	2.6			2144	2.8
8 M	0442	8.1		**23** TU	0351	7.9
	1100	2.6			1010	2.7
	1655	8.4			1610	8.4
	2324	2.1			2236	2.1
9 TU	0520	8.6		**24** W	0439	8.6
	1139	2.1			1100	2.0
	1733	8.8			1658	9.0
					2324	1.5
10 W	0000	1.8		**25** TH	0524	9.2
	0555	9.2			1147	1.4
	1215	1.7			1745	9.5
	1808	9.1				
11 TH	0035	1.6		**26** F	0010	1.0
	0628	9.1			0608	9.6
	1248	1.6			1233	1.0
	1841	9.2			1829	9.8
12 F	0105	1.6		**27** SA	0054	0.8
	0659	9.2			0650	9.9
	1318	1.6			1317	0.8
	1911	9.1			1913	9.9
13 SA	0133	1.7		**28** SU	0136	0.8
	0728	9.1			0732	9.9
	1346	1.7			1400	0.9
	1940	9.0			1956	9.7
14 SU	0158	1.9		**29** M	0217	1.2
	0754	8.9			0814	9.6
	1412	2.0			1442	1.3
	2006	8.7			2039	9.2
15 M	0221	2.3		**30** TU	0258	1.7
	0819	8.6			0855	9.1
	1436	2.4			1525	1.9
	2032	8.3			2123	8.6
				31 W	0341	2.4
					0940	8.4
					1612	2.6
					2212	7.8

NOVEMBER

Day	Time	m		Day	Time	m
1 TH	0431	3.2		**16** F	0332	3.4
	1033	7.7			0940	7.6
	1712	3.3			1606	3.4
	2317	7.1			2210	7.2
2 F	0539	3.8		**17** SA	0421	3.8
	1145	7.2			1036	7.3
	1835	3.7			1706	3.6
					2314	7.0
3 SA	0051	6.8		**18** SU	0532	4.0
	0714	4.1			1148	7.2
	1321	7.0			1827	3.6
	2009	3.7				
4 SU	0219	7.0		**19** M	0033	7.0
	0841	3.8			0704	3.9
	1438	7.2			1310	7.3
	2117	3.3			1949	3.3
5 M	0320	7.4		**20** TU	0157	7.3
	0939	3.4			0826	3.4
	1534	7.6			1426	7.7
	2206	2.9			2059	2.8
6 TU	0405	7.8		**21** W	0305	7.8
	1024	2.9			0931	2.8
	1619	8.0			1529	8.2
	2247	2.6			2159	2.3
7 W	0444	8.2		**22** TH	0402	8.4
	1104	2.5			1027	2.2
	1658	8.4			1625	8.7
	2324	2.3			2252	1.8
8 TH	0520	8.6		**23** F	0453	8.9
	1140	2.2			1120	1.7
	1734	8.6			1718	9.1
	2358	2.1			2343	1.5
9 F	0553	8.8		**24** SA	0542	9.3
	1214	2.0			1210	1.3
	1808	8.7			1808	9.4
10 SA	0030	2.0		**25** SU	0032	1.3
	0626	8.9			0629	9.6
	1246	1.9			1259	1.1
	1841	8.8			1856	9.4
11 SU	0100	2.0		**26** M	0119	1.3
	0657	8.9			0715	9.6
	1317	2.0			1347	1.2
	1912	8.7			1944	9.3
12 M	0128	2.2		**27** TU	0205	1.5
	0727	8.8			0801	9.4
	1347	2.1			1434	1.4
	1943	8.5			2031	9.0
13 TU	0157	2.4		**28** W	0250	1.8
	0756	8.6			0846	9.1
	1417	2.4			1520	1.8
	2013	8.3			2117	8.6
14 W	0225	2.7		**29** TH	0335	2.3
	0825	8.3			0932	8.6
	1447	2.7			1608	2.3
	2045	7.9			2205	8.0
15 TH	0256	3.1		**30** F	0422	2.9
	0858	7.9			1021	8.1
	1522	3.1			1659	2.8
	2122	7.6			2258	7.5

DECEMBER

Day	Time	m		Day	Time	m
1 SA	0516	3.4		**16** SU	0417	3.1
	1117	7.6			1025	7.9
	1757	3.3			1653	2.9
					2254	7.6
2 SU	0000	7.1		**17** M	0511	3.3
	0619	3.7			1121	7.7
	1223	7.2			1750	3.0
	1902	3.5			2354	7.4
3 M	0111	7.0		**18** TU	0616	3.4
	0732	3.8			1226	7.6
	1333	7.1			1856	3.1
	2011	3.6				
4 TU	0219	7.1		**19** W	0103	7.4
	0840	3.7			0731	3.3
	1438	7.2			1338	7.6
	2111	3.4			2009	3.0
5 W	0315	7.3		**20** TH	0218	7.6
	0936	3.4			0849	3.0
	1532	7.4			1451	7.8
	2200	3.2			2121	2.7
6 TH	0401	7.7		**21** F	0328	8.0
	1022	3.1			0958	2.6
	1618	7.7			1559	8.1
	2243	2.9			2226	2.4
7 F	0442	8.0		**22** SA	0429	8.4
	1103	2.8			1100	2.2
	1659	8.0			1700	8.5
	2322	2.7			2325	2.1
8 SA	0521	8.3		**23** SU	0525	8.8
	1141	2.5			1157	1.8
	1739	8.2			1756	8.8
	2358	2.5				
9 SU	0558	8.5		**24**	0019	1.8
	1219	2.3			0617	9.2
	1817	8.5			1251	1.5
					1849	9.0
10 M	0034	2.4		**25** TU	0110	1.6
	0634	8.6			0707	9.4
	1256	2.2			1341	1.3
	1854	8.4			1938	9.1
11 TU	0109	2.3		**26** W	0158	1.5
	0709	8.7			0754	9.4
	1333	2.2			1428	1.3
	1930	8.4			2025	9.0
12 W	0144	2.4		**27** TH	0243	1.6
	0744	8.6			0838	9.3
	1409	2.3			1512	1.4
	2005	8.3			2107	8.8
13 TH	0219	2.5		**28** F	0324	1.9
	0819	8.5			0920	8.9
	1445	2.4			1554	1.8
	2042	8.1			2148	8.4
14 F	0254	2.7		**29** SA	0404	2.3
	0856	8.3			1000	8.5
	1523	2.6			1633	2.3
	2120	8.0			2227	8.0
15 SA	0333	2.9		**30** SU	0443	2.8
	0937	8.1			1040	8.0
	1605	2.7			1713	2.8
	2204	7.7			2307	7.5
				31 M	0525	3.2
					1123	7.5
					1755	3.3
					2353	7.1

Chart Datum: 5·06 metres below Ordnance Datum (Local)

TIDES

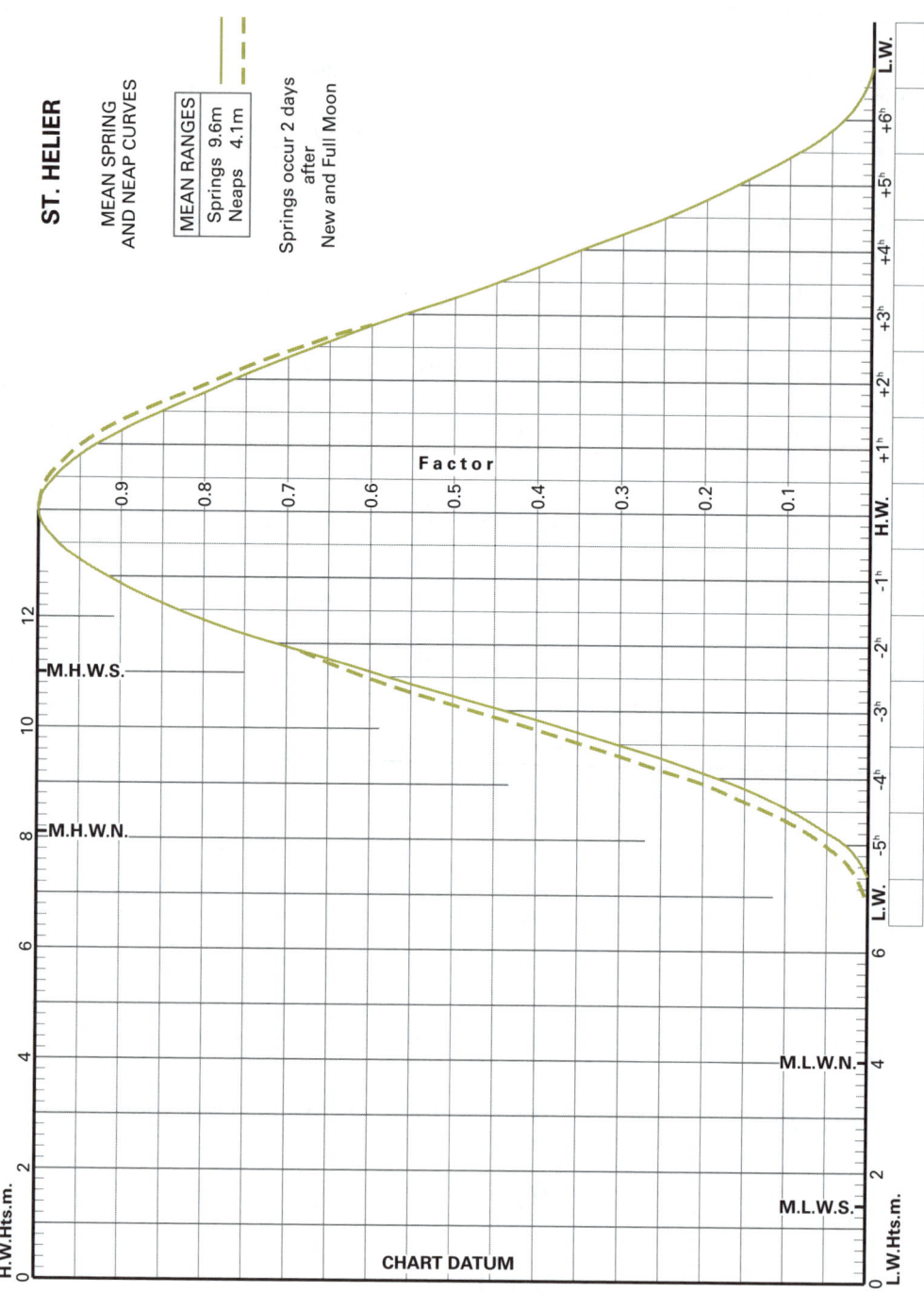

ST. HELIER

MEAN SPRING
AND NEAP CURVES

MEAN RANGES
Springs 9.6m
Neaps 4.1m

Springs occur 2 days
after
New and Full Moon

Factor

0.9 0.8 0.7 0.6 0.5 0.4 0.3 0.2 0.1

L.W.

+6ʰ +5ʰ +4ʰ +3ʰ +2ʰ +1ʰ H.W. -1ʰ -2ʰ -3ʰ -4ʰ -5ʰ L.W.

M.H.W.S.

M.H.W.N.

M.L.W.N.

M.L.W.S.

H.W.Hts.m.

L.W.Hts.m.

CHART DATUM

CHANNEL ISLES – ST HELIER

LAT 49°11'N   LONG 2°07'W

TIMES AND HEIGHTS OF HIGH AND LOW WATERS

2007

TIME ZONE (UT)
For Summer Time add ONE hour in **non-shaded areas**

Dates in amber are **SPRINGS**
Dates in yellow are **NEAPS**

JANUARY

Day	Time m	Time m	Time m	Time m
1 M	0410 9.3	1053 2.8	1645 9.4	2319 2.7
2 TU	0508 9.7	1152 2.4	1741 9.8	
3 W ○	0015 2.4	0558 10.1	1246 2.1	1830 10.1
4 TH	0104 2.2	0644 10.4	1333 1.9	1914 10.2
5 F	0148 2.1	0726 10.5	1415 1.9	1955 10.2
6 SA	0227 2.1	0804 10.4	1453 2.0	2031 10.0
7 SU	0302 2.3	0840 10.2	1527 2.2	2105 9.8
8 M	0334 2.6	0913 9.9	1557 2.6	2137 9.4
9 TU	0404 2.9	0945 9.5	1626 2.9	2210 9.0
10 W	0435 3.3	1019 9.1	1658 3.3	2245 8.6
11 TH ◑	0511 3.7	1057 8.6	1735 3.8	2327 8.2
12 F	0556 4.1	1144 8.1	1824 4.1	
13 SA	0024 7.8	0657 4.4	1250 7.7	1932 4.4
14 SU	0141 7.7	0815 4.4	1412 7.7	2054 4.3
15 M	0258 8.0	0933 4.1	1526 8.1	2206 3.9
16 TU	0400 8.5	1037 3.5	1627 8.6	2305 3.3
17 W	0453 9.2	1132 2.8	1720 9.2	2357 2.7
18 TH	0541 9.8	1223 2.2	1808 9.8	
19 F ●	0045 2.2	0627 10.3	1311 1.8	1853 10.3
20 SA	0131 1.8	0711 10.8	1356 1.4	1937 10.7
21 SU	0214 1.5	0754 11.1	1440 1.1	2019 10.9
22 M	0255 1.4	0836 11.2	1521 1.1	2101 10.9
23 TU	0336 1.4	0918 11.1	1602 1.3	2141 10.6
24 W	0417 1.7	0959 10.7	1642 1.7	2222 10.1
25 TH ◐	0458 2.2	1042 10.1	1723 2.3	2305 9.5
26 F	0542 2.8	1129 9.3	1811 3.0	2356 8.9
27 SA	0638 3.4	1229 8.6	1913 3.6	
28 SU	0105 8.4	0754 3.8	1353 8.2	2036 3.9
29 M	0234 8.3	0925 3.8	1527 8.2	2203 3.7
30 TU	0359 8.6	1048 3.3	1642 8.8	2315 3.2
31 W	0503 9.2	1152 2.7	1738 9.4	

FEBRUARY

Day	Time m	Time m	Time m	Time m
1 TH	0011 2.6	0553 9.8	1243 2.1	1824 9.9
2 F ○	0058 2.2	0636 10.3	1326 1.8	1903 10.2
3 SA	0138 1.9	0714 10.5	1403 1.6	1938 10.4
4 SU	0212 1.8	0748 10.6	1435 1.6	2010 10.4
5 M	0242 1.8	0819 10.6	1503 1.7	2039 10.2
6 TU	0309 1.9	0847 10.4	1528 2.0	2106 10.0
7 W	0335 2.2	0914 10.0	1552 2.3	2132 9.6
8 TH	0401 2.6	0941 9.6	1616 2.8	2158 9.2
9 F	0428 3.1	1008 9.0	1642 3.3	2226 8.6
10 SA ◐	0500 3.7	1040 8.4	1716 3.9	2303 8.1
11 SU	0545 4.2	1128 7.8	1808 4.5	
12 M	0007 7.6	0700 4.6	1252 7.4	1942 4.7
13 TU	0156 7.5	0843 4.4	1446 7.5	2128 4.3
14 W	0331 8.0	1008 3.8	1607 8.3	2242 3.6
15 TH	0434 8.9	1113 2.9	1705 9.1	2340 2.7
16 F	0526 9.8	1207 2.0	1754 10.0	
17 SA ●	0031 1.9	0613 10.6	1258 1.3	1839 10.7
18 SU	0118 1.3	0657 11.3	1344 0.8	1922 11.2
19 M	0202 0.9	0740 11.7	1426 0.5	2003 11.5
20 TU	0243 0.6	0820 11.8	1506 0.4	2042 11.5
21 W	0321 0.7	0900 11.6	1543 0.7	2119 11.1
22 TH	0358 1.1	0938 11.0	1619 1.4	2156 10.5
23 F	0434 1.8	1016 10.2	1654 2.2	2233 9.7
24 SA ◑	0513 2.7	1058 9.2	1735 3.2	2318 8.8
25 SU	0603 3.6	1154 8.2	1834 4.0	
26 M	0027 8.0	0725 4.2	1332 7.6	2013 4.4
27 TU	0219 7.8	0920 4.1	1528 7.8	2200 4.0
28 W	0355 8.3	1047 3.4	1638 8.6	2310 3.3

MARCH

Day	Time m	Time m	Time m	Time m
1 TH	0455 9.1	1143 2.6	1727 9.3	
2 F	0000 2.5	0540 9.8	1228 2.0	1807 9.9
3 SA ○	0042 2.0	0618 10.3	1306 1.7	1842 10.3
4 SU	0117 1.7	0652 10.6	1339 1.5	1914 10.5
5 M	0148 1.5	0723 10.7	1407 1.4	1942 10.6
6 TU	0215 1.5	0752 10.7	1432 1.5	2009 10.5
7 W	0241 1.6	0818 10.6	1456 1.7	2034 10.3
8 TH	0306 1.9	0843 10.3	1519 2.0	2057 10.0
9 F	0330 2.2	0906 9.8	1542 2.5	2119 9.5
10 SA	0355 2.6	0930 9.2	1605 3.1	2142 9.0
11 SU	0423 3.4	0957 8.6	1632 3.8	2212 8.4
12 M ◑	0500 4.0	1038 7.9	1716 4.4	2305 7.7
13 TU	0609 4.5	1157 7.3	1847 4.8	
14 W	0100 7.4	0758 4.5	1414 7.4	2051 4.5
15 TH	0302 7.9	0938 3.8	1544 8.2	2216 3.6
16 F	0411 8.9	1048 2.7	1643 9.3	2316 2.5
17 SA	0504 10.0	1144 1.8	1732 10.2	
18 SU	0008 1.6	0551 10.9	1235 1.0	1817 11.0
19 M ●	0056 0.9	0635 11.6	1321 0.4	1859 11.5
20 TU	0140 0.5	0718 12.0	1404 0.2	1939 11.8
21 W	0222 0.3	0759 12.0	1443 0.3	2018 11.7
22 TH	0300 0.5	0838 11.6	1520 0.7	2055 11.2
23 F	0337 1.0	0916 10.9	1555 1.5	2130 10.5
24 SA	0413 1.7	0953 9.9	1630 2.4	2207 9.6
25 SU ◑	0452 2.8	1036 8.9	1710 3.4	2252 8.6
26 M	0543 3.7	1136 7.9	1811 4.3	
27 TU	0006 7.8	0711 4.3	1328 7.4	2000 4.6
28 W	0208 7.6	0909 4.1	1514 7.8	2145 4.1
29 TH	0336 8.3	1027 3.4	1616 8.6	2248 3.3
30 F	0431 9.0	1117 2.7	1701 9.3	2333 2.6
31 SA	0514 9.7	1158 2.1	1738 9.8	

APRIL

Day	Time m	Time m	Time m	Time m
1 SU	0012 2.1	0550 10.1	1234 1.8	1811 10.2
2 M ○	0046 1.8	0623 10.4	1305 1.6	1842 10.4
3 TU	0116 1.6	0653 10.5	1333 1.5	1910 10.5
4 W	0144 1.5	0721 10.6	1400 1.5	1937 10.5
5 TH	0211 1.6	0748 10.4	1425 1.7	2002 10.4
6 F	0238 1.8	0813 10.2	1450 2.0	2025 10.1
7 SA	0304 2.1	0838 9.8	1514 2.5	2049 9.7
8 SU	0331 2.6	0903 9.3	1540 3.1	2114 9.1
9 M	0401 3.2	0934 8.7	1610 3.7	2148 8.6
10 TU ◑	0442 3.8	1019 8.0	1659 4.2	2245 7.9
11 W	0549 4.2	1142 7.5	1824 4.5	
12 TH	0034 7.6	0727 4.2	1344 7.7	2015 4.2
13 F	0227 8.1	0903 3.5	1511 8.5	2141 3.4
14 SA	0338 9.1	1014 2.6	1611 9.4	2243 2.4
15 SU	0433 10.1	1111 1.7	1702 10.3	2337 1.6
16 M	0523 10.9	1203 1.0	1748 11.0	
17 TU ●	0027 1.0	0609 11.4	1252 0.6	1832 11.5
18 W	0114 0.6	0653 11.7	1336 0.5	1913 11.6
19 TH	0157 0.5	0736 11.6	1418 0.6	1953 11.5
20 F	0239 0.7	0817 11.2	1457 1.1	2032 11.0
21 SA	0318 1.3	0858 10.5	1535 1.8	2110 10.3
22 SU	0358 2.0	0939 9.6	1613 2.7	2150 9.4
23 M	0441 2.9	1026 8.7	1657 3.6	2240 8.6
24 TU ◑	0535 3.7	1129 7.9	1800 4.3	2353 7.9
25 W	0657 4.1	1304 7.6	1934 4.5	
26 TH	0134 7.8	0831 4.0	1432 7.9	2102 4.1
27 F	0254 8.2	0942 3.5	1533 8.5	2204 3.4
28 SA	0350 8.8	1033 2.9	1620 9.0	2251 2.9
29 SU	0434 9.3	1114 2.5	1659 9.5	2331 2.4
30 M	0513 9.7	1151 2.2	1734 9.9	

Chart Datum: 5·88 metres below Ordnance Datum (Local)

CHANNEL ISLES – ST HELIER

LAT 49°11'N   LONG 2°07'W

TIMES AND HEIGHTS OF HIGH AND LOW WATERS

TIME ZONE (UT)
For Summer Time add ONE hour in **non-shaded areas**

Dates in amber are **SPRINGS**
Dates in yellow are **NEAPS**

2007

MAY

Day	Time m	Day	Time m
1 TU	0006 2.1 0547 10.0 1806 10.1	16 W	0542 10.9 1221 1.2 1805 11.0
2 W	0040 1.9 0619 10.1 1257 1.9 ○ 1837 10.2	17 TH	0047 1.1 0630 11.1 1310 1.1 1850 11.2
3 TH	0112 1.8 0650 10.2 1328 1.9 1906 10.3	18 F	0136 1.0 0717 11.0 1356 1.2 1933 11.1
4 F	0144 1.8 0720 10.1 1358 2.0 1934 10.2	19 SA	0221 1.2 0802 10.7 1439 1.6 2016 10.7
5 SA	0214 1.9 0750 9.9 1427 2.2 2002 10.0	20 SU	0306 1.6 0846 10.2 1521 2.1 2058 10.2
6 SU	0245 2.2 0820 9.7 1456 2.6 2032 9.7	21 M	0349 2.1 0931 9.5 1603 2.8 2141 9.5
7 M	0317 2.6 0853 9.3 1527 3.0 2105 9.3	22 TU	0434 2.8 1018 8.8 1648 3.4 2229 8.8
8 TU	0353 3.0 0932 8.8 1606 3.4 2149 8.8	23 W	0524 3.4 1112 8.3 1741 3.9 ◐ 2327 8.3
9 W	0439 3.4 1025 8.3 1659 3.8 2251 8.4	24 TH	0623 3.8 1218 7.9 1847 4.1
10 TH	0543 3.6 1141 8.0 1813 4.0 ◐	25 F	0039 8.1 0730 3.9 1329 8.0 1958 4.1
11 F	0018 8.2 0703 3.6 1310 8.2 1941 3.8	26 SA	0151 8.1 0836 3.7 1433 8.2 2102 3.8
12 SA	0146 8.6 0824 3.2 1429 8.7 2100 3.2	27 SU	0253 8.4 0932 3.4 1527 8.6 2155 3.4
13 SU	0258 9.2 0934 2.5 1532 9.4 2205 2.5	28 M	0345 8.7 1021 3.1 1613 9.0 2242 3.0
14 M	0358 9.9 1035 1.9 1627 10.1 2303 1.9	29 TU	0429 9.1 1104 2.8 1653 9.4 2325 2.7
15 TU	0452 10.5 1130 1.4 1717 10.7 2356 1.4	30 W	0510 9.4 1145 2.5 1731 9.7
		31 TH	0005 2.4 0547 9.6 1224 2.4 1806 9.9

JUNE

Day	Time m	Day	Time m
1 F	0044 2.2 0624 9.7 1301 2.3 ○ 1840 10.0	16 SA	0123 1.5 0705 10.4 1342 1.7 1921 10.7
2 SA	0122 2.1 0700 9.8 1337 2.3 1915 10.1	17 SU	0212 1.5 0753 10.3 1429 1.8 2006 10.5
3 SU	0158 2.1 0736 9.8 1412 2.3 1950 10.0	18 M	0258 1.7 0837 10.1 1512 2.1 2048 10.2
4 M	0234 2.2 0814 9.7 1447 2.5 2028 9.9	19 TU	0341 2.0 0919 9.7 1552 2.5 2128 9.8
5 TU	0312 2.3 0854 9.5 1525 2.7 2110 9.7	20 W	0421 2.4 0959 9.2 1631 2.9 2208 9.3
6 W	0353 2.5 0939 9.2 1608 2.9 2157 9.4	21 TH	0459 2.9 1040 8.8 1709 3.3 2250 8.9
7 TH	0440 2.7 1029 9.0 1659 3.2 2251 9.1	22 F	0538 3.3 1124 8.4 1752 3.7 ◑ 2339 8.4
8 F	0535 2.9 1128 8.8 1759 3.3 ◑ 2355 8.9	23 SA	0622 3.6 1217 8.2 1844 3.9
9 SA	0637 3.0 1234 8.7 1907 3.3	24 SU	0037 8.1 0716 3.8 1320 8.0 1945 4.0
10 SU	0105 8.9 0745 3.0 1344 8.9 2019 3.1	25 M	0143 8.0 0819 3.9 1424 8.1 2051 3.9
11 M	0216 9.1 0854 2.7 1452 9.2 2128 2.8	26 TU	0247 8.1 0922 3.7 1523 8.4 2152 3.6
12 TU	0322 9.4 0959 2.4 1554 9.6 2232 2.4	27 W	0345 8.4 1019 3.4 1614 8.8 2246 3.2
13 W	0424 9.4 1101 2.1 1651 10.1 2332 2.0	28 TH	0436 8.8 1110 3.1 1659 9.2 2335 2.8
14 TH	0522 10.1 1158 1.9 1744 10.4	29 F	0522 9.1 1157 2.8 1742 9.6
15 F	0029 1.7 0615 10.4 1253 1.7 ● 1834 10.6	30 SA	0021 2.4 0605 9.5 1242 2.5 ○ 1823 9.9

JULY

Day	Time m	Day	Time m
1 SU	0106 2.1 0647 9.7 1324 2.3 1904 10.1	16 M	0205 1.5 0742 10.3 1419 1.8 1953 10.6
2 M	0148 1.9 0728 9.9 1404 2.1 1945 10.3	17 TU	0246 1.6 0821 10.3 1457 1.9 2031 10.5
3 TU	0229 1.8 0810 10.1 1443 2.1 2026 10.4	18 W	0323 1.7 0857 10.1 1531 2.1 2106 10.2
4 W	0309 1.8 0852 10.1 1524 2.1 2108 10.4	19 TH	0354 2.0 0929 9.8 1602 2.4 2138 9.8
5 TH	0351 1.8 0934 10.0 1606 2.2 2151 10.2	20 F	0423 2.4 1001 9.4 1631 2.8 2210 9.4
6 F	0433 2.0 1018 9.7 1650 2.4 2237 9.8	21 SA	0450 2.9 1033 8.9 1702 3.3 2244 8.8
7 SA	0519 2.3 1105 9.4 1738 2.8 ◑ 2327 9.4	22 SU	0522 3.4 1110 8.4 1740 3.7 ◑ 2325 8.3
8 SU	0609 2.7 1158 9.0 1834 3.1	23 M	0602 3.9 1159 8.0 1831 4.1
9 M	0026 9.0 0707 3.0 1302 8.8 1941 3.3	24 TU	0022 7.8 0700 4.2 1310 7.7 1942 4.3
10 TU	0137 8.8 0817 3.2 1415 8.8 2057 3.3	25 W	0142 7.6 0819 4.3 1432 7.8 2104 4.2
11 W	0255 8.8 0933 3.2 1529 9.0 2213 3.0	26 TH	0305 7.8 0939 4.1 1541 8.3 2214 3.7
12 TH	0410 9.1 1044 2.9 1637 9.5 2322 2.5	27 F	0410 8.3 1043 3.5 1637 8.8 2312 3.1
13 F	0515 9.5 1148 2.5 1735 9.9	28 SA	0504 8.9 1137 3.0 1725 9.5
14 SA	0023 2.1 0610 9.9 1245 2.1 ● 1826 10.3	29 SU	0004 2.5 0551 9.5 1226 2.4 1809 10.0
15 SU	0118 1.7 0658 10.2 1335 1.9 1912 10.6	30 M	0052 2.0 0635 10.0 1312 2.0 ○ 1852 10.5
		31 TU	0138 1.5 0717 10.4 1355 1.6 1934 10.9

AUGUST

Day	Time m	Day	Time m
1 W	0220 1.2 0758 10.7 1435 1.4 2015 11.1	16 TH	0254 1.5 0827 10.4 1501 1.8 2036 10.6
2 TH	0300 1.1 0838 10.8 1515 1.4 2055 11.1	17 F	0319 1.8 0855 10.2 1527 2.1 2103 10.2
3 F	0339 1.1 0917 10.7 1553 1.5 2135 10.8	18 SA	0343 2.2 0921 9.8 1551 2.5 2129 9.7
4 SA	0417 1.5 0956 10.3 1633 1.9 2215 10.3	19 SU	0406 2.7 0946 9.3 1618 3.0 2155 9.1
5 SU	0456 2.0 1037 9.8 1714 2.5 ◐ 2258 9.6	20 M	0431 3.2 1013 8.7 1648 3.6 ◐ 2225 8.4
6 M	0539 2.7 1123 9.1 1803 3.2 2352 8.8	21 TU	0502 3.9 1047 8.1 1731 4.2 2308 7.8
7 TU	0633 3.4 1223 8.5 1911 3.7	22 W	0551 4.5 1144 7.6 1840 4.6
8 W	0107 8.2 0750 3.9 1350 8.2 2041 3.8	23 TH	0029 7.3 0717 4.8 1338 7.4 2019 4.6
9 TH	0247 8.1 0922 3.8 1524 8.5 2212 3.4	24 F	0232 7.4 0904 4.5 1516 7.9 2147 4.0
10 F	0413 8.6 1044 3.3 1636 9.1 2324 2.7	25 SA	0351 8.1 1021 3.8 1617 8.7 2251 3.1
11 SA	0515 9.3 1147 2.6 1731 9.8	26 SU	0446 8.9 1117 3.0 1706 9.6 2344 2.3
12 SU	0020 2.1 0603 9.9 1238 2.1 ● 1817 10.4	27 M	0533 9.8 1207 2.2 1751 10.4
13 M	0108 1.7 0645 10.3 1322 1.7 1857 10.7	28 TU	0033 1.6 0616 10.5 1254 1.6 ○ 1834 11.0
14 TU	0149 1.4 0723 10.5 1400 1.6 1933 10.8	29 W	0119 1.1 0657 11.0 1337 1.1 1915 11.5
15 W	0224 1.4 0756 10.5 1433 1.6 2006 10.8	30 TH	0202 0.7 0738 11.3 1418 0.9 1955 11.7
		31 F	0241 0.6 0816 11.4 1457 0.9 2034 11.6

Chart Datum: 5·88 metres below Ordnance Datum (Local)

TIME ZONE (UT)

For Summer Time add ONE hour in **non-shaded areas**

Dates in amber are **SPRINGS**
Dates in yellow are **NEAPS**

2007

SEPTEMBER

Day	Time m	Day	Time m
1 SA	0319 0.8 / 0854 11.2 / 1534 1.2 / 2113 11.1	16 SU	0305 2.1 / 0842 10.1 / 1516 2.3 / 2052 9.8
2 SU	0355 1.3 / 0931 10.6 / 1611 1.8 / 2151 10.4	17 M	0328 2.6 / 0904 9.6 / 1541 2.9 / 2115 9.2
3 M	0431 2.1 / 1008 9.9 / 1650 2.6 / 2232 9.4	18 TU	0351 3.3 / 0927 9.0 / 1609 3.5 / 2141 8.6
4 TU	0512 3.0 / 1052 9.0 / 1736 3.4 / ◗ 2326 8.4	19 W	0418 3.9 / 0955 8.4 / 1647 4.2 / ◗ 2217 7.9
5 W	0607 3.9 / 1155 8.2 / 1854 4.1	20 TH	0501 4.6 / 1041 7.7 / 1753 4.7 / 2332 7.3
6 TH	0056 7.7 / 0738 4.6 / 1344 7.9 / 2044 4.2	21 F	0628 5.0 / 1239 7.3 / 1939 4.7
7 F	0257 7.9 / 0926 4.1 / 1528 8.4 / 2217 3.5	22 SA	0200 7.3 / 0828 4.7 / 1448 7.8 / 2117 4.1
8 SA	0413 8.6 / 1042 3.3 / 1631 9.2 / 2317 2.7	23 SU	0326 8.1 / 0953 3.9 / 1551 8.8 / 2223 3.1
9 SU	0504 9.4 / 1136 2.5 / 1718 9.9	24 M	0420 9.1 / 1050 2.9 / 1640 9.8 / 2317 2.2
10 M	0005 2.0 / 0546 10.0 / 1220 2.0 / 1758 10.5	25 TU	0507 10.0 / 1140 2.0 / 1726 10.7
11 TU	0046 1.6 / 0622 10.5 / 1258 1.7 / ● 1834 10.8	26 W	0006 1.4 / 0550 10.8 / 1227 1.3 / ○ 1808 11.4
12 W	0121 1.4 / 0655 10.7 / 1331 1.6 / 1906 10.9	27 TH	0052 0.9 / 0631 11.4 / 1312 0.9 / 1850 11.8
13 TH	0151 1.4 / 0725 10.7 / 1400 1.6 / 1935 10.8	28 F	0135 0.6 / 0712 11.6 / 1354 0.7 / 1931 11.9
14 F	0217 1.5 / 0753 10.6 / 1426 1.7 / 2003 10.7	29 SA	0216 0.6 / 0751 11.6 / 1434 0.8 / 2012 11.7
15 SA	0241 1.5 / 0818 10.4 / 1451 1.9 / 2028 10.3	30 SU	0254 0.9 / 0829 11.3 / 1513 1.2 / 2051 11.0

OCTOBER

Day	Time m	Day	Time m
1 M	0332 1.6 / 0907 10.7 / 1551 1.9 / 2131 10.2	16 TU	0257 2.7 / 0833 9.7 / 1514 2.9 / 2047 9.3
2 TU	0409 2.4 / 0945 9.8 / 1633 2.8 / 2215 9.1	17 W	0323 3.3 / 0857 9.2 / 1544 3.5 / 2116 8.7
3 W	0452 3.4 / 1031 8.9 / 1718 3.8 / ◗ 2315 8.1	18 TH	0353 3.9 / 0929 8.6 / 1623 4.0 / 2157 8.1
4 TH	0554 4.2 / 1142 8.1 / 1852 4.3	19 F	0438 4.4 / 1019 8.0 / 1727 4.5 / ◗ 2311 7.5
5 F	0100 7.6 / 0735 4.6 / 1342 7.9 / 2042 4.2	20 SA	0558 4.8 / 1201 7.6 / 1902 4.5
6 SA	0248 8.0 / 0916 4.1 / 1512 8.4 / 2200 3.4	21 SU	0115 7.5 / 0746 4.6 / 1402 8.0 / 2036 3.9
7 SU	0352 8.7 / 1022 3.3 / 1609 9.2 / 2252 2.7	22 M	0245 8.3 / 0913 3.8 / 1512 8.9 / 2146 3.1
8 M	0438 9.4 / 1109 2.6 / 1652 9.9 / 2335 2.2	23 TU	0344 9.2 / 1014 2.9 / 1606 9.8 / 2242 2.2
9 TU	0517 10.0 / 1150 2.1 / 1730 10.3	24 W	0433 10.1 / 1107 2.1 / 1654 10.7 / 2333 1.5
10 W	0012 1.8 / 0551 10.4 / 1225 1.9 / 1803 10.6	25 TH	0519 10.8 / 1156 1.4 / 1740 11.3
11 TH	0045 1.7 / 0623 10.6 / 1257 1.8 / ● 1834 10.7	26 F	0021 1.0 / 0603 11.3 / 1243 1.0 / ○ 1825 11.6
12 F	0114 1.7 / 0652 10.6 / 1325 1.7 / 1903 10.7	27 SA	0107 0.8 / 0645 11.6 / 1328 0.9 / 1909 11.7
13 SA	0141 1.8 / 0719 10.6 / 1352 1.8 / 1931 10.5	28 SU	0150 0.9 / 0727 11.5 / 1412 1.0 / 1952 11.4
14 SU	0207 1.9 / 0745 10.4 / 1419 2.0 / 1957 10.2	29 M	0232 1.3 / 0808 11.2 / 1455 1.4 / 2035 10.8
15 M	0232 2.3 / 0809 10.1 / 1447 2.4 / 2022 9.8	30 TU	0313 1.9 / 0849 10.6 / 1538 2.1 / 2119 9.9
		31 W	0355 2.7 / 0932 9.8 / 1625 2.9 / 2208 9.0

NOVEMBER

Day	Time m	Day	Time m
1 TH	0443 3.5 / 1022 8.9 / 1722 3.6 / ◗ 2310 8.2	16 F	0345 3.6 / 0927 8.9 / 1616 3.6 / 2158 8.5
2 F	0546 4.2 / 1131 8.3 / 1841 4.1	17 SA	0432 4.0 / 1020 8.5 / 1713 3.9 / ◗ 2304 8.1
3 SA	0038 7.9 / 0713 4.4 / 1307 8.1 / 2008 4.0	18 SU	0538 4.3 / 1136 8.2 / 1828 4.0
4 SU	0207 8.0 / 0837 4.1 / 1430 8.4 / 2118 3.6	19 M	0028 8.1 / 0702 4.2 / 1306 8.4 / 1949 3.7
5 M	0311 8.6 / 0941 3.6 / 1529 8.9 / 2211 3.1	20 TU	0152 8.4 / 0824 3.7 / 1423 8.9 / 2101 3.1
6 TU	0359 9.1 / 1030 3.0 / 1615 9.4 / 2254 2.6	21 W	0259 9.1 / 0933 3.1 / 1526 9.6 / 2203 2.5
7 W	0440 9.6 / 1111 2.6 / 1654 9.8 / 2332 2.4	22 TH	0356 9.8 / 1031 2.4 / 1621 10.2 / 2259 1.9
8 TH	0516 10.0 / 1147 2.3 / 1730 10.1	23 F	0448 10.5 / 1126 1.8 / 1714 10.8 / 2352 1.5
9 F	0006 2.2 / 0549 10.2 / 1221 2.2 / 1803 10.2	24 SA	0537 10.9 / 1218 1.4 / 1804 11.1 ○
10 SA	0038 2.1 / 0620 10.4 / 1253 2.1 / 1834 10.2	25 SU	0042 1.4 / 0624 11.2 / 1309 1.3 / 1852 11.1
11 SU	0109 2.1 / 0650 10.4 / 1325 2.1 / 1905 10.2	26 M	0131 1.4 / 0710 11.2 / 1358 1.3 / 1939 10.9
12 M	0139 2.2 / 0718 10.3 / 1356 2.2 / 1934 10.0	27 TU	0217 1.6 / 0755 11.0 / 1445 1.6 / 2026 10.5
13 TU	0209 2.5 / 0747 10.1 / 1427 2.4 / 2004 9.7	28 W	0303 2.0 / 0840 10.6 / 1532 2.0 / 2113 10.0
14 W	0238 2.8 / 0816 9.8 / 1458 2.8 / 2036 9.3	29 TH	0348 2.6 / 0925 10.0 / 1620 2.6 / 2200 9.3
15 TH	0309 3.2 / 0848 9.4 / 1533 3.2 / 2112 8.9	30 F	0435 3.2 / 1012 9.3 / 1710 3.2 / 2251 8.7

DECEMBER

Day	Time m	Day	Time m
1 SA	0526 3.7 / 1106 8.8 / 1806 3.7 / ◗ 2350 8.3	16 SU	0427 3.2 / 1017 9.3 / 1700 3.1 / ◗ 2248 8.9
2 SU	0627 4.0 / 1210 8.4 / 1910 3.9	17 M	0519 3.5 / 1111 9.0 / 1756 3.3 / 2347 8.7
3 M	0058 8.1 / 0734 4.1 / 1322 8.3 / 2014 3.9	18 TU	0621 3.7 / 1217 8.8 / 1901 3.4
4 TU	0207 8.3 / 0840 4.0 / 1429 8.4 / 2113 3.7	19 W	0056 8.6 / 0734 3.6 / 1330 8.6 / 2013 3.3
5 W	0306 8.6 / 0937 3.6 / 1526 8.7 / 2204 3.4	20 TH	0210 8.8 / 0849 3.4 / 1444 9.1 / 2124 3.0
6 TH	0356 9.0 / 1026 3.3 / 1615 9.0 / 2250 3.1	21 F	0319 9.3 / 0959 2.9 / 1552 9.5 / 2230 2.6
7 F	0439 9.3 / 1110 2.9 / 1657 9.3 / 2331 2.8	22 SA	0422 9.8 / 1103 2.4 / 1655 10.0 / 2331 2.2
8 SA	0518 9.7 / 1150 2.6 / 1736 9.6	23 SU	0519 10.3 / 1203 1.9 / 1752 10.4
9 SU	0009 2.6 / 0554 9.9 / 1229 2.4 / 1812 9.8	24 M	0028 1.9 / 0612 10.7 / 1300 1.6 / ○ 1844 10.6
10 M	0046 2.5 / 0628 10.1 / 1306 2.3 / 1848 9.9	25 TU	0121 1.7 / 0701 11.0 / 1352 1.4 / 1933 10.7
11 TU	0121 2.4 / 0702 10.1 / 1342 2.3 / 1922 9.9	26 W	0210 1.6 / 0748 11.0 / 1440 1.4 / 2019 10.6
12 W	0155 2.5 / 0736 10.1 / 1417 2.3 / 1958 9.8	27 TH	0256 1.7 / 0831 10.8 / 1525 1.7 / 2101 10.3
13 TH	0229 2.5 / 0812 10.0 / 1452 2.5 / 2035 9.7	28 F	0338 2.1 / 0912 10.4 / 1606 2.1 / 2141 9.8
14 F	0304 2.8 / 0849 9.8 / 1530 2.6 / 2114 9.4	29 SA	0417 2.5 / 0951 9.9 / 1644 2.6 / 2220 9.3
15 SA	0343 3.0 / 0930 9.6 / 1612 2.9 / 2158 9.2	30 SU	0454 3.0 / 1030 9.4 / 1720 3.1 / 2259 8.8
		31 M	0532 3.5 / 1113 8.8 / 1800 3.6 / ◗ 2346 8.4

TIDES

Chart Datum: 5·88 metres below Ordnance Datum (Local)

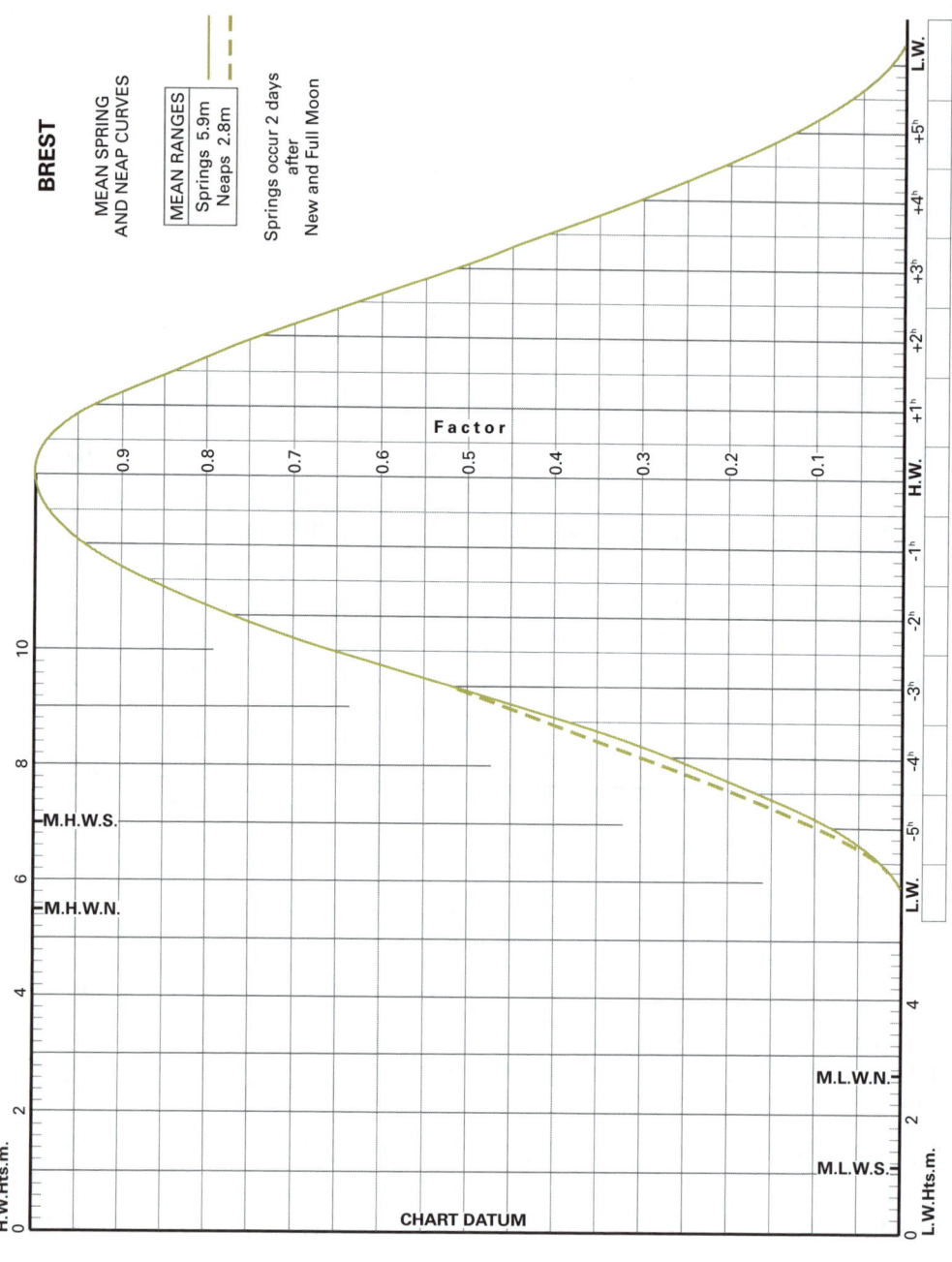

BREST

MEAN SPRING
AND NEAP CURVES

MEAN RANGES
Springs 5.9m
Neaps 2.8m

Springs occur 2 days
after
New and Full Moon

Factor

0.9 0.8 0.7 0.6 0.5 0.4 0.3 0.2 0.1

H.W.

L.W.

M.H.W.S.

M.H.W.N.

M.L.W.N.

M.L.W.S.

CHART DATUM

H.W.Hts.m.

L.W.Hts.m.

TIME ZONE -0100
(French Standard Time)
Subtract 1 hour for UT
For French Summer Time add
ONE hour in **non-shaded areas**

FRANCE – BREST

LAT 48°23'N   LONG 4°30'W

TIMES AND HEIGHTS OF HIGH AND LOW WATERS

Dates in amber are **SPRINGS**
Dates in yellow are **NEAPS**

2007

JANUARY

Time	m	Time	m
1 0251	6.2	**16** 0241	5.7
0915	2.0	0902	2.6
M 1519	6.4	TU 1508	5.7
2135	1.9	2125	2.4
2 0346	6.5	**17** 0333	6.1
1010	1.7	0953	2.2
TU 1612	6.5	W 1556	6.1
2227	1.8	2212	2.1
3 0435	6.7	**18** 0419	6.4
1059	1.5	1039	1.8
W 1659	6.6	TH 1640	6.4
○ 2313	1.7	2257	1.8
4 0519	6.8	**19** 0502	6.8
1144	1.4	1122	1.4
TH 1742	6.6	F 1723	6.7
2356	1.6	● 2340	1.5
5 0600	6.9	**20** 0545	7.1
1226	1.4	1205	1.2
F 1822	6.6	SA 1805	6.9
6 0039	1.6	**21** 0025	1.3
0639	6.8	0627	7.2
SA 1305	1.5	SU 1247	1.0
1900	6.5	1846	6.9
7 0116	1.7	**22** 0107	1.2
0715	6.7	0709	7.3
SU 1342	1.7	M 1330	1.0
1935	6.3	1928	6.9
8 0153	1.9	**23** 0151	1.2
0749	6.5	0751	7.2
M 1418	1.9	TU 1413	1.1
2010	6.1	2011	6.7
9 0229	2.1	**24** 0235	1.4
0824	6.2	0835	6.9
TU 1454	2.2	W 1459	1.4
2047	5.8	2056	6.4
10 0306	2.4	**25** 0323	1.7
0900	5.9	0922	6.5
W 1532	2.5	TH 1548	1.8
2127	5.6	◑ 2146	6.1
11 0347	2.7	**26** 0415	2.1
0942	5.6	1016	6.1
TH 1616	2.8	F 1643	2.3
◑ 2215	5.4	2245	5.8
12 0435	2.9	**27** 0518	2.5
1035	5.3	1123	5.7
F 1710	3.0	SA 1750	2.6
2317	5.2	2359	5.6
13 0537	3.1	**28** 0634	2.7
1144	5.2	1247	5.5
SA 1817	3.1	SU 1909	2.7
14 0030	5.2	**29** 0130	5.6
0650	3.1	0759	2.6
SU 1300	5.2	M 1412	5.6
1928	3.0	2027	2.6
15 0140	5.4	**30** 0245	5.9
0801	2.9	0911	2.3
M 1410	5.4	TU 1518	5.9
2032	2.7	2130	2.3
		31 0343	6.2
		1007	1.9
		W 1609	6.2
		2221	1.9

FEBRUARY

Time	m	Time	m
1 0430	6.5	**16** 0402	6.5
1053	1.6	1021	1.6
TH 1652	6.5	F 1625	6.5
2305	1.7	2240	1.6
2 0510	6.8	**17** 0446	7.0
1134	1.4	1106	1.1
F 1730	6.6	SA 1707	6.9
○ 2343	1.5	● 2323	1.1
3 0546	6.9	**18** 0528	7.4
1210	1.3	1148	0.7
SA 1804	6.7	SU 1748	7.2
4 0020	1.5	**19** 0005	0.8
0619	6.9	0609	7.6
SU 1243	1.3	M 1229	0.6
1836	6.7	1828	7.3
5 0052	1.5	**20** 0049	0.7
0650	6.9	0650	7.7
M 1314	1.4	TU 1310	0.6
1905	6.6	1907	7.3
6 0124	1.6	**21** 0131	0.8
0719	6.7	0730	7.5
TU 1343	1.6	W 1352	0.8
1934	6.4	1947	7.1
7 0154	1.8	**22** 0214	1.1
0747	6.5	0812	7.1
W 1413	1.9	TH 1434	1.3
2003	6.2	2029	6.7
8 0225	2.1	**23** 0259	1.5
0816	6.2	0855	6.6
TH 1443	2.2	F 1520	1.8
2034	5.9	2115	6.2
9 0258	2.4	**24** 0349	2.1
0848	5.8	0946	6.0
F 1516	2.6	SA 1613	2.4
2111	5.6	◑ 2212	5.7
10 0337	2.7	**25** 0451	2.6
0927	5.5	1055	5.4
SA 1559	2.9	SU 1722	2.9
◑ 2201	5.3	2333	5.3
11 0429	3.0	**26** 0615	2.9
1025	5.1	1235	5.2
SU 1701	3.2	M 1854	3.0
2315	5.1		
12 0543	3.2	**27** 0123	5.3
1143	5.0	0755	2.8
M 1828	3.3	TU 1412	5.4
		2022	2.8
13 0052	5.1	**28** 0241	5.7
0716	3.1	0907	2.4
TU 1335	5.1	W 1513	5.8
1958	3.0	2123	2.3
14 0214	5.4		
0836	2.7		
W 1449	5.5		
2104	2.6		
15 0313	5.9		
0934	2.2		
TH 1540	6.0		
2154	2.1		

MARCH

Time	m	Time	m
1 0334	6.1	**16** 0247	6.0
0958	1.9	0908	2.1
TH 1558	6.2	F 1517	6.1
2209	1.9	2130	1.9
2 0416	6.5	**17** 0337	6.6
1039	1.6	0957	1.4
F 1636	6.5	SA 1602	6.7
2248	1.6	2216	1.3
3 0452	6.7	**18** 0422	7.1
1114	1.4	1042	0.9
SA 1709	6.7	SU 1644	7.1
2323	1.4	2300	0.9
4 0524	6.9	**19** 0505	7.5
1146	1.3	1125	0.5
SU 1739	6.8	M 1724	7.4
○ 2354	1.3	● 2342	0.7
5 0553	6.9	**20** 0546	7.8
1215	1.3	1206	0.4
M 1806	6.8	TU 1804	7.6
6 0024	1.3	**21** 0027	0.5
0620	6.9	0627	7.8
TU 1242	1.3	W 1247	0.5
1833	6.7	1843	7.5
7 0053	1.4	**22** 0109	0.6
0647	6.8	0708	7.5
W 1309	1.5	TH 1328	0.8
1900	6.6	1923	7.2
8 0121	1.6	**23** 0153	1.0
0714	6.6	0749	7.0
TH 1336	1.8	F 1411	1.3
1926	6.4	2004	6.7
9 0150	1.9	**24** 0238	1.5
0740	6.3	0834	6.4
F 1403	2.1	SA 1456	2.0
1954	6.1	2051	6.1
10 0221	2.2	**25** 0330	2.1
0809	5.9	0926	5.8
SA 1434	2.4	SU 1550	2.6
2027	5.8	◑ 2151	5.6
11 0259	2.6	**26** 0434	2.7
0845	5.6	1040	5.2
SU 1514	2.8	M 1702	3.0
2112	5.4	2318	5.3
12 0348	2.9	**27** 0602	2.9
0938	5.1	1225	5.0
M 1611	3.2	TU 1839	3.1
◑ 2224	5.1		
13 0458	3.2	**28** 0108	5.3
1108	4.9	0739	2.8
TU 1740	3.3	W 1356	5.3
		2005	2.8
14 0007	5.0	**29** 0221	5.7
0636	3.1	0846	2.4
W 1303	5.0	TH 1452	5.7
1926	3.1	2101	2.3
15 0144	5.4	**30** 0310	6.0
0807	2.7	0933	2.0
TH 1424	5.5	F 1533	6.1
2038	2.6	2145	2.0
		31 0350	6.4
		1012	1.7
		SA 1608	6.4
		2221	1.7

APRIL

Time	m	Time	m
1 0424	6.6	**16** 0353	7.1
1045	1.5	1013	0.9
SU 1640	6.6	M 1616	7.2
2254	1.5	2233	0.9
2 0454	6.7	**17** 0438	7.5
1115	1.4	1058	0.6
M 1708	6.7	TU 1658	7.4
○ 2324	1.4	● 2318	0.6
3 0522	6.8	**18** 0522	7.6
1143	1.4	1142	0.6
TU 1735	6.8	W 1740	7.5
2353	1.4		
4 0550	6.8	**19** 0002	0.6
1211	1.4	0605	7.5
W 1802	6.8	TH 1224	0.7
		1821	7.4
5 0023	1.5	**20** 0049	0.8
0617	6.7	0648	7.2
TH 1238	1.6	F 1307	1.1
1829	6.6	1903	7.1
6 0052	1.6	**21** 0135	1.1
0644	6.5	0732	6.8
F 1305	1.8	SA 1351	1.5
1857	6.5	1947	6.6
7 0122	1.8	**22** 0223	1.6
0712	6.3	0820	6.2
SA 1334	2.1	SU 1439	2.1
1926	6.2	2036	6.1
8 0156	2.1	**23** 0316	2.2
0744	5.9	0915	5.6
SU 1407	2.4	M 1534	2.6
2001	5.9	2138	5.7
9 0236	2.4	**24** 0420	2.6
0824	5.6	1027	5.2
M 1450	2.8	TU 1643	2.9
2049	5.5	◑ 2258	5.4
10 0328	2.8	**25** 0539	2.8
0920	5.2	1154	5.1
TU 1549	3.1	W 1807	3.0
◑ 2202	5.2		
11 0437	3.0	**26** 0029	5.4
1048	5.0	0700	2.7
W 1712	3.2	TH 1313	5.3
2337	5.2	1925	2.8
12 0606	2.9	**27** 0139	5.6
1230	5.1	0805	2.5
TH 1851	3.0	F 1411	5.6
		2023	2.5
13 0109	5.5	**28** 0230	5.9
0731	2.5	0854	2.2
F 1349	5.6	SA 1455	5.9
2004	2.4	2108	2.2
14 0213	6.1	**29** 0311	6.1
0834	1.9	0934	1.9
SA 1444	6.2	SU 1532	6.2
2059	1.8	2146	1.9
15 0306	6.6	**30** 0347	6.3
0926	1.4	1009	1.8
SU 1532	6.7	M 1605	6.4
2147	1.3	2220	1.8

Chart Datum: 3·64 metres below IGN Datum

TIDES

TIME ZONE -0100
(French Standard Time)
Subtract 1 hour for UT
For French Summer Time add
ONE hour in **non-shaded areas**

FRANCE – BREST

LAT 48°23'N   LONG 4°30'W

TIMES AND HEIGHTS OF HIGH AND LOW WATERS

Dates in amber are **SPRINGS**
Dates in yellow are **NEAPS**

2007

MAY

Time	m		Time	m
1 TU	0420 6.4 / 1041 1.7 / 1636 6.5 / 2253 1.6		**16** W	0413 7.1 / 1033 1.0 / 1634 7.2 / 2255 0.9
2 W ○	0451 6.5 / 1111 1.7 / 1705 6.6 / 2324 1.6		**17** TH	0501 7.2 / 1119 1.0 / 1719 7.2 / 2343 0.9
3 TH	0521 6.5 / 1141 1.7 / 1735 6.6 / 2356 1.6		**18** F	0547 7.1 / 1205 1.1 / 1804 7.1
4 F	0552 6.5 / 1211 1.7 / 1805 6.6		**19** SA	0034 1.0 / 0633 6.9 / 1250 1.3 / 1849 6.9
5 SA	0029 1.7 / 0622 6.4 / 1242 1.9 / 1836 6.4		**20** SU	0121 1.3 / 0720 6.5 / 1336 1.7 / 1935 6.6
6 SU	0103 1.9 / 0655 6.2 / 1316 2.1 / 1911 6.2		**21** M	0210 1.5 / 0809 6.1 / 1424 2.1 / 2025 6.0
7 M	0141 2.1 / 0733 5.9 / 1354 2.3 / 1952 6.0		**22** TU	0301 2.1 / 0901 5.7 / 1516 2.4 / 2120 5.8
8 TU	0225 2.3 / 0818 5.6 / 1441 2.6 / 2044 5.7		**23** W ●	0357 2.4 / 1000 5.4 / 1614 2.7 / 2223 5.6
9 W	0318 2.5 / 0917 5.4 / 1539 2.8 / 2152 5.5		**24** TH	0459 2.6 / 1105 5.3 / 1720 2.8 / 2330 5.4
10 TH ◑	0423 2.6 / 1033 5.3 / 1653 2.9 / 2310 5.5		**25** F	0604 2.7 / 1211 5.3 / 1827 2.8
11 F	0538 2.6 / 1154 5.4 / 1814 2.7		**26** SA	0037 5.5 / 0706 2.6 / 1312 5.4 / 1927 2.7
12 SA	0029 5.8 / 0653 2.3 / 1306 5.7 / 1925 2.3		**27** SU	0135 5.6 / 0800 2.5 / 1404 5.6 / 2019 2.5
13 SU	0135 6.1 / 0757 1.9 / 1407 6.2 / 2024 1.8		**28** M	0224 5.7 / 0847 2.3 / 1448 5.9 / 2104 2.3
14 M	0232 6.6 / 0853 1.5 / 1459 6.6 / 2117 1.4		**29** TU	0306 5.9 / 0928 2.1 / 1528 6.1 / 2145 2.1
15 TU	0324 6.9 / 0944 1.2 / 1547 6.9 / 2207 1.1		**30** W	0345 6.1 / 1006 2.0 / 1604 6.3 / 2223 1.9
			31 TH	0422 6.2 / 1042 1.9 / 1639 6.4 / 2259 1.8

JUNE

Time	m		Time	m
1 F ○	0458 6.3 / 1117 1.9 / 1714 6.5 / 2336 1.8		**16** SA	0536 6.7 / 1151 1.4 / 1753 6.9
2 SA	0533 6.3 / 1152 1.9 / 1749 6.5		**17** SU	0022 1.2 / 0623 6.6 / 1237 1.5 / 1838 6.8
3 SU	0014 1.8 / 0609 6.2 / 1228 1.9 / 1826 6.4		**18** M	0109 1.4 / 0708 6.4 / 1322 1.7 / 1922 6.6
4 M	0052 1.8 / 0648 6.2 / 1307 2.0 / 1906 6.3		**19** TU	0154 1.6 / 0751 6.2 / 1406 1.9 / 2006 6.4
5 TU	0134 1.9 / 0730 6.0 / 1349 2.1 / 1950 6.2		**20** W	0238 1.9 / 0835 6.0 / 1450 2.1 / 2050 6.1
6 W	0219 2.0 / 0816 5.9 / 1436 2.3 / 2040 6.1		**21** TH	0323 2.1 / 0919 5.7 / 1536 2.4 / 2136 5.8
7 TH	0309 2.1 / 0910 5.7 / 1529 2.4 / 2137 5.9		**22** F ●	0410 2.4 / 1008 5.5 / 1626 2.6 / 2228 5.5
8 F ◑	0405 2.2 / 1011 5.6 / 1630 2.5 / 2240 5.7		**23** SA	0502 2.6 / 1103 5.3 / 1721 2.8 / 2325 5.4
9 SA	0508 2.2 / 1117 5.7 / 1737 2.4 / 2346 5.9		**24** SU	0558 2.8 / 1203 5.3 / 1822 2.9
10 SU	0614 2.2 / 1224 5.8 / 1845 2.3		**25** M	0029 5.3 / 0657 2.8 / 1304 5.4 / 1923 2.8
11 M	0056 6.1 / 0720 2.0 / 1329 6.0 / 1950 2.0		**26** TU	0130 5.4 / 0755 2.7 / 1401 5.5 / 2021 2.6
12 TU	0200 6.3 / 0821 1.8 / 1429 6.3 / 2050 1.7		**27** W	0226 5.5 / 0848 2.5 / 1452 5.7 / 2112 2.4
13 W	0259 6.5 / 0919 1.6 / 1524 6.6 / 2147 1.5		**28** TH	0315 5.7 / 0935 2.3 / 1537 6.0 / 2157 2.2
14 TH	0355 6.6 / 1013 1.5 / 1616 6.8 / 2240 1.3		**29** F	0359 5.9 / 1017 2.2 / 1619 6.2 / 2240 2.0
15 F ●	0447 6.7 / 1103 1.4 / 1705 6.9 / 2330 1.2		**30** SA	0441 6.1 / 1058 2.0 / 1659 6.4 / 2320 1.8

JULY

Time	m		Time	m
1 SU	0521 6.2 / 1138 1.9 / 1738 6.5		**16** M	0009 1.3 / 0609 6.6 / 1223 1.5 / 1824 6.9
2 M	0000 1.6 / 0600 6.3 / 1217 1.7 / 1818 6.6		**17** TU	0052 1.3 / 0648 6.5 / 1303 1.5 / 1902 6.8
3 TU	0042 1.5 / 0640 6.4 / 1258 1.7 / 1859 6.7		**18** W	0130 1.4 / 0724 6.4 / 1340 1.7 / 1938 6.6
4 W	0124 1.5 / 0722 6.4 / 1340 1.7 / 1941 6.6		**19** TH	0206 1.7 / 0759 6.2 / 1416 1.9 / 2012 6.3
5 TH	0207 1.5 / 0805 6.3 / 1424 1.8 / 2026 6.5		**20** F	0242 1.9 / 0833 6.0 / 1453 2.1 / 2047 6.0
6 F	0252 1.6 / 0851 6.2 / 1511 1.9 / 2114 6.3		**21** SA	0318 2.3 / 0911 5.7 / 1531 2.4 / 2125 5.7
7 SA ●	0342 1.8 / 0942 6.0 / 1604 2.1 / 2208 6.1		**22** SU	0358 2.6 / 0954 5.4 / 1616 2.7 / 2212 5.4
8 SU	0437 2.0 / 1040 5.8 / 1703 2.3 / 2309 5.9		**23** M	0446 2.9 / 1050 5.2 / 1713 3.0 / 2314 5.1
9 M	0539 2.2 / 1145 5.8 / 1811 2.3		**24** TU	0549 3.0 / 1159 5.1 / 1822 3.1
10 TU	0022 5.8 / 0647 2.3 / 1257 5.8 / 1923 2.3		**25** W	0032 5.0 / 0701 3.0 / 1313 5.2 / 1937 3.0
11 W	0137 5.9 / 0758 2.2 / 1408 6.0 / 2034 2.1		**26** TH	0149 5.2 / 0811 2.9 / 1420 5.5 / 2043 2.7
12 TH	0247 6.0 / 0904 2.0 / 1512 6.2 / 2137 1.8		**27** F	0251 5.5 / 0909 2.6 / 1514 5.8 / 2136 2.3
13 F	0347 6.2 / 1002 1.8 / 1608 6.5 / 2233 1.5		**28** SA	0341 5.8 / 0957 2.2 / 1601 6.2 / 2221 1.9
14 SA ●	0440 6.4 / 1053 1.6 / 1658 6.7 / 2323 1.4		**29** SU	0425 6.1 / 1041 1.9 / 1643 6.5 / 2304 1.6
15 SU	0527 6.6 / 1140 1.5 / 1743 6.9		**30** M ○	0506 6.4 / 1122 1.6 / 1723 6.8 / 2344 1.3
			31 TU	0546 6.6 / 1202 1.4 / 1803 7.0

AUGUST

Time	m		Time	m
1 W	0026 1.1 / 0625 6.8 / 1242 1.2 / 1843 7.1		**16** TH	0059 1.3 / 0651 6.6 / 1308 1.5 / 1904 6.7
2 TH	0107 1.0 / 0704 6.8 / 1323 1.2 / 1923 7.1		**17** F	0130 1.5 / 0720 6.5 / 1339 1.7 / 1932 6.5
3 F	0147 1.1 / 0744 6.7 / 1405 1.3 / 2004 6.9		**18** SA	0159 1.8 / 0749 6.2 / 1410 2.0 / 2001 6.2
4 SA	0230 1.3 / 0826 6.5 / 1449 1.6 / 2048 6.6		**19** SU	0229 2.2 / 0819 5.9 / 1443 2.3 / 2032 5.8
5 SU ◑	0315 1.7 / 0912 6.2 / 1538 1.9 / 2138 6.2		**20** M ◑	0301 2.5 / 0912 5.5 / 1521 2.7 / 2109 5.5
6 M	0406 2.1 / 1006 5.9 / 1635 2.3 / 2238 5.8		**21** TU	0341 2.9 / 0940 5.3 / 1610 3.0 / 2203 5.1
7 TU	0508 2.4 / 1114 5.6 / 1745 2.5 / 2355 5.5		**22** W	0439 3.2 / 1053 5.0 / 1721 3.2 / 2330 4.9
8 W	0624 2.7 / 1239 5.5 / 1910 2.6		**23** TH	0605 3.3 / 1228 5.0 / 1854 3.2
9 TH	0131 5.5 / 0748 2.6 / 1404 5.7 / 2032 2.3		**24** F	0116 5.0 / 0739 3.1 / 1352 5.3 / 2016 2.8
10 F	0248 5.8 / 0900 2.3 / 1511 6.1 / 2136 2.0		**25** SA	0230 5.4 / 0845 2.7 / 1452 5.8 / 2113 2.3
11 SA	0345 6.1 / 0957 2.0 / 1603 6.5 / 2228 1.6		**26** SU	0321 5.8 / 0935 2.2 / 1539 6.3 / 2159 1.8
12 SU	0432 6.4 / 1044 1.7 / 1648 6.8 / 2312 1.3		**27** M	0405 6.3 / 1019 1.7 / 1621 6.6 / 2241 1.3
13 M ●	0512 6.6 / 1125 1.5 / 1727 6.9 / 2351 1.2		**28** TU ○	0445 6.6 / 1100 1.3 / 1702 7.1 / 2322 1.0
14 TU	0548 6.8 / 1202 1.4 / 1802 7.0		**29** W	0524 7.0 / 1141 0.9 / 1741 7.4
15 W	0027 1.2 / 0621 6.7 / 1236 1.4 / 1834 6.9		**30** TH	0002 0.7 / 0602 7.2 / 1221 0.8 / 1821 7.5
			31 F	0044 0.7 / 0640 7.2 / 1301 0.9 / 1900 7.4

Chart Datum: 3·64 metres below IGN Datum

TIME ZONE -0100
(French Standard Time)
Subtract 1 hour for UT
For French Summer Time add
ONE hour in **non-shaded areas**

FRANCE – BREST

LAT 48°23'N   LONG 4°30'W

TIMES AND HEIGHTS OF HIGH AND LOW WATERS

Dates in amber are **SPRINGS**
Dates in yellow are **NEAPS**

2007

SEPTEMBER

Day	Time m	Time m	Time m	Time m		Day	Time m	Time m	Time m	Time m
1 SA	0124 0.9	0719 7.1	1343 1.1	1940 7.2		**16** SU	0120 1.8	0710 6.4	1333 2.0	1923 6.3
2 SU	0206 1.2	0800 6.8	1426 1.4	2023 6.7		**17** M	0148 2.1	0738 6.1	1404 2.3	1952 5.9
3 M	0250 1.7	0845 6.3	1515 1.9	2113 6.1		**18** TU	0218 2.5	0810 5.8	1441 2.6	2026 5.5
4 TU	0341 2.3	0940 5.9	1614 2.4	2216 5.6		**19** W	0256 2.9	0853 5.4	1529 3.0	2117 5.1
5 W	0446 2.7	1056 5.5	1732 2.9	2347 5.2		**20** TH	0351 3.2	1004 5.1	1637 3.2	2245 4.8
6 TH	0614 3.0	1237 5.4	1910 2.8			**21** F	0518 3.4	1148 5.0	1814 3.2	
7 F	0136 5.4	0747 2.8	1404 5.7	2031 2.4		**22** SA	0043 5.0	0704 3.2	1320 5.4	1944 2.8
8 SA	0245 5.8	0855 2.4	1503 6.2	2128 1.9		**23** SU	0202 5.4	0816 2.7	1422 5.9	2043 2.3
9 SU	0334 6.2	0945 1.9	1549 6.5	2212 1.6		**24** M	0253 6.0	0907 2.1	1510 6.5	2130 1.7
10 M	0414 6.5	1026 1.6	1628 6.8	2251 1.4		**25** TU	0337 6.5	0951 1.6	1553 7.0	2213 1.2
11 TU	0449 6.7	1103 1.4	1703 7.0	2325 1.3		**26** W	0418 7.0	1034 1.1	1635 7.4	2255 0.8
12 W	0520 6.8	1136 1.4	1734 7.0	2356 1.3		**27** TH	0457 7.3	1115 0.8	1716 7.7	2336 0.6
13 TH	0545 6.8	1206 1.4	1802 6.9			**28** F	0537 7.5	1157 0.7	1756 7.7	
14 F	0026 1.4	0616 6.8	1235 1.5	1829 6.8		**29** SA	0020 0.6	0616 7.5	1239 0.7	1837 7.5
15 SA	0053 1.6	0643 6.6	1304 1.7	1856 6.6		**30** SU	0101 0.9	0656 7.2	1322 1.0	1919 7.1

OCTOBER

Day	Time m	Time m	Time m	Time m		Day	Time m	Time m	Time m	Time m
1 M	0144 1.3	0738 6.9	1408 1.5	2004 6.6		**16** TU	0118 2.2	0710 6.2	1338 2.3	1926 5.9
2 TU	0230 1.9	0825 6.3	1500 2.0	2057 6.0		**17** W	0151 2.5	0744 5.9	1417 2.6	2003 5.6
3 W	0323 2.5	0925 5.8	1603 2.5	2208 5.4		**18** TH	0232 2.8	0829 5.6	1506 2.9	2056 5.2
4 TH	0433 2.9	1049 5.5	1726 2.8	2345 5.2		**19** F	0328 3.1	0938 5.3	1611 3.1	2219 5.0
5 F	0606 3.1	1229 5.5	1901 2.7			**20** SA	0447 3.3	1113 5.2	1736 3.1	2359 5.1
6 SA	0123 5.4	0733 2.8	1347 5.8	2013 2.4		**21** SU	0622 3.1	1238 5.5	1901 2.7	
7 SU	0224 5.8	0834 2.4	1441 6.2	2104 2.0		**22** M	0121 5.5	0737 2.6	1343 6.0	2004 2.2
8 M	0309 6.2	0921 2.0	1524 6.5	2146 1.7		**23** TU	0217 6.1	0832 2.1	1435 6.5	2055 1.6
9 TU	0346 6.5	1000 1.7	1600 6.7	2222 1.5		**24** W	0304 6.6	0920 1.5	1522 7.0	2142 1.2
10 W	0419 6.7	1035 1.6	1633 6.8	2255 1.4		**25** TH	0348 7.1	1006 1.1	1607 7.4	2227 0.9
11 TH	0449 6.8	1106 1.5	1703 6.9	2325 1.4		**26** F	0431 7.4	1050 0.8	1651 7.6	2311 0.7
12 F	0518 6.9	1135 1.5	1731 6.8	2353 1.5		**27** SA	0513 7.5	1135 0.7	1735 7.6	2355 0.8
13 SA	0545 6.8	1205 1.6	1759 6.7			**28** SU	0555 7.5	1220 0.8	1819 7.4	
14 SU	0021 1.7	0613 6.7	1235 1.8	1826 6.5		**29** M	0042 1.1	0638 7.2	1306 1.1	1904 7.0
15 M	0049 1.9	0641 6.5	1305 2.0	1855 6.3		**30** TU	0127 1.5	0724 6.9	1355 1.5	1954 6.5
						31 W	0216 2.0	0815 6.4	1449 2.0	2050 5.9

NOVEMBER

Day	Time m	Time m	Time m	Time m		Day	Time m	Time m	Time m	Time m
1 TH	0311 2.5	0916 5.9	1552 2.5	2159 5.5		**16** F	0221 2.7	0822 5.8	1453 2.6	2049 5.5
2 F	0419 2.9	1033 5.6	1708 2.7	2321 5.3		**17** SA	0315 2.9	0923 5.6	1551 2.7	2157 5.3
3 SA	0539 3.0	1157 5.6	1828 2.7			**18** SU	0421 3.0	1037 5.6	1701 2.7	2315 5.4
4 SU	0044 5.4	0656 2.8	1309 5.7	1935 2.5		**19** M	0538 2.9	1152 5.7	1815 2.6	
5 M	0145 5.7	0758 2.5	1404 6.0	2027 2.2		**20** TU	0032 5.7	0651 2.6	1259 6.0	1921 2.2
6 TU	0232 6.0	0846 2.2	1449 6.2	2111 2.0		**21** W	0135 6.1	0753 2.1	1358 6.4	2019 1.8
7 W	0312 6.3	0928 2.0	1527 6.4	2148 1.8		**22** TH	0229 6.5	0848 1.7	1451 6.8	2111 1.4
8 TH	0347 6.5	1004 1.8	1602 6.6	2223 1.8		**23** F	0320 6.9	0940 1.3	1542 7.1	2201 1.2
9 F	0419 6.6	1038 1.7	1634 6.6	2255 1.7		**24** SA	0408 7.2	1030 1.0	1631 7.3	2250 1.0
10 SA	0450 6.7	1110 1.7	1705 6.6	2325 1.8		**25** SU	0455 7.3	1119 0.9	1719 7.3	2337 1.1
11 SU	0521 6.7	1142 1.7	1736 6.5	2356 1.9		**26** M	0542 7.3	1207 1.0	1807 7.1	
12 M	0552 6.6	1215 1.8	1807 6.4			**27** TU	0028 1.3	0629 7.2	1256 1.2	1856 6.8
13 TU	0028 2.0	0623 6.5	1248 2.0	1839 6.2		**28** W	0116 1.6	0716 6.9	1346 1.5	1945 6.5
14 W	0101 2.2	0656 6.3	1324 2.2	1914 6.0		**29** TH	0205 1.9	0806 6.6	1437 1.9	2038 6.1
15 TH	0138 2.4	0735 6.1	1405 2.4	1956 5.7		**30** F	0256 2.3	0900 6.2	1532 2.2	2134 5.7

DECEMBER

Day	Time m	Time m	Time m	Time m		Day	Time m	Time m	Time m	Time m
1 SA	0352 2.6	0959 5.9	1633 2.5	2237 5.5		**16** SU	0301 2.4	0904 6.1	1530 2.3	2131 5.7
2 SU	0455 2.8	1104 5.7	1737 2.7	2342 5.4		**17** M	0355 2.5	1001 5.9	1626 2.4	2233 5.7
3 M	0601 2.8	1211 5.6	1840 2.7			**18** TU	0457 2.6	1106 5.9	1730 2.4	2340 5.7
4 TU	0048 5.5	0705 2.8	1313 5.7	1938 2.6		**19** W	0605 2.5	1214 6.0	1838 2.3	
5 W	0145 5.7	0802 2.6	1406 5.8	2029 2.4		**20** TH	0052 5.9	0715 2.3	1322 6.1	1944 2.1
6 TH	0233 5.9	0851 2.4	1453 6.0	2113 2.3		**21** F	0158 6.2	0821 2.0	1427 6.4	2046 1.8
7 F	0315 6.1	0934 2.2	1533 6.1	2153 2.1		**22** SA	0258 6.6	0921 1.7	1526 6.7	2143 1.6
8 SA	0353 6.3	1013 2.1	1611 6.3	2230 2.0		**23** SU	0354 6.8	1017 1.4	1621 6.9	2236 1.4
9 SU	0429 6.5	1050 1.9	1646 6.3	2305 2.0		**24** M	0446 7.1	1110 1.2	1712 7.0	2327 1.3
10 M	0505 6.6	1126 1.9	1721 6.4	2340 2.0		**25** TU	0535 7.2	1159 1.1	1800 7.0	
11 TU	0539 6.6	1201 1.8	1756 6.4			**26** W	0019 1.3	0621 7.2	1247 1.1	1847 6.8
12 W	0016 2.0	0615 6.6	1238 1.8	1832 6.3		**27** TH	0105 1.4	0706 7.0	1333 1.3	1931 6.6
13 TH	0053 2.0	0652 6.5	1315 1.9	1910 6.2		**28** F	0149 1.6	0750 6.8	1417 1.6	2014 6.3
14 F	0131 2.1	0731 6.4	1356 2.0	1951 6.0		**29** SA	0233 1.9	0832 6.5	1502 1.9	2058 6.0
15 SA	0213 2.3	0815 6.2	1440 2.1	2038 5.9		**30** SU	0317 2.2	0915 6.1	1547 2.3	2143 5.7
						31 M	0403 2.5	1002 5.8	1636 2.6	2235 5.5

Chart Datum: 3·64 metres below IGN Datum

TIDES

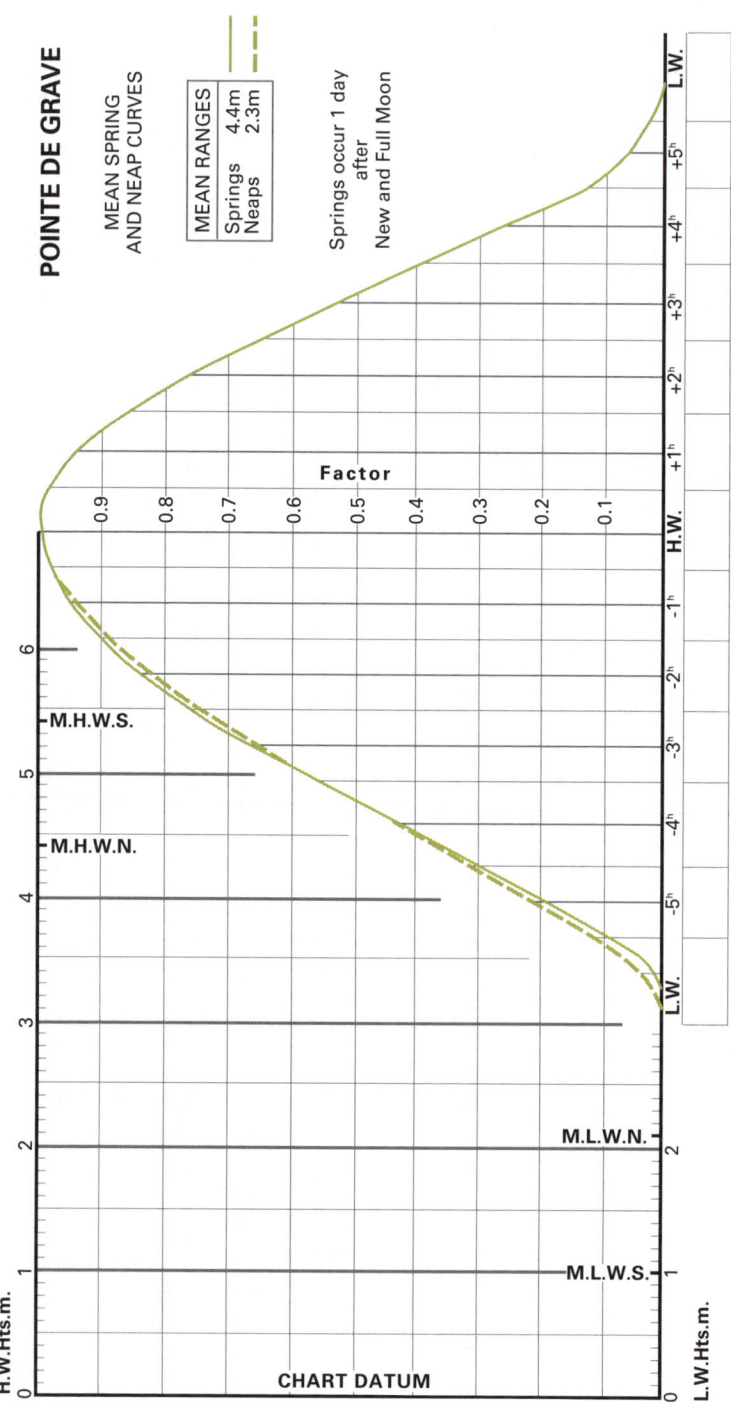

POINTE DE GRAVE

MEAN SPRING
AND NEAP CURVES

MEAN RANGES	
Springs	4.4m
Neaps	2.3m

Springs occur 1 day
after
New and Full Moon

Factor

TIME ZONE -0100
(French Standard Time)
Subtract 1 hour for UT
For French Summer Time add
ONE hour in **non-shaded areas**

FRANCE – POINTE DE GRAVE

LAT 45°34'N   LONG 1°04'W

TIMES AND HEIGHTS OF HIGH AND LOW WATERS

Dates in amber are **SPRINGS**
Dates in yellow are **NEAPS**

2007

JANUARY

#	Day	Time m	Time m	Time m	Time m		#	Day	Time m	Time m	Time m	Time m
1	M	0305 5.0	0900 1.6	1535 5.0	2121 1.6		16	TU	0253 4.6	0848 2.0	1524 4.6	2114 2.0
2	TU	0357 5.1	0957 1.5	1626 5.1	2213 1.5		17	W	0339 4.9	0939 1.8	1609 4.8	2200 1.7
3	W	0444 5.3	1047 1.3	1712 5.2	2300 1.5		18	TH	0423 5.1	1027 1.5	1652 5.0	2245 1.5
4	TH	0527 5.4	1133 1.3	1754 5.2	2343 1.4		19	F	0505 5.4	1113 1.3	1733 5.2	2329 1.3
5	F	0608 5.4	1216 1.3	1833 5.1			20	SA	0547 5.5	1157 1.1	1814 5.3	
6	SA	0025 1.5	0645 5.3	1254 1.4	1908 5.0		21	SU	0014 1.2	0630 5.6	1240 1.0	1855 5.3
7	SU	0102 1.5	0719 5.2	1331 1.5	1941 4.9		22	M	0057 1.2	0713 5.6	1322 1.0	1937 5.3
8	M	0139 1.6	0752 5.1	1407 1.6	2015 4.7		23	TU	0140 1.2	0757 5.5	1404 1.1	2021 5.1
9	TU	0217 1.8	0827 4.9	1445 1.8	2052 4.6		24	W	0223 1.3	0844 5.4	1447 1.3	2108 4.9
10	W	0257 1.9	0907 4.7	1525 2.0	2137 4.4		25	TH	0310 1.4	0935 5.1	1535 1.5	2203 4.7
11	TH	0340 2.1	0954 4.5	1612 2.2	2234 4.3		26	F	0404 1.7	1036 4.8	1630 1.8	2314 4.5
12	F	0432 2.3	1055 4.3	1709 2.3	2345 4.2		27	SA	0509 1.9	1153 4.6	1738 2.0	
13	SA	0535 2.4	1211 4.2	1819 2.4			28	SU	0040 4.4	0626 2.0	1318 4.5	1857 2.1
14	SU	0058 4.2	0645 2.4	1328 4.2	1926 2.3		29	M	0158 4.6	0747 2.0	1434 4.6	2014 2.0
15	M	0200 4.4	0751 2.2	1432 4.4	2024 2.2		30	TU	0303 4.8	0857 1.8	1537 4.8	2117 1.8
							31	W	0356 5.0	0954 1.6	1626 4.9	2208 1.6

FEBRUARY

#	Day	Time m	Time m	Time m	Time m		#	Day	Time m	Time m	Time m	Time m
1	TH	0440 5.2	1042 1.4	1706 5.1	2252 1.5		16	F	0407 5.2	1011 1.4	1637 5.1	2230 1.4
2	F	0518 5.3	1123 1.3	1741 5.2	2331 1.4		17	SA	0450 5.5	1057 1.1	1717 5.4	2314 1.1
3	SA	0551 5.4	1201 1.2	1812 5.2			18	SU	0532 5.7	1141 0.9	1757 5.5	2356 0.9
4	SU	0008 1.3	0622 5.4	1234 1.2	1841 5.1		19	M	0614 5.9	1222 0.7	1836 5.6	
5	M	0041 1.3	0651 5.3	1305 1.3	1908 5.1		20	TU	0041 0.8	0655 5.9	1303 0.8	1916 5.5
6	TU	0112 1.4	0719 5.2	1335 1.4	1936 5.0		21	W	0121 0.9	0737 5.7	1342 0.9	1956 5.3
7	W	0143 1.5	0748 5.0	1405 1.6	2005 4.8		22	TH	0202 1.0	0820 5.4	1423 1.2	2038 5.1
8	TH	0215 1.6	0819 4.8	1437 1.8	2039 4.6		23	F	0247 1.3	0907 5.1	1507 1.5	2127 4.7
9	F	0249 1.8	0854 4.6	1512 2.0	2121 4.4		24	SA	0338 1.6	1006 4.7	1600 1.9	2240 4.4
10	SA	0330 2.1	0940 4.3	1555 2.3	2221 4.1		25	SU	0443 2.0	1135 4.3	1710 2.2	
11	SU	0425 2.3	1051 4.1	1702 2.5	2351 4.1		26	M	0023 4.3	0610 2.2	1315 4.3	1843 2.4
12	M	0546 2.5	1201 4.0	1834 2.5			27	TU	0153 4.4	0742 2.1	1435 4.4	2009 2.2
13	TU	0122 4.2	0713 2.4	1405 4.2	1953 2.4		28	W	0300 4.7	0852 1.8	1533 4.7	2109 1.9
14	W	0229 4.5	0824 2.1	1505 4.5	2053 2.1							
15	TH	0321 4.8	0921 1.8	1554 4.8	2144 1.7							

MARCH

#	Day	Time m	Time m	Time m	Time m		#	Day	Time m	Time m	Time m	Time m
1	TH	0349 4.9	0943 1.6	1615 4.9	2156 1.6		16	F	0256 4.9	0856 1.7	1529 4.9	2119 1.6
2	F	0427 5.1	1026 1.4	1648 5.1	2236 1.4		17	SA	0344 5.3	0946 1.3	1612 5.3	2206 1.3
3	SA	0459 5.3	1103 1.2	1717 5.2	2311 1.3		18	SU	0428 5.6	1032 0.9	1653 5.5	2250 1.0
4	SU	0527 5.4	1136 1.2	1744 5.2	2344 1.2		19	M	0510 5.9	1116 0.7	1733 5.7	2334 0.7
5	M	0554 5.4	1206 1.2	1809 5.2			20	TU	0552 6.0	1158 0.6	1813 5.7	
6	TU	0014 1.2	0620 5.3	1234 1.2	1835 5.2		21	W	0019 0.7	0633 5.9	1238 0.7	1852 5.6
7	W	0042 1.2	0646 5.2	1301 1.3	1900 5.1		22	TH	0100 0.7	0715 5.7	1318 0.9	1932 5.4
8	TH	0110 1.3	0713 5.1	1328 1.5	1928 4.9		23	F	0141 0.9	0758 5.4	1358 1.2	2014 5.1
9	F	0139 1.5	0741 4.9	1355 1.6	1957 4.7		24	SA	0225 1.3	0846 4.9	1442 1.6	2104 4.8
10	SA	0210 1.7	0812 4.6	1427 1.9	2033 4.5		25	SU	0316 1.7	0949 4.5	1536 2.0	2219 4.4
11	SU	0248 1.9	0851 4.3	1506 2.2	2123 4.2		26	M	0423 2.0	1127 4.2	1649 2.4	
12	M	0337 2.2	0956 4.1	1603 2.5	2249 4.1		27	TU	0006 4.3	0555 2.2	1306 4.2	1826 2.4
13	TU	0453 2.4	1152 3.9	1741 2.6			28	W	0136 4.4	0727 2.1	1419 4.4	1949 2.2
14	W	0041 4.1	0637 2.4	1336 4.1	1919 2.4		29	TH	0240 4.7	0831 1.9	1511 4.7	2046 1.9
15	TH	0159 4.5	0757 2.1	1440 4.5	2026 2.1		30	F	0326 4.9	0919 1.6	1549 4.9	2130 1.7
							31	SA	0401 5.1	0958 1.4	1619 5.0	2209 1.5

APRIL

#	Day	Time m	Time m	Time m	Time m		#	Day	Time m	Time m	Time m	Time m
1	SU	0430 5.2	1033 1.3	1645 5.1	2243 1.3		16	M	0401 5.6	1002 0.9	1625 5.5	2223 0.9
2	M	0457 5.3	1105 1.2	1711 5.2	2315 1.3		17	TU	0445 5.8	1048 0.8	1707 5.6	2308 0.7
3	TU	0524 5.3	1134 1.2	1737 5.2	2344 1.2		18	W	0529 5.9	1131 0.7	1749 5.7	2353 0.7
4	W	0551 5.3	1202 1.3	1804 5.2			19	TH	0613 5.8	1213 0.8	1831 5.6	
5	TH	0013 1.2	0617 5.2	1228 1.3	1831 5.1		20	F	0039 0.8	0658 5.5	1255 1.0	1915 5.4
6	F	0041 1.3	0644 5.0	1255 1.5	1859 5.0		21	SA	0122 0.9	0744 5.2	1337 1.3	2001 5.1
7	SA	0110 1.4	0713 4.8	1324 1.6	1930 4.8		22	SU	0208 1.3	0834 4.8	1423 1.7	2054 4.8
8	SU	0143 1.6	0746 4.6	1357 1.8	2007 4.6		23	M	0300 1.7	0939 4.4	1518 2.0	2204 4.5
9	M	0222 1.8	0830 4.4	1438 2.1	2100 4.4		24	TU	0405 2.0	1107 4.2	1628 2.3	2334 4.4
10	TU	0312 2.1	0939 4.1	1536 2.4	2220 4.2		25	W	0527 2.2	1234 4.2	1753 2.3	
11	W	0425 2.3	1123 4.0	1706 2.5	2359 4.3		26	TH	0056 4.4	0650 2.1	1342 4.4	1909 2.2
12	TH	0601 2.2	1300 4.2	1839 2.3			27	F	0200 4.6	0753 1.9	1432 4.6	2008 2.0
13	F	0122 4.6	0721 1.9	1405 4.6	1949 2.0		28	SA	0247 4.7	0841 1.7	1510 4.8	2054 1.8
14	SA	0223 4.9	0822 1.6	1457 5.0	2045 1.6		29	SU	0324 4.9	0922 1.6	1541 4.9	2134 1.6
15	SU	0314 5.3	0915 1.2	1542 5.3	2135 1.2		30	M	0356 5.0	0957 1.5	1610 5.0	2209 1.5

Chart Datum: 2·83 metres below IGN Datum

TIDES

TIME ZONE -0100
(French Standard Time)
Subtract 1 hour for UT
For French Summer Time add
ONE hour in **non-shaded areas**

FRANCE – POINTE DE GRAVE

LAT 45°34'N   LONG 1°04'W

TIMES AND HEIGHTS OF HIGH AND LOW WATERS

Dates in amber are **SPRINGS**
Dates in yellow are **NEAPS**

2007

MAY

	Time	m		Time	m
1 TU	0426	5.1	16 W	0423	5.6
	1030	1.4		1020	1.0
	1639	5.1		1644	5.5
	2243	1.4		2245	0.9
2 W	0456	5.1	17 TH	0511	5.6
	1101	1.4		1107	0.9
	1708	5.1		1730	5.5
	2314	1.4		2333	0.9
3 TH	0525	5.1	18 F	0558	5.5
	1131	1.4		1152	1.0
	1738	5.1		1816	5.5
	2346	1.3			
4 F	0555	5.0	19 SA	0022	0.9
	1200	1.4		0646	5.3
	1809	5.1		1236	1.2
				1903	5.3
5 SA	0018	1.4	20 SU	0108	1.1
	0626	4.9		0734	5.0
	1231	1.5		1321	1.4
	1841	5.0		1951	5.1
6 SU	0051	1.4	21 M	0155	1.4
	0659	4.8		0824	4.8
	1303	1.6		1408	1.7
	1917	4.9		2042	4.9
7 M	0127	1.6	22 TU	0245	1.6
	0738	4.6		0919	4.5
	1341	1.8		1500	1.9
	2000	4.7		2138	4.7
8 TU	0209	1.7	23 W	0341	1.9
	0828	4.4		1024	4.3
	1426	2.0		1559	2.1
	2056	4.6		2243	4.5
9 W	0302	1.9	24 TH	0445	2.0
	0935	4.3		1135	4.2
	1525	2.2		1706	2.2
	2205	4.5		2353	4.4
10 TH	0410	2.0	25 F	0554	2.1
	1059	4.6		1241	4.3
	1642	2.2		1814	2.2
	2325	4.5			
11 F	0528	2.0	26 SA	0057	4.4
	1220	4.4		0659	2.0
	1800	2.1		1336	4.4
				1915	2.1
12 SA	0042	4.7	27 SU	0152	4.5
	0641	1.8		0753	1.9
	1326	4.7		1420	4.6
	1908	1.8		2008	2.0
13 SU	0146	5.0	28 M	0239	4.6
	0744	1.5		0839	1.8
	1421	4.9		1459	4.7
	2008	1.5		2053	1.8
14 M	0242	5.2	29 TU	0319	4.7
	0840	1.3		0919	1.7
	1511	5.2		1535	4.8
	2103	1.3		2133	1.7
15 TU	0334	5.4	30 W	0356	4.8
	0932	1.1		0956	1.6
	1558	5.4		1610	4.9
	2155	1.0		2211	1.6
			31 TH	0432	4.9
				1031	1.5
				1645	5.0
				2248	1.5

JUNE

	Time	m		Time	m
1 F	0506	4.9	16 SA	0549	5.2
	1106	1.5		1137	1.2
	1719	5.1		1806	5.4
	2325	1.4			
2 SA	0541	4.9	17 SU	0010	1.1
	1140	1.5		0637	5.1
	1755	5.1		1223	1.3
				1852	5.3
3 SU	0002	1.4	18 M	0057	1.2
	0617	4.9		0722	5.0
	1216	1.5		1307	1.4
	1832	5.0		1937	5.2
4 M	0041	1.4	19 TU	0141	1.3
	0655	4.8		0804	4.8
	1253	1.6		1351	1.5
	1913	5.0		2019	5.0
5 TU	0121	1.5	20 W	0225	1.5
	0738	4.7		0846	4.6
	1335	1.7		1436	1.7
	1958	4.9		2102	4.8
6 W	0205	1.5	21 TH	0310	1.7
	0827	4.6		0930	4.4
	1421	1.8		1523	1.9
	2050	4.8		2147	4.6
7 TH	0255	1.6	22 F	0359	1.9
	0924	4.5		1021	4.3
	1516	1.8		1616	2.0
	2149	4.7		2240	4.4
8 F	0352	1.7	23 SA	0453	2.0
	1030	4.5		1122	4.2
	1618	1.9		1714	2.1
	2253	4.7		2341	4.3
9 SA	0456	1.7	24 SU	0554	2.1
	1140	4.5		1226	4.2
	1724	1.8		1816	2.2
10 SU	0002	4.8	25 M	0048	4.3
	0602	1.6		0656	2.1
	1247	4.6		1326	4.3
	1831	1.7		1916	2.1
11 M	0111	4.9	26 TU	0150	4.3
	0707	1.6		0752	2.0
	1349	4.8		1418	4.5
	1935	1.6		2011	2.0
12 TU	0214	5.0	27 W	0244	4.4
	0808	1.4		0841	1.9
	1445	5.0		1504	4.6
	2036	1.4		2100	1.9
13 W	0313	5.1	28 TH	0331	4.5
	0906	1.3		0925	1.8
	1539	5.1		1546	4.8
	2134	1.2		2145	1.7
14 TH	0408	5.2	29 F	0413	4.7
	0959	1.2		1007	1.7
	1629	5.3		1626	4.9
	2228	1.1		2228	1.6
15 F	0500	5.2	30 SA	0452	4.8
	1050	1.2		1047	1.5
	1718	5.4		1705	5.0
	2320	1.0		2310	1.4

JULY

	Time	m		Time	m
1 SU	0531	4.9	16 M	0622	5.1
	1127	1.5		1211	1.2
	1744	5.1		1835	5.3
	2351	1.3			
2 M	0609	4.9	17 TU	0042	1.1
	1207	1.4		0659	5.0
	1824	5.2		1250	1.3
				1912	5.2
3 TU	0034	1.3	18 W	0120	1.2
	0649	4.9		0733	4.9
	1247	1.4		1328	1.4
	1905	5.2		1946	5.1
4 W	0115	1.2	19 TH	0157	1.3
	0730	4.9		0805	4.8
	1329	1.4		1405	1.6
	1949	5.1		2019	4.9
5 TH	0157	1.2	20 F	0233	1.5
	0814	4.8		0839	4.6
	1412	1.4		1443	1.7
	2035	5.1		2055	4.7
6 F	0241	1.3	21 SA	0311	1.7
	0902	4.7		0919	4.4
	1459	1.5		1525	1.9
	2126	5.0		2137	4.4
7 SA	0329	1.4	22 SU	0354	1.9
	0957	4.6		1009	4.2
	1552	1.6		1613	2.1
	2224	4.8		2230	4.2
8 SU	0424	1.5	23 M	0446	2.1
	1101	4.5		1114	4.1
	1653	1.7		1713	2.2
	2329	4.7		2339	4.1
9 M	0526	1.7	24 TU	0553	2.3
	1213	4.5		1231	4.1
	1800	1.7		1824	2.3
10 TU	0043	4.6	25 W	0102	4.0
	0635	1.7		0704	2.3
	1325	4.6		1341	4.2
	1911	1.7		1933	2.2
11 W	0156	4.7	26 TH	0213	4.2
	0746	1.7		0807	2.1
	1431	4.8		1438	4.4
	2021	1.6		2032	2.0
12 TH	0303	4.8	27 F	0309	4.3
	0851	1.6		0900	1.9
	1530	5.0		1526	4.7
	2125	1.4		2124	1.8
13 F	0403	4.9	28 SA	0356	4.6
	0950	1.5		0947	1.7
	1623	5.1		1609	4.9
	2222	1.2		2211	1.5
14 SA	0455	5.0	29 SU	0437	4.8
	1041	1.3		1031	1.5
	1711	5.3		1649	5.1
	2313	1.1		2255	1.3
15 SU	0541	5.1	30 M	0516	5.0
	1128	1.3		1113	1.3
	1755	5.3		1729	5.3
	2358	1.1		2337	1.1
			31 TU	0555	5.1
				1154	1.2
				1809	5.4

AUGUST

	Time	m		Time	m
1 W	0020	1.0	16 TH	0052	1.1
	0633	5.2		0656	5.0
	1234	1.1		1259	1.2
	1849	5.5		1907	5.1
2 TH	0100	1.0	17 F	0123	1.4
	0712	5.2		0723	4.9
	1314	1.1		1330	1.4
	1931	5.4		1935	5.0
3 F	0139	1.0	18 SA	0153	1.4
	0752	5.1		0752	4.7
	1355	1.1		1402	1.5
	2014	5.3		2006	4.7
4 SA	0220	1.1	19 SU	0224	1.7
	0835	4.9		0825	4.5
	1438	1.3		1436	1.8
	2101	5.1		2041	4.5
5 SU	0303	1.3	20 M	0258	1.9
	0924	4.7		0906	4.3
	1526	1.5		1515	2.0
	2156	4.8		2126	4.2
6 M	0354	1.6	21 TU	0339	2.2
	1027	4.5		1004	4.1
	1625	1.7		1607	2.3
	2304	4.5		2234	3.9
7 TU	0456	1.8	22 W	0442	2.4
	1149	4.4		1131	4.0
	1738	1.9		1728	2.5
8 W	0031	4.4	23 TH	0016	3.9
	0613	2.0		0615	2.5
	1315	4.4		1304	4.1
	1902	1.9		1858	2.4
9 TH	0154	4.4	24 F	0145	4.1
	0737	2.0		0735	2.3
	1429	4.6		1411	4.3
	2021	1.7		2008	2.1
10 F	0305	4.6	25 SA	0246	4.3
	0849	1.8		0835	2.0
	1529	4.9		1503	4.7
	2124	1.5		2102	1.8
11 SA	0401	4.8	26 SU	0333	4.6
	0945	1.5		0925	1.7
	1618	5.1		1546	5.0
	2216	1.3		2149	1.5
12 SU	0446	5.0	27 M	0415	4.9
	1032	1.3		1009	1.4
	1659	5.3		1627	5.3
	2301	1.1		2233	1.2
13 M	0524	5.1	28 TU	0453	5.2
	1114	1.2		1052	1.2
	1736	5.3		1707	5.5
	2341	1.1		2314	1.0
14 TU	0558	5.1	29 W	0531	5.3
	1152	1.2		1133	1.0
	1809	5.3		1746	5.7
				2355	0.8
15 W	0019	1.1	30 TH	0609	5.4
	0628	5.1		1213	0.9
	1227	1.2		1826	5.7
	1839	5.3			
			31 F	0037	0.8
				0648	5.4
				1253	0.9
				1907	5.6

Chart Datum: 2·83 metres below IGN Datum

TIME ZONE -0100
(French Standard Time)
Subtract 1 hour for UT
For French Summer Time add
ONE hour in non-shaded areas

FRANCE – POINTE DE GRAVE

LAT 45°34'N   LONG 1°04'W

TIMES AND HEIGHTS OF HIGH AND LOW WATERS

Dates in amber are **SPRINGS**
Dates in yellow are **NEAPS**

2007

SEPTEMBER

Day	Time m	Time m	Time m	Time m
1 SA	0116 0.9	0727 5.3	1333 1.0	1950 5.4
16 SU	0113 1.5	0711 4.9	1324 1.5	1924 4.8
2 SU	0155 1.1	0808 5.0	1416 1.2	2037 5.1
17 M	0141 1.7	0742 4.7	1355 1.7	1954 4.5
3 M	0238 1.4	0855 4.8	1504 1.5	2134 4.7
18 TU	0212 1.9	0817 4.4	1430 2.0	2034 4.2
4 TU	0328 1.7	1002 4.5	1604 1.8	◑ 2253 4.3
19 W	0250 2.2	0907 4.2	1517 2.3	● 2140 3.9
5 W	0434 2.1	1141 4.3	1726 2.1	
20 TH	0345 2.5	1034 4.0	1632 2.5	2334 3.8
6 TH	0034 4.2	0603 2.3	1315 4.4	1903 2.1
21 F	0522 2.6	1221 4.1	1820 2.5	
7 F	0159 4.4	0735 2.1	1427 4.7	2021 1.8
22 SA	0113 4.0	0658 2.4	1337 4.4	1937 2.2
8 SA	0303 4.6	0842 1.9	1522 4.9	2115 1.5
23 SU	0215 4.4	0802 2.1	1432 4.8	2032 1.8
9 SU	0350 4.8	0932 1.6	1605 5.1	2200 1.3
24 M	0302 4.7	0854 1.7	1517 5.1	2119 1.4
10 M	0427 5.0	1014 1.4	1639 5.3	2239 1.2
25 TU	0344 5.1	0940 1.4	1559 5.5	2203 1.1
11 TU	0458 5.1	1052 1.2	1722 5.3	● 2315 1.1
26 W	0424 5.3	1024 1.1	1640 5.7	○ 2246 0.9
12 W	0525 5.1	1127 1.2	1737 5.3	2348 1.1
27 TH	0503 5.5	1107 0.9	1721 5.8	2327 0.8
13 TH	0552 5.1	1158 1.2	1804 5.3	
28 F	0542 5.6	1149 0.8	1802 5.8	
14 F	0019 1.2	0618 5.1	1227 1.3	1830 5.2
29 SA	0009 0.8	0622 5.5	1231 0.8	1845 5.7
15 SA	0046 1.3	0644 5.0	1255 1.4	1856 5.0
30 SU	0051 1.0	0703 5.4	1312 1.0	1930 5.4

OCTOBER

Day	Time m	Time m	Time m	Time m
1 M	0132 1.2	0747 5.1	1356 1.3	2021 5.0
16 TU	0108 1.8	0712 4.8	1326 1.8	1926 4.5
2 TU	0216 1.6	0839 4.8	1446 1.6	2124 4.6
17 W	0141 2.0	0748 4.6	1403 2.0	2007 4.3
3 W	0309 2.0	0954 4.5	1550 2.0	◑ 2254 4.3
18 TH	0221 2.2	0839 4.4	1449 2.2	2114 4.1
4 TH	0420 2.3	1136 4.4	1717 2.2	
19 F	0316 2.4	0958 4.2	1558 2.4	● 2257 4.0
5 F	0033 4.2	0553 2.4	1305 4.5	1854 2.1
20 SA	0440 2.5	1135 4.2	1734 2.4	
6 SA	0148 4.4	0719 2.2	1412 4.7	2003 1.9
21 SU	0032 4.2	0611 2.4	1254 4.5	1853 2.1
7 SU	0243 4.7	0829 1.9	1503 5.0	2053 1.6
22 M	0136 4.5	0720 2.1	1353 4.9	1952 1.8
8 M	0325 4.9	0907 1.7	1541 5.1	2134 1.4
23 TU	0226 4.8	0815 1.7	1443 5.2	2043 1.4
9 TU	0357 5.0	0948 1.5	1612 5.2	2211 1.3
24 W	0311 5.2	0906 1.4	1529 5.5	2130 1.1
10 W	0424 5.1	1024 1.4	1639 5.3	2244 1.3
25 TH	0353 5.4	0954 1.1	1613 5.7	2215 1.0
11 TH	0450 5.2	1057 1.3	1705 5.3	● 2315 1.3
26 F	0435 5.6	1040 0.9	1657 5.8	○ 2259 0.9
12 F	0517 5.2	1127 1.3	1732 5.2	2344 1.4
27 SA	0518 5.6	1125 0.8	1742 5.8	2343 0.9
13 SA	0544 5.2	1156 1.4	1759 5.1	
28 SU	0601 5.6	1210 0.9	1829 5.6	
14 SU	0012 1.5	0612 5.1	1225 1.4	1826 5.0
29 M	0029 1.1	0647 5.5	1255 1.1	1918 5.3
15 M	0040 1.6	0641 5.0	1254 1.6	1854 4.8
30 TU	0113 1.4	0737 5.2	1342 1.3	2013 4.9
31 W	0200 1.7	0833 4.9	1435 1.7	2119 4.6

NOVEMBER

Day	Time m	Time m	Time m	Time m
1 TH	0256 2.0	0945 4.7	1537 2.0	◑ 2241 4.4
16 F	0207 2.1	0830 4.6	1436 2.1	2102 4.3
2 F	0404 2.3	1112 4.5	1655 2.2	
17 SA	0301 2.3	0935 4.5	1537 2.2	2221 4.2
3 SA	0005 4.3	0524 2.4	1233 4.6	1818 2.2
18 SU	0410 2.3	1052 4.5	1650 2.2	2342 4.3
4 SU	0115 4.4	0641 2.3	1338 4.7	1926 2.0
19 M	0525 2.2	1207 4.7	1803 2.0	
5 M	0208 4.6	0743 2.1	1429 4.8	2017 1.8
20 TU	0052 4.6	0634 2.0	1312 4.9	1907 1.8
6 TU	0248 4.8	0833 1.9	1508 4.9	2100 1.7
21 W	0148 4.8	0735 1.8	1409 5.2	2004 1.5
7 W	0320 4.9	0915 1.7	1540 5.0	2137 1.6
22 TH	0239 5.1	0832 1.5	1501 5.4	2057 1.3
8 TH	0350 5.0	0952 1.6	1609 5.1	2212 1.5
23 F	0327 5.3	0926 1.2	1552 5.6	2147 1.2
9 F	0419 5.1	1026 1.5	1638 5.1	2244 1.5
24 SA	0414 5.5	1017 1.1	1641 5.6	○ 2236 1.1
10 SA	0450 5.2	1059 1.5	1708 5.1	● 2314 1.5
25 SU	0501 5.6	1107 1.0	1730 5.6	2323 1.1
11 SU	0520 5.2	1130 1.5	1738 5.0	2344 1.6
26 M	0550 5.6	1156 1.0	1820 5.5	
12 M	0551 5.1	1203 1.5	1808 4.9	
27 TU	0012 1.3	0640 5.5	1244 1.1	1911 5.3
13 TU	0015 1.7	0623 5.0	1235 1.6	1840 4.8
28 W	0100 1.5	0730 5.3	1333 1.4	2004 5.0
14 W	0048 1.8	0658 4.9	1310 1.7	1916 4.6
29 TH	0149 1.7	0823 5.1	1423 1.6	2101 4.7
15 TH	0124 1.9	0738 4.8	1349 1.9	2001 4.4
30 F	0240 1.9	0920 4.9	1517 1.9	2204 4.5

DECEMBER

Day	Time m	Time m	Time m	Time m
1 SA	0337 2.1	1024 4.7	1617 2.1	◑ 2312 4.4
16 SU	0247 1.9	0913 4.8	1516 1.8	2145 4.5
2 SU	0441 2.2	1133 4.6	1724 2.2	
17 M	0342 2.0	1014 4.8	1613 1.9	2254 4.5
3 M	0018 4.4	0548 2.3	1240 4.5	1832 2.2
18 TU	0445 2.0	1122 4.8	1717 1.9	
4 TU	0115 4.5	0653 2.2	1338 4.6	1931 2.1
19 W	0005 4.6	0552 2.0	1232 4.8	1824 1.8
5 W	0202 4.6	0749 2.1	1426 4.7	2020 2.0
20 TH	0113 4.7	0659 1.8	1339 4.9	1929 1.7
6 TH	0243 4.7	0838 2.0	1507 4.8	2103 1.9
21 F	0214 4.9	0804 1.6	1442 5.1	2031 1.5
7 F	0320 4.9	0920 1.9	1544 4.8	2141 1.8
22 SA	0310 5.1	0906 1.4	1540 5.3	2128 1.4
8 SA	0356 5.0	0959 1.8	1620 4.9	2217 1.7
23 SU	0403 5.3	1004 1.2	1634 5.4	2222 1.3
9 SU	0430 5.1	1036 1.7	1654 4.9	● 2251 1.7
24 M	0454 5.5	1058 1.1	1725 5.4	○ 2313 1.3
10 M	0505 5.1	1112 1.6	1727 5.0	2326 1.7
25 TU	0544 5.6	1149 1.1	1814 5.4	
11 TU	0539 5.2	1149 1.6	1801 4.9	
26 W	0001 1.3	0632 5.6	1236 1.1	1901 5.3
12 W	0001 1.7	0615 5.1	1225 1.6	1836 4.9
27 TH	0050 1.4	0717 5.5	1321 1.2	1945 5.1
13 TH	0038 1.7	0652 5.1	1303 1.6	1914 4.8
28 F	0134 1.5	0800 5.3	1405 1.4	2028 4.9
14 F	0116 1.8	0733 5.0	1342 1.7	1956 4.7
29 SA	0218 1.6	0841 5.1	1448 1.6	2110 4.7
15 SA	0159 1.8	0819 4.9	1426 1.7	2046 4.6
30 SU	0303 1.8	0924 4.8	1534 1.9	2157 4.5
31 M	0352 2.0	1013 4.6	1626 2.1	◑ 2255 4.3

Chart Datum: 2·83 metres below IGN Datum

TIDES

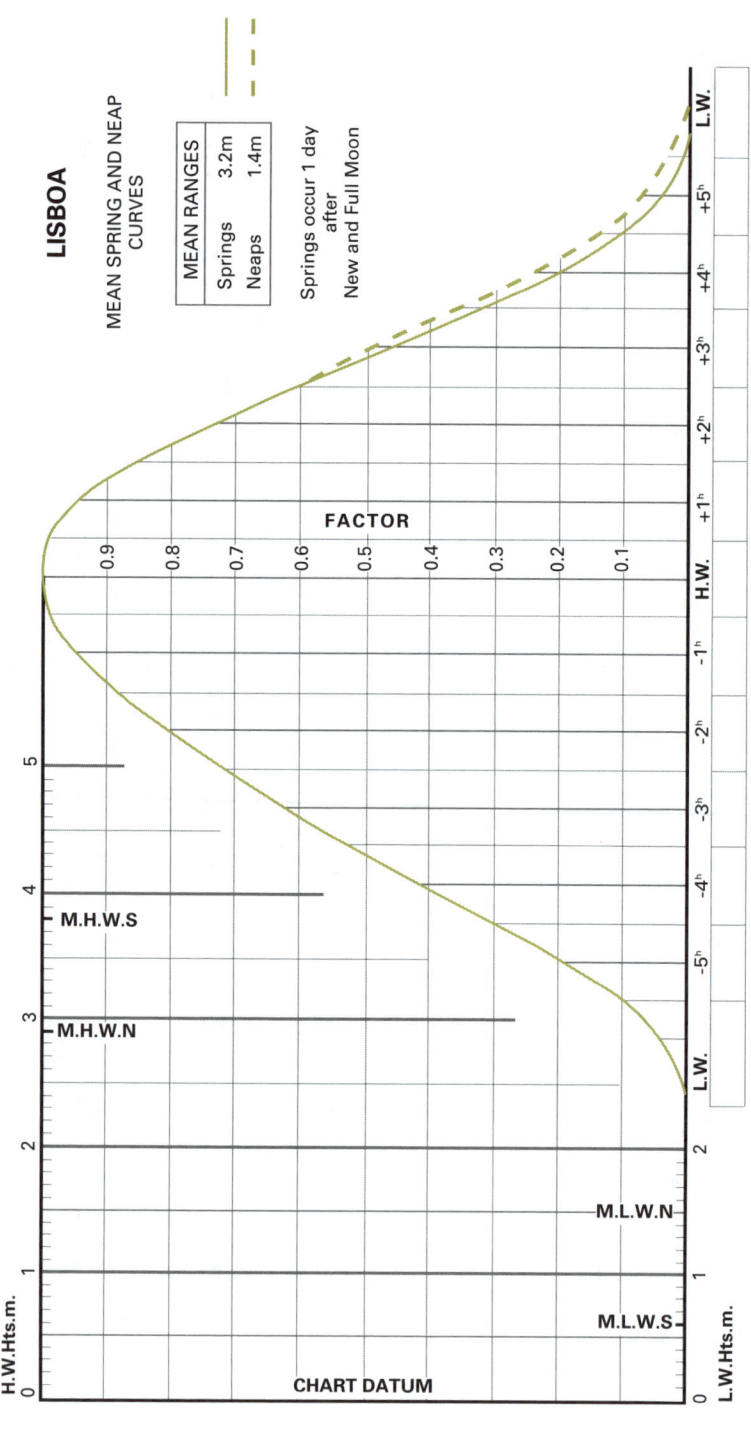

LISBOA

MEAN SPRING AND NEAP
CURVES

MEAN RANGES	
Springs	3.2m
Neaps	1.4m

Springs occur 1 day
after
New and Full Moon

FACTOR

0.9
0.8
0.7
0.6
0.5
0.4
0.3
0.2
0.1

H.W.

+1^h +2^h +3^h +4^h +5^h L.W.

-1^h -2^h -3^h -4^h -5^h

M.H.W.S
M.H.W.N
M.L.W.N
M.L.W.S

L.W.

H.W.Hts.m.
L.W.Hts.m.

CHART DATUM

PORTUGAL – LISBOA

LAT 38°43'N   LONG 9°07'W

TIMES AND HEIGHTS OF HIGH AND LOW WATERS

Dates in amber are **SPRINGS**
Dates in yellow are **NEAPS**

2007

JANUARY

Time	m		Time	m
1 0105	3.4		**16** 0053	3.1
0704	0.9		0657	1.2
M 1335	3.3		TU 1320	3.0
1924	0.9		1913	1.1
2 0159	3.5		**17** 0142	3.3
0759	0.7		0744	1.0
TU 1429	3.4		W 1409	3.2
2014	0.8		1957	0.9
3 0249	3.6		**18** 0228	3.5
0848	0.7		0828	0.8
W 1518	3.4		TH 1455	3.3
○ 2059	0.8		2040	0.8
4 0335	3.7		**19** 0313	3.7
0933	0.6		0910	0.6
TH 1602	3.4		F 1540	3.5
2140	0.8		● 2122	0.6
5 0417	3.7		**20** 0357	3.8
1013	0.6		0952	0.4
F 1642	3.4		SA 1623	3.6
2218	0.8		2204	0.5
6 0455	3.6		**21** 0440	3.9
1050	0.7		1033	0.4
SA 1719	3.3		SU 1705	3.6
2254	0.9		2246	0.5
7 0530	3.5		**22** 0523	3.9
1125	0.8		1115	0.4
SU 1752	3.2		M 1748	3.6
2329	0.9		2328	0.5
8 0602	3.4		**23** 0606	3.8
1200	0.9		1158	0.5
M 1825	3.1		TU 1831	3.5
9 0006	1.1		**24** 0013	0.6
0635	3.3		0651	3.7
TU 1237	1.0		W 1243	0.6
1900	3.0		1917	3.3
10 0045	1.2		**25** 0101	0.8
0713	3.1		0741	3.5
W 1319	1.2		TH 1333	0.9
1943	2.9		○ 2010	3.2
11 0132	1.3		**26** 0157	1.0
0759	3.0		0838	3.2
TH 1410	1.3		F 1432	1.1
◑ 2038	2.8		2114	3.0
12 0231	1.5		**27** 0306	1.2
0858	2.8		0950	3.0
F 1513	1.4		SA 1545	1.2
2145	2.7		2231	3.0
13 0342	1.5		**28** 0432	1.2
1010	2.8		1112	2.9
SA 1624	1.4		SU 1707	1.3
2256	2.8		2349	3.1
14 0458	1.5		**29** 0558	1.1
1123	2.8		1230	3.0
SU 1730	1.4		M 1822	1.2
2359	2.9			
15 0603	1.4		**30** 0058	3.2
1226	2.9		0707	1.0
M 1826	1.3		TU 1334	3.1
			1921	1.1
			31 0154	3.4
			0800	0.8
			W 1426	3.2
			2009	0.9

FEBRUARY

Time	m		Time	m
1 0242	3.5		**16** 0212	3.5
0843	0.7		0812	0.6
TH 1509	3.3		F 1440	3.5
2050	0.8		2025	0.7
2 0324	3.6		**17** 0257	3.8
0920	0.6		0854	0.4
F 1547	3.4		SA 1523	3.7
○ 2126	0.7		● 2107	0.4
3 0400	3.7		**18** 0340	4.0
0953	0.6		0934	0.3
SA 1621	3.4		SU 1605	3.8
2159	0.7		2148	0.3
4 0432	3.7		**19** 0423	4.1
1024	0.6		1014	0.2
SU 1651	3.4		M 1645	3.9
2230	0.7		2228	0.3
5 0502	3.6		**20** 0504	4.1
1054	0.6		1054	0.2
M 1720	3.4		TU 1726	3.8
2300	0.7		2308	0.3
6 0531	3.5		**21** 0545	4.0
1124	0.7		1134	0.4
TU 1748	3.3		W 1806	3.7
2331	0.8		2350	0.5
7 0600	3.4		**22** 0628	3.8
1155	0.9		1216	0.6
W 1818	3.2		TH 1850	3.5
8 0004	1.0		**23** 0036	0.7
0631	3.2		0715	3.5
TH 1228	1.0		F 1302	0.9
1853	3.0		1939	3.3
9 0041	1.2		**24** 0130	1.0
0708	3.0		0811	3.1
F 1307	1.2		SA 1358	1.2
1935	2.9		◐ 2042	3.0
10 0125	1.4		**25** 0244	1.3
0755	2.8		0929	2.9
SA 1356	1.4		SU 1518	1.5
◐ 2032	2.7		2209	2.9
11 0229	1.5		**26** 0426	1.4
0900	2.7		1107	2.8
SU 1509	1.5		M 1659	1.5
2148	2.7		2341	3.0
12 0400	1.6		**27** 0603	1.3
1028	2.6		1231	2.9
M 1639	1.5		TU 1821	1.4
2313	2.8			
13 0529	1.5		**28** 0052	3.2
1156	2.7		0705	1.1
TU 1755	1.4		W 1329	3.1
			1916	1.2
14 0025	3.0			
0636	1.2			
W 1302	2.9			
1853	1.2			
15 0122	3.3			
0727	0.9			
TH 1354	3.2			
1941	0.9			

MARCH

Time	m		Time	m
1 0144	3.4		**16** 0059	3.4
0750	0.9		0703	0.9
TH 1413	3.3		F 1333	3.4
1957	1.0		1920	0.9
2 0227	3.6		**17** 0149	3.7
0826	0.8		0748	0.6
F 1450	3.4		SA 1418	3.7
2032	0.8		2003	0.6
3 0303	3.7		**18** 0235	4.0
0857	0.7		0830	0.4
SA 1523	3.5		SU 1500	3.9
○ 2104	0.7		2045	0.4
4 0335	3.7		**19** 0318	4.2
0926	0.6		0910	0.2
SU 1553	3.6		M 1541	4.0
2134	0.7		● 2126	0.3
5 0405	3.7		**20** 0400	4.3
0954	0.6		0950	0.2
M 1621	3.6		TU 1621	4.1
2203	0.7		2206	0.2
6 0433	3.7		**21** 0442	4.2
1022	0.6		1029	0.3
TU 1648	3.6		W 1702	4.0
2231	0.7		2247	0.3
7 0500	3.6		**22** 0524	4.1
1050	0.7		1109	0.5
W 1715	3.5		TH 1743	3.9
2300	0.8		2330	0.5
8 0528	3.5		**23** 0607	3.8
1118	0.9		1151	0.7
TH 1744	3.4		F 1826	3.6
2330	0.9			
9 0558	3.3		**24** 0017	0.6
1147	1.0		0655	3.4
F 1816	3.2		SA 1237	1.1
			1916	3.4
10 0003	1.1		**25** 0115	1.1
0631	3.1		0754	3.1
SA 1220	1.2		SU 1335	1.4
1853	3.0		◐ 2022	3.1
11 0042	1.3		**26** 0235	1.4
0713	2.9		0919	2.8
SU 1301	1.4		M 1503	1.6
1942	2.9		2154	3.0
12 0139	1.5		**27** 0424	1.5
0813	2.7		1102	2.8
M 1407	1.4		TU 1651	1.7
◐ 2055	2.8		2327	3.0
13 0313	1.6		**28** 0550	1.4
0947	2.6		1217	3.0
TU 1554	1.7		W 1806	1.5
2233	2.8			
14 0458	1.5		**29** 0033	3.2
1132	2.8		0644	1.2
W 1727	1.5		TH 1308	3.2
2358	3.1		1855	1.3
15 0611	1.2		**30** 0121	3.4
1241	3.0		0723	1.0
TH 1830	1.2		F 1347	3.3
			1932	1.1
			31 0200	3.6
			0756	0.9
			SA 1421	3.5
			2005	0.9

APRIL

Time	m		Time	m
1 0233	3.7		**16** 0207	4.0
0826	0.8		0802	0.4
SU 1452	3.6		M 1432	4.0
2036	0.8		2019	0.4
2 0305	3.7		**17** 0252	4.2
0855	0.7		0844	0.3
M 1521	3.7		TU 1515	4.1
○ 2106	0.8		● 2102	0.3
3 0334	3.7		**18** 0336	4.2
0923	0.7		0925	0.3
TU 1550	3.7		W 1557	4.1
2135	0.8		2145	0.3
4 0403	3.7		**19** 0420	4.1
0951	0.7		1006	0.4
W 1618	3.7		TH 1639	4.1
2204	0.8		2229	0.4
5 0432	3.6		**20** 0505	3.9
1019	0.8		1047	0.6
TH 1647	3.6		F 1723	3.9
2233	0.9		2315	0.6
6 0501	3.5		**21** 0551	3.7
1047	0.9		1131	0.9
F 1716	3.5		SA 1809	3.7
2304	1.0			
7 0532	3.3		**22** 0006	0.9
1116	1.1		0642	3.3
SA 1748	3.3		SU 1220	1.2
2337	1.2		1901	3.4
8 0607	3.2		**23** 0106	1.2
1148	1.3		0744	3.0
SU 1826	3.2		M 1320	1.5
			2006	3.2
9 0019	1.3		**24** 0225	1.4
0650	3.0		0905	2.8
M 1232	1.5		TU 1444	1.7
1915	3.0		◑ 2130	3.0
10 0118	1.5		**25** 0355	1.5
0751	2.8		1033	2.8
TU 1340	1.7		W 1616	1.7
◑ 2027	3.1		2253	3.1
11 0247	1.6		**26** 0509	1.4
0925	2.7		1141	3.0
W 1523	1.7		TH 1726	1.6
2203	3.0		2356	3.2
12 0425	1.5		**27** 0603	1.3
1104	2.9		1231	3.2
TH 1655	1.5		F 1816	1.4
2327	3.2			
13 0537	1.2		**28** 0044	3.3
1212	3.2		0644	1.1
F 1759	1.2		SA 1310	3.3
			1857	1.2
14 0029	3.5		**29** 0123	3.5
0632	0.9		0719	1.0
SA 1303	3.5		SU 1345	3.5
1850	0.9		1932	1.1
15 0121	3.8		**30** 0158	3.5
0718	0.6		0751	0.9
SU 1349	3.8		M 1418	3.6
1936	0.6		2005	1.0

TIDES

TIME ZONE (UT)
For Summer Time add ONE hour in **non-shaded areas**

PORTUGAL – LISBOA

LAT 38°43′N   LONG 9°07′W

TIMES AND HEIGHTS OF HIGH AND LOW WATERS

Dates in amber are **SPRINGS**
Dates in yellow are **NEAPS**

2007

MAY

Day	Time m	Time m		Day	Time m	Time m
1 TU	0232 3.6 / 0823 0.9 / 1449 3.6 / 2037 0.9		**16** W	0227 4.0 / 0818 0.5 / 1451 4.0 / 2042 0.5 ●	
2 W	0304 3.6 / 0853 0.9 / 1520 3.7 / 2109 0.9 ○		**17** TH	0315 4.0 / 0902 0.5 / 1536 4.0 / 2129 0.5	
3 TH	0335 3.6 / 0923 0.9 / 1551 3.6 / 2140 0.9		**18** F	0403 3.9 / 0946 0.6 / 1623 4.0 / 2217 0.6	
4 F	0407 3.5 / 0952 1.0 / 1622 3.6 / 2212 1.0		**19** SA	0452 3.7 / 1031 0.8 / 1709 3.8 / 2306 0.7	
5 SA	0440 3.4 / 1022 1.0 / 1656 3.5 / 2246 1.0		**20** SU	0541 3.5 / 1117 1.0 / 1757 3.7 / 2357 0.9	
6 SU	0515 3.3 / 1055 1.1 / 1732 3.4 / 2325 1.1		**21** M	0632 3.3 / 1206 1.2 / 1847 3.5	
7 M	0555 3.2 / 1133 1.3 / 1814 3.3		**22** TU	0053 1.1 / 0727 3.0 / 1301 1.4 / 1943 3.3	
8 TU	0011 1.3 / 0643 3.0 / 1223 1.4 / 1906 3.2		**23** W	0155 1.3 / 0829 2.9 / 1407 1.6 / 2047 3.1 ◑	
9 W	0111 1.4 / 0746 2.9 / 1330 1.5 / 2013 3.1		**24** TH	0302 1.4 / 0938 2.9 / 1518 1.6 / 2156 3.0	
10 TH	0228 1.4 / 0907 2.9 / 1456 1.6 / 2134 3.2 ◑		**25** F	0407 1.4 / 1044 2.9 / 1626 1.6 / 2300 3.1	
11 F	0348 1.3 / 1029 3.0 / 1616 1.4 / 2251 3.3		**26** SA	0505 1.4 / 1139 3.0 / 1724 1.5 / 2354 3.1	
12 SA	0458 1.1 / 1135 3.3 / 1721 1.2 / 2354 3.5		**27** SU	0554 1.3 / 1225 3.2 / 1813 1.3	
13 SU	0555 0.9 / 1229 3.5 / 1817 0.9		**28** M	0039 3.2 / 0637 1.1 / 1305 3.3 / 1856 1.2	
14 M	0048 3.7 / 0646 0.7 / 1318 3.7 / 1907 0.7		**29** TU	0120 3.3 / 0715 1.1 / 1342 3.4 / 1935 1.1	
15 TU	0139 3.9 / 0733 0.6 / 1405 3.9 / 1955 0.6		**30** W	0158 3.4 / 0751 1.0 / 1418 3.5 / 2011 0.9	
				31 TH	0235 3.4 / 0825 1.0 / 1453 3.5 / 2047 1.0	

JUNE

Day	Time m		Day	Time m
1 F	0312 3.4 / 0858 1.0 / 1558 3.5 / 2122 0.9 ○		**16** SA	0354 3.6 / 0933 0.8 / 1612 3.8 / 2209 0.6
2 SA	0349 3.3 / 0931 1.0 / 1605 3.4 / 2159 0.9		**17** SU	0442 3.5 / 1019 0.8 / 1658 3.8 / 2256 0.7
3 SU	0427 3.3 / 1007 1.0 / 1643 3.5 / 2237 0.9		**18** M	0528 3.4 / 1103 1.0 / 1742 3.7 / 2341 0.8
4 M	0508 3.3 / 1046 1.1 / 1724 3.5 / 2320 1.0		**19** TU	0612 3.3 / 1147 1.1 / 1825 3.5
5 TU	0551 3.2 / 1129 1.1 / 1809 3.5		**20** W	0025 1.0 / 0656 3.1 / 1231 1.2 / 1908 3.3
6 W	0007 1.0 / 0640 3.1 / 1219 1.2 / 1900 3.4		**21** TH	0111 1.1 / 0741 3.0 / 1320 1.4 / 1953 3.2
7 TH	0101 1.1 / 0736 3.1 / 1318 1.3 / 1958 3.3		**22** F	0201 1.3 / 0831 2.9 / 1414 1.5 / 2046 3.0 ◑
8 F	0203 1.1 / 0840 3.1 / 1425 1.3 / 2104 3.3		**23** SA	0257 1.4 / 0930 2.8 / 1517 1.5 / 2147 2.9
9 SA	0309 1.1 / 0949 3.1 / 1534 1.3 / 2212 3.3		**24** SU	0358 1.4 / 1033 2.9 / 1623 1.5 / 2251 2.9
10 SU	0415 1.1 / 1055 3.2 / 1642 1.1 / 2317 3.4		**25** M	0458 1.4 / 1131 3.0 / 1725 1.4 / 2350 3.0
11 M	0517 1.0 / 1154 3.4 / 1744 1.0		**26** TU	0553 1.3 / 1222 3.1 / 1820 1.3
12 TU	0018 3.5 / 0614 0.9 / 1249 3.6 / 1843 0.8		**27** W	0041 3.0 / 0640 1.2 / 1308 3.2 / 1907 1.2
13 W	0115 3.6 / 0707 0.8 / 1342 3.7 / 1937 0.7		**28** TH	0128 3.1 / 0722 1.1 / 1350 3.3 / 1949 1.1
14 TH	0210 3.7 / 0758 0.7 / 1433 3.8 / 2030 0.6		**29** F	0212 3.2 / 0801 1.0 / 1431 3.4 / 2029 1.0
15 F	0303 3.7 / 0846 0.7 / 1523 3.8 / 2120 0.6 ●		**30** SA	0254 3.2 / 0839 1.0 / 1511 3.5 / 2109 0.9 ●

JULY

Day	Time m		Day	Time m
1 SU	0336 3.3 / 0918 0.9 / 1553 3.6 / 2148 0.8		**16** M	0428 3.5 / 1004 0.8 / 1642 3.8 / 2237 0.6
2 M	0418 3.3 / 0957 0.9 / 1634 3.7 / 2229 0.7		**17** TU	0507 3.4 / 1043 0.8 / 1720 3.7 / 2314 0.7
3 TU	0500 3.4 / 1038 0.8 / 1717 3.7 / 2311 0.7		**18** W	0543 3.3 / 1119 0.9 / 1754 3.6 / 2349 0.8
4 W	0543 3.4 / 1121 0.9 / 1800 3.7 / 2355 0.8		**19** TH	0616 3.3 / 1155 1.0 / 1828 3.4
5 TH	0628 3.3 / 1207 0.9 / 1846 3.6		**20** F	0025 1.0 / 0651 3.1 / 1233 1.1 / 1903 3.2
6 F	0041 0.8 / 0716 3.3 / 1256 1.0 / 1936 3.5		**21** SA	0104 1.1 / 0729 3.0 / 1316 1.3 / 1943 3.1
7 SA	0133 0.9 / 0809 3.2 / 1352 1.1 / 2032 3.3		**22** SU	0150 1.3 / 0817 2.9 / 1409 1.5 / 2035 2.9 ◑
8 SU	0231 1.0 / 0910 3.1 / 1456 1.1 / 2136 3.3		**23** M	0247 1.4 / 0919 2.8 / 1516 1.6 / 2141 2.8
9 M	0335 1.1 / 1017 3.2 / 1608 1.2 / 2246 3.2		**24** TU	0356 1.5 / 1030 2.8 / 1634 1.6 / 2256 2.8
10 TU	0444 1.1 / 1125 3.2 / 1721 1.1 / 2357 3.2		**25** W	0507 1.5 / 1138 2.9 / 1746 1.5
11 W	0551 1.0 / 1230 3.4 / 1830 1.0		**26** TH	0006 2.8 / 0608 1.4 / 1236 3.0 / 1844 1.3
12 TH	0103 3.3 / 0653 1.0 / 1330 3.5 / 1932 0.8		**27** F	0104 2.9 / 0658 1.3 / 1326 3.2 / 1931 1.1
13 F	0203 3.4 / 0748 0.9 / 1425 3.7 / 2026 0.7		**28** SA	0154 3.1 / 0742 1.1 / 1412 3.4 / 2014 0.9
14 SA	0256 3.5 / 0838 0.8 / 1515 3.8 / 2114 0.6 ●		**29** SU	0239 3.3 / 0824 0.9 / 1456 3.6 / 2054 0.7
15 SU	0345 3.5 / 0923 0.8 / 1601 3.8 / 2157 0.6		**30** M	0322 3.4 / 0904 0.8 / 1538 3.8 / 2134 0.6 ○
			31 TU	0403 3.5 / 0944 0.6 / 1620 3.9 / 2213 0.5

AUGUST

Day	Time m		Day	Time m
1 W	0444 3.6 / 1024 0.6 / 1701 3.9 / 2253 0.5		**16** TH	0508 3.5 / 1047 0.8 / 1720 3.7 / 2310 0.8
2 TH	0525 3.6 / 1105 0.6 / 1743 3.9 / 2333 0.5		**17** F	0537 3.4 / 1119 0.9 / 1749 3.5 / 2341 0.9
3 F	0606 3.6 / 1146 0.6 / 1825 3.8		**18** SA	0606 3.3 / 1151 1.0 / 1819 3.3
4 SA	0016 0.7 / 0650 3.5 / 1231 0.8 / 1911 3.6		**19** SU	0014 1.1 / 0640 3.2 / 1227 1.2 / 1854 3.1
5 SU	0102 0.8 / 0738 3.3 / 1323 1.0 / 2003 3.4 ◑		**20** M	0051 1.3 / 0720 3.0 / 1311 1.5 / 1938 2.9 ◑
6 M	0156 1.0 / 0836 3.2 / 1426 1.1 / 2108 3.2		**21** TU	0139 1.5 / 0813 2.8 / 1412 1.6 / 2039 2.7
7 TU	0302 1.2 / 0947 3.1 / 1547 1.3 / 2228 3.0		**22** W	0249 1.7 / 0927 2.8 / 1543 1.7 / 2206 2.7
8 W	0423 1.3 / 1108 3.1 / 1716 1.2 / 2352 3.0		**23** TH	0422 1.7 / 1054 2.8 / 1716 1.6 / 2339 2.8
9 TH	0544 1.3 / 1223 3.3 / 1833 1.1		**24** F	0540 1.6 / 1208 3.0 / 1822 1.4
10 F	0103 3.2 / 0651 1.1 / 1326 3.5 / 1933 0.9		**25** SA	0045 3.0 / 0637 1.3 / 1304 3.3 / 1911 1.1
11 SA	0200 3.3 / 0745 1.0 / 1418 3.7 / 2020 0.8		**26** SU	0136 3.2 / 0723 1.1 / 1352 3.5 / 1953 0.9
12 SU	0247 3.5 / 0829 0.9 / 1503 3.8 / 2101 0.6 ●		**27** M	0220 3.5 / 0805 0.9 / 1436 3.8 / 2033 0.6
13 M	0328 3.5 / 0908 0.8 / 1542 3.8 / 2136 0.6		**28** TU	0301 3.7 / 0845 0.6 / 1518 4.0 / 2112 0.5 ○
14 TU	0405 3.6 / 0943 0.7 / 1618 3.8 / 2209 0.6		**29** W	0341 3.8 / 0924 0.5 / 1559 4.1 / 2150 0.4
15 W	0437 3.6 / 1016 0.7 / 1650 3.8 / 2240 0.7		**30** TH	0421 3.9 / 1003 0.4 / 1639 4.2 / 2229 0.4
			31 F	0501 3.9 / 1043 0.4 / 1720 4.1 / 2308 0.5

TIME ZONE (UT)
For Summer Time add ONE hour in **non-shaded areas**

LAT 38°43'N   LONG 9°07'W
TIMES AND HEIGHTS OF HIGH AND LOW WATERS

Dates in **amber** are **SPRINGS**
Dates in **yellow** are **NEAPS**

2007

SEPTEMBER

Day	Time m	Day	Time m
1 SA	0541 3.8 / 1124 0.5 / 1802 3.9 / 2349 0.7	**16** SU	0529 3.5 / 1116 1.1 / 1743 3.4 / 2332 1.1
2 SU	0623 3.7 / 1208 0.7 / 1848 3.7	**17** M	0600 3.3 / 1148 1.3 / 1816 3.2
3 M	0034 0.9 / 0711 3.5 / 1300 1.0 / 1941 3.3	**18** TU	0004 1.4 / 0637 3.1 / 1227 1.5 / 1856 3.0
4 TU	0127 1.2 / 0810 3.2 / 1408 1.3 / ◑ 2052 3.1	**19** W	0044 1.6 / 0725 3.0 / 1323 1.7 / ◐ 1955 2.8
5 W	0241 1.5 / 0930 3.1 / 1544 1.4 / 2226 2.9	**20** TH	0149 1.8 / 0836 2.8 / 1458 1.8 / 2127 2.7
6 TH	0419 1.6 / 1103 3.1 / 1725 1.4 / 2356 3.0	**21** F	0338 1.8 / 1014 2.9 / 1645 1.7 / 2313 2.8
7 F	0547 1.5 / 1220 3.3 / 1835 1.2	**22** SA	0511 1.7 / 1139 3.1 / 1754 1.4
8 SA	0100 3.2 / 0648 1.3 / 1317 3.5 / 1924 1.0	**23** SU	0021 3.1 / 0611 1.4 / 1238 3.4 / 1843 1.1
9 SU	0148 3.4 / 0733 1.1 / 1403 3.7 / 2003 0.8	**24** M	0110 3.4 / 0658 1.1 / 1326 3.7 / 1926 0.8
10 M	0228 3.6 / 0811 0.9 / 1442 3.8 / 2037 0.7	**25** TU	0153 3.7 / 0740 0.8 / 1410 4.0 / 2006 0.6
11 TU	0303 3.7 / 0845 0.8 / 1517 3.9 / ● 2108 0.7	**26** W	0234 3.9 / 0820 0.6 / 1452 4.2 / ○ 2045 0.4
12 W	0335 3.7 / 0916 0.7 / 1548 3.9 / 2137 0.7	**27** TH	0315 4.0 / 0900 0.4 / 1534 4.3 / 2124 0.3
13 TH	0405 3.7 / 0946 0.7 / 1618 3.8 / 2206 0.7	**28** F	0355 4.1 / 0940 0.3 / 1615 4.3 / 2203 0.4
14 F	0433 3.7 / 1016 0.8 / 1646 3.7 / 2234 0.8	**29** SA	0435 4.1 / 1021 0.4 / 1657 4.2 / 2243 0.5
15 SA	0501 3.6 / 1045 0.9 / 1713 3.6 / 2303 1.0	**30** SU	0517 4.0 / 1104 0.6 / 1741 3.9 / 2325 0.8

OCTOBER

Day	Time m	Day	Time m
1 M	0601 3.8 / 1151 0.8 / 1830 3.6	**16** TU	0531 3.4 / 1121 1.3 / 1749 3.2 / 2331 1.4
2 TU	0011 1.1 / 0651 3.5 / 1247 1.1 / 1928 3.3	**17** W	0608 3.2 / 1202 1.5 / 1831 3.0
3 W	0108 1.4 / 0754 3.3 / 1403 1.4 / ◑ 2047 3.0	**18** TH	0012 1.6 / 0655 3.1 / 1257 1.6 / 1930 2.8
4 TH	0230 1.7 / 0921 3.2 / 1547 1.5 / 2225 2.9	**19** F	0116 1.8 / 0804 3.0 / 1424 1.7 / ◐ 2100 2.8
5 F	0416 1.7 / 1054 3.2 / 1718 1.4 / 2346 3.1	**20** SA	0258 1.8 / 0937 3.0 / 1604 1.6 / 2239 2.9
6 SA	0536 1.5 / 1204 3.4 / 1817 1.2	**21** SU	0431 1.7 / 1102 3.2 / 1715 1.4 / 2347 3.2
7 SU	0041 3.3 / 0629 1.3 / 1256 3.5 / 1900 1.1	**22** M	0535 1.4 / 1204 3.5 / 1808 1.1
8 M	0124 3.5 / 0710 1.1 / 1337 3.7 / 1935 0.9	**23** TU	0038 3.5 / 0625 1.1 / 1254 3.8 / 1853 0.8
9 TU	0200 3.6 / 0745 1.0 / 1414 3.8 / 2007 0.8	**24** W	0122 3.7 / 0710 0.8 / 1340 4.0 / 1936 0.6
10 W	0233 3.7 / 0817 0.9 / 1446 3.8 / 2037 0.8	**25** TH	0205 4.0 / 0753 0.6 / 1425 4.2 / 2017 0.4
11 TH	0303 3.8 / 0848 0.8 / 1517 3.8 / ● 2106 0.8	**26** F	0247 4.1 / 0835 0.4 / 1509 4.2 / ○ 2058 0.4
12 F	0333 3.8 / 0919 0.8 / 1546 3.8 / 2134 0.8	**27** SA	0330 4.2 / 0919 0.4 / 1553 4.2 / 2140 0.5
13 SA	0401 3.7 / 0948 0.9 / 1615 3.7 / 2202 0.9	**28** SU	0413 4.1 / 1003 0.4 / 1639 4.0 / 2222 0.6
14 SU	0430 3.6 / 1017 1.0 / 1644 3.5 / 2230 1.0	**29** M	0458 4.0 / 1050 0.6 / 1727 3.8 / 2307 0.9
15 M	0459 3.5 / 1048 1.1 / 1715 3.4 / 2259 1.2	**30** TU	0545 3.8 / 1141 0.9 / 1819 3.5 / 2356 1.2
		31 W	0638 3.6 / 1240 1.1 / 1919 3.2

NOVEMBER

Day	Time m	Day	Time m
1 TH	0056 1.5 / 0742 3.3 / 1355 1.4 / ◑ 2035 3.0	**16** F	0000 1.5 / 0642 3.2 / 1245 1.4 / 1917 2.9
2 F	0214 1.6 / 0901 3.2 / 1523 1.5 / 2200 3.0	**17** SA	0100 1.6 / 0744 3.1 / 1356 1.5 / ◐ 2032 2.9
3 SA	0345 1.7 / 1023 3.2 / 1641 1.4 / 2312 3.0	**18** SU	0220 1.6 / 0901 3.1 / 1515 1.4 / 2154 3.0
4 SU	0459 1.6 / 1130 3.3 / 1739 1.3	**19** M	0342 1.5 / 1019 3.2 / 1627 1.3 / 2303 3.2
5 M	0006 3.2 / 0554 1.4 / 1222 3.4 / 1823 1.2	**20** TU	0451 1.3 / 1124 3.4 / 1726 1.1
6 TU	0049 3.4 / 0637 1.2 / 1304 3.5 / 1901 1.1	**21** W	0000 3.4 / 0548 1.1 / 1219 3.6 / 1818 0.8
7 W	0126 3.5 / 0715 1.1 / 1341 3.6 / 1934 1.0	**22** TH	0050 3.6 / 0639 0.8 / 1310 3.8 / 1906 0.7
8 TH	0200 3.6 / 0749 1.0 / 1415 3.6 / 2006 0.9	**23** F	0137 3.8 / 0726 0.6 / 1400 3.9 / 1952 0.6
9 F	0233 3.7 / 0822 0.9 / 1448 3.6 / ● 2037 0.9	**24** SA	0224 4.0 / 0816 0.5 / 1449 4.0 / ○ 2037 0.5
10 SA	0304 3.7 / 0854 0.9 / 1520 3.6 / 2107 0.9	**25** SU	0310 4.0 / 0904 0.4 / 1538 3.9 / 2122 0.6
11 SU	0335 3.6 / 0926 1.0 / 1551 3.5 / 2137 1.0	**26** M	0358 4.0 / 0953 0.5 / 1627 3.8 / 2208 0.7
12 M	0406 3.6 / 0958 1.0 / 1623 3.4 / 2207 1.1	**27** TU	0446 3.9 / 1042 0.6 / 1718 3.6 / 2255 0.9
13 TU	0438 3.5 / 1031 1.1 / 1658 3.3 / 2239 1.2	**28** W	0535 3.8 / 1132 0.8 / 1809 3.4 / 2345 1.1
14 W	0513 3.4 / 1108 1.2 / 1736 3.2 / 2315 1.3	**29** TH	0626 3.6 / 1228 1.0 / 1903 3.2
15 TH	0553 3.3 / 1151 1.3 / 1820 3.0	**30** F	0039 1.3 / 0721 3.4 / 1328 1.2 / 2003 3.0

DECEMBER

Day	Time m	Day	Time m
1 SA	0140 1.5 / 0822 3.2 / 1432 1.3 / ◑ 2109 2.9	**16** SU	0044 1.2 / 0725 3.3 / 1326 1.1 / 2001 3.0
2 SU	0249 1.5 / 0930 3.1 / 1539 1.4 / 2216 2.9	**17** M	0144 1.3 / 0825 3.2 / 1428 1.2 / ◐ 2107 3.0
3 M	0359 1.5 / 1036 3.1 / 1641 1.4 / 2316 3.0	**18** TU	0252 1.3 / 0932 3.2 / 1536 1.1 / 2216 3.1
4 TU	0502 1.5 / 1134 3.1 / 1735 1.3	**19** W	0403 1.2 / 1041 3.3 / 1642 1.0 / 2320 3.2
5 W	0006 3.1 / 0556 1.3 / 1224 3.2 / 1821 1.2	**20** TH	0511 1.1 / 1146 3.4 / 1744 0.9
6 TH	0050 3.3 / 0642 1.2 / 1307 3.3 / 1902 1.1	**21** F	0019 3.4 / 0613 0.9 / 1246 3.5 / 1840 0.8
7 F	0129 3.3 / 0723 1.1 / 1346 3.3 / 1939 1.0	**22** SA	0114 3.6 / 0711 0.7 / 1343 3.6 / 1934 0.7
8 SA	0206 3.4 / 0800 1.0 / 1424 3.3 / 2013 1.0	**23** SU	0208 3.7 / 0806 0.6 / 1438 3.6 / 2024 0.6
9 SU	0241 3.5 / 0836 1.0 / 1500 3.3 / ● 2046 1.0	**24** M	0300 3.8 / 0858 0.5 / 1530 3.7 / ○ 2113 0.6
10 M	0315 3.5 / 0911 0.9 / 1535 3.3 / 2119 1.0	**25** TU	0349 3.9 / 0947 0.4 / 1620 3.6 / 2200 0.7
11 TU	0351 3.5 / 0946 0.9 / 1612 3.3 / 2153 1.0	**26** W	0437 3.9 / 1035 0.5 / 1707 3.5 / 2245 0.8
12 W	0427 3.5 / 1022 0.9 / 1650 3.2 / 2229 1.0	**27** TH	0523 3.8 / 1120 0.6 / 1752 3.4 / 2328 0.9
13 TH	0506 3.5 / 1101 1.0 / 1730 3.2 / 2309 1.1	**28** F	0606 3.6 / 1204 0.8 / 1835 3.2
14 F	0547 3.4 / 1143 1.0 / 1814 3.1 / 2353 1.1	**29** SA	0011 1.0 / 0649 3.4 / 1248 1.0 / 1918 3.1
15 SA	0633 3.3 / 1231 1.1 / 1903 3.0	**30** SU	0057 1.2 / 0733 3.2 / 1334 1.1 / 2005 2.9
		31 M	0147 1.3 / 0822 3.0 / 1426 1.3 / ◑ 2101 2.8

TIDES

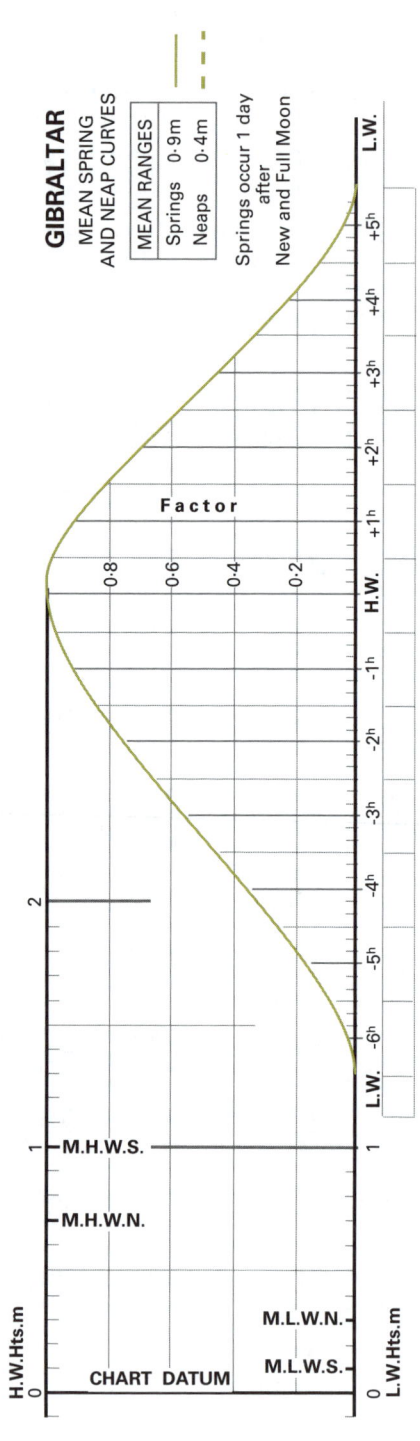

GIBRALTAR
MEAN SPRING
AND NEAP CURVES

MEAN RANGES

Springs	0·9m
Neaps	0·4m

Springs occur 1 day
after
New and Full Moon

TIME ZONE -0100
(Gibraltar Standard Time)
Subtract 1 hour for UT
For Gibraltar Summer Time add
ONE hour in **non-shaded areas**

GIBRALTAR

LAT 36°08′N   LONG 5°21′W

TIMES AND HEIGHTS OF HIGH AND LOW WATERS

Dates in amber are **SPRINGS**
Dates in yellow are **NEAPS**

2007

JANUARY

Date	Time	m	Time	m	Time	m	Time	m
1 M	0110	0.8	0654	0.2	1321	0.9	1930	0.1
2 TU	0202	0.8	0741	0.1	1412	0.9	2015	0.1
3 W	0250	0.9	0825	0.1	1501	0.9	○ 2058	0.1
4 TH	0335	0.9	0908	0.1	1547	0.9	2137	0.1
5 F	0417	0.9	0949	0.1	1630	0.9	2214	0.1
6 SA	0457	0.9	1028	0.1	1710	0.9	2250	0.1
7 SU	0535	0.9	1107	0.2	1750	0.9	2324	0.1
8 M	0612	0.8	1146	0.2	1829	0.8		
9 TU	0000	0.2	0651	0.8	1228	0.2	1909	0.7
10 W	0038	0.2	0732	0.7	1315	0.3	1952	0.7
11 TH	0123	0.3	0818	0.7	1409	0.3	◑ 2040	0.7
12 F	0219	0.3	0910	0.7	1514	0.3	2138	0.6
13 SA	0336	0.3	1013	0.7	1633	0.3	2251	0.6
14 SU	0502	0.3	1122	0.7	1745	0.3		
15 M	0004	0.7	0603	0.3	1222	0.7	1837	0.2
16 TU	0100	0.7	0649	0.3	1313	0.8	1920	0.1
17 W	0147	0.8	0729	0.2	1400	0.8	2000	0.1
18 TH	0230	0.8	0808	0.2	1446	0.9	2039	0.1
19 F	0312	0.9	0849	0.1	1530	0.9	● 2119	0.0
20 SA	0353	1.0	0931	0.1	1613	1.0	2159	0.0
21 SU	0434	1.0	1014	0.1	1655	1.0	2238	0.0
22 M	0516	1.0	1057	0.1	1739	0.9	2318	0.0
23 TU	0559	0.9	1142	0.1	1824	0.9		
24 W	0001	0.1	0646	0.9	1232	0.1	1914	0.8
25 TH	0049	0.1	0738	0.9	1327	0.2	◑ 2009	0.8
26 F	0146	0.2	0836	0.8	1434	0.2	2113	0.7
27 SA	0300	0.3	0945	0.8	1603	0.2	2234	0.7
28 SU	0437	0.3	1106	0.7	1742	0.3		
29 M	0003	0.7	0600	0.2	1222	0.8	1847	0.2
30 TU	0112	0.7	0658	0.2	1323	0.8	1936	0.1
31 W	0206	0.8	0744	0.1	1414	0.8	2018	0.1

FEBRUARY

Date	Time	m	Time	m	Time	m	Time	m
1 TH	0250	0.8	0825	0.1	1459	0.8	2055	0.1
2 F	0330	0.9	0903	0.1	1540	0.9	○ 2129	0.0
3 SA	0405	0.9	0939	0.1	1616	0.9	2200	0.0
4 SU	0438	0.9	1013	0.1	1651	0.9	2230	0.0
5 M	0509	0.9	1045	0.1	1724	0.8	2259	0.1
6 TU	0539	0.8	1117	0.1	1756	0.8	2326	0.1
7 W	0609	0.8	1148	0.1	1828	0.8	2355	0.1
8 TH	0641	0.8	1221	0.2	1904	0.7		
9 F	0025	0.2	0718	0.7	1301	0.2	1946	0.7
10 SA	0102	0.3	0806	0.7	1355	0.3	◑ 2039	0.6
11 SU	0157	0.3	0907	0.6	1526	0.3	2149	0.6
12 M	0359	0.4	1030	0.6	1722	0.3	2323	0.6
13 TU	0544	0.3	1156	0.7	1824	0.2		
14 W	0038	0.7	0636	0.3	1258	0.7	1908	0.1
15 TH	0130	0.7	0718	0.2	1348	0.8	1948	0.1
16 F	0215	0.8	0758	0.1	1434	0.9	2026	0.0
17 SA	0257	0.9	0839	0.0	1517	0.9	● 2105	0.0
18 SU	0338	1.0	0920	0.0	1600	1.0	2144	0.0
19 M	0418	1.0	1001	0.0	1642	1.0	2222	-0.1
20 TU	0459	1.0	1042	0.0	1724	1.0	2300	0.0
21 W	0541	1.0	1124	0.0	1808	0.9	2339	0.0
22 TH	0625	1.0	1207	0.1	1855	0.9		
23 F	0022	0.1	0713	0.9	1257	0.1	1948	0.8
24 SA	0113	0.2	0810	0.8	1401	0.2	◐ 2051	0.7
25 SU	0227	0.3	0921	0.7	1549	0.3	2217	0.6
26 M	0433	0.3	1056	0.7	1749	0.3		
27 TU	0001	0.6	0606	0.3	1226	0.7	1848	0.2
28 W	0112	0.7	0658	0.2	1325	0.7	1930	0.1

MARCH

Date	Time	m	Time	m	Time	m	Time	m
1 TH	0159	0.8	0738	0.1	1410	0.8	2005	0.1
2 F	0238	0.9	0813	0.1	1448	0.8	2037	0.1
3 SA	0311	0.9	0846	0.1	1522	0.9	2107	0.0
4 SU	0342	0.9	0918	0.0	1554	0.9	○ 2135	0.0
5 M	0411	0.9	0948	0.0	1625	0.9	2203	0.0
6 TU	0438	0.9	1018	0.0	1654	0.9	2229	0.1
7 W	0504	0.9	1046	0.1	1723	0.8	2254	0.1
8 TH	0531	0.8	1113	0.1	1753	0.8	2320	0.1
9 F	0600	0.8	1142	0.1	1827	0.7	2347	0.2
10 SA	0635	0.7	1214	0.2	1908	0.7		
11 SU	0019	0.3	0720	0.7	1259	0.3	2002	0.6
12 M	0106	0.3	0823	0.6	1428	0.3	◐ 2111	0.6
13 TU	0259	0.4	0948	0.6	1654	0.3	2245	0.6
14 W	0521	0.3	1130	0.6	1800	0.2		
15 TH	0010	0.7	0617	0.2	1239	0.7	1844	0.1
16 F	0105	0.8	0659	0.1	1329	0.8	1924	0.1
17 SA	0150	0.9	0740	0.1	1414	0.9	2002	0.0
18 SU	0233	1.0	0820	0.0	1457	1.0	2041	0.0
19 M	0314	1.0	0902	-0.1	1540	1.0	● 2120	-0.1
20 TU	0356	1.1	0943	-0.1	1622	1.0	2159	0.0
21 W	0437	1.1	1023	-0.1	1705	1.0	2237	0.0
22 TH	0519	1.0	1103	0.0	1750	0.9	2316	0.1
23 F	0604	0.9	1144	0.1	1838	0.9	2359	0.1
24 SA	0653	0.8	1231	0.2	1932	0.8		
25 SU	0050	0.2	0751	0.8	1336	0.3	◐ 2037	0.7
26 M	0209	0.3	0904	0.7	1538	0.3	2202	0.7
27 TU	0427	0.3	1045	0.6	1731	0.3	2342	0.7
28 W	0555	0.3	1214	0.7	1825	0.2		
29 TH	0047	0.7	0640	0.2	1308	0.7	1902	0.2
30 F	0132	0.8	0715	0.2	1347	0.8	1934	0.1
31 SA	0207	0.8	0747	0.1	1422	0.8	2004	0.1

APRIL

Date	Time	m	Time	m	Time	m	Time	m
1 SU	0239	0.9	0818	0.1	1454	0.9	2033	0.1
2 M	0308	0.9	0849	0.1	1525	0.9	○ 2102	0.1
3 TU	0337	0.9	0920	0.0	1555	0.9	2131	0.1
4 W	0404	0.9	0949	0.1	1624	0.9	2158	0.1
5 TH	0432	0.9	1017	0.1	1654	0.9	2225	0.1
6 F	0500	0.8	1045	0.1	1725	0.8	2252	0.2
7 SA	0531	0.8	1114	0.2	1801	0.8	2321	0.2
8 SU	0607	0.7	1147	0.2	1845	0.7	2356	0.3
9 M	0654	0.7	1232	0.3	1941	0.7		
10 TU	0049	0.3	0758	0.6	1403	0.3	◐ 2048	0.6
11 W	0238	0.4	0920	0.6	1611	0.3	2211	0.7
12 TH	0440	0.3	1057	0.7	1721	0.2	2332	0.7
13 F	0544	0.2	1209	0.7	1809	0.2		
14 SA	0030	0.8	0630	0.1	1301	0.8	1850	0.1
15 SU	0118	0.9	0713	0.1	1347	0.9	1930	0.0
16 M	0202	1.0	0755	0.0	1431	0.9	2011	0.0
17 TU	0246	1.0	0838	0.0	1516	1.0	● 2052	0.0
18 W	0330	1.0	0920	0.0	1600	1.0	2133	0.0
19 TH	0414	1.0	1002	0.0	1645	1.0	2214	0.0
20 F	0458	1.0	1043	0.0	1732	0.9	2256	0.1
21 SA	0545	0.9	1125	0.1	1822	0.9	2341	0.2
22 SU	0636	0.8	1213	0.2	1919	0.8		
23 M	0036	0.3	0736	0.7	1319	0.3	2023	0.7
24 TU	0155	0.3	0847	0.7	1500	0.3	◐ 2137	0.7
25 W	0345	0.3	1012	0.7	1636	0.3	2258	0.7
26 TH	0511	0.3	1134	0.7	1736	0.3		
27 F	0002	0.8	0601	0.3	1229	0.8	1817	0.2
28 SA	0048	0.8	0638	0.2	1311	0.8	1851	0.2
29 SU	0125	0.8	0712	0.2	1346	0.8	1924	0.2
30 M	0158	0.9	0745	0.1	1419	0.8	1955	0.2

Chart Datum: 0·25 metres below Alicante Datum (Mean Sea Level, Alicante)

TIDES

TIME ZONE -0100
(Gibraltar Standard Time)
Subtract 1 hour for UT
For Gibraltar Summer Time add
ONE hour in **non-shaded areas**

GIBRALTAR

LAT 36°08'N   LONG 5°21'W

TIMES AND HEIGHTS OF HIGH AND LOW WATERS

Dates in amber are SPRINGS
Dates in yellow are NEAPS

2007

MAY

Day	Time m	Time m	Time m	Time m		Day	Time m	Time m	Time m	Time m
1 TU	0229 0.9	0818 0.1	1452 0.9	2027 0.2		16 W	0218 1.0	0816 0.0	1452 0.9	●2027 0.1
2 W	0301 0.9	0850 0.1	1524 0.9	○2058 0.2		17 TH	0305 1.0	0901 0.0	1540 0.9	2112 0.1
3 TH	0332 0.9	0922 0.1	1556 0.9	2129 0.2		18 F	0353 1.0	0945 0.0	1628 0.9	2157 0.1
4 F	0404 0.9	0953 0.1	1629 0.9	2200 0.2		19 SA	0441 0.9	1029 0.1	1717 0.9	2242 0.1
5 SA	0436 0.8	1024 0.2	1704 0.8	2231 0.2		20 SU	0530 0.9	1112 0.1	1808 0.9	2330 0.2
6 SU	0511 0.8	1056 0.2	1744 0.8	2306 0.3		21 M	0622 0.8	1200 0.2	1903 0.8	
7 M	0551 0.8	1134 0.2	1829 0.8	2348 0.3		22 TU	0024 0.3	0719 0.8	1259 0.3	2001 0.8
8 TU	0640 0.7	1224 0.3	1924 0.7			23 W	0130 0.3	0821 0.7	1409 0.3	☽2101 0.8
9 W	0048 0.3	0741 0.7	1345 0.3	2026 0.7		24 TH	0245 0.3	0925 0.7	1520 0.3	2202 0.7
10 TH	0216 0.3	0854 0.7	1517 0.3	☽2136 0.7		25 F	0359 0.3	1033 0.7	1625 0.3	2303 0.8
11 F	0347 0.3	1016 0.7	1628 0.2	2249 0.8		26 SA	0503 0.3	1136 0.7	1720 0.3	2354 0.8
12 SA	0459 0.2	1130 0.7	1725 0.2	2351 0.8		27 SU	0554 0.3	1225 0.7	1806 0.3	
13 SU	0556 0.1	1227 0.8	1813 0.1			28 M	0037 0.8	0635 0.2	1307 0.8	1844 0.2
14 M	0043 0.9	0644 0.1	1317 0.9	1858 0.1		29 TU	0115 0.8	0713 0.2	1344 0.8	1921 0.2
15 TU	0131 1.0	0730 0.0	1405 0.9	1942 0.1		30 W	0151 0.8	0750 0.2	1421 0.8	1956 0.2
						31 TH	0227 0.9	0825 0.2	1457 0.8	2031 0.2

JUNE

Day	Time m	Time m	Time m	Time m		Day	Time m	Time m	Time m	Time m
1 F	0304 0.9	0900 0.2	1533 0.9	○2106 0.2		16 SA	0339 0.9	0936 0.1	1616 0.9	2146 0.1
2 SA	0342 0.9	0935 0.2	1610 0.9	2141 0.2		17 SU	0428 0.9	1019 0.1	1703 0.9	2232 0.1
3 SU	0420 0.9	1010 0.2	1648 0.9	2218 0.2		18 M	0516 0.9	1100 0.1	1751 0.9	2316 0.2
4 M	0459 0.8	1046 0.2	1729 0.9	2258 0.2		19 TU	0604 0.8	1142 0.2	1838 0.9	
5 TU	0541 0.8	1127 0.2	1814 0.8	2344 0.3		20 W	0003 0.2	0653 0.8	1226 0.2	1926 0.8
6 W	0629 0.8	1215 0.2	1904 0.8			21 TH	0053 0.2	0744 0.8	1315 0.3	2015 0.8
7 TH	0039 0.3	0724 0.8	1316 0.2	2000 0.8		22 F	0147 0.3	0835 0.7	1409 0.3	☽2104 0.8
8 F	0147 0.3	0827 0.7	1425 0.2	☽2101 0.8		23 SA	0245 0.3	0930 0.7	1508 0.3	2156 0.7
9 SA	0259 0.3	0936 0.7	1534 0.2	2206 0.8		24 SU	0349 0.3	1030 0.7	1613 0.3	2251 0.7
10 SU	0411 0.2	1049 0.8	1640 0.2	2312 0.8		25 M	0459 0.3	1133 0.7	1718 0.3	2346 0.8
11 M	0521 0.2	1155 0.8	1741 0.2			26 TU	0559 0.3	1227 0.7	1810 0.3	
12 TU	0011 0.9	0621 0.1	1252 0.8	1834 0.2		27 W	0034 0.8	0646 0.2	1313 0.8	1853 0.3
13 W	0105 0.9	0714 0.1	1345 0.9	1924 0.1		28 TH	0119 0.8	0727 0.2	1355 0.8	1933 0.3
14 TH	0156 0.9	0803 0.1	1436 0.9	2012 0.1		29 F	0201 0.8	0805 0.2	1435 0.8	2010 0.2
15 F	0248 0.9	0850 0.1	1527 0.9	●2100 0.1		30 SA	0244 0.9	0842 0.2	1515 0.9	○2049 0.2

JULY

Day	Time m	Time m	Time m	Time m		Day	Time m	Time m	Time m	Time m
1 SU	0326 0.9	0919 0.1	1554 0.9	2128 0.2		16 M	0415 0.9	1004 0.1	1646 0.9	2217 0.1
2 M	0407 0.9	0956 0.1	1633 0.9	2208 0.2		17 TU	0458 0.9	1039 0.1	1725 0.9	2255 0.1
3 TU	0447 0.9	1034 0.1	1713 0.9	2249 0.2		18 W	0538 0.9	1113 0.1	1803 0.9	2333 0.2
4 W	0529 0.9	1113 0.1	1755 0.9	2333 0.2		19 TH	0618 0.8	1147 0.2	1841 0.9	
5 TH	0614 0.9	1156 0.2	1841 0.9			20 F	0011 0.2	0659 0.8	1223 0.2	1920 0.8
6 F	0021 0.2	0704 0.8	1245 0.2	1931 0.9		21 SA	0052 0.2	0741 0.7	1302 0.3	2000 0.8
7 SA	0117 0.2	0800 0.8	1342 0.2	2027 0.9		22 SU	0138 0.3	0828 0.7	1350 0.3	☽2045 0.7
8 SU	0220 0.2	0903 0.8	1447 0.3	2128 0.8		23 M	0234 0.3	0922 0.7	1454 0.4	2139 0.7
9 M	0332 0.2	1015 0.8	1603 0.3	2238 0.8		24 TU	0351 0.3	1030 0.7	1622 0.4	2246 0.7
10 TU	0457 0.2	1132 0.8	1721 0.3	2348 0.8		25 W	0523 0.3	1146 0.7	1741 0.4	2356 0.7
11 W	0613 0.2	1239 0.8	1825 0.2			26 TH	0624 0.3	1246 0.7	1833 0.3	
12 TH	0050 0.9	0711 0.1	1338 0.8	1919 0.2		27 F	0053 0.8	0707 0.2	1333 0.8	1914 0.3
13 F	0147 0.9	0800 0.1	1430 0.9	2007 0.1		28 SA	0142 0.8	0746 0.2	1415 0.9	1953 0.2
14 SA	0240 0.9	0845 0.1	1519 0.9	●2053 0.1		29 SU	0226 0.9	0823 0.1	1455 0.9	2032 0.2
15 SU	0330 0.9	0926 0.1	1604 0.9	2136 0.1		30 M	0309 0.9	0900 0.1	1534 1.0	○2112 0.1
						31 TU	0351 1.0	0937 0.1	1613 1.0	2153 0.1

AUGUST

Day	Time m	Time m	Time m	Time m		Day	Time m	Time m	Time m	Time m
1 W	0431 1.0	1014 0.1	1652 1.0	2233 0.1		16 TH	0505 0.9	1038 0.1	1722 0.9	2258 0.1
2 TH	0512 1.0	1052 0.1	1733 1.0	2315 0.1		17 F	0538 0.9	1107 0.2	1752 0.9	2330 0.1
3 F	0555 1.0	1132 0.1	1816 1.0	2358 0.1		18 SA	0610 0.8	1136 0.2	1823 0.9	
4 SA	0642 0.9	1215 0.2	1903 1.0			19 SU	0002 0.2	0645 0.8	1207 0.3	1856 0.9
5 SU	0047 0.2	0735 0.9	1306 0.2	☽1956 0.9		20 M	0038 0.2	0728 0.7	1243 0.3	☽1938 0.8
6 M	0146 0.2	0837 0.8	1410 0.3	2057 0.8		21 TU	0125 0.3	0821 0.7	1336 0.4	2033 0.7
7 TU	0303 0.3	0952 0.8	1539 0.3	2213 0.8		22 W	0243 0.4	0931 0.7	1521 0.5	2147 0.7
8 W	0454 0.3	1122 0.7	1719 0.3	2339 0.8		23 TH	0450 0.4	1101 0.7	1715 0.4	2320 0.7
9 TH	0618 0.3	1239 0.8	1828 0.3			24 F	0601 0.3	1218 0.7	1813 0.4	
10 F	0050 0.8	0711 0.2	1337 0.9	1918 0.2		25 SA	0031 0.8	0645 0.2	1309 0.8	1854 0.3
11 SA	0147 0.9	0754 0.1	1425 0.9	2001 0.2		26 SU	0122 0.9	0722 0.2	1351 0.9	1933 0.2
12 SU	0235 0.9	0832 0.1	1507 0.9	2041 0.1		27 M	0206 0.9	0758 0.1	1430 1.0	2012 0.1
13 M	0317 0.9	0906 0.1	1544 1.0	●2118 0.1		28 TU	0248 1.0	0834 0.1	1510 1.0	○2051 0.1
14 TU	0355 0.9	0939 0.1	1619 1.0	2153 0.1		29 W	0330 1.1	0911 0.1	1549 1.1	2132 0.1
15 W	0431 0.9	1009 0.1	1652 1.0	2226 0.1		30 TH	0411 1.1	0949 0.1	1629 1.1	2212 0.0
						31 F	0452 1.1	1027 0.1	1709 1.1	2252 0.1

Chart Datum: 0·25 metres below Alicante Datum (Mean Sea Level, Alicante)

GIBRALTAR

LAT 36°08'N   LONG 5°21'W

TIMES AND HEIGHTS OF HIGH AND LOW WATERS

Dates in amber are SPRINGS
Dates in yellow are NEAPS

2007

SEPTEMBER

Time	m		Time	m
1 0534	1.0		**16** 0526	0.9
1106	0.1		1057	0.2
SA 1751	1.1		SU 1735	0.9
2333	0.1		2320	0.2
2 0620	1.0		**17** 0559	0.8
1147	0.2		1125	0.3
SU 1837	1.0		M 1807	0.8
			2351	0.3
3 0018	0.2		**18** 0640	0.8
0713	0.9		1158	0.4
M 1236	0.3		TU 1848	0.8
1929	0.9			
4 0115	0.3		**19** 0031	0.4
0816	0.8		0736	0.7
TU 1342	0.4		W 1245	0.4
◑ 2034	0.8		◐ 1947	0.7
5 0244	0.4		**20** 0147	0.4
0937	0.8		0847	0.7
W 1532	0.4		TH 1436	0.5
2159	0.8		2105	0.7
6 0502	0.4		**21** 0419	0.4
1120	0.8		1018	0.7
TH 1723	0.4		F 1646	0.4
2343	0.8		2246	0.7
7 0615	0.3		**22** 0532	0.3
1237	0.8		1143	0.8
F 1824	0.3		SA 1745	0.4
8 0052	0.8		**23** 0006	0.8
0659	0.2		0615	0.3
SA 1327	0.9		SU 1237	0.9
1906	0.2		1828	0.3
9 0140	0.9		**24** 0058	0.9
0734	0.2		0652	0.2
SU 1407	1.0		M 1320	1.0
1943	0.2		1907	0.2
10 0219	0.9		**25** 0142	1.0
0806	0.2		0728	0.1
M 1443	1.0		TU 1401	1.1
2017	0.1		1946	0.1
11 0254	1.0		**26** 0223	1.0
0836	0.1		0805	0.1
TU 1515	1.0		W 1442	1.1
● 2050	0.1		○ 2026	0.1
12 0327	1.0		**27** 0305	1.1
0905	0.2		0842	0.1
W 1545	1.0		TH 1522	1.2
2122	0.1		2106	0.0
13 0358	1.0		**28** 0347	1.1
0934	0.1		0921	0.1
TH 1614	1.0		F 1604	1.2
2153	0.1		2147	0.0
14 0428	1.0		**29** 0429	1.1
1002	0.1		1001	0.1
F 1641	1.0		SA 1645	1.1
2222	0.1		2227	0.1
15 0457	0.9		**30** 0512	1.1
1029	0.2		1041	0.2
SA 1707	0.9		SU 1728	1.1
2251	0.2		2308	0.2

OCTOBER

Time	m		Time	m
1 0559	1.0		**16** 0527	0.9
1123	0.2		1057	0.3
M 1815	1.0		TU 1737	0.9
			2353	0.2
2 0653	0.9		**17** 0609	0.8
1213	0.3		1131	0.4
TU 1910	0.9		W 1820	0.8
3 0049	0.3		**18** 0000	0.4
0759	0.8		0705	0.8
W 1327	0.4		TH 1222	0.4
◑ 2019	0.8		1920	0.8
4 0232	0.4		**19** 0112	0.4
0924	0.8		0815	0.7
TH 1528	0.5		F 1407	0.5
2151	0.8		◐ 2036	0.7
5 0445	0.4		**20** 0334	0.4
1104	0.6		0936	0.8
F 1709	0.4		SA 1602	0.4
2335	0.8		2207	0.7
6 0550	0.4		**21** 0450	0.4
1214	0.9		1058	0.8
SA 1803	0.3		SU 1707	0.3
			2331	0.8
7 0036	0.8		**22** 0539	0.3
0630	0.3		1158	0.9
SU 1300	0.9		M 1755	0.3
1841	0.3			
8 0118	0.9		**23** 0027	0.9
0703	0.2		0619	0.2
M 1337	1.0		TU 1246	1.0
1914	0.2		1837	0.2
9 0153	0.9		**24** 0113	1.0
0732	0.2		0657	0.2
TU 1409	1.0		W 1329	1.1
1946	0.2		1918	0.1
10 0225	1.0		**25** 0156	1.0
0801	0.2		0735	0.1
W 1440	1.0		TH 1412	1.1
2018	0.1		1959	0.1
11 0255	1.0		**26** 0239	1.1
0831	0.2		0815	0.1
TH 1508	1.0		F 1455	1.1
● 2049	0.1		○ 2042	0.0
12 0324	1.0		**27** 0323	1.1
0900	0.2		0856	0.1
F 1537	1.0		SA 1539	1.1
2120	0.1		2120	0.1
13 0353	1.0		**28** 0408	1.0
0929	0.2		0938	0.1
SA 1605	1.0		SU 1624	1.1
2150	0.2		2206	0.1
14 0422	1.0		**29** 0454	1.0
0958	0.2		1021	0.2
SU 1633	1.0		M 1710	1.0
2219	0.2		2249	0.2
15 0452	0.9		**30** 0542	1.0
1026	0.3		1107	0.3
M 1703	0.9		TU 1800	1.0
2249	0.3		2335	0.3
			31 0638	0.9
			1201	0.3
			W 1857	0.9

NOVEMBER

Time	m		Time	m
1 0034	0.4		**16** 0643	0.8
0743	0.8		1213	0.4
TH 1317	0.4		F 1902	0.8
◑ 2005	0.8			
2 0207	0.4		**17** 0049	0.4
0901	0.8		0745	0.8
F 1459	0.4		SA 1336	0.4
2127	0.8		◑ 2008	0.8
3 0353	0.4		**18** 0230	0.4
1023	0.8		0854	0.8
SA 1626	0.4		SU 1508	0.4
2256	0.8		2124	0.8
4 0503	0.4		**19** 0352	0.3
1132	0.9		1008	0.8
SU 1723	0.3		M 1620	0.3
			2244	0.8
5 0000	0.8		**20** 0453	0.3
0549	0.3		1115	0.9
M 1221	0.9		TU 1718	0.2
1805	0.3		2351	0.8
6 0045	0.9		**21** 0543	0.2
0625	0.3		1210	1.0
TU 1259	0.9		W 1808	0.2
1841	0.2			
7 0121	0.9		**22** 0043	0.9
0658	0.3		0628	0.2
W 1333	1.0		TH 1259	1.0
1915	0.2		1854	0.1
8 0153	1.0		**23** 0132	1.0
0730	0.2		0711	0.1
TH 1404	1.0		F 1346	1.1
1949	0.2		1939	0.1
9 0224	1.0		**24** 0219	1.0
0801	0.2		0754	0.1
F 1435	1.0		SA 1433	1.1
2022	0.2		○ 2025	0.1
10 0255	1.0		**25** 0306	1.0
0833	0.2		0839	0.1
SA 1506	1.0		SU 1521	1.1
● 2055	0.2		2110	0.1
11 0326	1.0		**26** 0353	1.0
0904	0.2		0925	0.1
SU 1538	1.0		M 1610	1.0
2127	0.2		2155	0.1
12 0358	0.9		**27** 0441	1.0
0935	0.3		1012	0.2
M 1611	0.9		TU 1659	1.0
2158	0.2		2240	0.2
13 0432	0.9		**28** 0531	0.9
1007	0.3		1100	0.2
TU 1645	0.9		W 1750	0.9
2230	0.2		2327	0.2
14 0509	0.9		**29** 0624	0.9
1041	0.3		1154	0.3
W 1723	0.9		TH 1845	0.9
2305	0.3			
15 0552	0.9		**30** 0020	0.3
1120	0.4		0722	0.9
TH 1807	0.8		F 1258	0.3
2347	0.3		1944	0.8

DECEMBER

Time	m		Time	m
1 0126	0.3		**16** 0028	0.3
0825	0.8		0717	0.8
SA 1412	0.3		SU 1305	0.3
◑ 2048	0.8		1942	0.8
2 0242	0.4		**17** 0133	0.3
0930	0.8		0816	0.8
SU 1525	0.3		M 1417	0.3
2156	0.7		◑ 2045	0.8
3 0354	0.4		**18** 0247	0.3
1035	0.8		0922	0.8
M 1630	0.3		TU 1530	0.3
2306	0.8		2158	0.7
4 0457	0.3		**19** 0401	0.3
1132	0.8		1032	0.8
TU 1725	0.3		W 1642	0.2
			2314	0.8
5 0003	0.8		**20** 0510	0.2
0547	0.3		1138	0.9
W 1219	0.8		TH 1747	0.2
1810	0.3			
6 0048	0.8		**21** 0020	0.8
0628	0.3		0608	0.2
TH 1259	0.9		F 1237	0.9
1851	0.2		1842	0.1
7 0127	0.8		**22** 0116	0.9
0705	0.3		0659	0.1
F 1336	0.9		SA 1330	0.9
1928	0.2		1933	0.1
8 0202	0.9		**23** 0208	0.9
0740	0.2		0747	0.1
SA 1411	0.9		SU 1422	1.0
2004	0.2		2022	0.1
9 0237	0.9		**24** 0259	0.9
0815	0.2		0835	0.1
SU 1447	0.9		M 1513	1.0
● 2040	0.2		○ 2108	0.0
10 0311	0.9		**25** 0347	1.0
0848	0.2		0922	0.1
M 1524	0.9		TU 1603	0.9
2114	0.2		2153	0.0
11 0346	0.9		**26** 0434	1.0
0922	0.2		1008	0.1
TU 1601	0.9		W 1651	0.9
2148	0.2		2235	0.1
12 0421	0.9		**27** 0520	0.9
0957	0.2		1054	0.1
W 1638	0.9		TH 1738	0.9
2223	0.2		2317	0.1
13 0459	0.9		**28** 0606	0.9
1034	0.3		1140	0.2
TH 1716	0.9		F 1825	0.9
2259	0.2		2359	0.2
14 0539	0.9		**29** 0654	0.9
1115	0.3		1228	0.2
F 1758	0.8		SA 1914	0.9
2339	0.2			
15 0625	0.9		**30** 0044	0.2
1204	0.3		0743	0.8
SA 1846	0.8		SU 1322	0.2
			2004	0.8
			31 0136	0.3
			0835	0.8
			M 1420	0.3
			◑ 2057	0.7

Chart Datum: 0·25 metres below Alicante Datum (Mean Sea Level, Alicante)

TIDES

INDEX

Abbreviations 5
Admiralty chart symbols .... Back cover
Beaufort scale 75
Brest tidal coefficients 143
Coastguard, HM. Channel Is, SAR 133
  Eire 134
  Denmark 135
  Germany, Netherlands 136
  Belgium, France 137
  Spain, Portugal, Azores 139
Coast Radio Stations 112
Communications, Chapter 3 101
Contents 4
Conversion table 72
Distance off dipping lights, Table of 71
Distress call .... Front cover
First Aid 124
  Essential information 124
  General medical information 125
  First Aid kit 127
Flags, International Code .... Inside front cover
GMDSS 128
Helicopter rescue 123
IALA Buoyage .... Inside front cover
Light recognition .... Inside back cover
Lights, buoys and waypoints (selected)
  1 SW England 12
  2 S Central England 16
  3 SE England 19
  4 E England 20
  5 E Scotland 24
  6 NW Scotland 27
  7 SW Scotland 30
  8 NW England, Wales and E Ireland 32
  9 SW England, S Wales and S Ireland 35
  10 Ireland 37
  11 W Denmark 40
  12 Germany 41
  13 Netherlands and Belgium 44
  14 N France 46
  15 N Central France and Channel Islands 48
  16 N & S Brittany 51
  17 S Biscay 45
  18 N & NW Spain 56
  19 Portugal & The Azores 59
  20 SW Spain, Gibraltar & Morocco 62
Lights for small craft .... Inside front cover
MAYDAY calls, Relay 122
Medical help (see also First Aid) 124
Morse code .... Inside front cover
Moonrise & moonset 65
National Coatchwatch Institution 121
Navigation, Chapter 1 8
Navtex 79

Port radio stations
  S England 104
  E England 105
  Scotland 108
  W England and Wales 109
  Ireland 110
  Denmark 110
  Germany 110
  Netherlands 111
  Belgium 114
  N France 114
  Channel Islands 115
  W France 115
  Spain 116
  Portugal 116
  Gibraltar 116
Radio data 101
  HF radio 103
  Marine VHF band 103
  MF radio 103
  Silence periods 103
  Traffic lists 103
Radio operation 101
  Phonetic alphabet/numerals 101
  Prowords 102
Safety, Chapter 4 121
Secondary port tidal differences 152
  Aberdeen 203
  Avonmouth 208
  Belfast 209
  Brest 215
  Cherbourg 214
  Cobh 210
  Cuxhaven 212
  Dieppe 213
  Dover 200
  Dublin 209
  Dunkerque 213
  Esbjerg 211
  Galway 210
  Gibraltar 217
  Greenock 206
  Helgoland 211, 212
  Holyhead 207
  Immingham 202
  Le Havre 213
  Leith 203
  Lerwick 204
  Lisboa 216
  Liverpool 206
  London Bridge 201
  Lowestoft 202
  Milford Haven 208, 209
  Oban 205
  Plymouth 199

Pointe de Grave 216
Portland 199
Portsmouth 199, 200
River Tyne 202
St Helier 214
St Malo 214
Sheerness 200, 201
Shoreham 200
Southampton 200
Stornoway 204
Ullapool 205
Vlissingen 212
Walton-on-the-Naze 201
Wick 203, 204
Wilhelmshaven 212
Sound signals & shapes 115
Speed, time & distance table 58
Standard Port curves & predictions
Aberdeen 286
Avonmouth 326
Belfast 334
Brest 398
Burnham-on-Crouch 264
Cherbourg 382
Cobh 342
Cuxhaven 354
Dartmouth 226
Dieppe 374
Dover 250
Dublin 330
Dunkerque 370
Esbjerg 346
Falmouth 218
Galway 338
Gibraltar 410
Greenock 310
Helgoland 350
Holyhead 318
Hoek van Holland 362
Immingham 274
Le Havre 378
Leith 282
Lerwick 294
Lisboa 406
Liverpool 314
London Bridge 258
Lowestoft 270
Milford Haven 322
Oban 306
Plymouth 222
Pointe de Grave 402
Poole 234
Portland 230
Portsmouth 242
River Tyne 278
St Helier 394

St Malo 386
St Peter Port 390
Sheerness 254
Shoreham 246
Southampton 238
Stornoway 298
Ullapool 302
Vlissingen 366
Walton-on-the-Naze 266
Wick 290
Wilhelmshaven 358
Sunrise & sunset 64
Tides, Chapter 5 141
Bournemouth to Selsey Bill,
instructions and curves 148
Calculations 144
Coefficients, Brest 143
Dover range & HW times 142
Tidal gates
Irish Sea 195
Menai Strait 197
Scotland 193
Southern England 190
Tidal streams
Channel Islands 166
English Channel & S Brittany 152
Isle of Wight 160
North Sea 172
Portland 158
Scotland 178
West UK & Ireland 184
VHF direction finding 131
Vocabulary, general 6
Weather 98
Weather, Chapter 2 75
BBC Radio 4 broadcasts 78
Belgium, CRS broadcasts 92
Channel Islands, forecasts 87
Denmark, CRS broadcasts 89
Denmark, forecast areas 89
France, forecasts and areas 92
Germany, CRS broadcasts 90
Gibraltar forecasts 98
HMCG broadcasts 84
Irish CRS broadcasts 88
Navtex 79
Netherlands CG & local radio broadcasts 92
Portugal, forecasts and areas 96
Sources 84
Spain, forecast areas, CG broadcasts 96, 98
Terminology 75
UK, shipping forecast areas/record 76
UK, telephone forecasts 81
UK, fax forecasts 82
UK, mobile phone forecasts (SMS) 83
Vocabulary in five languages 98

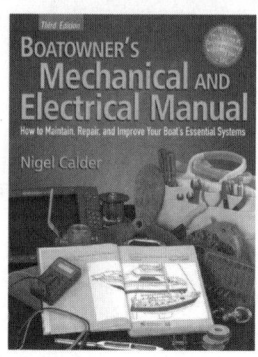

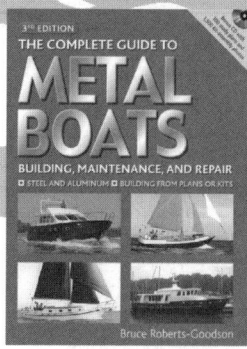